McGRAW-HILL SERIES IN MANAGEMENT

CONSULTING EDITORS
Fred Luthans
Keith Davis

Arnold and Feldman: Organizational Behavior

Bartol and Martin: Management

Bernardin and Russell: Human Resource Management: An Experiential Approach

Boone and Bowen: Great Writings in Management and Organizational Behavior

Boone and Kurtz: Management

Bounds, Yorks, Adams, and Ranney: Beyond Total Quality Management: Toward the Emerging Paradigm

Bovée, Thill, Wood, and Dovel: Management

Cascio: Managing Human Resources: Productivity, Quality of Work Life, Profits

Daughtrey and Ricks: Contemporary Supervision: Managing People and Technology

Davidson and de la Torre: Managing the Global Corporation: Case Studies in Strategy and Management

Dess and Miller: Strategic Management

Dilworth: Operations Management: Design, Planning, and Control for Manufacturing and Services

Dilworth: Production and Operations Management: Manufacturing and Services

Dobler, Burt, and Lee: Purchasing and Materials Management: Text and Cases

Feldman and Arnold: Managing Individual and Group Behavior in Organizations

Fitzsimmons and Fitzsimmons: Service Management for Competitive Advantage

Frederick, Post, and Davis: Business and Society: Corporate Strategy, Public Policy, Ethics

Gaynor and Kirkpatrick: An Introduction to Time Series Modeling and Forecasting for Business and Economics

Hodgetts and Luthans: International Management

Hoffman and Moore: Business Ethics: Readings and Cases in Corporate Morality

Jauch and Glueck: Business Policy and Strategic Management

Jauch and Glueck: Strategic Management and Business Policy

Jauch and Townsend: Cases in Strategic Management and Business Policy

Katz and Kochan: An Introduction to Collective Bargaining and Industrial Relations

Beyond Total Quality Management

Toward the Emerging Paradigm

Koontz and Weihrich: Essentials of Management

Kopelman: Managing Productivity in Organizations: A Practical, People-Oriented Perspective

Kuriloff, Hemphill, and Cloud: Starting and Managing the Small Business

Levin, Rubin, Stinson, and Gardner: Quantitative Approaches to Management

Luthans: Organizational Behavior

Luthans and Thompson: Contemporary Readings in Organizational Behavior

Miles: Theories of Management: Implications for Organizational Behavior and Development

Miles and Snow: Organizational Strategy, Structure, and Process

Mills: Labor-Management Relations

Mitchell and Larson: People in Organizations: An Introduction to Organizational Behavior

Molander: Responsive Capitalism: Case Studies in Corporate Social Conduct

Monks: Operations Management: Theory and Problems

Newstrom and Davis: Organizational Behavior: Human Behavior at Work

Newstrom and Davis: Organizational Behavior: Readings and Exercises

Pearce and Robinson: Corporate Strategies: Readings from Business Week

Porter and McKibbin: Management Education and Development: Drift or Thrust into the 21st Century?

Prasow and Peters: Arbitration and Collective Bargaining: Conflict Resolution in Labor Relations

Quick and Quick: Organizational Stress and Preventive Management

Rue and Holland: Strategic Management: Concepts and Experiences

Rugman, Lecraw, and Booth: International Business: Firm and Environment

Sayles: Leadership: Managing in Real Organizations

Schlesinger, Eccles, and Gabarro: Managing Behavior in Organizations: Text, Cases, and Readings

Schroeder: Operations Management: Decision Making in the Operations Function

Steers and Porter: Motivation and Work Behavior

Steiner: Industry, Society, and Change: A Casebook

Steiner and Steiner: Business, Government, and Society: A Managerial Perspective, Text and Cases

Steinhoff and Burgess: Small Business Management Fundamentals

Sutermeister: People and Productivity

Walker: Human Resource Strategy

Weihrich: Management Excellence: Productivity through MBO

Weihrich and Koontz: Management: A Global Perspective

Werther and Davis: Human Resources and Personnel Management

Wofford, Gerloff, and Cummins: Organizational Communications: The Keystone to Managerial Effectiveness

Yoffie and Gomes-Casseres: International Trade and Competition: Cases and Notes in Strategy and Management

Beyond Total Quality Management

Toward the Emerging Paradigm

Greg Bounds
University of Tennessee

Lyle Yorks
Eastern Connecticut State University

Mel Adams
University of Alabama in Huntsville

Gipsie Ranney
University of Tennessee

McGraw-Hill, Inc.

New York St. Louis San Francisco Auckland Bogotá Caracas
Lisbon London Madrid Mexico City Milan Montreal New Delhi
San Juan Singapore Sydney Tokyo Toronto

Beyond Total Quality Management
Toward the Emerging Paradigm

 This book is printed on recycled, acid-free paper containing a minimum of
50% total recycled fiber with 10% postconsumer de-inked fiber.

1 2 3 4 5 6 7 8 9 0 DOH   DOH 9 0 9 8 7 6 5 4 3

ISBN 0-07-006678-7

This book was set in New Baskerville by Monotype Composition Company.
The editors were Lynn Richardson, Josh Pincus, and Joseph F. Murphy;
the production supervisor was Annette Mayeski.
The cover was designed by Carla Bauer.
R. R. Donnelley & Sons Company was printer and binder.

Library of Congress Cataloging-in-Publication Data

Beyond total quality management: toward the emerging paradigm / Greg
    Bounds . . . [et al.].
        p.   cm.—(McGraw-Hill series in management)
    Includes bibliographical references and index.
    ISBN 0-07-006678-7
    1. Total quality management.   I. Bounds, Gregory M.   II. Series.
    HD62.15.B49   1994
    658.5'62—dc20   93-38388

About the Authors

Greg Bounds is a Research Associate in the College of Business Administration at the University of Tennessee. He earned a B.A. in Psychology at Davidson College, Davidson, North Carolina, and a Ph.D. in Industrial and Organizational Psychology at the University of Tennessee, Knoxville. Before completing his Ph.D., Dr. Bounds did managerial and nonmanagerial work as Branch Office Manager with the federal government; Advertising Sales Team Manager and Salesman; Program Analyst; Line Worker and Shift Supervisor in a Food Processing Plant; and Work Crew Supervisor in agricultural industries. Dr. Bounds has engaged in consulting, training, and applied research with a variety of organizations.

In his tenure at UT, Dr. Bounds has managed a research program focused on the transformation of companies toward the new paradigm; served as a member of intervention teams at the University of Tennessee's world-renowned Management Development Center; and helped found the Center for the Advancement of Organizational Effectiveness at the University of Tennessee, which sponsors interdisciplinary research focused on the themes of the new paradigm. Dr. Bounds is a cocreator and co-author of many of the principles that are taught in the Institutes of the Management Development Center. Dr. Bounds is a coeditor and contributing author for 15 of the 34 chapters for *Competing Globally through Customer Value* (Westport Conn.: Quorum, 1991), a book recommended by the Total Quality Forum.

Lyle Yorks is Professor of Management Sciences at Eastern Connecticut State University, where he coordinates the Master of Science in Organizational Relations program. He is also a member of the faculty of the Executive Development Program at the University of Tennessee. He is also a Principal of the Marshall Group in Scottsdale, Arizona. His consulting work and research focuses on organizational restructuring and the development of effective work groups in support of corporate strategy. He has more than 20 years' experience in developing high-involvement work systems and processes. His articles have appeared in professional journals such as the *Academy of Management Review,* the *California Management Review, Planning Review* and *Personnel.* Included among the companies he has worked with are Arizona Public Service, American Express, General Electric, General Motors, Coopers & Lybrand, Florida Power & Light, and Eastman Chemical.

Mel Adams is Assistant Professor of Management at the University of Alabama in Huntsville. He received his Ph.D. in Business Administration from the University of Tennessee, where he was elected to Beta Gamma Sigma. He previously managed program development for Oak Ridge Associated Universities, a Department of Energy prime contractor, where he worked closely with many major U.S. energy companies. Dr. Adams is the recipient of several research grants and contracts and the author of several publications in journals and proceedings. He has also consulted with Fortune 500 firms and many small businesses on strategic planning and continuous process improvement. He also has experience in management development, training, and training program management, and he has been recognized for his teaching and assistance to small businesses.

Gipsie Ranney is a consultant in system improvement and statistical methodology. She was a member of the statistics faculty of the University of Tennessee for fifteen years. While at the University, she was a founder of The Institute for Productivity through Quality. In 1988, she joined the General Manager's staff of the General Motors Powertrain Division. Subsequently, she was Director of Statistical Methodology for General Motors' Powertrain Group. Dr. Ranney is a member of the Board of Directors of the Ohio Quality and Productivity Forum. She serves as consultant to the Westmoreland County Deming Study Group in Pittsburgh. She is a member of the Board of Directors of the Physical and Mathematical Sciences Foundation of North Carolina State University. Dr. Ranney has developed and conducted numerous seminars for engineers and managers on theory and methods for organizational improvement. She has coauthored a variety of publications on statistical methods and managing for improvement. She has consulted with managers in both manufacturing and service organizations for more than a decade, in addition to collaborating with researchers in education and health care. Dr. Ranney holds a B.S. in Mathematics from Duke University and a Ph.D. in Statistics from North Carolina State University.

Contents

Preface   *xix*

CHAPTER 1   **Global Competitiveness and the Emerging Paradigm   1**

Chapter Outline   1
Chapter Overview   2
An Accepted Definition of Total Quality Management   2
Pervasive Change and Paradigm Shifts   5
The Nature of Paradigms and Paradigm Shifts   6
Stages of the Managerial Paradigm Shift   7
The Stage of Normalcy for Management   10
Traditional Management   10
The Diversions of the Cold War   11
The Stage of Anomalies for Management   13
Evidence of a Shift   13
Explanations for the Anomalies   14
Sources of Japanese Competitiveness   16
Competitive Response to Anomalies   21
The Role of the Baldrige Award in the Shift   26
Small and Midsize Companies Seize the Challenge   27
The Stage of Replacement: A New Paradigm   28
Themes of the New Paradigm   29
Theme 1: Customer Value Strategy   29
Theme 2: Organizational Systems   30
Theme 3: Continuous Improvement   32
The Message of This Text   34
Concluding Comments   36
Summary of Key Points   37
Key Terms   38
Discussion Questions   38

Experiential Exercise   38
References   38

CHAPTER 2   **TQM and the Foundation of the Emerging Paradigm   40**

Chapter Outline   40
Chapter Overview   41
Introduction   41
The Concept of Quality   44
The Transcendent View of Quality   45
A Critique of the Transcendent View of Quality   45
The Evolution of Quality Approaches   46
The Inspection Era   47
The Statistical Quality Control Era   48
The Quality Assurance Era   55
The Strategic Quality Management Era   59
Total Quality Management   60
Strategy, Quality, and Customer Value   63
The Continuous Improvement Philosophy   66
The Total View of Quality   79
Beyond Total Quality Management   80
The Nature of the Paradigm Shift   82
Concluding Comments   83
Summary of Key Points   84
Key Terms   84
Discussion Questions   85
Experiential Exercise   85
References   85

CHAPTER 3   **Organizational Culture and Paradigm Shift   87**

Chapter Outline   87
Chapter Overview   88
Introduction   89
Toward a Culture Supporting the Emerging Paradigm   89
Key Principles   90
Culture and Organizational Purpose   96
The Rational View of Organizations   97
The Cultural View of Organizations   98
What Is Culture?   100
Culture Defined   101
A Holistic View of Culture   101
An Example of Culture Change for Control Theory   104
The Interrelatedness of Cultural Levels   111

Why Culture Emerges   112
Achieving External Adaptation   112
Achieving Internal Integration   113
How Culture Develops   114
The Role of Founders and Leaders   114
Mechanisms for Developing Culture   116
Cultural Development as a Learning Process   119
Shared Understandings   120
Culture as a Guide to Behavior   121
Group Nonconformity   122
Individual Nonconformity   123
Strong Culture and Nonconformity   124
Where to Begin Culture Change   124
Summary of Key Points   125
Key Terms   126
Discussion Questions   126
Experiential Exercises   126
References   127

CHAPTER   4   **Management Role Responsibilities   130**

Chapter Outline   130
Chapter Overview   131
The Importance of Managerial Roles   131
Role Responsibilities and Managerial Performance   133
Culture and Role Systems   134
A Managerial Role Responsibilities Framework   135
Traditional Management Roles   136
A Shift to a New Agenda for Continuous Improvement   138
Diversity of Role Accomplishments   139
A Framework Combining Types and Domains of Accomplishments   139
Types of Accomplishments for Continuous Improvement   141
Domains of Accomplishments for Superior Customer Value   145
Using the MAT Framework for Role Systems   153
Role Responsibility Differences   154
Depicting Managerial Role Responsibilities   154
Consequences of Gaps: Role System Inadequacy   160
The Nature of Managerial Role Responsibilities   162
The Key to Culture Change   166
Summary of Key Points   166
Key Terms   166
Discussion Questions   167
Experiential Exercise   167
References   167

CHAPTER 5   **Concepts of Customer Value   170**

Chapter Outline   170
Chapter Overview   171
Introduction   172
The Concept of Value   172
Monetary Value   172
Buyer Value   173
Customer Value   175
Customers Identified and Defined   178
Market Segmentation   178
Improving Match by Refinement of Market Segments   178
Who Uses the Product or Service?   180
A Broader Use Process   181
Customer Value as a Means/End Relationship   183
Concern for End Use   184
Product Attributes and Characteristics   185
Consequences as Benefits or Sacrifices   186
End States and Evaluative Criteria   186
Customer Value Processes   188
Realized Value versus Anticipated Value   188
Individual Valuation Process   189
Organizational Valuation   192
Abbreviated Attitude Formation   195
Abbreviated Valuation Processes   196
The Influence of Norms on Choice (Intention to Buy)   198
Purchase Behavior (Actual Buying)   199
Use Experience   200
Customer Value Strategy   201
Examples of Revitalized Demand   202
Implementing a Customer Value Strategy   203
Concluding Comments   203
Summary of Key Points   204
Key Terms   204
Discussion Questions   204
Experiential Exercise   205
References   205

CHAPTER 6   **Strategic Management and the Emerging Paradigm   209**

Chapter Outline   209
Chapter Overview   211
Introduction   211
The Growing Role of Strategic Management   211
Defining Strategy   213
Who Is Involved in Strategic Management?   215
The Emerging Paradigm and Strategic Management   215

Strategic Management of Customer Value   **216**
Defining the Business   **218**
Writing a Mission Statement   218
Vision Statement   220
Using Market Opportunity Analysis to Define the Business   221
Stakeholder Analysis   224
Corporate Values/Philosophy/Principles   226
External Analyses   **227**
Remote Environment Analysis   227
Industry Analysis   228
Competitor Analysis   230
Forecasting and Prioritizing the Opportunities and Threats   231
Internal Analysis   **232**
Performance Analysis   232
Function, Activity, and Process Analyses   233
Portfolio Analysis   235
Defining Key Problems and Strategic Issues   **235**
Root Problems versus Symptoms   235
Strategic Alternatives   **237**
Goals and Objectives   237
Long-Term Strategies   239
Competitive Strategy versus Cooperative Strategy   240
Evaluating Strategic Alternatives   241
Strategic Choice and Strategy Implementation   **241**
Annual Goals and Objectives   242
Action Plans and Policies   242
Leadership and Management   244
Systems and Structure   245
Organization Culture   246
Human Resource Management   246
Evaluation of Strategy Implementation   **247**
Summary of Key Points   **248**
Key Terms   **248**
Discussion Questions   **249**
Experiential Exercises   **249**
References   **250**

CHAPTER   7   **Measuring Customer Value**   **253**

Chapter Outline   **253**
Chapter Overview   **254**
Focusing on Customer Value   **254**
Customer Needs, Product Quality, Customer Value, or Satisfaction?   255
Customer Value and the Garbage Business   258
Service Quality at North American Phillips   259
A General Methodology for Learning about Customer Value   259

Techniques for Measuring Customer Value   263

Techniques for Measuring Consumer Value   263

Techniques for Measuring Commercial Customer Value   268

Principles of Measurement   270

Avoiding Value Measurement Errors   272

Using Customer Value Measures   273

Translating Learning into Strategy and Systems   273

Methods for Improving System Performance   275

Quality Function Deployment   276

Implementing the QFD Process   278

Improvement of Systems and Processes   281

Satisfaction and Dissatisfaction Measurement   282

Measures of Customer Satisfaction   282

The Dynamics of Value and Implications for Measurement   286

Refining Satisfaction and Dissatisfaction Measurement   287

Implications for Strategy   289

Summary of Key Points   291

Key Terms   291

Discussion Questions   291

Experiential Exercises   292

References   292

CHAPTER 8   **Organizing to Improve Systems   296**

Chapter Outline   296

Chapter Overview   297

Introduction   298

The System View   299

Aligned Subsystems of the Organization   301

Horizontal Work Flows to Serve Customers   302

Systems of Combined Horizontal and Vertical Flows   303

Key Elements of Systems   304

Hierarchical Management   307

Problems with Hierarchical Management   308

The Inadequacy of Hierarchical Teams   310

Growing Complexity   311

Building Horizontal Linkages to Patch the Hierarchy   313

Ad Hoc Teams   315

Committee Structure   317

Internal Customers   317

System Ownership   318

Matrix Management   319

Cross-Functional Systems Approach   320

Systems Focused on Products   325

Systems Focused on Customers   328

The Advantages of System Ownership   332

The Limitations of System Ownership Approaches   336
Beyond Structural Change   337
Summary of Key Points   338
Key Terms   338
Discussion Questions   339
Experiential Exercise   339
References   339

CHAPTER 9   **Variation: Interpreting its Meaning   342**

Chapter Outline   342
Chapter Overview   343
Introduction   343
Recognizing and Interpreting Variation   345
Key Ideas   345
Effects of Variation   348
Variation in Consumer Products   348
Variation in Consumer Services   349
Variation in Organizational Inputs   349
Variation in Future Conditions   350
Variation Produced inside the Organization   351
Theories for Interpreting the Meaning of Variation   352
Ignoring Variation   353
Imposing Arbitrary Standards   354
Overreacting to Variation   356
Shewhart's Theory and Method to Interpret Variation   357
Stable versus Unstable Variation   357
The Statistical Control Chart   358
Interpreting Control Charts   363
Constructing Control Charts   365
Use of the Information Contained in Variation   392
Other Tools for Analysis of Data   393
Remarks on the Use of Tools   397
Summary of Key Points   397
Key Terms   398
Discussion Questions   398
Experiential Exercises   399
References   399

CHAPTER 10   **Variation: Understanding Causes   401**

Chapter Outline   401
Chapter Overview   402
Introduction   402
Key Ideas   403
Variation Linked to Causes   404

Example: Product Quality   404
Example: Corporate Accounts Payable   412
Example: Sales Promotions   418
Interpreting Results   421
Treating Results Produced by Common Causes as if They Came from a Special Cause   422
Arbitrary Targets   423
Action on Special Causes   425
Interdependence of Organizational Results: A Hypothetical Factory   426
Evaluating Performance of Systems and People   432
Learning and Action for Improvement   435
Elements of a System for Organization-wide Improvement   435
Systematic Learning: PDSA   439
Summary of Key Points   441
Key Terms   441
Discussion Questions   442
Experiential Exercise   442
References   442

CHAPTER 11   **Strategic Linkage of Operations through Employee Involvement   444**

Chapter Outline   444
Chapter Overview   445
Introduction   445
Definition of Employee Involvement   447
Establishing Employee Involvement within a Strategic Context   447
Establishing the Context: Utilizing the MAT Framework   447
Improving Operational Proficiency   450
A "Pull" Model of Employee Involvement   451
The Organizational Forms of Employee Involvement   452
Mistakes to Be Avoided When Implementing Employee Involvement   466
Human Resource Implications of Employee Involvement   467
Summary of Key Points   471
Key Terms   472
Discussion Questions   472
Discussion Exercise   473
References   473

CHAPTER 12   **Cultural Change and Organizational Learning   476**

Chapter Outline   476
Chapter Overview   477
Introduction   477
TQM at Advanced Computer Technology: Journey into Cultural Change   478
Change and Organizational Culture   480
The Difficulty of Triggering Change   481

Cultural Change as a Paradigm Shift   482
Causing a Transformational Change   483
The Baldrige Award as a Trigger for Change   483
The Critical Path of Change   487
Frame-Breaking Change   489
Leverage Points for Driving Transformational Change   490
The Importance of Sensitivity to Cultural Impediments to Transformational Change   495
Assessing Organizational Culture   497
Who Should Do the Cultural Analysis   497
Data Gathering   498
Organizational Learning and Transformational Change   501
Espoused Theory and Theory in Use   503
Double Loop versus Single Loop Learning   503
Continuous Improvement Requires Continuous Learning   504
Conclusion   505
Summary of Key Points   505
Key Terms   506
Discussion Questions   506
Discussion Exercise   507
References   507

Case Studies   511

Federal Express: The Vision Made Real   511
IBM Rochester: The Seasons of Change   538
John Young: Hewlett-Packard's Champion of Change   575
St. Mary's Continuous Quality Improvement   596
Toyota, Part I: The Standardization of Culture   620
Toyota, Part II: Customer Satisfaction Measurement   642
Toyota, Part III: Toyota Production System and *Kaizen*   663
Toyota, Part IV: The Culture of Standardization   678
Xerox, Part I: Establishing the Vision   710
Xerox, Part II: Realizing the Vision   731
Xerox, Part III: Accomplishing Behavioral Change   754
**Xerox, Part IV: Xerox 2000: Putting It Together
                         "Building the New Xerox"   755**
Glossary   791
Indexes
Name and Company Index   799
Subject Index   805

Preface

When we started drafting *Beyond Total Quality Management: Toward the Emerging Paradigm,* some of our colleagues scoffed and asked us why we should bother to write a textbook for a market that does not yet exist. At that time, only a few business and engineering schools offered courses on Continuous Improvement or Total Quality Management (TQM). Many professors regarded these topics as passing fads (and some still do). Working closely with industry, however, we came to believe that the organizations of the future would need managers who have been educated on these topics. Today, our vision has been realized. Industry now demands that schools of business and engineering educate students on the continuous improvement of business processes and systems to provide superior customer value. As authors, we have anticipated our own customers' needs and have provided a means to meet those needs. This customer focus embodies one key principle in what we describe as a new, emerging paradigm for management.

We wrote this text for use in any class designed to prepare students for management in the coming decades. But because the philosophies and practices discussed in this book go well beyond the traditional rubric of management, this text will also be useful in marketing and industrial engineering courses which address the emerging quality paradigm as a natural part of their content coverage. One would be likely to find this text in courses ranging from "Contemporary Issues in Management" to "Strategy Formulation and Implementation." Some schools have created new courses on TQM or Continuous Improvement, while others have kept an existing course title but revamped the content to focus on the themes of this text. By whatever means, and by whatever label, almost all schools of business and engineering are incorporating the quality themes of this text into their curriculum. We hope that this text will be useful for years to come in helping you educate students on these important topics.

This text is suitable for use at both the undergraduate and graduate/ MBA level. While the concepts are challenging, undergraduates should find the book readable and accessible. In our classroom tests of the material, we have found that students enjoy the conceptual rigor because it gives them a taste of the challenge that real managers face every day. Through studying this text students will be better prepared for the demands they will encounter as managers in the future.

▶ THE EMERGING PARADIGM

In simple terms, a *managerial paradigm* can be defined as the way people think and act in conducting business. It provides rules and standards as well as accepted examples of managerial practice, laws, theories, applications, and instrumentation.

To educate the reader on the new, emerging paradigm, we have created an original framework of ideas that integrates various topics that were previously treated as separate issues. These topics include systems theory, strategic management, managerial roles, organizational culture, variation theory, marketing research and measurement, and quality improvement. We have attempted to exemplify this integrative framework with current, comprehensive case studies, but we have also addressed connections to existing theories of management. Our text is integrated by three themes of the emerging quality paradigm that are addressed in every chapter: customer value strategy, organizational systems, and continuous improvement.

Theme 1—*Customer Value Strategy:* Customer value is defined as a combination of benefits derived from using a product or service and the sacrifices required of the customer. The customer value strategy is the company's plan for offering value to customers, including product characteristics, attributes, mode of delivery, support services, and so on.

Theme 2—*Organizational Systems:* Organizational systems are the means that provide customer value. These systems cut across functional and departmental boundaries and broadly include material and human inputs, process technology, operating methods and work practices, streams of work activity, information flows, and decision making.

Theme 3—*Continuous Improvement:* To keep pace with the changes in the external environment, managers have to change the organization. Managers have always made improvements. However, with rates of change increasing in the external environment, managers must improve differently and at a greater rate than in the past. They must pursue continuous improvement, which is a constant striving to learn, change, and make things better. Such relentless change can help create the company's future through both radical and incremental improvements in products, processes, and systems.

▶ KEY MESSAGE OF THE TEXT

From this text students will learn that Total Quality Management, properly implemented, can never be just another program or a managerial style or a motivational gimmick for application at the lowest level of the organization. Rather, TQM should be a cultural transformation that is driven by the redefinition of managerial roles. The notion of paradigm shift implies a change of theory (or rationale) and action in the practice of management. This means that managers have to change the way they think about and do their work. It is not enough for them to be supportive of such change by their subordinates. They must change themselves. This managerial change cannot be accomplished by simply using quality tools and techniques. It requires a fundamental change in the values, beliefs, and assumptions about how business should be conducted.

▶ RATIONALE FOR THE TITLE: *Beyond Total Quality Management*

First, what is Total Quality Management? TQM is often used to refer to any collection of changes, techniques, and programs that managers choose to institute in the name of improvement. To somewhat more thoughtful managers, the word *total* conveys the idea that all employees, throughout every function and level of an organization, pursue quality. The word "quality" applies to every aspect of the organization. This begins with the strategic management process and (in the case of a manufacturing organization) extends through product design, manufacturing, marketing, finance, and so on. In short, TQM is as much about the quality process as it is about quality results or quality products.

Second, what does it mean to go *beyond* TQM? In a nutshell, it means that a paradigm shift is a more fundamental change than the programmatic approach often designated as TQM. We see TQM as a convenient label for the thoughts and practices currently being adopted that are different from traditional management. In the period of paradigm shifting, managers often use a label to signify that they are doing something different. Once the shift to the new paradigm is complete, the buzzword will no longer be needed. Managers will simply refer to these new ideas and practices as *management*. In the interim, it may be useful to think of TQM as simply an important milestone in an ongoing evolution of the field of management. Total Quality is a buzzword that marks the beginning of a new era in which managers will focus on customer value, cross-functional systems, and continuous improvement, the three themes of this text. Viewing TQM as another step in the evolution of management reminds us to continue seeking improvement, to go beyond current TQM theory and practice, rather than settling into another period of preserving the status quo.

▶ SIGNIFICANT FEATURES OF THIS TEXTBOOK

1—*Case Studies:* One of the most important features of the text is the inclusion of original, in-depth case studies. Each case is current and describes the managerial practices of a leading company that is shifting to the emerging paradigm as we approach the twenty-first century. The cases are diverse in their coverage of both service and manufacturing organizations. The service sector is represented by companies like Federal Express and St. Mary's Medical Center, while manufacturing companies like Toyota, Hewlett-Packard, and IBM Rochester are also featured. The cases are also diverse in their coverage of managerial issues. For example, the four-part Toyota case describes how they focus on customer satisfaction to guide improvements throughout their company's manufacturing and logistical systems. Meanwhile, the Federal Express case describes the managerial systems they have put in place to support their strategy for serving customers.

2—*Quality in Action:* Each conceptual chapter contains a special feature called *Quality in Action: A Message to the Student.* These twenty-two messages (one or two per chapter) were commissioned exclusively for this text and were written by recognized professional leaders in the quality movement such as Paul Allaire, Chairman and CEO of Xerox. These messages are intended to (1) inspire the student to learn about the concepts and techniques of management that will be an unavoidable part of managerial practice in the future, and (2) educate the student on the thoughts and practices of recognized leaders. *Quality in Action* gives students a unique chance to learn directly from the people who are building the foundations of the emerging paradigm—from Edwin Artzt, Chairman and CEO of Procter and Gamble, to Owen Bieber, President of United Auto Workers, to Curt Reimann, Director of the Malcolm Baldrige National Quality Award.

3—*Pedagogical Features:* The concepts presented throughout the text should be intellectually challenging, while also captivating for the student because of the real world flavor given by the examples and cases. Every chapter and case study contains questions and exercises that require the student to think critically about the material, for example, by analyzing the case studies using the models and principles presented in the chapters. Students are also asked to suggest what the company should do next, based upon the concepts and principles learned in other cases and chapters. The discussion questions and experiential exercises require the student to communicate analyses in both oral and written form. Other useful pedagogical features include chapter overviews, summaries of key points, lists of key terms, and an end-of-book glossary.

4—*Authorship:* Each author is both a practitioner and a theorist. This text was written by people who are actively engaged in helping public and private organizations (large and small) to integrate these philosophies and methods into everyday practice. In addition, we are all actively developing and publishing the theoretical basis for the emerging quality paradigm. While practitioners should find the text enlightening, students will find that the authors' practical experiences have provided the solid foundation of an accessible approach aimed at their special educational needs.

5—*Classroom Testing:* *Beyond Total Quality Management* was thoroughly classroom-tested. All four authors of this text have been teaching the principles of the emerging paradigm in both academic and industrial settings for years. Most of the chapters and cases were used repeatedly as reading material in graduate and undergraduate business classes at three universities. We actively engaged our customers, more than 300 students, in the product development process. They gave us invaluable feedback on our writing and on the pedagogical features of this text.

6—*Currency:* The rates of change in the field of management are increasing, which makes it important for this text to be current in its coverage. To make it as up-to-date as possible, we have drawn recent examples from the popular press and trade journals as well as from our own experiences with companies attempting to make the shift. The case studies were all written in the 1990s and describe the issues and approaches that are of vital importance in today's environment.

7—*International Focus:* This textbook includes extensive coverage of international issues. Chapter 1 is devoted entirely to the global competitive context. Many of the *Quality in Action* messages refer to international competition. For example, the message from Chairman and CEO Donald V. Fites of Caterpillar describes how global competition inspired culture change in the company. There are many examples within the chapters that allude to international competition. Most of the cases feature companies that operate globally and discuss numerous issues in international management. For example, the Xerox case explicitly addresses a "globally integrated supply chain."

8—*Ethical Foundations:* The text prescribes a value system that can guide managers in decision making. For example, improving the efficiency of resource utilization is a socially responsible thing to do in an era of dwindling resources and population explosion. The focus on customer value provides an important decision criterion for ethical decisions. The emphasis on teamwork and long-term investment leads managers not to abuse employees for short-term gains, and to avoid taking short-term gains at the expense of long-term prosperity and job security. In fact, the entire book emphasizes that managers must build systems that serve customers and thereby serve all stakeholders (internal and external to the organization) over the long term. What could be more appropriate as a guiding framework for ethical decision making and social responsibility?

9—*Instructor's Supplements:* We are pleased to offer adopters a complete Instructor's Manual for use with this text. The Instructor's Manual was prepared by Dr. Kim Melton of Virginia Commonwealth University, an experienced classroom instructor and professional consultant in the field of quality management. In addition to traditional teaching aids, the instructor's manual offers a tools and techniques supplement for instructors whose quality course has a more quantitative and technical orientation. Dr. Melton also provides instructors with numerous suggestions for connecting the concepts covered in the theory chapters with related real world applications in the case studies. Finally, the Instructor's Manual features a complete Test Bank which, true to the spirit of the emerging paradigm, contains questions that force students to think critically about the material they have learned and apply the theories and methods within a creative learning context. A computerized version of the Test Bank is also available to adopters.

10—*Customization:* The entire book is available on PRIMIS, McGraw-Hill's electronic custom publishing system. PRIMIS allows you to take selections from this text and combine them with a wide variety of articles, case studies, and other McGraw-Hill textbook chapters to create a unique text tailored to your specific classroom needs. For further information on this option, please contact your local McGraw-Hill sales representative.

▶ OVERVIEW OF CHAPTER CONTENT

Chapter 1 focuses on *Global Competitiveness* and gives readers an appreciation for the pervasiveness of change that organizations face and why a shift to the continuous improvement paradigm is important. It explains the popular but often misunderstood terms "paradigm" and "paradigm shift" and also summarizes the major contrasts between the new and old paradigms of management.

Chapter 2 discusses the *Foundations of TQM* and overviews the field of quality and continuous improvement to give the reader a historical perspective and basic understanding of popular terms and authors. A key feature of this chapter is the explanation of the term "Total Quality Managment."

Chapter 3 provides students with the foundations for *Understanding Organizational Culture* and describes the culture of organizations pursuing the new paradigm. It prepares the student for learning about the specific methods, tools, and approaches which accompany the core concepts of the new paradigm. The first section of the chapter elaborates on the "key principles" of the emerging paradigm.

Chapter 4 focuses on designing *Managerial Roles* and overviews the network of interrelated managerial roles and provides and integrative framework for role elaborations in the remainder of the textbook. It also sets the stage for Chapters 5 to 10, which emphasize that a customer-focused strategy should be the starting point for continuous improvement and the purpose that guides the design of managerial roles and responsibilities.

Chapter 5 examines *Customer Value Concepts* and defines customer value in terms of the combination of benefits enjoyed and sacrifices required of customers. It also explains how the concept of customer value compares to other notions of "value" such as Porter's ideas about the "value chain" and "buyer value."

Chapter 6 is devoted to *Strategic Management* and provides a model of the strategic management process that is based on customer value and that thrives on continuous improvement. This chapter also relates traditional concepts of strategy to a firm's customer value-based strategy and reviews some key managerial tools for strategic planning.

Chapter 7 highlights *Customer Value Measurement* and develops a model for measuring quality, customer value, and customer satisfaction. It reviews various marketing research methods for learning about what customers need and translating those requirements into products and processes. It also teaches the reader how to use survey and other measurement techniques to monitor a firm's success in providing value to customers.

Chapter 8 focuses on *Understanding and Improving Systems* and emphasizes the importance of integrating across functional and departmental boundaries to overcome hierarchical management and provide superior customer value. This chapter reviews the benefits and drawbacks of various approaches to managing and improving the systems of an organization.

Chapter 9 covers the key issues in *Interpreting the Meaning of Variation* and provides an introduction to concepts and methods that improve the manager's ability to understand variation and interpret the messages it contains about the causes that produce it.

Chapter 10 continues this discussion by providing students with a basis for *Understanding the Causes of Variation.* This chapter illustrates the complex cause and effect relationships that combine to produce organizational results. It also provides insight on how systems thinking and understanding of variation can improve managerial practice.

Finally, Chapters 11 and 12 address the transformation of an organization toward the emerging paradigm.

Chapter 11 stresses the importance *Employee Involvement* and discusses how to link strategy and operations through employee involvement.

Chapter 12 focuses on *Cultural Change and Organizational Learning* and discusses the concepts of transformational change and continuous learning that will be necessary for the new paradigm.

▶ ACKNOWLEDGMENTS

The help of many capable reviewers has made an immeasurable contribution to the book. We wish to acknowledge the contributions of the people who reviewed earlier drafts of our chapters and cases:

Paul Bobrowski, Syracuse University
Albert J. Cole, Senior Logistics Officer, Central Intelligence Agency
Stefanie Fenton, Quality Improvement Networks Manager, The Healthcare
    Forum
Stephen Haag, University of Minnesota—Duluth
Barbara Hastings, University of South Carolina—Spartanburg
Janelle Heineke, Boston University
Gary M. Kern, Indiana University—South Bend
David A. Lewis, University of Massachusetts—Lowell
Joe Sparks, Director of Continuous Process Improvement, Teledyne-Brown
    Engineering
Robert Stottle, President/Founder, Thermal Corporation
Mark Treleven, John Carroll University

We also appreciate the contributions of the industry leaders who were
gracious enough to contribute pieces for our "Quality in Action: A Message
to the Student" feature:

Paul A. Allaire, Chairman and CEO, Xerox Corporation
Edwin L. Artzt, Chairman and CEO, The Procter & Gamble Company
Thomas E. Bennett, President and CEO, Ingersoll-Dresser Pump Company
Owen F. Bieber, President, United Automobile Workers
James L. Broadhead, Chairman and CEO, Florida Power & Light Company
James M. Brogden, President, Master Industries
Fujio Cho, President and CEO, Toyota Motor Manufacturing, U.S.A., Inc.
Albert J. Cole, Senior Logistics Manager, Central Intelligence Agency
Donald V. Fites, Chairman and CEO, Caterpillar Inc.
Roger E. Handberg, Executive Vice President, Ceridian Corporation
Kenneth Iverson, Chairman and CEO, Nucor Corporation
Donald R. Keough, President and COO, The Coca-Cola Company
Robert J. Kohler, Vice President and General Manager, TRW Avionics &
    Surveillance Group
Tom Martin, Vice President, Marketing, Dell Computer Corporation
J.S. Mayo, President, AT&T Bell Labs
Roy Merrills, Chairman, Northern Telecom Inc.
Masaki Morita, Former Chairman, Sony Corporation of America
Sharon A. Ostby, Manager, Quality & Information Systems, Ceridian Cor-
    poration
Curt W. Reimann, Director, Malcolm Baldrige National Quality Award
Stephen B. Schwartz, Senior Vice President, IBM Market-Driven Quality
Thomas W. Sidlik, Vice President, Customer Satisfaction & Vehicle Quality,
    Chrysler Corporation
Ray Stata, Chairman and CEO, Analog Devices Inc.
Kenneth L. St. Cyr, Corporate Director, Apple Quality Management, Apple
    Computer Inc.

We are also grateful to the industry leaders who contributed epigraphs and discussion questions to this text:

Nolan D. Archibald, Chairman and CEO, The Black and Decker Corporation

Thomas F. Clarkson, Assistant Vice President, Quality Development, Allstate Insurance Company

Robert W. Coggin, Senior Vice President, Marketing, Delta Airlines

L. D. DeSimone, Chairman, Minnesota Mining & Manufacturing Company (3M)

Christopher B. Galvin, Senior Executive Vice President, Motorola Inc.

R. L. Heidke, Vice President and Director, Corporate Quality, Eastman Kodak Company

Michael J. McKenna, President, North American Division, Crown Cork and Seal Company

Alex Trotman, President and COO, Automotive Group, Ford Motor Company

We thank everyone at McGraw-Hill for their support and dedication to this textbook. We are particularly grateful for the efforts of the following people: Lynn Richardson, Josh Pincus, Becky Kohn, Joe Murphy, and Annette Mayeski.

We also thank the students who endured the earlier drafts of this text for the past four semesters. They gave us many helpful comments for improvement. We are particularly indebted to the following very special students: Chris Bolton, Zach Davidson, John Harmon, Gary Hunter, Pat Kruczek, Karl Manrodt, Anne Marie Ricardi, Jerry Williams, Tim Williams, and Sharon Yarbrough.

We thank all of those individuals of the College of Business Administration at the University of Tennessee who supported this project. In particular, we appreciate the support of Warren Neel, Dean of the College, and John Riblett, Director of the Management Development Center. Without their faith in us and constant goading, we may not have written this text. We are particularly thankful for Al Cole's many helpful questions and comments on our early drafts of many of these chapters and cases. We thank Larry A. Pace for contributing ideas in the early stages of preparing this textbook. We also thank Kim Melton for her invaluable contributions to this project and the ancillary package.

Finally, we acknowledge our families and friends for their patience and assistance. We dedicate this work to Greg's wife, Tuck, for her patience and love, and sons, buddy Matthew and partner Joseph; to Lyle's wife Joanne for her faithful support, and his children, Lyle Jr., Tracy, and Russell; to Mel's patient and loving daughter, Melody, and his parents for their prayers and support; to Judy Snow, Statistics Department secretary at the University of Tennessee, for her help and support, and to the memory of Gipsie's father, Raymond B. Bush—a businessman who understood the meaning of customer value; and finally, to our team's battle cry, WUDA!

Greg Bounds
Lyle Yorks
Mel Adams
Gipsie Ranney

Beyond Total Quality Management

Toward the Emerging Paradigm

chapter **1**

Global Competitiveness and the Emerging Paradigm

Both the theory and practice of Western management have created a drag on our forward motion. It is the principles of management that are in need of reform.

C. K. Prahalad and G. Hamel *

▶ CHAPTER OUTLINE

Chapter Overview

An Accepted Definition of Total Quality Management

Pervasive Change and Paradigm Shifts

The Nature of Paradigms and Paradigm Shifts
Stages of the Managerial Paradigm Shift

The Stage of Normalcy for Management

Traditional Management
The Diversions of the Cold War

The Stage of Anomalies for Management

Evidence of a Shift
Explanations for the Anomalies

---

* C. K. Prahalad and G. Hamel, "The Core Competence of the Corporation," *Harvard Business Review*, May–June 1990, p. 80.

Sources of Japanese Competitiveness
Competitive Response to Anomalies
The Role of the Baldrige Award in the Shift
Small and Midsize Companies Seize the Challenge

The Stage of Replacement: A New Paradigm

Themes of the New Paradigm
Theme 1: Customer Value Strategy
Theme 2: Organizational Systems
Theme 3: Continuous Improvement

The Message of This Text

Concluding Comments

Summary of Key Points

Key Terms

Discussion Questions

Experiential Exercise

References

► CHAPTER OVERVIEW

U.S. managers have enjoyed being part of the most productive and powerful economy in the world, but they have encountered intense global competition in the last few decades. While U.S. managers were enjoying a stage of normalcy, with business as usual, global competitors shifted to a different paradigm of management, a new framework for managerial thought and action. As a result, U.S. managers moved from a stage of normalcy to a stage of anomalies, where nothing seemed to work like it used to. Global competitors had rewritten the rules of the economic game. Competitors and customers now challenge U.S. managers to shift to a new paradigm or be left behind by these changes. This new paradigm is still emerging; however, its central idea is that *managers must think and act to improve organizational systems to provide superior customer value.*

► AN ACCEPTED DEFINITION OF TOTAL QUALITY MANAGEMENT

Total Quality Management (TQM) is a hot topic in business and academic circles.[1] Business managers are fervently trying to figure out how to do it,

---

1. According to Mary Walton (1990), the name "Total Quality Management" was first suggested by Nancy Warren, a behavioral scientist in the United States Navy.

An Exciting Time to Start a Career in Management

It was May 1946. After studying till 2 a.m. and dreaming his way through a brief night of sleep, John woke with thoughts of his new job, just one final exam away. He dashed across campus to his last collegiate class. He paused for a moment at the threshold of the hall. Momentarily overwhelmed by exuberance, anticipation, and adrenaline, John strained to suppress his emotions.

John's excitement stayed with him in the following weeks. He was lucky to be part of the postwar economic boom. Driven by unprecedented domestic and foreign demand, U.S. industrial organizations were growing exponentially. Like many other companies, John's new employer could sell virtually everything it produced. With a degree in management under his belt, John felt that his opportunities were boundless.

It is now May 1986. John wakes with arthritic pain knifing through his hips and knees. Having long abandoned his youthful exuberance, John bemoans the curses of old age, grumbling to the familiar figure in the mirror. On the verge of retiring as a respected corporate executive, John has achieved a comfortable prosperity for himself. But he is doubtful about his grandchildren's future. Although they enjoy a high standard of living compared to many in the world, their future holds daunting challenges. The U.S. companies in John's industry, like many others, face formidable foreign competition. His company withstood bankruptcy proceedings twice, and now enjoys only mediocre profits, primarily marketing foreign products under its own label.

A plaque on John's wall says, "Time will pass quickly, and stops for no one. You can make either good or bad of it." As John reads the plaque, he wonders how he and his generation of managers might have done better. Collectively, they have played a large part in the current economic environment: lost leadership in many markets, growing national debt, eroded national infrastructure, and slipping technological and educational status. Deep down, John knows that he and other managers should have done something differently, and that future managers will have to change their practices to avoid the failures he has witnessed. Managers of the next generation will have to shift to a new managerial approach more suitable to today's economic challenges. The approach being advocated in today's management circles is frequently referred to as Total Quality Management or, simply, Total Quality.

It is not too late for John's company to be transformed with an approach like Total Quality Management. In fact, there is a great deal of excitement among his managers and employees over the company's TQM efforts. Young recruits from business and engineering schools have offered the company a new and vigorous generation of managers who are educated on new concepts and methods of management. All employees are engaged in the improvement process. John's company is launching new products and services in burgeoning markets with improved organizational systems and methods of management. The results of growth in market share and profitability have not yet materialized, but everyone is optimistic. John's managers continue to learn about new methods of management and incorporate them as they evolve their managerial practices. The processes of change and learning are not easy, and the results are not guaranteed. After all, there are many other companies pursuing similar standards for excellence. Life as a manager in John's company is certainly challenging. It is indeed an exciting time to start a career in management.

while academicians are trying to determine what it is. None of them completely agree upon either the definition of TQM or how to put the concept into practice. This disagreement should be expected. First, TQM is an evolving concept that is changing as new concepts and methods are developed. Second, different organizations are in different stages of transforming to TQM. Third, different organizations may require different forms of TQM.

One notable exception to this pervasive disagreement over the concept of TQM is the definition offered by the participants in the Total Quality Forum, a consortium of business and academic leaders who come together annually to study TQM and disseminate their learnings. A study group of the 1992 Total Quality Forum defined *Total Quality* as:

. . . a people-focused management system that aims at continual increase in customer satisfaction at continually lower real cost. TQ is a total system approach (not a separate area or program), and an integral part of high-level strategy. It works horizontally across functions and departments, involving all employees, top to bottom, and extends backwards and forwards to include the supply chain and the customer chain. . . . [Rampey and Roberts, 1992]

Not everyone will agree with this definition, although it seems general enough to cover many variations of TQM. Some people refuse to even talk about TQM. For example, when asked about Total Quality Management, W. Edwards Deming, who is widely regarded as a leading "quality guru," responds that TQM is not in his vocabulary. "What is that?" he asks. Others who do talk about TQM may feel that this definition is not specific enough or that it leaves out important concepts.

Despite these reservations, the above definition is the most concise one available and agreeable to both business and academic leaders. It also separates the underlying principles from the tools and techniques that are often mistaken for the concept. This separation reveals an important insight into the reason that many managers fail to achieve their expectations with TQM.

The purpose of presenting this definition here is not to offer it as a framework for this text. Rather, it is simply to introduce the reader to the topic. This text is actually devoted to taking the reader beyond Total Quality Management.

We suggest that managers must go beyond Total Quality Management not because the above definition is deficient. Any definition of an evolving concept will be deficient at a fixed point in time. It is bound to be improved in the future. The purpose of going beyond Total Quality Management is to ensure that managers continue to learn about the themes, concepts, and methods that compose the new approach. They should continue to evolve their thinking about TQM as they attempt to implement it. Also, as the definition suggests, TQM should not be a separate area or program. It should be a way of life. The inclusion of the phrase "not a separate area or program" in the above definition should communicate to the reader that managers have a tendency to regard TQM as just another program and that they must be reminded not to do so. As soon as managers decide to "implement TQM," they are doomed to fail in transforming their organization.

For managers not currently practicing TQM or some other variant of this new approach as a way of life, a transformation is required to shift to new managerial practices. For this reason, we emphasize the importance of making the shift, which can be profound. Many people refer to this shift as a paradigm shift, a term that conveys the idea of profound transformation on a personal level and an organizational level. Within an organization, these changes can also be described as culture change. Paradigm shift is much broader than just the shift of isolated companies to a new culture. Paradigm shift involves the shift of the whole field of management. Managers who shift their organizations are participating in a broader phenomenon.

As you will see in the examples and case studies contained in this book, managers in different companies use different words to refer to the new ways of thinking and acting. Some managers use the term "Total Quality Management," and some do not. For example, IBM refers to Market-Driven Quality. For this reason, in our chapters we refer to the specific themes, concepts, and methods that make up the emerging paradigm, rather than refer to a general term like Total Quality Management. There is no consensus, and may never be, on what makes up the theory and practice of TQM. However, managers are beginning to realize the need for a paradigm shift.

We discuss below the stages of the paradigm shift and why it is important for managers to make this paradigm shift. We describe the nature of the emerging paradigm in terms of three themes: customer value strategy, cross-functional systems, and continuous improvement. These three themes are interwoven throughout every chapter of this text. The central idea is that *managers must think and act to improve organizational systems to provide superior customer value.* This managerial responsibility constitutes the core of the emerging paradigm. This chapter provides the basis for understanding the nature of the paradigm shift. The following chapter explains what it means to go beyond Total Quality Management.

► PERVASIVE CHANGE AND PARADIGM SHIFTS

Over time, managers have faced a growing intensity of global competition and pervasive change. The big three in the American automobile industry have lost market share to determined Japanese competitors like Toyota. Boeing and McDonnell Douglas have lost market share to their new European rival, Airbus. Relentless advances in technology open and close markets as products rapidly move through ever-shorter life cycles. In the mid-1980s, compact disk (CD) players replaced phonographic record players almost overnight, and advances in laser technology may soon replace CDs.

Better communications and logistical innovations have increased accessibility to even the remotest corners of the earth. As technological and economic development continues, the number of global competitors will continue to increase. Customers now expect more because competitors offer more.

Managers are realizing that traditional approaches to management are inadequate for keeping up with these changes. Traditional approaches simply do not provide managers with the means or the incentives to continuously make the required improvements. In an effort to do things differently, managers have tried implementing quality improvement programs. They have even tried to practice Total Quality Management. Many managers expected instant gratification from these efforts. Unfortunately, many of them have been disappointed.[2]

The reason for the disappointment with TQM is that managers often treat it as just another program to be implemented. Facilitators are assigned, training is offered, goals are set, and managers expect quick results. Implementing another program with a three-letter acronym is not the way to stay competitive. Rather, transformation is required. Traditional managers must think and act differently. The changes required of them are profound. Managers do not need another *program*, but another *paradigm*.

The Nature of Paradigms and Paradigm Shifts

The word "paradigm" is popular these days, but managers may fail to appreciate the power of the concept. The notion of "paradigm" and "paradigm shift" is one of the keys to managing change. Thomas Kuhn defined paradigm as the "universally recognized scientific achievements that for a time provide model problems and solutions to a community of practitioners" (1962). Although Kuhn applies the concept of paradigm to the development of science, the concept also applies to organizations and management.

Defining Paradigm and Paradigm Shift   For managers, *paradigm* consists of the organizational realities (such as values, beliefs, traditional practices, methods, tools, etc.) that members of a social group construct to integrate the thoughts and actions of its members. A paradigm provides rules and standards as well as accepted examples of managerial practice, laws, theories, applications, and instrumentation. To put it very simply, a *managerial paradigm* consists of the way people think and act in conducting business. Such a simple statement is memorable, but it may induce people to overlook other important points about paradigm and paradigm shift which are summarized below.

Kuhn argued that science does not progress through piecemeal accumulation, in which earlier knowledge and techniques provide a foundation for later elaborations. This approach would yield a constellation of observations, facts, laws, theories, and methods that would all be compatible. In fact, earlier scientific "truths" are not always permanent contributions. For example, Aristotelian dynamics or phlogistic chemistry are incompatible with the scientific views of today. However, old views are not unscientific simply because they have been discarded. Nor do they reflect human idiosyncrasy more than today's views. Current views are simply regarded as more valid or "truthful."

As science progresses, it shifts from one paradigm to another.[3] The

---

2. The difficulties many companies experience in implementing Total Quality were suggested in *Newsweek*, Sept. 7, 1992, pp. 48–49.
3. Classical examples of such scientific revolutions are seen in the work of Copernicus, Newton, Lavoisier, and Einstein.

same can be said of management. For example, in *The Machine That Changed the World*, James Womack alludes to the shift from production by craftsmen to mass production, and a more recent shift from mass production to lean production. Other shifts include Henry Ford's assembly line, and the time and motion studies of Frederick Taylor and Frank Galbraith.[4]

Although the work of Newton and Einstein used scientific method, their perceptions of the world, and consequently their ways of practicing science, differed dramatically. Similarly, managers who advocate mass production and those who advocate a lean production system like that of Toyota think and act differently. Their different practices, beliefs, values, and assumptions define their different paradigms.

Education and Paradigm Shifts   The education that prepares managers for professional practice reflects a particular management paradigm. It provides managers with beliefs about (1) the fundamental entities of business, (2) how these entities interact, (3) questions that should be asked, and (4) what techniques should be employed in seeking solutions. As managers shift from one paradigm to another, their beliefs will change and so will their actions. This shift may require reeducation about management thought and practice. For new managers just completing a management education, adopting the emerging paradigm described in this text may seem more natural, as they have fewer habits to break.

Stages of the Managerial Paradigm Shift
When many beliefs and actions change in concert within an organization, the transformation is referred to as a **paradigm shift**. We describe the nature of the shift toward the emerging paradigm beyond TQM in the last section of this chapter. First, we identify three stages to the scientific paradigm shift: normalcy (working within a paradigm), anomalies (events that contradict the paradigm), and replacement (changing the paradigm).

Normalcy   During the stage of **normalcy**, managerial practices are firmly based upon principles or truths that the management community believes in. Thought and action proceed as normal. Within a given paradigm, normal managerial practice represents a puzzle-solving activity, a cumulative endeavor wherein managers steadily extend the scope and precision of managerial knowledge. For example, in the traditional push system of production, managers developed computerized material requirements planning (MRP) systems to help them fulfill master schedule plans for production. The MRP was an advancement within the traditional mass production paradigm, which helped managers deal with intransigent problems of production scheduling and inventory control.

---

4. See Robert Reich's book *The Reindustrialization of America* for further review.

The Toyota Production System

The Toyota Production System is a revolutionary approach that has been adopted by many Japanese companies in the aftermath of the 1973 oil shock. The primary purpose of the Toyota Production System is to eliminate unnecessary elements in production to achieve cost reduction and satisfy consumer needs at the lowest possible cost. To achieve cost reduction, the system must achieve three **subgoals:**

1. Quantity control, which enables the system to adapt to daily and monthly fluctuations in demand in terms of quantities and variety.
2. Quality assurance, which assures that each process will supply only good units to subsequent processes.
3. Respect for humanity, which must be cultivated while the system utilizes human resources to attain its cost objectives.

There are several **key concepts** in the Toyota Production System:

1. Just-in-time manufacturing, which means to produce the kind of units needed, at the time needed, and in the quantities needed. Just-in-time eliminates unnecessary intermediate and finished product inventories, and allows Toyota to quickly adapt to demand changes.
2. Autonomation (*Jidoka*, in Japanese), which means autonomous defects control. Autonomation never allows defective units from a preceding process to flow into and disrupt a subsequent process, because automatic stopping devices are attached to the production machines.
3. Flexible workforce (*Shojinka*), which means varying the number of workers to accommodate demand changes.
4. Creative thinking or inventive ideas (*Soikufu*), which means capitalizing on worker suggestions.

The Toyota Production System establishes the following **subsystems and methods** (the means) to make these four concepts real and accomplish the goals listed above:

1. *Kanban* system, which is an information system that controls the production of the necessary products in the necessary quantities at the necessary time in every process of a factory and also between companies. *Kanban* cards ensure that a work process withdraws parts from the preceding process only as needed (a pull system), rather than allowing all processes to produce parts only according to a master schedule (a push system).
2. Production smoothing, which means a production line is no longer committed to the manufacture of a single type of product in vast lot sizes. Instead, a single line produces many varieties each day in response to varying customer demand. Production smoothing is achieved through both monthly and daily adaptation to demand changes.
3. Shortening of setup time, which reduces the overall production lead time across the entire process. Setup time is the amount of time needed to change a fixture on a machine and prepare the production line to produce a different model. For example, in 1970, Toyota succeeded in shortening the setup time of an 800-ton punch press to three minutes. Toyota has achieved one-touch setup, less than one minute, on many operations.
4. Standardization of operations, which minimizes the number of workers by balancing the operations on the line. It ensures that each operation requires the same cycle time to produce one unit of work. The worker follows a standard operations routine and maintains a standard quantity of work-in-process inventory.
5. Machine layout and the multifunction worker, which allows for a flexible workforce. The range of jobs for which each worker is responsible can be widened or narrowed very easily by laying out machines in a U-shaped line, ensuring that workers are well trained and versatile through job rotation, and continuously evaluating and revising standard operations routines.
6. Improvement activities, which are aimed at reducing costs, improving productivity, reducing the workforce, and improving employee morale. Improvements are accomplished through small groups and suggestion systems.
7. Visual control system, which monitors the state of the line and the flow of production. Foolproof systems, for example, a light or some other type of signal, indicate an abnormality in production. Other visual controls include the standard operations sheets, *Kanban* cards, digital display panels, and storage and stock plates.
8. Company-wide quality control, which promotes improvement in all departments, so the actions of one department are reinforced by other departments. Special boards of department directors meet to ensure that communication and cooperation occur and to address company-wide problems (Monden, 1983).

Anomalies During the stage of **anomalies**, unexpected events challenge management's assumptions about business. Normal conditions are disrupted. The facts violate the accepted paradigm, as when a company's traditional approach to product development creates a product that flops in the marketplace. People often overlook anomalies that threaten to subvert the accepted paradigm. However, anomalies cannot be ignored forever, particularly if a conventional solution using known rules and procedures does not solve a problem that it has previously remedied. For example, a manager may find that cost cutting fails to reverse declining profitability or a new sales promotion fails to regain market share. Some industries have experienced the challenges of global competition earlier than others. For example, companies in the automobile, consumer electronics, and microchip industries suffered declining profitability and lost market share. If anomalies persist and are further analyzed, managers may come to regard the accepted paradigm as inadequate and begin to look for a new one.

Replacement Companies either move from the stage of anomalies to replacement of the management paradigm, or they suffer the economic consequences. During the stage of **replacement**, new theories, principles, and practices replace the old ones. Managers achieve a new consensus on the fundamentals of business and management, the questions that should be asked, and the techniques that should be employed in seeking solutions. Replacement does not mean all elements of the past paradigm are invalid, but they are at least reconfigured. For the new paradigm to be accepted, it must seem better than alternative paradigms at explaining business phenomena and resolving problems. Replacement with a new paradigm implies dramatic change, but over time a new paradigm comes to be taken for granted and shared among managers. This initiates a new sequence of stages for a subsequent paradigm shift.

The remainder of the chapter elaborates on each of the three stages for the managerial paradigm shift described in this text. The purpose of this discussion is to help the reader appreciate the context for the emerging paradigm which is described in subsequent chapters. Specifically, managers in the 1990s are in the midst of a paradigm shift. It is taking place all around them. Those managers who intend to be global competitors will have to participate in the shift. If they choose not to participate, they will be left behind by those who do. By understanding the context of the paradigm shift, managers will be better equipped to transform their organizations and shift to the emerging paradigm.

▶ THE STAGE OF NORMALCY FOR MANAGEMENT

In the stage of normalcy, managers think and act in ways considered traditional and acceptable. Expectations are clear, rules are known, and results are predictable. First, we will look at the most recent period of normalcy for U.S. managers. Then, we will suggest how managers failed to attend to global economic changes that led to the stage of anomalies.

Traditional Management

Twentieth-century management in the United States has been strongly influenced by Taylor's scientific management and Weber's theory of bureaucracy. These approaches have led managers to work within functional hierarchies, with their responsibilities divided according to specialized activities, such as accounting, marketing, engineering, and manufacturing. Economic principles for competing in well-defined markets emphasized economies of scale, efficiencies, mass production, and technological innovation.

While there had been competition, competitors often played according to a "live and let live" strategy. Because monopolies were precluded by law, companies had little incentive to completely drive competitors from the marketplace. For example, relative market share among the big three automobile makers was stable for many years. As long as Ford made no major move, General Motors and Chrysler were content to conduct business as usual. And they all made a lot of money. Despite the publicity of the "cola wars," a similar situation seems to exist with Pepsi and Coke.

Even when new product technologies created new markets, such as plastics in the 1950s, management practices changed very little. Managers set goals for productivity, efficiency, and profitability, using management by objectives (MBO) to link strategy and operations through the hierarchy. Managers motivated employees to fulfill those goals by inducements such as profit sharing, stock options, and bonuses, or other rewards such as job enrichment or participative management. However, the job of management remained much the same: set goals, define roles, provide technologies, and motivate employees. Accounting, marketing, engineering, and manufacturing practices also did not change. Occasionally, new techniques were introduced within the traditional functions, such as quality control in manufacturing. But such changes went largely unnoticed by the rest of the organization.

No one challenged this approach to management as long as it served society well. While managers in other countries were rewriting the rules of business practice and management, U.S. managers continued in the stage of normalcy. The United States, and western society in general, was focused on another agenda: the cold war.

The Diversions of the Cold War

As an economic superpower, the United States could channel vast resources into the cold war, a four-decade effort to stem the tide of communism. No leader better epitomized the resolve of the United States to resist and defeat communism than President Ronald Reagan. One of his

1984 campaign ads best summarized the rationale for expending vast resources on military deterrence and preparation for battle:

> There is a bear in the woods. For some people, the bear is easy to see. Others don't see it at all. Some people say the bear is tame. Others say it is vicious and dangerous. Since no one can really be sure who's right, isn't it smart to be as strong as the bear—if there is a bear.

The logic was compelling and played to people's fears. The perceived threat was not unfounded. However, with the dawning of the 1990s, the bear suddenly disappeared. The Berlin Wall fell, East and West Germany united, democracy and capitalism arrived in Eastern Europe, the Warsaw Pact was abrogated, the Soviet Union dissolved, and communism ended in Europe, its birthplace. Democracy and capitalism had won (Thurow, 1992). The cold war was over, but at what price to the victor?

The United States stands alone as the only military superpower in the early 1990s. However, during the decades that the U.S. was preoccupied with winning the cold war, Germany and Japan were emerging as the new economic superpowers. The world gradually shifted from being a single polar economic world revolving around the United States, to a tripolar world anchored in the United States, Japan, and the European Community.

Certainly, the U.S. was not oblivious to these economic developments; they were the results of programs designed to help war-torn and undeveloped countries catch up with the United States.[5] The assumption, largely proven true, was that economic prosperity fosters democracy and, hence, world security. However, while others were catching up, the United States neglected its own economic development that would ensure it remained a superpower in the new economic order. The cold war diverted the United States from its own development in two ways: the diversion of monetary investments and the diversion of attention from the changing rules of the game.

Diversion of Money The United States has discovered it is difficult to remain both a military superpower and an economic superpower, especially when others concentrate on being just an economic superpower. Japan and Germany were constitutionally restricted from massive military buildups, while the United States channeled vast resources into the military. Unfortunately, while military spending did prop up the U.S. economy and produced some marketable R&D (research and development) inventions, military spending alone cannot guarantee long-term global competitiveness for U.S. firms.

---

5. These programs include the Marshall Plan and the post-World War II rules governing international economic competition, the GATT (General Agreement on Tariffs and Trade)–Bretton Woods system.

Diversion of Attention The rules of the economic game have changed, and much of the United States has not kept pace. The new economic superpowers continue to create new and different strategies. In the century to come, the United States will be just one among other superpowers engaged in an economic competition with rules increasingly written by others.

In many industries, new process technologies have become relatively more important than new product technologies. Industries of the future will increasingly rely on brainpower rather than endowments of natural resources and capital. In the last two decades, U.S. managers started to see some of the effects of these changing global conditions. We have gradually entered the stage of anomalies: old approaches to management do not seem to work and old ways of thinking no longer explain what is happening in dynamic world markets.

▼

QUALITY IN ACTION: A MESSAGE TO THE STUDENT
Donald V. Fites, Chairman and Chief Executive Officer, Caterpillar Inc.

Caterpillar Inc. has been a leading producer of construction machines and engines since it was formed in 1925. Threatened in the 1980s by determined competitors like Komatsu of Japan, Caterpillar seemed in danger of permanently losing its reputation as a global market leader. Caterpillar Chairman and Chief Executive Officer Donald V. Fites reveals how such a challenge can inspire a cultural shift.

Back in the good old days, it used to be enough to define quality in terms of zero defects on the assembly line. All we had to do was keep our "quality" products coming, because people would always buy them. Most of the time, we couldn't build them fast enough. But as the years passed, we began to lose our sense of urgency about quality. We assumed that we were still light-years ahead of the competition, that we were still improving quality at an acceptable rate, and that we were consistently satisfying customers' value expectations.

When the 1980s hit, we were jolted out of our complacency. After fifty years of growth and prosperity, the bottom dropped out of our markets. Suddenly, our customers weren't buying our products like they used to. And to make matters worse, we had a whole host of new, aggressive non-U.S. competitors to contend with—most with an obsession for quality.

This was, of course, a major impetus for change. For the balance of the 1980s and on into the 1990s, we began making changes throughout the organization to improve quality, lower costs, and provide better customer value. We modernized our facilities worldwide, we began a new product introduction process that's cutting development time by more than half, and we reorganized our old functional corporate structure from the ground up to make it more competitive in a global marketplace. Driving all these changes has been a new appreciation for continuous quality improvement, which has permeated every aspect of our culture and operations. Now, everything we do reflects our customers' definition of what quality means—to encompass design, performance, and after-sale service and support.

We're proud to say that our attention to total quality has kept us in a global leadership position. Now that the world is becoming a borderless economy, continuous quality improvement—no matter what the label—is an absolute necessity for survival.

▲

▶ THE STAGE OF ANOMALIES FOR MANAGEMENT

Over the last four decades, there has clearly been a shift from producer power, with less competition, to consumer power, with increased global competition that offers consumers more choices (Case, 1989). How has this shift from producer power to consumer power happened?

Evidence of a Shift

Once dominated by the United States, the global economy is increasingly led by another force, Japan.[6] The trade deficit initially went negative for the United States, with imports exceeding exports, in 1971. This means that Americans are buying more goods from abroad than they are able to sell there, which is an indicator of global competitiveness. Since 1976, the trade deficit has remained negative.[7] In fact, it grew from $22 billion in 1980 to a peak of nearly $160 billion in 1987.

Although the trade deficit has shrunk some in recent years, the United States has already lost industrial leadership in many areas, as reflected by market share trends. The worldwide market share held by United States firms in a number of industries has fallen precipitously. Market share losses have occurred in autos, machine tools, textiles, steel, shoes, and consumer electronics. Even more alarming are the declines in high-technology industries, the seed industries of future commercial markets, such as customizable chips, DRAMs (Dynamic Random-Access Memory chips), floppy disks, and hard disks. Furthermore, by the end of the 1980s, the United States led in just ten of the twenty-two technologies the Pentagon considered vital to U.S. security. While holding its own in four, the United States lagged in eight of the twenty-two technologies. These eight are biotechnology, gallium arsenide semiconductors, high-power microwaves,

---

6. Public recognition of this change has been documented in the United States, for example, in *The Wall Street Journal*, Jan. 19, 1990, p. 1.
7. For updates, see the *International Trade Statistics Yearbook*, published by the United Nations.

integrated optics, machine intelligence and robotics, microchips, pulsed power, and superconductors (*Fortune*, Jan. 1, 1990).

Market share trends for products may show an incomplete picture of the erosion of the U.S. manufacturing base. Many U.S. manufacturers are becoming hollow corporations that sell products manufactured elsewhere under a U.S. label. Companies like General Electric, Zenith, and many others in the electronics industry have suffered significant erosion in manufacturing. Even the big three automobile producers are increasingly selling cars made by non-U.S. based companies, and many models assembled in the United States have a high proportion of foreign-made parts. The aerospace industry may soon confront the same challenges faced by the automobile industry in the 1980s. In fact, Boeing's new 777 will contain a high percentage of parts made in Japan and elsewhere.

Some managers suggest the apparent "hollowing out" simply reflects a benign trend toward globalization. Others believe that it represents a natural progression away from manufacturing toward a service-based economy. However, hollowing out may reflect a shift in relative managerial capability among global competitors and the survival of the fittest in an unforgiving process of industrial Darwinism.

Having abandoned markets that may be costly to recapture, the United States faces daunting challenges in the 1990s. Foreign firms have raised the level of competition in U.S. markets by establishing beachheads, a market position gained as a secure starting point for further growth. U.S. firms have fallen behind in research and development and capital spending, which are necessary to ensure a flow of new products, processes, and capabilities needed to remain competitive. These are symptoms of a problem that may cause U.S. competitiveness to decline even further. How did this happen?

Explanations for the Anomalies

One explanation attributes diminished competitiveness to factors outside the organizations themselves, as *normal responses to the macroeconomic climate.* Another explanation says the U.S. decline is due to *poor management.*

Normal Responses to the Macroeconomic Climate   The difficulties U.S. industry is experiencing may be normal responses to the macroeconomic climate. Businesses experienced external shocks like the energy crisis and higher fuel prices, and the maturation of older "sunset" industries. Transition to a "postindustrial" service-dominated economy added to the shocks. Federal debt, high interest rates, inflation, and an overvalued dollar have created a miserable macroeconomic climate. Other policies make the situation worse, including tax incentives that favor consumption and borrowing over saving and investing, and residential construction over industrial modernization; and trade and industrial policies that hinder coherent responses to countries that target specific industries for development.

Since the decline in U.S. market share in the early to mid-1980s coincided with the rise in the value of the dollar, it is tempting to attribute lost market share to the rising dollar. After all, the increased purchasing power that comes with a rising dollar stimulates domestic consumption and increased demand for imports. When the dollar is higher, prices of foreign goods and services seem more attractive.

If we believe that the rising dollar caused U.S. producers to lose market share, we could argue that there is nothing really wrong with U.S. competitiveness, and that we simply need to get the dollar back down. But this argument assumes that consumer decisions are made purely on the basis of price, and that other factors like quality and customer value are either equal across product alternatives or irrelevant.

Empirical evidence doesn't support the argument. For example, during the 1970s, the dollar declined greatly against the yen.[8] However, U.S. market share did not correspondingly rise. More recently, from about 1985 to 1990, the drop in the dollar again failed to produce any significant reversal of market share trends, although some companies were helped.

In the mid- to late 1980s, the United States compelled the Japanese to help devalue the dollar against the yen, but Japanese companies took steps to overcome the unfavorable yen/dollar exchange. They dramatically increased market share, despite the growing strength of the yen. You might expect that in order to do so the Japanese would have to cut prices and, therefore, raise wages by less than the productivity growth. However, the opposite was true. Wages rose along with market shares, as the Japanese continued to improve efficiency and quality. Monetary exchange rates are important to a firm's competitiveness, but they do not fully determine it.

Some industry observers believe that U.S. firms need progressively cheaper labor costs to hold onto markets because of their declining lead in technology and a growing notoriety for inferior product quality (Krugman and Hatsopoulos, 1987). However, the cheapening of U.S. goods and the fall of the dollar simply will not reverse the unfavorable trends in the trade balance and market share, particularly where high-technology products and processes are involved and high quality is demanded. The continued success of Japanese firms in the face of unfavorable exchange rates shows us the weakness of relying exclusively on a devalued dollar. Again, monetary exchange rates are important, but there are other factors to be considered. Managers of U.S. firms must learn to compete on another basis.

Poor Management Another school of thought acknowledges the need to correct obvious inconsistencies and imbalances in macroeconomic and industrial policies, but argues that these measures alone will not restore U.S. competitiveness. U.S. firms must improve the value of their products

---

8. For data, see the U. S. Bureau of Labor Statistics, *International Comparisons of Manufacturing Productivity and Labor Cost Trends*, 1985.

and services to attract more domestic and overseas customers. According to this school, the United States has lost its competitiveness because of an internal factor: poor management (Hayes, Wheelwright & Clark, 1988). It is believed that good management is required at both the micro and macro levels of the economy, and that management at these two levels should be mutually supportive.

Saying that the U.S. industrial decline is due to poor management does not mean that it was inherently poor, but poor relative to the competition. At one point, U.S. business practices were adequate, when there was less challenging competition. What made them poor was that global competitors started doing better.

Head-to-Head Competition   From a macroeconomic point of view, the competitive battle could be seen as one between countries, and their industrial and economic policies. Lester Thurow (1992) describes it as "head-to-head" competition, wherein various countries or regions with relatively equal levels of technology and economic development compete to dominate the same high-wage industries. In fact, officials in all three economic superpowers often speak of their competition in these terms. Ask managers in Japan, Germany, and the United States to name the industries that will be vital to a high standard of living in the future, and they offer remarkably similar lists: microelectronics, biotechnology, the new materials-science industries, telecommunications, civilian aviation, robotics and machine tools, and computers and software (Nomura Research Institute of America, 1990).

The stage of anomalies for U.S. management has arisen because global competitors, particularly the Japanese, are playing according to a different set of rules. To understand how relatively poor management in this head-to-head competition caused the anomalies that U.S. firms have experienced, we have to examine the practices of these global competitors.

Sources of Japanese Competitiveness

At first glance, it might appear that Japanese business success results from a work ethic. Japanese white-collar workers are notorious for working six-day weeks and sixteen-hour days. The work ethic certainly thrives, but the Japanese also manage by a different set of rules. A three-year study of nearly 1,500 large manufacturers in western Europe, North America, and Japan led researchers to conclude:

> . . . in America and Europe, almost regardless of the competitive priorities set for the company, the manufacturing managers continue to be under direct and short-term pressure to perform well on costs. The Japanese, on the other hand, seem to consider that costs will be reduced in the long term if they concentrate on quality improvement, process technology, and finding qualified supervisors and

Europe Pulls Together

The formation of the European Economic Community has removed impediments to trade among its members, and promises to stimulate broader economic growth. Eastern European countries, such as the Czech Republic, Slovakia, Hungary, Poland, and even the nations of the former Soviet Union, are abandoning centrally planned economic systems in favor of deregulated, market-based, competitive economies. These formerly communist countries certainly have a long way to go to catch up with even western standards for quality and customer value (Forker, 1991). However, their potential should not be ignored. One day, these countries may also join the EEC. If the EEC continues to expand, it could create a European economy more than twice as large as those of Japan and the United States combined.

Companies outside the EEC have expanded investments in the region to maximize their "insider" status.

Such investments strengthen the EEC's global competitiveness. The EEC's *local content rule* requires its companies to acquire 40 percent of their parts and components from EEC companies or pay a *dumping tax* on all parts imported for assembly. This dissuades investors from setting up assembly shops fed by the free flow of imported parts, which would not be much different from importing the product in the first place. To encourage the transfer of technology to Europe's semiconductor industry, and to provide better-paying, high-skilled jobs for its workers, the EEC imposes a high tariff on imported silicon wafers not produced within the EEC (*Tokyo Business Today*, April 1989).

In the future, U.S. companies will face technologically capable European firms that are supported with the macroeconomic policies, infrastructure, and labor force skills needed to be more competitive.

workers to run their operations. This interpretation suggests that the time frames and indeed the basic paradigms for strategic planning and action in Japan and in the West are substantially different. . . . [Ferdows, Miller, Nakane, and Vollmann, 1987, p. 12]

These researchers further observe that the Japanese firms aim at a predetermined sequence of priorities in manufacturing:

1. High quality
2. Delivery reliability
3. Lower production costs
4. Increased production flexibility

Many Japanese firms have passed the first two stages and now are focusing on stages three and four. To achieve leadership in flexible manufacturing, a firm must develop technologies in-house as well as assimilate technology from outside suppliers, and must make quantum breakthroughs as well as incremental improvements. The Japanese have been better at in-house incremental improvements than scientific and technological breakthroughs. By contrast, American firms tend to rely on quantum breakthroughs and overlook opportunities to simplify processes and systems through incremental improvements. Americans tend to build sophisticated information systems to conform to already overly complicated production systems (Ferdows et al., 1987).

This research suggests Japanese managers enact a different paradigm than U.S. managers, with macroeconomic factors to support it. In other words, at the microeconomic level, within organizations, the Japanese are continuing to refine managerial approaches that optimally fit with macroeconomic strategies. The Japanese integrate technology and economic planning through a number of institutional mechanisms, including technology strategies, collective industrial strategies through *keiretsu* industrial groupings, governmental agencies such as the Ministry of International Trade and Industry (MITI), and professional organizations such as the Japanese Union of Scientists and Engineers (JUSE). Let's look at each.

Technology Strategies   The Japanese improve technology through investments to upgrade manufacturing facilities, and improve quality because of severe interfirm competition, short product life cycles, and fast obsolescence of facilities. The development of technological skills emphasizes engineering, innovation, and technology assimilation. A world technology scanning system, technology-oriented information systems, and networking arrangements are widely used.

The Japanese are famous for taking products invented elsewhere and producing them better and cheaper than anyone else through process improvements. For example, in the past two decades the Japanese have taken control of the markets for three leading new products: the video camera/recorder and the fax, both invented by Americans, and the CD player, invented by the Dutch.

They were able to do so because they devote two-thirds of their research and development expenditures to new process technologies. With continuous improvements by a knowledgeable and skilled work force, they produce the product better and cheaper, taking the market away from the inventor. American firms do just the opposite: they spend more on new product technologies, hoping to get monopoly power to set higher prices and earn higher profits on a new product.[9] As low-cost, high-quality competitors enter the market, the American firms abandon the market in pursuit of new product markets (Thurow, 1992).

Japanese government organizations monitor, forecast, analyze, plan, and coordinate strategic industrial development. They encourage technology development and innovation, as well as the design and engineering that translates basic innovations into marketable products. They even administer a national examination system for engineering consultants. A number of factors interact to contribute to a national technology-oriented climate, including a commitment to science, a high value on quality, and willingness to take risks (Bowander and Miyake, 1990). These technology strategies are supported by collective industrial strategies organized

---

9. While Japanese versus U.S. total R&D expenditures may be comparable, the R&D numbers do not reflect a competitive situation as good as it may look. The Japanese government invests primarily in civilian production first and military second. By contrast, the U.S. invests in military first.

through *keiretsu* groupings of companies throughout all major Japanese industries.

Keiretsu Industrial Groupings In support of these practices, groups of Japanese firms, known as *keiretsu*, are financially interlocked and work together to strengthen each other (Yoshida, 1992). There are two types of *keiretsu* in Japan, vertical and horizontal. A *vertical keiretsu* typically consists of a large manufacturing company, such as Toyota, Nissan, Hitachi, or Toshiba, and many of its suppliers, producers, distributors, and retailers which work together in a cooperative group. This provides the basis for stable relationships with mutual benefits to all companies in the group. Suppliers continuously improve with management methods and technologies provided by the parent company, and the parent gets better quality, reduced costs, and just-in-time deliveries.

A *horizontal keiretsu* involves a main bank, an insurance company, a trust banking company, a trading company, and a few dozen large manufacturing companies under which small manufacturing companies are grouped. The member companies remain independent, but they share information and financial risk. For example, when the Mitsubishi *keiretsu* launches a new large-scale enterprise, such as Space Communication Corp., the group's satellite services venture, all twenty-eight group members invest their capital. While each individual company's risk is minimal, as a group they have tremendous resources to take swift, bold, and decisive action.

Similar collective strategies exist in Germany. For example, the Deutsche Bank group intervened on behalf of the German economy to buy up shares of Mercedes-Benz when Arab investors threatened to take it over. This type of intervention frees managers from emphasis on quarterly profits and concerns over short-term performance in the stock market. Bank ownership helps firms plan corporate strategies and helps them raise the money to carry out these strategies to enhance the company's long-term prospects.

Government Cooperation and Leadership In Japan, government and industry cooperate to achieve desired societal objectives. For example, the Ministry of International Trade and Industry coordinates *keiretsu* groups through industrial policy to benefit all Japanese. When Fifth Generation Computer was developed, MITI included within it electronics firms from all six of the *keiretsu* groups, so the results of their cooperative research would be broadly disseminated. As a result, individual consumers and workers get both stability in employment and improved products.

MITI officials also maintain close relationships with the major industrial trade and business associations, such as the Electronics Industries Association of Japan and the Japan Chamber of Commerce and Industry. These relationships offer two-way communication. Complaints, suggestions, proposals, and other grassroots actions can be easily communicated to MITI, and MITI can communicate its societal objectives to companies throughout Japanese industries (Yoshida, 1992).

Global Cooperation   Despite U.S. objections, the two biggest business groups in the world (the Mitsubishi and the Deutsche Bank groups) met in March 1990 in Singapore to talk about a global alliance. Among other topics, they discussed their interest in expanding their market share in civilian aircraft production and further breaking the American monopoly. This meeting portends an ominous future for American free trade principles and American companies. For example, McDonnell Douglas's market share has been cut in half, down from 30 to 15 percent, since Airbus entered the market sponsored by the British, French, German, and Spanish governments. In 1990, Boeing's share dropped below 50 percent for the first time in decades (Thurow, 1992).

Response to Pressure   The Japanese respond to internal and external pressures to minimize the effects of any constraints. Japanese problems include high population density, low natural resource endowments, high imported dependence on energy, shortage of skilled personnel, and isolation from other countries. They respond by pursuing micro-miniaturization, resource conservation, space conservation, high-density living, intense communication links, high levels of teamwork, high productivity, innovative skills, and information access through continuous scanning of world technological advances. The result of these practices in business is rapid technological growth and high industrial competitiveness (Bowander and Miyake, 1990).

The Japanese ability to compete under duress was never more evident than during the *endaka* (high yen/low dollar) crisis of the mid-1980s. The United States needed help to lower the value of the dollar and reduce its trade deficit by lowering the relative cost of U.S. exports. Conversely, a powerful yen would induce Japan to import more, curb its exports, and reduce its trade surplus. Japan went along with the plan, but not only did the plan fail, it seemed to backfire. The Japanese yen doubled in value, along with Japanese real estate and all other yen-based assets. Yet exports continued to grow, because the Japanese cut costs, upgraded facilities, and streamlined management. The steel industry illustrates the effect.

Because it exported more than 30 percent of its output, the Japanese steel industry was vulnerable to a high yen. Its relative costs increase dramatically with the value of the yen. As a result, during this time, the net customer value of Japanese steel and its global competitiveness were reduced to almost nothing, despite its reputation for high quality. The country's five largest blast furnace operators posted operating losses of 400 billion yen in 1986. Nippon Steel declared war on its fixed costs and publicly vowed to slash them by 1 trillion yen, or 30 percent, by 1990. They closed blast furnaces, slashed wage rolls, consolidated production centers, and expanded multipurpose units. By the end of fiscal 1987,

Nippon achieved 40 percent of the planned reduction, and one year later, the figure was 60 percent. The improvements continued. Domestic demand started to pick up, Japanese steel exports were reduced, and global prices soared. Japanese steelmakers soon recovered their ability to be price leaders, and they are now much more able to weather the market cycles because their costs have been reduced (*Tokyo Business Today*, March 1989).

Competitive Response to Anomalies

How should U.S. managers respond to business anomalies such as lost market share, diminished profitability, and the failure of strategies that used to work? A glib answer is that they should take a proactive stance to do whatever is necessary to ensure the survival and prosperity of their organizations. Sometimes the response just takes the form of "Japan bashing." For example, concerns over an American backlash against the Japanese success in capturing 30 percent of the U.S. car market have led Toyota to drop its "Global 10" promotional campaign among dealers. The goal was to grab 10 percent of the world car market. By dropping the campaign publicly, Toyota seems less like a steamroller, but it remains relentless in its dedication to the pursuit of perfection (*Business Week*, "Japan's Sharp Turn," Mar. 2, 1992, p. 32). Competitors must respond to remain in the race.

Too often, however, the answer "whatever necessary" translates into protectionism. Indeed, many managers prescribe U.S. protectionism as an appropriate response to what they perceive to be unfair practices by others. For example, U.S. managers often regard a collective strategy like *keiretsu* as "closed" systems, unfair and even illegal, in violation of antitrust and banking laws. U.S. laws do not permit banks to own industrial firms, and prevent industrial firms from jointly planning business strategies behind closed doors.

U.S. officials have often attempted to negotiate with the Japanese to "level the playing field" and change the closed system to get the Japanese to comply with the principles of free trade and free competition. Such attempts imply that the Japanese closed system is old and unfair, and must be replaced by the new and fair American system. Many Americans regard the *keiretsu* as just an informal trade barrier (*Newsweek*, "Japan: All in the Family," June 10, 1991). However, the Japanese regard their system as one of close cooperation, not closed or exclusionary. Further, the Japanese might ask, "Why would anyone want to change a system which is so effective and efficient?" (Yoshida, 1992).

It is unlikely that the Japanese or anyone else will always submit to U.S. rules for economic competition. In the future, successful companies and successful societies will be those who give up their national allegiance in order to identify with international economic rules. A new world trading system is emerging. The United States would probably be better off by taking part in helping to shape it, as a participant that knows how to play within its rules (Stevens, 1990; Kindel, 1991). Japanese companies like Toyota and Nissan have already brought these practices to America to support their production facilities here.[10]

Many U.S. companies are starting to learn from Japanese cooperative techniques. For example, after attempting to vertically integrate, but failing to master the production process of Excel Industries, Inc., a supplier of car windows, in 1985 Ford Motor Company opted for a *keiretsu*-type arrangement. Ford bought 40 percent of Excel and agreed to buy 70 percent of its windows from Excel for the next several years. Excel's revenues grew fourfold, which allowed a $4 million investment in new manufacturing systems. Now there is not only an environment of trust, but Excel and Ford can introduce new models faster than ever. Similar examples of cooperation among American companies exist in research, design, financing, production, and marketing (for review, see *Business Week*, "Learning from Japan," Jan. 27, 1992, pp. 52–60).

In addition to being open to the changing rules of global competition, American managers must be more aware of the global context. In the past, they have been ignorant of global developments. For example, 48 percent of the senior executives in 254 U.S. companies with annual sales between $10 million and $500 million have never even heard of ISO 9000 standards, the international quality standards endorsed by the United States, the members of the EEC, and others around the world (Miller, 1993). U.S. response to anomalies must be grounded in better understanding of the context, the potential causes of the lack of competitiveness abroad, and a resolve to act on those causes.

Responding with broad-scale protectionism would represent a form of economic warfare that parallels the military approach, with trade blockades and isolationism. In the long run, such an approach would do more harm than good. It would cut off opportunities for trade and deprive all consumers of access to the most valued products in the world. However, the most insidious danger of protectionism is the narcotic effect of government support; that is, it tends to isolate companies from pressures to improve.

Unlike military competition, economic competition is not destructive to human welfare. Rather, it focuses efforts on ways to make life better. The winner in an economic competition builds the world's best products and enjoys the world's highest standard of living. But the "losers" also enjoy a higher standard of living than before. Some American companies are responding to the anomalies of lost competitiveness in productive ways. For example, after years of lagging behind the Japanese, American computer chip makers like Intel, Motorola, and Texas Instruments are, according to Jack Beedle, president of In Stat Inc., "building devices for their uniqueness and [creating] new markets, neither of which the Japa-

---

10. See *Fortune*, "Why Japan Keeps On Winning," July 15, 1991; *The Wall Street Journal*, vol. 228, p. 49, "Japanese Auto Makers Help U.S. Suppliers Become More Efficient."

nese do so well" (*Fortune*, "Chipper Days for U.S. Chipmakers," May 6, 1991, pp. 91–96).

Economic competition ultimately benefits all consumers because the competitors seek to answer these questions: Who can make the best products? Who expands their standards of living most rapidly? Who has the best-educated and best-skilled work force? Who leads the world in investment—plant and equipment, R&D, infrastructure? Who manages the best organizations? Who has the best institutional support—government, education, and business? For companies to be forced to improve in these areas is good for all consumers (Thurow, 1992).

As many Japanese companies have shown, market share and profit will result from winning in this competition. U.S. managers must adjust their thoughts and actions to fit into the emerging paradigm of management, one which is more aptly described as cooperative competition than as free market competition. Cooperation among government, industry, and organizations is the order of the day. If U.S. managers do not shift to a new paradigm, the period of anomalies will continue for them.

▼

QUALITY IN ACTION: A MESSAGE TO THE STUDENT

Curt W. Reimann, Director, Malcolm Baldrige National Quality Award, U.S. Department of Commerce, National Institute of Standards and Technology

Since 1987, the Malcolm Baldrige National Quality Award has served as both a performance gauge and a competitive stimulus for American industry. Award director Curt W. Reimann describes the award and its program strategy.

The Malcolm Baldrige National Quality Award (MBNQA) was created by the U.S. Department of Commerce to enhance U.S. competitiveness. The purpose of the Award is threefold:

- to promote awareness of quality as an increasingly important element in competitiveness,
- to improve understanding of the requirements for quality excellence, and
- to foster sharing of information on successful quality strategies and the benefits derived from implementation of these strategies.

The Award Program strategy has two basic, interrelated elements—one conceptual and the other institutional.

I. The Conceptual Model

The conceptual part of the strategy is built around the Award criteria—the values underlying the criteria, their structure, and their design characteristics. Specifically, the Award criteria are designed to support dual, results-oriented goals, as follows: (1) delivery of ever-improving value to customers, and (2) improvement of overall company operational performance. These goals reflect a key point with respect to the criteria: They are aimed as much at overall organizational performance as at product and service quality. Or, stated in another way, product and service quality excellence and operating performance excellence both derive from overall excellence in process management.

Core Values

The criteria are built upon a set of ten core values and concepts, as follows:

- customer-driven quality
- leadership
- continuous improvement of all processes
- employee participation and development
- fast response
- design quality and prevention
- long-range outlook
- management by fact
- partnership development
- corporate responsibility and citizenship

Note that these values and concepts relate to all customer, operational, human resource, supplier, and public responsibility issues.

The Criteria Structure

Core values and concepts, though essential to guide the creation of criteria, would not constitute a meaningful or reliable basis for evaluating Award applications. Nor would they provide a useful device for addressing the other, more important purposes of the Award Program. A conceptual model was needed for embedding the core values to produce a useful instrument. At the time the Award was created, there was no such generally recognized and accepted model or instrument.

To devise the model, we reviewed the management literature and the experiences of many practicing managers. The analysis showed that the major requirements could be grouped in seven areas, as follows: (1) strong customer focus; (2) effective, hands-on leadership; (3) good systems for acquiring, analyzing, and using information; (4) a strategic, longer-range outlook toward quality; (5) focus on human resource development and excellence; (6) effective process management; and (7) focus on a variety of results indicators. Interestingly, these requirements appeared equally valid for businesses and non-businesses, including health care organizations, government agencies, and education organizations. Thus the model offered the potential for cross-sector communications sharing, and networking.

A framework was created from the seven basic areas—each area consisting of two or more specific, actionable requirements. This seven-category model has evolved since 1987, and now incorporates a total of twenty-eight requirements—called examination items in the Award criteria.

Though created to serve the needs of the Award Program, the seven-category framework structure was conceived as a new stage in the evolution of quality management from values, tools, and principles to a discipline structure—a basis for defining all requirements, relationships among requirements, and for creating and extending a meaningful body of knowledge. In effect, this approach subordinates tools and techniques that often "get in the way" of efforts to focus on customers and operational requirements.

Criteria Characteristics

There are several important characteristics of the Award criteria that determine their utility and also their limitations:

- The criteria are directed toward results, as measured by a composite of indicators. The composite includes customer-related and performance-related indices as well as those related to employees and suppliers. This broader interpretation of results creates important commonalities among otherwise diverse organizations.
- The criteria framework links processes to results. The framework is basically a comprehensive process improvement model incorporating dynamic feedback—the basis for institutional learning.
- The criteria are nonprescriptive. That is, the criteria do not prescribe tools, techniques, systems, or organizations. Thus the criteria imply wide latitude in approaches to meeting basic requirements.

The criteria are nonprescriptive for three important reasons:

1. The criteria's focus is on requirements that produce results, not on preset procedures, tools, or organizations. Through this approach, companies are encouraged to develop and demonstrate creative, adaptive, and flexible approaches to meeting basic requirements. The nonprescriptive nature of the requirements thus supports incremental and major ("breakthrough") improvement.
2. Selection of tools, techniques, systems, and organizations usually depends upon many factors such as business size, business type, the company's stage of development, and employee capabilities.
3. Focus on common requirements within a company rather than on specific procedures fosters better understanding, communication, and sharing, while encouraging diversity and creativity in approaches.

II. Institutional Strategy

The institutional part of the strategy concerns itself with how a very small program may "multiply" its effects broadly throughout the U.S. economy. This is pursued in three ways: (1) communications; (2) assessment capability; and (3) broad involvement in the Program.

Communications

The Award criteria focus on *generic* requirements, and are thus intended to foster communication across organizational lines and among different sectors of the economy. This is important as much communication and sharing takes place locally, and locally there is usually a diverse mix of organizations (manufacturers, service providers, schools, hospitals, government agencies, etc.). The ability to communicate tends to foster the creation of sharing networks. The approach taken by the Award Program assumes that the focus on similarity of requirements offers a better means for cooperation than focus on tools and techniques which may differ appreciably among organizations.

The Award winning companies play a major role in communications. In the first five years, these companies made more than 10,000 presentations, reaching all sectors of the economy.

Assessment Capability
The Award criteria and scoring system offer an assessment capability, including self assessment. Such assessments may be carried out by organizations whether or not they are interested in awards or are eligible for awards. This feature helps to extend the "reach" of the Award Program manyfold.

Broad Involvement in the Award Program
The Award Program's institutional strategy operates through broad involvement by individuals from many organizations. The Program seeks participation from all sectors, geographical areas, and organizations. Through partial annual turnover in its Boards, the Program extends its reach and its linkages. Those serving on Boards are also a major part of the Program's communications strategy.

The MBNQA philosophy regards the Award as much more than a contest. It is a symbol of a national effort to promote fundamental changes in how our institutions work and how they relate to one another. The Award Program is fostering higher expectations, cooperation, and sharing of information. The Award criteria have become a working tool for many organizations.

In my view, success of the national effort depends heavily upon adoption and adaptation by the education sector. Though we are making some progress, very much remains to be done. There is now a need for business schools and academic researchers to build upon the learnings emerging from the Award Program, and to drive their learning into the educational curriculum for our future managers.

The Role of the Baldrige Award in the Shift
Many companies are using the criteria of the Malcolm Baldrige National Quality Award to guide their transformation into the emerging paradigm. Many companies swear by it. Others criticize it. The critics have listed the following problems with the Baldrige:

- It requires too much time and money to follow the forty-page set of instructions, write an application (up to seventy-five pages), and support the requirements to disseminate or tell the story after winning.

- Bureaucracy can creep in and it can cost hundreds of thousands or even millions of dollars to apply and compete.
- Winners do it just to boast of the win in their advertisements.
- Companies get too caught up in winning rather than in achieving quality and solving their business problems (which is what the Baldrige Award is all about).
- The award doesn't guarantee that a company's products are superior, or that it will succeed financially. (For example, Baldrige Award winner Wallace Co., a Houston oil-supply company, filed for Chapter 11 bankruptcy protection.)
- The award does not address innovation, financial performance, or long-term planning (*Fortune*, "Is the Baldrige Overblown?" July 1, 1991, pp. 62–65).

As with any tool or set of guidelines, the value of the Baldrige Award process is determined by how intelligently it is used. The Baldrige Award is not perfect; it is still evolving. Despite its deficiencies, however, the Baldrige Award is better than what many companies have had, namely, a bagful of tricks and programs sold to them by consultants who lack a vision of how to put it all together and avoid the bureaucracy of traditional "program implementations." To make the Baldrige useful, companies need leaders with a vision and knowledge, an element the Baldrige cannot provide. These leaders must figure out how the Baldrige fits their vision, select the parts that do, discard the parts that do not, and supplement the areas of deficiency. In this context, the Baldrige can be quite useful.

The International Quality Study jointly conducted by Ernst & Young and the American Quality Foundation examined over 900 management practices in over 500 organizations around the world. Their research confirms that employing a set of "quality practices" can help improve performance and competitive advantage. However, the usefulness of any practice depends on the starting point of the company. For example, low performers need to concentrate on the fundamentals—building the organization's capacity to develop and deliver reliable products and services. They might do this by building the human resource infrastructure, listening to customers to get better at what they already do (rather than trying to create new markets), and redesigning business processes. However, some of the highly touted practices, such as benchmarking, employee empowerment, and externally oriented planning tools, only work in higher-performing companies.[11]

Small and Midsize Companies Seize the Challenge

Much of our concern over American competitiveness gets focused on the layoffs and shutdowns of our industrial behemoths like General Motors

11. For additional information about the International Quality Study, contact the National Director, Operations and Quality Management, Ernst & Young, 1600 Huntington Building, Cleveland, Ohio 44115.

and IBM. Most of the winners of the Malcolm Baldrige National Quality Award are large companies or divisions of large companies. However, small companies now vie for the Baldrige Award in unprecedented numbers. Representing only 18 percent of the entries in 1988, small companies now represent about half of the entries for the award. Large companies are driving this growth by pressuring their suppliers to prove their quality credentials by shooting for the Baldrige Award. For example, Motorola gave its suppliers until 1994 to apply for the award or risk being dropped. Many states, such as Delaware, Maine, Nevada, New York, and North Carolina, have initiated quality programs to support the improvement efforts of their small businesses.

The Minnesota Council for Quality has had financial support from companies like 3M, Honeywell, and IBM for activities such as seminars, meetings, local councils, and annual competitions, "Baby Baldriges," patterned after the Baldrige Award. While the state competition requires less documentation than the national award, it can serve as a dress rehearsal for the big dance. For example, Zytec Corporation in Eden Prairie won the first state competition and won the Baldrige Award the same year. The improvement efforts inspired by the competition can bring fortune to small companies. After failing to win the first year it applied for the Baldrige, Hutchinson Technology, Inc., a maker of components for computer disk drives, spent the next twelve months working on its deficiencies. Hutchinson's president, Wayne M. Fortun, credits these efforts for a 40 percent jump in annual earnings, to $13 million, on a revenue gain of 12 percent, to $160 million.

Small companies must join their bigger cousins in the challenge to shift to a new paradigm in order for the U.S. to remain a vital part of the global economic community. Small and midsize companies account for about half of the total value added by U.S. manufacturing, produce nearly half of all U.S. exports, and employ more than half of all factory workers. From computers to industrial machinery, large manufacturers often rely on smaller suppliers for 50 percent or more of the value of finished products (*Business Week*, "Special Report: Quality," Nov. 30, 1992, pp. 66–75). Managers of smaller firms must be just as devoted to learning about and shifting to a new paradigm. In fact, the success of many of the larger firms depends on it.

▶ THE STAGE OF REPLACEMENT: A NEW PARADIGM

The stage of replacement means shifting to a new paradigm. Managers must shift to a new paradigm for managing organizations because of the anomalies that threaten their survival and prosperity. To make this shift, however, they must understand the new paradigm and how it differs from

Figure 1

Description of old paradigm and new (emerging) paradigm on topics for the theme of customer value strategy

Topics	Old paradigm	New (emerging) paradigm
Quality	Meeting specifications, inspected into product, make tradeoffs among quality, cost, schedule	One component of customer value, managed into process, seek synergies among quality, cost, schedule
Measurement	Internal measures of efficiency, productivity, costs, and profitability, not necessarily linked to customers	All measures linked to customer value
Positioning	Competition	Customer segments
Key stakeholder	Stockholder, boss (other stakeholders are pawns)	Customer (other stakeholders are beneficiaries)
Product design	Internal, sell what we can build	External, build what customers need

the old paradigm. To initiate this understanding, we will contrast the new (but still emerging) paradigm with the old paradigm.

Themes of the New Paradigm

The differences between the new and the old paradigms are organized around three themes: customer value strategy, cross-functional systems, and continuous improvement. You will find these themes interwoven throughout every chapter of this book. In brief, the central idea of this book is that *managers must think and act differently than in the past to improve organizational systems to provide superior customer value.* In the interest of conceptual clarity, we discuss each of the themes below separately. However, they are, in practice, often inseparable.

Theme 1: Customer Value Strategy

Customer value is defined as the combination of benefits derived from using a product (or service) and the sacrifices required of the customer. The *customer value strategy* is the business plan for offering value to customers, including product characteristics, attributes, mode of delivery, support services, and so on. The theme of customer value strategy may be addressed in many topics, including quality, measurement, positioning, key stakeholder, and product design (see Figure 1).

Quality   In the old paradigm, managers define quality in terms of meeting specifications. Quality is assured by weeding out the "bad" products before they are shipped to customers. Managers make tradeoffs among quality, cost, and scheduling under the assumption that relationships among these outcomes are fixed. By contrast, in the new paradigm, managers recognize that product quality is only one component of customer value, and managers seek synergies among quality, cost, and schedule, not just tradeoffs. For example, improving quality by reducing variation in outputs reduces defects, reduces costs, and makes performance to schedule more predictable. Further, quality is more broadly defined than just product quality. Quality applies to every aspect of the organization. It must be managed into processes and systems, and not just inspected into products.

Measurement   In the old paradigm, measurement systems are focused on internal measures of efficiency, productivity, costs, and profitability. This is the tradition of management by objectives. Managers do not necessarily understand how these internally focused measures are related to customer value. In the new paradigm, managers may use internally focused measures, but they are linked to customer value in a broader measurement system. Managers interpret measures in terms of the impact on customer value in the long term and short term.

Positioning   In the old paradigm, managers make strategic positioning decisions based primarily on warfare models focused on the competition. In the new paradigm, managers make strategic positioning decisions with a focus on market segmentation and customer needs.

Key Stakeholder   In the old paradigm, the key external stakeholder is the stockholder, and the key internal stakeholder is one's boss. All other stakeholders, such as customers, employees, suppliers, and business partners, are pawns to serve the goals of the key stakeholders. In the new paradigm, the key stakeholders are customers, both internal and external customers. Providing value to customers is the key to serving all other stakeholders over the long term.

Product Design   In the old paradigm, the product design process is internally driven, based on the assumption that "we know what is best for the customer." Managers enact a "push" strategy that aims to "sell what we can build." In the new paradigm, managers develop products after first determining what customers need. Managers both react to improve products in existing markets and actively seek to create new markets with new products.

Theme 2: Organizational Systems

Organizational systems are the means that provide customer value. These systems broadly include material and human inputs, process technology, operating methods and work practices, streams of work activity, information flows, and decision making. The approaches to managing these systems in the old and new paradigms are discussed below according to these topics: cross-functional approach, technology, employee involvement, human resource management, role definition, culture, and structure (see Figure 2).

Figure 2

Description of old paradigm and new (emerging) paradigm on topics for the theme of organizational systems

Topics	Old paradigm	New (emerging) paradigm
Cross-functional approach	Negotiation across functional interfaces to obtain cooperation	Cross-functional systems defined, owned, and optimized
Technology	To deal with complexity, to eliminate people problems	To reduce complexity, source of optimization for customer value
Employee involvement	Focused on hygiene factors	Focused on strategic factors
Human resource management	Regarded as a staff responsibility, administration of personnel hiring, firing, and handling complaints	Regarded as a critical resource, managed as system input
Role definition	Task and job descriptions set limits	Vision inspires flexibility
Culture	Social and emotional issues are suppressed, politics and power dominate	Connect with individual sense of purpose, emotions, and social meaning
Structure	Specialization, tall hierarchy with functional emphasis	Integration, flat hierarchy with team emphasis

Cross-Functional Approach   The old paradigm does not acknowledge systems that cut across functional or unit boundaries. Managers simply negotiate across functional interfaces to obtain minimal cooperation. In the new paradigm, managers define, own, and optimize cross-functional systems for customer value.

Technology   In the old paradigm, managers use technology to help them deal with the overly complex systems that have grown up in the organization. Also, they use technology to eliminate people problems (robots don't talk back). In the new paradigm, managers prefer to eliminate complexity rather than automate it or computerize it. Managers use technology only to optimize systems for customer value.

Employee Involvement   In the old paradigm, employee involvement programs are implemented without a focus to contribute to systems. Employee involvement in improvement programs tends to focus on quality of worklife issues and some limited operational changes. In the new paradigm, employee involvement is strategically focused and contributes to system purposes.

Human Resource Management   In the old paradigm, managers regard human resource management (HRM) as a staff responsibility. HR specialists process paperwork to hire and fire, and handle personnel complaints.

In the new paradigm, line managers regard human resources as critical resources and strategically manage them as inputs to systems.

Role Definition In the old paradigm, managers use task and job descriptions to prescribe and set limits to personal responsibilities. In the new paradigm, managers convey a vision to lead and inspire flexibility. Employees participate in any activities required to provide superior value to customers.

Culture In the old paradigm, managers suppress social and emotional issues that are regarded as irrational and sources of distraction away from goals and objectives. Power and politics dominate the culture, with individuals jockeying for personal gain. In the new paradigm, managers connect organizational mission and purpose with each individual's sense of purpose, emotions, and social meaning. Individuals channel their needs for pride in workmanship toward strategic purposes.

Structure In the old paradigm, organizational structure is based on specialization of tasks. The hierarchy is tall, with many levels of managers, and it emphasizes functional lines of authority. In the new paradigm, the hierarchy is flat, with fewer levels of managers, and it emphasizes teamwork to serve superordinate objectives.

Theme 3: Continuous Improvement

To keep pace with the changes in the external environment, managers have to change the organization. Managers have always made improvements. However, with rates of change increasing in the external environment, managers must improve differently and more frequently than in the past. They must pursue *continuous improvement*, which is a constant striving to change and make things better. Approaches to improvement are contrasted in the following topic: occasion, approach, response to error, decision-making perspective, managerial roles, authority, focus, control, and means (see Figure 3).

Occasion In the old paradigm, the occasions for improvement were primarily new product development and reaction to salient problems. Managers mostly looked for big breakthroughs to get improvement. In the new paradigm, the occasions for improvement are everywhere, every day. Managers improve proactively at every opportunity, even in the absence of salient problems. Managers improve all aspects of the organization's systems through both big breakthroughs and small steps.

Approach In the old paradigm, managers accomplish improvements through trial and error. In the new paradigm, managers use the scientific method to study proposed changes and their effects.

Figure 3

Description of old paradigm and new (emerging) paradigm on topics for the theme of continuous improvement

Topics	Old paradigm	New (emerging) paradigm
Occasion	Focused new product development, episodic, reactive to problems, big breakthroughs only	Focused on broader systems, unending, proactive to opportunities, big breakthroughs and small steps
Approach	Trial and error	Scientific method
Response to error	Punish, fear, cover-up, seek people fix, employees are responsible	Learning, openness, seek process/system fix, management is responsible
Decision-making perspective	Individual political expediency, short term	Strategic, long-term, purposeful for organization
Managerial roles	Administer and maintain status quo, control others	Challenge status quo, prompt strategic improvement
Authority	Top-driven via rules and policies	Customer-driven through vision, enablement, and empowerment
Focus	Business results through quotas and targets	Business results through capable systems, means tied to results
Control	Scoring, reporting, evaluating	Statistical study of variation to understand causes
Means	Delegated by managers to staff and subordinates	Owned by managers who lead staff and subordinates

Response to Error   In the old paradigm, if they care at all, managers are intolerant of error. They regard error as a personal failure, and they respond with punishment to instill fear in those blamed. The result is fear and cover-up in the future. In the new paradigm, error is not desired; however, managers view error as an opportunity for learning. People openly acknowledge error because managers do not assign personal blame, but seek to fix a process or system.

Decision-Making Perspective   In the old paradigm, managers make decisions that are politically expedient or that serve short-term personal objectives. In the new paradigm, managers make decisions that serve long-term strategic purposes.

Managerial Roles   In the old paradigm, managers primarily administer existing systems and maintain the status quo. In the new paradigm, managers challenge the status quo for strategic improvement to meet future demands. At the same time, they consistently execute existing systems to meet current demands.

Authority   In the old paradigm, managers impose authority from the top down via rules and policies. In the new paradigm, top managers still hold authority, but they impose it by communicating a vision, enabling people with systems, and empowering them to make the vision real.

Focus   In the old paradigm, managers focus on improving business results through the imposition of quotas and targets. They delegate responsibility, often without giving real authority to change broader systems that constrain results. In the new paradigm, managers focus on improving business results through improving the capabilities of systems. They focus on the means as well as the results, because they have retained responsibility for improving systems.

Control   In the old paradigm, managers control the organization through scoring individual performance, reviewing regular reports, and evaluating performance as either good or bad. In the new paradigm, managers statistically study variation to understand the causes of poor performance and make changes in systems to improve performance.

Means   In the old paradigm, managers delegate the means of improvement to staff and subordinates who must figure out how to meet established targets. In the new paradigm, managers assume responsibility for the means of improvement. They lead improvement by staff and subordinates.

The Message of This Text

The new paradigm outlined above represents an ideal toward which many managers are now striving. Many managers have tried to move toward this new paradigm by implementing programs, such as quality circles, quality improvement teams, just-in-time manufacturing, quality function deployment, and total quality initiatives. They often achieve moderate gains, but they usually fall short of expectations. Managers must recognize that piecemeal program implementation will never suffice. Special programs will realize their full potential only in the context of a broader paradigm shift. It requires a fundamental culture change to move from an old paradigm to a new paradigm.

Many managers have also discovered that a paradigm shift is easier said than done. They espouse the behaviors, values, and beliefs described above in the new emerging paradigm; however, they do not always live up to what they say. These managers and their organizations are in the transitional stage, somewhere in between the old and the new. To some of their frustrated members, these organizations may seem hopelessly stuck in transition.

It can take a long time to change habits. The shift cannot be made all at once. Managers must learn new ways of thinking and acting. Then they have to practice these new ways and discover for themselves what works or does not work. Further, if the whole organization is to act in concert, the members have to come to some social agreement about what works and what does not work. This cultural learning can take years. Just like inertia for physical objects, the larger the organization, the more difficult it is to make the shift. Unfortunately, many U.S. organizations are not shifting fast enough to keep up with change in the external environment. Others are blazing ahead.

For students of management, it is an exciting time. You have the opportunity to take part in and perhaps even help lead a paradigm shift. Part of the excitement comes from the fact that the new paradigm is continuing to evolve as the concepts of the new paradigm are being refined. The new paradigm is indeed still emerging in two senses of the word. First, the concepts are evolving continuously. Second, more and more organizations are attempting to make the shift.

This text intends to educate the reader on the thoughts and actions expected of managers in the emerging paradigm. It does so in three parts, as shown in Figure 4. The three circles displaying each of the three parts of the text imply that the parts in the smaller circle can only be fully understood in the context of the larger circles.

The four chapters in the first part generally discuss the nature of the paradigm shift. Chapter 1, "Global Competitiveness and the Emerging Paradigm," which you have just read, describes the three stages of the shift and provides a context for understanding the need for a paradigm shift. Chapter 2, "TQM and the Foundation of the Emerging Paradigm," reviews the history of managerial approaches to quality to provide the conceptual foundation for the new paradigm. Chapter 3, "Organizational Culture and Paradigm Shift," introduces the concept of culture to explain how a paradigm arises through cultural learning to determine the thoughts and actions of managers. Thus, a paradigm shift requires cultural transformation. Chapter 4, "Management Role Responsibilities," overviews how the network of managerial roles should be integrated and focused on accomplishing improvement.

The six chapters in the second part specifically discuss the nature of the new paradigm. The core concepts and methods described in this part provide the basis for managerial thought and action in the new paradigm. Chapter 5, "Concepts of Customer Value," describes the concept of customer value to provide a basis for integrating strategic management and continuous improvement, which is the topic of Chapter 6. Chapter 7, "Measuring Customer Value," overviews methods for determining what customers value, translating that information into a customer value strategy, and setting up measurement systems to assess the organization's performance in providing customer value. Chapter 8, "Organizing to Improve Systems," overviews concepts and methods for understanding and improving the systems that provide customer value. Chapters 9 and 10, on "Variation," overview concepts and methods for the statistical study and improvement of systems that cause variation.

The two chapters in the third part discuss how to make the paradigm shift real in organizations. Chapter 11, "Strategic Linkage of Operations through Employee Involvement," reveals how the concepts and methods must be applied throughout an organization in order to link a customer value strategy to operations that deliver the strategy to customers. Chapter

Figure 4

Organizing framework for *Beyond Total Quality Management*

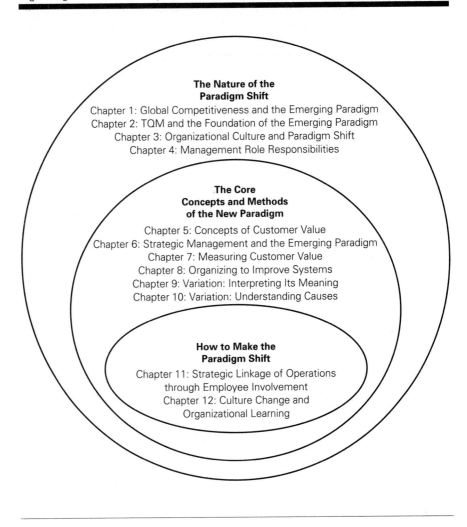

**The Nature of the
Paradigm Shift**

Chapter 1: Global Competitiveness and the Emerging Paradigm
Chapter 2: TQM and the Foundation of the Emerging Paradigm
Chapter 3: Organizational Culture and Paradigm Shift
Chapter 4: Management Role Responsibilities

**The Core
Concepts and Methods
of the New Paradigm**

Chapter 5: Concepts of Customer Value
Chapter 6: Strategic Management and the Emerging Paradigm
Chapter 7: Measuring Customer Value
Chapter 8: Organizing to Improve Systems
Chapter 9: Variation: Interpreting Its Meaning
Chapter 10: Variation: Understanding Causes

**How to Make the
Paradigm Shift**

Chapter 11: Strategic Linkage of Operations
through Employee Involvement
Chapter 12: Culture Change and
Organizational Learning

12, "Culture Change and Organizational Learning," suggests a model and methods for managers to use to transform their culture toward the new paradigm.

In addition to the core conceptual chapters, the text offers a number of case studies to illustrate how managers in diverse industries are attempting to make the theory a reality.

Concluding Comments

This chapter has briefly discussed the macroeconomic context within which managers of organizations must operate. To keep up with global developments, U.S. managers must change certain societal institutions, such as those provided in macroeconomic governmental policy, laws governing industrial practices, and professional organizations for coordinating industrial development. We may briefly touch some of these issues in coming chapters; however, this book primarily addresses the new paradigm at the microeconomic level of the economy: the management of business organizations.

The competitive battle that managers face can be seen as one between management teams, each vying for global market share in head-to-head competition. However, to spark improvement, it is best for managers to view competitiveness and global market share as results of the competitive battle. To achieve these results, managers must have a good process for competing. The new paradigm suggests a process that requires managers to square off for a battle with themselves, rather than to simply focus on competitors and react to their moves. The battle must be driven by continuous improvement of the organization to better serve the rising standards of customers. Customers are the Darwinian force that determines which companies are the most fit for survival. Managers in the new paradigm must continuously assess their capabilities and make changes to provide what customers value. The management teams that do the best job of this type of self-improvement will win the competitive battle to best serve customers.

▶ SUMMARY OF KEY POINTS

1. To keep up with increasing rates of change in their environments, managers may have to make radical changes in their thoughts and actions.
2. These changes are likely to be part of a *paradigm shift* to a new approach to management.
3. Three stages to a paradigm shift include: *normalcy* (things work as expected), *anomalies* (things do not work as expected), and *replacement* (expectations are changed).
4. In the 1970s and 1980s, many U.S. managers slipped from the stage of normalcy into the stage of anomalies, with lost market share, declining profitability, and failures of strategies that used to work.
5. The anomalies were created by global competitors who thought and acted according to a different managerial paradigm.
6. In the 1980s, many U.S. managers responded to the anomalies by implementing programs that had disappointing results, rather than attempting to understand and enact the new paradigm.
7. To make the paradigm shift, managers must understand how the old paradigm differs from the new paradigm.
8. The new emerging paradigm has three interwoven themes: *customer value strategy, organizational systems,* and *continuous improvement.*
9. Managers must think and act differently than in the past to improve organizational systems to provide superior customer value.

▶ KEY TERMS

anomalies   paradigm
continuous improvement   paradigm shift
customer value   replacement
customer value strategy   Total Quality Management (TQM)
managerial paradigm   Toyota Production System
normalcy
organizational systems

▶ DISCUSSION QUESTIONS

1. How has the nature of competition changed over the last few decades?

2. Briefly describe the three stages of paradigm shift and discuss why a dramatic change in management is necessary in many U.S. firms.

3. How are the three themes of the new paradigm interrelated?

4. Is the new paradigm described in this chapter compatible with the cooperative strategies of global competitors such as the Japanese and the Germans?

5. What changes will the U.S. have to make at a macroeconomic level of society to support the microeconomic paradigm shift within industrial organizations?

▶ EXPERIENTIAL EXERCISE

• Compare and contrast the content of the Malcolm Baldrige National Quality Award (MBNQA) summarized in the Message to the Student from Dr. Curt W. Reimann with the content of the new emerging paradigm, which is summarized in Figures 1 through 3. Create three lists.

To indicate the similarities:
(1) list the content items of the new emerging paradigm under seven areas of the MBNQA Criteria Structure.

To indicate the differences:
(2) list separately the unique features of MBNQA.
(3) list separately the unique features of the new emerging paradigm.

▶ REFERENCES

B. Bowonder and T. Miyake, "Technology Development and Japanese Industrial Competitiveness," *Futures*, 1990.

J. Case, "Competitive Advantage," *Inc.*, April 1989, pp. 33–34.

"Challenge and Dilemma for Corporate Japan: The EC Gears Up for 1992," *Tokyo Business Today*, April 1989.

F. W. Davis and K. B. Manrodt, "Service Logistics: An Introduction," *International Journal of Physical Distribution & Logistics Management*, vol. 21, no. 7, 1991, p. 9.

K. Ferdows, J. G. Miller, J. Nakane, and T. E. Vollmann, "Evolving Global Manufacturing Strategies: Projections into the 1990s," *International Journal of Operations and Production Measurement*, January 1987.

L. B. Forker, "Quality: American, Japanese, and Soviet Perspectives," *Academy of Management Executive*, vol. 5, no. 4, 1991, pp. 63–74.

"Getting High Tech Back on Track," *Fortune*, Jan. 1, 1990, p. 74.

Oren Harari, "Ten Reasons Why TQM Doesn't Work," *Management Review*, January 1993, pp. 33–38.

R. H. Hayes, S. C. Wheelwright, and K. B. Clark, *Dynamic Manufacturing: Creating the Learning Organization*, The Free Press, New York, 1988.

S. Ishihara, *The Japan That Can Say No: Why Japan Will Be First among Equals*, Simon & Schuster, New York, 1991, p. 50.

Stephen Kindel, "The New Corridors of Power," *Financial World*, Mar. 5, 1991, pp. 22–25.

"Kohl to Reassure Soviets on Unification," *The Boston Globe*, Feb. 9, 1990, p. 2.

P. R. Krugman and G. N. Hatsopoulos, "The Problem of U. S. Competitiveness in Manufacturing," *New England Economic Review*, January/February 1987.

Thomas S. Kuhn, *The Structure of Scientific Revolutions*, The University of Chicago Press, 1962.

M. M. Lele and J. N. Sheth, *The Customer Is Key*, John Wiley & Sons, New York, 1987.

Cyndee Miller, "U.S. Firms Lag in Meeting Global Quality Standards," *Marketing News*, vol. 27, no. 4, Feb. 15, 1993, p. 1.

Yasuhiro Monden, *Toyota Production System: Practical Approach to Production Management*, Industrial Engineering and Management Press, Norcoss, Ga., 1983.

Nomura Research Institute of America, *New Directions in Corporate Management and the Capital Market*, The Institute, New York, 1991, p. 1.

A. Parasuraman, V. Zeithaml, and L. Berry, "A Conceptual Model of Service Quality and Its Implications for Future Research," *Journal of Marketing*, Fall 1985, pp. 41–50.

C. V. Prestowitz, *Trading Places: How We Allowed Japan to Take the Lead*, Basic Books, New York, 1988.

J. Rampey and H. Roberts, "Perspectives on Total Quality," *Proceedings of Total Quality Forum IV*, Cincinnati, Ohio, November, 1992.

Candice Stevens, "Technoglobalism vs. Technonationalism: The Corporate Dilemma," *Columbia Journal of World Business*, no. 25, 1990, pp. 42–49.

"Super-Industrialism and the New Japan," *Tokyo Business Today*, March 1989.

L. Thurow, *Head to Head: The Coming Economic Battle among Japan, Europe, and America*, William Morrow and Company, Inc., New York, 1992.

M. Walton, *Deming Management at Work*, Perigree Books, New York, 1990.

Kosaku Yoshida, "New Economic Principles in America—Competition and Cooperation: A Comparative Study of the U.S. and Japan," *Columbia Journal of World Business*, vol. 26, no. 4, Winter 1992, pp. 2–15.

chapter **2**

TQM and the Foundation of the Emerging Paradigm

Preoccupation with the past is a serious drag on originality of action. The tendency is to take action by refining the past rather than by redesigning for the future; by grafting some change onto an existing system without rethinking the system.

*Joseph M. Juran**

▶ **CHAPTER OUTLINE**

Chapter Overview

Introduction

The Concept of Quality

The Transcendent View of Quality
A Critique of the Transcendent View of Quality

The Evolution of Quality Approaches

The Inspection Era
The Statistical Quality Control Era
The Quality Assurance Era

The Strategic Quality Management Era

Total Quality Management
Strategy, Quality, and Customer Value

---

* Joseph M. Juran, *Managerial Breakthrough*, McGraw-Hill, New York, 1964, p. 164.

The Continuous Improvement Philosophy
The Total View of Quality
Beyond Total Quality Management
The Nature of the Paradigm Shift
Concluding Comments

Summary of Key Points

Key Terms

Discussion Questions

Experiential Exercise

References

► CHAPTER OVERVIEW

Approaches to the management of quality have evolved tremendously over the last century. In the new paradigm, managers are shifting away from methods of inspection that catch defects before they reach customers. They are moving toward proactive improvement to reduce variation around targets that match customer needs. This approach helps managers provide superior customer value as a strategy for competing in today's globally competitive environment. In the new paradigm, all managers are involved in quality improvement for the purpose of customer value. Quality is not just the responsibility of staff experts or a single department. It results from a team effort. It is led by top managers as a part of strategic management of the organization.

► INTRODUCTION

In the last decade, managers became interested in quality. Federal initiatives such as the U.S. Department of Commerce's Malcolm Baldrige National Quality Award, and local initiatives such as the Madison, Wisconsin, Quality Improvement Network, were launched. Prominent figures such as Deming, Juran, and Ishikawa started to appear in the popular press. Managers began to suspect that they must do something different, and many responded. Despite the good intentions, these responses have often been inadequate or inappropriate.[1] Programs to improve quality proliferated. They started with great fanfare and then fizzled. Quality circles popped up in every industry. They achieved only modest improvements which were often unrelated to the firm's strategy. Armies of good soldiers

---

1. A recent article in *The Wall Street Journal* (Fuchsberg, 1992) summarizes the results of a major study by the American Quality Foundation that suggests that the quality movement is faltering.

marched off to training in Statistical Process Control, Just-in-Time Manufacturing, and Total Quality Management. The trainees returned well versed, but with no plan for putting the training into practice. There are many reasons for these failures, including the following:

- The efforts were too narrowly focused, as with statistical applications on the shop floor.
- The efforts were misfocused, limited to improving only "quality of worklife" issues for employees rather than also addressing issues of strategic concern.
- The managers relied on traditional methods and assumptions, and were not equipped with the right tools, techniques, and theory to improve quality.
- The managers were too focused on tools and techniques, and did not understand how to transform themselves, their employees, and the organization.
- The managers were too impatient, with a short-term focus, and unwilling to stay the course, overcome initial barriers, and wait for long-term gains.

Consider the following ten reasons why TQM "programs" do not work for many companies (for review, see Harari, 1993):

1. *TQM focuses people's attention on internal processes rather than on external results.* An asset of TQM is that it gets managers to attend to internal processes. But taken to an extreme, managers can get too preoccupied with internal issues such as the controversial issue of performance measurement and ignore shifting perceptions and preferences of customers.
2. *TQM focuses on minimum standards.* Zero defects and no rework efficiency distract people from adding value and excitement to customers' lives.
3. *TQM develops its own cumbersome bureaucracy.* Organizational charts and reporting systems with interlocking committees, councils, and improvement teams imply a linear and predictable improvement process, rather than the chaotic and disruptive rebuilding that is often necessary.
4. *TQM delegates quality to quality czars and "experts" rather than to "real" people.* Quality shouldn't be delegated, but lived in the strategy of the company and roles of the managers.
5. *TQM does not demand radical organizational reform.* Real quality improvement requires structural change (perhaps flattened structures), and liberation of people from stifling control systems and the tyranny of functionalism which precludes teamwork.
6. *TQM does not demand changes in management compensation.* If rewarded on short-term financial gains, managers will not be likely to attend to quality measures.

7. *TQM does not demand entirely new relationships with outside partners.* This deficiency results from the above conditions. Managers fail to enact nonlegalistic relationships based on trust and mutual support.

8. *TQM appeals to faddism, egotism, and quick-fixism.* Although they will not admit it, many managers have applied for awards, like the Baldrige, for reasons of personal aggrandizement and corporate public relations, or for quick and painless profitability. In reality, quality requires a never-ending pursuit of improvement.

9. *TQM drains entrepreneurship and innovation from corporate culture.* Too much emphasis on standardization and routine precludes the constant shifting needed to keep up with external changes.

10. *TQM has no place for love.* Though this comment seems a bit precious, it means that the analytical, detached, and sterile programs put in place to ensure quality are often devoid of the human emotion and soul that inspire attachment to the company by employees and to the products by customers.[2]

Certainly, not all TQM programs are characterized by all of these deficiencies. But many of the TQM failures suffer at least a few of these major problems. Business papers and magazines often criticize TQM and offer advice on TQM programs, some good and some not so good.[3] Before heeding any advice on how to fix something that seems broken, managers should seek to understand the underlying cause.

The underlying cause of all these TQM deficiencies is that managers failed to understand the concept of *quality*. Some managers define quality too narrowly as "meeting specifications." Others do not define quality at all, but rely on the claim, "I know it when I see it." We define quality as a principle that encourages excellence in everything: products, strategies, systems, processes, and people. As you will see, there are many ways that quality can be pursued and realized. This chapter reviews some of the specific approaches that help managers realize the general principle of excellence.

To inspire purposeful change for improvement, managers must have a clear understanding of quality. They must understand how it relates to their roles, and how it must be integrated and connected to the organization's strategy for providing value to customers. This integrated approach brings quality into the mainstream of managerial practice. In this chapter, we will review the concept of quality and the evolution of approaches to quality. We will look at the work of some world-renowned advocates of quality improvement and discuss the implications for revolutionizing the practice of management.

---

2. For a good debate on the validity of these reasons, see the articles by Selwyn W. Becker and Oren Harari in *Management Review*, May 1993, pp. 30–36.
3. For examples, see *The Wall Street Journal*, Feb. 24, 1992, and May 14, 1992.

QUALITY IN ACTION: A MESSAGE TO THE STUDENT
J. S. Mayo, President, AT&T Bell Labs

AT&T Bell Laboratories was instrumental in initiating the modern era of quality in the United States. President J. S. Mayo explains how AT&T's approach to quality has evolved out of a narrow "zero defects" orientation into a holistic philosophy based on customer value.

Quality and Total Quality Management have seen significant evolution. The mechanization of the AT&T network after World War I required the introduction of equipment of unprecedented complexity and reliability. The success of AT&T in this time frame was helped through the contributions of such leaders in quality as Walter A. Shewhart. The quality thrust at that time was mainly inspection and quality assurance, which had its genesis in statistical quality control. These fundamentals are still applicable to the technology evolution that has occurred in fields such as microelectronics, fiber optics, and software.

However, the world has changed and progressed, and the scope of quality technology has been expanded beyond performance parameters of products and services to include all aspects of business. The competitive environment demands attention to the important concept of "value to the customer." This concept requires more than just producing zero defects to meet engineering specifications. AT&T, to be a leader in the extremely competitive information market worldwide, has expanded its quality focus to embrace what is called "Total Quality Management," a more holistic approach to quality. Through a passion for understanding, controlling, and continuing to improve all of our processes, we have been able to achieve better focus on our customers, our people, as well as our products and services. Our business and the world are dynamic, demanding, and changing; therefore, at AT&T, quality is a journey to be the best in everything we do.

▶ THE CONCEPT OF QUALITY

While managers have shown interest in the concept of quality, many have been frustrated by its elusiveness. They find diverse and often conflicting definitions in professional books, journals, and news media. Despite common themes such as continuous improvement, customer focus, and excellence, different people emphasize different things. For example, in a 1991 public television special, "Quality or Else," executives, managers, workers, academics, and others defined quality variously as follows:

- A pragmatic system of continual improvement, a way to successfully organize man and machines
- The meaning of excellence
- The unyielding and continuing effort by everyone in an organization to understand, meet, and exceed the needs of its customers

- The best product that you can produce with the materials that you have to work with
- Continuous good product which a customer can trust
- Producing a product or service that meets the needs or expectations of the customer
- Not only satisfying customers, but delighting them, innovating, creating

Your own sample of definitions would probably reveal similar variety. Different companies, and even different people within the same company, often disagree on the definition of quality. Sometimes the disagreements are merely due to semantics. Sometimes they are the result of focusing on different dimensions of quality. Other times the differences are more profound, implying conflicting courses of action and approaches to management. Here we look at several views of quality and then offer a definition that should help to integrate managerial efforts to improve quality throughout an organization.

The Transcendent View of Quality

The concept of quality has often been defined, from a *transcendent view*, as "innate excellence" (see Garvin, 1988, for a review). This view implies that high quality is something timeless and enduring, an essence that transcends or rises above individual tastes or styles. It often regards quality as an unanalyzable property that people learn to recognize through experience, just as Plato argued that beauty can be understood only after exposure to a series of objects that display its characteristics.

Reflecting this view, in his book *Zen and the Art of Motorcycle Maintenance*, Robert M. Pirsig (1974, pp. 185, 213) writes: "Quality is neither mind nor matter, but a third entity independent of the two.... [E]ven though Quality cannot be defined, you know what it is." Others who advocate a transcendent view of quality define it with examples, listing the "best" in categories such as the best hamburger, the best national park, the best zoo. (For example, see Passell and Ross's book *The Best* [1975].) In their book *Quintessence: The Quality of Having It*, Cornfeld and Edwards (1983) discuss the "quintessence" of products as diverse as the Volkswagen Beetle, Crayola crayons, Swiss Army knives, and Hershey's chocolate Kisses, and suggest that what they have in common is that "they each exhibit a rare and mysterious capacity to be just exactly what they ought to be."

A Critique of the Transcendent View of Quality

Walter A. Shewhart, the father of modern-day statistical quality control, offered the following criticism of the transcendent view of quality:

> Dating at least from the time of Aristotle, there has been some tendency to conceive of quality as indicating the goodness of an object. The majority of advertisers appeal to the public upon the basis of the quality of product. In so doing, they implicitly assume that there is a measure of goodness which can be applied to all kinds of product, whether it be vacuum tubes, sewing machines,

automobiles, Grape Nuts, books, cypress flooring, Indiana limestone, or correspondence school courses. Such a concept, is, however, too indefinite for practical purposes. [Shewhart, 1931, p. 37]

The transcendent view of quality essentially tells a manager "you will know it when you see it" and does not inform managers how to pursue excellence. Certainly the notion of excellence is an important and inspirational component of quality. However, future managers must have a better understanding of the concept. The definition of quality must be more pragmatic, more objective, and more tangible. It must inform managers about how to make improvements. There are at least three views of quality that provide these insights for managers: product-based, manufacturing-based, and user-based views of quality. We discuss below how these various views of quality fit into the concept of customer value and how a total view of quality forms the basis of the evolving concept of Total Quality Management.

To better understand how this total view of quality impacts managerial practices, it is useful to understand how managerial approaches to quality have evolved from a narrow view, focused on inspection and conformance to specified standards, toward a broader view, focused on organizational strategy for providing superior customer value. We now discuss the evolution of quality approaches.

▶ THE EVOLUTION OF QUALITY APPROACHES

The shift to Total Quality Management and beyond will be revolutionary for many managers because the tenets of the new paradigm are so radically different from past managerial practices. It will require both a thought revolution and a behavioral revolution. Approaches to quality have evolved through a series of gradual refinements over the last century. The shift seems dramatic and revolutionary to many managers because they have not kept up with the evolving approaches to quality.[4] These managers who have been left behind may have tinkered with various quality approaches over the years. However, they have not defined their managerial roles in terms of the latest advancements.

In the next few sections, we will review the evolution of quality through four distinct eras: inspection, statistical quality control, quality assurance, and strategic quality management (Garvin, 1988). Figure 1 provides an overview. Each quality era builds on its predecessor.

---

4. The new paradigm involves all functions and departments of the organization. Since they have been primarily held responsible for quality in traditional managerial practice, manufacturing and production departments may have kept up with the evolving concept of quality more than other departments such as marketing, finance, and engineering.

Figure 1

The four major quality eras

Identifying characteristics Date of inception	Stage of quality movement			
	Inspection (1800s)	Statistical quality control (1930s)	Quality assurance (1950s)	Strategic quality management (1980s)
Primary concern	Detection	Control	Coordination	Strategic impact
View of quality	A problem to be solved	A problem to be solved	A problem to be solved, but one that is attacked proactively	A competitive opportunity
Emphasis	Product uniformity	Product uniformity with reduced inspection	The entire production chain, from design to market, and the contribution of all functional groups, especially designers, to preventing quality failures	The market and consumer needs
Methods	Gauging and measurement	Statistical tools and techniques	Programs and systems	Strategic planning, goal-setting, and mobilizing the organization
Role of quality professionals	Inspection, sorting, counting, and grading	Troubleshooting and the application of statistical methods	Quality measurement, quality planning, and program design	Goal-setting, educaton and training, consultative work with other departments, and program design
Who has responsibility for quality	The inspection department	The manufacturing and engineering departments	All departments, although top management is only peripherally involved in designing, planning, and executing quality policies	Everyone in the organization, with top management exercising strong leadership
Orientation and approach	"Inspects in" quality	"Controls in" quality	"Builds in" quality	"Manages in" quality

Reprinted from D. Garvin, *Managing Quality*, 1988, p. 37.

The Inspection Era

Until the nineteenth century, skilled craftsmen manufactured goods in small volume. They handcrafted and fit together parts to form a unique product that was only informally inspected. Population growth and industrialization brought about production in larger volume.

Mass Production and Inspection   In the 1800s, increased specialization, division of labor, and mass production required more formal inspection. Parts had to be interchangeable. Inspectors examined products to detect flaws and separate the good from the bad. They used gauges to catch deviant parts and make sure parts fit together at final assembly. The gauging system made inspections more consistent than those conducted solely by eye, and gave inspection a new respectability.

Formalizing the Inspection Function   By the early 1900s, gauging had become more refined, and inspection was even more important. It was prominent in Henry Ford's moving assembly line and Frederick W. Taylor's system of shop floor management. In 1922, G. S. Radford formally linked inspection to quality control. For the first time, quality was regarded as an independent function and a distinct management responsibility. Radford (1922, p. 5) defined quality in terms of conformance to "established requirements" and emphasized inspection. He also suggested some lasting quality principles, such as getting designers involved early, closely coordinating various departments, and achieving the quality improvement results of increased output and lower costs. Through the 1920s, however, quality control was most often limited to inspection and focused on activities such as counting, grading, and rework, which is antithetical to Total Quality Management's emphasis on prevention to avoid defects. Inspection departments and quality professionals were not required to troubleshoot, to understand and address the causes of poor quality, until the 1930s, with the creation of statistical quality control.

The Statistical Quality Control Era

In 1931, Walter A. Shewhart gave quality a scientific footing with the publication of his book *Economic Control of Quality of Manufactured Product.* Shewhart was one of a group of people at Bell Laboratories investigating problems of quality.[5] The statistical quality control approach that Shewhart advocated is based on his views of quality. *Statistical quality control* requires that numbers derived from measures of processes or products be analyzed according to a theory of variation that links outcomes to uses.

Shewhart's Views of Quality   Shewhart offered a pragmatic concept of quality: "The measure of quality is a quantity which may take on different numerical values. In other words, the measure of quality, no matter what the definition of quality may be, is a variable" (p. 37). For example, since the shape of a Hershey's chocolate Kiss is very important, its configuration quality may be expressed numerically in terms of three variables: height, width, and symmetry. Shewhart's emphasis on measurement in his definition of quality obviously relates to his prescriptions for statistical quality control, which requires numbers. Below, we further discuss Shewhart's view of quality in terms of three categories of definitions: product-based, manufacturing-based, and user-based definitions.

---

5. Engineers at Bell's manufacturing arm, Western Electric, were seeking greater standardization and uniformity in the nation's telephone network.

Product-Based Shewhart explains that the word "quality," in Latin, *qualitas*, comes from *qualis*, meaning "how constituted" and signifies a thing's basic nature. Emphasizing a *product-based view of quality*, Shewhart argued that the quality of a manufactured product may be described in terms of a set of characteristics. Product-based definitions of quality suit engineers because they are concerned with translating product requirements into specific components and physical dimensions that can be produced. For example, measurement of capacity, inductance, and resistance may be used to define the quality of a relay. So, according to this view, quality is a precise and measurable variable: differences in quality reflect differences in the quantity of an attribute the product possesses (Garvin, 1988). For example, high-quality rugs have a large number of knots per square inch. Quality in a rug can be seen as an inherent characteristic that can be assessed objectively. Since quality reflects the quantity of attributes contained by a product, and because attributes are costly to produce, high quality means higher cost. In this view, a Cadillac loaded with a number of amenities is a higher-quality car than a stripped-down Chevrolet.

The product-based view has some merit, but it does not accommodate differences in individual tastes and preferences. Some people prefer a Chevrolet to a Cadillac.

Manufacturing-Based Another meaning of the word "quality" is "the degree of excellence that a thing possesses" once it is manufactured. The *manufacturing-based view of quality* focuses on manufacturing and engineering practices, emphasizes conformance to specified requirements, and relies on statistical analysis to measure quality. As you will see, it contradicts the notion that higher quality necessarily corresponds to higher cost. Returning to the example of a relay, Shewhart suggests the overall quality of a relay can be further expressed in terms of whether it meets engineering specifications for product-based characteristics (qualities), such as capacity, inductance, and resistance. To simplify, let's just consider two dimensions, resistance and inductance. Upper and lower bounds on each dimension would form a rectangular region defining conformance to specifications (see Figure 2).

The quality or degree of excellence of a product (represented by a point or a set of two measurements) falling within the rectangular region would be characterized as good or satisfactory. A product with quality outside the region, not conforming to specifications, would be characterized as bad or unsatisfactory. Of course, real manufacturing processes produce a stream of products. Ideally, each individual product has quality that conforms to specifications. However, variation in the production process may produce some products that are outside the specifications.

Shewhart suggested that the fraction of nonconforming items produced by a manufacturing process can be studied statistically to assess

Figure 2

Measurements of two quality variables for an electronic
relay as an example of Shewhart's views of quality

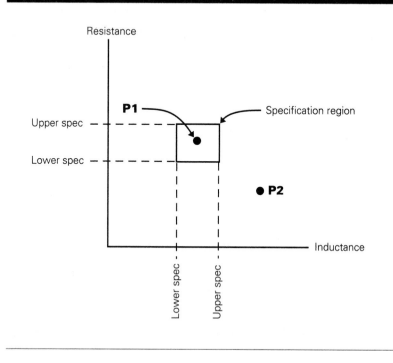

quality.[6] The knowledge gained from statistical studies can be used to improve the control of quality, thus ensuring that a larger fraction of the products conform to specification. By stabilizing and reducing variation in the process, managers can ensure that product quality is always within specification. Such improvement would mean fewer defects, less scrap, less rework, and consequently, less cost.

Numerical measurement allows managers to compare the quality of product for a given period with that of another period and determine whether or not the differences are greater than should be left to chance. Shewhart devotes the bulk of his 1931 book to this statistical approach to analyzing quality. His process control charts provide the foundation for modern approaches to statistical quality control.[7]

---

6. Shewhart also suggests that quantitative measures of quality on various dimensions of a manufactured product could be combined into an overall measure of quality to measure the "degree of excellence," a variable which could also be studied statistically.

7. Shewhart's disciple W. Edwards Deming taught these methods to Japanese executives and engineers beginning in 1950, and emphasized reducing variation and improving quality beyond just meeting specifications. In the 1980s, Deming again told U.S. managers about these statistical approaches to quality improvement.

For decades, American managers have relied on a manufacturing-based approach to quality. But in recent years, managers have found this approach too limiting because it is internally focused, concerned more with engineering and production control than with the customer's perception of quality. Managers are increasingly adopting a broader concept of quality, conceived in terms of the product's user.

User-Based The user-based perspective does not abandon manufacturing quality as a strategic objective, but provides a context for it. As Shewhart says, "The broader concept of economic control naturally includes the problem of continually shifting the standards expressed in terms of measurable physical properties to meet best the shifting economic value of these particular physical characteristics depending upon shifting human wants" (1931, p. 54). The *user-based view of quality*, popular with people in marketing, presumes that quality rests in "the eye of the beholder," the user of the product, rather than an engineer's specified standards.

Returning again to the example of the relay, the user-based view suggests that quality is described by the match, or the discrepancy, between the product (point P1 in Figure 2) and the customer's needs (point P2 in Figure 2). The closer the match, the smaller the discrepancy between the product and the customer's needs, the higher the quality. Shewhart hinted at this more subjective approach, but he did not fully explore its implications. This user-based view of quality was largely ignored in favor of Shewhart's approach to statistical quality control. Refinement of this view came later.

Process Variation and Control Shewhart recognized that *variation*, or fluctuation in events or outcomes over time, was a fact of industrial life: no two parts were likely to be manufactured exactly alike even if produced by the same operator using the same equipment. The issue of quality became one of acknowledging variation and using principles of probability and statistics to distinguish acceptable (normal) variation from unacceptable (abnormal) variation. Shewhart's analytical techniques for determining the range of acceptable variation were based on his concept of statistical control: "A phenomenon will be said to be controlled when, through the use of past experience, we can predict, at least within limits, how the phenomenon may be expected to vary in the future. Here is it understood that prediction means that we can state, at least approximately, the probability that the observed phenomenon will fall within the given limits" (1931, p. 6).

Plotting data graphically with statistical limits enabled managers to assess whether the numbers fell within the acceptable range (see a sample process control chart in Figure 3).[8] Shewhart's approach also suggested

8. Deming (1986) later reconceived this "acceptable" variation as "common cause" variation.

Figure 3

An example of a statistical process control chart

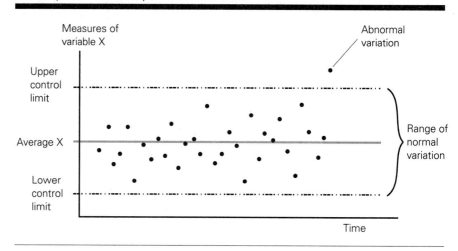

drawing samples of output throughout the production process, rather than waiting until after final assembly.

Sampling Techniques Two other Bell Labs scientists, Harold Dodge and Harry Romig, also made advances in sampling techniques. They recognized that 100 percent inspection to sort good from bad products was inefficient. But a more efficient alternative, checking only a limited number of products in the lot to decide whether the entire lot was acceptable, entailed certain risks. An inspector could possibly accept a lot that contained a large number of defects or reject a lot that was within the acceptable boundaries for quality.[9]

To deal with these risks, Dodge and Romig developed *acceptance sampling* plans to check a certain number of items for a specified lot size, count the number of defective items, and consult sampling tables (based on probability theory) to decide whether or not the entire lot should be rejected.[10] Acceptance sampling was a tolerable and even useful approach to quality in an era when companies could afford defects. In today's competitive environment, in the emerging paradigm, this sampling approach is no longer adequate. It does not provide a means to continuous improvement through the study and reduction of variation. It does not encourage managers to continuously improve as does Shewhart's approach to statistical quality control.

---

9. Deming (1986, Chapter 15) argues that acceptance sampling actually maximizes total cost when there is stable variation in inputs to the sampling process.

10. The Average Outgoing Quality Limit (AOQL) showed the relationships of product quality, lot size, sampling rules, and the outgoing quality for the entire manufacturing process.

These apparent advances in statistical quality control helped the Bell System improve the quality of its telephone equipment and service for customers. However, neither the sampling techniques nor the process control charts had much impact outside the Bell System, until World War II created the need for large volumes of munitions.

The Impact of World War II When faced with the problem of providing the Ordnance Department of the U.S. Army with large quantities of high-quality arms and ammunition from multiple suppliers, the War Department considered two alternatives: (1) train contractors to use process control charts, or (2) develop a system of acceptance sampling procedures to be applied by government inspectors. The War Department selected the second alternative, acceptance sampling, and in 1942 it established a Quality Control Section staffed largely with Bell Labs statisticians. The staff soon developed a new set of sampling tables to apply the concept of acceptable quality levels (AQL), the maximum percent defects allowable for a supplier to still be considered satisfactory.

These techniques relieved the primary bottleneck, the understaffed inspection process, which was slowing the production of war materials. Suppliers who recently satisfied AQL criteria were inspected less frequently, while those failing AQL criteria were scrutinized more extensively. Not only were inspectors more productive, but product quality levels also improved. Although the War Department sought to disseminate these techniques to other branches of industry through training courses and seminars for executives, engineers, inspectors, and other practitioners, most early trainees did not use what they had learned. However, some trainees did achieve impressive results and shared them through local societies for quality control. By 1946, several of these local groups had banded together to form the American Society for Quality Control (ASQC), which still exists today.

After the war, some of the most significant developments in the evolution of quality were launched in Japan, where "quality management" evolved along a somewhat different course. Americans largely ignored these developments until Japanese products started to earn a reputation for high quality and Japanese firms began to realize increased market share and profitability in industries traditionally dominated by U.S. firms.

Developments in Postwar Japan The Japanese course of action was influenced by Americans like W. Edwards Deming, Joseph M. Juran, and Armand V. Feigenbaum. Deming, a leading disciple of Walter A. Shewhart, was the first to arrive in Japan, and at the invitation of the Japanese Union of Scientists and Engineers (JUSE), he taught executives and engineers to study and reduce variation through process control charts. In contrast to the acceptable quality levels (AQL) approach, which tolerates a certain level of defects and does not encourage continuous improvement, Deming's

Figure 4

The Plan, Do, Study, Act (PDSA) cycle, also known
as the Shewhart Cycle or Deming Cycle

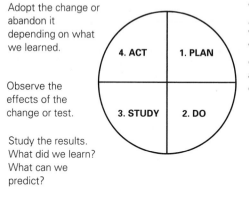

Adopt the change or
abandon it
depending on what
we learned.

Observe the
effects of the
change or test.

Study the results.
What did we learn?
What can we
predict?

What could be the most important
accomplishments of this team?
What changes might be desirable?
What data are available? Are new
observations needed? If yes, plan
a change or test. Decide how to use the
observations.

Carry out the change or test decided
upon, preferably on a small scale.

Step 5. Repeat Step 1, with knowledge accumulated.
Step 6. Repeat Step 2, and onward.

Adapted from Deming, *Out of the Crisis*, MIT/CAES, 1986, p. 88.

approach emphasized management's responsibility for continuous improvement of systems of production.

Deming taught the Japanese Shewhart's principles of scientific thinking embodied in the *Plan, Do, Study, Act* (PDSA) cycle, which the Japanese
soon referred to as the *Deming Cycle* (see Figure 4). The PDSA cycle provides
managers with a scientific method for learning how to make improvements.
Deming introduced the Japanese to modern approaches to consumer
research and suggested methods for relating the research to continuous
improvement. While Americans seemed to discount these approaches as
wartime efforts not relevant to a booming postwar economy, the Japanese
subscribed to them as the means of rebuilding their country.[11] They continued to develop and apply methods for continuous improvement with an
emphasis on quality. And they advanced the concept of quality, as you
will see below.

Under the intellectual leadership of prominent business leaders like
Kaoru Ishikawa, the Japanese continued to refine the Shewhart/Deming
approach to continuous improvement. They introduced other techniques
to support an approach to continuous improvement which focused on
the means (the causes) and not just the ends (the results). For example,

11. Deming's approach was recognized nationally when Emperor Hirohito awarded him the
Second Order Medal of the Sacred Treasure and when JUSE established the Deming Prize, which
is awarded to individuals and companies for statistical applications and quality improvements.

Ishikawa developed the *cause/effect diagram* or *fishbone diagram* as a format for documenting ideas about cause/effect relationships.

The efforts of Deming and JUSE succeeded in making statistical quality control, with process sampling and charting techniques, fashionable in Japanese factories in the 1950s. However, as Ishikawa explains, "Quality control remained a movement among engineers and workers in the factories. Top- and middle-level managers did not show much interest"[12] (1986, p. 19). Ishikawa suggests that the turning point for the Japanese came with the arrival of two other Americans, Joseph M. Juran and Armand Feigenbaum, who encouraged them to make quality control a tool of management.

By the late 1940s, quality control was an established discipline in the United States. However, its methods remained largely inspection-based applications on the factory floor. Then several publications in the 1950s and early 1960s ushered in the next quality era.

The Quality Assurance Era

During the *quality assurance* era, the concept of quality in the United States evolved from a narrow, manufacturing-based discipline to one with implications for management throughout a firm. Statistics and manufacturing control remained important, but coordination with other areas, such as design, engineering, planning, and service activities, also became important to quality. While quality remained focused on defect prevention, the quality assurance era brought a more proactive approach and some new tools. Four elements of the quality assurance era are discussed below: quantifying the costs of quality, total quality control, reliability engineering, and zero defects.

Costs of Quality   Until the 1950s, managers assumed it was important to improve quality because defects were costly. But they had no idea just how costly defects were and consequently did not know how much they should improve. They had no yardstick for measuring the costs of quality. In addition to emphasizing management's role in quality, Joseph Juran gave managers a means of answering a critical question which remained in their minds: "How much quality is enough?" (See the 1951 edition of *Juran's Quality Control Handbook.*)

Juran divided the costs of achieving a given level of quality into *avoidable costs* and *unavoidable costs.* Unavoidable costs are those related to preventing defects. These include inspection, sampling, sorting, and other quality control initiatives.[13] Avoidable costs are related to defects and product failures. These include scrapped materials, labor hours required for rework

---

12. Deming's first lectures were to CEOs representing 80 percent of the capital in Japan. He established many committed followers among these industrial leaders. For example, Shoichiro Toyoda, CEO of Toyota Motor Company, reportedly referred to Dr. Deming as his "teacher."
13. We know now that even these costs can be avoided if quality is improved enough.

and repair, complaint processing, and financial losses resulting from unhappy customers. Juran called avoidable costs "gold in the mine" because investment in quality improvement can sharply reduce them and lead to substantial savings. With Juran's cost of quality concept, managers could calculate when additional expenditures on prevention were justified. Juran's cost of quality approach also illustrated the important principle that early decisions, as in engineering design, affected the quality costs incurred later on, in both the factory and the field.[14]

Total Quality Control   In 1956, Armand Feigenbaum extended this principle by suggesting that high-quality products are more likely to be produced through total quality control than when manufacturing works in isolation:

> The underlying principle of this total quality view . . . is that, to provide genuine effectiveness, control must start with the design of the product and end only when the product has been placed in the hands of a customer who remains satisfied . . . the first principle to recognize is that quality is everybody's job. [Feigenbaum, 1956, pp. 94, 98]

Feigenbaum's message reinforced Juran's emphasis on managerial responsibility. To make total quality control work, many companies developed matrices or relationship charts, like the one in Figure 5. The chart lists functions (departments or groups) across the top and required activities down the side, and shows responsibility relationships in each cell. The considerable overlap among functions means that cross-functional teams are needed to ensure required communication and collaboration, for example, in assessing the "manufacturability" of a design and debugging new manufacturing techniques through pilot runs.

Both Juran and Feigenbaum acknowledged that statistical methods and manufacturing control were still important. However, they also felt total quality control would require new management skills to deal with areas such as new product development and vendor selection. Managers also would be required to engage in activities such as quality planning and coordinating cross-functional teamwork. Despite the emphasis on teamwork, Feigenbaum's TQC matrix suggests that more than half of the primary responsibilities for quality belong to the quality control department, another practice that is antithetical to modern Total Quality Management.

Reliability Engineering   While total quality control was emerging, another branch of the quality discipline, *reliability engineering*, was developing with even more heavy reliance on probability theory and statistics. Because

---

14. Notice that this model is completely antisystemic. It is based on accounted costs and captures only scrap, rework, warranty and the ways people traditionally "improved" quality, namely, inspection and purchase of new equipment. By contrast Deming (1986) suggests a chain reaction whereby improved quality leads to lower cost.

Figure 5

Feigenbaum's total quality control matrix or relationship chart applied to product quality

Areas of responsibility	General manager	Finance	Marketing	Engineering	Manager–manufacturing	Manufacturing engineering	Quality control	Materials	Shop operations
Determine needs of customer			(R)						
Establish quality level for business	(R)		C	C	C				
Establish product design specs				(R)					
Establish manufacturing process design				C	M	(R)	M	M	C
Produce products to design specs			M	C	C	C	C	C	(R)
Determine process capabilities					I	C	(R)	M	C
Qualify suppliers on quality							C	(R)	
Plan the quality system	(R)		C	C	C	C	(R)	C	C
Plan inspection and test procedures						C	(R)	C	C
Design test and inspection equipment						C	(R)		M
Feed back quality information			C	C	I	M	(R)	C	C
Gather complaint data			(R)						
Analyze complaint data			M	M			(R)		
Obtain corrective action			M	C	C	C	(R)	C	C
Compile quality costs		(R)	C	C	C				
Analyze quality costs		M					(R)		
In-process quality measurements							(R)		C
In-process quality audit				C		C	(R)		
Final product inspection			C	C	M	C	(R)		

Code: (R) = Responsible; C = Must contribute; M = May contribute; I = Is informed

Reprinted from A. Feigenbaum, *Total Quality Control*, 1961, p. 61.

complex electronics, missiles, and aerospace equipment were not performing reliably during the Korean War in the early 1950s, the military supported the development of reliability engineering. Further driven by postwar growth of the aerospace and electronics industries, reliability engineering sought to assure acceptable product performance over time. Engineers developed mathematical models for predicting equipment performance over time for different products under different operating conditions.[15]

Increased testing did not necessarily help companies improve to meet reliability objectives, so, in addition to prediction, improvement programs were initiated in engineering and manufacturing. Engineers attempted to improve reliability and reduce failure rates over time through a variety of techniques, including:

- *Failure mode and effect analysis* (FMEA), a method for systematically reviewing the ways a product could fail and proposing alternative designs
- *Individual component analysis*, a way of analyzing failure of key components and seeking to correct the weakest
- *Derating*, the requirement that parts be used below their specified stress levels
- *Redundancy*, the practice of using parallel systems as backups in the event that important components fail[16]
- *Monitoring of field failures*, with laboratory testing and analysis of failed parts[17]

Zero Defects Both total quality control and reliability engineering aimed to prevent defects and emphasized engineering skills and attention to quality throughout the design process. By contrast, zero defects focused on management expectations and human relations. The zero defects approach was developed in 1961–1962 at the Martin Company, which was building Pershing missiles for the U.S. Army. Rather than rely on massive inspection to achieve high quality, as it had previously done, Martin established an ambitious schedule to deliver a defect-free missile. It offered workers incentives to lower defect rates and build the missile exactly right the first time, with no hardware problems, no document errors, and all equipment set up and fully operational ten days after delivery (rather than the normal ninety days). The program focused on workers' motivation and awareness, with the goal to "promote a constant, conscious desire to do a job (any job) right the first time" (Halpin, 1966, p. 5). The missile arrived on time and was fully operational in less than twenty-four hours.

---

15. These models seek to make predictions using a theory appropriate for description, which partially explains their disappointing results.

16. Sometimes the addition of redundancies added new failure modes and did not increase overall reliability as expected.

17. Analysis of failures provided information on failure modes but ignored the fact that the same system generated nonfailures. Sometimes "fixes" involved misinterpretation of the results and did not solve problems as anticipated.

From this experience, managers concluded that the project's success was primarily a result of their own changed attitude. James F. Halpin, the Director of Quality at Martin Company, explains: "The reason behind the lack of perfection was simply that perfection had not been expected. The one time management demanded perfection, it happened! Like everyone else in the world, management had accepted as a fact the theory that mistakes are inevitable. By its very actions—setting acceptable quality levels and trying to keep rework costs down to a preset level—management was saying: 'We expect a few defects now and then, just as long as they are kept within reasonable limits.' Actually, the very emphasis on extensive inspection led many workers to reason: 'If I miss it, the inspector will catch it. That's what he's paid for' " (1966, p. 15).

The zero defects program was heavy on philosophy, motivation, and awareness, and lean on specific proposals and problem-solving techniques. While the zero defects movement overemphasized the importance of enhancing employee attention to perfection, Martin did challenge the prevailing assumption that some non-zero level of defects, an acceptable quality level (AQL), was good enough. Martin initiated a fight against historical quality control approaches which continues today, for example, through the writings of Philip B. Crosby, who worked at Martin in the 1960s and who authored the popular books *Quality Is Free* (1979) and *Quality Without Tears* (1984). Crosby's approach to quality improvement intends to get everyone to "do it right the first time." Crosby (1986, pp. 58–86) summarized his approach to management in what he refers to as the *Absolutes of Quality Management*, which answer the following questions:

1. What is quality?
2. What system is needed to cause quality?
3. What performance standard should be used?
4. What measurement system is required?

ANSWERS

1. *The First Absolute*: The Definition of Quality Is Conformance to Requirements.
2. *The Second Absolute*: The System of Quality Is Prevention.
3. *The Third Absolute*: The Performance Standard Is Zero Defects.
4. *The Fourth Absolute*: The Measurement of Quality Is the Price of Nonconformance.

The quality assurance era significantly expanded the involvement of all other functions through total quality control, and inspired managers to pursue perfection actively. However, the approaches to achieving quality remained largely defensive. Controlling quality still meant acting on defects. Quality was something that could hurt a company if ignored, rather than a positive characteristic necessary in obtaining competitive advantage. This view started to change in the 1970s and 1980s, when managers started to recognize the strategic importance of quality.

▶ THE STRATEGIC QUALITY MANAGEMENT ERA

The present quality era, *Strategic Quality Management*, incorporates elements of each of the preceding eras, particularly the contributions of Shewhart, Deming, Juran, and Feigenbaum. So many elements of previous eras are incorporated into Strategic Quality Management that the last two decades may at first appear to be just a repackaging of old ideas. There are, however, dramatic differences from earlier eras. For the first time, top managers began to view quality positively as a competitive advantage, and to address it in their strategic planning processes, which are focused on customer value (Steingraber, 1990).

Because quality started to attract the attention of top managers, it impacted management throughout the organization. Quality was not just for the inspectors or people in the quality assurance department to worry about. This era marks the emergence of a new paradigm for management. A number of developments were brought together and reconfigured into a new approach to management in all departments and specialties.

A variety of external forces brought quality to the attention of top managers. They began to see a link between losses of profitability and poor quality. The forces that brought this connection to their attention included a rising tide of multimillion-dollar product liability suits for defective products and constant pressure from consumer advocates like Ralph Nader. Top managers also felt pressures from the government on several fronts, including closer policing of defects, product recalls (a recall in the late 1970s cost Firestone Tire and Rubber $182 million), and "lemon laws" to provide automobile consumers recourse for recurrent defects. Perhaps the most salient external force was the growing market share incursions from foreign competitors, particularly the Japanese, in such diverse industries as semiconductors, automobiles, machine tools, radial tires, and consumer electronics.

Producing products with superior quality, lower cost, and more reliable delivery, Japanese firms gained market shares and achieved immense profitability. The onslaught of these events in the mid-1970s and 1980s seemed rather sudden. However, Japanese firms had been building their industrial capabilities for decades, developing and refining approaches to quality grounded in the principles taught to them by Americans after World War II. Managers and theorists have been captivated by "Japanese management" over the last two decades. Indeed, the Strategic Quality Management era borrows a number of its elements from the developments that quietly took place in Japan at the same time as the quality assurance era in the United States. We now discuss how some of these elements fit into Total Quality Management.

Total Quality Management

Just as the definition of quality has been a source of confusion, so has the definition of Total Quality Management. There is no consensus on what constitutes TQM. Almost every organization defines it differently or calls it something other than TQM. Japanese writers (e.g., Ishikawa, 1985, and Imai, 1986) often use Feigenbaum's term "Total Quality Control" (TQC) and the Japanese term for their approach, "Company-Wide Quality Control" (CWQC), to label approaches to management that are quite similar to what American managers call "Total Quality Management."

In the United States, *Total Quality Management* is often used to refer to the management approaches being developed in the current era of Strategic Quality Management while the new paradigm is emerging. Ideally, managers in the Strategic Quality Management era regard Total Quality Management as something more than a "program," and take it beyond all the deficiencies mentioned earlier. In this context, the word "total" conveys the idea that all employees, throughout every function and level of an organization, pursue quality. The word "quality" suggests excellence in every aspect of the organization. "Management" refers to the pursuit of quality results through a quality management process. This begins with strategic management processes and extends through product design, manufacturing, marketing, finance, and so on. It encompasses, yet goes beyond, all of the earlier definitions of quality by pulling them together into a never-ending process of improvement. In short, Total Quality Management is grounded in the broad concept of quality which was discussed earlier. Accordingly, TQM is as much about the quality process as it is about quality results or quality products. It begins with people, particularly managers.

Total Quality Management was profoundly influenced by developments in Japan, but it is not a phenomenon that can be branded "Made in Japan." As we have seen, TQM has many of its roots in America. Many of its elements are rooted in theories and practices of management that were developed in America. Schmidt and Finnigan (1992) suggest that TQM's roots include:

1. *Scientific Management*: Finding the best one way to do a job.
2. *Group Dynamics*: Enlisting and organizing the power of group experience.
3. *Training and Development*: Investing in human capital.
4. *Achievement Motivation*: People get satisfaction from accomplishment.
5. *Employee Involvement*: Workers should have some influence in the organization.
6. *Sociotechnical Systems*: Organizations operate as open systems.
7. *Organization Development (OD)*: Helping organizations to learn and change.
8. *Corporate Culture*: Beliefs, myths, and values that guide the behavior of people throughout the organization.
9. *The New Leadership Theory*: Inspiring and empowering others to act.
10. *The Linking-Pin Concept of Organizations*: Creating cross-functional teams.
11. *Strategic Planning*: Determining where to take the organization, and how and when to get there.

Schmidt and Finnigan also suggest that certain American theories and practices are dysfunctional and antithetical to TQM. These include:

1. *Bureaucratic Management*: Direction from the boss, compliance from the subordinate.
2. *Caveat Emptor*: Let the buyer beware.
3. *MBO and MBR*: Management by objectives and management by results.
4. *Internal Competition*: Encouraging each department to be number one.
5. *The Strategy of Organizational Stability*: "If it ain't broke, don't fix it."
6. *Antagonism toward Unions*: Workers' interests are basically different from managers' interests.
7. *Bottom-Line Driven*: Profit is the first test for every decision and action.

While its roots are in American management theories and practices, TQM attempts to reconfigure these into a whole approach to management that is more than the simple sum of its parts. These parts may have existed before the Strategic Quality Management era and the popularity of TQM. However, they were not usefully configured into an integrated approach that is focused on the themes of the emerging paradigm. This holistic approach makes TQM fundamentally different from past traditions of management.

TQM may yet be regarded as a passing fad. However, the underlying themes of management being addressed by those who are striving to define and move to a new paradigm are not fads. These themes include the importance of understanding customer needs, formulating strategies to provide value to customers, and continuously improving organizational systems to provide that value. Let's take a closer look at each of these themes.

QUALITY IN ACTION: A MESSAGE TO THE STUDENT
Stephen B. Schwartz, IBM Senior Vice President, Market-Driven Quality

Companies that enjoy immense prosperity, such as IBM, often grow into bloated bureaucracies, with excessive layers of management and overly complex business processes. Despite their technical capabilities and great resources, they become less able to compete with smaller, more nimble competitors, particularly in the dynamic computer industry. Stephen B. Schwartz, Senior Vice President, Market-Driven Quality, explains how IBM plans to transform itself and remain a major player in this highly competitive industry.

Since the late 1970s, close to 50 percent of the companies on the U.S. Fortune 500 listing have been displaced. The business environment is rapidly changing, and IBM, as much as any other company, is faced with new challenges and new levels of customer expectation. At IBM, we have evolved a Total Quality Management (TQM) approach to meet these challenges that we are convinced will ensure a transformation of the company, linked to positive business results.

We call our quality approach Market-Driven Quality or MDQ. At its center is a focus not just on customer satisfaction, but on customer delight. MDQ has emerged as the implementation plan for our corporate business strategy. Our MDQ approach has come to mean more than the reliability and price/performance of a computer. We've made it more than a program. Now MDQ encompasses every aspect of customer satisfaction improvement, including the continuous improvement of all our business processes, the elimination of defects, the speed of delivering and implementing a solution, its usability, the availability of support, the efficiency of service, and even the simplicity of bills and prompt, courteous telephone service. MDQ is becoming a completely integrated part of the way we do business.

The understanding of Total Quality Management principles is so important to IBM's future and the future of America that we have sponsored a multimillion-dollar partnership with nine colleges and universities to teach it in their curricula, especially in business and engineering courses. Our intent is to ensure that graduates of these courses are ready to apply the principles of quality management from the first day they are on the job.

Strategy, Quality, and Customer Value

Producing defective products (not conforming to design specifications) is certainly antithetical to quality. However, preventing defects has not captured the strategic interests of top managers. Top managers in the United States tend to see defect prevention as an element of control, a managerial responsibility they typically delegate to subordinates. Unfortunately, this view regards quality only as something that will hurt the company if neglected. By focusing on the customer in the new paradigm, managers view quality as a means of achieving competitive advantage by providing value to customers.

The Concept of Customer Value Value-based approaches expand on the user-based view of quality by incorporating the notion of "price or costs." Regarding value-based approaches, Garvin (1988, p. 45) suggests "a quality product is one that provides performance or conformance at an acceptable price or cost. By this reasoning, a $500 running shoe, no matter how well-constructed, could not be a quality product, for it would find few buyers." In support of this view, researchers have demonstrated a positive relationship between market share and value-based measures of quality (Curry and Faulds, 1985). Other examples contradict this value-based approach which assumes that lower cost always means higher value to the customer. Designer dresses that sell for $5,000, or luxury cars that cost more than a home, suggest that there is another dimension of value. The definition of customer value offered below expands on this value-based definition of quality. In fact, the customer value concept encompasses all of the foregoing definitions of quality.

Figure 6

Quality improvement for customer value

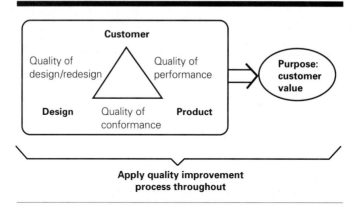

We define *customer value* as a combination of benefits and sacrifices occurring when a customer uses a product or service to meet certain needs. Those consequences that contribute to meeting one's needs are benefits, while those consequences that detract from meeting one's needs are sacrifices.

For example, a person who purchases a large luxury car to satisfy a need for pleasurable travel might enjoy such benefits as comfort, restfulness, and audio entertainment. On the other hand, the person also has to make certain sacrifices, such as paying for the vehicle, difficulties in parking a large vehicle, and fuel and maintenance costs. These sacrifices detract from meeting customer needs. For example, if the car owner lives in a town that doesn't have a dealership for the luxury car, he or she will incur costs such as frustration, time, and the inconvenience of going to another town for service.

The concept of customer value encompasses the benefits and sacrifices associated with the customer's use process throughout the life cycle of product ownership. As Deming (1986, p. 176) suggests: "Quality must be measured by the interaction between three participants: (1) the product itself; (2) the user and how he uses the product, how he installs it, how he takes care of it (example: customer [permitting] dirt to fall into [a] roller bearing), what he was led (as by advertising) to expect; and (3) instructions for use, training of customer and training of repairman, service provided for repairs, and availability of parts."

The concept of customer value also encompasses all the definitions of quality mentioned so far (see Figure 6). To provide value to customers, managers must ensure the following:

1. *Quality of Design/Redesign*: Product designs conform to customer needs (product-based and user-based quality). For example, automobile producers design car seats to conform to the contours of the driver's back.

2. *Quality of Conformance*: Products manufactured conform to product designs (manufacturing-based quality). For example, each car seat produced meets the targeted design specifications.
3. *Quality of Performance*: Products manufactured conform to customer needs by performing in the field (user-based quality). For example, the car seats maintain their shape after years of use.

All of these dimensions of quality should be managed through a quality improvement process that enhances customer value. Placing quality in the broader context of customer value counteracts the tendency of people with different functional orientations within an organization to take different views of quality (Garvin, 1988). For example, marketing people tend to have a user-based and product-based view that focuses on matching product characteristics with customer perceptions. Engineers, on the other hand, tend to take a product-based view that focuses on defining product characteristics. Manufacturing people tend to view quality as conformance to specifications and targets.

Each of these views is important, and has a role in executing a strategy for customer value. But taken alone, each concept of quality also has blind spots and limitations. Quality improvement programs that are focused on one specific function tend to be disappointing because they do not coordinate with the efforts of others. When functional managers do not show sensitivity to the other perspectives of quality, they miss opportunities for gaining competitive advantage. For example, Kentucky Fried Chicken could make the best fried chicken in the world (in terms of conformance to specs), but with the changing attitudes of consumers toward fried foods, the company had to change its product and its image. Now it goes by the name "KFC" and has introduced "light and crispy," skinless chicken to minimize the "sacrifice" for health-conscious consumers.

Achieving strategic objectives for customer value requires that the organization's activities be integrated at every level and across every function. Each manager must know how his or her work fits with that of others. To gain this understanding, managers need an even broader view of quality.

A Strategic Customer Focus Certainly, managers must ensure quality through conformance to design specifications. But quality of conformance should be a secondary issue, pursued only after they have seen that design conforms to the needs of the customer (quality of design). Thus, managers in the new paradigm regard quality as an important element to strategy formulation and planning: deciding which markets to enter, which customers to serve, which products and services to offer, and how to provide value to customers and outperform competitors in doing so. Market research becomes an important tool for understanding how the many dimensions of quality affect customer value. As Ishikawa suggests, it requires a consumer, rather than a producer, orientation; managers must "know how consumers use their products" (1985, p. 107).

Strategic managers must be market-oriented; however, they must not make the mistake that Ford Motor Company made in rejecting the minivan because the market did not yet exist. Hal Sperlich developed the idea of the minivan because he had a mission in mind: to create a vehicle for the housewife which was more user-friendly than the station wagon, with the height, width, and handling to make it practical for grocery shopping and carpooling. When Ford rejected it, Sperlich took the idea to Chrysler, which subsequently created and temporarily cornered the market.

A Strategic Quality Focus Once top managers decide to compete on the basis of particular dimensions of quality, they enter the realm of strategic planning. The issue of quality of conformance to the strategic plans becomes a matter for their direct attention. This means assuming personal responsibility for continuously improving the systems and processes that provide valued goods and services for customers. Strategic quality managers believe that concern for quality offers a means of strategically positioning the firm, first, by determining the dimensions of quality important to customers, and second, by conforming to and continually improving on the design specifications. In addition, they ask themselves how they can use quality to better serve customers. If quality and profitability are strategically linked, then why just match the quality levels of competitors? Competitive advantage comes from exceeding the quality levels of competitors. In a dynamic marketplace where each competitor seeks to reach the highest quality level and serve the changing needs of customers, managers must continuously improve.

The Continuous Improvement Philosophy

Some approaches to quality implicitly constrain continuous improvement. For example, as we have seen, Juran provided managers with measures for the avoidable and unavoidable costs of quality. This seemed to allow managers to determine a maximum desirable amount of quality. As Juran explains, "The basic quality problem is to strike the correct balance between cost of quality and value of quality for each quality characteristic" (1962, Section 1, p. 10). Figure 7 depicts how this balance is determined. In general, as unavoidable costs go up, avoidable costs go down. In other words, when managers spend more on quality control (unavoidable costs), the number of defects go down (avoidable costs). The point of lowest total cost of quality (avoidable plus unavoidable costs) is where the two lines for these costs intersect. This point then dictates how much quality is enough, in Juran's terms.

While managers should be concerned with costs, Juran's approach to balancing quality and costs offers managers an excuse for less than excellent performance and for not implementing continuous improvement. This cost-focused approach to quality can be antithetical to a continuous

Figure 7

The Economics of Quality of Conformance,
Juran's answer to the question "How much quality is enough?"

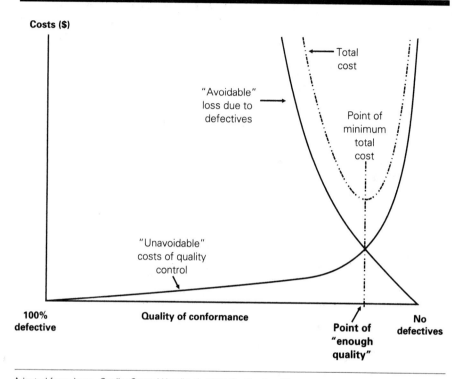

Adapted from Juran, *Quality Control Handbook*, 1962, Section 1, p.10.

improvement strategy focused on customer value.[18] There are several flaws in this thinking. First, it defines quality only in terms of "conformance to specifications" and suggests that money is lost only when defects occur. Second, it allows managers to assume that there is always a tradeoff between quality and cost based on predictable cost curves. Third, it assumes that managers can accurately and completely measure the costs of quality. Fourth, it assumes that to minimize costs, managers should be content to determine a maximum amount of "necessary quality" rather than the amount of quality that will meet customers' needs. The theme of continuous improvement attacks each of these assumptions.

Defining Continuous Improvement   In our view, constant reaching for continuous improvement may be achieved through big steps (breakthroughs)

18. Juran's approach appears to contradict the philosophies of zero defects and continuous improvement. However, the contradiction disappears when managers pursue the Japanese

Figure 8

Features of *kaizen* and innovation

	Kaizen	Innovation
1. Effect	Long-term and long-lasting, but undramatic	Short-term, but dramatic
2. Pace	Small steps	Big steps
3. Time frame	Continuous and incremental	Intermittent and non-incremental
4. Change	Gradual and constant	Abrupt and volatile
5. Involvement	Everybody	Select few "champions"
6. Approach	Collectivism, group efforts, systems approach	Rugged individualism, individual ideas and efforts
7. Mode	Maintenance and improvement	Scrap and rebuild
8. Spark	Conventional know-how and state of the art	Technological breakthroughs, new inventions, new theories
9. Practical requirements	Requires little investment, but great effort to maintain it	Requires large investment, but little effort to maintain it
10. Effort orientation	People	Technology
11. Evaluation criteria	Process and efforts for better results	Results for profits
12. Advantage	Works well in slow-growth economy	Better suited to fast-growth economy

Reprinted from M. Imai, *Kaizen*, 1986, p. 24.

and little steps (increments). Some authors have made a similar distinction between Japanese and Western approaches to improvement. Imai (1986) suggests American managers tend to rely on *breakthroughs*, the innovative one-shot deals that achieve dramatically better levels of performance (or discontinuous leaps). Juran advocated such innovation in his 1964 book, *Managerial Breakthrough*. By contrast, Imai suggests, Japanese managers tend to accomplish improvement through *kaizen*, a number of undramatic and subtle improvements gradually and cumulatively raising the level of performance without interruption (or continuous advancement).[19]

kaizen approach to incremental improvement, because the costs of improvement become more transparent. For more discussion of this idea, see Schneiderman (1986).

19. Some managers use the phrase "continuous improvement" to convey this more specific notion of incremental improvement. We use it more broadly to emphasis continuous or relentless effort.

Figure 9

Ideal versus actual pattern for innovation

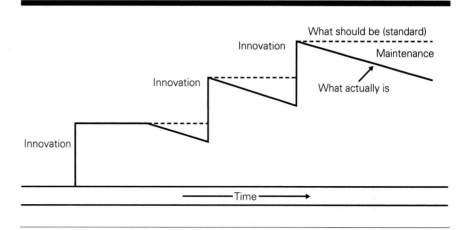

Adapted from M. Imai, *Kaizen*, 1986, p.26.

Imai contrasts *kaizen* and innovation (1986, pp. 25–27). Figure 8 shows that innovation, the Western approach, achieves dramatic or discontinuous jumps, primarily through technological advances and large sums of money spent on research and development. After reaching a new standard, however, performance decays while managers simply await the next innovation (see Figure 9). By contrast, *kaizen* does not necessarily require sophisticated technologies, but relies on people to apply simple techniques and some common sense to continue to upgrade the standard of performance.

The most powerful approach would be to combine *kaizen* and innovation (see Figure 10). Between the big jumps, repeated small steps would ensure perpetual progress with no backsliding. This motion is what we mean by "continuous improvement."

Global competitors are increasingly pursuing improvement through both innovation and incremental changes. Contrasts between Japanese and American approaches often reinforce our emphasis on continuous improvement as relentless, constant reaching. For example, the following quote from *The Deming Guide to Quality and Competitive Position* illustrates the contrast between IBM and a Japanese supplier:

> Apparently the computer giant decided to have some parts manufactured in Japan as a trial project. In the specifications they set out that the limit of defective parts would be acceptable at three units per 10,000. When the delivery came in there was an accompanying letter. "We Japanese have a hard time understanding North American business practices. But the three defective parts per 10,000 have been included and are wrapped separately. Hope this pleases." [Gitlow and Gitlow, 1987, p. 32]

Figure 10

Progress through both *kaizen* and innovation

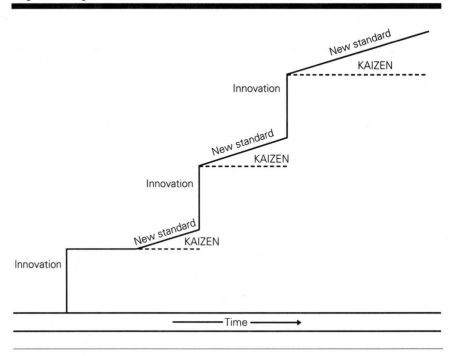

Adapted from M. Imai, *Kaizen*, 1986, p.27.

Historical quality approaches that induce complacency, such as "acceptable quality levels" (AQL), are obsolete in this type of competitive environment. Even the zero defects plea for workers to "do it right the first time" must be regarded as inadequate. The product design may be entirely wrong for the market. Even when the design specifications are right, managers should seek to reduce variation within the specifications that define defects and nondefects. It's not enough to "just do it right the first time."

Reducing Variation The zero defects campaigns of the 1960s and 1970s advanced the quality concept beyond the AQL approach by disavowing complacency with any level of defects. However, for some organizations, zero defects could be achieved by just meeting specifications and going no further. For example, a grinding operation should grind steel rods to meet the engineering specifications for length of six inches, plus or minus ten one-hundredths of an inch (6 + or − .10). Any part within the range of 5.9 to 6.1 inches in length meets the specification and is "not defective." All parts produced by grinding operation A, shown in Figure 11, are good. Operation A meets the zero defects goal. Presuming that the design

Figure 11

Frequency distributions of output from two grinding operations

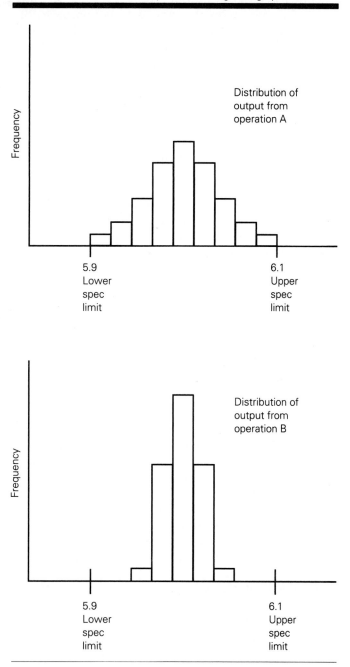

specifications conform to customer needs, these parts should meet customer needs. But they may not.

In contrast to the zero defects approach, Shewhart's approach to statistical quality control, as taught to the Japanese by W. Edwards Deming in the 1950s, challenges managers to disavow complacency with just meeting specifications. Deming taught the Japanese to study and continuously reduce variation in systems to consequently reduce variation in the output (such as for operation B in Figure 11).

The importance of continuous improvement can be seen in the simple example of the grinding operation. Productivity and cost can be improved by reducing variation. A part ground to the length of 5.9 inches meets the specification as a "good" part, but it requires extra labor, tools, and machine time to grind the part down .10 inch shorter than the target of six inches. Further, grinding the .10 inch off the steel rod wastes .10 inch of steel. If the operation were to simply grind rods down to the target of six inches, with virtually no variation, all previously wasted labor, machine, and material costs could be saved. Even better, why not improve the cutting operation, so the steel rods are cut closer to six inches, and totally eliminate the subsequent grinding operation.

The impact of variation on customers should also be considered. Again, all parts from the grinding operation may meet engineering specifications, but that does not mean that all parts equally meet customers' needs. A part 5.9 inches long may not meet the customers' needs as well as one 6.0 inches long. For example, the 5.9-inch steel rod fits into a machine assembly and works "perfectly" at first. However, over time, as it gets worn with use by the customer, it will more quickly wear to the point of no longer meeting customer specifications (i.e., less than 5.9 inches long). The short life of the rod may compromise the performance of the machine and may even cause a breakdown that interrupts the customer's activities. The part fails to meet the customer's need for reliability, an important dimension of quality. For an industrial customer, this could mean the shutdown of an entire production line while costly repairs are done.

Taguchi (1986) suggests that there is increasing loss, for the producer, the customer, and society, associated with increasing variability, or deviation from a target value that reflects the "ideal state." This relationship to variability can be expressed as a loss function, as shown for the distribution of rods from grinding operation C, in Figure 12. The greater the variability, deviation from target, the greater the loss.

Traditional specifications, used in the manufacturing-based approach to quality, define conformity in terms of upper and lower specification limits. For example, steel rods should meet the engineering specification for length of six inches, plus or minus 10 one-hundredths of an inch (6 + or − .10). This approach tends to allow complacency concerning variation within that range. It assumes that a product just barely meeting

Figure 12

Taguchi's loss function: loss increases as a function of variation

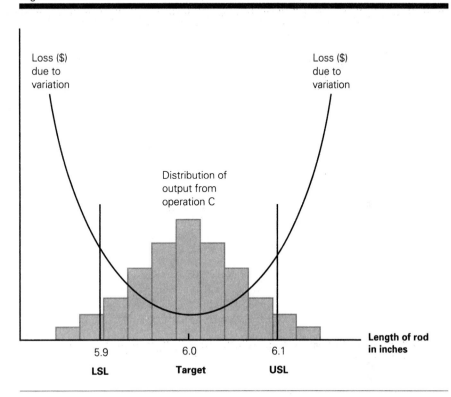

specifications, just within the limit, is just as "good" as one right in the middle, but one just outside the limit is "bad." Taguchi questions these assumptions, and suggests the degree of "badness" or "loss" increases gradually as the deviation from the target value increases. Although managers may choose to do the right thing (the target), in order to provide superior value to customers through superior "quality," they must also continuously improve their systems and reduce variation to meet the target.[20] In the 1980s, Motorola committed to a campaign called Six Sigma, which is one way of saying reduce variation so much that the chance of producing defects is down to about 3.4 defects per million, or 99.99966 percent perfect.

Deming suggests that a chain reaction results from quality improvement through reduced variation. He notes that the following chain reac-

---

20. The concepts and methods for doing so, including statistical process control (SPC) and design of experiments (DOE), are discussed later.

Figure 13

Deming's "Condensation of the 14 Points for Management"

1. Create and publish to all employees a statement of the aims and purposes of the company or other organization. The management must demonstrate constantly their commitment to this statement.
2. Learn the new philosophy, top management and everybody.
3. Understand the purpose of inspection, for improvement of processes and reduction of cost.
4. End the practice of awarding business on the basis of price tag alone.
5. Improve constantly and forever the system of production and service.
6. Institute training.
7. Teach and institute leadership.
8. Drive out fear. Create trust. Create a climate for innovation.
9. Optimize toward the aims and purposes of the company the efforts of teams, groups, staff areas.
10. Eliminate exhortations for the work force.
11. a. Eliminate numerical quotas for production. Instead, learn and institute methods for improvement.
    b. Eliminate M. B. O. Instead, learn the capabilities of processes, and how to improve them.
12. Remove barriers that rob people of pride of workmanship.
13. Encourage education and self-improvement for everyone.
14. Take action to accomplish the transformation.

tion was on the blackboard of every meeting with top management in Japan from July 1950 onward:

- Improve quality ⇒
- Costs decrease because of less rework, fewer mistakes, fewer delays, snags: better use of machine time and materials ⇒
- Productivity improves ⇒
- Capture the market with better quality and lower price ⇒
- Stay in business ⇒
- Provide jobs and more jobs (1986, p. 3)

Deming has formulated a management theory centered around system improvement, the reduction of variation to meet customer needs, and the humane and intelligent management of people. Deming's Fourteen Points are elements of his theory for management, which calls for management to assume leadership and personal responsibility to put it in place (see Figure 13).

Management Responsibility for Systems and Processes Associated with the emphasis on continuous improvement and redesign of the system is the management responsibility for leading and carrying out this work. As Deming says, "Any substantial improvement must come from action on the system, the responsibility of management" (1986, p. 7). Deming out-

Figure 14

Deming's view of production as a system

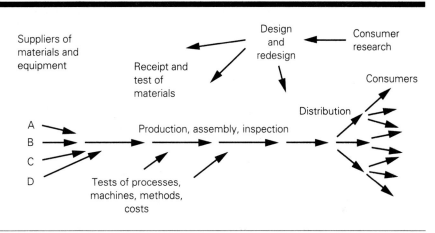

About this figure (which is reprinted from *Out of the Crisis*, 1986, p.4), Deming states: "Improvement of quality envelops the entire production line, from incoming materials to the consumer, and redesign of product and service for the future. This chart was first used in August 1950 at a conference with top management at the Hotel de Yama on Mount Hakone in Japan. In a service organization, the sources A, B, C, etc., could be sources of data, or work from preceding operations, such as charges (as in a department store), calculation of charges, deposits, withdrawals, inventories in and out, transcriptions, shipping orders, and the like."

lined this management responsibility for the Japanese when he defined production as a system (see Figure 14):

> Mere talk about quality accomplishes little. It was necessary to go into action. The flow diagram [in Figure 14] provided a start. Materials and equipment come in at the left. It would be necessary, I explained, to improve incoming materials. Work with your vendor as a partner on a long-term relationship of loyalty and trust to improve the quality of incoming materials and to decrease costs. The consumer is the most important part of the production line. Quality should be aimed at the needs of the consumer, present and future. Quality begins with the intent, which is fixed by management. The intent must be translated by engineers and others into plans, specifications, tests, production. [pp. 4–5]

Fulfilling this responsibility for systems and processes ensures that managers take action to reduce variation and achieve continuous improvement. These ideas are intimately connected. Later we explore in detail how managers study system and process variation and its causes to determine appropriate actions for making improvements.

Juran also emphasizes managerial responsibility for improvement to meet customers' needs, but he does not use the term "system" to describe this managerial responsibility. Instead, Juran uses the term "macroprocesses" to refer to cross-functional systems which encompass the "microprocesses" within functions (1992, p. 334). Further, *Juran's Trilogy* is an ap-

Figure 15

The Juran Trilogy diagram

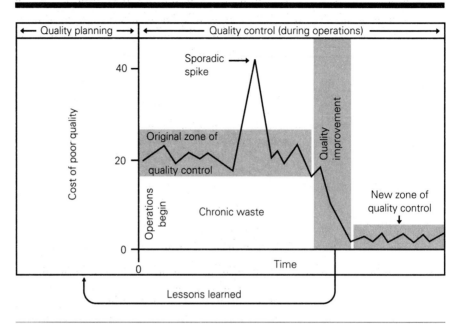

Reprinted from J. M. Juran, *Juran on Quality by Design*, 1992, p. 17.
Note: Juran's Trilogy diagram shown above relates to product deficiencies, which is one way Juran defines quality. Specifically, the "cost of poor quality" shown on the vertical scale exhibits such units of measure as error rates, percent defective, and service call rate. On this scale, perfection is at zero. A shift up is bad, and a shift down is good. The Trilogy diagram can also display product features, or "product salability," on the vertical dimension. Product salability defines quality in terms of meeting customer needs. On this scale, a shift up is good, and a shift down is bad.

proach to cross-functional management that is composed of three managerial processes: planning, control, and improvement (see Figure 15).

Quality planning

This is the activity of developing the products and processes required to meet customers' needs. It involves a series of universal steps which can be abbreviated as follows:

- Establish quality goals
- Identify the customers—those who will be impacted by the efforts to meet the goals
- Determine the customers' needs
- Develop product features that respond to customers' needs
- Develop processes that are able to produce those product features
- Establish process controls, and transfer the resulting plans to the operating forces

Quality control

This process consists of the following steps:

- Evaluate actual quality performance
- Compare actual performance to quality goals
- Act on the difference

Quality improvement

This process is the means of raising quality performance to unprecedented levels ("breakthrough"). The methodology consists of a series of universal steps:

- Establish the infrastructure needed to secure annual quality improvement
- Identify the specific needs for improvement—the improvement projects
- For each project establish a project team with clear responsibility for bringing the project to a successful conclusion
- Provide the resources, motivation, and training needed by the teams to:
  - Diagnose the causes
  - Stimulate establishment of remedies
  - Establish controls to hold the gains [Juran, 1992, pp. 14–16]

To accomplish quality improvement depicted in the Trilogy, Juran suggests the following:

- Top managers are responsible for designing for quality by making quality planning (goal setting) a part of business planning.
- Quality goals or quality improvement projects should be deployed down through the hierarchy by breaking them into subgoals ("bite-size" projects) at lower levels.
- In the case of macroprocesses that have no ownership and cannot be broken into pieces and deployed, top managers should form quality councils that establish and oversee project teams to improve macroprocesses.

Whether you adopt Deming's approach or Juran's approach to improvement, you will hear similar messages on managerial responsibility. They both suggest that a manager's responsibility for improving systems and processes goes beyond the traditional responsibility for achieving results or "getting things done through others."[21] In different ways, both Deming and Juran suggest that managers act as leaders, first by setting the vision for those who work within the system, then by providing and constantly improving the means by which they can achieve that vision. However, Deming's approach is more consistent with what we describe as the emerging paradigm.

---

21. The terms "system" and "process" appear to be used interchangeably in this discussion. We make a distinction between a system and a process, designating the former as a more broad and strategic concept that encompasses processes.

This latter focus on the means of achieving the result is referred to as "process-oriented management" by writers who describe Japanese management approaches (e.g., Imai, 1986, p. 16). Process-oriented management attempts to identify and improve the underlying causes of results, by "managing upstream." For example, Imai (p. 50) suggests that "asking why several times will dig out several causes, one of which is usually the root cause."

According to Ishikawa, Japanese managers enhance this process-oriented approach with an *internal customer orientation*, which means that within the organization "the next process is your customer" (Ishikawa, 1985, p. 107). As Imai (1986, pp. 51–52) suggests: "If quality is to be maintained and improved in the production process, there must be smooth communication among all the people at every production stage. . . . Assuring quality to each customer at each stage will assure quality in the finished product." This ideal may not always be achieved, but the customer orientation does provide a focus for cross-functional improvement.

The Japanese have also combined process-oriented and internal customer-oriented approaches with Feigenbaum's Total Quality Control to yield an even more powerful approach to managing systems. Many Japanese managers use the term "Company-Wide Quality Control" to designate their approach to total quality (Ishikawa, 1985). Company-Wide Quality Control involves all divisions and all employees in an integrated approach to accomplish superordinate objectives for quality, cost, and scheduling (quantity and delivery).

Company-wide quality control goes beyond Feigenbaum's notion of TQC in that it does not assign most of the primary responsibilities for quality to a quality control department. According to Ishikawa, policy deployment cascades improvement targets and links means and ends throughout every function and level of the organization. Cross-functional teams integrate everyone's actions to meet these common objectives.

Imai (1986, p. 125) summarizes this approach: "The cross-functional goals of QCS (quality, cost, and scheduling) are clearly defined as superior to such line functions as design, production, and marketing. Therefore, the positioning of cross-functional goals as superordinate goals necessitates a new systems approach to decision making. . . . Within this context, 'quality' is concerned with building a better system for quality assurance; 'cost' is concerned both with building a system for identifying cost factors and with reducing costs; 'scheduling' refers to building a better system for both delivery and quantity." Ishikawa (1985, p. 109) adds: "Sectionalism has to be broken down, and the company has to be ventilated so that everyone can enjoy a breath of fresh air. Everyone must be able to talk to each other freely and frankly."

The power of this *cross-functional systems approach* to management is that it integrates activities throughout the organization for improving toward strategic objectives. It raises everyone's attention to a higher level, above functional concerns, toward a holistic view of the organization and its purpose to serve customers. In this text, however, we argue that managers in this era should use the concept of cross-functional systems flexibly. They should define the domain and boundaries of systems as needed to accomplish any specific improvement objective, beyond the general categories of quality, cost, and scheduling.

System Improvement, Problem Solving, and Crisis Resolution Managers often complain that they do not have time to do systems improvement, that they cannot afford to analyze and reflect upon systems because they are too busy responding to crises, and that they have to deal with the same crises over and over. These managers do not realize that the crises merely reflect their failure to solve problems permanently by improving systems. The distinction between system improvement, problem solving, and fire fighting is clarified:

Crisis resolution or *fire fighting* represents fixing the immediate situation just so normal operations can continue. For example, a sander belt may jam the sanding machine. Removing the belt and unjamming the machine puts out the fire for now, but the fire may recur. *Problem solving* represents finding the cause of the problem and addressing the cause so that the problem does not return. For example, problem solving may entail ensuring that the belt is of the right size and quality, and operated at the prescribed speed, or repairing a malfunctioning sander. Thus, problem solving involves removing the source of the fire, the smoldering embers. Note, however, that both crisis resolution and problem solving are prompted by deficiencies in the current system. By contrast, *system improvement* requires rethinking of the system. The system is not just repaired and maintained, but changed, perhaps by redesigning the system to eliminate belts or redesigning the part or previous processes to eliminate the need to sand. Managers do not wait for a crisis or a problem (a fire) before they take action (Bounds and Dobbins, 1991, p. 139).

Recognizing the difference between these ideas can make a big difference to a company. Based on his firm's research, the chairman and CEO of A.T. Kearney, Inc., Fred G. Steingraber, estimates that in service industries as much as 40 percent of costs is spent on fixing problems that shouldn't have happened (1990). By redefining managerial roles for system improvement rather than just problem solving, a typical service company can save a lot of money, and serve customers better at the same time.

The Total View of Quality

The concept of customer value represents a dramatic improvement over the traditional approach to quality, the "conformance to specified standards" approach. It extends the concept of quality to include user perceptions and use consequences. However, it still falls short of the concept of Total Quality, which stresses the importance of quality in every aspect of an organization.

Perhaps the Japanese best express this broader and more holistic view of quality. Ishikawa (1985, p. 45) states: "Narrowly interpreted, quality means quality of product. Broadly interpreted, quality means quality of work, quality of service, quality of information, quality of process, quality of division, quality of people, including workers, engineers, managers, and executives, quality of system, quality of company, quality of objectives, etc." This view of quality may at first seem to be too idealistic. However, managers who are committed to this view of quality have pragmatic solutions for translating the word "quality" into organizational realities.

As Imai (1986, p. xxiii) suggests, it all begins with the "quality of people." He states:

> There is very little agreement on what constitutes quality. In its broadest sense, quality is anything that can be improved. When speaking of "quality" one tends to think first in terms of product quality. When discussed in the context of *kaizen* strategy nothing could be further off the mark. The foremost concern here is with the *quality of people.* The three building blocks of a business are hardware, software, and "humanware." Only after humanware is squarely in place should the hardware and software aspects of a business be considered. Building quality into people means helping them become *kaizen* conscious.

This total view of quality includes all of the above quality themes we have already seen, integrating them into a comprehensive approach to continuous improvement.

Beyond Total Quality Management

Quality has evolved from a discipline relegated to inspectors and technical experts to a strategic focus and a process-oriented approach to management that commands the attention of all employees, from the top to the bottom of the organization, from the CEOs and presidents to the front-line workers. The popular term "Total Quality Management" conveys the comprehensive nature of this approach, with emphasis on the word "Total" and a broad definition of "Quality." As mentioned earlier, labeling this new approach by any name, such as TQM, may imply a uniformity in all the approaches that go by the name. But this is not true. "TQM" approaches vary from company to company. And similar approaches often have different names.

No one model from the strategic quality management era will work for every organization. First, in the Strategic Quality Management era, we are participating in the emergence of a new paradigm. Our understanding of the new paradigm is continuing to evolve. We are currently in a stage of experimentation, with organizations shifting and managers inventing and testing new approaches to management to help define a new paradigm. Second, every organization faces unique circumstances and must vary its approach accordingly. Each organization must develop its own specific approach to suit its own internal and external circumstances.

To maintain their sanity in this type of environment, managers (and students) must have a high tolerance for ambiguity. They must be prepared to receive confused and often conflicting messages from consultants, authors, and other "experts." Some conflicts inadvertently result from semantic differences when conceptual differences are minimal. Others result from conceptual differences, grounded in real disagreements over definitions and approaches, even when these differences might be masked by semantics similarities. Most importantly, we must be prepared to go beyond TQM. The implications of doing so are profound. They include going beyond programs, moving toward customer value and toward normalcy of the new paradigm.

Beyond Programs To go beyond TQM implies that managers should not "do quality" by implementing programs. This is not an indictment of the definition of TQM, but of the typical approach that managers take in doing TQM.[22] In many organizations, managers regard TQM as a sideline activity, a corporate program which requires only a few hours each week. Collateral quality activities are established apart from the normal management process, rather than blended in as a way of life. Additionally, managers often mistakenly believe that the use of certain tools and techniques constitutes Total Quality Management, a belief often associated with the program mentality. The definition of TQM developed by the working council of the Total Quality Forum dispelled this misconception by separating the underlying principles from the tools and techniques that are often used to apply the principles. This is the way it should be once we reach the period of normalcy for the new, but still emerging paradigm.

As managers go beyond TQM, the fundamental principles of the emerging paradigm become a natural part of daily management processes, rather than something that managers are preoccupied with implementing or worried about putting in place. Managerial practices unconsciously flow from the fundamental principles that firmly reside in the minds of managers, taken for granted as the assumed way of doing business. The emerging paradigm becomes central to the manager's role and not an extra duty that requires conscious attention and directed effort.

Toward Customer Value Initial efforts to implement TQM programs encouraged managers to improve quality in each and every function of the organization. As managers evolve their thinking away from a program mentality and toward a paradigm mentality, they realize that they must do even more. Since the various functions of an organization may each define quality according to different dimensions, top managers must ensure that each function defines and improves quality in a way that integrates

---

22. Writers of trade books reinforce this approach by prescribing steps to implement plans. For example, see *Quality in America: How to Implement a Competitive Quality Program*, by V. Daniel Hunt, Homewood, Ill.: Business One Irwin, 1992.

with the activities of all other functions to optimize the whole. The concept of customer value provides the organizational purpose for integrating quality improvement efforts throughout an organization. Managers must go beyond the product-focused concept of quality and understand how all of its dimensions must be managed in order to meet superordinate objectives for the organization's customer value strategy. This integration must not be left to chance, but purposefully managed and continuously improved. Otherwise, managers may jeopardize the organization's survival and prosperity.

Toward Normalcy of the Paradigm As managers and organizations go beyond TQM toward a paradigm driven by customer value and beyond a "program implementation" approach to quality, they approach a period of normalcy after the period of paradigm shift. In this context, the answer to the question, "Is TQM a fad?" has to be "Yes, it had better be a fad." In the period of normalcy for the new paradigm, when it is accepted as the "proven" way of managing organizations, the term will no longer be needed. The fundamental principles of the emerging paradigm will have become synonymous with the practice of management.

In the period of normalcy, we may just speak of management rather than a buzzword like Total Quality Management. However, we are now still in a transitional period, with some organizations/industries experiencing anomalies and just now sensing the need for change, and with some organizations/industries currently making the paradigm shift. In this transitional period, we can expect such labels to be commonplace, and perhaps useful for some organizations to sustain attention and motivation for the change effort. People seem to need a label to designate the new approaches to management as different from those of the past.

In the new period of normalcy, managers will continue to refine the paradigm, testing new tools, techniques, and concepts which fit in with the now accepted paradigm, and further perfecting its practice. This new period of normalcy will last until it is time for yet another paradigm shift, as revealed again by the existence of anomalies and events inexplicable within the accepted paradigm.

The Nature of the Paradigm Shift

In general, the shift from traditional approaches to the new paradigm will often highlight contrasts in management practices. Certainly, the contrast of the old paradigm versus the new, emerging paradigm represents extremes, and most organizations fall somewhere in the middle ground. Thus, shifting to a new paradigm will mean different things for different organizations and for different managers within an organization. For managers who have kept up with the evolutionary developments in quality, the required shift will not be as dramatic. They may simply have to rearrange and integrate some of the diverse elements or quality programs into an integrated whole, or develop new cultural values and beliefs to support the new paradigm.

To the extent that the current organizational culture is already compatible with the new concepts, methods, and techniques, the shift will be much easier. Some managers will have to start from scratch, not only developing understanding of the concepts, methods, and techniques, but also developing a set of cultural beliefs, values, and assumptions to sustain the practice of the new paradigm. Some managers have not even kept up with advancements in management concepts that occurred independently of the evolution of quality, e.g., participative management and transformational leadership. Those managers who are behind in these areas will find it even more difficult to make the shift, because approaches and concepts of the new paradigm are still emerging.

The irony of achieving normalcy in the new paradigm is that it contains a built-in component that undermines the state of normalcy itself: it requires continuous improvement. Nothing can remain normal for long, because people constantly challenge the status quo. The new paradigm bears within it the seed of its own destruction. However, the destructive and reconstructive process will be evolutionary during this period of normalcy, as people continuously improve the paradigm itself, constantly shifting it into newness.

Concluding Comments

The reader should not infer from the foregoing discussion of the Strategic Quality Management era that all managers are practicing the themes of the emerging paradigm in the same way or even to the same extent. As with all other quality eras, a number of companies and managers may be doing parts of it, only a handful may actually be doing most of it, and none are doing all of it. The current era of strategic quality management presents managers with an ideal conception of "quality" toward which they must strive. There have certainly been many failures among those attempting to make changes in managerial practices. We shouldn't scoff at their failed attempts, but seek to learn from their mistakes and improve future management practice from the lessons learned.

Managers have recognized the strategic importance of quality. They have attempted to make the shift to strategic quality management, or Total Quality Management, or whatever term you choose. But many have failed because they have tried to do so with a less than comprehensive approach, piecing together various elements from past quality eras into a patchwork of quality programs. Returning to the reasons for failure cited earlier in this chapter, the common thread to almost every failed quality program is the lack of knowledge and the lack of managerial leadership. Top managers failed to lead a *strategic* quality management effort, which requires a customer-focused vision, personal commitment to continuous improvement, and a cultural transformation to integrate the efforts of the entire organization toward the leader's vision. It draws the best elements (e.g., human relations, design for quality, learning through study of variation, total quality integration, cross-functional teamwork) from all of the foregoing quality eras, and combines them into an approach tailored to meet the organization's competitive challenges and opportunities. Only top managers can successfully lead this kind of approach to quality.

Success also requires a personal transformation, particularly for the leaders, through knowledge and understanding of the new paradigm, and skill in role modeling the newly required behaviors, methods, and techniques for the rest of the organization. This text seeks to equip managers of the future with the knowledge and understanding they will need to practice management in this emerging paradigm and contribute to its continued evolution.

▶ SUMMARY OF KEY POINTS

1. For quality to be a useful concept, managers must define it appropriately.
2. Existing views of quality include product-based, manufacturing-based, and user-based views, and a total quality view which incorporates all of these.
3. Total Quality refers to product quality, and process and system quality. These all begin with people quality.
4. Approaches to managing quality have evolved over the last century through several stages.
5. Earlier stages in the evolution of quality include the inspection, statistical quality control, and quality assurance eras.
6. Most recently, the Strategic Quality Management era put together concepts developed in the earlier eras with a strategic focus on customer value.
7. This evolution has led to an emerging new paradigm for management.
8. In the new paradigm, the themes of focusing on customer value, continuous improvement, and system management are commonly accepted as the normal way to manage organizations.
9. When the new paradigm becomes the accepted way of thinking and acting, a way of life for managers, and is not thought of as something special or deserving a special name or three-letter acronym, they will have gone beyond TQM.

▶ KEY TERMS

acceptance sampling
breakthroughs
crisis resolution
cross-functional systems approach
Deming Cycle (Plan, Do, Study, Act)

inspection
internal customer orientation
Juran's Trilogy
kaizen
manufacturing-based view of quality

problem solving

product-based view of quality

quality

quality assurance era

reliability engineering

statistical quality control

strategic quality management era

system improvement

Total Quality Management

transcendent view of quality

user-based view of quality

variation

zero defects

▶ DISCUSSION QUESTIONS

1. Drawing on the chapter, list as many different definitions of quality as you can, and note the drawbacks and benefits of each definition.
2. How are the various definitions integrated in the concept of Total Quality Management?
3. What are the primary elements from earlier quality eras that are most important to managers in the strategic quality management era?
4. Compare and contrast the philosophies underlying Figure 7: The Economics of Quality of Conformance, and Figure 12: Taguchi's Loss Function.
5. What does it mean to go "Beyond Total Quality Management"?

▶ EXPERIENTIAL EXERCISE

Deming's Bead Exercise. (Details provided in Instructor's Manual.) For description of the exercise, see Mary Walton's *The Deming Management Method*, Perigree Books, New York, 1986.

▶ REFERENCES

G. M. Bounds and G. H. Dobbins, "The Manager's Job: A Paradigm Shift to a New Agenda," in M. J. Stahl and G. M. Bounds (eds.), *Competing Globally through Customer Value: The Management of Strategic Suprasystems*, Quorum Books, Westport, Conn., 1991, pp. 116–145.

B. Cornfeld and O. Edwards, *Quintessence: The Quality of Having It*, Crown Publishers, New York, 1983.

Philip B. Crosby, *Quality Is Free*, Mentor/New American Library, New York, 1979.

Philip B. Crosby, *Quality Without Tears: The Art of Hassle-Free Management*, McGraw-Hill, New York, 1984.

D. J. Curry and D. J. Faulds, "The Measurement of Quality Competition in Strategic Groups," in J. Jacoby and J. C. Olson (eds.), *Perceived Quality: How Consumers View Stores and Merchandise*, Lexington Books, Lexington, Mass., 1985, pp. 269–293.

W. E. Deming, *Out of the Crisis*, Massachusetts Institute of Technology, Cambridge, Mass., 1986.

G. Fuchsberg, "Quality Programs Show Shoddy Results," *The Wall Street Journal*, May 14, 1992, pp. B1, B9.

D. A. Garvin, *Managing Quality: The Strategic and Competitive Edge*, The Free Press, New York, 1988.

Howard S. Gitlow and Shelley J. Gitlow, *The Deming Guide to Quality and Competitive Position*, Prentice-Hall, Englewood Cliffs, N.J., 1987.

James F. Halpin, *Zero Defects*, McGraw-Hill, New York, 1966.

Oren Harari, "Ten Reasons Why TQM Doesn't Work," *Management Review*, January 1993, pp. 33–38.

M. Imai, *Kaizen: The Key to Japanese Competitive Success*, Random House, New York, 1986.

K. Ishikawa, *What Is Total Quality Control? The Japanese Way*, Prentice-Hall, Englewood Cliffs, N.J. 1985.

J. M. Juran (ed.), *Quality Control Handbook*, McGraw-Hill, New York, 1951.

J. M. Juran (ed.), *Quality Control Handbook*, 2d ed., McGraw-Hill, New York, 1962.

J. M. Juran *Juran on Quality by Design: The New Steps for Planning Quality into Goods and Services*, The Free Press, New York, 1992.

J. M. Juran, Frank M. Gyrna, Jr., and R. S. Binghan, Jr. (eds.), *Quality Control Handbook*, 3d ed., McGraw-Hill, New York, 1974, pp. 2–9.

Thomas S. Kuhn, *The Structure of Scientific Revolutions*, The University of Chicago Press, 1962.

P. Passell and L. Ross, *The Best*, Pocket Books, New York, 1975.

Robert M. Pirsig, *Zen and the Art of Motorcycle Maintenance*, Bantam Books, New York, 1974.

"Quality or Else, Program One: The Global Marketplace," Films Incorporated, Chicago.

G. S. Radford, *The Control of Quality in Manufacturing*, Ronald Press, New York, 1922.

Frank Rice, *Right Every Time: Using the Deming Approach*, Marcel Dekker, Inc., New York, 1990.

Warren H. Schmidt and Jerome P. Finnigan, *The Race without a Finish Line*, Jossey-Bass, Inc., San Francisco, 1992.

Arthur M. Schneiderman, "Optimum Quality Costs and Zero Defects: Are They Contradictory Concepts?" *Quality Progress*, November 1986, pp. 28–31.

W. A. Shewhart, *Economic Control of Quality of Manufactured Product*, D. Van Nostrand Company, New York, 1931.

Fred S. Steingraber, Chairman and CEO, A. T. Kearney, Inc., "Total Quality Management," speech delivered to the Institutional Investor CEO Roundtable, Naples, Fla., Jan. 19, 1990.

Genichi Taguchi, *Introduction to Quality Engineering: Designing Quality into Products and Processes*, Asian Productivity Organization, Tokyo, 1986.

chapter **3**

Organizational Culture and Paradigm Shift

We have found that the principles of TQM which we practice at Eastman Kodak Company are just as applicable to hospitals, schools, and local government. We believe the basics of TQM are universal, and they include Customer Focus, Teamwork, Analytical Approach to Process Management and Decision Making, Management Leadership and Continuous Improvement. Application of these principles is not something one does in addition to their regular work, it is the way they do their work. When that is realized, the quality journey has begun.

R. L. Heidke, Vice President and Director, Corporate Quality, Eastman Kodak Company

▶ **CHAPTER OUTLINE**

Chapter Overview

Introduction

Toward a Culture Supporting the Emerging Paradigm

Key Principles

Culture and Organizational Purpose

The Rational View of Organizations
The Cultural View of Organizations

What Is Culture?

Culture Defined
A Holistic View of Culture
An Example of Culture Change for Control Theory
The Interrelatedness of Cultural Levels

Why Culture Emerges

Achieving External Adaptation
Achieving Internal Integration

How Culture Develops

The Role of Founders and Leaders
Mechanisms for Developing Culture
Cultural Development as a Learning Process
Shared Understandings

Culture as a Guide to Behavior

Group Nonconformity
Individual Nonconformity
Strong Culture and Nonconformity
Where to Begin Culture Change

Summary of Key Points

Key Terms

Discussion Questions

Experiential Exercises

References

▶ CHAPTER OVERVIEW

To make a paradigm shift in management, managers must change the thoughts and practices of people throughout the organization. The concept of culture provides managers with a powerful means of understanding behavior in organizations. Our definition of culture provides managers with an understanding of what culture is, why it emerges, and how it develops. A good understanding of culture informs managers about how to change behaviors to implement the principles of the emerging paradigm of management.

▶ INTRODUCTION

A student from Hong Kong was invited to dinner. He had asked someone if there was a customary gesture a dinner guest should make to show his gratitude for the invitation. He was told to bring a bottle of wine; the guest arrived with a gallon jug. As another example, President Bill Clinton unwittingly insulted the people of South Korea by publicly placing an interpreter between himself and the South Korean head of state.

When we enter strange social situations, we all try to figure out what is expected of us by attending to the language and customs. We feel exhilarated when we cope successfully, and miserable when we behave inappropriately. These feelings are part of the dynamics of what may be called "culture." Incidents like those described above indicate how culture influences human behavior. Yet we seldom pause to consider how this powerful force shapes our actions and provides meaning to our lives. Culture influences how we interpret events and provides answers to social questions. It enables us to interact effectively with each other, to behave in expected patterns. What managers must realize is that cultural forces operate within organizations just as in the larger society.

We are all aware of the extreme variety that exists among cultures of the world. Patterns of thought and action in a Yanomami tribe of Brazil are quite different from those in an English village. Similar cultural diversity exists among industrial organizations. The cultural patterns of thought and action can vary widely. The emerging paradigm requires an organizational culture very different from traditional organizations.[1] The field of management is in the process of shifting to a newly emerging paradigm. Shifting an organization to this emerging paradigm requires new thoughts and actions by managers, in other words, a new culture. We discuss in this chapter some of the cultural features that best promote the emerging paradigm.

▶ TOWARD A CULTURE SUPPORTING THE EMERGING PARADIGM

Each organization's culture will be unique according to its own circumstances and history. However, there are common features of the cultures that promote the emerging paradigm. Some key principles for these cultures are discussed below.[2]

---

1. The terms "paradigm" and "culture" are often used interchangeably, but we draw an important distinction. Paradigm refers to the ways of thinking and acting prescribed by a professional field, such as management, or a scientific field, such as chemistry. Culture refers to the ways of thinking and acting that are characteristic of a particular social group or organization.
2. Cultures that promote the new paradigm are just beginning to evolve, and therefore we cannot provide a comprehensive list of all the elements. Even as these cultures evolve, it is unlikely that a prescription could be written for all the elements of an ideal culture.

Key Principles

Some key principles in a culture that supports the new paradigm include:

- The importance of determining what customers value as opposed to what management thinks they need.
- A customer versus an organizational focus.
- A focus on optimizing organizational performance rather than maximizing functional end results.
- A focus on the processes and systems that cause results and not the results themselves.
- The importance of experimentation for knowledge and openness to new information.
- Mistakes that lead to organizational learning are acceptable.
- The importance of continuous improvement versus working to specification or adherence to the status quo.
- Performance improvement comes from process/system improvement and not just improving people.
- To improve processes/systems, managers must seek out root causes of problems.
- Continuous improvement is demanded at every level of the organization.

The following section contrasts these key principles with traditional management.

The Importance of Determining What Customers Value as Opposed to What Management Thinks They Need   This is perhaps one of the most telling cultural indicators. Too often managers assume that they know what customers value, when they really do not. For example, Ricoh Company of Japan recently found that nearly 95 percent of its customers never used three keys specifically put into its fax machines to make them more appealing to customers (*Business Week*, Apr. 29, 1991, p. 59). David Kelly, president of DKD, a top industrial design firm, notes: "The guys who are designing most of these complex technological products are such techies that they think it's natural for everybody to hold down four buttons and twiddle a knob at the same time" (*Business Week*, Apr. 29, 1991, p. 60).

In a culture that supports the emerging paradigm, managers determine what customers value beginning with strategy, through design, engineering, and right down to each operation. Conversations are infused with specific references to what customers value. In one company, product innovations were met by intense questioning about their effect on customer value. This questioning was directed toward ensuring that innovations went far enough in providing such value, a subtle but impressive indicator of the culture.

A Customer versus an Organizational Focus   In many organizations today, lip service is paid to customer focus, but discussions within the organization center on criteria important to the organization itself. For example,

Thomas Pirelli, head of Enterprise Systems, a customer of IBM, stated to *Fortune* magazine that he had three different sets of IBM managers visit him. "They never asked about our needs. They don't listen. All they do is talk and show you the charts they've brought along" (*Fortune*, July 15, 1991, p. 54). When managers are focused on internal issues more than on their customers, they also tend to focus on functional objectives rather than on how the relationships between functional areas contribute or detract from specific aspects of customer value. In such organizations, departments completing a task often feel they can "toss it over the wall," meaning that they can now wash their hands of it. Problems belong to the "catching" department, which in turn seeks to get it "over the wall" as quickly as possible.

Ultimately, one source of this problem is that senior managers identify with their "functional team" and their subordinates are reluctant to appear disloyal. Accordingly, they are hesitant to work collaboratively with other functions unless their own functional interests are well protected. They assume that if they do not guard their own interests, others will take advantage of them and punish them. Managers who demonstrate an interest in customer value independent of functional identity foster a culture that is more likely to facilitate competitive gains.

Humans have a natural need for meaning in their lives. Participating in organizations offers one way for people to obtain this meaning. Unfortunately, organizations very easily become inwardly focused, with their members seeking to preserve the status quo because it serves their egos, provides security, or is personally meaningful. They make the organization itself more important than the organization's purpose (Schwartz, 1985).

As stated above, the primary purpose of organizations should be to provide customer value. Those organizations that succeed at providing superior customer value will survive and prosper; those that fail will not. Placing customers as top priority assumes that the interests of other constituents (investors, suppliers, employees) will be better served over the long term. This orientation requires the evolution of a culture that defines "superior customer value" as the foundation for group meaning, for serving other constituents, and ultimately, for its own survival and prosperity. This orientation can still be meaningful and fit with a general set of values that might be described in terms of "pride in workmanship."

Organizations with this new culture are very appealing to employees because of the human need to be part of something meaningful. In these organizations, employees take pride in workmanship and providing superior customer value. What a contrast this is to organizations that just focus on productivity gains and efficiency reports. A culture that embodies this feature can provide welcome meaning to the lives of its members.

Our field research tells us that a focus on customers inspires change more readily than any corporate initiative to enhance profits, efficiencies, or other internally oriented goals. Thus the emerging paradigm offers as a central tenet a customer focus, which can inspire a culture shift.

A Focus on Optimizing Organizational Performance rather than Maximizing Functional End Results   It is possible to maximize the performance of each functional area in an organization and still suboptimize the performance of the organization. Measures of performance must be carefully chosen to avoid this result. For example, optimizing productivity in manufacturing can lead people to ignore quality and compromise customer value. It does not have to be this way, but the tendency for managers to pursue their own functional agendas is quite prevalent in traditional hierarchical organizations. This often happens when the various functions of an organization have each developed their own distinct group identities and corresponding subcultures. The problems of functional isolation within an organization can resemble the problems of nationalism and tribalism that plague many countries trying to hold together diverse peoples.

A Focus on Processes and Systems That Cause Results and Not the Results Themselves   This requires a fundamental shift in beliefs about quality and productivity from those found in many companies. In the new culture, people understand that quality, productivity, and customer value are byproducts of the performance of the work that managers do in improving systems. If they are by-products, they can not be specifically worked on. One should manage causes (i.e., the means, systems, or processes), not by-products. Thus the critical questions become: "What are the critical means, and how do we improve them?"

When managers throughout an organization think in terms of process and system improvement for customer value rather than just functional objectives, the diverse functional subcultures may start to blend. As each group assimilates the superordinate values of a "customer orientation," integrated efforts among the functions become more likely and more strategically purposeful. Envision a company that has no quality department because "we don't work on quality." This might be precisely the attitude at a company that assumes quality is everyone's business, because management truly understands the significance of quality being a byproduct as well as a way of life for everyone in the organization.

The Importance of Experimentation for Knowledge and Openness to New Information   This value is reflected in people seeking to improve both products and processes on a regular basis. This is not just permissive tinkering. Rather, these efforts are grounded in ongoing efforts to test and supplement intuitive and experiential efforts by a systematic process of learning about cause and effect. People have been specifically trained in systematic building of knowledge and have the analytical tools and resources available to them to systematically improve. People recognize the transient nature of "solutions" when systems and variation are fully understood. Suggestions for improvement are welcomed, discussed, and tested. Furthermore, this type of behavior is recognized and valued. "Don't rock the boat" is not an acceptable piece of advice.

Mistakes That Lead to Organizational Learning Are Acceptable   When people experiment with alternative courses of action, sometimes they do not achieve desirable results. In the new culture, mistakes are viewed as opportunities for learning. Even mistakes that result from carelessness rather than planned experimentation are triggers for assessing what happened and learning how to prevent it. Mistakes are not occasions for attributing personal blame. Not only do people need to feel secure in risk-taking and experimentation, they need to feel secure in revealing mistakes so that learning, rather than a cover-up, can take place.

The Importance of Continuous Improvement versus Working to Specification or Adherence to the Status Quo   In many organizations, people work to specification and feel that as long as their work is within specifications or standard, it should be accepted as satisfactory. The expression "if it ain't broke, don't fix it" epitomizes this approach to management. One implication of this expression, namely, "if it is broke, fix it," makes sense; when problems arise, they should certainly be solved. However, continuous improvement goes well beyond problem solving, which corrects the causes of deviation from standard.

Continuous improvement assumes that something is "broke" if it has variation that can be reduced around the target desired by customers. Continuous improvement, of course, becomes progressively more difficult as the more obvious improvements are made and more challenging issues remain. However, the challenge must be met. "If you're standing still, you are losing ground" is more indicative of the values of continuous improvement.

A metaphor from high jumping, "the bar is always raised," expresses the value that one cannot rest on one's laurels.[3] Each success, achievement, or breakthrough simply sets the standard higher. The Lexus slogan, "The Relentless Pursuit of Perfection," conveys such a commitment to continuous improvement. While standards of achievement may be raised by customers, managers should not be content to just meet those standards; rather, they should lead and establish new standards, raising customer expectations with enhanced capabilities to deliver valued products and services.

Performance Improvement Comes from Process/System Improvement and Not Just Improving People   Many organizations devote considerable time to teaching managers to "deal with the problem employee," and "corrective performance counseling." Improvement of knowledge and skills of the work force is important, but these efforts are focused on fixing special causes and not on systematically building work force capabilities. Also, these approaches implicitly assume that individual employees, not larger

---

3. We are indebted to Jeff Peters for this metaphor.

systems, are primarily responsible for performance problems. In the new culture, managers assume that performance problems are due to managerial systems, not just employee attitudes and skills. This assumption is reflected in the response of supervisors and managers to performance problems. Initial questions aim to identify causes in processes and systems as opposed to determining "who is at fault."

To Improve Processes/Systems, Managers Must Seek Out Root Causes of Problems Rather than seek out root causes, managers are often content to solve the problems that result from them. Sometimes the problem solving is a quick fix that is ultimately irresponsible to customers. For example, work crews and supervisors in a department making grinding wheels were having a problem with voids in the wheels that were the result of the type of materials being used. To get the product out according to schedule, they filled the voids in the wheels with resin, which may appear hard, but doesn't last very long in a customer's grinding operations. In other cases, problem solving offers a responsible quick fix, such as when manufacturing people receive designs that aren't buildable and reengineer them on the spot to make them work.

In the examples above, the problems were due to root causes that could be found only by looking outside the area where the problem was manifested. The poor materials quality that was causing voids in grinding wheels was due to purchasing and production practices. The unbuildable design was due to engineering practices. Purchasing and engineering are among the many factors that make up the larger systems that generate problems. The design of products and production processes is frequently responsible for problems that pop up later in time, far removed from the root cause. Fixing these problems downstream costs more than preventing the problem with a good system in the first place, and ultimately it drains resources away from the building of good systems. Since systems are multifunctional, people cannot build and improve them without teamwork.

Continuous Improvement Must Be Demanded at Every Level of the Organization Robert Galvin of Motorola has said that "quality is a personal responsibility." Unfortunately, many managers view quality and continuous improvement as something to delegate. Managers delegate responsibility for continuous improvement under the guise of empowerment. Many do not realize that empowerment without enablement is a lie. Managers can enable workers only by providing them systems that work. Managers throughout the organization, particularly those at the top, must take responsibility for continuous improvement. If it does not start at the top, it is not likely to thrive at other levels of the organization. The U.S. work force in a Japanese joint venture reflected this principle in a survey. When asked who they would rather work for, the overwhelming majority responded that they would rather work for the Japanese because "they do what they say they will do." Under Japanese management, the employees in this joint venture are renowned for continuous improvement.

In continuously improving organizations, rather than delegating the responsibility, managers lead the effort at every level, beginning with strategy and systems, and down to operations. Every aspect of the organization is subject to change for improvement, and all employees are responsible for playing appropriate roles in continuous improvement.

Managers are particularly responsible for building the kind of culture described above. The concept of culture offers managers a means of understanding the causes of behavior within the organization so they can take appropriate action to shift to the emerging paradigm. In the remainder of this chapter, we define culture and look at how culture in an organization emerges, develops, and influences behavior in the shift to the emerging paradigm.

QUALITY IN ACTION: A MESSAGE TO THE STUDENT
Sharon A. Ostby, Manager, Quality and Information Systems,
and Roger E. Handberg, Executive Vice President, Ceridian Corporation

Leaders often communicate important cultural values to employees through vivid imagery. Roger E. Handberg and Sharon A. Ostby of Ceridian Corporation use the sport of auto racing to symbolize the constant attention required to successfully compete. Formerly a part of Control Data Corporation, Ceridian Corporation was established in 1992 to provide businesses with services such as payroll processing, media and market research, and networking. They also provide technology-based services and products to government customers worldwide.

Continuous improvement does not sound very exciting at first.

Images in the mind can make the relentless pursuit of quality sound rather dark and without reward. The thrill of a quantum leap, a paradigm shift, and a magnificent turn more often captures the imagination and pervades the literature on business improvements. In a culture that reveres the start-up, the start-over, the overnight success, life cycles of 18 months, and quarterly profits, it is difficult to keep our attention on the daily, measurable, manageable improvements that ultimately matter. But it is in this constancy of purpose that the customer is ultimately served and retained.

The sport of auto racing provides an analogy. At the starting line, the driver sits in a splendid machine, the result of careful design and planning, and starts the engine. The engine roars; the crowd roars; each driver is confident of a win. The flag is dropped, and the race is on. As the laps unfold, the drivers implement their winning strategies. Fuel is monitored and braking timed perfectly to achieve that balance between taking the curve and keeping control. Pit stops have been rehearsed so that time lost is kept to a minimum. Passing an opponent is planned and executed, sometimes with ease, but often with the thinnest of margins. A thousand small corrections are made by the driver and crew that go unnoticed by the spectators. The best cross the finish line out front, and their customers applaud and shout and vow to come again next time. The teams that consistently field winners are those that immediately and constantly review their performance for any and all improvements that can be made to gain an advantage next time, even while the current race is on. Before the customers have gone home, engines will be torn apart and the enhancements begun.

The ultimate satisfaction is in striving toward ever-increasing standards of performance. It is the essence of providing value to the customer. It is what the customer demands and deserves.

At Ceridian, we have a focus on employees, customers, and shareholders, and our values revolve around people, quality, and profitability. Our competitive advantage is achieved by meeting our customers' needs through best practices, developed by continuous improvement of all our processes. The rewards of profitability are the result. Our employees have developed that passion to deploy total quality management principles in everything they do to ensure we will successfully compete in the worldwide economy of the future.

▲

▶ CULTURE AND ORGANIZATIONAL PURPOSE

The concept of culture was first applied to organizations by *Organization Development (OD)* practitioners (Jacques, 1952; Harrison, 1972). OD typically seeks to make an organization more adaptive to its environment by changing its culture. For example, OD encourages people to openly question their values, beliefs, and behavioral norms, and to become more receptive to change.[4]

OD was widely popularized by consultants in the 1970s and 1980s, but many of their interventions were disappointing. They frequently focused on the process of doing OD and failed to ensure that their goals fit the organization's mission or purpose. With increasing global competition in the 1990s, and more pressures for organizations to change continuously and to improve, the OD theme of change has again become important. However, we have learned that OD interventions must be focused to achieve specific goals. Managers must use the concept of culture to accomplish rational purposes, such as goals for survival and prosperity. In doing

---

4. Popular OD techniques include team building, sensitivity training, and transactional analysis (French, Bell, and Zawacki, 1983).

so, however, they must go beyond what has traditionally been considered "rational management." We discuss how the rational and cultural views can be combined to help managers move into the emerging paradigm.

The Rational View of Organizations

Organizations are created to accomplish collective purposes (Deal and Kennedy, 1982). When members pursue the organization's purposes or goals, their behavior may be described as "rational management." The professional manager's job is to make sure the organization achieves its purposes. The rational manager strives to achieve the organization's purposes by focusing on goals, formal roles, technologies, and combinations of these elements (Thompson, 1967; Perrow, 1979; Scott, 1981). Managing these elements might seem quite straightforward; the manager needs only to establish goals, clarify employee roles to fulfill the goals, give employees the required technologies, and reward their performance. Traditional management by objectives (MBO) programs attempted to do just that. Unfortunately, as we explain below, it is not that easy.

Born during the Industrial Revolution, the rational view of organizations has continued to develop over the last 200 years. In the nineteenth and early twentieth centuries, engineers such as Charles Babbage (1792–1871), Frederick W. Taylor (1856–1915), and Frank B. Gilbreth (1868–1924) emphasized *specialization* and *division of labor* in the quest for "efficiency." The work of these fathers of *scientific management* gave rise to functionalism and hierarchical forms of organization. Also influential was the work of German sociologist Max Weber (1864–1920). Weber advocated "bureaucracy" as a highly efficient model of organization based on hierarchy and formal authority (see Gerth and Mills, 1946, 1973). According to Weber, the characteristics of a well-developed bureaucracy include specialization of tasks, appointment by merit, promotion on the basis of ability and experience, planned career opportunities, routinization of activities, rules and regulations to guide behavior, a clear chain of command, specification of authority and responsibility, and a rational, impersonal climate that imposes a sense of duty. Although the ideal bureaucracy has probably never existed, Weber believed that the closer an organization could approach this model, the more efficient it would be.

Many of the current practices of industrial engineering and industrial psychology follow the traditions of scientific management and fit into this rational view. For example, engineers conduct scientific time and motion studies with the goal of increasing efficiency and productivity. Industrial psychologists determine how factors such as individual knowledge, skills, and abilities relate to particular tasks so that organizations make a good fit between individuals and job designs. Behavioral psychologists study how to manipulate individual performance with rewards and punishments.

These quantitative approaches can be useful to goal-oriented managers. Unfortunately, these approaches also treated people as cogs in a machine. They are inadequate when other dimensions of human experience are ignored, as in Weber's bureaucracy (Ouchi and Wilkins, 1985). To manage and change human behavior in organizations, managers must understand what the roles, goals, and technologies mean to individuals.

Weber's bureaucracy operates like a machine with structures and rules designed to overcome or minimize the effect of human "frailties." Once established, however, organizations take on a life of their own. Sometimes they appear chaotic, irrational, at odds with formal goals and roles (Ouchi and Wilkins, 1985). Bureaucratic machines seek to suppress social and emotional dynamics, working against the impulses of human nature. After all, people do become emotionally involved with their work, and with their co-workers; they seek meaning in their work activities and interactions with colleagues. Workers become attached to their organizations.

When managers refer to the social and emotional side of organizational life as "irrational," they imply that it has no sensible explanation, no logical order, and no clear relevance to organizational goals. Goal-oriented managers may fail to understand these realities because they ignore cultural issues, such as the meaning and feeling that people experience in organizations (Barnard, 1938; Arnold, 1935; Selznick, 1957). However, the organization's survival and prosperity depend upon managers understanding culture, since there are cultural elements other than goals, formal roles, and technologies which guide behavior (Wallach, 1983).

The Cultural View of Organizations

Adopting a *cultural view of organizations* does not mean managers will be less concerned with achieving the organization's purpose. Rather, they will pursue the organization's purpose in a more enlightened way and acknowledge the realities of human nature. This is particularly important for managers attempting to transform to the emerging paradigm, because the transformation requires changing thought and actions. The emerging paradigm is focused on continuously improving customer value. It is very purposeful.

The cultural view helps managers understand the causes of human behavior. To change the way people think and act, managers must understand how the thoughts, interpretations, expectations, and habits that people have are developed and maintained. This understanding gives managers insight into how to change them.

The rational view of organizations suggests that to accomplish change managers should establish goals, clarify employee roles to fulfill the goals, give employees the required technologies, and reward their performance. Many organizations attempting to do Total Quality Management have taken this approach with disappointing results. For example, one company took a very rational approach to TQM. It set product quality improvement targets to reduce defect levels to less than 100 parts per million and achieve 100 percent customer satisfaction. Managers and employees were trained in statistical process control, and quality improvement and problem-solving techniques. The PCs and software needed to do statistical analyses were provided. Facilitators were trained and assigned to process action teams. Managers and employees from different departments were told to work together. They were even promised a bonus if they achieved the improvement goals.

These actions were not inherently bad. However, the managers failed to transform the organization through these means. Some impressive improvements were quickly attained, but these came from uncovering obvious problems which were easy to fix. The more intractable problems associated with the long-standing culture of the organization were not fixed, and the TQM program fizzled and disappeared after about 10 months. These were some of the problems: People in different departments still distrusted one another. They perceived things differently and almost always proposed conflicting solutions. Employees had for so long resented managers ignoring their input that they participated only half-heartedly. They also feared that the statistical analyses would be used to evaluate them and take corrective action, so they falsified data on some occasions.

The managers had learned new tools and techniques; however, they did not fully understand the theory and philosophy underlying them. So they were often at a loss for how to use them. Even worse, they sometimes used their old mind-set in applying the new tools. For example, the manager of the maintenance department used statistical charting to monitor the downtime of machines in the production department. He evaluated his maintenance people on how long it took them to make repairs and get the line running again, a measure that was ingrained in his mind as an indicator of his contribution to the organization's purpose. Unfortunately, this encouraged the maintenance people to avoid stopping the line to do preventive maintenance, which anticipates problems and takes corrective action before defective products are ever produced. This actually caused more defects to be produced because repairs were not done until the machine actually broke.

These problems were culturally based. They were due to the mindsets of the people, their traditional philosophy, their values and beliefs about how things work, and their habits of conducting business. The cultural view can help managers to change these important causes of human behavior. To shift to the emerging paradigm, managers must change the mind-sets as well as the actions of the people in the organization. The concept of culture provides insights about making these changes. Shifting to a new paradigm means changing many things in concert. Just implementing the use of a new tool or technique, or redefining employee roles, does not constitute a paradigm shift. To accomplish a paradigm shift, managers must change many elements of culture; they must understand the concept of culture.

▶ WHAT IS CULTURE?

Over time, writers have defined the concept of culture to suit their own needs (Brown, 1976; Kuhn, 1962; Morgan, 1980; Deal and Kennedy, 1983). This has led some definitions to focus on the values and beliefs that cause a certain behavior, while others focus only on the behavior itself. Adding to the confusion is the popular use of terms such as "organizational culture" and "corporate culture" which writers rarely define.

The concept of culture must be clearly defined, because the definition determines how one investigates, manages, and changes culture. Here we seek to define culture in a way that helps explain the causes of behavior. This definition will best help managers to use organizational culture in furthering the organization's goals.

There are two opposing notions of how to view culture: the outward view and the inward view. The *outward view of culture* focuses on behavior and those things about culture that are directly observable, such as artifacts, patterns of behavior, speech, formal laws, and technical know-how (Kroeber and Kluckhohn, 1952; Spradley and McCurdy, 1975; Barnouw, 1979; Mitchell, 1973). When CEO John Young describes technical innovation at Hewlett Packard, he lists things that are observable:

> To encourage innovation at HP, we've tried to create a climate that fosters creativity. We begin by recruiting a diversity of technical talent, people from all around the world, with expertise in varying disciplines, and with degrees from several different universities. We provide them with a very rich set of tools, including a great deal of computing power. We encourage people from different disciplines and different projects to share their ideas freely. We ask our engineers to communicate regularly with key customers. We also want them to talk to suppliers, so that our designs incorporate parts whose performance and reliability are well known to us. The work environment makes communication very easy. Our offices are very open, and people can trade ideas over the partition. Our electronic mail system has a special bulletin board for R&D engineers, as well as links to key customers and suppliers. [See "Remarks by John Young to Samsung Managers," Apr. 8, 1991, case study section of this text.]

You could walk into HP and find the outward parts of culture that John Young refers to above. What you cannot see directly, but is also evident in his words, is the mind-set at HP, or the inward side of culture. For example, Young seems to value and believe in technical innovation (". . . that's the engine that will drive future growth. Because innovation creates new markets that never existed before"). Further, he assumes that the way to achieve innovation is through fostering a climate of creativity, with technical talent, tools, and open communication.

The *inward view of culture* stresses the process through which behavior is learned, and the ideas, beliefs, symbolism, and evaluative aspects of culture (Linton, 1936; Parsons, 1951; Triandis, Vassilou, Vassilou, Tanka, and Shanmugan, 1972). From this inward perspective, culture is the set of implicit rules that govern behavior (Radcliffe-Brown, 1957). If it were not for the values, beliefs, and assumptions about innovation (inward culture), people at HP would not have acted to put in place the behaviors and systems to support innovation (outward culture). Thus, the inward and outward parts of culture are interrelated.

Culture Defined

We can begin to formulate our definition of culture with a list of factors that most definitions of the term have in common:

- Culture is a social construction: the elements of culture, such as values, beliefs, and understanding, are held in common by all group members.
- Culture provides members with a way of making sense of events.
- Culture contains customs or traditions.
- Within a culture, patterns of values, beliefs, expectations, understanding, and behaviors emerge and evolve over time.
- Culture guides behavior: customs or traditions are the glue that holds an organization together and ensure that members behave according to norms.
- Each organization's culture is unique. (Buono, Bowditch, and Lewis, 1985; Ott, 1989)

Building on these common factors, we define *culture* as *a pattern of artifacts, behaviors, values, beliefs, and assumptions that a group develops as it learns to cope with internal and external problems of survival and prosperity.* Our definition encompasses both the outward and inward views. As we saw in the example of Hewlett Packard, each view tells us something important about an organization's culture.

A Holistic View of Culture

Looking at culture from both the inward and outward views gives us a *holistic view.* Edgar H. Schein (1985) reconciled these perspectives by subdividing culture into three levels, all working together. As shown in Figure 1, artifacts (Level 1) correspond to the outward view. Values and beliefs (Level 2) and underlying assumptions (Level 3) reside in the minds of people, and together they correspond to the inward view.

First-Level Elements Schein's first-level elements, *artifacts,* can be broken down even further into Levels 1A and 1B (Martin and Sehl, 1983). Level 1A consists of the *products of behavior* (i.e., technologies, language, office layouts, and physical arrangements). Level 1B consists of the actual *patterns of behavior* (i.e., habits, norms, rites, and rituals). The elements of Level 1 are easily observed, but the meanings of these elements depend on the two deeper levels of culture (Ott, 1989; Sathe, 1985).

Figure 1

Three levels of organizational culture and elements that reflect each level

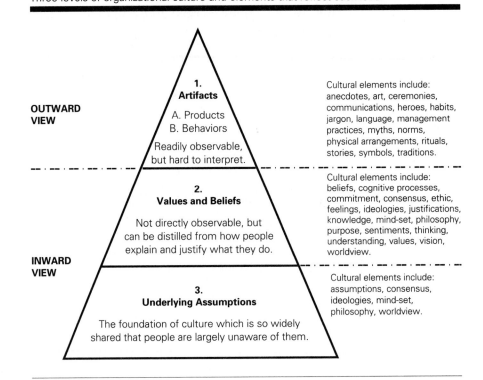

OUTWARD
VIEW

1.
Artifacts

A. Products
B. Behaviors

Readily observable,
but hard to interpret.

Cultural elements include:
anecdotes, art, ceremonies,
communications, heroes, habits,
jargon, language, management
practices, myths, norms,
physical arrangements, rituals,
stories, symbols, traditions.

2.
Values and Beliefs

Not directly observable, but
can be distilled from how people
explain and justify what they do.

Cultural elements include:
beliefs, cognitive processes,
commitment, consensus, ethic,
feelings, ideologies, justifications,
knowledge, mind-set, philosophy,
purpose, sentiments, thinking,
understanding, values, vision,
worldview.

INWARD
VIEW

3.
Underlying Assumptions

The foundation of culture which is so widely
shared that people are largely unaware of them.

Cultural elements include:
assumptions, consensus,
ideologies, mind-set,
philosophy, worldview.

Based on Schein, 1985, and Ott, 1989.

Second-Level Elements   Second-level elements consist of *values* and *beliefs*. Beliefs are perceived associations between two or more objects, events, attributes, or outcomes. For example, one might believe that engineers are perfectionists, and that perfectionists delay the work of others with obsessive attention to detail. These beliefs link the object "engineer" to the attribute "perfectionist" to the event "obsessive attention to detail" to the outcome "delay the work of others."

Such beliefs can affect an individual's behavior toward the engineer. However, the behavior also depends on the individual's values. A cultural value states what is important or conveys a sense of what "ought to be." For example, if top managers feel the contributions of engineers more important than those of any other group, they may encourage the engineer's obsessive attention to detail. Together, beliefs and values help determine people's attitudes and intentions to behave in certain ways (Fishbein and Ajzen, 1975).

Values and beliefs are often expressed in the form of ideologies, moral codes, and philosophies that guide decision making and behavior in certain situations. For example, Apple Computer is committed to what it calls Apple Quality Management (AQM) as a way of doing business. The fundamental philosophy underlying the practices of AQM is summed up in the following principles:

- Focus on customers and constantly exceed their expectations.
- Develop, document, and improve processes.
- Give Apple employees the power to change the way they work.
- Make decisions based on data.
- Foster teamwork and encourage cross-functional teams.
- Take responsibility.

Philosophy statements are useful for summarizing the values and beliefs of a company. However, explicit statements of values (espoused values) may not coincide with what group members actually do (Argyris, 1975; Argyris and Schon, 1978; Deutscher, 1966, 1973). It is important to keep this in mind when assessing a group's culture. Informants may misinform others about their group's values in order to appear socially desirable. Espoused values may also represent aspirations for the future rather than current reality (Schein, 1985). Investigators cannot simply rely on what group members say about the group, even if espoused values appear to be consistent with behavior and other artifacts.

Third-Level Elements   Over time, fundamental values and beliefs may become so taken for granted that they are assumed true and never questioned. We speak of these as underlying *assumptions*. At this most inward level, these basic assumptions are accepted as unquestionable truths about the way the world works. Over time, certain values and beliefs may prove so successful in solving problems, in coping with an uncertain world, or otherwise repeatedly affirmed, that they are eventually considered unquestionably valid. These assumptions are so taken for granted, so shared that they may even slip from the conscious awareness of the members (Geertz, 1973; Schein, 1984, 1985).

Such assumptions act as "theories in use" to guide decision making and behavior, and indicate appropriate perceptions, thoughts, and feelings (Argyris, 1976). They serve as a sort of "automatic pilot" to guide our actions without demanding our full attention (Wilkins, 1983). Core elements act as the foundation for other aspects of culture. That is why until a change in the underlying assumptions takes place, many behavior changes (such as those induced through rewards, job demands, and formal controls) are temporary.

Schein provides the following example of how stated values can unwittingly contradict underlying assumptions, and how failure to address these assumptions hinders behavioral change. A management group decided to act as consultants for themselves and diagnose their own culture. A newly hired employee in this group noted that "one of the interesting features of the [company's] culture was the tendency to assume that only people who had been in the company a long time could understand how it really operated; as a result, recently arrived employees found it difficult to make any contribution. The senior person in the group . . . turned on the young consultant and said angrily: 'How can you sit there and make a statement about the [company's] culture when you have been here barely one year? You are completely wrong. We accept the ideas of new employees' " (1985, pp. 23–24).

Here is yet another example of the effect of assumptions on behavior. During a meeting of first-line supervisors and managers, a supervisor raised her hand and quite sincerely asked, "When will this be over?" This was several months into an effort to change the organization's culture toward a new paradigm. The author asked what she meant by "over." "Every two years or so, we do something like this," she replied. "Several years ago we did sensitivity training, then we did MBO, then team building, then job enrichment. I just wanted to tell my people when this will be over." These people shared an assumption that "processes" are "programs" which will end. They expected the change effort to be transitory. This explained why people were not making any commitment to sustain the effort over the long term, despite senior management speeches and pronouncements to the contrary.

Assumptions about the external environment can determine the economic fate of organizations. For example, Montgomery Ward assumed that the market would not be good after World War II, and they decided not to expand. As a result, Sears Roebuck captured market dominance. This example leads to the important point that managers and their organization's culture must adapt to survive in changing external environments. Managers will face many critical incidents in the evolution of their culture. At these points, they must engage in searching, probing, testing, and making difficult choices on alternative courses of action in order to adapt (Taylor, 1987). One of the keys to developing a culture that supports the emerging paradigm is the nature of the control process that managers put in place. To ensure the learning and adaptability needed in this new context, managers must adopt a modern approach to control that fits this agenda.

An Example of Culture Change for Control Theory

The field of management starts to ingrain a paradigm in the minds of managers through formal education. Business schools teach future managers about theories and practices of management. One of the old theories that conflicts with the emerging paradigm is traditional control theory. We devote several pages to this issue because it is central to a culture that supports the emerging paradigm. As you read below, notice how control theory pervades all three levels of culture: artifacts (products and behaviors), values and beliefs, and assumptions.

Traditional Control Theory The role of controlling has been described in management literature for decades (see Fayol, 1949). *Traditional control*

Figure 2

Traditional control process

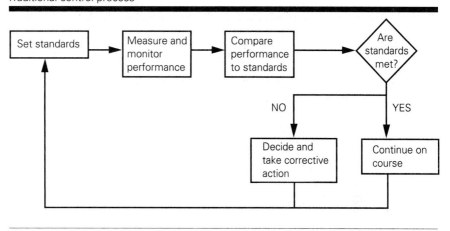

theory defines *controlling* as "a systematic effort by business management to compare performance to predetermined standards, plans, or objectives to determine whether performance is in line with these standards and presumably to take any remedial action required to see that human and other corporate resources are being used in the most effective and efficient way possible in achieving corporate objectives" (Mockler, 1970, p. 14). Based on this definition, there are at least four discernible steps to the traditional controlling process:

1. Set predetermined standards, plans, or objectives.
2. Measure and monitor performance.
3. Compare performance to the predetermined standards.
4. Make a decision and take corrective action.

Check almost any introduction to management text and you will find a model of traditional control theory similar to the one in Figure 2.

Deficiencies of Traditional Control Theory The modern approach to controlling performance that we advocate is based on the idea that managers are responsible for systems and they must understand the theory of variation to understand how to address the causes of performance. In comparison to this modern approach, there are a number of deficiencies in the traditional approach to controlling performance. The deficiencies begin at the first step: managers tend to develop standards without considering what must be done to enable people to meet the standards. The traditional control theory does not acknowledge the manager's responsibility to attend to systems to make sure people have the high-quality equipment, raw materials, training to do the job, methods of work, and cooperation from team members who are working toward compatible standards.

The deficiencies of traditional control theory extend to the last step, where managers decide to take corrective action. In traditional control, managers use the rule of *managing by exceptions,* which means they pay little attention to outcomes that conform to standard. Only the *significant deviations,* or exceptions, attract their attention. It is natural to attend only to deviations from standards because they are easily spotted. It also saves time to focus one's investigative efforts on the events that are problematic and ignore those that are not. However, by doing nothing unless standards are violated, managers (1) fail to develop knowledge and (2) fail to continuously improve, two imperatives in the emerging paradigm. By acting on "exceptions," so judged by arbitrary standards, rather than considering the capability of the system to meet the standard, managers also can make results worse than they might be if they did nothing.

Knowledge Development The key to controlling is that managers must have knowledge of the causes of deviations in order to take action to correct them. The traditional approach does not inform managers about the causes. It encourages managers to assume deviations are discrete events, isolated in time. The modern approach of the emerging paradigm encourages managers to view deviations as a part of a pattern of variation over time that can be studied statistically. The statistical approach informs managers about how to meet standards by informing them about the causes of performance, which can be acted upon.

Continuous Improvement The modern approach of the new paradigm encourages managers to go beyond the minimal requirements of current standards to continuously improve performance, and not just fix problems to return performance to normal. In other words, it goes beyond the "if it ain't broke, don't fix it" mentality. It even goes beyond the idea of preventing deviations. It is based on the premise that managers must continuously reduce variation in performance by acting on the system of causes and raise the level of performance by system design and redesign.

The Modern Control and Improvement Process The *modern control and improvement process* of the emerging paradigm, shown in Figure 3, incorporates some of the elements of the traditional control process along with the statistical approach to the study of variation and its causes (Deming's Plan, Do, Study, Act Cycle). The modern control and improvement process is built around four basic building blocks that very simply describe the *process of performance.* These building blocks are *input, transformation, output,* and *customer value* (or some other stakeholder).

Every output has a customer or some other stakeholder, whether internal or external to the organization. The customer either makes use of the output, or in some way benefits or makes some sacrifice because of the output. The output also has an identifiable transformation process that produced it. Before the transformation process can occur, however, various inputs have to be prepared. The strategy, structure, product designs, machinery, plant layout, policies, procedures for work, rules for

Figure 3

A modern approach to control and improvement based on the study of variation

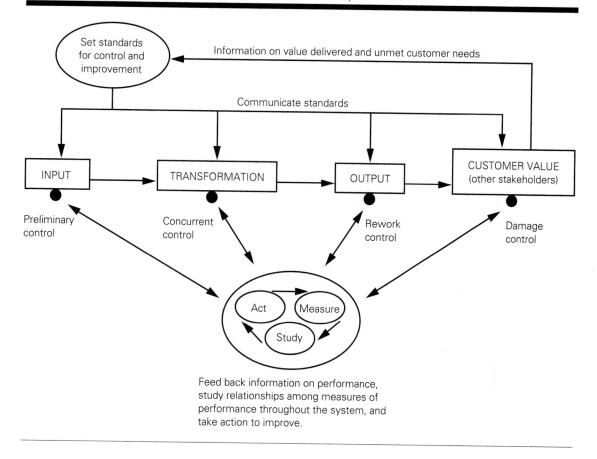

Feed back information on performance, study relationships among measures of performance throughout the system, and take action to improve.

conduct, materials, and human resources all have to be put in place before anything can be done to transform inputs into outputs for customers. Managers are responsible for the work to control and improve the system inputs which ultimately determine outputs.

The basic elements of the modern control and improvement process include the following four steps, which are represented in the ellipses in Figure 3.

1. *Set standards for control and improvement.* This step requires managers to go beyond the traditional approach to set standards that do not have waste embedded and do not encourage complacency. For example, traditional product specifications often tolerate a range of variation around a target, whereas an emphasis on continuous improvement encourages the reduction of variation around a target. It also requires managers to match targets to evolving customer needs and to reduce variation to better meet targets.

The nature of the standards will also be different in a modern control and improvement process. For example, managers will carefully consider the impact of quotas on workers and eliminate them. Managers will lead and inspire by setting a purpose and articulating a vision. Managers do not assume that unmotivated workers with poor attitudes are the source of problems. Rather, they assume that poor attitudes are the product of the systems managers put in place.

Specific quantitative goals and objectives are only established when managers also articulate the means of achieving them. Standards are no longer used as exhortations for workers to do better. They are not used as yardsticks to evaluate and judge individuals. Rather, they are used to communicate the vision. Furthermore, standards are not set as lofty objectives independent of what the current systems are capable of producing. Rather, they are realistic and based upon feedback about current performance capabilities.

2. *Measure.* This step means that appropriate measures are developed and data are collected to assess performance, much like the traditional control process.

3. *Study.* This step means that managers analyze the data using statistical methods and other tools and techniques to understand the causes of variation. It also requires managers to study the relationships among measures to understand the impact of their actions on performance throughout the organization. This is a significantly different control activity from the traditional activity of "compare performance to predetermined standards." It places a priority on knowledge development rather than evaluating and assigning blame for deviations. Furthermore, it does not assume, as does the traditional approach to control, that managers already know the cause of the deviation.

4. *Act.* This step means taking corrective action on the basis of knowledge obtained through the study of feedback. Depending on the situation, corrective action may mean crisis management, problem solving, or system improvement to attack root causes.

As mentioned earlier, standards and measures used in controlling performance are spread throughout the organization. When the performance process and the control and improvement process are combined, you get a picture of the modern control and improvement process, as shown in Figure 3 above. Standards and measures may be established at points corresponding to each of the four blocks and communicated to relevant people throughout the organization. In addition to setting standards and measuring at each of these four blocks, managers also take corrective action at each of these blocks.

The action taken at any one block may be based on information feedback from the study of measures at that point, or from other points in the performance process. Ideally, the action taken is based upon the statistical study of measures to understand the causes of variation. Application of the measure-study-act sequence at each of these four points constitutes four different aspects of performance control: (1) preliminary control of inputs, (2) concurrent control of the transformation process, (3) rework control to correct flawed outputs, and (4) damage control to smooth relations with customers who receive flawed outputs. These actions to control performance are listed in order of their effectiveness. Preliminary control is most effective, and damage control is least effective.

Managers achieve *preliminary control* by making projections about the future and anticipating needed changes. Preliminary control is both preventive, to avoid undesirable outcomes, and proactive, to achieve improved outcomes. The most important part of preliminary control is the job of improving the system of causes, as we have repeatedly stressed in this text. It is here that managers attack root causes. By changing and improving inputs, managers exert a great deal of control over the performance of downstream events, including transformation, output, and customer value. It is easier to control and improve downstream activities in transformation if managers control and improve upstream processes to provide good inputs.

Concurrent control is done on a real-time basis, as workers execute the tasks to transform inputs into outputs. Concurrent control consists of fine tuning and making course corrections to execute work according to the designs, procedures, and steps determined at the stage of inputs. Corrective actions may involve making adjustments to machine settings, redistributing time and energy, or changing behavior. Concurrent control may be described as operational control or steering control. A good analogy is driving a car. Ideally, the driver vigilantly monitors road and traffic conditions and makes adjustments to ensure safe arrival at his or her destination.

Rework control is necessary when the previous two forms of control, preliminary and concurrent control, have failed. In other words, defective or off-target output has been produced that must be reworked before it can be passed on to customers. Consider some examples. A defective shaft must be reground to meet the specification for length before it can be included in a sub-assembly. A financial report must be rewritten before it is presented to the board of directors because its calculations were based upon some faulty numbers. Sometimes rework is not even possible. The output may have to be discarded or sold for salvage. In some cases, managers just have to accept the output and make the best of it. For example, financial results, like sales volume and profitability, are difficult to rework, despite the determined efforts of many creative accountants.

Managers should not rely exclusively on rework control, because it is more costly to do things twice than it is to "do it right the first time" by ensuring preliminary and concurrent control, the mainstays of the emerging paradigm. Relying on rework to control performance increases all kinds of costs. It wastes resources, such as materials, machines, and labor, that could be used elsewhere. Inspectors have to be hired to check for defects. It makes delivery schedules unpredictable and requires that inventory be built as safety stock. And too often, defective products slip through inspection undetected and get into the marketplace to customers. This is particularly problematic with services, which are delivered as they are produced, so there is no time for inspection.

If defective or off-target output does get into the hands of customers (or other stakeholders), then managers have to engage in *damage control*. They must minimize the negative impact on customers. There are many ways they might do this, including apologizing, refunding money, replacing the product, performing the service again (a form of rework), and promising to do better in the future. The five-year/50,000-mile warranty on new automobiles represents a form of damage control. Other forms of damage control seek to minimize the perception of damage by the customer, which might be referred to as image management. For example, a young man buys his first car, a Mazda station wagon, from a used car dealer. When he notices that the car smokes more than it should, the car salesman insists, "It's not a Mazda if it doesn't smoke a little." Another example is not charging a dissatisfied customer for a meal.

Work on Upstream Control The most important point about damage control is that it happens when all the previous approaches to control, including preliminary, concurrent, and rework control, have failed. The damage has taken place, and all managers can do is hope to minimize it or get customers to forget about it. In the emerging paradigm, managers seek to prevent failure and ensure success in the future through *upstream control*, which emphasizes taking action on systems and processes. The further upstream they can go in taking action, the better. At times, all four approaches to control are necessary. However, if managers devote more time and effort to preliminary control, less time and effort will be required downstream in the other forms of control. In simple terms, prework avoids rework.

Feedback information is critical to this modern approach to control. It does not change what has been done in the past, but informs people about past performance and unmet customer needs. Feedback from the study of customer needs ensures the right standards are set in the first place. Then feedback on performance reveals whether those needs were met. If studied, feedback information can aid understanding how to improve future performance. Notice in Figure 3 that feedback flows in both directions, upstream and downstream. This two-way flow ensures that corrective actions are based on feedback information from both upstream and downstream measures. For example, with downstream feedback, the engineers designing a new manufacturing process as an input study the impact of the new process on workers in the transformation process, the output products and services, and the customers who acquire and use these outputs. With upstream information, engineers notify workers of process changes and inform them how best to conduct concurrent control during the transformation process (a form of feedforward control).

The two-way flow of information also implies that managers study the relationships between measures at various stages of the performance process. Statistical methods are available for investigating these relationships. Consider some examples. The Cadillac division of General Motors, like all other automobile producers, conducts market tests of various prototype designs (input) to see what customers like. Process engineers study the effect of computer control algorithms (transformation) on the physical characteristics of chemical products at DuPont. Georgia-Pacific salespeople study the impact of variation in thickness and surface characteristics of particleboard (output) when it is laminated to manufacture ready-to-assemble furniture (customer value). When managers take this approach to control, they use information gathered downstream to guide "corrective actions" upstream. Their top priority is to control and improve the inputs that compose the system, because all subsequent performance depends upon how well they do this job.

It is easy to see how control theory is reflected at all three levels of culture. In order to shift to the concepts and methods of the emerging paradigm, managers must change their thoughts and actions at all three levels.

The Interrelatedness of Cultural Levels

The three levels of culture are dynamically interrelated; each level influences the others. This explains why managers often fail to change culture. Many attempts to change culture focus on surface-level artifacts without changing deeper levels. Such changes are doomed to be temporary. For example, a top management team in a Fortune 500 company sought to change its culture toward Total Quality Management. A highly placed OD professional led the effort. Unfortunately, the management team spent untold hours manipulating symbols, language, myths, jargon, and other surface-level elements of culture, without really confronting underlying assumptions, values, and beliefs. They never developed an understanding of the new themes and concepts of the emerging paradigm. As a result, the actions of top managers frequently did not coincide with the symbols and rhetoric (espoused values and beliefs).

One example is this company's guiding principle, which states, "We improve the quality of our business by recognizing the interdependencies among functional units and all components of our business." However, when cost-cutting objectives are occasionally stressed, each manager retreats to functionalism, fighting for his or her own turf and attacking others. Another principle, "Trust and respect are fundamental to our organizational behavior," is frequently contradicted by micromanaging, second-guessing decisions of subordinates, and tinkering with budgets.

When top managers are inconsistent, the surface-level manipulations become objects of derision among the rest of the organization. For example, workers may inscribe uncomplimentary graffiti on posters touting "Quality." To the workers, the graffiti is no more disrespectful than the managerial actions that contradict and undermine the message of the poster.

The following parable points out the fundamental problem of manipulating surface-level aspects of culture in an effort to achieve a deeper change:

> A Peace Corps volunteer was assigned to teach mathematics to family groups in a region of a third world country. However, when the volunteer arrived, he discovered that many of the family groups already knew something about mathematics. Furthermore, the family groups had questions about mathematics. Unfortunately, the volunteer had simply memorized all the answers in the book he was using and did not understand the theories of the mathematics he was supposed to be teaching. He could deliver his prepared lectures, but he could not answer their questions.

When top management simply memorizes all the answers, they can't help change the culture. Speaking the words at formal presentations sounds good, but it's not enough. Only when managers really understand and believe the themes of the emerging paradigm can they make their actions consistent with it and respond to variations on the themes. When the themes become taken-for-granted assumptions in the minds of its people, then the organization has accomplished a profound shift. Making the themes stick at the deepest level of culture is important, because the underlying assumptions serve as the foundation for all other levels. To better understand these dynamic relationships between the levels of culture, it helps to know why and how culture emerges.

▶ WHY CULTURE EMERGES

Culture emerges in organizations because of the organization's need to deal with the external and internal problems of survival and prosperity. As an organization shifts to a new paradigm, managers may have to revisit their old cultural solutions to these problems. What exactly are these problems and why does the emergence of culture help solve them? We discuss these problems as external adaptation and internal integration.

Achieving External Adaptation

An organization's survival and prosperity depend on its ability to effectively interact with its environment and achieve *external adaptation*. The organization must not only serve its customers, but also its investors, suppliers, regulators, other social institutions, and benefactors. Organizations face many options, influences, and constraints as they interact with different external groups. Organizations must be able to cope with the environment by developing cultural solutions for adapting, including:

1. A sense of mission or purpose
2. Goals for fulfilling the mission
3. Means for accomplishing the goals
4. Measurements to assess how well they are doing
5. Procedures for making corrections and changing courses of action to fulfill the mission and goals (Schein, 1985)

Consider how IBM Rochester had to adapt to changing market conditions in order to survive. A major player in the mid-range computer market, IBM Rochester had for years relied on a particular product development process. This process was dominated by engineers doing what they knew to be best for the market and took four to five years to bring a new product to the market. In the mid-1980s, IBM Rochester was faced with either reducing the development cycle to about two years or risking failure in an increasingly competitive market. To bring out a new product in such a short period, they had to accept new goals, means of meeting the goals, and measures of their progress. For example, to develop over three times as many lines of programming code in half the normal time, they "tore up" old processes, simulated new approaches, developed new models for removing software defects, and even brought in customers to collaborate on product development in the early stages. IBM Rochester adapted to the environment by changing its culture. They have labeled their new culture "Market-Driven Quality."

Achieving Internal Integration

Internal integration refers to the cohesion of a group, how members are able to work together to fulfill the group's mission (Tichy, 1982, 1983). A group achieves internal integration by developing cultural solutions to address these issues:

1. A common language
2. Specific group boundaries (criteria for inclusion and exclusion)
3. Power and status
4. Intimacy, friendship, and love
5. Rewards and punishments
6. Ideology and religion (Schein, 1985)

As consensus develops on these issues, the group derives learned solutions for achieving internal integration that become a part of the organization's culture. Good internal integration permits the development of cultural solutions that facilitate external adaptation.

Having cultural solutions for internal integration allows people to interact and behave comfortably. Members know the rules of the game and can predict and understand what is going on. For example, at Toyota Motor Sales, U.S.A., Inc., when cross-functional change is planned, the consensus process gets informally initiated early in the planning process. Prior to ever entering a formal meeting, most participants have at least heard the issues, and probably have been asked for input. Because proposals are developed and discussed so thoroughly among the departments involved, consensus is built informally before the meeting.

Culture emerges in an organization because of the need for solutions to business problems. The solutions for external adaptation and internal integration provide group members a means of dealing with problems of survival and prosperity that are inherent to most social groups. As the environment changes, so too must the solutions. If these issues are not addressed as an organization shifts to a new paradigm, the group will not survive and prosper.[5]

▶ HOW CULTURE DEVELOPS

We have discussed the elements that make up culture, and why culture emerges. Next, we will examine how a culture develops. The most important factors are the founders and leaders of the organization, the learning process, and shared understandings. By knowing how culture develops, managers are better able to influence culture's continued development and change toward a new paradigm.

The Role of Founders and Leaders

Organizations are usually formed by a founder who assembles a group of people in order to achieve certain purposes or goals. This group, led by the founder, develops the mission statement and vision for the organization. When this founding group begins to bring in others, a common history begins and so does the development of the organization's culture (Schein, 1985). A wonderful example is Sam Walton, the founder of WalMart. Walton established a single store in Rogers, Arkansas, and grew his company into a multibillion-dollar retail chain with over 1,720 outlets in 42 states, before his death in 1992, with a continued growth of 150 stores per year. Regarded as a master at developing an organizational culture, Walton imbued WalMart with his down-home touch. He would show up unannounced at his retail stores to offer advice on pricing and merchandising, and lead the employees in cheers like "Give me a W . . . give me an A . . ." Most important, Walton instilled in WalMart successful systems and approaches to retailing. He taught people to think as he thought. He gave them a philosophy of treating the customer like a king

---

5. Adaptation is important, but it may not be enough for some organizations. For a "learning organization," it is not enough just to survive through "adaptive learning." It must also continually expand its capacity to create its future through "generative learning" (Senge, 1990, p. 14).

or queen, empowering the worker to do what is right, and sharing the rewards of hard work with everyone who contributes.[6]

The founders and leaders of an organization affect the development of culture in many ways. Their position of authority permits them to impose their values, beliefs, and favorite solutions. For example, when Tom Watson, Sr., founded IBM in 1914, he incorporated his personal beliefs into the company's culture, including *respect for the individual, the best customer service, and pursuit of excellence.*[7] Watson believed that:

- A company must respect individual employees and help them respect themselves. This means letting the employees know they make a difference, rewarding superior performance, promoting from within, and creating a democratic environment.
- The customer must be given the best possible service. Companies must let customers know how important they are and satisfy their requirements. To give the best possible service, every employee's job description must be related to this goal, and every employee must receive appropriate training and education on how to reach it.
- Excellence and superior performance must be pursued. A company must strive to avoid defects in products and services. To ensure excellent products and superior performance, a company must hire motivated individuals and then provide the necessary training and environment conducive to excellence.

These quality values are intended to provide the foundation for all of IBM's business activities. However, founders and subsequent leaders must continue to evolve and build the organization's culture for it to remain vibrant. For example, several years ago the leader of one of IBM's larger clients told IBM's chairman of the board that IBM wasn't doing a good job because they weren't listening to their customers. This opened the eyes of IBM's executives and prompted them to renew their commitment to IBM's basic principles with a new approach, "Market-Driven Quality."

In addition to their position of authority, many founders and leaders rely on the quality known as "charisma" to develop culture. Charisma arises from things such as self-confidence, conviction, interpersonal skills, creativity, perspective, and energy. This quality can be a compelling force for leaders, particularly in the early stages of group development (Bennis, 1983). When formal authority and charisma are combined with other more concrete mechanisms, the founders and leaders can have a profound effect on culture.

---

6. See *Fortune*, "Hall of Fame," Mar. 23, 1992, p. 113; *Fortune*, "What Sam Walton Taught America," May 4, 1992, pp. 104–105.
7. For more information, see the book by T. J. Watson, Jr., *A Business and Its Beliefs: The Ideas That Helped Build IBM*, McGraw-Hill, New York, 1963.

Mechanisms for Developing Culture

The primary mechanisms that leaders have for developing culture are:

- What they choose to emphasize, measure, and attempt to control
- Reactions to critical incidents and crises
- Deliberate role modeling, teaching, and coaching
- Criteria for allocation of rewards and status
- Criteria for recruitment, selection, promotion, retirement, and dismissal

Secondary mechanisms that further assist in embedding culture include:

- The organization's design and structure
- Organizational systems and procedures
- Design of physical space, facades, and buildings
- Stories, legends, myths, and parables about important events and people
- Formal statements of organizational philosophy, creeds, and charters

When these secondary mechanisms are consistent with the primary mechanisms, they build ideologies and bolster the primary mechanisms. If inconsistent, they will either be ignored or a source of conflict until they are rectified (Schein, 1985).

These mechanisms continue to be available to subsequent leaders of the organization after the founder passes from the scene. New leaders may try to preserve the current culture, seeing it as the psycho-social "glue" that holds the organization together. However, new leaders may also be charged with "reinventing" the organization, taking a different strategic direction or moving into another stage of development. This is typically the case with organizations struggling to adopt a new paradigm. During these periods of transition, the organization can become a battleground as conflicts erupt over the direction the organization will take.

These mechanisms reinforce new cultural values, beliefs, and behaviors. For example, Xerox recently attempted to integrate its supply chain worldwide, which meant reducing logistics costs, reducing inventory supply levels, and improving customer satisfaction. To accomplish these goals, Xerox changed the performance measures for its managers. One of the change agents responsible for promoting the integrated supply chain at Xerox's Department of Central Logistics and Asset Management stated:

> ... the USMG [marketing] vice-president and the head of manufacturing share a common metric. They used to be trying to minimize their respective days of supply at the expense of the other fellow. Now manufacturing has to be concerned about producing things that are not needed, to reduce finished goods, but also to be responsive. Since inventory is to be reduced throughout the chain, he can't rely on safety stock. . . . Global optimization is top priority.

To accomplish the goals of the integrated supply chain vision, Xerox had to get cooperation among its various units around the globe. Xerox's culture of isolationism and selfishness by managers had to change. Establishing new performance measures was one change Xerox made to promote the new values of cooperation and sharing.

QUALITY IN ACTION: A MESSAGE TO THE STUDENT

Paul A. Allaire, Chairman and CEO, Xerox Corporation

Leadership is a key to transforming an organization's culture toward the emerging paradigm. In the following message, Chairman and CEO Paul A. Allaire describes the vision that will lead Xerox into the future.

In preparing this message, I could not help but ponder how different the world is today than 30 years ago when I was in your position. Back in the '50s and '60s, the United States was easily the world's leading economic power. No longer. Today we are locked in a battle for global economic supremacy. Let me give you a few facts to make this point. As recently as 1960, Japan accounted for only 2 percent of the world's economy. Today, it is 15 percent. In that same time frame, America controlled some 35 percent of the world's economy. Our portion today is about 27 percent. Between 1984 and 1987, we went from being the largest creditor nation in the world to the largest debtor nation, a dubious position we still hold.

These are fundamental issues for American society, with enormous impact on our way of life, our standard of living, and our ability to create meaningful employment. This is the environment in which you will be working and living. There are two other critical points I want to make briefly. First, technology will continue to be the key driver of growth and wealth creation and the overall quality of life. Second, the world is now one competitive marketplace, and we must be the best in the world, not just in the United States. Your standard of living and that of your children depend on it.

What this means for Xerox is that to be successful in this global competitive environment, Xerox will have to intensify its focus on the customer and get ready to change more in the next five years than it has in the last ten years. And we have changed plenty in the past ten years. During the decade of the eighties, we focused on quality to turn Xerox around and to begin to recapture market share from our foreign competitors. While the quality story is a tremendous one for us, during the past few years we have started to think about what comes next. We continue to work relentlessly on total quality, and we view it as a race without a finish, a never-ending process of continuous improvement. However, we have been asking ourselves if quality will be enough to make us truly successful in the nineties.

An important part of this self-examination was the work we did on Xerox 2000. It was a year-long process that involved my senior team in weeks of learning. We took time out to take stock of global trends in our technologies and our markets. We heard from a wide variety of industry experts. We spent days meeting with our customers. That process gave us a clear direction of where we are heading. It is capsulized in our Strategic Intent:

> "Xerox, The Document Company, will be the leader in the global document market, providing Document Services that enhance business productivity."

The Xerox 2000 process made it clear that we had significant market opportunity. But it also made it clear that "we can't get there from here." We need to change, and change dramatically, to realize these opportunities. Specifically, we need to:

- Focus efforts more on customers, marketplace, competition
- Give people "end-to-end" accountability, with a clear line of sight to customers
- Provide people with the capacity to act; reward based on performance
- Enable Xerox people to manage their business segment
- Simplify business processes
- Unleash the entrepreneurial spirit
- Radically increase the "clock speed" to reduce time to market

It also be came clear to us that *massive* change was the order of the day. There are three elements to this change strategy upon which we have embarked. These include *organizational structures* focused on the customer; *behavior* that is team-oriented, creative, entrepreneurial, and devoted to open communication and learning; and *people* who are the best in the industry, with skills, knowledge, and experience supported by training and rewards.

We've embarked on a bold new journey. We are putting in place the hardware (the new organization) and the software (new ways of managing and working) to enable us to seize the opportunities identified by the Xerox 2000 work. But more needs to be done. All of the work we have done in the past few years has set the stage for realizing a vision for a new Xerox.

What is the Xerox I envision? I see an enterprise that has very special and unique qualities—an organization that is looked to when people want to figure out what will be effective management in the next century, much as they do today when they want to understand Total Quality Management. I see a company that values and celebrates the diversity of its employee body and creates an environment where each individual feels motivated to apply his or her creative energies to the work at hand. I also see a company made up of teams and communities of people who have the capacity to manage their own piece of the business, who have the freedom to use their own judgment and creativity, and who share in the risks and the rewards. Finally, I see a company that is a learning organization—a company in which learning is pervasive and second-nature, a company in which learning becomes the norm, not the exception. The company I envision will enable and depend on continuous learning throughout the organization—a company in which failures are seen as opportunities, where successes are studied with an eye to improvement, where new ideas are nurtured and implemented, where learning is defined as doing things differently.

We're off to a very good start! We are already one of the most diverse work groups in the world. Our work on quality has given us a leg up on empowering our work force and working together effectively as teams. Our presidential reviews and training infrastructure are important ingredients of a learning organization. We are on track to achieve the new Xerox—and it is the right track. So, much of the "it" is already in place or being put into place. The critical ingredient now is putting it together. To me, that means management. I have become more and more convinced that managing the "it"—putting it together—is the last big frontier of competitive advantage and the most powerful lever to productivity growth.

That brings us back to you. You are America's secret weapon in the global competition battle. No matter what you do in your career, you will be a key competitive component. In planning for a career in this competitive environment, you must learn about the concepts and methods that help management fulfill its important role in putting it together.

▲

Cultural Development as a Learning Process

As suggested earlier, organizations are often built around the values, beliefs, and assumptions of it founders and leaders. But culture also develops through a *learning process.* Through trial and error and experimentation, members learn which solutions appear to work and which do not in solving problems of external adaptation and internal integration.

Behavioral Learning   When a particular course of action solves a problem, removes a need, or earns a reward, that behavior is reinforced and will likely be tried again in similar circumstances. With repeated apparent success of the solution, group members will begin to share a belief in it as a way to accomplish positive outcomes. People also learn to avoid circumstances that create fear, dread, or insecurity (Schein, 1984, 1985; Solomon and Wynne, 1954). For example, in her first publishing job, an editor discovered that making a spelling mistake had such terrible consequences (public humiliation for making the mistake, followed by a feeling of inferiority and inadequacy), even the most terrible speller learned to do better.

The learning that occurs through anxiety/pain avoidance is very stable. Once something works, it may be repeated indefinitely, even if the source of the anxiety no longer exists. The behaviors may persist because they appear to continue to work, and may even evolve into a ritual (Schein, 1985). For example, in practicing traditional control theory, managers tend to assume that individual workers are the primary cause of deviations from standards. Subordinates who have been raked over the coals in management meetings learn to be prepared for similar occasions. These authors have talked to many subordinates who react defensively, by covering up or even falsifying data to avoid reprisal. When this is not possible, they generate extensive reports, with supporting data, to excuse their poor performance and explain why it will not happen again. When subordinates are asked to change the way they collect and analyze data to uncover root causes, they are distrustful and persist in their old habits.

Learning Abstract Concepts   Learning can also occur abstractly, as when we learn from being told something or by reading. If many people repeatedly tell a new member of an organization that the way to succeed is to "know the right people and win political favor," the person may come to believe it regardless of whether it is true. In this way, we learn a great deal about how to think, act, and feel in organizations. When values and beliefs learned abstractly are reinforced through behavioral experience, they are even further ingrained.

Shared Understandings

Culture also develops through *shared understandings*. Over time, the members of a group begin to build a communication system with shared meaning (Schein, 1985). This communication system involves not only a common language, but also common beliefs, values, attitudes, emotions, and viewpoints. Shared understandings emerge through critical incidents and the process of socialization.

Critical Incidents   Throughout a group's history, certain important events occur that in retrospect are seen as "critical." These events may have come about as a result of a major obstacle, threat, or opportunity. Members will look back on the event as a milestone or marker of the group's historical progress. *Critical incidents* lead a group to shared understandings by providing a focus. They are a shared learning experience that embody the new values and beliefs. Appropriate emotional responses, as well as behavior, are learned.

A critical event, like IBM Rochester's crisis in the mid-1980s, tends to get everyone's attention. At Rochester, everyone shared common emotions of fear over losing the mid-range computer market, and elation over successfully coping with the threat. Everyone talked about the problem, the solution, and the results. These conditions of sharing prompted social learning that pervaded the entire organization. The Market-Driven Quality culture that evolved at Rochester will for years be linked to this critical incident. Stories and legends about heros from the era will continue to influence IBM Rochester culture for years to come.

Process of Socialization   Critical incidents are not the only context for all group learning. Individuals learn through positive accomplishment, anxiety/pain avoidance, or abstract learning during their day-to-day work lives. But how does this transfer to the group? Individual learning becomes shared as people help each other interpret and understand events. This is known as the process of *socialization*.

When a new member enters an organization, socialization begins immediately. For this new member, it means "learning the ropes." This is done formally through orientation sessions and training programs. Informally, it occurs through chats at the water fountain or talks over lunch. For example, Toyota employees learn the approach to consensus decision making informally. When a rookie manager proposes something to a veteran who knows the Toyota approach, the veteran asks the rookie to discuss it with certain others. Somebody always asks the rookie, "Have you talked to everybody involved?" Veterans may even ask other veterans this question.[8]

The socialization process extends beyond bringing new members into the group. Throughout the life of the group, members continue to "learn the ropes" and reinvent "the ropes." *Formal socialization* continues through such things as training programs, educational seminars, and formal communications (memos and announcements). *Informal socialization* becomes even more apparent through nonverbal communications (pats on the back, icy stares) and other symbols (rituals, ceremonies, stories, heroes, logos, decor), and actual day-to-day experiences at work. Informal socialization is probably more effective than formal socialization. It occurs more spontaneously and may be viewed as more credible and relevant (Sathe, 1983).

▶ CULTURE AS A GUIDE TO BEHAVIOR

Culture can serve as both an asset and a liability for an organization (Sathe, 1985). As an asset, culture can make organizational life very efficient. Shared understandings make communication easier, since certain things "go without saying" and people share certain cues and guidelines for interpreting messages. Where there is strong culture, people are able to make good decisions when no one else can be consulted and there is no written rule. In this way, culture serves as a basis for confident action (Pettigrew, 1979).

Without cultural *consensus* on core values, beliefs, and assumptions, each employee would work on whatever he or she thought was important, without regard to the work of others. Rigid rules and regulations would be

---

8. Japanese companies may have an advantage in socializing their members because of the importance of *ningen kankej*, or social relationships, and establishing social harmony through information sharing and teamwork (Cooney, 1989). However, this approach works in America, too. In fact, this Toyota example is drawn from the Toyota Motor Sales company in the United States.

the only way to guide behavior. By contrast, a strong culture, with consensus on expected behaviors, values, beliefs, and assumptions, allows autonomy and discretion for employees. When managers also fulfill their responsibility to provide vision, build good systems, and educate employees on these, then employees tend to make the right decisions, in the interest of the whole organization because they all share the same cultural foundation.[9]

Though a strong culture has many advantages, it is not likely that large organizations will have perfectly uniform culture. People have diverse experiences in other groups (families, communities, churches, schools, and so on) that they do not leave behind completely when they enter their work lives. An organization's culture is a result of all of the cultural influences the members bring (Goffman, 1961; Gregory, 1983). Although organizations attempt to socialize new members into their own culture, subcultures may also emerge as certain groups do not conform to the dominant culture.

Group Nonconformity

It is very common for *subcultures* to develop in organizations that consist of many subgroups (divisions, functions, departments). A subculture is a culture specific to a subgroup. The more isolated a subgroup is within the organization, the more likely it is to develop its own culture. As groups become more internally cohesive, it may become more difficult to achieve plant-wide integration across them (Whitsett and Yorks, 1983). These are natural social processes that occur within groups of people that are isolated or have conflicting goals. Managers must build systems within the organization to counteract these tendencies.

A group's subculture may isolate it from the rest of the organization. For example, in one corporation the finance department developed such "strange" beliefs and practices that when they gave general reports in management meetings, no other managers understood their logic or attached any value to their reports, since they were seen as fictional accounts with no basis in reality. Not only did the rest of the organization regard the finance department as "stupid" or "crazy," some of their own people did. One young, but fairly high-placed financial officer admitted that after having gotten an MBA at a reputable school, he wondered if he had learned all the wrong things about accounting and financial analysis. Everything done at the corporation seemed at odds with what he had learned in school. After about three years, he decided it was the finance department that was confused.

The effect of subcultures on the achievement of the overall organization's purpose depends on how compatible the subculture is with the

---

9. This promotes efficiency in operations through what Ouchi (1980) has referred to as clan control. In effect, shared values, traditions, and beliefs function as substitutes for bureaucratic rules and controls.

larger culture. Subcultural variations may be described as either *enhancing*, *orthogonal*, or *countercultural.* Enhancing subcultures embrace the dominant culture even more fervently than the rest of the organization. Orthogonal subcultures accept the values of the dominant culture as well as any non-conflicting set of values that it considers its own. Countercultures directly challenge the core values of the dominant culture and express support for an alternative set of values (Duncan, 1989; Martin and Shiel, 1983). In some cases, subcultures may become so prominent that there appears to be no one dominant culture, a situation that undermines constancy of purpose.

The existence of subcultures has at least two important implications for shifting to the emerging paradigm: one deals with the horizontal dimension of the hierarchy, and the other deals with the vertical dimension. Horizontally, if functional departments each develop autonomous self-images and cultures that place functional goals above company goals, it is hard to accomplish the ideals of the emerging paradigm. Recall that cross-functional teamwork is an important element in the emerging paradigm. Vertically, if management and labor are in cultural conflict, it is hard to accomplish the integration of strategy and vision into the operational realities of the workplace. The leadership and communication processes that are key to the emerging paradigm are disrupted.

The managerial subculture is key to making a paradigm shift, since it determines the culture of the rest of the organization. Managers have the power and authority to determine the organization's vision, goals, systems, policies, and standard operating procedures. As role models, they set expectations for thought and action. The employee subculture develops within this context. If managers are good leaders, employees are likely to be good followers. If managers are poor leaders, employees are likely to be poor followers. Managers must take responsibility for leading employees to good attitudes, desirable behaviors, and commitment to the organization's purpose.

Despite management's diligent efforts to establish a "desirable" culture within the organization, not everyone will conform to it. Beyond the dominant culture (or subculture) of a group, other influences on individual behavior include the environment, organization circumstances, and individual personality characteristics. Due to these forces, individuals may not conform to the group's culture.

Individual Nonconformity
In addition to group nonconformity, individuals may deviate from organizational norms on a personal basis. Not all individual nonconformity is bad for the organization. An individual who does not show concern for the good of the organization, does not share its values and norms of behavior, might be called a *rebel.* Rebels generally are just out for themselves. However, someone who does care for the organization, but chal-

lenges the behavioral norms to make it better might be called a *maverick* (Sathe, 1983, 1985). Organizations often need mavericks to help accomplish a shift and to continuously improve. The maverick may find behavioral nonconformity easier than the rebel because he or she may at least be perceived as having concern for the organization's best interests and values. The more deviant an individual is, the more imagination, determination, and marshaling of personal and organizational resources will be required for the individual to succeed.

To enhance the chances of success, the behavioral nonconformist might rely on two basic strategies: *cultural insurance* and *self-insurance.* Cultural insurance is obtained by gaining support from powerful others, especially the *good soldiers* who adhere to the dominant culture. Self-insurance involves building a reservoir of social credits, on the basis of one's own track record, personal power, and credibility (Hollander, 1978). To sustain this strategy, one must be able to replenish the social credits by demonstrating success, social repayment, and contribution to the organizational purpose. Over time, a successful nonconformist can acquire the reputation as one who "gets away with murder," but is respected either for consistent performance or promoting positive changes (Sathe, 1983).

Strong Culture and Nonconformity

A strong culture tends to impose conformity. Since nonconformity, or deviation from the status quo, is what leads to change, a strong corporate culture can be a liability, particularly when it has become dysfunctional or misfocused. There are many examples of companies that failed because their flawed perception of reality prevented them from responding to new competitive challenges. A strong culture makes it difficult for leaders to turn an organization in a new direction, even when survival depends upon such a shift. Since culture provides the lens for perceiving and giving meaning to events, it can prevent organization members from recognizing competitive and operational opportunities and threats (Barney, 1986; Crozier, 1964; Porter, 1980; Riley, 1983; Tichy, 1983).

Individuality should not be stifled just for the sake of having a strong culture. Individuality can be a benefit. It can prompt change, be a source of new ideas, methods, and strategies. This is not to say that a weak, fragmented culture is desirable. Rather, a strong culture that values new ideas, challenges the status quo, and continually looks for ways to increase customer value is likely to be the most successful. Managers must strike a balance between strong culture and nonconformity to have a culture supportive of the emerging paradigm.

Where to Begin Culture Change

How do managers develop the type of culture that supports the emerging paradigm? This question leads us into an old debate in the field of management and organizational change: Should we initially focus change efforts on the deepest levels of culture, through bringing to the surface the underlying assumptions? Or do we more effectively change behavior by changing and sustaining organizational structure and systems?

Traditionally, organizational development (OD) practitioners have sought to enhance the adaptive mechanisms of organizations by intervening in the core of culture (Levels 2 and 3 of the Schein model). They have encouraged people to question the values and norms under which they operate. Ideally, cultural intervention would make people more receptive to change and allow a more beneficial realignment of the organization with the environment (see French, Bell, and Zawacki, 1983, for a review of traditional OD techniques).

This approach has been challenged by those who argue that values and norms result from the interactions of people channeled by formal structures and systems (Wohlking, 1970). OD has since broadened its perspectives to include structural interventions, as participants on both sides of the debate have come to realize the problem of change is more complex than originally formulated (Beer, 1980). Still, this "chicken or egg" issue remains a puzzle for many seeking to transform organizations. The puzzle highlights why managers must have a clear understanding of culture.

Let's consider a much newer question: how does the transformation of organizations relate to the learning experiences of their members? The links between individual, team, and organizational learning (Marsick, 1988; Dechant and Marsick, 1991) are clearly relevant to the question of culture change, especially change in the core of culture. Sincere and profound adherence to the new paradigm may enable the leaders of even the most cursed organizations to overcome the damage of the 1980s. Companies that find it necessary to establish such a culture will face the challenge of transformational change.

▶ SUMMARY OF KEY POINTS

1. Rational managers attempting a paradigm shift must understand and change their organization's culture.
2. A holistic view of culture provides managers an understanding of the causes of behavior in organizations.
3. Culture emerges as a response to internal and external problems which members of the organization must learn to solve.
4. Culture develops as leaders instill their vision in the organization and as members learn solutions to internal and external problems.
5. Culture guides behavior within the organization and ensures conformity.
6. Conformity has both benefits and drawbacks for organizations that must shift to a new paradigm.
7. Shifting to the emerging paradigm requires cultural transformation for traditional organizations.

▶ KEY TERMS

artifacts

assumptions

beliefs

critical incidents

cultural view of organizations

culture

external adaptation

internal integration

inward view of culture

modern control and
  improvement process

outward view of culture

rational view of organizations

shared understanding

socialization

strong culture

subcultures

traditional control theory

upstream control

values

▶ DISCUSSION QUESTIONS

1. Why do organizational change programs aimed at only one level of culture tend to fail?

2. Why do training programs focused on imparting skills to individuals have limited impact in changing culture? Does the distinction between training and education have implications for changing culture? How does cultural learning differ from traditional classroom/seminar education, and what are the implications for changing culture?

3. Write a culture change "to do" list for leaders of an organization attempting to achieve paradigm shift. If change is required at all levels of culture, where do you start? Is there any role for a special "quality program" in making the shift?

4. What are the benefits and drawbacks of strong culture for organizations interested in making a paradigm shift?

5. Explain why the key principles listed in this chapter are important parts of the new paradigm.

6. A vice president of a Fortune 500 firm recently defined culture as "the way we do business today." When asked later, "Why do you do business this way?", the executive responded, "Because of our culture." What is wrong with this definition?

▶ EXPERIENTIAL EXERCISE 1

Obtain an audiotape or CD of the Elvis Presley song "Return to Sender." Everyone should listen to the facts of the case while the instructor plays it for the class. After listening to the facts, write a story that tells the background and details of the drama; for example, why the letter was repeatedly sent back. Write the story as if it would be used as a script for a novel or a daytime soap opera. Also propose a solution, as if you were a counselor and had to resolve the social problem. After ten minutes of writing, volunteers will read aloud their stories and solutions.

▶ EXPERIENTIAL EXERCISE 2

Break the class into groups of five or six people. Each group should pick any three of the key principles of the new paradigm (discussed early in the chapter). Describe how each of these key principles would be expressed at each of the three levels of Schein's model of culture:

Level 1: Artifacts and Behaviors
Level 2: Values and Beliefs
Level 3: Underlying Assumptions

After fifteen to twenty minutes of discussion, have each group present their work for one of the key principles.

▶ REFERENCES

C. Argyris, "Theories of Action That Inhibit Individual Learning," *American Psychologist*, Vol. 31, 1976, pp. 638–654.

C. Argyris and D. A. Schon, *Organizational Learning: A Theory of Action Perspective*, Addison-Wesley, Reading, Mass., 1978.

T. Arnold, *The Symbols of Government*, Yale University Press, New Haven, Conn., 1935.

C. I. Barnard, *The Functions of the Executive*, Harvard University Press, Cambridge, Mass., 1938, 1968.

J. B. Barney, "Organizational Culture: Can It Be a Source of Sustained Competitive Advantage?" *Academy of Management Review*, Vol. 11, No. 3, 1986, pp. 656–665.

V. Barnouw, *Culture and Personality*, Dorsey Press, Homewood, Ill., 1979.

Warren Bennis, "The Artform of Leadership," in Suresh Scrivastva and Associates (eds.), *The Executive Mind: New Insights on Managerial Thought and Action*, Jossey-Bass, San Francisco, 1983.

Michael Beer, *Organizational Change and Development: A Systems View*, Goodyear Publishing Company, Santa Monica, Calif., 1980.

R. H. Brown, "Social Theory as Metaphor," *Theory and Society*, Vol. 3, 1976, pp. 169–197.

A. F. Buono, J. L. Bowditch, and J. W. Lewis III, "When Cultures Collide: The Anatomy of a Merger," *Human Relations*, Vol. 38, No. 5, 1985, pp. 477–500.

Barry D. Cooney, "Japan and Culture," *Training and Development Journal*, August 1989, pp. 58–61.

M. Crozier, *The Bureaucratic Phenomenon*, University of Chicago Press, 1964.

T. E. Deal and A. A. Kennedy, *Corporate Cultures*, Addison-Wesley, Reading, Mass., 1982.

Kathleen Dechant and Victoria J. Marsick, "In Search of the Learning Organization: Toward a Conceptual Model of Collective Learning," *Proceedings*, May 1991, Eastern Academy of Management, Hartford, Conn.

I. Deutscher, "Words and Deeds," *Social Problems*, Vol. 13, 1966, pp. 235–254.

I. Deutscher, *What We Say/What We Do: Sentiments and Acts*, Scott, Foresman, Glenview, Ill., 1973.

W. J. Duncan, "Organizational Culture: 'Getting a Fix' on an Elusive Concept," *The Academy of Management Executive*, Vol. 3, No. 3, 1989, pp. 229–235.

H. Fayol, *General and Industrial Management*, Pitman, New York, 1949.

M. Fishbein and I. Ajzen, *Belief, Attitude, Intention and Behavior: An Introduction to Theory and Research*, Addison-Wesley, Reading, Mass., 1975.

W. L. French, C. H. Bell, and R. A. Zawacki, *Organization Development: Theory, Practice, and Research* (rev. ed.), Business Publications, Inc., Plano, Tex., 1983.

C. Geertz, *The Interpretation of Cultures*, Basic Books, New York, 1973.

H. Gerth and C. W. Mills, *From Max Weber: Essays in Sociology*, University Press, Oxford, 1946, renewed 1973.

E. Goffman, "The Characteristics of Total Institutions," in *A Sociological Reader on Complex Organizations*, 2d ed., A. Etzioni (ed.), Holt, Rinehart & Winston, New York, 1961.

K. L. Gregory, "Native-View Paradigms: Multiple Cultures and Culture Conflicts in Organizations," *Administrative Science Quarterly*, Vol. 28, 1983, pp. 359–376.

R. Harrison, "Understanding Your Organization's Character," *Harvard Business Review*, Vol. 5, No. 3, 1972, pp. 119–128.

E. P. Hollander, *Leadership Dynamics: A Practical Guide to Effective Relationships*, Free Press, New York, 1978.

E. Jacques, *The Changing Culture of a Factory*, Dryden Press, New York, 1952.

A. L. Kroeber and C. Kluckhohn, *Culture: A Critical Review of Concepts and Definitions*, Vintage Books, New York, 1952.

Thomas S. Kuhn, *The Structure of Scientific Revolutions*, The University of Chicago Press, 1962.

R. Linton, *The Study of Man*, Appleton-Century-Crofts, New York, 1936.

Victoria J. Marsick, "Learning in the Workplace: The Case for Reflectivity and Critical Reflectivity," *Adult Education Quarterly*, Vol. 38, No. 4, 1988, pp. 187–198.

J. Martin and C. Shiel, "Organizational Culture and Counterculture: An Uneasy Symbiosis," *Organizational Dynamics*, Autumn 1983, pp. 52–64.

G. D. Mitchell, *A Dictionary of Sociology*, Routledge & Kegan Paul, London, 1973.

R. J. Mockler (ed.), *Readings in Management Control*, Appleton-Century-Crofts, New York, 1970.

G. Morgan, "Paradigms, Metaphors, and Puzzle-Solving in Organization Theory," *Administrative Science Quarterly*, Vol. 25, 1980, pp. 605–622.

J. S. Ott, *The Organizational Culture Perspective*, Brooks/Cole Publishing Co., Pacific Grove, Calif., 1989.

W. G. Ouchi, "Markets, Bureaucracies, and Clans," *Administrative Science Quarterly*, Vol. 25, 1980, pp. 129–141.

William G. Ouchi and Alan L. Wilkins, "Organizational Culture," *Annual Review of Sociology*, Vol. 11, 1985, pp. 457–483.

T. Parsons, *The Social System*, Free Press, Glencoe, Ill., 1951.

C. Perrow, *Complex Organizations*, Scott Freeman, Palo Alto, Calif., 1979.

A. M. Pettigrew, "On Studying Organizational Cultures," *Administrative Science Quarterly*, Vol. 24, 1979, pp. 570–581.

M. Porter, *Competitive Strategy*, Free Press, New York, 1980.

A. R. Radcliffe-Brown, *A Natural Science of Society*, Free Press, Glencoe, Ill., 1957.

P. Riley, "A Structurationist Account of Political Cultures," *Administrative Science Quarterly*, Vol. 28, 1983, pp. 414–437.

V. Sathe, "Implications of Corporate Culture: A Manager's Guide to Action," *Organizational Dynamics*, Autumn 1983, pp. 5–23.

V. Sathe, *Culture and Related Corporate Realities*, Irwin, Homewood, Ill., 1985.

E. H. Schein, "Coming to a New Awareness of Organizational Culture," *Sloan Management Review*, Winter 1984, pp. 3–16.

E. H. Schein, *Organizational Culture and Leadership*, Jossey-Bass, San Francisco, 1985.

H. S. Schwartz, "The Usefulness of Myth and the Myth of Usefulness: A Dilemma for the Applied Organizational Scientist," *Journal of Management*, Vol. 11, No. 1, 1985, pp. 31–42.

W. R. Scott, *Organizations: Rational, Natural and Open Systems*, Prentice-Hall, Englewood Cliffs, N.J., 1981.

P. Selznick, *Leadership in Administration*, Harper & Row, New York, 1957.

R. L. Solomon and L. C. Wynne, "Traumatic Avoidance Learning: The Principles of Anxiety Conservation and Partial Irreversibility," *Psychological Review*, Vol. 61, 1954, p. 353.

J. P. Spradley and D. W. McCurdy, *Anthropology: The Cultural Perspective*, Wiley, New York, 1975.

Lauren P. Taylor, "Management: Agent of Human Cultural Evolution," *Futures*, October 1987.

J. D. Thompson, *Organizations in Action*, McGraw-Hill, New York, 1967.

N. M. Tichy, "Managing Change Strategically: The Technical, Political, and Cultural Keys," *Organizational Dynamics*, Autumn 1982, pp. 59–80.

N. Tichy, *Managing Strategic Change: Technical, Political, and Cultural Dynamics*, Wiley, New York, 1983.

H. D. Triandis, V. Vassilou, G. Vassilou, Y. Tanka, and A. V. Shanmugan, *The Analysis of Subjective Culture*, Wiley-Interscience, New York, 1972.

Ellen J. Wallach, "Individuals and Organizations: The Cultural Match," *Training and Development Journal*, February 1983, pp. 29–36.

L. White, *The Science of Culture*, Grove Press, New York, 1949.

David A. Whitsett and Lyle Yorks, "Looking Back at Topeka: General Foods and the Quality-of-Worklife Experiment," *California Management Review*, Vol. 25, No. 4, 1983, pp. 93–109.

A. L. Wilkins, "The Culture Audit: A Tool for Understanding Organizations," *Organizational Dynamics*, Autumn 1983, pp. 24–38.

Wallace Wohlking, "Attitude Change, Behavior Change: The Role of the Training Department," *California Management Review*, Vol. 13, No. 2, 1970.

chapter 4

Management Role Responsibilities

Over the last several years, we have grown fourfold through acquisitions of other companies. We have brought several cultures together using the basic premise that quality, total quality management, and all that entails, is the cornerstone of our business philosophy. We are bringing together our suppliers, our customers, and our employees to form a partnership for ongoing continuous improvement in every single work process in every factory and office. It is a complex task accomplished by one small step at a time, no improvement considered too small.

Michael J. McKenna, President, North American Division, Crown Cork and Seal Company

▶ **CHAPTER OUTLINE**

Chapter Overview

The Importance of Managerial Roles

Role Responsibilities and Managerial Performance
Culture and Role Systems

A Managerial Role Responsibilities Framework

Traditional Management Roles
A Shift to a New Agenda for Continuous Improvement

Diversity of Role Accomplishments
A Framework Combining Types and Domains of Accomplishments
Types of Accomplishments for Continuous Improvement
Domains of Accomplishments for Superior Customer Value

Using the MAT Framework for Role Systems

Role Responsibility Differences
Depicting Managerial Role Responsibilities
Consequences of Gaps: Role System Inadequacy
The Nature of Managerial Role Responsibilities
The Key to Culture Change

Summary of Key Points

Key Terms

Discussion Questions

Experiential Exercise

References

▶ CHAPTER OVERVIEW

Traditional approaches to management are inadequate because they have failed to specify a purpose. Management curricula have too often taught students process skills without mentioning the organization's purpose for customer value. As a result, students graduate with the delusion that if they work diligently enough with their social process skills or technical skills, they will succeed as managers of competitive organizations. Certainly, these skills and traditional managerial roles, such as planning, organizing, leading, and monitoring, are important, but they must be applied for a purpose. The emerging paradigm specifies the purpose. Role responsibilities for the emerging paradigm require managers to accomplish change and stable execution of their strategies, systems, and operations. And these accomplishments must be tightly integrated to achieve continuous improvement in customer value.

▶ THE IMPORTANCE OF MANAGERIAL ROLES

Managers have often relied on new technology or structural changes to provide fast, comprehensive improvements in their organizations. In the emerging paradigm, improved technologies and structures may be required, but managers do not stop here. Instead, they introduce improvements throughout the organization. Furthermore, all of these changes are integrated, mutually supportive, and strategically directed toward providing value to customers. Such comprehensive improvement requires leaders to put in place the right set of role responsibilities and define what people *should* accomplish. In brief, people will not shift from old practices until their roles are redefined. This chapter introduces a framework for role accomplishments that makes the themes of the emerging paradigm come to life. And it discusses the use of the framework of role responsibilities.

▼

QUALITY IN ACTION: A MESSAGE TO THE STUDENT

Albert J. Cole, Senior Logistics Manager, Central Intelligence Agency (CIA)

When learning new role behaviors, it helps to have role models. Albert J. Cole, Senior Logistics Manager with the Central Intelligence Agency, suggests that we rediscover the successful entrepreneur as one role model for the emerging paradigm.

During the past year, I have met many senior managers from both industry and government. I often ask them to describe their fundamental role in their organization. There is always a moment of silence, and usually a glance that tells me that if I were smart, I wouldn't be asking such a question, because I should already know what the traditional managerial roles are. However, they rarely define their role in terms of continuous improvement. Now, I have to confess, with an MBA and some 30 years of experience doing managerial kinds of things in both government and industry, until now I too had no idea what the true managerial role should be. After two years of intense study on the issues discussed in this book, I now know what managers should be doing, and how customers and stakeholders should measure their performance.

We know that traditional hierarchical management creates barriers that inhibit the organization's ability to serve customers. Many senior managers think that making their budget and staff grow bigger is their primary role, and it often takes priority over the needs and values of customers and stakeholders. They are rewarded with increases in job grade pay when they succeed in doing this. Such an inward focus builds up organizational cost for activities that have no value to the customer. For example, a large government office commissioned a process action team to analyze service delivery in its motor pool. The team found it was spending close to $1 million for in-house maintenance services when the same services could have been contracted out at less than 30 percent of the in-house cost. In general, I estimate that 20 to 40 percent of the cost in private industry and government adds absolutely no value for customers. Stated another way, for every $100 of operating budget, $20 to $40 is wasted on non-value-added activity. Think about this every time you open your pocketbook to purchase products and services, or better yet, when you pay your taxes.

Globally competitive markets require managers to rethink their roles. We can no longer solve our problems with a continuous flood of dollars like I have seen done so many times during my government career. Even incompetent managers can accomplish their goals if given enough money. Having worked with founders and having founded several businesses of my own, what always strikes me is that founders and entrepreneurs have a completely different mind-set than what I observe in professional managers. Successful founders and entrepreneurs exude their principles and values; they lead by example and pull the best from people who work with them. They almost never dwell on organization charts, for they are too busy satisfying the needs of their customers. They enjoy working in an environment which encourages risk taking, collaboration, and a diversity of ideas. They respect the people working with them and are always willing to share information on all aspects of the business. Professional managers, on the other hand, often seem to focus on their personal goals and power structure. They withhold vital information which enables them to manage from a position of fear while attempting to control behavior through policies, procedures, and organizational design. In several organizations I have worked with, when the entrepreneur's position was taken over by the professional manager, the organization started to go downhill. In two cases, a thriving organization went out of business.

Managers of the 21st century will have to think and act more like founders and entrepreneurs. They will create and continuously improve organizational designs and systems composed of minimum, necessary sets of activities to provide superior customer value.

Role Responsibilities and Managerial Performance

Roles are important determinants of managerial performance for managers throughout the organization. *Roles* are the responsibilities, behaviors, or performance accomplishments expected of a person in a particular position. *Formal roles* are prescribed in job descriptions, which list task requirements and responsibilities. After a person begins a new job, however, *informal roles* evolve to suit social and personal preferences, which may differ from formal roles (Katz and Kahn, 1978; Graen, 1976; McGrath, 1976). For example, because of his proclivity to take copious notes at all meetings, John acquired the informal role of secretary on each of the three quality improvement teams of which he is a member. He has neither a formal title nor job responsibility, yet he keeps records on all meetings, collects the progress reports between meetings, and distributes memos to group members. Both formal and informal roles should direct the actions of diverse people toward desired purposes.

If managers perceive themselves incompetent for a role, they will avoid it (Bandura, 1977). Leaders are responsible for putting in place *systems* that ensure people are competent for continuous improvement responsibilities. These include systems for selection, placement, education, coaching, and ongoing development. But even when these systems for individual competency are in place, other systems may prevent a competent person from fulfilling a role. An individual's apparent failure to perform as in-

Figure 1
The relationship of roles and culture

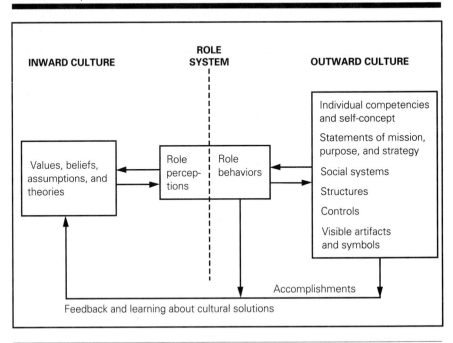

tended may be the result of lack of facilitators or the presence of inhibitors in broader systems (Deming, 1986; Peters, O'Connor, and Eulberg, 1985). Facilitators and inhibitors include resources such as raw materials, technologies, tools, and methods, as well as the social system of interrelated roles and culture.

Culture and Role Systems
Managerial roles can be the starting point for leaders intent upon transforming the culture. Role perceptions give people a vision of what they are supposed to do. The various levels of culture are dynamically interrelated. Values, beliefs, and assumptions lead people to behave in certain ways, and behavior leads people to think in certain ways. Thus, the culture sustains itself. The relationship between core thought and behavior creates a loop: thought causes behavior, which causes thought. This loop presents an enigma for managers who must change the culture to shift to the emerging paradigm. It is so difficult to break into or overcome this cycle that managers attempting the shift have often failed because of it. How do managers break the loop and shift to the emerging paradigm?

The answer is to attack the middle ground, the *role systems,* which are the interrelated role perceptions and behaviors; the bridge between the inward and outward sides of culture (see Figure 1). *Role perceptions* reside in the minds of people (inward) as beliefs about what one is responsible for doing. If conditions are right, these perceptions lead to *role behaviors* (outward), which are actions to accomplish the role perceptions.

The nature of systems is such that all parts are interrelated. Managers cannot change one part in isolation. The behavior of any one person relates to, affects, results from, or coordinates with the behavior of others (Katz and Kahn, 1978, p. 189). To create an atmosphere that facilitates change, leaders must inspire everyone in the organization with a vision of what they should be accomplishing to improve customer value. There must also be an interrelated system of role responsibilities for this agenda.

If managers, particularly top managers, do not make sure their roles are consistent with the emerging paradigm, it is difficult to develop a culture supportive of it. For example, managers may issue statements of principles, create slogans and posters to symbolize their commitment to "Quality," set lofty objectives to be number one in customer satisfaction, and put in place committee structures to oversee projects and monitor progress. However, if managers do not change their fundamental assumptions about how to do business, inconsistencies will emerge in their actions. For example, while managers espouse "Quality" and "Customer Satisfaction," their resource allocations undermine long-term efforts to improve. When managers only manipulate surface-level manifestations of culture, they ultimately fail to "walk the talk," as managers often say. When employees perceive these inconsistencies, they infer that the managers really are not committed, that managers are manipulating them or implementing another "program of the month."[1]

Managers must get away from a program mentality to shift to the emerging paradigm. Establishing an appropriately focused role system for managers is the first step in making the paradigm shift. *Responsible management* accomplishes an integrated set of outcomes for strategically focused *continuous improvement* in *cross-functional systems* for *superior customer value.* These three themes of the emerging paradigm are made operational in the framework of role responsibilities presented in this chapter.

► A MANAGERIAL ROLE RESPONSIBILITIES FRAMEWORK

Competing to provide customers with superior value in a global economy will require managers to continue to improve their organization and consistently execute a customer value strategy. This creates a challenge: continuous improvement requires change, but consistent customer value requires

---

1. They may even use these inconsistencies as an excuse for not changing. Inconsistencies can not only dampen people's motivation for change, they can offer real impediments (e.g., the lack of skills, resources, appropriate measurements, and social support), even when motivated people are willing to overlook the inconsistencies.

stability. Over the long term, customers expect products to get better. We expect more from our automobiles now than 10 years ago. But over the short term, customers also expect products to be the same. If we rent a Ford Taurus in Toledo this week, we expect it to be just as good as the one we rented last week in Miami.

Unfortunately, traditional management approaches frequently fail to achieve a purposeful balance between change and stability. In traditional organizations, the over-control that is intended to maintain stability often precludes healthy strategic change. Cultural forces for stability include the social system of roles, structures, and controls. In the emerging paradigm, however, managers must be willing to change all of these forces when necessary. To provide the best customer value, managers must engage in a mix of role activities to achieve two seemingly contradictory objectives: change and stability. Traditional managerial roles are inadequate for this agenda.

Traditional Management Roles

In 1916, Henri Fayol introduced what became the predominant frame of reference for managers: *planning, organizing, commanding, coordinating, and controlling* (1949). These terms are defined below:

- *Planning* (both the short- and long-term): Determining in advance what should be accomplished and how it should be accomplished. It requires managers to set goals and strategies.
- *Organizing:* Prescribing relationships between people and resources, and grouping activities and resources in a logical fashion in order to accomplish goals.
- *Commanding:* Influencing or affecting the behavior of others to get members of the organization to work effectively to accomplish the organization's goals.
- *Coordinating:* Adjusting the activities of independent groups to ensure harmonious action. Coordination is essential to blend the independent work of groups and accomplish the organization's overall goals and objectives.
- *Controlling:* Comparing actual performance with standards and taking any necessary corrective action.

Fayol's framework is commonly used to organize and teach management principles (Bounds and Dobbins, 1993; Carrol and Gillen, 1987). However, it falls short for several reasons. As Mintzberg has pointed out, the framework provides only vague managerial objectives:

> When he is called and told that one of his factories has just burned down, and he advises the caller to see whether temporary arrangements can be made to supply customers through a foreign subsidiary, is he planning, organizing, coordinating, or controlling? How about when he presents a gold watch to a retiring employee? Or when he attends a conference to meet people in the trade? Or on

returning from that conference, when he tells one of his employees about an interesting product idea he picked up there? (1975, p. 49)

As an alternative to Fayol's framework, Mintzberg proposes ten roles: three interpersonal roles (*Figurehead, Leader, Liaison*), three informational roles (*Monitor, Disseminator, Spokesman*), and four decisional roles (*Entrepreneur, Disturbance Handler, Resource Allocator,* and *Negotiator*). These are defined below:

- *Figurehead:* Performs ceremonial duties or "makes appearances."
- *Leader:* Inspires people to fulfill the unit's purpose; similar to Fayol's "commanding," except that leaders also provide vision and ensure workers' needs are met.
- *Liaison:* Contacts people outside the vertical chain of command and builds up an information system and network of relationships that serve his or her agenda.
- *Monitor:* Gathers information from a network of contacts, such as subordinates, peers, superiors, and people outside the organization.
- *Disseminator:* Shares and distributes this information to subordinates who need it.
- *Spokesman:* Sends information to people outside his or her work unit, including peers, customers, suppliers, business partners, etc., through various oral and written media.
- *Entrepreneur:* Looks out for new ideas and makes decisions to improve the unit and adapt to changing conditions; acts as a voluntary initiator of change.
- *Disturbance Handler:* Responds to pressures and problems.
- *Resource Allocator:* Decides who will get what resources, and clarifies who can make what decisions about which resources.
- *Negotiator:* Balances individual needs by negotiating solutions between opposed parties; sometimes acts as intermediary and sometimes acts on his or her own behalf.

The interpersonal roles arise from a manager's formal authority and put the manager in a position to fulfill the informational roles, which derive from the information gathering accomplished by the manager as a liaison. Interpersonal and informational roles support the decisional roles, which require managers to use information as an input to decision making. Just like Fayol's roles, Mintzberg's roles can be used to describe almost any manager's job.

Unfortunately, both Fayol's and Mintzberg's frameworks fail to relate managerial work to the themes of the emerging paradigm: customer value strategy, systems management, and continuous improvement. For example, Mintzberg's role of entrepreneur suggests that managers introduce change, but it does not make managers responsible for continuous improvement as defined in earlier chapters. Nor does Mintzberg integrate all managerial roles around the strategic purpose of accomplishing superior customer value.

In Fayol's traditional framework, the activities of organizing, commanding, coordinating, and controlling are based on the primary activity of planning Managers first plan by setting goals, objectives, and strategies, and then organize, command, coordinate, and control to successfully implement the plans. The emerging paradigm departs from traditional managerial approaches in the first step, planning. In Fayol's approach, planning is not explicitly aimed at providing customer value. It makes no value judgment about the strategic priority of customer value. Without a customer value focus, a manager's plans are often inwardly focused on productivity, efficiency, or profit.

In traditional frameworks, planning entails establishing a roadmap for administering existing strategies, systems, and policies. There is nothing indicating a need for improvement. Without explicit requirements for improvement, the organization's control mechanisms may dampen the creative urges of individuals. Fayol's lack of emphasis on change and improvement is understandable within his historical context. The environment was more friendly in his day, with fewer competitors and fewer regulations. Today, however, managers cannot afford to use a static framework in thinking about their activities.

A Shift to a New Agenda for Continuous Improvement

Carrying out continuous improvement of customer value means that managers must *plan* to improve systematically. These improvements should not be narrowly focused on one of the many dimensions of customer value (for example, cost reduction) or concentrated in one area of the organization (for example, the shop floor). All aspects of the organization must be part of the plan. Rather than resting content with existing arrangements, managers must continue to ask the purpose of each managerial role to focus attention on the sense of imperatives in the emerging paradigm.[2]

Behavior can be studied at many levels, ranging from a more microanalytical level to a broader organizational level. It might be studied as *behavioral roles*, such as those suggested by Fayol and Mintzberg. For example, a leadership role may be composed of several behaviors: deciding on a vision for the organization, writing a memo, making a speech. Further, specific behaviors might be studied and broken down into *component motions*, such as movements, as done in time and motion studies earlier this century, or tasks, as in detailed job analysis. For example, finger, hand, and arm movements may compose the behavior of typing a memo.

This chapter does not address microanalysis of role behaviors, but rather how they relate to managerial responsibilities for more purposeful

---

2. The traditional meaning of the word "role" itself does not convey the sense of imperatives. For this reason, we emphasize the words "responsibility" and "accomplishment" to convey the importance of strategic purpose in the new managerial agenda. Continuous improvement is not optional in the emerging paradigm.

role accomplishments. For example, the traditional roles of negotiation, leadership, and planning may be required to accomplish a breakthrough. This view of role behavior defines the purpose of management in the emerging paradigm. Finally, each of these accomplishments might be further described in terms of how it relates to the *organizational purpose* of providing superior customer value. Many accomplishments are required to fulfill this purpose, including breakthrough, incremental improvement, standardization, routinization, maintenance, and execution. We discuss each of these accomplishments below.

Diversity of Role Accomplishments

We describe the *role accomplishments* (the outcomes of role behavior) for this new managerial agenda using two dimensions: *type* and *domain* (Bounds and Pace, 1991). *Type of accomplishment* categorizes the outcomes of role behavior according to the degree of change involved. The types of accomplishment range from consistent execution (no change in systems) to breakthroughs (unprecedented, radical change in systems).[3] These types of accomplishment include (1) breakthrough, (2) incrementalism, (3) standardization, (4) routinization, (5) maintenance, (6) execution.

Domain of accomplishment refers to the object or the part of the organization that is being acted upon. A domain may be narrow in scope, such as a single technique of work execution or a hand movement within a task. Or it may be as broad as the organizational structure or strategic systems of the organization, spanning many functions and departments. The domains discussed below range from strategy, through systems, to operations. To provide superior customer value, there must be a good fit among all domains, including (1) customer value strategy, (2) design strategy, (3) systems, (4) policies, (5) motivators, (6) processes, (7) technology, (8) operations.

A Framework Combining Types and Domains of Accomplishments

Combining the types and domains of accomplishments creates a two-dimensional layout we call the *Management Accomplishment Topograph (MAT)* (see Figure 2). The layout in Figure 2 shows all possible combinations of the listed types and domains of managerial role accomplishments. For example, Position 1 indicates the combination of "breakthrough" and "customer value strategy." Combining these two categories specifies the managerial role accomplishment "breakthrough improvement of customer value strategy." Within an organization, managerial role responsibilities can be defined in terms of the positions on this grid.[4]

---

3. Monitoring and measuring provide information to assist in these accomplishments.
4. Note that the listing order of these types and domains of change is not intended to convey their worth or value to the organization. Each is necessary, important, and valuable to the organization.

Figure 2
The MAT (Management Accomplishment Topograph)

Type of Accomplishment	Customer value strategy	Design strategy	Systems	Policies	Motivators	Processes	Technology	Operations
Breakthrough	1							2
Incrementalism								
Standardization							5	
Routinization								
Maintenance								
Execution	4							3

Domain of Accomplishment

Different role responsibilities can be described by this framework. For example, although they may engage in similar *types* of activities, there are clear differences between the *domains* of a frontline operator and the president of the company. The operator may make creative improvements, but the domain will probably be narrow in scope and concrete, focused on physical activities or work processes. The operator accomplishes "breakthrough on operations" at Position 2 on the MAT in Figure 2, while the president accomplishes "breakthrough on customer value strategy" at Position 1. Similarly, the president "executes customer value strategy" at Position 4 on the MAT, and the operator "executes operations" at Position 3.

The MAT provides a visual demonstration of how role accomplishments are interconnected throughout an organization. It implies the competitive strength of an organization with interconnected managerial accomplishments is much greater than one aggregating loosely connected and largely autonomous accomplishments. This framework emphasizes the fact that superior customer value should come from improvement throughout the organization. The significance of this framework will be more clear after discussion of the details. Each of the elements of the MAT framework is discussed below.

Types of Accomplishments for Continuous Improvement

In the emerging paradigm, managers move quickly and easily from *accomplishments for improvement* (breakthroughs, incrementalism, and standardization) to the *accomplishments for stabilization* (routinization, maintenance, and execution), and then back to accomplishments for improvement. These are an integrated set of accomplishments necessary for continuous improvement. Let's look at some examples of each of these accomplishments.

Breakthrough *Breakthrough* means a big improvement is accomplished through radical departure from past practices. A breakthrough may come through *creativity*, when an old system is disregarded or scrapped. Creators synthesize and develop ideal systems with a clean slate. Because of this fresh approach, they can overcome the old prejudices, limitations, and intractable problems of existing systems.[5] Pure creativity is probably never achieved, but just approached. In creating a new system, it is very difficult to discard the old completely. For example, in progressing from the horse and buggy to the "horseless carriage," while the source of horsepower changed from animal to mechanical, the structure of the carriage very much resembled that of the horse-drawn buggy. Similarly, few managerial accomplishments are purely creative. For example, Henry Ford's advances in mass production systems were a creative shift that transformed industrial manufacturing practices. However, Ford did incorporate production methods from existing systems.

Most managerial breakthroughs are the result of *innovation*. In innovation, existing technologies, processes, or components of existing systems are recombined and reassimilated in novel ways. The innovated system as a whole fundamentally differs from that which existed before. For example, consider Sony's product innovation incorporating computer technology and a microphone to produce a filmless camera that offers a soundtrack to accompany each frame. The camera records images on a reusable floppy disk that can be played back instantly on any television set. This combination of existing technologies resulted in a superior means of quickly recording, re-experiencing, and sharing memorable images. As another example, when Paul H. O'Neill took over at Alcoa, he showed that he has a penchant for "bucking the system." He decentralized the

---

5. Classical examples include the paradigm shifts from Ptolemy's belief that the sun revolves around the earth to the Copernican view that the earth revolves around the sun, and from Newtonian physics to Einstein's relativity and quantum theories. Such philosophical and theoretical shifts change the way people perceive reality. They also require different methods and practices.

company and encouraged managers to pursue unconventional thinking and go after the big breakthroughs. This became Alcoa's strategy for improvement (*Business Week*, "The Recasting of Alcoa," Sept. 9, 1991, pp. 62–64).

Incrementalism   In incrementalism, small improvements are accomplished. Incrementalism may result from creativity or innovation; however, it most often results when existing systems are adjusted and modified by *slight alterations*. The accumulation of a number of relatively small incremental improvements can have a tremendous impact. Employees at Hughes Aircraft demonstrated the value of incrementalism through their effort to build satellites in a more cost-effective manner. They began by mapping out every step, from design to delivery. Working in multidiscipline teams composed of workers from design, manufacturing, purchasing, and marketing, the Hughes employees identified 131 steps that were candidates for improvement. They then focused on thirty of the most urgent. By making a series of seemingly small changes, such as moving a hole a quarter of an inch so an inspector could insert a testing probe more easily, Hughes cut the time it took to build a satellite control processor—the brains of the machine—from forty-five weeks to twenty-two weeks. The changes saved millions of dollars (*Fortune*, Apr. 9, 1990, p. 48). Whether incremental or breakthrough, improvements are not accomplished unless proposed changes are put in place. This requires standardization.

Standardization   Our use of the term "standardization" is not limited to meaning imposed standards such as specifications, protocols, rules, and procedures, or the uniformity of materials, parts, products, machines, dies, tools, etc. (see Shingo, 1988). Standards are an important part of standardization, but they must be considered in a broader context. In standardization, managers verify the operability and performance of new systems before releasing them for use. Standardization requires the manager to transmit information about the system's purpose and architecture, educate people who work with the system, and demonstrate that the system works as intended. The resulting standardized system displays the right strategic focus, statistical capability, and predictability for stable, on-target system performance. Our definition resembles that of Ishikawa and Lu (1985, p. 62), which states, "If a person determines a method, he must standardize it and make it into a regulation, and then incorporate it into the company's technology and property . . . [the method] must be useful to everyone and free of difficulty."

The following manufacturing scenario illustrates standardization for a simple work task.[6] On an assembly line, operators assemble parts onto frames that move along the conveyor. Upon completing each assembly,

---

6. The example is based on an experience of President Nemoto of Toyoda Gosei, but was modified to fit the purposes of this chapter.

the worker marks the frame to indicate it is ready to go to the next workstation. When he has free time, the worker reaches up the conveyor to mark frames coming from the previous process, prior to assembling the parts. But on one occasion, the worker marked a frame just before the line stopped for the lunch break. After lunch, the worker forgot that he marked the frame before assembling it and so sent it to the next station. The defect was caught at a final inspection of the completed unit, and the unit had to be redone.

This problem occurred because the supervisor failed to do two things. He did not communicate the importance of marking the frame only after it has been assembled. Nor did he initially verify and observe the worker's activities to ensure that the task was consistently and correctly performed. This failure of standardization resulted in a defect, which may not always be detected before shipping the unit to a customer. Such defects add cost to the product, in the form of rework, inspection hours, lost capacity, and lower customer value. Similar failure to standardize broader systems results in costs and sacrifices that diminish customer value on an even larger scale. Standardization represents a critical managerial activity to ensure that proposed changes are implemented.

In addition to the necessity of standardization in manufacturing, service industries also benefit from standardization. McDonald's employees assemble unique orders upon customer requests, but they do so using protocols (procedures and rules) established and confirmed by management. For example, the burgers and fries are cooked a predetermined amount of time, and temperatures of the grill and frying vat are monitored and adjusted to produce optimal results. As a result of standardization, customers know what they will get at any McDonald's.

Lack of standardization can lead to more than burnt fries. Consider the following experience that happened when a small child was hospitalized for dehydration due to a virus. The doctor prescribed intravenous fluids for rehydration. After some effort, the nurses finally succeeded in finding a vein that would sustain the IV needle. The needle was taped and wrapped, and everyone thought the most traumatic part of the hospital visit was over. But several hours later, the needle was dislodged and the whole thing had to be repeated. When the child's parents asked why the needle came out, the nurse responded, "Well, look at how [the nurses on the earlier shift] taped this thing. This technique just doesn't work as well." The parents then asked why the most effective technique wasn't standard practice, to which the nurse responded, "You know better than that, Dad. Every cook stirs the pot in her own way." Unfortunately, while this laissez faire attitude allowed nurses to enjoy a certain measure of freedom and creative expression, it caused undue hardship for the patient. Of course, not all activities can be fully standardized, particularly in the service sector. For example, medical personnel must often use their creative abilities in devising solutions to unanticipated and unusual problems. But clearly, some degree of standardization is desirable.

Standards should not simply be imposed arbitrarily from above (Ohno, 1988). Rather, they should be developed in conjunction with those who must use them. McCormick & Company, Inc., a producer of seasonings, flavorings, and specialty foods in Hunt Valley, Maryland, is using statistical process control to develop work standards based on historical study and understanding of variation. Managers at McCormick have found that the workers accept the new standards more readily than the arbitrarily set standards previously imposed. Computerized charting and real-time monitoring of data also provide more motivation for adhering to and improving against standards than in the past (Boyle and Kahan, 1991). Collaboration on developing the standards that are a part of standardization forms the initial learning that is the basis of routinization.

Routinization   In routinization, systems are fine-tuned, balanced, and mastered by those subordinates responsible for operating the system. The "bugs are worked out" of the system, so execution becomes more predictable, and initial performance variations are explained and reduced over time (Yin, 1979). The benefits of routinization are observed in what trainers refer to as the "learning curve" that reflects noticeable mastery of a task or shaping of behavior through successive approximations (Millenson, 1967). Not only does routinization imply an expectation for smoother and more accurate performance with each repetition, it also implies repetition at appropriate times. Thus, routinization has cyclical characteristics both in the content of the activity and its placement in a schedule (Schriber and Gutek, 1987). Over time, the system becomes second nature to those working within it.

Routinization can be interpreted as a subordinate activity that complements standardization. Standardization is a superior's responsibility for working on the system to institutionalize change. Routinization is a subordinate's responsibility for working in the system.

Maintenance   In maintenance, the manager fully sustains and controls the existing system (and mode) of execution, with no changes in its architecture. The purpose of maintenance is to ensure that the system consistently produces valued goods and services for customers. Unanticipated events often create crises that managers must resolve immediately to maintain system performance. Maintenance also involves preventive actions to avoid problems and to ensure consistency in the future.

Consider an example of an unanticipated or special event observed in the industrial wood products industry. During routine maintenance, an operator accidentally adjusted a valve that controlled the flow of wax to wood particles that were to be processed into pressed board. Decreasing the flow of wax prior to pressing causes boards to fail to bond during the pressing operation. As soon as the press operator saw the decreased wax flow, he looked for the cause. When he discovered the valve had been adjusted, he made the correction, notified the maintenance operator of his error, and established procedures to prevent such events in the future.

Execution   In execution, managers take action to directly accomplish their intended purpose. A system owner executes a strategic system, while an operator executes an operational task within that system. The operator will execute a task through physical manipulation of tools; the system owner will execute the system through manipulation of information, using such vehicles as memoranda, personal directions and requests, master schedules, and orders.

Consider how work is executed in service organizations. The customer contact person may have to assess the individual customer's needs and then configure a network of resources and protocols to deliver the service. As a simple example, a submarine sandwich shop employee takes an order and builds a sandwich to specifications, within given parameters. It may be that the shop has six- or twelve-inch buns, six types of meat, four types of cheese, and fifteen other toppings, and that the owner has prescribed weight limits for each option. The employee will create "any" sandwich you want within these parameters. Thus, the employee creatively customizes the value offering while executing operations to deliver the service.

In practice, managers should flow from creation to execution and integrate these diverse accomplishments to provide superior customer value. After managers introduce a new production system, they must standardize, maintain, and execute the system in order to consistently produce valued outputs for customers. After making incremental or innovative improvements, managers must again standardize and maintain the modified system to ensure consistent performance throughout the organization.

Domains of Accomplishments for Superior Customer Value

To ensure improvement and consistent performance throughout an organization, managers have to address many different *domains,* areas of activity or objects being acted upon. The examples above alluded to various domains: Sony's filmless camera, Hughes Aircraft's satellite production system, an assembly line work procedure, a technique for inserting and securing IV needles, a wax flow valve, and a submarine sandwich. All managerial accomplishments in the emerging paradigm are driven by the organization's mission or purpose, which is to competitively execute a customer value strategy through a matching design strategy. Managers then develop the systems, policies, and motivators that ensure work is done through the processes, technology, and operations to fulfill the strategies. Managers must accomplish continuous improvement in all of these domains.

In the emerging paradigm, managers generally intend to provide customer value, by meeting a general area of needs or desires. However, there are many ways they might choose to do so in order to provide superior value. To specify competitive strategy, managers must address two integral components: (1) customer value strategy, and (2) design strategy.

Customer Value Strategy   A customer value strategy is a plan for providing superior value to customers through specific product and service offerings. Value is an outcome for the customer, a function of the sacrifices required for all benefits realized in the acquisition and use of a product or service.

In the broadest sense, decisions about market participation determine what value the organization intends to provide to customers. For example, in recent years General Motors decided to get into the credit card business, and Toyota decided to produce luxury automobiles and full-size trucks. Within these broad strategic decisions lie the details about the configuration of the product or service to meet customer needs. These details involve benefits and sacrifices associated with product functionality, ease of use, raw materials, components, configurations of raw materials and components, appearance, reproducibility, consistency, flexibility, image, availability, deliverability, transportability, durability, longevity, price, and many other benefits and sacrifices for customers.

A customer value strategy must be grounded in specific and detailed understanding of what customers value. The arduous process of determining what customers value is an important managerial activity. Customer value strategies should not be taken for granted or based on untested assumptions about customers, but must be explicit and consciously matched with customer needs on a continual basis, because customer needs change.

Managers attempting to meet certain needs or desires of a specified market or market segment may provide value through a variety of offerings. They are at liberty to emphasize particular combinations of benefits and sacrifices to compete in that market. For example, in the audio market, they may choose to promote a low-cost, convenient, and transportable Walkman-type radio. This requires some sacrifice in terms of musical fidelity, but offers value through its other qualities. They may, on the other hand, specialize in top-of-the-line speakers. The available combinations of different sacrifices and benefits seem to be infinite.[7]

A customer value strategy must also be intertwined with design strategy decisions, regarding current and future organizational capacities and capabilities.[8] For example, Coca-Cola chose an overall European strategy for closer relationships with retailers, bolder merchandising, cheaper prices, and faster delivery. To implement this strategy and better control their capability, Coca-Cola added to its traditional role as image marketer and supplier of secret ingredients to local independent bottlers by buying local

---

7. For another example, see *Business Week*, cover story, Apr. 29, 1991.
8. Capacity is the constraint on volume and schedule. From the point of view of demand, capability is the constraint on how much variation in customer needs can be handled. From the point of view of supply, capability is the variation produced on the value delivered.

bottlers and managing production themselves (*Fortune*, Aug. 13, 1990, p. 68).

Design Strategy   The second component of competitive strategy involves organizing the means of producing and delivering value. For example, some corporations, such as Reebok and Sun Microcomputers, primarily design, market, and distribute products manufactured by others. They do not have manufacturing capabilities and so are known as "hollow corporations" or "virtual corporations." Many who do manufacture their own products will utilize outside sources for certain components rather than purchase and manage a production plant.

Whatever combination of different organizational design components is selected, it should be intertwined with the customer value strategy. This can be seen in the way Conner Peripherals integrated its customer value and design strategies in the market for compact hard disk drives. In dynamic, high-technology markets, managers must do in a few months what their counterparts in other markets often take years to accomplish. Decision speed and response time spell the difference between prosperity and bankruptcy. Some competitors invest heavily in research and development to produce the smallest and fastest drives, which they sell at premium prices. These competitors may bring out advanced products, but risk finding no buyers for them. Other competitors choose to be commodity producers by supplying high volumes of a standard disk drive, which they sell at a lower price. These competitors risk sinking a lot of money into factories that can be outmoded and surpassed by rapidly changing technology or more efficient competitors.

Conner follows neither of these strategies. It sells first, then designs and builds. This approach allows them to provide a product that closely matches customer needs. The cornerstone of Conner's manufacturing strategy is flexibility. Conner forgoes the cost advantages of manufacturing its own components. It buys nearly all its parts from others and leases the factory space it needs to assemble and test its drives, which keeps capital investment low. For every dollar in plant and equipment, Conner has $7.17 in sales, compared with $3.59 for Seagate, a leading competitor. This approach gives Conner Peripherals flexibility to respond to shifts in demand. In 1988, for example, Conner pounced on the fastest-growing market segment, disk drives for laptop and notebook computers (*Fortune*, Aug. 13, 1990, p. 51).

Conner avoids many of the problems traditionally associated with research and development, ownership of factories, and bureaucracy, yet it listens to customers, and develops and manufactures products rapidly upon demand. Conner chose a value strategy for quick response time to customer needs, with frequent and on-demand innovation. Conner's design strategy, including sales, product design, and manufacturing capabilities, serves to implement the company's value strategy. Conner Peripherals might be called a virtual corporation. This strategy is increasingly being used by companies that want to combine the flexibility, speed, and entrepreneurial spirit of the small company with the expansive reach and capital resources of the large corporation. Companies like AT&T, Matsushita, Apple, Sony, and Corning are putting together such alliances. TelePad Corporation of Reston, Virginia, has developed more than two dozen collaborative alliances to bring out its new pen-based computer, with manufacturing by IBM, design and development by GVO, engineering by Intel, and paychecks for its fourteen employees by Automatic Data Processing, Inc. (*Business Week*, Feb. 8, 1993, pp. 98–103).

Systems Systems are integrated collections of personnel, knowledge, abilities, motivations, equipment, machinery, methods, measures, processes, and task activities. Systems provide customer value through diverse cross-functional activities, in a horizontal flow across the organizational hierarchy. They are the means through which the customer value strategy is carried out. Activities include design, development, material acquisition, physical transformation, assembly, packaging, logistical movement, distribution, and selling of products and services, as well as related consumer education. Systems may also be seen as composed of all the following domains listed on the MAT: policies, motivators, processes, technology, and operations.

Managers define systems according to their particular situation.[9] The multifunctional nature of systems means the manager will have to orchestrate and integrate contributions from and to various functions, such as product engineering, process engineering, accounting, marketing, logistics, procurement, maintenance, and production. For example, consider how president Shoichiro Toyoda of Toyota Motors reorganized product development to improve an already excellent production system. As head of the council that now directs long-range product strategy, Toyoda created the position of chief engineer and redefined the roles of the chief to encompass systematically broad responsibilities.

The chief engineer has charge of everything associated with the development of a car. First, he determines its physical dimensions, suitability for its potential market, how it will be made, and who the suppliers will be. He helps design marketing strategies and even talks frequently with car buyers. The chief engineer also stays on top of social, political, and environmental trends. The chief engineer system differs sharply from Detroit's traditional approach to product development, where a new-model boss has narrowly defined responsibilities and limited power, works under specific instructions from the product planning and marketing

---

9. For service organizations, a system may be more ad hoc in nature, like a network, rather than a fixed set of elements, with predetermined and fixed routines and sequences of activities. Service employees arrange a temporary system of resources and protocols in response to specific customer needs. They creatively absorb the natural variation in customer needs as they customize a service. The enabling resources, protocols, and parameters within which the service employee operates are derived from more permanent systems of the organization.

departments, and rarely has direct contact with dealers and customers (*Fortune*, Nov. 19, 1990, p. 72).[10]

System owners, like Toyota's chief engineer, may find it useful to identify subsystems within their larger system, and enlist subordinates to manage them. (Some companies refer to this as a "cross-functional process.") Like larger strategic systems, subsystems transcend functional and departmental boundaries. They are part of the collection of cause factors that provide customer value. For example, raw material availability is a subsystem of a plant that involves activities in production planning, purchasing, accounting, logistical movement, receiving, and temporary storage.

Policies Policies are general statements or principles intended to guide individual thinking, decision making, and action, or define the domain of decision making by designating authority and limitations. Policy-makers must consider the effect of their formal statements, and the implicit principles that subordinates infer from managerial decisions and actions. Whether formal or informal, ideal policies ensure that decisions contribute to organizational purpose.

Policies differ in their breadth of coverage. The broadest policies are *corporate policies*; these apply to everyone and form the foundation for more specific policies. In contrast, a specific department such as procurement may have *departmental policies* that are not relevant to any other department workers.[11] Policies provide guidelines for individual action and may remove the necessity to repeatedly analyze similar situations. However, since situations do vary, policies should allow for some individual discretion, particularly in services where customer contact personnel draw on networks of resources to serve individual customers. Managers must achieve a balance between a need for flexibility and a need for order. Too much flexibility and individual discretion leads to chaos, while inflexibility leads to stagnation and bureaucratic over-control.

An organization's policies should be consistent with its strategy and systems to ensure that employees do what is necessary to provide superior customer value. When inconsistencies occur, customer value is compromised. For example, buying only from low-cost bidders may undermine managerial efforts to ensure consistent product quality. Some companies attempt to regulate the conditions under which employees may speak with each other or with customers. Such policies discourage the informal communication that fosters a customer-oriented culture. Some organizations, such as the Tennessee Valley Authority, have slashed corporate policy manuals down to ten or twenty general statements, relying on less formal ways to guide individual actions. Such streamlining eliminates the

---

10. For other examples, see Womack, *The Machine That Changed the World*, 1990.
11. Although operators may be involved in their creation, these more specific policies are not listed as a discrete domain.

need for employees to fight "the system" in order to do their jobs and makes sure that policies are used as tools rather than straitjackets (Pascale, 1985).

Motivators Motivators are organized activities for inspiring, directing, and sustaining appropriate employee behavior to fulfill the purpose of the strategic systems. Motivators include formal mechanisms such as progress reporting requirements, evaluations, appraisals, rewards, authority structures, information systems, resource allocation and control systems, and job design, selection, and promotion criteria. Informal mechanisms include specific aspects of organizational culture, such as role systems, group norms, group values, and individual beliefs. Since motivators reinforce all other role accomplishments, they must be improved along with other domains. Motivators help build the link between strategy and operations by attempting to ensure that people behave appropriately to execute the strategy.

Processes A process represents a flow of activities across multiple operations which transforms input into output for customers. There are at least two types of processes: *production processes* and *business processes* (Harrington, 1991). Production processes produce output that is sold to customers in the form of goods and services, for example, motorcycles and overnight package delivery. Business processes produce output for administrative purposes, such as a quarterly financial report or a completed purchase order. Together, production and business processes make up larger systems that encompass multiple functions.

In the case of a traditional manufacturing line, production processes are the flow of products or production material from one worker or operation to another. Each worker or operation transforms the materials in some way and then sends it on to the next operation.

Processes are not simply the sum of operations. Other important characteristics of a process are (1) the transport of materials or products between operations, and (2) the delays that occur between operations (Shingo, 1988). So, to improve processes continuously, managers must consider the steps *within* as well as the flow *across* operations. For example, when managers of the Toyota Production System synchronize (across) operations and make batch sizes smaller, they reduce both process delays and work-in-process inventories. This process improvement also requires that each of the operations (within) reliably produces high-quality parts.

Similar flows exist in business functions, such as development, distribution, financial accounting, financial planning, purchasing, and personnel. For example, in the development function at IBM, there are processes such as records management, design and material review, component qualification, tool design, and engineering change management. Business processes in the financial accounting department at IBM include accounts receivable, accounts payable, and cost accounting (Harrington, 1991).

These business processes involve the flow of paper and information rather than the flow of material and products. Nevertheless, just like production processes, these business processes consist of a flow across operations and the transport and delays associated with that flow.

Technology Technology includes the elements of applied science needed for doing the work to provide value in the goods and services produced. Through technology, an organization uses its resources to convert inputs into outputs. This broad definition of technology includes two components: *knowledge* and *tools.*

Depending upon the particular applications and markets served, knowledge may pertain to:

- the design of new products or product components, such as an optical scanner;
- the transformation of raw material properties into products, such as plastics and synthetic fibers;
- the use of energy, such as nuclear and laser technologies;
- the extension of human sensation, such as through the use of an electron microscope and ultrasound imaging; or
- the organization and management of human activities, such as through the use of statistical thinking for understanding variation.

The power of knowledge cannot be harnessed without the second component of technology: tools. Tools include the instruments, machines, algorithms, or programs that are used to execute the work to provide valued goods and services. A diversity of tools exist in the application of science. They encompass a wide range of complexity and type, including hand tools (such as a hammer), automated machinery (such as numerically controlled robotics), computer software (such as CAD/CAM), production hardware (such as a metal-cutting lathe), and so on. Organizational and managerial tools include fishbone diagrams, statistical control charts, budgets, portfolio models, and so on.

Technology represents a vastly important component of strategic systems for customer value. It can even create new markets. Consider the burgeoning field of laser chemistry. The potential value to be derived from the marriage of knowledge and tools in this field is astounding. "Laser chemists are employing such exotic gambits as 'laser traps' and 'optical tweezers' to grab, slow, and manipulate bits of molecules of living cells. In the process, they are discovering better techniques for such diverse tasks as etching circuits on silicon and unraveling the inner workings of cells" (*Business Week,* July 16, 1990, pp. 160–162). Future applications of this process technology can create entirely new markets and provide unforeseen value to customers.

A survey by Ernst & Young confirmed that the primary reason banks will use technology in the future is to meet customer expectations, beyond the traditional objectives of cost reduction and increased revenue. For example, Bay Banks, a highly successful regional bank in the northeast, was the first in their market to employ a saturation strategy for deploying off-premises and advanced-function ATMs. They were also first to offer ATM access to statements of cleared checks and deposits, and to make available image statements (Teixeira and Ziskin, 1993).

Operations An operation transforms input into output. For example, a worker grinds an engine block to the right dimensions. But recall that an operation is only one part of a larger process flow. Grinding is one operation performed in a production process that transforms raw materials into engine blocks. Operations can be further broken down into the *operational tasks* performed to transform input into output and the *operating methods* guiding that work.

An operational task is the group of mental and physical activities of people and machines doing work. Operational tasks include such diverse activities as thinking about and planning for work, preparing materials and machines, transforming or transporting materials through manual manipulation of tools or through automated machines, delivering services, and monitoring and measuring work outcomes.

Operational tasks may be broken down into component motions, such as observable, physical, behavioral movements, and unobservable, intangible, mental "movements." The work of technological tools, for example, of computers and automated machine tools, may be considered operational motions. Examples of operational motions include hand movements to control a forklift or to measure board thickness with a micrometer, signals to communicate to an airline pilot, mental calculations and analysis of statistical data, verbal signals to communicate with co-workers on an oil drill, manual lifting and placement of subassemblies on an assembly line, and visual input and mental interpretation to read a micrometer measurement and collect data for a control chart.

Operating methods are the ways of using the available technology, that is, knowledge and tools, and other assets to do the work of the strategic systems. Operating methods include the standard rules, procedures, protocols, and arrangements of tasks that individuals use to guide the regular and orderly execution and measurement of work. Operating methods are critical in providing customer value, because they determine whether process technology and material, mechanical, and human assets are optimally utilized.

The way individuals or groups of workers use knowledge and tools at their disposal depends on their operating methods. For example, because of their operating methods, work crews in two different plants achieve different results using identical equipment. One work crew operates by a standard procedure to turn off all machines for a shift changeover, and does preventive maintenance prior to producing any parts. By contrast, the second shift stops their machines only for maintenance when something goes wrong. The crew that does preventive maintenance avoids many of the difficulties (longer downtime and poor quality) which are brought on by machine breakdowns.

The domain of operating methods also includes interpersonal and group social processes. These can be as important to the physical transformation of material and labor into goods and services as physical operating methods. These methods help ensure that groups function as a team. For example, Milacron employees devised a rule to ensure that members of their interdisciplinary product development team participate fully in team activities. Their rule states that team members should not discuss their deliberations with nonteam members so no one would fear saying something others would make fun of outside the group (*Fortune*, May 21, 1990).

▶ USING THE MAT FRAMEWORK FOR ROLE SYSTEMS

A typology represents reality in an organized form to make real events easier to talk about and think about. However, typologies rarely acknowledge all the complexity of real events, and the events are not always so discretely categorized. A change may appear to be both breakthrough and incremental improvement. These accomplishments can easily blur together.

This was true when Heinz managers began to question long-held assumptions about cost reduction. With some innovative thinking they call "paradigm busting" and low-tech incremental improvements, engineers at the Ore-Ida factory in Plover, Wisconsin, greatly improved customer value and returns to the company. They had been puzzled for years by the frequent breakage of frozen French fries. They decided to challenge their production "paradigm" by examining every step of the production process, from the bays where trucks full of whole potatoes unload, through plant operations, where the potatoes are skimmed along conveyors, sliced, and ultimately packaged. The process permitted uncooked potatoes to undergo 3- to 14-foot drops routinely as they tumbled along the production line. Although they weren't breaking or bruising, internally the potatoes were developing microscopic fault lines. These fault lines caused the fries to fracture. The solution was simple: they eliminated potato free-fall by installing a few metal slides, saving $300,000 annually (*Fortune*, Apr. 9, 1990, pp. 46–48). The changes were small; the improvement was big.

Was this change at Ore-Ida a breakthrough or simply an incremental improvement? In one sense, it doesn't matter, since Ore-Ida succeeded. However, categorizing accomplishments can help provide a model to enlighten and inspire managers to do things they might otherwise not think of. The MAT framework plays this inspirational role in helping managers shift to a new role system for the emerging paradigm.

Role Responsibility Differences

In the emerging paradigm, employees at all levels and in all positions should pursue various types of accomplishments in several of the domains displayed on the MAT. Managers should avoid thinking that only higher-level managers engage in the conceptual and creative work, while lower-level employees only execute orders without need of thought. By participating in continuous improvement of customer value, the often illusory promise of "job enrichment" can materialize for all employees.[12]

This broad participation blurs the traditional distinction between "manager" and "worker," but distinctions do remain. Obviously, employees at different levels differ in authority and scope of responsibility. Different types of employees will pursue continuous improvement in different domains. Recall the responsibility differences between the president and the operator. Top managers may focus on improving value and design strategies rather than worry about day-to-day execution of operations. Line workers may focus on improving the operational methods of executing their own work. The work of these two groups concentrates in different corners of the MAT.

Depicting Managerial Role Responsibilities

To illustrate the application of the MAT, Figures 3, 4, and 5 depict managerial role accomplishments for *strategic leaders, middle managers*, and *operators*. Individuals in each group spend time working to accomplish different things, represented by the cells of the MAT. A third dimension, "time spent," is depicted with varied intensity of shading, as in Figure 3. Heavier shading indicates more time spent. As the shading indicates, the role accomplishments are different for each of these groups of employees. They concentrate on different types and domains of accomplishments. The MATs in Figures 3, 4, and 5 collectively illustrate a role system that is the foundation for a culture that supports the emerging paradigm.[13]

The role responsibilities prescribed on the MAT in Figure 3 require strategic leaders to continuously improve customer value strategy, design strategy, and the systems that allow the organization to realize those strategies. This strategic leadership is the cornerstone of the emerging paradigm. Paul Allaire, chairman and CEO at Xerox, describes this role of redesigning the organization as "organizational architecture," which goes well beyond just reorganization and restructuring. It encompasses all aspects of culture change (Howard, 1992). It provides a context for the work of middle managers who must put in place these strategies and systems, continuously improve them, and ensure their stable execution (see Figure 4). When strategic leaders and middle managers are engaged in this new role system,

---

12. For foundations of the concept of job enrichment, see Paul, Robertson and Herzberg (1969); and Hackman and Oldham (1976).
13. These are stereotypical roles. Each organization must determine how responsibilities for specific role accomplishments should be distributed.

Figure 3
The MAT for managerial leaders

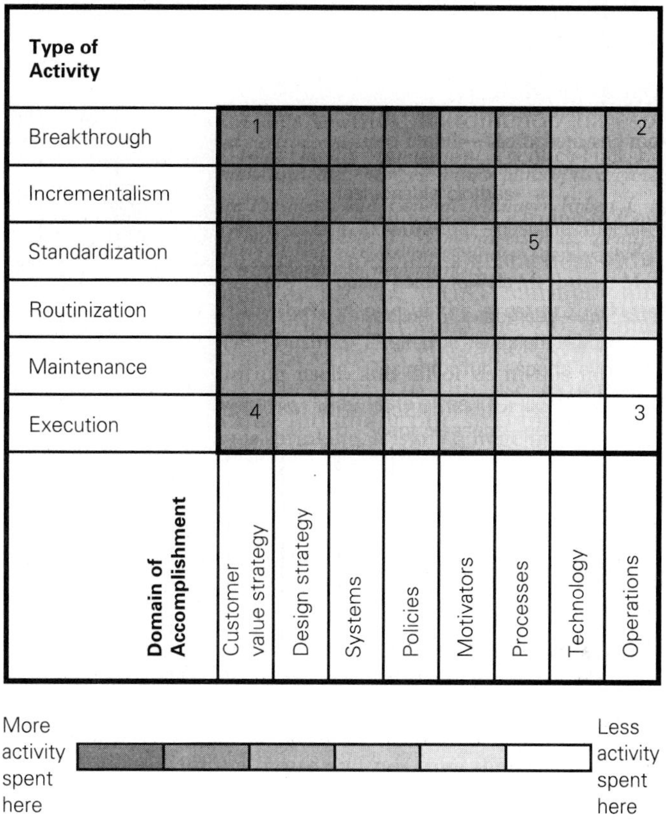

Type of Activity	Customer value strategy	Design strategy	Systems	Policies	Motivators	Processes	Technology	Operations
Breakthrough	1							2
Incrementalism								
Standardization							5	
Routinization								
Maintenance								
Execution	4							3

Domain of Accomplishment

More activity spent here ▮▮▮▮▮□ Less activity spent here

Copyright © 1990 by Gregory M. Bounds.

they provide vision and the means of achieving the vision. Then the role responsibilities of operators are easily focused on executing the systems and processes that are put in place, as depicted in the MAT in Figure 5. Operators may be given autonomy to make improvements in their areas, and they may contribute ideas for improving broader systems. Job enrichment becomes real, and operational activities are strategically focused.

Strategic Leaders versus Operators We have seen that strategic leaders spend more time creating value strategy than operational motions (see Figure 3). Figure 3 generally suggests that strategic leaders concentrate on the creation, innovation, incremental improvement, and standardization of competitive strategy, strategic systems, and corporate policies.

By contrast, operators (as shown in Figure 5) concentrate on routinization, maintenance, and execution of process technology, operating meth-

Figure 4
The MAT for middle managers

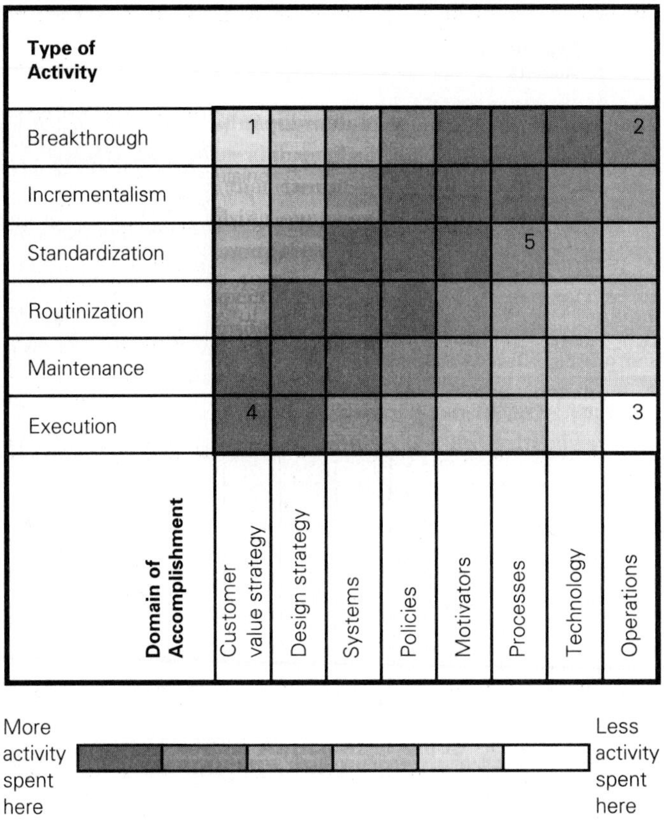

Type of Activity								
Breakthrough	1							2
Incrementalism								
Standardization						5		
Routinization								
Maintenance								
Execution	4							3
Domain of Accomplishment	Customer value strategy	Design strategy	Systems	Policies	Motivators	Processes	Technology	Operations

More activity spent here ▬▬▬▬▬▬ Less activity spent here

Copyright © 1990 by Gregory M. Bounds.

ods, and operational tasks. When they do participate in other regions, it is more likely to be initiated by a manager who is responsible for accomplishments in that area. However, operators engaging in creative activities may provide input to system managers through suggestions, team meetings, presentations to task forces, or even through temporary membership on task forces.[14] Superiors who own responsibility for strategy must integrate diverse subordinate contributions for customer value. The ultimate architects of all domains are the strategic leaders, who hold overall responsibility for strategy development and deployment.

Other Positions In addition to the role responsibilities depicted for strategic leaders, middle managers, and operators, other positions can be de-

---

14. For guidelines on how Japanese companies set up suggestion systems, see *The Idea Book*, by Lee Ann James (1988).

Figure 5

The MAT for operators

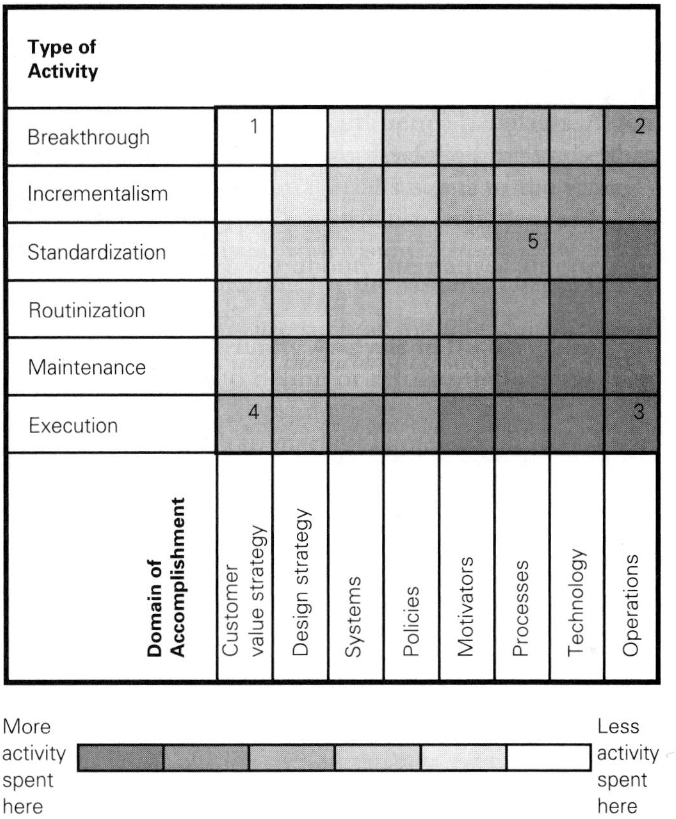

Type of Activity	Customer value strategy	Design strategy	Systems	Policies	Motivators	Processes	Technology	Operations
Breakthrough	1							2
Incrementalism								
Standardization						5		
Routinization								
Maintenance								
Execution	4							3

Domain of Accomplishment

More activity spent here ▮▮▮▮▮▮ Less activity spent here

scribed with the MAT. For example, many organizations have positions labeled *foreman* or *first-line supervisor*. These people focus more on standardization and routinization than execution of operational tasks and motions. As shown in Figure 6, the activities of a foreman may concentrate in regions of the MAT somewhere between those of middle managers and operators.

Some organizations do not assign one person to the position of supervisor or foreman. Rather, they develop *autonomous work groups* or *self-managing teams* composed of operators who perform their own supervisory activities. The role responsibilities of autonomous teams may even encompass regions of the MAT formerly covered by middle managers. For example, Cindy Ransom, a middle manager at Clorox, asked her workers at a 100-person plant in Fairfield, California, to redesign the plant's operations. With minimal guidance from Ransom, a team of hourly workers established training programs, set work rules for absenteeism, and reorganized the

Figure 6

The MAT for supervisor/foreman

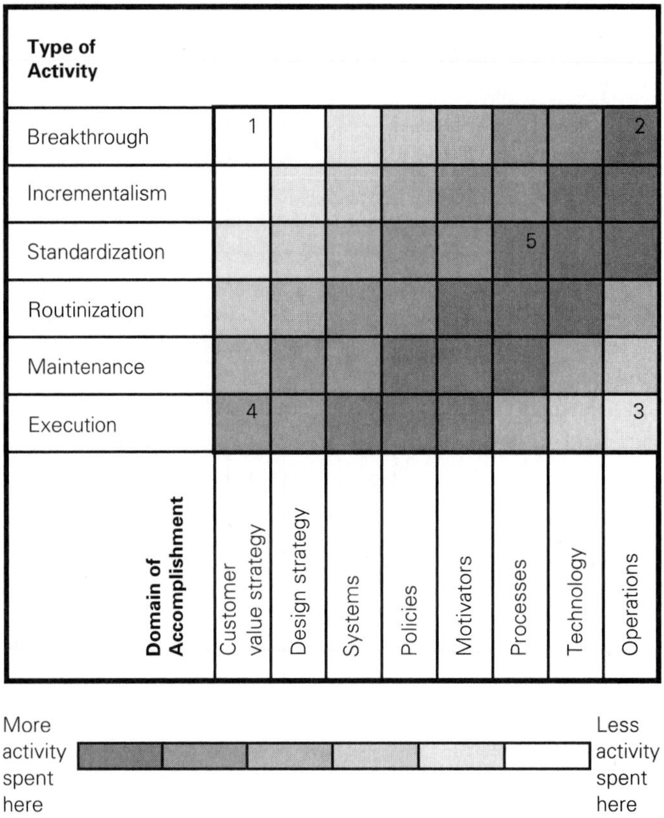

Type of Activity	Customer value strategy	Design strategy	Systems	Policies	Motivators	Processes	Technology	Operations
Breakthrough	1							2
Incrementalism								
Standardization						5		
Routinization								
Maintenance								
Execution	4							3

Domain of Accomplishment

More activity spent here ▮▮▮▮▮▮ Less activity spent here

Copyright © 1990 by Gregory M. Bounds.

once traditional factory into five customer-focused business units. Relieved from these traditional managerial responsibilities for "operations," Ransom used her free time to attend to the needs of customers and suppliers (*Fortune*, "The New Non-Manager Managers," Feb. 22, 1993, pp. 80–84).

Many positions in middle management simply go away with the cast-off layers of the hierarchy, or they are reabsorbed into teams that manage cross-functional systems and processes. In fact, organizational designs of the future may be much less hierarchical, more streamlined and tailored to match business systems and processes.

The role responsibilities of *support staff* and *specialists* can also be depicted on the MAT. MAT profiles can help convey to support staff and specialists the context and purpose of their work, and aid their integration into strategic systems. For example, the MAT in Figure 3 suggests that strategic leaders spend relatively more time on accomplishing breakthroughs on customer value strategy. They make decisions about value offerings based on the information generated by a team of assistants, like design engineers, marketing analysts, and other specialists. These support specialists do the research and design work to create, innovate, and incrementally improve the configurations of value components for products and services.[15]

Role Differences within the Stereotype   Not every individual within a stereotyped group will necessarily pursue all the accomplishments prescribed in these MAT examples. For example, some operators may devote almost all of their time to executing motions for operational tasks, at the position numbered 3 on the MAT in Figure 5. Other operators, in similar jobs, may spend relatively more time creating improved operations, at the position numbered 2 on the MAT. While each individual MAT profile may look very different, the role responsibilities of the group of individual operators as a whole may look very much like the MAT profile depicted in Figure 5.

Prescribing Team Role Responsibilities   The MAT can also be used to prescribe role responsibilities for teams. The teams may be composed of members from diverse levels and functions within the organization. Given the cross-functional nature of managerial work in the emerging paradigm, prescribing team accomplishments may be more appropriate. In general, the MAT should be used flexibly, at any level of analysis, whether it be individual, work group, departmental, functional, divisional, or cross-functional team.

Responsibility for Prescribing Role Responsibilities   The MAT in Figure 3 suggests that strategic leaders own the responsibility for improving an organization's design strategy. This task involves determining the role responsibilities for each employee, and specifying how each will contribute to customer value. The profiles presented in Figures 3 through 6 provide strategic leaders with a starting point. These profiles will not fit every organization; managers need to prescribe managerial role responsibilities in accordance with the demands of their external environment, competitors, suppliers, customers, societal pressures, legal factors, technological trends, and employees.[16]

Since the MAT should be used flexibly, the domains listed on the MAT should not be treated as an exhaustive list of rigid classifications. Other domains might usefully be included on a MAT. For example, a

---

15. Many organizations are reducing the number of staff personnel and assigning their roles to managers and other line employees, which further breaks the traditional division between thinking and doing. However, specialists will remain as important assets to competitive organizations.

16. There are likely to be contingencies not expressed in this discussion, such as size or technology.

category labeled "product technology" might be treated as a separate and more specific component of the value strategy domain.

The MAT can be used to compare current accomplishments (what is done now) with ideal accomplishments (what should be done in the future). The comparison could reveal the following: (1) areas of redundancy, which represent wasted time and energy as well as excess cost; (2) opportunities for correcting role conflicts; and (3) gaping holes or voids that may jeopardize customer value.[17] Gaps could reflect that current human resources need further development or that available resources may simply need to be appropriately allocated.

Consequences of Gaps: Role System Inadequacy

Having such gaps can be detrimental to customer value and extremely frustrating for employees. The most striking example in the history of continuous improvement is the failure of *quality circles*, which are teams of employees established for the purpose of learning about and improving quality in their work areas. The failure can be readily explained in terms of the MAT.

The Failure of Quality Circles   When appropriately focused, quality circle accomplishments reside in the upper right-hand corner of the MAT, namely, breakthrough, incremental improvement, and standardization of process technologies and operations. For example, a quality circle may be assigned to devise new work methods to fit a new flexible manufacturing system.

Quality circles often fail because they are not appropriately focused; their accomplishments in these domains are not integrated with strategy. For example, quality circles were established by a Fortune 500 company in the chemicals industry, but they were not focused on strategic purposes. The circles made a few workplace improvements and changed some operational methods. However, management rejected many of their proposals as either "too costly" or "unnecessary." Reports were ignored, requests for funding denied, and many attempts to make local changes were squashed. With the members demoralized, the quality circles soon fizzled. Those that were not disbanded were used to play cards and socialize. In this organization, quality circles were doomed to fail because of a lack of strategic leadership, a big gap in an important area of the MAT. General Motors learned this lesson the hard way in 1982 when top management issued an edict that the company was to "get out there and get into this quality improvement," but they failed to provide much more direction than that. All the divisions went in different directions, each following an anointed guru like Deming or Crosby, each talking a different language,

---

17. The MAT may also be useful in organizations that are down-sizing and flattening their hierarchies, wherein important managerial responsibilities are often lost or forgotten during personnel cuts.

and none really linked to an overall strategy. As a result, GM lost several years pursuing a fragmented approach while competitors took away market share (Rohan, 1990).

Lack of Leadership   Consider another example of the consequences of gaps. A manager of a human resources department in a medium-sized firm asked one of the authors about a communication and information system problem that involved a number of different departments. None of the departments wanted to devote the resources and the time to attack it, or take the political risk, or expend the mental anguish to fight about it with other departments. The manager explained, "We have been caught between the lower level of the organization and top managers. Top managers are too busy doing whatever they do. All we get from them are statements of goals and objectives. The lower level doesn't have the ability to do what the top has asked, so we have been told to fix it."

The manager eventually set up a project team to address this cross-functional and multilevel problem. But this solution was just a quick fix, while the real need was to pursue the long-term agenda of transforming the top managers into strategic leaders. The project team may be allowed to proceed, and they may even fix the problem short term. However, to try to "fix" the whole organization with this "project by project" type of remedy driven at a low level of the organization would be like nurses giving aspirin to a cancer patient. The problems would continue to arise, since this is a fundamentally sick organization that needs more radical therapy. The human resources department in the above example needs to develop a strategy for long-term improvement of its human resources and get top managers to adopt it as a part of their organizational strategy.

Consider how much easier and more productive it would be for cross-functional participants if their managers really enacted the role system described in this chapter. The culture would be very different. When cross-functional project teams are used in a culture that supports the emerging paradigm, the participants do not feel like they are patching up a hopeless case. Rather, they feel as though they are significantly contributing to a vibrant and purposeful organization. The MAT suggests the comprehensive approach that managers must take to build such an organization.

The manner in which the manager pursues this agenda should be flexibly determined to suit individual strengths and idiosyncratic styles of leadership. While they should have appropriate autonomy for "style," managers should not be distracted from accomplishing their purpose. As Zaleznik (1989, pp. 61, 64) warns, "too many managers put interpersonal matters, power relations, and pouring oil on troubled waters ahead of real work," and "the cost of this game is the demise of learning as well as the abandonment of any hope for creativity." We define real work as continuous improvement in customer value.

Loss of Market Opportunities   Another way that gaps in the MAT affect performance is that they can cause managers to lose market opportunities. For example, creative ideas from employees are of no use if managers are not open to them. For seven years, the Chrysler Corporation ignored one of its managers, Ron Zarowitz, who had the idea of installing fold-out car seats in minivans. Chrysler leaders did not think the market wanted them. As soon as they decided to give the idea a shot and they released models with fold-out car seats, Chrysler could not make enough of them to meet the phenomenal market demand. Chrysler leaders were out of touch with the market (Dumaine, 1991).

Waste of Resources   Managers should use the MAT as a source of inspiration, and perhaps as an assessment tool to help develop a role system focused on "real work," not wasted work. The role system described in the MAT requires much more of leaders than traditional TQM programs in which top managers delegate the work to a TQM department, or some other staff group, and its "Quality Czar" and band of facilitators. For example, Florida Power and Light, a winner of the Deming Prize, found that its "quality program" became a big bureaucracy in itself and distracted managers from doing real work to serve customers. TQM programs that do not comprehensively address all aspects of an organization's culture produce problems that can waste valuable time and delay transformation. For instance, Polaroid faced problems when implementing its TQM program, and they did not make much progress until they wrestled through some cultural issues. The Polaroid scientists felt that the emphasis placed on incremental improvement might dampen their approach to seeking big breakthroughs (*Business Week*, "Where Did They Go Wrong?" Oct. 25, 1991, pp. 34–38).

In the emerging paradigm, every manager has role responsibilities for personally accomplishing continuous improvement. The MAT is not a simple recipe for success, but a vision of a challenging set of role responsibilities. For companies that really try to change their culture, the business results can be impressive. Ames Rubber Corporation embarked on culture change in 1985 to get managers to engage in the process of improvement rather than implement a program. In 1992, Ames was a finalist in the small business category of the Baldrige Award. Since 1987, when the changes really started to take hold, Ames managers have reduced finished product rejects by over 50 percent, reduced in-process defects from 30,000 to 200 parts per million, and achieved record profits in 1991 and 1992, in the midst of a recession (Shelton, Winter 1992/1993).

The Nature of Managerial Role Responsibilities

The nature of managerial work changes with its purpose. We overview some of these changes below.

Teamwork for Continuous Improvement   In executing this new managerial agenda, some managers are assigned ownership for customer value determination. Others own strategic systems and subsystems that transcend traditional unit boundaries. System and subsystem owners will not simply coordinate functional interfaces through conflict resolution and negotiation, but will design and build systems to contribute to customer value. Under the guidance of system and subsystem managers, others oversee process technology and operational tasks in traditional functions, to ensure consistent contribution to systems. Some managers bear responsibility for a mixture of these activities. While their role responsibilities may vary, managers should work together as a team with a common purpose to continuously improve customer value. Teamwork requires that all managers in the organization be appropriately focused on their responsibilities, otherwise teamwork is undermined.

Motorola has made teamwork an important part of its strategy for competing. It even holds an annual competition for improvement teams from its facilities around the world. For example, Motorola's Codex subsidiary in Mansfield, Massachusetts, cut $13 million from inventories, saving $1.3 million in carrying costs, and cut the average time it takes to get its supplies from eight weeks to three. The team eliminated much of the paperwork in the supply chain by automatically exchanging electronic forecasts, orders, and invoices with customers and paying them by computer without human intervention. Costs were cut and customers were served better. Motorola estimates that the savings from all of its team improvements are about $2.2 billion annually. These estimates do not take into account the advantages gained in the marketplace from improved strategies and higher-quality products (Feder, 1991).

Flexible Team Participation System owners and operational owners will flexibly pursue accomplishments, as needed, in many domains of the organization. Traditional job descriptions do not adequately describe the flexible roles of managers in this new type of organization. Leaders will inspire through vision and role modeling and rely less on formal job descriptions that imply limits to responsibility. The content and focus of an individual's work may change frequently as the situation and system owners demand in order to provide the best customer value. As a result, the context of the managerial job will be less individualistic, less hierarchical, and less predefined. Managers will not work exclusively with immediate subordinates and immediate superiors, which are defined by hierarchical relations. Rather, they will do much of their work with managerial work teams focused on the domains of the MAT.

Integration for Synergy In this flexible organization, the lines of authority, communications, and interaction may seem blurred compared to traditional hierarchies. However, the purpose of customer value remains clear and serves as the unifying thread, an integrative mechanism, for all managerial role responsibilities. Such an organization may initially appear chaotic and disordered, just as the thickly matted tangles of a braided rug or mat might appear from a close vantage point. However, a broader view of this approach to managing reveals that the tangles are skillfully interrelated to create a whole that accomplishes an intended purpose greater than the simple sum of individual parts.

Wal-Mart's success is related to its relentless focus on satisfying customer needs and the way it translates a strategic vision into reality. Wal-Mart's goals are to provide customers access to quality goods, to make these goods available when and where customers want them, to develop a competitive cost structure, and to build and maintain a reputation for absolute trustworthiness. The means to achieving these goals include a largely invisible logistics technique called "cross-docking." Goods never spend valuable time sitting in a warehouse, but are continuously delivered to Wal-Mart's docking facilities, where they are selected, repacked, and dispatched to stores in less than 48 hours. With cross-docking, Wal-Mart achieves economies of purchasing full truckloads while avoiding the usual inventory and handling costs. To run the cross-docking system, Wal-Mart has made strategic investments in interlocking support systems, including:

- A private satellite-communication system to allow contact among distribution centers, suppliers, and every point of sale in every store
- Its own fleet of 2,000 trucks to ensure a fast and responsive transportation system
- A decentralized control system premised on frequent, informal cooperation among stores, distribution centers, and suppliers to support a "pull" system for providing products when and where customers need them
- The role of senior management aimed not at directing store managers what to do, but encouraging them to learn from the market and from each other
- A video link connecting all stores to corporate headquarters for video conferences to exchange information
- A human resource system with programs like stock ownership and profit sharing to make personnel more responsive to customers
- Division of each store into 36 merchandise departments (compared to five at Kmart) to allow more focused and effective training of employees and to be more in touch with specific customer segments (Stalk, Evans, and Shulman, 1992)

QUALITY IN ACTION: A MESSAGE TO THE STUDENT

Kenneth Iverson, Chairman and CEO, Nucor Corporation

Nucor Corporation is the sixth-largest producer of steel and steel products in the United States. Though America's steel industry has been hit hard by global competition, Nucor has remained competitive with high-quality, low-cost products. In the last twenty years, Nucor has increased its paid dividend every year, has never posted a quarterly loss, and has never laid off an employee for lack of work. Chairman and CEO Kenneth Iverson explains how

Nucor has integrated various domains within the organization to support its overall strategy and maintain a competitive edge.

Nucor's success in the steel industry has come from adhering to the following principles.

- Operate with few management layers. The fewer you have, the more effective it is to communicate with employees and the easier it is to make rapid and effective decisions. Nucor has only four levels above the hourly employees: (1) Chairman CEO/President COO, (2) Vice President/General Managers, (3) Department Managers, and (4) Foreman/Area Supervisor.

- Push decisions down, let the people doing the work decide how it should be done, avoid staff. In many cases, staff people do not help make better decisions nor do they accelerate decisions. Our corporate headquarters consists of twenty-one people. We have no centralized purchasing, marketing, engineering, or research. These functions are all done at the division level.

- All of Nucor employees have a significant part of their compensation based on productivity or profitability. There are no discretionary bonuses. Bonuses are formalized, and every employee knows what bonus he will receive for an increase in productivity or an increase in profitability of his division.

- Remember, good managers can make bad decisions, even at the top.

- Encourage new technology. When a division manager wants to try something new, we almost never turn him down even when we don't think it will work. Nucor is known for adopting new technologies, but it's not widely known that at least 50 percent of what we try doesn't work and is abandoned.

- Try to make as little distinction as possible between management and other employees in the company. Destroy the hierarchy of privilege and perks that are so prevalent in many corporations. How do we do this at Nucor?
  Everyone has the same group insurance.
  Everyone has the same holidays.
  Everyone has the same vacation.
  Everyone wears the same color hard hat.
  No reserved parking places.
  No company cars.
  No executive dining room.
  No company airplane.
  No company boats.
  No company hunting lodges.
  Everyone travels economy class.

- Above all, take care of your employees. They are, by far, the most valuable asset the company has. Nucor has some unusual benefits. The company pays $2,000 per year for four years of college, or four years of vocational training past high school, for every child of every employee in the company.

Adhering to these principles creates the teamwork and creative spirit that we need to stay ahead of competitors and serve customers better.

The Key to Culture Change

The MAT provides a vision of the role responsibilities fulfilled by managers in the emerging paradigm. It requires much more of leaders than traditional TQM programs. Leaders do not just offer their "support" by paying for training, hiring special staff to run a TQM program, sitting in on a few steering committee meetings, and paying overtime to operators who attend quality circles. It requires fundamental change in each manager's role responsibilities. Only through changing managerial roles will managers ever accomplish a culture that supports the emerging paradigm. Managerial role perceptions and role behaviors, thought, and action must change. As these change, the culture will be transformed as a natural result of continuous improvement in every domain of the organization.

▶ SUMMARY OF KEY POINTS

1. The role systems embedded within an organization's culture determine the accomplishments of managers.
2. Traditional frameworks describing managerial role responsibilities are inadequate in the emerging paradigm because they fail to provide managers with purposeful responsibilities.
3. Managerial role accomplishments must be prescribed to ensure both change for improvement and stable execution for superior customer value.
4. If change is not standardized, improvements cannot be executed, and the organization will jeopardize customer value.
5. Managers must accomplish continuous improvement throughout all domains of the organization, from planning through operations.
6. A customer value strategy must be supported by systems, policies, processes, technologies, methods, and tasks to make it a reality.
7. In the emerging paradigm, all managerial role responsibilities must be focused on this agenda.
8. These role responsibilities require continuous learning about the constituents and the systems of the organization.
9. The nature of managerial roles will shift toward teamwork for continuous improvement, flexible team participation, and integration for synergy.

▶ KEY TERMS

breakthrough	maintenance
customer value strategy	Management Activity Topograph
design strategy	(MAT)
domains of accomplishment	operations
execution	policies
incrementalism	processes

role accomplishments
role behaviors
role perceptions
role systems
roles

routinization
standardization
systems
technology
types of accomplishments

▶ DISCUSSION QUESTIONS

1. What are the deficiencies of traditional managerial roles according to the role system described on the MAT?

2. What are the deficiencies of traditional management programs (such as MBO, participative management, quality circles) according to the role system described on the MAT?

3. Compare the major points of this chapter with Deming's 14 Points. How does this chapter address each of the 14 Points? Are there any deficiencies in either the chapter or the 14 Points?

▶ EXPERIENTIAL EXERCISE

• Provide each member of the class with a blank MAT, which they will use to describe their past or present employment experiences. Each person should shade in the regions that reflect the role accomplishments that are typical of one of the following:

(1) My job.
(2) My boss.
(3) My employing organization as a whole.

Then shade the regions of the MAT that represent what should have been accomplished, as in the emerging paradigm (or imagine your ideal or dream for these things, job, boss, or organization). Note the deficiencies, which are revealed by the lack of overlap from the actual to the ideal.

What are the implications of these gaps?

What symptoms resulted in the organization due to these gaps?

▶ REFERENCES

A. Bandura, "Self-Efficacy: Toward a Unifying Theory of Behavioral Change," *Psychological Review*, Vol. 84, 1977, pp. 191–215.

G. M. Bounds and G. Dobbins, "Changing the Managerial Agenda," *The Journal of General Management*, Vol. 18, No. 3, Spring 1993, pp. 77–93.

G. M. Bounds and L. A. Pace, "Management Activity for Competitive Capability," in M. J. Stahl and G. M. Bounds (eds.), *Competing Globally through Customer Value: The Management of Strategic Suprasystems*, Quorum Books, New York, 1991.

D. Boyle and G. Kanan, "Work Standards—The Quality Way," *Production and Inventory Management Journal*, Second Quarter 1991, pp. 67–73.

S. J. Carroll and D. J. Gillen, "Are the Classical Management Functions Useful in Describing Managerial Work?" *Academy of Management Review*, Vol. 12, 1987, pp. 38–51.

W. E. Deming, *Out of the Crisis*, Massachusetts Institute of Technology, Cambridge, Mass., 1986.

B. Dumaine, "Closing the Innovation Gap," *Fortune*, Dec. 2, 1991, pp. 56–62.

H. Fayol, *General and Industrial Management*, Pitman, New York, 1949.

Barnaby J. Feder, "At Motorola, Quality Is a Team Sport," *New York Times*, Jan. 21, 1993, p. C1.

G. Graen, "Role-Making Processes within Complex Organizations," in M. D. Dunnette (ed.), *Handbook of Industrial and Organizational Psychology*, Rand McNally College Publishing Company, Chicago, 1976.

J. R. Hackman and G. R. Oldham, "Motivation through the Design of Work: Test of a Theory," *Organizational Behavior and Human Performance*, Vol. 16, 1976, pp. 250–279.

H. J. Harrington, *Business Process Improvement: The Breakthrough Strategy for Total Quality, Productivity, and Competitiveness*, McGraw-Hill, New York, 1991.

R. Howard, "The CEO as Organizational Architect: An Interview with Xerox's Paul Allaire," *Harvard Business Review*, September–October 1992.

K. Ishikawa and D. Lu, *What Is Total Quality Control? The Japanese Way*, Prentice-Hall, Englewood Cliffs, N.J., 1985.

Lee Ann James, *The Idea Book*, Productivity Press, Stamford, Conn., 1988.

D. Katz and R. L. Kahn, *The Social Psychology of Organizations*, John Wiley & Sons, New York, 1978.

J. E. McGrath, "Stress and Behavior in Organizations," in M. D. Dunnette (ed.), *Handbook of Industrial and Organizational Psychology*, Rand McNally College Publishing Company, Chicago, 1976.

J. R. Millenson, *Principles of Behavioral Analysis*, Macmillan, New York, 1967.

H. Mintzberg, "The Manager's Job: Folklore and Fact," *Harvard Business Review*, Vol. 53, No. 4, 1975, pp. 49–61.

Kenichi Ohmae, "Getting Back to Strategy," *Harvard Business Review*, November–December 1988, pp. 149–156.

Taiichi Ohno, *Toyota Production System: Beyond Large-Scale Production*, Productivity Press, Cambridge, Mass., 1988.

R. Pascale, "The Paradox of 'Corporate Culture': Reconciling Ourselves to Socialization," *California Management Review*, Winter 1985, pp. 26–41.

W. J. Paul, K. B. Robertson, and F. Herzberg, "Job Enrichment Pays Off," *Harvard Business Review*, Vol. 47, No. 2, 1969, pp. 61–78.

L. H. Peters, E. J. O'Connor, and J. R. Eulberg, "Situational Constraints: Sources, Consequences and Future Considerations," *Research in Personnel and Human Resources Management*, Vol. 3, 1985, pp. 79–114.

T. M. Rohan, "New Crisis in Quality," *Industry Week*, Oct. 15, 1990, pp. 11–14.

J. B. Schriber and B. A. Gutek, "Some Time Dimensions of Work: Measurement of an Underlying Aspect of Organization Culture," *Journal of Applied Psychology*, Vol. 72, No. 4, 1987, pp. 642–650.

James E. Shelton, "Survival Code: A Willingness to Change," *The Quality Management Forum*, American Society of Quality Control, Vol. 18, No. 4, Winter 1992/1993, pp. 2–5.

Shigeo Shingo, *Non-Stock Production*, Productivity Press, Cambridge, Mass., 1988.

G. Stalk, P. Evans, and L. E. Shulman, "Competing on Capabilities: The New Rules of Corporate Strategy," *Harvard Business Review*, March–April 1992.

D. Teixeira and J. Ziskin, "Achieving Quality with Customer in Mind," *The Bankers Magazine*, January/February 1993, pp. 29–35.

James P. Womack, *The Machine That Changed the World*, Rawson Associates, New York, 1990.

R. K. Yin, *Changing Urban Bureaucracies*, Lexington Books, Lexington, Mass., 1979.

Abraham Zaleznik, "Real Work," *Harvard Business Review*, January–February 1989, pp. 57–64.

Business Week, July 16, 1990, pp. 160–162, "The New World's Lasers Are Conquering."

Fortune, Apr. 9, 1990, pp. 40–49, "Cost Cutting: How to Do It Right."

Fortune, May 21, 1990, pp. 67–72, "The Soul of an Old Machine."

Fortune, Aug. 13, 1990, pp. 48–54, "America's Fastest-Growing Company."

Fortune, Aug. 13, 1990, pp. 68–73, "Coke Gets Off Its Can in Europe."

Fortune, Nov. 19, 1990, pp. 66–69, "Why Toyota Keeps Getting Better and Better."

chapter **5**

Concepts of
Customer Value

The concept of quality transcends product performance and encompasses all aspects of customer satisfaction. Customers not only want a product that performs exactly to their requirements, they want that product to come on time, they want information on time, and they want their orders to be handled as efficiently as possible. Continuous improvement of quality and customer satisfaction is essential in today's marketplace. In many cases it's not just a success factor, it's a survival factor.

L. D. DeSimone, Chairman, Minnesota Mining and Manufacturing Co. (3M)

▶ **CHAPTER OUTLINE**

Chapter Overview

Introduction

The Concept of Value

Monetary Value
Buyer Value
Customer Value

Customers Identified and Defined

Market Segmentation
Improving Match by Refinement of Market Segments

Who Uses the Product or Service?
A Broader Use Process

Customer Value as a Means/End Relationship

Concern for End Use
Product Attributes and Characteristics
Consequences as Benefits or Sacrifices
End States and Evaluative Criteria

Customer Value Processes

Realized Value versus Anticipated Value
Individual Valuation Process
Organizational Valuation
Abbreviated Attitude Formation
Abbreviated Valuation Processes
The Influence of Norms on Choice (Intention to Buy)
Purchase Behavior (Actual Buying)
Use Experience

Customer Value Strategy

Examples of Revitalized Demand
Implementing a Customer Value Strategy

Concluding Comments

Summary of Key Points

Key Terms

Discussion Questions

Experiential Exercise

References

▶ CHAPTER OVERVIEW

The concept of customer value gives managers a focus for providing products and services that meet customer needs. The closer the match between the product and the customer's needs, the higher the customer value, and higher customer value increases the likelihood that customers will continue to purchase and use the product in the future. Thus, customer value is an integral concept for focusing a manager's strategic decisions and continuous improvement efforts. By understanding customer valuation and use processes, managers will make better strategic decisions and will achieve a better focus for their continuous improvement efforts to better serve customers. They may even improve their own buying behavior as customers.

▶ INTRODUCTION

A sixteenth-century observer, Diego de Bobadilla, provided the following account of an enterprising but somewhat unrealistic Chinese trader:

> A Spaniard who had lost his nose through a certain illness sent for a Chinaman to make him one of wood, in order to hide the deformity. The workman made him so good a nose that the Spaniard in great delight paid him munificently, giving him 20 *escudos*. The Chinaman, attracted by the ease with which he had made that gain, loaded a fine boatload of wooden noses the next year and returned to Manila. [*National Geographic*, September 1990, Vol. 178, No. 3, p. 16]

The trader understood one of the messages of the previous chapter: to survive and prosper, managers must implement a strategy to serve the needs of their customers. However, the trader overestimated the demand for wooden noses. He did not understand the market segment of "those with no nose."

In the emerging paradigm, managers continuously improve to better execute the organization's customer value strategy. The concept of customer value is the key to establishing this strategy and to continuously improving execution of the strategy. This chapter provides managers with a conceptual understanding of customer value to help them fulfill their responsibilities in the emerging paradigm.

▶ THE CONCEPT OF VALUE

The term "value" has many meanings and thereby produces confusion. The term can be applied in several contexts. Remember, customer value is defined as the summation of benefits and sacrifices that result as a consequence of a customer using a product/service to meet certain needs. In addition to customer value, we discuss personal values, cultural values, and role values. In these general uses, the term "value" denotes "a sense of what ought to be" or "that which is important." The customer value concept is developed below by building some fundamental equations that distinguish customer value from another popular concept, monetary value.

Monetary Value

One popular conception of value equates the value of something with its price:

Equation 1: value = price

Accordingly, one can infer the value people place on things by what they willingly give up for them. This logic means that "high value" corresponds to "high sacrifice." Conversely, low value corresponds to low sacrifice. This is often extended into the notion that something is valuable if it costs a lot of money. Definitions of value that rely on this concept of *monetary value* are by nature very limited and not useful to managers in the emerging paradigm.

Buyer Value

Michael Porter (1985, pp. 132–133), a writer whose ideas on competitive strategy captivated American managers in the 1980s, refines an economic definition of value in terms of two ideas: *value added* and *buyer value*. These ideas pertain to the industrial chain.

Products and services reach eventual end users through complex routes and relationships. The intermediate customers that make up the *industrial chain* are business organizations; some are producers and others are channels for producers to reach end customers. These include distributors, transporters, re-marketers, wholesalers, retailers, or manufacturing representatives. Although they are often remote, end users are indirectly responsible for demand, via supplier/customer linkages in the chain. Orders for paper at the copy machine ultimately pull down trees in the forest.

At each of the customer/supplier links throughout the industrial chain, something of economic value is delivered to the customer. Porter (1985, p. 39) defines *value added* as "selling price less the cost of purchased raw materials." Using this notion of economic value, one can distinguish end users from all others in the industrial chain according to whether they add value to the product as it passes along the chain or whether they consume value. The logger adds value by cutting down trees. The trucker adds value by transporting the trees to the paper processing plant. The paper processing plant adds value by converting wood into paper. The distributor, transporter, and retailer of the finished paper product add value by making the paper available for consumers. The end user, the office worker, consumes the paper by using it.[1] Porter's economic notion of value suggests that a product's bundle of attributes carries an inherent value. It can be used immediately or stored and used later.

Porter suggests *buyer value* is a function of buyer performance (in economic terms) and buyer cost.

Equation 2: value = economic performance minus cost

He suggests that a firm lowers buyer cost or raises buyer performance through the impact of a whole array of links between the firm's *value chain* and its buyer's *value chain*. (A value chain, as shown in Figure 1, disaggregates a firm into its strategically relevant activities to understand costs and sources of differentiation.)

---

1. With the practice of recycling, an end user can sometimes become a supplier. The end-user test remains valid since the cost of materials exceeds the selling price (salvage value); hence, no value was added.

Figure 1

Porter's value chain concept

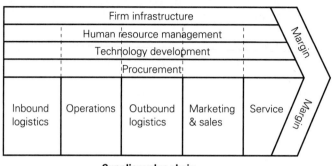

Reprinted from Porter (1985).

Porter (p. 135) suggests that a firm can lower its buyer's cost in a number of ways, including the following:

- Lower delivery, installation, or financing cost
- Lower the required rate of usage of the product
- Lower the direct cost of using the product, such as labor, fuel, maintenance, required space
- Lower the indirect cost of using the product, or the impact of the product on other value activities. For example, a light component may reduce the transport costs of the end product
- Lower the buyer cost in other value activities unconnected with the physical product
- Lower the risk of product failure and thus the buyer's expected cost of failure

Porter's emphasis on lowering buyer's cost is still too narrow because it addresses only one of the many sacrifices that customers have to make in using a product. There may be many more besides monetary sacrifices, for example, mental frustration in using a poorly designed product. Although he does not fully develop the idea, Porter recognizes that raising buyer performance also depends on understanding what is desirable performance from the buyer's viewpoint and "better satisfying needs" (p. 138). The concept of customer value builds on this idea and offers managers a concept more useful in guiding strategic planning and continuous improvement. Certainly all the firms in the industrial supply chain add value to the end product, or increase its economic worth, by engaging in costly activities. But whether these costly activities are instrumental to achieving superior customer value depends on how customers use the resulting products and services as means to attain certain desired end states.

Another deficiency in Porter's value chain is its sequential view of providing value to end customers, in contrast to the Japanese *keiretsu*. The *keiretsu* establishes collaborative business relationships to better serve the economic interests of the members, their customers, and society. Although many industries are still accurately described as chains of supplier-customer linkages, many American companies are experimenting with industrial partnerships managed as a system, orchestrated to provide superior customer value.[2]

Customer Value

Another popular conception of "value" assumes value is a function of both *benefits* and *sacrifices*. For example, an advertisement touts a product as a "good value" because it offers the purchaser a lot of benefits at a low price. In this case, "high value" accompanies "low price." According to this notion, *customer value* equals benefits minus sacrifices:

Equation 3: value = benefits minus sacrifices

This suggests that the higher benefits are relative to sacrifices, the higher will be the value (Zeithaml, 1988). The distinctions between customer value, monetary value, and buyer value are extremely important because continuous improvement activities should be driven toward the purpose of providing the best customer value, not just adding economic value.[3] Managers can increase the customer value of a product by increasing the benefits or decreasing the sacrifices. The concept of customer value moves away from the notion that value is something inherent to the product or service toward the notion that value is determined in the context of customer use. Thus, the customer does not value a product in a vacuum, but rather values the consequences of its use.

The *relationship* between the supplier and the customer can have a profound impact on perceptions of value. The following equation includes relationship as a significant additional component in value:[4]

Equation 4: value = (benefits minus sacrifices) * relationship

For example, medical services rendered by the long-time family doctor may be perceived as more valuable than equal services rendered by a stranger. Things such as trust, familiarity, devotion, and friendship may greatly affect perceptions of value.

---

2. The authors thank Al Cole for suggesting this line of reasoning.
3. The relationship between price and perceived value can be a bit tricky. In some cases, such as when a customer pays a high price for a piece of jewelry, the customer may indirectly derive a higher value by paying a higher price, such as in the joy of owning and showing off expensive jewelry. In such situations, monetary value interacts with customer value, not only through instrumental linkages to status as a social goal, but through the perceptual processes with which the customer perceives value. Or it may simply be that price is a benefit as well as a sacrifice in this case.
4. The authors thank Karl Manrodt for suggesting this component of value.

For managers to make use of the concept of customer value, they must first identify and define who their customers are.

▼

QUALITY IN ACTION: A MESSAGE TO THE STUDENT
Edwin L. Artzt, Chairman and Chief Executive, The Procter & Gamble Company

Procter & Gamble is one of the largest consumer products companies in the world. It is also a leading promoter of total quality in academia and industry. Chairman and Chief Executive Edwin L. Artzt explains the importance of customer value in Procter & Gamble's business strategy.

Understanding the concept of value is a must in today's marketplace, because consumers are changing the way they think about the balance between performance and price—the building blocks of value. While most consumers are still willing to pay more for exceptional quality, they're putting more emphasis on price than ever before. What they're looking for is "affordable quality"—better quality at a better price.

This represents perhaps the most fundamental challenge you'll face as a manager. When I first entered the workforce in 1953, we tended to think you could have better quality or better price, but not both. Surprisingly, most people in business continued to think that way until a few years ago, when customers' and consumers' persistent demands literally forced us to change the way we think about value. Fortunately, the principles of Total Quality gave us the ability to deliver both better quality and better price.

For example, TQ's parallel emphasis on continual improvement and systemic change has helped us at P&G to identify and drive out of our systems costs that don't deliver value to our consumers. In a company with more than 100,000 employees working at more than 200 locations in over 50 countries, this can be a seemingly impossible task. But we're doing it by following two basic Total Quality principles.

First of all, we've developed a thorough understanding of what contributes to our consumers' perceptions of value—and what doesn't.

In addition, we've focused on understanding and continually improving our systems—from suppliers to store shelves—to drive out non-value-added costs and improve service.

A good example from our business was our promotion and distribution logistics system. Like many manufacturers over the last couple of decades, P&G has increasingly resorted to short-term, deep-discount promotional deals to attract buyers. Price cuts of 30% to 40% off the regular shelf price for short periods of time are not unusual. In this environment, users who switch brands pay lower prices on the average. However, a brand's loyal users are penalized as they regularly pay a higher price for their favorite brands. These swings also create variability and massive inefficiency in the manufacturing and distribution system. To meet heavy, short-term demand, manufacturers must build raw material inventory, design peaks and valleys into their production schedules, and build up finished inventory. In addition, the proliferation of deals creates potential pricing errors and rework. Cash gets tied up in warehousing costs, excessive shipping rates, and handling costs. The bill for this inefficiency is staggering, up to 17% of our net revenue.

How did we let ourselves get into this situation? Well, it's simple. First of all, we weren't measuring how consumers rated the value of our brands. And we weren't precisely measuring what consumers—especially loyal consumers—were paying for our products. The second reason this happened was that we weren't looking at the total system implications of these promotional activities . . . and we didn't understand all the hidden costs that came with them. What we discovered, when we started looking at how this system was affecting our business, was that this complex system of deals and incentives wasn't being driven by the trade . . . or even by consumers shopping for bargain basement prices. We did it to ourselves.

So, we decided to simplify the system. That led us to a strategy we call value pricing. We're taking a portion of our trade promotion dollars, along with savings from increasing system efficiency, to fund reduced list prices. This provides more consistent, reliable pricing day-in and day-out, with smaller deal-to-deal swings. We've substantially reduced the variation in trade demand for the brands that have gone to value pricing—which has an inverse ripple effect back through the chain. Variations in volume forecasts, plant production, and raw materials supply have all been dramatically reduced. These reductions represent real cost savings—as much as $175 million a year when we start seeing the full benefits—savings that are then reinvested into providing better quality and better prices for our consumers. Let's take Dawn, our liquid dishwashing soap, as an example. Before value pricing, the price of a regular size bottle swung wildly from $.99 to $1.89. Now, under value pricing, it regularly sells for about $1.32. And it looks like our consumers appreciate the change. Since our move to value pricing on Dawn, the brand has achieved a record year in volume and share. And consumers are giving Dawn significantly higher ratings for being a good value.

This change in our promotion system is just one example, but it demonstrates clearly why Total Quality is critical to our business. It helps us focus on two important factors: understanding how value is perceived by our consumers, and understanding how our total system is—or isn't—contributing to superior value.

Total Quality Management is necessary because consumers have raised the bar. They're tired of paying for companies' inefficiencies. Add to that the growing competitive pressure that results from the globalization of the marketplace and you have perhaps the most challenging business environment we've ever known.

▶ CUSTOMERS IDENTIFIED AND DEFINED

Identifying customers is not a simple task. Most organizations do not have a single, typical customer; they have many customers within and outside the organization, each with their own set of needs. The first step in developing a customer value strategy is to understand how the structure of the market can be segmented.

Market Segmentation

Segmenting markets into groupings of customers represents a compromise between treating each customer as unique or all customers as the same. While each customer is unique, needs do overlap to some degree. Customers are grouped according to criteria that can differentiate the groups. *Market segments* may be determined with general information such as socio-economic status and specific information such as lifestyle preferences.[5] Ideally, *segmentation* yields groupings of customers that might be inclined to make choices in one particular way or another, for example, those who would buy a Ford Escort and those who would buy a Cadillac.

Improving Match by Refinement of Market Segments

Customer value is defined by the match or fit of the product to the customer's needs. For example, household cleansers vary in "cutting strength" and "the amount of scent." Figure 2 shows that individuals may vary in their needs for these features. A *mass market approach* tries to meet every person's need with one product, targeted perhaps at the X in the middle of the field. This product probably would meet few needs very well.

Through segmentation, products may be targeted (at the X) to better suit the needs of a certain segment of similar people within the mass market. The closer the match, the better the fit, the higher the customer value. The product targeted at Segment 1 matches person A better than B within the segment, and much better than C in the mass market.[6] To provide superior customer value, managers try to maximize the match or minimize the gap between what the product offers and what the customer needs. Person C may have to use the product targeted for Segment 1 if no product exists to better match his needs. But as soon as another product offers more value, he will likely use it instead.

At the opposite extreme of the mass market approach, each individual is considered a single market segment, and products are tailored to per-

---

5. For consumer goods, segmentation factors include demographics, socio-economics, personality, and psychographics. For industrial goods, these factors include organizational characteristics such as size, location, sales, and the information contained in the U.S. Standard Industrial Classification (SIC) coding systems.
6. We assume that production output conforms to targeted design.

Figure 2

Segmentation and match of product to customer need

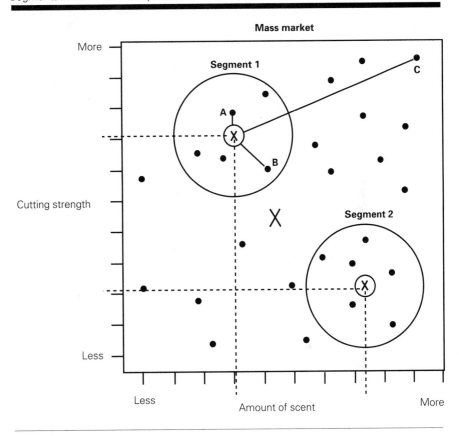

fectly meet the individual's needs.[7] Such an approach requires flexibility and responsiveness not possible in traditional mass production systems. By contrast, the supplier of tailored products and services builds networks of resources upon demand to deliver value to the customer. Indeed, the only limitation on "fit" or "match" for customer value is the degree of flexibility of the producer (Davis and Manrodt, 1991).

There are many ways to define market segments.[8] Garvin (1988) suggests eight *dimensions of quality*, each defined below:

---

7. Rather than segmentation, this approach implies market fragmentation. The effect is to shrink the size of the segments, and create many more target segments within a mass market (Robert, 1992).

8. Segmentation is an iterative and ongoing process. Managers may take a preliminary guess about segments so they can identify customers to study. Upon study, they may decide that they need to redefine the segments and study them further.

1. *Performance*: Primary operating characteristics of a product. Example: acceleration, handling, cruising speed, and comfort in an automobile.
2. *Features*: Enhancements that supplement a product's basic functioning. Examples: free drinks on a plane flight, permanent press cycle on a washing machine, automatic tuners on a color television set.
3. *Reliability*: Probability that a product will malfunction or fail within a specified period of time.
4. *Conformance*: Degree to which a product's design and operating characteristics meet pre-established standards.
5. *Durability*: Measure of a product's life.
6. *Serviceability*: Speed, courtesy, competence, and ease of repair of a product.
7. *Aesthetics*: Individual reactions to how a product looks, feels, sounds, tastes, or smells.
8. *Perceived quality*: Inferences drawn about product quality from various sources, such as tangible and intangible aspects of the product, advertising, brand image, and company reputation.

These dimensions represent options managers might choose in order to execute a particular strategy for customer value. For example, the Dodge Stealth appeals to the customer who wants excitement as a feature, and the Chrysler minivan appeals to the customer who wants convenient family travel. Continuous improvement along any of these dimensions of quality can enhance the customer value that managers plan to offer and ultimately deliver. However, to determine which dimensions are most important to customers, managers must have a clear understanding of customer needs. This begins with understanding customer concerns for end use of the product.

Who Uses the Product or Service?

Managers can refine their understanding of market segments by asking more questions about the users of their product. When a mother selects a breakfast cereal from the grocery store shelf, she has just made a decision as a customer of that retail outlet. When her child selects a cereal from the cupboard, the child can be seen as a more remote customer. What these customers value can also be very different. The mother may value low cost and nutrition, while the child values taste. The mother and child can be distinguished as the buyer and the ultimate consumer. Similar distinctions can be drawn in industrial purchasing, where one organization buys from another.

This way of looking at customer value leads to the following distinctions. A *consumer* is the person or organization that actually uses the product or service. A *decider* is the person or organization that selects, chooses, specifies, and authorizes payment for the product or service. A *beneficiary* is the person or organization that benefits from or makes a sacrifice because of the use of the product or service. In many situations, the customer may be all three. However, some cases are more complex. Consider, for example, the Watervliet Arsenal, which produces cannons for military use. The soldier (or military unit) may be viewed as a consumer, the acquisition agency (Department of Defense) as a decider, and the American public as a beneficiary. Making these distinctions allows Watervliet managers to refine the meaning of customer value. Each customer values different outcomes. Knowledge of these values is important because it provides information needed to set goals for system improvement (Carothers and Bounds, 1991).

Beyond this, managers sometimes find that finer distinctions are useful. For example, six different buying roles apply to purchasing processes for both consumer and industrial products:

1. *Initiator* (identifies the need for the product)
2. *Influencer* (has informational or preference input to the decision)
3. *Decider* (makes the final decision through budget authorization)
4. *Purchaser* (makes the actual purchase)
5. *Gatekeeper* (does analysis and makes recommendations)
6. *User* (consumes the product or service) (Bonoma, 1982; Lehmann and Winer, 1991)

Managers can use this detailed role list to make sure that important customers are not ignored. For example, Federal Express saw a benefit in making the user and the purchaser part of the same buying role. The company has achieved remarkable success in bypassing the shipping clerk, allowing the sender of an overnight package to purchase a shipping service directly. Using Federal Express, a sender can be assured that the package has left the building and is reliably en route to its final destination.

A Broader Use Process

In addition to the buying process, managers should also consider the entire *use process*: all of the activities that customers go through in using a product or service. The value of a product or service is determined by much more than just the act of *consumption* (i.e., using up the product or service). Rather, value derives from all aspects of the use process. Customers may have to find, acquire, transport, store, use, dispose of, and stop the ongoing use of a product or service, as defined below:

1. *Find.* A customer must locate a product or service to fulfill a need. This may require search, recognition, and choice.
2. *Acquire.* Acquiring may entail ordering, paying for, financing, transferring, and registering the ownership.
3. *Transport.* Once acquired, the customer (or the vendor) may have to move the product from where it is to where it can be further used.
4. *Store.* The customer may have to store the product prior to further use. Storage may be brief or long term, and may be repeated in different forms.

5. *Use.* At some point, the customer applies the product or service practically to fulfill the need.

6. *Dispose of.* Once utilized, the customer may have to dispose of the remainder or residue of the product.

7. *Stop.* The customer may at some time decide to stop using the product or service. (Bounds and Dobbins, 1993)

We use the acronym FATSUDS to remember these activities. This sequence applies to individual consumers and industrial organizations in the supply chain. (Transport, Store, and Dispose may not apply to some services.) One person may perform all of the *FATSUDS activities*, or, as with many industrial products, the activities may be divided among different people, teams of people, or departments.

These activities are listed in a logical order, but the actual process may not be so orderly. The sequence may be different, and some elements may be skipped, others repeated. For example, when someone seeks to find a product or service, he or she may not fully understand what to look for or the extent of the need. Rather than go shopping with a clear set of product specifications and expectations in hand, the customer may engage interactively with the supplier in assessing his or her need and in developing the specifications for the product.

To provide superior value, managers must determine what customers value throughout the FATSUDS sequence. Earl Conway, formerly Procter & Gamble's Corporate Quality Director (now retired), suggests how important disposability of products has become in recent years:

> We start with market research and determine what customers value. Traditionally, we focused on performance-related factors and aesthetics. But recently we are learning about other things that the customer considers important. For example, concern for the environment has made us attend to the biodegradability of our disposable diapers. No longer are we just concerned with absorbancy and fit. What happens to the diaper after it is used is important to consumers, and they will make buying decisions based on that. So we have to treat the consumer's concern for the environment just as seriously as we do the concern for absorbancy and fit.

Value derives from much more than using a product or service. Rather, it comes from each aspect of the use process. Other aspects of the use process, like ease of availability, quality of the service, and congeniality of the supplier, greatly impact the customer's perception of value. For example, in making a choice between two alternative products, the customer may have a preference for the physical attributes and characteristics of product A. However, this preference alone does not ensure that the customer will choose that product. A person may prefer the taste of a Tastee Freeze milk shake over that of a McDonald's milk shake. However, if the only Tastee Freeze in town is seven miles away, and McDonald's is one mile away, the ease of acquiring the McDonald's shake may be more attractive than the long drive.

As another example, consider how the military was faced with a choice between the General Dynamics F-16 and the Northrop F-17 fighter jets. The planes performed comparably, but the General Dynamics F-16 was selected. This was because General Dynamics had initiated preparation for production prior to winning approval for the contract, allowing them to promise faster availability. Further, the F-16 design included an engine already in production for other aircraft. This meant that the technical capabilities for maintaining the engine already existed and that spare parts would generally be available. Because of their existing product line, General Dynamics could take advantage of economies of scale and prior progress along the learning curve to produce quality engines. So the value of General Dynamics' F-16 was determined by more than just the performance of the aircraft.[9]

Managers might identify many opportunities to deliver superior customer value if they consider the whole use process. Hospitals are catching on to this idea. For example, the University of Michigan Hospital sought to cut the time it took to admit patients. Over a four-year period, a team of employees cut admitting time from a discouraging 2.3 hours to 11 minutes. Not only did this improvement increase value to customers, it eliminated wasteful jobs and saved an estimated $260,000 a year for the hospital (*Business Week*, "Quality," Dec. 5, 1991). Such improvements are valued by customers of hospitals because almost everyone values their time and loathes the frustrations of dealing with inefficient bureaucracy. Below, we discuss further how customer value is determined by the fit between the means of providing value (goods and services) and customers' needs.

▶ CUSTOMER VALUE AS A MEANS/ENDS RELATIONSHIP

Many factors influence what end states a customer values and the product he or she chooses. These include the *macroenvironment* (political, economic, technological, social, and cultural factors); *customer characteristics* (psychosocial characteristics, lifestyle, and needs); the *use process* (specific situations such as how, when, where, and by whom a product is bought and used, and the sequence of use activities); and the *relationships with supplier organizations* (whose systems actually provide the competing product or service alternatives).

The macroenvironment and customer characteristics combine to determine the customer's desired end states. The *means/ends model* in Figure

---

9. Certainly, there were many other factors that entered into this military decision. But the example reflects the importance of looking at customer value as part of each role in both the choice process and the use process. The people occupying these various roles or executing these activities may each value something different. They may even have conflicting values and competing agendas.

Figure 3

Means/ends model, concept and examples

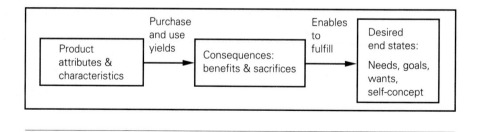

3 illustrates this process. In brief, the means/ends model suggests that customers buy products (means) to accomplish some purpose or fulfill a need (ends) (Brunswik, 1952; Gutman, 1982; Gutman and Alden, 1985; Howard, 1977; Myers and Shocker, 1981; Perkins and Reynolds, 1988; Levitt, 1969, 1984). Customer value increases with the *match* between product use consequences and customer needs. For example, the benefits women seek in shampooing their hair may be broken down into specific production requirements and related to personal needs, as the examples in Figure 4 show (Myers, 1978; Myers and Shocker, 1981).

Concern for End Use

The types of questions that cross customers' minds when they are buying a new product illustrate the general concerns that a customer has over use consequences:

Will it do what I want it to do?
What good is this particular feature?
How long will it last?
How much does it cost?
How soon can I get it?
How quickly can I learn to use it?
Is it easy to use?
Does it come in other colors or styles?
Does it break down often?
How expensive is it to fix?
Will my friends like it?

People do not buy a product for the sake of the product itself, but because of what the product can do for them. For example, you may buy a microwave oven to cook edible food that satisfies your hunger quickly. You may buy a plain car to provide a means of transportation, or you may buy a stylish car to get aesthetic pleasure, reinforce your self-concept, and gain social esteem among your peers.

Figure 4
Means/ends examples*

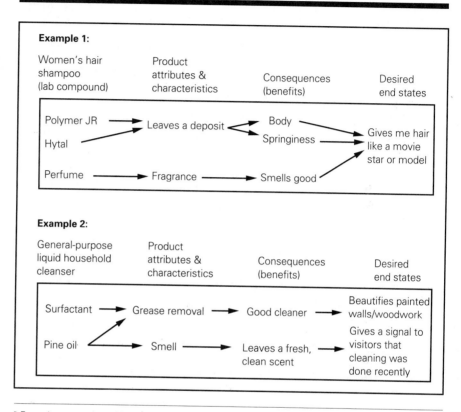

Example 1:

Women's hair shampoo (lab compound) → Product attributes & characteristics → Consequences (benefits) → Desired end states

Polymer JR → Leaves a deposit → Body → Gives me hair like a movie star or model
Hytal → Leaves a deposit
Springiness → Gives me hair like a movie star or model
Perfume → Fragrance → Smells good

Example 2:

General-purpose liquid household cleanser → Product attributes & characteristics → Consequences (benefits) → Desired end states

Surfactant → Grease removal → Good cleaner → Beautifies painted walls/woodwork
Pine oil → Smell → Leaves a fresh, clean scent → Gives a signal to visitors that cleaning was done recently

* Examples were adapted from Myers and Shocker (1981).

To make improvements that strategically enhance customer value, managers need *measurement systems* to help them determine what customers value, and assess the delivery of customer value. The measurement system should span the customers' perceptions of means/ends relationships, use processes, value delivered, and satisfaction and dissatisfaction. Armed with this knowledge, managers can design and deliver products of the best value. To develop such a measurement system, managers must understand all of the components of the means/ends model. Each of these is further discussed below.

Product Attributes and Characteristics
Products and services may be described in terms of shape, density, smell, texture, temperature, taste, etc., and time sequence and intervals between events. Realizations on these physical and temporal dimensions give the

product or service certain *attributes* and *characteristics*: such physical attributes as the degree or amount of shininess, thickness, strength, saltiness, and sharpness, and temporal characteristics, such as delivery timeliness and amount of repair time.[10]

In accordance with the means-ends perspective, customers are interested in attributes only if they perceive a relationship between the attributes and use consequences that will lead to desired end states. For example, a customer buys a down-filled parka to achieve warmth, not for the down filling.

Companies that supply hard goods to customers could learn from service companies about ways to provide value that go beyond just physical dimensions of the goods. Some notable service firms include: Delta Air Lines, Federal Express Corporation, UPS, J. B. Hunt Transport Services, Marriott Corporation, and The Walt Disney Corporation (for review, see Heskett, Sasser and Hart, 1992; and Zemke, 1989).

Consequences as Benefits or Sacrifices

Acquiring and using a product or service involves a certain degree of sacrifice. A sacrifice may require the customer to give up something, such as money, time, energy, sleep, or peace of mind. The customer may experience *benefits* and *sacrifices* during any of the FATSUDS activities. The combination of all these benefits and sacrifices represents the overall value of the product or service to the customer.[11]

End States and Evaluative Criteria

When a customer uses a product, he or she evaluates the use consequences as either benefits or sacrifices according to the effect on certain end states. People have a host of desired end states (needs, goals, wants, personal values, and self-concepts) that affect customer value. The term *"need"* is often used for brevity to refer to all of these. Defined more narrowly, need indicates a lack of something useful or required. We may have needs such as security, hunger, thirst, social acceptance, love, and accomplishment (Maslow, 1970; Alderfer, 1972). A *goal* represents an unfulfilled aspiration, aim, or objective. Common goals are those for prosperity, social status, and career accomplishments. *Want* indicates a lack of something desired or wished for, but not required. Wants include desires for intellectual stimulation, entertainment, or happiness. Figure 5 suggests some common use situations that reflect various needs, goals, and wants.

---

10. Some companies are adopting time as a key part of their competitive strategies for serving customers (see Stalk and Stout, 1990).

11. To understand customer value, you might need to consider not only what they buy (product attributes and characteristics), but where they buy it (location), and when they buy (time of year, month, and day; or during sales, price breaks, and rebates).

Figure 5

A general classification of use situations

Customer perception of product use situations	Examples
1. Current problem	a. Dry skin problems—soaps and creams b. Oily hair—shampoos and rinses
2. Potential problem	a. Bad breath—toothpaste and mouthwashes b. Lack of social approval—prestige products such as fashionable clothes
3. Normal depletion	a. Low on fuel—gasoline, fuel oil b. Low on cleaners—dishwashing soaps, scouring pads, paper towels
4. Interest opportunity	a. Feeling of expertise—wine, stereos, perfumes b. Desire for diversion—sports equipment, autos c. Desire for fun—sports events, shows, movies
5. Sensory pleasure opportunity	a. Taste pleasure—ice cream, gourmet foods, fruits b. Scent pleasure—perfumed soaps, wine, flowers
6. Product-related problem	a. Side effects from product use—buffered aspirin, hypoallergenic toiletries, ecologically safe laundry detergent b. Undesirable product characteristic—bad-tasting mouthwash, low-lead gasoline
7. Satisfaction/frustration	a. Dog owners may dislike the appearance/odor of dog food, but cannot find a brand that solves this problem b. Overweight people may feel that no foods are tasty, filling, and low calorie at the same time

Adapted from Geraldine Fennell, "Consumers' Perceptions of the Product-Use Situation," *Journal of Marketing*, Vol. 42, April 1978, pp. 40–43.

Personal values are general beliefs about what is personally important. These include the importance of independence, excitement, relationships with others, self-fulfillment, and so on (Rokeach, 1968, 1973; Kahle, 1983). In addition to these broad values, people might hold personal values that are particular to different domains (e.g., religion, family, work, consumption) (Scott and Lamont, 1973; Vinson, Scott, and Lamont, 1977). All of these personal values reside within the person, as opposed to the concept of customer value, which arises from the interaction between a person and a product.

A person's *self-concept*, or *self-image*, is another end state that one may seek to achieve through a product or service. One's self-concept, for example, a desire to see oneself as brave, daring, loving, or caring, can be a strong motivational force. The need for fulfillment of self-concept may be related to what Burns and Woodruff (1990) call the *"possession value"* of a product. They note that a product may produce value through the pleasure derived from proximity to and association with it, perhaps through its symbolic and aesthetic qualities.

Figure 6

Evaluative criteria ranked in order of importance for two restaurant use situations

Celebration use situation	Time pressure use situation
1. Atmosphere/decor	1. Fast service
2. Menu specialties	2. Convenient location
3. Reputation for fine cuisine	3. Tasty food
4. Efficient table service	4. Low price
5. Friendly personnel	5. Friendly personnel
6. Price	6. Decor

Adapted from Cravens, Hills, and Woodruff (1987).

▶ CUSTOMER VALUE PROCESSES

In seeking information about alternative products, customers try to learn what each product has to offer for their recognized "needs." For example, the importance of various criteria used to evaluate and choose a restaurant varies with the customer's needs, such as a celebration of an anniversary versus a time-pressured workday lunch (see Figure 6). A customer essentially compares "what the product offers" with "what I need."

Realized Value versus Anticipated Value

Customers may engage in this valuation process before, during, and after product purchase and use. So managers may be most interested in measuring customer perceptions of value at three points in time: (1) at the point of choice among alternative products, when the customer anticipates value; (2) during product use, and (3) after product use, when the customer evaluates the realized value.

It may help to distinguish between *realized value* and *anticipated value*, since these change over three points in time. *Anticipated value* is the value that customers predict they will get in the future if they purchase and use a particular product. Choice is often based upon anticipation of the benefits and sacrifices, and customers may make relative comparisons of product alternatives and choose the one that offers the best anticipated value.[12] Actual customer value is realized once the customer acquires and uses the product. Evaluation during and after use may result in satisfaction or dissatisfaction with the *realized value*, which in turn affects future anticipated value and subsequent choices.

---

12. Perhaps the customer does some type of net present value evaluation when the purchase decision is made.

Individual Valuation Process

Individual valuation is a mental process leading to some prepurchase behavior and postuse behavior. This process involves both rational and emotional elements. Managers need to understand the key activities of this *valuation process*, which concerns how the customer perceives product attributes and infers means/ends relationships, and then assimilates this information into memory to influence behaviors. A general model of the valuation process may involve the following steps when a person buys a car:

1. *Recognize the need* for a car.
2. *Search for information* about alternatives through brochures and test drives.
3. *Encounter physical cues,* such as the fabric in the interior.
4. *Perceive attributes and characteristics,* such as the softness of the seat and handling on curvy roads.
5. *Form beliefs about benefits and sacrifices,* such as safety and comfort.
6. *Form attitudes* about alternative cars by weighing all the benefits and sacrifices.
7. *Decide* to buy one of the cars.
8. *Actually buy and use* the car.
9. *Evaluate* the ownership and use experience.

This model is meant to be only an approximation of the valuation process. Each of these steps in the process is composed of many psychological components and subprocesses. On the other hand, in some cases, choosers do not engage in each step explicitly. Some steps may occur subconsciously and easily. Other steps may occur at widely separated intervals, such as when using memory of prior experiences to make a judgment. Further, some situations may not require extensive mental processing or the order of the activities may be different.

Attitudes Formed about Alternatives Attitudes involve evaluating an object or event as either good or bad, liked or disliked, positive or negative. In the case of customer choice, the match of the product with the customer's use situation, goals, needs, wants, and self-concept primarily determines whether the evaluation will be positive or negative. We feel good about things that help accomplish our goals and fulfill our needs. This match also determines the magnitude or strength of feeling.

The model in Figure 7 illustrates the relationship of *attitude formation* to the means/end model. A person's attitude toward buying a product depends upon his or her beliefs and evaluations of the means/ends relationship. For example, a father and son may react differently to a sports car in the showroom. The father says, "Oh, no," because he anticipates the car's power and fears for his son's safety. The son says, "Oh, yes," because he also anticipates the speed, and imagines how it would boost his image among peers.

Figure 7

Means/ends attitude formation process

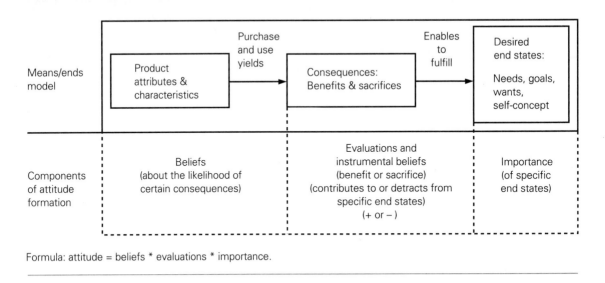

Formula: attitude = beliefs * evaluations * importance.

The view of the attitude formation process presented in Figure 7 suggests extensive mental processing and calculation. It is derived from expectancy theories of motivation, such as VIE theory (Vroom, 1964), and theories of attitude formation (see Fishbein and Ajzen, 1975). It suggests that attitudes are formed by the *beliefs* and *feelings* about the means/ends relationship. One's attitude toward a product is a function of (1) one's beliefs about whether the product attributes will produce certain benefits or sacrifices, and (2) the extent to which one believes these benefits or sacrifices contribute to or detract from need fulfillment.[13]

The strength of one's beliefs may vary. For example, customers may evaluate a consequence of using the product as a benefit (positive), but believe that the benefit will not contribute very much to the fulfillment of a particular need. Customers have many needs that vary in importance; this greatly affects attitude or anticipated value. One's attitude toward buying a product is the result of the combination of all benefits and sacrifices believed to follow from using it. Customer value increases as benefits come to outweigh sacrifices. A positive net customer value means that buying and using the product contributes to the fulfillment of customer "needs" more than it detracts. This attitude roughly corresponds to the anticipated value of the product in use.[14]

---

13. Benefits are judged as positive outcomes (indicating contribution to goal achievement), and sacrifices are judged as negative outcomes (indicating detraction from goal achievement).
14. Advertising and sales processes attempt to influence attitude formation by influencing need recognition, need priorities, perceptions of product attributes and characteristics, and perception of the product's match with recognized needs.

For example, if a product yields a benefit that contributes to an unimportant goal and a sacrifice that detracts from an important goal, the overall anticipated value of the product will be low.[15] The size of a car's engine and the corresponding tradeoff between power to accelerate and fuel economy is an example of how benefits and sacrifices relate differently to different goals. The relative importance of one's goals "to save time by driving fast" versus "to save money by driving economically" determines what value a particular size engine offers to that person. Further, the relative importance of one's goals, and corresponding weights attached to benefits and sacrifices, may change over time, which changes one's evaluation of a product. The criteria you use to evaluate a car is likely to change over time as your life changes.

Like or dislike are general responses that may or may not be accompanied by specific emotions. Specific emotions might include anger, jubilation, love, shame, remorse, guilt, joy, fear, or hate. Managers should seek to elicit strong positive emotional responses from customers, as well as generally positive attitudes, because strong emotions are motivating. The more positive emotions a customer has for a product, the more likely he or she is to repeat purchase and recommend the product to others.

The Relative Nature of Customer Value Customers determine benefits and sacrifices subjectively, changing over time as use situations, needs, standards of comparison, expectations, and norms change. For example, customer expectations about the speed of computer processing have continued to rise over the last couple of decades. It now seems intolerable to wait thirty seconds in front of a dormant monitor while the computer cranks out mathematical solutions that would have taken hours only a few years ago.

So there is really no such thing as the "absolute value" of a product. The customer value of a product is determined relative to the customer's perception of the product's contribution to need fulfillment, relative to customer standards, norms, and expectations at the time of the perceived need. When there are few competing alternatives, a product may be judged to be the "best" net value. Once competing alternatives become available, that same product may be assessed as low in value, requiring sacrifices that outweigh its benefits. This is why continuous improvement is so important in today's competitive environment.

Another important dimension of the relative nature of customer value springs from the concept of relative deprivation. This concept refers to the fact that people perceive themselves to be deprived to the extent that they perceive better alternatives are possible, but are inaccessible or unavailable to them (Aronson, 1980). When customers expand their

---

15. Conversely, the summative nature of the formula of attitude formation suggests that if a product requires a sacrifice in one area, it may be compensated with a benefit elsewhere. This assumption about compensation may be incorrect in some choice processes.

imaginations and perceive possibilities beyond their status quo, they raise their aspirations. This implies that managers may create demand through product and service innovation, where demand may not have existed before. For example, several decades ago, there was no apparent demand for the Sony Walkman, laptop computers, microwave ovens, and Nintendo games. These products were not yet imagined.

Idiosyncratic Nature of Customer Value Needs vary from one individual to the next, and so the anticipated value of a product may be very idiosyncratic or particular to each individual customer. Only those customers with similar needs are most likely to derive the same value from the use of the product. A product that one person thinks of as offering high value might be worthless to another. This *idiosyncratic* (or personally determined) nature of customer value suggests managers must understand how markets are segmented. That is, they need to know the uniformity within customer groups and the diversity across customer groups with regard to specific use situations.[16]

A caveat about attitude formation is in order. Attitudes may not be formed simply on the evaluation of use consequences. Products may elicit emotional responses from learned associative memory networks. Subconsciously, a person might react negatively or positively to certain cues of the product, without regard to use consequences. For example, colors and smells that are associated with happy childhood memories might elicit feelings of joy and contentment. Conversely, other cues associated with bad experiences might elicit feelings of fear and apprehension (Tolman, 1959; Rescorla, 1968). These kinds of emotional responses are highly idiosyncratic, particular to one's personal experiences. Only others with similar emotional experiences would react similarly. Such emotional reactions, although not logically related to use, might indirectly influence one's intentions toward the product. So managers may find it necessary to measure both evaluative reactions and emotions to fully understand customer responses to product use (Gardial, Clemons, Woodruff, Schumann, and Burns, 1991).

When the customer is an organization, the valuation process is even more complicated than when the customer is just one individual. Despite the increased complexity, the basic steps of individual valuation still apply to organizational customers. After all, organizations are composed of individuals.

Organizational Valuation

By definition, an *organization* consists of a group of people that endures over time, coordinates their activity, and serves some common purpose. Families are small groups with features similar to those of business organi-

---

16. As managers move away form the mass market approach toward tailored products and services, flexible and responsive organizations will offer maximum customer value, with no discrepancy in the match of products and needs.

zations (for example, membership rules that give identity and discriminate insiders from outsiders, and relatively long-term and purposeful social interaction). Virtually all types of organizations will purchase products and services, such as office materials, communication services, food, machinery, technical know-how, software, raw materials, component parts, subassemblies, and subcontracted labor.

The valuation process is always more complicated when the customer is an organization. The social and interpersonal dynamics that ensue when several people are involved is what makes *organizational valuation* complex. Social norms, peer pressure, interpersonal relations, bargaining and negotiation, bureaucratic and political processes all pervade organizational valuation. Issues of customer value also become intermingled with organizational strategy when the customers are wholesalers, distributors, retailers, and re-marketers. Each of these *channel customers* has an organizational strategy that involves end users.

The burden for improvement in the customer/supplier interface does not rest completely on the shoulders of suppliers, but with both customers and suppliers. Without inputs that meet their requirements, organizations will not be able to execute systems and processes to produce value for their customers. Large industrial organizations often create confusion for suppliers by presenting them with muddled purchasing processes and with competing and often contradictory "customer" voices. For example, one supplier in the aerospace industry received four different answers to the same question from the purchasing, quality assurance, engineering, and production departments of an aircraft producer. Suppliers must do their best to sort out the confusion that their customers present them. Customers also have an obligation to clarify their system to their suppliers.

Customers and suppliers in the industrial chain should work together to create customer value strategies that serve consumers and meet the company's needs for economic performance. Customer value strategies based on the preferences of engineers or marketing experts are not nearly as effective as those based on firm knowledge of what customers value. For example, Bill Jones, the owner of a retail music center in Knoxville, Tennessee, had the following experience. In the mid-1980s, a piano manufacturer introduced a new line of high-gloss, brilliantly colored pianos in contemporary styles at an annual meeting with its dealers. The dealers were shocked because they knew the market would not buy the pianos, and the manufacturer had not asked them for their opinions. The dealers told the manufacturer's sales representatives they did not want to order any of the designer pianos. However, the sales representatives threatened to start selling pianos to furniture stores and other decorator outlets, a move which would establish a new set of competitors in the hometowns of the dealers. Bill gave in to the pressure and ordered some of the designer pianos, which then sat on his display floor unsold for two years. After two years of listening to dealer complaints, the manufacturer's sales representative punched holes in the back of the designer pianos and authorized Bill to return them to the manufacturer as "defective." On his next trip to pick up stock from the manufacturer, Bill went inside the warehouse and found a sea of blue, green, red, and pink pianos all being returned because they were "defective."

To deliver value all along the industrial chain, managers should investigate and communicate with one another about customer value. Some of the factors affecting organizational valuation processes are discussed below.

Cultural Values The *cultural values* of the organization provide a context within which individual attitudes and behaviors are formed. Cultural values are shared among the members of a group and may offer a source of common meaning, identity, and cohesion for the members (Schein, 1985). Although cultural values can conflict with the individual values of group members, they are an important force in the valuation process. Some examples of cultural values include striving for excellence, service quality, risk taking, and human relationships (Badovick and Beatty, 1987; Wallach, 1983).

Role Values In addition to group cultural values, individuals may adopt *role values* that are unique to their job position or interpersonal role in the group (Badovick and Beatty, 1987; Kilpatrick, Cummings, and Jennings, 1963). Role values may differ from personal values and from other role values in a different group. For example, a person might value "getting recognition for my own work" in an industrial organization, but shun individual recognition in religious activities with his or her church.

As mentioned earlier, organizational choice processes may involve many diverse people playing several roles in customer choice: initiator, influencer, decider, purchaser, and user. Each of these roles may have different goals, needs, wants, and self-concepts, and thus different criteria for evaluating a product. The role of organizational "user" may also be differentiated according to the FATSUDS sequence of activities (finding, acquiring, transporting, storing, using, disposing of, and stopping). Each of these "use" activities may be engaged in by many diverse people in an organization. Simply knowing the technical specifications for products and services will not ensure that suppliers "provide value" to their organizational customers.

Thus, the questions of "who are the customers?" and "what value do they anticipate?" may yield several answers across the many individual faces of the organizational customer. Organizational processes for making choices will also vary across organizations and specific situations. For example, the buying situation may be described as either a *new task*, a *modified rebuy*, or a *straight rebuy* (Robinson, Faris, and Wind, 1967), as defined below:

- *New task*: The organization buys a product or service with which its members have practically no relevant buying experience. Considerable information is sought, and extensive effort is made to evaluate several alternatives.

- *Modified rebuy:* The organization buys a product or service that is intended to replace one they currently use. Since they are considering products or services other than the one now being used, information is gathered on these alternatives.
- *Straight rebuy:* The organization buys a product or service they have already bought often. The members of the organization may have considerable experience with the product and be so satisfied that they seek no information on alternatives. They simply reorder from the same supplier.

Further, some organizations may engage in "satisficing" on particular purchases, that is, spending little time analyzing alternatives, but simply and quickly picking anything that minimally meets requirements. Another organization may routinely use extensive analysis and procurement procedures.

A supplier must try to understand the specific valuation and choice processes of each customer organization: the bureaucracy, the politics, the social relations, and interpersonal dynamics, as well as the needs of various individual role players. Although the customer/supplier interface is much more complex when the customer is an organization, the general valuation process resembles that of individuals.

Abbreviated Attitude Formation

The above approach implies that attitude formation involves a lot of mental algebra and calculations for each available alternative, as if attitudes could be derived in an absolute sense, depicted with a numerical value.[17] In situations such as buying a car, where the number of product alternatives, attributes, benefits/sacrifices, and end-state "needs" is much greater, this approach seems beyond human capabilities.

Simplification of Mental Processing People often do not engage in all this information processing, particularly when they are very familiar with the product. Rather than form overall attitudes for each alternative, people often simplify the mental task of matching the product and their needs. Customers may translate the numerous specific product attributes into a smaller, and therefore more manageable, set of benefits and sacrifices which have meaning in relation to the primary desired end states (Clemons and Woodruff, 1992).

---

17. Consider what this would imply in even a simple situation: with only two product alternatives, each with attributes to consider, and with five benefits/sacrifices to consider, and two end-state "needs" to fulfill. That would entail many possible different belief combinations for these attributes, benefits/sacrifices, and needs.

Binary Decisions and Cutoffs   Customers may also reduce as many decisions as possible to simple binary decisions, yes or no, pass or fail. They may set cutoffs on key attributes to help them eliminate alternative products from consideration. For example, all cars that cost more than $10,000 may be eliminated from consideration. For all car models under $10,000, those which do not meet certain comfort, safety, fuel efficiency, or style criteria may be eliminated from consideration.

Prioritized Criteria   Once the alternatives are whittled down to a more manageable size, such as four models, the customer may further simplify the mental demands of attitude formation by determining which criteria are still important. For example, applying a fuel efficiency criterion of "better than 30 mpg" may mean that the chooser doesn't much care whether a car gets 33 mpg or 40 mpg. Further, the four models still being considered for choice may be perceived as relatively equal on safety. When there is no variation on a criterion, that criterion is of no further use in making the choice. The customer may now focus on style, and comfort, and price in forming his or her attitude toward buying and using the remaining alternatives. The customer may concentrate on making relative comparisons such as "this model is *more* comfortable than the others." Comparison judgments are often easier to make than absolute judgments. The application of these criteria and the attitude formation process are still very clearly related to customer needs, and in line with the means/ ends model.

Abbreviated Valuation Processes
Just as the attitude formation process may be abbreviated, so might the entire nine-step process of valuation listed earlier. Some of these shortcuts are discussed below.

The Effect of Familiarity and Involvement   Valuation processes can be quite simple in practice (Howard, 1977; Olshavsky and Granbois, 1979). The simple graphic in Figure 8 suggests two factors, *extent of involvement* and *familiarity with the product*, which might determine how extensive the customer's choice processes are. Extent of involvement refers to the personal significance that a product has in the customer's life. For example, cars, houses, and computers might tend to be considered high-involvement items, whereas candy bars, pencils, and toothbrushes might tend to be considered low-involvement items. Of course, individuals may differ in their levels of involvement with a product. Involvement is not a characteristic of the product or service, but a characteristic of the individual person in relation to the product or service (Cravens, Hills, and Woodruff, 1987; Assael, 1985).

   In general, less information processing will be required when a customer is more familiar with a product. The customer may already have engaged in the information search and mental processing (beliefs and

Figure 8

A classification of the extent of customer choice processing

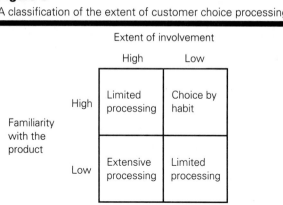

Extent of involvement

		High	Low
Familiarity with the product	High	Limited processing	Choice by habit
	Low	Extensive processing	Limited processing

Adapted from Cravens, Hills, and Woodruff (1987, p. 138).

evaluations). Alternatively, low familiarity requires the customer to engage in more extensive processing, particularly with high-involvement items. The customer engages in extensive processing to learn about the means/ends relationship, and establish the beliefs and evaluations necessary to form an attitude toward the alternatives.[18] For low-involvement items, the search process may be limited, even when the familiarity with the product is low. In such cases, people often engage in trial purchasing as a way of learning about the product. When the customer is highly familiar with a low-involvement item, such as chewing gum, it may be purchased out of habit, with virtually no information processing.

Learned Shortcuts These shortcuts do not invalidate the full valuation process. For example, even the biggest shortcut, habit buying, can be described in terms of the nine-step process. Habit or routinized buying still involves need recognition, for example, the anticipation of hunger at breakfast time which may prompt one to buy a favorite cereal when grocery shopping. However, the search for information about alternatives may be skipped. And since the means/ends relationship, beliefs, and evaluations are already well learned, and attitudes are already formed, all the customer must do is recognize the product on the shelf and select it. The chooser may even enact predetermined rules for choice (e.g., "when my old jeans wear out, I'll buy more Levi's"), particularly when he or she has a long-standing relationship with a supplier ("I always get haircuts from Linda").

---

18. There are exceptions that challenge this framework. For example, people often walk onto the sales lot of a car dealer or mobile home dealer and make high-involvement purchasing decisions that appear to be impulsive.

In habit buying, learning about the means/ends relationships occurred at an earlier time. Perhaps when the cereal was newly introduced and advertised, the customer became interested, investigated it, read the information on the box, and used it on a trial basis to learn more about the product. Once familiar with the product, and having reaffirmed product knowledge through repeated use, the customer doesn't have to engage in the mental processing to calculate the benefits and sacrifices in relation to his or her recognized need. He or she simply buys what works.

At some point, the chooser probably does engage in each of the nine valuation steps, although the engagements may be separated in time (as when one relies on the memory of last month's information search to make a choice today), and may vary in the amount of time devoted to each step. The order of the steps may even be altered, as in impulse buying, or when we encounter an innovative product, like the microwave oven. Need recognition occurs only after a person has encountered the product, perceived the attributes, and formed beliefs about the benefits and sacrifices. The mental calculations of beliefs and evaluations can occur very efficiently and outside the customer's consciousness. By contrast, the planned purchase of an important, expensive, nonroutine, unfamiliar product might entail conscientious execution of each valuation step.

Conditions for Extensive Valuation   In addition to the conditions of personal involvement and product familiarity, the valuation process may be more extensive (more deliberate, more effortful, more time consuming) when:

1. Many comparable alternatives exist
2. Many criteria must be considered in relation to multiple "needs"
3. There are tradeoffs among various criteria for each alternative (with potential for equal final results among alternatives), and relative comparisons cannot be directly made on each criterion
4. There is uncertainty about perceptions, beliefs, and/or evaluations, or some type of discomfort or lack of mastery which motivates attention to the choice process
5. There is conflict between rationality and emotionality, and/or between attitudes and subjective norms
6. Plenty of time is available
7. The benefits of extensive search outweigh the costs (such as price and opportunity loss)

The Influence of Norms on Choice (Intention to Buy)

Once attitudes and emotions are formed, by whatever process, the choice seems to be a simple matter of selecting the one alternative toward which one's attitude and emotions are most favorable. The choice seems to be a foregone conclusion, and quite simple on paper. As customers, sometimes our choices are easy and obviously correct to us, even when the stakes are high and the consequences highly important. However, at other times, even at the moment of choice, we agonize over it, reluctant to commit, perhaps because the differences between alternatives are very small, and there are tradeoffs among equally important criteria. We may also question the validity of our beliefs and evaluations. Such uncertainty makes us waver and reconsider our attitudes even at the moment of choice. In addition to our attitudes, another factor, subjective norms, can enter into the choice process to influence and complicate our choice.

The beliefs and evaluations that compose the attitude formation process are instrumental in nature, that is, concerned with fulfilling some goal, need, want, or self-concept. A person's intention to buy a product may also depend on beliefs and evaluations that are normative in nature, that is, concerned with what other people think should or should not be done. Although a person may hold certain normative beliefs, he or she may or may not be motivated to comply with any of these other people, which may depend on regard for the other person as a leader, role model, or expert. Normative beliefs and motivation to comply lead to normative pressures, the totality of which may be termed "subjective norm."[19] Along with attitudes, a person's subjective norms determine his or her intention to buy and use a product (Fishbein and Ajzen, 1975).

The introduction of subjective norms into a choice process can complicate one's decision, which otherwise might be clear and simple if based only on personal attitudes. Even at the moment of choice, some people will recap the choice process by writing down and reviewing the pros and cons of each alternative to help make the decision. Others will throw away the details and go with a "gut feeling." Some may even flip a coin when the differences between alternatives are slight. Whatever the case, the customer may eventually muddle through the moment of choice and then intend to purchase a particular product or service.

Purchase Behavior (Actual Buying)

As suggested by the FATSUDS sequence of activities, actually buying the product may be easier said than done. The would-be buyer may have difficulty with any one of the first three activities: finding, acquiring, and transporting. We have all had the experience of looking for something at the grocery store and not being able to find it. Customers can't buy what they can't find. Home Depot is fast becoming a household name as the largest retailer of do-it-yourself home-improvement products. Guaranteeing to beat any competitor's advertised price by 5 percent has helped Home Depot succeed; however, low pricing is just the tip of the iceberg. Home Depot makes the shopping experience enjoyable and more "valu-

---

19. The subjective norm seems to impact intentions in a way that goes beyond just the "instrumental" desire of gaining esteem, social acceptance, or favor among others. Sometimes it just seems to matter what other people think. Perhaps compelled to do the right thing, we accept the opinions of others in the belief that they have some special insight not accessible to us.

able" by staffing its stores with experienced tradespeople who give shoppers personal attention and help them select the product that fits their needs. At Home Depot, you might find a former electrician giving a shopper advice on how to rewire a light fixture, or you might find him delivering a free "how-to" clinic on rewiring for a group of interested patrons (Mason, 1992).

Problems with acquiring and transporting products may also impede one's intentions. For example, based on information in a mail-order catalogue, an expectant mother decided to buy a rocking chair through a local franchise. However, the local franchise had lost its fabric samples, so she couldn't place the order. It took the factory two months to send more samples, which was a month after the arrival of her baby. She bought another rocking chair elsewhere. Her original intention to acquire from the mail-order franchise was thwarted. In other special situations, such as ordering a product C.O.D. (collect on delivery) and industrial purchasing, delays in transporting a product can cause the customer to alter original intentions and to buy something else. The benefits and sacrifices of buying (e.g., finding and acquiring) help determine value and greatly impact repeat buying. Once a person successfully buys a product or service, he or she is then in a position to use it for its designed purpose.

Use Experience

The choice of a product or service involves anticipation of value. The use of a product or service, throughout all the FATSUDS activities, results in realization of actual value. The customer's use experiences involve some of the valuation activities discussed above: (1) encounter of physical cues, (2) perception of attributes and characteristics, (3) perception of use outcomes, and (4) formation of attitudes and emotions.

The realized value provides feedback to subsequent choice processes through learning. Customers may revise their expectations of value by altering both their beliefs and their evaluations of the consequences as either benefits or sacrifices, contributions or detractions. Further, their "needs" may change as a result of the product's use. For example, they may raise their goals and aspirations after having achieved former goals. Or they may lower their expectations because of poor performance of the product.

QUALITY IN ACTION: A MESSAGE TO THE STUDENT
Kenneth L. St. Cyr, Corporate Director, Apple Quality Management, Apple Computer, Inc.

To survive in the fast-paced computer industry, where fortunes seem to be made and lost overnight, a company must continuously improve to meet changing expectations for customer value. Corporate Director of Apple Quality Management Kenneth L. St. Cyr reveals how Apple Computer, Inc., is focusing on customer value as a strategy for competing in this dynamic industry.

Apple Computer has always had a reputation of having great, highly innovative products. When the personal computer industry was in its infancy, that alone was sufficient to propel Apple to the forefront of industry leadership.

But in recent years, both our customers and our competitors have told us that great products alone are not enough to be successful. All aspects of the customer experience—product, service, sales, and support—must be top notch in order for Apple (or anyone else) to succeed. Continuously and systematically improving these areas is essential. Even if you're number one today, the competition will see to it that you won't last long unless you're always improving.

Our total quality management journey, named Apple Quality Management (AQM), is built upon a fundamental belief that everything we do, every decision we make, is focused on exceeding customer expectations. As the personal computer industry has matured, so too has Apple Computer. We have rigorously employed quality management principles to reduce cycle time in product development, manufacturing, and administrative areas, improve product quality, reliability, and services, and achieve higher levels of customer satisfaction. Winning on the J. D. Powers Customer Satisfaction Survey in 1991 and again in 1992 reflects the results of that work.

Apple has been able to change (reinvent) itself as our customers' needs have changed and expanded. Using AQM principles, we've been able to effectively manage change to ensure that our customers' interests are continuing to be met. Customer satisfaction will continue to fuel our success into the 21st century.

▶ CUSTOMER VALUE STRATEGY

As we have seen, customer value is the combination of benefits and sacrifices that result as a consequence of a customer using a product or service to meet certain needs. The more closely a product matches the needs of the customer when it is used, the higher the customer value. Customer value affects customer choices prior to the use of a product, and determines postuse evaluations (satisfaction and dissatisfaction) and postuse behaviors (repeat purchasing, word-of-mouth advertising, and complaining). Over time, these evaluations and behaviors collectively determine the economic fate of organizations. Organizations cannot exist without customers, but providing the best customer value can achieve immense profitability (Narver and Slater, 1990). Thus, customer value is strategically important to every business.

Competing globally by providing superior customer value is an approach that has been touted for decades (Drucker, 1954; Webster, 1988; Narver and Slater, 1990). As a strategy it seems intuitively appealing, even obvious. However, the best way to achieve customer value is not so obvious. It may require managers to break new ground and deviate from the traditional rules of strategy and management (Hamel and Prahalad, 1989). To do so, they must first understand how their customers choose, use, and evaluate products. Having gained this understanding, they can then move on to choose the value to provide, strive to provide superior value in this realm, communicate the value to customers, and assess the delivery of value (Burns and Woodruff, 1990).

Every organizational activity should be directed toward customer value. For example, segmentation may suggest new customer groups, including customers who use a competitor's product and potential customers who are not currently using the product class. If done creatively, the manager formulating a customer value strategy may discover new market opportunities. The following examples illustrate how the concept of customer value can help revitalize demand for an organization's products.

Examples of Revitalized Demand

A company may serve customers by developing products and services in response to changing customer needs. For example, Stouffer's Lean Cuisine entrees fit American lifestyle trends, including growing concern for health and fitness, and less time spent on food preparation. Lean Cuisine offered nutritional, low-calorie meals, easy to prepare in a microwave or toaster oven, with attractive appearance, good taste, and a competitive price. The gourmet recipes appealed to sophisticated, young customers, and offered enough variety to encourage them to consume Lean Cuisine frequently. Sales of Lean Cuisine quickly reached $300 million (*Marketing News*, 1985).

A company may also please customers by innovating new products and services to meet stable, long-held customer needs. For example, by the mid-1980s, Yamaha had achieved 40 percent share in the piano market after years of persistent work. But demand started to dwindle by 10 percent a year. The market was saturated, with 40 million pianos in dens, living rooms, and concert halls around the world. With low-cost producers entering the market, it would have been easy for Yamaha managers to label the piano division a "dog" and divest quickly. However, Yamaha neither divested nor used one of the traditional approaches to retaining and gaining market share in head-to-head competition. (Traditional approaches include adding new models, buckling down, cutting costs, slicing overhead, and going upscale with luxury or specialty items.) Rather, Yamaha thought about the value customers might derive from the use of a piano. They achieved a broader view of the market, and thought in customer terms of providing "musical entertainment" and not simply in product terms of providing pianos. They recognized that more people were listening to music than ever before, and most people do not have the time to learn to play a piano. Then they recalled the idea of the player piano and incorporated optical technology to give it a pleasant sound. Unlike the old clunker in Grandma's parlor, the optical technology distinguishes ninety-two degrees of strength and speed of key touch, digitally records and reproduces keystrokes with great accuracy, and stores music on a 3.5-inch disk.

By equipping pianos with this technology, Yamaha has created a new product, the DiskLavier. Introduced in 1987, the DiskLavier enables people to invite Horowitz into their living room, practice the flute with piano accompaniment, transfer music over phone lines, and enjoy concerts through a mail-order club. Despite facing a stagnant market, Yamaha revitalized its business by creatively serving existing needs (Ohmae, 1988). By 1993, the DiskLavier contributed about 19 percent of Yamaha's profitability.

Managers must carefully consider whether to reinvest in or divest organizations that are serving stagnant markets. Some markets simply can't be revitalized. For example, with the arrival of the automobile, a buggy whip manufacturer had to anticipate declining demand in the early 20th century. Later, the carburetor manufacturer gave way to the maker of fuel injectors. Sometimes managers must shift resources to serve completely new markets. Other times they must shift resources to serve the same market in a different way. Miscalculation can transform valuable resources into useless inventory, like a shipload of wooden noses, and distract managers from more promising opportunities.

Implementing a Customer Value Strategy

The best way to ensure that customers choose your product or service is to provide more benefits and fewer sacrifices than competing alternatives. Start by selecting the right value to provide and create designs to serve *important* customer needs. Then provide the best value available by making products that conform to the design. To make "providing the best value" the *strategic intent* of the organization, managers must understand the phenomenon of customer value.

Concluding Comments

Managers must understand the concept of customer value. It provides a focus for strategic planning and continuous improvement efforts. It is the key to an organization's survival and prosperity. Managers must maintain relationships with customers for the purpose of market transactions. If managers provide customers with something they value, customers will continue to provide managers with the resources, primarily money, that sustain the organization's activities. The more value that managers provide customers, the more secure the relationship. The information provided in this chapter should help managers better understand the concept of customer value.

With this chapter, we have only initiated the understanding that managers must develop about customer value by providing a framework for further learning and some examples of how managers deal with customer value. The specific details required to understand specific customers and markets must be developed by managers themselves as they address strategic issues such as: What markets should the organization serve? What do customers in those markets value? How should the organization serve those markets? How should the organization measure its performance in serving those markets? Managers should use the concept of customer value as the guide to answering these questions.

▶ SUMMARY OF KEY POINTS

1. Customer value is the combination of benefits and sacrifices that results when a customer uses a product or service.
2. The degree of customer value is determined by how well product and service attributes and characteristics match the needs of customers.
3. Managers must carefully identify their customers in order to determine the value of their products and services.
4. Managers can understand the concept of customer value better and make better decisions if they understand the process through which customers derive value.
5. Customer value processes involve need recognition, information search, experience and use, perception, and attitude formation.
6. Sometimes the customer's valuation process is extensive and thoughtful. At other times, it is shortcutted and habitual.
7. Managers improve their strategic decisions when they consider the concept of customer value and clearly identify their customers and what those customers value.

▶ KEY TERMS

anticipated value	monetary value
attitudes	need
buyer value	realized value
cultural values	role values
customer value	segmentation
FATSUDS	use process
market segments	valuation process
mass market approach	value added
means/ends model	value chain

▶ DISCUSSION QUESTIONS

1. How is the concept of customer value different from the concept of quality?
2. Explain the importance of the means/ends model for strategic decision making.

3. How can organizations use the concept of customer value to direct their continuous improvement efforts?

▶ EXPERIENTIAL EXERCISE

- Describe a recent purchase experience in terms of the customer value processes described in this chapter. Note the shortcuts that you took in deciding what to purchase.

  Then list the benefits and sacrifices that you have realized as a result of purchasing and using the product or service. Map the use process according to the FATSUDS sequence to identify all the benefits and sacrifices associated with the broad use process.

  What market segment do you think you fit from the perception of the company that provided the product or service? Infer this from the match or mismatch of the product or service with your needs. How would you change their view of the market segment and the configuration of the product to better meet your needs? If the company responded to your input, how likely would it be that you would return to them for a repeat purchase?

▶ REFERENCES

K. Albrecht and L. J. Bradford, *The Service Advantage: How to Identify and Fulfill Customer Needs*, Dow-Jones Irwin, Homewood, Ill., 1990.

C. P. Alderfer, *Existence, Relatedness, and Growth: Human Needs in Organizational Settings*, Free Press, New York, 1972.

M. B. Arnold, *Emotion and Personality*, Vol. 1, *Psychological Aspects*, Columbia University Press, New York, 1960.

E. Aronson, *The Social Animal*, W. H. Freeman and Company, San Francisco, 1980.

H. Assael, *Marketing Management*, Kent Publishing, Boston, 1985.

G. J. Badovick and S. E. Beatty, "Shared Organizational Values: Measurement and Impact upon Strategic Marketing Implementation," *Academy of Marketing Science*, Vol. 15, No. 1, Spring 1987, pp. 19–26.

T. V. Bonoma, "Major Sales: Who Really Does the Buying?" *Harvard Business Review*, May-June 1982, p. 113.

G. M. Bounds and G. Dobbins, "Changing the Managerial Agenda," *Journal of General Management*, Vol. 18, No. 3, Spring 1993, pp. 77–93.

E. Brunswik, *The Conceptual Framework of Psychology*, University of Chicago Press, 1952.

M. J. Burns and R. B. Woodruff, "Value: An Integrative Perspective," *American Psychological Association Proceedings*, 1990.

E. R. Cadotte, R. B. Woodruff, and R. L. Jenkins, "Expectations and Norms in Models of Consumer Satisfaction," *Journal of Marketing Research*, Vol. 24, November 1987, pp. 305–314.

D. S. Clemons, *Expanding the Model of Consumer Satisfaction and Dissatisfaction: The Means-Ends Disconfirmation Model of CS/D*, a doctoral dissertation, Department of Marketing, Logistics, and Transportation, University of Tennessee, 1993.

D. S. Clemons and R. B. Woodruff, "Broadening the View of Consumer (Dis)Satisfaction: A Proposed Means-Ends Disconfirmation Model of CS/D," *American Marketing Association Winter Proceedings*, 1992.

D. W. Cravens, G. Hills, and R. B. Woodruff, *Marketing Management*, Irwin, Homewood, Ill., 1987.

F. W. Davis and K. B. Manrodt, "Service Logistics: An Introduction," *International Journal of Physical Distribution and Logistics Management*, Vol. 21, No. 7, 1991, p. 9.

P. F. Drucker, *The Practice of Management*, Harper & Brothers Publishers, New York, 1954.

M. Fishbein and I. Ajzen, *Belief, Attitude, Intention and Behavior: An Introduction to Theory and Research*, Addison-Wesley Publishing Company, Reading, Mass., 1975.

S. F. Gardial, D. S. Clemons, R. B. Woodruff, D. W. Schumann, and M. J. Burns, "The Structure of Evaluations: Contrasting Consumer's Pre-Purchase, Post-Purchase, and (Dis)Satisfaction Experiences," *Working Paper Series*, University of Tennessee, 1991.

J. Gutman, "A Means-End Chain Model Based on Consumer Categorization Processes," *Journal of Marketing*, Vol. 46, Spring 1982, pp. 60–72.

J. Gutman and S. D. Alden, "Adolescents' Cognitive Structures of Retail Stores and Fashion Consumption: A Means-End Chain Analysis of Quality," in Jacob Jacoby and Jerry C. Olson (eds.), *Perceived Quality*, Lexington Books, Lexington, Mass., 1985, pp. 99–114.

G. Hamel and C. K. Prahalad, "Strategic Intent," *Harvard Business Review*, May-June 1989, pp. 63–76.

K. G. Hardy, "Add Value, Boost Margins," *Business Quarterly*, Summer 1987, pp. 63–64.

J. L. Haskett, W. E. Sasser, Jr., and C. W. L. Hart, *Service Breakthroughs*, Free Press, New York, 1990.

D. R. Hausknecht, "Measurement Scales in Consumer Satisfaction/Dissatisfaction," *Journal of Consumer Satisfaction, Dissatisfaction and Complaining Behavior*, Vol. 3, 1990, pp. 1–11.

T. J. Hayes and C. B. Tathum, *Focus Group Interviews: A Reader*, American Marketing Association, 1989.

J. A. Howard, *Consumer Behavior: Application of Theory*, McGraw-Hill, New York, 1977.

C. E. Izard, *Human Emotions*, Plenum Press, New York, 1977.

R. M. Johnson, "Trade-Off Analysis of Consumer Values," *Journal of Marketing Research*, Vol. 11, May 1974, pp. 121–127.

L. Kahle, *Social Values and Social Change: Adaptation to Life in America*, Praeger, New York, 1983.

F. P. Kilpatrick, M. C. Cummings, and K. Jennings, *Source Book of a Study of Occupational Values and the Image of the Federal Service*, The Brookings Institution, Washington, D.C., 1964.

B. King, *Better Designs in Half the Time*, Goal/QPC, Methuen, Mass., 1987.

D. R. Lehmann and R. S. Winer, *Analysis for Marketing Planning*, 2d ed., Irwin, Homewood, Ill., 1991.

M. M. Lele and J. N. Sheth, *The Customer Is Key*, John Wiley & Sons, New York, 1987.

R. Levitt, "Marketing Myopia," *Harvard Business Review*, July-August 1984, pp. 45–56.

R. Levitt, *The Marketing Imagination*, Free Press, Glencoe, Ill., 1986.

D. Locker and D. Dunt, "Theoretical and Methodological Issues in Sociological Studies of Consumer Satisfaction with Medical Care," *Social Science and Medicine*, Vol. 12, July 1978, pp. 283–292.

"Manufacturers Undaunted by Failures in Quest for New Product Successes," *Marketing News*, Nov. 22, 1985, p. 17.

A. Maslow, *Motivation and Personality*, 2d ed., Harper & Row, New York, 1970.

J. Mason, "Value: The New Marketing Mania?" *Management Review*, May 1992, pp. 16–21.

J. A. Miller, "Studying Satisfaction, Modifying Models, Eliciting Expectations, Posing Problems, and Making Meaningful Measurements," in H. Keith Hunt (ed.), *Conceptualization and Measurement of Consumer Satisfaction and Dissatisfaction*, Marketing Science Institute, Cambridge, Mass., 1976, pp. 72–91.

J. B. Miner, *Theories of Organizational Behavior*, The Dryden Press, Hinsdale, Ill., 1980.

J. H. Myers and A. D. Shocker, "The Nature of Product-Related Attributes," *Research in Marketing*, Vol. 5, 1981, pp. 211–236.

J. C. Narver and S. F. Slater, "The Effect of Marketing Orientation on Business Profitability," *Journal of Marketing*, Vol. 54, October 1990, pp. 20–35.

K. Ohmae, "Getting Back to Strategy," *Harvard Business Review*, November–December 1988.

F. Olander, "Consumer Satisfaction—A Skeptic's View," in H. Keith Hunt (ed.), *Conceptualization and Measurement of Consumer Satisfaction and Dissatisfaction*, Marketing Science Institute, Cambridge, Mass., pp. 409–454.

R. L. Oliver, "Effect of Expectation and Disconfirmation on Postexposure Product Evaluations: An Alternative Interpretation," *Journal of Applied Psychology*, Vol. 62, August 1977, pp. 480–486.

R. L. Oliver, "A Cognitive Model of the Antecedents and Consequences of Satisfaction Decisions," *Journal of Marketing Research*, Vol. 17, November 1980, pp. 460–469.

R. L. Oliver, "Processing of the Satisfaction Response in Consumption: A Suggested Framework and Research Propositions," *Journal of Consumer Satisfaction, Dissatisfaction and Complaining Behavior*, Vol. 2, 1989, pp. 1–16.

R. L. Oliver and J. E. Swan, "Equity and Disconfirmation Perceptions as Influences on Merchant and Product Satisfaction," *Journal of Consumer Research*, Vol. 16, December 1989, pp. 372–383.

R. W. Olshavsky and D. H. Granbois, "Consumer Decision Making—Fact or Fiction?" *Journal of Consumer Research*, Vol. 6, September 1979, pp. 93–100.

J. C. Olson and P. Dover, "Disconfirmation of Consumer Expectations through Product Trial," *Journal of Applied Psychology*, Vol. 64, April 1979, pp. 179–189.

A. Parasuraman, V. A. Zeithaml, and L. L. Berry, "SERVQUAL: A Multiple-Item Scale for Measuring Consumer Perceptions of Service Quality," *Journal of Retailing*, Vol. 64, No. 1, Spring 1988, pp. 12–40.

W. S. Perkins and T. J. Reynolds, "The Exploratory Power of Values in Preference Judgments: Validation of the Means-End Perspective," *Advances in Consumer Research*, Vol. 15, 1988, pp. 122–126.

M. Porter, *Competitive Advantage: Creating and Sustaining Superior Performance*, Free Press, New York, 1985.

R. A. Rescorla, "Probability of Shock in the Presence and Absence of CS in Fear

Conditioning," *Journal of Comparative and Physiological Psychology*, Vol. 66, 1968, pp. 1–5.

M. Robert, "Market Fragmentation versus Market Segmentation," *Journal of Business Strategy*, Vol. 13, No. 5, September–October 1992, pp. 48–53.

P. J. Robinson, C. W. Farris, and Y. Wind, *Industrial Buying and Creative Marketing*, Allyn & Bacon, Boston, 1967, chap. 2.

M. Rokeach, *Beliefs, Attitudes, and Values*, Jossey-Bass, San Francisco, 1968.

M. Rokeach, *The Nature of Human Values*, Free Press, New York, 1973.

M. J. Rosenberg, "Cognitive Structure and Attitudinal Affect," *Journal of Abnormal and Social Psychology*, Vol. 53, 1956, pp. 367–372.

E. H. Schein, *Organizational Culture and Leadership*, Jossey-Bass, San Francisco, 1985.

J. E. Scott and L. M. Lamont, "Relating Consumer Values to Consumer Behavior: A Model and Method for Investigation," in *Increasing Marketing Productivity*, American Marketing Association, Chicago, 1973, pp. 283–288.

M. J. Sirgy, "A Social Cognition Model of Consumer Satisfaction/Dissatisfaction," *Psychology and Marketing*, Vol. 1, 1984, pp. 27–44.

R. A. Spreng and R. W. Olshavsky, "A Desires-as-Standard Model of Consumer Satisfaction: Implications for Measuring Satisfaction," *Journal of Consumer Satisfaction, Dissatisfaction, and Complaining Behavior* (forthcoming).

George Stalk, Jr., and Thomas M. Stout, *Competing against Time*. Free Press, New York, 1990.

E. C. Tolman, "Principles of Purposive Behavior," in S. Koch (ed.), *Psychology: A Study of a Science*, Vol. 2, McGraw-Hill, New York, 1959.

D. E. Vinson, S. E. Scott, and L. M. Lamont, "The Role of Personal Values in Marketing and Consumer Behavior," *Journal of Marketing*, Vol. 41, 1977, pp. 44–50.

V. H. Vroom, *Work and Motivation*, Wiley, New York, 1964.

E. J. Wallach, "Individuals and Organizations: The Cultural Match," *Training and Development Journal*, February 1983, pp. 29–36.

F. E. Webster, "The Rediscovery of the Marketing Concept," *Business Horizons*, May-June 1988, pp. 29–39.

R. A. Westbrook, "A Rating Scale for Measuring Product/Service Satisfaction," *Journal of Marketing*, Vol. 44, Fall 1980, pp. 68–72.

R. A. Westbrook and M. D. Reilly, "Value-Percept Disparity: An Alternative to the Disconfirmation of Expectations Theory of Consumer Satisfaction," in Richard P. Bagozzi and Alice M. Tybout (eds.), *Advances in Consumer Research*, Vol. 10, Association for Consumer Research, Ann Arbor, Mich., 1983, pp. 256–262.

R. A. Westbrook and R. L. Oliver, "The Dimensionality of Consumption Emotion Patterns and Consumer Satisfaction," *Journal of Consumer Satisfaction*, Vol. 18, June 1991, pp. 84–91.

R. B. Woodruff, E. R. Cadotte, and R. L. Jenkins, "Modeling Consumer Satisfaction Processes Using Experience-Based Norms," *Journal of Marketing Research*, Aug. 20, 1983, pp. 296–304.

V. A. Zeithaml, "Consumer Perceptions of Price, Quality, and Value: A Means-End Model and Synthesis of Evidence," *Journal of Marketing*, Vol. 52, 1988, pp. 2–22.

Ron Zemke, *The Service Edge*, New American Library, New York, 1989.

chapter **6**

Strategic Management and the Emerging Paradigm

> *What I propose is a system of "market in" in which consumer requirements are to be of utmost concern. In practical terms, I propose that manufacturers study the opinions and requirements of consumers, and take them into account when they design, produce, and sell their products. When developing a new product, a manufacturer must anticipate consumers' requirements and needs.*

> *Kaoru Ishikawa**

▶ CHAPTER OUTLINE

Chapter Overview

Introduction

The Growing Role of Strategic Management
Defining Strategy
Who Is Involved in Strategic Management?
The Emerging Paradigm and Strategic Management

Strategic Management of Customer Value

---

* K. Ishikawa and D. Lu, *What Is Total Quality Control? The Japanese Way*, Prentice-Hall, Englewood Cliffs, N.J., 1985, p. 45.

Defining the Business

Writing a Mission Statement
Vision Statement
Using Market Opportunity Analysis to Define the Business
Stakeholder Analysis
Corporate Values/Philosophy/Principles

External Analyses

Remote Environment Analysis
Industry Analysis
Competitor Analysis
Forecasting and Prioritizing the Opportunities and Threats

Internal Analysis

Performance Analysis
Function, Activity, and Process Analyses
Portfolio Analysis

Defining Key Problems and Strategic Issues

Root Problems versus Symptoms

Strategic Alternatives

Goals and Objectives
Long-Term Strategies
Competitive Strategy versus Cooperative Strategy
Evaluating Strategic Alternatives

Strategic Choice and Strategy Implementation

Annual Goals and Objectives
Action Plans and Policies
Leadership and Management
Systems and Structure
Organization Culture
Human Resource Management

Evaluation of Strategy Implementation

Summary of Key Points

Key Terms

Discussion Questions

Experiential Exercises

References

▶ CHAPTER OVERVIEW

The emerging paradigm is reshaping the way managers think about strategy and the process for managing long-term strategy formulation as well as short-term strategy implementation. This chapter provides a strategic management model focused on developing managers and organizations driven by customer needs. The process of strategic management must be grounded in managers' knowledge of and priority on customer value, development of consensus on goals and objectives, and their focus on improving value-creating systems and employees. Before introducing the emerging strategic management model, we define the various concepts of strategy. Under the emerging paradigm, the most important strategy for a firm to specify is its long-term approach for discovering, creating, and improving customer value. This value-based strategy must be developed in concert with and drive managers' choice of long-term goals and generic, grand, and operating strategies that focus the entire organization on total quality, comprehensive excellence, and customer satisfaction. All corporate, business, and functional-level strategies support the firm's strategy for providing value to clearly defined target market segments.

▶ INTRODUCTION

How do successful managers determine the long-term direction of their company and make that direction a reality? What role did managers play in the success of such firms as Wal-Mart, Apple, Ford, Toyota, and Honda? Although many controllable and uncontrollable factors help determine performance, management process and leadership play key roles in any situation. For example, in a comparison of U.S. and Japanese auto firms, researchers found that managers' activities were the major source of productivity differences (Lieberman, Lau, and Williams, 1990). One of the key management activities in the emerging paradigm is strategic management.

The Growing Role of Strategic Management

As Figure 1 shows, planning approaches include simple annual budgeting, forecast-based planning, externally oriented planning, and comprehensive strategic management (Gluck, Kaufman, and Wallach, 1982). As managers found themselves in ever more complex and turbulent environments in the 1960s, their internally oriented, reactive approach gave way to an open systems view that required more external analysis and planning. By the 1980s, strategic management evolved from long-range planning by addressing strategy implementation as well as strategy formulation. Today, managers practicing strategic management attempt to create their organization's future. To do so, they must analyze both the internal and external situations in a well-defined strategic framework, and develop and manage

Figure 1

Types of planning

	Financial	Forecast-based	Externally oriented	Strategic management
Value system	Meet budget	Predict future	Think strategically	Create the future
Timeframe	Annual	Multiyear	Multiyear	Long-term
Components	Functional analysis	Gap analysis	Situation analysis Competitive analysis	Well-defined strategic framework
	Annual budget	Pro forma financial statements	Alternative evaluation	Strategic thinking
				Coherent reinforcing management processes
				Negotiated objectives
				Progress reviews
				Incentives
				Supportive value system and climate

F. Gluck, S. Kaufman, and A. S. Wallach, "The Four Phases of Strategic Management," *Journal of Business Strategy*, Vol. 2, Winter 1982, pp. 9–21.

value-creating processes and organizational cultures. The focus on customer value becomes the basis for strategic management.

Today, *strategic management* is the process managers use to formulate and implement strategies for providing the best customer value that will achieve the mission of the organization. Strategic management includes the analysis and major long-term decisions of strategy formulation as well as the short-term actions that implement the strategy through integrated annual action plans, policies, corporate culture, and ongoing attention to strategy and systems. While all managers should think and act strategically, most managers cannot dedicate their time solely to long-range planning. As owners of key processes, their role is to develop and improve these processes in relation to the other systems of the organization to create value and improve the organization's capabilities.

Although strategic management has generally improved firm performance (Rhyne, 1986; Fredrickson, 1984), even this modern approach has sometimes failed to satisfy customers and stakeholders as global competition has emerged (Pearson, 1992). During the 1970s and 1980s, Japanese firms changed the competitive front and the determinants of success in many industries by making quality a strategic imperative. Now, to compete in Europe, firms must meet the requirements of International Standards Organization (ISO-9000), a series of operating standards for products, services, quality systems, etc., that managers use to standardize quality systems throughout their firms.

These changes have made managers at all levels of many profit, not-for-profit, private, public, manufacturing, and service organizations increasingly aware of the strategic importance of relentless quality improvement. In the last few years, many of the principles of quality management overlapped or replaced principles of management and strategic management (Little, 1992; Schonberger, 1992). For example, popular concepts of customer satisfaction, continuous improvement, benchmarking, cycle time, and teamwork are closely related to strategic concepts such as mission, objectives, environmental analysis, strategic choice, motivation, and corporate culture. These emerging principles (Kiernan, 1993) have focused managers on a new management paradigm involving leadership, organizational learning, core competences, firm architecture, and time-based strategy.[1]

The emerging paradigm emphasizes continuous improvement of customer value in every aspect of strategy formulation and implementation. Improving customer value requires a cross-functional approach to learning what is and will be valued, designing value, producing value, and improving the value-creating and delivering systems. Thus, continuous improvement of customer value becomes the basis for the firm's overall strategy.

Defining Strategy

There are many ways of looking at strategy,[2] and managers typically engage in several types of strategic formulation. As used in business, *grand strategy* refers to a firm's coordinated and sustained efforts to achieve its long-term goals. For example, Wal-Mart's grand strategy has relentlessly pursued market penetration and market development. Although grand strategy refers more to top managers' deliberate, intended plan of action, a grand strategy can usually be inferred from the pattern of managers' activities in an organization. Specific grand strategies to grow, maintain, and retrench are described later in this chapter.

A firm's grand strategy helps define an overall approach to growth, but it does not necessarily reflect the most fundamental basis on which an organization competes. The concept of *generic strategy* refers to achieving either the lowest total delivered cost or a highly differentiated offering with either a broad or narrow market focus (Porter, 1980). There are four generic strategies: broad low-cost, broad differentiation, focused low-cost, and focused differentiation. According to Porter, using one of these strategies can enable a firm to achieve superior competitive position and sustainable competitive advantage, while being "stuck in the middle" of an industry with no clear advantage lowers performance. For example, Wal-Mart's

---

1. Also see IBM Case, Figure 7, "The Quality Journey," for illustration of paradigm changes over time.
2. Since Chandler (1965) first applied the concept of strategy to business, various approaches have defined strategy as an overall plan, as a pattern of activity in an organization, as the position of a firm in a competitive environment, or simply as the perspective or character of an organization (Mintzberg and Quinn, 1991). Following Mintzberg and Waters (1985), who distinguished realized (probably emergent) strategy as more important than a firm's intended, deliberate plan, Thompson and Strickland (1992) defined *strategy* as "the pattern of organizational moves and managerial approaches used to achieve organizational objectives and pursue the organization's mission."

growth in discount retailing is based on broad low-cost through superior distribution, inventory management, and employee involvement. Nordstrom's has differentiated its upscale department stores with unmatched personal service. The Limited stores target specific niches with low-cost, trendy fashions. On the other hand, Sears has found itself stuck between the large discounters, specialty stores, and upscale department stores. The best-performing firms often achieve both low-cost and differentiation through highest relative quality and other factors (Galbraith and Schendel, 1983; Miller, 1987). These results are consistent with many experts' prescriptions concerning quality improvement as the most important source of competitive advantage (Deming, 1986; Imai, 1986; Ishikawa, 1985).[3]

Specifying the grand and generic strategies is only part of the manager's approach to the market. As part of their competitive strategy, managers in every firm have an implicit value strategy. A value strategy is the pattern of decisions and actions that constitute the firm's overall approach toward providing realizable net value to customers. But when managers focus on continuously improving customer satisfaction, they need more than an unintended, implicit value strategy. As Deming (1986) suggested, this strategy should be explicit and grounded in the mission and culture of the firm. This becomes a customer *value-based strategy*. A value-based strategy directs managers to take responsibility for (1) delivering products/ services that provide best value for defined needs, and (2) creating strategic systems to continuously improve that value and satisfy the obligations of the enterprise (Carothers and Adams, 1991). Generic strategy specifies the firm's emphasis on cost or differentiation. Grand strategy specifies how the firm will develop its market, grow, or retrench. The explicit value strategy identifies which customer needs and dimensions of value the firm will satisfy. Thus, the complete statement of a firm's overall strategy will include an internally consistent combination of its value-based strategy, generic strategy, and grand strategy.

Wal-Mart, Disney, Lincoln Electric, Motorola, and the leading Japanese car makers provide familiar examples of value-based strategies in which all systems are designed to maximize and improve customer satisfaction. Wal-Mart retains Sam Walton's stated intent to continuously improve customer value with everyday low prices on name brands to an ever-expanding market. Disney's films, theme parks, and consumer goods provide best-value family entertainment. Lincoln Electric has continuously improved quality and lowered the cost of its electric arc welders, the finest in the world. Motorola continuously improves the value of its cellular phones by making them smaller, reducing their cost, and improving performance.

---

3. Achieving best quality by statistical management of systems and empowerment of people often results in lowest delivered cost as redesign, scrap, rework, field failures, and customer complaints are eliminated. Further, superior quality leads to repeat purchases and differentiation based on customer satisfaction. The combination of lowest delivered cost and highest quality, of course, usually provides best value to consumers when pricing is based on cost.

Japanese car makers have gone beyond basic quality requirements (*atari-mae hinshitsu*—"taken for granted") to design cars that fascinate and delight customers (*miryokuteki hinshitsu*—"things gone right") (Woodruff, 1990). World-class Japanese firms (*kaisha*) provide best value with synergistic combinations of knowledge-based strategies, alliances, and productivity-based strategies (Smothers, 1990). These are sequentially deployed to penetrate and develop markets.

Who Is Involved in Strategic Management?

All managers and many line employees at the corporate, business, and functional levels in an organization help formulate and implement strategy. The top executives of every organization are ultimately responsible for the organization's performance. They usually make most of the key decisions about overall direction and allocate resources to achieve the key goals. Middle managers and employees in each business unit must identify and satisfy market needs effectively and efficiently by formulating their own strategies in a manner consistent with the organization's goals, building capability and integrating their efforts. Functional and department-level managers and employees must implement the business strategies efficiently. Gaining the employee commitment required for successful implementation generally happens either through visionary, exemplary leadership or through iterative participation in strategy formulation among all levels. In small firms, where the corporate and business levels overlap, key personnel play a larger role in both strategy formulation and implementation.

The Emerging Paradigm and Strategic Management

In the emerging paradigm, managers base strategy on continuously improving customer value.[4] Many of the principles for implementing this approach may apply universally to all organizations and settings (Schonberger, 1992). Results from 320 studies showed that improving key customer value variables such as product/service quality, R&D, and social responsibility nearly always enhanced profitability, growth, and financial stability[5] (Capon, Farley, and Hoenig, 1990). International research on quality practices indicates that explaining the strategic plan to employees, customers, and suppliers; improving and simplifying production and development processes; and shortening cycle times consistently benefit every organization (Fuchsberg, 1992b). But some quality practices such as benchmarking may be helpful only to firms with good leaders who know how

---

4. Many managers think their situation is unique. Other managers believe in a set of universal principles (e.g., BCG learning curve or PIMS market share "laws"). In the contingency approach, the current framework for strategy (Hofer, 1975), the appropriateness of a given strategy depends on the organization's competitive setting as defined by customer type (consumer vs. industrial), purchase frequency, stage of product life cycle, dollar importance to customer, technological change, and product differentiation (Hambrick and Lei, 1985).
5. Relative price and marketing expense were not significant.

to use such advanced techniques. Thus, an explicit value-based strategy focused on customer value may be required, but the actual implementation process may depend on organizational size and competitive position. In short, the emerging paradigm enhances the strategic management process by focusing managers on customer needs. Customer value, as the central driving force for strategic management, is a necessary condition for success. Since maximizing customer value requires total organizational commitment to excellence, quality, and satisfaction for all stakeholders, customer value may also be a sufficient organizing strategy for many firms.

▶ STRATEGIC MANAGEMENT OF CUSTOMER VALUE

Traditionally, the strategic management process has attempted to answer four basic questions: Who are we? Where are we now? Where do we want to be? How are we going to get there?[6] Most models of the process take a broad view of stakeholders, and are competitor-driven rather than customer-oriented. This chapter introduces a customer value-based model of strategic management (see Figure 2). With the focus on customer value, the basic questions change: For what customer need do we take responsibility? How can we provide best value to satisfy that need? and What can we expect in return? Given an organization in a complex environment, the strategic management process includes eight activities:

1. Defining the business in terms of management's vision, philosophy, values, and goals for meeting specified customer needs.
2. Assessing external opportunities and threats to improving customer value.
3. Assessing internal value capabilities, resourcefulness, and weaknesses.
4. Defining a key problem and strategic issues from the environmental analyses.
5. Identifying strategic alternatives in terms of long-term objectives and grand strategies.
6. Choosing one of the strategic alternatives.
7. Developing annual objectives, allocating resources, and implementing short-term plans.
8. Monitoring and improving customer value and value-providing systems.

In the following discussion, we look more closely at how managers can focus the strategic management process on creating value for the customer

---

6. There are at least three views of strategic management, none of which focus explicitly on customer needs. Linear flowchart models picture a *rational, analytical* approach to management decision making. The *intuitive/inductive* approach emphasizes less analytical, more informal and incremental decision making (Mintzberg and Quinn, 1990). In the *political/behavioral* approach, power and influence form the basis for decision making (Cyert and March, 1963).

Figure 2
Strategic management process model

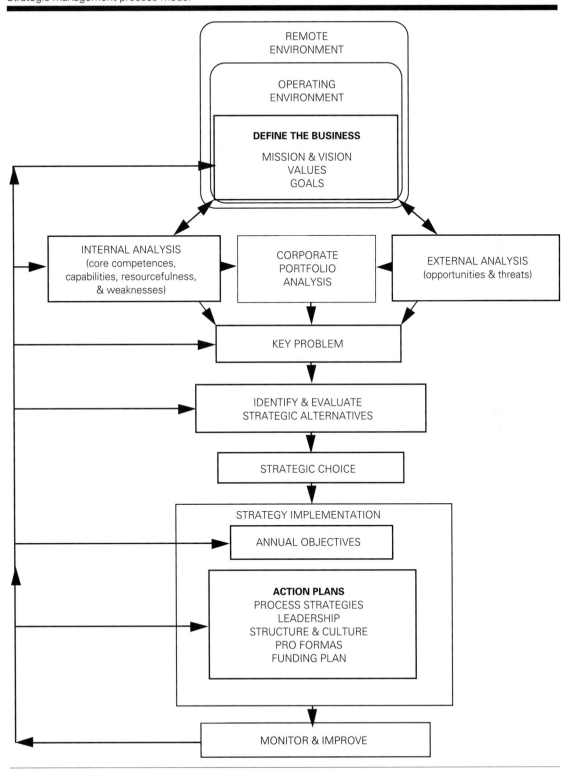

at each of these steps. Both customer value and continuous improvement begin with defining the business in terms of customer needs.

▶ DEFINING THE BUSINESS

Three things taken together provide the basic motivation for all employees and help focus efforts and resources on customer satisfaction: *mission or vision, corporate values and philosophy,* and *long-term goals.* The *mission* should describe the organization's current purpose in terms of what the organization will do over the near term. This statement should set the organization apart from those serving the same customer need. A *vision* statement outlines what purpose managers want the organization to serve over the long term and what the organization should become. Some organizations have both, some one or the other; only rarely does either include financial aspects. Mission and vision statements focus management efforts and provide the most basic, unifying logic for all stakeholders. *Corporate values and philosophy* state the principles that guide how the organization will do business. *Long-term goals* specify broad directions managers will take to fulfill the mission.

Writing a Mission Statement

Mission statements, especially those at the business level, define the domain and intent of the firm's activities. The mission outlines the *specific need* the firm's product or service meets, the *market* served, and the *technology* used to meet the needs of that market. A one-sentence statement should specify what customer need managers take responsibility for satisfying, who has this need, where these customers are, and how the need is served. The mission may also state the firm's customer value position or intent in terms of relative quality and price. In some firms, top management may define the business in terms of the firm's *core products, core technologies,* or *core competences* (Prahalad and Hamel, 1990; Reimann, 1992).

A *core product* is simply the product or service that the customers value most. A core product may be a key component which is protected by patent or proprietary position. Core products often carry the largest gross margin. A *core competence* is a distinctive competence that is a key means of providing value because it adds to the perceived benefits that customers value in the end product. The competence makes many more markets accessible, and it is usually difficult to imitate. For example, Wal-Mart's success is based on the core competences of logistics and human resource management. A *core technology* (also called core capability later in the chapter) is that combination of know-how, hardware, and software that is the basis of a core competence. The 3M company focuses on its core technologies in coatings and adhesives to make 50,000 different products; perhaps its greatest core competence is innovation management. Lincoln Electric defines itself in terms of a core product, the best electric arc welders in the world, but its leadership is based on the core competence of employee motivation.

▼

QUALITY IN ACTION: A MESSAGE TO THE STUDENT
Robert J. Kohler, Vice President and General Manager, TRW Avionics and Surveillance Group

In addition to automotive products and information systems, TRW produces an array of products for the space and defense industry, such as spacecraft, security systems, space communications, and electronic sensors. Facing a declining space and defense market, TRW has learned it must make dramatic changes in these parts of its organization. Incrementalism is not adequate. Vice President and General Manager Robert J. Kohler suggests that to transform TRW and make it viable, TRW managers must identify and focus on the core competences that are transferable to new markets.

My organization is involved in one of the greatest market shakeouts in history: we are in the defense business. The market is shrinking rapidly; the industry is drastically restructuring itself; and all of us in this industry are trying to find, create, and/or invent new lines of business for our organizations. Yet even while the defense market is shrinking, it is still a huge market. For a long time to come, the U.S. government will spend in excess of $200 billion on defense. So how to exist in our current market while inventing new markets in which to participate becomes a significant challenge.

But it is not as simple as finding new markets, and much of what we know or have learned from the past is simply irrelevant for us today. As we try to re-create ourselves, we have learned several lessons which I want to share with you. Speed of decision making is essential. The standard process of carefully thought-out and laborious strategic planning is no longer applicable. It is not that careful thought is irrelevant, it is simply that speed is mandatory. Further, it is important to create the future from the future and not from the past. Typical strategic planning is an extrapolation from the past, and, when you are trying to create a future that you currently cannot predict, it can only be done from the future.

To create the future, it is important to know your organization very well. This means understanding what the organization's core competences and core "incompetences" are. Where defense organizations have failed in the past, and will fail in the future, is trying to get into businesses for which they have no core competence. In our organization, for example, we concluded that one of our core competences was system engineering and system integration. This is a skill transferable to non-defense opportunities such as Intelligent Vehicle Highway Systems (IVHS)—a new emerging market.

You also need to understand those skills your organization has that are core competences and are actually harmful to doing something new. (I call these core incompetences.) For example, defense firms have developed a core competence in dealing with the U.S. defense establishment—understanding the rules, accounting systems, etc. The problem is that this way of doing business is actually detrimental to entering commercial markets.

But it can be done. The challenge is to be willing to change the organization to the degree and speed required. Total Quality Management has received considerable publicity and, in some quarters, is seen as the management system to save U.S. industry. Advocates of TQM usually emphasize the importance of continuously improving through small incremental steps. Such continuous improvement is not bad, but it is just not the solution to the problems that the defense industry faces. Incremental improvement is terrific if you are in a business that is "continuous" and susceptible to "improvement." We are in a business which is in a state of "discontinuity" and requires dramatic "transformation." In this setting, the leader must encourage breakthroughs in the organization and challenge the people to accomplishments that cannot be predicted. This requires a way of managing, leading, and involving our people that we have not done before. It is enrolling and empowering as opposed to manipulating and controlling.

In the end, I suspect that we in the defense sector are not really unique. All markets are susceptible to dramatic change and displacement. Any organization, to be successful over the long haul, must be willing to understand itself very well and challenge all of its basic assumptions about how to do business.

Although many formal mission statements specify these core dimensions, they often do not set the firm apart. Also, because these statements are often too long to be remembered, most fail to inspire employees. Highly successful firms have a simple purpose, to be the best at serving a particular need or to achieve one clear, simple goal (Pearson, 1992). For example, Xerox has assumed responsibility for being The Document Company. Management's single-minded purpose must be specific and competitively significant. In guiding their own and their employees' behaviors, managers cannot afford to ignore the practical significance of a concise, focused mission or vision statement. The challenge is to write a mission statement that is broad enough to facilitate growth yet narrow enough to focus the organization on what it does best.

Vision Statement

If a mission statement merely describes the current scope of activities without conveying a sense of opportunity, it may not engage managers or employees. The CEO must then lead by also articulating a vision of what is possible and desirable. A clear vision explicitly identifies management's strategic intent for the firm in terms of which needs will be satisfied and the scale on which it will be done. *Strategic intent* is management's "sustained obsession to achieve global leadership [in a specified market] at all levels" (Hamel and Prahalad, 1989). In terms of core competence, this intent means world leadership in design and development of a particular class of product or service functionality. For core products, the intent means dominant share of world manufacturing. This vision must be simple and compelling, certainly challenging, practicable, and realistic. Managers must internalize, articulate, and spread the vision. The following ten questions may help a manager to determine if an organization is vision-driven.

1. Do you have a simply defined but compelling "ideal state"?
2. Do you have vision "apostles"?
3. Have you fully thought through converting vision into a value-based strategy?
4. Have you connected the vision to outflanking your competitors?
5. Have you identified the skills and knowledge necessary to achieve the vision?
6. Are you conducting widespread training and education?
7. Have you linked managerial systems to the vision?
8. Are you displaying "constructive impatience"?
9. Are you advertising your vision?
10. Are you campaigning for the vision? (adapted from Brown, 1992)

Using Market Opportunity Analysis to Define the Business

Managers wanting to define or refocus their firm's mission and vision on current or potential customers' needs, wants, and values need to use a systematic approach to market segmentation. Market opportunity analysis (MOA) is a formal methodology that assesses macroenvironmental trends, customers, competitors, and distribution channels in order to focus on the needs of a market segment. Finalizing an organizational mission or vision is usually a learning process among managers and employees. The task is to agree on a fairly short, simple statement that everyone internalizes. The process usually begins with the top management team. An outside facilitator is often necessary to ensure equal airtime, to question assumptions, and to play devil's advocate. Managers often realize quickly that they do not know enough about their market to define their customers' needs nor do they have enough competitor intelligence to be able to set their firm apart. Market opportunity analysis provides a framework for this effort.

As shown in Figure 3, MOA helps managers understand what various customers value in a current or proposed product or service, what drives their purchase and use behavior, and what competitors will offer, so that the managers can evaluate opportunities for growth (Cravens, Hills, and Woodruff, 1987). The goals of the analysis are to define the aggregate market; then, to segment that market into groups with similar needs, benefits, or experiences in various usage situations; and finally, to determine which of the segments the managers intend to serve. Thus, MOA offers a systematic process for clarifying the basic purpose of the organization.

Given an opportunity idea, managers first define the structure of the market by drawing a product-market hierarchy. For example, Figure 4 shows the structure and rivals in the market for home monitoring services with two groups, latchkey children and the homebound elderly. Starting from the basic customer need underlying the opportunity (monitoring), a market hierarchy breaks down a *generic class* of products or services (monitoring services) into specific *product types*, then further into the various *brands* that are direct competitors within each product type. The

Figure 3

Market opportunity analysis

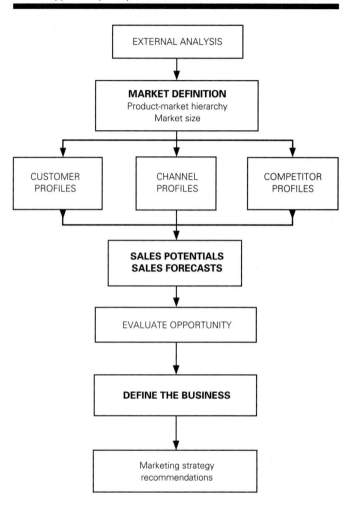

Adapted from Cravens, Hills, and Woodruff (1987), Chap. 4.

generic class consists of all the different product or service types that can meet the need. The various customer needs and behaviors within this generic class form the first basis for segmentation into distinct product types. In Figure 4, the types fall into three groups with similar needs based on the type and timing of contact. These types are further divided by the type of assistance required. Finally, within each product type, further segmentation usually occurs at the brand level as each competitor attempts to appeal to one or more unique groups of customers with a homogeneous need.

Figure 4

Segments within the product market hierarchy for home monitoring services

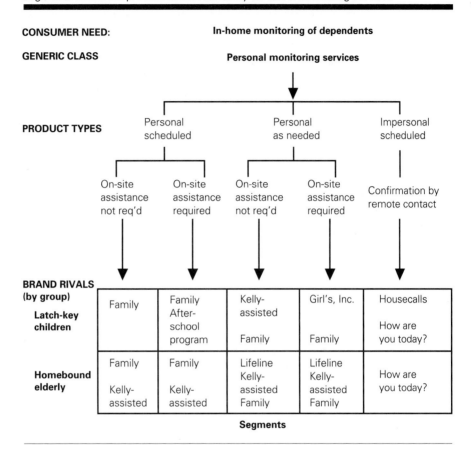

CONSUMER NEED: **In-home monitoring of dependents**

GENERIC CLASS   **Personal monitoring services**

PRODUCT TYPES	Personal scheduled		Personal as needed		Impersonal scheduled
	On-site assistance not req'd	On-site assistance required	On-site assistance not req'd	On-site assistance required	Confirmation by remote contact

BRAND RIVALS (by group)					
Latch-key children	Family	Family After-school program	Kelly-assisted Family	Girl's, Inc. Family	Housecalls How are you today?
Homebound elderly	Family Kelly-assisted	Family Kelly-assisted	Lifeline Kelly-assisted Family	Lifeline Kelly-assisted Family	How are you today?

Segments

Managers should decide the particular customer group and need they will serve. The hierarchy should reflect the structure of the market and provide managers with the full competitive context. Managers must avoid defining the product-market hierarchy and market segments with general demographic (age, income, etc.) or technology variables until after the market has been segmented on benefits the customers want or the customers' situation. Otherwise, managers and employees become disconnected from specific customer needs and behaviors. Segments based on general demographics or product similarity can also disguise competitors that offer alternative ways of satisfying those needs. Managers enhance their customer focus as they come to understand the benefits customers seek, their decision-making process for buying and using the firm's offering, and the situation in which customers realize these benefits.

Customers' behaviors include recognizing a problem and the need for a solution, searching for information and alternatives, evaluating alternatives, choosing and purchasing a solution, and dealing with any out-comes resulting from use of the product or service. If segments do not differ on at least one of these behaviors, on the benefits customers seek, or in the situations in which they use the product, then the segments are not different in a way useful to the firm. Thus, a target market must be an actionable segment, i.e., an opportunity to provide better value which offers the minimum volume necessary to serve the segment and reach the firm's objectives. Developing a company-wide understanding of the sacrifices that customers must make to use the product also improves customer orientation. Thus, managers can usually strengthen their organization's mission by developing complementary services that minimize customers' total sacrifice (to acquire, use, and dispose of the product) across all steps in their process of satisfying the need. Along with identifying customer needs, managers must also analyze the firm's key stakeholders as described below.

Stakeholder Analysis

The purpose and goals of a firm represent the consensus of all those who have a stake in the organization. The major stakeholders are usually categorized into two groups. *Internal stakeholders* include those with a direct financial interest in the firm: managers, stockholders, and employees (or members). *External stakeholders* include customers, suppliers, creditors, competitors, unions, regulators, government, social activists, and the communities in which the firm operates. Managers must balance the interests of all stakeholders to optimize organizational effectiveness (Anderson, 1982). Essentially, the long-term achievement of any single group's goals, especially stockholders or employees, depends on optimizing the results for all groups. Although strategic management models usually include stakeholder analysis as a key step in defining the business, few models prescribe which stakeholders are most important.[7]

The emerging paradigm requires that managers and employees put customers first on the list of stakeholders, because the value perceived by customers is the ultimate source of all opportunities to create new wealth. Managers must know what customers value, provide the best net value available, and continuously improve that value. After customers, the employees are next in importance. Stockholders and managers may benefit most over the long run when all internal stakeholders are focused on serving customers' needs. Firms are unlikely to achieve global leadership without this constant focus on the customer. Firm performance and stockholder gains are positively related to a firm's customer and market orientation (Narver and Slater, 1990). For example, Sony emphasizes creating benefits for customers, the company, and ultimately, the communities in which it operates, even if this does not maximize short-term profits. To

---

7. Some models for stakeholder analysis suggest methods for determining stakeholder strength and power (Daft, 1986).

enhance a customer-driven mission, managers often develop statements of corporate values.

QUALITY IN ACTION: A MESSAGE TO THE STUDENT

Masaki Morita, Former Chairman, Sony Corporation of America, Current Chairman and CEO, Sony Life Insurance, Ltd.

Sony Corporation is one of the premier consumer electronics firms in the world. Historically, Sony has used the strategy of trading short-term profits for long-term investment to serve customers and communities. Masaki Morita, former Chairman, Sony Corporation of America, explains how this principle has been formalized in Sony's policies and business practices.

Sony has a basic production policy, which I call our "3C Policy." This policy emphasizes creating benefits for our customers, our company, and ultimately, the communities in which we operate.

Our first priority is our customers. By making existing products close to our customers, we can quickly respond to their needs and given them the greatest benefit. We do our utmost to apply state-of-the-art manufacturing techniques and production technologies to the manufacturing process. By doing so, we can create reliable, quality products at a reasonable price and deliver them in a timely fashion. When our customers benefit, we increase sales and gradually generate profits.

Our second priority is to give benefits to our company. We generate profits so we can allocate resources effectively for the future. We make the greatest efforts to establish a good working environment and encourage our employees to develop their own abilities and creativity to the fullest extent. We also try very hard to build a positive corporate image, which attracts the most talented people to our company. With many motivated and capable people, we raise our technological potential to its highest level, ensuring future growth. If we become profitable with strong products and a positive corporate image by realizing our first and second priorities of benefitting our customers and company, then we will be capable of serving the community effectively.

Thirdly, good corporate citizenship has become an increasingly important part of Sony's business in America. To become a good corporate citizen, we pursue another policy to develop local suppliers and focus on environmental issues. Let me give a short example that illustrates our "3C" policy. We built a color television factory in San Diego, California, in 1972, when the exchange rate did not favor such a decision. In fact, many American companies—some that perhaps put only their immediate benefits and their profit first—had begun to invest in overseas manufacturing plants or were already receiving finished products from Asian suppliers.

While the San Diego plant produced high-quality products, manufacturing was not cost-effective at startup. Why then did Sony invest? Because Trinitron televisions were selling well in this country and we wanted to locate production within one of our main markets. We knew we had to be close to our customers to better meet their needs. Our decision was based solely on long-term growth goals and overall corporate strategies.

After years of hard work, our San Diego plant now produces over 1.8 million picture tubes and finished sets per year. Eighty percent of the material used in our picture tubes is sourced in the U.S. Currently, approximately 8,000 Americans are employed in Sony's ten factories and three R&D centers. Our local production totals about $1.6 billion in goods. Of this production, approximately $400 million of goods were exported.

Sony still faces many difficulties promoting local production. If we think only in terms of initial manufacturing costs, perhaps Sony should increase production in Asia. But that would be contrary to our philosophy, implemented in this country for over twenty years, of making products where we sell them. So we are striving to strengthen our U.S. manufacturing operations with our conviction to pursue manufacturing investments based on long-term growth goals and overall strategies. In spite of the many difficulties we face, we are committed to manufacturing in this country.

Corporate Values/Philosophy/Principles

The goals, strategy, and culture of an organization develop out of manager and employee values concerning the way their organization does business. Top managers usually have the greatest influence on the firm's values. Many successful older firms retain and promote the personal values of their founders. Because employees often treat their customers the way managers treat them, managers must explicitly and briefly state their relevant values as corporate values, philosophy, or principles. Many managers now document their corporate values concerning individual worth, social and environmental responsibility, innovation, safety, excellence, teamwork, etc. (Pearce and David, 1987). For example, Wheeling-Pittsburgh Steel Corp. has given each employee a one-page copy of twelve principles concerning quality, low-cost/high-quality production (see box for the first two principles), ethics, safety and health, employees' opportunity to contribute, drugs and alcohol, capital investment, processes improvements, compliance with laws, fiduciary duty, dividends, and community involvement.

Andrall Pearson, former CEO of Pepsico, suggests that many organizations suffer from a values gap, "the pervasive difference between what the

---

Wheeling-Pittsburgh Steel Corporation

Mission Statement

Our mission is to strive for excellence and prosperity for the mutual benefit of our customers, stockholders, employees, and communities. We are dedicated to being a progressive, integrated manufacturer of selected flat rolled, tin mill, and fabricated products and are committed to satisfying our customers' requirements through quality, service, and low-cost production.

(Sample) Principles

In the pursuit of our mission, Wheeling-Pittsburgh Steel Corp. espouses twelve principles which should guide

the actions of all employees in all circumstances.

I. *Quality.* We are dedicated to customer-driven quality. We constantly strive to improve our processes, products, and services, guided by understanding and satisfying changing customer needs.

II. *Low-Cost/High-Quality Production.* We recognize a direct and positive connection between high-quality products and services and low-cost production. Maintaining this connection is the best way to serve our customers.

---

company says it stands for and what it actually delivers. . . . This gap is the largest single source of cynicism and skepticism in the workplace today" (Pearson, 1992, p. 67). The organization's values must be relevant to the emerging competitive environment, and they must be reinforced often enough to be part of the common vocabulary. Clear values, focused vision, and sustainable core competences must be exciting and bold enough to change the way employees think about the organization from a production focus to customer service. Market definition and segmentation help drive this change by making the key customer needs and wants more visible to all employees.

▶ **EXTERNAL ANALYSES**

Strategy depends on foreseeable external conditions as well as the firm's own capabilities and vulnerabilities. External analyses complement the market opportunity analysis used to determine the organization's mission. Whereas MOA emphasizes customer trends, several types of external analyses attempt to determine the effect of external forces on the industry and firm to find specific opportunities and threats. External analysis begins with the broad underlying forces in the remote environment, then progressively narrows through industry analysis, looking at competitors and customers, and finally forecasts the strength and potential impact of the key driving forces in terms of the firm's opportunities and threats.

Remote Environment Analysis

Trends in the remote environment are the least controllable of all forces affecting an organization. Systematic analysis of the remote environment looks for the broadest relevant trends in five major arenas. *Social* trends include long-term changes in cultural attitudes, values, and behaviors such as permissiveness, conservatism, family structure, entertainment and leisure time patterns, health and environmental consciousness, educational achievement, cultural diversity, and so on. Broad *technological* trends include major technological drivers such as miniaturization, electronification, and automation which are making all activities more information intensive, speeding up innovation, and shortening product life cycles. *Economic* factors to be monitored include inflation, consumer confidence, the business cycle, interest rates, exchange rates, and globalization. The *political and regulatory* climate should be considered carefully for specific changes such as tax rulings, environmental regulations, safety requirements, labor regulations, and federal budget reallocations. *Ecological* trends include global warming, deforestation and desert formation, species declines, pollution level changes, and natural catastrophes such as earthquakes, floods, and storms.

These forces in the external environment have typically been analyzed for their impact on the firm or industry as a means of understanding the most basic driving trends. While such analysis can be useful, focusing on the *firm* often ignores the impact on *customers.* In the continuous improvement model, external analysis emphasizes how external trends affect customers' perceived and desired value, and the market rather than the industry. With such a view, many U.S. managers would have understood (perhaps even anticipated) the importance of customers' rising expectations for quality, value, and convenience, and competitors' actions to meet and raise those expectations.

Industry Analysis

The operating or task environment consists of the industry in which the firm operates, together with the forces directly affecting that industry which the firm may be able to influence but not control. Porter (1980) suggested that the level of profitability of a given industry is determined by the overall intensity of industry competition, which in turn derives from the industry structure and the level of five key forces. These are: (1) *threat of entry,* (2) *power of suppliers,* (3) *power of buyers,* (4) *impact of substitutes,* and (5) *intra-industry rivalry.* Analysis of the key forces driving an industry will reveal the inherent attractiveness of that industry. Porter's five forces model also suggests that a firm can build competitive advantage by reducing the combined pressure of these outside forces.

The threat of entry, which increases competition, is minimized by a firm's ability to erect *barriers to entry.* The most important barriers are based on high startup cost, economies of scale or scope, experience curve effects, differentiation, or a combination of these. Lincoln Electric has kept Japanese competitors from entering its markets by making the highest-quality electric arc welder while basing price on ever-declining total cost. Service firms frequently prevent entry through differentiation. For example, American Express remains the leader in travelers' checks based on its policy of nearly instant service worldwide. Japanese firms have used flanking, vertical integration, and cooperative strategies to provide superior value and reduce or overcome entry barriers (Smothers, 1990).

Suppliers and *buyers* exert pressure on an industry and a given firm in proportion to their size, order volume and frequency, margins, and so on. Managers have traditionally believed it to be in their best interest to reduce the power of these upstream and downstream stakeholders by reducing dependence on any one supplier or buyer. However, increasing the number of suppliers usually increases quality problems and transaction costs. The emerging paradigm builds dependent relationships with a few key suppliers to focus the firm on improving not only its own processes but also those of its suppliers. Many firms have dramatically reduced the number of suppliers to as few as one for each part. Although this makes the firm more dependent on its suppliers, it helps improve incoming quality, minimize inventory costs, and put just-in-time (JIT) systems into place. This raises output, productivity, quality, and customer value. Likewise, increasing the customer's cost of switching away from the firm helps control buyer pressure, but reducing customer power may lower customer satisfaction if improving value is deemphasized. Instead, managers may drive improvement by establishing a dependency relationship with each customer, just as with suppliers, usually through value-adding service.

As product extensions proliferate and brand loyalty fades, *substitutes* have become more important to industry analysis. Consumers now seek more variety through substitutes. In certain industries, the competition between product types may be more important than that within types. For example, in the entertainment product market, movie theaters compete with view-at-home videotapes, sporting events, and other live entertainment. Market opportunity analysis improves managers' perspectives by focusing on all products or services that customers consider to be alternative ways of satisfying their needs.

Rivalry has become intense in many industries, and the front has broadened from selected local markets to national, even international markets. Porter defines rivalry as jockeying for position and says it may range from gentlemanly to warlike. Rivalry results when two competitors have conflicting goals. One rival can attempt to change the game by altering the rules, influencing the balance of forces, or anticipating the direction of change first. Price wars, one way to influence the balance of forces, seldom benefit either rival since net profit margins quickly erode. Coke and Pepsi's long-running rivalry has expanded the soft drink market through rivalry in advertising and product innovation, while price competition has been restrained to temporary local skirmishes.

Rivalry on quality, not just price, is based on much more fundamental customer needs, combined with the ability to lower total delivered costs. Thus, the emerging paradigm provides a way of engaging in rivalry with a realistic chance of winning. A firm that can deliver superior net value to consumers and continuously improve that value has established leadership in the mind of the consumer and the ability to keep moving the target ahead of competitors. Japanese auto firms changed the basis of competition in the world auto industry from features and frills to higher product quality and reliability with lower operating costs. In fact, they are now attempting to change the front again by defining quality in psychological terms to capture the customer's emotions.

Managers can often intuitively establish the relative level of each of these five forces in their industry. However, because of the many determinants of each force, it is not easy to determine whether each major force is increasing or decreasing in strength. Industry analysis is most useful when it clarifies the driving forces and predicts the overall industry profitability. With this information in hand, managers' next step is to narrow the analysis to key competitors.

Competitor Analysis

As rivalry has intensified, threatened firms have become much more competitor-oriented and have adopted more formal, systematic competitor analysis. Yet defining a firm's competitors can be difficult. For markets in which a firm has an established position, the key competitors are those who sell to the same customers. If the firm is targeting new markets or segments, the key competitor may be either the market leader or the weakest firm in the market (depending on its strategy). A focus on key competitors, especially in intense rivalries, can cause a firm to ignore new entrants who will change the basis of competition. The competitor focus may also reduce customer orientation. Having defined key competitors in each segment, managers must understand each rival's goals, strategies, probable course of action, and strategies that might provoke retaliation. To gain market share without retaliation, managers must understand the rival's weaknesses better than the rival itself.

In this situation, the emerging paradigm has two advantages. First, the customer orientation keeps the true focus of long-term competition on satisfying the customer. New entrants successfully challenge market leaders precisely because they bring a new perspective to satisfying customer needs. Incumbents, bound by large investments, traditional channels, pricing policies, and complacent cultures, often become myopic and vulnerable. Second, the customer focus facilitates an often inconspicuous, nearly invisible array of tactics that incrementally but continuously improve delivered value. In effect, as customers' expectations are gradually exceeded, the firm providing best value can move beyond the capability of its rivals to meet the rising expectations. National differences in investments in R&D reinforce such resourcefulness (see box).

In the 1960s, the economy car segment (college students and young professionals who wanted basic yet reliable cars) was poorly served by American and European car makers. In 1959, Toyota entered this value-conscious segment. American car manufacturers responded with the Ford Falcon, Chevy Corvair, Chevy Vega, and Dodge Dart; all much larger "economy" cars with terrible repair records. Since U.S producers did not learn how to make adequate margins on these cars, they neglected the

---

Planned Obsolescence or Customer Satisfaction?

Japan's biggest consumer firms spend 20 percent more than their U.S. rivals on research and development. But how they spend the money is as important as the amount. Most U.S. firms concentrate on developing a new product and extending its life cycle to write off development costs. The Japanese believe it is better to introduce new products every six months. They have reorganized their R&D to create three generations of products at the same time. Japanese firms do not wait for the market to tell them when a product has died.

For example, engineers started working on the radio/cassette recorder when they were designing only a radio. While CDs were being developed, Sony engineers were designing smaller discs, the new minidisc

and recording Minidisc-Man. The Japanese say they are not deliberately making any product obsolete. They simply assume from the start that today's new product will eventually be replaced, and they want to control the timing of new product introductions, profits, and market share to push competition out of the market.

Planned obsolescence seems to be a negative term. It's really just trying to keep the market alive and bring something extra to add value to the consumer. In the Japanese view, everyone benefits. The customer gets something new, and the company makes more money.

ABC Evening News, Jan. 30, 1992.

---

needs of customers in this growing segment. In fact, they failed to take the foreign competition seriously until the early 1980s, well after the segment was lost and the Japanese had gone on to establish a strong position in the more profitable mid-size segment.

Competitor analysis must be pursued until one even knows the personalities of the key personnel in rival firms. Japanese firms analyze the competitors' top managers, their interests, activities, personalities, and decision patterns. Managers must understand key rivals' strategic intent, product developments, and probable actions in pricing, promotion, and distribution. Public information sources, industry insider information, and rumor can be pieced together, but this task often requires a systematic, comprehensive effort headed by trained analysts. Hence the need for a thorough, firm-wide approach which integrates competitor analysis with customer analysis to determine the next way to improve value.

Forecasting and Prioritizing the Opportunities and Threats

Having analyzed the remote, industry, and competitive environments, managers must forecast the *direction* and *magnitude* of the driving forces and translate these into opportunities and threats. Both quantitative and qualitative approaches should be used to improve the reliability and validity of forecasts. Opportunities must be clearly defined. Which new markets might be targeted, which technologies would improve products or processes and reduce costs, which needs should be satisfied first? Forecasting should also predict the size and growth rate of opportunities. To minimize the impact of forecasting error, many firms now compete with quick-response, flexible manufacturing or service delivery systems. This capability is a formidable competitive advantage that is based on meeting customer needs faster than competitors and reducing total costs.

Forecasting can also refocus on customer value. Too often, managers attempt to predict key industry trends or specific competitive actions without relating these to customer value. External analysis is most useful when forecasting leads to earlier, accurate prediction of changes in customer needs and behavior. The opportunities and threats must be prioritized from most to least important to the organization's success. The criteria used for this subprocess are derived from the mission, goals, and internal capabilities of the firm. Many managers try to use one criterion such as potential dollar volume or expected return on investment; a better approach is to use several criteria, including those related to customer satisfaction, vision, and strategic intent.

▶ INTERNAL ANALYSIS

The firm's internal situation is as important in determining strategic direction as its external opportunities and threats. When viewed from the perspective of customer satisfaction, the internal analysis should assess the firm's capability to meet current and future customer needs and its ability to build future capability (resourcefulness). The ability to build core competencies that generate unforeseen products faster and cheaper, and to consolidate technologies and skills into competencies that empower individuals to adapt quickly is the ultimate source of competitiveness (Prahalad and Hamel, 1990). Quantitative financial, competitive, and operating analyses must complement qualitative assessments of key functional areas.

Performance Analysis

Internal analysis often begins with understanding an organization's success quantitatively as indicated by financial ratios, competitive position, and measures of customer value. Traditional profitability, liquidity, leverage, and activity ratios can suggest key internal strengths and weaknesses, but only with knowledge of variation and clear organizational definitions. Measures of profitability include *gross margin, return on sales* (net margin), *return on total assets* (also called *return on investment*), and *return on equity.* Along with common size statements and growth charts, profitability ratios and revenue trends help establish historical performance patterns. Stock market performance measures include *earnings per share, price-earnings ratio,* and *dividend yield;* long-term shareholder value may be more important than any short-term measure (Pearson, 1992). Managers often evaluate performance against four standards: past performance, current objectives, industry averages, and rivals' performance. The overall pattern in the four types of comparisons is more important than any single measure. It is the variation over time that is the basis for interpretation of any measure of performance. These measures must be stable over time and conditions to be meaningful.

Most large and some small firms measure competitive position by market share or market rank. Again, a static snapshot using absolute share is usually misleading. Managers must understand the variation in market share over a specified timeframe in the context of the entire market's growth or shrinkage. Even dynamic measures of market position may ignore new markets. Accurate assessment of market share or rank depends on correctly defining the total market; it is important to include all current and emerging competitors without being too broad. Remember that the market definition identifies a group of target customers with a particular need; the competitors include all organizations trying to meet that same need in that same group. This performance measure is essential for evaluating how well one is meeting customer needs. Improving financial performance or growth may be good signs, but either can also disguise declining share.

Likewise, market share reveals little about how and why customers are delighted or dissatisfied. To evaluate performance against customer expectations, managers must use direct measures from the market. Managers should be market sensitive rather than financially sensitive. To evaluate firm performance, managers should regularly combine the results of surveys, product returns, customer calls, focus groups, order feedback forms, and customers' alternative product applications with ratio analysis, market share, and stock performance.

The emerging paradigm also measures performance concerning resourcefulness and responsiveness. Managers should measure how long it takes the firm to become aware of, then respond to, changes in the environment. Being able to anticipate changes starts an organization on the way toward meeting customers' needs faster and better than competitors.

Function, Activity, and Process Analyses

Function, activity, and process analyses help identify qualitative competitive advantages and disadvantages. A *distinctive competence* is any organizational function or skill that is superior to that of rivals. A *competitive advantage* is a distinctive competence that is important to customer satisfaction. Determining these requires a thorough qualitative assessment of strategies, tactics, and customer value. Traditionally, internal analysis focused on functional specializations (production/operations, marketing, finance/accounting, human resource management, management and leadership) and organization structure. But this means that functional analysis is limited to strengths and weaknesses within each function. Porter's value chain (1980) helps managers analyze the firm horizontally rather than vertically by measuring the value-added at each step of the firm's total process. Although markups or contribution margins at each step indicate the firm's cost position relative to rivals, activity cost analysis does not necessarily define value added from customers' point of view.

Competitive advantages often arise out of the ability to generate process synergies that increase customer value. In the emerging paradigm, internal analysis identifies and analyzes such cross-functional processes and systems. The managerial activity that bridges functions and connects processes into systems is sometimes referred to as "managing the white spaces" (Rummler and Brache, 1990). For example, Dell Computers has defined a new approach to computer manufacturing and sales. Dismissed as telemarketing by rivals, Dell went on to provide better product quality and service than retailers with custom orders by phone, unlimited calls to toll-free technical support, a thirty-day money back guarantee, and next-day, on-site service via independent contractors. Dell's traditional functions are much more efficient than those of its rivals, but superior customer value is based, not on low cost, but on its cross-functional customizing, quick response, and guaranteeing systems.

Internal analysis for the emerging paradigm depends on correctly identifying the firm's activities that impact quality, performance, delivery, and service attributes. These activities and the linkages between them must be identified as critical systems, processes, and capabilities. Managers should always focus on the actual behaviors and actions taken rather than on what individuals say their unit's strengths and weaknesses are. Finally, managers should evaluate each process and system for the capability to satisfy customers, now and in the future.

Managers with a strategic intent to be global leaders will develop the firm's ability to anticipate customer needs and take actions today to satisfy future needs. Strategic capabilities encompass the whole value-delivery system and include collective learning. A *core capability* is "a set of differentiated skills, complementary assets, and routines that provide the basis for a firm's competitive capacities and sustainable advantage in a particular business" (Teece, Pisano, and Shuen, 1990, p. 28). As a knowledge set, a core capability includes the content of (1) employee knowledge and skills as embedded in (2) technical systems, and the learning processes guided by (3) managerial systems, values, and norms (Leonard-Barton, 1992). Capability-based firms like Wausau Insurance, Rubbermaid, and Sun Microsystems have developed superior acuity, speed, innovativeness, and consistency (summary of G. S. Stalk's presentation, by B. C. Reimann, 1992). Measuring customer satisfaction and capability to improve value usually reveals problems and competitive disadvantages between functions rather than within a specific function. Such cross-functional problems may be the most frequent cause of poor customer satisfaction.

Competitive benchmarking is a new technique for evaluating internal processes. In this analysis, managers determine the firm's critical processes and outputs, baseline those processes, then compare the performance of each process against a standard outside the industry. If the goal is to improve a process to world-class quality, managers must find a firm that is recognized as one of the best in the world, not just within the industry.[8] Managers should use benchmarking wisely to inspire tailor-made solutions and not just mindlessly copy other organizations. They must know how to measure the important processes and how to interpret the measures.

---

8. See Xerox case for benchmarking process.

Portfolio Analysis

In this chapter, we have focused on internal analysis at the business level. For *multibusiness* corporations, internal analysis looks at the financial and market performance of each strategic business unit (SBU). Portfolio models based on industry or market attractiveness and relative business strength have dominated managers' thinking, but such models tend to be financially driven toward resource allocation decisions and profit maximization. The emerging paradigm suggests that corporate executives should view SBUs as a portfolio of core competences that span the SBUs and allocate talent as well as capital to build competences and improve capabilities.

In summary, internal evaluation is combined with the findings of external analysis to determine the key problems, strategic issues, and possible and desirable new goals and strategies. Traditional approaches emphasize the concept of environmental fit, in which managers build on the firm's competitive advantages to realize its external opportunities, while strengthening its weaknesses and minimizing threats. Customer-based approaches focus primarily on improving value to customers in the target market. Whichever approach is used, managers complete the analysis by determining key problems, strategic issues, and evaluation of strategic alternatives.

▶ DEFINING KEY PROBLEMS AND STRATEGIC ISSUES

Managers are problem solvers. Unfortunately, many spend their time solving the little daily problems and never get to the important system issues. Poor managers may explain, "I don't have time to manage!" Although dealing with issues under their control, this behavior usually puts quick fixes on symptoms within functions rather than curing the systemic problem. This is the opposite of strategic management. Because functional fixes often maximize the subunit performance at the expense of total system effectiveness, the resulting suboptimization may make the strategic situation worse. Poor financial performance, declining market share, employee turnover, and high defect rates are symptoms of a more fundamental strategic problem. When managers focus too heavily on financial measures, they often ignore the means that create those outcomes.

Root Problems versus Symptoms

The remedy for fixing symptoms is to define and solve the root problems. A root problem represents the basic underlying cause of symptoms such as poor performance, employee turnover, or customer dissatisfaction. One way to isolate a root problem is to group all symptoms that seem to be related, then try to determine the underlying source of these related problems. This type of analysis nearly always requires cross-functional system assessment. Although it is important to understand the extent to which problems are driven primarily by external or internal factors, whenever possible, root problems should be stated in terms of controllable internal factors. Blaming uncontrollable external forces like competitors, the economy, or the government will not help achieve solutions. The first step is to determine whether the objectives were realistic. Then, evaluate whether the problem arose from poor strategy formulation or inadequate strategy implementation. Establish the timeframe of the problem; even long-term solutions require short-term actions. Determine whether the problem is technical or behavioral; technically trained managers often try to solve behavioral problems with technical fixes, since it is easier to change technology than behavior. Without pointing fingers, establish whether the problem is at the corporate, business, or functional level.

The emerging paradigm often changes a manager's view of this problem-definition process. It forces a long-term, market-driven orientation and helps to reveal the firm's process shortcomings. Some of the tools of continuous improvement such as Pareto analysis, cause-effect charts, and SPC (statistical process control) may help make this problem-definition activity more systematic and efficient for all processes. These tools usually force managers to be more responsive.

Managers often use *gap analysis* to help define the key problem; financial or market performance under the current strategy is plotted into the future and compared to long-term objectives. For example, if revenue has grown 10 percent per year, but the five-year plan calls for 15 percent revenue growth, managers must either reduce the growth objective or change their strategy to fill the gap. Since financial analysis tracks the results of satisfying customers, not customer satisfaction itself, focusing exclusively on financial measures can lead to bad decisions. Gap analysis on customer satisfaction can show improvement in market position before financial results improve. By selecting appropriate measurements, managers can analyze the potential gaps in product or service quality, customer value, and customer satisfaction. For example, Motorola used benchmarking to perform gap analysis on product quality, process efficiency, and cycle times.

Having isolated the key problem(s), managers must also understand the most important strategic issues to address in solving the problem. In this step, managers draw on both the internal and external analyses to understand what factors need to be dealt with and where management must focus attention. Strategic issues can be identified by looking for the match between the current strategy and industry-driving forces, future key success factors, competitive vulnerabilities, and the capabilities necessary to realize emerging opportunities. These strategic issues, combined with the key problem, should suggest whether the current strategic approach needs fine-tuning or major change. Then managers are ready to develop alternative long-term solutions to the key problem.

▶ STRATEGIC ALTERNATIVES

Managers need to define and evaluate alternative courses of action. A strategic alternative consists of a set of objectives and corresponding value-based, generic, and grand strategies. Each strategic alternative must offer the potential to solve the key problem, close the projected gaps in performance, and improve customer value. Strategic alternatives are not merely different arrangements of various quick fixes to the individual symptoms. Managers should begin developing strategic alternatives by specifying alternative long-term goals and objectives and the means to achieve them.

Goals and Objectives

Nearly all rational management models are based on the assumption that human behavior and organizational performance are enhanced by goal clarification and goal consistency. Strategic management takes this one step further by distinguishing between goals and objectives. *Goals* are the broad statements of intent reflecting what the organization would like to do. They indicate the overall direction to be taken, for example, to increase sales or profits, protect market share, diversify, or improve quality. *Objectives* are the specific long- and short-term targets the firm expects to reach in a specified timeframe. For example, if the long-term goal is to increase sales, the corresponding objective might be to reach $100 billion in total revenues by the year 2000. Goals provide direction, objectives provide the milestones anyone can use to measure progress toward the goals.

The traditional paradigm insists on quantified objectives for each organizational goal. However, some quality experts and top managers in excellent firms do not believe in setting specific targets (Schonberger, 1992; Deming, 1986). Instead, managers play a coaching role, setting one or two key goals (not quantified), and providing the resources to help subordinates meet these goals creatively. This debate is far from over. The choice between broad improvement goals and quantified targets may depend on the situation and the manager's level. If the organization needs to improve radically or change strategy, a select few quantified targets may be necessary to focus everyone on the seriousness of the situation. For example, Robert Galvin's original challenge to Motorola employees was to increase quality by a factor of ten. Xerox, however, focused only on a broad-based redefinition of logistical and inventory processes to meet a general improvement goal. Either approach can be difficult to implement. Setting objectives arbitrarily without a defined rationale and a means (strategy) for accomplishing them is at best meaningless and at worst destructive.

Without objectives to operationalize goals, managers and employees have only vague generalities to guide decision making, yet objectives are not the end themselves. Rather, objectives are the milestones to work toward to achieve the mission. Thus, for each goal there should be at least one quantified, measurable objective with a timeframe for its achievement.

If managers choose to set quantified organizational targets, then corporate and business-level objectives should be defined and prioritized for those key results that drive the organization. Internally focused or competitor-focused firms usually set specific objectives for *total revenues, competitive position, profitability,* and *diversification.* More comprehensive managers often add *customer satisfaction, quality, technological position, employee development,* and *social responsibility* targets. Managers should not translate high-level financial objectives to units below those which have profit and loss responsibility. The objectives for competitive or technological position may quantify the firm's strategic intent. For example, Toyota Motor Corporation, under intense international and domestic pressure, recently scaled back its plans to achieve 10 percent of the world vehicle market by the end of the century, a corporate objective never before acknowledged (White and Chandler, 1992). In the emerging paradigm, however, customers are ranked first, and managers must specify the firm's first objective in terms of what they expect to do for customers that they are not currently doing. For example, managers may seek to improve customer satisfaction to 99 percent within five years or to reach 95 percent on-time delivery of all orders. Questions to consider include: What level of quality will be achieved, what level of customer satisfaction, and how much additional value can be created?

Writing objectives is critical to strategic management, yet this step is fraught with traps. For example, in an attempt to stimulate growth, long-term sales objectives are frequently stated as an average annual growth rate in percentage terms rather than the absolute level of revenue desired in, say, the fifth year. But only the absolute number makes the size of the task visible to all. Most important, quality and value improvement targets should be stated in statistical terms. Using statistically based measures maintains an unbiased understanding of process performance.

Managers must help focus employees and other resources by deciding the minimum set of objectives and by exploring any resulting tradeoffs. Since no organization or group of employees can focus on more than about three things in a given period of time, managers must prioritize and reduce the list of objectives to a meaningful set of three to five key targets. This set should include, in this order, customer satisfaction or value improvement, growth, profitability, and competitive position. Without a target for each, managers must understand the tradeoffs and synergies among these objectives.

All types of firms can benefit by simultaneously improving quality and reducing cycle times. For example, Cyrix has shortened the development cycle for advanced microprocessor chips to eighteen months and can predict when it will introduce new chips before Intel, the market leader whose development cycle is still two to three years (*Business Week*, Sept. 14, 1992, p. 62). Regardless of whether managers choose to set objectives, they must work on designing and implementing predictable strategies.

Figure 5
Grand strategies

Build and grow	Definition
Market penetration	(same products, same markets)
Product development	(new products, same markets)
Market development	(same products, new markets)
Diversification	(new products, new markets)
Concentric	(related products, markets, or technologies)
Conglomerate	(unrelated products, markets, or technologies)
Integration (acquisition)	
Horizontal	(buy competitors at same stage in activity chain)
Vertical—backward	(buy operations with activities upstream)
—forward	(buy operations with activities downstream)
Joint venture	(form separate new corporation jointly owned)
Innovation	(fast new product development)
Hold and maintain	(improve existing practices and market position)
Retrenchment	
Turnaround	(downsize and improve)
Divestiture	(sell assets as operating concern)
Liquidation	(close operations and sell assets piece by piece)

Long-Term Strategies

As shown in Figure 5, the grand strategies are grouped into "build and grow," "hold and maintain," and "retrenchment" strategies. Ansoff (1965) conceptualized the build-and-grow strategy as a simple combination of current or new products targeted at current or new markets: *market penetration/concentration, market development, product development, diversification*. Rumelt (1980) distinguished related from unrelated diversification based on the degree of fit with the firm's existing products or markets. Others have added horizontal and vertical *integration* (either by merger or acquisition), *joint venture*, and *innovation*.

A hold-and-maintain strategy is frequently characterized by emphasis on current operations with minimal investment. Managers of firms in low-growth, high-profit markets often protect or reinforce their position by doing many little things better. Retrenchment grand strategies include *turnaround, divestiture* and *liquidation*. All three forms of retrenchment usually involve some form of downsizing to reduce the company to a set of profitable core operations. A turnaround strategy pares excess costs by eliminating non-value-adding activities and reinvests in value-added operations with growth potential. Some businesses, plants, or operations with value to someone else as a turnaround prospect can usually be divested. Unprofitable operations with little potential for turnaround and no prospective buyers may have to be liquidated for the salvage value of each individual asset.

Customer versus Competitor Orientations

To many western managers, the Japanese competitive achievement provides hard evidence that a hallmark of a successful strategy is the creation of sustainable competitive advantage by beating the competition. If it takes world-class manufacturing to win, you have to beat competitors with your factories. If it takes rapid product development, you have to beat them with your labs. If it takes mastery of distribution channels, you have to beat them with your logistics system. No matter what it takes, the goal of strategy is to beat the competition. After a decade of losing ground to the Japanese, managers in the U.S. and Europe have learned this lesson very well. As a guide to action, it is clear and compelling. As a metric of performance, it is unambiguous. It is also wrong.

Winning the manufacturing or product development or logistics battle is not a bad thing. But it is not really what strategy is—or should be—about. When the focus of attention is on ways to beat the competition, strategy inevitably gets defined primarily in terms of the competition. For instance, if the competition has recently brought out an electronic kitchen gadget that slices, dices, and brews coffee, you had better get one just like it into your product line—and get it there soon. . . . When you go toe-to-toe with competitors, you cannot let them build up any kind of advantage. You must watch their every move. Or so the argument goes.

Of course, it is important to take the competition into account, but that should not come first in making strategy. First comes painstaking attention to the customers' needs and close analysis of a company's real degrees of freedom in responding to those needs. The willingness to rethink what products are and what they do, as well as how to organize the business system that designs, builds, and markets them, must follow. Competitive realities are what you test possible strategies against; you define them in terms of customers. Tit-for-tat responses to what competitors do may be appropriate, but are largely reactive. They come second, after your real strategy. Before you test yourself against competition, your strategy should encompass the determination to create value for customers.

It should also encompass the determination to avoid competition whenever and wherever possible. As the great philosopher Sun Tzu observed five hundred years before Christ, the smartest strategy in war is the one that allows you to achieve your objectives without having to fight. Nintendo's "family computer" sold 12 million units in Japan alone, during which time it had virtually no competition at all. . . .

. . . in my experience, managers too often and too willingly launch themselves into old-fashioned competitive battles. It's familiar ground. They know how to fight. They have a much harder time seeing when an effective customer-oriented strategy could avoid the battle altogether.

Kenichi Ohmae, *The Borderless World: Power and Strategy in the Interlinked Economy*, Harper Business, New York, 1990.

Competitive Strategy versus Cooperative Strategy

Most approaches to business strategy adopt a competitor orientation and prescribe various ways to build sustainable competitive advantage(s). The unstated assumption is that success is based on some monopoly power that is to a large degree controllable by managers. In the early 1980s, military strategy was explored for relevance to business (Reis and Trout, 1984; Kotler, 1984; James, 1984). Offensive strategies include frontal assaults, flanking attacks, encirclement, and guerrilla warfare. Defensive strategies include preemptive moves, entrenchment, and counterattack. However, leading Japanese managers insist that they pay little attention to competitors, but rather focus on defining and satisfying customer needs (Maruta, 1990; Matsushita, 1988). (See box.)

Cooperative strategies have recently gained importance as a basis for survival (Hamel, Doz, and Prahalad, 1989). In particular, joint ventures between global firms, foreign and domestic, as well as between large and small firms are now common. Rather than vertically or horizontally integrating, some industries, particularly in apparel and electronics, have established networks or collective strategies to maximize responsiveness and minimize cost (Shephard, 1991).

Strategists have also pursued two other divergent approaches to customer value. Global strategy attempts to define one product that will be acceptable in most markets using the same promotion; globalization pushes the broad low-cost strategy to its limit. In the other approach, a transnational firm attempts to meet the unique needs of each local market with focused differentiation. Although cooperative strategies have become essential to either approach, managers must protect the firm's core competences and technologies. Erosion of competitive position often begins with granting access to core products through licensing or outsourcing which exposes key customer needs to aggressive rivals. Thus, cooperative strategies must be carefully managed for both sides to benefit.

Evaluating Strategic Alternatives

The strategic alternatives must be thoroughly evaluated by identifying the key advantages and disadvantages of each as well as the assumptions on which each is based. Since managers will shape action plans around these assumptions, they must explicitly recognize and test their assumptions about the economy, the industry, consumer behavior, and new technology and entrants. Decision-making studies show that devil's advocacy is the best method primarily because it clarifies assumptions better than other approaches like brainstorming and dialectic discussion (Schweiger and Sandberg, 1988). There are several criteria for evaluating strategies (Rumelt, 1979). *Internal consistency* means that the action plans support each other. *Realistic* means the plan is achievable, even if it is challenging. *Focused on problem solving* means the plan solves the key problem and addresses the key strategic issues. *Capable of solving key subproblems* means that most of the symptoms are also addressed. We would add another criterion, *customer benefit,* which means that the plan must improve value to the customers. The decision-making process should ensure that each alternative meets these criteria. With clear understanding of the assumptions, pros, and cons of each alternative, managers can choose one for the firm's long-term strategic decision.

▶ STRATEGIC CHOICE AND STRATEGY IMPLEMENTATION

The choice of long-term objectives and strategy is often influenced by recent performance under the firm's historical strategy, the values and attitudes of top managers concerning risk and investment, and the structure and culture of the organization. If managers change strategy too often, or test tactics that are inconsistent with the grand or generic strategies, they lose focus. Generic strategy is usually very stable; grand strategy may change more often as resources become available. The criteria for choosing a particular strategy should be clearly defined.

To implement strategy, managers must address all devices (such as systems, policy, structure, culture) used to install new strategy or reinforce existing strategy. To implement long-term strategy, top management must set annual objectives, put in place action plans and policies, improve the organization's cross-functional systems, and provide the leadership and management to focus the corporate culture on the customer.

Annual Goals and Objectives

Given a set of long-term corporate or business-level objectives, top and middle managers determine the corresponding short-term (first year) objectives (along with the means to reach them) that will mark progress toward the overall goals of the organization. These are also firm-level, not functional objectives. Again, the quality and improvement objectives rank first, followed by the financial or competitive position targets. Managers can minimize confusion by focusing the organization on the one to three most important targets and drive toward their achievement within the next year. Common short-term objectives emphasize cycle time reduction, quality improvement, customer satisfaction, new products, response time, process improvements, and employee participation.

The management challenge is to develop objectives that are realistic, yet challenging, and that unify the organization. For high-achieving organizations, the objectives may be incremental improvements over the previous year. For low-performing but capable units, radically ambitious objectives may be required to refocus managers and employees alike. For weak units, more modest objectives that demonstrate success may help build confidence and cohesion. Once goals are agreed upon, managers' primary responsibility in strategy implementation is providing the leadership and management of systems to remove the cross-functional barriers to implementation.

Action Plans and Policies

For most managers, making the plan work is more difficult than formulating the plan. There is nothing magic in objectives, no guarantee of success; quantifying targets merely clarifies how success will be defined and measured. The real key to success is in implementing the short-term action plans. To implement customer value, grand, and generic strategies, managers specify annual plans and resources for each system, process, or function, then coordinate policies and structure the organization and its processes to implement these plans. Although short-term plans are often determined by function, process, and project managers, top management usually approves, facilitates, or modifies these plans. Whether top-down or bottom-up, it is top management's responsibility to see that strategy is

Figure 6

Policy development

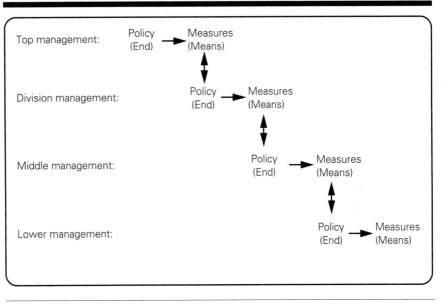

consistent across the organization, that resources are allocated appropriately, and that all systems focus on improving customer value. *Policies* are management's formal and informal rules for routine behaviors. Such rules standardize routine decision making so that subordinates can perform tasks more efficiently. All policies should help maximize customer value and satisfaction or improve processes, not just benefit the functional specialist. For example, travel policies should make it easy for employees to serve customers and measure the value of travel, not just control the travel budget.

One systems-oriented process model for developing goal consensus throughout the organization is *hoshin* planning (also called policy deployment). As shown in Figure 6, policy deployment develops the short-term action plans (the means) at each level to be consistent with the overall strategy by linking these plans to the measures derived from the policies (ends, i.e., the objectives) established with the managers above. While quality function deployment (QFD) focuses on cross-functional or horizontal integration, *hoshin* planning is a highly participatory, vertical, top-down and bottom-up process used primarily as a coordinating/linking activity in the organization. In fact, policy deployment places more emphasis on process than on outcome (Imai, 1986; King, 1989). Also known as *management by policy* or *management by planning* (MBP), in contrast to management by objectives (MBO), policy deployment has no direct link with personnel practices such as promotion or salary decisions. *Hoshin* planning places great emphasis on individual autonomy and self-management at the managerial level:

> In an autocratic organization, the boss sets the target. In a participative organization, the boss and subordinates sit down together and come to some agreement as to what the targets will be. In *hoshin* planning, the subordinate sits down by himself or herself and decides what he or she thinks the target ought to be, and then gets together with others in the organization to align those targets. This system focuses on the individual developing his own ideas of what needs to be done, and then integrates them. Goals are measured by the individual manager who sets them for himself or herself. [King, 1989]

While individual organizations have adapted variations of policy deployment, *hoshin* planning typically includes the following (adapted from Huge, 1990):

1. Develop a five-year vision for the company.
2. Determine an annual policy in support of the vision.
3. Deploy the policy throughout the organization through participative planning.
4. Implement the policy.
5. Audit the process and plans monthly.
6. Conduct annual audits by top management.

The process is recursive, and the results of the annual top management audit form a partial basis for the policy development phase for the next year (Huge, 1990). At first glance, the policy deployment process would appear to run counter to the view of system improvement presented in this book. In the old paradigm, *hoshin* planning is often translated through management by objectives without concern for the means, and without maintaining a customer focus. This is not true in the new paradigm. In fact, the highly participatory process of individual goal-setting described above takes place only in the context of a customer-value-oriented, top-down vision of the organization's purpose. Managers pay close attention to coordination and integration at all organizational levels. Within this context, participative planning is consistent with system improvement.

Leadership and Management

Once plans are set, top management must drive them down to the operating level in terms everyone can understand. Leadership involves setting clear goals, involving subordinates to work toward those goals, and providing systems and resources to reach the goals. Managers' actions must be consistent with their words. With skilled employees, higher performance usually results when individuals and groups can creatively define how they will accomplish those goals. Managers' job descriptions usually need to be refocused on system change or improvement (leadership) rather than

---

Sam's Rules for Building a Business

1. Commit to your business.
2. Share your profits with all associates, and treat them as partners.
3. Motivate your partners.
4. Communicate everything you possibly can to your partners.
5. Appreciate everything your associates do for the business.
6. Celebrate successes. Find some humor in failures. Don't take yourself so seriously.
7. Listen to everyone in your company. And figure out ways to get them talking.
8. Exceed your customer's expectations.
9. Control your expenses better than your competition.
10. Swim upstream. [Walton, 1992]

---

employee supervision (administration). Sam Walton used many of these principles to build Wal-Mart (see box).

A key to implementation is process and system ownership by a team or an individual. Ownership means the team or individual has taken responsibility for and is willing to be held accountable for improving the performance of the process. An individual or team can claim ownership or top management may assign ownership; either way, a leader must take charge of process definition and improvement for each critical process. After deciding which process a leader owns, managing means improving that process and improving the links between that process and others before it, after it, and parallel with it. As a result, managers' behavior will usually change. With a different concept of their job, managers will lead by asking questions more than by giving orders; they will get directly involved with customers, suppliers, and subordinates; and they will encourage workers to question every practice, submit suggestions, and innovate (Pearson, 1992; Schonberger, 1992).

Once processes are in control, leaders are also responsible for improving customer value by improving the process. Managers and employees can do this only if they know who the customers are, have met and talked with them directly at the customer's location, systematically collect data on what customers value, and can infer what the customer will value even before the customer knows this. All managers must be capable of talking with customers and transmitting customer values to employees. In conjunction with market opportunity analysis, managers must also build an innovative, entrepreneurial culture that is focused, responsive to customers, and flexible enough to take advantage of related opportunities.

Systems and Structure

Implementation plans often begin with reorganization, a structural approach. While structure should follow and fit the strategy, structure is often the biggest barrier to system improvement and strategic change. Many quality problems can be traced to overspecialization and the resulting suboptimization by departments or functions. An organization's structure must resolve the inherent conflict between the need for specialization at the functional level and the need for integration across the business. Setting up departments or functions helps employees specialize on tasks and helps managers focus resources, develop expertise, and gain synergies. However, when managers are rewarded for expanding staff or cutting costs and employees carry out parochial policies, formal structure often gets in the way of process integration across functions. Most organizations have a difficult time maintaining cross-functional integrating mechanisms, so managers resort to liaisons, ad hoc task forces, troubleshooters, and endless meetings. These Band-Aid approaches nearly always succumb to the inertia of the formal structure.

There are several top and middle management barriers that managers must overcome: lack of openness, short-term focus, and authority and power. Each of these contributes to fear in employees that inhibits improvement (Deming, 1986). Many managers have to be trained to be more open. Top management has to develop a reward system that is consistent with long-term objectives rather than short-term quotas, then reinforce improvement by middle managers, not just administration of the function. Middle managers often need assistance in learning that employee empowerment enhances managerial effectiveness.

Organization Culture

An organization's culture is determined by values and assumptions about the way business is done that organizational members hold in common. Many barriers to implementing customer-value strategies are due to managerial (not employee) values and attitudes ingrained over many years. With analysis and feedback, managers can learn to manage both the substance and symbolism in four areas that influence corporate culture: rituals, communications, reward systems, and ethics. Managers' personal behaviors speak loudest and are hardest to change. Managers must personally and collectively develop knowledge of customer value and improvement techniques. Each manager must obtain feedback directly, yet anonymously, from both employees and customers. Further, managers should analyze rituals and practices such as meetings, communications, and recognition and reward systems to identify dysfunctional and inconsistent behaviors. Successful managers creatively and publicly motivate individual contributions to continuous improvement and celebrate group achievements of short-term objectives. Finally, managers must set ethical standards, provide exemplary ethical leadership, and enforce ethical standards throughout the organization.

Human Resource Management

Perhaps the most important key to implementation is human resource management (HRM). Team building, a common starting point, must be part of a systematic change program led by top management. Recruiting, selecting, and training procedures should be modified to provide a work force oriented to and capable of cooperatively understanding customer needs, creating value, and improving value systems. Managers in continuously improving organizations will identify skills needed to compete in emerging technologies that redefine customer value and recruit highly qualified people to develop into core capabilities or competences (Pearson, 1992). Job descriptions should define each employee's responsibility for improvement, not just task performance. Cross-training in job tasks, statistical training (SPC), and team building are essential. All managers and employees must learn to work together, deal with customers, break down barriers between functions, and continuously improve all aspects of the organization so as to deliver better value.

That employees need frequent, accurate, and consistent feedback is certain. SPC enables employees to understand the processes they work with and provides them with immediate feedback. It also makes employees more aware of managers' responsibility for system improvements. If managers are not willing to act on process information to improve systems, a program of continuous improvement should never be started. Managers must be trained to listen, respond to cross-functional issues, help employees become responsible for and develop ownership of their part of the process, and deal with suggestions in a positive, timely way.

Managers must create performance development and reward systems to focus work on what is and will be important to improving customer value, to encourage the right balance of individual and collective effort, and to motivate changes in behavior. Many change programs fail early because managers and employees do not get a strong signal that improvement and customer satisfaction are paramount. The CEO must use HRM systems to redefine the culture and convince employees that continuous improvement is not another fad, that customers and management really do expect *continuous* improvement.

▶ EVALUATION OF STRATEGY IMPLEMENTATION

Planning is key to good implementation, but managers must then monitor the action plans as they unfold. Strategic control systems focus on two questions: (1) Is the strategy being implemented as planned? and (2) Is the strategy working (is it achieving the intended results)? Just as with operating control systems, managers should specify the standard for strategic performance, establish a system for monitoring that performance, and take corrective action when deviations exceed trigger points. Managers tend to monitor operating performance better than strategic progress because their personal reward system is tied to short-term financial results and because they have not empowered employees to be responsible for the operating system. Thus, strategic control systems should be separated from operating control systems.

Most managers, familiar with traditional operating control systems, rely on budgets and schedules. Traditional controls, though, may be counterproductive. Budgets were designed as a resource allocation tool, not a control tool. If the customer is most important, strategic control must put quality improvement and system improvement ahead of the financial goals. In fact, Robert Galvin, former CEO of Motorola (now retired), reversed the usual reporting order in executive committee meetings by putting quality improvement updates first on the agenda. To further emphasize the importance of customer satisfaction, he then left the room before financial results were reported. Roger Milliken, CEO of Milliken and Co., quit focusing on variance reports in order to spend all his time on quality issues. Neither example illustrates systemic, multidimensional management (focused on means and results). However, these leaders did dramatize the importance of focusing on customer value. In short, to fulfill the organization's purposes managers must focus on satisfying internal and external customers and continuously improve processes and capabilities that impact customer value.

▶ SUMMARY OF KEY POINTS

1. Customer-driven strategic management has become essential at all levels of an organization.
2. The emerging paradigm refocuses each step of the strategic management process on the customer.
3. The mission and vision focus on specific customer needs and values in defined target segments.
4. External analyses focus on identifying the influences on customer value, while internal analyses assess the systems providing that value relative to customers' future needs and the emerging competitive situation.
5. The emerging paradigm ranks goals and objectives for quality, customer satisfaction, and process improvement ahead of financial targets.
6. A customer-value orientation helps ensure that strategy implementation integrates leadership and management, cross-functional system improvement, culture change, and motivation, performance appraisal, and reward systems.
7. Improvements in effectiveness are much more likely to be based on process improvements that improve customer satisfaction than on financial results (Lieberman, Lau, and Williams, 1990).

▶ KEY TERMS

core capability	goal
core competence	grand strategy
core product/service	implementation
core technology	market segmentation
cross-functional system	mission
generic strategy	objective

policies
resourcefulness
strategy

strategic management
value-based strategy

▶ DISCUSSION QUESTIONS

1. What are the key tasks in the strategic management process?
2. What must a manager specify to define the business? How can a manager avoid the trap of defining the business in terms of a specific product?
3. What analyses should be done before deciding long-term objectives and strategy?
4. Which is more important and why: core products, core technologies, or core competences?
5. What are the levers for managers who want to change an organization?
6. What are some of the key differences between the traditional strategic management process and the emerging paradigm?

▶ EXPERIENTIAL EXERCISES

1. Look in a recent issue of *Forbes* or *Fortune* for a cover story on a leading firm. On a copy of the article, underline and label the firm's:
   • Mission
   • Strategic intent
   • Long-term goals
   • Specific objectives
   • Opportunities and threats
   • Competitive advantages and capabilities
   • Key strategic problems or issues
   • Generic and grand strategies
   • Short-term action plans

   Write one sentence on how the firm's managers define customer value. Write one page on the role of quality, continuous improvement, and systems management in the firm's strategic management process.

2. In a personal message to the student, Alex Trotman, president and chief operating officer of Ford Motor Company's Automotive Group, states: "Successful individuals, like successful organizations, need to have clear, well-defined visions of where they're going and what they're going to be. Then they need to develop strategies to get there. Total Quality Management is an important part of Ford's strategy for being the best supplier of customer value in the automotive industry. One of the most important strategies for an individual has to be getting a good education, and then to make life a constant learning experience. Getting a good education on the themes discussed in this text will provide you with the vision needed to be a successful

manager in the future. You should make this education a part of your personal strategy to succeed."

One of the advantages of studying management is that the principles you learn often apply to your personal life. With reference to specific principles in this chapter, write a strategic plan for your personal success. Include a vision statement, a definition of success, and a statement of how to make the vision real.

▶ REFERENCES

P. Anderson, "Marketing, Strategic Planning, and the Theory of the Firm," *Journal of Marketing*, Vol. 42, Spring 1982, pp. 15–26.

I. Ansoff, *Corporate Strategy*, McGraw-Hill, New York, 1965.

T. Brown, "Is Your Company Vision-Driven?" *Industry Week*, May 18, 1992, p. 11.

T. Brown, "Are You Vision-Driven?" Part II, *Industry Week*, June 1, 1992, p. 11.

N. Capon, J. U. Farley, and S. Hoenig, "Determinants of Financial Performance: A Meta-Analysis," *Management Science*, Vol. 36, No. 10, 1990, pp. 1143–1159.

G. H. Carothers and M. Adams, "Competitive Advantage through Customer Value: The Role of Value-Based Strategies," in M. Stahl and G. Bounds (eds.), *Competing Globally through Customer Value*, Quorum, New York, 1991.

A. Chandler, *Strategy and Structure: Chapters in the History of American Industrial Enterprise*, MIT Press, Cambridge, Mass., 1962.

D. Cravens, G. Hills, and R. Woodruff, *Marketing Management*, Irwin, Homewood, Ill., 1987.

R. M. Cyert and J. G. March, *A Behavioral View of the Firm*, Prentice-Hall, Englewood Cliffs, N.J., 1963.

R. Daft, *Organization Theory*, West, St. Paul, Minn., 1986.

W. E. Deming, *Out of the Crisis*, MIT (CAES) Press, Cambridge, Mass., 1986.

J. W. Frederickson, "The Comprehensiveness of Strategic Decision Processes: Extensions, Observations, Future Directions," *Academy of Management Journal*, Vol. 27, No. 3, 1984, pp. 445–466.

G. Fuchsberg, "Quality Programs Showing Shoddy Results," *Wall Street Journal*, May 14, 1992, p. B1.

G. Fuchsburg, " 'Total Quality' Is Termed Only Partial Success," *Wall Street Journal*, Oct. 1, 1992b, p. B1.

J. Galbraith and D. E. Schendel, "An Empirical Study of Strategy Types," *Strategic Management Journal*, Vol. 4, 1983, pp. 153–173.

D. A. Garvin, *Managing Quality*, Free Press, New York, 1988.

F. Gluck, S. Kaufman, and A. S. Wallach, "The Four Phases of Management," *Journal of Business Strategy*, Vol. 2, Winter 1982, pp. 9–21.

D. C. Hambrick and D. Lei, "Toward an Empirical Prioritization of Contingency Variables for Business Strategy," *Academy of Management Journal*, Vol. 28, No. 4, 1985, pp. 763–788.

G. Hamel, Y. L. Doz, and C. K. Prahalad, "Collaborate with Your Competitors and Win," *Harvard Business Review*, January–February, 1989, pp. 133–139.

G. Hamel and C. K. Prahalad, "Strategic Intent," *Harvard Business Review*, May–June 1989, pp. 63–76.

C. W. Hofer, "Toward a Contingency Theory of Business Strategy," *Academy of Management Journal*, Vol. 18, No. 4, 1975, pp. 784–810.

E. C. Huge, *Total Quality: An Executive's Guide for the 1990s*, Dow-Jones Irwin, Homewood, Ill., 1990.

K. Imai, *Kaizen*, McGraw-Hill, New York, 1986.

K. Ishikawa and D. Lu, *Total Quality Management*, Prentice-Hall, Englewood Cliffs, N.J., 1985.

M. J. Kiernan, "The New Strategic Architecture: Learning to Compete in the Twenty-first Century," *Academy of Management Executive*, Vol. 7, No. 1, 1993, pp. 7–21.

B. King, *Better Designs in Half the Time*, Goal/QPC, Methuen, Mass., 1989.

D. Leonard-Barton, "Core Capabilities and Core Rigidities: A Paradox in Managing New Product Development," *Strategic Management Journal*, Vol. 13, 1992, pp. 111–125.

M. Lieberman, L. J. Lau, and M. D. Williams, "Firm-Level Productivity and Management Influence," *Management Science*, Vol. 36, No. 10, pp. 1193–1215.

J. H. Little, "Variation, Knowledge, and the Quality Movement," presented at 1992 Academy of Management Annual Meeting, Las Vegas, Nev., 1992.

Y. Maruta, "The Kao Corporate Philosophy," speech to the European Institute of Business Administration (INSEAD), Fontainebleau, France, May 9, 1989.

K. Matsushita, *Not for Bread Alone: A Business Ethos, A Management Ethic*, PHP Institute, Inc., Tokyo, 1988.

H. Mintzberg and J. Quinn, *The Strategy Process*, 2d ed., Prentice-Hall, Englewood Cliffs, N.J., 1991.

H. Mintzberg and D. Waters, "Of Strategies, Deliberate and Emergent," *Strategic Management Journal*, Vol. 6, 1985, pp. 257–272.

J. C. Narver and S. Slater, "The Effect of Market Orientation on Firm Performance," *Journal of Marketing*, 1990.

I. Nonaka, "The Knowledge-Creating Company," *Harvard Business Review*, November–December 1991, pp. 96–104.

J. Pearce and F. David, "Corporate Mission Statements: The Bottom Line," *Academy of Management Executive*, Vol. 1, No. 2, 1987, pp. 109–116.

J. A. Pearce II and R. Robinson, *Strategic Management: Strategy Formulation and Implementation*, Irwin, Homewood, Ill., 1991.

A. E. Pearson, "Corporate Redemption and the Seven Deadly Sins," *Harvard Business Review*, May–June, 1992, pp. 65–75.

M. Porter, *Competitive Strategy*, Free Press, New York, 1980.

C. K. Prahalad, "Globalization: The Intellectual and Managerial Challenges," *Human Resource Management*, Vol. 29, No. 1, 1990, pp. 27–37.

C. K. Prahalad and G. Hamel, "The Core Competence of the Corporation," *Harvard Business Review*, May–June 1990, pp. 79–91.

B. C. Reimann, "The 1992 Strategic Management Conference: The New Agenda for Corporate Leadership," *Planning Forum*, Vol. 20, No. 4, 1992, pp. 38–46.

L. Rhyne, "The Relationship of Strategic Planning to Financial Performance," *Strategic Management Journal*, Vol. 7, 1986, pp. 423–436.

R. P. Rumelt, "Evaluation of Strategy: Theory and Models," in D. E. Schendel and C. W. Hofer (eds.), *Strategic Management: A New View of Business Policy and Planning,* Little, Brown, Boston, 1979.

G. Rummler and A. T. Brache, *Improving Performance: How to Manage the White Space on the Organizational Chart,* Jossey-Bass, San Francisco, 1990.

R. J. Schonberger, "Is Strategy Strategic: Impact of Total Quality management on Strategy," *Academy of Management Executive,* Vol. 6, No. 3, 1992, pp. 80–87.

D. Schweiger and W. Sandberg, "The Utilization of Individual Capabilities in Group Approaches to Strategic Decision-making," *Strategic Management Journal,* Vol. 10, No. 1, 1988, pp. 31–43.

J. Shephard, "Entrepreneurial Growth through Constellations," *Journal of Business Venturing,* Vol. 6, No. 5, 1991, pp. 363–373.

N. Smothers, "Patterns of Japanese Strategy: Strategic Combinations of Strategies," *Strategic Management Journal,* Vol. 11, No. 7, 1990, pp. 521–533.

G. P. Evans Stalk and L. E. Shulman, "Competing on Capabilities: The New Rules of Corporate Strategy," *Harvard Business Review,* March–April 1992, pp. 57–69.

Sun Tzu, *The Art of War,* S. B. Griffith (ed.), Oxford University Press, London, 1963.

D. Teece, G. Pisano, and A. Shuen, "Firm Capabilities, Resources, and the Concept of Strategy," Consortium on Competitiveness and Cooperation, Working Paper #90-9, University of California at Berkeley, Center for Research in Management, 1990.

A. Thompson and A. Strickland, *Strategic Management: Concepts and Cases,* 6th ed., BPI Irwin, Homewood, Ill., 1992.

S. Walton, *As Sam Walton: Made in America, My Story,* 1992.

J. B. White and C. Chandler, "Pressed by All Sides, Hard-Driving Toyota Trims Back Its Goals," *Wall Street Journal,* May 19, 1992, p. A1.

D. Woodruff, "A New Era for Auto Quality," *Business Week,* Oct. 22, 1990, pp. 84–96.

chapter **7**

Measuring Customer Value

Until recently, the Civil Aeronautics Board required commercial airlines to work within fairly limited parameters regarding which services we could offer to our customers, thus defining quality in the industry. In today's environment, deregulation has given us the opportunity to let the customer redefine quality through methods such as market research and customer partnering. This kind of customer focus is central to effective total quality management and is reflected in the words of our founder, C. E. Woolman: "Delta has always tried to operate by the Golden Rule—to put ourselves on the other side of the counter and treat our customers as we would like to be treated ourselves."

Robert W. Coggin, Senior Vice President, Marketing, Delta Airlines

▶ **CHAPTER OUTLINE**

Chapter Overview

Focusing on Customer Value

Customer Needs, Product Quality, Customer Value, or Satisfaction?
Customer Value and the Garbage Business
Service Quality at North American Phillips
A General Methodology for Learning about Customer Value

Techniques for Measuring Customer Value

Techniques for Measuring Consumer Value
Techniques for Measuring Commercial Customer Value
Principles of Measurement
Avoiding Value Measurement Errors

Using Customer Value Measures

Translating Learning into Strategy and Systems
Methods for Improving System Performance
Quality Function Deployment
Implementing the QFD Process
Improvement of Systems and Processes

Satisfaction and Dissatisfaction Measurement

Measures of Customer Satisfaction
The Dynamics of Value and Implications for Measurement
Refining Satisfaction and Dissatisfaction Measurement
Implications for Strategy

Summary of Key Points

Key Terms

Discussion Questions

Experiential Exercises

References

▶ **CHAPTER OVERVIEW**

The emerging paradigm requires that a customer-value orientation be driven into all parts of the organization. To do this managers must develop a comprehensive approach to measuring customer needs, quality of products and services delivered, customer value, and customer satisfaction. They should begin with developing a customer value strategy using methods of market research. They must then translate the strategy into operations. One method for doing this translation is quality function deployment. Finally, they should assess the level of customer value delivered with direct measures of outcomes and with measures of customer satisfaction. These methods are important in providing information as a basis for future organization strategy and continuous improvement. Patterns in customer value data can be traced to systems and processes that are candidates for improvement.

▶ **FOCUSING ON CUSTOMER VALUE**

Focusing on customer value can yield big results. Managers, in their efforts to continuously improve, make choices about what to measure. In the initial phase of quality initiatives, managers often begin by focusing on improving output, so they measure product quality at the end of the manufacturing line. Others focus on a market outcome and measure customer satisfaction. Whether measured with an overall score or on specific dimensions of quality or satisfaction, neither output nor outcome measures necessarily lead to better understanding of what customers really value. Yet, today's customers are more value-conscious than ever and more able to make informed judgments about what provides good value. Rather than prestige, image, positioning, or low price, value today means real performance, delivering what was promised so that the customer gets the right combination of product quality, fair price, and good service (Power, 1991). Thus, delivering value as defined by the customer has become paramount. In a survey of high-scoring Baldrige Award applicants, the U.S. Government Accounting Office (GAO) found that customer satisfaction, quality, cost, financial performance, and competitive position generally improved with the adoption of quality management practices (Government Accounting Office, 1991). Measurement of quality and customer satisfaction was key to tracking this improvement in performance.

To provide superior value to customers, managers and employees must meet customers' needs, yet exceed their expectations. Studying customer needs can reveal many opportunities to improve value. Earl Conway, former corporate quality director, Procter & Gamble, Inc., explained that his company is driving into its culture a principle adopted from leading Japanese companies: "Study real people, in real situations, with real products." This suggests that it is imperative for managers to think like customers in order to better please them, and that managers must understand the uses as well as the users to be able to improve value. For example, in using traditional toothpaste tubes, customers must put up with the mess from dropped toothpaste. When P&G managers finally adopted the imperative to "improve customer value by increasing benefits and reducing sacrifices," they developed a squeeze dispenser that minimized the dropped toothpaste mess through the recoil suction of the dispenser pump.

Implementing this managerial imperative of measuring and improving customer value can be quite difficult. For example, many Japanese automakers study a person's eye movements in a car to discover needs that customers will not express verbally. Such in-depth, scientific study can produce insights leading to superior value for customers. After briefly reviewing the managerial imperative to focus on value and presenting a general model for determining customer value, this chapter details some techniques for measuring customer value and customer satisfaction. These measurements are key to formulating and assessing an organization's strategy.

Customer Needs, Product Quality, Customer Value, or Satisfaction?

To realize the benefits of a customer value strategy, the concept of customer value must be made operational. One way to render the concept operational is to devise methods to measure value and use the information

Figure 1

A general model of the antecedents, usage consequences, and realized end states of customer satisfaction and value

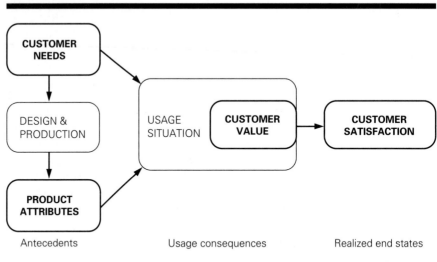

to make better strategic and operational decisions (Schonberger, 1992). To meet this imperative, managers must develop a comprehensive system to measure each point of the customers' means-ends model (antecedents, usage consequences, and realized end states—see Figure 1). This suggests that managers, to clearly understand their market and opportunities to improve, should measure separately each of the different aspects of this model: customers' needs/wants/preferences, product/service quality, customer value, and customer satisfaction. This comprehensive approach usually leads to much better understanding of unmet needs, important quality attributes, the relative value of various dimensions of product and service to the customer, and any (dis)satisfaction customers derive from dealing with the firm.

As shown in Figure 2, customers' needs must be understood and used to design the products and services offered. The experience customers have with the product or service in a given situation determines the value they realize. Customer (dis)satisfaction is the outcome of providing value that meets or does not meet the customer's need in that situation. Managers must measure product quality as an antecedent to both customer value and satisfaction, measure the value perceived by customers during usage, and measure the satisfaction or dissatisfaction that is the realized end state.

The task of measurement is not a simple one. In addition to understanding which aspect (needs, quality, value, satisfaction) is being mea-

Figure 2

Various dimensions of cost, quality, and value by product/service category

Category	Cost components	Value components	Quality components
Bank	Service charges; interest rates	Variety of services; ease of understanding	Financial stability; personal interest in customers
Building product	Low cost	Training seminars; easy to install	Easy to work with; durable
Coffee shop	Low prices; specials	Hours open; take-out items	Cleanliness; taste of food
Convenience store	Reasonable prices	Items easy to find; variety	Clean; attractive interior
Discount store	Sales/clearances; low prices	Easy return; check cashing	Selection; well-known brands; pleasant atmosphere
Family steakhouse	Low prices; coupons	Salad bar; kids' menu	Taste of steak; atmosphere
Furniture maker	Low price; range	Quick response to requests; on-time delivery	Nationally known brands; patterns available
Furniture store	Credit policies; low prices; price range	Delivery; display method	Well-known brands; knowledgeable salespeople
Gas station	Low prices	Windshield cleaners; pump speed	No alcohol in gas; octane rating
Ice cream	Low cost; specials; coupons	Container size	Taste; richness; amount of flavor; creaminess
Jewelry store	Sales; low prices; low interest rates	Personal interest in customer; fast service	Unique jewelry; custom designing
Pizza restaurant	Specials; coupons; promotions; low prices	Fast service; home delivery; take-out; variety	Hot product; taste; consistent product
Psychiatric hospital	Low-cost treatment	Comfortable rooms; visitor accommodations	Experienced physician; innovative treatments
Specialty tune-up clinic	Reasonable cost; specials	Car ready when promised; fast service	Fixed right first time; qualified mechanics
Supermarket	Low prices	Well-stocked; check cashing	Clean; selection; specialty departments
Temporary employment service	Reasonable cost	Performance guarantee; follow-up	Competence of temps; understands what is needed
Auto parts store	Low cost; sales; private label	Parts variety; fast service	Parts in stock; knowledgeable salespeople

T. C. Ragland, "Consumers Define Cost, Value, and Quality," *Marketing News*, Sept. 25, 1989, p. 20.

sured, managers must identify the dimensions of each aspect that are most important to customers. Some marketers erroneously define value to mean low cost or a price cut (Power, 1991). While value always has a cost component, consumers usually define value to include other things they want beyond the basic product or service. As shown in Figure 2, the determinants of value (the critical dimensions) differ for each product or service category. To the degree that managers successfully differentiate their offering, these critical dimensions may also differ for each firm in an industry. Measures of overall satisfaction do little to help managers understand their customers' key decision criteria or how to improve (Garvin, 1988). Specific measures of customer value can be used by managers in all types of businesses, as the following two examples illustrate.

Customer Value and the Garbage Business

The experience of Browning Ferris Industries, Inc., a garbage collection company, illustrates just how complex this can be. A narrow output view of service performance quality might have focused on how often Dumpsters were emptied on schedule. Likewise, a narrow view focused on outcomes might have confined itself to customers' overall satisfaction with garbage pickup. Instead, BFI first focused on understanding what its customers valued beyond the emptying of a Dumpster. The results of this research on customers' real needs and those attributes of service valued by customers were then used to develop an index of service quality and a customer satisfaction measurement system.

Both Browning Ferris and Waste Management, Inc., are spending millions of dollars to reduce customer "churn," the loss each year of about 14 percent of their customer base. Each hauler's customers can be easily targeted by spotting the blue BFI or maroon WM Dumpsters. Then, only customer loyalty resulting from good service prevents the rival from undercutting with a lower price. When William Ruckleshaus took over Browning Ferris in 1988, he was shocked to learn that his firm was losing almost as many customers each month (4,000–5,000) as it was gaining (6,000). His complacent managers believed this was "the way the industry works." However, as growth slowed, competition increased for the existing customers, and minimizing customer loss by improving customer satisfaction with better service became key to continued growth.

A university expert in customer satisfaction surveyed 30,000 BFI customers to design a satisfaction index that rates each of BFI's 200 hauling districts. In addition, each month the firm now asks thousands of customers to respond in writing to questions about service. From this data, Browning Ferris is beginning to understand what people value in their garbage service. First, driver lateness, messiness, and noise irritate many people. Second, Dumpsters must be placed out of the way of customers' back doors, driveways, and the view, and care taken that they don't get blown into parking lots or parked cars. Third, Dumpsters must be in good condition, with weathertight lids and bottoms, and painted. Fourth, the company must help manage obnoxious neighbors who spill garbage or whose uncovered garbage attracts rats to the customer's property. If Browning Ferris installs locks, its drivers must get out of the truck and relock the Dumpsters. Finally, large price increases should be accompanied by better service. With this improved understanding of its customers, Browning Ferris has already cut its churn to about 12 percent (Bailey, 1993).

Service Quality at North American Phillips

As shown in Figure 3, the service quality survey from North American Phillips suggests how many questions may need to be asked and the amount of analysis that may be required for each step in the customer's chain of behavior. This survey, which addresses only the quality of repair service rendered by a company-authorized local repair center, measures the customer's situation (section A), the quality of service provided (section B), the timeliness of service (section C3), the perceived value of the service (section C4), performance (section C5), overall satisfaction (section D1), and the customer's intention to buy again (section D2). This comprehensive approach can yield strategic insights into what customers value and how to improve only when results are linked to the full complement of potential causes.

A General Methodology for Learning about Customer Value

In some situations (like waste management), managers initially may find that improving value is as easy as listening to customer feedback and taking appropriate action. In other situations, determining value requires sophisticated data-gathering techniques and statistical analysis. One general approach to learn about what customers value involves a cycle of four activities: *projecting, invalidating, discovering,* and *confirming* (Carothers and Bounds, 1991). In the first step, projecting, managers make an educated guess (hypothesis) of what customers value. In the second step, invalidating, managers assume their guess is correct, then attempt to disprove it. In the third step, discovering, managers state what was found to be erroneous about their hypothesis, and further articulate customers' needs, wants, preferences, and value drivers. In the last step, confirming, managers examine customer behavior throughout the purchase decision, use, and disposal process to determine any discrepancy between what customers value and what the firm provides. Managers should use these successive activities to continuously challenge their assumptions about what customers value. This methodology helps managers to break from existing frames of thought. Executing successive cycles of these steps produces a more sophisticated and refined understanding of what customers value. This knowledge is then used to determine value strategy and continuous improvement priorities.

In each situation, managers must determine the level of sophistication necessary to improve customer value by recognizing the trade-offs between the costs of thoroughness and the costs of superficiality. The more thoroughly managers study customer value, the more time and money it will cost. The more superficially, the more likely they are to lose opportunities and act on mistaken assumptions. Some large firms have taken a new approach that combines these four steps and eliminates the heavy, up-front investment in customer research before going to market. Instead, with flexible manufacturing systems and multiple potential designs, they *design for quick response* after market introduction. This approach uses quick

Figure 3

QUALITY OF SERVICE SURVEY

Please rate the service you recently received from our national service network on your Magnavox, Philco, Sylvania, or Philips consumer electronics product. Consider all service calls required for this particular problem. Indicate your answers by checking the appropriate box for each question.

A. TYPE OF SERVICE CALL

1. Was your product:
   - Repaired in your home...☐   (Please complete ONLY sections B and D)
   - Picked up at your home but repaired in our service center ....☐   (Please complete ONLY sections B and D)
   - Carried in or mailed in by you to our service center...............☐   (Please complete ONLY sections C and D)

B. IN-HOME SERVICE

	YES	NO
1. When you called for service were you able to get through on the first call without getting a busy signal?	☐	☐

	YES	NO
2. When you called, were you placed on hold?	☐	☐

	YES	NO
3. Did the person you talked with on the phone give you the feeling that he/she really cared about your problem?	☐	☐

	SAME DAY	NEXT DAY	3RD DAY	4TH DAY	LATER
4. What day was your appointment scheduled for?	☐	☐	☐	☐	☐

	YES	NO
5. Was this the day you most preferred?	☐	☐

	SAME DAY	NEXT DAY	3RD DAY	4TH DAY	LATER
6. If not, what day would you have most preferred?	☐	☐	☐	☐	☐

	AM 8-12	PM 12-5	Evening After 5	All Day 8-5
7. When was the technician scheduled to arrive?	☐	☐	☐	☐

	YES	NO
8. Was this the time of day you most preferred?	☐	☐
9. Did the technician come on the scheduled day?	☐	☐
10. Did the technician arrive during the scheduled time period?	☐	☐
11. Did the technician give you the feeling he/she really cared about your problem?	☐	☐
12. Did the technician seem to be knowledgeable and competent about your problem?	☐	☐
13. Did the technician explain what was done to fix your problem?	☐	☐
14. Were the charges on the invoice explained to you?	☐	☐

15. Considering the service you received, how would you rate the charges for:

	No Charge Involved	Very Reasonable	Reasonable	Unreasonable	Very Unreasonable
-LABOR (incl. home call)	☐	☐	☐	☐	☐
-PARTS	☐	☐	☐	☐	☐
-TOTAL CHARGE	☐	☐	☐	☐	☐

	1	2	3	4	More Than 4
16. How many trips were required to complete the repair?	☐	☐	☐	☐	☐

adaptability to obtain customer information directly from sales patterns and then adjust the product mix (Zangwill, 1993).[1] For example, Sony introduced several dozen versions of the Walkman, then reduced the number of versions based on sales patterns. The customer value processes are discussed in detail below.

Projecting   To project value, a manager must hypothesize about customer value for each customer group. If managers accept this initial projection as truth without investigating customers' perceived value, they risk serious

1. Without knowledge of variation, this approach may create internal variation and increase cost.

Figure 3 (Continued)

	Excellent	Good	Fair	Poor
17. Overall, how would you rate our technician?	☐	☐	☐	☐

	Available on Service Truck	Mailed To You	Brought Back Later By A Technician	No Part Needed
18. If a part was needed to complete the repair, was the part:	☐	☐	☐	☐

	No Part Ordered	Same Day	1-4 Days	5-9 Days	More Than 9 Days
19. If a part was ordered, how many days did it take for you to get the part?	☐	☐	☐	☐	☐

(PLEASE SKIP TO SECTION D: Overall Rating)

C. PRODUCTS CARRIED OR MAILED TO OUR SERVICE CENTER:

1. When your product needed repair, did you:
   -Carry your product into our service center? ☐
   -Mail your product into our service center? ☐

2. If you carried your product into our service center:	YES	NO	N/A
-Were our hours of operation convenient for you?	☐	☐	☐
-Was our service center attractive?	☐	☐	☐
-Did our counter person give you the feeling he/she cared about your problem?	☐	☐	☐
-Was the repair completed on the day we promised?	☐	☐	☐

	Very Satisfied	Satisfied	Neither Satisfied/ Dissatisfied	Dissatisfied	Very Dissatisfied
3. How satisfied were you with how quickly your product was repaired?	☐	☐	☐	☐	☐

4. Considering the service you received, how would you rate the charges for:

	No Charge Involved	Very Reasonable	Reasonable	Unreasonable	Very Unreasonable
LABOR	☐	☐	☐	☐	☐
PARTS	☐	☐	☐	☐	☐
TOTAL CHARGE	☐	☐	☐	☐	☐

	YES	NO
5. Was your product properly repaired the first time it was brought/sent to our service center?	☐	☐

(PLEASE COMPLETE SECTION D: Overall Rating)

D. OVERALL RATING: ALL SERVICE CALLS:

	Very Satisfied	Satisfied	Neither Satisfied/ Dissatisfied	Dissatisfied	Very Dissatisfied
1. Considering all these questions, how satisfied are you with the overall service you received?	☐	☐	☐	☐	☐

	Definitely Would Buy	Probably Would Buy	Might or Might Not Buy	Probably Would Not Buy	Definitely Would Not Buy
2. If you needed to replace the product you had repaired, how likely would you be to buy another product from our company?	☐	☐	☐	☐	☐

3. Please add any comments you have about the service you received.

_____

_____

_____

---

error. The initial hypothesis is only a starting point for understanding customers. To complete the step, the manager should: (1) state assumptions about the context of customer value (the strategic plans of customer organizations, rates of change in market conditions, and anticipated competitors); (2) assess the benefits and sacrifices associated with product use; (3) estimate the value customers have been led to expect through advertising, proposals, and past performance; and (4) infer from customer behaviors what they truly value (for example, a customer will avoid a fast food restaurant if the line is over four cars long). If customers' needs and preferences are unknown, as is usually the case in emerging markets, managers may have to start with product benefits and avoided sacrifices.

Invalidating   To invalidate the conjectured value, managers test their guess by collecting data from current or potential customers. Managers should genuinely intend to disprove their projected value. This means being careful to choose subjects for study that will not simply confirm their ideas; such manipulation only harms the overall process of improving customer value. To invalidate their guesses, managers should talk to those who have selected (current customers), those who might need (qualified prospects), and those who have rejected the organization's products and services (lost customers). They must (1) analyze similarities and differences in the perceptions of each group of customers and target segments; (2) characterize the differences in value provided by their organization compared to that of competitors; and (3) record the order and significance of the various elements of value. This step is key to overcoming the manager's or engineer's mindset that they already know what is best for the customer.

Discovering When the invalidating stage has revealed flaws in the initial hypothesis, managers must then describe the adjusted imperatives for customer value. Discovering activities should determine: (1) the basic functions customers expect from the product/service; (2) the relative value the product must provide to exceed competing alternatives; (3) the minimum criteria (in order of importance) that customers use in making choices; (4) the value expectations that determine continued customer choice or a switch to competing alternatives; (5) the macroenvironmental factors (cultural, economic, social, and political) that might affect customer choices; and (6) the personal factors (goals, wants, social values, and situations) that might influence customer value. Organizational flexibility is the key to meeting these new/adjusted imperatives.

Confirming The ultimate indicator of customer value is found in customer behaviors that confirm whether or not an organization has provided superior value. The ultimate goal is to attract and retain loyal customers. Continuous reselection by customers may mean that they find the product/service to be of superior value. Customers usually switch brands if they perceive better value elsewhere. As the Browning Ferris example showed, even when easy undercutting would tend to minimize loyalty and lead to high churn rates, a comprehensive view of the total service may lead to superior value and prevent price competition. In some product arenas, customers may also switch simply for variety or curiosity; for example, brand loyalty to a specific cold cereal suffers whenever buyers seek variety.

A customer's purchase behavior may represent one of the following increasing levels of perceived value: sampling (experimenting), rational brand loyalty (preference based on objective current criteria), favoritism (preference based on subjective, historical evaluation), and exclusive reliance (routine selection). Customers' word-of-mouth testimonials or complaints may also demonstrate these various levels of perceived value. Managers should group customers according to their purchase behaviors to study the reasons for those behaviors. What components of value (both benefits and sacrifices) lead to these behaviors? Then, for strategy, what components of value are important in increasing perceived value? To answer such questions, managers need to know how to measure customer value and customer satisfaction. The next sections describe some techniques that are often used for these measures.

▶ TECHNIQUES FOR MEASURING CUSTOMER VALUE

The ability to define and measure customer value depends heavily on the type of customer. Measuring industrial or commercial customer value often requires a different set of techniques or a focus on different value drivers from those used to quantify consumer value for market segments in the general public. This section presents techniques for measuring customer value for each type of customer.

Techniques for Measuring Consumer Value

Many managers use scaled measures (such as 1 to 5 ratings) of relative customer satisfaction instead of absolute measures of customer value (such as estimates of time saved in ordering or reduced repair time). There are many techniques that fit the means-ends model better than scaled customer satisfaction measures. Managers can use these techniques to learn specific details about customer value. For example, in *behavioral analysis*, managers go on site, observe how customers use the product or service, and ask probing questions about the use process. Data from behavioral analysis must ultimately be translated into information that can be communicated to managers who plan products and set priorities for continuous improvement.

Many marketing research techniques have been developed to capture information on customer value. However, these techniques have been applied more often at the level of physical characteristics in the means-ends model, and less often to the consequences of use that determine value. For example, marketing managers often test prototype products by having customers keep journals or diaries on their perceptions of product attributes. Feedback questionnaires also usually focus on the attribute level. Early attitude measures (e.g., Rosenberg, 1956) focused on the "realization of valued states," but were often implemented at the attribute level. The concreteness of the attribute level (the touchable and seeable nature of products) attracts managers to that level of analysis, away from the more intangible level of desired end states.

When assessing customer value, managers must remember that they are trying to determine the relative importance of benefits and sacrifices to customers. To keep focused on customer value, managers must continually ask themselves, "Important to what end?" In addition to asking questions about the attributes of a product, they must understand how these attributes relate to the key consequences of use and desired end states.

Rokeach (1968, 1973) developed measures of personal values that reflect generally desired end states that people pursue. While such general information can be useful, more specific information might be gathered from marketing techniques, including personal interviews, focus group interviews, laddering, and trade-off analysis.

Personal Interviews The most direct approach to measuring what customers value is to ask them in personal interviews, one-on-one, in on-site meetings, telephone calls, or teleconferences. The content of the discussion should be guided by a structured set of questions to ensure that its coverage and flow meet the objectives of the interview. Some questions should be open-ended to probe for unanticipated responses. Interviews can focus on all components of the means-ends relationships of customer value. Excerpts from in-depth interviews designed to elicit a customer's thoughts about a product use experience often reveal individual concerns for certain end states and their beliefs about means-ends relationships. Consider the following example (Woodruff, Schumann, Clemons, Burns, and Gardial, 1991, p. 14):

Investigator: Okay. What else can you tell me about the car that is of interest?

Respondent: Very safe car. Uh, handles great in the rain. Handles great in the snow.

Investigator: What is your reaction to it being safe and handling great?

Respondent: Well, there's no play in the steering wheel. When you turn, you turn. You can hold it steady on the road with one finger. Uh, as far as safe. In the rain, I guess, is what gets me. I don't drive that often in the snow. But in the rain, course I know a lot of it has to do with your tires. But it's a heavy, you know, good heavy car. To where, you know, I have two kids in the car, I don't feel you're going to slide all over the road. You know, fishtail, or . . .

Investigator: What's that like, knowing or feeling that you're not gonna . . . ?

Respondent: Well, it means when it comes to pouring rain, you know, that I don't pull over to the side of the road or I'm not frightened to get in the car. You know, I feel like I can always go anywhere I want to go.

Protocol Analysis *Protocol analysis*, which is sometimes called *content analysis*, can be used to make sense of verbal data gathered through open-ended interviews or discussions (Locker and Dunt, 1978; Westbrook, 1980). The researcher first records the conversation and transcribes it, then develops a coding system for patterns in the responses. Like the blind men who each felt a different part of the elephant and perceived very different beasts, the protocol analyst only captures pieces of the phenomenon and may misinterpret or overgeneralize the data. People tend to verbalize only 10 to 15 percent as many thoughts about consequences in the means-ends chain as they do the product/service attribute level.

Interviewers may have to probe deeply to elicit information on abstract consequences and desired end states. Customers may be reluctant to reveal "hidden" motivations. For example, they may be more comfortable stating they bought a Cadillac because of the quality reputation than because of their need for social status (Gardial, Clemons, Woodruff, Schumann, and Burns, 1991).

Focus Groups The *focus group technique* uses an unstructured interview to encourage a group of customers to discuss their feelings, attitudes, and perceptions about a particular topic. The focus group technique, one of the qualitative marketing research techniques developed in the 1950s, is based on the assumption that people who share a problem will be more likely to discuss it among others who share their thoughts and feelings. Focus groups can be used:

1. To generate hypotheses that can be studied quantitatively
2. To generate information for structuring consumer questionnaires
3. To provide overall background information on a product category
4. To get impressions on new product concepts for which there is little information
5. To stimulate new ideas about older products
6. To generate ideas for new creative concepts
7. To interpret previously obtained quantitative results[2]

Focus groups work best when they are composed of eight to twelve people scientifically selected to represent a specific segment of customers, and who have some common interest to develop rapport (Hayes and Tathum, 1989). Managers may wish to conduct multiple focus groups to broaden the range of observation and reduce the possibility of unintended bias, to test reliability, or to probe special issues that arise. Focus groups are relatively easy to set up, but are often difficult to conduct. Although there is no one best way to conduct a focus group, some general principles apply. For example, since the focus group offers managers a chance to learn about value directly from customers in their own words, the facilitator should be as nondirective as possible. The focus group needs some guidance, but it must be facilitated without imposing ideas on the group. To be sure that responses are genuine and spontaneous, group members should not be forced to participate. When conducted well, the focus group is perhaps the only technique that can lead to chains of responses, synergies, and creative ideas.

The data from focus groups are difficult to interpret. Analysts usually examine tapes or transcripts of the sessions and classify bits of information according to whatever categories they determine are most relevant to their research question. They try to detect patterns and significant clues to

---

2. See Bellenger, Bernhardt, and Goldtucker, in Hayes and Tathum (eds.) (1989), who reviewed the literature on focus group interviews.

customer value relationships. The subjective nature of this analysis means that managers must guard against the tendency to use focus groups to confirm preconceived ideas.

Laddering *Laddering* provides a method for identifying the needs, desires, wants, or values of customers, and the product attributes instrumental in serving them (see Gutman, 1982; Gutman and Alden, 1985). Managers using this technique attempt to probe all aspects of customer value and the means-ends relationships. Laddering is most often used in individual interviews, but can be used in focus groups (Clemons, 1993).

Laddering is an associative procedure for relating verbal responses to uncover relationships among the components of customer value. The interviewer might ask the customer to respond to a question about the use of a product, perceptions of a product category, or some underlying need. The interviewer listens to the response and then probes further by asking, "What's important about that?" "What comes to mind?" or "Why?" until the customer can no longer answer. The interviewer should probe all aspects of the conversation to avoid the bias of focusing on particular aspects that might confirm the interviewer's preconceptions.

While the interviewer should generally focus on the product and its use, he or she should not prematurely cut off any additional conversation that might lead to unexpected learning. On the other hand, open-ended discussion can waste time. In the interest of brevity, the interviewer should try to focus the conversation on the components of the means-ends model.

Trade-Off Analysis Once a set of attributes has been identified as potential components of product or service value, managers need to determine the relative importance of each. Techniques such as *trade-off analysis* might be useful in this regard (Johnson, 1974). Trade-off analysis uses a matrix format to have customers make relative comparisons among the set of attributes and to indicate which attributes are most important to them. One of the drawbacks of trade-off analysis is that the attributes are already determined, so customers can respond only to the structure provided by the researcher. If open-ended techniques are used to identify the set of attributes, this drawback can be minimized. Another drawback is that the technique usually focuses on the attribute level of the means-ends model. It does not help to establish linkages among attributes, consequences, and desired end states. So, trade-off analysis should be used in conjunction with other techniques to determine the most important desired end states of customers.

Market Test New product development processes usually include a stage for market testing. A *market test* always involves having target customers try the product, usually under the same circumstances in which they would use similar products. *Beta test* is a term used in the software and other industries for the final phase of market research immediately preceding full commercialization. Current customers with a known level of expertise are used to test the latest version of the product with the purpose of trying to detect all flaws that might remain. In software development, this step is particularly important, since the software may be required to operate on several different platforms and interface with several other software programs written by other developers to different standards. A market test provides the best way to understand product performance and sources of value from the customers' viewpoint.

Direct Observation Customer value is driven by needs throughout the decision-making and use process. Managers can often improve their understanding of value by directly observing the customers at each stage of decision making and use of the product or service. Learning behavior, shopping behavior, usage behavior, disposal behavior, and the situational influences on each of these may lead to new uses of the product, new product attributes, new packaging, or new information to help improve the value of the product to the customer. Direct observation can be either intrusive or nonintrusive. Nonintrusive is better because the data are most reliable and valid when the data collector does not influence the respondent, but managers should use techniques that probe the customer's thinking. Managers sometimes observe focus groups directly from behind one-way glass, or videotape the groups and infer from the lab to the actual usage situation. In-store observation from a remote distance and videotape in the home or workplace are the least-intrusive observation techniques.

Other Sources of Data on Customer Value There are several other data sources and techniques for collecting data on customer value that have traditionally been used by managers. Some of these techniques provide better understanding of customer value, particularly when the customer may be unable to verbalize the unmet need or desired value. Unfortunately, managers have tended to rely exclusively on these sources rather than use them to confirm the results of primary customer data. The *jury of expert opinion* involves the use of sales personnel, top managers, or experts in the field to provide understanding of customer value. Other *third-party sources* such as universities and market research databases may lend insight into what customers value. *Employees* (particularly customer contact personnel) often understand more about customer needs and value than managers realize. Managers should develop a formal, systematic process for employees to record customer contacts and marketing insights. Finally, *call records* (information requests, requests for quotes, etc.) are an important source of data. Customer calls reveal unmet value improvement opportunities that are often overlooked by managers. Receptionists should be trained and equipped to collect such data. Computers can now gather some information automatically. Managers should combine data from the above methods for directly determining customer value with data from current customers. Such data should be analyzed at least monthly for emerging trends, out-of-control special causes, and critical incidents.

After-Sale Feedback   Most managers have a wealth of untapped data on customer value at their fingertips in customers' postsale communications with the firm about product deficiencies. Managers usually collect complaint, returns, and warranty data from several key subgroups, including customer service, manufacturing, and channel members. *Complaint data* are expressed in phone calls, comment cards, and other unstructured responses; *returns data* and *warranty claims* usually concern specific performance shortcomings that derive from design deficiencies. The key task for managers include designing and implementing a cross-functional information system that will collect and report the data as useful information to the key decisionmakers in each cross-functional process.

Techniques for Measuring Commercial Customer Value

Many of the techniques used to measure consumer value can also be used to measure commercial customer value. However, there are some unique features to be considered. Managers in firms serving other commercial or industrial organizations have usually relied on engineered specifications for product quality to determine what they need to produce. Yet customer value results from more than just the product attributes, and the intangibles of the use process must also be considered. Managers hoping to enhance the value of their product and firm should thoroughly analyze how their commercial customer uses the product, study how the two organizations interact, and not simply rely on specifications from their own engineering department. For example, managers should use behavioral analysis, go on-site to observe the use processes of customers, and ask probing questions about the processes. If managers understand customers' use processes, the consequences and the desired end states, they can often conceive better products that may displace current offerings.

The "customers" in a commercial firm include people other than individual end-users, such as the purchasing specialists and engineers administering the contract (who often do not fully understand the end-users' needs). To ensure that value is provided to these other customers, the value of a firm's product or service to the commercial customer must be analyzed in terms of benefits realized, costs saved, and the relative competitive advantage the customer gains.

For a commercial customer, design is key to building in product quality; however, satisfaction cannot be guaranteed by engineering. Managers may enhance the value of the firm's product/service through training and education, application, and consultation. Value can also be differentiated by making it greater than a competitor's, by making value flow to the customer faster or sooner, or by providing more certainty about the product and service (Hanan and Karp, 1991).

QUALITY IN ACTION: A MESSAGE TO THE STUDENT

Thomas E. Bennett, President and Chief Executive Officer, Ingersoll-Dresser Pump Company

In 1992, the pump divisions of Ingersoll-Rand and Dresser Industries merged to form the Ingersoll-Dresser Pump Company. This new venture produces pumps for such diverse industrial applications as petroleum refineries, water treatment facilities, and Navy battleships. President and CEO Thomas E. Bennett explains the importance of focusing improvement efforts on performance drivers connected to customer value.

The key to focusing a new organizational culture on strategic improvement is to establish performance drivers that are critical to the success of the business, readily understood by employees worldwide, and supported by literally thousands of initiatives. At Ingersoll-Dresser Pumps, we have determined that three performance drivers are essential to our ultimate success as a world-class performer. They are response, availability, and delivery. First, we want our employees to develop a keen sense of the need to improve the quality of their responses, not only to external, but to internal customers as well. Second, we know that a large measure of our success depends upon having certain products and spare parts available for immediate delivery or within a few weeks of the customer's order. Finally, we know that customers all over the world depend upon the integrity of our delivery schedules to complete their planning. Making our deliveries on time, every time, will help us differentiate our performance from that of the competition and give us that much-needed special edge to secure the next order. Response, availability, and delivery are the performance drivers that we're communicating to our associates all over the world with the expectation that their improvement activities will be prioritized to focus on these critical areas.

One way to be a value-adder is to help customers control one or more of their critical costs, or exploit one or more of their critical revenue sources. At every opportunity to add value, managers can ask:

1. Where are cost savings and productivity improvements possible?
2. Where are volume and margin increases possible?

Answering these two questions will help managers understand customer value in the present and the future, by business functions and by lines of business. Managers must also assess customers' needs and (dis)satisfaction.

For example, the founder (an engineer) of a successful small heater manufacturer decided to adopt and implement quality management and continuous improvement. He first attempted to measure customer satisfaction among the mechanics, chief engineers, purchasing agents, and machine operators who were his customers in the plastics industry. A self-addressed comment card enclosed with every order failed to generate more than 1 percent response. Next, a survey of 800 firms on his mailing list revealed that most respondents did not know his firm and that his mailing list was terribly out-of-date. Then, even with established relationships, his salespeople could not get their contacts to evaluate the firm. In visits to his top sixty customers, he learned first-hand that most appreciated his outstanding, delivered-as-promised service. An anonymous questionnaire he left behind confirmed that 80 percent of his key customers valued his superior delivery and service.

Finally, for a sample of his potential customers, local university students measured possible sources of value. First, they found that customers' average cost of downtime was over $400/hour. Even though only 2 percent of downtime was caused by heater failure, he was able to assure same or next day delivery. Next, for those customers who made at least two phone calls to order a heater, the founder had an opportunity to lower their ordering costs. In addition, few customers knew their heater inventory cost. Several years' experience suggested that most customers carried about twice as many heaters in inventory as they needed. Using this collected information on gains from less downtime, faster ordering and order processing, and inventory reductions, the founder was able to determine that, on average, he could save customers between 10 and 30 percent of their annual heater costs. His salespeople modified their selling approach to use a combination of data on relative value and customer satisfaction, brochures and catalogs, and information about the company's internal processes.

Principles of Measurement

There are several principles managers should follow when measuring customer value. These include:

1. Use multiple measures of each construct
2. Focus on behavior over attitudes or purchase intentions
3. Use both direct and indirect measures of key constructs
4. Validate results of intrusive methods with nonintrusive techniques
5. Confirm and understand quantitative results with qualitative studies
6. Measure customer satisfaction and value at the appropriate time

Each of these principles is discussed below.

Use Multiple Measures of Each Construct   Managers must use more than a single measure of customer needs, customer value, and customer satisfaction. If managers are completely willing to solicit, accept, and act upon customers' honest feedback, the firm's own measures will provide the best understanding of customer value. Without openness or in highly competitive situations, managers may gain better understanding by validating internal data with data from an objective, independent third party.

This principle of multiple measures also means that questions on the same general topic should be asked in several different ways. For example, a fast-food restaurant might use the following measures of customer satisfaction: satisfaction ratings from customer comment cards on the tables, number of customer complaints, and the number of customers leaving the drive-through line prematurely. The same restaurant could measure customer value by tracking the percentage of sales from repeat customers, average frequency of visits, and customers' perceived value relative to competitors as reported to an objective, third-party research group.

If customers are using several measures of quality or performance, managers may need to combine the results of the key independent rankings of products, each of which measures different aspects of quality. For example, one rating of cars on mechanical problems, operating cost, and safety combined the results of the J. D. Power Initial Quality Survey (initial defects), the *Consumer Reports* Trouble Index (consumers' reported frequency of repairs), the *Consumer Reports* Cost Index (consumers' reported cost of vehicle operation), and the Highway Loss Institute Insurance Injury Report (safety) (see Miller, 1992). This calculated value indicated that Asian cars were highest on quality, American cars were best on overall cost, and European cars were safest, but lower in quality than Asian and American vehicles.

Focus on Behavior over Attitudes or Purchase Intentions The quickest, least expensive data on customer value usually focus on attitudes toward the product/service or the prospect's intention to buy. More reliable, but expensive measures of customer satisfaction and value can be obtained from observing (1) customer behavior at the place of purchase, (2) behavior while using the product, (3) the usage situation, and (4) behavior after use (other product applications, referral, disposal, etc.). In general, attitude and intention measures should be used only when highly correlated with purchasing behavior. Even when the customer has difficulty imagining the benefits from the new product attributes, behavior analysis will still yield insight. For example, the 20-year adoption period for the microwave oven might have been shortened significantly if managers had understood how many changes the new technology would require in a cook's behaviors throughout food preparation, serving, consumption, and cleanup.

Use Both Direct and Indirect Measures of Key Constructs Ask questions that evaluate the product attribute or performance directly, but supplement these with questions that probe customer behaviors indirectly. For example, in response to a direct opinion question on a marketing survey by university students, only one-sixth of the adult respondents in a random sample considered themselves to be at high personal risk from sexual activity. In response to an indirect behavioral question, however, at least one-third of the sample reported being involved in nonexclusive relationships. In this example, the indirect question about type of relationship provided a better measure of the real level of customer need for protection.

The direct question about perceived risk provided valuable information about the marketing strategy (awareness campaign) that would be required to meet that need.

Validate Results of Intrusive Methods with Nonintrusive Techniques Attempts to measure customer satisfaction and value directly are always intrusive if any contact is made with the customer, since the intrusion may influence the respondent. Mail and phone surveys, interviews, simulations, experiments, and focus groups also assume that the respondent's statements accurately reflect behavior. The results of these methods should be validated with measures obtained through nonintrusive methods such as store observations, reports by coworkers or relatives, showrooms, videotapes of usage situations, focus groups observed from behind one-way mirrors, etc. The Japanese use of neural engineering cited earlier (eye movements in cars) may have provided nonintrusive data on customers' reaction to new car features.

Confirm and Understand Quantitative Results with Qualitative Studies Researchers' attempts to quantify, analyze, and graph data may disguise key results that lead to real interpretation into what customers really want and value. Qualitative information should be collected in the earliest and latest stages of research to deepen understanding of how customers really think about the product in each situation. Open-ended interviews, focus groups, and customer complaint data are particularly useful as sources of qualitative responses. Both qualitative and quantitative data should be collected systematically to facilitate later analysis and interpretation.

Measure Customer Satisfaction and Value at the Appropriate Time Customer *value* should be measured at the time of usage, when the customer can express most clearly the relative performance, utility, and benefits of the product or service. Overall customer *satisfaction* should be measured at time of use and again several weeks or months after purchase to allow time for evaluation of the experience. U.S. automakers have relied on initial satisfaction measures instead of value measures, then ignored customers' growing dissatisfaction as later repair problems mounted. For products or services that are consumed immediately, short-term measures of both value and satisfaction may be most useful while the user still remembers the experience.

Avoiding Value Measurement Errors
Failure to provide superior value is often the result of a manager's mistake in value determination or system management. The greatest mistake is asking only superficial questions or avoiding the relevant, tough questions. The bases for most mistakes include:

- Incorrectly identifying customer values
- Ordering customers' priorities for these values incorrectly

- Misinterpreting the significance (the weight) customers place on specific values
- Inappropriate systems design
- Poor execution of the firm's strategy

To improve value, managers must find and correct the systemic causes of these mistakes. The results of all value determination activities, especially the confirming activities, serve as the basis for realigning the firm's value strategy and making system improvements. That is why managers need good value measurements throughout the organization and system design and redesign to improve value.

Managers are often faced with these common mistakes, most of which are related to inadequate understanding of the basic dimensions of quality or value (Garvin, 1988). Perhaps the greatest mistake is to pursue values that are not important to customers. Another error is to rely on the wrong measurement standard for quality, value, or satisfaction. Also, if the yardstick is too crude to detect subtle differences in perceived value, managers will miss opportunities to improve value. Measurements can be so limited that managers completely miss key customer criteria or value. For example, reliance on warranty claims or complaints may cause managers to ignore the much larger population of customers who switched to a rival's product without complaining. A related mistake is to continue using historical metrics even though the environment and customer preferences have changed. American carmakers continued to focus on performance and features even as Japanese carmakers gained market share by emphasizing the reliability that customers valued more.

If needs, quality, value, and satisfaction have been measured correctly, managers must use the measures in designing the systems and products that will deliver that value. The next section describes how managers can translate value measurements into strategy. Quality function deployment is one method managers can use to avoid the value measurement errors discussed above.

▶ USING CUSTOMER VALUE MEASURES

Translating Learning into Strategy and Systems

Ultimately, managers must prioritize and focus their value strategies to match customer needs. They must translate their detailed knowledge about customer value and means-ends linkages into action to improve the organizational systems that deliver the value. This requires collaboration between managers with value determination activities and those in product and process design and engineering. As Earl Conway, formerly of Procter & Gamble says, "We have to translate consumer research into products. To do that, there has to be a strong link between marketing, product development, and production, and we have to ensure that what is measured is relevant to customers. A few years back, we discovered that we weren't doing such a good job of this. For example, there was not enough communication between researchers and manufacturing process designers, so manufacturing measurement systems were designed that didn't measure what consumers valued."

Even if managers use the typical quality tools to reduce variation and produce defect-free products, the product may still not meet customers' need for value. Managers must continuously improve customer value by doing the *right things* right, and not just by doing *something* right.[3] The abacus, slide rule, and calculator illustrate the importance of customer value in ensuring that improvements are strategically effective.[4] What is the customer need behind all three devices? One answer is the need for "hand-held computation." Measuring characteristics like speed, accuracy, and the ability to do complex functions, managers could perhaps determine the value of each technology and brand product in satisfying this need. Certainly, advancing from abacus to slide rule to calculator improves performance on these key characteristics that drive customer value. The electronic calculator provides much greater accuracy and convenience than the mechanical slide rule.

To use customer value as the basis for strategy during the slide rule era, managers should redesign and improve the slide rule by making it easier to handle or otherwise refining the product. They should also improve their production system, lower total cost, and thus improve the value of slide rules. Unfortunately, technological change usually means that such actions are insufficient to meet customers' real or changing needs. For example, making the slide rule round greatly simplified use, but did little for accuracy. Too often, managers frame their definition of the customer need around their present product or service, like the slide rule. They often focus so intently on improving the slide rule to enhance customers' satisfaction with slide rules that they get passed by. To make the jump to the next generation of products, like the calculator, managers must constantly search for new technologies that improve value in ways the customer may not yet imagine. Managers can no longer assume that customers have broad generic needs that can be met with generic products in mass markets. Customers are becoming more discriminating, and prefer to be pampered with products and services that fit their individual needs. Today, for example, calculators come in all sizes, colors, and price ranges, with different functions, button sizes, covers, thicknesses, and power supplies, for many different business, financial, technical, scientific, home, and professional applications.

---

3. The danger in using the term "Total Quality Management" is that people forget to put the emphasis on the word "Total," ending up with a constrained approach to continuous improvement with limited strategic implications.
4. The example of the abacus, the slide rule, and the calculator was provided by Tom Nolan, a consultant with Associates in Process Improvement. For other examples, see T. Nolan and L. Provost, "Understanding Variation," *Quality Progress*, May 1990.

For techniques used in stimulating and managing radical (breakthrough) technological change, we refer the reader to texts in innovation management and new product development. For continuous improvement, we turn next to methods invented by the Japanese for translating value into system requirements.

▼

QUALITY IN ACTION: A MESSAGE TO THE STUDENT
Tom Martin, Vice President, Marketing, Dell Computer Corporation

Michael Dell started selling personal computers from his University of Texas dorm in 1985. Before competitors caught on, Michael Dell built Dell Computer into a Fortune 500 company that today designs, develops, manufactures, services, and supports a complete line of personal computers compatible with industry standards in more than 120 markets worldwide. Tom Martin, Vice President, Marketing, explains how Dell is using customer satisfaction measures to get potential customers to perceive superior value in its products and services.

It doesn't take a rocket scientist to figure out Dell Computer Corporation's winning equation: quality products, plus outstanding service and support—divided by competitive prices—equals satisfied customers. With this "total value equation," Dell has won customer satisfaction awards from Dataquest, Reliability Ratings, and J. D. Power and Associates. Focus groups indicated that customers like comparative data on competing products, so we use the data to achieve certain advertising objectives. For example, in our ads we have displayed comparative data from independent surveys which show that Dell is number one in specific categories such as service, technical support, price, reliability, upgradeability, functionality, and overall satisfaction. The purpose of customer satisfaction ads is not to close the deal and sell a computer, but to raise customers' overall knowledge of Dell products. Side-by-side comparisons of products increase Dell's credibility in its claims and reinforces customers' beliefs about Dell's high performance and quality service. While satisfaction studies provide information useful in advertising strategies, these studies do not *cause* increased customer satisfaction. To increase customer satisfaction we must continually improve performance and service. The real measure is continually exceeding customers' expectations.

▲

Methods for Improving System Performance
The emerging paradigm requires managers to integrate diverse activities to serve the purpose of superior customer value. With a few notable exceptions, the traditional U.S. approach to functional integration has historically involved three basic components:

1. *Structural devices,* such as matrix organization, self-contained business units, hybrid organizations, or any of a variety of coordinating mechanisms like task forces, committees, or liaison roles. Managers seeking to integrate and align the functions through artificial means know how unsuccessful such approaches typically are. Without changing managerial roles, learning, and culture to focus on system improvement, these approaches are seen as add-ons or extras, rather than as the way work should be done.

2. Introduction of a *superordinate goal* strategy, stressing such themes as "Quality Is Job One," "Zero Defects," and the like. Such slogans may set impossible targets, be overly simplistic, or be unsupported by any reasonable action plan.

3. Management exhortation to *do the right thing the right way the first time.* Deming (1986) insists that such exhortations merely accuse the employee of, at best, not trying hard enough, or at worst, trying to do things wrong. Although it may help focus attention, this approach often presumes that employees can and should fix the processes for which management is responsible.

These approaches are subtly elitist (Cole, 1989). They assume that managers or executives can bring about quality improvement and functional integration while resting comfortably in the same position from which they started, namely, in power and in control. Managers and executives like to hear that quality is "free." However, these reassuringly simple approaches usually fail to take into account the multiple linkages among the systems and subsystems of the organization. In contrast, quality function deployment (QFD) provides a natural, ongoing way to integrate the "voice of the customer" throughout the systems and processes of the organization.[5]

Quality Function Deployment

Quality function deployment was developed in Japan by Mitsubishi's Kobe Shipyards in 1972, and adopted by Toyota in 1978. More recently, many Japanese organizations, from manufacturers of electronics and appliances to designers of swimming pools and apartment layouts, have used QFD to improve processes and build competitive advantage (Hauser and Clausing, 1988). In the U.S., since Ford Motor Company adopted QFD in 1983 to counter Toyota, such notable companies as Procter & Gamble, General Motors, Digital Equipment Corporation, Hewlett-Packard, and AT&T now use QFD to improve communication, product development, and measurement processes and systems.

As developed by the Japanese, QFD is a highly structured format used to translate customer value requirements into specific product and service characteristics, and ultimately into the processes and systems that provide the valued products and services. The aim of QFD is to translate customer needs or wants into detailed technical requirements, and to set priorities using competitive data. QFD should help organizational processing activi-

---

5. If not done in a disciplined manner, QFD can be excruciatingly complex.

Figure 4

House of quality

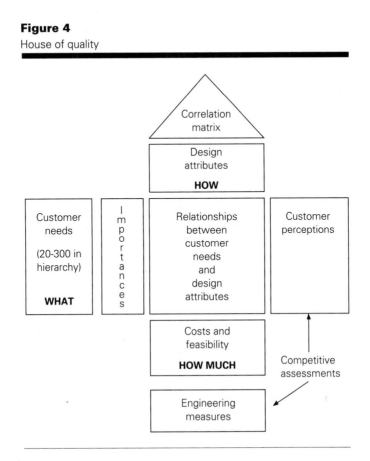

ties and outputs match customer wants (Cole, 1989). As shown in Figure 4, QFD employs a "what-how" matrix listing customer wants (the "what"), technical requirements (the "how"), and competitive assessments using customers' subjective perceptions and the firm's own objective engineering measurements (King, 1989). Thus, QFD provides a way to integrate and subordinate specialized functions and departments into coordinated, collaborative activity that provides customer value. While many organizations will choose not to use such a structured technique, they will have to write operational definitions that clearly articulate the means of providing value to customers. These definitions will have to be translated into processes and operations to produce the products and services. QFD simply provides the structured methodology that promotes communication among the specialized experts (marketing, engineering, and manufacturing staff) who must do this work.

There is more to QFD than simply filling out a "house of quality" matrix. It involves implementing a customer-oriented philosophy (Hauser and Clausing, 1988). In a 1950 visit to a steel plant, Dr. Ishikawa (1985) discovered strong sectionalism that mitigated against cross-functional co-operation to eliminate defects. He coined a key phrase to help explain the need for cooperation: "You must imagine that the next process is your customer" (JUSE, quoted in Cole, 1989, p. 241). This is not mere rhetoric. In QFD, the voice of the customer, both internal and external, is translated into concerted action on the part of the organization to fulfill customers' requirements:

> Of particular importance here is the development of quality function deployment systems (QFDS). This involves the development of checking systems (forms to be filled out) for ensuring that employees from different departments, initially marketing and R&D with design, will work together to collect data that match up customer wants and needs on specific dimensions with engineered specifications. These matrices ensure this outcome by requiring data collection to measure the fit between the two areas. When deviations occur, the relevant personnel from the different departments must work out ways to eliminate them. Data are also collected on the performance of competitors, and their fit is compared to one's own performance. This same process is next applied to measuring the fit between engineering specifications and manufacturing processes. [Cole, 1989, p. 242]

The chief advantage of the QFD approach over other mechanisms is that it integrates, at a system level, different departmental activities through common task requirements. This minimizes deviation from customer wants throughout the product design and production cycle (Cole, 1989). Companies that use QFD can achieve a competitive advantage by delivering the products and services customers want. These outputs will be efficiently and effectively designed and delivered more quickly than those of competitors. For example, Toyota has claimed that QFD nearly eliminated warranty claims concerning rust and helped reduce development costs and time to market by as much as 40 percent (Sullivan, 1986a, 1986b). In a recent study of U.S. firms, the use of QFD yielded several process improvements in product development, such as structuring the decision-making process across functional groups, building a well-organized, highly motivated team, and moving information efficiently from its origin to the ultimate user (Griffin, 1992). Thus, QFD may improve long-term process performance more than short-term product gains.

Implementing the QFD Process

As shown in Figure 5, the QFD house of quality is merely the first in a series of such matrices that translate the customers' needs into product and system requirements and specifications. The measures of customer needs and values are translated first into design attributes which are in turn the basis of product/service features. These required features are based directly on measures of customer needs. The features are then used to define the processes and operating conditions that are required to deliver value to the customer. Each step of the process in the house of quality, design matrix, operating matrix, and control matrix is based on

Figure 5

The flow of communications in translating customer needs into operations using QFD interaction matrices

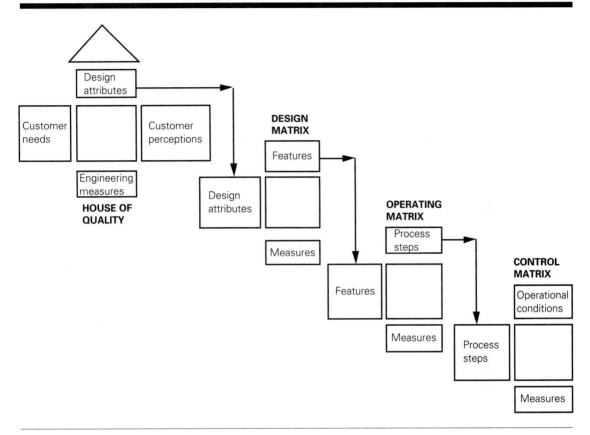

clearly defined measures that incorporate customers' needs and values. The data produced in one stage of the development process are explicitly related to the decisions that must be made in the next stage.

As shown in Figure 6, the matrices centralize and make very visible and concise the data needed to generate product definition, design, production, and delivery decisions. The customers' requirements on the vertical dimension are individually matched with the design requirements on the top horizontal dimensions of the matrix. A coding scheme of circles, periods, triangles, etc., is then used to indicate the degree and direction of influence of the most important requirements of the design. Each decision's assumptions are clearly defined and linked to the customers' needs. The actual use of the charts makes information needs obvious. Because the matrices also store the product plan, the loss of details is less likely. And the matrices improve communication between managers, team members, decision makers, and decision implementers (Griffin, 1992).

Figure 6
Example of QFD house of quality

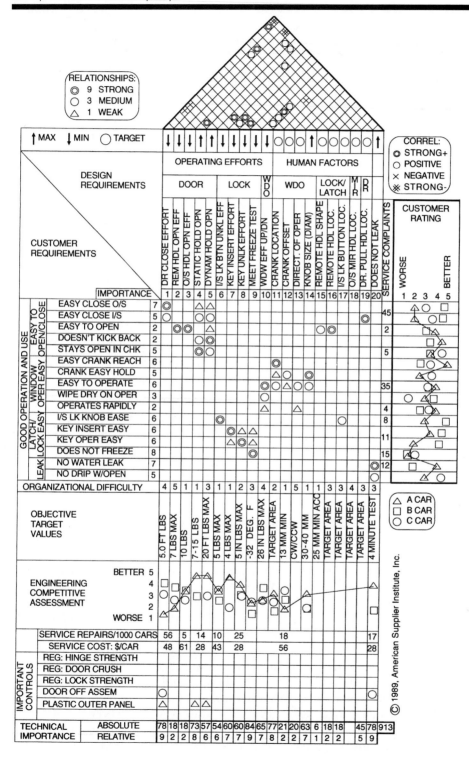

The house of quality is the first step in negotiating what managers agree the design will achieve for customers. It defines those cost-effective design attributes that can be delivered to achieve customer perceptions of value. QFD has stages similar to the traditional U.S. phase-review development process. However, with the simultaneous consideration of customer needs, engineering capabilities, and process design, QFD can contribute continuous cross-functional participation from start to finish and generates consensus decisions about trade-offs (Griffin, 1992). The QFD process helps managers in each function or department to (1) understand what the external customer values, and (2) understand their contribution to the systems and processes that provide the value. This understanding provides a basis for cross-functional teamwork and collaboration.

Policy deployment provides the larger strategic context for QFD. Imai (1986, pp. 144–145) illustrated the value of the policy deployment approach by contrasting it with the traditional alternative:

> The president of an airline company proclaims that he believes in safety and that his corporate goal is to maintain safety throughout the company. This proclamation is prominently featured in the company's quarterly report and advertising. Let us further suppose that the department managers also swear to a firm belief in safety. The flight crews say they believe in safety. Everyone in the company practices safety. True? Or might everyone simply be paying lip service to the idea of safety?
>
> On the other hand, if the president states that safety is a company policy and works with his division managers to develop a plan for safety that defines their responsibilities, everyone will have a very specific subject to discuss. Safety will become a real concern. For the manager in charge of catering services, safety might mean maintaining the quality of food to avoid customer dissatisfaction or illness. How does he ensure that the food is top quality? What sorts of control points and checkpoints does he establish? How does he ensure there is no deterioration in food quality in flight? Who checks the temperature of refrigerators or the condition of the oven while in the air?
>
> Only when safety is translated into specific actions with specific control and checkpoints established for each employee's job may safety be said to have been truly deployed as a policy. Policy deployment calls for everyone to interpret policy in light of his own responsibilities and for everyone to work out criteria to check his success in carrying out the policy.

One can substitute the words "quality," "TQM," or "customer value" for the word "safety" in the above quote to describe an approach that many American organizations would find beneficial.

Improvement of Systems and Processes

Many companies use QFD just on new product/service development. However, in the emerging paradigm, managers continue to use the philosophy underlying QFD to improve existing systems and processes. QFD is quite

Runyon, Quality, and the U.S. Postal Service

Marie Kiehl usually picked up her employer's mail at the local post office. Often it was not available at the 8:30 pick-up time. After she complained to the central office, her local postmaster met her one morning to explain that she had no right to complain since the firm had not paid a "caller" fee for the privilege of picking up the mail early rather than having it delivered later. When she asked, "Will paying the fee improve our service?" the postmaster replied, "No. It will give you the right to complain" (*Reader's Digest*, April 1993).

This incident merely suggests the monumental challenge that Marvin Runyon faced when he accepted the position of Postmaster General of the United States. Along with other factors, such managerial attitudes had contributed to rising postal rates and declining volume. To stem the losses, he embarked on a three-point plan: reducing postal overhead and bureaucracy, improving service quality, and stabilizing rates for two years. First,

an early retirement program streamlined the structure by eliminating 30,000 overhead and 16,000 line positions, yet maintained delivery. Second, higher first class service goals were monitored by Price Waterhouse each quarter. Runyon also developed ways to help postal employees listen to customers. An independent system measured postal service satisfaction among households. Training complemented employee empowerment, trouble-shooting teams, and efforts to make services more user-friendly and accessible with expanded retail hours. Pricing was simplified and customers' suggestions for new products and services were seriously considered. From a $50 million loss in July 1992, these initiatives helped the Postal Service improve to a $500 million profit by the end of the fiscal year in September 1992, and savings of $700–$800 million in 1993 (Runyon, 1993).

useful in both of these applications since it promotes cross-functional communication and the translation of customer needs into operational realities. For example, organizations often assign process action teams to improve processes. One of the first steps in improving processes is to identify the customers and determine what they value. This initial work provides a focus for the improvement efforts of the process action team. It explicitly connects measures of customer value to the systems and processes that are to be improved. All of the market research techniques discussed earlier can be used by these process action teams.

Once a customer value strategy is designed and implemented, managers must observe the results of their efforts in delivering customer value. Such observation provides information about whether their strategy and improvement efforts have been successful. Traditional approaches include satisfaction and dissatisfaction measurement. These approaches are discussed below, along with suggestions for improvement.

▶ SATISFACTION AND DISSATISFACTION MEASUREMENT

Measures of Customer Satisfaction

Thus far, you have learned the importance of measuring customer needs, product quality, and customer value. Many managers, however, begin at the end of the buyer behavior model by measuring customer satisfaction. Managers often use measures of customer satisfaction and dissatisfaction to assess their firm's performance in providing value, rather than to plan a value strategy, learn customer needs, or measure product quality (Albrecht and Bradford, 1990; Hausknecht, 1990). Managers should use customer satisfaction measurement, but not rely on it exclusively.

Although satisfaction and dissatisfaction measures are becoming more popular, managers remain confused about the meaning and comparability of the various types of measures (see Figure 7 for examples). More than thirty different measures of the phenomenon have been documented (Hausknecht, 1990).

Reactions to Perceived Value One of the outcomes of customers' use experience might be satisfaction or dissatisfaction with the product. Customers do not frequently use the terms "satisfied" and "dissatisfied" to describe their use experiences, but when they do, the meanings are closely related to the concept of value. A customer's valuation process attaches a valence (positive or negative) to the use experience. Satisfaction or dissatisfaction is a value judgment one step further as the customer compares the use experience (realized value) to some customer-generated standard of anticipated or expected value (Oliver, 1980; Woodruff, Cadotte, and Jenkins, 1983). Satisfaction or dissatisfaction depends on (1) the affective response (an arousal of pleasantness or unpleasantness) to the discrepancy, and (2) the extent to which the "good/bad for me" evaluation met, exceeded, or fell below the standard (Oliver, 1989).[6]

The standard might be an expectation such as what the value was "predicted to be" prior to purchase and use.[7] In this case, satisfaction or dissatisfaction would result from the extent to which the expectation was disconfirmed (Oliver, 1977, 1980) (see item 1 in Figure 7). However, this expectancy disconfirmation theory is somewhat incomplete, because customers probably employ multiple standards either in combination (e.g., Cadotte, Woodruff, and Jenkins, 1987) or over time (e.g., Miller, 1977).

Types of Standards Pre-use expectations are not the only standards customers use. The list of possible standards include:

- Predicted performances (Olson and Dover, 1979)
- Experience-based norms (Woodruff, Cadotte, and Jenkins, 1983)
- Equity (Oliver and Swan, 1989)
- Values (Westbrook and Reilly, 1983)

---

6. Some writers make distinctions between satisfaction with specific events and an overall attitude which results over time from many incidents of satisfaction. For example, a multi-item scale called SERVQUAL measures "perceptions of service quality," which is defined as "the degree and direction of discrepancy between consumers' perceptions and expectations" (Parasuraman, Zeithaml, and Berry, 1988; Cronin and Taylor, 1992).

7. A standard may not necessarily be a point along some performance dimension, but may be a range of indistinguishable levels, that is, a "zone of indifference." Further, the zone may vary across customers for the same dimension, and across dimensions for the same customer (Woodruff, Cadotte, and Jenkins, 1983).

Figure 7

Examples of different types of measures of customer (dis)satisfaction, emotional reaction, and intentions

Measures of Satisfaction/Dissatisfaction

1. My expectations were:

Too high: It was poorer than I thought		Accurate: It was just as I expected		Too low: It was better than I thought
1	2	3	4	5

2. Overall, how satisfied have you been with this _____ ?

100% Completely satisfied	90	80	70	60	50	40	30	20	10	0% Not at all satisfied

3. How satisfied were you with _____ ?

Very dissatisfied	Somewhat dissatisfied	Slightly dissatisfied	Neither	Slightly satisfied	Somewhat satisfied	Very satisfied
_____	_____	_____	_____	_____	_____	_____

4. I am satisfied with _____ .

Agree |__|__|__|__|__|__|__|__|__|__| Disagree

5. Here is a picture of a ladder. At the bottom of the ladder is the worst _____ you might reasonably expect to have. At the top is the best _____ you might expect to have. On which rung would you put _____ ?

9	Best I could expect to have
8	
7	
6	
5	
4	
3	
2	
1	Worst I could expect to have

6. Likert scales (summed)

	Strongly agree				Strongly disagree
a. I am satisfied with _____	1	2	3	4	5
b. If I had it to do all over again, I would _____	1	2	3	4	5
c. My choice to _____ was a good one.	1	2	3	4	5
d. I feel bad about my decision concerning _____	1	2	3	4	5
e. I think that I did the right thing when I decided _____	1	2	3	4	5
f. I am not happy that I did what I did about _____	1	2	3	4	5

Measures of Emotional Reaction

7. Mark on one of the nine blanks below the position which most closely reflects your satisfaction with _____ .

Delight	Pleased	Mostly satisfied	Mixed	Mostly dissatisfied	Unhappy	Terrible	Neutral	Never thought about it
_____	_____	_____	_____	_____	_____	_____	_____	_____

Figure 7 (Continued)

Examples of different types of measures of customer (dis)satisfaction, emotional reaction, and intensions

8. The question and scales below can be used to measure separate emotions, for example, those captured by the adjectives "loading" on each of the following ten emotional dimensions. (1) interest—excitement, (2) enjoyment—joy, (3) surprise—startle, (4) sadness—anguish, (5) anger—rage, (6) disgusted—revulsion, (7) contempt—scorn, (8) fear—terror, (9) shame—shyness, (10) guilt—remorse.

Please indicate the extent to which each word describes the way you feel with respect to _____ .

1	2	3	4	5
Very slightly or not at all	Slightly	Moderately	Considerably	Very strongly

Measures of Behavioral Intentions

9. How likely are you to use (play with) _____ in the future?

Very unlikely	Unlikely	Likely	Very likely
1	2	3	4

10. Knowing what you know now, what are the chances in ten (10) that you would choose to use the _____ again?

0	1	2	3	4	5	6	7	8	9	10
No chance										Certain

For complete review, see D. R. Hausknecht, "Measurement Scales in Consumer Satisfaction/Dissatisfaction," *Journal of Consumer Satisfaction, Dissatisfaction and Complaining Behavior*, Vol. 3, 1990, pp. 1–11.

- Ideal (Miller, 1977; Sirgy, 1984)
- Minimum tolerable (Miller, 1977)
- Deserved (Miller, 1977)
- Desires (Spreng and Olshavsky, 1991)
- Sellers' promises (Woodruff et al., 1991)[8]

The source of the standards might be the information used in the search process, such as experience with alternative products or the same product, advertising promises, the experiences of others, or one's own logical inference from product information. Further, pre-use and post-use valuation may entail the use of different mixes of standards. For example, before the purchase, customers might attempt to maximize their choice based on which alternative most closely matched their "ideal." But after purchase, customers may acknowledge that the ideal cannot be met, and may be content to confirm that the chosen product performs better than the alternatives not chosen (Gardial et al., 1991). Managers must determine what standards people use to rate their satisfaction or dissatisfaction (e.g., the tough work of segmentation), so they can better understand the meaning of their measures and take appropriate action to improve.

---

8. These constructs are not mutually exclusive. For example, experience-based norms involve the deserved notion, but temper it with customer knowledge of what is possible performance.

Meaning of Measurements Quantitative data from rating scales are often gathered through surveys that measure satisfaction and dissatisfaction. However, given the complexity of the phenomenon (e.g., varying standards over time and individuals, or role of emotions), as described above, it may be difficult to gather meaning from the data. The same scale of values on a typical bipolar measurement scale may have different meanings to different people. As Olander (1977, p. 415) states, "There is seldom, if ever, a yardstick which is common to different groups or which stays put over time." In responding to generic satisfaction scales, people may use whatever standard or frame of reference that comes to mind, leaving managers to guess about the meaning of the responses.

The way satisfaction questions are framed on a questionnaire may influence what standard customers select. Questions may be phrased to specify the standard(s) the customer should consider, for example, "compared to your ideal . . ." or "compared to other brands. . ." But even that approach has drawbacks. When there are many possible standards, it is usually not clear how to determine which standards are appropriate for different situations and different people. Usually, the researcher has to assume that a given segment will have the same frame of reference. Further, the use of multiple scales, one for each type of standard, imposes lengthy and tedious work for respondents (Woodruff et al., 1991). Managers should identify and focus on the few standards judged most important by customer groups.

The Dynamics of Value and Implications for Measurement

Given a set of standards, if product performance meets or exceeds customer expectations, the customer is likely to be satisfied. If not, the customer is likely to be dissatisfied. Even a dissatisfied customer, if handled properly, can be converted into a satisfied customer. For example, Whirlpool discovered that the customers most likely to buy again were those who initially were dissatisfied over a problem, complained, and had their problem quickly and courteously fixed. Perhaps this phenomenon has to do with building a relationship and its impact on perceptions of value. Customer value is certainly a dynamic event during the ownership and use of a single product, and over time across multiple products.

Satisfied customers are more likely to buy again and to advise others to buy again, because of the anticipation of value to be gained. However, the factors that lead to customer satisfaction are also quite dynamic. Even satisfied customers may not buy again if their needs or standards change, or if alternative products are available. Given dynamic markets, customer needs, and standards, managers should not assume that satisfaction levels are stable or comparable over time. Rather than relying on satisfaction measures as the only performance indicator, managers might find direct measures of value delivered and perceived to be more useful. This direct measurement process must study competing alternatives to compare value offerings.

Choosing Competitive Benchmarks The existence of multiple standards of comparison across individuals and situations raises the question of who managers must identify as "the competition" (Gardial et al., 1991). The answer to this question has serious implications for orienting continuous improvement activities. For example, if managers accept "brand experience" or "other brands" as the standard, they may be content to simply benchmark and ensure that they are a little better than competing alternatives, rather than understanding the underlying customer value. If managers take the customers' needs as the "ideal" standard, they might be motivated to create and innovate product and process breakthroughs which achieve quantum leaps in improved value. To do so, managers must know the means-ends relationships of the customer value chain.

Relative Value Even comparisons based on customer ideals may not anticipate future innovations. Reliance on satisfaction and dissatisfaction measures may encourage managers to remain within the current paradigm or framework of current offerings.

Satisfaction and dissatisfaction measures may be useful for assessing value within a given paradigm, and these consequence measures may also reveal when a company has been left behind by a competitor's shift to a new paradigm. For example, this occurred with the decline in demand for typewriters at the onset of the age of personal computers. However, satisfaction and dissatisfaction measures do not inspire managers to lead a paradigm shift, because the key data on customers are collected at the end of the process. Managers may aspire to create dissatisfaction with current products, by envisioning new possibilities with improved products, as Yamaha revitalized demand for its products in the entertainment market by rethinking the market in terms of customer needs and not in terms of existing piano products.

Refining Satisfaction and Dissatisfaction Measurement

Managers must continuously seek to improve satisfaction and dissatisfaction measurement. Some areas for improvement are suggested below.

Qualitative Measures In addition to the complexity introduced by the possibility of multiple standards, the terms "satisfaction" and "dissatisfaction" as anchors may not capture the meanings that accompany the vast range of customers' cognitive and emotional reactions (Westbrook and Oliver, 1991; Gardial et al., 1991). Given these potential deficiencies in the use of satisfaction and dissatisfaction scales, managers should have a system of measurement that comprehensively encompasses the means-ends concept of customer satisfaction, perhaps using qualitative data along with quantitative survey data. The scale values might reveal areas of strength or weakness, while the qualitative data help provide interpretation of the numbers and a richer knowledge base for managerial action (Woodruff et al., 1991).

Assessing Specific Objects/Attributes   For satisfaction and dissatisfaction measures to be useful, they must offer specific information. Customers may be highly satisfied with one aspect of their experience and not with another. High overall satisfaction may accompany high dissatisfaction with one particular aspect. For example, on a hospital visit you encounter many objects (doctors, administrative staff, nurses, technicians, facilities, equipment), and each object may have multiple attributes (friendliness, expertise, modernity, efficiency). You may be highly satisfied with everything except the friendliness of one nurse. So it is essential to specify the focus for satisfaction responses, perhaps by having customers assess each aspect individually. Such specific feedback should lead to specific improvements because managers directly control product attributes through design and operations, and because they can usually influence customers' standards.

Assessing Means-Ends Relationships   Exclusive measurement of objects/attributes ignores the instrumental relationship of attributes to use consequences and desired end states. To directly assess what customers value (i.e., goal-related consequences), managers must not just measure perceived attributes or perceived consequences, they must also measure customer evaluations and emotional reactions to those perceptions (see items 7 and 8 in Figure 7). Managers must understand customer perceptions of these means-ends relationships, including causal beliefs, attitudes, and emotions, due to the effects that these mental events can have on subsequent motivation and intention to buy and use the product (Izard, 1977; Arnold, 1960). See items 9 and 10 in Figure 7 as examples of measures of behavioral intentions.

Tailored Measurement Systems   There is no universal prescription for a measurement system that will always provide useful information. Managers must develop measurement systems using their own judgment and understanding of the means-ends relationships for their specific customers. The concepts and suggestions contained in this chapter should be adapted and enlisted to support managerial creativity and ingenuity.

Cross-Functional Participation   The responsibility for determining what customers value and assessing the delivery of customer value is not simply a job for marketing managers. This work must be done by every manager of the organization for internal, channel, and end-user customers. The best measurement systems are derived from cross-functional efforts and participation, and every activity of the organization should be directed toward providing and enhancing value for customers. Appropriately focused measures must be used for each process. Certainly, the frequency and type of measures used will vary with the purpose and scope of activity in each process. Ongoing process measures may be gathered and charted every few minutes or hours within a manufacturing plant, but customer surveys will likely be conducted less frequently.

Implications for Strategy

The process of determining customer value must accompany broader market opportunity analysis for new technologies in emerging large markets as well as for further differentiated products/services in ever-smaller market segments. The most extreme form of market segmentation, sometimes called *market fragmentation*, defines each customer as a segment with unique needs to be met through responsive and flexible organizational systems (Robert, 1992). Flexible manufacturing systems driven by QFD may enable a firm to meet the needs of ever-smaller market segments. Managers must understand the latent, emerging needs and value sought by their current and potential customers, not just current product quality. Thus, customer value is the centerpiece measurement between customers' needs, quality attributes, and customer satisfaction. Marketing becomes part of the system and integrated strategy for delivering value to customers (Power, 1991). Consider how Advanta Corporation does this with its credit cards.

The traditional way of issuing credit cards is to mail out offers for credit cards to anyone with a good credit record. This mass marketing approach means blitzing the nation with 30 to 40 million pieces of mail offering the same interest rates and annual fees to everyone. For example, Citicorp grew to be the nation's largest issuer of credit cards by offering only two types: the *Classic* for the general population and the *Preferred* for more affluent customers. In a saturated market, Advanta has been enjoying double-digit growth in revenues and profits by tailoring the cards to carefully chosen customers.

Advanta reduces its costs by keeping its MasterCards and Visas out of the hands of potential problem customers. For example, after culling creditworthy names from generally available credit bureau lists, Advanta puts potential card holders through more than two dozen other proprietary databases that narrow the target group even further. Among the screens are total debt outstanding, debt on other credit cards, and what the customer pays for the other cards. Most card issuers only look at two criteria: income and bill-paying history.

Based on extensive analysis, Advanta tailors the pricing to the selected customers, which often results in better interest rates, more favorable terms, and larger credit lines than its competitors. Advanta reduces its credit losses because its customers tend to pay their bills more promptly. Advanta customers also tend to use the Advanta credit cards more than others, and to maintain outstanding balances and pay finance charges. (For the past four years, Advanta's credit card receivables have grown at a rate of 35 to 40 percent a year, outstripping the industry growth rate of 6 percent). Advanta even analyzes the customer's credit record to reveal whether a customer typically pays bills at a certain time of the month. If so, Advanta can time its billing cycle to coincide with the customer's habits. Advanta's president, Richard Greenawalt, explains, "We get enough information about the customer to know what doesn't satisfy them about the credit cards they have. We try to play off that dissatisfaction" (Pae, 1993).

At Advanta, marketing research plays a central role throughout strategy formulation and implementation. In the emerging paradigm, marketing research must lead the effort to determine the customers' requirements and competitive drivers in the beginning of the process, as well as measuring the outcomes of customer value and customer satisfaction. Marketing strategists must segment the market and identify target segments that can be better served, then develop a strategy to deliver, perhaps exceed, the value required by customers and meet the firm's objectives. To do this, measurements of customer value and satisfaction must be communicated throughout the organization; they must be used to unite the entire organization in the pursuit of total customer satisfaction, and to reach the organization's goals.

Market measurements also drive the particular marketing mix that determines the perception of value by the customer. In addition to translating the measures of customer requirements into product and system designs and features, QFD also relates these to cost, thus influencing the price. Customer needs, values, and satisfaction are the primary driving force behind distribution and promotion strategy and tactics. As Wal-Mart and Dell Computer Corporation have shown with their low-cost, direct distribution systems, understanding what the customers really want often enables managers to shorten the distribution channel, increase value and satisfaction, and lower costs.

Value and satisfaction measurements should also be used to help design the theme of awareness campaigns, help educate customers on new evaluation criteria, and reinforce beliefs about the customer orientation of the organization and the value of the product/service. A poll of 24,000 consumers by Video Storyboard Tests, Inc., found that value was the most compelling reason consumers recalled ads in 1989.[9] Sears, Kmart, and J. C. Penney made the top ten most memorable ads for the first time by stressing value with low prices in the ads, with copy like, "Your money's worth and a whole lot more." Many ad campaigns in the top fifty stressed value.

It is important for the organization to measure customer value and define the total organizational strategy around delivering value to the target customers. Continuous improvement efforts must also be directed by the information gained through measuring customer value. Ongoing measurement of customer value and satisfaction provides an assessment

---

9. "Pitches on Value Stick in Consumers' Minds," *Wall Street Journal*, June 4, 1990, p. B1.

of value delivered and reveals opportunities for enhancing value with improved products and services, and with improved systems for producing and delivering them. When all managers and employees are working together toward the common goal of superior customer value and are regularly measuring customers' needs and responses across the means-ends model, the organization is truly customer-driven.

▶ SUMMARY OF KEY POINTS

1. Managers must stay close to their customers to provide superior customer value.
2. Managers can stay close to their customers only by measuring what they value.
3. A general process for learning about customer value involves projecting, invalidating, discovering, and confirming what customers value.
4. Marketing research techniques may be used to measure what customers value and help plan strategy.
5. Quality function deployment can be used to promote communication that translates customer needs and wants into product and service features, process designs, and operations.
6. Once products and services are delivered to customers, their value must be assessed.
7. Measurements of customer satisfaction and dissatisfaction can be used to measure customer reactions to value delivered.
8. Managers must use measurements of customer value and (dis)satisfaction to formulate customer value strategies and to continuously improve implementation.

▶ KEY TERMS

behavioral analysis

customer needs

customer satisfaction

customer value

focus group technique

laddering

market test

Protocol analysis

quality function deployment (QFD)

trade-off analysis

▶ DISCUSSION QUESTIONS

1. How would you explain the difference between customer needs, product quality, customer value, and customer satisfaction? Use one example to illustrate the differences in these concepts.
2. How should managers collect market data when time to market is critical? What are the risks of the various trade-offs they must make to shorten the time to market? How would you suggest they determine the optimal approach to meet customers' needs better than competitors?

3. Should managers do their own market research or hire an outside firm? To do their own, what would they have to know how to do? If they had no experience in these tasks, what would you suggest they do? Should a manager start with product quality, customer needs, customer value, or customer satisfaction measures? How does the organization's situation affect your answer?

4. How is customer value linked to managers' decisions about strategy?

▶ **EXPERIENTIAL EXERCISES**

1. Compare the value and satisfaction measurement strategies of two similar local small businesses, one a nationally franchised operation, the other a sole proprietorship. For example, you might pick up the customer feedback card at a fast-food chain restaurant, then do the same at a nearby non-chain fast-food restaurant. Quick-copy shops, auto repair services, and electronic stores are also potential candidates. How does each operation measure quality, value, and satisfaction? Which of these does the customer feedback card emphasize? Ask the manager how often the data are collected and analyzed, how the information is used, and what difference it has made in the firm's operations. Has the firm improved its customer satisfaction? What should each firm be measuring? What three recommendations would you make to improve each firm's measurement of customer needs, service or product quality, customer value, or customer satisfaction?

2. Look in the library for recent issues of *Consumer Reports, Stereo Review, MacWorld, PC Magazine,* or *Runners World.* Find an article that evaluates competing brands within the same product category. How did they measure product quality, subjectively with rating scales or objectively with quantified measurements of physical characteristics? Did they report customer (user) satisfaction? If so, how was satisfaction measured? Which publication(s) report on customer value? How did they define value and determine what particular brand provided best value? What three recommendations would you make to improve the measurement process?

▶ **REFERENCES**

K. Albrecht and L. J. Bradford, *The Service Advantage: How to Identify and Fulfill Customer Needs,* Dow-Jones Irwin, Homewood, Ill., 1990.

M. B. Arnold, "Emotion and Personality," *Psychological Aspects,* Vol. 1, Columbia University Press, New York, 1960.

J. Bailey, "Why Customers Trash the Garbage Man," *Wall Street Journal,* Mar. 17, 1993, pp. 81A, 81B.

E. R. Cadotte, R. B. Woodruff, and R. L. Jenkins, "Expectations and Norms in Models of Consumer Satisfaction," *Journal of Marketing Research,* Vol. 24, November 1987, pp. 305–314.

G. H. Carothers and G. M. Bounds, "Customer Value Determination and System Improvement Cycles," *Competing Globally through Customer Value: The Management of Strategic Suprasystems,* Greenwood Press, Westport, Conn., 1991.

G. A. Churchill, Jr., "A Paradigm for Developing Better Measures of Marketing Constructs," *Journal of Marketing Research*, Vol. 16, February 1979, pp. 64–73.

D. S. Clemons, *Expanding the Model of Consumer Satisfaction and Dissatisfaction: The Means-Ends Disconfirmation Model of CS/D*, unpublished doctoral dissertation, Department of Marketing, Logistics, and Transportation, University of Tennessee.

R. E. Cole, "Large-Scale Change and the Quality Revolution," in A. M. Mohrman, S. A. Mohrman, G. E. Ledford, T. G. Cummings, E. E. Lawler III, and Associates (eds.), *Large-Scale Organizational Change*, Jossey-Bass, San Francisco, 1989.

J. J. Cronin, Jr., and S. A. Taylor, "Measuring Service Quality: A Reexamination and Extension," *Journal of Marketing*, Vol. 56, No. 3, 1992, pp. 55–68.

W. E. Deming, *Out of the Crisis*, MIT (CAES) Press, Cambridge, Mass., 1986.

S. F. Gardial, D. S. Clemons, R. B. Woodruff, D. W. Schumann, and M. J. Burns, "The Structure of Evaluations: Contrasting Consumers' Pre-Purchase, Post-Purchase, and (Dis)Satisfaction Experiences," *Journal of Consumer Research*, March 1994.

D. A. Garvin, *Managing Quality*, Free Press, New York, 1988.

Government Accounting Office, *Management Practices: U.S. Companies Improve Performance through Quality Efforts*, GAO/NSIAD-91-190, Gaithersburg, Md., 1991.

A. Griffin, "Evaluating QFD's Use in U.S. Firms as a Process for Developing Products," *Journal of Product Innovation Management*, Vol. 9, 1992, p. 171–187.

J. Gutman, "A Means-End Chain Model Based on Consumer Categorization Processes," *Journal of Marketing*, Vol. 46, Spring 1982, pp. 60–72.

J. Gutman and S. D. Alden, "Adolescents' Cognitive Structures of Retail Stores and Fashion Consumption: A Means-End Chain Analysis of Quality," in J. Jacoby and J. C. Olson (eds.), *Perceived Quality*, Lexington Books, Lexington, Mass., 1985, pp. 99–114.

M. Hanan and P. Karp, *Competing on Value*, American Management Association, AMACOM, New York, 1991.

J. R. Hauser and D. Clausing, "The House of Quality," *Harvard Business Review*, May–June 1988, pp. 63–73.

D. R. Hausknecht, "Measurement Scales in Consumer Satisfaction/Dissatisfaction," *Journal of Consumer Satisfaction, Dissatisfaction and Complaining Behavior*, Vol. 3, 1990, pp. 1–11.

T. J. Hayes and C. B. Tathum, *Focus Group Interviews: A Reader*, American Marketing Association, Chicago, 1989.

M. Imai, *Kaizen*, McGraw-Hill, New York, 1986.

K. Ishikawa, *Total Quality Management*, D. Lu (ed.), Prentice-Hall, Englewood Cliffs, N.J., 1985.

C. E. Izard, *Human Emotions*, Plenum Press, New York, 1977.

R. M. Johnson, "Trade-Off Analysis of Consumer Values," *Journal of Marketing Research*, Vol. 11, May 1974, pp. 121–127.

B. King, *Better Designs in Half the Time*, Goal/QPC, Methuen, Mass., 1989.

D. Locker and D. Dunt, "Theoretical and Methodological Issues in Sociological Studies of Consumer Satisfaction with Medical Care," *Social Science and Medicine*, Vol. 12, July 1978, pp. 283–292.

J. A. Miller, "Studying Satisfaction, Modifying Models, Eliciting Expectations, Posing Problems, and Making Meaningful Measurements," in H. K. Hunt (ed.), *Conceptual-*

ization and Measurement of Consumer Satisfaction and Dissatisfaction, Marketing Science Institute, Cambridge, Mass., 1977, pp. 72–91.

L. Miller, "Blending Auto Surveys to Cut through Clutter," *Wall Street Journal*, July 31, 1992, pp. 81A, 81B.

F. Olander, "Consumer Satisfaction—A Skeptic's View," in H. K. Hunt (ed.), *Conceptualization and Measurement of Consumer Satisfaction and Dissatisfaction*, Marketing Science Institute, Cambridge, Mass., 1977, pp. 409–454.

R. L. Oliver, "Effect of Expectation and Disconfirmation on Postexposure Product Evaluations: An Alternative Interpretation," *Journal of Applied Psychology*, Vol. 62, August 1977, pp. 480–486.

R. L. Oliver, "A Cognitive Model of the Antecedents and Consequences of Satisfaction Decisions," *Journal of Marketing Research*, Vol. 17, November 1980, pp. 460–469.

R. L. Oliver, "Processing of the Satisfaction Response in Consumption: A Suggested Framework and Research Proposition," *Journal of Consumer Satisfaction, Dissatisfaction, and Complaining Behavior*, Vol. 2, 1989, pp. 1–16.

R. L. Oliver and J. E. Swan, "Equity and Disconfirmation Perceptions as Influences on Merchant and Product Satisfaction," *Journal of Consumer Research*, Vol. 16, December 1989, pp. 373–383.

J. C. Olson and P. Dover, "Disconfirmation of Consumer Expectations through Product Trial," *Journal of Applied Psychology*, Vol. 64, April 1979, pp. 179–189.

P. Pae, "Advanta Finds Edge with Careful Customer Screening," *Wall Street Journal*, Apr. 8, 1993, p. B2.

A. Parasuraman, V. A. Zeithaml, and L. L. Berry, "SERVQUAL: A Multiple-Item Scale for Measuring Consumer Perceptions of Service Quality," *Journal of Retailing*, Vol. 64, No. 1, 1988, pp. 12–40.

C. Power, "Value Marketing," *Business Week*, Nov. 11, 1991, pp. 132–140.

T. Ragland, "Consumers Define Cost, Value, and Quality," *Marketing News*, Sept. 25, 1989, p. 20.

M. Robert, "Market Fragmentation vs. Market Segmentation," *Journal of Business Strategy*, Vol. 13, No. 5, 1992, pp. 48–53.

M. Rokeach, *Beliefs, Attitudes, and Values*, Jossey-Bass, San Francisco, 1968.

M. Rokeach, *The Nature of Human Values*, Free Press, New York, 1973.

M. J. Rosenberg, "Cognitive Structure and Attitudinal Affect," *Journal of Abnormal and Social Psychology*, Vol. 53, 1956, pp. 367–372.

M. Runyon, "Delivering Customer Satisfaction: Address by Address, Coast to Coast,' speech to the Economic Club of Detroit, Nov. 16, 1992, *Vital Speeches*, Vol. 59, No. 7, Jan. 15, 1993.

R. J. Schoenberger, "Is Strategy Strategic: Impact of Total Quality Management on Strategy," *Academy of Management Executive*, Vol. 6, No. 3, 1992, pp. 80–87.

M. J. Sirgy, "A Social Cognition Model of Consumer Satisfaction/Dissatisfaction," *Psychology and Marketing*, Vol. 1, 1984, pp. 27–44.

R. A. Spreng and R. W. Olshavsky, "A Desires-as-Standard Model of Consumer Satisfaction: Implications for Measuring Satisfaction," *Journal of Consumer Satisfaction, Dissatisfaction, and Complaining Behavior*, 1991.

L. P. Sullivan, *QFD Benefits*, American Suppliers Institute Publication IC, 1986a.

L. P. Sullivan, "Quality Function Deployment," *Quality Progress*, Vol. 19, No. 6, 1986b, pp. 36–50.

R. A. Westbrook, "A Rating Scale for Measuring Product/Service Satisfaction," *Journal of Marketing*, Vol. 44, Fall 1980, pp. 68–72.

R. A. Westbrook and M. D. Reilly, "Value-Perception Disparity: An Alternative to the Disconfirmation of Expectations Theory of Consumer Satisfaction," in R. P. Bagozzi and A. M. Tybout (eds.), *Advances in Consumer Research*, Vol. 10, Association for Consumer Research, Ann Arbor, Mich., 1983, pp. 256–262.

R. A. Westbrook and R. L. Oliver, "The Dimensionality of Consumption Emotion Patterns and Consumer Satisfaction," *Journal of Consumer Satisfaction*, Vol. 18, June 1991, pp. 84–91.

R. B. Woodruff, E. Cadotte, and R. Jenkins, "Modeling Consumer Satisfaction Processes Using Experienced-Based Norms," *Journal of Marketing Research*, Vol. 20, August 1983, pp. 296–304.

R. B. Woodruff, D. W. Schumann, D. S. Clemons, M. J. Burns, and S. F. Gardial, "The Meaning of Consumer Satisfaction and Dissatisfaction: A Themes Analysis from the Consumer's Perspective," unpublished research paper, 1991.

W. I. Zangwill, "When Customer Research Is a Lousy Idea," *Wall Street Journal*, Mar. 8, 1993. p. A14.

chapter **8**

Organizing to Improve Systems*

To manage a company by monitoring the functional aspects of an organization is not the most effective way to manage today. Instead, you need to optimize the business processes that make up your company, and these processes typically cut across functional boundaries. The methods used to manage business processes will be a major factor in determining the survival of corporations in the coming decade.

Nolan D. Archibald, Chairman and Chief Executive Officer, Black & Decker Corporation

▶ **CHAPTER OUTLINE**

Chapter Overview

Introduction

The Systems View

Aligned Subsystems of the Organization
Horizontal Work Flows to Serve Customers
Systems of Combined Horizontal and Vertical Flows
Key Elements of Systems

* The authors thank Tuck Bounds and Jim Reeve for their assistance in preparing this chapter and Larry Pace for contributing ideas to the chapter.

Hierarchical Management

Problems with Hierarchical Management
The Inadequacy of Hierarchical Teams
Growing Complexity

Building Horizontal Linkages to Patch the Hierarchy

Ad Hoc Teams
Committee Structure
Internal Customers

System Ownership

Matrix Management
Cross-Functional Systems Approach
Systems Focused on Products
Systems Focused on Customers
The Advantages of System Ownership
The Limitations of System Ownership Approaches
Beyond Structural Change

Summary of Key Points

Key Terms

Discussion Questions

Experiential Exercise

References

▶ CHAPTER OVERVIEW

Hierarchical structures slice the organization into vertical and specialized units. With traditional management, this leads to a number of problems that jeopardize customer value. These problems include excessive control, narrow accountability, social isolation, constrained communication, imposed results with delegated means, lack of cross-functional responsibility, and incidental treatment of customer value. Hierarchical work teams fail to overcome these problems, and systems grow more complex, fragmented, and less focused on improving customer value. Systems approaches encourage managers to view the organization as an integrated whole. They organize managers to address the horizontal flows of activities to serve customer value. Approaches that patch the hierarchy include ad hoc teams, committee structures, and internal customers. Other approaches go further by assigning ownership for cross-functional systems, systems focused on products, and systems focused on customers. When used together, these systems approaches avoid many of the problems associated with hierarchical management and encourage managers to continuously improve to provide superior customer value.

▶ INTRODUCTION

One of the three primary themes of the emerging paradigm is the management of cross-functional systems. In this chapter we distinguish the systems approach from an approach called "hierarchical management," then we elaborate on the specific approaches to making these concepts a reality for managers.

Hierarchical structures divide the work of an organization into a sequence of separate and narrowly defined tasks, and reaggregates the people performing those tasks into departments. This results in an organization that is divided into specialized functions or units. The people in each of these units tend to focus on their specialized tasks and objectives. Each reports to a boss whose activities and objectives are also relatively specialized. This approach developed during the industrial revolution to replace inefficient cottage industries. During this era of explosive industrial growth, the main concern was growing fast without going broke. So managers focused on cost, growth, and control. Control systems funneled information up the hierarchy to decision makers who were supposed to ensure that all the specialized parts fit together to accomplish the organization's mission (Hammer, 1990).

Hierarchical management is more than just a structure. Managerial attitudes, responsibilities, approaches, objectives, and rewards are also fragmented. The core problem is that managers do not work collaboratively as team members to address the systems and processes that flow across functional boundaries. They each just do their own thing. As General Motors (GM) discovered in the 1980s, this approach can contribute to a company's demise in competitive markets.

In 1984, GM reorganized itself, wiping out the Fisher Body Division and General Motors Assembly Division (GMAD), which seemed to have been slowing the efforts to improve vehicle quality. An interviewer from *Forbes* asked why Roger Smith, then GM chairman, couldn't have simply threatened to fire the top executives from the divisions if the situation didn't improve. Smith responded:

> Okay, we could do that, and it's the way we used to do it. But he [the Fisher executive] says, "Wait a minute. I did my job. My job was to fabricate a steel door, and I made a steel door, and I shipped it to GMAD. And it's GMAD's fault." So you go over to the GMAD guy and say, "Listen, one more lousy door and you're fired." He says, "Wait a minute. I took what Fisher gave me and the car division's specs and I put them together, so it's not my fault." So you get the Chevrolet guy, and you say, "One more lousy door," and . . . "Wait a minute," he says. "All I got is what GMAD made." So pretty soon you're back to the Fisher guy, and all you are doing is running around in great big circles. [*Forbes*, Aug. 24, 1987, p. 33]

This example illustrates how specialized units tend to pass off the responsibility for the value of the ultimate product. Contrast this GM example with the example of system ownership at Toyota where the Toyota chief engineer integrates specialized knowledge and skills throughout broad systems. The chief engineer is responsible for everything associated with the development of a car, including initial market studies, design for manufacturability, development of marketing strategies, and analysis of customer feedback after the product is launched.

The hierarchical approach to management still pervades almost every industry. But it has created significant problems. Certainly complex organizations must be partitioned in some way and delegated to individual "owners" of the parts. But the way in which the organization is partitioned makes a difference. The partitioning determines the nature of the responsibilities of the managers who own the parts. In hierarchical management, the organization is sliced vertically. Each manager is responsible for his or her *vertical slice*, or silo, whether it is a business unit, division, function, department, work unit, or some other "piece" of the organization. This approach creates barriers that inhibit integrated efforts to serve customers.

If hierarchical management isn't working anymore, what should replace it? In this chapter, we look at the specific shortcomings of hierarchical management and then see how the newer systems approaches remedy many of its problems. We generally describe the systems view of organization, explain the deficiencies of hierarchical management in light of the systems view, and then discuss specific systems approaches managers have used to remedy these deficiencies. The remedies seek to change the way managers view the organization, and determine how managers organize their efforts to improve systems and processes.

▶ THE SYSTEMS VIEW

Rather than just suffer the fragmentation and complexity of hierarchical management, many managers are beginning to think of their organizations as a system rather than an aggregation of separate functions. The *systems view* describes an organization as an *open system* in flux with its environment through a work flow of input, conversion, and output (Katz and Kahn, 1978; Pasmore, 1988; Schein, 1970; Senge, 1990). The word "open" means that the system has multiple interactions with its environment, through exchanges with suppliers, business partners, investors, regulators, and customers. Within the organization, a *system* consists of an integrated collection of personnel, knowledge, abilities, motivations, equipment, machinery, methods, measures, processes, and task activities. There are many ways to view systems, as described below.

Ishikawa's Cause and Effect Diagram

Ishikawa uses the terms "process" and "system" interchangeably to represent the collection of cause factors that produce valued goods and services

Figure 1

Ishikawa's cause and effect diagram

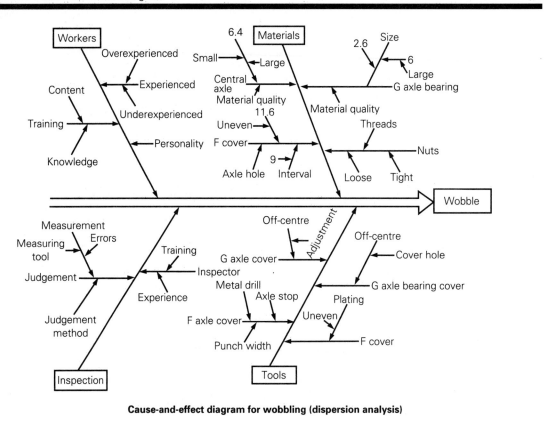

Cause-and-effect diagram for wobbling (dispersion analysis)

Ishikawa (1982).

(Ishikawa and Lu, 1985, p. 63). These factors include material, machine, measurement, method, and manpower (the five Ms). According to Ishikawa, process encompasses any work relating to design, purchasing, sales, personnel, and administration. The 5-M causes dispersed throughout the organization all potentially affect customer value.

Ishikawa's cause and effect diagram (or fishbone diagram) is used to represent the relationship between some "effect" and all the possible "causes" that influence it. For example, wobble during machine rotation is responsible for factory defects. In order to eliminate the wobble, the managers must understand its causes. The cause and effect diagram in Figure 1 illustrates how the effect, wobble, relates to a number of possible causes, which are organized under four categories (or branches of the diagram): workers, materials, inspection, and tools (Ishikawa, 1982).

Potential causes are written onto each of the twigs on a branch of the diagram to answer the question, "Why did this happen?" Even quantitative information can be included. For example, the diagram in Figure 1 records answers to these questions:

1. Why does the machine wobble occur? Because of variation in the materials. "Materials" is written on the diagram as a branch.
2. Why does variation in materials occur? Because of the variation in the G axle bearing. The G axle bearing becomes a twig on the branch.
3. Why does variation in the G axle bearing occur? Because of the variation in the size of the G axle bearing. Size becomes a twig on another twig.
4. Why does variation in the size of the G axle bearing occur? Because of the variation at the 2.6mm point. The 2.6mm point thus becomes a twig on a twig on a twig. (Ishikawa, 1982)

The cause and effect diagram captures the knowledge of a team of people and puts it into a form that is easily communicated and understood. It can help a team decide where to focus their investigative efforts to improve a system. However, it does not capture the complexity of many organizational systems. It suggests direct linear relationships and does not imply interdependencies or interactions.

Systems may be seen as composed of all the following domains: policies, motivators, processes, technology, and operations. In a sense, a system is everything that affects customer value, a view which is not very useful for managers who must take specific actions to accomplish continuous improvement. Managers need a more organized view of these elements. We discuss two ideas for organizing these elements, including aligned subsystems and horizontal flows to serve customers.

Aligned Subsystems of the Organization

The systems view in Figure 2 partitions an organization into *subsystems*, including strategic, technological, human-cultural, structural, and managerial. Accordingly, it implies that these subsystems, or themes, pervade every part of the organization. These subsystems are in dynamic interaction with each other; changes in one subsystem are likely to "spill over" and affect the behavior of other subsystems (Van Gigch, 1978). Managers in the managerial subsystem are responsible for the interfaces among the other four subsystems to ensure the quality of transformation of input into output.

Since these subsystems are interdependent, they should fit together to optimize the larger system. The notion of subsystems *alignment* is useful, but by itself is not enough to overcome hierarchical management. Each owner of a functional silo could simply work to ensure subsystem fit within their silo, e.g., marketing strategy fits marketing technology. Each division of GM could have managed a perfect fit among these subsystems within each division, yet still have the problem of poor fit across the divisions.

Figure 2

An organization as an open system with interrelated subsystems

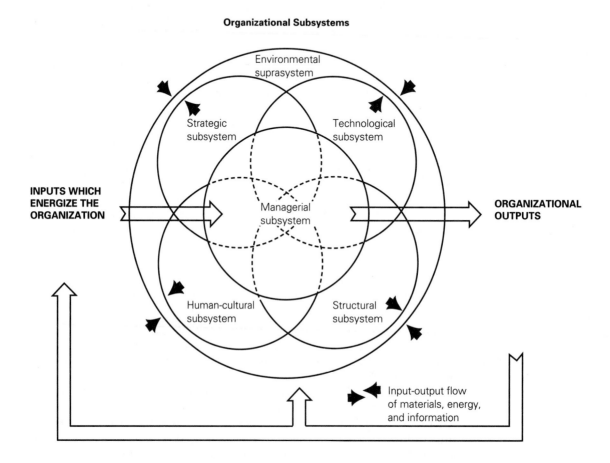

Adapted from *Contingency Views of Organization and Management* by Fremont E. Kast and James E. Rosenzweig.
©1973, Science Research, Inc. Reprinted by permission of the publisher.

Horizontal Work Flows to Serve Customers

An organization becomes an *open system* when there is a transactional exchange of input or output with the external environment: suppliers, investors, customers, and so on. The key to going beyond hierarchical management is to define managerial roles and responsibilities in terms of the *horizontal flows* of inputs, conversion, and outputs which span all the subsystems in Figure 2. W. Edwards Deming suggests that the system of production is a horizontal flow of work extending from suppliers to consumers. It involves consumer research, design and redesign, receipt and test of materials, production, assembly, inspection, distribution, and tests of processes, machines, methods, and costs. The flow in Deming's system is circular, with feedback from customers driven into all other activities. This flow represents a *horizontal slice* of the organization, but it is different from the idea of subsystems. It maps the flow of work and resources. For example, when a new product is developed and launched, designs are translated into engineering specifications. Parts and materials are purchased from suppliers for manufacturing and assembly. Once completed, the final product is promoted and sold, then packaged and shipped to customers. Consumer research initiates a new cycle of production.

If managers look for these horizontal flows in their organization, they will find many of them in the flow of work from one department to another. The hierarchy groups the people who perform these specialized activities separately into departments or functions. This separation leads to problems in hierarchical management because the activities are planned and managed sequentially as if they are independent. Viewing the organization as an open system helps to overcome what Peter Senge (1990) suggests is our human tendency to focus on snapshots of isolated parts of the system without understanding their interrelatedness.

Systems of Combined Horizontal and Vertical Flows

This focus on horizontal flows is key to achieving the cross-functional teamwork needed to provide superior customer value. However, the vertical flows of information and work between layers of management should not be ignored. In attending to the vertical flow of work, managers must realize that work that flows up and down the chains of the hierarchy does not create value for customers. When managers become focused on the vertical flows, they are distracted by issues of power and politics, rather than focused on providing systems that produce superior customer value. Vertical flows of work, such as unnecessary paperwork and reporting, should be minimized or eliminated unless they are key to providing customer value or sustaining the organization over the long term. Many companies, such as Nucor Steel, have realized this and have flattened their hierarchies by eliminating layers of middle managers.

While the layers of middle managers may be diminished, they still play an important role in integrating the various parts of the organization no matter which way it is sliced. If we simply define the systems view in terms of horizontal flows, we may be guilty of *horizontal reductionism*, partitioning the organization along cross-functional systems, but not attending to how those systems are integrated to form a whole organization. This may result in an organizational state of health that is just as bad as the disease it was intended to cure, namely a *vertical reductionism* that slices the organization along the flow of the hierarchy, the functional boundaries. In this chapter, we focus on cross-functional systems approaches; however, managers should not forget their responsibility to ensure all the parts fit together to optimize the performance of the entire organization. Otherwise, the performance of the whole organization will be less than the sum of the parts no matter which way you slice it.

Viewing an organization as one large open system means that managers must address how to integrate horizontal and vertical flows of work and information. The customer value strategy developed by strategic leaders must be deployed throughout all levels of the organization down to operations. The flow should be two-directional, because strategic plans and investment decisions must be based on knowledge of operational capabilities. The concept of open systems helps managers to integrate organizational resources to fulfill the customer value strategy. It encourages managers to view their own roles in the vertical flow as supportive of the horizontal flows that serve customers. To focus on these systems, managers must understand what they are.

Key Elements of Systems

There are many different ways to view the systems of the organization. Each has its merits. As mentioned earlier, Ishikawa suggested that the systems of the organization include the collection of cause factors. Ishikawa implies that the system can be improved by improving each separate component. This is useful when solving problems and improving the inputs of a system. However, there are other ways of organizing our thoughts about systems. Below, we focus on the cross-functional and holistic nature of systems. We make several distinctions and define the key elements of systems, including processes, operations, policies and motivators, and technology. These all combine to make up an organizational system.

Processes versus Operations Process and operation exist on distinct dimensions (Shingo, 1988, p. 232). *Operation* is work performed by people and machines on materials or information. A manufacturing worker operates a cutting lathe. An office worker operates a computer to issue payroll checks. A fast-food worker operates a grill to cook hamburgers. A market analyst operates with information to advise strategic planners. An operation is a discrete stage at which a person may work on different products at a particular workstation over time. *Process* refers to the flow of products, materials, or information from one worker or workstation to another, the flow across operations. For example, the strategic planning process may involve many operations, including forecasting, market analysis, financial analysis, and customer analysis. As another example, operating a cutting lathe may be one operation in a process that transforms wood into finished furniture.

As F. B. Gilbreth first observed in 1921, processes are composed of four phenomena: *processing* (or machining), *inspection, transport,* and *delay.* To improve a process, one cannot simply improve the machining operations, or the inspection operations or the transport operations, that are a part of the flow. For example, a division manager at FACOM in France used a machine-type layout, in which the same types of machines were grouped together. When someone noted that his choice of layout had the disadvantage of increasing the need for transport of material from one machine group to another, he replied, "That's not a problem. We have chain conveyors set up between processes" (Shingo, 1988, p. 6). Certainly, conveyors may represent an improvement in transport operations, but this did not necessarily improve the overall process at FACOM. Improving the overall process for better cycle time, for example, would require a just-in-time (JIT) approach that eliminates the need to transport batches of material from one machine group to another.

It is important to distinguish between processes and operations. An example taken from one American office equipment manufacturer demonstrates why. Noticing difficulty in getting orders for parts from inventory to the assembly line, the manufacturer automated the warehousing function by installing robots to pick up and deliver the parts to the workers. The cost of the high-rise automated warehousing operation was over $40 million. The new system was considered a technological marvel. Later, when the manufacturer moved to a JIT approach and worked with its suppliers to deliver components directly to the assembly process, the entire automated warehousing operation was found to be unnecessary. It added costly *transport* and *delays* to the manufacturing process.

By thinking of processes in terms of material flows across diverse operations, managers can envision ways of improving processes that do not consist simply of improving operations. For example, they might discover it is better to eliminate the need for inspection than to improve inspection operations. It is better to eliminate the need for transport than to improve the means of transporting. Eliminating the need for inventory is better than improving the means of storage and retrieval of parts. This view can also help managers focus on eliminating delays and complexities that characterize the overgrown systems of a hierarchical organization.

Production versus Business Processes Processes exist in many business functions. *Production processes* are characterized by flows of material across operations. In contrast, *business processes* are characterized by flows of information across certain decision points, or the flow of paper from one operation to another.[1] For example, the process for expediting the delivery of parts within the purchasing function requires the flow of paper and information across multiple operations, including phone calls to check availability and prices, filling out forms, and getting signatures.[2] Business processes can be found in every function. Some of the processes identified by IBM for various functions include:

- *Distribution* processes of receiving, shipping, storage, parts expediting, and transportation

---

1. The term "administrative processes" might also be used here to convey that all types of organizations, not just industrial organizations, are composed of processes.
2. Expediting can be a symptom of system deficiency.

- *Financial planning* processes of cost estimating, transfer pricing, and contract management
- *Production control* processes of parts planning and ordering, scheduling management, and new product planning
- *Purchasing* processes of alteration and cancellation, expediting, and invoicing and payment (Harrington, 1991)

Systems versus Processes   Processes and operations are clearly distinct. However, managers tend to confuse the terms "systems" and "processes," often using them interchangeably. There are significant advantages for managers who make the distinction. Keep in mind, though, that not all authors use the conceptual distinction that we make below.

In our view, a *system* differs from a process in several ways. The scope of systems is broader. A system is composed of multiple and diverse kinds of processes, such as those in marketing, production, engineering, and finance. Furthermore, the flow of work is not simply sequential, from one operation or process to another. Rather, the processes are interdependent and influence each other in what can be a complex tangle of relationships. Complex systems are not easy to characterize or diagram with flow charts.

Policies, Motivators, and Technology   Systems are also composed of policies, motivators, and technology (note the parallel to the aligned subsystems mentioned earlier). *Technology* includes the knowledge and tools needed for doing the work to provide value in the goods and services produced. *Policies* and *motivators* are means leaders use to communicate their vision and encourage people to behave appropriately. Leaders vary in their use of policies and motivators.[3] Some rely on only a few general policies, and others issue extensive rules of conduct. Some rely on intrinsic motivation through inspiration, and others use rewards and inducements to motivate people. In general, the better leaders are at providing employees with a vision and the knowledge, skills, and systems for doing their work, the less necessary are policies and intrinsic motivators to ensure appropriate behavior.

Without appropriate behavior, the pieces of the system, such as multiple processes, will not fit together optimally. As the GM example illustrated, in hierarchical management, policies and motivators encourage people to fit their processes together in ways that are suboptimal for the overall system. Improvements made in one process within the overall system may yield only marginally improved results because of constraints imposed by the rest of the system. A fragmented approach to improvement will always yield suboptimal results. Fragmentation is exactly what happens in hierarchical management.

---

3. Extrinsic motivators attempt to induce appropriate behavior through systems of rewards and penalties. Intrinsic motivation is enhanced by good management.

Systems Thinking The systems view can help managers overcome this fragmentation. Peter Senge suggests that *systems thinking* requires hierarchical managers to undergo a mind shift from viewing themselves as separate from the world to viewing themselves as connected to the world, from seeing problems as caused by someone or something "out there" to seeing how their own actions create the problems they experience. Senge states that:

> Systems thinking also needs the disciplines of building shared vision, mental models, team learning, and personal mastery to realize its potential. Building shared vision fosters a commitment to the long term. Mental models focus on the openness needed to unearth shortcomings in our present ways of seeing the world. Team learning develops the skills of groups of people to look for the larger picture that lies beyond individual perspectives. And personal mastery fosters the personal motivation to continually learn how our actions affect our world. Without personal mastery, people are so steeped in the reactive mindset ("someone/ something else is creating my problems") that they are deeply threatened by the systems perspective. [1990, p. 12]

Senge's approach encourages organizational learning, which is a prerequisite to effective change. To build a better appreciation for how the systems view helps managers overcome fragmentation, we discuss some of the problems of hierarchical management.

▶ HIERARCHICAL MANAGEMENT

Hierarchical *structure* breaks systems into functions or departments with managers assigned responsibility for each. Hierarchical structure is not inherently bad. In fact, some form of hierarchy, with different levels of power and authority, will probably always exist in all organizations. What is bad is the culture and approach to management that hierarchical structure encourages. It is this approach, the managerial behaviors, not the structure, that we call *hierarchical management*.

Hierarchical management treats the organization as a machine and emphasizes *analytical methodology* (things are understood by taking them apart) and *reductionism* (the parts of things are themselves understood by taking the parts apart until fundamental elements can be discovered) (Morgan, 1986; Ackoff, 1981). According to this approach, the performance of the organization will be optimized if the individual functions are optimized. The whole is managed by its parts.

The advantages to hierarchical management include:

- It can be efficient since it supports economies of scale where resources can be shared across many customers or products.
- It groups experts with similar backgrounds and provides a pool of knowledge and skills capable of completing tasks in that discipline.

- It supports tight control, which may be necessary when the workforce is uneducated.

Hierarchical management can appear to be very successful in a stable world.[4] However, today's business environment is marked by rapid technological advances, ever-shorter product life cycles, increasing customer demands, and an increase in the number of competitors willing to meet those customer demands. The world is no longer stable. Tight control, isolated task mastery, and economies of scale are not sufficient. Managers will need improved systems. For example, some organizations will benefit from flexible manufacturing systems that allow them to make smaller batches of a wider array of products (*Fortune*, Apr. 20, 1992, p. 52).

Certainly, hierarchical managers have attempted to foster teamwork within their organization. Likert (1961) suggests that managers should use *hierarchical teams* and rely on the "linking pin" role of middle managers to ensure integration. A hierarchical team consists of a manager and his or her immediate subordinates. Hierarchical teams exist at all levels of the organization. They are interlocked (or linked) across levels of the organization because all employees, except the person at the very top and those at the bottom, are members of two teams. As *linking pins*, middle managers play different roles in each team. They serve as leaders in one group and as subordinate members, along with peers at their same level, in the other group. To be effective in this linking-pin role, the middle manager must exert influence upward on his or her own boss as well as downward to lead subordinates in their own work group. Unfortunately, the problems outlined below keep hierarchical teams from achieving integration.

Problems with Hierarchical Management

There are seven problems typically associated with hierarchical management. These are briefly summarized below.

Excessive Control As defined by Fayol (1949), *control* means "seeing that everything occurs in conformity with established rule and expressed command." Control is important, but too much of it breeds inflexibility and precludes change for improvement.

Narrow Accountability When each manager is evaluated specifically on the performance of his or her department, each will attend to his or her objectives in the narrowest sense, as in the GM example above. This is a ridiculous requirement for people working in a complex system filled with interdependencies. It creates "breeding grounds for tunnel vision, as people tend to substitute the narrow goals of their particular department

---

4. Things are not always what they appear to be in a complex system like the global economy. There are time delays and intricate relationships which make it difficult to infer causal relationships at any one point in time (Senge, 1990).

for the larger goals of the process as a whole" (Hammer, 1990, p. 108). Managers are not responsible for their tunnel vision. They are merely reacting rationally to the irrational evaluation policies put in place by their superiors. For example, a manufacturing department that measures unit costs encourages managers to create overlong production runs and stacks of unsold goods.

Social Isolation Experts grouped into a function may work well together as a team to fulfill their own mission. However, sectionalism may result; they may not work well with other groups of experts if they are isolated (Ishikawa and Lu, 1985). For example, in one consumer products firm the departments involved in new product development are located in different buildings. So they tend to pass paperwork among themselves through the mail, with little personal interaction. Under these conditions, people may feel *caged* off from next and prior processes (Schonberger, 1990, p. 61).

Constrained Communication In hierarchical management, communication between functions is like trying to get from the left ankle to the right by going up one leg and down the other. The taller the hierarchy, the longer the trip. Coordinating even the simplest improvements under these circumstances can be frustrating. Constrained communication interferes with continuous improvement because the more important problems and biggest opportunities for improvement are mainly interdepartmental (Juran, 1964).

Imposed Results, Delegated Means Typical hierarchical organizations lay out goals and objectives for specific business units or departments, but do not plan the means for achieving them. When leaders are detached from working on the means of achieving results, subordinate managers pursue their goals and objectives independently. Efforts are not integrated and lack synergy; they may even conflict.

Lack of Cross-Functional Responsibility When subordinates are measured and controlled through narrowly defined goals and objectives, superiors tend not to hold any of them responsible for cross-functional responsibilities. It is difficult to deploy strategic goals for improvement in this context. To some degree, managers can deploy strategic goals along hierarchical lines: corporate to division, division to functional department, etc. However, this arrangement fails when goals relate to systems that are cross-functional in nature.[5] When there is no single "owner" of the system, there is no obvious answer to the question: "Deployment to whom?" (Juran, 1992, p. 39).

The problems that arise within a given department (or function)

---

5. Juran (1992) refers to these systems as interconnecting networks of macroprocesses, for example, new product launching, billing, bidding for business.

are relatively easy to handle. The managers concerned usually have the authority and resources to handle them. However, implementing cross-functional improvements involves interdepartmental (intersectional or interdivisional) activities. Job descriptions usually confine a manager's responsibility to a particular function or department, which restricts the freedom of the manager to address cross-functional and interdepartmental issues. Hierarchical management also usually lacks internal reporting relationships among the different departments (Imai, 1986).

Customer Value Is Incidental   As a result of the above problems, customer value gets treated as something incidental to specialized work. Hierarchical management assumes that if individuals each optimize their own part of the business, the performance of the whole will be optimal for customers. Unfortunately, when no one "owns" and manages the entire system, results for customer value may be disappointing. Managers simply assume customer value is delivered downstream.

The system of causes exists even in a hierarchically structured organization. The key problem in hierarchical management is that the people working in these systems are partitioned into vertical slices (such as design, production, or distribution), and managers tend to focus only on the work in their slice. They have little control over activities upstream or downstream. They are not often held responsible or concerned about what happens downstream. Like Humpty Dumpty, an organization with hierarchical management is reduced, divided, and broken into pieces, but no one ever puts it back together again to optimally serve customers. At best, the head of each slice seeks to coordinate and resolve conflicts with other slices. Typically, "customer service" is relegated to a department which must compete with the rest for the attention of senior managers.

The Inadequacy of Hierarchical Teams

Cross-functional problems are supposed to be resolved within the hierarchical teams (a manager and his or her immediate subordinates). But these teams are inadequate because the seven problems outlined above lead to value conflicts and goal conflicts within the teams. These conflicts lead to bargaining for mediocre standards and objectives, or incessant politicking, power brokering, and turf battles. Superiors become driven by crisis, managing reactively by fighting every daily brushfire. Within this context, the superior who leads the work team is cast in the role of being a negotiator who responds to the functionally focused initiatives of the subordinates. The boss spends too much time satisfying immediate concerns and not enough optimizing performance of the system. The real work of making and marketing goods and services gets ignored (Zaleznik, 1989). When goals and objectives are internally focused and defined in terms of profitability or costs, and managers are preoccupied with coordination and control, they may ignore the effect of their actions on customers. Customer value is suboptimized.

Only in organizations whose cultures are driven by a systems view will hierarchical teams be able to achieve the integration needed to optimally serve customers. Unfortunately, hierarchical organizations tend not to develop these types of cultures unless they have extraordinary leaders.

Growing Complexity

In the less competitive markets of the past, hierarchical organizations have been successful and have grown over time. With growth and size comes complexity and the associated wastes and inefficiencies.[6] Managers do not intentionally design complexity into organizations; the complexity tends to grow up in piecemeal fashion. This explains why an electronics company could spend $10 million a year to manage a field inventory worth $20 million. At one time, the inventory was worth $200 million, and managing it cost $5 million. Since then, warehousing costs have escalated, components have become less expensive, and better planning has minimized units in inventory. But the complex inventory procedures remain (Hammer, 1990, p. 110). Since they've been managing functions instead of systems, when managers start looking for systems, they are likely to find them overgrown, inefficient, and misfocused.

Unfortunately, the waste and inefficiencies associated with complexity are compounded in large hierarchical organizations, where complexity tends to spread across various functions and no one manager takes responsibility for reducing it. Managers simply manage their tasks and pass the work on down the line. Every manager merely tries to make the best of his or her situation, complexity and all. Four examples of unnecessary complexity are presented below.

Example 1: Marketing Promotions   A sales promotion is like "Old Faithful" for the marketing manager required to maximize sales. It produces a predictable and pronounced, yet temporary, upswing in sales. Because of the negative impact on scheduling and delivery, inventory levels, overtime, and product quality, such erratic variation in demand creates nightmares for production people. These production costs usually outweigh the sales benefits. However, the marketing group, measured only in terms of sales, seem not to care about such production problems. They are only behaving rationally toward the system of rewards that does not encourage any interest in the effects of their actions on other departments.

Example 2: Procurement Practices   If superiors evaluate the procurement department on the basis of purchase price variance, they have an incentive to focus their efforts on this performance measure. To take advantage of quantity discounts, procurement may purchase in quantities greater than

---

6. Suzaki (1987) defines waste as "anything other than the minimum amount of equipment, materials, parts, space, and worker's time, which are absolutely essential to add value to the product."

needed. These raw material inventories add costs to the system in terms of obsolete materials, remnants, carrying charges, and material management. The procurement group may maintain multiple vendors to ensure price competition and keep prices down. But downstream, production will be subject to variations among vendors, which degrades overall system performance.

Example 3: Implementing Just-in-Time Strategies Hierarchical management can interfere with the implementation of new systems that are inherently multifunctional and interdepartmental. Consider, for example, a just-in-time (JIT) manufacturing strategy. A demanding approach to manufacturing, JIT requires shortened lead times, inventory minimization, equipment reliability, balanced flows, and predictable performance throughout the system. Rather than focus on one function or operation, managers must focus on the overall system. The production department must stabilize and reduce variation in processes, eliminate unnecessary inventories, reduce the time required to set up machines, and do production changeovers. Purchasing must ensure that incoming materials are delivered on time, in the right quantity, and with consistent quality, rather than simply granting contracts to low-bid suppliers to meet cost objectives. This is very different from simply working to maintain standards for scrap, rework, efficiencies, and utilization of machinery.

Just pressing traditional functions to "do better" does not provide the conditions needed for successful JIT, especially when traditional control systems are still in place. Unilateral action by either purchasing or production to move toward JIT can be punished with poor evaluations on traditional performance measures. Even when manufacturing is able to introduce new systems like JIT, the results may be minimal because of the constraints imposed by larger systems.

Example 4: Upstream Processes Impede Improvement In the early 1980s, a heavy-equipment manufacturer began improving its manufacturing facility. But they discovered that the results of their efforts were constrained by upstream activities. The company offered customers many optional product features, and most orders were unique. Custom engineering to fill these orders required work by many departments. All the parts of the order came together on the factory floor, where production people worked overtime to coordinate thousands of details, resolve crises, and complete the order. The work environment was hectic. Customers changed orders that were already being built. Engineers delivered drawings late. Salespeople promised shorter lead times to get a large order from an important customer. Purchasing failed to provide parts needed to assemble orders.

The company took action to reduce overtime costs and improve productivity, including JIT, quality circles, employee involvement, computer integrated manufacturing, single-minute exchange of dies, automated inventory control, and sophisticated robotics. After investing significant capital and many hours of overtime to develop flexible manufacturing, everyone felt good about what they had achieved. They had reorganized the factory floor around process flows, with all machines needed to manufacture a product line co-located. These actions significantly reduced setup time, achieved a batch size of one, and eliminated work-in-process inventory at every step. Inventory could no longer be used to keep sloppy activities upstream from disrupting downstream activities, so every step in the manufacturing process became critical.

The results of their efforts were disappointing: average manufacturing time dropped 33 percent, from twelve to eight hours, and productivity increased 10 percent, but only 50 percent of customers' orders were shipped on time, rework dropped only 5 percent, overhead was still too high, and the next product was introduced late. At first, the managers were sure their efforts would pay off over time as everyone learned the new system. But several years later, they were frustrated to see only modest additional improvements. Senior management blamed manufacturing for not delivering on its promises. But they soon discovered the people in manufacturing were victims of events outside their control. They still could not stop changes to customer orders or prevent improperly specified orders from reaching the factory floor. They could not get engineering to provide drawings on time or make designers stop changing the specifications of new products once they came to manufacturing.

Despite all the obvious improvements in manufacturing, the performance of the overall system was still suboptimal for customers. Unimproved upstream processes were constraining the performance of the manufacturing process. No manager had envisioned the performance of the organization in terms of a larger system with integrated parts. Rather, each manager tried to perform his or her own function well and leave to chance the performance of the larger system of which that function was a part.

▶ BUILDING HORIZONTAL LINKAGES TO PATCH THE HIERARCHY

The deficiencies of hierarchical management are rooted in management's failure to think of the organization in terms of cross-functional systems, the horizontal flows of work that serve customers. How do managers actually organize their efforts to turn system concepts into reality? Several approaches are discussed below. Some approaches simply patch the hierarchy by building horizontal linkages across the organization. Other approaches reconceive managerial roles and responsibilities to give ownership for systems and thereby change the manager's view of the organization. Some of these approaches also change the structure of the organization. We discuss these in the next section. Figure 3 overviews all of these approaches, their intended benefits, and usual drawbacks.

Organizational Learning Disabilities

Peter Senge suggests that hierarchical managers may never learn to manage their organization as an open system because they suffer from seven organizational learning disabilities:

1. *"I am my position."* People trained to be loyal to their jobs may confuse the job with their identity. They focus only on their position and have little sense of responsibility for the results produced when all positions interact.

2. *"The enemy is out there."* People tend to find someone or something outside themselves to blame when things go wrong. They focus on their own position, "in here," and do not see how their own actions extend beyond the boundary of that position, "out there." When those actions have consequences that come back to hurt them, they misperceive these new problems as externally caused. Consequently, by failing to realize that "out there" and "in here" are part of the same system, they fail to detect the leverage they can use "in here" on problems that straddle the boundary between them and "out there."

3. *"The illusion of taking charge."* Being proactive by taking action against an enemy "out there" is frequently seen as an antidote to being reactive—waiting until a situation gets out of hand before taking a step. However, if people simply become more aggressive in fighting the enemy, they are reacting, regardless of what they call it. True proactiveness comes from seeing how they contribute to their own problems.

4. *"The fixation on events."* People are conditioned to see life as a series of events, and for every event, they think there is one obvious cause. The problem with fixation on events is that the primary threats to organizational survival come not from sudden events,

but from slow, gradual processes. Focusing on events, people are preoccupied with reacting, and they never learn to create their own futures.

5. *"The parable of the boiled frog."* If you place a frog in a pot of boiling water, it will immediately jump out. But if you place it in a pan of cool water and gradually raise the temperature to boiling, the frog will become groggier and groggier until it is unable to climb out of the pot. For organizations, this means managers must learn to see slow, gradual processes by paying attention to the subtle as well as the dramatic.

6. *"The delusion of learning from experience."* People learn best from experience, but never directly experience the consequences of many of their most important decisions in organizations. For managers, the most critical decisions have systemwide consequences that stretch over years or decades, including decisions about research and development, investments in capital, and selection of leaders. Attempting to deal with the complexity of their decisions, managers break organizations into functional hierarchies, which makes analysis of the most important problems in a company a perilous or nonexistent exercise.

7. *"The myth of the management team."* When they have to face complex problems, management teams break down under pressure. Taught in school to never admit they do not know an answer, people are threatened by collective inquiry. They reward those who excel in advocating their views, not inquiring into complex issues. They protect themselves from appearing ignorant, and this blocks out any new understandings and disables organizational learning.

(Adapted from Senge, 1990, pp. 18–25.)

Aware of the deficiencies of hierarchical management, many managers have tried to fix it. For example, managers have often built lateral relationships among specialized units through such means as direct contact, liaison roles, task forces, teams, integrating personnel, integrating departments, and matrix organization (Galbraith, 1973, 1979). Organizations attempting to implement Total Quality Management or continuous improvement programs have used similar approaches, including ad hoc teams, committee structure, and internal customers. These approaches are implemented within hierarchical organizations and do not significantly change the organizational structure. The functions remain intact. Further, the roles and responsibilities of managers remain primarily functionally defined.

Figure 3

Various approaches to systems, their intended benefits, and usual drawbacks

	Approach	Intended benefits	Usual drawbacks
	Hierarchical teams	Linkage through middle management Build teamwork	Limited horizontal communication Functional allegiance
Three approaches establishing horizontal linkages to patch up the hierarchy	Ad hoc teams	Cross-functional teamwork Solve problems	Problem focused and reactive Lacks coordination among teams
	Committee structure	Coordinate improvement efforts	Encourages detachment and passivity by leaders
	Internal customer concept	Promote teamwork Prevent problems from being passed on	Ensures only minimal compliance Allows suboptimization
	Matrix management	Expedite and coordinate across functional interfaces	Doesn't encourage improvement of systems Complexity of hierarchy still in place Lacks integration between product/projects
Three approaches establishing system ownership	Cross-functional systems	Establish system ownership Promote teamwork for improvement Focus on customer value	Complexity of hierarchy still in place Overwhelming for traditional managers Requires mature culture
	Systems focused on products	Reduces functionalism Reduces complexity Builds teamwork and flexibility Flattens hierarchy	Lacks economies of scale May not fit need for specialization Does not integrate with other systems May lack customer focus
	Systems focused on customers	Reduces functionalism Reduces complexity Builds teamwork and flexibility Flattens hierarchy More responsive to customer	Lacks economies of scale May not fit need for specialization Does not integrate with other systems

©Bounds, Bounds, and Reeve, 1992, *Understanding and Improving Systems for Customer Value.*

Ad Hoc Teams

Managers may put *ad hoc teams* together to address specific cross-functional problems. Ad hoc teams are usually considered temporary, not permanent additions to the structure, although they may remain together if the team achieves success. The general term "cross-functional" is used here, but other terms, such as cross-divisional, cross-departmental, or cross-unit, might also be used. Each organization has its own name for these teams, such as process action teams and quality improvement teams, which can

---

Harrington's Twelve Cornerstone Tools to Streamlining

---

1. *Bureaucracy elimination.* Removing unnecessary administrative tasks, approvals, and paperwork.
2. *Duplication elimination.* Removing identical activities that are performed at different parts of the process.
3. *Value-added assessment.* Evaluating every activity in the business process to determine its contribution to meeting customer requirements. Real-value-added activities are the ones that the customers would pay you to do. For example, a customer is willing to pay for the meal served on an airplane (real-value-added), but does not care whether you keep records on employees who are on vacation or who come in late.
4. *Simplification.* Reducing the process's complexity.
5. *Process cycle-time reduction.* Determining ways to compress cycle time to meet or exceed customer expectations and minimize storage costs.
6. *Error proofing.* Making it difficult to do the activity incorrectly.
7. *Upgrading.* Making effective use of capital equipment and the working environment to improve overall performance.
8. *Simple language.* Reducing the complexity of the way we write and talk; making our documents easy to comprehend by all who use them.
9. *Standardization.* Selecting a single way of doing an activity and having all employees do the activity that way all the time.
10. *Supplier partnerships.* The output of the process is highly dependent on the quality of the inputs it receives. The overall performance of any process improves when its suppliers' input improves.
11. *Big picture improvement.* This technique is used when the first ten streamlining tools have not provided the desired results. It helps look for creative ways to drastically change the process.
12. *Automation and/or mechanization.* Applying tools, equipment, and computers to boring, routine activities to free employees for more creative work.

---

be assigned at different levels of the organization. These teams can be given a variety of tasks which involve improving flows of work across functions. Sometimes these teams are given specific projects or objectives to accomplish, for example, the developmental launch of a new product. Such a team could consist of product design experts, representatives from manufacturing to assure designability, and of course, a team leader responsible for pulling the various efforts together.

Groups can also be put together for the purpose of fixing a salient problem, such as reducing defects that are reaching the customer. In organizations using process teams to do "continuous improvement," often the assignment is the general task of eliminating waste and inefficiency, also referred to as *streamlining*. Harrington (1991, p. 131) defines streamlining as "the trimming of waste and excess, attention to every minute detail that might lead to improved performance and quality. It suggests contouring to provide the smoothest flow, the least resistance to progress and performance with the minimum amount of effort" (see box).

There are two major problems with the ad hoc team approach typically used in hierarchical organizations. The first is that it represents a reactive approach. Teams are usually formed in order to react to a particular problem, rather than to enact improved strategies or systems. This reactive tendency is reflected in Harrington's advice that "big picture improvement" be step eleven. From a systems view, this advice begs the question, "Why not address the big picture first?"[7]

---

7. Hammer and Champy (1993) note that beginning by attacking bureaucracy may lead to chaos because it has been the glue that holds together the fragmented processes of traditional

The second, and more serious, problem is that managers often take a haphazard and uncoordinated approach to assigning ad hoc teams, especially when any set of managers can form a team to address any issue. Certainly, managers need to be free to initiate improvement. However, when there is no coordination, there will likely be no integration between groups. If there is no unifying or coordinating management, using ad hoc teams represents a "patchwork" approach to addressing systems. The teams will miss opportunities for synergy, or worse, they may even work toward incompatible goals. Valuable resources may be wasted. In order to overcome these problems of integration, some hierarchical organizations use a committee structure.

Committee Structure

Committees provide a forum for communication, coordination, and participation (Juran, 1962). When used appropriately, a *committee structure* provides a coordinating body to guide ad hoc teams and make sure their work fits together well enough to serve the organization's purposes. For example, a *steering committee* (or cross-functional board of executives) may establish, resource, and oversee teams that work on issues such as quality, cost, and scheduling. Companies implementing Total Quality Management or continuous improvement programs frequently use steering committees. Committee structures can be useful in this capacity.

A member of the committee may also be actively involved as a leader or member of one of the ad hoc teams. However, a committee structure may actually encourage detachment. The committee members may infer that their only role is to act as facilitators and provide support for others to do the work of improvement. Having served on the committee, they may feel they have fulfilled their responsibility for accomplishing improvement. They may never find time for actually improving systems. The committee structure can encourage managers to think improvement is a part of a particular project or a sideline activity, rather than a way of life. This result breeds passive managers who respond to the initiatives of others rather than actively engage in improvement on a daily basis.

Internal Customers

Another way that managers have tried to address the horizontal flow of work within hierarchical organizations is by identifying *internal customers*. This approach encourages people to think of the next process as the customer. As we have seen, the people who create problems are often not directly inconvenienced by it. The internal customer approach encourages people to be sensitive to problems or inconveniences they cause others downstream. To break the vicious circle of passing the buck from one person to another, the internal customer approach requires every individual to resolve never to pass on a problem to the next process. It helps to

organizations. They also suggest that managers should first reengineer these fragmented processes.

break down the walls of sectionalism and promotes cooperation (Imai, 1986; Ishikawa, 1985).

By focusing on the needs of internal customers, managers and workers expand their viewpoint beyond their own area of work, and start to build teamwork and communication. The internal customer concept makes sure that managers attend to the horizontal flow of work as a part of their daily life and integrate their work into the systems of the organization. For example, since designs must be manufacturable, design engineers should regard the people in manufacturing as customers for the designs they produce.

Within a hierarchical management approach, the internal customer concept has its limitations. Managers may enact a contractual arrangement and bargain to minimize what they deliver to "internal customers." Formal requirements may be stated in terms of specifications, to which "internal suppliers" may only minimally comply, particularly if their performance objectives are functionally focused. Another deficiency of the internal customer approach is that problems that are caused by internal suppliers far upstream in a sequence of work activities may be difficult to resolve. For example, customer service in the field is far removed from design engineering, which may not regard it as an internal customer. It is difficult to get the attention of people far upstream, because each of the internal customer-supplier linkages do not extend beyond "the next process" in the sequence. If the hierarchy still dominates the culture, the downstream customer can be left with little recourse other than trying to go up through the chain of command or trying to push feedback through all the multiple internal customer-supplier linkages.

This internal customer concept may be an improvement for some organizations, but falls short of partnership between all participants in a system. Furthermore, the internal customer concept is not adequate to ensure that overall system flows are appropriately focused and integrated to optimally serve the external customers. If not combined with other system approaches, it preserves the old adversarial model that is inherent to the hierarchical approach.

Approaches such as ad hoc teams, committees, and internal customers might be most useful when used in combination. For example, the internal customer stuck with a problem caused far upstream may seek recourse through a committee structure that seeks input on cross-functional problems. But these approaches designed to build horizontal linkages may be even more effective when combined with the system ownership approaches.

▶ SYSTEM OWNERSHIP

In contrast to hierarchical management, *system ownership* approaches acknowledge the existence of cross-functional systems and redefine managerial roles and responsibilities accordingly. This approach gives a manager or team of managers ownership of a specific system. System ownership should overcome many of the deficiencies of hierarchical management.[8] If no manager owns responsibility for the systems of an organization, they will remain unimproved, will grow more complex, and will produce suboptimal results for customer value. In today's competitive marketplace, how managers manage these systems will spell the difference between success and failure.

Because of the interdependencies within an organization as an open system, these cross-functional systems are best managed by teams of owners. Unfortunately, both teamwork and ownership issues get ignored in hierarchical management. So, many managers are organizing in new ways to manage horizontal systems. In the emerging paradigm, managers must be prepared to take ownership of systems that cut across the organization horizontally. Below, we describe several approaches that establish ownership for systems and improve teamwork.

Because the systems approach resembles matrix management, we will first look at matrix management and its inadequacies. After this, we will move on to see how the other system approaches go well beyond matrix management.

Matrix Management

Unlike hierarchical management, *matrix management* assigns responsibility for cross-functional flows. Matrix structure leaves the hierarchy in place, but superimposes a horizontal structure in order to achieve some coordination and integration (see Figure 4) (Galbraith, 1973, 1979; Child, 1977). This horizontal structure may be defined in terms of products or projects (example, products 1 through 4). A product or project manager assumes responsibility for the horizontal flow. He or she coordinates, integrates, and expedites work among the functions. Matrix structures vary in terms of how power and authority are divided between functional managers and product/project managers.

There are two primary problems associated with typical matrix structures. First, the purpose of the product/project managers is to either help administer or to circumvent existing systems, but they are not traditionally given the responsibility to improve systems. They simply resolve crises and foster communication across functions. Thus, the complexity of the functional organization remains. Of course, there are exceptions. For example, improvements were accomplished in the complex structure of the Canon Production System (Productivity Press, 1987). Second, even when managers are given such power, the projects/products still share resources, facilities, and equipment, and managers may start to compete with each other for resources and fail to cooperate to optimize their performance for all customers. A matrix structure redefines the product/

---

8. To get improved results for customers, as Deming (1986, p. 49) points out, managers must "improve constantly and forever the system of production and service."

Figure 4

The matrix organization

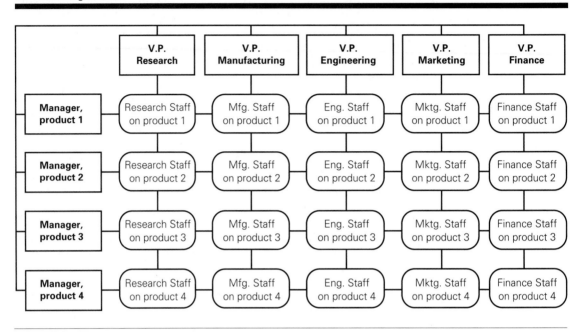

project manager's job in terms of a horizontal flow. However, it can still suffer suboptimization and fail to address systems (Bartlett and Ghoshal, 1990).

Cross-Functional Systems Approach

The cross-functional systems approach is a general approach that gets expressed in many forms. It is based on our earlier definition of systems as horizontal flows of work and resources that serve customers. The key to the *cross-functional systems approach* is to assign ownership which redefines managerial roles and responsibilities in terms of systems. The system owner does not just bear responsibility for controlling a vertical slice of the organization, but must integrate a collection of system elements scattered throughout the organization.

Cross-functional management seeks to have every function pursue the same superordinate goals. The cross-functional matrix in Figure 5 lists quality, cost, and scheduling as *superordinate goals* or goals for *kaizen-strategy deployment*, which is popular with Japanese companies such as Toyota. In this approach, managers from these different functions work as a team to make cross-functional improvements for each of these goals (Imai, 1986; Ishikawa and Lu, 1985).[9]

9. Where there is a strong correlation between actions and goals (as shown in Figure 5), the managers of the department take more responsibility for managing the cross-functional issues.

Figure 5

A Japanese approach to cross-functional management

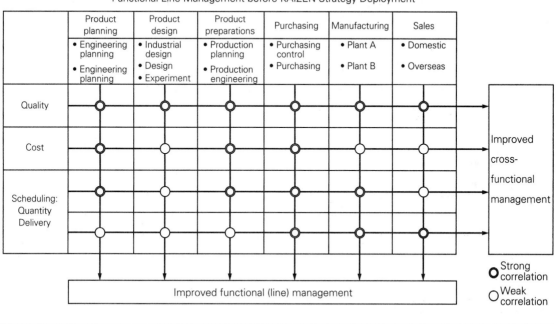

Functional Line Management before KAIZEN-Strategy Deployment

	Product planning	Product design	Product preparations	Purchasing	Manufacturing	Sales
	• Engineering planning • Engineering planning	• Industrial design • Design • Experiment	• Production planning • Production engineering	• Purchasing control • Purchasing	• Plant A • Plant B	• Domestic • Overseas

Rows: Quality; Cost; Scheduling: Quantity Delivery

Improved cross-functional management

○ Strong correlation
○ Weak correlation

Improved functional (line) management

Imai (1986), *Kaizen*, p, 130.

These are not new goals for organizations. However, managers have traditionally worked toward these goals within functions. For example, the marketing department improves the quality, cost, and scheduling of its own work. Improvement within a function is not bad, but it is deficient when the organization really needs system improvement across functions. Consider the earlier example of the limited impact of just-in-time manufacturing when broader systems are not addressed.

Managers could define systems in terms of superordinate goals for quality, cost, and scheduling. Toyota did this for its Delivery Quality Improvement Program. The first objective was to reduce damage rates from 0.36 percent in 1990 to 0.28 percent in 1991. The damage rate objective was further reduced in 1992 to 0.21 percent. Toyota also decided to achieve an estimated annual repair cost savings of $300,000 through the reduction of damage for 1991, a figure derived from the 0.28 percent damage rate. Accomplishing these objectives required cross-functional improvement of the logistical systems for delivering vehicles.

Managers should use the cross-functional system approach flexibly and should define systems in whatever way necessary to improve customer value. Systems will look very different from one organization to another. Three examples of cross-functional systems are presented below.

Example 1: Provisioning Systems of the Watervliet Arsenal   The Watervliet Arsenal in Watervliet, New York, builds military weaponry such as cannons under the command of the Army Armament, Munitions, and Chemical Command. To provide managers and workers in manufacturing with what they need to build high-quality cannons, Watervliet Arsenal managers must integrate the efforts of diverse functions, such as engineering, procurement, operations, and quality assurance. They have achieved this through focusing management efforts on three cross-functional systems:

Acquiring material: The system that specifies, chooses, and communicates requirements, audits delivery, and actually receives shipment of raw material for cannon production.

Designing for manufacturability: The system that assesses manufacturability in degrees of difficulty, translates that understanding within the design process, and confirms and validates the design in actual replication.

Equipping the operation: The system that provides and assures [that] the adequate manufacturing process components of tools, machines, sufficiently informed and trained operators, N/C computer program and raw material are positioned at the operation so that each production component can be replicated consistently within engineering specifications. [Conway and Carothers, 1991, pp. 777–778]

▼

QUALITY IN ACTION: A MESSAGE TO THE STUDENT

Thomas W. Sidlik, Vice President, Customer Satisfaction and Vehicle Quality, Chrysler Corporation

Intense global competition in the automobile industry has inspired managers to come up with new ways to organize their improvement efforts. The following message from Thomas W. Sidlik explains how Chrysler is integrating the ideas of customer focus and cross-functional systems in new product development.

Chrysler Corporation doesn't build vehicles, it provides customer satisfaction in transportation. Beginning in the 1980s, continuous quality improvement activities aimed at increasing customer satisfaction became a clear business focus at Chrysler. In the 1990s, Chrysler's business plan incorporates breakthrough quality improvements in all-new models by restructuring the company into platform teams. Platform teams consist of all of the company functions—engineering, design, finance, manufacturing, sales, and marketing—working together as a team to develop new products that provide customer satisfaction. The platform teams seek input from customer research and benchmarking to create basic new designs and new processes.

We have established four platform teams at Chrysler, one for each major product class: (1) large car, (2) small car, (3) mini-van, and (4) jeep/truck. The leader, or general operations manager, of each platform team is a vice president who also has normal line responsibilities. These cross-functional platform teams overcome the traditional barriers that used to keep people from working toward the common objective of customer satisfaction. For example, the general operations manager for the large-car team is the vice president of procurement and supply, and he has people from other functions, like product planning, reporting to him. This new approach to product development provides the means to achieve customer satisfaction and make Chrysler competitive on a global scale.

Example 2: Product Design/Redesign Systems at Cadillac In the mid-1980s, Cadillac Motor Co., the luxury car division of General Motors, faced declining market share and profitability. Cadillac's traditional approach to product design/redesign was a sequential flow of functional activities, from concept to assembled vehicle. Each functional group, such as design, engineering, materials management, and manufacturing, worked largely in isolation from other groups. But Cadillac needed to quickly introduce new models that would meet customer needs more closely, with higher quality and with lower cost to the company. The old approach was no longer adequate.

Cadillac managers reconceived their vehicle design/redesign system and implemented what they call the *simultaneous engineering* (SE) approach (what other companies may call "concurrent engineering"). In simultaneous engineering, functional activities are done simultaneously as much as possible, with all participants working as a team. Further, since customers are a part of the team, the "voice of the customer" is driven into every stage of the vehicle development process, beginning with design. This means that departments such as marketing, design, engineering, and manufacturing have to quickly translate customer needs into designs and engineering specifications that are manufacturable. Manufacturing processes are being developed while designs are being translated into engineering specifications. Designers and engineers do not just toss their completed drawings over to manufacturing, which has to build the product. They all work together as a team even after the new model is brought to the marketplace. This approach reduces development time, improves product quality, reduces costs, and enhances customer value.

Example 3: Value-Specific Systems at Georgia-Pacific Systems may be defined to serve specific elements of customer value. For example, Georgia-Pacific supplies particleboard (chemically bonded wood particles) to furniture manufacturers who use it in items such as tabletops. The furniture manufacturers machine the board and laminate the surface to give it a finished look. Furniture manufacturers need boards compatible with their machining processes. One characteristic important to them is a smooth surface. Specifically, furniture manufacturers prefer not only a smooth surface across the face of a board, but consistent smoothness from one board to the next. Consistent smoothness reduces variation in the lamination process and yields higher quality, reduced scrap, less downtime, reduced costs, and ultimately a better tabletop for the consumer.

To meet customer needs, one particleboard plant created a system called "Smooth Surface" and assigned a team of managers to improve it. Improvement required teamwork because smoothness results from the actions of many departments throughout the plant. Procurement had to ensure consistent wood chip quality, and notify production departments about variation to allow them to adjust their downstream operations. The milling and drying department had to grind the chips down to the appropriate fiber length, thickness, and density, and then dry the fibers to achieve the right moisture content. The blending and forming department had to apply the right amount of resin and other chemicals to match the moisture content and fiber quality, and then form an evenly distributed and layered mat of fibers. The pressing department had to "cook" the mat under the right conditions, temperature, pressure, and time. The finishing department had to trim and sand the board and inspect it for defects. The shipping department had to ensure the boards were properly stacked and loaded for transport to the customer. The maintenance department had to understand the operations of all departments to perform repairs correctly and do preventive maintenance.

Clearly, these various departments had to manage their interrelationships. For example, increased moisture content coming from milling and drying required adjustment in resin application, which required adjustment in press temperatures and timing to achieve consistent smoothness. However, the team of managers improving this system also discovered that plant policies, such as appraisals and rewards, were essential elements that needed to be revised. For example, procurement managers could no longer be rewarded only for holding down costs by buying cheap chips. Maintenance people could no longer be evaluated on machine downtime, because such an appraisal policy discouraged preventive maintenance to reduce variation in operations.

The Smooth Surface team also discovered that the concept of system can be raised or lowered to several levels within an organization: corporation, business unit, division, plant, and so on. For example, the division consists of several production plants. Due to capacity limitations and demand fluctuations, a customer may receive shipments of particleboard from a plant in Georgia one month and from a plant in Virginia the next month. So, to ensure smooth surface availability to customers, the system must encompass sales and production planning across all geographically dispersed plants.

To ensure the availability of product, a divisional manager may need to build a system that permits one plant to take over for another in cases where there is an unanticipated shutdown or lack of capacity. To ensure a consistently smooth surface for the customer, regardless of which plant in the division supplies the board, division managers must enact uniform standards of performance across plants. If this division-wide system is managed appropriately, the customer can receive consistent smoothness from the division no matter which plant supplies it (Tasma and Martin, 1991).

Cross-Functional Systems and the Hierarchy   Cross-functional systems are defined and assigned to managers who must own and improve them. If several of these systems are defined and depicted on a graph as flowing across the traditional functional hierarchy, the structure of managerial responsibilities may appear to be a matrix organization. It is a matrix structure in the sense that is requires functionally specialized managers and workers to have a dual allegiance and contribute to an explicit superordinate purpose, for example, Smooth Surface from Georgia-Pacific. However, it is not product-focused as in the matrix structure, but rather focused on achieving specific cross-functional improvements.

Unfortunately, in a cross-functional system, the complexity of the hierarchy remains in place. Issues of power, authority, resource allocation, goals/objectives, and reporting relationships may complicate efforts to improve systems. This approach can also be overwhelming for traditional managers, particularly if they are assigned the task of improving the complex systems that have grown up under the auspices of hierarchical management. It also requires that managers be able to envision their organization in new ways. Succeeding with this approach to improving the systems of the organization requires a culture devoted to the themes of the emerging paradigm. For example, managers must assume that if they do something for the good of the company, but which hurts their performance on functional goals, it will be good, not bad, for their careers. Managers must be devoted to customer value rather than the traditional hierarchy. The cultural transformation often required may take years to accomplish.

Systems Focused on Products
The approaches described below go further than the cross-functional systems approach to overcome the problems of the hierarchy and matrix management. They actually dismantle the hierarchical organization and establish systems that match horizontal flows. These flows may be organized around products or around specific customers. This approach breaks the organization down into smaller, more manageable systems with a specific product or customer focus. Organizing in this matter combines the best features of big corporations, including access to large amounts of capital, the means to make substantial investments in basic research, and the ability to attract and keep the most talented managers, with the best features of a small business, namely, focus, flexibility, and speed (*Fortune*, Apr. 20, 1992, p. 51).

Organizing systems around products means simplifying the horizontal flows that are often overly complex in large organizations and dedicating them to specific products. Schonberger (1990, p. 44) describes these *product-focused systems* as "unsnarled flow paths," which is a new twist on an old theme of "focused factories" (see Skinner, 1974). Schonberger suggests that building these unsnarled flow paths is something like converting common roadways to freeways. It eliminates many of the numerous routes on and off the ordinary road, and upgrades others to create a limited-access highway. The flows of work and information are smooth and predictable in focused systems.

Prioritizing Products   Most plants have too many products for each product to have its own unsnarled flow path. As a compromise, the first step to unsnarling product flows is to group products into families that follow about the same flow path and use about the same resources. Thus, systems may be built around these product families. Managers should identify the few products that do serve their own pathways. The Pareto principle suggests that most organizations have a small number of products that produce most of the revenue, or, at the component level, draw on most of the resources. Each of these products may have enough volume to justify its own resources arranged into a cell or flow line (Schonberger, 1990).

Using the Pareto principle to prioritize can help managers achieve "a focus strategy." It helps to name the players in the focus strategy and categorize products according to their importance to the organization's marketing strategy. These categories might be called stars, starlets, and extras, as described below.

1. *Stars:* Dominant revenue-earning (or resource-using) products. They get their own resources (as movie stars get their own dressing room, fan club, etc.); we pamper them and serve them first.
2. *Starlets:* Intermediate revenue-earners. They share reserved resources with other starlets and get served after the stars.
3. *Extras:* Low revenue-earners. They wait in line for resources of uncertain quantity and availability, and are served last. [Schonberger, 1990, p. 44]

Examples of organizing diverse work activities around products are easy to conceive within a manufacturing facility. Instead of organizing manufacturing around tasks (fabrication, drilling, pressing, and finishing), there would be focused factories built around products, with a line dedicated to each product (or product family). A team of workers and managers would be responsible for improving and executing each flow. However, to really improve the systems of the organization, the flow must be extended beyond the factory floor. Two examples of systems focused on products are presented below.

Example 1: The Order Flow System   One functionally organized company found that an average order spent ninety days in its order flow system, and a complex order could be there for as long as 225 days. Less than 1 percent of this time was actually spent processing the order. The system was overwhelmingly complex: an average order encountered thirty-two handling steps, and many orders passed through these steps four times.

Each department performed several steps, then passed the order to the next department, with little consideration of other departments. During its journey, the order was moved twenty-two times, shuttling between five states. Senior management was surprised when they uncovered the complexity of the order flow system, because they thought manufacturing was the cause of the slow responses customers had experienced.

To eliminate the complexity and improve response time, the company organized its order flow systems around products. Each product line had its own flow cell that included pricing, specification, and engineering. The members of the cells were co-located so that hand-off time was reduced and communication increased. Each order was handled by only one to three people beyond the sales organization. The only specialization was engineering versus non-engineering. Each member could become familiar with his or her particular product line, allowing distributors to call directly to a cell and obtain all the information needed about a particular product line. In addition, compensation was based on performance of each cell, measured by accuracy, timeliness, customer satisfaction, and profitability.[10]

In the five years since the company reorganized the order flow factory, the results have been astounding. The average time to process orders dropped from 90 to 25 days. This significantly increased customer satisfaction and reduced the number of changes the factory had to deal with. Cost (as measured by the number of people required to do the work) dropped by over 40 percent. The number of orders going through the order flow factory correctly the first time rose from virtually zero to 85 percent (Nicol and Sirkin, 1991). This example illustrates that building systems that are dedicated to products can eliminate complexity, reduce costs, and serve customers better.

Example 2: An Insurance Company Manufacturing organizations are not the only ones that can organize systems around products. The approach can be extended to other types of organizations. For example, an insurance company could organize around products rather than tasks. A marine department, or cell, might include all the tasks needed to support marine products: underwriting, risk analysis, quotes, etc. When one task hands off to the next, they are right next to each other. The amount of paperwork in process is reduced, and process delays are eliminated. The faster throughput makes the company more responsive to customers.

Example 3: Hallmark Cards Hallmark Cards provides another good example of a company establishing a focused system. Card companies survive on their ability to put out new material. At Hallmark, the system of bringing out new cards had become a nightmare: it took two years to complete the cycle of introducing new cards. To remedy this problem, Hallmark reorganized around particular market segments, creating systems for par-

---

10. Compensation systems such as this ignore the effects of the broader organizational system and the external environment, such as market demand fluctuations.

ticular holidays. They also had separate systems for birthdays and get-well cards. A team with members involved in creating, manufacturing, and marketing is assigned to each holiday. Team members work near each other so that work flows directly from one part of the system to the next. The reorganization cut cycle time in half, saved money, and made the company more responsive to changing tastes (*Fortune*, May 18, 1992).

Systems Focused on Customers

One of the most dynamic ways to organize horizontal flows of work is around customers. In focused systems, employees with different skills are grouped to accomplish a complete piece of work. For example, when a mortgage loan officer, title searcher, and credit checker sit and work together, rather than sequentially, information moves straight to where it's needed, unfiltered by a hierarchy. If an employee has a problem with workers upstream, he or she can talk to them directly, rather than ask his or her boss to talk to theirs (*Fortune*, May 18, 1992). Integration is achieved more quickly since the team is smaller, more identifiable, and more committed to specific customer-focused objectives. Customer-focused systems are dedicated to specific customers or market segments. As with the product focus, a customer-focused system can be achieved with any type of organization.

Example 1: Procter & Gamble   Procter & Gamble used to have many different representatives calling on each customer. Now they define a customer-focused system for each major account, such as Wal-Mart. This approach makes everyone working in the system "closer to the customer." It formally links the horizontal flow of activities. Workers and managers are more allegiant to serving their customer rather than to their function or specialized discipline.

Example 2: Mutual Benefit Life (MBL)   Processing insurance applications at Mutual Benefit Life required that an application go through as many as thirty steps, across five departments and involving nineteen people. Typical turnarounds ranged from five to twenty-five days, during which information passed from one department to the next, including credit checking, quoting, rating, underwriting, and so on.

MBL's rigid, sequential approach created many problems for customers. The president of MBL, wanting to improve customer service, demanded a 60 percent improvement in productivity. MBL did this by removing departmental boundaries and creating a new "case manager" position. Case managers have total responsibility for an application from the time it is received to the time a policy is issued. Unlike clerks who perform a fixed task repeatedly under supervision, case managers work autonomously. As a result, MBL can now complete an application in as little as four hours, and average turnaround takes only two to five days (Hammer, 1990, pp. 106–107).

Creating Focused Systems When managers decide to shift to focused systems from a traditional hierarchical structure, they are making a radical change. They are often starting with a clean slate to create a new system. One approach that can be used to make this shift is the visual technique called *storyboarding.* It was introduced hundreds of years ago by Leonardo da Vinci as a means of constructing large murals. Leonardo would create hundreds of small drawings which he would assemble on a wall for study. Walt Disney used storyboarding by having his artists pin their drawings to a cork-lined wall to develop the plot and sequence of animation in his movies. In the 1970s, General Electric started using storyboards with teams of managers to solve business problems. Each person would jot down ideas on small cards and pin them to a wall. After brainstorming, the cards would be sorted and resorted under various headings until the group was satisfied with the structure of the ideas. A similar technique, the *affinity diagram,* was developed in Japan as one of the "Seven New QC Tools" (for review, see Mizuno, 1979; and Brassard, 1989). Storyboarding, or the affinity diagram, helps to provide structure to the creative process.

In creating a focused system, managers might start by storyboarding to identify all of the inputs, processing activities, and outputs delivered to customers (assuming customers have already been identified and what they value determined). Once all ideas are sorted into related groupings of inputs, activities, and outputs, managers might create a flow chart (or set of flow charts) to lay out the work flows. While creating the focused system, the team of managers should be conscious of the streamlining principles listed earlier in this chapter so they do not build into the system unnecessary complexity or non-valued-added work. Once the structure of the focused system is created, the managers must then bring it to life with the human resources and technologies needed to do the work. Once the system is brought on line, the manager or team of managers must continue to improve it and refine its design.

Advantages of Customer-Focused Systems In an age of "customer focus," focused systems offer significant advantages over hierarchical management. When you wrap systems around the customers, the system is embedded with people who know all of the products a particular customer might be interested in. Organizing systems around the customer allows for great flexibility in meeting customers' desires and demands. It permits different service levels or packages of services for different customers. For example, it may be necessary to keep accounting records for some customers on a daily basis. If accounting is within each customer-focused system, this tailoring is possible.

Focused systems have advantages over the cross-functional systems approach described earlier. As we have seen, in a cross-functional systems approach, the hierarchy is left in place, and although the roles of some managers are redefined to give them system ownership, the complexity inherent to large hierarchical organizations is not fully eliminated. This approach can seem overwhelming to managers. Customer-focused systems overcome complexity by obliterating the functional organization. Each system becomes a mini-organization attempting to recapture the vitality of the small entrepreneurial organization with teamwork, cross-training of workers, multiple-skilled managers and workers, flexible participation, common objectives, and intense focus on the customer. Integration is easier because the hurdles characteristic of functional divisions simply do not exist. The continuous improvement process is easier because smaller organizations with team-based cultures are usually more adaptable. Furthermore, in smaller and simpler systems, solutions may come easier because the causes are more easily identified.

Using Focused Systems Flexibly Organizations must be creative when organizing around customers. In the case of MBL, the system owner also executed all the work of the system. Some organizations may use combinations of product-focused systems for manufacturing purposes, and customer-focused systems at the marketing interface with customers. For example, a production system team may be in charge of all the plants that produce Tide detergent. However, the customer interface people are not Tide specialists (as in a product focus). Rather, they are customer specialists, for example, a Wal-Mart specialist that sells all of Procter & Gamble's products to Wal-Mart. This approach gives Procter & Gamble one point of entry, one contact, one system owner for each customer.

Focused systems are not possible for every organization. Each organization will manage systems in different ways. However, the message is clear: to competitively serve customers in the 1990s, one way or another, managers must address the horizontal systems of the organization. In general, the system ownership approaches discussed above offer significant advantages to managers who want to address these systems.

▼

QUALITY IN ACTION: A MESSAGE TO THE STUDENT
Roy Merrills, Chairman, Northern Telecom Inc.

Northern Telecom Inc. started building telecommunications equipment seven years after Alexander Graham Bell invented the telephone. Today, Northern Telecom produces and markets telecommunications products and services around the world. Chairman Roy Merrills explains how Northern Telecom pursues excellence by improving major business processes.

In today's highly competitive, global marketplace, it takes more than superior products and services to be successful. At Northern Telecom, we have a vision of global industry leadership in telecommunications—and a road map for getting there. It begins with putting the customer first and being obsessed with customer satisfaction. It means exceeding our customers' expectations in *everything* that we do. Inside Northern Telecom, and with our customers, we call this our "Excellence!" initiative.

The pursuit of excellence across Northern Telecom is being driven on two fronts. First, and the more visible, are the quality efforts of some 1,200 continuous improvement (CI) teams, involving participation of employees in every part of the world. These CI team activities are bringing improvement to every aspect of our business—from on-time product introduction to answering telephones on time.

Complementing these efforts, our senior executive team has launched projects to radically improve, and, in some cases, completely redesign, the company's major business processes. These global process teams are looking at specific business processes; customer requirements, corporate planning, financial planning, research and development, marketing, product introduction, sales, sales order flow, manufacturing, distribution, installation, billing, and service. And they are following the same methodology familiar to the CI teams around the world. These teams will:

- Identify their customers and determine what they consider important
- Establish baseline measurements for the way we do business today
- Decide what changes to make
- Execute the change
- Verify the results
- Refine and standardize the change at all Northern Telecom locations around the world

The key business process teams have the potential to make major breakthroughs by focusing on the bigger picture that crosses functional and organizational boundaries. It's a lot more than rationalizing what we are currently doing or eliminating bottlenecks in a particular area. Instead, we are rethinking what we are doing as a company, and why we are doing it. As these teams discover better ways to do business and implement process improvements on a global basis, we can anticipate a quantum leap in our ability to satisfy our customers' needs and improve customer satisfaction.

We also will be looking for ways to exploit the power of information technology (IT) as an element in process change. Business process design and information technology are natural partners. When combined, they can have a major influence in the way an entire process evolves. Except in manufacturing, information technology typically has been used to automate or simplify functions. Using IT to reshape entire business processes is a fairly new concept. The handful of companies that have exploited it are high on the results.

Northern Telecom is on a journey to become a company that consistently delights our customers. Achieving Total Quality Management and customer satisfaction is not something we will do and then return to "business as usual." Being the world-class leader of our industry demands a long-term commitment to continuously improving everything we do, to "Excellence!"

The Advantages of System Ownership

With the various system ownership approaches just described, cross-functional integration is not left to informal communication, the "old faithful" of a hierarchical manager. In hierarchical management, people in different areas are pitted against one another, so informal communication produces negotiations and bickering. By contrast, real integration and teamwork can occur under a systems approach. For this to happen, owners of these systems must believe the approach is not a fad, "the flavor of the month," or a temporary assignment to be terminated once a report is filed. When top managers commit to the system ownership approach, several advantages result: responsibilities for the improvement process are clarified, an eclectic approach overcomes deficiencies in particular approaches, and managers create their own realities. These advantages are discussed below.

Responsibilities for the Improvement Process Are Clarified By simply focusing on operations or processes buried within functions, managers ignore vast opportunities for system improvement. A major advantage to the system ownership approach is that it ensures that someone in the organization takes responsibility for improving systemwide performance. Systems become subjects open to change, rather than constraints that have to be accepted as given and worked within. The first step in improving a system is to assign ownership. For example, the systems of the Watervliet Arsenal discussed above each have a system owner responsible for improvement. These owners are responsible for leading team members through an improvement process like that listed below:[11]

1. Identify a system owner and team members for each critical system.
2. Describe the system under study.
3. Identify all subsystems that contribute to the critical system.
4. Define the interdependencies of the subsystems.
5. Prioritize the subsystems as to their contribution to the critical system.
6. Develop a detailed "as is" description of the critical system. This includes identifying the interfaces between all system components as well as expanding the level of detail for major contributing subsystems.
7. Identify obvious system deficiencies.
8. Identify possible causes of system deficiencies.
9 Establish "baseline" measures for the system and major subsystems.
10. Assess the performance of the system and major subsystems.
11. Develop a "should be" description of the system and subsystems.
12. Recommend changes to improve system and subsystem performance (this may mean creating a new system).

---

11. Some of the "advanced" tools that are used to manage cross-functionally include the "Seven New QC Tools," also known as the "Seven Management and Planning Tools" or "7 MP Tools" in the U.S. These are summarized and illustrated in Mizuno (1979) and Brassard (1989).

13. Make changes to specific subsystems and confirm that the changes generate improved performance. [Kirby, 1991, p. 239]

Companies practicing continuous improvement often organize their efforts around a structured improvement process like the one listed above. Each one may be different. For example, AT&T advocates the following management and improvement steps for ensuring process (system) quality.

Step 1: Establish process management responsibilities:

- Review owner selection criteria
- Identify owner and process members
- Establish review responsibilities of owner and process members

Step 2: Define process and identify customer requirements:

- Define process boundaries and major groups, outputs and customers, inputs and suppliers, and subprocesses and flows
- Conduct customer needs analysis
- Define customer requirements and communicate your own requirements to suppliers

Step 3: Define and establish measures:

- Decide on effective measures
- Review existing measures
- Install new measures and reporting system
- Establish customer satisfaction feedback system

Step 4: Assess conformance to customer requirements:

- Collect and review data on process operations
- Identify and remove causes of abnormal variation
- Compare performance of stable process to requirements and determine chronic problem areas

Step 5: Investigate process to identify improvement opportunities:

- Gather data on process problems
- Identify potential process problem areas to pursue
- Document potential problem areas
- Gather data on subprocess problems
- Identify potential subprocess problems to pursue

Step 6: Rank improvement opportunities and set objectives:

- Review improvement opportunities
- Establish priorities
- Negotiate objectives
- Decide on improvement projects

Step 7: Improve process quality:

- Organize team and develop action plan
- Determine root causes (diagnostic journey)

- Test and implement solution (remedial journey)
- Hold the gains
- Perform periodic process review[12]

Like Deming's Plan, Do, Study, Act (PDSA) Cycle, such improvement processes are just formalized applications of basic scientific method. These structured approaches provide useful guidelines to system owners who are learning to lead the improvement process. The stepwise nature of these improvement processes may seem dryly analytical. However, the process must be conducted in the context of facilitated change to address all aspects of the culture, not just the work flows and work behaviors. To accomplish and sustain improvements, individual thought processes, values, beliefs, and assumptions must also change.

As they mature in practicing continuous improvement, managers might find a structured process too constrained and time consuming. They may want to cast off the structure and just do the work. At this point, the improvement process has become a natural part of managerial practice, well learned and requiring less conscious attention. When it is a part of their cultural fiber, managers may move though the improvement process more efficiently, in a more creative and freewheeling fashion.

An Eclectic Approach Overcomes Deficiencies in Particular Approaches
When managers are committed to improving the systems of the organization, they can consciously use an *eclectic approach* and draw from all the approaches discussed above. As shown earlier in Figure 3, each approach has its benefits and drawbacks. For example, if a large organization is split into various smaller focused systems, the top managers still have the task of integrating across these focused systems. System managers may fight for resources and attention from top managers. The focused system alone has no mechanism for achieving integration.

Managers should seek every opportunity to build horizontal linkages across the organization to serve customers. However, not all systems will be managed the same way. Not all specialized units or functions within the organization will be dissolved and dispersed into product-focused or customer-focused teams. Managers should use a mixture of approaches as needed.

Some activities may still be best managed within a function, or centralized, to take advantage of economies of scale. Some companies may maintain a single purchasing function in order to save money on administration. The information system departments of most organizations may remain centralized because of the impracticality of having multiple mainframe computers throughout the organization. (This assumes people must have

---

12. For a review of these steps and the tools and techniques that can be used to do this work, see AT&T's book *Process Quality Management and Improvement Guidelines*. To order a copy, contact AT&T's Customer Information Center, Order Entry Department, Indianapolis, Ind.

access to a mainframe rather that PC networks.) The basic research and development at companies like 3M will likely remain functionally organized and administered, although they may become more customer-driven.

Even though certain activities remain functionally organized or centralized does not mean the work cannot be managed to contribute to system optimization. On the contrary, enlightened systems managers will integrate functional activities and make them subservient to the needs of customers. They will do so by flexibly drawing upon any of the approaches to managing systems as needed. They may use a combination of a committee structure, customer-focused systems, cross-functional systems, or ad hoc teams to achieve specific customer value goals. For example, under the auspices of its customer satisfaction committee, Toyota Motor Sales, U.S.A., relied on superordinate goals, subcommittees, ad hoc teams, informal communications, and its unique culture to engage many departments in a collaborative effort called the Delivery Quality Improvement Program. The organization remained functionally organized and relied on a centralized department, customer relations, to provide customer satisfaction data.

An eclectic approach allows managers to comprehensively cover the major systems of the organization and overcome specific deficiencies. Consider some examples. A committee structure can provide oversight of the diverse systems, and establish common purposes, priorities, and integration among system owners. Assigning system owners ensures that systems are managed on a daily basis and optimized to serve customers. When a functional culture needs to be changed to achieve integration, customer-focused systems can help build teamwork and yield JIT advantages.

In general, when the systems of the organization are being managed eclectically, workers and managers are team-oriented, flexible, and focused on customer value. People are more capable of very quickly changing (reactively and proactively) to meet customer demands.

Managers Create Their Own Realities   There is no one best way to coordinate work in all organizations. Managers have to study the needs of customers, select a strategy, craft an organization to execute the strategy, and continuously improve all phases of this managerial work. Unless the systems of the organization are identified and owned by managers, they will most likely appear chaotic, unfocused, and inefficient. With system ownership, the systems of the organization will approach the ideal characteristics that Harrington (1991, pp. 15–16) suggests are common to all well-defined and well-managed processes and systems:

- Someone held accountable for how well the process/system performs (the owner)
- Well-defined boundaries (the process/system scope)
- Well-defined internal interfaces and responsibilities

- Documented procedure, work tasks, and training requirements
- Measurement and feedback controls close to the point at which the activity is being performed
- Customer-related measurements and targets
- Known cycle times
- Formalized change procedures
- Managers know how good they can be

The Limitations of System Ownership Approaches

No approach to partitioning the organization will serve as a panacea for an organization's competitiveness woes. Even customer-focused systems will not completely cure hierarchical management. For example, General Motors was organized along customer-focused lines, with marketing divisions like Chevrolet and Cadillac devoted to different market segments. To make any approach to systems viable as a means of providing superior customer value, managers must attend to the whole system, not just the cross-functional flows. As mentioned earlier, this means changing the organization's culture and managerial role responsibilities. This requires managers to challenge old assumptions about their business and to accept responsibility for accomplishing continuous improvement throughout the organization.

If managers establish customer-focused systems as mini-organizations, but fail to address these other important elements of the organization, the results will be disappointing. They will lose one of the primary benefits of hierarchical management and functional specialization, namely, economies of scale, but fail to realize the benefits of systems management, namely, optimization of the system to provide superior customer value.

Some managers must own the entire organization as a system. They must address the cultural dimensions as well as the architecture of the work systems within the organization. Attending only to the horizontal or vertical flows of work, without addressing the culture, would be like designing, building, and furnishing a house for optimal flow of household activity without worrying about how the family will function as a social unit. In other words, the way the systems of an organization are defined is important, and so we have presented many approaches as models for defining systems. However, shifting to the emerging paradigm requires much more.

These approaches for organizing managers to improve systems must be combined with new ideas on culture, managerial role responsibilities, theories of management, the improvement process, and approaches to organizational learning. Establishing system ownership is only one aspect of the emerging paradigm. Without broadly attending to all elements of an organization as an open system, just restructuring work flows and reporting relationships amounts to reshuffling the deck chairs on the *Titanic:* a futile exercise over the long term.

Managers must seek to understand their organization as a part of an even bigger system. This broader perspective leads them to manage systems that extend to relationships outside the boundaries of the organization. The Japanese *keiretsu* is an example of managing larger economic systems. Consider the dream of some visionaries to develop a nationwide factory network. For example, Nimble carmakers could take an order, then build and deliver custom-made, defect-free cars in only three days. Cars assembled from modular components could later be upgraded with the latest technology. To fulfill this dream, the following support systems might be developed:

- A satellite and computer network that functions like a huge base of diversified suppliers
- Concurrent engineering processes to encourage collaboration of design, production, marketing, purchasing, and service departments—either within the same company or among corporate partners
- Flexible factories with standardized machines, software, and processes
- A capital-gains tax indexed to the length of time an investment is held to stimulate spending on manufacturing (*Business Week*, Dec. 6, 1991)

These kinds of arrangements are years away, if they ever materialize. However, the vision does illustrate the importance of thinking in terms of systems to serve customers.

Beyond Structural Change

Sometimes structural change will be necessary to overcome the deficiencies of hierarchical management. Gail Hering, CEO of Atmospheric Processing, Inc., a small firm in Holland, Michigan, describes the deficiency of hierarchical management: "That mentality dooms a company. . . . Doing the work was about the last thing on my managers' minds. They were too busy looking over everyone else's shoulders and hiring more and more people to build their fiefdoms and give their own careers a boost." To break away from hierarchical management, Hering has reconceived the organization chart, not in terms of the traditional pyramid, but in terms of a wheel, with customer satisfaction at the hub, and key activities like planning, scheduling, training, maintaining, and processing as the spokes. Functional departments are not drawn on the chart, and top management is shown as the outer rings of the wheel to support their fellow employees (*Inc.*, October 1992, pp. 147–149).

Such examples are inspiring; however, the way the organizational chart is drawn is not what is important. What is important is how the work gets done to serve customers. To this end, Gail Hering has also led a cultural change to make customer satisfaction her company's top priority and to redefine managerial roles as change agents who lead continuous improvement. No matter what the reporting structure or the arrangement of boxes on an organizational chart, what is most important is how the managers view their work, their roles, their place within a broader system that serves customers. The systems view helps to establish this managerial responsibility in the emerging paradigm. The approaches outlined above suggest how managers can organize differently and reconceive their responsibilities to make the systems view a reality.

▶ **SUMMARY OF KEY POINTS**

1. Hierarchical management is fragmented management behavior.
2. Hierarchical management evolves from a structure that partitions the organization into vertical slices devoted to specialized tasks and narrow objectives.
3. The problems associated with hierarchical management lead to suboptimal performance for customer value.
4. Hierarchical management performs suboptimally because it fails to recognize and improve the systems of the organization.
5. The systems view conceives of the organization in terms of horizontal flows that cut across functional specialties which must be integrated for optimal performance of the whole system.
6. There are many approaches to organizing managerial efforts to improve these systems.
7. Some approaches to managing these systems consist of patching up the hierarchy. These include ad hoc teams, committee structures, and the internal customer concept.
8. Other approaches to managing these systems resemble the matrix structure, but go beyond it by assigning ownership for systems. These include cross-functional systems, systems focused on products, and systems focused on customers.
9. These systems approaches offer significant advantages over hierarchical and matrix approaches, particularly if used together.

▶ **KEY TERMS**

ad hoc teams	matrix management
committee structure	operation
cross-functional system approach	process
customer-focused system	product-focused system
eclectic approach	streamlining
hierarchical management	subsystem
hierarchical structure	system
hierarchical teams	system ownership
internal customers	systems view
linking pins	

▶ DISCUSSION QUESTIONS

1. What is hierarchical management?
2. What are the problems associated with hierarchical management?
3. How is the systems view conceptually different from hierarchical management?
4. What are the proposed benefits and usual drawbacks of the various approaches to managing the systems of the organization?
5. Why would you use an eclectic approach to managing systems?
6. How does the shift to a systems view relate to changing a culture toward the emerging paradigm?
7. How do the various system approaches help managers overcome the organizational learning disabilities listed by Peter Senge?

▶ EXPERIENTIAL EXERCISE

- In groups of five or six people, prepare an "owner's manual" for the managers assigned ownership of the systems of an organization. You might list some general principles, goals, or purposes to guide their actions, and suggestions for combining various approaches to manage the systems of the organization.

▶ REFERENCES

R. L. Ackoff, *Creating the Corporate Future*, John Wiley and Sons, New York, 1981.

C. A. Bartlett and S. Ghoshal, "Matrix Management: Not a Structure, a Frame of Mind," *Harvard Business Review*, July–August 1990, pp. 138–145.

G. M. Bounds and G. H. Carothers, "The Role of Middle Management in Improving Competitiveness," in M. J. Stahl and G. M. Bounds (eds.), *Competing Globally through Customer Values: The Management of Strategic Suprasystems*, Quorum Books, New York, 1991.

M. Brassard, *The Memory Jogger Plus+*, GOAL/QPC, Methuen, Mass., 1989.

Canon Production System, Productivity Press, Stamford, Conn., 1987.

J. Child, "The Shape of Organization-Grouping Activities," *Organizations: A Guide to Problems and Practice*, Harper and Row, London, 1977, pp. 72–94.

G. J. Conway and G. H. Carothers, "Application to Government: U.S. Army, Watervliet Arsenal," in M. J. Stahl and G. M. Bounds (eds.), *Competing Globally through Customer Values: The Management of Strategic Suprasystems*, Quorum Books, New York, 1991.

W. E. Deming, *Out of the Crisis*, MIT Center for Advanced Engineering Study, Cambridge, Mass., 1986.

H. Fayol, *General and Industrial Management*, Pitman, New York, 1949.

"Fiddling with Figures while Sales Drop," *Forbes*, Aug. 24, 1987, pp. 33–35.

J. Galbraith, *Organization Design*, Addison-Wesley, Reading, Mass., 1973.

J. Galbraith, "Matrix Organization Designs: How to Combine Functional and Project Forms," in R. E. Hill and B. J. White (eds.), *Matrix Organization and Project Management*, Michigan Business Papers, Ann Arbor, Mich., No. 4, 1979, pp. 43–59.

M. Hammer, "Reengineering Work: Don't Automate, Obliterate," *Harvard Business Review*, July–August 1990, pp. 107–108.

M. Hammer and J. Champy, *Reengineering the Corporation*, HarperCollins, New York, 1993.

H. J. Harrington, *Business Process Improvement*, McGraw-Hill, New York, 1991.

M. Imai, *Kaizen: The Key to Japan's Competitive Success*, Random House, New York, 1986.

"Is Big Still Good?" *Fortune*, Apr. 20, 1992, p. 52.

K. Ishikawa, *Guide to Quality Control*, Asian Productivity Organization, 1982, available through UNIPUB, White Plains, N.Y.

K. Ishikawa and D. Lu, *What Is Total Quality Control? The Japanese Way*, Prentice-Hall, Englewood Cliffs, N.J., 1985.

J. M. Juran, *Juran on Quality by Design: The New Steps for Planning Quality into Goods and Services*, Free Press, New York, 1992.

J. M. Juran, *Managerial Breakthrough: A New Concept of the Manager's Job*, McGraw-Hill, New York, 1964.

D. Katz and R. L. Kahn, *The Social Psychology of Organizations*, John Wiley and Sons, New York, 1978.

K. E. Kirby, "Organizational Change: The Systems Approach," in M. J. Stahl and G. M. Bounds (eds.), *Competing Globally through Customer Values: The Management of Strategic Suprasystems*, Quorum Books, New York, 1991.

P. R. Lawrence and J. W. Lorsh, *Organization and Environment: Managing Differentiation and Integration*, Irwin, Homewood, Ill., 1969.

R. Likert, *New Patterns of Management*, McGraw-Hill, New York, 1961.

H. Mintzberg, *The Structuring of Organizations*, Prentice-Hall, Englewood Cliffs, N.J., 1979.

S. Mizuno, *Management for Quality Improvement: The Seven New QC Tools*, Productivity Press, Cambridge, Mass., 1979.

G. Morgan, *Images of Organization*, Sage, Beverly Hills, Calif., 1986.

R. Nicol and H. Sirkin, "Manufacturing Beyond the Factory Floor: The White Collar Factory," *Target*, Winter 1991, pp. 28–35.

W. A. Pasmore, *Designing Effective Organizations: The Sociotechnical Systems Perspective*, John Wiley and Sons, New York, 1988.

E. H. Schein, *Organizational Psychology*, 2d ed., Prentice-Hall, Englewood Cliffs, N.J., 1970.

R. J. Schonberger, *Building a Chain of Customers*, Free Press, New York, 1990.

P. M. Senge, *The Fifth Discipline: The Art and Practice of the Learning Organization*, Doubleday, New York, 1990.

S. Shingo, *Zero Quality Control: Source Inspection and the Poka-Yoke System*, Productivity Press, Cambridge, Mass., 1986.

S. Shingo, *Non-Stock Production: The Shingo System for Continuous Improvement*, Productivity Press, Cambridge, Mass., 1988.

W. Skinner, "Focused Factory," *Harvard Business Review*, May–June 1974.

T. A. Stewart, "Are You Flat, Lean, and Ready for a Bold New Look? Try High-Performance Teams, Redesigned Work, and Unbridled Information," *Fortune*, May 18, 1992, p. 96.

K. Suzaki, *The New Manufacturing Challenge: Techniques for Continuous Improvement*, Free Press, 1987.

C. Tasma and S. Martin, "Georgia-Pacific Corporation Industrial Wood Products–Particle Board Division," in M. J. Stahl and G. M. Bounds (eds.), *Competing Globally through Customer Values: The Management of Strategic Suprasystems*, Quorum Books, New York, 1991.

J. P. Van Gigch, *Applied General Systems Theory*, Harper and Row, New York, 1978.

A. Zaleznik, "Real Work," *Harvard Business Review*, January–February 1989, pp. 57–64.

chapter **9**

Variation: Interpreting Its Meaning

Variation is the product of any system . . . management's job is to study variation, with the proper theory, to unravel the message that the variation is trying to tell us about how to improve the process.

W. Edwards Deming*

▶ **CHAPTER OUTLINE**

Chapter Overview

Introduction

Recognizing and Interpreting Variation

Key Ideas

Effects of Variation

Variation in Consumer Products
Variation in Consumer Services
Variation in Organizational Inputs
Variation in Future Conditions
Variation Produced inside the Organization

Theories for Interpreting the Meaning of Variation

Ignoring Variation

* B. Carlson and G. Ranney, "Deming's Point Seven," *Commentaries on Deming's Fourteen Points for Management*, Ohio Quality and Productivity Forum, Piqua, Ohio, 1989.

Imposing Arbitrary Standards
Overreacting to Variation

Shewhart's Theory and Method to Interpret Variation

Stable versus Unstable Variation
The Statistical Control Chart
Interpreting Control Charts
Constructing Control Charts
Use of the Information Contained in Variation

Other Tools for Analysis of Data

Remarks on the Use of Tools

Summary of Key Points

Key Terms

Discussion Questions

Experiential Exercises

References

▶ CHAPTER OVERVIEW

Variation in systems, processes, people, and the results they produce is a source of valuable information for improvement. The aim of this chapter is to provide an introduction to concepts and methods that improve the ability to understand variation and interpret the messages it contains about the causes that produce it.

▶ INTRODUCTION

We live with variation in every aspect of our lives. Consumption of power for heating or cooling and the demand for power generation vary daily from one location to another. An adult's weight varies day to day and year to year. Variation in a patient's physiological characteristics occurs through the course of an illness. The physician learns from that variation about the effectiveness of his treatment. The time it takes to travel from home to work or school varies, depending upon weather conditions, time of departure, speed, and traffic density. The personalities and capabilities of the people we know are different. When one or more characteristics of any collection of items or individuals are evaluated, the results are not all the same; that is, they exhibit *variation*.

Figure 1

A run chart showing variation in a series of results

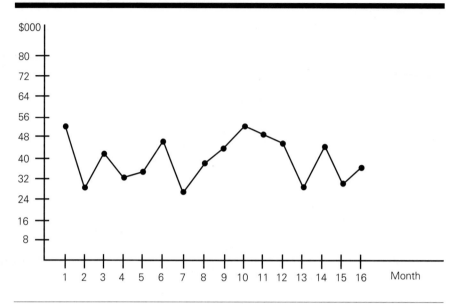

Managers encounter variation in many forms. There is variation in the materials purchased for production.[1] There is variation in the time of delivery of services and in the quality of the service delivered. The quantity of human, material, and financial resources used to produce a product or service varies over time. Figure 1 shows a production unit's monthly overtime costs in thousands of dollars, plotted in time sequence.[2] The variation in labor required to produce the product is reflected by the variation of these costs. The needs of customers vary, as do their perceptions of products or services. Variation in economic conditions over time affects markets for products and services and affects the ability of organizations to acquire capital and other resources. These and other forms of variation affect the manager's work.

The ability to create superior value for customers requires at least three kinds of knowledge: (1) customer knowledge—knowledge of cus-

---

1. The existence of variation in materials led to the practice of establishing engineering tolerances for characteristics of components to be used in assembly. Mass production relies on the use of interchangeable parts. In recognition of the fact that all parts of a certain kind would not be exactly alike, engineers established tolerances to define how much variation could exist in a stream of parts coming to assembly and still have successful assembly of component parts.
2. A plot of series of results such as the one shown in Figure 1 is usually called a run chart. The chart has a horizontal scale representing time, a vertical measurement scale, and plotted points representing the individual results. The vertical dispersion of the points represents the time-to-time fluctuation, or variation, in the series.

tomer needs and desires, and knowledge of how customers use products or services; (2) subject matter knowledge—scientific, engineering, and social knowledge required to be able to produce the product or service; and (3) self-knowledge—knowledge of the capabilities of the organizational system to deliver value, and knowledge of how that system works and might be improved. The existence of variation in customers and their uses of products or services increases the difficulty of developing a strategy to fulfill their needs and desires. Subject matter knowledge in the physical, biological, and social sciences is built through the development and testing of theories of cause and effect. Variation in test results due to sources not accounted for in the theory renders interpretation of experimental results more difficult. Systems produce variation and are affected by variation in their inputs and in the external environment. Assessing organizational capabilities and building knowledge of how systems actually work are rendered more difficult by the existence of variation. The difficulties created by variation can be lessened if appropriate methods are consistently used to interpret results that vary over time and conditions. Variation in results carries messages concerning the process or system that generates them, if there is a means to receive and interpret the messages. If managers have a rational theory and method to interpret variation, they are better able to guide the development and use of all of the kinds of knowledge that are needed to survive and prosper.

▶ RECOGNIZING AND INTERPRETING VARIATION

To manage for improvement, managers need to recognize variation, interpret the messages it contains about the organization, and act according to the implications of those messages. Some key ideas concerning variation and theory and methods to interpret it are discussed in this chapter.

Key Ideas

- Time and resources used in coping with undesirable variation do not contribute to the creation of value. One of the aims of improvement work is to reduce the amount of undesirable variation present in the system, its inputs, and its outputs.
- By studying variation and acting on its sources, managers can achieve greater uniformity of product and more timely and predictable service—and thereby improve the economic well-being of the enterprise.
- By observing the ways in which managers cope with or react to variation, at least three theories employed to interpret variation can be identified: (1) Variation should not exist. (2) All variation is the result of something exceptional to be minutely analyzed and acted

on. (3) Variation exists in results as a consequence of actions of the causes that produce the results. This is a theory originated by Walter Shewhart.

- Shewhart's theory of variation is most consistent with modern concepts and practices of system management and is most useful in interpreting the meaning of variation.
- Shewhart made a distinction between stable (statistically controlled) variation and unstable variation in a series of results. He devised the statistical control chart to provide a consistent method to study variation and link it to its causes.
- The control chart and its rules for interpretation provide the manager with a means to make a clear and repeatable judgment of the state of statistical control of variation in the results.
- A primary advantage of using a control chart is to minimize the economic loss that comes from mistakes that occur in interpreting the meaning of variation. The loss occurs when these mistakes lead to inappropriate actions for improvement.
- Study of variation, with the appropriate theory, leads to understanding the system of causes and helps to inform managers where and when action on the system could produce improvement of future results.
- Tools can be misused if they are not integrated into a framework of theory and practice that ensures their appropriate use.

QUALITY IN ACTION: A MESSAGE TO THE STUDENT
James M. Brogden, President, Master Industries

Master Industries is a medium-sized Ohio company that develops, manufactures, and assembles technically demanding thermoplastic components. Its customers include automobile manufacturers and other producers of durable goods. President James M. Brogden explains why it is important for managers at Master Industries to understand variation.

At Master Industries our mission is: "to provide the best in quality and value of service and goods, recognizing and promoting the person, as consumer, customer, and producer, with opportunity for each to realize his or her highest potential." We believe this will result in: "loyal customers, committed associates, the highest return on investment, and business continuity through the generations." Our mission statement clearly indicates that our values are multiple and holistic in nature. We believe that optimization for Master Industries will be achieved when all those affected by our company benefit from its existence. While it is true that we wish to achieve a good return on investment and business continuity, we do not wish to accomplish these aims without achieving the other key aims of having loyal customers and committed associates.

About a decade ago, I first encountered the concepts of variation in products, processes, and people originated by Shewhart and further developed by Dr. Deming. Our first attempts to use those concepts were focused on our manufacturing processes and our products. We have continued to teach our employees (associates) about variation and the methods they can use to learn about the effects of our operating practices and other factors on the output. Much of the training Master associates receive now is done while they participate in project teams established to study and recommend ways to improve processes and to redesign our systems for improved effectiveness. The work of improvement teams is periodically reviewed by management in a formal review process. The purpose of the review sessions is to help employees with the logic and methods of process study and to emphasize the importance of systematic learning and improvement. Our long-term objective is to integrate the practice of building knowledge for improvement into the daily work of all associates in the company.

My staff and I have gained in our abilities to manage for sustainable improvement by learning about variation. We have learned to avoid reacting to individual events and performance indicators. We now realize that reacting to each result without taking variation into account leads to waste of valuable time and resources and leads, more often than not, to changes that produce no improvement. Our knowledge of variation helps us to keep our managerial efforts focused on the systems we have created and have a responsibility to improve.

Although the use of knowledge of variation has brought us benefit by improving our effectiveness as designers and producers, the greatest benefit has been the change it has produced in our approach to managing the people of Master Industries. As a small, family-owned company, Master Industries had never adopted a formal system for rating employee performance. When we learned about systems and variation, we realized that performance rating systems are founded on a set of assumptions that are inconsistent with our beliefs and values. Performance rating systems confuse the effects of the system with the performance of the individual. These widely used systems create competition and demoralize people, and are of no benefit in providing feedback that will help people develop their capabilities. Instead, we concentrate on providing leadership and coaching to our associates so that they can grow as individuals and as associates of Master Industries. Our job as leaders is to optimize the unique talents and skills of all our associates.

We have come to understand that many widely used personnel policies and practices are founded on the belief that all people are alike and cannot be trusted to make wise decisions about their work. One of our first steps away from such an approach was to revise our education reimbursement policy. In the past, we required that a course must be clearly related to the employee's job in order to receive reimbursement for expenses. About five years ago, we adopted a policy of paying for any educational activity an associate wants to undertake. The benefits in terms of growth of the individuals we have supported to develop themselves have far outweighed the expense. We have also invested in training associates in a variety of areas ranging from injection molding technology to planned experimentation. We believe that the investment we make in people is repaid many times over in their enthusiasm for the company and for the work that they do.

▲

▶ EFFECTS OF VARIATION

The consumer is the ultimate recipient of variation introduced all along the chain of production of a product or service. Variation is directly manifested in the product or service, but it also makes its way into the final outcome through cost, timeliness, or availability. Variation created by the system of production or brought into it through incoming materials, services, and other inputs is a source of waste. Time and resources used in coping with undesirable variation do not contribute to the creation of value and constitute a loss to society. One of the aims of improvement work is to reduce the amount of undesirable variation present in the system, its inputs, and its outputs.

Variation in Consumer Products

The consumer experiences the effects of variation in products in the form of errors, delays, poor performance, reduced reliability, unpredictable delivery, lack of availability, and lack of uniformity. These are all aspects of quality. Whether the consumer sees these attributes as a pattern or as a collection of isolated incidents depends somewhat on the frequency of purchase and use of a product or service. The producer is better able to see these attributes as variation in the repetitive production of units of product or service or in the repeated activities of internal processes.

When we go to the market and select cans of soup from the shelf, we expect our can of tomato soup to be full and to be the same as previous cans in taste, color, and consistency. That is, we expect uniformity in repeated purchase. The producer must produce little variation in these attributes from can to can in order to meet our expectations. We would not be likely to repeatedly buy a brand of tomato soup if each can we opened contained a surprise.

We accept variation in the form of lack of uniformity item to item in some kinds of consumer products, probably because no producer has changed customers' expectations by providing better uniformity at the same price. One example is mass-produced, relatively inexpensive garments, such as women's blue jeans. No two pairs of the same brand and style with the same size on the label can be expected to be the same size; that is, there is a large dimensional variation in women's jeans. The sacrifice the consumer makes as a result of that variation is having to try on each item before purchase. Lack of uniformity in results of dyeing processes means that purchasers of carpet, upholstery, and drapery fabric must be careful to get all their materials from the same dye lot. Otherwise, color variation will be noticeable. Lack of uniformity in quality of packaging processes may mean the consumer cannot assemble a child's toy on Christmas Eve because a part is missing. Excessive variation in dimensions of mating components of complex mass-produced machinery leads to impaired performance and reduced reliability for some percentage of the final product. The unfortunate purchaser then deals with the consequences of poor performance and product failure. Variation in product delivery schedules and schedule performance affects the consumer through uncertain availability of a product when he needs it.

Variation in Consumer Services

Variation also affects the consumer's experience with services. Through experience, consumers of services come to expect errors and misinformation in service. Lack of uniformity of training, lack of standardization of service delivery methods and procedures, and lack of communication all contribute to the variation that causes consumers to have that kind of experience. The effects of variation are often seen by the consumer of services as uncertainty of time of delivery. Someone who has an appointment with a physician has to plan his or her day knowing that waiting time in the physician's office could vary from fifteen minutes to several hours. Someone who needs to have an appliance repaired or telephone equipment installed knows he or she may as well take the day off from work because of the wide variation in possible arrival and completion times for the service.

The experienced airline traveler sees lack of uniformity of service in a variety of forms. Assessment of penalty charges associated with changes to itinerary in the midst of a trip varies from airline to airline, and from location to location and agent to agent within the same airline. The air traveler knows that enforcement of FAA rules about quantity and placement of carry-on articles depends on the flight attendant crew, as do attributes of food and beverage service. Attributes of landing of the aircraft vary from one landing to the next. Variation in departure and arrival times led to a federal requirement that airlines report their schedule performance (an attempt by the government to bring improvement through "management by result"). One major airline has advertised that it is an industry leader in on-time arrivals. It does not report that it has lengthened scheduled travel times to provide a buffer against variation.

Variation in Organizational Inputs

The organizational customer sees variation in purchased products and services in many of the same forms as consumers, but on a larger scale. Variation in service quality and delivery performance affects the organizational customer in terms of its impact on internal scheduling, communications, and logistics, and on distribution of its products to the marketplace. Variation in characteristics of purchased products and materials affects the producibility of the manufacturing organization's products, as well as their quality and reliability. Manufacturing, shipping and inventory costs, and schedule performance are often affected dramatically by the variation in incoming materials and component parts because of the rework and process changes necessary to adjust for that variation.

Procurement policies that require purchase of the same item from multiple suppliers or purchase on low bid contribute to the variation in organizational inputs. During the last decade, major manufacturers have begun to understand the importance of predictability and uniformity of supply, as well as other advantages of long-term relationships with suppliers, and have begun to move away from those policies. But much remains to be done to improve the actual working relationships that organizational customers have with their communities of suppliers to reduce incoming variation.

Variation in Future Conditions

Variation in possible future conditions is a source of uncertainty introduced into the planning process. Future demand must be predicted for existing products or services and for products or services yet to be developed. The organization must predict the future economic health of the markets in which it chooses to operate. The effects of future economic conditions on availability of financing and other resources must also be anticipated. The organization must predict future needs for human resources and anticipate the types of skills and knowledge that will be critical to the success of its activities in the future. The risks associated with adopting alternative market strategies and system designs must be evaluated. Variation in customer preferences over time combines with excessive time spent in product design, development, and testing to make prediction of market conditions at the time of introduction of a new product or service very difficult. The longer the development cycle, the further into the future predictions must be made, building in greater uncertainty.

Figure 2 shows a time-ordered plot of the number of requests for a service. Having the people and equipment available when they are needed to provide the service requires knowledge of the existence and magnitude of variation in demand. For example, there is variation in requirements for emergency services at a hospital and variation in the demand for elective surgery. Hotels in business and government centers have much lower occupancy rates on Fridays and Saturdays than they do during the rest of the week. The demand for service in a restaurant fluctuates hour to hour and day to day. The number of customers to be served at the end of a holiday season, such as Thanksgiving or Christmas, strains the capacity of the airlines, but the demand for air travel is less during January and February.

Variation of a magnitude like that shown in Figure 2 has important implications for the design of the system used to provide the service. One could choose to staff with sufficient full-time labor to meet the largest

Figure 2

Daily number of requests for a service

demand observed in the past. But that would create considerable idle time that would need to be filled with some type of alternative work. Or one could staff with full-time labor sufficient to meet a low, nearly guaranteed level of demand and then use part-time or temporary employees to fill any larger demand that occurs. But this creates the problem of choosing between training temporary employees well enough to be able to provide high-quality service, or allowing quality of service to deteriorate during periods of high demand. The effects of variation in demand on equipment capacity requirements must also be understood and accounted for in system design. Choice of equipment design affects skill requirements for employees, and so staffing decisions and equipment design decisions are interdependent. Intelligent selection of a particular system design involves predicting how variation in requirements placed on the capacity of a system of production or service will affect cost, quality, and timeliness of delivery. The enterprise cannot completely control the external sources of influence on its performance. But it can seek to accurately predict future events and govern its future through actions appropriate to those predictions.

Variation Produced inside the Organization

Variation is created while producing a product or service. Mechanical processes are not precisely repeatable; machines wear out over time and do not produce uniform results. Tooling wears and affects the output. Equipment breaks down, and production is interrupted. Employees vary in their skills and knowledge, so the results of their work are different. Methods of doing work are often not standardized, so there is variation in results produced and time and resources consumed. Environmental conditions change. Demands placed on equipment and people vary over time and affect the outputs. The amount of rework and correction of mistakes required varies and affects the workload. Variation in results of attempts to produce a product or service affects other aspects of business activity, such as planning, scheduling, acquisition and allocation of resources, and procurement. Once created, undesirable variation creates loss for the organization. The loss occurs internally as cost, waste, and lowered productivity, and externally through lack of competitiveness in the marketplace.

Variation in the many forms described above is a source of waste and damage to the economic well-being of both consumers and producers. To provide value to customers, an organization must be prepared to deal with variation in their needs. Managers should recognize the variation in backgrounds, knowledge, skills, and abilities of their employees and work to optimize the interactions among employees and the work they do. Processes and systems send messages about how they work in the form of variation in the results they produce. By studying and acting on the sources of variation, managers can achieve greater uniformity of product and predictable, timely service and thereby improve the economic well-being of the enterprise. Rather than risk unexpected damage to long-term objectives by seeking to manage results (costs, profits, ROI, employee turnover, etc.) directly, managers should seek to understand the system that generates them and act on that system to bring about sustainable improvement of future results.

▶ THEORIES FOR INTERPRETING THE MEANING OF VARIATION

Variation exists in the results produced by an organization and its subsystems. There are different theories used by managers to interpret the meaning of variation in process or system results.[3] Interpretation of information and events requires that there be a rationale or theory as a basis for the interpretation. Formal theories are sometimes employed for interpretation; for example, a theory of physics is used to interpret a physical phenomenon or a psychological theory is used to interpret human behavior. In other cases, the theory being used is implicit in the interpretation and the actions taken as a consequence; i.e., there is some rationale employed in the act of interpretation, even though it is not explicitly stated. Argyris (1990) refers to "Human Theories of Control" as follows:

> We can think of human beings as having been taught, early in life, how to act in ways to be in control . . . People transform these lessons into theories of action. The theories of action, in turn, contain rules that are used to design and implement the actions in everyday life. . . . Human beings have programs in their heads about how to be in control . . . These programs exist in the human mind in two very different ways. The first way is the set of beliefs and values people hold about how to manage their lives. The second way is the actual rules they use to manage

---

3. We use the term "theory" here in the sense of the Greek *theoria*, meaning view or speculation.

their beliefs. We call the first their espoused theories of action; the second, their theories-in-use.

By observing the ways in which managers cope with or react to variation, at least three theories employed to interpret variation can be identified. The three theories and the managerial behaviors they produce can be described as follows:[4]

1. Variation should not exist. Standards and practices should produce uniform results when they are rigidly followed. When variation does exist, it is the result of people's failure to adhere to those standards and practices. When this theory is used, managers either try to ignore the existence of variation or try to cause it not to exist by imposing rigid standards.

2. All variation is the result of something exceptional (usually, a single cause) to be minutely analyzed and acted on. When this theory is used, managers seek explanations for each event that occurs and tend to overreact by making changes in systems that often produce worse results than they would have seen if they had taken no action at all.

3. Variation in any kind of results exists as a consequence of actions and interactions of the causes that produce the results. Variation is created by two kinds of causes: (1) causes that act on every result and are part of the design of the system and the everyday practices and policies used to manage the system, and (2) causes that are special in that they act only at certain times or locations. This is the theory linking variation to causes originated by Walter Shewhart. Use of this theory leads to different methods of analysis of variation and actions by managers than the two previous ones.

The last alternative is the theory most consistent with modern concepts and practices of system management and improvement, and is most useful to interpret the meaning of variation. In this theory, variation is treated as a source of knowledge about how systems actually operate, so that knowledge can be used to redesign those systems for improvement. Before considering that alternative, we will explore the behaviors that exhibit use of the first two theories and some of the implications of those behaviors.

Ignoring Variation

If managers adopt the theory that variation should not exist, a method they can use to react to variation is to try to ignore it. Many personnel systems appear to have been established with the implicit assumption that all people are alike; i.e., there is no variation in people, or there should not be. Organizational policies that provide decision rules to be uniformly applied—for example, how many days employees can be absent for

---

4. Use of the three theories can be seen in the way we approach the management of our everyday lives. Their use is not restricted to business management.

Figure 3

Dot plot of transaction times for travel arrangements made by phone

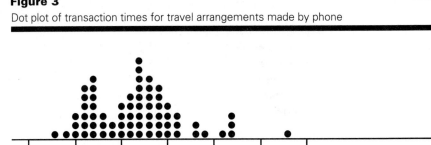

bereavement—appear to be founded on ignoring the existence of variation in the circumstances in which people find themselves. As an example of ignoring the existence of variation, we refer to Figure 3. It shows a dot plot of the amount of time required to complete each of about seventy telephone transactions to make travel arrangements at a travel agency. Variation in customers' needs—length of trip, number of travel segments, lodging requirements, needs for various forms of transportation—contribute to the variation in time required to complete the transaction.

Consider some results of ignoring variation such as that shown in Figure 3. Because there is variation in complexity of the job to be done with each travel transaction, it is unrealistic to set a fixed quota on the number of transactions a single agent should complete in a fixed period of time. When a quota is set, variation in time required to meet customers' needs to their satisfaction is ignored, and the existing variation is translated to other, more undesirable forms. Agents try to meet their quota and speed up their work, make mistakes and treat customers abruptly. The net outcome is rework to correct mistakes, deterioration in quality of service, and customer dissatisfaction, with inevitable poor results in the marketplace. In addition, agents are made to feel incompetent, damaging their self-esteem and enthusiasm to contribute to the organization.

Imposing Arbitrary Standards

In the belief that imposition of standards to be rigidly enforced will create desirable performance, managers establish standards, often with no knowledge of system capability to achieve those standards. Managing to arbitrary targets, rewarding or praising those who exceed them and penalizing or berating those who fail to meet them, is founded in the theory that variation should not exist. This approach ignores the existence of variation in the output of a dynamic system, and can produce surprising consequences. For example, a variety of automotive after-market products were produced in a plant. The plant manager made a practice of holding a weekly management meeting in which each area manager was praised or criticized, depending on whether he had met the previous week's production schedule for his area. An annual physical inventory count turned up a large disparity between the physical count of one type of product and the amount shown in the computerized inventory record. The physical count was short. The plant manager decided that thieves from the surrounding town must be stealing parts from the warehouse. He had a fence built around the company's property to prevent any more stealing. A physical inventory a few weeks later showed another short physical count. The plant manager decided that employees must be stealing from the warehouse, so he had a fence built around the warehouse and gates installed that could be locked. Another physical count showed that the problem still existed. The plant manager hired a detective to catch the thieves. During the night, the manager of the area that produced the product and two of his employees were observed hoisting boxes of the product over the warehouse fence and taking them back to the production area. For several months, the area manager had shown consistently good weekly schedule performance. He had managed to come up with a method that made his performance look good, so he didn't have to endure embarrassment and criticism in the weekly production meetings. When production problems occurred and the area manager saw he wouldn't be able to meet his schedule, he would "borrow" material from the warehouse. He would bring it back to the production area and then the material handlers who also logged production figures into the computer inventory record would move the material back into the warehouse. The area manager had thought he would be able to somehow make up the discrepancies before a physical count revealed them, but production problems continued to crop up. After he had begun his new method of "manufacturing" product, he found it difficult to stop, because he couldn't figure out a way to explain the sudden deterioration in performance that would occur if he stopped. The area manager's behavior may appear to the outside observer to have been irrational and foolish, but may have seemed entirely rational to the area manager, given the system within which he lived.[5]

The following example from Bounds, Reeve, and Gilbert (1991, pp. 369–370) is an illustration of results of the same type of behavior, most likely generated by similar beliefs about variation.

> The traditional concept of control revolves around meeting engineered standards. A department manager told one of the authors, "Yes, we're almost always in control. We meet standards every month." . . . This department manager discovered that production efficiency varies erratically from hour to hour and day to day. Efficiency was not predictable or stable over time, although on the average, over a period of a month, the department met engineered standards. For example, the manager frequently recognizes a projected shortfall in production numbers

---

5. Source: Dr. Brian Joiner, Joiner Associates.

near the end of the month. He then makes a long production run, a "gravy run," of an "unneeded" but easy-to-run part to get the monthly efficiency up to standard. . . . Instability and variation in production outcomes are important because of the ripple effects throughout the organization. Thus, a department may meet standards for accounting control, as aggregated over the period, and yet be out of statistical control, within the period, to the detriment of overall system objectives.

In both the cases described above, management acted in a way that is symptomatic of a belief that variation in the processes producing the product could be legislated out of existence. Attempts to cause that variation not to exist or to at least ignore the possibility of its existence led to translation of that variation into other undesirable, unanticipated forms. Standards were met, but other dimensions of performance, such as inventory cost, were unfavorably affected. Attempts to manage system results directly by use of arbitrary targets and rigid standards, rather than addressing the structure and dynamics of the system that generates those results, may produce temporary improvements in the dimension addressed, but can be expected to produce damaging effects over the long term.

Overreacting to Variation

Another way to react to variation is to try to explain every fluctuation in a series of outcomes as the result of a specific cause. This behavior is typified by intense media analyses of daily fluctuations of the stock market or of year-to-year fluctuations in ten-day sales figures for automobiles. Peter Senge (1990, p. 21) describes this kind of behavior in his book *The Fifth Discipline* as a "fixation on events":

> We are conditioned to see life as a series of events, and for every event, we think there is one obvious cause. Conversations in organizations are dominated by concern with events: last month's sales, the new budget cuts, last quarter's earnings, who just got promoted or fired, the new product or competitors just announced, the delay that just was announced in our new product, and so on. The media reinforces an emphasis on short-term events—after all, if it's more than two days old, it's no longer "news." Focusing on events leads to "event" explanations: "The Dow Jones average dropped sixteen points today," announces the newspaper, "because low fourth-quarter profits were announced yesterday." Such explanations may be true as far as they go, but they distract us from seeing the longer-term patterns of change that lie behind the events and from understanding the causes of those patterns.

Senge identifies the "fixation on events" as one of the seven "learning disabilities" that afflict organizations. Treating each outcome as if it were singular and explaining it as an isolated occurrence is overreacting to variation. By overreacting to variation, managers fail to address the past and present causes that combine to produce it.

None of the behaviors described above is likely to lead to increased understanding of the sources that act in combination to produce variation in process or system results. A better approach is to recognize the existence of variation and adopt an approach of interpreting it as a series of messages from the system about how it operates. Shewhart's theory is most useful for interpreting the messages in variation. When used in combination with appreciation for system structures and dynamics, and an understanding of the effects of managerial practices on people and their behaviors, use of Shewhart's theory can substantially increase the capability to improve the organization and its results. Shewhart's theory of variation will be discussed in the next section.

▶ SHEWHART'S THEORY AND METHOD TO INTERPRET VARIATION

Dr. Walter Shewhart worked for Bell Telephone Laboratories during the 1920s. He undertook work to improve uniformity of product produced by Western Electric, the manufacturing unit of AT&T. In the course of his work, Shewhart created a theory for interpreting variation and linking it to its causes. Shewhart developed his theory and method for the purpose of interpreting variation in measured characteristics of a series of items produced by a manufacturing process (1931). Deming extended Shewhart's theory by applying it to interpretation of a series of results produced by any type of causal system (1986). The series could be the results of service transactions, or managerial figures such as costs or accident rates, or they could be measures from large-scale systems, such as the annual figures on the U.S. balance of trade. Deming made the point that the concepts of variation created by Shewhart could be applied even in cases when there were no figures available for analysis. Shewhart's theory of variation provides a useful method to interpret the performance of a process or system, to relate observed variation to its causes, and to determine a course of action to bring about improvement.

Stable versus Unstable Variation

Shewhart made a distinction between *stable variation* and *unstable variation* in a series of results. The "results" could be a measured dimension of a series of manufactured parts, concentrations of some constituent in a succession of batches of chemical material, monthly unit costs for production of a product, daily number of requests for a type of service, or a wide variety of other possible streams of results. Stable variation is of a consistent magnitude, and the results fluctuate randomly around a steady average. Unstable variation can be seen in a series that has an inconsistent magnitude of variation, a changing average, or some kind of systematic pattern over time. Figure 4 illustrates stable variation in a series of results. The results show a steady magnitude of variation around a steady average, and

Figure 4

Stable variation in results

Result

Time

the up-and-down fluctuations in the series of values appear to be random.[6] Shewhart referred to stable variation as *"statistically controlled variation."*

Figure 5 illustrates three kinds of unstable variation in results. The results depicted in Figure 5a vary around a consistent level, or average, except during one period when a sudden shift to a different level (size) of results occurs. Some unusual event has occurred during that one period of time. Predicting the occurrence of similar episodes would require knowledge of the cause of the unusual variation.

Figure 5b depicts another kind of unstable variation. Rather than a single episode when unusual results are produced, the results in Figure 5b exhibit longer-term, erratic fluctuations in size. The short-term, result-to-result fluctuations are consistently of about the same magnitude around the shifting level of results.

The short-term variation shown in Figure 5c is of a steady magnitude, but the entire series shows growth over time in the size of the results. Without knowing something about the conditions that produced the series and something about likely future conditions, it would be virtually impossible to predict the behavior of future results with any degree of belief. Future results might level off, continue to increase, or show a downward trend. In other words, the variation in the series lacks statistical control.

The Statistical Control Chart

Walter Shewhart devised the statistical control chart to operationally define[7] the state of statistical control of variation in a series of results. Figure 6 depicts a *control chart* constructed from a series of results with *statistical*

---

6. For a specific example of a series of results that exhibits stable variation, the reader may refer to Figure 17, a chart showing counts of surface defects in a consumer product, or to Figure 31, a chart showing a series of monthly overtime costs.

7. An operational definition gives communicable meaning to a concept (in this case, statistically controlled variation) by describing how the concept is to be applied. Chapter 9 of Deming's book *Out of the Crisis* contains a discussion of operational definitions.

Figure 5
Unstable variation in results

(a) Short-term variation stable, episodic shift to a different level

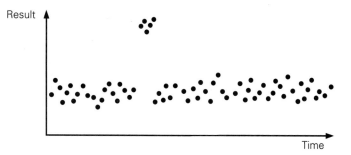

(b) Short-term variation stable, erratic fluctuation in level

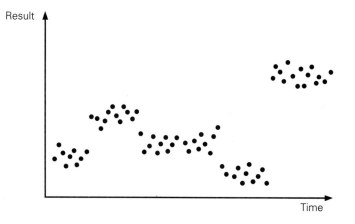

(c) Stable short-term variation, increasing level

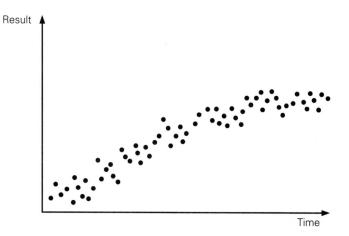

Figure 6

Statistical control

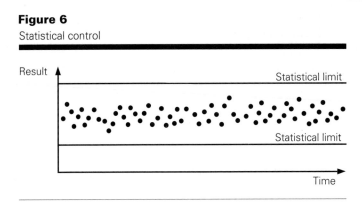

control limits. Statistical control limits are derived by applying appropriate statistical formulas to the observed results. There are a variety of control charts designed to be used for different kinds of data.[8] The general interpretation of the control chart is the same, regardless of the kind of chart being used.

The control chart and its rules for interpretation provide the manager with a means to make a clear and repeatable judgment of the state of statistical control of variation in the results. Statistical control limits, combined with rules for detecting systematic patterns, allow a manager to judge whether the variation in a collection of results produced by a process or system is stable and predictable, at least in the near term. They tell the manager how much variation to expect in the results from a stable system of causes—*common causes of variation.* Common causes are imbedded in the design and daily operating practices of the organizational system, and they are acted on only with change of system design and managerial policy and practice.

In Figure 7, some points lie outside the statistical control limits. These points provide a signal that the variation in the series is not statistically controlled. Statistically controlled variation is produced by a collection of constant or common causes that act on every result. The specific influence of these causes on the results may vary over time, but the causes are common to every result. The existence of signals of a lack of statistical control in the observed variation indicates that additional, *special causes of variation* act intermittently to produce variation in addition to that which would exist given the action of common causes.

A primary advantage of using Shewhart's theory is to minimize the economic loss that comes from two kinds of mistakes that occur when

---

8. Specific examples of control charts will be discussed in following sections. Figure 13 is an example of a *p* chart, Figure 16 is an example of a *u* chart, Figure 17 is an example of a *c* chart, Figures 22 and 23 show *X*-bar and *R* charts, Figures 30 and 31 illustrate the use of *X* and moving *R* charts. All of these examples rely on the same methods of interpretation, the subject of this section.

Figure 7

Lack of statistical control

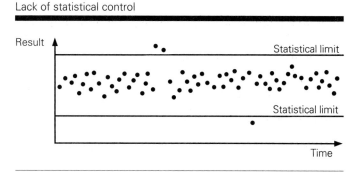

results are interpreted without distinguishing variation created by special causes from variation produced by common causes alone. The two mistakes are:

1. Interpreting a result that came from the effects of common causes as if it were affected by something special
2. Interpreting a result that was affected by something special as if it came from common causes

The economic loss occurs when these mistakes lead to inappropriate actions for improvement.

A few examples will illustrate the two kinds of mistakes. Deming refers to actions based on the first kind of mistake as "tampering." In manufacturing, tampering occurs when operators continually attempt to adjust the process to make the product uniform. Each fluctuation is treated as if it came from something special, and the dials or knobs are twisted to make the next result come out exactly on target. The net effect is to produce more variation in the stream of results.[9] At the level of the business unit, tampering occurs when explanations of each and every unfavorable deviation from plan or budget are intensely investigated to identify a single cause. This widespread practice wastes labor hours on a grand scale. Coincidental events are identified as causes for each movement up or down without consideration of all of the other actions and events that combined to produce the final outcome.

The second kind of mistake might be characterized in general as "we won't let that happen again." In a manufacturing plant, one employee

---

9. There are numerous other examples of tampering in manufacturing. Some poorly designed automatic feedback control systems react to each individual outcome as if it were a signal of a systematic change, alter processing factors to different levels, and produce more variation as a result. Some manual and automated inventory control systems are designed to adjust order sizes according to the most recent period's demand or usage. Some measurement systems are set up to recalibrate to a standard based on each observed deviation.

was caught putting gas from the pump used to fuel company vehicles into his personal car. As a result, an elaborate system for ensuring that wouldn't happen again was put into place. Each time an employee needs to fill the gas tank of a company vehicle, he must go through a procedure in which he completes a form to obtain a key to the pump, pumps the gas, and returns the key to the proper location. In this case, one incident has introduced additional paperwork and effort to every trip by every employee. When this practice was instituted, no one asked about whether misuse of company fuel was common or if the one event was exceptional. We see examples of this behavior throughout business organizations and government. Requirements and regulations are often instituted across the board in reaction to a single event. This is done without first determining whether the event that generated the supposed need for additional regulation is likely to occur again, or to occur frequently enough to warrant the additional time and effort used to meet the new requirement or regulation.

The preceding remarks are not intended to imply that all analysis and reactions to variation should be stopped, but some of those reactions may be, in fact, overreactions that introduce additional variation and waste. When a control chart is used, managers can consistently interpret the information contained in variation. They can make informed judgments about what needs to be changed and who carries primary responsibility for changing it in order to gain sustainable improvement. The individual who holds authority over the system generating the results has the responsibility to initiate and manage action on common causes. Common causes are part of the design of the system and the practices and policies used to manage the system. Even when special causes act to produce variation, those who work within the process or system often do not have authority to make the required changes to prevent future recurrence of their effects. The following paragraph addresses this from the viewpoint of manufacturing:

> Some special causes can be removed only by management. For example, production workers sometimes need engineering assistance to remove problems connected with malfunction of machinery in use. It is the responsibility of management to provide assistance when needed. Another instance of management's responsibility for special causes occurs in the current state of chaos in dealing with vendors. Production workers are sometimes forced to use unacceptable or inconsistent raw materials or parts. It is management's job to take corrective action to work with vendors to improve the quality of incoming materials, and to halt the practice of switching from one source to another. [Deming, 1986, p. 320]

The primary capability of people who work within a system lies in being able to provide information on changing conditions and input on what might be potential causes of the variation in results.

Figure 8

Statistical control

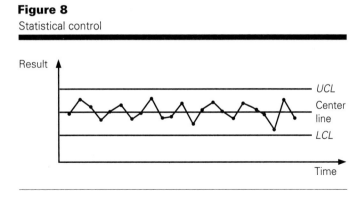

Interpreting Control Charts

The statistical control chart provides an operational definition of the state of statistical control of the variation in a series of results.[10] The control chart provides a means:

- To study and assess variation and to judge whether it is stable
- To maintain a continuous record of results so that the effects of changes to the system can be seen
- To receive signals of change
- To reveal through patterns of variation information about causes of that variation

The kind of control chart to be used in a given situation depends upon the kind of data to be examined. Although specific details of construction may vary from one type of chart to the next, the fundamental elements of analysis of variation are common to all control charts. A control chart with no points outside statistical control limits and no systematic patterns in the plotted points shows variation in a state of statistical control. In the example of a control chart shown in Figure 8, the symbols *UCL* and *LCL* refer to upper and lower statistical control limits. Statistical control limits are calculated according to formulas applied to the data plotted on the chart.[11] Limits derived by using specifications or target values are not statistical control limits.

---

10. An operational definition describes a method that brings communicable meaning to a concept.
11. Some texts state that statistical control limits are constructed to provide for a certain probability that points will fall outside control limits when there are no special causes acting on the results. Deming indicates that this viewpoint is incorrect in the following passage from his text *The New Economics for Industry, Government, Education.* "It is possible that a control chart may fail to indicate existence of a special cause when one is actually present. It may send us scouting to find a special cause when there is none. It is wrong (misuse of the meaning of a control chart) to suppose that there is some ascertainable probability that either of these failures will occur. We can only say that the risk to incur either failure is very small."

Figure 9
Signals of lack of statistical control

(a) A point outside statistical limits

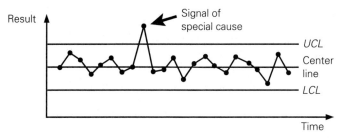

(b) A run of points on one side of the center line

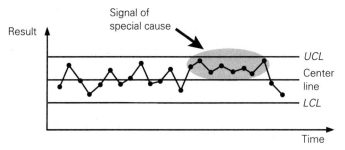

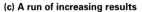

(c) A run of increasing results

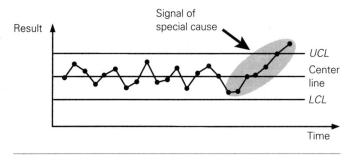

A point outside statistical control limits is taken to be an out-of-control signal indicating the effect of a special cause of variation (see Figure 9a).

If the data plotted on a control chart are time ordered, then their fluctuations up and down can be examined for systematic patterns. A wide variety of checks for systematic (nonrandom) patterns in sequences of time-ordered points are presented in various publications (see, for example, the Wheeler and Chambers book included in the references). The two simple checks that follow have the advantages of being easily committed to memory and easily applied. Other choices of checks for patterns might be made. Once a set of rules to check for systematic patterns has been selected, the same set should be applied consistently. If the data are not plotted in time sequence, it is not appropriate to apply the following two checks for systematic patterns.

1. Seven or more successive points (a run of points) on one side of the center line is taken to be an out-of-control signal (see Figure 9b for an illustration).

2. Seven or more successive points (a run of points) steadily increasing or decreasing is taken to be an out-of-control signal (see Figure 9c for an illustration).

Once a center line and control limits have been established, they can be extended, and additional new points plotted and examined for signals of change. Managers can use these signals to confirm whether their actions have produced the intended effect. The center line and control limits also provide a means to determine when it is appropriate to seek a specific explanation for a particular result, rather than relying on the usual damaging and wasteful practice of asking for explanations for all unfavorable fluctuations in results. Specific explanations should be sought when there are signals of the existence of special causes. Identification of the cause(s) of exceptional results provides a means to take appropriate action to either perpetuate causes of favorable results or eliminate causes of unfavorable results.

The center line and limits on a control chart are not altered until a signal of sustained change has been seen on the chart (usually a run of points above or below the center line) and the signal can be connected to a change in the process or its inputs. However, if the level or variation in results changes and the change is sustained over a variety of conditions, a change to center line and control limits may be made even if the cause has not been identified. Otherwise, the chart becomes useless for detecting further change. In no case are revisions made to center line and limits arbitrarily or according to some external criterion without knowledge of the subject matter; for example, with each new data point, every thirty points, every week, every month, and so on.

Constructing Control Charts

The appropriate type of control chart to be used in a particular application depends on the kind of data being studied. In traditional quality control, two types of data have usually been identified: attributes and variables. The distinction was made primarily to help distinguish between data that could be analyzed using X-bar and R charts and data that need to be given a different treatment. Four kinds of data are typically encountered when

Figure 10

Kinds of data and charts designed to analyze them

Kind of data	Type of control chart
Categorical data	p chart
Counts of events or occurrences in space or time	u chart
Variables data	X-bar and R chart, X and moving R chart
Ranks or ratings	Charts and other methods not discussed here

studying systems or processes. They are listed in Figure 10, along with the type of control charts designed to analyze them.

Categorical data are obtained by classifying each of a group of individuals, items, or events into one of two or more categories. The data are counts of how many were classified into each category. For example, engineering change notices are classified by the reason for the change, and the resulting data consist of counts by reason. Manufactured parts are classified as scrap, repair, or good, and the resulting data consist of the number of items in these three categories. When survey respondents are classified by their age, the resulting data consist of the number of respondents in each age category.

Counts of a different kind are obtained by observing *some type of "event" in space or time.* Typical quality control work has involved observing and counting the occurrences of defects or flaws in manufactured materials, such as various kinds of surface flaws in paint on an automobile body, pinholes in sheets of steel or aluminum, or impurities in a compound or food product. The counts are made for a surface area or volume of physical material and reflect the density and dispersion of the occurrences. Another situation in which counts arise from observation occurs when a particular kind of event is observed over a period of time. For example, power generators observe and record the number of service interruptions on a daily or monthly basis; providers of goods or services observe and record the number of customer complaints received in a day or a month; manufacturers concern themselves with the number of unscheduled processing interruptions in a production system; safety departments keep track of the number of recordable accidents that occur per month. In these cases, time is the frame of reference for examining the rate and pattern of occurrences of the event.

Variables data are produced by measuring a quantitative characteristic on some continuous scale, for example, length, weight, or time. A dimension of a part, weight of a part, time required to complete a task, flow rate of a liquid, unit cost of a manufactured product, length of time a service is interrupted—all of these measurements are data of the variables kind.

Ranks are created by ordering a collection of individuals or items from 1 to 20, for example, according to some criterion (best to worst, largest to smallest, least to greatest, etc.). Similar data arise by assigning a rating (excellent, good, mediocre, etc.) to an individual or item. Special statistical methods have been devised to deal with ranks or ratings. Those methods will not be discussed here, since their breadth of beneficial application is somewhat limited.

The p Chart   The p chart is used to analyze categorical data that consist of counts of number of items in two categories (good—not good, yes—no, etc.).[12] The points on a p chart represent the fraction of items in a given subgroup of items that fall into one of two categories (fraction good or fraction defective, fraction red or fraction not red, etc.). The subgroup size (number of items classified to produce a single point on the control chart) may not be constant. Figure 11 contains a description of the method for constructing a p chart. Interpretation of a p chart would proceed along the general lines for interpretation of control charts discussed earlier.

The following example illustrates use of a p chart to study variation in results of production. Although the example is concerned with manufacturing, the principles illustrated would also apply if the data came from a system producing a service, such as health care, lodging, or transportation. The only important difference that exists in production of a product and production of a service is that there is no opportunity to rework service transactions before they reach the customer as there is in manufacturing. In terms of system analysis and study of variation, there is no difference in manufacturing and service.

In our example, electronic modules are manufactured and then subjected to a functional test prior to packaging and shipping. Records are kept of the number of modules tested each day and the number of modules that pass the test. The data shown in Figure 12 are for twenty-three days of production.

Figure 13 shows the p chart constructed from the data shown in Figure 12. The total number of modules that passed the test (31,914) was divided by the total number tested (34,291) over the twenty-three days to obtain the center line shown on the control chart (.931). The line segments appearing at varying distances from the center line are the control limits; that is, the limits defining the magnitude of deviation of individual points around the center line, if the variation were in statistical control. The control limits vary due to the variation in subgroup size (number tested) on each day. The formulas for control limits for a p chart shown in Fig-

---

12. The mathematical model that forms the basis for analyzing the variation in a stream of categorical data is the Bernoulli model.

Figure 11
Method for constructing a *p* chart

- Subgroups of items are classified into two categories according to some criterion. Counts of number of items in each of the two categories are made.
- The number of items in one of the two categories in each subgroup and the number of items, *n*, in each subgroup are recorded.
- For each subgroup, calculate *p*, the proportion of items in the subgroup classified into one of the two categories:

$$p = \frac{\text{number of items in one category in subgroup}}{n}$$

where *n* is the number of items in the subgroup.
- Plot the values of *p* as points on the control chart.
- Calculate the center line for the chart as:

$$\bar{p} = \frac{\text{total number of items in the one category in all subgroups combined}}{\text{total number of items in all subgroups}}$$

where the totals are obtained from the data available.
- Calculate the control limits *for each subgroup* as:

$$UCL_p = \bar{p} + 3\sqrt{\frac{\bar{p}(1 - \bar{p})}{n}}$$

$$LCL_p = \bar{p} - 3\sqrt{\frac{\bar{p}(1 - \bar{p})}{n}}, \text{ if not negative}$$

If all subgroups have the same number of items, the control limits will be the same for all subgroups.

Figure 12
Data from functional tests of electronic modules

Day	Number tested (*n*)	Number passed	Proportion passed— yield (*p*)	Day	Number tested (*n*)	Number passed	Proportion passed— yield (*p*)
1	720	674	.936	13	1435	1347	.939
2	880	819	.931	14	1488	1389	.933
3	1420	1329	.936	15	1500	1406	.937
4	1460	1350	.925	16	1450	1357	.936
5	1430	1347	.942	17	1430	1308	.915
6	1450	1361	.939	18	1424	1336	.938
7	1440	1323	.919	19	1620	1535	.948
8	1480	1385	.936	20	1680	1543	.918
9	1490	1386	.930	21	1850	1693	.915
10	2160	1996	.924	22	1755	1639	.934
							.942
11	1430	1318	.922	23	1829	1723	
12	1470	1350	.918				
				Totals	34,291	31,914	.931

Figure 13

Control chart for daily proportion of electronic modules that pass a functional test

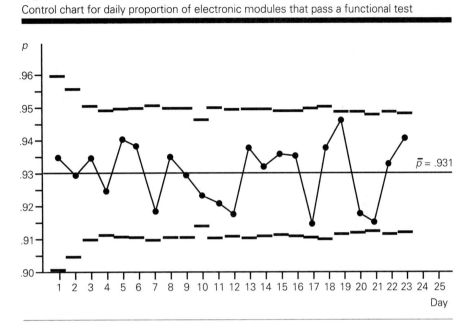

ure 11 indicate that limits of variation, given a particular average, depend upon the subgroup size. Examples of computations that led to the control limits shown are as follows:

For subgroup (day) 1, $n = 720$. The control limits are:

Upper control limit $UCL = .931 + 3\sqrt{\dfrac{.931(1 - .931)}{720}} = .931 + 0.28 = .959$

Lower control limit $LCL = .931 - 3\sqrt{\dfrac{.931(1 - .931)}{720}} = .931 - .028 = .903$

For subgroup (day) 10, $n = 2160$. The control limits are:

Upper control limit $UCL = .931 + 3\sqrt{\dfrac{.931(1 - .931)}{2160}} = .931 + .016 = .947$

Lower control limit $LCL = .931 - 3\sqrt{\dfrac{.931(1 - .931)}{2160}} = .931 - .016 = .915$

By examining the control chart, we conclude that the variation in yields, as measured by daily testing results, is stable, in statistical control, at an average yield of about 93 percent. Whatever the design of the product, the manufacturing processes, the procurement methods, and all of the attendant support and managerial processes and practices may be, they demonstrate through this period of time the capability to produce failed modules at a level of about 7 percent of production. This level of failure is, of course, due to the combined effects of the design, production, and support processes mentioned above and the functional testing process. All of these are candidates for study and redesign if sustainable improvement is to be made.

Given existing conditions, the average yield of 93 percent can be used as a basis to define limits of variation in yield at a given production level for use in scheduling and resource planning. For a given number of modules produced, n, the yield could be expected to vary in the range defined by:

$$n\bar{p} \pm 3\sqrt{n\bar{p}(1 - \bar{p})}$$

This formula defines control limits for variation in the number of modules that pass the functional test when n modules are submitted to test. In cases where n was constant, a control chart could be constructed (an np chart) for the number of modules that pass the test. When n varies from subgroup to subgroup, interpretation of such a chart is a more complex task, so construction of an np chart is not recommended.

The system that produced these results is stable, but that doesn't mean it produces desirable results. In fact, there are several reasons why managers would want to improve this system. On average, to obtain a given number, X, of good modules, it would be necessary to produce $X/(.931)$ modules. So an order for 1,000 modules would require producing roughly 1,074 modules, on average; filling an order for 2,000 modules would require producing 2,148. The variation in production requirements introduced by variation in quality of the results affects inventory costs, labor costs, administrative and record-keeping costs, and so on, and may have important implications for equipment capacity requirements to meet demand. In addition, the variation in production results produces a need to establish scheduling and inventory policies intended to achieve an appropriate balance among various kinds of costs and simultaneously meet customer demand. So reducing variation by improving quality reduces, in turn, the difficulty of attempting to balance the various dimensions of business performance. Sustained improvement in the system generating the results of Figure 13 would be seen as an upward trend in yields or a run of yields above the current average of .931. The increase in yield would be accompanied by reduced variation, as can be seen by examining the formulas for control limits shown in Figure 11. Reduced variation would produce, in turn, reduced costs that could be translated into better market position in terms of price, and a reduced need to trade off various dimensions of business performance and customer value.

Figure 14
Method for constructing a *u* chart

- The number of occurrences of an event is recorded for each of a series of periods of observation. Or the number of occurrences of an "event" such as a defect, flaw, or impurity is recorded as a result of examining a series of quantities of physical material. The data for each subgroup of information consist of a count of the number of occurrences of the event of interest and a record of the amount of area, volume, time, or work observed to make the count.
- A unit of area, volume, time, or work is defined for use as a means to make the plotted points comparable. This is called the "inspection unit" in traditional applications of *u* charts for counts of defects.
- The number of events counted, *c*, and the number of "inspection units," *n*, are recorded for each subgroup of information.
- For each subgroup, calculate *u*, the number of occurrences per unit:

$$u = \frac{c}{n} = \frac{\text{number of occurrences counted}}{\text{number of "inspection units" observed}}$$

- Plot the values of *u* as points on the control chart.
- Calculate the center line for the chart as:

$$\bar{u} = \frac{\text{total number of occurrences in all subgroups}}{\text{total number of units in all subgroups}}$$

- Calculate control limits for *each subgroup* as:

$$UCL_u = \bar{u} + 3\sqrt{\frac{\bar{u}}{n}}$$

$$LCL_u = \bar{u} - 3\sqrt{\frac{\bar{u}}{n}}, \text{ if not negative}$$

If all subgroups arose from observing the same amount of time or material, the control limits will be the same for all subgroups.

The *u* Chart   Variation in counts of events in space or time is analyzed for stability using a *u* chart.[13] The *u* chart is a chart of plotted points that consist of counts of the number of occurrences of a particular kind of event, appropriately scaled to account for the amount of time or material observed to arrive at each count. Figure 14 contains a description of the method used to construct a *u* chart. Interpretation of a *u* chart would generally proceed according to the earlier discussion on interpreting control charts.

An example of use of a *u* chart comes from the safety department of a small company that uses a molding process to produce parts used in a variety of consumer products. The molding process involves loading blanks into mold cavities, loading the mold into a press where the material is subjected to very high temperatures, and then unloading the molded

---

13. The mathematical model that forms the basis for analyzing the variation in a stream of counts of occurrences is the Poisson model.

Figure 15
Monthly counts of recorded accidents in production of molded parts

Month	Number of accidents (c)	Labor hours (1000s) (n)	Accidents per 1000 hours (u)	Month	Number of accidents (c)	Labor hours (1000s) (n)	Accidents per 1000 hours (u)
1	201	30.4	6.61	7	169	30.4	5.56
2	214	30.4	7.04	8	204	35.2	5.80
3	256	36.8	6.96	9	170	33.6	5.06
4	168	32.0	5.25	10	244	33.6	7.26
5	176	32.0	6.25	11	183	30.4	6.02
6	216	30.4	7.11	12	190	27.2	6.99
				Totals	2,391	382.4	6.25

Figure 16
Accidents per thousand labor hours

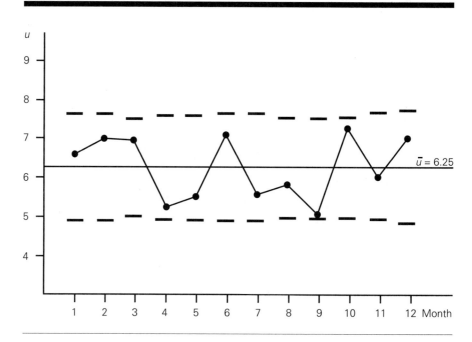

parts. The safety director was concerned with the rate of occurrence of accidents in production. He decided to analyze the data shown in Figure 15. The data consist of the number of recorded accidents and the number of thousands of labor hours worked for twelve months.

Figure 16 shows a control chart constructed from the data in Figure 15. The counts of accidents are counts of occurrences of an event.

The variation in these counts is appropriately analyzed through use of a u chart. The points plotted on the chart represent recorded accidents each month scaled by a unit intended to reflect the amount of opportunity for accidents to occur—the number of labor hours worked each month, in thousands. The unit selected to scale the counts is 1,000 hours of labor. The line segments on the chart are statistical control limits based on the formulas shown in Figure 14. Their distances from the center line vary, since the number of thousands of labor hours varies month to month. Examples of the computations used to obtain the control limits are as follows:

For subgroup (month) 3, the number of thousands of labor hours worked is $n = 36.8$ and the control limits are computed as:

$$UCL = \bar{u} + 3\sqrt{\frac{\bar{u}}{n}} = 6.25 + 3\sqrt{\frac{6.25}{36.8}} = 6.25 + 1.24 = 7.49$$

$$LCL = \bar{u} - 3\sqrt{\frac{\bar{u}}{n}} = 6.25 - 3\sqrt{\frac{6.25}{36.8}} = 6.25 - 1.24 = 5.01$$

For subgroup (month) 12, the number of thousands of labor hours worked is $n = 27.2$ and the control limits are computed as:

$$UCL = \bar{u} + 3\sqrt{\frac{\bar{u}}{n}} = 6.25 + 3\sqrt{\frac{6.25}{27.2}} = 6.25 + 1.44 = 7.69$$

$$LCL = \bar{u} - 3\sqrt{\frac{\bar{u}}{n}} = 6.25 - 3\sqrt{\frac{6.25}{27.2}} = 6.25 - 1.44 = 4.81$$

The safety director's first reaction to the control chart was to conclude that the variation in monthly accidents per thousand hours was in statistical control, so nothing could be done to reduce the rate of occurrence. This is, of course, an erroneous interpretation of the meaning of stable variation due to common causes. Improvement in the form of reduced variation or a change in the average result can be made; however, the improvement comes from redesign of process and operating practices if it is to be a sustained improvement and unexpected damage is not to be created elsewhere.

When he was asked about what might cause accidents, the safety director's response was that people don't pay attention to what they are doing and thus have accidents. After some discussion, he agreed that perhaps the conditions in which accidents could occur were built into the design of the process. He also commented that the majority of recorded accidents were burns that occurred when operators were unloading molds. Manufacturing engineers were asked to look into the possibility that equipment design and the method that had to be used to unload parts could be contributing to the occurrence of burns. Some equipment redesign led to a noticeable reduction in the rate of occurrence of burns.

This example illustrates addressing a common cause of variation—in this case, equipment design—as it affects variation in occurrences of

Figure 17

c chart for surface defects in a consumer product

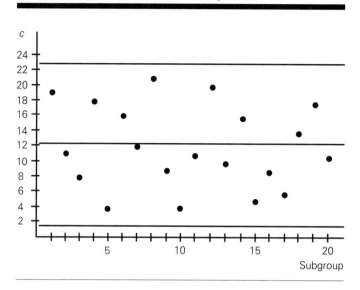

accidents. One might ask why processing equipment would not be designed to minimize risk of burns. This is not an exceptional case, and it illustrates a flaw in the process of designing equipment. A large proportion of the problems that show up downstream in the production process actually are created in upstream processes, such as design and procurement. Continual improvement activity must be extended to those upstream processes if economic and effective change is to be made without unnecessary cost and other forms of damage.

Traditionally, u charts have been used to examine data that consist of counts of defects or flaws of various kinds in manufactured products. Figure 17 shows a control chart constructed from counts of the number of surface defects found on subgroups of five units of a type of consumer product selected from the product produced on each shift for a period of ten days. The manufacturing plant ran for two shifts each day during that period. Since each subgroup contained five units of product, the "inspection unit" selected to construct the chart was five units of product, so that the number of units observed in each subgroup was one and the u values (defects per inspection unit) were the actual counts—the c values. The resulting c chart is shown in Figure 17.

The conclusion to be drawn from examining the control chart shown in Figure 17 is that the variation in counts of defects is produced by a collection of causes common to the entire period. Managers analyzed the occurrence of defects by constructing a *Pareto diagram* for defects by type, and they worked on the defect with the highest frequency. Several kinds of defects were typically noted in the product. Figure 18 shows Pareto diagrams constructed from counts of defects made during the two weeks of time covered by the c chart in Figure 17. The Pareto diagrams shown are simply bar graphs constructed from the counts, with the five most frequently occurring kinds of defects each given a separate bar, and the count of all other kinds of defects given a single bar.[14]

Figure 18a shows the Pareto diagram for the first week. According to plant practice, the focus of work would be Defect A, the type of defect occurring most frequently. But Figure 18b illustrates a pitfall associated with exclusive use of Pareto analysis to determine what should be worked on. Taken alone, Pareto analysis does not consider whether the data observed during a given period can be expected to be typical over a longer period; it does not consider the existence of variation in counts of occurrences. During the second week, there is a change in the frequencies for the various kinds of defects, and the ranking of frequencies for the defects changes. If the data from the second week had been used to choose what to work on, Defect B would have become the focus of attention. Note also that Defect E drops out of the top five and Defect G appears on the list. Relying purely on the Pareto analysis to determine what to work on could clearly lead to confusion, given the existence of variation.

X-bar and R Charts X-bar and R charts, or X and moving R charts, are used to analyze variables data. When groups of results are produced under conditions thought to be homogeneous, there is a rational basis for grouping (subgrouping) individual measurements into subgroups of two or more measurements. In this case, X-bar and R charts are employed to study the variation of measurements between subgroups and within subgroups. For a given subgroup of measurements, X-bar is the average of the measurements in the subgroup; R is the range of the measurements in the subgroup. The subgroup range is a measure of variation within the subgroup. When there is no rational basis for subgrouping the data, they are usually analyzed in the sequence in which they arose by means of a chart for individual measurements (X chart) and an accompanying chart consisting of ranges of contiguous measurements (moving R chart). Methods designed for use with variables data (X-bar and R charts, X and moving R charts, means, standard deviations, etc.) should not be applied to ranks or ratings.

Figure 19 contains a description of the methods to be used to construct X-bar and R charts. Figure 20 contains a table of constants for use in analysis of variables data.

The data shown in Figure 21 were obtained in the course of studying a machining process in a plant that manufactures a complex assembly

---

14. If the kinds of defects were flaws in the surface finish of a automobile body, the defects might be: A: dirt particles in the paint; B: sags in the paint; C: scratches; D: dents and dings; E: bubbles in the paint, and so on.

Figure 18
Pareto diagrams

(a) Counts of defects by type: first week

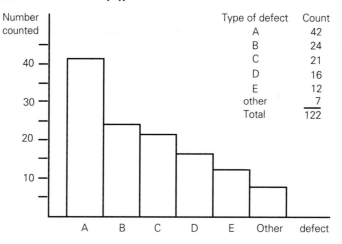

Type of defect	Count
A	42
B	24
C	21
D	16
E	12
other	7
Total	122

(b) Counts of defects by type: second week

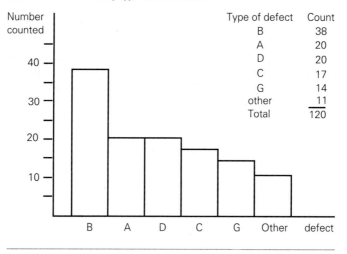

Type of defect	Count
B	38
A	20
D	20
C	17
G	14
other	11
Total	120

whose major components are produced by machining metal castings. Both the machining and the assembly are done in the factory. Excessive variation in a certain dimension of one of the assembly components was creating difficulties in assembly, and these data arose as a result of an effort to understand that variation and its sources. The dimension was created by a series of rough and final cuts made by a particular machine. The machine had a numerical controller that automatically adjusted the cutting tools to account for wear. The adjustment was made according to an algorithm

Figure 19
Method for constructing X-bar and R charts

- The data are organized in subgroups of n measurements each. The individual measurements in a subgroup are called X values.
- For each subgroup, the range and the average of the X values are calculated. The range of the X values is computed as:

R = (largest X value in the subgroup) − (smallest X value in the subgroup)

The average of the X values, X-bar, is computed as:

$$\overline{X} = \frac{\text{sum of } X \text{ values in the subgroup}}{n}$$

- Plot R for each subgroup as a point on the R chart.
- Calculate the average range, the center line for the R chart, as:

$$\overline{R} = \frac{\text{sum of the subgroup ranges}}{\text{number of subgroups}}$$

- Calculate control limits for the R chart:
  Upper control limit $UCL_R = D_4\overline{R}$
  Lower control limit $LCL_R = D_3\overline{R}$

  Refer to the table of control chart constants (Figure 20) to obtain the values of the constants D_3 and D_4. The appropriate constants are located in the table by selecting the row corresponding to the subgroup size, n. The convention we have used for control limits on an R chart is that there is no lower control limit for ranges if the number of measurements in a subgroup is 6 or less. Therefore, no D_3 value is provided for subgroup sizes of 6 or less.
- Analyze the range chart. The control limits for the corresponding X-bar chart are based on the average range. If the range chart shows signals of lack of statistical control, the control limits for the X-bar chart do not reflect a consistent magnitude of within subgroup variation. In such a case, it is recommended that control limits not be placed on the X-bar chart. If control limits are placed on the X-bar chart, they should be taken only as a rough approximation.
- Plot the $\overline{X}$ value for each subgroup on the $\overline{X}$ chart.
- Calculate the center line for the $\overline{X}$ chart as:

$$\overline{\overline{X}} = \frac{\text{sum of the subgroup } \overline{X} \text{ values}}{\text{number of subgroups}}$$

- Calculate control limits for the $\overline{X}$ chart:
  Upper control limit $UCL_{\overline{X}} = \overline{\overline{X}} + A_2\overline{R}$
  Lower control limit $LCL_{\overline{X}} = \overline{\overline{X}} - A_2\overline{R}$

that called for an adjustment every ten parts based on measurements of some of the parts by an automatic gauge in the machine. At the time the data were collected, no one in the plant seemed to know precisely how the algorithm worked, or the rationale for the frequency of adjustment. The data were obtained after some preliminary discussion about potential sources of variation. Production people suspected that the controller was creating some of the variation by overadjusting the position of the cutting

Figure 20

Constants for use in control chart calculations—variables data

Number of measurements per subgroup (n)	A_2	d_2	D_3	D_4
2	1.880	1.128		3.267
3	1.023	1.693		2.574
4	0.729	2.059		2.282
5	0.577	2.326		2.114
6	0.483	2.534		2.004
7	0.419	2.704	0.076	1.924
8	0.373	2.847	0.136	1.864
9	0.337	2.970	0.184	1.816
10	0.308	3.078	0.223	1.777

The appropriate constants to be used for a particular subgroup size (number of measurements in a subgroup) are located in the row containing that subgroup size (n) in the left column.

tool. A team of people from production decided that subgroups of parts would be selected so that the parts within the same subgroup came from one group of ten produced with the tool in a given position. Then the variation within a subgroup would not contain the potential effects of tool adjustment. The effects of tool adjustment would be expected to appear as additional variation between subgroups. Data were collected for a period of ten hours by selecting two subgroups of three parts each hour, making sure that each set of three came from a single tool position. The parts were then measured by a coordinate measuring machine available in the plant. The resulting data were analyzed using X-bar and R charts. The data in Figure 21 consist of each set of three measurements, along with

Figure 21

Measurements of a machined part dimension—subgroups of three measurements each

Subgroup	Individual measurements			$\bar{X}$	R	Subgroup	Individual measurements			$\bar{X}$	R
1	17	15	20	17.3	5	11	27	25	24	25.3	3
2	29	29	30	29.3	1	12	22	27	26	25.0	5
3	22	18	21	20.3	4	13	20	16	21	19.0	5
4	20	23	22	21.7	3	14	31	25	30	28.7	6
5	18	19	21	19.3	3	15	22	20	19	20.3	3
6	28	26	30	28.0	4	16	22	17	21	20.0	5
7	16	14	15	15.0	2	17	29	28	28	28.3	1
8	26	24	25	25.0	2	18	26	27	28	27.0	2
9	17	21	20	19.3	4	19	15	19	14	16.0	5
10	27	29	26	27.3	3	20	25	24	25	24.7	1
									Totals	456.8	67

Figure 22

Range chart for dimensions—subgroups of three machined parts

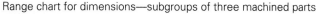

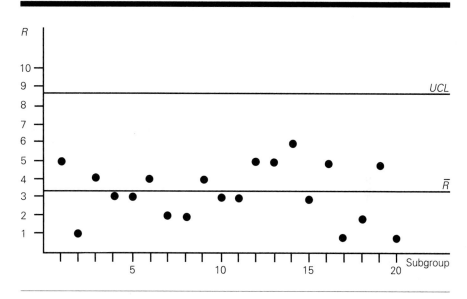

the average and range of those measurements; the data were coded to simplify arithmetic.

The subgroup ranges, reflecting the part-to-part variation within subgroups, are plotted on the R chart shown in Figure 22. The center line and control limits were obtained by use of the methods described in Figure 19. The center line on the chart is the average range, computed as:

$$\overline{R} = \frac{\text{sum of the subgroup ranges}}{\text{number of subgroups}} = \frac{67}{20} = 3.35$$

and the upper control limit is:

$$UCL_R = D_4\overline{R} = 2.574(3.35) = 8.62$$

Since the subgroup size is three, there is no lower control limit on the range chart. The variation in subgroup ranges is judged to be in a state of statistical control. This implies that the part-to-part variation in the dimension, for parts produced within the same tool setting, was of a consistent magnitude over the period of time data were collected.

The X-bar chart shown in Figure 23, constructed from the subgroup averages, has a center line computed as:

$$\overline{\overline{X}} = \frac{\text{sum of the subgroup averages}}{\text{number of subgroups}} = \frac{456.8}{20} = 22.84$$

Figure 23

X-bar chart for dimensions—subgroups of three machined parts

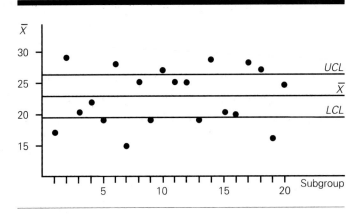

and control limits computed as:

$$UCL_{\bar{x}} = \overline{\overline{X}} + A_2\overline{R} = 22.84 + 1.023(3.35) = 22.84 + 3.43 = 26.3$$
$$LCL_{\bar{x}} = \overline{\overline{X}} - A_2\overline{R} = 22.84 - 1.023(3.35) = 22.84 - 3.43 = 19.4$$

There are numerous points outside the control limits on the X-bar chart. The control limits are based upon using the average range as a measure of common cause variation. A stable range chart provides support for the assumption that the variation within subgroups is produced by a collection of causes that are common to all results in a subgroup. By virtue of the subgrouping strategy used in this case, common cause variation was taken to be that variation existing in results produced with the same tool setting. The X-bar limits then define the amount of variation expected to be seen in the subgroup averages if results are consistently the same size, regardless of tool setting.

Figure 24 shows another way to picture the variation depicted in the range and average charts. This is a time-ordered plot of the individual measurements in each subgroup. Plots of individual measurements can sometimes be helpful in interpreting the behavior of summary statistics such as X-bar and R. In Figure 24, the three individual values are plotted with respect to the vertical scale in a horizontal position over the subgroup number. The subgroups of three measurements have been shaded to aid in seeing the pattern of variation in the data. The resulting picture reveals a shifting in general size of the numbers from one subgroup to the next that is large in comparison to the spread of numbers within the same subgroup. This particular plot of individual measurements simply confirms the messages about variation contained in the control charts.

The variation pictured in Figure 24 has implications for the creation of improved value for customers. Variation in the dimension was creating

Figure 24

Plot of individual dimensions of subgroups of three parts

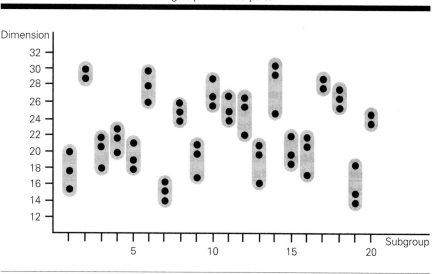

difficulties in assembly. Assembly difficulties have implications for manufacturing effectiveness in terms of scheduling, capacity, inventory, and other components and dimensions of the manufacturing system. Reduced manufacturing effectiveness leads to increased costs, which are translated into either lowered profitability or increased prices, and a damaged competitive position. But the variation in the dimension, given that assembly could be carried out, also shows up in product performance. Variation can lead to friction and wear, resulting in reduced reliability and impaired performance. Dimensions of customer value related to reliability and performance are directly affected by this variation, and so reducing it can be an important contributor to improved customer value.

The points outside the statistical limits on the X-bar chart indicated that there were causes producing longer-term change in process results from subgroup to subgroup, in addition to those that acted to produce the piece-to-piece variation reflected in subgroup ranges. One of those potential causes was the tool adjustment algorithm. However, there were other sources of variation that could have contributed to the change in results from one subgroup to the next. Some possibilities were variation in cutting surfaces of the tools, longer-term variation in hardness of castings, variation in machining feed rates and speeds, variation in coolant properties, and so on.

Figure 25 shows a *cause and effect diagram* (also known as a fishbone diagram or Ishikawa diagram) for causes of variation in the dimension. Constructing a cause and effect diagram is a useful way to gather and organize the theories about possible causes of observed results that exist

Figure 25

Cause and effect diagram, variation in a dimension of a machined surface

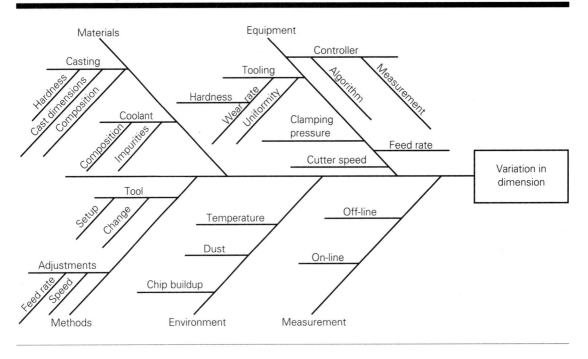

among people who work with and manage a process. The diagram consists of a box on the right containing the effect under consideration. Leading to the box is a main "bone" with smaller bones branching off. The diagram shown in Figure 25 is incomplete, since it represents current thinking about potential cause and effect relationships at the beginning of the improvement effort. The cause and effect diagram must be used with some caution, since it does not explicitly show possible effects of the causes on each other. Constructing a cause and effect diagram is an effective way to capture and organize the results of brainstorming efforts of a group working on a project or a problem. But when there can be interactions and feedback loops among various characteristics, there must be considerable additional thought and analysis beyond the kind of brainstorming and idea generation that typically takes place in the construction of cause and effect diagrams. For example, variation in hardness and dimensions of incoming castings may have a stronger effect in combination with the tool adjustment algorithm in use than if there were no automatic feedback adjustment method in place. The effect of feed rate on variation in the resulting dimension depends upon clamping pressure and cutter speed. The cause and effect diagram provides a means to begin the thought process. If there is to be a reasonable chance to make sustainable improvement in results, there must be, in every case, explicitly stated theories about cause and effect that can be investigated through observational and experimental studies.

In the effort to reduce variation in the machined dimension, additional observational and experimental studies were planned to clarify the effects of different sources of variation. Production personnel could deal internally with machine adjustments, feed rates, and speeds, and could attempt to address consistency of coolant and consistency of tool setting. Addressing the numerical control algorithm, uniformity of tooling, and uniformity of important characteristics of castings would require support and participation from engineering and purchasing. Without a fairly strong case that a significant portion of the problem with the dimension could not be addressed on the production floor, little or no action could be expected from other functions. The reward system in the organization did not support working on problems with existing products and processes when there were new products to be developed and new procurement contracts to initiate. This situation is typical of many in which direct producers of a product or service have little or no input regarding decisions concerning production process design and procurement, yet they must cope with problems that are created by other functions.

X and Moving R Charts X and moving R charts are used to analyze a time-ordered stream of variables data when measurements come one at a time (such as one per time unit) or when there is no rational basis for grouping the data into subgroups of two or more measurements. When one measurement of a characteristic is made per batch for material produced in large, presumably homogeneous batches of liquid or granular material, for example, there may be no obvious rationale for grouping the data into subgroups. Thus, the measurements appear for analysis as a sequence of individual readings. Administrative summaries are produced for which only one measurement is available per unit time (monthly, weekly, daily, etc.)

When measurements appear for analysis as a time-ordered sequence of readings, one per unit of time, a commonly practiced approach is to plot the individual measurements in time sequence as points on a chart. Statistical control limits are established by using ranges of pairs of contiguous measurements in the sequence. A series of ranges is produced by finding the range of the first and second measurements, the range of the second and third measurements, the third and fourth, the fourth and fifth, and so on, thus creating so-called "moving ranges." The reasoning behind the use of moving ranges is that contiguous results will be as nearly homogeneous and subject to the same causes as possible, and item-to-item fluctuations will be subject to the least possible influence from trends and other systematic effects acting on the data in the sequence. The use of moving ranges to establish an approximate level of "background" or common cause variation allows the effects of other influences to be seen

Figure 26
Method for constructing X and moving R charts

- Calculate moving ranges by finding the range of successive pairs of measurements and construct a range chart.
- Calculate the center line for the moving range chart as:

$$\overline{R} = \frac{\text{sum of the moving } R \text{ values}}{\text{number of moving } R \text{ values}}$$

Note: the number of ranges is one less than the number of X values.
- Calculate control limits for the moving range chart as:

Upper control limit: $UCL_R = 3.267\overline{R}$
Lower control limit: none
- Plot the X values.
- Calculate the center line for the X chart as:

$$\overline{X} = \frac{\text{sum of the } X \text{ values}}{\text{number of } X \text{ values}}$$

- Calculate control limits for the X chart as:

$$UCL_X = \overline{X} + 3\left(\frac{\overline{R}}{d_2}\right)$$

$$LCL_X = \overline{R} - 3\left(\frac{\overline{R}}{d_2}\right) \quad \text{where } d_2 = 1.128$$

through points outside control limits as well as by systematic patterns in the series. Figure 26 contains a description of the method used to construct and analyze X and moving R charts.

For about two decades, direct and indirect labor overtime was a way of life in one company that manufactures consumer products. The company could sell all the products it could make, so the primary problem of production was inadequate capacity. Management did not recognize that poor quality of production processes was a major factor in inability to meet production requirements during normally scheduled hours. Typically, overtime was scheduled during weekends to meet the production schedule for the week. As this practice persisted year after year, production workers began to see overtime as an entitlement and assumed a certain level of overtime pay as a part of their income. When new competitors with higher-value products entered the market, the company's sales volume began to decline. As the decline persisted, management's attention was drawn to production costs and overtime expense. Suddenly, production managers were expected to make substantial reductions in the cost of overtime. Little consideration was given to the factors that might help explain the difficulties of reducing overtime expense, such as poorly designed production processes, inadequate engineering support for production, fluctuations in schedules brought about partly by inadequate forecasting of sales volume and partly by production quality problems, and

Figure 27

Monthly accounted overtime cost in thousands of dollars for
a production unit

Month	Overtime cost	Month	Overtime cost
1	53.25	9	44.07
2	27.54	10	53.25
3	42.23	11	49.57
4	33.05	12	45.90
5	34.89	13	29.38
6	47.74	14	45.90
7	25.71	15	31.21
8	38.56	16	36.72
		Total	638.97

procurement practices and relationships with suppliers that contributed
to quality problems with supplier materials. Top management was attempting to manage costs directly, rather than to manage the system that
generated the costs, by demanding rapid decreases in line items of the
production budget. Production management tended to blame the problem of overtime on production labor, believing that labor was largely
responsible for lack of productivity and was deliberately resisting improvement in order to maintain their incomes. They failed to realize that laborers' dissatisfaction with reduced overtime was entirely reasonable, given
historical precedent. The labor force simply expected the future to be
like the past and did not recognize that changes in the marketplace were
creating a new set of conditions for the company. The labor force, unlike
management, recognized the barriers to improved productivity put in
place by managerial practices and inadequate production system and product design.

A manufacturing manager made a practice of reviewing performance
to budget on a monthly basis. Every month, each production manager
reported performance to an annual forecast using actual accounted costs
for past months and forecasted costs for the remaining months of the
budget year. The report was made by presenting figures in a table that
consisted of actual cumulative cost for past months of the budget year,
total forecasted cost for the remaining months, and current deviation
from the annual budget figure for each budget line item. Actual monthly
costs for prior periods were not made available in the report. Because of
top management's intense scrutiny of overtime costs, the manufacturing
manager had required that each production unit's budgeted overtime
cost for the current year be significantly lower than in past years.

The data shown in Figure 27 are monthly accounted overtime costs in
thousands of dollars for one production unit. The data cover the previous
budget year and the first four months of the current year. The data are
a stream of individual results of the variables type. They have been plotted

Figure 28

Run chart of monthly accounted overtime cost in thousands of dollars

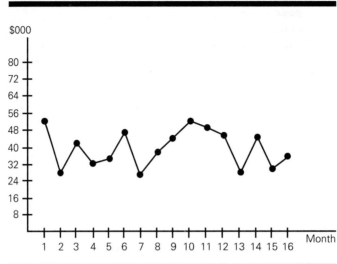

in time-ordered sequence on the chart shown in Figure 28. A time-ordered plot of a series of results such as this is called a *run chart* in quality control literature. The pattern of variation shown on the run chart suggests that overtime costs for this production unit have stayed at a steady level over the past sixteen months. There are no indications of either abrupt, sustained shifts in the level of costs or trends upward or downward.

To fully address the question of stability of the variation in the series, statistical control limits may be placed on the chart. Since the results come one at a time (monthly), and there appears to be no rationale for grouping

Figure 29

Monthly overtime costs and their moving ranges

Month	Overtime cost	Moving *R*	Month	Overtime cost	Moving *R*
1	53.25		9	44.07	5.51
2	27.54	25.71	10	53.25	9.18
3	42.23	14.69	11	49.57	3.68
4	33.05	9.18	12	45.90	3.67
5	34.89	1.84	13	29.38	16.52
6	47.74	12.85	14	45.90	16.52
7	25.71	22.03	15	31.21	14.69
8	38.56	12.85	16	36.72	5.51
			Totals	638.97	174.43

Figure 30

Moving range chart for monthly overtime costs

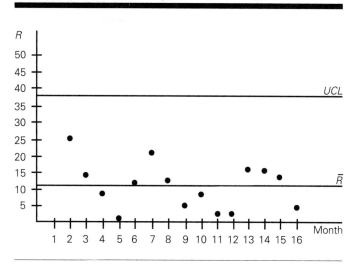

the data into subgroups, control limits are established using moving ranges. Figure 29 shows the computations of moving ranges, and the ranges are plotted on the moving R chart shown in Figure 30.

The center line and control limit for the moving ranges were obtained by use of the methods described in Figure 26. The center line on the moving range chart was computed as:

$$\overline{R} = \frac{\text{sum of the moving ranges}}{\text{number of ranges}} = \frac{174.43}{15} = 11.63$$

and the upper control limit is:

$$UCL_R = 3.267\overline{R} = 3.267(11.63) = 38.00$$

The conclusion to be drawn from examining the moving range chart is that the variation in overtime costs month to month is stable. The average range can be used to establish control limits for the monthly overtime costs.

The run chart of monthly overtime costs shown in Figure 28 is actually a plot of X values—individual measurements of the variables type. The run chart becomes an X control chart when control limits are placed on it. Using the method described in Figure 26, the center line for the X chart is computed as:

$$\overline{X} = \frac{\text{sum of the } X \text{ values}}{\text{number of } X \text{ values}} = \frac{638.97}{16} = 39.94$$

Figure 31

X chart of monthly overtime costs

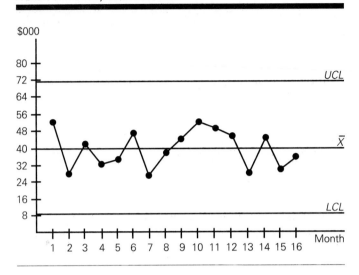

The control limits for the *X* chart are based on the average moving range and are computed as:

$$UCL_X = \overline{X} + 3\left(\frac{\overline{R}}{1.128}\right) = 39.94 + 3\left(\frac{11.63}{1.128}\right) = 39.94 + 30.93 = 70.87$$

$$LCL_X = \overline{X} - 3\left(\frac{\overline{R}}{1.128}\right) = 39.94 - 3\left(\frac{11.63}{1.128}\right) = 39.94 - 30.93 = 9.01$$

The resulting *X* chart is shown in Figure 31.

The variation in monthly overtime costs is stable over the entire sixteen-month period. The causes of the level of overtime cost and the variation in costs month to month are imbedded in the system of production—its design and daily operation. The control limits on the *X* chart define expected variation in monthly costs in the near-term future, given no change to the system of production. Overtime costs can be expected to be, on average, about $40,000 and could vary from about $9,000 to about $71,000. These limits of variation define the capability of the production system in terms of accounted overtime cost. Making no change to the design and operation of the system of production will result in a continuation of overtime costs at these levels.

The data analyzed in the preceding discussion were gathered from historical records at the end of the fourth month of the second year. The report to the manufacturing manager presented at the same time contained forecasts of overtime costs for the remainder of the second year. Those forecasted values are shown added to the *X* chart in Fig-

Figure 32

Actual accounted overtime costs for 16 months with forecasts for the
next 8 months added

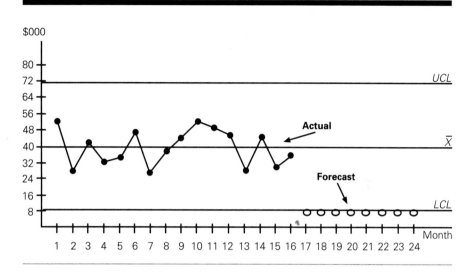

ure 32. An annual target for overtime costs had been set that was about
40 percent of the previous year's total overtime expense. As additional
months of actual costs were accumulated, the forecasts for the remaining
months of the budget year were revised downward to keep the actual-plus-
forecast budget expense on the annual target. The financial people in
the production unit had done this kind of manipulation for several years.
Since the manufacturing manager never looked at a chart such as the one
shown in Figure 32, he never fully comprehended the lack of reality in
the monthly reports he was receiving. The manager of the production
unit experienced extreme pain only once a year, at the year-end review—
an event anticipated with fear and quickly forgotten. The production unit
manager was probably grateful to the financial group for their manipulations, since his pain was of relatively short duration. This situation is typical
of the irrational forecasting and budgeting that come about when top
management attempts to manage system results without knowing the system, and sets arbitrary targets to be achieved without participating in the
system analysis and making the changes required to produce sustainable
change for improvement of system results.

The variation in a machined dimension studied earlier in this chapter
showed evidence of longer-term change in the form of out-of-control
points on the X-bar chart. The control limits on the X-bar chart were
based on the variation among measurements in the same subgroup and
reflected short-term variation among parts machined at a fixed tool setting.
The production personnel who worked on this project believed that the

Figure 33

X chart of subgroup averages, dimensions of machined parts

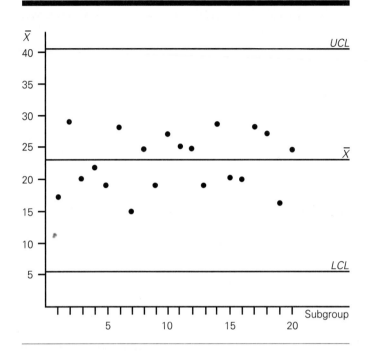

primary source of the longer-term variation was the numerical control algorithm that adjusted the tool setting every ten parts. However, they planned to do additional studies to clarify the effects of possible sources of variation. They intended to continue collecting data from the process while some of these studies were carried out. Their first step was to question whether the longer-term variation present in the dimensional results was stable. The control limits that had been placed on the original X-bar chart (Figure 23) reflected only the short-term variation in dimensions. To address the question of stability of longer-term variation, control limits had to be established that would reflect some stable, common cause level of longer-term variation. To do this, the subgroup averages (X-bars) shown in Figure 21 were treated as a succession of twenty individual measurements, and two-item moving ranges of the X-bar values were calculated. Using the methods described in Figure 26, the moving ranges were used to derive a new set of control limits for the subgroup averages. A chart of the X-bar values with the new limits ($LCL = 5.2$, $UCL = 40.5$) is shown in Figure 33. The new limits are considerably wider than those shown in Figure 23, since they reflect the subgroup-to-subgroup fluctuations in the X-bar values. The variation in X-bar values shows stability relative to these

Figure 34

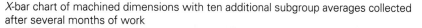

X-bar chart of machined dimensions with ten additional subgroup averages collected after several months of work

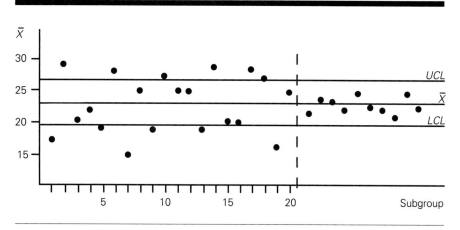

limits, leading to the conclusion that the longer-term variation in dimensions is produced by a collection of causes that lie within the normal operation of the process and its supply system.

Extensive work was done with the supplier of castings on achieving consistency of metallurgical properties of castings, lot to lot. Changes were made to the supplier's casting process as a result of a sequence of experiments aimed at determining and acting on important process and material factors affecting those properties. After considerable discussion and some conflict about tooling prices, it was agreed that perishable tooling purchases would be made from a supplier with demonstrated ability to provide tools of uniformly good quality. Production personnel carried out intensive studies of the coolant system, corrected a number of problems, and studied and improved coolant properties. Process engineers worked with operators to determine the appropriate settings for feed rates and speeds, and standard operating settings were established. Assembly problems and scrap levels were reduced by the reduction in variation achieved, and plant management began to support the project. A control engineer who could work on the control algorithm was located. Process engineers and the control engineer conducted several studies to arrive at a tool adjustment algorithm that would not add to variation, while maintaining the target dimension.

Averages of ten subgroups of three measurements collected after the new tool adjustment algorithm was put into place are plotted in Figure 34 on the original X-bar chart with the original limits based on within subgroup variation. The variation of the new X-bar values is clearly less than that of the earlier X-bars. Longer-term variation has been reduced enough so that it cannot be detected using the historical variation within subgroups as a measure of background variation. The ongoing use of control charts while improvement efforts are under way provides a means to confirm that changes have led to improvement.[15]

Use of the Information Contained in Variation

The preceding examples have been used to illustrate use of control charts to study and learn from variation. The variety of possibilities for patterns of variation in results is endless. One objective of characterizing the behavior of variation is to render a judgment of the state of statistical control of the variation, since that judgment provides an indication of whether future results are predictable. An equally important objective focuses on the causes of variation. If the variation in results is judged to be due to only common causes (the process or system is producing stable results), then any sustainable changes in results will be achieved by change in the fundamental operating practices and policies, structure, and design of the process or system. When the existence of special causes of variation is indicated, the special causes can be identified and actions can be taken to prevent their effects from being seen in the form of additional variation (over and above common cause variation) in the future. The specific kind of actions required to effectively remove or to nullify the future effects of special causes may have to be taken outside the boundaries of the process under study. The same may be true for common causes of variation. Variation seen in a process at the local level is often created by policies and practices enacted at some earlier time in some other process.

Operationally, use of information on variation may serve as the basis of two kinds of activities:

1. Monitoring process results and taking actions to intervene in the process upon statistical signal of change so the process is brought back to its former condition
2. Use of the information contained in observed variation to develop an increasing understanding of its causes, so improved knowledge of cause and effect relationships can be used to change the process and improve future results

The intent of the first kind of activity listed above is to achieve and maintain a steady state, i.e., a steady level of variation around a steady average. Once a state of statistical control is achieved with current operating practices, no further improvement or reduction of variation is likely with the first kind of activity. The second kind of activity is intended to identify opportunities for change to the process and its inputs, which are expected to improve all future results. This implies use of process data as a part of

---

15. The reader who wishes to learn more about study of variation using control charts and other methods may refer to the books authored by Burr; Deming; Shewhart; Moen, Nolan, and Provost; and Wheeler and Chambers listed in the references.

practice of the Shewhart cycle (referred to by Deming as PDSA: Plan, Do, Study, Act) for continual learning and improvement. Thus, theories concerning cause and effect relationships are continually developed and systematically investigated through a process of planned experimentation and sampling designed to reveal the effects of various potential sources of variation.

Study of variation, with the appropriate theory, leads to understanding the system of causes, and helps to inform managers where and when action on the system of causes could produce improvement of future results. Reduced variation around target outcomes, based on a clear understanding of customer needs and desires, provides for simultaneous improvement of customer value and organizational effectiveness.

▶ OTHER TOOLS FOR ANALYSIS OF DATA

When data collection and analysis for the purpose of quality improvement became popular in the early 1980s, considerable attention was focused on Japan's *"seven tools for quality control."* In his book on Japanese methods for continuous improvement, Imai (1986) lists the seven tools as Pareto diagrams, cause and effect diagrams, histograms, control charts, scatter diagrams, graphs, and check sheets. Numerous examples of these and other tools for data collection and summary can be found in Ishikawa's book *Guide to Quality Control* (1976), as well as in a variety of other books on quality and statistical analysis. Examples of control charts, Pareto diagrams, and the cause and effect diagram are shown earlier in this chapter.

These tools can be very helpful, provided they are used appropriately. Too often, a tool for data analysis is used for its own sake, out of the context of systematically building knowledge and taking action for improvement. This may be done in the mistaken belief that the tool is able to lead the user to ask the right questions about the process. Unfortunately, no tool is able to provide a rationale for analysis or a substitute for thought. In the following, Pareto analysis and histograms will be used as examples to provide some cautionary remarks about the use of tools for data analysis.

Pareto analysis of frequency of occurrence of failures or defects by type can help managers to prioritize work. But managers must be sure to take into account the importance of each kind of failure and focus on the processes generating the failures, rather than on the results. To be effective, Pareto analysis of defects or failures by type should be accompanied by three essential activities:

1. Relate the defects or failures to locations or stages in the process where they would most likely be generated.
2. A multifunctional group should construct an enumeration of possible causes that might act alone or in combination to produce the problem.
3. Use control chart analysis to guard against misidentification of causes.

Without these activities, the solutions enacted may institute additional inspection steps or costly quick fixes that do not address the sources of the problem. Actions directly on defects will not dry up the sources of future defects.

Pareto analysis or any other tool for data analysis should be used in conjunction with subject matter knowledge and knowledge of variation to prevent the kinds of mistakes described in the two examples that follow. Both involve attempts by plant personnel to improve the quality of incoming materials. In the first case, managers used counts of defective items found in production to determine which suppliers should be singled out for improvement. One supplier was identified as "the plant's worst supplier" on the basis of those counts. No one in the plant had noted that the supplier in question supplied roughly twenty times as many parts as the next highest volume supplier of parts. When the data were scaled by volume, the worst supplier turned out to have a much lower rate of occurrence of defective parts than several other suppliers. In addition, no one had considered the question of stability of variation week to week in the occurrence of defects, or the possibility that the rates of occurrence of defective material for all suppliers could show variation due to common causes alone. If all suppliers' results, taken as a group, showed only common cause variation, the place to look for improvement was in the system of procurement. It would not be rational to select a few suppliers as special cases to single out and subject to special treatment.

In the second case, a supplier of parts to a plant was singled out for special treatment as a result of a single incident. During one month, several thousand parts were rejected for a particular kind of dimensional defect. In the several years that the plant had used this supplier, they had never previously rejected any of the supplier's materials. Yet, as a result of this incident, the supplier was put on the list of "bad suppliers." When a team of personnel from the supplier's plant visited the customer's plant, they learned that a newly designed automatic assembly machine had recently been installed to insert their part into an assembly. In the past, the part had been inserted by hand and operators were able to make adjustments for variation in a certain dimension of the supplier's part. The automatic assembly machine was not able to make the adjustment, and so the dimension had become critical to successful assembly. The supplier had not been informed of the change and was not aware that the dimension in question was now a critical one. The supplier was able to correct the problem quickly by making changes in production of the part. Getting removed from the "bad supplier" list took months of negotiation, since no one in the customer plant wanted to admit that they had played a part in the supplier's problem. Both of the preceding examples illustrate use of analytical tools without employing knowledge of the subject matter and knowledge of the history of variation in making judgments about where to focus improvement efforts.

Figure 35

Frequency histogram constructed from the coded values of
dimensions of 60 parts

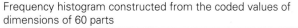

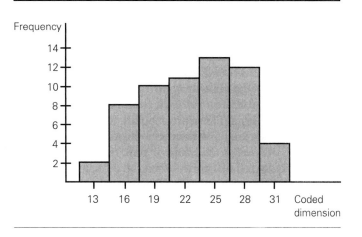

Figure 35 shows a frequency *histogram* constructed from the coded
values of individual part dimensions displayed in Figure 21. The histogram
was produced by arbitrarily constructing a set of contiguous, equal-length
intervals on the scale of measurement and then counting the number of
measurements in the set of data that fell in each of the intervals. The
horizontal scale on the histogram is the scale of measurement, and the
vertical scale represents frequency, or relative frequency, of occurrence.
Vertical bars are drawn over the intervals of a height corresponding to
the frequency or relative frequency of occurrence in the collection of
measurements. Most textbooks on applied statistics contain descriptions
of methods to use in constructing histograms.

A histogram provides a graphical description of the distribution of a
collection of measurements. Histograms can be quite useful in providing
a picture of the shape of distribution of data, but they must be used with
considerable caution. In the case of the data on dimensions, the histogram
shown in Figure 35 obscures the information that connects the observed
variation to the chronology of results and process structure. Those connections were made in the *X*-bar and *R* charts and the time-ordered dot plot
of the same data shown earlier. The histogram does depict the variation
in the collection of numbers, but it conveys no information about stability
of variation. Figure 36 illustrates this drawback for histograms. The picture
shows two sets of data plotted in time sequence and histograms of the data.
The histograms are rotated so that the scales of measurement coincide with
the time-ordered plots. The loss of time-related information produced by
constructing the histograms is apparent. In terms of the pattern of variation

Figure 36
Same histogram, two different messages about variation

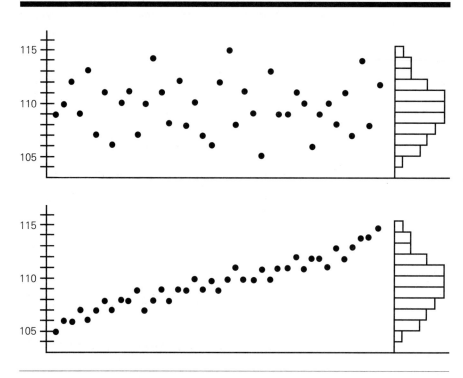

shown in the sequence, the time-ordered plots in Figure 36 convey entirely different messages about stability of variation. The plot of the first set of data provides no basis for believing that there is important change occurring in results; the variation in the second set of data carries the message that change is occurring—something is causing the results to grow in size. This message would, at least, generate some questions as to what the cause for the trend might be. Yet, both sets of data contain the same numbers, so histograms constructed from the data using the same intervals on the scale of measurement are the same. The histograms do not preserve the most important information in the two series—the pattern of variation over time.

Many descriptive statistical tools and graphical techniques, such as histograms, means, standard deviations, and variances, are designed to summarize data and efficiently preserve the information contained in the individual measurements. But they do not preserve all the information contained in a collection of data observed in time sequence. The information related to the time sequence is destroyed by the summary. This is a drawback to be considered when using these tools and techniques to describe variation in results of a dynamic process or system. Tools and methods that preserve the information connected to time order are most appropriate for studying process variation.

▶ REMARKS ON THE USE OF TOOLS

In the early 1980s, numerous trips to Japan by American industrialists led to the "discovery" of Japan's "seven tools of quality control." The seven tools were taught to employees of Japanese firms and used extensively in quality circles to solve problems and identify and test possible process improvements at the local level. The Americans did not recognize that those Japanese firms were managed to engage everyone in appropriate activities to improve quality and performance of the enterprise, each according to his area of responsibility. They concluded that quality circles and the seven tools were all that was needed to achieve organization-wide improvement. Although the seven tools were brought back to America and swept through company after company, they did not produce much long-term effect. Managers simply expected the hourly work force to use those tools to solve the problems that the managers didn't themselves know how to solve.

Managers' attempts to learn from other organizations and cultures are often afflicted by this kind of trap in thinking. A manager sees the tool, practice, or technology and believes that it possesses intrinsic value that will cause it to have positive effects whenever it is used. He then attempts to copy the tool or practice in his own environment with high expectations of great results. More often than not, there is an initial flurry of activity, followed by less frequent usage, and, finally, the tool disappears from use. The manager fails to realize that the value of the tool is derived from the conditions of use. If the environment does not provide a set of conditions in which it is rational and beneficial to use the tool, then it will not be seen as having value and will not be used.

Even if the environment encourages use of particular tools, tools can be misused if they are not integrated into a framework of theory that provides guidance on their appropriate use. A theory and method for interpreting variation takes on value if it enables rational linkage of ob-served variation in results to the causal factors that create it and thus enables learning and action for sustainable improvement. Shewhart's the-ory of variation provides a means to interpret the messages contained in process and system data within a conceptual framework that comprehends the system view.

▶ SUMMARY OF KEY POINTS

1. Undesirable variation damages the enterprise. Reducing the amount of undesirable variation present in the system, its inputs, and its outputs is a purpose of improve-ment work.

2. By studying variation and acting on its sources, managers can achieve greater uniformity of product or service and improve the enterprise.

3. If managers use a rational theory and method to interpret variation, they are better able to manage and to guide the development and use of the knowledge needed to survive and prosper.

4. A primary advantage of using a control chart is to minimize the economic loss that comes from mistakes that occur in interpreting the meaning of variation.

5. Study of variation leads to understanding the system and helps managers take better actions in their efforts to produce improvement.

► KEY TERMS

categorical data

cause and effect diagram

common causes

control chart

counts of events in space or time

histogram

p chart

Pareto diagram

run chart

seven tools for quality control

special causes

stable variation

statistical control limits

statistically controlled variation

u chart

unstable variation

variables data

X and moving R charts

X-bar and R charts

► DISCUSSION QUESTIONS

1. From your personal experience, provide some examples of the two kinds of mistakes that can be made in interpreting variation. For each example, determine which kind of mistake might have been made. If you have data to support your belief that a mistake was made, include it, along with an analysis and interpretation.

2. Explain why imposing arbitrary standards to get rid of variation is not an effective means to manage variation. How are employees affected by the imposition of arbitrary standards?

3. What are the advantages of using a control chart to interpret variation in a series of results?

4. Given the control chart for monthly overtime costs shown in Figure 31, what would you predict overtime costs to be in the next month? What are some of the causes of overtime? Are the causes you mentioned likely to be common or special?

5. A businessman drives two miles on city streets and seven miles on a freeway from his home to his office. Make a cause and effect diagram for causes of variation in the time it takes him to drive to work in the morning. Which of the causes would be likely to be common and which special?

6. Why are managers better able to manage for improvement if they use Shewhart's theory and method to interpret variation?

▶ EXPERIENTIAL EXERCISES

1. Go to the library and obtain the figures for the U.S. balance of trade for the past twenty years. Alternatively, select some other measure that is reported annually by the federal government. Note whether the figures are indexed to a particular year and, if so, to what year. Construct a control chart from the data and interpret the results. What are your conclusions about the series?

2. Go to the library and obtain the annual reports of a large company for the past fifteen to twenty years. Select a type of performance indicator from the annual report that appears for each year (dollars profit, ROI, etc.). Construct a control chart from the data and interpret the results. What are your conclusions?

3. Select an activity that you perform every day (for example, driving to school, getting dressed in the morning, going through the cafeteria line at lunch). Make a daily measurement of the time it takes for you to complete the activity for a period of three or four weeks. You should clearly define how you will measure the time and how you will keep the resulting records. Construct a simple cause and effect diagram for factors that may create variation in the times day to day. Determine what additional information you might record in addition to the times to help you understand the variation. When you have collected the data, construct a control chart and interpret the messages it contains about the variation in the times you recorded. Alternatively, you might choose some other kind of information to collect and analyze.

4. Bring to class a newspaper article that contains an example of "fixation on events" and "event" explanations, as described by Senge. The financial page is a good place to look for examples. Discuss the example with the class. Point out other factors that might have affected the result being explained, in addition to the explanation noted in the article.

▶ REFERENCES

Chris Argyris, *Overcoming Organizational Defenses*, Allyn and Bacon, Boston, 1990.

G. M. Bounds, J. M. Reeve, and K. C. Gilbert, "Managerial Performance Measurement," in M. Stahl and G. Bounds (eds.), *Competing Globally through Customer Value*, Quorum Books, New York, 1991, pp. 369–370.

I. W. Burr, *Statistical Quality Control Methods*, Marcel Dekker, New York, 1976.

W. E. Deming, *Out of the Crisis*, MIT Center for Advanced Engineering Study, Cambridge, Mass., 1986.

W. E. Deming, *The New Economics for Industry, Government, Education,* MIT Center for Advanced Engineering Study, Cambridge, Mass., 1993.

Masaaki Imai, *Kaizen*, Random House Business Division, New York, 1986.

K. Ishikawa, *Guide to Quality Control*, Asian Productivity Organization, Tokyo, 1976.

R. D. Moen, T. W. Nolan, and L. P. Provost, *Improving Quality through Planned Experimentation*, McGraw-Hill, New York, 1991.

Peter M. Senge, *The Fifth Discipline*, Doubleday, New York, 1990.

W. A. Shewhart, *Economic Control of Quality of Manufactured Product*, Van Nostrand, New York, 1931.

W. A. Shewhart, *Statistical Method from the Viewpoint of Quality Control*, Dover, New York, 1986.

M. J. Stahl and G. M. Bounds (eds.), *Competing Globally through Customer Value*, Quorum Books, New York, 1991.

D. W. Wheeler and D. S. Chambers, *Understanding Statistical Process Control*, 2d ed., SPC Press, Knoxville, Tenn., 1992.

Variation: Understanding Causes

There is a fundamental mismatch between the nature of reality in complex systems and our predominant ways of thinking about that reality. The first step in correcting that mismatch is to let go of the notion that cause and effect are close in time and space.

*Peter M. Senge**

▶ **CHAPTER OUTLINE**

Chapter Overview

Introduction

Key Ideas

Variation Linked to Causes

Example: Product Quality
Example: Corporate Accounts Payable
Example: Sales Promotions

Interpreting Results

Treating Results Produced by Common Causes as if They Came from a Special Cause
Arbitrary Targets
Action on Special Causes
Interdependence of Organizational Results: A Hypothetical Factory
Evaluating Performance of Systems and People

* Peter M. Senge, *The Fifth Discipline*, Doubleday, New York, 1990.

Learning and Action for Improvement

Elements of a System for Organization-wide Improvement
Systematic Learning: PDSA

Summary of Key Points

Key Terms

Discussion Questions

Experiential Exercise

References

▶ CHAPTER OVERVIEW

The aim of this chapter is to illustrate the complex structures of cause and effect relationships that combine to produce organizational results, and to provide insight on how system thinking and understanding of variation can improve managerial practice.

▶ INTRODUCTION

To increase capability to improve customer value, three important areas for learning are (1) the organization—its systems, managerial practices, methods, technologies, (2) the external environment—market trends, strategies and practices of competitors and other organizations, new technologies and operational methods, (3) customers—their needs and their use of products and services. Most of this chapter will be devoted to internal learning. Interdependencies among components of a system and among results on various dimensions of performance are illustrated. Use of Shewhart's theory of variation to improve interpretation of organizational results and judge performance of systems and people is discussed. The chapter concludes with a discussion of learning and action for improvement.

The examples used in the chapter are based on experience in manufacturing enterprises, but the principles they illustrate apply to the management of any organization. Some publications on quality improvement suggest that theory and methods used for improvement in manufacturing organizations do not apply to service or government. This viewpoint comes from interpreting quality improvement in manufacturing as being confined to activities that directly affect a product with measurable physical characteristics. There are three limitations to this view. First, any service, administrative, or managerial activity produces a product—the result of the activity. The important characteristics of service products may be different from material products, and they may require use of different methods for study, but they are nevertheless products. Second, the products of any organization are produced by the combined actions of the organization's systems. The quality of products is a result of the quality of those systems and the methods used to manage them. Restricting quality improvement work to processes at lower levels of an organization, such as production or assembly processes or service delivery processes, guarantees that the kinds of improvements achieved will be limited and will contribute little to the long-term effectiveness and survival of the enterprise. Third, major systems of service or governmental organizations are very similar to the kinds of systems in manufacturing organizations, and they are typically managed using the same methods. The general principles of system dynamics and of variation presented here apply to any system, regardless of its final product.

Key Ideas

Some key ideas discussed in this chapter are:

- Since there are interdependencies among the parts of an organization, optimization of individual parts of the organization may constitute suboptimization for the whole. If managers appreciate the existence of interdependencies among functions, units, and processes of an organization, they will recognize the need to manage for system-wide optimization, rather than to suboptimize one dimension of performance or maximize the performance of single components.
- An important principle for understanding systems is that causes and effects are often not close in time and location.
- The greatest leverage for improvement at a rate large enough to ensure survival lies in recognizing the existence of systems, understanding them, and acting to change them. These are all managerial responsibilities.
- Organizational results are necessarily linked or interdependent since they are generated by the same system. The relationships among results are determined by the system structure and dynamics that create variation and time lags of various lengths between causes and effects. Sincere but misguided attempts to change organizational performance in one dimension at a time create unintended effects. The interactions of components within the system generate unanticipated results in other dimensions of performance.
- Without understanding that variation is an attribute of results on various dimensions of performance and that there are interactions among system components in producing results, we are led into "event explanations" of cause and effect.
- Improvement of a kind and at a rate to ensure organizational survival and prosperity can be accomplished by making process and system improvement a part of the organization's strategy and creating a system for improvement.

- Since new knowledge is the basis of action for improvement, learning is critical to the capability to improve. A systematic method designed to improve the efficiency and rate of learning is scientific method. Deming has described use of scientific method in an organizational setting in his "cycle for learning and for improvement," the Plan, Do, Study, Act (PDSA) cycle.

▶ VARIATION LINKED TO CAUSES

An entire organization can be managed as a system to accomplish its long-term purpose, or it can be managed as a collection of independent parts (functions, activities, processes) with the expectation that decisions and practices intended to optimize the parts will optimize the whole organization. Such nonsystematic management is based upon the assumption that the parts are independent and the result for the whole organization will be the sum of the results of the individual parts. Since there are *interdependencies* among the parts of an organization, *optimization* of the individual parts may constitute *suboptimization* for the whole. Three examples are discussed below. They illustrate interdependencies among parts of an organization and connections between variation and often unrecognized causal factors.

Example: Product Quality

The first example deals with a production quality problem.[1] Production quality problems are often symptoms of systemic flaws that exist elsewhere in the organization. Work to address a problem in production is usually focused at the local level, and no one in the organization recognizes causes of the problem that lie elsewhere in the system. Figure 1 shows a control chart (a *c* chart) for the occurrence of assembly errors.[2]

Each assembly has a build tag attached to the main body of the assembly showing a list of part numbers to be assembled onto the body. Assemblies are inspected and functionally tested at the end of the assembly line. Inspectors record information on the occurrence of missing parts and

1. The actual case that formed the basis for the example involved a complex assembly process in which several different parts were added to the assembly at each workstation. The situation has been simplified to include only one workstation where two components are added to an assembly. This example is typical of numerous situations in high-volume assembly operations where different products are built on the same assembly line. For example, in one portion of the assembly line in an automotive assembly plant, electronic components are assembled into the vehicle: battery, wiring harnesses, sensors, radio, electronic displays, heat and air conditioning controls, fuses, interior and exterior lighting, and so on. Different vehicles have different option packages and call for different combinations of electronic components. Vehicles are often built in a mixed sequence.
2. A *c* chart is a special case of the *u* chart. It is used when the time of observation or the amount of material inspected to arrive at a count of occurrences is the same for all counts used to construct the control chart.

Figure 1

Assembly errors recorded in inspection of collections of 100 assemblies

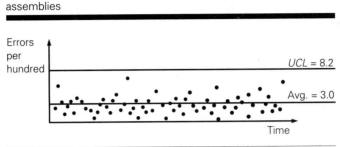

incorrect part numbers found in assemblies. Inspection records are summarized and used to produce a report on assembly quality showing the number of errors (missing and incorrect parts) for production lots of 100 assemblies. The method of summarizing the information from inspection is purely arbitrary, as is often the case. There is no rationale used for summarizing the data that would permit managers to learn something about the potential sources of assembly problems by analyzing the variation in the results.

In spite of these limitations on usefulness for learning about the sources of assembly problems, the control chart in Figure 1 does tell us something about the occurrence of assembly errors. Given the methods used to gather and organize the data on assembly errors, the fact that the variation shows a state of statistical control leads to the conclusion that assembly errors are a chronic problem. From the viewpoint of statistical control, stable variation in occurrences of errors is the result of a collection of causes that are common to all outcomes of the assembly process. The control chart provides an operational definition for an excessive number of errors given the system in place: a point above the upper control limit. There are no points above the upper control limit on the chart in Figure 1. Without the knowledge to properly interpret variation in the number of errors, managers in the assembly area would react to what appeared to be excessively high occurrences of errors, such as the last point on the chart. They would focus their attention on the people who made the errors and remind them of the need to not make mistakes. Any subsequent reduction in the number of errors would be interpreted as evidence that the reminders were effective, since the existence of a steady level of variation in number of errors would not be taken into account. The same sequence of events would continue to be repeated: the occurrence of an apparently large number of errors followed by actions to improve the workers' efforts and subsequent reduction in the number of errors reinforcing the managers' belief that their actions had improved results. Managers often focus on people who do the work at the local level as the

Figure 2

Combinations of body, Part A, and Part B produced in an
assembly process

Body number	Part A number	Part B number
B72436AC793	943B98	1563C62
B72463AC793	943B98	1563C92
B72436AC893	943B88	1563C92

source of problems because they fail to recognize that the local process is an outcome of the methods used to manage the entire organization. Methods used to produce the product and process designs and the practices employed to put the materials, equipment, methods, people, and supervision in place at the local level determine the quality and effectiveness of the local process. The focus on people as the source of most problems is indicative of an unstated managerial assumption that the only source of mistakes is the people who make them.

To understand the causes of assembly errors, we will analyze one important part of the assembly process. In this part of the process, Part A and Part B are assembled onto a body. There are three assemblies produced in the assembly process, each with a particular combination of part numbers for body, Part A, and Part B. Figure 2 shows the combinations that are produced on a regular basis.

The three assemblies are produced in a mixed sequence, rather than in batches. An assembly error has occurred if either of the two parts is missing or if the wrong part of either kind is assembled onto a body with a given number. Nominal mating dimensions[3] for all combinations of the bodies and versions of Part A are the same, so that it is possible to assemble any part number for Part A to any part number for the body. The same is true for Part B. So, if the part number for Part A, Part B, and the body are not the correct ones for a given assembly, an assembly error has occurred. Incorrect assemblies produced at this stage must be disassembled and reworked later in the production process. To completely address the problem of misassembly, we would need further information about the rates of occurrence of specific kinds of errors. However, analysis of the assembly process structure reveals some general themes.

Figure 3 shows the assembly process as conceived by the designer. This is the *"formal" process* shown on process documentation. The *"informal,"*

---

3. Component parts in assemblies have dimensions that must match for proper assembly. As a simple example, consider the fit of the barrel and the cap of a pen. The inside diameter of the cap and the outside diameter of the barrel at the points of contact between cap and barrel must be of certain sizes to ensure proper fit of cap to barrel. These diameters are called mating dimensions, and there are nominal values and tolerances specified for each.

Figure 3
Assembly process as designed and documented

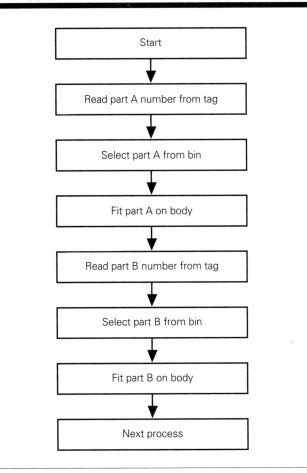

actual, *process* is considerably more complex. A simple *logic flow diagram* of the actual process is shown in Figure 4. One operator assembles both Part A and Part B to the body. The body comes down the assembly line with a tag attached containing the body number, the Part A number, and the Part B number required for the assembly. Two bins, each labeled with a Part A number, contain the two different varieties of Part A; two labeled bins contain the Part B numbers. The bins are filled by material handlers who support the assembly line. To carry out his part of the assembly process, the operator reads the Part A number from the tag on the body, selects a Part A from one of the two bins, and attempts to assemble it onto the body. There is sufficient variation one part to the next in the mating dimensions of both body and Part A so that a fit is not guaranteed. If the operator cannot fit the selected Part A onto the body, he puts it

Figure 4

Logic flow diagram of actual assembly process

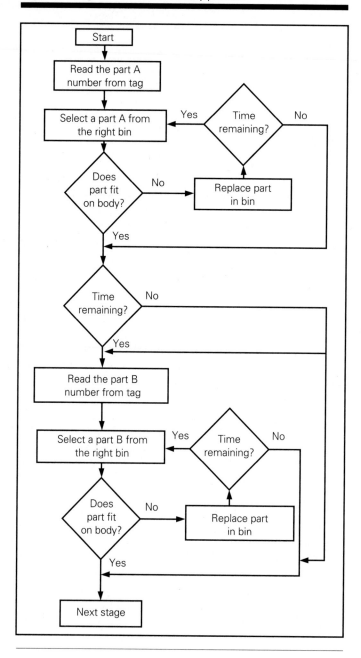

back into the bin and selects another. This activity continues until the operator either finds a Part A that will fit, or the body has moved so far down the line that the operator can no longer reach it. In that case, the body proceeds on without a Part A or a Part B attached. If there is time left to attempt assembly of a Part B to the body, the operator reads the Part B number from the tag and goes through the same process as he did with Part A—attempting to find a Part B that will fit.

Knowing the process logic and the information about part number combinations and the layout of parts in bins, we can enumerate some possible causes or conditions that lead to assembly errors in this part of the production process. In an environment where a formal process for analysis and learning exists, analysis of possible causes would be done by a team of people, including product and process designers, purchasing personnel, production managers, and operators. The team might construct a cause and effect diagram for assembly errors after having constructed the flow diagram shown in Figure 4. Having personnel on the team from functions other than production and from production management would ensure that people with the capability to address causes appropriately would be involved in the improvement activity. In the actual situation on which this description is based, a single engineer conducted the analysis and presented a case to management that changes needed to be made in the product design and the design of the assembly process. No formal activity to analyze and improve processes or systems existed in the company. Management reacted to problems when they occurred by expecting the work force and their immediate supervisors to solve them. The engineer persisted in pressing his case for over a year before any change was actually made.

The first opportunity for an assembly error to occur exists in reading part numbers from the tag. An operator might have difficulty recognizing and remembering the part numbers from the tag, as can be seen by inspecting Figure 2. Body numbers are an alphanumeric string of eleven characters, and differences exist only in the fifth, sixth, and ninth characters. Two of the body numbers differ only in that the fifth and sixth characters are reversed. Similar problems exist with Part A and B numbers. The complexity and small differences between part numbers, combined with small print on the tags, increase the likelihood that recognition errors will occur. Vision problems or insufficient lighting could compound the problem.[4]

Selection of a part from the "right" bin presents further opportunities for error. The operator could recognize the part number correctly, but select the wrong bin. Stock in the bins could be mixed, with wrong part

---

4. Workers in service and administrative activities often encounter the problem of deciphering unreadable written or printed material. Workers who deal with this problem include pharmacists, airline baggage handlers, postal service employees, bookkeepers, order fillers, teachers, and cooks. Blaming the worker for mistakes is typical in these situations.

Figure 5

Local assembly problems and their causes

Local problem	Cause	Sources
Common mating dimensions across part numbers	No error-proofing	Product design methods and standards
Variation in mating dimensions	Part production variation	Upstream production processes
Complex, confusing part numbers	Assignment of part numbers with no consideration of needs of user in production	Part number assignment process
Unreadable part numbers	No consideration of user in production	Tag design and printing processes
Operators with visual problems or dyslexia selecting and assembling parts	No consideration of required skills in job assignment	Personnel selection and assignment processes
Mixed part numbers in bins	Material mixed in inventory or handling	Material storage and handling processes
Placement of bins prevents efficient and accurate selection of parts	No consideration of human factors in process layout	Process design methods and standards
Line speed contains no allowance to make multiple tries at assembly	Line speed based on formal process; no failure modes analysis	Process design methods and standards

numbers in one or more bins. Once a part is selected, it could fail to fit because of dimensional problems of one or both mating parts. The operator could replace a part that has failed to fit into the wrong bin. Because the assembly line runs at too great a rate to allow for multiple tries at assembly, successive failures to fit could lead to assemblies with missing parts.

The potential errors we have just noted are commonly attributed to the operator when they occur. But the operator interacts with the product and process designs, the materials, and the process layout in committing those errors. The causes or conditions that provide the opportunity for errors to occur are common to all outcomes—they exist as part of the process. Two possible exceptions are operators' visual acuity and ability to recognize patterns in the part numbers and unstable variation in dimensions of the mating parts. The extent to which these influence the probability of an error depends on variation of operators and incoming materials. But the stable variation seen in Figure 1 implies that these sources did not affect the results enough to produce out-of-control signals during the time period covered by the data.

The common causes of assembly errors mentioned above are introduced into the assembly process from sources external to that process. Figure 5 shows some of the problems that exist locally and indicates causes and process sources of these problems. By the time the assembly process goes into operation, all of the causes shown in Figure 5 have already been put into place. There is nothing the operator can do directly to remove the conditions that increase the likelihood of errors. Meanwhile, product and process design engineers and purchasing personnel are using the same faulty practices of design and procurement to create the next product and process designs and issue contracts for material supplies. People in the personnel function are using the same faulty methods to select production workers and assign them to jobs. By continued use of faulty practices, people in other functions are creating new opportunities for symptoms of those practices to show up in production in the future.

Responsibility for perpetuating the existence of flawed design, procurement, and personnel processes lies with the managers who manage the systems that include these processes. Without a systemic viewpoint that recognizes the interdependencies among production results and the causes that lie elsewhere in the organizational system, managers will likely continue to focus on the frontline worker. The worker cannot do anything to correct the problems created elsewhere nor see the connections between other functional activities and the production process. As a result, *local solutions* to problems tend to consist of building in additional inspection or rework steps that are ineffective and add cost.

In a sequence of steps that form the core of a system, the leverage for improvement is greater upstream than downstream. In the assembly situation described above, upstream steps include product and process design, procurement, and personnel selection and assignment. Improvements to these processes will improve numerous downstream processes at the same time. Addressing the causes of problems, rather than continually working on the problems after they have been created, is a far more effective use of resources. This does not mean that daily problem solving should not be done. Once created, there is no choice but to solve problems at the local level to meet the needs and expectations of customers. Managers must react to prevent poor-quality products from reaching the customer. But downstream problem solving only returns the process to the state it was in before the problem occurred. Problem solving at the local level does not prevent new problems of the same type from occurring in the future. Only managers at higher levels in the organization have the authority to change systems that cut across functional and other group boundaries. Personnel at lower levels do not have the perspective to see, in total, those systems and their interconnected but widely dispersed components.

There are numerous examples of the kinds of system problems illustrated in the example above. Managers often do not consider how the existing system affects the ability of people to do what is required. When they are asked about why errors in processing might occur (whether the processing is manufacturing or an administrative or service activity), managers typically say that errors occur because "people don't concentrate on their work," or "people aren't careful," or "people don't care about the quality of their work." They act on this belief by exhorting the work force to improve with slogans, such as "Be a quality worker" or "Quality depends on you."

Example: Corporate Accounts Payable

The XYZ Corporation has three divisions and several operating units. At one time, certain financial activities were carried out locally at each of the three divisions. One of those local activities was processing accounts payable and paying suppliers. As part of an effort to increase efficiency and reduce the cost of financial labor, the accounts payable activity was centralized and the record-keeping system was automated. Purchasing and ordering activities were still done locally. Information required to process and pay supplier invoices was transmitted from the divisions to the corporate computer, and suppliers sent their invoices to corporate accounts payable for processing.

Information contained in the central computer system for a given supplier included authorized part numbers, authorized shipping quantities, piece prices, and payment terms. Whenever changes were made in contractual items that affected payment, the local division would send a change notice for that supplier to the central computer. When an invoice arrived, the computer would edit the information for discrepancies based upon the current supplier information in the computer record. If there was any type of mismatch between the information in the computer record and on the invoice, a discrepancy record would be generated. Mismatches could occur due to delays in entry of contractual change notices, errors of other kinds in the computer record, or errors on the invoice. Discrepancies were investigated and resolved by hand. Any necessary corrections would be entered into the computer record so that the central record was up to date and the invoice could be paid. Only a few years after the centralization occurred, the company was employing forty people in the corporate accounts payable department to resolve invoice discrepancies.

A manager in the financial group recognized the waste and loss involved in resolving invoice discrepancies and was building a case for redesigning the accounts payable activity. He compiled records to describe the magnitude of the discrepancy problem. A chart similar to the one shown in Figure 6 was constructed based upon records of number of invoices processed and number of invoices containing at least one discrepancy.[5] Data from all three divisions were combined to produce the chart. The control chart shows instability of variation in percentage of discrepant invoices. To determine whether the discrepancy problem was localized in one of the divisions, the data were subsequently stratified by division and

5. The control chart was constructed by treating the monthly percentages as a series of individual, quantitative values, so that the chart is an X chart. The control limits were based upon moving ranges of successive percentages. The reader may refer to the book by I. W. Burr listed in the references for a discussion of similar X chart applications.

Figure 6

Control chart for monthly percentage of invoices with at least one discrepancy

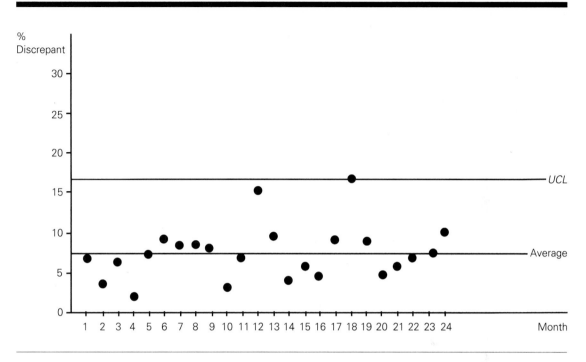

separate control charts were constructed for each division. Figure 7 shows the individual charts. The point beyond the upper control limit on the corporate chart corresponds to a point beyond the upper control limit on the chart for Division 1. The data for Divisions 1 and 2 have roughly the same average. However, a point above the upper control limit on the chart for Division 1 indicates that the variation in percent discrepant is unstable. The data from Division 3 indicate a lower occurrence of discrepant invoices and stable variation. Noticeable differences in the behavior of the results for the three divisions suggest that part of the discrepancies are being created in the divisions and their respective supplier communities, and are not generated exclusively in the corporate accounts payable group. Internal divisional practices, processes for dealing with suppliers, and the invoicing practices of each supplier community contribute to these differences. Divisional practices that may produce discrepancies include methods and frequency of pricing changes, frequency of engineering changes and related changes in part numbers, methods of scheduling and expediting shipments, policies concerning responsibility for shipping costs for expedited materials, as well as methods and frequency of communicat-

Figure 7

Control charts for percentage of discrepant invoices by division

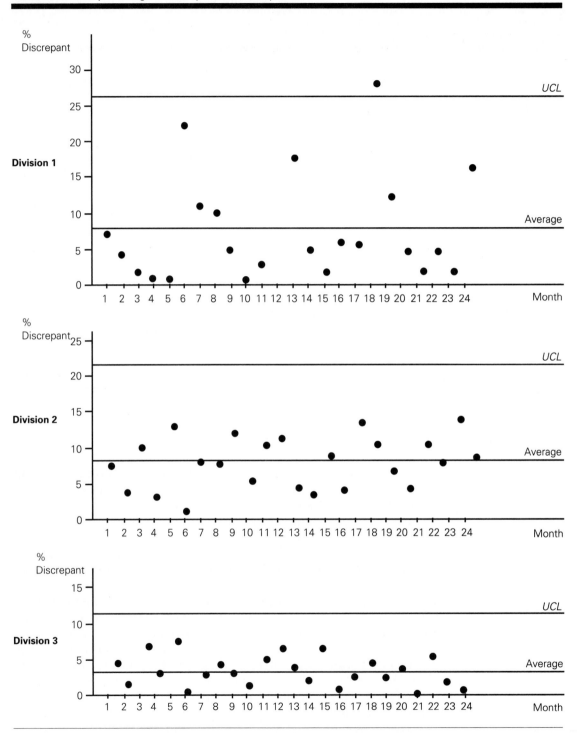

ing changes to the corporate record-keeping system. To reduce the occurrence of discrepant invoices, managers should:

- Learn about specific divisional practices
- Determine what would constitute improved standard practice
- Negotiate to establish standard practices
- Change numerous processes required to support the change in each of the divisions

Like the assembly error example, the invoice discrepancy problem is an example of a valiant attempt to address symptoms. Many of the important sources of invoice discrepancies lie in upstream processes. The leverage for improvement is relatively low in the accounts payable process, since the problems have already been created upstream and will continue to be created there until upstream sources are addressed. Both this example and the assembly error example illustrate an important principle for understanding systems: causes and effects are often not close in time and location. Failure to recognize the separation of cause and effect is an important barrier to learning for improvement.[6] Figure 8 shows accounts payable as the location of problems generated elsewhere in the system—in processes that reside in purchasing, engineering, manufacturing, and in processes that involve interface with suppliers. There is a time delay, as well as a change in organizational location, before the symptom—a discrepancy—appears in the financial accounts payable process. Resources are expended in attempting to correct the specific symptom, while the processes that generate the problems continue to create additional problems that will appear later. This dynamic structure reinforces itself by consuming resources for problem solving and decreasing the capability to invest in upstream work to remove causes of problems. We can see the same structure at work in production situations where problems caused by faults in upstream design and procurement processes are addressed in production.

There is a severe limitation placed on the ability to improve when improvement efforts are restricted to having the frontline work force attempt to be better problem solvers. The greatest leverage for improvement at a rate large enough to ensure survival lies in recognizing the existence of systems, understanding them, and acting to change them. These are all managerial responsibilities. Most likely, the centralized accounts payable process in the XYZ Corporation was created to improve efficiency. Costs for financial labor reflected in traditional cost accounting reports for each division may have appeared to be excessive. Centralizing and automating that process at the corporate level appeared to be a way

---

6. Senge describes dynamic system structures in *The Fifth Discipline.* Cause and effect relationships among factors that create change over time are understood by creating "causal loop diagrams" that describe reinforcing and balancing feedback processes and delays between cause and effect.

Figure 8

Causes and effects separated in time and location: accounts payable is
the location of problems created elsewhere

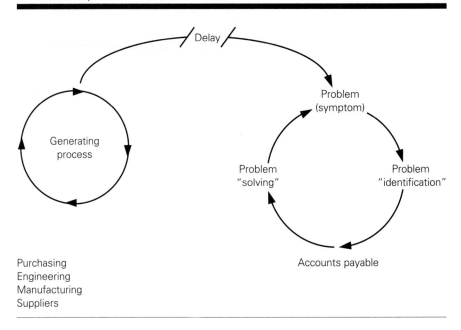

Purchasing
Engineering
Manufacturing
Suppliers

to reduce labor cost. But managers creating the new system did not consider the interdependencies of accounts payable activities and other divisional processes. Figure 9a shows the accounts payable activity as it existed in a system of related divisional activities prior to centralization. (Corporate financial was not part of that system.)

Figure 9b shows the centralized system. Centralization led to the addition of communication paths in the accounts payable activity to input the original supplier information to the computer and to make changes in pricing, build authorizations, and other items as they were made at the divisional level. The net result was to add additional possibilities for the occurrence of delays, errors, and communication failures. Centralization also meant that information in the computer system was less likely to be consistent with that submitted by suppliers on invoices. Management attempted to improve a single dimension of performance (labor cost) and failed to understand the relationships among various parts of the system of communication required to pay invoices.

The invoice discrepancy problem illustrates the complexity of cause and effect relationships in a large organization. In a small entrepreneurial enterprise, tasks are accomplished informally with knowledge of nearly all affected parties. For example, invoices are paid without the use of a complex system of communication and data processing. In a large,

Figure 9

Accounts payable system

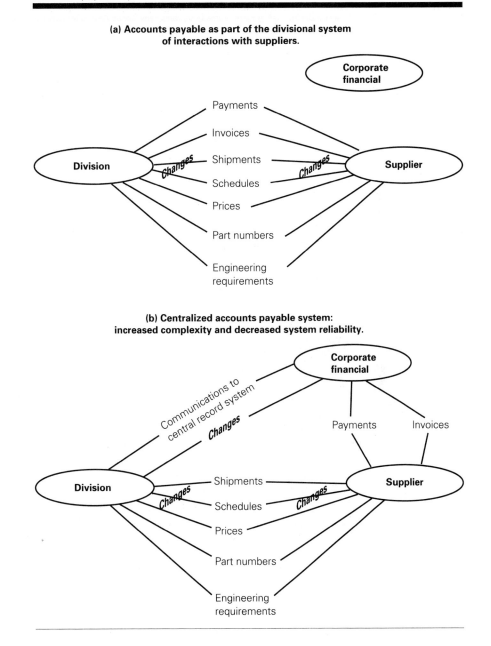

(a) Accounts payable as part of the divisional system of interactions with suppliers.

(b) Centralized accounts payable system: increased complexity and decreased system reliability.

Figure 10

Sales volume in a stagnant market: results that would be seen
without action to increase sales

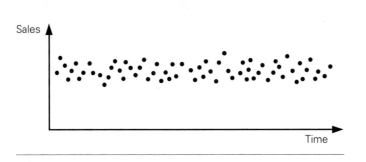

bureaucratic organization, those who carry out particular tasks have virtually no knowledge of the effects of their actions on distant processes and
individuals. Systems develop without any planning, often in reaction to a
sequence of events, each of which appears to demand some new addition
or change to the system for carrying out the work. As organizations grow,
managers tend to add patches and additional structure and regulation to
the system. As a result, large organizations tend to become hopelessly
complex and burdened with wasteful activity. In such cases, the risk of
creating system-wide paralysis by a massive redesign adds to the inertia for
maintaining the status quo. But complete redesign may have the greatest
likelihood of accomplishing a noticeable improvement in effectiveness.
When attempting a system redesign, managers must clearly understand
the linkages of the system in question to other organizational components;
otherwise, paralysis will be a likely outcome, at least in the near term.

Example: Sales Promotions

The following example illustrates the suboptimization that can occur when
functional objectives are set and functions are managed as if they were
independent enterprises. Traditionally, managers have not been expected
to consider the effects of their actions on other components of the organization. Figure 10 shows a time series (run chart) of sales volume that
might exist if the sales function took no action to temporarily increase sales.
The individual points might be daily, weekly, or monthly sales volume. The
series might reflect underlying demand for either a product or a service
in a stagnant market. For example, the figures might represent sales of a
staple food item or a household cleaning item, or seasonally adjusted sales
volume for automobiles or air travel. Alternatively, they might represent
restaurant sales volume or volume of business done by a home cleaning
service.

Sales volume affects labor and equipment capacity requirements for production of the product or service. The variation in sales volume shown in Figure 10 implies that there is variation in the equipment and labor capacity required to produce the product or service, but the variation is within predictable limits. Predictable demand allows economic decisions to be made concerning the means by which requirements will be met in production,[7] and allows managers to plan and schedule resources for future production using reliable predictions of near-term future demand.

If a business organization is not managed as a system with a common purpose, it is likely that the sales department will be expected to increase sales without regard for the effects of fluctuations in sales on other areas of the business. The sales manager will be rewarded for meeting sales targets, or at least for showing short-term increases in sales. Figure 10 shows a pattern of sales volumes that could exist if the sales department took no action to increase sales volume in the short term; Figure 11 depicts a pattern of sales volumes that might be seen when the sales department makes increasing sales in the immediate future their top priority, regardless of the effects of variation in sales volume on the rest of the business. The sales department stages a promotion or sales incentive, offering the product or service at a lower price or with a rebate.[8] Consumers adjust their buying patterns to take advantage of lower prices. In the case of staples, they simply stock up on items that can be stored for a long period of time. In the case of services, they adjust their calendars to take advantage of the opportunity to save money.[9]

When considered over the long term, the net effect of this sales strategy is not necessarily an increase in sales volume. It may simply change the

---

7. Any service activity includes a production function. The actions of people and equipment that transform inputs into the resulting service can be viewed as production, just as the transformation of material, equipment, energy, and labor inputs into material goods is production. For example, in the commercial airline industry, one of the services delivered is the transport of travelers from the departure gate in one airport to the arrival gate in another. The production process includes moving travelers into the airplane, flying them from one destination to another, and moving travelers from the airplane to the arrival gate. These are activities involved in *producing* the service. In a restaurant, one portion of the production function is to prepare food. In a hospital, performing diagnostic tests, filling prescriptions and administering drugs to patients, performing surgical procedures, and feeding patients can all be viewed as production activities. The fact that there is no material product as an outcome of the transformation does not prevent seeing any activity that transforms inputs into results as a form of production. The two noticeable distinctions between production activities in service and in manufacturing may be (1) poor-quality service results cannot be reworked or scrapped without the customer's direct knowledge as they often can in manufacturing, and (2) results of service production activities usually cannot be inventoried to dampen the effects of fluctuating demand. At least 10 percent of employee hours consumed in a manufacturing organization are devoted to service activities. Service functions include financial, personnel, procurement, maintenance, data processing, and materials management.
8. Examples include rebates on cars and trucks, bargain airline ticket prices, and sales promotions on food items in grocery stores.
9. There may be justification for promotions to level demand in highly seasonal markets with technical constraints on production of the product or service.

Figure 11

Sales volume in a stagnant market: results that would be seen
with action to increase sales[10]

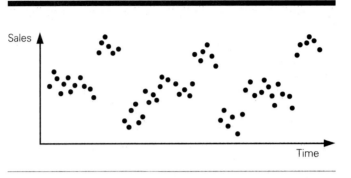

pattern of purchases over the short term.[11] In terms of production of the
product or service, this increases the overall level of variation that must
be accommodated. Fluctuations in requirements for labor and equipment
increase. To accommodate these fluctuations, the size of the full-time
labor force could be increased to provide the capability to meet maximum
levels of demand. But alternative work must be found to fill idle labor
capacity during times when demand is at a low level. Alternatively, increased labor requirements at times of peak demand could be met by
working overtime or by taking on temporary employees. In either case,
the quality of the product or service may be affected. Wide fluctuations
in demand for manufactured products pose the same dilemmas for equipment capacity; either capacity is put into place to meet high demand
levels, or inventory is built up during times of low demand to buffer
against insufficient capacity during high demand periods. In the first case,
equipment would stand idle during times of low demand; in the second,
additional inventory and storage costs would be incurred. In the case of
service, having equipment on hand to meet maximum levels of demand
results in underutilization of equipment during periods of low demand;
having equipment sufficient to meet only low to medium demand levels
implies that sales will be lost during times when demand exceeds capacity.

A focus on organization-wide optimization would lead managers to
consider the ripple effects of variation that sales promotions and incentives

10. Note that neither this chart nor the preceding one is a statistical control chart. They are
simply run charts to depict variation. The use of knowledge of variation in an organization
extends beyond the mere application of "SPC [statistical process control] tools" to analyze
process results. In this case, knowledge of variation and its effects is useful in evaluating the
overall benefits of certain sales practices.
11. Long-term increases in sales volume for an existing product or service are achieved by
expanding the market by improving net value or by finding new markets. Simply affecting the
time of purchase through incentives and promotions does not produce any sustainable increase
in the size of the market.

cause and to consider the long-term net return from such actions. Variation, once introduced into a system, is translated into many forms and may have widespread effects on several dimensions of business performance, including quality and cost and, ultimately, profitability and customer value. No single function or unit in a business enterprise consisting of highly interdependent components should be managed as if it were an independent entity, with no effect on other functions or units.

The preceding examples link results seen on various dimensions of performance to causes that are primarily related to interdependencies among functions, units, and processes within the larger organizational system. If managers appreciate those interdependencies, they will recognize the need to manage for system-wide optimization, rather than to suboptimize one dimension of performance or maximize the performance of single components. Some examples of integrating the activities and objectives of different functions and breaking down departmental barriers are emerging. A division of an automobile manufacturing company has reorganized its operations into product teams. Each team has a cross-functional leadership group with responsibility to jointly manage all of the activities involved in designing and producing the product and managing the work force. In another company, the responsibilities of design engineers have been enlarged to include introduction of their products into the production system. Design engineers work in production until good-quality product is being produced at normal production volumes. They return to their design activities with improved knowledge of design factors that affect the company's ability to manufacture the product. A manufacturer of consumer products has organized teams consisting of engineers, production managers, and production operators to work with major suppliers on improvement of incoming supplies. The supplier is asked to form a team with similar composition to work with the company's team. A manufacturer of household products has stopped offering coupons and price incentives. It was determined that the total cost of these practices was much greater than any apparent benefit gained by temporary increases in sales. A large distributor of electronic equipment has put its entire sales force on salary to change the focus of salespeople from attempting to maximize their income by any means available (a natural behavior when there are bonuses available) to serving the needs of customers.

▶ INTERPRETING RESULTS

As they react to present conditions and plan for the future, managers review and interpret the meaning of various *indicators of organizational performance*. They review results to determine how well their organization is functioning, and they act to bring about change in future results. Fundamental causes are often separated in time and location from the results

Figure 12

Stable variation in costs

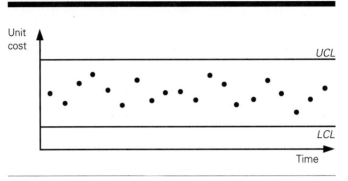

Figure 13

Judging a current result by comparing with the previous result

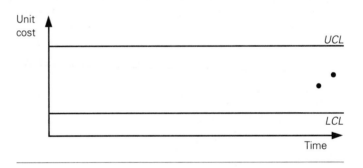

reviewed by managers. Actions to improve future results would be more likely to produce their intended effects if results were reviewed with an understanding of variation and an understanding of systems and how they work.

Treating Results Produced by Common Causes as if They Came from a Special Cause

At all levels of the organization, measures of the outcomes of work fluctuate over time. Implicit in a manager's interpretation of these fluctuations is a theory of variation. Shewhart's theory is considered most useful for interpreting variation in system and process results. Figures 12 and 13 contrast use of Shewhart's theory to interpret system results with another, more prevalent, mode of thinking. The figures refer to unit costs, but the discussion that follows would apply to a variety of organizational results at various levels, including figures for productivity, throughput, safety, customer satisfaction, customer complaints, schedule performance, scrap costs, inventory costs, overtime costs, operating efficiencies, and so on.

Figure 12 shows a history of costs for production of a product or service, converted to a per unit basis. The variation in unit costs is stable. Using Shewhart's theory, a unit cost that lies within the statistical control limits (*UCL* and *LCL*) is taken to be produced by a collection of causes that are common to every result. In terms of the factors that produced it, the last unit cost shown on the graph does not differ from any of the others shown. There is no rational basis for attributing the current period's increase in unit cost to one particular cause.

Figure 13 illustrates the limited information frequently used by managers to interpret results.[12] In order to judge performance, the manager compares the current result to the one that immediately preceded it. The change from the previous period to the current one is seen as having been produced by a single cause, so managers ask their subordinates to explain the reason for the change, particularly if it is unfavorable. Subordinates make valiant attempts to link the change to increases in some of the components of cost, while ignoring downward fluctuations in other components. Typical analyses focus on identifying increases in overtime costs, scrap costs, or any other component of cost that fluctuates over time, and identifying an event that happened to coincide with the unfavorable fluctuation in the component. Managers then use these explanations to determine what they need to work on next. When there is stable variation in a series of results, this approach to interpreting results leads managers to a series of actions that produce no sustained improvement, and may, in fact, create additional waste and render the system more ineffective.

This practice is damaging in another way as well. It leads managers to confuse coincidence with cause and effect and to develop faulty theories about the effects of their actions. They ignore the fact that there are time delays between causes and their effects, and develop a belief that the current result is produced by actions of the immediate past. With frequent changes of position, they seldom have the opportunity to see the long-term effects of their actions. Managers could improve their interpretations of the meaning of results by taking the history of variation in the results into account.

Arbitrary Targets

Figures 14 and 15 illustrate another kind of misinterpretation of results. Although the charts and the following discussion focus on analysis of unit

---

12. In many organizations, SPC has been adopted as standard practice, so managers have become accustomed to seeing statistical control charts for product characteristics. However, they have not recognized that the concept of stable variation produced by common causes applies to variation in other kinds of results.

Figure 14

Desired result outside the capability of the system
generating results

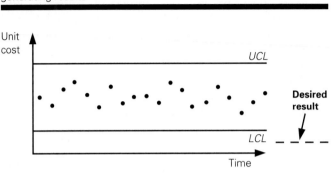

Figure 15

Results will be better than desired about half the time

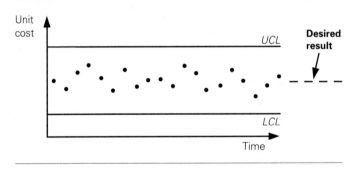

costs, the same discussion could be applied to a variety of other kinds of
organizational results. A manager establishes, often arbitrarily, a target
value for some kind of result, such as unit cost.[13] The organization is
expected to achieve the target within a certain period of time. Competitive
analyses often provide the basis for the target.[14] Managers believe that
establishing these targets will motivate the organization to do what is
necessary to achieve them. Frequently, managers set numerical targets
on several different dimensions of performance without recognizing that

---

13. Some examples are: 50 percent reduction in warranty cost, 10 percent reduction in the
number of salaried employees, 1,000 TQM projects completed, defects per million units reduced
to less than two, product development time reduced to six months, market share increased
to 35 percent.
14. For example, analysts produce a number that is taken to be the competitor's unit cost.
The analysts do not report whether the number is an average over some time period or whether
the competitor's costs are stable, increasing, or decreasing over time.

results on various dimensions are not independent and are generated from a common system of causes. Sincere but misguided attempts to change results in one dimension at a time creates unintended effects. The interactions of components within the system generate unanticipated results in other dimensions of performance.

Managers compare actual results for a particular time period to the numerical targets they have set. They criticize or praise their subordinates, depending on how the current result compares to the target. Figure 14 shows a series of monthly unit costs that exhibit statistically controlled variation. The upper and lower statistical control limits (*UCL* and *LCL*) define the capability of the system that generates the results. In the example shown in Figure 14, the conclusion one would draw by examining the picture is that the existing system is not capable of producing the product or service at a unit cost as low as the target (the desired result). The manager who established the target might continuously question subordinates about why they have not achieved this target. The manager would do better to recognize that he is the manager of the system generating the costs and so is responsible for the capability of that system. Achieving a sustained reduction in unit costs will require a system redesign and a change to the policies and practices used to manage the system and the people who work in it. No improvement will occur until the causes of cost are understood by the manager who is responsible for managing the system.

Figure 15 illustrates a case in which the kind of result desired by the manager falls within the capability of the system, roughly in the center of the range of possible outcomes that system could produce without any change. About half the time, unit costs will fall above the target, and about half the time, below. As long as neither the target nor the system is changed, celebrations upon achieving the target and reprimands for not achieving it will alternate in a random sequence.

Action on Special Causes

The point above the upper control limit in Figure 16 is a signal of the action of a special cause on the result. Unlike the situation in which the manager attempts to identify single causes for the random fluctuations in a series of results produced by common causes, this signal provides a rational basis for attempting to identify a cause for the unusual increase and to take appropriate action. In seeking to identify a cause, managers might examine their own actions first. For example, suppose the results shown in Figure 16 were percentage of orders shipped late. To reduce production costs, a manager may have set a numerical target for overtime cost without attempting to understand why production units must work overtime. Subordinates do their best to meet the target, but the production system is not capable of meeting the shipping schedule without overtime. The overtime target is met, but schedule performance deteriorates.

The results in Figure 16 could be overtime costs. A sales manager

Figure 16

A signal of the existence of a special cause

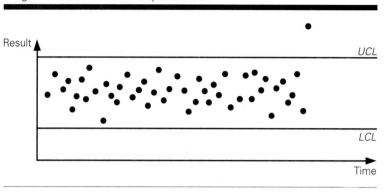

instructs the sales force to increase sales to unprecedented levels. The sales increase is achieved, but the capacity to meet new levels of orders without increasing overtime does not exist. The results plotted in Figure 16 might be warranty costs for an organization's products and the out-of-control point might be affected by warranty claims for a new product recently introduced into the firm's product line. A manager may have insisted that the product be introduced on schedule in spite of engineers' protests that the product should not be introduced without further testing. Results in one part of an organization are often symptoms of actions and practices used somewhere else. Organizational results are necessarily linked, or interdependent, since they are generated by the same system. The relationships among results are determined by the system structure and dynamics that create variation and time lags of various lengths between causes and effects.

Some writers on the subject of statistical process control state or imply that special causes of variation always exist at the local level and can be addressed locally. According to this view, the responsibility to take appropriate action on the special cause lies with the local work force. Process operatives see day-to-day occurrences that come at them from somewhere else; the chance of their being able to connect those occurrences to some generator of disturbance in another unit or function is remote. To act on another unit or function's activities is entirely beyond their authority. With the range of actions available to them to address problems that are generated somewhere else in the system, it is not surprising that their solutions sometimes consist of building in various forms of waste, such as excessive inspection and other kinds of adjustments to accommodate problems.

Interdependence of Organizational Results: A Hypothetical Factory

The following example illustrates relationships among results in different dimensions of performance. The example contains data obtained by simulating some of the activities that take place in a typical factory.[15] An assembly is produced in the factory for a particular customer. The factory regularly receives orders for 100 assemblies from the customer. Factory experience in filling the orders has varied over time. Figure 17a shows a control chart of some history of filling orders from the customer. The plotted figures are the number of assemblies that reached final inspection in order to get 100 acceptable assemblies to fill the order. For example, the first point plotted on the control chart is 108. Thus, 108 assemblies were produced and inspected at final inspection; eight of the assemblies were rejected for some reason and redirected to salvage and repair processes. The 100 that passed final inspection were shipped to the customer. The actual sequence of acceptances and rejections of assemblies is not known. It might have been that a production run of 100 was scheduled, some of the assemblies produced during that run were rejected, and additional runs and inspections were scheduled until 100 good assemblies were finally available. Internal production and inspection costs produced by poor production quality are not addressed directly in the data shown in Figure 17a, but the implications for the magnitude of those costs and others are clear. Figure 17b shows results seen after sources of the special cause variation in Figure 17a have been addressed and prevented from recurring. The chart in Figure 17c shows results after additional changes have been made to the production system and its inputs to improve the results that arrive at the final inspection process. Product and process redesign and change of operating practices in upstream processes have led to the improvements shown.

Figures 18 and 19 show the effects of internal quality improvements on two other dimensions of organizational performance when a given production scheduling and ordering policy is followed. The initial production schedule for the customer's next order will call for production of the number of assemblies that were produced to fill the previous order, less finished goods inventory on hand. If additional assemblies are required to fill the order, additional builds will be scheduled. Similarly, orders to suppliers will authorize shipment of enough material to produce the initially scheduled build, and additional materials will be expedited, if required. This policy is not optimal in any sense. It simply provides a means to show the effects of variation in product quality on some other dimensions of performance. Figure 18 shows the variation in sizes of orders to suppliers. The three run charts correspond directly to the control charts shown in Figure 17. The order sizes are in units representing the inputs required to make one assembly. The process of generating the figures in each run chart was begun with order two. Variation in the sizes of orders to suppliers shows the effect of production quality in the factory on the

---

15. The full details of the situation and several simplifying assumptions are discussed in the original paper from which the following was extracted: Gipsie B. Ranney, "The Implications of Variation," *Quality Progress*, Vol. 23, No. 12, December 1990, pp. 71–77.

Figure 17

Factory experience filling orders from a customer for an assembly: number of assemblies produced to have 100 accepted for shipment

(a) History prior to improvement.

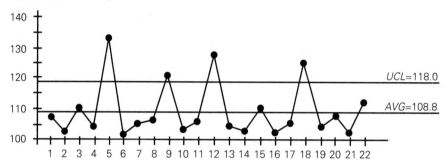

(b) Results after special causes are removed.

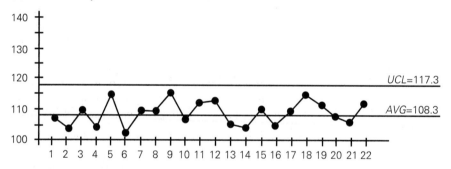

(c) Results after further actions are taken to improve quality.

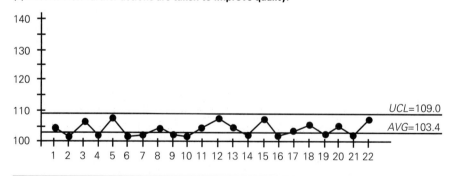

order sizes is purely a function of the factory's internal quality; there is no fluctuation in the size of orders from the factory's customer.

Often, people who work within a production system believe that most of their troubles are generated somewhere else. A typical reaction to trouble is to blame difficulties in production on fluctuations in demand for the product and unpredictable customer orders. This example illus-

Figure 18

Factory experience filling orders from a customer for an assembly:
sizes of orders to suppliers

(a) History prior to improvement.

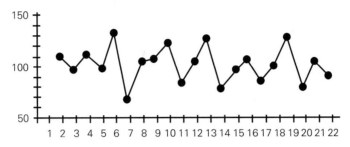

(b) Results after special causes are removed.

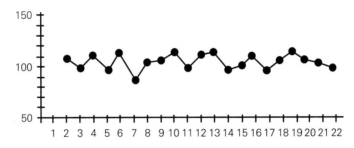

(c) Results after further actions are taken to improve quality.

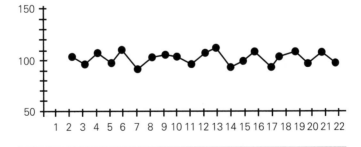

trates that considerable trouble can be created inside the walls of the
factory without any fluctuations in orders. Factory quality improvement is
shown to reduce variation in order sizes. This reduction in variation would
benefit suppliers directly and the customer indirectly. Faced with extreme
and unpredictable variation in order sizes, suppliers will do one of the
following: (1) maintain large finished goods inventories, so that variation
in orders will not affect their own production system, (2) allow their own
production schedules and orders to their suppliers to fluctuate in response
to the variation in order sizes, or (3) allow their own production schedules

Figure 19

Factory experience filling orders from a customer for an assembly:
finished goods inventory

(a) History prior to improvement.

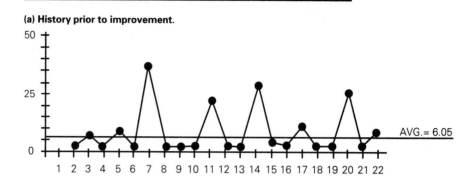

AVG.= 6.05

(b) Results after special causes are removed.

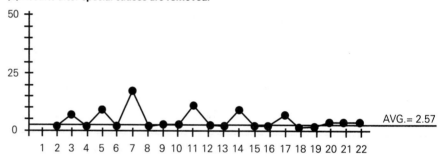

AVG.= 2.57

(c) Results after further actions are taken to improve quality.

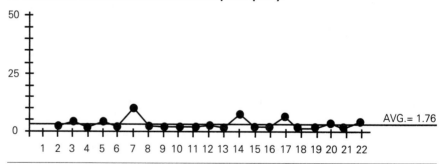

AVG.= 1.76

to vary, but buffer their suppliers from the disturbance produced by variation in order sizes by maintaining large incoming materials inventories.
Variation in order sizes to suppliers is an indicator of organizational performance that is probably judged to have little importance unless the effects
of that variation are recognized. Large and unpredictable variation in
order sizes affects supplier costs and other dimensions of supplier perfor-

mance, such as quality and delivery, and ultimately affects the company's ability to provide value to customers.

Figure 19 shows the effects of factory quality improvement on the factory's finished goods inventory, given use of the scheduling and ordering policy described earlier. The run charts shown correspond directly to the control charts shown in Figure 17. The figures plotted are the number of assemblies remaining after the customer's order is filled. Those assemblies are then held in inventory until the next order and shipment. The effect of improvement is to decrease variation in the size of finished goods inventory. Also, the average number of units held in inventory from one order to the next is decreased. More than a 50 percent reduction in the average size of inventory is seen as a result of bringing the production system into statistical control.[16]

This example establishes a direct link between the levels of finished goods inventories, and thus their costs, and the quality of the production system, as indicated by the quality of its output. There are numerous costs linked to and affected by production quality. Among them are costs for material handling, inspection, space, energy, overtime, and supervision. Similar problems with other products in the factory would combine to produce variation in requirements for financial resources, affecting financial planning. Due to the inability to measure and link portions of costs to the problem of inadequate design and production, the implications of variation and poor quality are not appreciated beyond a surface attention to product quality as it reaches the marketplace. The lack of ability to measure does not imply that the effects of variation and poor quality of products and systems cannot be recognized, understood, and addressed.

In the preceding example, inventory costs are linked to product quality and the quality of the production system. There are two distinctly different approaches to addressing organizational results. Typical managerial practice has been to attempt to manage organizational results directly by setting short-term numerical objectives and admonishing the organization to achieve the objectives. The difficulty with this practice lies with the systemic implications of meeting those targets.

Inventory exists not because the organization set out to create inventory, but rather to buffer the production system and the customer from variation in production results and requirements. Inventory serves as a form of insurance against failure of the production system. Direct action on inventory cost by removing finished goods, in-process and incoming materials inventories will temporarily reduce inventory costs, but the effects of doing so will be felt and seen in other dimensions of performance— ability to meet schedules, product quality, overtime costs, and so on. Failure to address problems of systemic quality implies that inventory will return to its former levels over time, or performance will deteriorate in other

---

16. It should be noted that this is one specific example and not a rule for the magnitude of improvement that might be expected in other cases.

dimensions. Organizational results are, indeed, results. They are *caused* by the interaction of systemic elements or components. Attempts to manage results directly may produce negative effects in other dimensions, perhaps with a time delay. Action directly on results can produce temporary improvement in the dimension being considered, but produce unintended effects in other dimensions and no sustained improvement. Understanding and managing causes of those results can bring sustainable improvement.

Evaluating Performance of Systems and People

The concepts of variation and of systems introduced in the preceding pages have implications for evaluation of performance. Without understanding that variation is an attribute of results on various dimensions of performance and that there are interactions among system components in producing results, we are led into *event explanations*[17] of cause and effect. These event explanations amount to confusing coincidence with cause and effect. For example, IBM was identified in the book *In Search of Excellence* as one of the so-called "excellent" companies and has been seen over the years as exemplary of good management. Yet IBM posted the largest one-quarter loss in history for the fourth quarter of 1992 and has been faced with continuing reductions in its labor force. If the same practices existed at IBM over the entire period, there is a strong possibility that several other factors contributed to IBM's results of the past, as well as those of the present. It seems fairly obvious in the case of IBM that a number of global economic, political, and market factors have combined to influence results. A rational analysis of the practices and decisions in General Motors over the past several decades would lead to an understanding that the factors contributing to General Motors' current performance are the result of actions taken over those decades, rather than due to the actions of a single chief executive in a single year. Understanding system dynamics, the internal interactions of the components of any system, and the effects of factors in the environment external to the system, and recognizing the existence of stable variation in results over time and conditions renders attempts to ascribe performance results of almost any kind solely to the contribution of a single individual or single component of a system irrational. The systemic view calls into question the practice of annual ratings of performance based on current results at any level in an organization. This practice is based upon the assumption that there are no effects on results from any source other than the individual being rated, or that the effects are constant for every individual and constant over time. The practice of ranking individuals or divisions of companies, or any other collection of entities, according to short-term performance measures is a result of failure to understand the nature of systems and variation.

---

17. The term is used by Senge in his book *The Fifth Discipline*.

Although rating individual performance on the basis of coincident system results is an irrational exercise, managers do have the responsibility to optimize the skills and abilities of their employees and to provide guidance on development. This guidance includes feedback, but it should be directed toward identifying areas in which the employees could use support and further training, education, and other kinds of developmental experience. Those managerial responsibilities and the skills required to fulfill them are different from those required to act as a judge, rather than as a mentor of continually learning and developing employees.

System thinking also brings the realization that actions can produce effects in multiple dimensions, and that various dimensions of performance are not independent of one another. It is common managerial practice in some organizations to segment analysis of various dimensions of performance into different agenda items, so that cost is considered separate from quality, ability to meet schedules, and so on. Improved practice would entail focus on methodology and system analysis, and a multivariate judgment of system performance indicators, rather than the traditional univariate approach.

▼

QUALITY IN ACTION: A MESSAGE TO THE STUDENT
Ray Stata, Chairman and CEO, Analog Devices, Inc.

Analog Devices, Inc., produces semiconductor integrated circuits which process measures of temperature, pressure, velocity, and other real-world phenomena. Manufacturers of computers and microprocessors use this technology for a wide variety of industrial and military applications. Analog Devices has the largest market share in about 75 percent of its product lines. However, as chairman and CEO Ray Stata explains, leaders at Analog Devices are not content with past success. Instead, they use systems thinking to promote continuous learning and improvement.

The rates of change that we face in technology and markets is exponential. To meet these challenges, we have to accelerate our rates of improving and of learning, two sides of the same coin. It is possible to think of quality improvement as a way to achieve customer satisfaction through continuous improvement in the way we work. But quality improvement is much more than this. I like to think of it as a system for learning which takes place on four levels: individual, team, company, and society. To ensure that individual learning is reflected in changed behaviors, skills, and attitudes, we educate and train our people just in time, on the job. Team and organizational learning is rooted in dialogue—how we communicate to each other what's going on in our minds and what's going on in reality. Quality improvement encourages team members to distinguish between facts and opinions and to build consensus by combining diverse observations into a shared view of reality.

At Analog Devices, we promote organizational learning by clarifying and envisioning where and how we want learning and improvement to occur. The success stories that result from quality improvement activities are diffused through QIP Fests (quality improvement program conferences) to get people across the organization to share what they are learning. To accomplish this mutual learning, for example, between our semiconductor plants in Ireland and Massachusetts, we need standardized language and definitions. People need to speak the same language and use the same definitions and terms for information exchange to be effective. Our quality improvement efforts are helping to improve standardization.

Analog Devices is a highly decentralized company, so detailed strategic planning usually takes place within divisions. To overcome the barriers to learning that are inherent to this structure, we formed fifteen corporate-wide product, market, and technology task forces that drew together 150 top professionals from throughout the company. After twelve months of deliberation, these task forces delineated some imperatives for change (including integrated customer response, world-class manufacturing, shared technology and manufacturing resources, time to market, and shift in market position), as well as specific recommendations for how to bring about those changes. This organizational learning exercise revised some of our basic beliefs and assumptions.

Societal learning requires communication among organizations. In the Boston area, we have created the Center for Quality Management to provide a network for member companies to freely share with each other. A course provides members with a common conceptual framework and language. Roundtables, seminars, and workshops promote ongoing learning.

At Analog Devices, we have learned some important lessons about quality improvement. First, we learned that it is harder to manage a company so that people feel good about themselves than to learn the seven tools of quality. However, the human, motivational side of the equation is more important than the analytical, problem-solving side. It provides a platform for incremental improvement and innovative breakthroughs. Employee satisfaction is key to customer satisfaction.

Second, we learned that we must transform managers into leaders. In the early 1980s, when Analog was doing wonderfully, my approach to managing change was naive—"Here are the books; you're smart guys, so read them and make it better. Quality's free; just do it!" Three years after the speeches and slogans, of course, nothing had happened. In the mid-1980s, when Analog was facing tougher times, we hired a vice president of quality to fix the situation. He did a wonderful job of convincing the organization of the value of quality improvement methods, but we were in a period of "picking the low-hanging fruit." There were so many problems out there that any effort to improve would yield progress. Finally, in 1990, after most of the low-hanging fruit was gone, I came to realize that making it happen was my job, not the vice president of quality's job. I had to become knowledgeable enough and skilled enough to lead the process.

Third, we learned what it means to be leaders. Historically we referred to leaders as "captains of the ship" to denote their role in operating the vessel entrusted to their care. But leaders of the 1990s must be both designers and operators. They must shape the design of the organization structure and policies so as best to fulfill the corporate mission. The leader will be a facilitator of change—a learner and teacher, a coach and counselor, a role model, a diagnostician, a designer of new systems and organizational structures, and a master of dialogue. A special role for the leader at the top of the organization is to be an iconoclast. The biggest impediment to change is your assumptions and beliefs; nothing fails like success. You have to identify the beliefs and assumptions that used to work, but are now getting in your way. In companies with strong cultures, that's a hard knot to unravel.

Finally, we learned that systems thinking is one of the keys to organizational learning and improvement. Organizations are like giant networks of interconnected nodes. Changes intended to improve performance in one part of the organization can affect other parts of the organization with surprising, often negative consequences. Decisions based solely on information at the local level, which is often the only information available, can be counterproductive to the system as a whole. Using analytical tools, we can learn about organizational behavior and show how the structure and policies of companies generate undesirable performance. We can also use these tools to build better systems. However, system change is blocked unless the major decision makers learn together, come to share beliefs and purpose, and are committed to take the actions necessary for change. I'm excited and challenged by how much I have to learn to provide the leadership Analog Devices needs. Every day I learn a little bit more, and every day I learn just how much more I have yet to learn. To lead, you must continue to learn.

▲

▶ LEARNING AND ACTION FOR IMPROVEMENT

Learning is an essential element for improvement. Without new knowledge, there is no basis to see that the current way the organization functions is not desirable. Learning provides a rational basis for action, a second essential element for improvement.

Elements of a System for Organization-wide Improvement

The rate and magnitude of improvement can be increased by making process and system improvement a part of the organization's strategy and creating a system for improvement. The system should take into account the existing knowledge, capabilities, and culture of the organization and should provide for integration of improvement activity into all aspects of organizational work. It should provide for development of skills and knowledge for improvement by all organizational members. Some important considerations in designing a system for organization-wide improvement are discussed below.

Education   If organizational members are to be committed to any effort for improvement, they must understand the reasons why improvement is necessary—the strategic importance of improvement. They must understand how they and the other stakeholders of the enterprise will benefit from redesign of organizational systems, processes, and methods of doing work. Their work must be grounded in concepts that enable them to see the effects of their work differently and allow them to better interpret the information they use to carry out their work. A plan for education of organizational members in the concepts of improvement should begin with education of management.

Modeling by Managers   Engagement by organizational members in learning and working for improvement will be more likely to occur if managers model the expected behaviors themselves. Many unsuccessful quality improvement programs have been marked by delegation of education, training, and responsibility for improvement to lower levels of the organization or to improvement specialists, while managers continue to carry on business as usual. Faulty systems and faulty practices by management continue to create conditions within which sustainable improvements cannot be made. Perpetuation of faulty practices by management while the work force is expected to change breeds cynicism in that work force.

Clear Understanding of Responsibility   All job descriptions should be altered to include a statement that learning and improvement work are expected, as well as a statement indicating the employee's responsibility to users of the outputs of the job. For example, the job description for process engineers in a Japanese-American joint venture manufacturing company states explicitly that the first responsibility of the process engineer is to "support the operator." This means that the process engineer must continually work to find ways to enable the operators on the production line to do high-quality work efficiently with a minimum of effort. Job descriptions for managers should include a statement of responsibility for improvement of the systems they manage.

Improvement Identified as Having Strategic Importance   The organization's strategic plan should state that improvement of system, process, and product or service quality is an organizational strategy. If improvement work is not of sufficient importance to be considered strategic, it will occur only as a result of isolated efforts, and improvement of the kind and at the rate required for survival and prosperity will not occur.

Identification and Prioritization of Improvement Activities   Some managers have expected to see significant improvement occur by simply asking people to volunteer for improvement teams and pick something to work on. Without any guidance by management, the cumulative result of these volunteer efforts may be little change in organizational effectiveness. To achieve significant improvement, improvement activities should be selected for their potential impact on customer value and achievement of the organization's purpose. Improvement activities at the highest level of the organization should be focused on design and redesign of systems. At lower levels, process improvement activities can be selected on the basis of their contribution to improving process outputs used by other organizational members and to improving the internal quality and effectiveness of processes. As a general rule, improvement activities should not be selected in response to single events. A supplier of a large manufacturing company made a practice of setting up an improvement team each time there was a customer complaint. Since the customer's supply line was long, the problem had usually disappeared by the time the complaint was raised. Since the problems were typically sporadic and most likely were produced by special causes, teams had great difficulty identifying causes of problems, were not able to reproduce the conditions that produced the problems, and were not able to confirm that changes made would prevent the problems from recurring. Teams were frustrated, and little improvement took place. The supplier then changed the basis for formation of improvement teams. Teams were formed to study and recommend improvements to organizational processes that produced products of strategic importance. The new teams were able to systematically plan and test their improvement ideas. Significant improvements were made, and team members expressed enthusiasm for continuing their improvement work.

A Systematic Method for Improvement Work When learning to use new concepts and methods for improvement, teams need guidance on how to proceed with the work. A process for improvement will be discussed later in this section.

Training Training and guidance in the use of tools and methods for improvement should be provided to organizational members while they are working on improvement projects so that the training will be reinforced by immediate application and appropriate applications in context are provided. The ability to provide just-in-time training requires that a plan for developing and deploying qualified trainers must be put in place.

Review of Improvement Work Managers are accustomed to reviewing results—figures on costs, quality, productivity, schedule performance, customer complaints, and so on. The message often conveyed by these reviews is that the method for achieving the result is of no importance. When only results continue to be reviewed, there is no reinforcement to organizational members that they should change the methods or the rationale by which they do their work.

A small manufacturing company in Ohio has begun using a process of reviewing the work of improvement teams.[18] When the need for an

---

18. The process being used by the company is modeled on the "Review and Inquiry Process" developed by Peter Scholtes of Joiner Associates.

improvement team is identified, team members representing functions that affect the product, process, or system to be improved are identified by managers of those functions. The level of team members depends upon the scope of the work identified. A formal statement describing the purpose of the work, expectations of the team, and boundaries to the scope of the work is written. An initial team meeting is held in which managers discuss the improvement activity with the team and answer questions. The team receives training in teamwork skills, and an improvement specialist provides the team with guidance on proper use of tools for study of processes. Team meetings are held regularly and are part of the work responsibilities of team members. Quarterly review sessions are held in which the team presents a report on their work to a review team consisting of the president of the company and members of his management staff. A formal procedure is followed for the review. The team presents their work, and the reviewers ask questions focused on the rationale and methods used by the team to carry out their work, rather than focusing primarily on the results. Judgmental comments and criticism of the team's work are not allowed. The reviewers make suggestions for further work and for improvement of methods and rationale. The president of the company and the other reviewers have received training in appropriate methods of reviewing, asking questions, and making suggestions to a team, as well as in the concepts and methods of improvement. The review is observed by a team of improvement specialists who provide feedback to the review team.

A process of review serves a variety of purposes. Formal review by top management emphasizes the importance of improvement work. Organizational members receive the message that improvement work is valued and expected. Since participation on improvement teams is not voluntary, improvement work is considered to be a part of the normal activity of organizational members. Attention to the rationale and methodology for improvement serves to educate team members and encourage them to continue learning. Since they must review teams and their review is in turn observed by specialists, managers are encouraged to improve their own skills and knowledge. The formality of the review process, with specific rules against use of judgmental language and threatening or critical behavior, gives both managers and team members the opportunity to participate in learning new modes of conduct and new ways of thinking, while preventing managers from reverting to old patterns of reviewing results without regard for the methods used to achieve them. The review process enables team members to gain recognition for their work and provides support for new roles for managers as teachers and developers of people. Adoption of such a process requires that several conditions be put into place: (1) managers must understand the concepts and methods for process and system improvement, (2) management must have made the decision to change their role from judging results to participating in improvement and developing the knowledge and capabilities of the people they manage, and (3) management must have sufficient belief that the process will yield improved long-term performance so that they will support organizational members as they learn and develop.

Identification of Barriers to Improvement A review process such as the one described above provides a means for managers to learn about organizational policies and practices that hamper the ability to improve. A process to learn about barriers to improvement will be successful only if organizational members are convinced by the actions of managers that they will not be punished for honest, open discussion of organizational problems.

Mechanisms to Share Learning A variety of methods have been proposed to increase the rate of improvement by sharing learning across an organization. One organization has established "centers of expertise." The organization has a number of manufacturing plants and engineering and administrative facilities. Representatives from a functional area, such as product engineering or manufacturing, meet on a regular basis to learn from each other and from recognized experts about improved methods, and to establish recommended practices for the organization. Some organizations hold meetings devoted to reports by teams on their improvement work. Other organizations publish newsletters or papers devoted to discussions of improvement projects and methods for process study.

Systematic Learning: PDSA

Since new knowledge is the basis of action for improvement, learning is critical to the capability to improve. A systematic method designed to improve the efficiency and rate of learning is scientific method. Use of scientific method in the organizational setting was described by Shewhart and further elaborated by Deming in his "cycle for learning and for improvement." Repeated use of the *PDSA (Plan, Do, Study, Act) cycle*[19] is a method for systematically developing knowledge of the cause and effect relationships that exist in systems and processes, and for developing and testing new products and new methods of doing work. When the PDSA cycle is applied as a methodology for learning within a system for improvement, the probability of improvement is increased beyond what would occur by relying on chance.

Use of the PDSA cycle by improvement teams[20] begins with stating the aim of the improvement activity: what is the team trying to accomplish? The aim of the improvement activity is further clarified by describing the kind of improvements that might be seen as a result of the team's activities. The next step is establishing a baseline of existing knowledge about the

---

19. Other authors refer to a cycle for improvement as Plan, Do, *Check*, Act. Deming uses the term "Study" to emphasize the importance of learning in improvement.
20. The reader can find a complete discussion of use of the PDSA cycle by improvement teams in the book by Moen, Nolan, and Provost shown in the references at the end of this chapter.

process or system under study. The team identifies the inputs to the process and their suppliers, and the outputs of the process and their users. They develop a flow diagram of the process and construct run charts or control charts as a history of variation in important characteristics of the process and its outputs. The team then develops a list of ideas for improvements to be investigated and establishes a plan for initial applications of the improvement cycle.

The team then begins the improvement cycle. The first phase of the cycle is to establish a *plan* for the cycle. The planning phase involves describing a study to be conducted, a test of a process change, or an experiment that will be carried out in the next phase of the cycle. The plan includes a list of all the steps required to conduct the study or test, including who will carry out each step, when each step will be carried out, what data and other records will be recorded, who will inform and gain the cooperation of other members of the organization to be affected by the test, and what training is needed and who will do it. If a test or experiment is planned, the theory that forms the basis for the experiment is stated. (The theory could be widely accepted scientific theory or simply a belief about causes of variation in process results.) A prediction of the results expected from the test is stated, along with methods to be used to collect and analyze the data of the test or experiment.

The study or test is carried out in the *do* phase of the cycle. Any failures to follow the plan are recorded for use in the analysis. The third phase of the cycle is *study*. Results of the "do" phase are compared to predictions made during the planning phase. If the results do not agree with what was predicted, the theory laid out during the planning phase may be revised. If the results agree with the prediction, the team determines how the conditions of the study might differ from conditions that might be seen in the process or system in the future. These differences may require further testing to extend the range of conditions under which the theory can be expected to apply. During the *act* phase of the cycle, the team decides what actions are appropriate, given the results of the three previous phases. Action may consist of change to the process or system under study, or the team may determine that further testing is required before making any substantial changes. The "act" phase also includes deciding what should be the focus of the next cycle. Practice of the PDSA cycle provides a discipline for systematically learning and using the knowledge gained to make changes for improvement.

Use of the PDSA cycle to conduct studies of planned changes is a helpful practice for large-scale system changes that are contemplated by management, as well as for smaller-scale processes. Small-scale testing provides a means by which problems can be discovered prior to putting changes that carry the risk of large-scale failure into effect. For example, the centralized accounts payable system described in an earlier section of this chapter could have been tested prior to putting it into effect by running a simulation of the centralized system parallel with the normal operations of the decentralized system for a subset of accounts in one division. It is doubtful that the centralized system would have been put into place, without redesign of the processes supporting the system, if such a test had been carried out.

The ability to improve is enhanced and ensured by learning about customer needs, advances in technology and market conditions, and the system that generates organizational results. Knowledge of the concepts of variation and use of appropriate methods to unravel the messages contained in variation increase the ability to learn. However, no amount of internal or external learning is a substitute for managerial action on the basis of what is learned to optimize the capability of the organization to create value for customers.

► SUMMARY OF KEY POINTS

1. There are interdependencies among the parts of an organization. Optimization of individual parts of the organization may suboptimize the whole.
2. The greatest leverage for improvement at a rate large enough to ensure survival lies in recognizing the existence of systems, understanding them, and acting to change them.
3. An important principle for understanding systems is that causes and effects are often not close in time and location.
4. Managers who do not understand variation due to common causes are led into event explanations of cause and effect.
5. Organizational results on various dimensions of performance are linked, or interdependent, since they are generated by the same system. Attempts to change organizational performance in one dimension at a time can create unintended effects.
6. Improvement of a kind and at a rate to ensure organizational survival and prosperity can be accomplished by making process and system improvement a part of the organization's strategy and creating a system for improvement.
7. The Plan, Do, Study, Act cycle is a systematic method designed to improve the efficiency and rate of organizational learning.

► KEY TERMS

event explanations	local solutions
formal process	logic flow diagram
indicators of organizational	optimization
performance	PDSA cycle
informal process	suboptimization
interdependencies	

▶ **DISCUSSION QUESTIONS**

1. Provide some examples of optimizing the performance of a single component of an organization, but suboptimizing the entire organization.

2. In his book *Out of the Crisis* Deming describes the chain reaction that begins with quality improvement: "Improve quality. Costs decrease because of less rework, fewer mistakes, fewer delays, snags; better use of machine-time and materials. Productivity improves. Capture the market with better quality and lower price. Stay in business. Provide jobs and more jobs." The chain reaction links improved quality with reduced costs. Numerous other authors have described a relationship of quality and cost that is the opposite of Deming's; that is, higher quality is accompanied by higher costs. Explain the reasons behind the difference.

3. An analyst reports that your competitor produces his product for $10 per unit. What would you ask the analyst in order to understand the meaning of this number? What would you seek to know about the competitor's organization to understand the number?

4. Suppose you are a plant manager. A salesperson for a software company proposes to sell you a software system that will automate scheduling of production, inventory control and management, and ordering of parts from suppliers. What would you do to weigh the benefits of purchasing the software? What kinds of analyses and tests would you conduct? Why?

5. Explain the following statement:
   An important part of management is planning. Planning requires prediction of the results of actions. Prediction requires a theory of cause and effect. Therefore, management requires use of theory.

6. List components of the system that produces student grades in a course. Comment on how those components might be interrelated and affect each other. Try to explain the underlying rationale for the practice of grading. What other dimensions of student learning might be affected by the need to achieve a grade?

▶ **EXPERIENTIAL EXERCISE**

- Select a process that you use to accomplish a daily or weekly activity, such as scheduling and carrying out your studies or getting dressed for the day. What are important quality characteristics of the process and its products (results)? What would constitute an improvement to the results of the process? If you sought to change the process for improvement, how would you know that an improvement had been made? List some of the possible causes of variation or poor quality in the process and its results. Write a plan for conducting one or two repetitions of the PDSA cycle to improve the process and its results. If you currently have a job, you might choose to do the tasks described above for a process in your workplace.

▶ **REFERENCES**

I. W. Burr, *Statistical Quality Control Methods*, Marcel Dekker, New York, 1976.

W. E. Deming, *Out of the Crisis*, MIT Center for Advanced Engineering Study, Cambridge, Mass., 1986.

W. E. Deming, *The New Economics for Industry, Government, Education*, MIT Center for Advanced Engineering Study, Cambridge, Mass., 1993.

R. D. Moen, T. W. Nolan, and L. P. Provost, *Improving Quality through Planned Experimentation*, McGraw-Hill, New York, 1991.

P. M. Senge, *The Fifth Discipline*, Doubleday, New York, 1990.

W. A. Shewhart, *Economic Control of Quality of Manufactured Product*, Van Nostrand, New York, 1931.

W. A. Shewhart, *Statistical Method from the Viewpoint of Quality Control*, Dover, New York, 1986.

Strategic Linkage of Operations through Employee Involvement

We are committed to Customer Focused Quality as a business strategy to exceed customer expectations. All of our employees have received training in quality process skills and building quality customer relationships. Allstate has a formalized structure to manage our quality efforts, which consist of Quality Councils and Improvement Teams. Because of our commitment to Customer Focused Quality and the training our employees have received, our work force is empowered to make the necessary decisions to improve customer satisfaction in all aspects of our businesses.

Thomas F. Clarkson, Assistant Vice President, Quality Development, Allstate Insurance Company

▶ **CHAPTER OUTLINE**

Chapter Overview

Introduction

Definition of Employee Involvement
Establishing Employee Involvement within a Strategic Context
Establishing the Context: Utilizing the MAT Framework
Improving Operational Proficiency
A "Pull" Model of Employee Involvement
The Organizational Forms of Employee Involvement

Mistakes to Be Avoided When Implementing Employee Involvement

Human Resource Implications of Employee Involvement

Summary of Key Points

Key Terms

Discussion Questions

Discussion Exercise

References

▶ CHAPTER OVERVIEW

Employee involvement is an essential element of the emerging paradigm. It is the process through which employees are empowered to make decisions relevant to their level of the organization that will positively impact on the organization's ability to provide value to the customer. However, employee involvement is only meaningful when management creates a proper context. Just as the emerging paradigm is more than a collection of tools and methods, employee involvement is more than activities in which employees participate. This chapter defines employee involvement, examines its role within the strategic context and the MAT framework of managerial roles, discusses the various forms of employee involvement, and looks at some of the more common mistakes made in implementing it. The implications for human resource practices are also addressed.

▶ INTRODUCTION

Creating an organization dedicated to the emerging paradigm requires a strong connection between strategic focus and operational reality. In many organizations, this link has been poorly made. Employees, managers, and nonmanagers alike must accept responsibility to make this connection. Employee involvement is the process through which this crucial link is made. For employee involvement to be effective, there must be a consistent alignment of effort between employees at all levels of the organization. The word "employee" does not just refer to workers or operators. It includes managers.

Consistent alignment is achieved through a focus on the cross-functional systems and processes that deliver customer value. Managers must focus employee involvement efforts on maintaining, operating, and improving these systems and processes. In one company, for example, management identified product design and manufacturing engineering as two places where improvements would immediately impact the customer.

Employee involvement in action

Plaspac[1] is a highly profitable division of a large diversified corporation. The company's product line consists predominantly of flexible plastic packaging materials, used in both food and nonfood applications. During the past twenty-five years, Plaspac has always returned profits that met or exceeded corporate expectations, a record of performance that allowed divisional management the luxury of operating with substantial autonomy in its dealings with the parent corporation. This success has been built by providing high customer value in terms of low price and high-quality products and services. Plaspac's commitment to innovation and continuous improvement has made it a tough competitor.

Plaspac has often adopted methods like statistical process control, enriched job design, and teams. However, the organization is selective in the new practices it adopts, making sure they comprise a coherent and integrated approach to management which is linked to the company's strategy.

Since 1970, Plaspac has gradually but persistently applied principles of enriched job design throughout its operations. The identification of manufacturing process variables and their required control has been part of Plaspac's productivity strategy since 1976. Originally, this control process was based on a variance analysis process adapted from socio-technical systems theory (Davis and Cherns, 1975). In the late 1970s, this variance analysis process was supplemented by statistical process control.

In 1982, plans were initiated for the creation of a new and technologically advanced production line in the company's southeastern plant complex. The new production line was to utilize the latest technology, including computerized controls. From the beginning, several managers advocated a team concept to structuring the work on the new line. These managers envisioned a work structure in which a team of operators deployed themselves as necessary across the line. In addition, the team could assume many indirect labor and management functions.

A steering committee composed of plant management dealt with issues of funding, policy variances, and the establishment of a management philosophy relative to the new line. A design team reporting to the steering committee was formed. It consisted of three operations employees from the plant (two production workers and one from maintenance), an experienced supervisor, the plant superintendent, a process engineer, a member of the human resources staff, and a controller. A consultant with experience in team designs was retained to work with the design team.

Meeting twice weekly throughout the summer of 1985, the design team analyzed each potential job, the equipment, and potential staffing requirements. The result was a system of three operators and three helpers who are responsible for the entire line, including extrusion, racking, slitting, and packaging. (Each of these processes is a separate function on a traditional line.) The considerable cross-training involved results in a highly flexible work group. The team is also responsible for many traditional supervisory functions. On a traditionally staffed line, there would be six or possibly seven direct labor people and thirteen indirect labor people. In addition to their operational tasks, each member is assigned responsibility for coordinating one of six team tasks: (1) quality control, (2) housekeeping and safety, (3) maintenance auditing, (4) performance advising, (5) personnel scheduling, or (6) production scheduling and reporting. A pay-for-knowledge compensation system was put in place which links pay to skills.

The use of enriched job design, SPC, problem-solving task forces, and teams within Plaspac has become an essential element of the company's competitive strategy and, consequently, crucial to its competitive advantage. What is striking about Plaspac is that it has avoided implementing a series of disjointed programs which compete with each other, run their course, and disappear. These initiatives have all come out of a small group of people working closely with line managers. Employee involvement within Plaspac is directed toward specific tasks the company needs accomplished, with the focus on empowering employees to more effectively perform their jobs.

---

1. Plaspac is a pseudonym for a company that was extensively researched by one of the authors under the constraint that the company not be identified by name (Yorks and Whitsett, 1989).

Employee involvement efforts focused on key processes in these areas. Cross-functional teams consisting of people from both areas of the company worked with customer input to design a product that was easier to use and maintain while providing features desired by customers. Development time was reduced, costs lowered. The value of employee involvement is that employee knowledge is marshaled toward improvements which impact the customer.

Definition of Employee Involvement

Employee involvement is "a process for empowering members of organizations to make decisions and solve problems appropriate to their levels in the organization" (Pace, 1989). This process may involve realigning power, knowledge, and information to lower levels in the organization, but it may not. Providing superior customer value is the criterion that determines the nature of employee involvement, rather than a philosophy of employee involvement for its own sake. A critical link for translating strategic intention into action, employee involvement takes various forms. Work teams, job enrichment, quality circles, task forces, and labor-management action teams are among the more common organizational manifestations.

Establishing Employee Involvement within a Strategic Context

Employee involvement is only meaningful when a strategic context has been established through leadership, systems, and processes which are supplemented with the appropriate tools. The Plaspac case is instructive (see box), as Plaspac used teams to execute a productivity strategy which provides customer value.

Rushing to establish employee involvement processes with little consideration as to how these mechanisms will relate to the rest of the organization, or how the organization must be prepared to change and adapt to employee involvement, can short-circuit the best-intended efforts. This is especially true when there is more form than substance to the program (Cole, 1989). Effective use of employee involvement requires clear role relationships between managers and other employees.

Top managers must be responsible for determining what customers value and developing strategic systems that provide customer value. Once these systems are standardized, middle-level managers have significant responsibility for improving various component subsystems. This involves giving operational employees or operators specific assignments for the maintenance and routinization of tasks and getting them involved in the ongoing efforts of managers for improvement. We can gain understanding of how the roles of various members of the organization link up through the management accomplishment topograph (MAT).

Establishing the Context: Utilizing the MAT Framework

The MAT model is composed of two dimensions: type and domain of accomplishment (see Figure 1). When employee involvement is practiced

Figure 1
The MAT (management accomplishment topograph)

Type of accomplishment								
Breakthrough								
Incrementalism								
Standardization								
Routinization								
Maintenance								
Execution								
Domain of accomplishment	Customer value strategy	Design strategy	Systems	Policies	Motivators	Processes	Technology	Operations

within the MAT framework, the efforts of employees are aligned with those of management.

In the emerging paradigm, managers must create the context for employee involvement by directing their activities toward the appropriate domains of accomplishment. Management owes employees the systems, policies, motivators, processes, technology, and operations that are capable of providing customer value. Top managers are responsible for making breakthroughs and improvements in customer value and corresponding systems. Middle management works to standardize and routinize these systems, while creating motivators, processes, technology, and operations that translate them into productive practices that deliver customer value. Operators must routinize the changes introduced in their work areas and then focus their attention on maintenance and execution of operations, while also helping to continuously improve them.

Employees working at the operational level of the organization have key roles to play within the domains with which they are most familiar: processes, technology, and operations. Most of the time, operators will routinize, maintain, and execute work tasks. However, they will also create improved ways of performing operations, or will make innovations in technology and processes. There are many ways to organize for such employee involvement. Consider some examples.

In the contractor division of Rain Bird Sales, Inc., an irrigation company in California, the decision was made to target engineering and manufacturing functions of the organization because improvements in these areas would significantly impact the business's customers. Part of the effort was directed toward stabilizing key engineering and manufacturing processes. Management was targeting the areas of the business that would have a strategic payoff. Employees were involved in making improvements based on their hands-on knowledge of the processes involved (Chang, 1993).

Del Norte, a Texas-based manufacturer of electronic security systems, has gradually changed its traditional, top-down hierarchy to a three-tiered form of organization. At the center of this structure is the quality steering committee which is responsible for setting corporate direction and communicating that direction. The second tier is a corrective team composed of middle managers and supervisors who provide resources to work teams and provide for interdepartmental communication. Members from this team also periodically form ad hoc task teams to work on specific cross-functional issues. Membership of these ad hoc task teams is selected from among members of the work teams which make up the third tier. These standing work teams perform specific tasks and seek to improve the activities in the third tier (Schneider, Schneider, and Riley, 1991). This type of organization can work because each tier is essentially focused on the appropriate level and domain of accomplishment.

Employees must understand customer value, the various components of the systems that provide it, and how customer value is defined and measured. This understanding gives meaning and direction to their specific activities, enabling them to act in terms of providing customer value. Based on their understanding, operators should be prepared to operate the systems and processes provided to them by managerial leaders and middle management. Additionally, they must maintain current performance to provide a stable base from which to launch further improvements.

These types of activities are part of the responsibilities of the work teams on the new manufacturing line at Plaspac. In operating the line, operators must coordinate with each other to synchronize activities or make joint decisions to develop compatible schedules. In addition to bearing the primary responsibility of executing operational tasks, the team must also monitor the performance of these activities to ensure they are producing product that meets the criteria of providing customer value. This monitoring requires employees to observe, measure, and record. Operational adjustments are made based on this monitoring. The monitoring also provides information needed by both the team and management for the improvement of work activities. When special events occur that jeopardize the execution of operational activity, team members have to take corrective action in order to return line operations to normal functioning.

Improving Operational Proficiency

Improvement implies that current performance is not only maintained, but enhanced. Improvement through both breakthroughs and incrementalism is the ultimate goal of all employees. Operational-level employees can improve operational proficiency through several activities, specifically, reducing variation, adjusting averages, suggesting changes, and implementing changes. These improvement activities provide employees with opportunities to use their creativity and thinking ability to improve the strategic capability of their company. These improvements are most likely to be made within the domains of processes, technology, and operations. However, employees should also be encouraged to contribute ideas for improving all other domains, as well.

Reducing variation yields system-wide benefits in terms of increased predictability, reduced costs, conformance to the design target, and reduced sacrifice for a multitude of internal and external customers. Employees must engage in incremental and continuous improvement of their work activity to achieve reduction of variation in their work outcomes.

Adjusting averages may have to be accomplished if the average value of what is provided is going to equal the target around which variation is reduced. In a service setting, adjusting averages may involve improving cycle times. Bill Arnold, CEO of Centennial Medical Center in Nashville, Tennessee, notes productivity in the hospital is really cycle time. This is true in providing the patient service and in processing paperwork. Breakthrough ideas and continuous improvement suggestions from people in accounts receivable have helped reduce accounts receivable turnaround from seventy-eight days to forty-four days over three years (Judge, 1992).

Through *suggesting changes* based on their experience with resolving crises, problem solving, and reducing variation, employees can help improve the systems within which they work. Since employees are not the owners of these systems, they may not have insight into all the causes of the symptoms they have observed. Some improvements will not be possible without making changes in other parts of the system. Bill Arnold points out that leadership requires that senior managers be with people, not over them. To achieve this objective it is essential that management avoid focusing on the bottom line, and instead have a clear understanding of the system and processes that contribute to the bottom line. Arnold holds open forums with his employees once a month, five meetings in one day. These meetings provide a wealth of information for improving systems and processes.

Whenever improvements or breakthroughs in strategic systems are possible, employees must effectively *implement change*. This requires that they understand the rationale for the changes and be flexible in adopting new methods.

Once again, the Plaspac example is illustrative. Within their team, operators on the new manufacturing line continually work to improve performance through reducing variation and raising the average of what is produced. Ideas for improvements that go beyond their ability to influence the organization are passed on to management as part of the ongoing effort toward improvement. At times these suggestions lead to the establishment of task forces to address complicated issues. Change in processes, technology, and work methods is a way of life.

A "Pull" Model of Employee Involvement

For employee involvement to deliver on its potential for improving organizational performance, it must be integrated into a larger context of managerial responsibility for systems improvement, as conceptualized in the MAT. The effective performance of managerial roles creates the context for a "pull" system of appropriate employee involvement (Pace, 1989). When managers are involved in the creation of a customer value strategy, and in the systems and policies that give this strategy operational meaning, they can create an environment where employees are routinely included in continuous improvement. A pull model aligns employee involvement efforts with the strategic direction of the organization. The notion of a pull approach contrasts with "pushing" employee involvement as an end in itself. This pushing often leads to a focus on activities, rather than improvements that impact the customer.

With a pull system, top management leads toward system integration through its own involvement. Participation in system improvement is the job of everyone in the organization. As suggested by the MAT, when people at each level of the organization concentrate their activities toward the appropriate domain of accomplishment, integration will naturally occur. Said another way, managers create processes of participation when they fulfill their roles in system improvement.

Xerox learned in the early 1980s that it was necessary to integrate employee involvement with a top-down focus on company objectives. Problem-solving teams and other efforts at getting hourly workers, technicians, engineers, and first-line supervisors involved in problem solving and decision making focus on getting things done through working together. Employees at the work unit level are responsible for knowing who their customers are and satisfying their customers' requirements. These efforts have been integrated into a strategic focus on customer satisfaction through continuous improvement. This strategy involves concerted efforts to improve the managerial systems at Xerox so they reflect a consistent focus on internal and external customer satisfaction. The resulting pull

Figure 2

Integrated "pull" approach to systems improvement

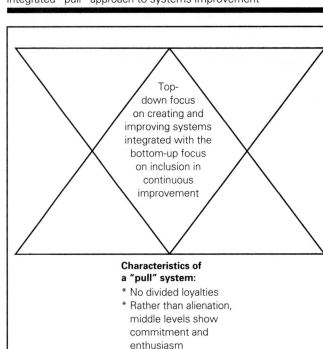

Top-down focus on creating and improving systems integrated with the bottom-up focus on inclusion in continuous improvement

Characteristics of a "pull" system:
* No divided loyalties
* Rather than alienation, middle levels show commitment and enthusiasm
* System improvement is everyone's job

Adapted from Pace, 1989.

model integrating this top-down focus on TQM with operational-level efforts of employee involvement is presented in Figure 2 (Pace, 1989).

This pull model contrasts sharply with the push approach exemplified by an employee involvement program implemented in the manufacturing division of a company as a bottom-up process without specific direction from the corporation. The employee involvement activities were focused primarily on quality of work life (QWL) issues rather than on system improvement. Meanwhile, managers in the manufacturing division were not consulted in the development of the corporation's strategy for Total Quality Management. The resulting lack of integration is illustrated in Figure 3.

The Organizational Forms of Employee Involvement

Once it becomes part of how an organization operates, employee involvement takes various forms. These include work teams, job enrichment, quality circles, task forces, and labor-management action teams. As we

Figure 3

Push approach for Total Quality Management
and employee-focused programs

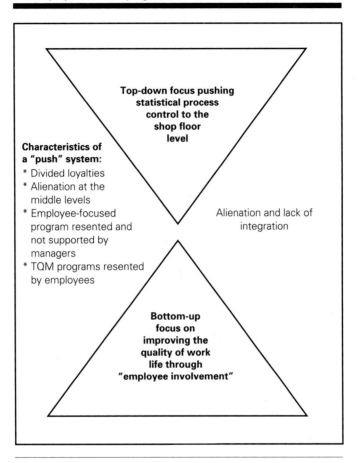

Adapted from Pace, 1989.

discuss these forms, remember that the focus within each is on maintaining, operating, and helping to improve the key processes for which they are responsible. These methods for employee involvement have evolved over the past several decades as management has learned how to create structures and processes for employee involvement. As the examples given below illustrate, companies are learning how to recast these ideas in order to integrate employee involvement into the emerging paradigm.

Work Teams Work teams are groups of employees who are collectively responsible for some carefully delineated, complete piece of the work process. Sometimes they are referred to as self-directed work teams (Wellins, Byham, and Wilson, 1991), autonomous work groups, or self-regulating work groups. These labels are somewhat misleading since, although team members are typically empowered to make many more decisions and exert much more control over their work than has historically been the case for employees, they do so within very real organizational constraints. For that reason, some writers call them "semi-autonomous work teams" or simply "work teams" (Lawler, 1986). John Kelly, of the Industrial Relations Department at the London School of Economics, has argued that such groups should be called "flexible work groups" since "flexibility, not autonomy, provides a key concept in understanding this form of job redesign" (1982, p. 112).

Ideally, all the members of the team become capable of performing the full range of tasks that fall under the team's area of responsibility. Building this team capability requires a significant amount of cross-training. One of the primary advantages of teams is that a small number of people assign themselves to the work that needs to be done, rather than working at a set task until reassigned by a supervisor. Members of self-directed teams may also assume functions normally performed by supervisors or specialized professionals, such as dealing with performance issues, purchasing supplies and equipment, and revising work methods. The pay system of the organization must usually change to reflect the fact that workers can perform a number of tasks (Lawler, 1986, p. 105). This is necessary both to reward people for developing the full range of skills needed by the team, and to permit the flexible deployment of people to those tasks that need to be done at any given moment.

One application of the team concept is found at NUMMI, the joint venture of General Motors and Toyota in Fremont, California. All employees in the plant are organized into teams ranging from five to eight members (Brown and Reich, 1989). There is one job classification for all production workers in the plant, and the match between production needs and skills (as opposed to seniority) is the primary criterion for making job assignments. Team leaders are responsible for the duties of first-line supervisors in a traditionally organized plant. Many team leaders are also union representatives. Three or four teams constitute a group. Group leaders are the first line of management. Problems on the production line are handled as much as possible by the team members. Jobs are rotated among team members, who decide how frequently such rotation should take place. Teams meet periodically to discuss work methods, how to improve quality, simplify the work, and similar issues.

This form of job design makes it possible for employees to contribute to both stabilizing and improving the work process. However, maintaining positive group dynamics becomes an important issue for work teams. Team members must recognize their dependence on each other, exercise self-direction and self-control, and be willing to accommodate other team members (Truell, 1991). People who enjoy being "solo performers" are often ineffective or disruptive in work team situations. Core competencies for people working in teams, in addition to their knowledge and technical abilities, include listening, interpersonal communication, information gathering, and problem-solving skills.

To become cohesive units, teams typically go through four stages of development: forming, storming, norming, and performing (Tuckman, 1965). Organizations that are successfully integrating teams into the emerging paradigm (such as Saturn, which is discussed below) recognize that developing cohesive teams takes time and anticipate the need for facilitating them through the four stages.

The *forming stage* involves tentative behavior on the part of members of the team as they test out the role of the group and their places in it. For example, in one company, teams frequently checked with managers before finalizing or implementing their decisions. This behavior reflected their previous dependence on management. Managers must be careful to avoid reinforcing dependent behavior during this stage. Role relationships between management and supervision should be effectively worked out and agreed upon.

During the *storming stage*, members of the team may enter into conflict with each other. This often occurs once the relationship with management has been resolved and the attention of team members turns inward. Team members must be trained to constructively confront this conflict through the use of collaborative influencing and conflict resolution skills (e.g., Thomas, 1976). Team building facilitated by an external organization development person is often helpful. Skillful facilitation can help the team move through this difficult stage to the *norming stage*, in which productive group norms are established.

Assuming the norms which emerge are aligned with corporate goals, norming leads to a high level of performance in the *performing stage* (see Figure 4).

Although there is no set time for how long it takes a group to work through these stages, certain factors can influence the timing. Groups that are homogeneous, interdependent, and whose members work in close physical proximity will work through these stages more quickly. With good group dynamics, these groups will tend to be cohesive. Further, if the group's norms fit company objectives, cohesive groups are more effective than less cohesive ones (Magjuka and Baldwin, 1991).

Many employees in General Motors' Saturn car company are organized into self-managed work teams. When a team is first organized, Saturn takes specific steps to help them through the four stages. Each new team has two advisors, one from the UAW and one from management. A "charter member" assumes the responsibilities traditionally given to a supervisor. This charter member orchestrates the hiring of other team members and is responsible for teaching them Saturn's mission, the core values of the company, and the competencies necessary for successfully performing the team's tasks. During this forming stage, the charter member works closely with the two advisors.

Figure 4

Stages of group development (based on Tuckman, 1965)

Stage	Characteristics	Management action
Forming	Tentative behavior, checking with management to verify decisions and testing limits of the group's authority	Role clarification, provide information, avoid involvement in processes which are within the group's domain; emphasize the customer value strategy and their role in it
Storming	Internal group conflict, personality and style issues emerge, power struggles may surface	Provide facilitation, develop interpersonal competence among members
Norming	Patterns of behavior form, group culture emerges	Continue emphasis on customer value, pull group into process improvement efforts
Performing	Strong cohesiveness among members, concern for improving performance	Operate within the MAT framework

At Saturn, the charter member is charged with facilitating any conflicts which emerge during the storming stage. This person receives extensive training in facilitation skills. During the norming stage, the charter member moves away from the central facilitator role. Once the team has reached the performing stage, a work unit leader is elected by the team. This leader may or may not be the charter member. If a significant change in membership occurs, say two or three people at once, the team may have to return to the third, or even the second, stage and take steps to reaffirm itself as a self-managed team. This requires the team leader to take a more active facilitation role.

There is no personnel department at Saturn. Team members determine how many people are needed on the team and make hiring decisions from an established pool of applicants. Both NUMMI and Saturn, as well as many other facilities within General Motors, Ford, and Chrysler, operate with philosophical support from the UAW. Owen Bieber, president of the UAW, communicates his thoughts on employee involvement in his message to the student.

▼

QUALITY IN ACTION: A MESSAGE TO THE STUDENT

Owen F. Bieber, President, UAW

Nonmanagerial employees, laborers or workers, have an important role to play in the emerging paradigm. They also have an important stake in the success of their company. Owen F.

Bieber, president of the United Automobile Workers, explains what employee involvement can mean to employees when managed appropriately.

When workers are involved in the decisions that affect their lives on the job, everyone benefits. Work becomes safer and more satisfying. Quality and productivity go up, making customers happier and keeping workers' jobs and incomes secure. I'm proud that the UAW and other unions have helped spur American business toward greater employee involvement.

Good examples abound. In a series of moves that would have been unheard of just a few years ago, UAW members are taking charge of product quality. Workers in auto assembly plants are dealing directly with car buyers, and following up on problems with dealers and suppliers. We have won the right to shut down machines that are producing defective parts, and to file official complaints about poor quality.

Unfortunately, not every "employee involvement" program is worthy of the name. Involvement means nothing if workers aren't also given the power to make real changes in their plants, offices, and other workplaces. It's important to move beyond glib buzzwords, and recognize that true worker involvement means a fundamental change in the way businesses are managed in this country.

▲

Job Enrichment Job enrichment is a form of innovative job redesign that seeks to provide employees with jobs that enhance intrinsic motivation. This is done through designing the job so that each employee has more responsibility, receives recognition, and has more achievement potential (Herzberg, 1966).

Typically, enriched job design is accomplished through first combining tasks so that more skill variety is required to perform the job. Task combination also makes the job more meaningful to the employee because it creates a more complete, or holistic, piece of work which produces a definable product or service. The job is also made more complete by organizing the workflow so that each employee provides this product or service to a specific set of internal customers. For example, machine operators channel their output to a specific set of operators at the next step of the production process, rather than having their output pooled and randomly distributed among these "downstream" operators.

This completeness makes it possible to build more responsibility into the job. This results in the employee having control over how he or she executes that complete piece of work. Finally, feedback loops on the work performed are strengthened so that the employee has direct knowledge of results based on the quality of his or her performance (Whitsett, 1975; Hackman, Oldham, Janson, and Purdy, 1975; Yorks, 1979).

An example of this model is found in the policy coder job in an insurance company. Policy coders process the insurance application after it has been approved by an underwriter. Before enriched job design, each coder handled one line of business, either automobile, homeowner, or marine insurance. Further, they worked in a strict production mode doing a minimal number of tasks, specific to coding applications for insurance which had been approved by the underwriters. Any problems were set aside to be resolved at the direction of a supervisor. Insurance agents called the supervisor with any questions. Since several coders did each line of insurance, policies within that line were randomly assigned to coders in batches regardless of which insurance agency sold the insurance. Productivity and quality measures were maintained on a work unit basis.

Following job enrichment, the auto, homeowner, and marine coding functions were combined into a single job. Coders were cross-trained to perform all the coding functions. Each coder was assigned a set of insurance agencies. Business from a set of agencies always went to the same coder, and agents called the coder directly with questions. In other words, work was assigned to coders on a client basis (agency-set) rather than by type of insurance. All coders worked on auto, homeowner, and marine insurance, but for their set of agencies. (This also meant that coders were teamed with underwriters, since their work was assigned on the same basis.) Additionally, feedback was given directly to each coder through a variety of means. As jobs conform to this particular model of design, employees have a greater sense of meaning about their work, enhanced sense of responsibility, and knowledge of results, three psychological states which increase satisfaction and enhance commitment to quality (Hackman et al., 1975).

Job enrichment has had a somewhat checkered history (Lawler, 1986). This approach to job design was widely publicized in the 1960s and 1970s, when it became a management fad (Hackman, 1975). Although job enrichment lost its popular appeal during the late 1970s, it did not disappear (Hackman and Oldham, 1980). In their study of employee involvement and Total Quality Management practices among Fortune 1000 companies, Lawler, Mohrman, and Ledford (1992) found that job enrichment is widely used as an employee involvement strategy; respondents cited job enrichment as being used more often than self-managing work teams.

There are, of course, limitations in the degree to which individual jobs can be enriched. Some tasks may not be able to be combined because of the layout of existing technology which cannot be retooled. In other instances, cross-training might not be feasible because of the complexity of the tasks involved. Teams may be a more appropriate alternative in these situations.

Teams are most effective in situations requiring the flexibility of a small group of employees who can switch tasks to match the needs of a work process. In some ways, a team is a group of employees who collectively have an enriched job.

Job enrichment may be a better approach than teams in task settings where an individual employee can perform a discrete set of tasks for a specific set of clients. In such cases, the job enrichment design permits the establishment of individual responsibility for well-defined work outcomes. Employees can have individual responsibility for stabilization of their complete piece of work and also work with system owners on improvement issues.

Job enrichment may seem contradictory to the emphasis placed by the MAT on standardization, routinization, and stabilization in operator jobs. These three activities may seem to imply that the employee is only called upon to repeatedly and reliably execute a predetermined task. This is not the case. When integrated into the MAT framework, enriched job design is likely to have long-term meaning and prove sustainable.

To standardize a system, a manager verifies that it is operable, and demonstrates statistical capability and on-target performance. Standardization may involve both uniformity of materials, parts, and tools (Shingo, 1988, 1990), and the standardization of methods so that they are free of difficulty (Ishikawa, 1985). This requires a high level of cooperative effort between operators, manufacturing engineers, and the managers who own the systems. Standardization is the responsibility of managers, but is the product of collaboration with those who use the system (Ohno, 1988). Routinization, another key activity for stabilization, is an employee's responsibility. Employees must fine-tune the system, working out the bugs and reducing performance variation.

Although some tasks in a stabilized process may be perfectly scripted, others might require operator decision making and immediate responses to problems in dynamic situations. This is especially true in environments in which all contingencies cannot be anticipated. For example, in a customer service position, a worker may have to make judgments about the best way to serve a customer's needs; this could include making a referral, providing information, or resolving a problem. On the assembly line of one of General Motors' highest quality producing engine plants, the engine stops in front of the employee while he or she completes the prescribed operations. Because the engine moves on to the next workstation only after the employee releases it, the worker has more autonomy than in a traditional assembly line arrangement. If the employee finds a problem, he or she must decide whether to correct it or put the engine aside to be worked on later.

Plaspac has developed enrichment in some of its machine operator jobs. Operators are given a complete set of tasks, including inspection and quality responsibilities and routine maintenance. They can also request help from maintenance experts for more complex problems. As much as possible, production runs for a particular customer are given to the same operator. The operators receive a wide range of data on their production runs, for both stabilization and improvement purposes.

Quality Circles   Quality circles are another method of employee involvement. A quality circle is a group of employees from the same work unit who volunteer to meet regularly to solve productivity and quality problems, or to improve the existing level of product quality in their work area.

Generally the number of participants ranges from six to twelve, plus a facilitator. A circle will typically meet between four and six hours each month, usually on company time. Recommendations for improvements are made to management, which must approve any changes.

Quality circles are parallel structures, separate and distinct from the organization's regular ongoing activities. Because of this, quality circles can often be initiated with a minimum of disruption to the normally functioning organization and without posing a threat to its overall authority structure. However, circles may encounter resistance from certain functions in the company, such as staff specialists who may feel threatened that suggested improvements reflect poorly on their own performance. Resistance to circles often comes from middle management (Lawler and Mohrman, 1987).

The idea of quality circles originated in Japan and was widely adopted throughout American industry in the latter part of the 1970s and the early 1980s. Unfortunately, American managers misused the practice as an attempt to find a quick fix for deep-rooted strategic problems. This same tendency to look for a quick fix has been apparent in the attempts of many companies to utilize statistical process control.

Companies using quality circles tended to begin with a small number. Because they had participants who were strongly motivated to produce results, the circles achieved significant gains. After this initial period of success, quality circles usually spread throughout the organization and managers then came to believe that a larger number of circles corresponded to a larger number of improvements (Lawler and Mohrman, 1987, p. 43). The first circles usually received considerable attention from management and were implemented with great care; later circles were implemented more mechanically. An entire administrative structure could be created to supervise the proliferation of circle activity.

The idea that quality circles alone lead to improvements in system performance was naive because it ignored the larger systems of the organization which management, not the worker, creates and maintains. This allowed managers and others to believe that their company was doing something about productivity and quality without really doing much at all. Perhaps American industry was so intent on focusing on quality circles because the circles created an illusion of a tangible organizational solution. It was comfortable for the existing organizational power structure, and gave the appearance of constructive action. A mid-level manager could be made responsible for setting up a quality circle, complete with a formal office for purposes of coordination.[1]

Problems emerged as quality circles diffused into an organization-wide activity. These problems included managers becoming more interested in the number of employees participating in the circles instead of the significance of the results, managers often taking too long in responding

---

1. Unfortunately, managers tend to believe that organizational structures can solve their problems.

to suggested improvements, resistance from staff experts who felt employees were intruding on their turf, and a lack of focus on areas of improvement which would add value for the customer. Most companies were unable to sustain quality circles on a broad scale (Lawler and Mohrman, 1987; Cole, 1989). Despite difficulties, in one survey 66 percent of the responding companies still made some use of quality circles, although typically only a limited number of employees were involved (Lawler, Mohrman, and Ledford, 1992). However, the study also reported that "quality circles are seen as less successful than survey feedback and participation groups" (p. 58). Lawler, Mohrman, and Ledford conclude that American companies are not having success with quality circles as a long-term approach to employee involvement. In part, they attribute this to the faddish implementation of circles during the 1980s and speculate that "it is possible that some of the drop in their success rating is due to overuse and misuse" (p. 58). If this is correct, perhaps, like job enrichment, quality circles will quietly reemerge in American business in a more carefully conceptualized and implemented form.

Japanese companies still widely invest in quality circles, and Japanese quality control experts routinely recommend circles as part of a Total Quality system (Ishikawa, 1985). Throughout the 1970s, surveys conducted by the Japanese Ministry of Labor consistently indicated that approximately 40 percent of companies with over 100 employees reported using quality circles. Almost three-quarters of the firms with over 1,000 employees had circles (Japan, Ministry of Labor, 1973, 1977). By 1984, 60 percent of the firms with more than 100 employees and 84 percent of firms with over 5,000 employees engaged in quality circles (Japan, Ministry of Labor, 1985). Quality circles have spread to both the nonmanufacturing operations of Japanese manufacturing companies and to service-sector firms, including restaurants and nightclubs. In use for more than twenty years, and spreading throughout the economy, quality circles seem to have been institutionalized in Japan (Cole, 1989).

Toyota Motor Manufacturing, U.S.A., Inc., in Scott County, Kentucky, has an active quality circle program. Meetings are usually an hour in length, held after normal work hours for first- and third-shift workers and before the start of the second shift. Up to one hour per week of overtime pay is provided for participants. Prizes and awards are given in recognition of cost savings produced by circles.

Although participation is voluntary, management strongly encourages it. The company's intention is for everyone to want to participate and help pursue *kaizen*, or constantly seek improvement. Problems addressed by the circles can fall under the categories of safety, cost reduction, productivity, workability, and quality. However, certain other areas are off limits, specifically wages and salaries, benefits, company operating principles, human resources policies, supplier selections, new model design, sales and marketing policies, and personalities.

Toyota's quality circle program does not function in a vacuum. It is part of a much broader management system supported by a philosophy of management. This philosophy is perhaps best communicated by Fujio Cho, president and CEO of Toyota Motor Manufacturing, U.S.A., Inc., in his message to the student.

▼

QUALITY IN ACTION: A MESSAGE TO THE STUDENT
Fujio Cho, President and CEO, Toyota Motor Manufacturing, U.S.A., Inc.

Toyota Motor Company in Japan has been renowned for its consistent performance in ratings of product quality and customer satisfaction. In the last decade, Toyota has duplicated this success with manufacturing facilities in America. One of Toyota's keys to success has been its emphasis on employee motivation. President and CEO Fujio Cho explains how Toyota Motor Manufacturing, U.S.A., Inc., achieves employee motivation.

Toyota Motor Manufacturing, U.S.A., Inc., began commercial production of Camrys at Georgetown, Kentucky, in July 1988. Since that time, we have matched the quality of our sister plant, the Tsutsumi Plant in Japan. We are approaching our sister plant's performance in productivity. Our Kentucky team members (as we call our employees) are extremely enthusiastic, and they have met all of our challenges. Less than 2 percent of our work force is Japanese. These Japanese are here in the capacity of advisors/coaches to their American counterparts. In other words, the workers on our plant floor are all Americans, and the American team members are running the show even in the area of production engineering and office functions. The Toyota production system does work in America with American workers.

Four main factors for plant operation in a manufacturing company may be expressed as the four Ms. They are: machinery, material, method, and man/woman. The first two are obvious components of any production system. With today's communication and distribution systems, anyone with money can buy state-of-the-art machinery and newly developed material. So, the other two Ms, methods and man/woman, are relatively more important to the success of present-day manufacturing industries. The Toyota production system relies on *kaizen* to continuously improve our methods of work. Managers must ensure that all four Ms are developed in a production system; however, the key M is the human factor.

When I was put in charge of our new plant in Kentucky, I felt that whether the American work force was motivated or not would determine our success or failure in America. At the same time, I also held a firm belief that once we provided a proper environment, American team members would be able to produce the same quality as their counterparts in Japan. I cannot stress enough the fact that, in order to produce high-quality goods at a reasonable cost to satisfy our customers, it is essential that we motivate our work force. How are human beings to be motivated in the workplace? In order to consider this question, we need to think about why people lose their motivation in the workplace.

There are many factors that diminish motivation and make people lose their will to work hard, but one typical case is to make people do as they are told without letting them think. People are often treated as unthinking robots. The ability to think, I believe, is the major difference between human beings and other animals. If we were to treat the workers as mere laboring machines, then there is no difference between the workers and the beasts of burden. It is no wonder that they lose interest in their jobs and the motivation to do a good job.

People tend to lose their motivation:

- when they are not involved
- when they cannot participate in decision making
- when they are not informed of relevant information
- when they do not have any responsibility or authority
- when their work or contribution is not recognized, and so forth

It is our task, then, to find out ways to introduce these motivating factors on the manufacturing floors. In order to do this, we at TMM are taking a two-pronged approach. One is a direct approach in which we spell out necessary measures in the company's basic policy and human resources policy. The other approach is to scatter various motivating elements in our production methods and in the actual workplace. We may call this an indirect approach. As for the direct approach, in our team member handbook we tell the team members that "people are our most important resource and are the most important factor in the success of our organization." Based on this premise, we have taken concrete measures to ensure full communication, to treat everyone fairly, to stress continual education, and so forth. You may already be familiar with this because this kind of thinking and these measures are often called the Japanese management system and are widely publicized. In my opinion, the indirect approach is much more important. My reasoning is this. Our team members in the plant do the same work for eight hours every day, repeating job tasks about 450 times. If jobs are not meaningful to the workers or tend to disregard their dignity as human beings, the psychological damage to the workers could be devastating.

We at Toyota are trying to avoid such situations. The Toyota production system is based on the philosophy of respecting human dignity. In a more concrete sense, this is manifested in the following thoughts:

- Do not make people do work they do not find meaningful.
- *Muda*, or work that does not add value to the product, is a typical example of this. We must eliminate *muda*.
- People use machines, and not the other way around.
- Take measures so that problems are apparent to everyone and encourage team members to correct them.
- Always leave room for people to make decisions in their work.

Achieving employee motivation through the Toyota production system and the philosophy of respect for human dignity are key parts of Toyota's manufacturing strategy for the 1990s. Employee motivation is necessary for Toyota to be number one in customer satisfaction.

▲

Tennessee Eastman's facility in Kingsport, Tennessee, employs almost 8,000 workers who produce more than 300 different chemical, plastic, and fiber products. During the 1980s, the company established quality improvement teams throughout the facility. By the beginning of the 1990s, these teams had evolved into an interlocking structure involving every employee at every level of the complex. In their research on quality circles in the United States, Lawler and Mohrman (1985, 1987) found that those efforts that had a long-term impact on the organization evolved from circles to functioning teams in a manner similar to the Eastman experience. They argue that this is characteristic of the pattern of success for quality circle efforts in United States companies.

Task Forces and Cross-Functional Teams   Task forces are mechanisms for addressing problems and making decisions that have multifunctional implications, i.e., the solution or result must meet different sets of constraints. Further, the expertise for resolving the problem resides somewhere in the organization other than the top. Task forces are very useful mechanisms for resolving some of the cross-functional issues of systems and subsystems. The design team for the new manufacturing line at Plaspac was a task force.

To be effective, a task force must be characterized by the following (Galbraith, 1973):

- Members must be knowledgeable representatives of their functional organization's needs.
- Members must be in a position to speak with authority on behalf of their functional organization.
- Members must have the skills necessary for making decisions on the basis of information and expertise and must not be preoccupied with questions of formal authority.
- Generally, task force activity should be a substantial job obligation for only a few members, while the majority remain more focused on their home department obligations, albeit maintaining a meaningful commitment to the task force.
- Assignment to a task force must be viewed as a sign of being a highly valued employee, with participation being a recognized and rewardable activity.

To succeed, the members of a task force must be committed to resolve the issue in a manner that works for everybody with a stake in the decision. Unfortunately, in many companies people come to task forces with the mind-set of simply protecting their functional department's interests. The result is gridlock. Further, being assigned to task forces must be seen as a signal of the value of a person's potential contribution. This is in contrast to the "who can I spare" mentality many managers have when assigning people to participate.

General Electric is one company with a strong culture of task force participation. People are assigned to task forces very early in their careers with the company. If a young manager is not assigned to any important task forces, it is probably a sign that his or her contributions are not highly valued. Very quickly, new employees pick up the skills of effective task force participation.

In today's business environment, many task forces involve participants from various levels of the organization. The design team for the Plaspac manufacturing line is an example. The team included production workers, a process engineer, a human resources specialist, a supervisor, the plant superintendent, and the plant controller. The necessary expertise from various functions is often found at different levels of the organization. Members must respect each other for their expertise and contributions, not for their formal rank. In an American automobile company, a task force was created to resolve a drivetrain problem. One manager assigned an engineer with the proper expertise to the task force. However, once the manager found out that higher-level people from other departments were participating, he replaced the engineer with himself. This manager was not familiar with the problem and missed several meetings. Not surprisingly, this was not a particularly effective task force; in fact, the incident itself reveals a culture that does not deal well with task force mechanisms.

Senior executives who accept ownership for systems and middle managers who focus on their component subsystems, rather than on functional turf, are important elements in creating a culture that supports task force involvement. One of the more naive actions management can take is assigning subordinates to task forces with the instruction to cooperate even while management continues to argue over functional issues.

Del Norte Technology's ad hoc task teams are asked to solve specific problems, often across functional lines. They are successful because each task team is formed by a member of a corrective action team composed of middle-level managers. This corrective action team is in close communication with the quality steering committee which determines corporate strategy and direction. These task teams are functioning within a climate that supports their cross-functional objectives.

Labor-Management Action Teams   Management must forge a partnership with employees which recognizes the role of any unions that represent the workers. Building this new relationship may not be easy in an organization with a history of an adversarial relationship between management and labor. Considerable doubt will exist on both sides which may take a period of years to overcome.

One employee involvement mechanism through which this partnership relationship manifests itself is in labor-management action teams. Such action teams are temporary parallel problem-solving units which acknowledge the role of the union.

Xerox established such teams as part of its strategy to reduce its decline during the 1980s (Lazes, Rumpeltes, Hoffner, Pace, and Costanza, 1991). The company and the Amalgamated Clothing and Textile Workers Union (ACTWU) Local 14-A, which represents the hourly workers at Xerox, embarked on a cooperative effort to reduce costs and compete effectively. The ACTWU requested that management set up a joint labor-management study/action team to find ways to restructure and reduce costs in the departments in which its members worked. As a consequence, labor-management teams were established. Team members, which included engineers, managers, and hourly employees, were relieved of their regular jobs for six months to concentrate full-time on investigating a specific economic or business problem that affected their work area. As might be expected, problems occurred throughout the process, some of which were addressed as the teams completed their tasks. Other problems of labor-management relations remain. However, important gains were achieved. Management and labor must be prepared for a long-term sustained effort as they learn new ways of working together.

Mistakes to Be Avoided When Implementing Employee Involvement

Employee involvement is not a panacea. Nor is it an end in itself. Employee involvement makes sense when it is part of a systemic effort directed toward helping an organization improve the value it provides to its customers. Effective employee involvement takes patience on the part of management, as does the implementation of the customer value strategy itself. Here is a checklist of some common mistakes to be avoided, with some suggestions about how to avoid making them:

- Initiating a lot of activity in the absence of a systematic strategy and long-term implementation plan linking employee involvement to customer value gains.
  Suggestion The most significant gains are made in systems and processes which, when improved, will deliver immediate gains to the customer. Management should target employee involvement efforts toward those systems and processes.
- Initiating employee involvement activity without active, hands-on leadership from management.
  Suggestion Senior management must do more than mandate employee involvement. It must function as a team itself, modeling and teaching the skills wanted at lower levels of the organization. Frequent interaction with employees must occur.
- Counting activity (such as the number of quality improvement teams meeting) rather than measurable improvements.

Suggestion Rather than broad-scale implementation, focus initial efforts on high-leverage areas. Identify and measure the indicators of process or system performance.

- Unrealistic plans and expectations.
  Suggestion Select a few companies that started from a comparable point, employee relations history, management history, etc., and have successfully involved employees in improvement at all levels. Study their experiences. If such companies cannot be found, take the initial timeline and double it. Then double it again. Ask if management is prepared to stay the course.

- Using training as a measure of progress.
  Suggestion Training is critical, but it is a means to an end. Training is more effective if used immediately and perceived as relevant. Therefore, do not let training get ahead of actual implementation.

- Expecting it to be finished.
  Suggestion Continue to state, every day, that employee involvement is a key method in a strategy that requires continuous work and improvement. Methods may evolve, but the job is never done.

Human Resource Implications of Employee Involvement

If improving customer value is to prove effective, the systems and processes that are put in place in order to operationalize this strategy must be staffed by highly qualified people. People must be regarded as critical system elements who are managed and developed for quality and consistency (Pace and Bounds, 1991). System owners must assume primary responsibility for ensuring that this occurs. The human resources (HR) department has to come to view system owners as their primary internal customers and, accordingly, learn how to understand and provide value to them. This will require human resource professionals to create HR subsystems which deliver value to system owners by assisting them in achieving their strategic objectives. Like everyone else in the company, HR will have to stabilize and continuously improve their subsystems.

The Traditional Human Resource Perspective: Focus on the Individual   Traditionally, the human resources department has viewed its contribution to organizational performance through the functions of selection, performance appraisal, compensation and rewards, and development. These generic functions have been described as:

> *selecting* people who are best able to perform the jobs defined by the structure, *appraising* their performance to facilitate the equitable distribution of rewards, motivating employees by linking *rewards* to high levels of performance, and *developing* employees to enhance their current performance at work as well as to prepare them to perform in positions they may hold in the future. [Devanna, Fombrun, and Tichy, 1984, p. 41]

In executing these functions, HR practices have focused almost exclusively on the individual. Individually focused criteria define the job, and people are selected and evaluated accordingly. Rewards are administered to the individual based on his or her performance. Developmental needs are determined based on this appraisal of current individual performance.

Bounds and Pace (1991) have identified six assumptions implied by this individualistic approach:

1. The individual is largely in control of his or her own performance variation.
2. Supervisors can accurately distinguish individual performance.
3. Individual contributions to system performance are reflected in individual job performance criteria.
4. The administration of contingent rewards and punishments at the individual level ensures future performance.
5. Differentiating among individuals with regard to levels of performance, compensation, and status serves important organizational purposes.
6. These traditional functions of selecting, appraising, rewarding, and developing individuals are adequate vehicles for managing organizational change, enhancing systemic performance, and creating customer value.

These assumptions can all be seriously questioned in light of the new paradigm. Deming (1986) has made the argument that it is the systems provided by management that determine employee performance. If these systems are poorly designed and managed, the employee cannot perform up to expectations. An HR manager at Plaspac made that point by saying: "We punished people for years because of poor performance, while deep in our hearts we knew they could not do any better. They were victims of circumstances and management failure."

These assumptions also reflect a reductionistic perspective which holds that aggregated individual performance ensures overall system performance. Yet system performance depends on individuals directing their efforts toward optimizing the end product of customer value, not optimizing their own individual performance. In fact, sometimes it is necessary for the individual to sacrifice individual activity in support of the overall system.

The New Human Resources Focus As organizations shift toward a paradigm that embraces systems and teams, human resources departments will also have to focus on providing value to their customers through supporting the systems developed to provide customer value. HR professionals must become consultants, coproducers, and collaborators in the creation and improvement of organizational systems. Schuler (1990) has identified several emerging roles for HR, including business person, shaper of change, consultant to the line organization, strategy formulator and implementor, talent manager, and asset manager.

This change in perspective has proven difficult for many human resource professionals. Many HR managers are struggling with how to redefine the relationship between the organization and the employee. Where a few years ago HR professionals could present an employee with a defined career path, today they must serve to help employees stay abreast of the future needs of the organization in terms of the competencies and skills required by evolving organizational systems. Their primary client is now the organization, rather than employees or their superiors.

In one insurance company, the human resources function was completely reorganized. Responsibility for most human resource activity was shifted to the line organization. HR practitioners in the field were placed into generalist roles from which they were to serve as consultants or advisors to the line organization. Removed from their technical specialties, many of these HR professionals were experiencing significant anxiety about their ability to channel their expertise toward business goals. This concern was rooted in uncertainty about their ability to establish and maintain effective relationships with line managers.

In the emerging paradigm, the primary responsibility for managing human resources rests with the system owners and middle managers of the organization (Pace and Bounds, 1991). This requires not only significant adjustment on the part of HR professionals, but line managers as well. Line managers have often treated people as disposable commodities, regarding development as a necessary evil and seeking to minimize the costs of training and education. This approach to human resources significantly inhibits efforts to "pull" employees into making contributions to system performance.

Human Resource Practices Employee involvement requires innovation in human resource practices. Monetary rewards over and above base salary/wages should be tied to organizational accomplishment. Additionally, skill-based compensation systems become a basis for determining compensation based on *potential* contribution to the organization. A person is paid on the basis of certified skills. Usually tiers of skill clusters are established. A new employee is paid at an entry-level pay rate when he or she first enters a work unit. Once capable of performing a basic set of functions, the employee receives the next higher rate. A third tier is reached when the employee can perform all the tasks or functions within the work unit or team. A fourth tier might reflect special skills which are periodically needed at the work site. This is in contrast to traditional job-based compensation systems which pay the individual employee based on the specific job he or she is actually doing at a particular point in time. Skill-based pay encourages the development of a range of skills and rewards employees for the flexibility they provide the work unit.

Companies that have instituted these types of compensation systems report them to be quite successful (Lawler, Mohrman, and Ledford, 1992). A survey of Fortune 1000 companies indicated that companies are much more likely to increase rather than decrease their use of skill-based pay (Lawler, Ledford, and Chang, 1992). This survey confirmed that organizations attempting to use Total Quality Management are significantly more likely to use skill-based pay. Skill-based pay is expected to be an important element of the emerging paradigm.

Cross-training becomes a significant issue in employee involvement. It must be effective and available to employees. Making development a high priority is a major human resource issue. In organizations making extensive use of teams, the development of technical and team competencies is a team responsibility. Usually a team member is responsible for ensuring that other team members have access to training.

At Plaspac, one member of the new production line team is responsible for scheduling training for team members, ensuring that the content of the training meets current task requirements, and verifying the competency of each member of the team. At Saturn, training is initially the responsibility of the charter team member. As the team enters the norming stage of group development, this responsibility is absorbed into the team, with monitoring by the charter members.

Managers should be careful how they link this team responsibility for training to the pay-for-skills concept. At Cormetech, a joint venture between Corning and Mitsubishi to produce catalytic converters for power plants, under the pay-for-skills system three team members must certify that a worker has achieved the required skill level in order for the worker to qualify for a pay-level increase. Unfortunately, this approach can put people into conflict and invite political turmoil.

While striving for continuous improvement, organizations find their staffing requirements to be highly fluid. Making breakthroughs in processes often involves the redesign of work in a way that streamlines operations. This is especially true for financial services companies like Banc One, First Bank System, and others who are scrambling to utilize new technology to streamline their back-office operations. This redesign often involves a combination of functions, having a number of tasks simultaneously completed in a single operation. Estimates are that redesign of work processes in commercial banks and thrift institutions will reduce staffing needs by 30 to 40 percent by the end of the century (*Wall Street Journal*, Mar. 3, 1993, "Price of Progress"). This kind of change significantly alters the employment relationship. Instead of security, companies must now offer employees *employability security*; opportunities for them to develop those competencies that will enable them to maintain employability within or outside the company. Companies must regularly highlight those competencies that are highly valued by the organization and the larger workplace, and provide opportunities for people to acquire and demonstrate these abilities. These opportunities include on-line training, special job assignments, and rotational job assignments. Companies must also put in place processes that ensure staffing decisions are made based on demonstrated competencies.

Unfortunately, human resource development can present an interesting dilemma. Companies are relying increasingly on teamwork, even as companies are reducing the "roster" size of the team, and people are competing for places on teams. Group versus individual tensions present an ongoing challenge to management. Human resource professionals are struggling with how to handle this dilemma. Quite literally, human resource management is undergoing a transformation. The nature of this transformation is just beginning to emerge.

Developing and integrating these and other human resource methods becomes an important human resource role. The above are all examples of support systems that must be effectively linked to customer value systems. This must be done in collaboration with system owners (senior managers).

The role of human resources professionals at Plaspac provides an excellent example. They work with managers who are having difficulty or struggling with the human resource element of their systems, helping them to create, improve, and stabilize human resource subsystems. The success of these subsystems is measured in terms of contribution to strategic goals.

Rather than developing and promoting programs, a small core of human resources professionals keeps abreast of innovations in other companies. They seek to structure opportunities for managers at Plaspac to learn about these experiences firsthand. However, instead of advocating imitation, they encourage discussion and reflection about how these practices would fit into the strategic efforts of the company. This is the human resources role of the future.

▶ SUMMARY OF KEY POINTS

1. Employee involvement is a process for empowering members of organizations to make decisions and solve problems appropriate to their levels in the organization.
2. Employee involvement is not an end in itself, but a vehicle for improving and stabilizing organizational systems that provide customer value.
3. Employee involvement must be established within a strategic context in which system owners and middle managers "pull" employees into the process.
4. Employee involvement will not work if operational-level employees are charged with making improvements while management remains disengaged. Employee

involvement efforts at various levels of the organization must be aligned with each other. This alignment is accomplished through a focus on key systems and processes, and concentrating on improving those elements that impact the customer.

5. Managers and operational employees each have their own domains to which they must commit their talents to achieve superior customer value.

6. Employee involvement takes many different forms, including teams, job enrichment, task forces, quality circles, and labor-management action teams. These methods have been developed over several decades. They acquire new meaning within the context of the emerging paradigm.

7. Teams go through stages of development before they become cohesive, high-performing units. This process of development must be facilitated.

8. Although the emerging paradigm emphasizes standardization, routinization, and stabilization in operational jobs, these require a high level of cooperative effort between employees and the managers who own systems. Employees must fine-tune systems. Further, employees must make decisions in dynamic situations. These efforts give meaning to job enrichment.

9. The idea of quality circles originated in Japan. Unfortunately, American managers misused the practice in an attempt to find a quick fix for deep-rooted strategic problems. Some organizations, however, continue to use them effectively. They are widely used in Japan.

10. Employee involvement requires the creation of innovative human resource practices. These include pay-for-skills compensation systems, peer review systems, cross-training, and the redefinition of the relationship between the organization and its employees. Human resource departments must develop practices that provide value to their client departments.

▶ KEY TERMS

employability security
employee involvement
job-based compensation systems
job enrichment
labor-management action teams
pull model of employee
  involvement

push model of employee
  involvement
quality circles
skill-based pay
task forces
teams

▶ DISCUSSION QUESTIONS

1. What is employee involvement and how does it contribute to customer value?
2. What is a "parallel structure" and what issues does it raise for management?

3. What are the differences between how quality circles were implemented in the United States and how quality circles function in Japan?
4. What are the implications of the MAT for employee involvement?
5. How can job enrichment be compatible with stabilization of work processes?
6. What are each of the following organizational manifestations of employee involvement and how are they different from each other? Teams, job enrichment, quality circles, task forces, and labor-management action teams.
8. How is the human resource function being impacted by employee involvement and the move toward the emerging paradigm?

▶ DISCUSSION EXERCISE

- Working within a group of five or six other students, have each member think of a work experience. How could employee involvement methods been used to improve the value being delivered to the customer? What method(s) would have been appropriate? What would management's role have to be for this method to work? How do your observations about the potential for employee involvement fit with the "pull" model discussed in this chapter? Prepare a summary of your conclusions about employee involvement.

▶ REFERENCES

G. M. Bounds and L. A. Pace, "Human Resource Management for Competitive Capability," in M. J. Stahl and G. M. Bounds (eds.), *Competing Globally through Customer Value: The Management of Strategic Suprasystems*, Quorum Books, New York, 1991.

C. Brown and M. Reich, "When Does Union-Management Cooperation Work? A Look at NUMMI and GM-Van Nuys," *California Management Review*, Vol. 29, No. 4, 1989, pp. 26–44.

R. Y. Chang, "When TQM Goes Nowhere," *Training and Development*, Vol. 47, No. 1, 1993, pp. 25–29.

R. E. Cole, *Strategies for Learning: Small-Group Activities in American, Japanese, and Swedish Industry*, University of California Press, Berkeley, Calif., 1989.

L. E. Davis and A. B. Cherns, "Transition to More Meaningful Work," in Davis, Cherns, and Associates (eds.), *The Quality of Working Life*, Vol. 2, *Cases and Commentary*, Free Press, New York, 1975, pp. 270–283.

E. Deming, *Out of the Crisis*, MIT Press, Cambridge, Mass., 1986.

M. A. Devanna, C. J. Fombrun, and N. M. Tichy, "A Framework for Strategic Human Resource Management," in C. J. Fombrun, N. M. Tichy, and M. A. Devanna (eds.), *Strategic Human Resource Management*, Wiley, New York, 1984.

J. R. Galbraith, *Designing Complex Organizations*, Addison-Wesley, Reading, Mass., 1973.

J. R. Hackman, "Is Job Enrichment Just a Fad?" *Harvard Business Review*, Vol. 53, No. 5, 1975, pp. 129–138.

J. R. Hackman and G. R. Oldham, *Work Redesign*, Addison-Wesley, Reading, Mass., 1980.

J. R. Hackman, G. R. Oldham, R. Janson, and K. Purdy, "A New Strategy for Job Enrichment," *California Management Review*, Vol. 17, No. 4, 1975, pp. 57–71.

F. Herzberg, *Work and the Nature of Man*, World, New York, 1966.

K. Ishikawa, *What Is Total Quality Control?* translated by David J. Lu, Prentice-Hall, Englewood Cliffs, N.J., 1985.

J. M. Judge, "Bill Arnold: TQM Champion," *Health Care Financial Management.*, Vol. 6, No. 9, 1992, pp. 20–24.

J. E. Kelly, *Scientific Management, Job Redesign and Work Performance*, Academic Press, New York, 1982.

E. E. Lawler III, *High-Involvement Management*, Jossey-Bass, San Francisco, Calif., 1986.

E. E. Lawler III and S. Mohrman, "Quality Circles: After the Fad," *Harvard Business Review*, Vol. 63, No. 1, 1985, pp. 65–71.

E. E. Lawler III and S. Mohrman, "Quality Circles: After the Honeymoon," *Organizational Dynamics*, Vol. 15, No. 4, 1987, pp. 42–54.

E. E. Lawler III, G. E. Ledford, and L. Chang, "Who Uses Skill-Based Pay, and Why They Use It," *CEO Publication G 92-17 (220)*, Center for Effective Organizations, School of Business Administration, University of Southern California, Los Angeles, 1992.

E. E. Lawler III, S. Mohrman, and G. E. Ledford, Jr., *Employee Involvement and Total Quality Management*, Jossey-Bass, San Francisco, Calif., 1992.

P. Lazes, L. Rumpeltes, A. Hoffner, L. Pace, and A. Costanza, "Xerox and the ACTWU: Using Labor-Management Teams to Remain Competitive," *National Productivity Review*, Vol. 10, No. 3, 1991, pp. 339–349.

R. J. Magjuka and T. T. Baldwin, "Team-Based Employee Involvement Programs: Effects of Design and Administration," *Personnel Psychology*, Vol. 44, No. 4, 1991, pp. 793–812.

T. Ohno, *Workplace Management*, The Productivity Press, Cambridge, Mass., 1988.

L. A. Pace, "Moving toward Systems Integration," *Survey of Business*, Vol. 25, No. 1, 1989, pp. 57–61.

L. A. Pace and G. M. Bounds, "Linking Human Resource Management and Customer Value," unpublished working paper, 1991.

H. L. Schneider, C. Schneider, and D. Riley, "Clearing a Hurdle to Quality," *Quality Progress*, Vol. 24, No. 9, 1991, pp. 39–41.

R. S. Schuler, "Repositioning the Human Resource Function: Transformation or Demise?" *Academy of Management Executive*, Vol. 4, No. 3, 1990, pp. 49–60.

S. Shiba, "Japan, Today and Yesterday: Its Search for a Successful Development," paper presented at the Manila Hilton Hotel, Nov. 25, 1983 (cited in Cole, 1989).

S. Shingo, *Non-Stock Production: The Shingo System for Continuous Improvement*, The Productivity Press, Cambridge, Mass., 1988.

S. Shingo, *The Shingo Production Management System: Improving Process Functions*, The Productivity Press, Cambridge, Mass., 1990.

K. W. Thomas, "Conflict and Conflict Management," in M. D. Dunnette (ed.), *Handbook of Industrial and Organizational Psychology*, Rand McNally, Chicago, 1976, pp. 889–935.

G. F. Truell, *Employee Involvement: A Guidebook for Managers*, PAT Publications, Buffalo, N.Y., 1991.

B. W. Tuckman, "Developmental Sequence in Small Groups," *Psychological Bulletin*, Vol. 54, 1965, pp. 229–249.

R. S. Wellins, W. C. Byham, and J. M. Wilson, *Empowered Teams: Creating Self-Directed Work Groups That Improve Quality, Productivity, and Participation*, Jossey-Bass, San Francisco, Calif., 1991.

D. A. Whitsett, "Where Are Your Unenriched Jobs?" *Harvard Business Review*, Vol. 53, No. 1, 1975.

L. Yorks, *Job Enrichment Revisited*, AMACOM, New York, 1979.

L. Yorks and D. A. Whitsett, *Scenarios of Change: Advocacy and the Diffusion of Job Redesign in Organizations*, Praeger, New York, 1989.

chapter **12**

Cultural Change and Organizational Learning

There is nothing more difficult to carry out, nor more doubtful of success, nor more dangerous to handle, than to initiate a new order of things.

Machiavelli, The Prince

▶ **CHAPTER OUTLINE**

Chapter Overview

Introduction

TQM at Advanced Computer Technology: Journey into Cultural Change

Change and Organizational Culture

The Difficulty of Triggering Change
Cultural Change as a Paradigm Shift

Causing a Transformational Change

The Baldrige Award as a Trigger for Change
The Critical Path of Change
Frame-Breaking Change
Leverage Points for Driving Transformational Change
Cultural Impediments to Transformational Change

Assessing Organizational Culture

Who Should Do the Cultural Analysis
Data Gathering

Organizational Learning and Transformational Change

Espoused Theory and Theory in Use
Double Loop versus Single Loop Learning
Continuous Improvement Requires Continuous Learning

Conclusion

Summary of Key Points

Key Terms

Discussion Questions

Discussion Exercise

References

▶ **CHAPTER OVERVIEW**

Transformational change is very difficult to effect in organizations. Recent research suggests that change "programs" and extensive studies and discussions about an organization's culture usually do not lead to meaningful change. Changing roles and responsibilities is the key to successfully initiating change. This chapter examines different approaches to change and identifies some of the significant levers which help effect it. Although discussions about culture do not lead to change, culture is important. An organization's culture can impede change toward the emerging paradigm. Therefore, it is important that managers leading change have a valid understanding of their culture in order to facilitate the change process. This chapter presents methods for assessing an organization's culture while the organization is changing. Finally, the importance of adopting a posture of organizational members learning their way through change is discussed.[1]

▶ **INTRODUCTION**

Over the centuries, Machiavelli's observation about the difficulty of change has been supported repeatedly. Companies attempting to implement quality, Total Quality, or continuous improvement programs have found this process difficult and have met with limited success. Of 500 executives at major U.S. companies surveyed in 1992, only 36 percent believed their quality programs had improved their competitiveness (Arthur D. Little

---

1. This chapter was written from a managerial perspective of changing the organization. It does not adequately address other important issues, such as how individual employees deal with change.

Consulting, 1992 survey). In another survey of ninety-five corporations, 88 percent gave their quality efforts a failing grade (Rath and Strong Consulting, 1992 survey). Perhaps, these results are primarily due to how managers have pursued quality.

Do these surveys reflect the failure of the concepts and techniques, or the failure of the implementors? Or perhaps the problem is the impatience of managers to see their programs through? Certainly all of these elements contribute. But one of the primary reasons such efforts fail is that managers approach the change process from the perspective of implementing a program. The program approach is inadequate because moving the organization toward a comprehensive new approach such as the emerging paradigm is not the same as adding a new program to employee training. Rather, it requires a transformation of the organizational culture through a process of ongoing organizational learning. If managers understand the implications of transformational change for the organizational culture, they are more likely to avoid the disappointing failures of program implementation.

This chapter examines and provides methods and tools for confronting and resolving the many paradoxes of transformational change and the creation of a new organizational culture that supports the emerging paradigm. We will begin by looking at a detailed example of the difficulties of implementing transformational change.

▶ TQM AT ADVANCED COMPUTER TECHNOLOGY: JOURNEY INTO CULTURAL CHANGE

Advanced Computer Technology (ACT) is a niche computer manufacturer of on-line systems.[2] The company's products have proven highly successful in carving out a market in large and mid-range system applications for the retail industry and banking and financial services, among others.

As the industry became more competitive, CEO Frank Williams became convinced that managing quality was going to become a critical competitive factor in the 1990s. The industry was in the throes of a massive shakedown. Wang, a major player, seemed to be on the verge of bankruptcy. Digital was struggling through consecutive downsizings, and IBM was about to initiate its first major staffing reduction. A sluggish market was squeezing profits. ACT entered into strategic alliances with other firms, and found itself representing a quality standard that it did not control. The shift in the industry's landscape had been subtle, but had monumental effects. Williams believed that ACT was playing in an entirely different arena.

In 1990, Williams called his division managers together and told them to initiate a push for installing a "contemporary quality program." He gave them copies of suggested readings and hired a consultant to work with the group.

---

2. Advanced Computer Technology is a pseudonym.

Although there was an initial flourish of activity, a year later the effort had produced little visible progress. Most of the division heads were not convinced of a need for change and were simply going through the motions while putting their energies into tasks on which they placed a high priority.

Realizing that nothing was going to happen, Williams scheduled an off-site management meeting for all senior and key upper middle management employees. Williams then established a quality council consisting of himself, the five division heads, and a vice president who was given the assignment of coordinating the quality effort. After these initiatives, support among the division heads still varied, but it was clear that they would be required to engage in the process.

The quality council was responsible for strategic and annual tactical plans, formulating a vision built on quality, identifying critical success factors and indicators, and providing resources. Five teams were established, each supervised by a division head, and were charged with developing and monitoring a specific critical success factor assigned by the quality council. Facilitator training was provided to senior executives and members of the teams.

Following the completion of these activities, each division established a quality implementation team and a series of process improvement teams. Meanwhile, the company opened a greenfield site plant in Europe.[3] Key members of the management team who had been active in trying to put together a process for the major U.S. production facility volunteered to go to Europe in the hope that they would be more successful there.

The European plant has been successful, leading to some changes in the U.S. operation. However, progress remains slow and difficult. As ACT struggles to implement its program, it has become clear that certain elements of its culture are inhibiting the effort. In the product development department, ACT's policy had been to hire the most talented person it could find to head up a project, expecting that person to carry out the job with little or no involvement with other groups. This fostered a culture that ran counter to a team approach. The product development processes that evolved from this approach are not documented, and efforts to get them documented are met with tremendous resistance. On the production side of the company, individualism also seems to be the dominant management mode.

The way people are recognized in the organization also presents a significant cultural inhibitor of change. People who respond quickly to trouble spots, especially where customers are involved, are recognized and rewarded. This aspect of the culture encourages ambitious crisis managers to find a spark, fan it into a small fire, and then rush in to put it out. For

---

3. A greenfield site is a new work facility which is specifically created according to a particular management philosophy or model, often to demonstrate the viability of that model. The facility is located, planned, and staffed according to the principles of the model (in this case, Total Quality Management) and is shielded as much as possible from the influence of the traditional organizational culture and practices.

example, a fire may be a bug in the software, which is first escalated, then eliminated. Efforts to implement a continuous improvement attitude with a goal of eliminating fires is therefore counter to this process through which people become recognized for handling crises.

In the status hierarchy of the company, product development is the elite. The lead person of a product development team is greatly associated with the end product. The other members of the team receive some recognition. Input from other areas of the company to product development is given little recognition. This focuses attention on key individuals and is counter to efforts to emphasize cross-functional systems.

Because these entrenched ways of functioning have come into conflict with the emerging effort toward Total Quality Management and, more recently, a focus on cross-functional process geared to providing and enhancing customer value, progress has been stalled.

ACT's experience illustrates the important role of culture when making a transformational change. For most organizations, managers and employees alike must collectively build new knowledge and learn new skills and come to a new way of defining the meaning of their work. This cannot be imposed, but should grow out of a process involving all members of the organization in creating a new cultural framework. The power of the existing culture can seriously impede this process. Moreover, because those initiating the change are also part of this culture, their own instincts and actions will often work against what they are trying to accomplish. At ACT, Williams tried to initiate change without changing his own style of operating. Little happened until Williams himself changed his behavior.

▶ CHANGE AND ORGANIZATIONAL CULTURE

Organizations are constantly changing. Procedures change, approved ways of executing work are altered, products are modified, and people are reassigned. Much of this change goes unnoticed because it occurs within the context of the core culture; existing power relationships remain intact, there are no new demands to upset the major existing skill sets, and existing behavior patterns remain functional. Over time, the cumulative impact of these changes may be substantial. However, because the process occurs so slowly, people are rarely upset by it.

These ongoing evolutionary changes do not necessarily change those elements of the core culture that are thoroughly learned and taken for granted (Schein, 1984, 1990). Basic assumptions and core values and beliefs stabilize and preserve the fundamental cultural paradigm of the organization, and guide and constrain the evolutionary change that takes place. A strong, well-developed core culture is not easily changed. Before further considering the process of change, it will be instructive to consider just how difficult this process can be.

The Difficulty of Triggering Change

The stabilizing function of an existing core culture can counteract modest efforts toward transformational change. ACT has provided us with a good example, especially in how the recognition process works. The positive reinforcement of receiving individual recognition worked against efforts at moving toward a new paradigm. As the ACT case demonstrates, transformational cultural change can be difficult to achieve. Part of this difficulty arises from the taken-for-granted nature of the assumptions that make up the cultural paradigm. Among the assumptions shared by people throughout ACT is the idea that a high level of company performance is ensured by depending on the individual talents of particular people. Another assumption is that customer value is generated mostly in the inventive aspects of the product development process. Still another is that those people who should advance in the organization will emerge through taking advantage of crises. This last assumption places the primary focus on individual responses, rather than the systemic causes of a particular crisis.

These cultural assumptions represent trusted solutions for dealing with external and internal relationships. As a group develops a shared history, cultural assumptions tend to become aligned with one another, forming a mutually reinforcing pattern or paradigm. At ACT, the practice of hiring the best individuals and letting them develop product with little input from other groups was aligned with the cultural norm that the way to get recognized was to develop a reputation as a "good firefighter." Both rested on a deep-seated cultural value of individualism.

General Motors is another example of an organization that had a strong culture which blinded it to the competitive challenges of the global marketplace. Executives and managers throughout the company initially failed to take seriously the threat of Japanese carmakers, with their different approach to the importance of quality and methods for achieving it. GM was also slow to realize the extent to which domestic competitor Ford Motor Company was changing. Once GM recognized the challenge, following significant financial and market share losses, changing the systems and processes through which the company functioned proved difficult. In 1993, after several years of trying, the company was still struggling with change. General Motors' experience is consistent with the findings of Dennison (1990) that cultures which were less strong and less coherent at one time were correlated with greater organizational effectiveness in the future. Conversely, some strong cultures eventually led to a deterioration in organizational performance. This is reflective of an interesting dilemma: Organizations with strong cultures which reinforce success under a certain set of business conditions find it difficult to change when the paradigm changes. A strong culture can drive success. It can also impede transformational change.

Transformational change often occurs only when a series of events external to the organization cause people at all levels to examine their basic assumptions, a process known as *unfreezing* (Lewin, 1951). The experience of losing market share, suddenly finding that the market does not automatically respond to the company's new products or services, or confronting an emergent competitor can precipitate such reflection and examination. Beer, Eisenstat, and Spector (1990) found that the greatest change most often occurs in those work units confronted by severe competitive challenge, although they suggest that executives can create similar challenges in the absence of such conditions. Most of the companies who are recognized as pioneering the emerging paradigm, including Motorola, Inc., and Xerox, became committed to change when they believed they were on the verge of failure.

One of the paradoxes of organizational life is that the time to begin changing is before a competitive crisis emerges. When an organization is in a position of strength, resources are available to support the change effort and time is on the side of the organization (Yorks and Whitsett, 1989). By the time a crisis is recognized, it is difficult, and sometimes impossible, to regain a meaningful competitive advantage.

Unfortunately, managers and employees don't want to change when things appear to be going well. "If it's not broke, don't fix it" is an attitude that breeds complacency and ignores the fact that the leader in any competition is everyone else's target. In a competitive market, an organization that is not improving is losing ground. In fact, improving is not enough; to gain ground one has to be improving at a faster rate than the competition.

Cultural Change as a Paradigm Shift

Paradigms provide the model problems, methods, and style of explanation that guide the scientific enterprise at any one particular point in time. Organizational culture serves as a paradigm for members of the organization; it is used to determine which problems receive attention, to interpret events, and as a common language. A shared scientific paradigm provides a consensus about the rules and standards for how a particular research tradition is continued and extended. Similarly, an organization's cultural paradigm allows its members to confront problems from a common and accepted perspective.

Culture is a social paradigm. A paradigm has three characteristics, each of which holds important implications for changing organizations:

1. A *social matrix* consisting of everyone who accepts a certain way of looking at the world, and the practices consistent with that view.
2. A *way of looking at the world* consisting of the *cognitive approaches* and *emotional responses* of the social matrix, such as images of the organization and beliefs about how things work in it.
3. A *way of doing things* consisting of *methods* and *practices* exemplifying ways of doing things (Ledford, Mohrman, Mohrman, and Lawler, 1989; Mohrman and Lawler, 1985).

A manager advocating change must address each of these points as it relates to his or her organization. Changing a paradigm involves a shift in mental frameworks, as well as a search for new approaches, methods, and technologies.

The leverage points for change are found in the role relationships and in the various systems of the organization. These provide the primary context within which social and interpersonal dynamics are shaped. Changes in these elements of the organization need to be accompanied by processes of learning. People need to examine their assumptions because the organization's existing culture can inhibit or even defeat efforts toward implementing the emerging paradigm. Devising a strategy that overcomes these points of contradiction between the existing culture and the emerging paradigm is essential to a successful change effort. In turn, cultural change requires an accurate understanding of the existing culture. Later in this chapter, we will address some methods that are useful for assessing an organization's culture. First, however, we consider the change process itself.

▶ CAUSING A TRANSFORMATIONAL CHANGE

Organizational development professionals have long wrestled with the question of whether managers should focus on structures and systems or culture in trying to effect change. The quick answer is, simply, both. However, this requires intense, focused, and prolonged attention to the managerial leadership task. This task includes establishing those systems, processes, practices, and roles necessary for implementing a customer value strategy. These system changes, along with the behaviors they require, must drive the change process. The changes need to be supported by the appropriate tools so that people throughout the organization can put the strategy into practice. However, a strategy for change must be devised. How a management team goes about changing an organization is as important as the actual changes being put in place.

Various approaches are advocated in the management literature. These include the Baldrige award, the critical path of change model, and the frame-breaking change model.

The Baldrige Award as a Trigger for Change

The Malcolm Baldrige National Quality Award is sponsored by the Department of Commerce. Through a formal application process, each year a board of examiners is selected to review applications from companies applying for the award. The board of examiners consists of more than 250 quality professionals from business, professional, and trade organizations, accrediting bodies, universities, and government agencies. Companies compete in one of three categories: manufacturing, service, or small business. The review process is extensive and involves a series of stages, including site visits by examiners. Selection criteria are divided into seven "pillars" which together comprise the Baldrige quality framework: leadership, information and analysis, strategic quality planning, human resource development and management, management of process quality, quality and operational results, and customer focus and satisfaction (Hart and Bogan, 1992).

Some management teams have challenged their organizations to compete for the Baldrige award. The value of winning the award has become a topic of controversy within the management community (see Garvin, 1991, and Debate, *Harvard Business Review*, 1992). Supporters of the award argue that it has significantly raised the consciousness of executives about the importance of quality issues in the global marketplace and has provided a comprehensive framework for measuring quality efforts. Robert Galvin, chairman of Motorola's executive committee, maintains that the Baldrige award "*is* the most important catalyst for transforming American business" (1992, pp. 136–137). Others maintain that the award fails to provide an adequate conceptualization of quality and uses poor and out-of-date criteria. Crosby observes that companies nominate themselves for the award (unlike awards such as the Nobel and Pulitzer prizes). Furthermore, Crosby argues, the only opinions that count in quality are those of the customers (1992). He further reports that senior management is passing the criteria package to committees in their company and backing away from the process (p. 128). Deming (1992, p. 134) argues that the Baldrige award criteria do not address the management of quality, and transgress what he teaches. The results for a given period measured by the award criteria can be, Deming notes, purely a function of chance.

A skillful leader can utilize an award like the Baldrige as one leverage point for change. However, the award should not become the primary focus of the change effort, nor should its criteria displace meaningful indicators of performance in terms of customer value. Should senior management choose to utilize the award competition as a lever for change, it must remain actively engaged in the process of pursuing it. Further, senior management must ensure that the award not become an end in itself. There is no guarantee that winning an award contributes to a company's strategic purpose. This has been the attitude of Florida Power and Light's CEO, James Broadhead. Even though the company won the Deming Prize the previous year, in 1990 Broadhead set out to restructure the organization. He felt the company had become too laden with a staff bureaucracy which had grown out of the company's initial efforts toward winning the Deming Prize. Broadhead set out to continuously improve without maintaining extensive staff support. The restructuring was directed toward transforming the organization and its culture. In the restructuring, responsibility for quality performance was embedded into a lean-line organization.

In the aftermath of the worst hurricane in recent memory, Hurricane Andrew, 1.5 million of FPL's 5 million customers lost electricity. FPL's customers whose power could be restored were back on line within thirty days. (There were about 75,000 customers who had sustained such damage to their homes that electricity could not be turned on.) Larry Kelleher, vice president of human resources at FPL, says that one of the keys was that the leaner bureaucracy empowered field personnel and front-line managers to make important decisions in the field. One VP could now take control of the resources he needed, whereas before that VP might have depended on six different officials to get resources together. Meetings, phone calls, and check-on procedures would have been required (*Redeployment Issues*, 1993).

▼

QUALITY IN ACTION: A MESSAGE TO THE STUDENT
James L. Broadhead, Chairman and CEO, Florida Power and Light Company

In 1989, Florida Power and Light Company won the coveted Deming Prize, which was created by the Japanese Union of Scientists and Engineers (JUSE) to recognize outstanding quality management. In the meantime, FPL became almost too enthusiastic about quality. FPL's quality initiative itself became an overgrown bureaucracy, more focused on the quality process than on serving customers. Chairman and CEO James L. Broadhead explains how FPL has streamlined its approach to quality and refocused its business.

The rapid development of technological improvements and the emergence of new managerial techniques over the past several decades have distracted many major corporations from the most basic fundamentals of business—the importance of understanding your customers, your competition, and developing and utilizing the skills and knowledge of front-line employees.

The refocusing of organizations back to these basic business fundamentals has recently been packaged in an approach labeled "Total Quality Management." We at Florida Power and Light Company (FPL) call it "QIP" (i.e., Quality Improvement Process), or more simply, the "systematic application of common sense."

These business basics are embodied in the four principles of our QIP, which are:

1. *Customer satisfaction*: Quality is judged by the customer. Therefore, FPL must meet and surpass customer requirements and remain constantly on the alert to emerging customer trends. Quality includes all service and product attributes that contribute value to the customer and influence customer satisfaction and preference.

2. *Continuous improvement*: This means that FPL cannot stand still. The level of quality that was acceptable in the past must be raised to new levels. New products, better service, error reduction, better responsiveness, improved productivity, and more effective use of resources are some of the results

of a philosophy of continuous improvement. The overall goal is to raise performance to a higher level that distinguishes FPL from its competitors.

3. *Management by fact:* All employees must manage their work responsibilities based upon reliable information. This requires objective data collection and appropriate analyses which result in solutions to problems and decisions that properly consider the associated risks.

4. *Employee development:* Each individual is valuable to the organization. Education and training courses, together with on-the-job coaching, enable FPL employees to grow in their jobs by acquiring additional skills and advancing their careers. The company's working environment empowers employees to make decisions and to accept reasonable risks in performing their jobs.

To fully incorporate these principles into our organization, we use a framework that integrates the tools and techniques of QIP (such as quality improvement teams and process improvement) into all our business activities and directly supports our corporation's vision and strategies.

It is important for you as future managers to learn and understand how to apply the quality tools and techniques such as Pareto charts, cause and effect diagrams, etc. However, we at FPL also recognize that QIP is not the end objective, but rather is a means for moving the organization toward its business objectives.

Awards should be incidental by-products, not the focus of strategy. This was the case with Globe Metallurgical, Inc., which in 1988 was the first small company to win the Baldrige. None of the company's managers had even heard of the award until a vice president in the company picked up an application and asked CEO Arden Sims what he thought about applying for the competition. This was one week before the deadline for entries. Sims and a few of his officers wrote the sixty-three-page application over the weekend. They pretty much forgot about it until they were notified of a site visit. A few weeks later, they learned they had won the award. Globe did not use the Baldrige as a way to learn about total quality. Sims describes the award as "more of a reward for our efforts than a learning experience" (Rayner, 1992). Sims had introduced the first quality initiative into one of the company's plants in 1985. Key customers such as Ford were demanding certification of the processes of their suppliers. Convinced that quality and providing customer value were critical to the company's survival, Sims continued to search out new ideas that would help the company's operations. He adapted them and continued to drive them into the organization until they became part of the company's culture. Over time, he found that he and his management team had created a new company.

The most important award is succeeding in the global marketplace, and the criteria for achieving this are continually evolving to match changing customer values. Succeeding demands cultural change on the order of a paradigm shift. By December 1990, Globe Metallurgical had captured 20 percent of the European ferroalloy market. In April 1991, the company entered the Japanese market with a twenty-ton test order.

The Critical Path of Change

Beer, Eisenstat, and Spector (1990) argue that spending a significant amount of senior management time on discussions about culture and seeking to indoctrinate people into a new vision are not effective approaches to effecting transformational change. In one case, they note that an extensive "culture change" program rolled out over a period of two years came to a halt with little visible progress. According to one senior human resource executive in the firm, "We spent a lot of time discussing what values we should have, but not enough time discussing how to make them real in the organization" (pp. 28–29).

According to Beer, Eisenstat, and Spector, a critical path to corporate renewal begins with a redefinition of roles, responsibilities, and relationships. This addresses informal behavior at the organizational level, and then moves toward the coaching, training, team building, and process interventions at the individual and group level. (See Figure 1.)

In a glass company they studied, a new plant manager found himself faced with a situation in which meeting the demands of substantially improved quality and lower costs would require a fundamental change in how his plant operated. He also understood that the existing culture, which was the product of a highly centralized and functionally oriented plant structure, was a major barrier to change. Particularly strong conflicts characterized the relationship between the "hot end" of the production process in which the glass was molded and the "cold end," which inspected the glass once it cooled.

The plant manager created a quality committee chaired by the manager responsible for the cold end. Other members included heads of departments having direct effects on product quality and the supervisors for both the hot and cold ends. Discussions with the sales force identified twenty quality problems which strongly impacted on the marketability of the plant's products. The committee started with the top three. Interdepartmental coordination and cooperation began to increase. The focus shifted to the processes which impacted on quality problems. Task forces were established to address particular issues that emerged as the group worked to improve these processes. The head of quality control no longer felt isolated. Increasingly, discussions throughout the plant centered on customer quality issues, not functional department concerns. Defects dropped, productivity increased, and reinspection costs were reduced.

Figure 1

The critical path to renewal: sequencing interventions for learning

	Level of focus	
	Unit level	Individual or group level
Intervention seeks to modify	(1) Redefinition of roles	(2) Coaching/counseling Training
Informal behavior	Responsibilities Relationships	Process consultation Team building
Formal design	(4) Compensation system Information systems Organizational structure Measurement system	(3) Replacement Recruitment Career pathing Succession planning Performance development

The plant manager did not call for an in-depth study of the organization's culture, nor did he send all his people to a training program. Rather, he created ad hoc vehicles such as the quality committee and task forces which demanded changes in the roles, responsibilities, and relationships of both the management team and employees throughout the plant. Coaching, training, and team building could take place within the context of these ad hoc structures.

Both phases in this sequence seek to change informal behavior in the organization. The first phase must take place within the context of mobilizing energy and engaging in a participative process of creating a "task-aligned vision." This vision is formulated through the development of an informal, ad hoc structure that changes roles, responsibilities, and relationships across the organizational unit that is responding to a competitive crisis. The new behaviors demanded by these roles become the focus of the personal development efforts carried out in the second phase. People in this organizational unit are more likely to be motivated to learn the new way of operating because they see it as clearly relevant to the success of the business. Beer and his associates argue that if coaching, training, and facilitation interventions precede this phase, employees will not perceive these interventions to be directly related to making the organization more effective.

Following these first two phases come the "harder" interventions of phases three and four. Phase three involves the replacement of those employees who fail to modify their behavior or develop the skills their new roles demand. Recruitment, career and succession planning, and performance development systems are coordinated during this phase. Finally, in phase four, the ad hoc structure is formalized based on the experience of the preceding phases. This means a modification in organizational structure, compensation systems, and information systems.

In the glass company plant discussed above, as the various ad hoc structures carried out their tasks, the need for changes in organization systems and functions emerged. The kinds of competencies required to work in the emerging environment might lead to changes in selection criteria, for example.

Successful corporate revitalization tends to begin in individual units, often moving from remote and relatively isolated units into the corporate core. Additionally, senior management needs to walk a very delicate line, being tough in expectations, yet demonstrating flexibility in permitting managers to evolve workable means. This is perhaps the essence of empowerment. As Beer, Eisenstat, and Spector suggest, the value of placing an initial focus on roles and evolving an ad hoc approach is that it minimizes the threat often associated with formal structural change. It permits learning to take place prior to demanding that people adopt a new, fixed organizational structure. It also permits small-scale trials of changes.

Frame-Breaking Change

Transformational change should be driven by shifts in business strategy. Tushman, Newman, and Nadler (1988) define frame-breaking changes as "revolutionary changes *of* the system as opposed to incremental changes *in* the system" (p. 115). They approach such change from a system-wide perspective, talking about the need for redefined mission and core values. A central point in their analysis is the need for abruptly upsetting the existing equilibrium of the organizational system. This requires discontinuous shifts in the utilization of people, their roles, and processes. They go on to argue that in making such change occur executives need to use multiple levers to reinforce the changes. "Structure, systems, people, and processes must be concurrently managed so that they work together to support the new organization" (p. 121).

The frame-breaking model places emphasis on transforming an entire organization through changes initiated by top management. Tushman et al. observe that the series of changes which are made vary by time, industry, and executive vision. However, they argue that the content of a successful frame-breaking change must be linked to critical environmental success factors. Getting these success factors right hinges on the judgment of management and the information it gets from others. Correctly identifying the elements of customer value is an example of such success factors.

Generally, Tushman et al. see frame-breaking change beginning with a redefined mission and redefined core values. Alterations must be made in the balance of power and status among functions within the organization, accompanied by structural reorganization. These changes must disrupt business-as-usual behavior. Following the structural reorganization, the organization works on establishing the revised patterns of interaction through changes in roles, procedures, and systems.

Both the critical path model and the frame-breaking model place emphasis on changing how things are done in the organization. Change is pushed in a way that is significantly different from how the organization has been functioning. Little time is invested in initially analyzing the culture. Rather, changes are linked to the competitive needs of the business. However, unlike the critical path model, the frame-breaking model focuses on structural reorganization preceding the changes in roles and responsibilities. The frame-breaking model is a more centralized, top-down approach. In both models, roles and responsibilities are the key to impacting the culture of the organization.

The recent reorganization of Florida Power and Light approximates the frame-breaking model. In 1990, a new CEO, James Broadhead, determined that even though the company had won the Deming prize, significant changes were necessary if the company was to continue to be an industry leader. Deregulation and the feasibility of power companies from outside the FPL service area providing power to the company's industrial customers raised the specter of direct competition. Broadhead felt the company had to focus on providing customer value through being the provider of choice at the lowest possible cost.

Following a strategic assessment, a massive restructuring was initiated in early 1991. This reorganization began right at the top, with the senior management group being streamlined and functions throughout the organization being regrouped. One of the critical competencies looked for in selecting staff for the new organization was the ability to work across functions.

Leverage Points for Driving Transformational Change

The key to driving transformational change is top management persistence and relentless insistence on learning how to make the new strategy operational. Change must be rooted in the business needs of the organization. People must be placed in new roles which require them to rethink how they function.

The initial levers of change are to be found in the roles people play throughout the organization and in the methods, tools, and systems which provide the working content of these roles. Using these levers to produce a new organization, and ultimately a new organizational culture, is a difficult and complex task.

Disconfirming experiences create opportunities for management to reinforce the culture it is creating by causing people to question the validity of their assumptions. Such experiences need to happen periodically. They help to unfreeze the organization by causing people to question the validity of their assumptions about how the organization works. However, they need to take place within the context of an ongoing process of change.

Figure 2

Leverage points for change

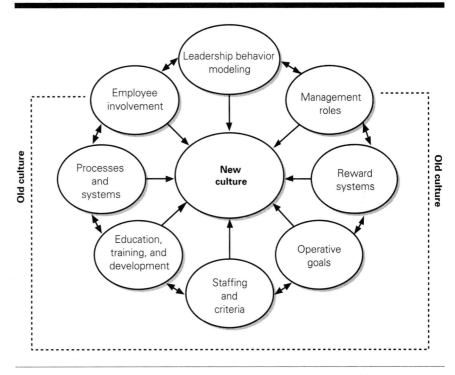

This change process must be firmly focused on providing customer value. Without this focus, unfreezing the system might actually increase variation in system performance (Adams, 1992). The leverage points for this process of change are systems that support the new strategy; the roles managers are expected to play as described by the MAT framework; the criteria used for staffing decisions; education, training, and development efforts targeted toward members of the organization; reward systems reworked and linked to the strategy; the leadership and behavior modeling provided by key executives and managers; employee involvement processes; and the operative goals of the organization.

Figure 2 summarizes these leverage points. As demonstrated in the figure, they initially strive to function within the old organizational culture, which can easily subvert them. Three things can help counteract this influence of the old culture. The first are the aforementioned disconfirming experiences. Creating these can be considered to be important leadership behavior. The second is the cumulative influence of all these leverage points being used simultaneously. The third is ongoing analysis and discussion of cultural issues, not as the primary intervention for change, but taking place within the context of implementing change through the leverage points. Over time, the cumulative effect of these efforts produces a new culture which supports the emerging paradigm.

▼

QUALITY IN ACTION: A MESSAGE TO THE STUDENT
Donald R. Keough, President and Chief Operating Officer, The Coca-Cola Company

Leaders who genuinely embrace the themes of the emerging paradigm are often passionate about it. They do not simply regard it as another coldly analytical approach to management or as a promotional gimmick. This spirited commitment to the theme of continuous improvement is evident in the message from Donald R. Keough, President and Chief Operating Officer, The Coca-Cola Company.

One of my firm beliefs is that "success is not a destination, but a journey." That belief speaks to a corporate culture that treats contentedness as anathema. The Coca-Cola Company owes its greatest successes to innovation and evolution. Even with great achievements, we cannot be content. What was good yesterday will not be good enough tomorrow.

But amid our creative discontent, our most basic goal is serving our customers with a passion. The business that loses its focus and lets that passion wane invites disaster. When a company is the leader, it is easy to begin to believe that people are lucky to do business with you. Instead, we must earn our right to do business with them, every day.

Satisfied customers and consumers are the lifeblood of The Coca-Cola Company. They pay our salaries; they feed our families. Every day, we must serve them with a passion born of the knowledge that without them, our company would quickly close its doors.

▲

A quick examination of Figure 2 will reveal that many of these points of leverage are key elements in the emerging paradigm. The comments below elaborate on the model.

Operative Goals In a sense, operative goals are reflected in many of the various leverage points in the model. However, because the concept of operative (as opposed to official) goals is so important to facilitating change, we give it explicit recognition in the model.

Operative goals "designate the ends sought through the actual operating policies of the organization; they tell us what the organization actually is trying to do regardless of what the official goals say are the aims" (Perrow, 1961, pp. 855–856). Management will often make pronouncements about the organization being committed to continuous improvement in providing customer value, but the actual operating policies of the organization imply different goals. For example, if managers are rewarded for maintaining quotas, product modifications to enhance customer value might be resisted. These modifications might disrupt existing operating procedures and require significant investment of resources, threatening the ability of managers to meet their quotas.

Sensitivity to operative goals is fundamental to assessing organizational culture. Operative goals tend to persist and become the standards around which decisions are made (Hall, 1987, p. 271). Thus, they reflect choices between competing values that may impede change. Changing operative goals through consistent and persistent practices and actions is basic to sustaining organizational change.

Efforts at organizational transformation have failed in part because the new philosophy of management was inconsistent with the operative goals and the reward structure of the organization (Blackler and Brown, 1980). However, linking the change agenda to operative goals facilitates organizational change (Yorks and Whitsett, 1989).

Operative goals are reflected in what management attends to, controls, and measures. The idea that the structure of most accounting and control systems may be inhibiting competitiveness (Kaplan, 1984) is slowly gaining currency in the U.S. business community (*Business Week*, June 6, 1988, pp. 100–115). A comment by a finishing foreman in one organization studied by the authors illustrates the problem. "The bottom line, unit costs, is driving production to run things poorly. The rules about running things are not followed. They put anything they have into the [product] without regard to quality, just to get the [product] out the door. The foreman will tell people to do things wrong just to get production out." The plant manager in the same plant stated he is supportive of improvements when "financially feasible." Culture cannot be shaped in directions not supported by the cost management system of the organization.

People throughout an organization are very sensitive to what management emphasizes. In one organization, meetings at which supervisors were to address a number of quality-related issued were canceled because management wanted to minimize costs during the fourth quarter. In another organization, emphasis was placed on hitting production quotas once market demand for their product started to strengthen. This was done regardless of the impact on factors valued by the customer.

Periodic use of the critical incident analysis method, described in the following section on assessing culture, is one way management can monitor its behavior in this regard. Even lost opportunities can become chances for organizational learning if management is willing to engage employees as equals in open dialogue, and if management is willing to learn. For example, management can periodically ask employees throughout the organization to describe a critical incident that reinforced the company's commitment to quality. Those same employees can next be asked to describe a critical incident that undermined the company's commitment to quality. These responses can be written anonymously. The responses can then be analyzed to provide insight into how management's behavior during critical incidents is being interpreted by the rest of the organization. They can also be analyzed in terms of the assumptions held by management which are in fact shaping its response to these incidents, giving insight into the culture which is being established.

The Criteria Used for Allocating Rewards and Status   People shape their behavior according to the organization's reward structure. Apart from shaping behavior, rewards are a method of communication. They are one of the clearest expressions of what managers value. The characteristics of the formal systems in which this takes place are obviously very important levers of change, a point made earlier in this chapter. However, how managers *use* the system is also important.

An interview with a manager in a leading consumer products company explored the relationship between measurement systems (discussed above) and the allocation of rewards. The manager explained, "If your rewards are set by your functional manager, whose goals are cost containment, and your business needs quality improvement, what are you going to work on? You will work on cost containment." This example illustrates the traditional approach to the relationship between quality and cost.

The Criteria Used for Staffing Decisions   One way to change an organization is through staffing decisions (Porter, Lawler, and Hackman, 1975, p. 442). Seeding the organization with managers who demonstrate behaviors consistent with the customer value strategy is fundamental to diffusing its tenets throughout a company. Yorks and Whitsett have reported data that demonstrate the impact of seeding on the change process (1989, pp. 69–70, 93, 150, 159–160). The organizations in their study facilitated the diffusion of change by placing supervisors and managers experienced with employee involvement and other quality methods in new work units. These people then suggested changes in their new work sites which helped the spread of these ideas. They were also open to change and helped convince others of the usefulness of these innovations. Indeed, positioning people throughout the organization who share one's values and goals is a time-honored, pragmatic way of gaining control of an organization. Reluctance to do so is one sign of lack of commitment to change. Of course, placing managers who demonstrate an ability and willingness to support change in key positions is a way of rewarding them as well.

In one company studied by the authors, an employee told us, "I don't know of one person in our company who has been promoted and progressed through the organization by working on these things." Yet another stated, "Maybe the formal performance appraisal criteria are in line with TQ [total quality], but I've never seen anyone promoted based upon those criteria. Working in the informal structure of the old culture is what gets you ahead." This company was not making much progress toward change.

Too much indiscriminate rotation of managers is disruptive to the change process, especially when it is linked to counterproductive criteria. In the same organization mentioned above, we were also told, "People are rotated every one to two years and are rewarded on what they come in and change to immediately yield a result. Later, another manager comes in and changes it back to the way it was."

Education, Training, and Development   New competencies must be developed throughout the organization. Some of these competencies are technical in nature, such as learning how to study variation. Others are behavioral, such as working across functions, and working with self-directed teams.

Most important, the education, skills, and competencies learned should be immediately applied on the job. Making sure this happens is a crucial leadership responsibility. Implementing a customer value strategy is *not* a training exercise. The training and development work must be linked to work-related expectations throughout the organization.

Cultural Impediments to Transformational Change

Earlier we noted that some recent research suggests that spending a lot of time talking about a "new culture" is not an especially effective way of changing an organization. Beer (1988) has described how setting out to change the culture of an organization prior to implementing changes in roles, systems, and processes fails "to stimulate significant change, despite top management's involvement in examining the old culture and defining the new one." Involving the organization in an elaborate "culture design project" just doesn't work.

Rather, for transformational change to take hold, it must be clearly and convincingly linked to the core strategic issues of the organization (Nadler, 1988). Managing to continuously improve customer value is such a strategy. However, this doesn't mean that culture per se can be ignored.

When a strategy of continuously improving customer value represents a dramatic shift for managers, it will be countercultural for the organization. However, most organizational cultures are highly resilient and can co-opt new managerial approaches. For example, people in the organization can adopt new buzzwords, but continue to function largely as before. Staff groups can take over responsibility for new systems, asserting themselves as experts. Line managers can treat the new approaches as the domain of the staff experts, thus removing primary responsibility for results from themselves. Gradually, new initiatives become slotted into the existing bureaucracy so that change takes place in only a very superficial way.

A good example of this kind of conflict comes from a situation in a large public utility. Senior management was striving to create a more customer-focused and responsive organization, cutting levels in the organization, seeking to empower middle- and lower-level line managers and their employees, and encouraging risk-taking behavior. Staff groups repeatedly sought to impose their interpretation of these changes on the line, creating complex programs and procedures around many of the strategic concepts. These programs, plus the tendency of the staff groups to "manage" the company, were indicative of the very culture management was seeking to change.

The point is that management must recognize the old culture and how it might impede the new strategy. This is why a thorough assessment of the existing organizational culture is so important. Initially, the problem is one of breaking the culture's hold on people throughout the organization. Breaking this hold requires repeating events that cause people throughout the organization to question their ability to predict management's response to situations. Such episodes function as "disconfirming experiences" or "disorienting dilemmas" which can cause people throughout the organization to question their assumptions. These periods of questioning provide windows of opportunity to emphasize new values and assumptions. Over time, the new culture which emerges represents the "glue" which institutionalizes the strategy of customer value.

Every crisis is an opportunity for disavowing the old culture, while reinforcing those values and assumptions which are part of the desired culture. Failure to do so sends a strong message that management is not serious about changing and that it is "business as usual." In times of crisis, employees see very clearly what it is that management pays attention to. In turn, cultural factors are either reinforced or changed.

A few years ago, one of the authors was touring an automotive engine assembly plant. During a downturn in the economy, the plant had been modernized. Each assembler had some control over the pacing of work. All were trained in statistical process control and received regular data on their work. Management and the union had jointly agreed on innovative procedures focusing on quality. When a remark was made as to how impressive all this was, an employee responded, "We haven't yet experienced capacity demand. Once the market comes back and we can sell everything we produce, then we'll see whether they are serious about all this." This employee, like most of his colleagues, was enthusiastic, but cautious, adopting a wait-and-see attitude. He was waiting for the first crisis.

Routine management processes can provide opportunities for management to generate disconfirming experiences as well. In one company, managers were told to budget for the level of expenditures it needed to provide adequate funding for change-related training and implementation in their divisions. Corporate management said the budgets, supplemented by plans, would be approved without questioning. However, many managers were skeptical, believing they would end up negotiating or justifying their request. As one manager put it, "They always take 10 to 15 percent off the top." However, in this instance, management did exactly what it said would be done: the budgets were approved and sent back with instructions to go to work. There was no negotiating, no justifying individual items; they just sent the budgets and plans back approved as submitted. Many in field management, especially the skeptics, were stunned; it was a disconfirming experience.

Recognizing and acting on opportunities for creating disconfirming experiences requires a high level of sensitivity to the traditional culture of the company. Developing this sensitivity demands a willingness to take a serious and critical look at how the company, and especially its management, functions. It requires members of management to engage in critical self-reflection on how their behavior manifests the culture they are trying to change, and the signals their behavior sends to the rest of the organization.

▶ ASSESSING ORGANIZATIONAL CULTURE

Because organizational cultures are complex, there is no easy way to assess them. Some of the challenges faced when analyzing culture include describing and categorizing cultural elements such as values, symbols, and beliefs (Barley, 1983). Perhaps even more challenging is determining what about the culture is valuable to the organization. Gaining useful insight into cultural phenomena requires a systematic and well-grounded approach. Critical to such an approach is having the proper people conduct the analysis.

Who Should Do the Cultural Analysis

Because analyzing a culture is a complicated task, it should be overseen by someone who has been specifically trained. Only a joint effort between an insider and a trained outsider can decipher a cultural paradigm (Schein, 1985).

A joint effort between outsiders and insiders helps to avoid the *subjectivity bias*, or systematic errors that accompany any one person's perspective. Both the insider and the outsider impose their own categories of meaning onto the events they observe. The outsider is less likely to understand the culture because he or she has not had time to learn the social matrix, the semantic nuances, how meanings are translated into behavior, and how behavioral rules vary situationally. So, initially, the outsider only learns about surface aspects of the culture. It takes some time to overcome *internal invisibility*, taken-for-granted meanings that are widely shared among members of the culture, but are not readily apparent to nonmembers (Schein,

1985). A dialogue between a trained outsider and trained insiders can help facilitate the analysis.

The insider should have some knowledge of behavioral science and be able to make distinctions between his or her observations and established beliefs about the organization. The person should be open to dialogue, and willing to question personal beliefs about the organization. In fact, through mutual probing insiders often reveal to outsiders the basic assumptions that have escaped their conscious awareness. The insider achieves awareness by explaining the cultural elements to the outsider, or by correcting the outsider's mistaken interpretations. "The nature of this work can be likened to trying to bring to the surface something that is hidden but not concealed deliberately. It is so taken for granted that it escapes notice, but it is perfectly visible once it has surfaced into consciousness" (Schein, 1985, p. 113).

One way of accomplishing this analysis is through the establishment of a collaborative inquiry process, in which a group of analysts from both inside and outside the organization jointly pursue an analysis of the organization's culture over time, even while changes are being initiated (Marshall and McLean, 1988). This can be accomplished through a process in which inside participants gather data on the organization's culture while for the most part executing their normal job responsibilities. The outside analysts also engage in data-gathering activities. Periodically, the group meets to engage in critical analysis of their data.

Senior managers cannot detach themselves from the cultural analysis. Ideally, an ongoing dialogue about culture should be established with key managers and executives with the purpose of making them more aware of their assumptions about the organization. The research team and managers should continue to observe the culture throughout the change effort. Indeed, some of the deeper, more subtle aspects of the organizational culture will be revealed through how the organization responds to the change process. A valid understanding of an organization's culture is developed through systematic use of appropriate data-gathering methods.

Data Gathering

The dialogue about the organization's culture must utilize data. Anthropologists known as ethnographers have developed highly specialized tools for analyzing culture. Typically, a long residence (at least a year) and participant observation provide the foundation of their research efforts (Pelto, 1970; Wolcott, 1975; Sanday, 1979). However, in rapidly changing environments, management does not have the luxury of time. Managers must begin to make immediate progress toward developing a new cultural paradigm.[4] We have already noted that this cannot be accomplished through discussions of the organizational culture. The cultural assessment

---

4. While organizations must move quickly, Senge (1991) warns that "faster can be slower" if managers act in haste, without knowledge, and put in place things that are inappropriate.

is conducted in order to bring impediments to the surface in order to change and provide insight into the dynamics of the organization. To speed up the process, the team can use other members of the organization to help gain many of the deeper insights that extended participant observation would have eventually revealed. These methods include observation, individual interviews, critical incident analysis, group self-analysis, and questionnaires. Properly utilized, these methods can enlist a significant portion of the organization in the analysis of culture, a process which will raise the level of awareness throughout the organization, facilitating the change process. Let's look briefly at each method.

Observation Careful observation is the starting point of any cultural analysis (Jorgensen, 1989; Fetterman, 1989). Initial observations should concentrate on achieving a relatively unfocused, preliminary impression of what is happening (Jorgensen, 1989). This involves attending meetings and observing people in their work activities. These observations are guided by general questions such as: How are people organized or arranged in the work setting? How do they respond to one another? Who does which tasks? What is the demographic composition of the group (gender, race, age, etc.)? How is the work space organized? As the observer becomes more familiar with the setting, observations become more focused on phenomena of particular interest. Because previous experience may blind an insider to the importance of certain cultural artifacts, often the observations of an outsider will provide more useful data.

It is extremely important to record observations (Fetterman, 1989). A written record of observations, or field notes, provides the basis for future analysis. With time, memory fades and subsequent observations overshadow earlier ones. The process of recording, reviewing, and reorganizing allows patterns of data to emerge.

Individual Interviews Information gathered through interviews with insiders supplements the observational data. Skilled "critical questioning" is an effective means of bringing assumptions to the surface. It is concerned not so much with eliciting information as with prompting reflective analysis (Brookfield, 1987, p. 93). This method of interviewing has been widely used in ethnographic research (Dobbert, 1982). Critical questioning invites individuals to examine their actions and explore the collective assumptions and values they share.

The key to critical questioning is framing questions that are insightful, specific to particular events or actions, and yet easily understood (Brookfield, 1987, pp. 93–94). For example, the interviewer might ask the respondent to "think back over the past few weeks. Has there been a particular time when you felt you were being especially effective in meeting your work unit's objectives? Tell me about it." Or "I noticed in the meeting yesterday afternoon you questioned the sales department's right to make a commitment to [a particular customer]. Tell me why you confronted them on this." A careful listener will usually be able to identify assumptions in the answers that describe particular events. Critical questioning can take place within the context of a formal interview or as part of a more casual conversation.

Schein (1985) advocates interviews that explore critical incidents in an organization's history as a way of developing meaningful insights. *Critical incidents*, also referred to as *social dramas* (Pettigrew, 1979), offer the analyst a look at the growth, evolution, and transformation of the organization.

To explore critical incidents, the interviewer attempts to get a reconstruction of the group's history to discover key historical events, how they were handled, and which kinds of solutions worked repeatedly and thus became embedded as a part of the culture. Critical questioning becomes an integral part of this kind of interview.

Critical Incident Analysis Another method of gaining insight into the core values and assumptions of an organization's culture is through critical incident analysis. *Critical incident analysis* prompts respondents to identify an incident that for some reason was of particular significance to them. The researcher provides a set of instructions on what kind of incident is to be identified, and respondents are then asked to write a paragraph or two describing the incident (Brookfield, 1987). For example, the instructions might read as follows:

> Think back over the past three months in your work. Identify an event in which you felt caught in a particularly difficult dilemma between the demands being placed on you by management and the priorities of performing your job. Write down, in no more than half a page, a brief description of the incident. Be sure your description includes the following details: (1) when and where it occurred, (2) who was involved (roles and job titles rather than personal identities may be given), (3) the exact nature of the dilemma, (4) how you resolved it, and (5) your reasoning for resolving it this way.

Written as specifically as possible, the responses generally reflect assumptions tied to the organization's culture. Assumptions become especially apparent when the analyst compares the responses of several people.

Group Self-Analysis Insiders can gain insight into their own culture without requiring an outsider or a joint team to go through a formal process of analysis. A group interview or group discussion can require the participants to diagnose where they fall along a given cultural dimension. After introducing the participants to the concept of culture as underlying assumptions, and illustrating for them some specific dimensions, they can be given a set of instructions for analyzing themselves (Schein, 1985).

Questionnaires A well-constructed questionnaire can be a valuable tool for measuring beliefs, values, and ideologies, especially if supplemented by interviews and participant observation methods. The resulting statistical profile can also be used as a baseline measure against which changes in the culture can be monitored through subsequent application of the questionnaire.

The consciousness-raising impact of the survey process can also be used to facilitate the change process. During data feedback sessions, participants provide those conducting the cultural assessment additional insight into the organizational culture by examining more critically the assumptions implied by the data. They also begin the process of "unfreezing" some of their thinking patterns by becoming more aware of how these assumptions impact their behavior in the organization.

Bounds and Dewhirst (1991) have specifically designed a survey instrument in terms of cultural dimensions that support the emerging paradigm. Their assessment questionnaire measures three organizational elements: individual managerial variables, organizational culture, and organizational management systems. The individual managerial variables are measures relating to competence and role perception. The cultural measures in the questionnaire assess values necessary for supporting the customer value strategy: customer orientation, cross-functional cooperation, crisis orientation, and historical change orientation. The system measures provide data relevant to profiling the authority structure, information systems, reporting systems, reward systems, and resource allocation systems. When scored, the responses provide a profile of the organization along these elements.

A thorough understanding of an organization's existing culture is important for devising a strategy of change. This understanding supports the change process, but is not the primary focus of it. Ongoing monitoring of the culture as the change strategy is implemented will lead to further insights about an organization's culture. Schein (1985) has observed that often the best way to understand an organizational culture is through the process of helping to change it. Lewin (1951) also suggested that one never understands a system before trying to change it. Managers should be prepared to go through cycles of analysis. Each cycle is likely to bring new insights into the organizational culture and how it is either facilitating or impeding the emergence of a new paradigm. This is part of the learning process that must be included in the change effort.

▶ ORGANIZATIONAL LEARNING AND TRANSFORMATIONAL CHANGE

Culture change requires that people in the organization learn. To return to points made by Ledford, Mohrman, Mohrman, and Lawler (1989), and Mohrman and Lawler (1985), they must change their way of looking at the world, including their cognitive approaches and emotional responses toward the social matrix, such as images of the organization and beliefs about how things work in it. In their daily lives, people continue to assimilate new experience in a way consistent with their past experience. This

Figure 3

Learning as a mediating process of cultural transformation

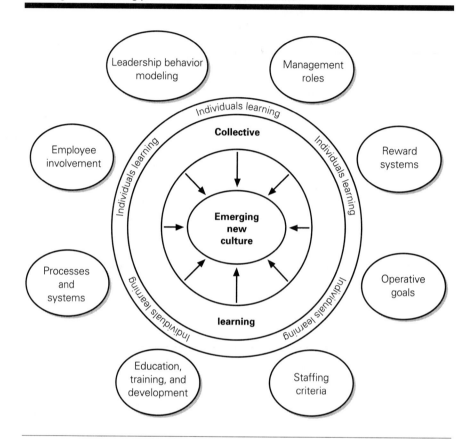

process reflects the power of the cultural paradigm. When they transform this paradigm, they come to a new interpretation of their experiences, both current and past. This arriving at a new interpretation of how the organization operates represents learning. Figure 3 depicts how learning mediates between the leverage points of change and the emerging organizational culture.

As individuals learn through challenging their past assumptions and in dialogue with each other, they change their individual perspectives on the organization and how they give meaning to the events taking place in the organization. As these new meanings are shared, they come to be manifested in the culture of the organization. In a very real sense, organizational culture is the product of collective learning. The process of learning mediates between the experiences members of the organization share and the culture which is established. If people experience new things, but continue to interpret these experiences in the old way, no change occurs in the organization's culture. The concept of collective learning is important. A new culture cannot be thought up by a small group of executives and imposed on the organization. A culture is created by those who live and interpret their collective experience in a certain way. A new culture cannot be taught. It is the product of collective learning. In a sense, one can say that organizational learning occurs when the lessons learned by individuals become part of the organization's memory by becoming part of its culture.

Cultural change, then, emerges from collective learning. Dechant and Marsick (1991, p. 225) note that "for organizational learning to occur, it must go beyond the learning process and outcomes of a single individual; it must be 'collective' in nature. Collective learning involves some degree of shared sense making." Argyris and Schon (1978, p. 19) add: "In order for *organizational* learning to occur, learning agents' discoveries, inventions, and evaluations must be embedded in organizational memory. They must be encoded in the individual images and the shared maps of organizational theory-in-use from which individual members will subsequently act. If this encoding does not occur, individuals will have learned, but the organization will not have done so." What Argyris and Schon are describing is a change in organizational culture.

Espoused Theory and Theory in Use

Chris Argyris and Donald Schon (Argyris, 1982; Argyris and Schon, 1978; Argyris, Putnam, and Smith, 1985; Schon, 1983) have done much of the seminal work linking change with learning. They make a distinction between *espoused theories* and *theories in use*. Essentially, espoused theories are what people say they do; theories in use are what people actually do. Obviously, what people say they do reflects in part the normative values in the organizational culture. Behavior is driven by many things, including organizational systems, the skills and behaviors with which a person is most comfortable, personality, and elements of the deep, level-three assumptions of organizational culture.

When problems in organizational performance are rooted in the gap between espoused theory and theory in use, detecting the source of "errors" is difficult because the factors governing action are taken for granted. If these taken-for-granted variables are collectively shared as part of a culture, or what Argyris and Schon call an *organizational theory in use*, uncovering them can be particularly difficult. A process of "double loop learning" (Argyris and Schon, 1978), in which underlying assumptions are brought out into the open and challenged, is required.

Double Loop versus Single Loop Learning

Single loop learning is instrumental in nature. Essentially, it involves correcting variance in known cause and effect relationships so that a desired outcome is achieved. *Double loop learning*, on the other hand, occurs when the assumptions and context within which instrumental action takes place are challenged. It is transformative in nature because it alters the socially construed meanings people share (Mezirow, 1991).

Organizational learning is both single looped and double looped, although the former is the most common. Double loop learning demands the creation of an organizational climate that helps make these assumptions public and open to public inquiry. Significant change in an organization's culture requires that people feel comfortable in developing the systems and processes through which this kind of learning can take place. As Marsick and Watkins (1990, p. 241) note, developing these kinds of processes means that members of the organization must share with each other the flaws they learn about the organization's learning system.

The implications for changing an organization's culture are significant. In addition to uncovering the hidden assumptions which are the content of the organizational culture, the hidden connections between the culture and the characteristics of the organization's learning system that inhibit the learning process must be considered. Said another way, double loop learning consists of both a change in the norms and assumptions which comprise an organization's culture and the "particular sort of inquiry into norms which is appropriately described as learning" (Argyris and Schon, 1978, p. 22). Since the processes of communication people feel comfortable with are shaped by both personal and cultural factors, this is often an important point of intervention for dealing with an organization's culture in a meaningful way.

Continuous Improvement Requires Continuous Learning

An important element in the strategy for managing for customer value is continuously striving to improve. This demands that people throughout the organization continue to challenge the assumptions that are becoming part of the organization's culture. Change becomes a constant, and learning is its handmaiden. The one taken-for-granted value is that nothing else is taken for granted.

Managers must emphasize measures of customer value on an ongoing basis. Further, system owners must engage people throughout the organization in discussions of system and process effectiveness. Emphasizing the roles people play in the MAT provides a continuous expectation of change. The content of what the organization is doing must continuously evolve, and on occasion change dramatically. The processes through which change is introduced must remain predictable. This way, people know where to look for change and are able to anticipate it.

Managers must keep people informed of the competencies required by the organization, so people can take the initiative in developing them. These competencies become an important element of human resource management in the customer value–oriented organization. Career development no longer is represented by a series of stable steps through a set career ladder. Rather, it becomes a process of enhancing competencies for creating customer value. As staffing levels change, processes for assessing and reassigning talent must be clear and visible to everyone. People will be expected to take the initiative in developing these competencies; the organization will have to support their initiatives and guarantee everyone fair consideration of their abilities. Thus, continuous improvement is supported by a dynamic staffing model (Marshall and Yorks, 1992).

▶ CONCLUSION

Culture has a strong, stabilizing effect on organizations. Accordingly, it can counteract efforts toward transforming how an organization functions. It is important for managers to understand their organization's existing culture and recognize when it is inhibiting change.

Understanding an organization's culture is not an easy thing. Outsiders can easily misinterpret events, while insiders may fail to recognize their own assumptions which are rooted in the culture itself. Analysis of an organization's culture is best accomplished by a team of insiders and outsiders working together and using a variety of methods. Understanding of the culture may only come about as the change process itself makes the deep-rooted assumptions of the culture evident to managers. The extent to which the culture has or has not changed is often reflected in how managers react to critical incidents in the operation of the organization.

The leverage points for changing an organization's culture are management's behavior, reward systems, operative goals, staffing criteria, training and development efforts, processes and systems, and employee involvement efforts. Changing a culture requires learning; people must come to a new understanding of what effective performance means. This learning is ongoing as the organization continuously seeks to improve customer value.

▶ SUMMARY OF KEY POINTS

1. Programs are inadequate for implementing a strategy of managing for customer value in most companies; a transformation of the organizational culture is required.
2. Culture plays a stabilizing role in organizations. Thus it tends to initially counteract efforts toward transformational change. It is important for managers to understand their existing culture and recognize when it is inhibiting change.
3. Culture change is required for traditional organizations to participate in a paradigm shift.
4. Changing roles and work processes is key to transformational change. As important as culture is to transformational change, the focus of the change effort must be on changing how things get done in the company.

5. The leverage points for changing an organization's culture are management's roles and behavior, reward systems, operative goals, staffing criteria, training and development efforts, processes and systems, and employee involvement efforts.

6. Assessing organizational culture is best accomplished through the efforts of a team consisting of outsiders and insiders to the organization. The team should use a variety of methods for gathering data.

7. Culture change requires learning. Organizational culture is the product of collective learning.

8. Continuous improvement in customer value requires continuous learning in the organization.

▶ KEY TERMS

Baldrige award

critical path to change

double loop learning

espoused theories

frame-breaking change

leverage points for change

single loop learning

theories in use

transformational change

▶ DISCUSSION QUESTIONS

1. Some organizations have spent a lot of time discussing cultural change and the kind of culture they are trying to create. Other organizations focus on changing the roles and responsibilities people perform. Which approach is more likely to lead to change? What is the basis for your answer?

2. Why is a knowledge of culture important in trying to implement the emerging paradigm?

3. What are the pros and cons of using the Baldrige award to initiate organizational change toward the emerging paradigm?

4. What are the similarities and differences between the critical path model and the frame-breaking model of change?

5. Describe why and how outsiders and insiders should collaborate to analyze culture.

6. How can the three models of change discussed in this chapter (i.e., Baldrige, critical path, and frame-breaking) be used in combination to transform an organization?

7. What is the difference between single loop and double loop learning? Which is critical if cultural change is going to occur? Why?

8. Chris Galvin, senior executive vice president and assistant chief operating officer, Motorola, Inc., states: "Seeking renewal and adapting instantaneously to change is a prerequisite for survival. The timing of making such change is counter-intuitive. The more one's associates protest that change is unnecessary or would be too uncomfortable, the more value there is in the proposal for change. The faster the experiment with renewal, the greater the competitive advantage." What does this statement mean in terms of cultural change? Is it good advice? Why or why not?

▶ DISCUSSION EXERCISE

- Form a small group in order to develop a plan for creating cultural change within your college or university. Assume you and your colleagues are administrators in your school (deans and associate deans or president and other academic officers) and you want to effect a transformational change toward the emerging paradigm. What aspects of the existing culture would be likely to impede change? How could you put people into new roles and responsibilities which would start the change process? What leverage points can be changed to help drive the change process? Present your conclusions in the form of an initial plan for changing the school in the direction of the new paradigm.

▶ REFERENCES

M. Adams, "TQM: OD's Role in Implementing Value-Based Strategies," in C. N. Jackson and M. R. Manning (eds.), *Intervening in Client Organizations*, Organizational Development Annual, Vol. IV, 1992, American Society for Training and Development, Alexandria, Va.

C. Argyris, *Reasoning, Learning, and Action: Individual and Organizational*, Jossey-Bass, San Francisco, Calif., 1982.

C. Argyris and D. A. Schon, *Organizational Learning: A Theory of Action Perspective*, Addison-Wesley, Reading, Mass., 1978.

C. Argyris, R. Putnam, and D. M. Smith, *Action Science*, Jossey-Bass, San Francisco, Calif., 1988.

S. R. Barley, "Semiotics and the Study of Occupational and Organizational Cultures," *Administrative Science Quarterly*, Vol. 28, 1983, pp. 393–413.

M. Beer, "The Critical Path for Change: Key to Success and Failure in Six Companies," in R. H. Kilmann, T. J. Covin, and Associates (eds.), *Corporate Transformation: Revitalizing Organizations for a Competitive World*, Jossey-Bass, San Francisco, Calif., 1988, pp. 17–45.

M. Beer, R. A. Eisenstat, and B. Spector, *The Critical Path to Corporate Renewal*, Harvard Business School Press, Boston, Mass., 1990.

F. H. M. Blacker and C. A. Brown, *Whatever Happened to Shell's New Philosophy of Management?* Saxon House, Westmead, England, 1980.

G. M. Bounds and H. D. Dewhirst, "Assessing Progress in Managing for Customer Value," in M. J. Stahl and G. M. Bounds (eds.), *Competing Globally through Customer Value: The Management of Strategic Suprasystems*, Quorum Books, New York, 1991, pp. 307–339.

S. D. Brookfield, *Developing Critical Thinkers*, Jossey-Bass, San Francisco, Calif., 1987.

P. B. Crosby, in debate: "Does the Baldrige Award Really Work?" *Harvard Business Review*, Vol. 70, No. 1, 1992, p. 128.

Debate (1992). "Does the Baldrige Award Really Work?" *Harvard Business Review*, Vol. 70, No. 1, pp. 126–147.

K. Dechant and V. J. Marsick, "In Search of the Learning Organization: Toward a Conceptual Model of Collective Learning," *Proceedings: Eastern Academy of Management*, Annual Meeting, Hartford, Conn., May 1991.

W. E. Deming, in debate: "Does the Baldrige Award Really Work?" *Harvard Business Review*, Vol. 70, No. 1, 1992, p. 134.

D. R. Dennison, *Corporate Culture and Organizational Effectiveness*, Wiley, New York, 1990.

M. L. Dobbert, *Ethnographic Research: Theory and Application for Modern Schools and Society*, Praeger, New York, 1982.

D. M. Fetterman, *Ethnography: Step by Step*, Sage Publications, Newbury Park, Calif., 1989.

R. Galvin, in debate: "Does the Baldrige Award Really Work?" *Harvard Business Review*, Vol. 70, No. 1, 1992, pp. 136–137.

D. A. Garvin, "How the Baldrige Award Really Works," *Harvard Business Review*, Vol. 69, No. 6, 1991, pp. 80–93.

R. H. Hall, *Organizations: Structures, Processes, and Outcomes*, 4th ed., Prentice-Hall, Englewood Cliffs, N.J., 1987.

C. W. L. Hart and C. E. Bogan, *The Baldrige: What It Is, How It's Won, How to Use It to Improve Quality in Your Organization*, McGraw-Hill, New York, 1992.

D. L. Jorgensen, *Participant Observation: A Methodology for Human Studies*, Sage Publications, Newbury Park, Calif., 1989.

R. S. Kaplan, "Yesterday's Accounting Undermines Production," *Harvard Business Review*, Vol. 62, 1984, pp. 95–101.

T. S. Kuhn, *The Structure of Scientific Revolutions*, University of Chicago Press, 1962.

G. E. Ledford, Jr., S. A. Mohrman, A. M. Mohrman, Jr., and E. E. Lawler III, "The Phenomenon of Large-Scale Organizational Change," in A. M. Mohrman, Jr., S. A. Mohrman, G. E. Ledford, Jr., T. G. Cummings, E. E. Lawler III, and Associates (eds.), *Large-Scale Organizational Change*, Jossey-Bass, San Francisco, 1989.

K. Lewin, *Field Theory in Social Science*, Harper, New York, 1951.

R. Marshall and L. Yorks, "Positioning People for Profits and Performance," *Financial Management Network's Video Magazine Series, Subscriber's Guide*, Vol. 53, October 1992.

V. J. Marsick and K. E. Watkins, *Informal and Incidental Learning in the Workplace*, Routledge, New York, 1990.

J. Mezirow, *Transformative Dimensions of Adult Learning*, Jossey-Bass, San Francisco, Calif., 1991.

M. B. Miles and A. M. Huberman, *Qualitative Data Analysis: A Source Book of New Methods*, Sage Publications, Beverly Hills, Calif., 1984.

A. M. Mohrman, Jr., and E. E. Lawler III, "The Diffusion of QWL as a Paradigm Shift," in W. G. Bennis, K. D. Benne, and R. Chin (eds.), *The Planning of Change*, 4th ed., Holt, Rinehart & Winston, New York, 1985.

D. A. Nader, "Organizational Frame Bending: Types of Change in the Complex Organization," in R. H. Kilmann, T. J. Covin, and Associates (eds.), *Corporate Transformation: Revitalizing Organizations for a Competitive World*, Jossey-Bass, San Francisco, Calif., 1988, pp. 66–83.

M. Q. Patton, *Qualitative Evaluation and Research Methods*, 2nd ed., Sage Publications, Newbury Park, Calif., 1990.

P. J. Pelto, *Anthropological Research: The Structure of Inquiry*, Harper and Row, New York, 1970.

C. Perrow, "Goals in Complex Organizations," *American Sociological Review*, Vol. 26, 1961, pp. 854–865.

A. M. Pettigrew, "On Studying Organizational Cultures," *Administrative Science Quarterly*, Vol. 24, 1979, pp. 579–581.

J. I. Porras and P. O. Berg, "The Comparative Impact of Different OD Techniques and Intervention Intensities," *Journal of Applied Behavioral Science*, Vol. 15, 1978, pp. 156–178.

C. W. Porter, E. E. Lawler III, and J. R. Hackman, *Behavior in Organizations*, McGraw-Hill, New York, 1975.

B. Rayner, "Trial-by-Fire Transformation: An Interview with Globe Metallurgical's Arden C. Sims," *Harvard Business Review*, May–June 1992, pp. 117–129.

Redeployment Issues, "Hurricane Andrew Puts Florida Power and Light's Redeployment to the Ultimate Test," The Marshall Group, Scottsdale, Ariz., Vol. III, No. I, 1993.

P. R. Sanday, "The Ethnographic Paradigm(s)," in J. Van Mannen (ed.), *Qualitative Methodology*, Sage Publications, Beverly Hills, Calif., 1979, pp. 19–36.

E. H. Schein, "Coming to a New Awareness of Organizational Culture," *Sloan Management Review*, Vol. 23, 1984, pp. 55–68.

E. H. Schein, *Organizational Culture and Leadership*, Jossey-Bass, San Francisco, Calif., 1985.

D. A. Schon, *The Reflective Practitioner*, Basic Books, New York, 1983.

A. Strauss and J. Corbin, *Basics of Qualitative Research*, Sage Publications, Newbury Park, Calif., 1990.

M. L. Tushman, W. H. Newman, and D. A. Nadler, "Executive Leadership and Organizational Evolution: Managing Incremental and Discontinuous Change," in R. H. Kilmann, T. J. Covin, and Associates (eds.), *Corporate Transformation: Revitalizing Organizations for a Competitive World*, Jossey-Bass, San Francisco, Calif., 1988, pp. 102–130.

A. L. Wilkins, "Organizational Stories as Symbols Which Control the Organization," in L. R. Pondy, P. J. Frost, G. Morgan, and T. C. Dandridge (eds.), *Organizational Symbolism*, JAI Press, Greenwich, Conn., 1983, pp. 81–92.

H. Wolcott, "Criteria for an Ethnographic Approach to Research in Schools," *Human Organization*, Vol. 34, 1975, pp. 111–128.

L. Yorks and D. A. Whitsett, *Scenarios of Change: Advocacy and the Diffusion of Job Redesign in Organizations*, Praeger, New York, 1989.

Case Studies

Federal Express: The Vision Made Real*

▶ A BRIEF AND VAUNTED HISTORY

The next time a teacher gives your most creative paper a grade of C, just remember, that was the same grade Frederick W. Smith received for a Yale undergraduate paper which contained early plans for an overnight air express venture, the original blueprints for Federal Express. Vision is the root of leadership, and Smith's plans were certainly visionary. However, succeeding in business (and making better than a C at Yale) requires more than vision. A leader's vision must also be well executed, else the vision remains only a dream, not a reality.[1]

After a tour of duty as a Marine Corps pilot in Vietnam, Smith returned to fulfill his dream. He and his business partners commissioned two independent market research studies which suggested a market niche for a reli-

able, time-definite overnight delivery service. Then they executed the vision. The engines of the Federal Express eight-plane fleet first hummed on April 17, 1973, marking the birth of a new company and the genesis of a new service industry, overnight air express.

Seven of the eight packages shipped that first night were trial runs addressed from one Federal Express salesperson to another. This was an inauspicious beginning for a startup that would become the only U.S. company to top $1 billion in revenues within its first 10 years. Although competitors have flocked to the market, Federal Express remains the unquestioned leader in overnight air express, with 45 percent market share and about $8 billion in 1992 revenues. Federal Express commands the world's largest air cargo fleet, 420 aircraft, and more than 94,000 employees worldwide to move nearly 300 million packages each year to and from customers in nearly 170 countries. To crown these business successes, in 1990, Federal Express became the first winner of the Malcolm Baldrige National Quality Award in the Service Company category.

What is the secret to such business success? Patented business school answers include: first

* This case was prepared by Greg Bounds.
1. The author thanks Fred Smith, CEO of Federal Express, for his gracious contributions and Anne Manning, senior specialist, corporate relations, for her assistance in preparing this case. For more details on how Federal Express executes its vision, see one of the key sources of information for this case, *Blueprints for Service Quality: The Federal Express Approach*, American Management Association Membership Publications Division, New York, 1991.

entrance to the market, product differentiation, innovative systems, leading technological capability, and reliable, high-quality service. These answers are all true; for example, Federal Express pioneered the "hub and spoke" pickup, sorting, and delivery network that allowed it to be the first to transport small packages and documents for customers door-to-door, from one U.S. location to another, overnight. However, the fundamental principle underlying all of these answers, and leading to Federal Express's business success and 1990 Baldrige award, was stated quite simply in its 1991 annual report: "Since our first day of operations, an intense focus on the needs of our customers and an absolute commitment to continuous quality improvement have defined Federal Express."

CEO Smith reiterated the conceptual simplicity of business success in a keynote speech before a national conference on quality and leadership held in conjunction with the Baldrige award ceremonies: "There is no secret to whatever success Federal Express has enjoyed. What we do is all in the books. Our secret, if there is one, is just doing what they say." In other words, the key to a leader's success is execution of the vision. To provide a context for a discussion of how Federal Express refines and executes its vision, we now briefly review Federal Express's current service strategies and systems for executing these strategies.

▶ CURRENT SERVICE STRATEGIES AND SYSTEMS

The current Federal Express service strategies were summarized in its 1991 annual report: "Our strategies are long-term and focused on one mission—to provide our customers with totally reliable, competitively superior global air/ground transportation of high priority goods and documents that require rapid, time-certain delivery." To provide superior service in an overnight air express market maturing with competition and globalization, Federal Express must continuously improve its service strategies and matching systems.[2] Some recent improvements are discussed below.

Integrated Sales Force

In recent years, Federal Express fully integrated its global sales force to sell all of its services discussed below. Additional resources were added to its global sales force of 17,000 to support this strategy (e.g., 250 extra sales professionals in fiscal 1991). Customers are contacted in a coordinated fashion by a single account team responsible for understanding and responding to their unique needs.

Standard Overnight Service

The FedEx Standard Overnight Service in the United States (SOS), with deliveries to most addresses next business day by 3 p.m., was initially limited to five pounds. In 1990, Federal Express expanded the five-pound limit to 150 pounds. This service offers customers next-afternoon delivery at a price that is highly competitive with all other next-day services in the marketplace. This lower-cost option provides customers with a choice: early morning delivery with FedEx Priority Overnight Service, or delivery later in the day at a money-saving price. The customer response exceeded the forecast and self-dilution (FedEx customers shifting from Priority Overnight to SOS) occurred at an acceptably low rate.

Overnight Freight Service

The FedEx Overnight Freight Service (OFS) was launched in 1991 in the United States to provide next-day-by-noon delivery for individual packages weighing up to 500 pounds. With advance arrangements, Federal Express will ac-

---

2. For more details on these service strategies and systems, see the sources from which these descriptions were lifted: Federal Express Annual Reports, supporting documents, and marketing brochures.

cept packages of virtually any weight for OFS delivery. Federal Express continues to offer a two-day freight service with a delivery commitment of 4:30 p.m. Demand for both services has outstripped pre-launch forecasts.

Powership Systems

A Powership system consists of a computer and accompanying devices installed at customer locations. The system allows customers to speed up the shipping process by eliminating the need for airbills. The system also performs numerous shipping tasks—label preparation, on-line package tracking, daily self-invoicing, and even international paperwork preparation—more quickly and easily than manual methods. The use of Powership systems by customers has grown dramatically over the last few years (e.g., by 60 percent in fiscal 1991). Federal Express plans to continue installing several thousand Powership systems each year. Over one-third of its volume and revenue each day is processed through Powerships, saving customers time and saving Federal Express money.

EXPRESSfreighter

In August 1989, a merger with Flying Tigers was completed. As Federal Express integrated two very different businesses, the company's international strategy gained a clearer focus. The schedule and route structure that Flying Tigers flew and Federal Express utilized after the merger were based on a complicated system of collecting and consolidating heavy freight at key terminals around the world. Central to this system was the concept of allocations, which gave each flight a certain amount of transcontinental space allocated to each terminal it served. While this system worked fairly well in the less time-sensitive markets previously served by Flying Tigers, it proved to be counterproductive in most cases to the time-definite high-value market thought by Federal Express to have the greatest long-term potential.

In January 1991, Federal Express launched a totally new concept called EXPRESSfreighter to change forever the way international shippers look at the airfreight market. The concept capitalizes on Federal Express strengths: global route authorities, enormous lift capacity, worldwide integrated information network, and growing sales and marketing capability throughout the world.

EXPRESSfreighter combines the cargo capacity of the Federal Express wide-body fleet (including thirteen new MD-11 wide-bodied jets) with the speed and reliability of international express services to substantially reduce transit times on intercontinental routes. The first EXPRESSfreighter flight linked Hong King nonstop to Anchorage, then on to the continental United States and Europe. By using a later departure, in the early evening, Federal Express can now offer Hong Kong customers late cutoff times, daily frequencies, and overnight service by 10:30 the next morning to the United States, Canada, portions of Mexico, and Caracas, Venezuela. Federal Express has added EXPRESSfreighter service to Singapore, Penang in Malaysia, Osaka in Japan, Frankfurt, and London, with direct flights into Federal Express North American hubs.

Federal Express renamed its International Distribution Service to call it FedEx International EXPRESSfreight Service (IXF), a high-yielding, time-definite service for shipments of virtually any size and weight. The service is available two ways: as a time-definite airport-to-airport service, with freight forwarders, brokers, or freight agents handling pickup, delivery, and customs clearance; or as a time-definite airport-to-airport service with customs clearance provided by Federal Express.

FSTCLEAR System

Federal Express offers customers using its International Priority Service and International EXPRESSfreight Service the advantage of a worldwide electronic customs clearance system that speeds up the process of clearing dutiable goods. The FSTCLEAR system has revolutionized the way declared items are cleared through customs. The process starts almost immediately after the package leaves the origin station, and most shipments have been precleared before they reach the destination clearance point. Through electronic manifesting, customs agents can "see" the shipments electronically before they ever arrive, and decide which can be cleared and which need additional examination.

These are some of the recent service strategy and system improvements made by Federal Express to continuously improve the value of its services to customers. These strategy and system improvements are important; however, to make the vision real and make the strategies and systems work, Federal Express seeks to improve every facet of its organization. The driving force for all of this continuous improvement at Federal Express is its leadership.

▶ LEADERSHIP FOR THE FUTURE

A seventeen-year path to service excellence seemingly came to fruition when Federal Express won the Baldrige award in 1990. Federal Express leaders could have been content to view the award as a symbol of their arrival at the end of their journey to service excellence. However, CEO Fred Smith recognized the award as one of many fruits to be earned on the never-ending journey of continuous improvement when he called the award "our license to practice." The award was simply a confirmation that Federal Express was putting in place a quality process to continuously improve every facet of the company. It confirmed that Federal Express was on the right path, not that they had arrived.

More evidence of progress on that path came in fiscal 1991, when Federal Express achieved its best performance ever on its service quality indicators (SQIs), setting records for daily, weekly, and monthly service. Through quality action teams (QATs) making improvements throughout the company, operating costs were driven down while quality performance went up. In fact, head count during the year grew at only half the rate of package volume. As a result of all the productivity and quality improvements, overall customer satisfaction with Federal Express service increased 12 percentage points from the previous year.

Though he is perhaps too modest to admit it, Fred Smith realizes that such improvements result only from capable leadership. Below, you will read Fred Smith's own words describing the Federal Express vision of how to "provide our customers with totally reliable, competitively superior global air/ground transportation of high priority goods and documents that require rapid, time-certain delivery." Supplementary comments (in brackets) and figures elaborate on some of Smith's key points about continuous improvement, such as the SQIs and QATs mentioned above.

▶ FRED SMITH ON EXECUTING THE VISION[3]

This is a speech entitled "Surviving the Global Market" given by Frederick W. Smith, Chairman and Chief Executive Officer, Federal Express Corporation, in Seattle, Wash., and Portland, Ore., on Nov. 12 and 13, 1991.

Now, I'd like to begin by telling you the story of a lady by the name of Margaret Jane who lives near Portland, Oregon, where, to this day, the townspeople talk about her vacation to Cannon Beach. Well, one bright, sunny day she took her son, little Jamie, to play in the surf at the water's edge. The sun was relentless, so she put lots of Coppertone 52 on his back and protected his little head with a Portland Trailblazers cap. They were digging in the sand in the shallow water when suddenly a *huge* wave swept over them, carrying Jamie out to sea, cap and all. Margaret Jane tried to save him, but to no avail. In desperation, she fell to her knees on the sand and cried, "Dear Lord, *please* return my son . . . I'll do anything . . . just bring my little boy back. If I can just see his sweet face one more time, I *promise* I'll never ask for another thing."

No sooner had she stopped praying when, out of

the blue, another gigantic wave plopped Jamie on the sand before her. She grabbed him in her arms, kissed his startled face, and took a long, hard look at him. She raised her face to the sky, narrowed her eyes, furrowed her brow and demanded, "OK, Lord, *where* is that Trailblazers cap!?!" Some people are just never satisfied.

Oh, well, who was it who said, "You can't please all the people all of the time"? We've hidden behind that adage for years, haven't we? After all, we in business have developed the best products we can. We engineered them to our highest quality standards. We've tried to give our customers what *we* think they want. Isn't that enough? No, it is not.

Customer satisfaction is *everything.* "Quality" means nothing if the product we make or the service we give is not exactly what the customer wants. Federal Express was based on that premise from the very beginning of the company. Now, I have to be up front with you. What we do at Federal Express is nothing new, nothing original. We just read the Demings, the Kantors, the Druckers, and work very, very hard to follow their advice. It's not easy.

While we were greatly honored to win the 1990 Malcolm Baldrige National Quality Award, we still have a long journey ahead of us. And so, Total Quality Management will continue to be Federal Express's single greatest management task into the 90s. It has to be, because "quality" is absolutely the only road to a satisfied customer at the end of each and every transaction. Our mission, our strategy, our definition of service are all focused on that one goal, a 100 percent completely satisfied customer, service to *his* standards, and not ours. And that has been our goal from day one.

And so, the Federal Express story is not a typical Malcolm Baldrige winner's story. It is not a dramatic story, like Xerox's, of a giant turnaround and reclaiming of market share from the Japanese. From the beginning, ours has been a story of continuous improvement, of an intense effort to eradicate errors and to reach 100 percent customer satisfaction, and nothing less.

In striving for that goal, we have become convinced that customer satisfaction *begins* with employee satisfaction. The processes and programs supporting this concept were noted by the Baldrige examiners as

strengths in our application. Our winning in the service category, I hope, emphasizes the necessity of a highly motivated workforce in achieving customer satisfaction. Unquestionably, the efforts, the talents, the commitment of our people are at the forefront of our customers' perception of our quality.

Each positive daily interaction with a customer is priceless, and absolutely impossible to measure. The fact is, interactions with customers are transient. We can't "re-call" a bad experience, like we can a faulty part, fix it and put it back into service so it works right the second time. All the more reason to create a workplace that responds to the human desire to be a part of a greater mission, one in which everyone can contribute and make a difference.

For that reason, we've tried to communicate to our people in a variety of ways that their company's goals are very much in line with their personal goals. We try to do that by answering a set of essential questions:

> What's in it for me?
> What do you expect of me?
> Where do I go if I need help?
> Where do I go to get justice if I have a problem involving my career?
> Is there opportunity to grow, to be challenged, and to get ahead?

When answers to these questions are reinforced with action, the next question will be from our people and most likely will be, "How can I help?" Our corporate philosophy, "people, service, profit," is at the heart of those answers. Three simple words, easy to say, easy to remember, hard to do. Putting people first in every action, every planning process, every business decision requires a tremendous commitment from every manager, indeed, every employee. But because customer satisfaction clearly does start with employee satisfaction, we can't let anything distract us.

Here's the message we try to communicate to our people: the purpose of a business is to gain and keep customers. A courier's job, for example, is to work directly for the customer. Our front-line manager's job is to make the courier's job easier, and her manager's job is to make the front-line manager's job easier, and so on until, for example, you get to me, and

Figure 1

Maintaining a "flat" organizational hierarchy

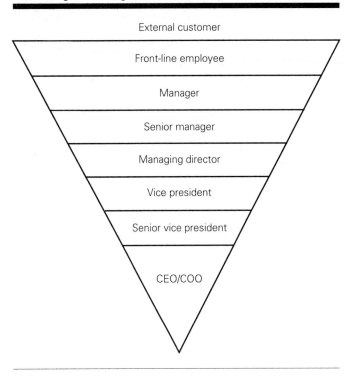

External customer

Front-line employee

Manager

Senior manager

Managing director

Vice president

Senior vice president

CEO/COO

my job is to do whatever it takes to help all of our people do their best. The concept is called "servant leadership."

One reason that task is somewhat easier at our company is that we adhere to five layers of management between our nonmanagement people and the executive suite. Now, the way those five layers look is not what you might expect. We have truly made an effort to invert the traditional hierarchical pyramid and put the emphasis where it belongs, where the rubber meets the road, with our customer-contact people. If you look at your organization chart that way, everyone in this room is your top officer's customer [See Figure 1.]

Do you see what happens when you invert the pyramid? Customers are right on top, where they have to be if our companies are to remain on top. If we're going to expect our people to be the best they can be, to demonstrate a people-first attitude in everything

they do, and to treat every fellow employee as a customer, then we must maintain an environment that encourages it. This is critical to the way our business runs, or any company runs, for that matter. The Malcolm Baldrige examiners cited our people-first philosophy and the processes that demonstrate it as a primary reason for our winning the service award.

The whole idea of servant leadership and the internal customer concept have been practiced from the early days at FedEx, even before they became buzzwords. Of course, there was really no other way we could operate. Consider what we do. We're like a Broadway play. Our curtain goes up on a new performance every night. Unfinished work cannot be postponed, thus, we can't postpone "the last act." This imperative is supported by 92,000 people who perform according to a finely tuned scenario in which timing is everything.

A late plane out of Brussels will affect operations

in New York, Anchorage, the far east, and nearly every place in between, and we have over 400 planes in the air every night. Mechanics must maintain these aircraft in top condition so that our pilots arrive on time at airports, where our couriers must sort and deliver those packages, documents, and freight, *on time*, to hundreds of thousands of customers around the world, every day. Customer service agents on five continents must be able to help our customers with their first shipment, or their bulk shipment or their overdue shipment, every day. And they must all work together to make good on our promise to our customers of absolutely, positively on-time delivery, every time.

And adding to that daily challenge are elements beyond our control, a hurricane in England, of all places, volcanic eruptions in Alaska, an earthquake in San Francisco, not to mention the usual rain, fog, sleet, or snow. These are the times when we have to rely on contingency plans, and backup contingency plans, and sometimes no contingency but the human ingenuity to make the right decision on the spot, and to *act* expediently, every time. In short, every employee must be empowered to do what has to be done in the name of customer satisfaction.

We've learned that you've got to let people take appropriate risks to serve customers once in a while, even if it means making a mistake or two once in a while. Well-intentioned efforts are just as important as successes. And, if you hang your sales or customer support people for trying to do something that doesn't quite work, you'll just get people who won't try anything. That's why we make our customer satisfaction policy quite clear:

- Take any step necessary to solve customer problems.
- Arrange the most expeditious delivery.
- Arrange a prompt refund or credit.

Of course, we must pay much more than lip service to empowerment. For example, our customer service agents can solve a customer's shipping problem on the spot for up to $250. And they know how to take care of the unusual; for instance, it was a customer service agent who initiated the special Federal Express delivery of a pump to Waco, Texas, where it saved the life of the little girl in the well, Jessica McClure. Our executive services people can do whatever it takes to expedite a shipment, hire a Lear jet to deliver one package if that's what it takes. And our first-line billing agents can arrange a refund or credit for up to $2,000 while on the phone with a customer. In fact, just one phone call to a managing director will allow an agent to refund up to $10,000. That's a lot of customer satisfaction for a few minutes on hold.

Setting clear goals and reinforcing them by word and action is at the heart of empowerment. Our people/service/profit philosophy guides our goal-setting process and we put teeth in our corporate goals by making management bonuses contingent upon our achieving them. If the goals are not met, no manager, no matter how high, gets a bonus, including me. It tends to keep everybody "reality-focused." [The Federal Express organization effectiveness department consults with managers and professionals using the audit checklist shown in Figure 2 to help improve their approach to goal setting.]

Our measurable people goal is the continuous improvement of our management leadership index score, which is drawn from our annual survey feedback action program. You'll hear more about that later. Our service standard is total customer satisfaction: 100 percent on-time deliveries, 100 percent accurate information. But as I'll describe in more detail later, we use customer-focused service quality indicators to measure our service failures in absolute numbers. We call it our "SQI process." Guided by daily reports from the SQI process, we focus on reducing those failures. Progress is reflected in reduced SQI points. The profit goal is to improve profit margins by a specified percentage.

Do we put our money where our mouth is? 1990 was the year we won the Malcolm Baldrige award. It was also the first year that no management bonuses were given. But to actually make the goal-setting process work in a large organization, everyone has to understand thoroughly the corporate mission and goals, and that requires keeping everyone well informed as to how the company's doing.

In addition to our formal communication channels, we employ a variety of programs that encourage two-way communication. The Baldrige examiners cited two in particular: our survey feedback action program (we call it "SFA") and the guaranteed fair

Figure 2

Audit checksheet for improving the approach to goal setting

	Does objective support corporate/ division/ department objectives?	Does objective support department key strategies?	Does objective reflect appropriate scope for this position?	Is it —specific —measurable —time bound —sufficient challenge?
Obj. 1				
Obj. 2				
Obj. 3				
Obj. 4				
Obj. 5				
Obj. 6				
Obj. 7				
Obj. 8				
Obj. 9				
Obj. 10				

                                                                            Yes   No

Does this participant's entire set of objectives:
  —appear to be appropriately aligned with internal and external work units?
  —reflect highly leveraged objectives?
  —reflect an appropriate balance of people/service/profit objectives?
  —avoid duplication of effort within his/her organization?

COMMENTS: _____

treatment procedure, our internal grievance process. SFA has been a part of our quality process for eleven years. This annual survey gives people an opportunity to express attitudes about the company, management, pay and benefits, and our service. In many ways, it's not unlike most companies' satisfaction surveys. [See the survey questions listed in Figure 3.]

What is different is the focus of the first ten statements, the statements that comprise the leadership index that determines annual bonuses. Those ten statements do not evaluate how closely managers supervise their people, nor do they assess how well they manage their budget. Instead, the leadership index reveals how well managers support their people and how well they empower them, *as perceived by each manager's customers*, the people who report to him. Allow me to cite three of those questions: "My manager asks

for my ideas about work," "I can tell my manager what I think," and, "My manager tells me when I do a good job."

I think you can see that the value we place on our people's opinions is very high, and we send that message in a variety of ways. SFA is just one of them. While individual responses are kept confidential, overall results are passed on to all managers, who must then meet with their work groups to develop an action plan for resolving any problem surfaced. To ensure that this part of the SFA process really works, we've added Statement 29: "The concerns identified by my workgroup in last year's survey feedback have been addressed."

I think you can see how SFA encourages strong, even-handed leadership and open communication, as does our guaranteed fair treatment process. The aim

Figure 3

Questions for survey feedback action (SFA) program

1. I feel free to tell my manager what I think.
2. My manager lets me know what's expected of me.
3. Favoritism is not a problem in my workgroup.
4. My manager helps us find ways to do our jobs better.
5. My manager is willing to listen to my concerns.
6. My manager asks for my ideas about things affecting our work.
7. My manager lets me know when I've done a good job.
8. My manager treats me with respect and dignity.
9. My manager keeps me informed about things I need to know.
10. My manager lets me do my job without interfering.
11. My manager's boss gives us the support we need.
12. Upper management (directors and above) lets us know what the company is trying to accomplish.
13. Upper management (directors and above) pays attention to ideas and suggestions from people at my level.
14. I have confidence in the fairness of management.
15. I can be sure of a job as long as I do good work.
16. I am proud to work for Federal Express.
17. Working for Federal Express will probably lead to the kind of future I want.
18. I think Federal Express does a good job for our customers.
19. All things considered, working for Federal Express is a good deal for me.
20. I am paid fairly for the kind of work I do.
21. Our benefit programs seem to meet most of my needs.
22. Most people in my workgroup cooperate with each other to get the job done.
23. There is cooperation between my workgroup and other groups in Federal Express.
24. In my work environment, we generally use safe work practices.
25. Rules and procedures do not interfere with how well I am able to do my job.
26. I am able to get the supplies or other resources I need to do my job.
27. I have enough freedom to do my job well.
28. My workgroup is involved in activities to improve service to our group's customers.
29. The concerns identified by my workgroup during last year's SFA feedback session have been satisfactorily addressed.

of the GFT process is to maintain a truly fair environment, in which anyone who has a grievance or concern about his or her job or who feels that he or she has been mistreated (for whatever reason) can have these concerns addressed through the management chain. In fact, every week our chief personnel officer, two rotating senior VPs, and I meet to review GFT cases that have progressed through the three-step internal process to the final stage, the appeals board.

Both the survey feedback action program and the guaranteed fair treatment process promote open communication. These are just two more ways we encourage people to take part, offer suggestions for improvement, question decisions, and surface concerns.

Through in-house surveys, we confirmed the notion that most people in the workplace prefer their immediate manager as their primary information source. And so we focus our communications effort on our frontline managers.

As we've expanded across international borders, that strategy has made very good sense. In our case, global dispersion and rapid expansion to 135 countries complicates communications tremendously. So we've established a live television network, FXTV, that, so far, reaches our people throughout the United States, Canada, and Europe. FXTV was implemented as an aid to quality deployment with no apparent ROI in dollars.

"FedEx Overnight" airs live every morning and is taped at receiving locations for viewing throughout the day. "FedEx Overnight" reports how well we did the night before, recapping operations worldwide. The regular telecast helps our people respond to problems our customers may be experiencing. This program and others fully dedicated to the quality topic give us the opportunity to demonstrate the commitment of our senior management to quality. In fact, each one of our senior officers has had a lead role at some time or other, including me.

The FXTV network has proven invaluable to our managing major changes. We announced our acquisition of Flying Tigers, for example, to our employees immediately after informing the wire services. Then, throughout the integration and final merger process, we used FXTV for live phone-in question-and-answer sessions between senior management and employees. We "go live" with our senior officers any time there is a major event that may affect our people, for example, the day after the gulf war began, or a few days after our cost containment memos were distributed.

A little over a year ago we had a unique occasion to use FXTV. ABC's Friday night program "20/20" concocted a story about FedEx based on reports by two former couriers. We didn't know how they would treat the story. We just knew it was going to be *bad*. So Jim Barksdale, our former COO, and Tom Oliver, then senior vice president of sales, went on the air live at noon the day ABC's Federal Express story was to be shown on "20/20." All we wanted to do was tell our employees the facts so when they went to work Monday morning, they wouldn't be blind-sided by customers' questions. FXTV has returned an inestimable return on our investment in people. The Malcolm Baldrige report noted its effective use in the training process along with our extensive use of sophisticated interactive video.

All customer contact people receive extensive training before they assume their jobs. For example, our call center agents are given six weeks of intensive classroom and hands-on training before taking their first call. Then we expect our people to hit the ground running with the ability to handle any customer situation. We want every customer inquiry to be handled by the first person customers talk with. Just think for a minute how frustrating it is to be passed around a company for an answer.

That is why every six months couriers, service agents, and customer service agents participate in a job knowledge testing program. These tests are online and can be taken at any computer terminal. This recurrent training has been part of our pilots' FAA requirement for years. And just as the FAA requires pilots who fail the tests to be taken off the line until they can pass, so are our couriers and customers agents. Pass or fail, each person receives a personalized "prescription" that targets areas requiring review with recommended resources, training materials, and interactive video lessons to help them get back up to speed.

We then try to catch people doing something right. We seek ways to reward individual and team quality efforts, and we generally don't have to look very far. For example, the "Circle of Excellence" award, presented monthly to the best performing Federal Express station, underscores teamwork. The winning station has its group photo placed in the lobby of corporate headquarters.

Our "Golden Falcon" is awarded to employees who go above and beyond to serve their customers. For example, Stephanie Flores, in southern Louisiana, hiked through flood water up to her knees to deliver one company's payroll. Maurice Jan't (pronounced Jana) scanned all of the packages he was picking up on the ninth floor of an office building in the middle of the San Francisco earthquake. Then he carried them nine floors down a rubble-strewn staircase so he could get to the airport on time. And do you know how we found out about Stephanie and Maurice? Their customers wrote to tell us about them, as they do about hundreds of other FedEx employees.

The "Bravo Zulu" (a Navy term for "well done") program gives managers the option of awarding a dinner, theater tickets, or cash to any employee who's done a particularly outstanding job.

But what is becoming increasingly more obvious to us is that, for most employees, the job itself is the reward: the autonomy and empowerment to make on-the-spot decisions to meet our customers' needs, the opportunity to design one's job, as our customer service agent task force was able to do, the opportunity to share with engineers the benefit of experience to make new technology work better, as our couriers did when we rolled out the SuperTracker, a vital link in our computer tracking system, COSMOS. COSMOS allows real-time process control of every transaction, 24 hours a day. That means we can capture more than 99 percent of customer data on all packages shipped, and remember, that's over 1.5 million a day.

Briefly, here's how our tracking system works: when a call comes into one of our twenty-four global customer service centers, a courier is dispatched to pick up the package. He or she scans the bar code on the package with the SuperTracker. Then the bar code is scanned again each time the package changes hands: at the station before it leaves your city, in one of our sorting centers before it is placed in a container to be loaded on a plane, at the destination station, before it's placed in a van, and finally, when it is delivered to our customers.

As our couriers are picking up and delivering their packages, they are continually informed through the computer in their vans about other packages to be picked up. The computer is called a DADS unit, and it automatically arranges the pickups in the most efficient order. Upon returning to his van the courier places his SuperTracker in a "shoe" in the DADS unit, immediately downloading the information into the COSMOS system. In this way, our customers can be updated on a real-time basis about the location of their packages.

Data collected through this process allows us to measure our service in absolute numbers, something we realized we'd have to do if we were serious about 100 percent customer satisfaction. As I mentioned earlier, we've been able to maintain service levels of 98 to 99 percent for several years now. However, as our volume grew from thousands of packages to over 1.5 million a day, 98 percent just wasn't good enough in absolute terms.

Just consider what we, as customers, would have to settle for from some of our most important services if things were done correctly even 99.9 percent of the time: two unsafe landings a week at Chicago's O'Hare Airport, 20,000 incorrect drug prescriptions per year, 500 bungled surgical operations each week, fifty new-born babies dropped at birth each day, and 22,000 checks deducted from the wrong bank account each hour. Can you imagine accepting that kind of performance? Why, we'd never get off the ground. We would drive everywhere, keep our money in a shoebox, and practice celibacy the rest of our lives.

We don't want our customers to settle for anything less than 100 percent error-free service from us either. So, starting in 1987, we put the full court press on refining our quality processes. We forgot about percentages and began to look at actual numbers of failures. We identified twelve major causes of customer aggravation, weighting each according to the customer's frustration level. Let me explain.

If you are expecting an important package today, say, a report from one of your international clients that has to be revised before a 10:00 meeting tomorrow morning, and it hasn't arrived by 10:30 a.m. today, as we promised, you might be worried. Maybe enough to call us. Upon hearing that the package is in Portland and will arrive by 11:30 today, you relax. Just an hour later than we promised, just an hour lost. We call this a "Right Day Late" and weight it one point because the "hassle factor" for you is minimal. By the way, we would have chalked up a "Right Day Late" error even if that document were only one minute late.

However, if your report doesn't arrive until tomorrow, the day of your meeting, and your deadline is breathing down your neck, the hassle factor increases substantially. We call that a "Wrong Day Late" and give it five points. But should we lose your report, heaven forbid, and you can't begin to prepare for your meeting, then you are really upset and so are a whole lot of other people around you. That rates a ten and just the opposite from what a ten usually implies!

Every day, we add up the failure points and call the total our SQI, service quality indicator At current package volumes, weighted points give us 60 million chances to fail every day. The first year we instituted the SQI, we averaged 152,000 daily points. The monthly average for August 1991 was 99,959. Our goal is to reduce that number to 15,000 over the next three years. We've set annual SQI goals to help us meet our ultimate goal, and, when we reach that, we'll set them even lower. [For more information on the Federal

Express approach to measuring service quality, see Appendix I, "Taking the Measure of Quality."]

Our quality action team program, which currently involves 1,000 teams, known as QATs, all over the world, was cited for involving people at all corporate levels. Cross-divisional root cause teams, each led by a vice president, focus on each one of the twelve SQI indexes. Divisional and work group QATs solve hundreds of little problems and come up with solutions that improve our service *and* save money. For example, one quality action team in the hub came up with a plan to reduce the training time of our document sorters, with savings to us of $3,096,000 annually. [For more information on the Federal Express approach to continuous improvement, see Appendix II, "Quality Deployment."]

Through employee involvement, FedEx's Los Angeles metro district improved "Late on the Right Day" and "Late on the Wrong Day" SQI performance by 51 percent. Quite an accomplishment, as you might guess if you've tried to get around in L.A. By fostering strong customer-supplier relationships, our procurement department reduced the number of FedEx vendors from nearly 4,000 to 100, retaining only those who practice quality processes. They saved 40 million dollars over a three-year period. To put that in perspective, our sales division would need to generate equivalent revenue of $668.5 million to have the same effect on our profitability.

When you multiply those kinds of numbers throughout Federal Express around the world, the vital role of employees becomes abundantly clear. For us, it also represents one more extension of our "people first" philosophy. The question is: how do we know that "people first" management and state-of-the-art technology and the SQI error reduction process really work? How do we *know* that all this is making a difference where it really counts?

The final test of quality resides with our customers. So we survey them continuously. Every day, in fact, an independent company conducts telephone interviews with approximately 150 customers, about 2,400 a quarter. Every question has five possible responses, ranging from 5 for "completely satisfied," 4 for "satisfied," and so on down to 1 for "completely dissatisfied."

Now here's where we make it tough on ourselves. We count *only* the top box, the number of "5" responses, when reporting our customer satisfaction levels. We don't collapse the top two as most surveys do, because we believe there's a lot of room for improvement between satisfied and completely satisfied. For example, how many of you use Federal Express's service? [*show of hands*] Keep your hands up if you are satisfied with our service. Now, keep them up only if you're completely satisfied. You see, we still have a lot of work to do! Of course, we're very proud of the fact that 92 percent of our customers report being completely satisfied. But it's that 8 percent that will keep quality at the top of our mind until we reach 100 percent.

Do quality processes have any effect on customer satisfaction? You be the judge. [We have data that indicate] the more we reduce the number of errors, the higher customer satisfaction goes. Unquestionably, the factors that will continue to push those lines in opposite directions are the efforts, the talents, and the dedication of our people. Our people made all of this happen. Indeed, employee satisfaction does lead to customer satisfaction.

No matter what business you're in, we believe when people understand the corporate mission, know what is expected of them, and *believe* they can make a difference because they are listened to and are allowed to put their ideas to work, they *will* make a difference. They will go beyond our expectations, and great things will start to happen.

Dan Yankelovich coined the phrase "discretionary effort" and defined it as "the difference between the maximum of effort and care which an individual *can* contribute and the minimum amount necessary to avoid being punished or fired." Discretionary effort is totally within each employee's control, to contribute or withhold as he or she chooses. Our challenge is to create organizations that encourage every person to *use* discretionary effort. We found that the more people are empowered in this way, the more they will freely choose to exert extra effort, and the more ordinary people will produce extraordinary performance.

And the customers? Well, they just keep coming back.

▶ CONCLUDING COMMENTS

In summary, Federal Express leaders have a vision, along with the service strategies, systems, and an approach to continuous improvement that can make the vision real. They believe that as global communities grow more closely aligned, politically, economically, and culturally, the demand for time-definite, reliable, cost-efficient transportation of high-value goods and documents will grow at a quickening pace. And they intend to offer "totally reliable, competitively superior" services in this overnight air express market, a market that they feel holds "the greatest potential for long-term growth and meaningful returns on our investment." In executing the company's vision, Federal Express leaders continuously improve the company's ability to meet this growing demand with a worldwide network of service, linked with modern aircraft and vehicle fleets, a comprehensive information network, and a highly motivated and focused group of employees.

▶ DISCUSSION QUESTIONS

1. Describe Federal Express in terms of its:
   a. Vision
   b. Strategies for service
   c. Systems
   d. Approach to continuous improvement (including methods and measurements)

   Note the synergies among these four aspects of Federal Express. How does each aspect either support or operationalize the others?

2. What incongruities are there between Federal Express's vision, strategies, systems, and approaches to continuous improvement?

3. As a consultant to Federal Express, what changes would you propose to eliminate these incongruities?

4. The industry in which Federal Express operates is increasingly competitive. What should Federal Express do to ensure that it provides superior value to customers in the future?

Taking the Measure of Quality

We believe that service quality must be mathematically measured.
—Frederick W. Smith, Chairman and CEO, Federal Express

If there still exists a service company that believes quality measures can only apply to manufacturing processes, Federal Express is not it. A commitment to clear, frequently repeated quality goals—followed up with continuous measurement of progress against these goals—forms the foundation of the Federal Express approach to quality.

The company's two ambitious quality goals are straight-forward and unequivocal: 100 percent customer satisfaction after every interaction and transaction, and 100 percent service performance on every package handled. While at first blush the "100 percent" language seems to smack of half-time pep talks, it nevertheless represents the kind of quality goal statement that is fundamental to fostering daily, incremental, continuous quality improvement within an organization.

Federal Express's leadership recognized early on the allure—and the danger—of settling for a quality commitment that was less than 100 percent. A difference of 2 percentage points hardly seems worth worrying about. But if the temptation to shave off a few points is great, the pitfalls are greater. In other words, if each person, department, and division within a service organization handles its assigned task at a 98 percent level of satisfactory performance, the end result won't be a 98 percent service level for the entire system, but something closer to 94 percent.

That is, problems, mistakes, delays, and inefficiencies get passed along from one operation to the next, in linear fashion, following an almost inexorable course leading to a compounded decrease in performance when viewed in the aggregate. For that reason, early in its history, Federal Express established what might have seemed an idealistic, but hopelessly naive target—the "100 percent service level" goal on all deliveries within the time commitments pledged to customers.

It took somewhat longer for the company to grasp all the implications of its other long-standing corporate quality goal, 100 percent customer satisfaction after each interaction and transaction. Company leaders insist their commitment to satisfied customers was there from the beginning—even before the beginning—as evidenced by the two preemptive market research studies conducted by the founders. Those studies persuaded FedEx that the world just might need a time-definite express delivery service and also suggested some of the measures by which a customer would value and judge such a service.

But from the first days of FedEx's operation until well into the late 1980s, the primary gauge by which the company measured service performance and customer satisfaction was percentage of on-time delivery—the number of packages delivered on time as a percentage of total package volume. By the late 1980s, Federal Express officials began to recognize that percentage of on-time delivery was, in reality, an internal or introspective measure of customer satisfaction using the company's own standards, not an external measure of customer satisfaction using the customer's standards.

Federal Express had by no means completely ignored the customer's perception of its performance. Quite the contrary. The company has cataloged customer complaints since the early '80s and has used that information to evaluate internal systems, change procedures, and tighten policies in order to eliminate the causes of frequently occurring complaints.

Dubbed the "Hierarchy of Horrors" by CEO Smith, the eight most common complaints were: wrong day delivery (a package delivered on a day later than that promised), right day late delivery (a package delivered on the promised day, but after the promised deadline—even one minute after), pick-up not made (failure to make a pick-up on the day requested), lost package, customer misinformed by Federal Express (mistaken or inaccurate information on rates, schedules, etc.), billing and paperwork mistakes (invoice errors, overcharges, missed proof-of-delivery documents), employee performance failures (courtesy, responsiveness, etc.), and damaged package.

To this day, Federal Express continues to react to and track customer complaints. The company has instituted a complaint-handling process in which complaint letters addressed to the CEO or COO are answered in writing, or by personal phone call, within 24 hours. Telecommunications experts and the customer service department are currently collaborating on a system that would allow the company to track and store data on all complaints, then sort the data by customer account number and geographic region, to pinpoint recurring problems and come up with solutions.

In addition to its catalog of "Horrors," the company also conducts customer satisfaction surveys regularly in an attempt to divine shortfalls in its overall performance. But at the same time as the Hierarchy of Horrors offered valuable insight into customer ex-

pectations and disappointments, it also served to illustrate the fallacy of measuring customer satisfaction primarily in terms of on-time delivery.

Company officials came to see, as all service companies must, that even when a company meets the "bottom line" of a service commitment—the service is rendered professionally, on time, and within price expectations—the customer may still wind up disappointed and disgruntled for any number of service-related reasons.

In other words, even when Federal Express couriers, pilots, and sorters handle a package flawlessly, on time, and with no damage, a customer might still be irritated at finding a mistake on an invoice or at hearing an impatient edge in a customer service agent's telephone voice.

The "Horrors" also failed to differentiate among various sorts of complaints as to their relative impacts on customer satisfaction. As the manager's guide explains:

> The frequency of a particular complaint does not necessarily reflect the impact a particular "Horror" has on the customer's perception of our services, nor does it indicate the extent to which a particular service factor influences the customer's overall perception. For example, when no proof of delivery is available, an on-time delivery loses some of its value.

Moreover, both the "Horrors" and the customer satisfaction surveys were deficient in one key area—they did not elicit the kind of information that would give management the capacity to be proactive—that is, anticipating and eliminating customer complaints before the letter or call comes in. With some customer service studies suggesting that 70 percent or more of all customers who have a "beef" with a company never voice their complaints, the statistical implications of a large company measuring customer satisfaction solely on the basis of on-record complaints is staggering.

On a typical day, for example, when 1.5 million packages travel through the Federal Express system, and 99 percent of all those packages reach their destination on time, undamaged, with accurate paperwork, the remaining one percent could represent 15,000 unhappy customers. Not all customers with a late package are unhappy. But if all 15,000 are unhappy, the company still may hear from only 4,500.

Over time, some key components of a feasible approach to measuring customer satisfaction and service performance began to emerge at Federal Express.

Here is an effective "do" list:

- Define service quality from the perspective of the customer, not by internal standards
- Develop a means for measuring actual service failures, not simply overall percentages of service achievement
- Weight each category of service failure to reflect its relative impact on customer satisfaction
- Continually track and measure performance against the 100 percent customer satisfaction and service performance goals
- Tie the customer satisfaction/service quality gauge to the service component of the people/service/profit corporate objectives
- Provide accurate, immediate feedback so that employees can spur action and innovation toward the company's 100 percent customer satisfaction and service performance goals

In June 1988, at the onset of fiscal year 1989, Federal Express adopted what it saw as a more comprehensive, proactive, customer-oriented measure of overall customer satisfaction and service quality. They called it the service quality indicator (SQI).

Service Quality Indicator (SQI)

Rather than replace the Hierarchy of Horrors, SQI's creators borrowed from it, also using feedback from customer focus groups, in developing a twelve-item statistical measure of customer satisfaction and service quality from the customer's viewpoint.

Figure 1 illustrates the twelve SQI items and the relative weighting factor assigned to each. Federal Express tracks these every day, both individually and in total. Note that the greater the weight factor, the greater the impact on customer satisfaction. A customer, for instance, will be less dissatisfied with a pack-

Figure 1

Federal Express service quality indicators

Indicator	Weight
Abandoned calls	1
Complaints reopened	5
Damaged packages	10
International	1
Invoice adjustments requested	1
Lost packages	10
Missed pick-ups	10
Missing proofs of delivery	1
Overgoods (lost and found)	5
Right day late deliveries	1
Traces	1
Wrong day late deliveries	5

age delivered late on the right day than with a damaged or lost package.

Here is a brief description of each SQI item:

- **Abandoned calls** Any phone call not answered by a customer service agent (i.e., the caller does not speak with an agent, but hangs up after ten seconds from the receipt of the call).
- **Complaints reopened** Any customer complaint reopened after an unsatisfactory resolution of the initial complaint.
- **Damaged packages** Packages with visible or concealed damage, or weather or water damage.
- **International** A composite score of service quality indicators from the company's international operations. Along with many of the SQI categories listed here, the international SQI also includes customs clearance delays.
- **Invoice adjustments requested** The number of packages on which customers request invoice adjustments. Federal Express includes invoice adjustments granted, as well as those requested but not granted, because an adjustment request indicates the perception of a problem by the customer.
- **Lost packages** Missing packages, and pack-

ages that have contents missing through pilferage.

- **Missed pick-ups** The number of requested package pick-ups that failed to occur.
- **Missing proofs of delivery** The number of invoices that do not include proof-of-delivery paperwork. (Federal Express promises customers proof of delivery with each bill.)
- **Overgoods (lost and found)** Packages that lack, or have lost, identifying labels for the sender and the addressee and are sent to the overgoods department.
- **Right day late deliveries** Packages delivered after the delivery commitment time (even one minute after) on the right date.
- **Traces** The number of "proof of performance" requests from customers that cannot be answered through data contained in a computer system called COSMOS (Customers, Operations and Services Master On-Line System) IIB, the main computer system used to track a package's movement throughout delivery. In other words, traces indicate that a Federal Express employee did not electronically scan a package's identifying bar code into COSMOS IIB at each point in the delivery process.
- **Wrong day late deliveries** Packages delivered after the commitment date.

Federal Express has established a goal to reduce by 90 percent the failure points recorded when the company instituted SQI in 1988. It is shooting for 1993 as the target date, five years after SQI start-up. (The initial SQI point figure was approximately 150,000,

which represents actual failures within each SQI, multiplied by the weighting factor, then totaled.) The company expects to achieve the goal despite annual increases in package volume.

During the first year under SQI, Federal Express reduced actual service failures by 11 percent, despite the fact that package volume had grown by 20 percent. By the first quarter of 1991, the company's average daily SQI score had been significantly reduced toward the five-year, 90 percent goal.

Each year, the company's service goal has been a set degree of progress toward that five-year SQI reduction goal. Determining exactly the amount of that progress is part of executive management's MBO goal-setting process. To invite widespread employee involvement in the continuous pursuit of lower SQI figures, management reports weekly results to employees via FXTV news programs.

As said earlier, all twelve indicators represent what CEO Smith describes as "critical points in the value chain." In following the Federal Express approach to improving service quality, each service organization must:

- Identify its own critical points
- Implement the necessary information-management tools to manage and track actual service performance and customer satisfaction for each point
- Work to eliminate root causes of service failures through an ongoing quality improvement process

The remainder of this appendix outlines other methods and systems the company uses to manage and track service performance and customer satisfaction.

▶ STRATEGIC DATA SYSTEMS WITHIN FEDERAL EXPRESS

To appreciate how far a company can go to manage and track service quality once it has identified its own critical value points, a brief overview of the Federal Express package-delivery process may be helpful.

The company offers its customers the benefit of positive tracking. Regardless of where in the system a package is—in the back of a delivery van traveling

along an L.A. freeway, or inside the belly of a cargo jet crossing the Sea of Japan—a customer service agent can provide real-time confirmation of the package's status and location.

The company can offer this added service and sense of security because of a sophisticated on-line computer system called COSMOS IIB. Beginning when a courier picks up a package, and repeated each time that package changes hands within the delivery-process, a Federal Express employee uses a hand-held SuperTracker computer to scan an identifying bar code preprinted on the package's airbill. The Super-Tracker automatically records the time and date of each scan and downloads the information to COSMOS IIB. When the package is delivered, the delivery courier performs a proof-of-delivery scan of the bar code, while entering the first initial and last name of the person who signed for the package.

Thus, when a customer calls to inquire "Where is my package?" "Who signed for it?" or "What time did it arrive?" a customer service agent can assess COS-MOS IIB to describe the package's complete history—provided each scan was completed as prescribed. Even if the package was delivered just minutes before, the customer service agent will be able to confirm where and at what time the package arrived, and who received it.

The COSMOS IIB system is just one of several information management systems (IMS) used by Federal Express to track, trace, and check service performance. COSMOS IIB, for example, enables the company to monitor its own delivery-time commitments. This information helps the company understand and manage its right day late and wrong day late SQI failures.

Other sophisticated systems monitor billing and proof-of-delivery statistics, lost and damaged packages (risk management), unanswered phone calls, and other critical points on a daily, hourly, and even min-ute-to-minute basis. Many, if not most, of the company's major information management systems have a direct impact on the company's ability to track service quality and performance.

Federal Express expends 5 percent of its annual gross revenues on developing and enhancing these management and customer information systems, and the effort is not limited to operational matters. The on-line job skills training and testing systems for couriers and customer service agents and the GFTPTrak computer system for tracking grievances are other examples of a fundamental commitment to the goal of measuring internal processes.

Federal Express sees its IMS investment as yet another demonstration of its commitment to valuing and empowering employees. The company believes that in spending millions of dollars to install a computer system that tracks a package in real-time on a round-the-world journey, it is demonstrating the value it places on the work performed by people who handle that package, scan its history into that system, and use that system to answer customer inquiries.

It may be that few service corporations will have operations that lend themselves to the extent of information management practiced by Federal Express. On the other hand, company leaders maintain that all service companies interested in delivering superior quality must be prepared to develop systems for measuring and tracking quality.

▶ CUSTOMER SATISFACTION SURVEYS

SQI notwithstanding, customer satisfaction surveys continue to be a significant barometer of performance. They represent a "reactive" tool for measuring service quality and as such are used to monitor improvement gains within Federal Express.

The company's marketing research department analyzes its customer base by many subsets and niches, including shippers versus consignees, document versus nondocument shippers, domestic versus international, overnight versus second-day service users, package generators (the individuals who want a package shipped) versus service implementors (the persons who actually call Federal Express for service).

Each year, the company conducts numerous customer satisfaction surveys, which consist of the following five major tracking studies.

The Customer Satisfaction Study
This is a quarterly telephone survey of 2,100 customers, chosen at random, with phone calls conducted on a daily basis. By contrast, some large service organizations conduct only one customer satisfaction survey

Figure 2
Customer satisfaction ratings and SQI trends

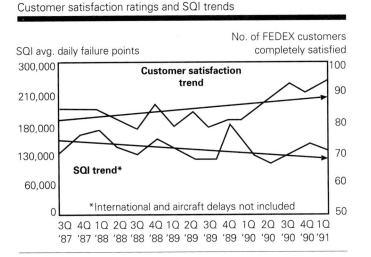

annually, interviewing a few hundred customers in the process.

The Federal Express quarterly survey covers four market segments: base business (by far the largest group, comprising the typical customer who phones in a request for pick-up service), U.S. export customers (domestic customers who ship overseas), manned-center customers (those who drop packages at the company's store-front service centers), and dropbox customers (those who drop packages in unmanned receptacles).

During a ten-minute interview, each customer's satisfaction is gauged against a fifty-item list of service attributes. Results also are relayed to senior management on a quarterly basis.

In January 1990, Federal Express took the aggressive step of changing its base business customer survey to a five-point satisfaction scale (completely satisfied, somewhat satisfied, neither satisfied nor dissatisfied, somewhat dissatisfied, completely dissatisfied). The five-point scale replaced a rating system that asked customers to rate their satisfaction on a percentage scale where 0 represented completely dissatisfied and 100 completely satisfied.

Federal Express officials say the new scale (see Figure 2) is not only easier to interpret and communicate, but also better aligns with the corporate objective of 100 percent customer satisfaction. Unlike some companies, where "completely satisfied" and "somewhat satisfied" responses might be blended into a single satisfaction rating, Federal Express also has chosen to use "completely satisfied" *alone* as its primary measure of improvement in customer satisfaction.

In a first-quarter 1991 survey, the company achieved a 94 percent completely satisfied rating, the highest rating yet under its new five-point system. If it had combined "completely" and "somewhat," the percentage of satisfied customers would have surpassed 99.6 percent.

Says one Federal Express market researcher: "We've decided that if we combine the completely satisfied and somewhat satisfied, that won't leave much room for improvement. This new survey format puts us on track to pursue 100 percent, *complete* customer satisfaction, which is really our main corporate goal."

Targeted Customer Satisfaction Studies
The company conducts a total of 10 targeted studies on a semiannual basis. Each direct-mail survey is designed to measure the satisfaction of customers who, within the previous three months, had an experience with one of 10 specific Federal Express processes, including complaint handling, claims handling, Saturday delivery, and invoice adjustments.

Federal Express goes so far as to survey customers on their satisfaction with its credit-collections handling process. It targets the studies because a random sampling of customers typically would not include a statistically valid sample of those that had recent experience with the process in question. Response rates average between 8 and 18 percent.

Federal Express Center Comment Cards

Each Federal Express store-front business service center invites customer reaction via comment cards. Staff collects and tabulates the cards twice a year and forwards the results to managers in charge of the business service centers.

Customer Automation Studies

Federal Express equips roughly 7,600 of its largest customers with Powership shipping and billing computer systems. The systems allow customers to print airbills and shipping labels automatically, track and confirm package delivery, generate shipping-volume and shipping-management reports, and receive invoices electronically. Powership users account for about 30 percent of the company's total package volume. The annual direct-mail survey, designed to gauge satisfaction with the automated devices, has garnered response rates as high as 45 percent.

Canadian Customer Study

Outside the United States, Canada represents the largest source and destination of Federal Express shipments. Once a year, by phone and direct mail, those customers are surveyed in much the same manner as the Customer Satisfaction Survey.

Just as analysts track quality over time at Federal Express, they track trends that surface from data derived form customer satisfaction surveys, with an eye toward identifying root causes of dissatisfaction. Consequently, the studies often lead directly to major changes in policy or procedure. When the results of a recent targeted study of Canadian customers revealed they were not satisfied with the geographic convenience of dropbox and business service center locations, the company embarked on a major expansion effort to add dropbox sites in the Canadian market.

By way of summary, those who oversee the Federal Express customer-survey process cite the following components as contributing to meaningful measurement:

- Consistent performance of the survey process over time, so results can be compared to identify trends.
- Customer segmentation to a meaningful level.
- Measurement by service attributes that are detailed enough to be actionable. (Professionalism, for example, is not sufficiently detailed. Cleanliness or speed in answering the phone, however, are detailed enough to be acted on.)
- Telephone surveys, as opposed to direct mail, when feasible.

Quality Deployment

If someone called Federal Express asking for the person in charge of quality, I would hope they could speak with anyone.
—*James L. Barksdale, Chief Operating Officer, Federal Express*

If Federal Express managers and employees thought they were in for a quality holiday after winning the Malcolm Baldrige National Quality Award, they may have had a rude awakening.

"It is critical that each of us understands that receiving the Nobel Prize for quality only marks the beginning of another level in our quest for 100 percent customer satisfaction," wrote Barksdale shortly after FedEx received the award. His statement appeared in an October 29, 1990, newsletter directed at executive management. "The continued success of Federal Express," he stressed, "depends on how well we as individuals buy into the quality-improvement process and use it to strive for our goal of having a satisfied customer at the end of every transaction."

With the building blocks of its people-first environment in place to empower people, and with SQI, Hierarchy of Horrors, and customer satisfaction surveys to measure and track service quality improvements or failures, the final piece of Federal Express's quality puzzle becomes, as Barksdale's comments sug-

gest, the ultimate quality challenge for any organization: to equip employees with a common quality language and a toolbox of problem-solving skills in order to pursue continuous service quality improvement on an ongoing basis.

Federal Express describes this final, never to be fully realized step as the "quality improvement process" (QIP).

While most of the people-first philosophies, initiatives, and service quality measures described earlier were developed in-house at Federal Express, much of the company's QIP language and many of the problem-solving techniques described in this appendix come from a quality-management consulting firm and were introduced in the company within the past few years.

Before delving further into the specific QIP strategies and techniques practiced by Federal Express, a brief overview of the Federal Express quality organization is in order.

▶ QUALITY STRUCTURE

The company has created a lean and decentralized quality deployment organization.

At the upper level, the company's leading quality overseer, the vice president of internal audit and quality assurance, has a direct reporting relationship to CEO Smith. Reporting to the vice president is a five-person quality department, responsible for research and development of new quality improvement techniques, as well as for overseeing major, high-level quality improvement efforts and activities with other organizations.

Along vertical lines, the company's twelve divisions are encouraged to take ownership of quality[1] by establishing yearly divisional quality deployment plans, linking their divisional quality objectives with the company's people/service/profit corporate goals.

Virtually every division employs a quality administrator, a point person with direct access to senior division management. The quality administrator is responsible for fostering and overseeing quality initiatives within the division, for managing quality award programs, and for serving as a quality resource to employees within the division. The larger divisions also employ several employee-involvement facilitators. These professionals have been trained in quality improvement techniques and in facilitating quality problem-solving meetings. They also train other employees in those same QIP skills.

Administrators and facilitators share information and quality improvement successes horizontally, across division lines, in biweekly meetings of the quality advisory board (QAB). A similar organization, the executive quality board (EQB), is designed to promote and maintain participation in QIP at the director and senior management levels. The EQB is chaired by the vice president of quality assurance, and includes at least one representative from each division.

Briefly stated, Federal Express has decentralized its quality structure by vesting quality autonomy within divisions while providing horizontal mechanisms (the QAB and EQB) for sharing information and quality successes across organizational lines within the corporation.

Even just a brief description of the Federal Express quality hierarchy would not be complete without the company's often-repeated caveat: a service quality improvement process should not, cannot, be imposed or instilled from on high within an organization and be expected to flourish long term. Instead, the objective is to set clear quality goals for all employees, provide as many people as possible with a uniform set of quality terms, skills, and tools, then allow each of those employees to evolve into what one Federal Express manager described as a "quality zealot."

▶ QUALITY TRAINING

To convey a uniform set of quality terms and tools to its work force, the company has developed curricula to teach quality theory and skills training to management and hourly employees alike.

The Leadership Institute (LI) offers training for management employees and quality administrators and facilitators, with courses developed by both the company's quality consulting firm and internal sources. To hasten the spread of the quality "gospel"

across its broad employee base, Federal Express has created a Quality Academy (QA) to provide similar training to nonmanagement employees.

A typical quality-training regimen covers such topics as the meaning of quality, the cost of quality, continuous improvement, and problem-solving processes. Specific courses within LI or QA might include statistical process control, quality management skills, skills in leading teams, and facilitator skills.

The extent to which all management and non-management employees receive quality training varies by division, once again in accordance with the Federal Express theory that decisions about quality administration are best made "close to home" within functional

---

1. To complete the voluminous Malcolm Baldrige award application, Federal Express also had each division prepare its own application, then merged their submissions into an overall corporate application.

business units. Overall, Federal Express's training programs are having their intended organizational impact—to open the same quality dictionary and the same quality toolbox to the greatest number of employees possible.

For instance, 95 percent of all telecommunications employees have received quality training, as have 96 percent of management and 65 percent of nonmanagement in the finance division. In customer service and sales—two key customer-contact groups—the training penetration is 90 percent for management and 60 percent for nonmanagement.

Quality administrators within each division have been charged with conducting quality improvement surveys of employees who receive training, gauging from their responses the value of the training materials, methods, and instructors. The results of these surveys are used to customize training courses to the needs of each division.

What are all these Federal Express employees learning about quality? Within the company's QIP, employees master important process-analysis techniques and problem-analysis/solution tools. It bears repeating that virtually all of the company's QIP techniques, terms, and tools have been imported and adopted from existing management theory and quality literature, or from an outside quality consulting firm. As CEO Smith noted, "What we do is all in the books. Our secret, if there is one, is just doing what they say."

▶ THE FEDERAL EXPRESS "TOOLBOX" FOR QIP

Quality Action Teams (QATs)

Also described as root cause teams and service teams, the quality action team (QAT) is the primary QIP technique taught in Federal Express's quality-training programs, then practiced hundreds of times throughout the company day in and day out.

At its core, the QAT is typically a four- to ten-member problem-solving team, often comprising both management and hourly employees drawn from multiple work groups or divisions. QATs are formed on either an ad hoc or ongoing basis to identify persistent service-quality problems, pinpoint "root causes," develop action plans to solve problems, then implement and track the effectiveness of solutions.

At any given time, more than 1,000 ongoing QATs focus on matters as local and specific as transporting packages from the Phoenix airport to a nearby sorting station by a more expeditious route, or as global as making major software enhancements to the company's main COSMOS IIB on-line package-tracking system.

"From our quality action teams we've learned," says Barksdale, "that success is seldom the result of a few big, technological or conceptual breakthroughs, but rather, hundreds of small innovations and improvements throughout the organization."

Each QAT follows a four-step problem-identification, assessment, and solution process known as FADE:

Focus, Analyze, Develop, and Execute. More specifically, the FADE process involves the steps described in Figure 1. All employees are permitted—Federal Express would say "empowered"—to initiate and participate in a QAT. And although QAT is primarily a team problem-solving process, employees are reminded through quality training and by quality facilitators that FADE can apply to an individual's professional and personal circumstances as well.

Significantly, corporate quality action teams have been formed for each of the company's 12 SQI items. Each team, headed by a corporate officer, is charged with tracking and analyzing actual failure data for one of the critical points of value in Federal Express's service process, and then using FADE and other quality tools and techniques to seek improvement in SQI results. One Federal Express official estimates that the corporate QATs focusing on two of the company's SQI measures—wrong day late and right day late—actually have a network of more than 1,000 employees involved in "sub-QAT" activities at all levels of the corporation.

Hundreds of smaller, fairly autonomous QATs also function within divisions, guided in their task by quality administrators and facilitators. To acknowledge QATs that have performed well, employees are encouraged to submit success stories within each division to the divisional quality administrators. Each administrator, in turn, passes along a success story to a

Figure 1
Focus * Analyze * Develop * Execute (FADE)

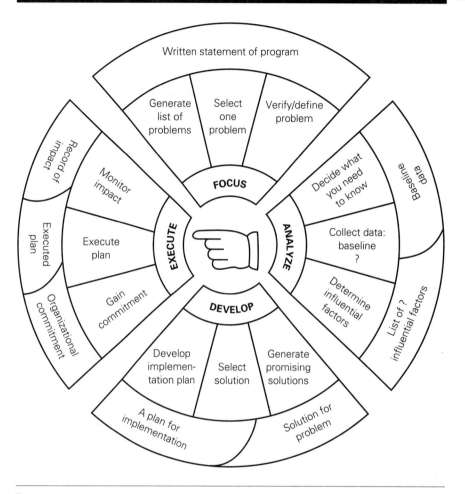

Focus
The focus phase represents the first major task in problem solving: selecting, verifying, and defining a problem on which to work. A QAT selects a single "critical" problem, often from a list of related problems that need to be resolved. Once the problem is identified, the QAT must verify and define it. The end product of the focus phase is a clear, written problem statement, which becomes the foundation for the remaining phases of the process.

Analyze
The goal of the analyze phase is to understand the primary contributing factors, or root causes, that lie at the problem's source. Typically, this analysis includes gathering and evaluating related data stored in myriad information management systems within the company.

Develop
At the development phase, a QAT builds on its analysis to brainstorm promising solutions to eradicate permanently all or part of the problem. Employees evaluate one solution against another, and develop an implementation plan for the most promising one.

Execute
The team seeks commitment to its solution from within the organization, then executes the plan and monitors its effectiveness.

committee of the QAT, which reviews all submissions. Once approved, the QAT has the opportunity to present its problem-solution story to executive management during a quarterly quality success story award presentation. Figure 2 presents examples of two successful QATs.

Customer-Supplier Alignments

In a perfect world, marriage, company—name any environment where human beings interact—the left hand would always know what the right hand is doing.

To promote better hand-to-hand coordination, Federal Express is using a quality improvement process widely known as "customer-supplier alignments," designed to build effective working relationships and encourage clear communication of needs and expectations among individuals, workgroups, and divisions, and with external customers as well. As one Federal Express quality administrator put it, customer-supplier alignment is an essential communication tool to ensure that employees, in their relationships with other employees, workgroups, and vendors, are "doing the right things right."[2]

Consistent with the company's "inverted pyramid" model, in which the employee is customer and the manager is supplier, customer-supplier alignments invite all employees to view themselves as suppliers and to envision others as customers. Employee A is a customer when she obtains material, information, or services from Employee B or Vendor C. At the same time, Employee A is a supplier when she provides these items or services to others.

FedEx wanted to implement customer-supplier alignments frequently and on an ongoing basis as a way to establish clear performance expectations throughout the company. To this end, the company developed a workbook designed to walk two parties through a series of three key alignment questions. The process culminates in a written document, which spells out both the customer's expectations and the supplier's service guarantees. These are established during the discussion, negotiation, and compromise that typically occur during each alignment.

---

2. Source: Organizational Dynamics Incorporated.

The three key questions a supplier asks the customer are:

- What do you need from me?
- What do you do with what I give you?
- What are the gaps between what I give you and what you need?

A Federal Express quality facilitator described the following hypothetical alignment between the managing director of personnel services, which sets corporate benefit policies, and the managing director of legal, which, as one of its functions, provides legal analysis of proposed personnel policies:

> Personnel services requires legal interpretation and feedback within a reasonable time frame on a proposed benefit policy change. When the length of time required for legal's response becomes unmanageable, personnel services requests a customer-supplier alignment. Legal inquires: "What do you need from me?" to which personnel services responds by offering examples of the various policy-analysis services it requires and the time constraints it faces.
>
> Personnel services also answers "What do you do with what I give you?" by noting that legal analysis is used to set clear, fair, enforceable, timely personnel policies that are consistent with the Federal Express people-first commitment.
>
> Personnel services explains that legal's typical three-week response time is too long. Legal, now equipped with a better understanding of the importance of its services to this particular customer, and the time constraints under which the customer must operate, agrees to a ten-day service guarantee, then puts that guarantee in writing.

Customer-supplier alignments are intended to occur spontaneously over time at all levels of the corporation. To get this relatively new quality ball rolling, executive management made the completion of five customer-supplier alignments a mandatory MBO for all directors and officers during fiscal year 1991.

"When you stop to think of all the ways people rely on one another throughout our operation, you can see that everyone's job is to support others so they can keep their 'customers' satisfied within the

Figure 2

QAT case studies

___

Hub Recycling

In 1989, when the Federal Express SuperHub sorting facility in Memphis began recycling aluminum cans to raise money for charity, a can recycler noted that the company might be missing other, potentially profitable, recycling opportunities.

Employees formed a QAT, the SuperHub Recycle Quality Action Team, including both management and hourly representatives. During the focus phase, the QAT identified several products with recycle or reuse value—including steel, batteries, paper, wood, plastic, oil, and tires—that the company was paying to have removed by refuse haulers.

In the analyze phase, the QAT identified the root causes of missed recycling opportunities as lack of awareness vis-à-vis the monetary value of such items and absence of a system for monitoring recyclable materials.

The team developed a quality action plan, which suggested performing a number of tasks:

- Draw up a comprehensive list of items with recycle, or second use, value
- Establish collection points for recyclable materials within the SuperHub
- Create a manual system for tracking the monthly volume and monetary value of all recycled or reused materials
- Identify vendors to either purchase the materials or provide disposal services free in return for the right to resell or reuse materials
- Implement a recycling awareness communication program, which would, among other things, post notices on SuperHub bulletin boards, submit articles to the SuperHub newsletter, and produce segments on HTV (a regularly scheduled SuperHub news program on FXTV)

With approval from the vice president of hub operations, the QAT's plan was executed. For fiscal year 1990, the first year of the SuperHub recycling effort, the program returned more than $196,000 to the company's bottom line.

The QAT team has summarized its experience in a booklet that is now available to divisional quality facilitators and to the managing directors of other Federal Express facilities. Leaders of the QAT are advising others within the company who may be interested in pursuing similar recycling opportunities.

Better Back Safety

In January 1989, the Federal Express safety department's regularly published "Worst First" rankings of the most injury-prone work areas placed the SuperHub's input and non-conveyable area at the top of the list.

Employees in the area handle and sort large, awkward packages and hazardous-materials shipments. Back injuries were the major problem, with the work area averaging three lost-time back injuries per month.

A QAT was formed to focus on reducing the number of back injuries. Analysis of pertinent accident reports revealed that most back injuries resulted from lifting strain, and that employees who had been with the company less than one year were most susceptible. Of the thirty employees who had suffered back injuries during the study period, twenty had been employed for less than twelve months. The QAT identified a number of root causes: ineffective new-hire orientation, poor work habits and lifting techniques, and absence of a safety-training course designed specifically for this operational area.

The QAT developed an action plan that included:

- Refining general safety training programs to include specific back hazards posed by the input and non-conveyable area
- Creating a "new-hire checklist" to ensure comprehensive orientation of new hires
- Publishing a safety manual specifically targeted to input and non-conveyable work
- Implementing a seven-exercise "Stretch 'N' Flex" workout before each work shift
- Developing an employee tracking report for monitoring improvements

The company succeeded in getting the QAT's action plan in place by March 30, 1990. Over the next two months, there were no back injuries reported in the area.

organization," Barksdale says. "As a result, when the product or service reaches the external customer, quality is built in at every step and becomes a permanent fixture."

Root Causes

It bears repeating that throughout the Federal Express QIP, the primary emphasis is on identifying critical value points within a process or organization, then locating and eliminating the root causes of failures at those points (service failures, communications failures, training failures, safety failures, etc.).

This quest for root causes is drummed home time and again, in innumerable ways, within the company. Often the concept is restated as "working on the main thing." In other instances it's framed in the context of the 80/20, or Pareto, principle, which separates problems into the significant few (those that deserve the most attention and hold promise for the greatest positive impact) and the trivial many (those which, even if solved, will not improve the problems in direct proportion to their numbers). The extraordinary concentration of QAT teams focused on two of the most numerous SQI failures is just one example of how Federal Express directs its quality improvement efforts based upon the Pareto principle. Even when root causes are found to be slightly, or even completely, outside of human control, Federal Express looks for alternative procedures and back-up systems to prevent or reduce service failures. For example, each night the company stations "hot spare" aircraft and flight crews at airports located strategically throughout its distribution system. These aircraft stand ready to be summoned on a moment's notice to compensate for regularly scheduled aircraft that are delayed by weather or mechanical failure. Even when a local sorting station has exhausted all possible options to trim the transit time from the airport to the sorting station, a Federal Express employee might strap himself into a seat in the cargo area of the truck and begin sorting packages while en route from the airport.

Techniques and Unique Terms

Virtually all the problem-analysis and solution-generating techniques used by Federal Express employees are readily found throughout quality-management literature and are widely in use at other corporations. A representative list of those techniques includes: brainstorming, selection grids, workflow analysis, Pareto charts, "fishbone" cause-and-effect diagrams, cost-benefit analyses, and force-field analyses.

To help employees develop a QIP mind-set, Federal Express quality leaders have introduced certain verbal paradigms and buzz-phrases that, while far from unique to the company, represent a few of the more significant messages Federal Express has gleaned from existing quality-management theory and terminology. Two of these primary QIP messages are:

The 1-10-100 Rule[3] Roughly translated, the rule suggests that the longer a problem goes unidentified or unaddressed, the more expensive it is to fix. If a problem or mistake is identified and fixed immediately, it costs $1 to fix. If the problem is caught downstream, it might cost as much as $10 to correct. And if it reaches the customer, it could cost as much as $100—or worse, cost the company.

As COO Barksdale frequently points out to employees, "At least 15 percent of the cost of any product or service is spent on rework or repair. Federal Express spends an estimated $800 million annually to undo missorted packages, deal with delayed airplanes, take care of invoice adjustments, and resolve other errors. And that doesn't even include the lost customers our errors cost us."

Continuous Improvement Interpreting "continuous improvement" for Federal Express means: "If it ain't broke, fix it." In other words, service-quality improvement calls for developing ways to do better work on a continuous basis. The "If it ain't broke, don't fix it" theory has no place in QIP. Instead, continuous improvement means: "Fix it now!" "Prevent problems before they happen," and "Look for new ways to meet customer needs."

---

3. Source: Organizational Dynamics Incorporated.

IBM Rochester: The Seasons of Change*

The Winter of Market Contentment

The rolling plains of southeastern Minnesota, blanketed in layers of snow and crisply clear coldness, are tranquil, yet uninviting to the IBM corporate fathers. Thus, the IBM employees at Rochester, Minnesota, toil through the winter, as usual, undisturbed by unannounced visitors from corporate Big Blue. Even if the golf courses were not buried in the same whiteness of the golf ball, the corporate fathers would have had to dig deep to find excuses to pop into Rochester. Immensely successful and ever-diligent in executing corporate strategy in the mid-1980s, the IBM Rochester employees appeared to have good reasons to be undisturbed.

In January 1986, IBM Rochester still made the System/36 and System/38 mid-range computers, which were distributed worldwide. In fact, IBM was selling as many System/38s in Japan as in the United States. Sixty percent of their install base was non-U.S. and growing every year. They had revenue growth every year; profit growth every year; improved return on assets every year. So why be disturbed? The customer satisfaction surveys corroborated the financial measures: IBM Rochester was a solid business. In some ways, it was as solid as a block of ice in the Minnesota winter, locked into the status quo.

The Fort Knox Fiasco

When an ice cube is removed from the freezer and suddenly plunged into a warm glass of tea, it crackles with tiny fissures pervading the formerly smooth interior, even though it remains intact. The event that cracked IBM Rochester's contentment was a failed product development project called "Fort Knox," which attempted to bring five different architectures within the IBM corporation together on one base for mid-range computers.[1] IBM wanted to converge these niche products into one to optimize their development resources across their five separate development labs. However, the multisite development effort failed miserably.

From a cost reduction perspective, it seems rational for IBM to focus and coordinate its resources, but the strategy was a bad deal for customers. IBM Rochester was developing a product that was too general to specifically meet diverse market needs. It would cost too much for the small business, because it had a lot of functionality for the big business. And it

---

* This case was prepared by Greg Bounds.

1. Fort Knox intended to combine the System/36, System/38, the 8100, the Series 1, and the 4300.

was not functional enough for the big business, because it controlled the cost for the small business. Thus, IBM Rochester was not matching any one segment very well.

At the time it would have taken Fort Knox between four and five years to develop the product.[2] Fort Knox started development in 1982. Three years into that cycle, and untold dollars later, it was canned, in 1985. Fort Knox died slowly because of IBM's seemingly unmitigated pressures for conformity. In their book, *The Silverlake Project,* Roy Bauer, Emilio Collar, and Victor Tang (Oxford University Press, New York, 1992, pp. 22–24) explain that "the biggest problem was that IBM never got its troops to buy in to Fort Knox. Resistance mounted—and actually accelerated as Fort Knox looked more and more iffy. IBM Rochester may have been the pocket of stiffest opposition. A few among us had the temerity to come forth and criticize the project to top management. Some of those who did paid a price; they were dispatched from the project and sent on assignment to the equivalent of Siberia . . . Pete Hansen, an experienced engineer and programmer at IBM Rochester . . . tried to convince IBM that Fort Knox wouldn't work. His prescience was rewarded by being removed from the project through a job promotion— one of those instances where 'heads roll up.' "

In that time frame, IBM Rochester squandered a product development cycle and failed to put out a new product. It was left with only senior products on the market. The Systems/ 36 and 38 were three to five years into their cycle, a ripe old age for computers. This was particularly disturbing since Rochester employees feared not getting out a new product for four more years. Market share was gradually eroding. People wondered how they would hold on to customers with technology and mar-

kets changing so fast. Experts speculated that IBM would abandon the mid-range market.

The Spring Thaw and New Life

Like many of the eventual Baldrige winners, IBM Rochester was not yet in a crisis in 1986; although they could have been today had they not recognized and redirected their errant course. IBM Rochester was shaken by the Fort Knox fiasco. One of the major breakthroughs came with the Silverlake project, which began as a "skunk works" effort led by none other than Pete Hansen and some of the programmers and engineers of the Fort Knox project. These people saw that the Fort Knox project was doomed, and its demise left them feeling they had something to prove. They enlisted the support of key managers they knew they could trust for secrecy, such as Dave Schleicher, the head of programming for the IBM Rochester development lab. And they clandestinely began to develop and test the feasibility of another market strategy. They initially went outside the existing product development systems and organizational controls, hidden from the rest of the organization. But they eventually won approval to scrap the Fort Knox project and formally initiate another development cycle.

IBM always assigns code names to development projects, mostly for security reasons, but also to build esprit de corps. Hansen's group found the code name "Silverlake" quite close to home. The Zumbro River meanders through Rochester and forms a lagoon which doubles as a power plant cooling reservoir. Filled with heated water from the power plant, the lagoon never freezes. Locals have named the lagoon Silver Lake.

The skunk works team picked the name because it conjured up images of the computer they had in mind, "a shimmering, almost heavenly, work of creation." The code name serendipitously reflects the culture change at Rochester better than it does the lofty dreams of the product developers. For example, when

---

2. For example, the System/36 took four years, and the System/38, an earlier project with quite different technology, took seven or eight years to develop.

Hansen's crew went to work on a prototype for Silverlake in the spring of 1985, IBM's desperation gave Hansen a certain mandate he didn't hesitate to assert. And all of a sudden, IBM employees loosened up and started breaking the rules. "When he requested a special piece of hardware, the engineering manager in charge said it would take three months. Hansen sat the man down and explained that he didn't have three months, and neither did anyone at IBM Rochester. Everyone's job was at stake, Hansen said, as he laid out the dire consequences of failure. If there were no engineers, he reminded the manager, there damn well wouldn't be much need for an engineering manager. Hansen had his hardware within a week" (Bauer, Collar, and Tang, 1992, pp. 25–26).

The Silverlake project was blessed by IBM's top executive management when an outsider, Tom Furey, was brought in as the new lab director to orchestrate the project's success. Tom Furey was another heavy rock tossed into Rochester's solidly frozen pool of contentment. Furey was a visionary straight out of Big Blue territory. He didn't know anything about Rochester's business, and nobody in Rochester knew him from Adam. Yet as soon as the people at Rochester started working with Furey, they realized he had business savvy. He not only was technologically competent, but he could think strategically. As one Rochester manager said of Furey, "He is one of the few [people] I've ever worked with who I truly believe could run a major corporation."

At first, the questions that quickly followed Furey into IBM Rochester fell like pebbles upon the frosted ears of the contented. "Who are our customers?" "What markets are the growth markets?" "What business are we in?" As Furey pressed for answers, the pebbles started to seem more like flaming meteorites, thawing the organization, making people question the fundamental nature of their business. Nobody knew the answers to these ostensibly simple questions. Everybody threw out anecdotes, but nobody really knew.

Furey conceded that Rochester had a good business, but admonished his people: "We must start understanding a little more about it." Furey put two task forces together, one to understand IBM Rochester's install-base demographics worldwide, and another to understand markets and market opportunity. It took three months to complete the reports, which showed that IBM Rochester was heavily penetrated in markets that weren't growing, and further, Rochester had lost two points of market share every year for the last ten years. IBM Rochester's director of market-driven quality and leader of the quest for the Baldrige award, Roy Bauer, states, "We were literally going out of business. Markets were exploding around us. Here we were, the leader by all the traditional quality measures in the world, and we were going out of business and didn't even know it."[3]

The Fort Knox fiasco fueled Furey's meteoric assault on IBM Rochester. The status quo was no longer as solid as it used to seem. Conditions were right for a thaw, and a transformation. Furey intuitively realized that the perception of crisis or imminent threat helps to rally people to shift to a new culture, and he took advantage of the perception.

The Silverlake Project

Furey and the other leaders of the Silverlake project determined that they needed a new line of products out in 1988 to remain a player in the mid-range computer market. To be out in 1988 meant cutting in half the development cycle time of previous products. They took it to their people and laid it on the table: "It's got to be 1988. If we don't turn this ship around, all

---

3. The author is extremely indebted to Roy Bauer for his insights, editorial advice, and support of this case study. Roy was hired at IBM Rochester in 1967, and since that time he has had diverse engineering and managerial experience, ranging from manufacturing and laboratory operations to corporate staff work. With a reputation as a hard worker, Roy is knowledgeable of many parts of IBM operations, and is a technically capable strategic thinker. Programming PCs for small business enhanced Roy's "end user" perspective.

of us will be looking for a new job. In order to do that, we've got to work harder. It's going to take a lot of work and commitment on your part, but we also have to change our development process, because hard work alone is not enough."

To get an idea of the challenge they faced, consider that IBM Rochester put two million lines of code in the System/36 computer, which took four years to develop. The Silverlake project required seven million lines of code in a two-year development cycle. IBM Rochester simply did not have the people, at the current productivity rates, to generate that much code. They had to do things differently.

Rochester leaders assigned teams to improve their engineering and programming processes to increase productivity, reduce defects, and optimize the work flow. Overtime work increased, but they also "tore up" old processes, simulated new approaches, did software defect removal modeling, and even brought in customers to collaborate on product development.

These changes amounted to a breakthrough, or a discontinuous shift in performance improvement, for IBM Rochester. They had aimed for two years, and they had the product out in twenty-eight months. And now the AS/400 mid-range computers are selling like gangbusters, growing in market share. IBM Rochester will never be the same.

The Silverlake project seems to have permanently changed IBM Rochester toward a market-driven culture. For years, IBM has been criticized for its bureaucracy, lethargy, and arrogance. IBM has sent messages to customers to the effect that, "We're IBM. We know what's best for you. Where would you be without us?" Other messages imposed conformity on IBM employees: "That's a creative thought, but that's not the IBM way."

This arrogance and self-contentment grew from the immense corporate success of IBM. But IBM Rochester now knows that past success is no guarantee to future success. And the changes at IBM Rochester have resulted in breakthroughs in their business vision and business practices. Rochester employees recognize that no one player will dominate the computer market, which is composed of diverse needs. Such a market requires informed positioning and continuously improved business processes to effectively serve those needs. IBM no longer relies on a traditional quality assurance organization. They build in quality on the front end, through strategic planning and product development processes, and then assure quality through process improvement.

This case study details a vision of market-driven quality at IBM Rochester. It illustrates that culture change requires much more than a statement of vision from leaders; the vision must be made real.[4]

▶ IBM ROCHESTER'S GLOBAL BUSINESS CONTEXT

The Rochester site reports to two of the seven lines of business in the IBM Corporation. It reports to the application business systems (ABS) line of business for its AS/400 family of products, and to the enterprise systems (ES) line of business for its hard disk drive family of products. In the United States, sales and service support is provided by the U.S. marketing and service line of business; and outside the U.S., this support is provided by the world trade organizations. Corporate quality guid-

4. This case study was written from material provided by IBM Rochester, particularly their publication, "Rochester Excellence . . . Customer Satisfaction," 2d ed., March 1991; a condensation of their application for the Malcolm Baldrige award; personal interviews and telephone conversations; and formal presentations. I am particularly indebted to Roy Bauer for his guidance and editorial contributions.

ance is provided to all IBM lines of business by the market-driven quality organization.

IBM Rochester Products

The AS/400 system software is translated into twenty-eight national language versions to support the more than 60 percent of AS/400 systems that are installed outside the U.S. The AS/400 system is sold directly by IBM as well as by over 7,000 independent business partners worldwide. The storage devices produced in Rochester include hard disk drives for the AS/400 and RS/6000 systems, and the PS/2 computer. Rochester also provides hard disk drives to other computer equipment manufacturers. These hard disk drives are leaders in their class in reliability, performance, and diagnostic capabilities.

The IBM Rochester Site

Although a very small part of the IBM Corporation, the Rochester site is the largest IBM facility in the world under one roof, employing 8,100 people, and occupying 3.6 million square feet of space on 586 acres. Rochester, Minnesota, is the principal development and manufacturing site for both IBM's hard disk storage systems and its ABS line of business. In addition, the Rochester site has prototype facilities for machining, plastic molding, heat treating, plating, and integrated circuit processing. IBM Rochester also has it own tool and model makers who build testing and processing equipment. In fact, 66 percent of IBM Rochester's 8,100-person work force is comprised of engineers, programmers, and other professionals.

IBM Rochester consists of more than just the Rochester site. It has worldwide development and U.S. manufacturing responsibility for the AS/400 computer system and hard disk storage devices. It has sister manufacturing facilities in Guadalajara, Mexico; Sumare, Brazil; Havant, England; Santa Palomba, Italy; and Fujisawa, Japan. IBM Rochester, as well as over twenty other IBM locations, provides programming development and support for the AS/400 system.

The Customer View

Although its facilities are obviously impressive, the heart and soul of IBM Rochester is its culture, which can be summed up as market-driven quality. Market-driven quality (MDQ) begins with understanding what is important to customers, covering all aspects of their relationship with IBM and its business partners, from products to support and after-sale service (see Figure 1). Satisfying customers requires superior and reliable solutions; administrative excellence; marketing and sales support; and delivery, maintenance, and service performance. Throughout its total enterprise—marketing, product development, manufacturing, and service—IBM's objective is to provide total customer solutions. These solutions demonstrate a knowledge of the customer's business and all other elements important to customer satisfaction.

Malcolm Baldrige Assessment Model

IBM Rochester continues to use the Malcolm Baldrige criteria as an assessment tool to sustain and improve its market-driven quality culture. Managers and staff do internal assessments, evaluate and assign points on the Baldrige scales, and recognize progress with awards. Rochester leaders feel that ongoing Baldrige assessment will help them "smoke out" those areas that need continuous improvement, as well as identify the next big breakthrough. The seven categories that comprise the Baldrige criteria provide a framework for describing IBM Rochester's approach to developing a market-driven quality culture (see Figure 2). These categories include: leadership, information and analysis, strategic quality planning, human resource utilization, quality assurance of products and services, quality results, and customer satisfaction.

Figure 1

Customer's view of IBM and elements important to satisfying
customers through market-driven quality

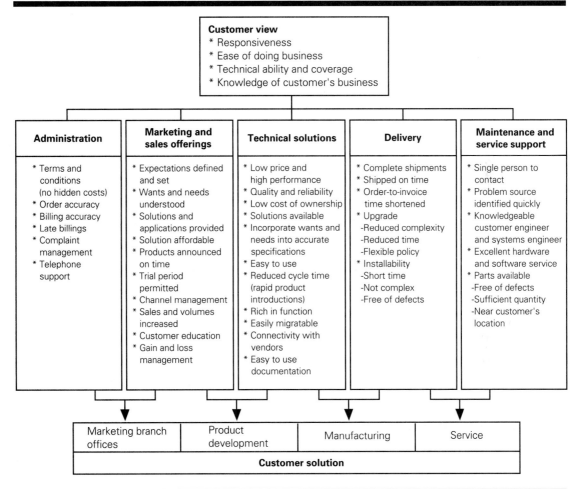

© IBM Corp., 1990, 1991.

▶ **LEADERSHIP**

The first Baldrige category, leadership, drives
all other aspects of MDQ. Although IBM Rochester values leadership and employee participation at all levels, it primarily requires that
leadership start at the top of the organization,
with site executives. At Rochester, some of the

elements of leadership are commitment to customer satisfaction and continuous improvement, and the creation of an environment for
teamwork, employee empowerment, enablement, excitement, and reward. However, the
most important part of leadership is the

Figure 2

IBM Rochester's view of the Baldrige framework

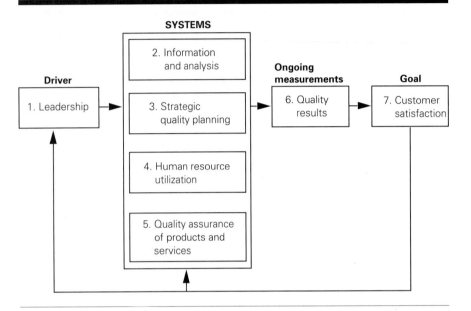

© IBM Corp., 1990, 1991.

establishment of a quality vision, and its deployment through policies, goals, and initiatives.

Vision Development

IBM Rochester's leadership process is depicted in Figure 3. Leadership begins with a thorough understanding of (1) IBM's quality values, and (2) markets/customers.

IBM's Quality Values and MDQ Principles The IBM Corporation seeks to adhere to the set of values provided by its founder Tom Watson, Sr.: *respect for the individual, the best customer service, and pursuit of excellence.* To do a better job of realizing these espoused values, IBM recently adopted market-driven quality (MDQ) principles to guide all of its business activities. These principles state: (1) the customer is *the final arbiter,* (2) we must understand our markets, (3) we must commit to leadership in markets we choose to serve, and (4) we must deliver excellence in execution across our enterprise.

These market-driven quality principles are expressed in corporate goals/policy instructions that provide guidance for implementing IBM's basic beliefs and serving IBM markets and customers. For example, corporate instruction (CI) 101 requires that all business processes, product and nonproduct, improve continually to make them more efficient, effective, and adaptable. CI 105 states that each new product must be superior in quality to previous products (of both IBM and competitors). Before announcing a product, each IBM development team must demonstrate to the corporate quality organization and other line executives that it complies with CI 105.

Rochester Executive Vision/Policy Based on the corporate goals/policy instructions and the MDQ principles, the Rochester site leaders develop their own executive vision/policy. The Rochester policy simply states that Rochester will settle for nothing but *Rochester excellence* in the continuous pursuit of *customer satisfaction.*

Figure 3

The leadership process at IBM Rochester

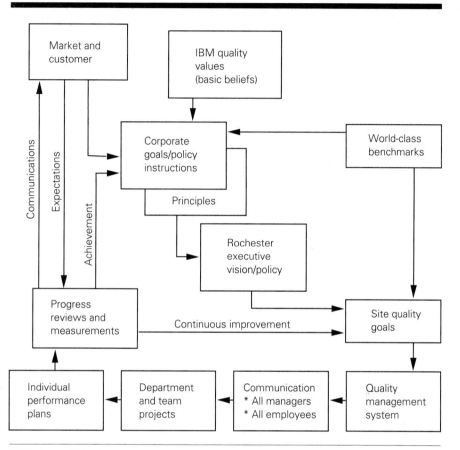

© IBM Corp., 1990, 1991.

Rochester's vision or site approach to this policy is summarized as:

1. Customer—The final arbiter
2. Products and services—First with the best
3. Quality—Excellence in execution
4. People—Enabled, empowered, excited, rewarded

Vision Deployment

Rochester managers do not simply formulate a vision without providing the means. IBM Rochester has identified six critical success factors to deploy its vision:

1. Enhance total product strategy and plans
2. Improve requirements definition process
3. Implement six-sigma defect-level quality strategy (3.4 defects per million)
4. Develop and implement an excellence in education plan
5. Enhance and enable employee involvement
6. Develop and implement total cycle reductions

IBM Rochester managers integrate these six critical success factors into a closed-loop, market-driven strategy cycle that represents their vision of how these factors will bring them

Figure 4

Vision of market driven quality cycle

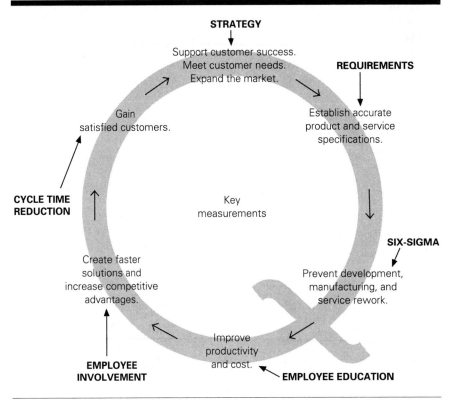

STRATEGY

Support customer success.
Meet customer needs.
Expand the market.

REQUIREMENTS

Gain
satisfied customers.

Establish accurate
product and service
specifications.

CYCLE TIME
REDUCTION

Key
measurements

SIX-SIGMA

Create faster
solutions and
increase competitive
advantages.

Prevent development,
manufacturing, and
service rework.

Improve
productivity
and cost.

EMPLOYEE
INVOLVEMENT

EMPLOYEE EDUCATION

success in the market and meeting customer needs (see Figure 4).

Experience with implementing these critical success factors has led Rochester managers to adopt certain beliefs, as represented by the arrows in Figure 4 above. First, meeting customer needs must serve as the foundation of the entire development process, and only by improving the requirements definition process can managers ensure that customer needs will be met. Second, progress through six-sigma quality goals reduces development, manufacturing, and service rework by ensuring that processes produce correct results the first time. Third, improving education and employee involvement increases productivity and reduces cycle times. Fourth, reduced cycle times

enable faster market response and an increased competitive advantage. Fifth, key measurements help to verify that processes are definable, repeatable, and predictable. And finally, continued engagement in this market-driven cycle of activities delights customers by providing solutions that help them achieve success in their business. Some of the means that IBM Rochester employees use to implement these beliefs are discussed below.

Site Quality Goals Rochester leaders formulate site quality goals, with input from stated policies and world-class benchmarks, and integrate those goals into the departmental and cross-functional team activities as well as into individual employee performance plans. The deployment activities are depicted in the lower half of the leadership process model in Figure 3 above.

Quality Management Systems While IBM Rochester hopes to infuse leadership throughout the organization and make it a part of daily activities and routine job responsibilities, they also impose a formal structure of committees and teams to guide, oversee, and monitor the success of these leadership activities. This structure, called the quality management system, provides a formal means of corporate control and integration. At the local level, functional quality teams address functional issues, which are overseen by a site quality steering committee composed of diverse site managers, which in turn is overseen by a Rochester management committee composed of site executives. The ABS executive steering committee oversees all site activities and is headed by the ABS general manager, and in turn is overseen by the customer satisfaction project office which crosses all lines of business at the corporate level.

This structure of committees does not constitute the heart of IBM Rochester's improvement activities. The heart of IBM Rochester's improvement activities is in daily team efforts within functions and across functions. However, the structure does ensure that managers (1) monitor the success of policy deployment (e.g., through monthly review of progress toward goals by the ABS executive steering committee), and (2) provide assistance, guidance, and integration (e.g., through working with various organizations, the corporate-level project office helps develop shared solutions). This structure also ensures that top managers help remove barriers to quality for the lower levels, to enable excellence and not just set goals.

Communication Through communication and education, employee performance plans are agreed upon by both the manager and the employee (see Figure 5). Although the manager and subordinate jointly develop individual performance plans, specific goals for quality improvement and customer satisfaction are not negotiable, but mandatory. All managers and employees participate in the development of employee performance plans.

Departments/Team Projects In addition to executing work to meet individual performance plans, employees participate in departmental and cross-functional team activities to continuously improve all aspects of the business.

Progress Reviews and Measurements Managers gauge the success of their policy deployment by monitoring the results. The "5-Up" measures that Rochester managers monitor are derived from their understanding of their markets and customers, and include:

- Customer satisfaction
- Defects at system test
- Software defects
- Cycle time
- System availability

Continuous improvement in performance on these 5-Up measures leads to revision of corporate and site goals.

The Quality Journey

To fully appreciate Rochester's vision of where the quality journey will take them in the coming years, it may help to see where it has already taken them. Figure 6 shows Rochester's evolving journey, the visions, initiatives, and goals, since 1981. Rochester's quality journey began in 1981 with the initiative called "People Responsibly Involved in Developing Excellence" (PRIDE), which focused on improving product reliability. In 1984, the quality journey was expanded to include process efficiency and effectiveness, and manufacturing cycle time improvements. While these initiatives were narrowly focused on business processes within departments, successes were not insignificant, particularly in manufacturing, where improvements yielded a 60 percent reduction in cycle time from the point of customer order to installation.

Figure 5

Quality values deployment

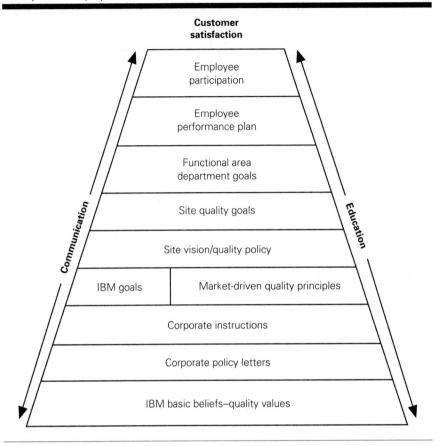

© IBM Corp., 1990, 1991.

However, Rochester managers soon realized that manufacturing improvements, no matter how impressive, would not ensure success in the market. In the mid-1980s, the failure of the Fort Knox project forced managers to broaden their conception of quality from "product quality" to "quality of all business activities, from strategy to operations." In 1986, the quality journey continued with planning and development cycle process improvements, and integration of suppliers and customers into development and production processes. The Silverlake project introduced the new line

of AS/400 mid-range computers in two years and ushered in a new era for continuous improvement in IBM strategy and operations. In 1989, Rochester's quality journey led to embracing market-driven customer satisfaction goals, focusing on total cycle time to the market, and extending customer involvement even further. In the 1990s, Rochester plans to implement an expanded set of initiatives that builds upon prior successes with the goal of becoming the undisputed leader in customer satisfaction.

The step-like progression for the years 1981, 1984, 1986, 1989, and 1990 (as shown

Figure 6

The quality journey

The quality journey continues ...

	Q 1981	Q 1984	1986	1989	Q 1990 – 1994
VISION	Product reliability	Process effectiveness and efficiency	Customer and supplier partnerships Competitive and functional benchmarks	Market-driven customer satisfaction Total business process focus Closed-loop quality/ management system	Customer — the final arbiter Quality — excellence in execution Products and services — first with the best People — enabled, empowered, excited, rewarded
INITIATIVES	Product performance improvement Cost of quality PRIDE	Process management Manufacturing cycle time improvement QFBP — quality focus in business processes	Customer and supplier involvement Benchmarks Development cycle time improvement	Total cycle time to market Prevention-based processes Functional integration Extending customer involvement	Critical success factors • Product strategy • Requirements • Six-sigma strategy • Education • Employee involvement • Cycle improvement Proactive customer satisfaction processes
GOALS	Zero defects	All processes rated	Best of competition	Total customer satisfaction	Undisputed leadership in customer satisfaction

in Figure 6) indicates breakthroughs in vision and performance for IBM Rochester. Each step has dramatically changed Rochester's view of quality and approach to managing the business. Managers have grown from viewing quality as a program toward viewing it as a way of life, from viewing it as ending with quality of products through conformance to standards toward viewing it as beginning with a customer-driven strategy.

The key to this quality journey has been vision. Leaders drive their organization toward business results by their vision, its match to the organization's environment (e.g., customers, competitors, and social and technological developments), and the successful deployment of that vision throughout the organization. IBM Rochester's quality journey will continue. The vision of its leaders and its market-driven culture will continue to evolve.

▶ INFORMATION AND ANALYSIS

To support effective communication, IBM Rochester has comprehensive, worldwide information and analysis systems available, as needed, to all employees. Rochester's electronic office system links employees worldwide, allowing real-time communication. Major information systems provide effective, powerful assistance within the company and externally. These systems cover the entire product cycle of design, development, manufacturing, marketing, and service. They promote contact with customers, suppliers, and business partners. Most importantly, they promote continuous improvement activities throughout the organization.

External Communications

To succeed in business, IBM Rochester knows it must have excellent external communications with suppliers, business partners, and customers. For example, electronic linkages to suppliers give Rochester employees instant access to information on supplier quality and material logistics. Further, the electronic office provides employees with an on-line log of phone calls from partners. Most importantly, the electronic office fosters the communication needed to provide customer solutions. For example, the order configuration system and the electronic customer support system discussed below are intended to enhance customer satisfaction with IBM's products and services.[5]

Order Configuration System Since there are over 3 million different configurations of the AS/400 available, ranging in price from $12,000 (including software) to $1 million, the

order process is critical to providing customer solutions. IBM Rochester's on-line order process electronically links customers to the AS/400 production process. A customer orders a system by working with a marketing representative to define the system configuration that meets the customer's needs. As data are entered at a branch office, the system validates the order configuration and data accuracy, preventing order errors.

The validated order is then transmitted directly into the plant manufacturing control system, where a build order and assembly sequence control information are generated and sent to the plant floor. Bar codes on the computer case and parts are wanded at each operation. The process routing contained on the bar codes enables the system to notify the operators of deviations from the prescribed build sequence. The finished product is then tracked through the distribution process en route to the customer. The electronic linkages with Rochester do not cease after the product is installed, but continue with service support. With this order configuration system, process steps and opportunities for translation problems are eliminated.

Electronic Customer Support Customer communication with IBM is enhanced by electronic customer support (ECS), which is provided with every AS/400 system. ECS provides an electronic connection to IBM for access to question and answer databases and IBM documentation. It also provides automatic problem identification, service requests, problem management, and software fixes, updates, and distribution. Through a modem provided with the AS/400, software engineers can remotely debug customer systems worldwide, and then share the fix with other customers, without leaving Rochester, Minnesota. ECS provides a real-time, closed-loop capability for IBM and its customers to communicate. Customers worldwide have on-line computer access to

---

5. Rochester employees have on-line access to customer satisfaction measurements, e.g., a monthly 90-day summary, monthly satisfaction track with concerns, monthly satisfaction track with total satisfaction, dissatisfied call-back status, and reasons for dissatisfaction. The measurement of customer satisfaction is further discussed in a subsequent section.

IBM Rochester, allowing them to work with IBM employees to interactively resolve problems.

Internal Communications

The electronic office ensures that Rochester employees have the information needed to make daily business decisions. Consider the following examples. Personnel systems provide information on such measures as sales and employee opinion surveys. Field data management provides information on defects at customer installations. Rapid communication with sales representatives, systems engineers, and field engineers aids in problem solving and communicating opportunities for improvement. Employees have instant access to technical information pertinent to development, manufacturing, and logistics.

Electronic information and analysis are critical for Rochester's manufacturing processes. The process of moving a product from development to manufacturing is highly automated. IBM Rochester translates design data into on-line manufacturing controls to improve the quality of manufactured parts. The central control point of the manufacturing processes is the manufacturing control system (MCS). As mentioned above, all production is controlled by the customer order. Customer orders are automatically transmitted from the branch office to the manufacturing control system and fed directly to the manufacturing assembly line. These on-line systems provide timely and consistent design information to worldwide manufacturing locations, eliminate opportunities for errors, and reduce process steps and time. Further, the assembly and sub-assembly areas provide process information to the manufacturing control system for analysis and review by cross- functional teams for root cause analysis and process improvements.

Improvement Activities

Information and data analysis are essential for improvement activities and ensure that the business is managed based on facts and not conjecture. When acquired, analyzed, and used appropriately, data can lead to more effective and trouble-free operation of internal processes, shorter cycle times, and improved customer satisfaction. Using data to make such improvements may require employees to engage in root cause analysis, statistical process control, and teamwork.

Root Cause Analysis If a process upset occurs, Rochester employees follow a disciplined approach called "root cause analysis" to find the causes of the upset. This approach consists of the following steps:

1. Confirm:
   Re-create problem
   Repeat failure
   Restate process deficiency
   Complete process review
   Visit supplier or customer location
2. Probe:
   Examine with electron microscope
   Examine checkpoints, dumps, and traces
   Examine vital product data
   Find last point before failure
3. Analyze:
   Determine frequency of occurrence (Pareto diagram)
   Review trend data (trend diagram)
   Review statistical process control charts
   Decide how exhibited and how found
   Evaluate single supplier versus multiple supplier
   Analyze execution path, system state, and environment
4. Correlate:
   Correlate supplier data, in-house data, and customer data
   Find indications of problems in other measures
   Identify recent process changes
   Determine batch, job lot, time stamp, and release level
5. Isolate:
   Isolate possible causes (fishbone diagram)
   Rank by probability

Perform additional testing

Perform experiment at suspected point of origin

Test for stress (heat, voltage, strength, life, etc.)

Test boundary conditions

On-line systems provide the data used in root cause analysis. This analysis is based on a fundamental ability to trace information back to its source. For example, information collected by the manufacturing control system can be analyzed to assess changes in new designs or to track a problem back through the process parameters of a particular operation.

Root cause analysis attempts to uncover the root cause of a problem, identifies required improvements for products or processes, and expands existing knowledge of the complex interrelationships involved in satisfying customer needs. It also helps ensure that improvement efforts are focused on the right areas. As one Rochester manager explains: "People often wonder why their businesses aren't successful after they've spent ten years working on quality improvement. It is probably because they have not focused on the high leverage points. Their problem may also come back to their goals. If you set goals and start looking at measurements, you must understand the measurements and how they are related to what you are trying to achieve. You shouldn't be measuring just for the sake of measuring."

Statistical Process Control Statistical process control (SPC) is used in critical operations throughout the Rochester site and its suppliers' sites. Employees from manufacturing get involved with a product early in its life cycle and work with development engineers to identify critical parts, parameters, or process steps that require continuous control through statistical monitoring techniques. Hard disk drive manufacturing lines are monitored using on-line process control. Operators and engineers continuously monitor production operations, observe the process capability levels, and assess the operation by comparing the last twenty-four hours of data with the established specification limits.

Rochester Improvement Teams Employees normally engage in cross-functional teamwork applying continuous improvement tools to improve outcomes such as product cycle time, efficiency, and communication. Process improvement teams, each led by a process owner responsible for ensuring high quality, are used extensively to simplify processes, create new defect prevention methods, and reduce cycle times in product and nonproduct processes. For example, the transformation of the engineering change process from the traditional printed copy method to an efficient on-line system was successfully completed by a quality improvement team. Working very closely with customers from across the site, the team began by modeling the process to identify bottlenecks and process inhibitors. By doing root cause analysis, the team determined what caused process upsets. The process flow was restructured and unnecessary steps were removed. To implement the new process, education and support were provided across the Rochester site. Improvements led to quick engineering change throughput and reduced product cycle time.

▶ STRATEGIC QUALITY PLANNING

IBM Rochester is seeking to integrate two previously separate planning processes: business planning and quality planning. This new strategic quality planning process is more market-driven than its traditional business planning used to be. The interrelationships of the major components in IBM Rochester's strategic planning process and its alignment with overall IBM corporate strategies are shown in Figure 7. The process is briefly described below.

Business Strategy Each year, IBM Rochester develops a five-year strategic plan, using information from market analysis, benchmarks of competitive and industry data, and innovations in new technology. The strategic planners attempt to understand the environment, e.g., where the growth markets and areas of economic depression are, and then make targeting decisions. Once decisions are targeted, planners attempt to understand the strategy of their competitors: How are companies like DEC, Unisys, Hewlett-Packard, and Fujitsu positioned? What are their strengths and weaknesses? Their likely strategic moves?

After targeting and gauging the competition, the planners seek to understand their critical success factors. Regarding these factors, one Rochester manager states, "Critical success factors are not just the products, but the application portfolio needed, the channels we sell through, the service and support, customers' views of us as a supplier, and how the solutions we offer customers meet target markets over the next five years."

The five-year plan also describes the long-term business and quality goals set by the IBM Corporation. Business and quality goals are addressed in iterative cycles to ensure they are consistent and measured appropriately at IBM Rochester. For example, the following five basic measures may be used to assess progress on business and quality goals: revenue, market share, return on assets, revenue per employee, and customer satisfaction.

Functional Strategies Manufacturing, development, marketing, service, and support teams develop functional strategies that contain the quality improvement plans required to achieve the business strategy. Functional strategies describe the human resources, capital, and expenses required to achieve the quality priorities and the business strategy.

Operating Plan Once this strategic plan is approved, an annual operating plan is developed with a two-year horizon. The operating plan is a detailed description of how to implement the strategy. It is also the vehicle used to commit resources to quality improvement. The strategy and operating plan owners ensure the planning process is continually reviewed and improved. The Rochester management committee (RMC), a cross-functional executive team, reviews and approves the Rochester strategy and operating plans.

The Planning Process A strategic planning department initiates the planning with information gathered from every area at the bottom of the organization, from engineers, programmers, manufacturing people, etc., for each line of business. Customers are included in the strategic planning process, providing product direction, and suppliers assist in the product sourcing strategy. Using this information, teams of employees develop a business strategy that includes product and business goals. The planners also compare resources and associated expenses to revenue and profit goals in order to balance the strategic plan.

Prioritizing Options Prioritization of strategic options is a challenge for IBM Rochester. The prioritization process that planners enacted in the past has been described by IBM employees as "lobbying by various functional and organizational advocates," or "a lot of emotional arm waving." One manager indicates a problem with the planning process as follows:

> Things often got put into the plan because of emotion, without good market analysis. Some executive would talk to a customer who was irritated because a product didn't have a certain function. The executive would make a decision based on this little bit of data. It didn't seem to matter that

Figure 7

Strategy planning: The interrelationships of company policy, business goals, business and functional strategies, and operating plans

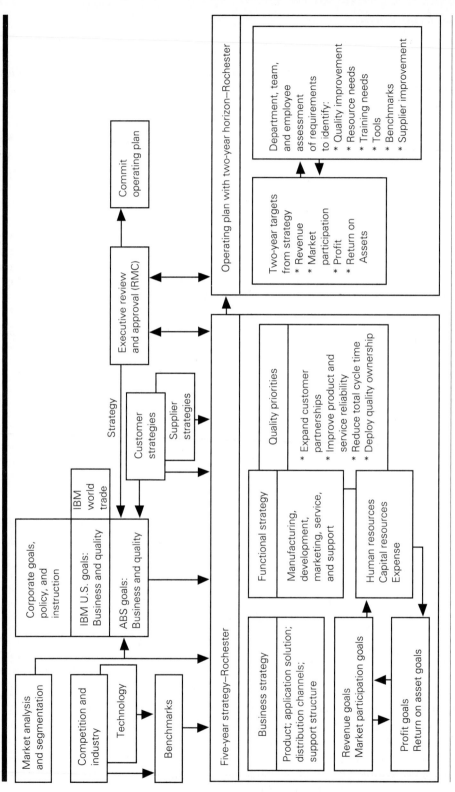

© IBM Corp., 1990, 1991.

this type of customer was only 1 percent of your install base. When we examined these kinds of planning practices, we found that Fortune 500 customers were heavily influencing the contents of our products, but they were less than 9 percent of our install base. So we were majoring on minors.

IBM Rochester planners now use a disciplined approach. It requires an understanding of market segments and uses a decision-making model and tools that structure trade-offs among competing objectives. For example, there are many trade-offs inherent in decisions about short-term versus long-term investments, particularly for competing objectives such as revenue versus market share, and customer satisfaction versus new technology. As one manager states, "You've got to decide how to spend your money: whether you spend 10 percent on customer satisfaction, or 20 percent or 80 percent. Whatever you spend it on, you're taking it away from something else. You can't just focus on the short-term customer satisfaction objectives. You have to also invest in new technology for providing future customer solutions. And you have to invest in growth markets."

Benchmarking and Strategic Goals

Benchmarking is rapidly becoming integrated into IBM culture. Corporate instruction 105 implicitly requires benchmarking. In order to ensure that every product's quality is "better than all predecessors," employees must know the quality of its predecessors. IBM Rochester does benchmarking through (1) the Tokyo systems evaluation lab, which does reverse engineering and cost analysis on competitor products, (2) the executive support system, which provides business investment, trade press, and consulting information on competitors, and (3) competitive analysis teams, which not only compare to competitor products and services, but build alliances in the marketplace to learn about technological processes and macrostrategies.

IBM Rochester applies benchmarking to all aspects of the business: products, services, and business systems and processes. The companies with which IBM Rochester engages in benchmarking may include noncompetitors, such as Merck, and competitors, such as Hewlett-Packard and Honeywell. Although it may be difficult to get approval to benchmark with competitors, the participants may decide to focus on *how* certain business processes are executed rather than on *how well.*

When Rochester planners are able to get specific benchmark data from world-class leaders, they use it to establish strategic goals and focus their improvement activities. They establish goals by developing a mythical competitor that comprises the best benchmarks for each element (e.g., cost, reliability, customer service, billing, and collection) from among the best companies in the world. This mythical competitor embodies realistic goals and also challenges employees to improve and to realize their ultimate goal to be the "undisputed leader in customer satisfaction." After setting goals, Rochester managers do root cause analysis, prioritize the drivers of quality results, and drive for six-sigma quality improvement.

Turning Strategic Plans into Customer Solutions

IBM Rochester's market-driven quality strategy dictates that the strategic planning process be driven by customers and market needs. The strategic purpose of IBM Rochester is to be the undisputed leader in customer satisfaction, and Rochester employees believe that if they succeed at this purpose, all other business goals, namely financial viability, will be realized. The strategic plans of IBM Rochester are turned into customer solutions, and ultimately customer satisfaction, through four phases of activity in a product cycle: (1) planning, (2) development, (3) manufacturing, and (4) marketing and service. Rochester's customer-driven product cycle is shown in Figure 8, and discussed below.

Figure 8

The customer-driven product cycle

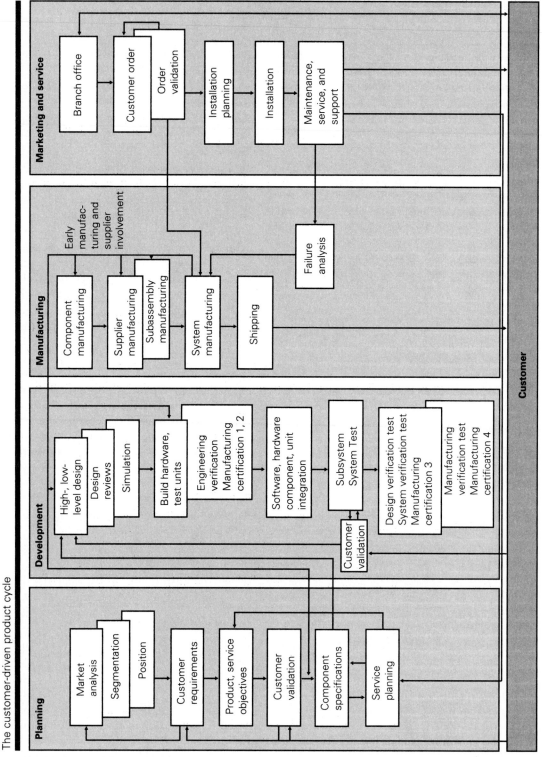

The four phases illustrated in Figure 8 are tightly linked to each other and to the customer. Cross-functional teams jointly shape the strategies and plans for the process. The planning process identifies customer needs and converts them into specifications. The development process takes the specifications through a rigorous series of design stages and verification activities, involving both manufacturing and customer evaluations. The manufacturing process engages suppliers and the product development team through joint decision-making activities early in the cycle. The marketing and service process tailors solutions to the customer's needs and represents the voice of the customer in defining new requirements. Marketing analysis and segmentation, the cornerstone of the product cycle, is discussed more thoroughly below.

Market Analysis and Segmentation

IBM Rochester begins its global market analysis and segmentation process by gathering data from sources in all geographic markets, such as consultant reports, government demographics, economic forecasts, university studies, and user group feedback. Each geographical area is segmented into small, medium, and large enterprises and establishments (see Figure 9). These enterprises and establishments are further segmented into industry, subindustry, and application opportunity market segments. For example, the distribution industry can be segmented into wholesale, specialty, and retail. Further, retail subindustries can be segmented into drug stores, auto parts, and hard-goods application opportunity market segments. Market analysis and segmentation can spell the difference between success and failure for a product. As one Rochester manager states: "It doesn't matter how perfect a product is from a quality standpoint. If you don't understand the targeted markets that you are going to play in, then your product will not be a success."

Selecting Target Markets

To select target markets, IBM Rochester evaluates market segments for their attractiveness and for the fit of its products and services within those segments. Segment attractiveness and segment fit comparisons are analyzed using the analytical hierarchy process. This process compares the relative strengths of each of the market segments with the ability to deliver solutions to those market segments. Segment attractiveness is gauged in terms of opportunity, growth, competition, executive vision, and business goals. Segment fit is gauged in terms of product fit, distribution channels, service and support, and application programs. From this analysis, target markets are selected and pursued.

Roy Bauer explains: "We figure out where the markets are going, and what segments we want to target. We first look at high-growth markets and see how well we fit in there. If we have a natural fit, we go after that market hot and heavy. If the market is high-growth, but our product doesn't fit well, there is likely a tremendous investment required in order to fit. We must decide whether we want to make that investment, or leave that market to somebody else. There are plenty of markets out there. We have to decide which niche to go after before talking about serving customers. And once we decide, we must then learn answers to the questions: What are the needs in this market? Who are the competitors? What differentiates us in the market? What are the barriers to entry? How do we best position in that market? etc."

Determining Customer Requirements

IBM Rochester performs detailed analyses of targeted markets to identify customer quality features and requirements. Plans are formulated and revised based on direct communication with customers. Tools like conjoint analysis are used to evaluate items within four strategic categories: product, applications, service, and channels. Each item is ranked for

Figure 9

Market analysis and segmentation

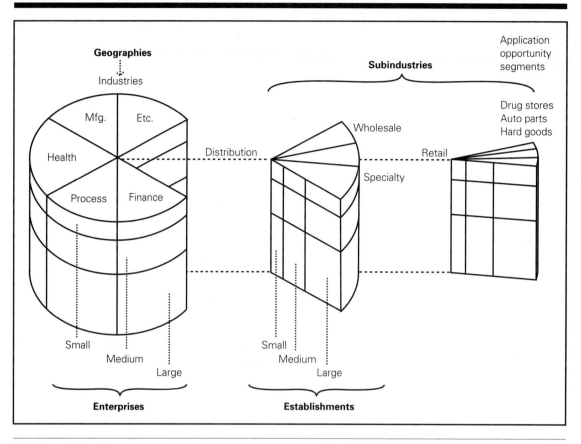

its importance within each category. Product quality features and requirements are weighed against the resources (both people and expenses) needed to achieve those requirements. To balance the plan, the items are prioritized into short-term (two-year) and long-term (five-year) projects. The plan is validated through customer councils, satisfaction surveys, consultants, business partners, industry comparisons, and field feedback.

In the Silverlake project, thorough analysis of customer requirements led IBM Rochester employees to a new understanding of their business. Without this new understanding, the AS/400 might not have succeeded in the market. IBM Rochester historically viewed itself as a supplier of computer hardware and operating systems. However, extensive study of the reasons for customer choices revealed that customers buy applications, or business solutions, with less concern for the hardware than hardware sellers like to think.

Customers evaluate maybe a half dozen applications and pick the one that best suits their business needs. If the application happens to run on an IBM computer, then IBM may sell a computer. As one Rochester manager states, "We are not in the business of selling operating systems. Our customers do not buy operating systems; they buy solutions. They don't care what the operating system is. They buy applications, and that's why our business partners are so important. They write most of the applications. And they understand our customers." So penetrating markets comes down to having the best applications. About 90 percent of the applications available in the AS/400 were written by third-party business partners.

To take advantage of this business reality, IBM Rochester decided that when it announced the AS/400, it would have the applications portfolio ready to go at the same time. The old practice of giving the hardware to the software-writing business partners close to announcement time would not enable immediate market penetration. When this is done, it may take six months to convert the software and provide the applications.

IBM Rochester decided that the applications should be ready as soon as the hardware was available. That meant the sales and support channels and all business partners had to be involved early in the product cycle. Roy Bauer explains what this means for product development: "It implies that you bring them into the development process on day one. The cross-functional team starts worrying about product announcement and product positioning on day one. You do not do it a few months before you are ready to announce the product. The early involvement of customers, suppliers, business partners, and channels helps you to make trade-offs and product development decisions throughout the cycle. So when you announce, you announce a solution."

▶ HUMAN RESOURCE UTILIZATION

As reflected in their basic belief, "Respect for the individual," IBM Rochester places tremendous value on its human resources and continues to invest in them.[6] Its strategy for utilizing human resources intends to not only implement the strategic business plan, but to also realize its "people vision" which derives from this basic belief. To accomplish their goals, Rochester leaders believe they must bring about a cultural shift through several people initiatives (see Figure 10).

People Vision

IBM Rochester's people vision intends to enable, empower, excite, and reward its work force within a market-driven culture. The term "enable" means to provide people with the assets needed to accomplish their goals. While the following discussion focuses on providing people with personal assets, such as knowledge and skills, the term "assets" includes all aspects of the systems, processes, work methods, information, tools, and materials through which Rochester's people satisfy customer requirements.

The term "empowered" does not mean licensed to be arbitrary. Rather, it means that people are given the ability to act *within guidelines* to achieve a goal. To empower people, managers must appropriately delegate ownership, responsibility, authority, and accountability, but not abdicate those things that are appropriate for themselves. While they must encourage risk taking, managers must not lose control of the processes they own. To do this, they must remain engaged and in touch with the systems, processes, and operations of the organization. Correspondingly, the people must respond to empowerment by working within policy, understanding the impact of

---

6. Expenditures for education are five times the national average for businesses, and equal about 5 percent of its payroll.

Figure 10

Human resource strategy

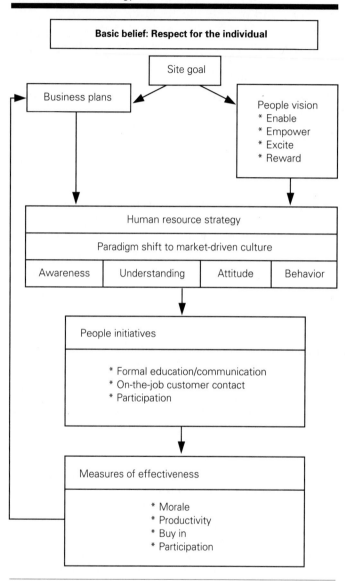

© IBM Corp., 1990, 1991.

their actions upon others, and thereby earn the privilege to be empowered.

The term "excited" implies that people are not just motivated to comply with market-driven requirements, but are enthusiastic about their work and have a sense of personal commitment to serving customers. As discussed later, behavioral measures of participation and surveys of employee satisfaction can reveal the level of excitement achieved.

These elements of the people vision are integral components and outcomes of a successful human resource strategy and cultural shift. Enablement and empowerment may lead to excitement, which may be sustained and reinforced through *rewards*, such as recognition and compensation.

Cultural Shifting

IBM Rochester's human resources strategy strives to bring about a cultural shift from a product-driven quality focus to a market-driven quality focus. This shift has caught as many people by surprise as did the site general manager when he peeled off his standard Big Blue attire and donned a superman-type outfit. He "flew" into the Mayo Civic Auditorium, as "Paradigm Man," with a red cape and a big Q on his chest, to discuss paradigm shift with the IBM Rochester employees attending leadership college.

In the past few years, IBM Rochester has shifted its culture to a new paradigm. The nature of the shift is summarized in the following pairs of terms.

Shift from:	Shift to:
Product-driven	Market-driven
Manage	Lead
Direct	Empower
Functional	Cross-functional
Action-oriented	Process-oriented
Individual contribution	Balance individual and team

As one Rochester manager stated, "We used to be very traditional managers who thought we could get by simply by telling people what they needed to do." The market-driven culture will require people to lead and empower rather than just manage and direct; to work cross-functionally rather than simply within functions; to engage in process improvements rather than simply taking action reactively to fix salient problems; and to balance individual efforts with team efforts. The emphasis on teamwork will be formally encouraged through more than just a "teamwork" line

item on performance ratings. Rather, common goals are defined so individuals will actually be rated on team results, and recognition systems have been changed to emphasize team achievements.

Key Lessons Learned   Critical events, like the Silverlake project, provide people with experiences that strongly affect their beliefs about how to conduct business. Listed below are the key lessons learned from the Silverlake project, which were acknowledged soon after its successful completion in 1989.[7]

1. Knowing our business and customers helped in targeting market segments.
2. Early involvement of customers and business partners throughout the process allowed us to calibrate the product to fulfill the real customer needs.
3. Designing quality at the component level elevated the quality of the entire product.
4. Managing the introduction of advanced technology into the marketplace provided us with knowledge of the customers and markets.
5. Creating an environment in which the employee is committed to the project and empowered to succeed is essential to reduce cycle time and increase quality.
6. Accuracy of market requirements led to a stable development/manufacturing process and reduced cycle time.
7. The executive steering committee management system permitted fast resolution of issues and reduced organizational complexity for the successful launch of the AS/400.
8. Early market positioning can help identify product strengths, but must be managed carefully to create proper market expectations. (If expectations are set higher than

---

7. Detailed in an unpublished case study, "The IBM AS/400: A Market-Driven Case," by Roy Bauer, Emilio Collar, and Victor Tang, presented at the 16th International Research Seminar in Marketing, La Londe Les Maures, France, May 17-19, 1989.

the company can meet, then customers may be less satisfied than they would otherwise have been.)

Challenging the Lessons Learned Certainly, the Silverlake project gave impetus to a cultural shift. However, Rochester employees continue to challenge their cultural principles. For example, Rochester managers went into the Silverlake project believing that definitions of customer requirements must be held stable from the beginning of a development cycle. Key lesson number six above suggests that the market requirements should be defined early in the development cycle and as accurately as possible to ensure stability throughout the remainder of the cycle. This stability allows simultaneous engineering based on a common and unchanging blueprint. If blueprints are changed frequently, because requirements were not accurate initially, then the work already done based on the old blueprint may become obsolete. Product and process engineers may have to go back to the drawing boards and do rework. Holding the blueprints stable avoids rework, and leads to more certain execution of designs in manufacturing, lower costs, and reduced cycle times.

Although the concept of accurate requirements may have served them well in developing the AS/400, IBM Rochester is not satisfied with it. Rochester employees are challenging themselves to hold blueprints stable when possible, but also to react quickly to incorporate customer input and technological advancements at later stages of the development cycle. Roy Bauer explains:

> Over the long term, involving customers reduces development time. Sure, you have to take resources off what you'd like to be doing and you put them on fixing some of the things that irritate customers. But it's easier to fix it now, during development, than later. And to fix something while you're developing it is endemic to the process itself, because most of these changes are part

of debugging. The time required to do it becomes almost transparent.

> Things change all the time. There is really no such thing as requirement stability because the market, the competition, the customers, and technology determine stability requirements. You can't control any of them. If in mid-cycle there's a new whiz bang deal out there in the market, because your competitor beat you to something, and you think you're going to introduce a product without it, I've got news for you. If you want your product to be successful, it's got to be there.

> Certainly, you must have an accurate requirements statement up front. But then you must have a process that's adaptable to change as you go through. The secret is shortening the cycle so you can afford to adapt, and improving your ability to adapt. Involving customers continuously can help you do it right the first time and shorten the cycle. So, please, work on the right problem; don't tell me about requirement stability.

IBM Rochester has not simply shifted to another cultural position which will remain in place for another decade or so. Rather, Rochester employees continue to challenge themselves, in order to perpetually shift and refine their culture. As one manager puts it, "We have an environment at this site that can be characterized as a 'healthy state of discontent.' This site just seems to be one that is never satisfied in where we are. We are always self-critical. Always learning from our experiences." IBM Rochester is continuously shifting its culture, sometimes with dramatic breakthroughs to progress in leaps and bounds, and sometimes with minor adjustments and reinterpretations to progress in many small steps that are cumulatively large and significant. They continuously strive to improve their thinking, their practices, and their goals, and to achieve integration among these. For example, to accomplish its six-sigma goals (3.4 defects per million by 1994), IBM Rochester has created hundreds of "10X teams," each charged to reduce defect levels tenfold and then a hundredfold.

Avoiding Cultural Regression Another reason IBM Rochester strives to improve its culture is that there are forces that may cause the culture to regress. For example, IBM tends to move its senior managers around. Replacement of experienced and committed leaders can interrupt the transformation process. As one manager states, "It's like taking two steps forward, and one step back." People who did not personally experience the transformation at Rochester certainly have less commitment to and understanding of its market-driven culture. IBM Rochester must continue to socialize new members into its market-driven culture. Ongoing use of the Baldrige criteria as an assessment tool helps IBM Rochester continue to develop its culture.

People Initiatives

IBM Rochester's human resources strategy will not shift the culture immediately. Permanent changes in behavior are likely to come only after individuals develop the awareness, the understanding, and the attitudes consistent with the market-driven culture. As illustrated in Figure 10, the human resources strategy entails three people initiatives intended to shift employee behavior to a market-driven culture: formal education/communication, on-the-job customer contact, and participation.

Formal Education/Communication IBM Rochester is continually educating employees and developing their skills. Individual discussion between managers and other employees is the most common and important communication channel. However, mandatory education through the following courses gives employees a basic foundation of knowledge and skills: transformational leadership, leadership college, manufacturing skills integration, market-driven quality, new manager training, new employee orientation, special focus modules, and customized area training. Other education

and communication avenues used to deploy Rochester's people vision include: faculty loan, cooperative education, technical interchange with universities, graduate work study, supplier education, job rotation, mentoring, technical assistant assignments, cross-functional assignments, executive interviews, roundtables, IBM TV network, bulletin board notices, IBM publications.

Customer Contact Although employee goals and objectives are customer-driven and educational activities encourage a customer orientation, some people may not "feel" market-driven since their jobs are isolated from direct customer contact. To remedy this isolation, IBM Rochester gives people on-the-job exposure to customers through a variety of assignments: as advocates through assignments in sales, through telemarketing and customer partnership calls to assess and monitor customer satisfaction, installation assessment teams, customer satisfaction action teams, and software partner labs. Some employees may be assigned to a marketing team to act as a junior engineer on customer visits, while others act as key account owners. Senior managers may take assignments to offer executive assistance to support a sales area.

Participation Initiatives The market-driven culture at IBM Rochester fosters participation and empowerment through many programs. Further, compensation and recognition programs ensure that people are rewarded for quality improvement and innovation (see Figure 11).

Measures of Effectiveness

Various measures are taken to assess the effectiveness of IBM Rochester's initiatives in accomplishing the people vision. For example, participation in technical vitality initiatives grew more than sixfold from 1986 to 1990, as measured by the number of articles in professional journals, patent applications, and inventions. IBM Rochester also monitors various in-

Figure 11
Initiatives for increasing participation

Empowerment decision making	Job flexibility	Recognition	Compensation
• Opinion survey • Speak-up process • Open door program • Suggestion plan • Roundtable discussions • Skip-level interviews • Development plans • Performance plans • Manufacturing skills integration	• Full employment • Volunteer temporary assignment • Flextime schedules • Internal transfer opportunities • Retraining	• Performance evaluation • Verbal thanks • Promotion • ABS quality awards • Team awards • ABS excellence awards • Management excellence awards • Management appreciation awards • Author recognition • Inventor recognition • Site-wide publicity	• Merit pay • IBM benefits plan • Voluntary tax-deferred savings plan • Voluntary stock purchase plan • Employee assistance program • A Plan for Life • Elder care referral • Child care referral • IBM club • Watson scholarship

©IBM Corp., 1990, 1991.

dicators of morale to reveal whether it has developed an excited work-force. For example, from 1987 to 1990, employee suggestions increased by 37 percent, and anonymous communications ("speak-ups") from employees to senior managers increased by 42 percent. While managers used to view such communications as negatively reflecting the existence of problems within the organization, they now view employee feedback as positive opportunities for improvement. The 94 percent voluntary participation in employee opinion surveys shows that the vast majority of employees believe their opinions are considered important.

Other measures reflect the excitement of the IBM Rochester work force: absentee rates are 48 percent below the industry average, turnover rates are 88 percent less than the industry average, and safety records are 57 percent better than the industry average. IBM Rochester's productivity also exceeds the industry average.[8]

▶ QUALITY ASSURANCE OF PRODUCTS AND SERVICES

At IBM Rochester, quality assurance does not simply mean adherence to engineered product specifications. Rather, it means meeting customer requirements and providing customer solutions to ensure customer satisfaction. The quality of IBM Rochester's products and services is assured through: early and continuing involvement of customers in the product cycle; process management to prevent defects, reduce cycle times and integrate the organization; and partnerships with suppliers for mutual benefit.

Continuing Customer Involvement
IBM Rochester used to be technology-driven, rather than customer-driven. As IBM's former

---

8. Measured in revenue per employee, IBM Rochester's productivity exceeds the industry average reported in *Forbes* magazine, Apr. 30, 1990.

CEO John Akers once said, "IBM has, for quite a long time, spent 90 percent of the time thinking about what's on our mind—exemplified by all of our products—instead of spending 90 percent of our time thinking about what's on the customer's mind."[9] IBM Rochester used to create technology and put it on the market, without involving customers in development of products and services. Now they realize customers are quite sophisticated and capable of assisting in the development of improved products and services. Customers are involved throughout the product cycle:

1. *Planning*: Customer and business partner councils
2. *Requirements*: User groups (like COMMON)
3. *Analysis and design*: Software partner laboratory
4. *Development*: Customer usability testing
5. *Build and test*: Early availability programs
6. *Support and feedback*: Customer partnership calls/surveys

Involving customers throughout the total product cycle, from planning requirements through support and feedback, not only ensures better products and services, it fosters a personal attachment by customers. As Charlie Bell, director of MIS at Jefferson Smurfit Corporation, states about the AS/400: "Do you realize that 90 percent of what I suggested last fall is now in the product? I feel like I'm part of the development team."

IBM Rochester brought customers into the development process through worldwide customer and business partner councils which review future product plans. Every day, customers visit an executive briefing center which is supported by development and manufacturing teams. An independent user group, COMMON, comprised of over 6,000 customers worldwide, holds regular local meetings to provide AS/400 requirements to IBM Rochester development and manufacturing. One Rochester employee describes the change in the new product development process as follows:

> In the old product development process, you would have a programmer sitting in the lab writing functions based on his perception of how the customer would use it. Then you would go through the whole development process and ultimately ship it somewhere down the road. Then you'd find out, in one of your user meetings, that none of your customers like the way you implemented that function. For example, you put this help screen in there with a bunch of defaults to help them so they don't have to key in all this information; however, you put the defaults in that customers never use. They always use this other set of defaults.

> Programmers that never worked in a customer environment before make guesses about what happens. When the guesses are revealed as wrong, the feedback about customer requirements would come back and go into the plan in the next cycle. If you were lucky, you got 50 percent of them in, and then the next cycle, one or two years later, the customer finally got what they really wanted. But you irritated them all along the way.

> Somebody finally asked: "Why don't we just bring in some customers and ask them the details up front?" The security department nearly went horizontal, fearing leaks and industrial espionage. But we overcame the fear and started the Software Partner Labs. We had early machines and programmers writing the code, and engineers trying to figure out how the function would perform. We brought customers in to use it and give us immediate feedback on what they liked and disliked, and what they would and would not use. And a programmer would go away and come back an hour later with changes. The process is real dynamic—flexible and adaptable to change.

The Software Partner Lab provides an opportunity for customers and business partners

---

9. See *Think*, February 1989.

to jointly develop new products and services. Customers validate that their requirements are being met, and they verify that their application programs will operate effectively on newly designed systems.

In addition, an extensive early availability program provides AS/400 systems to selected customers before they are available to the general public. These systems are monitored closely to ensure that customers are satisfied with the latest developments. Services and support procedures are also evaluated during this time. Customers are surveyed frequently to maintain an awareness of their satisfaction. They are contacted by IBM ninety days after receiving an AS/400 system. They are thanked for being an IBM customer and asked about their satisfaction with their new system. These ongoing partnerships and customer feedback provide input to plans for subsequent product development cycles.

Process Management Approach

Process management is key to achieving important objectives such as effectiveness, efficiency, adaptability, and continuous improvement. The steps in process management are: (1) identify key processes, (2) establish process ownership, (3) evaluate and measure, and (4) do root cause analysis.

Ownership is a key concept for process management at IBM Rochester. Process owners take responsibility for the steps of process management to address the causes of customer satisfaction. Process ownership is widespread at IBM Rochester. As one manager states: "Not every manager owns something, but key managers own key processes, and they have responsibility to improve them. There are a lot of subprocesses within the key processes, and these are owned by other managers who report to the key managers. Just about everybody is involved. It is fundamental to ask: 'Who owns that problem?' 'Who owns that opportunity?' and 'What are the commitment dates?' "

In the past, IBM Rochester has focused on production processes, attempting to optimize manufacturing. However, they have realized that to be the undisputed leader in customer satisfaction they must address all aspects of the business, and that each part of the organization cannot be optimized separately. So they have identified key processes which cut across functional and geographic boundaries to compose the Rochester business enterprise.

The key processes shown in Figure 12 are each assigned to a senior executive who heads a process management team composed of diverse members. Rather than just talk about the money made last quarter, these executives are actively involved in making the company better through process management. Within each enterprise process are subprocesses, each with process owners and process management teams. For example, the development software process is composed of twenty-seven subprocesses, one of which is microcode development. This subprocess has a corporate owner, and each site has an owner responsible for managing consistency and introducing new ideas across all IBM microcode sites.

Defect Prevention Strategy   Thus, IBM Rochester strives to prevent defects, rather than just detect them through inspection at various stages of the manufacturing line. When defects are prevented by continuously improving design tools and techniques, and by eliminating manual operations and errors in interpreting specifications, the design quality is improved, cycles are shortened, and costs are reduced. IBM Rochester estimates that if the cost of preventing a defect is X at the time of design, then a defect not prevented costs 13X at testing stage, and 92X at the stage of customer installation.

IBM Rochester used to spend about 75 percent of its capital on test and process control equipment for detecting defects in production. Moving from a detection to a prevention strategy has reduced that type of spending to only 25 percent of capital expenditures. The

Figure 12

Fifteen key enterprise processes

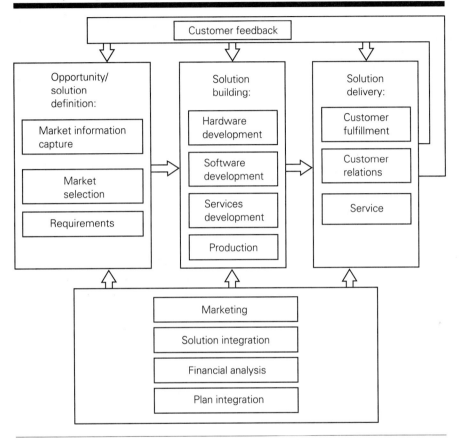

savings have been shifted to investments in productivity tools, defect removal tools, and prevention in the design phase of the product cycle. IBM Rochester spends more money on information technology; process management, ownership, and analysis; customer partnerships; high-function workstations to improve programmer quality and productivity in code writing; and education on empowerment, six-sigma, etc. Consequently, IBM Rochester has been able to do more with less, as reflected by the downsizing of the work force. The total site head count is down about 2,000 people since 1980, a 20 percent reduction, yet productivity and output are going through the roof.

Development Process As mentioned above, an iterative software development process involves customers in clarifying their requirements, identifying needed changes, and validating development decisions. Further, IBM Rochester's prevention-based design approach uses process management and simulation tools to remove defects before fabricating the hardware and integrating the software. Using the engineering verification engine (EVE) to simulate the system design, employees isolate and remove defects prior to building the hardware. EVE has resulted in 80 percent improvement in the time required to debug hardware, which eliminates excessive design iterations.

Process management has significantly reduced the development cycle time of computer systems and hard disks. The serial processes for producing the System/36 and the System/38 have been transformed to a parallel, continuous flow system for producing the AS/400 system (see Figure 13). Simulation, early manufacturing involvement (EMI), software component development, and parallel system tests have contributed to a 40 percent reduction in the development cycle time. Rather than working independently and sequentially, the functions of development, manufacturing, marketing, and service are integrated through concurrent and collaborative activities. Cross-functional EMI teams begin working in the early design stages to simultaneously develop hardware, software, and manufacturing processes, and work out details of product introduction, software installation, distribution logistics, customer service, and feedback systems. They also improve the manufacturing processes for continuous flow (as discussed below), to enable rapid, high-volume production capability. People from other worldwide IBM manufacturing sites participate on EMI teams to ensure that worldwide specifications are met.

Integration of Development and Manufacturing IBM Rochester has also improved the hand-off from design and product development to manufacturing. For example, errors due to manual translation of data are eliminated by sophisticated design tools that verify conceptual designs and then automatically translate them into detailed descriptions for production of chips, and processing instructions for such equipment as the automatic electronic component insertion machines that build printed circuit boards.

Before manufacturing begins, products are subjected to a series of verification tests that confirm both the product characteristics and the integrity of the development process. These verification tests serve as development checkpoints and are coordinated with the design of the manufacturing processes. An independent assurance organization certifies readiness at each checkpoint and verifies adherence to government regulations, industry standards, and corporate instructions.

Continuous Flow Manufacturing The ability to be flexible and responsive is key to excellence in manufacturing processes and the achievement of undisputed leadership in customer satisfaction. So process owners implement continuous flow manufacturing (CFM) to further reduce cycle times. CFM integrates all elements of its production and nonproduction support processes to reduce cycle time, reduce cost, and prevent defects. Order sizes, improvements in tooling, and changes to process flow are some of the factors affecting CFM cycle time reduction.

CFM begins with an examination of the total process, from a customer order to raw material gathering through manufacturing and customer installation. Cross-functional teams of employees, suppliers, customers, and business partners use process management techniques to make improvements and remove steps from the process. Employees frequently provide input to improve their jobs and key processes through department meetings, project teams, and cross-functional teams. Cooperative projects with suppliers also help to improve business results for IBM and suppliers.

Supplier Partnerships
IBM Rochester's 700 production suppliers account for about 30 percent of its production

Figure 13

Comparison of the System/3X with AS/400 in terms of cycle-time benefits realized through hardware simulation and a new software development process

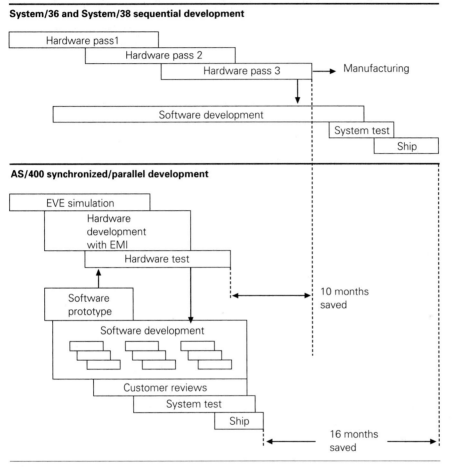

System/36 and System/38 sequential development

Hardware pass1

Hardware pass 2

Hardware pass 3 → Manufacturing

Software development

System test

Ship

AS/400 synchronized/parallel development

EVE simulation

Hardware development with EMI

Hardware test

Software prototype

Software development

10 months saved

Customer reviews

System test

Ship

16 months saved

© IBM Corp., 1990, 1991.

output. To ensure reliable and high-quality input from these suppliers, IBM Rochester trains, audits, and certifies its suppliers, and requires them to submit quality plans. Just like customers and business partners, suppliers are engaged early in product development, such as planning for logistics, deciding on hardware tooling, and selecting technologies. IBM Rochester supports its alliance partners with education, such as CFM training, ongoing assess-

ments, and recognition of progress.[10] By working with these alliance partners, IBM Rochester has eliminated the need for receiving inspection for many supplied parts. Further, sharing of technology and expertise benefits both IBM and its suppliers.

---

10. The number of production suppliers has been reduced by 44 percent since 1985, and 69 percent of production dollars are now spent with alliance suppliers.

▶ QUALITY RESULTS

IBM Rochester has achieved many quality improvement results. Some of these are listed below:

IBM Rochester Quality Improvement Results

Quality Improvement Trends since 1984

- Product reliability, 4X improvement in mean time to failure for hard disks and 3X improvement for computer systems.
- Reduction of write-offs (scrap) by 55 percent.
- Reduction of engineering costs by 45 percent.
- Reduction of total cycle time by 60 percent.

World-Class Benchmarks

- The average failure rate per circuit better than the industry average and better than the best worldwide competitor.
- The product development cycle for new computer systems reduced from about five years to around two years, which is less than that of competitors.

Process Excellence

- With less rework and scrap being required, manufacturing capacity has increased fivefold since 1986.

- Systems manufacturing cycle time reduced 80 percent and inventory reduced 50 percent since 1984.
- Storage products cycle time reduced 76 percent and inventory reduced 55 percent since 1984.
- Warehouse space reduced 30 percent.
- Space savings in systems manufacturing reduced 42 percent since 1986.
- Assembly line time has been cut in half since 1986.
- Energy use as a percentage of output has been reduced from 1.7 to less than 1 percent since 1982.
- CFC emissions have been eliminated at year-end 1991.

Supplier Partnership Results

- Suppliers' lead time has been reduced by 80 percent since 1988.
- Suppliers' defect rates on incoming parts have improved 58 percent since 1988.
- Improved employee satisfaction with purchased services, such as travel, cafeteria and vending, and cleaning, since 1988.
- Customer satisfaction has improved 8 percent since 1988.

▶ CUSTOMER SATISFACTION

IBM Rochester customers expect to be provided with solutions to their business problems. They expect responsiveness, ease of doing business, technical ability and coverage, and knowledge of their business. They expect these things from every point of contact with their provider, from the first administrative encounter to last service call. Only by comprehensively providing customer solutions will

IBM Rochester achieve its goal of being the undisputed leader in customer satisfaction.

The foregoing categories of leadership, information and analysis, strategic quality planning, human resource utilization, and quality assurance entail the activities used to provide customer solutions and satisfaction. IBM Rochester also obtains feedback on the success of these activities in achieving customer satisfac-

Figure 14

Customer partnership calls process

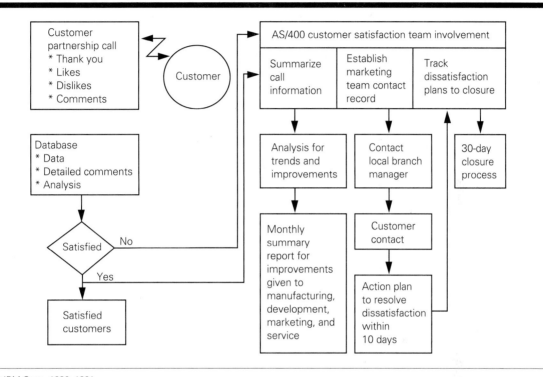

tion. Three important sources of information feedback are discussed below: customer partnership calls, surveys, and complaints. Other methods to ensure leadership in customer satisfaction include hotlines, field feedback, independent consultant reviews, and industry-accepted reports. Such communication with customers provides feedback to the development process about product quality and service requirements.

Customer Partnership Calls

The customer partnership call process thanks customers for purchasing an AS/400 system (see Figure 14). A Rochester employee calls the customer ninety days after a system is

shipped to get feedback from the customer. The comments are placed in a database, analyzed, and distributed monthly to engineering, programming, marketing, manufacturing, and service teams for evaluation. Dissatisfied and concerned customers are contacted by marketing to understand the details of their concerns. Pareto analysis has revealed several categories of reasons for dissatisfaction, each of which is tracked over time to make sure that actions taken yield improvements. These categories include: performance, service and support, features and function, migration/usability, partnership, applications, and other miscellaneous reasons. The customer satisfaction project office receives notification of the results of the customer contact. Thirty days later, the

Figure 15

AS/400 satisfaction/dissatisfaction survey results

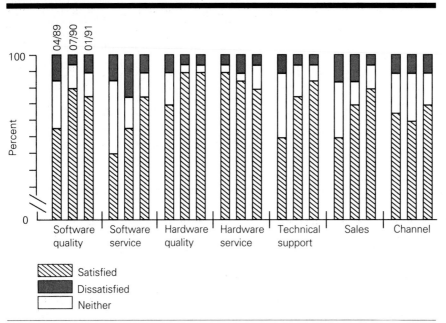

© IBM Corp., 1990, 1991.

same customers are called back to ensure they are satisfied.

Customer Surveys

IBM Rochester uses many different types of surveys annually, quarterly, and monthly to understand customer satisfaction worldwide. These types of surveys include: marketing and service general marketplace, competitive market tracking, AS/400 product/service, marketing and service customer executive opinions, AS/400 market tracking, and non-U.S. surveys. As an example of its content, the AS/400 product/service satisfaction survey asks about software quality, hardware quality, administration, channels, sales, software service, hardware service, and systems engineering.

Important Parameters For all surveys, several important parameters are addressed to ensure that customer feedback yields useful data, that is, data that can be translated into useful information. First, the data from the global installation base of customers must be collected in such a way that it can be grouped by customer type (e.g., end users, operators, programmers, decision makers, business partners, and large, medium, and small customers); by geographic region; by segment (e.g., distribution, manufacturing, process, state and local government, health, and finance); and by prior experience of customer group (e.g., migrate, competitive, and new/additional). Second, the data must be timely, as needed, either daily or yearly. Third, the sample size must be adequate to ensure statistically significant representation of the installation base. Fourth, the data must be unbiased to allow internal and external competitive comparison. Fifth, the data must be organized and distributed to allow it to be consolidated, analyzed, correlated, and directed to those who need it. Finally, the data must provide information about cause and effect relationships to inform continuous improvements.

Improvement over Time   IBM Rochester tracks survey data over time to assess satisfaction trends. For example, the results of the AS/400 product/service satisfaction/dissatisfaction survey reveals improvements and areas of opportunity (see Figure 15).

Complaint Management Process
To achieve the goal of being the undisputed leader in customer satisfaction, IBM Rochester has established a complaint management process that tightly links marketing and service teams to development and manufacturing teams. Complaints are received from customers by either the Rochester site general manager, the ABS general manager, or any of the executives in the IBM Corporation. The complaints are managed by the customer satisfaction management team working with the branch office closest to that customer. An investigator is assigned to examine and understand the specific details of the complaint, which must be resolved within two weeks. Feedback from the complaint is sent to the customer satisfaction management team, where it is recorded, assimilated with other information, and correlated for use in reports to the customer satisfaction council, and used to make product and service quality improvements.

From 1988 to 1990, the time required to resolve complaints was reduced from thirty-four to twelve days. This improvement helps IBM Rochester employees better serve customers after problems have been identified; however, they prefer to avoid creating problems in the first place. Data on complaints indicate that they are doing just that. Complaints are steadily decreasing and dropped by more than 50 percent from 1987 to 1990.

▶ CONCLUSION

In the past few years, IBM Rochester has achieved tremendous success with the management approach described above. IBM Rochester is now one of the most vibrant parts of IBM, and in many ways an industry benchmark.[11] Sales of AS/400s and disk drives are progressively growing. IBM Rochester is achieving the kind of success that earned its reputation as a "solid business."

The challenge IBM Rochester now faces is to continue with business success, but avoid the seemingly seasonal dip into complacency, self-satisfaction, and comfort with the status quo. As IBM Rochester almost illustrated, freezing into a status quo can eliminate you from contention in vital and turbulent high-technology markets. IBM Rochester is striving to carefully exist in a state of flux, with its culture and business practices balanced between fluid adaptability and structured predictability.

Thus, Rochester employees maintain a healthy state of discontent. They continue to seek the next breakthrough that will rally people to another energy-filled spring of market opportunity and business success. And they always look for small improvements that continuously shift them toward their objective to be the undisputed leader in customer satisfaction.

---

11. However, it remains to be seen whether IBM can duplicate Rochester's success throughout the whole corporation.

▶ DISCUSSION QUESTIONS

1. Break the class into work groups of five or six people. Each group should:
   A. Describe how IBM Rochester's culture changed by providing examples of change at these three levels of culture:
      Level 1: Artifacts and behaviors
      Level 2: Values and beliefs
      Level 3: Underlying assumptions
   B. Describe how change at one level of culture is reinforced or expressed at other levels of culture.

After fifteen to twenty minutes of discussion, have each group present their work for one example at each level.

2. What aspects of IBM Rochester's culture did not change in accordance with the principles of the emerging paradigm?

3. What lessons about organizational learning and transformation are illustrated in the IBM Rochester case?

John Young: Hewlett-Packard's Champion of Change*

Working in a rented Palo Alto garage, the partnership of William Hewlett and David Packard hooked its first big customer, Walt Disney Studios, in 1939. Disney purchased eight audio oscillators from Hewlett-Packard to develop and test an innovative sound system for the classic animated movie *Fantasia*. Since then, HP has become the world's leading manufacturer of electronic test and measuring instruments for scientists and engineers, and has grown to be a $13 billion company, and America's thirteenth-largest exporter.[1]

In fact, more than half of HP's business is generated outside the U.S. Two-thirds of HP's foreign sales go to Europe. And unlike most of its Silicon Valley competitors, HP has also achieved significant success in Japan. Substantial HP exports go through Yokogawa-Hewlett-Packard, a 30-year-old, billion-dollar company based in Tokyo with a staff of 4,000. Yokogawa-HP started out as a joint venture between Yokogawa Electric Corporation and HP, and is now the largest contributor to HP's business outside the U.S. As you will read below, HP's Asian joint ventures such as Samsung-HP and Yokogawa-HP have significantly influenced HP's culture.

HP's expanding global presence is not limited to Japan. HP markets products in 100 countries, with sales and support offices and distributorships on six continents, and research and manufacturing facilities in the U.S., Europe, Japan, Latin America, and Canada. HP's trend toward globalization, not only of its markets, but of all parts of its organization, has continued into the 1990s. For example, in 1990, HP moved the headquarters of its PC business to Grenoble, France, established new subsidiaries in Thailand, Turkey, and Portugal, and set up sales organizations in central and eastern Europe.

Such global expansion is matched only by HP's growing diversity of product offerings. HP markets 12,000 products, primarily computing and electronic measuring equipment, to serve customers in not only industry (primarily aerospace, telecommunications, aircraft, and automotive), but also science, engineering, health care, and education. By competing in such dynamic markets as electronics, where nothing stays the same very long, HP employees always face interesting

* This case was prepared by Greg Bounds and John Young.
1. Renowned for its management philosophy and style as well as for its innovative technology, HP has made the "best" lists of countless surveys on working environments, was chosen as one of the forty-three "excellent" companies in the best-selling *In Search of Excellence,* and was among eighteen firms praised for its strong commitment to values in *Corporate Cultures.*

new challenges. For example, half of HP's orders generated in 1990 were from products introduced in the preceding two years. Since its inception, HP has created its future by innovating and introducing a variety of new products. HP's breakthroughs over the years include the following:[2]

- The high-speed frequency counter, which reduces from ten minutes to two seconds the time needed to accurately measure high frequencies. Introduced in 1951, radio stations continue to use this product to accurately set frequencies to comply with FCC regulations.
- The world's first scientific hand-held calculator, which made the engineer's slide rule obsolete. Introduced in 1972, it was heralded as the "electronic slide rule."
- The HP9000, the world's first desktop mainframe computer. Unveiled in 1983, it was a computer small enough to fit on a desktop while having the same power as the room-size computers of the 1960s.
- The world's first hand-held computer to combine personal computer power with the capabilities of Lotus 1-2-3. Built into a device the size of a business calculator, the 11-ounce palmtop computer works alone or as a companion to desktop and laptop PCs. The HP95LX—code named Jaguar—has the computing power of an IBM XT, a 23-pound PC. Jointly developed by HP and Lotus, it was introduced in April of 1991. Such innovative products were once conceded to offshore manufacturers, particularly the Japanese.

The man who leads this far-flung Hewlett-Packard enterprise is president and chief executive officer John Young. A U.S. Air Force veteran with a B.S. in electrical engineering from Oregon State University and an M.B.A. from Stanford University, Young joined HP's marketing-planning staff in 1958. Young subsequently served as a regional sales manager, a member of the corporate finance staff, and general manager of the former Microwave Division, became a vice president in 1968, and then a director and executive vice president in 1974. In 1978, Young became HP's president and CEO.

Young has won many awards and been honored by foreign governments, universities, publications, the National Science Foundation, and the American Electronics Association. He has also served as a director, trustee, member, fellow, or chairman of thirty different organizations, associations, and universities. The Japanese so highly regarded Young that they granted him the distinguished Prime Minister's Trade Award, an award given to individuals who have contributed significantly to building mutual understanding in commerce between Japan and other countries.

Evidently, Young seems to be something of a kindred spirit to the Japanese. He not only maintains strong relationships with Canon, Hitachi, Mitsubishi, and other Japanese companies, he also shares the Japanese perspective that U.S competitiveness problems are largely of the U.S.'s own making, such as underinvesting and failure to build for the future. Young believes that since the economic activities of the world's largest trading nations are so inextricably interconnected, they should work closely together to coordinate their economic policies. On the other hand, Young also argues that the Japanese markets should be more open and easily accessible and encourages the Japanese to be more responsive as a trading nation.

Within HP, Young constantly battles company practices such as excessive bureaucracy, reviews, and controls that can discourage people from unleashing their competitive potential. For example, in 1990, Young eliminated the executive committee, which was formed

---

2. Northwest's *Compass Readings Magazine*, "John Young Proves Innovation Hewlett-Packard's Lifeblood," November 1991, pp. 30–36.

in 1974 as HP's primary policy-setting body, because he considered it an unnecessary layer in decision making. To encourage innovation, the lifeblood of HP, Young's company tries to recruit the very best people with a diversity of technical talent, provide them with a rich set of tools and a lot of computing power, and promote a climate that fosters creativity. While HP defines the goals of a product and the standard interfaces with which it must comply, it also allows its people to be creative.

Young's strategy for improving Hewlett-Packard's ability to compete in world markets includes investing heavily in research and development (R&D) ($1.4 billion in 1990, about 10 percent of its annual net revenue), innovating to create new markets, shortening product development cycles, and improving product quality. Young strongly advocates the application of total quality control (TQC) principles to implement this strategy. TQC has helped HP achieve a manufacturing productivity annual growth rate of 15 percent for the past five years, reduce warranty costs by $800 million over the past decade, and save hundreds of millions of dollars in inventory. HP also applies TQC principles outside manufacturing to get more accurate invoices, increase productivity in order processing, speed up turnaround in customer service, increase sales time with customers, and shorten product development cycles.

Outside HP, Young advocates more government action to develop, commercialize, and protect technology, and particularly, more government investments in R&D aimed at generic, precompetitive technologies like logic chips, fiber optics, advanced materials, and flexible manufacturing.[3] Young considers this focus on generic technologies a far wiser course of action than the government trying to decide which industries or products to support.

Young advocates tax credits for R&D investments because the resulting advances and benefits extend far beyond the firm that achieves the technological breakthrough. He also advocates recycling some of the U.S. defense R&D activities of the 725 federal laboratories to get a lot more value out of the enormous sums spent there. While advances derived from R&D investments in defense and space technologies, which account for over two-thirds of the U.S. government's R&D spending, may find some commercial applications, most are commercially irrelevant. Young frequently points out that, between the public and private sector, the U.S. spends 1.8 percent of GNP on commercially relevant technologies, while the Japanese are at 3.0 and the Germans at 2.8. And the U.S. trend is dead flat, while the others are going up.

In 1983, President Reagan appointed Young to chair the President's Commission on Industrial Competitiveness, which was chartered to explore means of improving the competitive posture of U.S. industry at home and abroad. In that role, Young helped convince the U.S. Commerce Department to sponsor the Malcolm Baldrige National Quality Award. Over the last decade, John Young has devoted considerable time and attention in serving as a missionary for the cause of improving quality and competitiveness. John Young not only thrives on the excitement and challenge of positioning Hewlett-Packard for competing in the twenty-first century, but also thrives on the duty of educating his peers and students, the managers of the future.

Young's beliefs about improvement and competitive strategy are explored and elaborated in the following transcripts. The first of these transcripts is an interview with John Young, which was specifically structured to explore some of the issues taught in this text. The other transcript is a presentation wherein Young clearly articulates to Samsung managers the details of Hewlett-Packard's approach to competing globally.

---

3. Pre-competitive refers to R&D activities that sufficiently reduce technical uncertainties and permit some assessment of the technology's commercial potential, but do not develop specific applications or prototypes.

► THE YOUNG AND BOUNDS INTERVIEW

This interview was conducted by Greg Bounds with John Young at Hewlett-Packard's corporate offices in Palo Alto, California, on September 26, 1991.

GB: I have a quotation here from one of your competitors. This person said, "I can show HP to anyone in this organization and scare them. They're good. They seem to know every move we make, they position themselves well in the market, and they always seem to do well. All their customer satisfaction numbers are as good as ours, and in some cases better than ours." This quotation clearly shows this person has identified HP as a benchmark competitor. Let me ask you to identify HP's best competitors and benchmarks. What organizations would you like to have HP pattern its processes and systems after?

JY: We have a broad base of business at Hewlett-Packard. We're in analytical measurements, medical electronics, tested measurement, computers, computer peripherals, and there isn't another company that looks like Hewlett-Packard. So when it comes to benchmarking, I think you find more of a menu than any one company. In test and measurement, some very small companies can be the world-class competitors, companies you would never recognize, like Tatron, Tekelek, and Shimatzu from Japan. Tectronix is our largest competitor, but we don't think they're necessarily the best competitor in the marketplace. You'll find that everybody at HP has got their short list of who the class operators are, and we watch their moves pretty carefully in a lot of ways. And we do benchmarking with companies that aren't direct competitors. Just looking at competitors may not be the best thing to do. They may not be world class in some things, like paying their bills. So we have spent a lot of time trading data with companies to benchmark things like accounts payable and some really interesting things have shown up. We've also benchmarked production activities like surface mount placement costs at Toshiba. They do huge volumes in consumer goods, and they are a far better world-class benchmark, one easier to get because they are not a competitor. So benchmark data is wherever you can get it. The important thing, I think, is to have a systematic look at your own processes and then decide where to get the best process information. It may not be just from your competitors.

GB: What are the keys to remaining as competitive as the above quotation implies you are?

JY: I think being competitive in today's marketplace is a challenging job. One of the things I have come to believe over the last decade or so, and I don't think this was true before that, is that you have to literally budget, set aside, some real part of your time, energy, and intelligence to simply improve your ability to compete. I think that in the old days you just turned the handle faster, and if you could turn your handle a little faster than the next guy, maybe you would win. But now you have to rethink what processes need re-engineering and put energy into doing it. For example, right now we've got a lot of pressure on improving our costs. But at the same time, we launched an over-10-million-dollar new program on how to write defect-free software, which will play a big role in the future. It's something we didn't have to do, but we have more than half our engineers writing software as their principal job. Writing better software, thinking about object technology, the right kind of frameworks; this is the kind of payoff you have to have.

Talking about accounts payable a minute ago, we're changing all that from a decentralized process to having a processing center for accounts payable in Colorado Springs. We can go from 1,200 to 300 people and pay all of our bills with one-fourth the number. You have to really get out in front of those kinds of things from an operations point of view. For example, our surface mount activities are very different. We only have 2,000 parts versus the tens of thousands of parts we used to have. We got on top of it early and decided change was coming up, and to be more competitive we were going to have to drive those things to get the unit cost down.

I think the other thing we have to do is be even more aggressive in looking at management understanding of user needs from a fresh perspective. And I think sometimes companies, including HP, get into very bad habits. The PC business is a perfect example of just following along in the wake of the leaders and offering the same kind of barely differentiated products, instead of backing up and asking what people are doing with these things on their desks. And are we sure that we don't have some new technology and more powerful circuits that allow them to solve problems some other way, a way that's going to be friendlier, easier to use, with all of the things that people desire. Lo and behold, when you can get people to do that, you find some fresh ideas that work even in a seemingly mature and hard-to-differentiate market. As long as the technology is changing, and electronics technology is actually increasing its rate of change, you have to use all the tools at your disposal to make things happen and take advantage of change. Breaking out of the mold of "same old way" thinking is the hardest thing to do.

GB: That leads perfectly into the issue of strategy. Some organizational leaders still believe they will have a good strategy if they analyze markets and meet existing needs with existing capabilities. Whereas I think an improved strategy paradigm is to forecast new markets, create new technology, and improve organizational capabilities, to create new needs and not just to meet existing ones. An example is HP's laser-jet printer. HP sorted out customers' potential needs and decided that you were going to create the capabilities to meet them.

JY: Right, exactly. Also consider the new Palm-tel, 95LX. It's 11 ounces, only as big as a calculator, and two and a half times as powerful as a PC XT. And it has spreadsheets in it, like Lotus 1-2-3. It costs less than some software, and it runs for months on two double-A batteries. It goes with you. But it's not a general purpose machine. You don't type letters on it. And that's good, because for the class of users targeted, we've made something that's simpler, friendlier, cheaper, and it does everything you want it to do. It fits that class of user like a tight suit. That's

where differentiation comes in. Instead of being the 73rd maker of a notebook computer, we backed up to find another way to cut the marketplace, or create a marketplace, around something we can do a little better than others.

GB: Can you elaborate some more on your perception of strategy, maybe your philosophy, the HP strategy process, or what HP strategy should be like in the future?

JY: We certainly do a lot to encourage that kind of thinking. We have strategy review once a year—we call it the business strategy summary, BSS—that we spend a lot of time on. It's a formal opportunity once a year to take a look at where the business is going. This review is very short on data and very long on "here's what I think and feel about our opportunities and where we're going to go." And it provides a good time to have some vigorous debates about that and stir things up. We do that, with every major organization, once a year, but, of course, more time gets spent on strategy generation. We've done more thinking around the ideas of the value chain. Mike Porter from Harvard Business School introduced the idea of value chains a while back. And we've found those interesting, particularly on something like the computer business. In fact, its a very interesting way to see and anticipate changes in the market and get yourself positioned. Which is, in a sense, what we try to do.

Now, think about the computer value chain. If you went back twenty to twenty-five years ago, it was a single chain by one company, IBM. Every part of it, starting with raw parts through CPUs through the operation system and networking applications, all was built around proprietary systems and products. An odd clone maker would try to get around the edges, but basically IBM owned the whole chain. Now the rise of standards allows you to break up that chain. And point competitors now can get in and set a very different competitive standard than might have been the case for an oligopolistic chain owner. So, that's an interesting idea, because if you take a look at information technology business largely, it's maybe a 750-billion-dollar business around the world. It's the biggest business there is. And it's locked to the GNP growth rates, plus 1 or 2 percent. In fact, if you look at the U.S. aggregate deployment of information technologies, broadly defined as a percent of producers' durable goods, they went from less than 15 percent twenty years ago up to about 35 percent in the mid-1980s. But it's actually come down by a percentage point or two, so that rising tide that was lifting all those boats has crested, and now you've got to struggle to find what's growing.

If you think about this value chain the averages are not so exciting. But there are plenty of niche markets in there, and these are big niches in many cases. You need partners to get into a chain segment, because you can't do all of these things alone. It requires you to buddy up with people to have access to budding technologies and that sort of thing. The value chain offers another way of thinking about strategy, and it's something HP uses quite a bit to check ourselves out. It's another way of thinking about spotting ideas, being out in front, giving you another kind of hook to think about real user needs. In fact, we have spent most of the last decade getting ourselves to compete in the most interesting parts of that value chain. It's the open systems rulebook, the revolution on the desktop, and we're going to drive everything to color.[4] If you went down that chain, and identified the most exciting things to do, that's what we are doing.

GB: In the future, I think competitive strategy will be driven more by direct linkages to user needs and not so much by a results orientation or financial orientation. But HP still advocates a management by objectives (MBO) process. How do you rationalize the traditional MBO emphasis upon results orientation versus an emphasis on continuous improvement as the means of meeting customer needs, that is, improving processes and

systems rather than simply deploying goals and objectives down through the organization?

JY: Well, I guess it depends on what you think the objectives are. I mean, our objectives are at an extremely high level. We have seven corporate objectives, and that is what we mean when we talk about management by objectives. What those objectives do is enfranchise the operating activities to have almost total freedom to pursue the results. So, if you're talking about a management by objective system which says "we're going to make 16 percent ROI and I don't care about anything else," it isn't that kind of system at all. It's a front-end system that talks in broad terms about our respect for people and our style of people management, about our obligations to the community, to make contributions in the business we're in, and to be profitable. But it doesn't say that 16 percent is the right number or 15 percent or that some family of numbers is right.

GB: It's certainly not a traditional MBO system of cascading goals and objectives?

JY: It's not traditional at all. It was done more than thirty years ago when we first had these corporate objectives written down. The idea is to have something to carry in your head that reminds you of the ideas the founders had. It ensures we run our business with the kind of style I want, but it has nothing to do with what business I'm going to be in or what range of results might be appropriate.

GB: How does continuous improvement fit into your strategy? Is it a strategic weapon, or is it simply something the staff people take care of?

JY: No, it's absolutely something that I have tried to institutionalize in every part of our business. Soon after I got to be the CEO in 1978, I started thinking about the strategic challenges for the decade of the 80s. I ended up writing down about ten of those things I thought we needed to worry about. I spent some time thinking about the fact that our products were changing from boutique kinds of instruments to volume manufactured computers and such things. I expected a lot of changes associated with that. Changing

---

4. By open systems, Young implies the movement away from proprietary products toward computer systems more like telephone companies, where you can easily pick up the phone in California and talk to someone in Tennessee, so all computers will be able to talk to each other, regardless of manufacturer.

expectations. Cost was going to be much more of a factor. With some of these instruments, you can make up the cost difference with extra features, but on other ones you can't. So I got to thinking about this. I thought that, for a variety of reasons, customer expectations about quality were changing, what good quality was, and about some of the practices that were changing. We were a very high quality company but I think we got there to a large degree from great workmanship and inspecting things in. And it was clear that other techniques were going to be important.

Secondly, I was persuaded that the best way to work on our costs was to start working on quality. That was not common wisdom in 1979, and we took a while to get things going. So we started thinking about those challenges, and that was one of my strategic issues. I set a goal for our company of cutting the failure rate of our products by a factor of 10 over the decade of the 80s. Now, that was a fortunate goal. I mean, if I had said 2 to 1, we wouldn't have done anything until 1988, because we would have just figured, hell, I can finesse that. But 10 to 1, we didn't know how to do. That made it hard. The other thing that was fortunate is that all of the operating activities we had at that time had warranty failure data. So we had a perfect metric that everybody had, and I could get everybody's attention. Measuring things is fundamental to get any results.

GB: Is that what really got you going?

JY: Well, we staggered around for the first year or two. We had a lot of teams that went to suppliers and to Japanese practitioners. Our Japanese joint venture company won the Deming prize in 1982, and we learned a lot more from that. And we began to make some real progress. At every general manager's meeting, we had success stories and I was selling this like you would sell soap, to be sure everybody knew this was the behavior we wanted, and we were going to make it very visible, and so forth. So once we got started, we got some real results, and one of the best stories we had on this thing was when the division just up the hill from where we're sitting got rid of their wave-solder machine (you run a PC board across a solder wave and it solders all these parts on). They got rid of this old stuff, sent it off to the Japanese joint venture company (Yokogawa-HP). We were looking at things like soldering defects, and in Japan (YHP) they were running, 5,000 parts per million. In fact, we in the U.S. had never even thought about dimensioning it in parts per million. It took the Japanese taking this cast-off wave-solder machine and systematically over about 18 months getting defects down to a hundred parts per million. The same equipment. By God, you can't explain that. There's something I've got to now understand differently than I understood before. These kinds of wins finally persuaded the organization that there is something there besides the same old way. But we're still doing that today. Everybody doesn't sign up and you're over it; we're still fighting the same-old-way mentality ten years later. But we've got to keep fighting. And now we've just gotten more and more sophisticated.

GB: How pervasive are the applications or improvements throughout the organization?

JY: We started in manufacturing and then we tried to move into administrative processes, how you schedule airplanes, how you collect the bills, or how you sell. We've had TQC programs on all of those. And now we're working on more complicated things that build on this learning, for example, trying to get our time to market down. Of course, that involves complex multifunctional processes, and everything in our company is organized by function. We've got sales, R&D, and manufacturing, but the innovation process crosses all three of those. Yet it's not a physical process, and nobody owns it. And we don't have an information system that describes it. So if you start working on some of these, boy, you start pretty far up the pipeline. You've got to say, "Gee, who could own this, and how are we going to get some descriptors of it. Because if I can't describe it and measure it, nothing's gonna happen." An awful lot of that kind of work has been going on to improve time to market, but, again, you go through the same kind of wins just like the PC soldering. I was just thinking about it because I was talking to a team of people working on improving the time to market.

GB: Is time to market a key measure for you?

JY: Yes. We have defined a metric called BET, break-even time. One day, you start with a product in engineering and you spend money on it. And then you get it into manufacturing, you spend more money on it. Then it comes out of manufacturing, and you start making some money back when you sell it. Well, the break-even time is the amount of time that it takes to get back money enough to break even with what was spent. Obviously, if I have a more efficient engineering process, I can get that done faster. If I design for manufacturability, I can build it more cheaply, rapidly, and cleanly. My objective is not just to have the fastest turkey ever spawned, but to have a winning product, which turns the cash flow up. We also have to market the right product, with all those support services and the training. So everything is hooked together. We want to cut BET in half. I was talking to one of our product development teams the other day and made a commitment to do this, and I was just laughing to myself when I got home. They showed all the elements of the same old way. At first, they said, "Gee, it's gonna cost more to put more energy on this BET program." But when they redefined things, it took a year out of the time to do it, and the total project cost went down. What a surprise.

GB: You have alluded to two ways to make improvements: incremental improvements and innovation for breakthroughs. How do you weigh those (breakthrough versus incremental improvement) in terms of their importance to implementing the strategy for serving customers better?

JY: Well, I think incremental improvement is something you've just got to do every day. That's part of improving your ability to compete, and sometimes there are bigger opportunities than others, but nevertheless, it's on your mind all day, every day. It's kind of a background mode, if nothing else. The breakthroughs you can do by *hoshin* planning or by inspiration when you're looking

at a value chain or brainstorming for ideas. You just have to jump on those things and do it. So they're not one or the other. These are kind of seamless things, for any manager has got all these balls in the air all of the time. You've just got to work all of them.

GB: Managing cross-functional systems to better serve customers implies two things to me. It implies that those managers who try to do so must have a broad perspective, that is, they can't simply be functionally oriented. And secondly, it implies continuous change in the organization, through incremental improvement and breakthroughs. Now, there are two factors that hinder this approach. I suggest that management development and promotion through specialization and narrowness which is reinforced by functional rewards is a hindrance. The second hindrance arises from the fact that in order to champion change, one must purposefully rock the boat. That is, you must challenge the status quo, you must be countercultural, you must be a persistent pest. And these kinds of behaviors typically are not rewarded. How do you counter or overcome these hindrances?

JY: You're right. You've got to attack this at a high enough level to accomplish it. If you're too far down, the cross-functional things just cannot work because you don't enfranchise it. One thing that I think is a real barrier, besides the ones you cited, is that nobody owns these processes.

GB: Exactly.

JY: Owners just don't exist. And there are no information systems to describe the processes. Most of those kinds of cross-functional processes are simply informational, not physical. And so an awful lot of work needs to go into this kind of base building before you can even go off and attack the processes. It's got to have high-level ownership by someone who overviews the right set of functions. And HP's got a lot of energy going into this. We've got corporate engineering working on information systems. That's a problem I have to own because of the resource deployment. And the culture change that has to go on with it has got to be driven at the highest possible level. Then you're going to get more and more owners.

GB: So you've taken ownership of what process?

JY: Cutting our time to market.

GB: And the people who report directly to you, your executives, do they have specific ownership of processes, cross-functional systems, that they're managing?

JY: Sure. The time-to-market problem is owned by everybody who does new product development, and everybody does new product development so, yes, it's a very broadly owned process. But it isn't something we can just pass down the line, because of the resource commitments and structural changes that have to be put in place in order to make this thing happen. Even if you wanted to, you couldn't make it happen if you don't have an information system that tells you what's going on. So a lot of those barriers are very real and have to be addressed at the right level.

GB: How are you overcoming the specialization problem? Specialization is necessary in order to get mastery of a particular area, function, or task, whatever. So it's an important part of organization, but taken to an extreme, I see it as an organizational impediment to cross-specialization or cross-functional types of work. How do you overcome that in terms of developing your managers?

JY: Process development, process management or process-oriented management, has a lot of built-in helps to solve that problem. Most people in management don't know how any of these processes work, because we're in our offices and have no idea what's going on unless we get involved. Even with the simplest TQC process, perhaps the most valuable thing that comes out of it is the fact that all the team members suddenly understand the whole process: here's what I do, here's what else goes on, here's what the dependencies are, and so forth. The same idea can happen at much higher levels of abstraction, and you've got to have a good team effort that's working on this total process. The marketing people have to work with the engineers to help them see these user needs and characterize the marketplace, the price sensitivity. And that's got to be interactive with the design teams and the manufacturing backup. No surprises here. This is a total team effort, and the more you communicate and learn about the other functions and their needs, the more you can understand how to optimize

the process outcome, not just your piece of the process.

GB: In addition to the communication and informal work on the process improvement to build cross-functional understanding, do you do any formal job rotation among functions?

JY: A lot. Particularly between engineering and manufacturing and some between engineering and marketing, because all these people for the most part are some kind of engineer. It's very typical for engineers to follow products out into the plant for a while.

GB: Typically, in organizations you learn that you can rise more quickly through the function if you stay specialized, that is, if you don't take those rotations. In some organizations, people perceive that taking a cross-functional rotation slows down their career progress. How do you overcome that perception at HP? Are people rewarded and promoted for getting the cross-functional experience?

JY: I think oftentimes what you say is true, but it may not quite be for the reasons you cite. My experience has been that often the people you send off to manufacturing are the poorest engineers whom you can spare from the R&D functions. They go out there and they don't come back, because the general manager doesn't think it's too important. So, it may look like there's no return path, but it's only because you didn't send the guys out there who could get back. In the old days, 1980s, we had the engineers in manufacturing on a lower scale than the R&D engineers. Well, you've already told them what you think about their relative values, so the best guys are not going to go from R&D to manufacturing. You've got to be brain-dead to miss that signal. So if you get these things on the right schedule and you are sure your best guys are persuaded to get out there, then there's no problem in getting them back. Managers are recruiting them to come back every day of the week.

GB: How do you encourage people to rock the corporate boat, to challenge the status quo?

JY: It's just sort of a style we grew up with here. We don't have any sacred cows, and I think the culture values and admires people who can step out and exhibit a lot of entrepreneurship. HP has a very high tolerance for that kind of thing. We have a lot of operating activities, fifty to sixty divisions that are more like small businesses. We tried to set up in a way to have maximum amounts of freedom to pursue our objectives, and that breeds entrepreneurial spirit, ownership, fast reactions that big company organizations just can't match. And it keeps that vitality, more like a start-up. Hopefully, it brings vitality together with the strengths of a big company, heavy-duty marketing, and some research backup that a small company doesn't have. It's not perfect. Nothing is perfect. But it's a set of trade-offs and we try to lean toward keeping that enthusiasm, that personal ownership, the vitality, finding those competitors out there and chasing them as hard as we can because it's life or death.

If you go to some other companies—you can probably imagine who they are—that are organized like "Big Companies," with huge functional organizations, it's almost impossible to keep that vitality. We've had to experiment from time to time as we get more into the systems business where these individual activities become much more interdependent. We can't very well go make CPUs and peripherals and write operating systems without talking with each other, and not only talking with each other, but having integrated strategy. So we tried several variations on keeping that ownership and enthusiasm and still having a systems discipline so that we get an optimum system at the end, not optimum pieces.

So it's again the process problem that we were talking about before. And we've done a number of things to try to fix that. The balance is always toward having that vitality, and every time we get toward big functions, things slow down. The committees grow up to talk about things, not a damn thing gets done, and the frustration level goes up enormously.

GB: So your strategy is to serve the customers through systems that cut across functions, and you deploy the strategy perhaps through an MBO process or hoshin. Tell me how you institutionalize strategy or

deploy strategy, and maybe mention some of the cross-functional measures, like the break-even time, which are used to guide systemic kinds of behaviors for system optimization rather than functional optimization of the pieces.

JY: Well, I don't know, that's a hard question to answer, because we don't quite go at it the way it sounds like you're asking.

GB: OK, tell me how you go at it.

JY: We're just trying to win in the marketplace. And we're trying to define strategy as we look for market opportunities that we can capitalize on and win. Then we think, "Well, what does it take, what are the ingredients it takes to win?" And with open systems, while the margins are going down and the value chain is sort of going away, we've got more competition, and so we've got to get our costs in line. And so we start driving all of these things as we see this is what it takes to compete. Then we start looking in our toolbox. How can we think about time-to-market? We know that's going to be a big competitive differential. Last year, a typical year, half of our orders came from products less than two years old, so we have a lot of product turnover. You don't have to be a genius to figure this one out. It used to be more like three years. We've gotten even better, so how do we drive that kind of thing? How do we encourage that kind of performance? Through metrics, talking to the teams, promulgating best practice through corporate people going around with training sessions. We use everything in our toolbox to try to get these jobs done. Maybe it's improving manufacturing by shifting surface mount. It may be a whole different set of things. I don't know that you would say that this is a strategy. It's more of what we think it takes to win. We start looking for ideas and benchmarks, how to drive things in a broad enough way, hard enough, to keep winning in the marketplace.

GB: Continuing to win often requires that you destroy old perceptions of what is right, old paradigms, if you will. The concept of paradigm shift has captured the imagination of managers. Do you think it's an important concept, and how do you personally manage the process of paradigm shifting?

JY: Well, I don't even know what paradigm shifting is. That's a word that's kind of gotten in vogue recently, but I don't really know what it is. I suppose paradigm shifting can easily be thought of as another way of thinking about getting rid of the same old way.

GB: If you considered a paradigm to be the same old way, or the status quo, it includes things like the current beliefs about the way things are, what factors are important, how those factors interrelate, and how you go about managing them, what methods or tools you use to succeed in business. A paradigm shift would be a realization that these factors aren't important, these relationships really aren't true, and maybe these methods aren't appropriate, so we need to dramatically change the way we view our world, the way we act in it. It seems that with continuous improvement and trying to compete in that dynamic marketplace, where half the products you produce came on line two years ago, you would have to continuously be shifting.

JY: Absolutely.

GB: Continuously challenging the status quo.

JY: It's sort of a way of life. That's why I don't think of it as so much a paradigm shift as continuing to challenge the same old way and to drive things ahead. It's not like you have a step function to do something else. It's much easier to set a cultural norm, if you can, in which change is expected. So I tell everybody, although a lot of times people complain, "Gee, if you don't like it, maybe you should be working for a beer company, because you know when the customer is born, they're going to start drinking, you know how many gallons per person, and the big deal is to go to light beer from regular. Your life is pretty much laid out for you, and if that's what suits you, that's what you ought to do."

But that's not our business. We make change happen. Our job is to turn dollars, a billion and three of engineering, into exciting new products. That's a transformation mechanism we call our company. And the rate of change of technology and so forth means that's a dynamic process. Now, if that doesn't suit you, you ought to do something else, but for most people who come here, that's why they came. It's fun. It's exciting. You've just

got to keep that going. And when it slows down, you get satisfied with the status quo. You start trying harder to find that next step, and that's when you get in trouble. So that's why I don't think about paradigm shifts from that point of view.

GB: You've already answered my follow-up question about whether shifting is an occasional event or a continuous way of life. It seems that it has to be continuous.

JY: It better be a continuous way of life, because if you get stuck at a point where you've got to have a gut-wrenching shift, you're probably so far behind the industry leaders, you're a dead duck anyway.

GB: So you can't wait for crisis to occur?

JY: Well, the U.S. automotive industry is probably a very good example of the difficulty you have when you have a culture that's same-old-way oriented, and whose same old ways are static. Democratic institutions have a way of needing a crisis to perturb them. You've got to lose enough market share, or have a sputnik go off, or something else to change your view. But if you're lucky enough to have set up your company and kept it going with change as the norm, you're so much better off. I don't kid anybody that it's an easy thing to do. You've got to work at that all the time.

GB: Regarding the requirement for continuous change to be a way of life, do you see any conflict between the need for continuous change versus the need for consistency and stability in delivery of value to customers, that is, the need to do things repeatedly the same way over time, from day to day, shift to shift, batch to batch?

JY: Continuous change versus the continuity it takes for customer satisfaction. Well, I don't see those as being all that inconsistent, because if you have processes under control, that's a base from which you can look at new things and build on that stable base. I don't think we do anything these days the same way time after time for very long. That isn't the hand we're dealt in our business. If we learn how to do surface mount and do it well, then we've got to have a flexible factory that builds on that—the extensions build on the fact that we can solder at a hundred parts per million defect rate or less. That's a basic know-how that I can now build on bigger boards, more layers, flexible factories. Our customer support, as noted in your opening remarks, is the best in the world. We know this from surveys with IBM, DEC, anybody. So getting customer satisfaction to release that dimension of full support is something we know how to do, and yet we continue to change dramatically how we do it. For example, with built-in diagnostics and telephone repairs, instead of having people go out, we troubleshoot on the phone. We can do all kinds of things we wouldn't even have thought of five years ago. We're radically transforming how it's done. Why does that rate of change not hurt our customer satisfaction? Because we have people who know how to change. The fundamental process that we started with is under control. And we can extend and add to something that we have under control in quite a variety of ways as long as we're sure we're not overdriving people's ability to assimilate and we don't lose the handle. That's what it seems like to me.

GB: Do you think customer satisfaction measures are adequate to really assess your performance in delivering value to customers?

JY: We have what we call a closed loop marketing. Lots of surveys all the time. We ask customers what they think about a variety of things. We capture every complaint, every phone call. In Boise alone, we take 60,000 calls a month on laser-jet and ink-jet printers. We strip that database every night. When something pops up that might be wrong, we'll know it in one or two days. We know which product to capture that might have something wrong with it. If there's something we can do, proactive things, we do it. Customers have been amazed. We send them a package with their name on it, "Here is your replacement printer, please put your old one in our box, seal it up, here's the label, prepaid, send it back to us." I get letters from people saying they can't believe it. So, I think we have very good metrics for our customer satisfaction. We keep working on getting even better on this front. Getting as close to the end user as you can is really important.

GB: In my studying of customer value, one thing I've learned is that as customer standards change over time, the satisfaction reports, the meanings of the numbers, change over time.

JY: Absolutely. And you can see that. Even though HP is number one in all of them, the absolute numbers of the whole group are slumping. So, even though we're continuing to improve, customer expectations are improving faster than we're improving. That's a problem we are always chasing.

▶ REMARKS BY JOHN YOUNG TO SAMSUNG MANAGERS, APRIL 8, 1991

I want you all to know how honored I am by your presence here this evening and by your interest in what I have to say.

As you may know, the relationship between Hewlett-Packard and Samsung began many years ago, in the late 1970s. Since the beginning, we have sought ways to help each other strengthen our relative positions in many different business areas. Our joint venture, Samsung Hewlett-Packard, continues to impress me very much by how it has expanded and prospered. It embodies many of the HP concepts I will be describing.

I know that the people at Samsung Hewlett-Packard have assisted many of your organizations in understanding these ideas and practices, and in helping you to adapt them to your own needs. More recently, we have begun to work together in developing a world-class workstation and the microprocessor and semiconductor processes associated with it. Our partnership is progressing well, from my perspective.

Last year, when I visited with Chairman Lee, he asked that I describe to you my thoughts on what is required to be a successful global company in the 1990s and into the next century. Today, I will describe some of the things HP is doing to prepare itself for the future. But I want you to know that I do so with some degree of doubt as to my ability to predict just what exact shape the future will take.

I believe that, in an industry like electronics, the pace of change is so fast that it becomes very difficult to see too far ahead. That's why, in my opinion, the best way to prepare for the future is to get in position, to prepare for what's ahead by building some basic strengths and by creating an organization and company culture that is very flexible and open to new ideas.

My talk today will cover five basic topics related to how we at HP are preparing ourselves:

- First, technical innovation. Because the successful companies of the next century will still be those that can apply advanced technology to meet customer needs.
- Second, quality. Because it will determine our ability to deliver products and services that earn long-term customer loyalty.
- Third, information. Because by using it more effectively, we can increase the value-added of our work and, by doing so, the wages we earn.
- Fourth, human resources. Because both innovation and productivity will depend so very much on what people think and do.
- Fifth and finally, access to global markets. Because the real strength in a brand or company name over time rests on the establishment of the business relationships, distribution channels, and reputation for good citizenship that are expected in host countries.

Technical Innovation

Let me begin with technical innovation, because that's the engine that will drive future growth. Because innovation creates *new* markets that never existed before. In other words, you make your own opportunities instead of relying on someone else to define the market, and the terms of competition, for you.

To encourage innovation at HP, we've tried to create a climate that fosters creativity. We begin by recruiting a diversity of technical talent, people from all around the world, with expertise in varying disciplines, and with degrees from several different universities. We provide them with a very rich set of tools, including a great deal of computing power. We encourage people from different disciplines and different projects to share their ideas freely.

We ask our engineers to communicate regularly with key customers. We also want them to talk to suppliers, so that our designs incorporate parts whose performance and reliability are well known to us.

The work environment makes communication very easy. Our offices are very open, and people can trade ideas over the partition. Our electronic mail system has a special bulletin board for R&D engineers, as well as links to key customers and suppliers. We make sure we're constantly exposed to new ideas from outside HP. We have a research board that includes leading scientists from around the world, who keep us abreast of promising technological developments. We also have very strong ties with the academic community. We invest heavily in research and development. In fiscal year 1990, we spent more than $1.3 billion, or about 10 percent of sales, on R&D.

Finally, we give our engineers a chance to really innovate. We define the goals of a product and the standard interfaces with which it must comply, and then we let people be creative.

Since we're working with you on HP's Precision Architecture-RISC technology as the basis for the workstations we are jointly developing, let me use its origins as a case in point. Our RISC program began with a straightforward directive from management: we wanted to work toward a single computer architecture to unify our product offerings over time.

We asked that the design meet specific requirements:

- It had to provide more computing power for a given price than machines from our competitors.
- It had to allow our customers to use the same software on a broad range of machines, so they could choose the exact price and performance they required.

- It had to be very reliable and give our customers a low cost of ownership.
- And it had to allow customers who already had HP computers to continue using their existing application software on the newly designed computers.

But we didn't tell our engineers *how* to achieve these goals. Our engineers started with very open minds. They decided to use HP's measurement expertise to learn how a computer really performs, not just how the theory says it should perform.

They measured literally billions and billions of computer instructions, both in our labs and at our customers' locations, in the widest variety of applications. After a lot of analysis, they chose to pursue an architecture based on what was then a relatively new idea called reduced-instruction-set computing, RISC.

HP was the first major computer vendor to develop commercial products with RISC technology. And at the time, our decision was described as either very brave or very foolish, depending on who you asked. Many people believed that HP was making a very big gamble. But we persevered and backed our engineers with the resources and support they needed to carry off this major development.

Today, RISC technology has been embraced as the new frontier that *all* computer vendors must explore. That's because RISC is making fundamental changes in the rate of improvement in computer-processing power.

The computer industry used to see a 30 percent annual decrease in the dollar cost per MIP, the speed of computing as expressed in millions of instructions per second. With RISC, the slope of that improvement curve has accelerated to a 50 to 70 percent annual decrease in the cost per MIP. And that's going to change the whole course of computing, with mainframe computer capabilities now available on people's desks.

In fact, we just introduced our new Series 700 workstation based on RISC, and it outperforms IBM's 3090 mainframe computer on some applications, especially numerically intensive ones. This kind of power on the desktop is changing both the way information is managed and the way people work in an organization.

I tell this story because I think it illustrates some of the key ingredients that make for innovation, at least at HP:

- The importance of understanding real customer needs
- The benefits of giving highly skilled and creative people the freedom to try new ways of meeting those needs
- Management's willingness to invest and take risks

HP may have a tradition of making significant advances in technology, but we've come to realize that innovation by itself won't be enough to win in the twenty-first century. The innovation process has two added dimensions: first, the rise of standards, and second, the need to shorten time to market. Let me discuss those two critical success factors, in that order.

For customers, standards provide investment protection by allowing them to add new capabilities without throwing out the equipment they already have. Standards also enable customers to move applications and data between different machines—a real boost to their organization's flexibility and responsiveness.

For software developers, standardized interfaces make it possible to write platform-independent code that can address wide markets. And that makes more applications available, which, in turn, spurs sales of more computers.

Standards have changed forever the *structure* of our industry, the rules of *competition*, and the rules of *cooperation*. Standardized interfaces have led to the proliferation of suppliers. Such standards enable highly focused niche competitors to offer just a single part of the entire customer solution, but a part that, thanks to standard interfaces, can fit into the overall systems solution. And because those niche competitors are so focused, they can refine and improve the single part they provide until it's a world-class product.

As a result, broad-based suppliers such as HP have to think carefully about where to invest their resources, the part of the entire customer solution where they can provide the best product or service, and what parts they should obtain by teaming up with other suppliers. Given this standards environment, we at HP intend to differentiate ourselves in two basic ways:

- First, we'll provide the best product offering, with leading-edge technology like RISC to differentiate our standards-based computer systems. On top of that, we'll provide innovative systems offerings that offer real customer benefits by making the systems easy to manage and use. In short, we want to help customers tap the full potential of information technology.
- But second, and no less important, we intend to stand out and above the pack because of the quality of our relationships and business dealings. In a standards world, integrity has become a very important factor in selecting a partner.

We think our engineers will also be challenged by a second consideration that will carry even more weight in the future than it does today, namely, the importance of bringing products to market very quickly.

Technology moves rapidly around the world, and the pace of change is accelerating. In addition, the new highly focused niche competitors I described earlier can move very quickly, putting real pressure on a larger, more broadly based organization. That's why, at HP, we've been working hard to shorten product development cycles.

In the best of TQC, we've chosen a breakthrough goal of *cutting in half* something we call break-even time, or BET. BET measures the amount of time it takes for the positive cash flow of a product after it begins shipment to equal the negative cash flow incurred during its development and transfer to manufacturing.

We chose BET because it measures the health of the *entire* innovation process: how well we've understood customer needs, the speed of our R&D cycle, and the ease with which we've been able to ramp up to volume manufacturing.

We're pursuing our BET goal with a number of initiatives:

- We've equipped our engineers with powerful workstations, which are linked to each other by high-speed networks.
- We've put R&D productivity managers in

each location. Their job is to facilitate change by identifying the best methods and tools available.
- But most important, we've changed how we manage the design process. Let me use a story of an HP division as an example of what's changed.

This particular division makes spectrum analyzers—electronic measuring devices—a product line for which HP has been the technology and market-share leader for decades. That's the kind of situation where it's easy to get complacent and to approach product development in a rather leisurely manner.

Like many divisions, this one used to approach the process as a series of steps done in a linear sequence. The idea probably started in the R&D lab . . . then moved to marketing . . . then to the model shop for prototyping . . . then back to R&D for development . . . then to test . . . then back to design . . . then to the manufacturing team . . . who maybe just at that point in time started talking to suppliers about parts requirements.

Well, this division got humbled back in 1985, when they saw new competitors on the horizon. So they decided to do things differently. They created a team of people who represented all the necessary functions, marketing, R&D, procurement, manufacturing, test. These people worked together in parallel, with manufacturing people in the R&D lab, for example. They even got their suppliers involved early on in the design process to make sure they could build the parts required with the quality, volume, and cost the division required.

The result was a product that took half as long to develop as its predecessor—cost about half as much, too—and which captured a 75 percent market share in Japan.

This kind of transformation is happening everywhere at HP. So we're not just innovating technologies; we're also developing new ways to manage the R&D process.

Quality

Increasingly, we're finding that the most critical processes—the ones that offer the greatest payback, like innovation—are those that cross organizational boundaries. To help us improve those processes, we've embraced total quality control, or TQC, as an important element of our overall management philosophy. We did it as a way of teaching ourselves how to compete more effectively.

In the late 1970s, we looked ahead to see what it would take to compete in the future. As part of that exercise, we did an internal study of our manufacturing costs. It showed us that fully 25 percent of our costs were related to quality problems, to finding and fixing problems that occurred during the design, manufacturing, and procurement processes.

I helped move people into action by setting what I called a breakthrough goal: to reduce our field-failure rates to one-tenth their current levels during the decade of the '80s.

Why did I choose a tenfold improvement as a goal? Because I wanted to force people to view their jobs in a different way.

TQC at HP has just a few simple aspects:

- We view every single activity we do as a process that can be documented and measured.
- We define and measure the quality of that process from the customer's point of view, including internal customers.
- We believe that every process can be improved, that perfection is the goal.
- And we demand total participation. TQC isn't something added on; it's the way we manage ourselves.

We started TQC in manufacturing, where the processes are the most physical and, therefore, easiest to measure. Let me share some of the results of these initiatives.

Companywide, our field-failure rates have decreased drastically. We fell just short of achieving our goal of a tenfold improvement in ten years, but we have specific plans to achieve that goal in one more year. But whether we achieved the exact goal or not—and we always knew it was a stretch—it's an effort that has no losers. Here are some paybacks we've seen already.

- Manufacturing productivity has risen dramatically, a 15 percent annual growth rate for the past five years.
- We've reduced warranty costs by $800 million over the course of the decade.
- And our inventory levels are down from representing 20.5 percent of revenue in 1979 to about just under 16 percent last year.

If we'd still been carrying inventory at the same level as we had in 1979, HP would have had $620 million more tied up in inventory than we had last year. Instead, we used that extra cash flow to improve our earnings.

Now we're applying TQC principles outside manufacturing. And we're seeing encouraging results. More accurate invoices. Increased productivity in order processing. Faster turn-around time in customer service. More sales time in front of customers. And shorter product-development cycles.

HP's chief operating officer is personally leading these efforts, because we know that passive management support just doesn't get the results required. TQC has to be the way we manage, not some extra program we do in our spare time.

Let me close this part of my discussion by saying that I have been pleased to see the progress SHP has made in implementing TQC throughout their organization. This is a fundamental institutional skill that will serve SHP well in the years ahead.

Information Systems

That point about measuring quality brings me to a third subject that all managers will have to deal with in the next century, and that's the power of data or information.

I've devoted a great deal of thought over the past few years to this whole subject of competitiveness, first as chairman of President Reagan's Commission on Industrial Competitiveness, and then as head of the Council on Competitiveness, which is a group sponsored by the private sector. My studies and conversations with business leaders around the world convince me that using information more effectively is perhaps the single most important source of competitive advantage that we can and should develop.

If we don't want to compete on the basis of low wages, then we have to compete on the basis of value-added. And that's where information technology fits in. It can help us be more productive than our competitors. Or it can help us be more creative, to use information to develop new products and services that command a premium price in world markets.

We run our business on some 2,900 minicomputers linked by a worldwide corporate network that transmits more than 15 billion characters of information each day. And we have more than 90,000 desktop devices, personal computers, workstations, and terminals. That's essentially one for each of our 91,000 employees. So the HP people responsible for competing in the marketplace have access to the information they need to do their jobs to the very best of their ability.

Our approach rests on the belief that you can't separate the management of information from management in general. In fact, I don't think we could have accomplished *any* of our business goals *without* the use of our information systems. The quality and productivity improvements I described earlier have been made possible by the use of information, because TQC is a methodology that relies on measurement and data.

Our information systems have also made it possible for us to establish closer ties with our suppliers. One of our global systems collects and aggregates parts requirements from divisions around the world and uses the total to negotiate and schedule volume purchases with our suppliers. Those suppliers with corporate contracts can, in turn, get access to our materials forecasts through an EDI (electronic data interchange) "mailbox" and use them to plan their own production runs.

This generates savings for vendors, which they pass on to us. In addition, we are often able to get on-time deliveries of key parts with much shorter lead times than other companies, which is the key to just-in-time (JIT) production. This is an area, by the way, in which Samsung's performance has really excelled.

We also use our information systems to track the quality of the parts we buy and how well the supplier meets the agreed-upon delivery schedules. We use the data to tell them where they need to improve their performance. And they've certainly done just that: since 1982, we've seen a 90 percent decrease in the number of defects contained in incoming parts.

Our engineering network does more than link design engineers to each other and to the remote computers they may require to do a particular task. The network also enables R&D engineers to get access to a database of preferred parts they may choose from, whose price, performance, and quality have been jointly approved by both R&D and manufacturing.

Finally, I think our information systems have played a key role in making HP more flexible and responsive to changes in the business environment. They provide us with up-to-the-minute information on orders and key financial results, making it possible for us to change course quickly, if necessary.

When HP managers come to work in the morning, they can get a graph of yesterday's worldwide orders—or year-to-date results, for that matter—viewed from whatever perspective they want: by product line, by geographical region, by distribution channel, you name it.

Our information systems also make it possible for us to respond quickly to change because they also allow us to bypass boundaries of rank, function, and geography. People don't have to go up the hierarchy to talk to someone else in the company. They just send that person a message over our electronic mail, bypassing layers of management.

Our information systems also make us more flexible. We can put together teams of people in different locations without having to move them all to one place. So part of the project might be done in the U.K., another in California, and a third in Korea, as is the case for some of the electronic instruments that SHP is working on.

In short, information has been the key to improving many of HP's basic business processes. In fact, for activities that aren't physical in nature, product development or customer support, for example, the information about that process is the *only* way to describe it.

Using information effectively is an integral part of managing at HP, and I think our experience shows what a powerful tool it can be.

Human Resources

Let me move on to the fourth critical issue for the future, and that's human resources. I've come to the conclusion that the challenge of competing has a very human dimension. Because being competitive isn't a goal in itself: it's just a means to an end.

At the national level, we compete to win a prize, and that prize is a rising standard of living for our people. So the benefits of being competitive are very personal in nature. They include more and better jobs and a confidence in the future. And businesses are, in essence, just groups of people. Their skills, flexibility, and commitment will determine our ability to compete in the future.

The first challenge we'll face will be to attract enough highly skilled job candidates. The demand for technically skilled people will continue to grow. So we'll need to work hard to make sure that we can hire the best people out of this very limited pool of talent and to support actions to increase the supply. That means our reputation as employers will be a critical factor in our ability to compete for scarce human resources.

HP is widely considered one of the best places to work. Our founders, Bill Hewlett and Dave Packard, built the company on trust and respect for the individual. The HP Way, as we call it, is based on the belief that people want to do a good job, and will do so if they have the tools and support they need. So management's job is to establish goals, gain consensus on them, and then provide people with great freedom of action in attaining those goals.

We encourage employees to be personally responsible. There are no time clocks for any employee. People manage their own personal time off, such as vacation and illness. We have a culture based on trust. There are few management privileges. No special dining room. No chauffeured cars. No fancy offices. In fact, no offices with doors. We encourage managers to be available, to get out of their offices and walk around, to talk to people and get the feel of what's really happening. We call it "management by wandering around."

We also have something called an "open door" policy, though that may be an inappropriate description, since we have no doors. What it means is simply this: any HP employee has the right to go talk to his manager's manager—or further up, even to the president, if necessary—with no fear about the consequences. The practice helps us to resolve problems and make sure that communication doesn't break down.

How will we keep these skilled people motivated? Well, I think a lot of that will depend on the very nature of the work itself:

- The ability to work in self-directed teams
- The knowledge that what you do makes a difference
- And the confidence that good work will be recognized and rewarded

We'll also have to keep beating back the demotivators: excessive bureaucracy, reviews, and controls. For example, last fall, we reorganized the company to simplify reporting relationships and push both decision making and accountability further down into the organization.

Reward systems will also play a role in motivating people. At HP, for example, we've made sure that all employees share in the company's success. We make it a practice to pay among the leaders in our field. And, in addition to these fully competitive salaries, twice a year we set aside 12 percent of our pre-tax earnings for a profit-sharing bonus. Everyone gets a check that represents the same percentage of their salary, whether he's a materials handler or a senior executive.

We also have a stock purchase program so employees can own part of the company. For every dollar an employee sets aside for stock purchase, the company contributes an additional 33 cents as a special incentive for ownership. These programs help keep everyone focused on the same goals: profitability and growth. They encourage both financial and emotional identification with the company.

But, in the future, financial rewards, although important, won't be enough to motivate people. There's an emotional side to work, too. And so we'll need to emphasize other kinds of recognition. Some will be very formal, such as awards to top performers. Others will be less formal, but perhaps more personal. People really value that phone call or note from a senior manager that says, "Thanks for a job well done."

To ensure our ability to attract and motivate talented people, we've made it a company goal to provide stability of employment. That goal has shaped our business strategies. We've chosen a mix of businesses and geographic locations that help balance different business cycles. If it's a boom-and-bust kind of opportunity, or a chance for a quick financial gain, but no future, we don't go for it. We manage our business with a view to its long-term prospects.

This approach has made HP people more willing to change because they know they're working for a company that will make every effort to provide them with a stable source of employment.

While HP employees feel confident they will have a job with the company, they also recognize that it might not be the same one they have today. They have to prepare themselves for new jobs by acquiring some new skills. Engineers will have to keep abreast of technology changes. Because after they've been out of college for five years, half of what they learned will have become obsolete. Production supervisors will need to learn new skills, too. Not just total quality control, but how to manage the total quality process that involves people from other functional areas, or how to move to entirely self-managed teams.

And so, we'll invest a lot in training and retraining HP people. And we'll search for innovative ways to deliver training courses to our employees. We're already using some interesting new approaches to lifelong learning. For example, HP engineers located in states thousands of miles away attend classes that originate from Stanford University in California. These engineers can take classes in their workplace, on company time. The classes are either broadcast live over television, or taped and then redistributed, and a local tutor coaches the students.

You may be interested to know that, on average, employees who have taken these recorded courses do significantly better in the classes than the full-time students.

Success in the next century, then, will continue to depend on some very basic things: the ability to hire the best people, to work with them to make sure they have the skills needed, and to earn their commitment to the company.

And from HP's perspective, at least, we know we'll have to accomplish these goals within a work force that will be much more diverse than it has been in the past. Because HP's operations are worldwide, our employees will represent a variety of nationalities and cultures. We have training programs specifically aimed at helping us manage that diversity, although I must say that there's no education as effective as the kind of experience Dick Warmington has been able to have here in Korea.

Access to Global Markets

That last comment brings me very neatly to the fifth and final subject I said I would discuss today: access to global markets.

In a technology business, access to global markets is vital because you need that broad base of customers in order to get a satisfactory return on your investments in engineering. At HP, we have embraced three basic strategies to help us tap the potential of diverse markets around the world.

First, we're seeking ways to ensure that HP does something more than just sell within a nation's borders. Instead, we must add some value back in terms of technology and economic development. This value-added presence, as we call it, has increasingly become a requirement for access to global markets. It's also a good way to grow your business. Because when you help develop a country's economy and technology base, you're also helping to develop a healthy market for your products.

There are many ways to add value. In the manufacturing area, this ranges from simple assembly at the lowest end of the value-added spectrum, and on up to—at the highest level of value-added—international entities that have worldwide R&D and manufacturing charters, and strong local management teams.

Samsung-Hewlett-Packard fits in this last category. They have developed power supplies and products in our line of electronic instruments which are distributed worldwide.

While global R&D and manufacturing represent

one very important form of value-added, another approach is to develop strong ties with local partners as suppliers. HP's purchase of DRAM memories and monitors from Samsung is an excellent example of this. Such purchases today represent a more than $50 million value-added presence annually.

Marketing is another area in which we'll be able to achieve local value-added, especially in the computer industry. Software and support will represent a growing portion of the final product, and these are the kinds of things that are best provided very close to the customer . . . in other words, locally.

We're moving a variety of marketing activities closer to the local markets in which our customers reside, including software localization, systems integration, and customer support. SHP, for example, has developed Hongul versions of HP's LaserJet and DeskJet printers.

These marketing activities bring me to a second thrust in our approach to global markets, and that is strategic alliances. Having a local partner, someone with a reputation for leadership and quality, is often a key to success. That's why HP is pursuing collaborative efforts with other companies. Besides the strength of our technology and products, we also intend to attract our allies by the quality of our relationships. We believe our business dealings must be characterized by complementary capabilities, mutual benefits, and mutual trust. And let me emphasize that our dealings with the Samsung Group certainly fit that description.

I've said that HP's global value-added presence and strategic relationships are the first two ingredients for access to global markets. Now let me move on to the third, which is the subject of distribution channels.

Just a decade ago, almost all of HP's products were sold by our direct sales force. That worked well, because the bulk of our sales went to other manufacturing companies. We understood their business, and so we could provide the expertise and complete solution to their problem.

Today, as we branch out into other areas, we're selling to companies whose business we don't understand so intuitively. And so we're teaming with other companies, software suppliers and value-added resellers, who know what specific customer needs are and who provide the applications and know-how to meet them.

In addition, customers are increasingly showing a preference for buying products like personal computers and printers from dealers. In response to these changes, we now use a variety of distribution channels to reach our customers: HP's direct sales force, especially for large accounts, third-party partners, and dealers.

This makes for a complicated sales process, and the challenge is to get all these channels of distribution to work together well. We have a channel-management program, with people specifically designated to work with each of these channels, both in our product divisions and in our field sales organization.

We recognize that we won't be successful unless our channel teammates succeed, and so we're investing a lot of time and energy to make sure that they do. For example, last year we put together a whole new program for dealers that enables them to choose from a range of HP support services, depending on their own particular business strategy.

Let me summarize now. I've spoken for quite some time, and you've been a very patient audience.

When I began these remarks, I said that I found it difficult to see too far into the future, given the rapid pace of change in the electronics industry. And I expressed my belief that the best way to prepare for what lies ahead is to get in position by having a strong foundation that puts the company in a position to capitalize on change and to seize the many opportunities ahead.

The issues I've discussed today make up that strong foundation:

- First, the ability to innovate and to implement technology very rapidly
- Second, a commitment to use total quality control to improve all our business processes
- Third, our ability to capitalize on the power of information
- Fourth, the skills, flexibility, and motivation of our work force
- Fifth and finally, access to global markets

through the best blend of value-added presence, strategic alliances, and distribution channels for each nation in which we do business

This foundation is just that: a place to begin. What gets built on top of that foundation, the exact size and placing of the rooms, that's harder to foresee.

As for HP, I believe that customers will be the architects of our future. Customers have needs we've yet to meet, which will be met by technologies we've yet to introduce.

So, for HP, we emphasize building the foundation. If we can make that strong, and remain responsive to changes in customer needs and in technology, I look forward to the future with confidence and anticipation.

And because I know that you at Samsung are also building a strong foundation—and because I know you are very responsive to the changes that are driving your marketplace—I believe you should feel very positive about your own prospects.

I know that the team at SHP is very interested in working with your organizations to assist in applying these concepts where you might see a fit with your own organization's needs. That interest is shared by the entire Hewlett-Packard organization, and let me close by expressing our enthusiasm for working with you in building the kind of business that will continue to thrive in the years ahead.

▶ DISCUSSION QUESTIONS

Break the class into groups of four or five for the following assignment. Describe the Hewlett-Packard approach to management in terms of three themes as follows:

- Theme 1: Customer value strategy, includes the following topics: quality, measurement, positioning, key stakeholder, and product design.
- Theme 2: Managing systems, includes the following topics: cross-functional approach, technology, employee involvement, human resource management, role definition, culture, and structure.
- Theme 3: Continuous improvement, includes the following topics: occasion, approach, response to error, decision-making perspective, managerial roles, authority, focus, control, and means.

Each group should be assigned one of the themes. Since some themes contain more topics than others, have each group select any five topics to focus on. About thirty minutes should be allotted for the groups to dig through the HP case and record their findings. After thirty minutes, have the groups share their ideas.

Take note of how these examples illustrate that the HP approach is consistent and integrated across all of the topics and themes. This illustrates the idea of a paradigm consisting of an integrated set of elements that are self-reinforcing and mutually supportive.

St. Mary's Continuous Quality Improvement*

In the 1990s, health care organizations face diminishing reimbursements and operating margins, rising consumer expectations and scrutiny, and intensified competition for services. A 1987 study by the American College of Health Care Executives indicated that quality in the health care industry will become a major focus in the competition for revenues. Also, the Joint Commission on the Accreditation of Health Care Organizations has refocused its accreditation review from structure to outcomes.

In an effort to cope with these challenges, St. Mary's Medical Center (SMMC) in Knoxville, Tennessee, recently initiated Total Quality Management. St. Mary's calls it "continuous quality improvement" (CQI). In this case, we describe St. Mary's initial efforts to transform its approach to management and make real the familiar terms "process improvement," "systems approach," "continuous improvement," "paradigm shift," and "culture change." These efforts are still in an early stage with much work to be done. The results are not evident yet, but St. Mary's has high hopes for the transformation process. This case discusses St. Mary's approach to Total Quality Management in terms of:

- Conceptual framework
- Schedule of implementation
- Operating structure
- Training and education

▶ ST. MARY'S ORGANIZATION AND MISSION

St. Mary's was established in 1929 as a not-for-profit organization. Today, St. Mary's is one of four major providers in east Tennessee. It has 531 licensed beds, a gross patient revenue of $229 million, and a staff of 2,000 employees.

Boards of directors oversee the activities of St. Mary's Health System, Inc., St. Mary's Medical Center, Inc., Health Dynamics, Inc., and St. Mary's Foundation, Inc. (see Figure 1). The medical staff is composed of 500 physicians in the disciplines of anesthesia, emergency medicine, family practice, medicine, obstetrics and gynecology, pathology, radiology, and surgery. The administrative council, which is also

* This case was prepared by Sharon Yarbrough and Greg Bounds.

Figure 1
St. Mary's Health System, Inc.

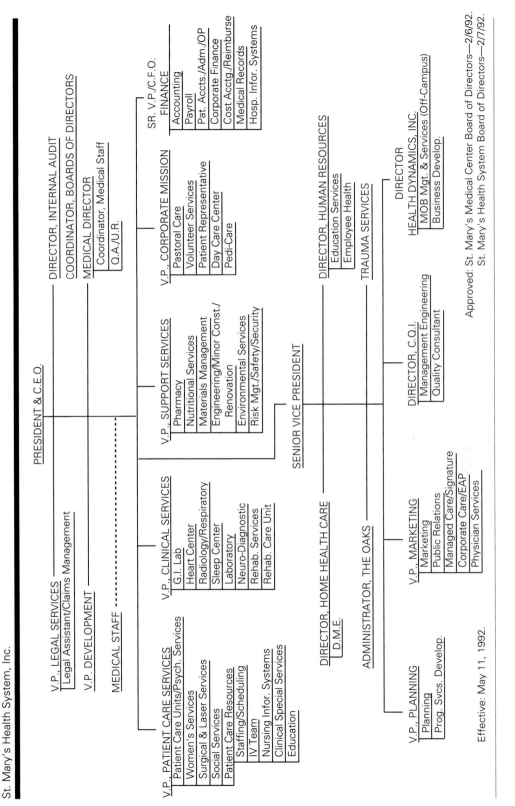

PRESIDENT & C.E.O.

DIRECTOR, INTERNAL AUDIT

COORDINATOR, BOARDS OF DIRECTORS

MEDICAL DIRECTOR
- Coordinator, Medical Staff
- Q.A./U.R.

SR. V.P./C.F.O.
FINANCE
- Accounting
- Payroll
- Pat. Accts./Adm./OP
- Corporate Finance
- Cost Acctg./Reimburse
- Medical Records
- Hosp. Infor. Systems

V.P. CORPORATE MISSION
- Pastoral Care
- Volunteer Services
- Patient Representative
- Day Care Center
- Pedi-Care

DIRECTOR, HUMAN RESOURCES
- Education Services
- Employee Health

TRAUMA SERVICES

DIRECTOR
HEALTH DYNAMICS, INC.
- MOB Mgt. & Services (Off-Campus)
- Business Develop.

V.P., LEGAL SERVICES
- Legal Assistant/Claims Management

V.P. DEVELOPMENT

MEDICAL STAFF

V.P. SUPPORT SERVICES
- Pharmacy
- Nutritional Services
- Materials Management
- Engineering/Minor Const./ Renovation
- Environmental Services
- Risk Mgt./Safety/Security

SENIOR VICE PRESIDENT

DIRECTOR, C.Q.I.
- Management Engineering
- Quality Consultant

V.P. CLINICAL SERVICES
- G.I. Lab
- Heart Center
- Radiology/Respiratory
- Sleep Center
- Laboratory
- Neuro-Diagnostic
- Rehab. Services
- Rehab. Care Unit

DIRECTOR, HOME HEALTH CARE
- D.M.E.

ADMINISTRATOR, THE OAKS

V.P., PATIENT CARE SERVICES
- Patient Care Units/Psych. Services
- Women's Services
- Surgical & Laser Services
- Social Services
- Patient Care Resources
- Staffing/Scheduling
- IV Team
- Nursing Infor. Systems
- Clinical Special Services
- Education

V.P., MARKETING
- Marketing
- Public Relations
- Managed Care/Signature
- Corporate Care/EAP
- Physician Services

V.P., PLANNING
- Planning
- Prog. Svcs. Develop.

Effective: May 11, 1992.

Approved: St. Mary's Medical Center Board of Directors—2/6/92.
St. Mary's Health System Board of Directors—2/7/92.

referred to as the "executive level," consists of the president and CEO, senior vice presidents of finance, health systems, medical affairs/medical director, medical services, support services, patient care services, planning, marketing, corporate mission, foundations, and legal services.

The following hospital mission statement reveals the organization's fundamental purpose:

> The mission of St. Mary's Medical Center is to continue the healing ministry of Jesus. Reaching out with courage and compassion in the spirit of Catherine McAuley—the founder of the Sisters of Mercy—St. Mary's seeks to serve the people and communities of east Tennessee. St. Mary's purpose is to enhance the quality of life by preventing illness, restoring and maintaining health, relieving suffering, and caring for the dying in a Christian atmosphere which affirms dignity and respect for each person.

St. Mary's accepts the challenge of modern medicine, and is often the first to provide the latest capabilities to customers. Old-fashioned caring, with the latest technological advancements, procedures, and equipment, reflects St. Mary's mission.

▶ INITIATION OF CONTINUOUS QUALITY IMPROVEMENT

Eli Matijevich, vice president of medical services, explains the initiation of the continuous quality improvement (CQI) program at St. Mary's:[1] "In 1988 or '89, a few of us at the executive level in the organization either had some background in CQI or had researched the literature with a natural curiosity. There was enough interest on the part of two or three of us that we went to a Deming course for a week to learn more about his approach. It seemed like a natural direction for the hospital to at least evaluate. I don't think any of us at that time were sure that this would really apply and translate directly to a hospital or a health care organization."

The health care industry is subject to the scrutiny of those who are currently "shopping" for quality health care. For example, businesses that have embraced quality improvement principles are increasingly seeking health care providers with the same orientation. However, St. Mary's did not initiate CQI just in response to external pressures. As Matijevich explains, St. Mary's leaders had "curiosity and the feeling that CQI might be something that would be really good for St. Mary's. With the exception of wanting to improve the esprit de corps and decrease turnover in patient care services among our nursing staff, which represents half the hospital staff, there wasn't a particular issue that pushed us into looking at Deming, or Juran, or Crosby."

▶ DEFINING QUALITY AT ST. MARY'S

From all their study of Total Quality Management, the executives of St. Mary's understood that quality is not just an attribute of products or services. They decided that St. Mary's CQI efforts would be founded on a definition of quality as a mindset, the soul of the organization itself, an all-pervasive drive of such intensity that it would define the corporate culture (Marchese, 1991). St. Mary's has established a quality mindset through executive commitment and a framework for CQI.

1. The authors of this case wish to express appreciation to Eli Matijevich, vice president of medical services, and Marty Margetts, director of continuous quality improvement, at St. Mary's Medical Center for their invaluable support; both graciously provided information used to write this case. Any inquiries about the CQI program at St. Mary's should be directed to Mr. Matijevich and/or Mr. Margetts.

Figure 2
Where to focus when defining quality health care

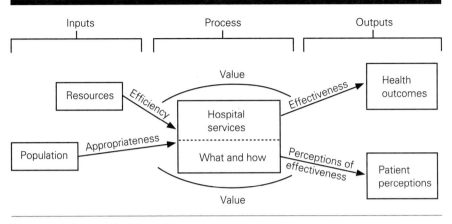

Lanning and O'Connor (1990), p. 42.

St. Mary's executives have also sought a broader understanding of product and service quality. Traditional health care quality models have focused on health status as the end result. St. Mary's executives prefer more recent models that have also considered the human interaction and consumer perceptions of quality (Lehtinen, 1983; Longest, 1977). In this approach, managers still relate quality to the structure of physical facilities, personnel, and organization, but they focus on the process of interaction between provider and consumer. This approach also focuses on how well the service interaction meets consumer expectations, which is a key outcome measure. Thus, outcomes in Figure 2 refer to the consequences of service delivery both in terms of health status (technical aspects) and patient perceptions (interpersonal aspects) in judging quality (Donabedian, 1980).

Quality Defined by Consumers
In the past, the role of health care consumers (patients, governments, payers) has been downplayed in determining what constitutes quality. It has been implied that consumers are not qualified to determine what truly constitutes quality with respect to the scientific and technical aspects of their clinical/medical needs (Demby, 1985; Donabedian, 1980). Now, however, interpersonal needs are increasingly recognized (Lanning and O'Connor, 1990). The data in Figure 3 illustrate that service quality is closely related to and determined by human performance in the interaction process. For example, "indifferent personnel" was frequently cited as a reason for poor service quality. This approach to defining service quality in terms of interaction with consumers presents a challenge because individual consumers vary tremendously in their desires, values, and expectations. It is difficult to anticipate and meet these varying needs.

Quality Defined by Payers
Payers of health services also provide an increasingly important perspective on the definition of service quality. Payers include insurance companies, governments, employers, and a variety of competitive health plans. Their emphasis on cost per unit service, or efficiency, is now being tempered with concerns for value—what they are receiving per dollar spent. Payers increasingly monitor individual encounters with the health care system through preadmission certification, concurrent review, and measures of cost per unit service to assure appropriateness and efficiency of

Figure 3

What consumers think of service quality based on those experiencing poor service

Reason service was poor	Type of service					
	Auto repair %	Banking %	Insurance %	Government %	Hospitals %	Airlines %
Work not done right	63	19	12	15	9	8
Too slow	19	29	31	40	23	8
Too expensive	26	7	18	0	20	0
Indifferent personnel	4	19	18	28	33	18
Unqualified personnel	7	14	14	9	10	10
Lack of courtesy	4	12	7	7	17	4

ASQC/Gallup Survey by John Ryan in the November 1985 issue of *Quality Progress*.

service. In addition, payers are working with aggregate data to find variations from a statistically defined norm of acceptable care (Lanning and O'Connor, 1990).

Quality Defined by Internal Customers

St. Mary's also defines service quality in terms of internal customers. In this internal customer approach, service quality means the service conforms to the requirements of people who work in the hospital. Whether the customer is a hospital department, a physician, a patient, or group from outside, St. Mary's is committed to improving the service each receives. This new customer orientation has been a challenge. Matijevich explains, "We didn't anticipate the complexity of CQI in an organization such as ours. It is a lot different than in a widgets shop where you are turning

out little widgets, where you can weigh them and measure them and test them; [here] the outcome measurement is something that is difficult for all of us. There are many more subtle places where things could go wrong. But understanding the processes is something we are getting better about. It has been beneficial for a lot of our areas. The customer focus has been good for the organization."

The executives at St. Mary's are convinced that the improvement of quality has a direct and measurable effect on their costs of doing business. They believe that improving service quality for all customers and reducing costs will help them fulfill St. Mary's mission. Achieving these improvements requires both executive commitment and a framework for CQI. We discuss these below.

▶ COMMITMENT FROM THE EXECUTIVE LEVEL

For approximately eighteen months, the Orion Partnership, a consulting firm from Seattle, Washington, facilitated many meetings, observing specific agendas and providing guidance and feedback. With Orion's help, St.

Mary's executives developed a continuous quality improvement strategy.

Figure 4 illustrates the importance of executive commitment to St. Mary's quality strategy. St. Mary's culture, and ultimately continu-

Figure 4

St. Mary's quality strategy

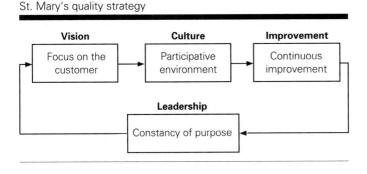

ous improvement itself, is driven by executive vision and leadership. Therefore, St. Mary's executives had to buy into CQI before it could succeed. They had to share the vision.

Matijevich explains: "... through a long evaluation period, we tried to decide whether executive management thought CQI was appropriate and could 'buy into it' and be comfortable with the management philosophy. We spent the first six to nine months of our evaluation process getting everybody to understand continuous quality improvement. The executives spent a lot of time in all-day sessions learning what CQI is all about, what the implications are for us and our methods for middle management, and how to start it. We developed the

first half of our current strategic plan without really being committed to CQI. Nine months into the process we got 'buy-in' to go on to the next step. Then we started to pilot some initial interdisciplinary teams to see what kind of reception it gets."

About this time the Joint Commission on Accreditation of Health Care Organizations was changing its evaluation format from a focus on structure to a focus on results or outcomes. This endeavor forced hospitals everywhere to adopt some process improvement models of assuring quality. It provided an additional source of motivation for St. Mary's CQI efforts.

▶ FRAMEWORK OF CONTINUOUS QUALITY IMPROVEMENT AT ST. MARY'S

The St. Mary's continuous quality improvement effort is based upon Deming's (1986) theory of management and Juran's (1979) team-based approach to solving chronic quality problems. CQI at St. Mary's is also based upon the following seven fundamental concepts and ten guiding principles. The seven fundamental concepts are:

1. *Quality Begins at the Top* Management supports quality improvements as a top-priority task and provides the driving force neces-

sary to support and sustain the operation of the system.

2. *Employee Must Be Involved* Successful quality programs are successful people programs. An all-encompassing people participation program will be one of the single most influential elements in the long-term success of quality improvement efforts at St. Mary's.

3. *Quality Is a Never-Ending Process* Successful programs in quality improvement are not one-shot efforts, but have become integral

parts of the organization's operational philosophy and culture. At St. Mary's, it means the continual evaluation by every person of how every job, every system, and every service or product can be improved.

4. *The Bottom Line Is Customer Satisfaction* Satisfying customers with quality and reliability at a reasonable price is the only way St. Mary's will remain competitive and stay in business.

5. *Quality Applies to All Functions, Including Administrative* Quality improvement is not a process that works only in line operations. It will be an important tool in keeping St. Mary's administrative systems focused and able to support quality health care.

6. *Quality Costs Less* The costs of waste and poor quality make up a substantial portion of hospitals' costs. Meeting customer requirements and doing the right thing correctly the first time will always cost St. Mary's less.

7. *Supplier Involvement Is Crucial* Quality medical care depends as much on the quality of the medical supplies and equipment as it does on the actions of the nurse, physical therapist, or lab technician. St. Mary's quality improvement effort will extend beyond the system under its immediate control in order to improve total quality.

The ten guiding principles are:

1. Quality service to our patients is the focus of everything we do.
2. Continuous improvement is essential to our success.
3. Commitment, involvement, and support by management are essential.
4. Teamwork and employee involvement are the foundation of our efforts to improve.
5. The best ideas for improvement come from those directly involved in the work.
6. Employees want to do their best, but work systems frequently make it difficult or impossible to do so.
7. Physicians, employees, and suppliers are our partners in the pursuit of quality.
8. All involved treat each other with fairness, trust, and respect.
9. Taking risks and learning from our mistakes are key elements in continuous improvement.
10. Problems are identified in order to find solutions, not to place blame.

▶ BENEFITS OF CONTINUOUS QUALITY IMPROVEMENT

The benefits of CQI for St. Mary's Health System are many. The most obvious benefit is better health care for the community. Central to the mission of the Sisters of Mercy is the pursuit of excellence in service. Also, the executive committee of St. Mary's developed a vision for the following benefits of CQI:

- Improved customer satisfaction leading to increased market share in the Knoxville and eastern Tennessee catchment area.
- Positioning of the organization to meet new Joint Commission on Accreditation of Health Care Organizations requirements.
- A system that will greatly enhance St. Mary's ability to attract and retain top-quality practitioners, administrators, and staff.
- An organization that, in its day-to-day operations, is highly congruent with the core values of the institution and the Mercy Health System.
- The market-responsive approach to managing necessary to support a pro-

gram of continuous quality improvement will also position St. Mary's to move more quickly to respond to the rapid pace of change found in the present health care environment.

- Reducing the cost and improving the quality of health care is part of St. Mary's social responsibility to the communities that it serves.
- A strong CQI effort will make a substantial contribution toward positioning St. Mary's as a preferential practice location for area physicians.

- Investment in a continuous improvement program will give St. Mary's a competitive advantage over other area health care institutions that delay addressing quality improvement.
- Creation of an attractive marketing advantage in relation to the growing numbers of companies that will demand a single health care supplier of demonstrable quality delivered at an acceptable price.

▶ CQI PROCESS AT ST. MARY'S

These fundamental concepts and underlying principles come to life in the St. Mary's improvement process. The improvement process has three basic elements which, when used in combination, allow the organization to continually evaluate and improve its business systems and practices. These three elements are: (1) department task analysis; (2) business process analysis; and (3) team-based problem solving. We discuss each of these below.

Department Task Analysis

Department task analysis helps clarify what a department does, who the department does it for, and who it is dependent upon for its own success. Clarifying these issues helps break down interdepartmental barriers that inhibit the smooth cross-functional flow of work. It also provides a foundation for the improvement process by determining why any given unit of the organization exists, who it serves, and who it is served by. The activities in the process serve to develop a definition of the department's mission, customers, suppliers, customer/supplier requirements, and feedback system to make certain that customer requirements are met.

Business Process Analysis

This analysis describes the organization's processes, both departmental and cross-functional, large and small, setting the stage for improvement as well as monitoring and effective control. Business process analysis describes the organization's processes to determine how they function and to locate potential areas for improvement. The analysis brings to light complexity, redundancy, and quality problems.

Team-Based Problem Solving

Team-based problem solving focuses teams of people on achieving practical, long-range solutions to specific key processes and systems. It is a structured approach focused on providing optimum solutions to specific problems. The problems may be identified by department task analysis, business process analysis, customer complaints, or manager/employee initiative.

Improvement may be driven by using any one or all of these three elements. Each manager decides where and when these approaches are to be applied. Used in combination, these elements provide a systematic approach to improving working relationships between units of the organization and improving work processes.

▶ IMPLEMENTATION OF CONTINUOUS QUALITY IMPROVEMENT

After determining the potential benefits of continuous quality improvement, St. Mary's developed an implementation plan that would be comprehensive and sustain a change in management style.

Installing an institution-wide continuous quality improvement program is a large, complex undertaking. Thus, St. Mary's plan takes a long-term view. It will take a number of years to fully implement all components of CQI. Initial installation is spread over the course of three years. Large-scale awareness and employee participation in the program will not be accomplished until sometime in the second year. This approach is recommended to enable the health system to plan and prepare for new skills and behaviors. It also allows cultural change to create a supportive environment for employee participation.

The major activities that make up this project are planning, education and training, department task analysis, business process analysis, and project-based improvement work. As a result of engaging in these activities, the following outcomes will be achieved:

- Management will have the information and tools to lead St. Mary's continuous quality improvement.
- A clear direction will be defined to guide the overall improvement effort and a detailed plan to guide continuous quality improvement implementation will be in place.
- A critical mass of St. Mary's employees will have the knowledge and skills to engage in solving quality problems.
- An organizational and managerial culture supportive of continuous quality improvement will exist.
- Improvement techniques will be in use in all functional organizations within the institution.

- Quality of care will be improved.
- Costs will be reduced and productivity will be increased.

The installation of CQI at St. Mary's was designed to take place in six phases: decision phase, organization phase, preparation phase, initial implementation phase, expansion phase, and integration/sustaining phase. Figure 5 presents the timeline for these phases.

Decision Phase
During this phase, the concepts of continuous improvement are introduced to senior management. Their purpose at this time is to determine not only their level of commitment to this concept, but also that of other parts of the organization.

Organization Phase
Planning for continuous improvement begins by establishing leadership structure, developing strategies to inform and involve the boards, physicians, and the Mercy Health System.

Preparation Phase
This phase finalizes the overall implementation plan. Pilot projects are identified, suppliers of training are selected, and a continuous improvement coordinator is appointed or hired. Orientation is held for the medical staff to introduce the continuous improvement process. Support systems for pilot projects are developed, while each division develops a distinct direction for continuous improvement. Also during this phase, senior managers prepare for roles required in the next phase. Activities that initiate culture change are set in motion. An employee survey is conducted.

Initial Implementation (Pilot Project) Phase
Pilot projects and teams are selected. As the teams are trained, the selected projects are undertaken, completed, and evaluated. Orga-

Figure 5

Timeline for project phases

	1990	1991	1992
	J F M A M J J A S O N D	J F M A M J J A S O N D	J F M A M J J A S

Decision phase
——— (1/90) (6/90)

Organization phase
——— (7/90) (1/91)

Preparation phase
——— (10/90) (12/91)

Initial implementation phase
——— (4/91) (10/91)

Expansion phase
———→ (10/91) (10/92)

Integration/sustaining phase
———→ (7/92)

nizational development begins at the division level.

The purpose of pilot projects is to develop and test the methods of quality improvement. In addition, they provide a basis to refine the implementation plan and define needed support resources. Pilot projects present an opportunity to begin orienting and training managers and initiating the culture change effort.

Expansion Phase

Broad orientation and training begins the roll-out of CQI to all employees. A support system is expanded to identify and prioritize opportunities for improvement activities. Teams begin to work on those quality problems and processes that have been identified as needing improvement. Supplier improvement programs begin and recognition and reward systems are established.

Integration/Sustaining Phase

This phase recognizes and communicates the successes of the program. Policies, procedures, and structures are modified to support the continuous improvement approach and to integrate CQI into all aspects of the organization. Teams continue to reduce waste and improve processes, which results in improved customer satisfaction and productivity.

St. Mary's continuous quality improvement is at the expansion phase of the timeline and is in the process of moving to the integration phase to evaluate the successes of their program.

▶ **COORDINATING CONTINUOUS QUALITY IMPROVEMENT**

The CQI strategic plan indicates that the tasks of improving quality and developing a culture of continuous improvement require special attention. The existing organization is not presently capable of providing the necessary attention or resources. Therefore, St. Mary's executive team has decided to develop a parallel organization structure devoted to continuous quality improvement. Such a structure will function hand-in-hand with the regular organization structure. At the same time, the parallel structure will give the CQI effort a high degree of visibility and send an important message to the entire organization.

Development of a parallel structure for managing and supporting continuous improvement will be an evolutionary process. Initially, due to the magnitude of the transformation, the structure will feature a fair degree of centralized control and coordination through steering committees. This is to ensure constancy of purpose and consistency of effort during the critical early stages of the change process.

Eventually, as the components of the improvement process and the elements of the new culture become anchored in the organization, more and more of the activities of the CQI steering committee may be decentralized. For example, the decentralized activities might eventually be placed with local steering committees at the division or business unit level.

The local steering committees would primarily take on the chartering and oversight responsibilities for improvement projects operating wholly within departments or functional areas under that organization. The corporate steering committee would maintain responsibility for all cross-functional improvement projects as well as the overall implementation and coordination of the CQI transformation.

Finally, the structure designed specifically to support continuous quality improvement will not dissolve or blend back into the regular structure until continuous improvement is integrated into the cultural fabric of the organization. For example, the CQI steering committee should not become one with the administrative council until CQI thinking and methodology is fully integrated into the behavior of the senior management group. These two committees have the same member composition, but different objectives.

▶ CONTINUOUS QUALITY IMPROVEMENT PROCESS ORGANIZATION STRUCTURE

The organizational structure for St. Mary's continuous quality improvement is structured as a hierarchy with the following elements: CQI steering committee, CQI department, quality guidance teams (QGTs), quality improvement teams (QITs), employee involvement committees (EICs), director of quality improvement, and quality team consultants/facilitators (see Figure 6). Each of these elements is briefly discussed below.

CQI Steering Committee

The purpose of the CQI steering committee is to provide direction and resources to ensure the successful implementation of the CQI process and the transformation to a culture of continuous improvement. Membership of this committee consists of the president and CEO, who chairs the committee, all members of the administrative council, the CQI coordinator, and designated technical specialists.

CQI Department

This group provides managers, supervisors, and employees with the educational, technical, and other support services necessary to accomplish the implementation of CQI. The CQI coordinator leads this group, which consists of St. Mary's employees who possess necessary skills or training. The CQI department uses the skills and resources of human resource development, patient care resources, quality

Figure 6

St. Mary's Health System: continuous quality improvement process—organization structure

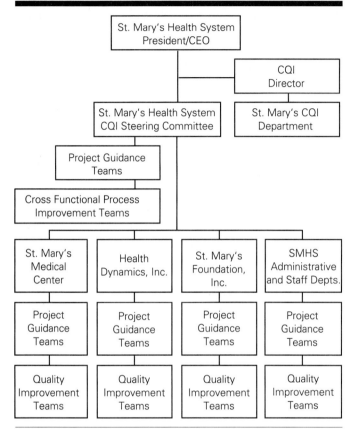

assurance, and other organizations and individuals within the St. Mary's Health System.

Project Guidance Teams

The objective of the project guidance teams is to oversee and support the activities of one or more project teams. Membership consists of managers and other key leaders with diverse skills and resources who have a stake in the improvement project and have the authority to make changes in the process under study. A member of the CQI steering committee chairs these teams.

Quality Improvement Teams (QITs)

The purpose of these teams is to rigorously apply the methodologies of quality improvement in order to solve specific quality problems. In addition, these teams will study the organization's systems and processes in order to discover ways to reduce waste and complexity within the organization, with the objective to improve quality and productivity. The organization of these teams consists of ad hoc work teams assigned to work on specific problems or processes in a given timeframe. Activities focus on two types of problem-solving activities. First, QITs address problems associated with processes not in statistical control or subject to special cause variation. The ad hoc membership consists of those employees who work closest to the problem. Secondly, the QITs work on reducing common cause variation found in processes that are in statistical control. Membership for this purpose consists of a mix of managers and employees who have specific knowledge or experience to contribute to the solution.

Cross-Functional Process Improvement Teams

These teams are assigned to study cross-functional processes. They are generally composed of managers who control the processes under study and others with specific knowledge or skills. They look at the ability of the process to meet customer requirements. These teams may undertake actual improvement projects or delegate specific problem areas to problem-solving QITs.

Example QIT Project: The Discharge Process

An example of a QIT project in St. Mary's Medical Center is changes implemented in the discharge process. Cross-functional representation for the team was composed of representatives from medical records, pharmacy, environmental services, admitting, unit clerk, and nursing. The team developed the following project statement: to decrease the amount of time between the patient leaving the unit and the patient name being discharged from active status on the computer. The seven-step method, seen in Figure 7, was used to analyze the discharge process. (This method is used in all projects.)

In step one, some of the customers (players) identified were patients being discharged, patients waiting to be admitted, cashiers for patient billing, housekeeping, medical records, admitting office, insurance companies, unit clerks, staff discharging patient, and ancillary departments such as lab, X-ray, pharmacy, dietary, nuclear medicine, CT,

ultrasound, and auxiliary. Measures were identified, and tools for the measurement were determined. Possible barriers were listed, and boundaries were established. A customer survey was developed and administered during this step.

Step two described the current discharge process with a flowchart (Figure 8). Key process indicators were identified and data were gathered and analyzed at this point. Selecting specific units to statistically evaluate was completed in step three. In addition, possible causes were identified, and a review of the causes and effects was conducted.

Various solutions were identified in step four. These possibilities were evaluated, barriers were identified, and solutions determined. Some of the solutions included designated discharges at all exits, utilizing a bar code scanner, discharge when patient leaves the room, and provide education for discharge nurse or nurse assistant. Step five studied the impact of the decisions in step four. Also, any deviations from the plan were projected.

The team presented the following potential processes in step six: standardization procedures throughout the organization, no additional staff required, no work flow interruptions, three-second procedure to scan the card, better use of health care professionals' time, and decrease the potential for delays in communication. Step seven recommendations were to continue to move forward with plans for implementation of the bar coding system, and continue QIT with same members until standardization was achieved throughout organization. The team also presented barriers and benefits of the problem-solving activity.

Employee Involvement Committee (EIC)

The purpose of this committee is a voluntary strategy that managers and supervisors may utilize at their option in order to provide local

Figure 7

The seven-step method

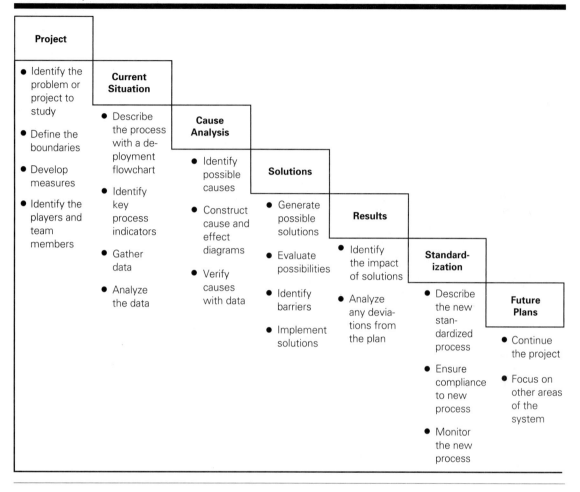

work groups with an opportunity to address problems that affect the quality of their work.[2] The organization of this committee is similar to the concept of a quality circle (a team of workers from the same work area or work group who meet on a regular basis over a defined period of time). The primary focus is human relations and the quality of work life. Quality improvement is a secondary focus.

Director of Quality Improvement

The director manages and provides direct support to the process of implementing organization-wide continuous quality improvement, supports and advises senior leadership through the transformation, and designs and carries out periodic evaluations of the process and results.

---

2. At the time this case was prepared, there was only one EIC functioning, in the pharmacy department.

Figure 8

Discharge process flowchart

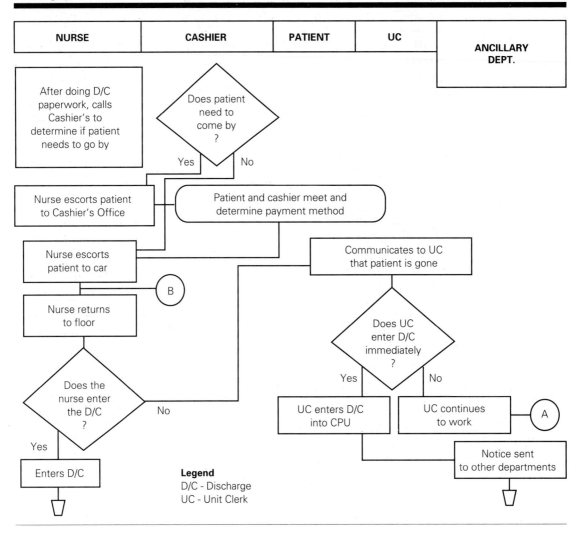

Quality Team Consultants/Facilitators

The role of these consultants is to provide training, facilitation, and consultation to quality improvement teams. The consultants are matrixed to the quality resource group on an as-needed basis and report to the CQI coordinator.

St. Mary's is in the process of evaluating and implementing procedures to further en-hance their CQI program. The CQI strategic plan stated that St. Mary's would offer courses to engage all the employees in CQI and have a set of internal facilitators guide team projects. The training is still under way. Once it is completed, training and support should yield a structured process of improvement in all functional units of the hospital.

► EXAMPLES OF CROSS-FUNCTIONAL SYSTEMS

Several cross-functional teams are focused on hospital-wide issues. St. Mary's has identified several systems that are key to its mission, including access/entry, diagnostic, intervention, value determination/relationships, return to community, resources, and remuneration/finance. The cross-functional teams flow-charted each of their assigned systems. By mak-

ing improvements in these key systems, St. Mary's hopes to see improvement in some key indicators: turnaround time in the operating room, waiting time in the emergency room, and reporting time of test results to outside physicians. These key indicators reveal how the hospital is performing in areas important to its customers.

Figure 9

St. Mary's key systems

The ***access/entry system*** begins with and includes all external points of origin, such as insurance companies, physicians, and general public sources. It encompasses internal processes for correct and timely access and entry to diagnostics and care.

System objective:
All customers will have satisfaction with access to St. Mary's Medical Center.

System measures:
- Customer satisfaction with accessibility to facility.
- Appropriate precertification and certification.
- Cycle time every entry. Out patient, Admissions, Women's Pavilion, ER (in and out).
- Inpatient room ready.

The ***diagnostic system*** begins with patient and environmental information, including external and internal laboratory procedures, external and internal communication of results, and development and communication of treatment plans, and extends through follow-up therapy and office and/or hospital visits.

System objective:
All diagnostic procedures will be obtained, processed, and communicated safely, effectively, and efficiently.

System measures:
- X-ray report turnaround time.
- Lab test turnaround time.
- Repeat x-rays.
- Resticks.
- Customer satisfaction survey. MD, patient.

Figure 9

St. Mary's key systems (Continued)

The ***intervention system*** includes all aspects of care while the patient is in the hospital, beginning with information from access/entry to discharge of patient.

System objective:
We will provide our patient customers appropriate, timely, indicated care.

System measures:
- Outcomes related to quality assurance/quality improvement multidisciplinary review.
- Comparisons of length of stay, average cost, average charge by drug-related group.
- Mortality rate.
- Patient satisfaction—how were you taken care of by the nurses and doctors?

The ***value determination/relationships system*** begins with the patient's world, including payers, medical establishments, and individual and group practices, and extends through patient, family, medical, and payer perception and value of services delivered.

System objective:
We will work with the community to provide needed services within economic constraints.

The ***return to community system*** involves planning and preparation of patients and families for the return to the community, including follow-up and ongoing care.

System objective:
All discharges are appropriately planned and patients and families are prepared for the return to the community.

System measures:
- Percentage of uncompleted/inappropriate discharges.
- Number of denied days.
- Returns to hospital within fourteen days.
- Delay days for Nursing Home placement.
- Patient satisfaction—are you satisfied that you came home with everything you need?

The ***resources system*** begins with the external world and includes human talent, skills, and abilities, information regarding technology, equipment, and associated needs and requirements, internal development of required professional and managerial skills and abilities, and reorientation, growth, and practice developing a value system.

System objective:
Services will be provided with the appropriate human and other resources.

Figure 9

St. Mary's key systems (Continued)

The **remuneration/finance system** starts with external financial processes, means, and methods, which include internal records, information sources for determining and informing of charges for equipment, personnel, medications, procedures, diagnostics, and supplies, preparation and presentation of the bill to the patient, family, and other parties. It also includes patient education regarding financial necessities and characteristics and collection arrangements.

System objective:
St. Mary's viability is related to appropriate charges and effective collections recognizing prudent, sound business practice.

With the assistance of Dr. Richard Sanders of the University of Tennessee, St. Mary's began to work on access/entry as a key system. The access/entry system begins with a decision by the doctor and the patient who enters the hospital through central admitting. It may also begin with the decision of a walk-in patient in the emergency room. The system ends when the incoming patient is secure in the nursing unit (room is available, clean, and appropriately supplied, and initial [admitting] orders are in place) or when outpatient is discharged. This system is supposed to provide swift and certain access to other hospital systems and services.

Access means appropriate diagnostic and health care executed and delivered.

Swift means within thirty minutes for admissions through a physician's office and within two hours for admissions through the emergency department.

Certain means pre-admission records are complete and final prior to patient presence in admissions; that financial and medical forms are correct; room and special equipment are available at time of call; and relevant staff expect the patient's arrival.

This system fails if:

- Any patient does not have access to diagnostics and care upon request by physician, RN, or patient requirement.
- Any patient does not have a room available as required.
- Any patient is not accompanied or preceded by appropriate medical, financial, and personal records.
- Any patient's medical, financial, and personal records contain errors.
- Any patient does not receive empathic care throughout the operation of the access/entry system.

▶ CONTINUOUS QUALITY IMPROVEMENT EDUCATION AND TRAINING

To accomplish culture change and give managers and employees the skills needed to accomplish CQI's vision, St. Mary's uses training and education to:

- Explain the need for improvement and create awareness of the importance of quality at all levels
- Communicate St. Mary's vision, values,

guiding principles, and strategic quality tools
- Develop a common language and understanding of concepts for communicating about quality
- Help define the structure and process through which CQI will take place
- Clarify responsibilities
- Provide managers and staff with the skills, knowledge, tools, and techniques they need to manage and improve the quality of their work
- Build teamwork throughout St. Mary's

St. Mary's approach to training and education for CQI is to make it an ongoing activity, starting with new employee orientation and extending through job skills training, continuing education, and retraining. St. Mary's will also stress education for suppliers and contractors. The content of St. Mary's training and education courses includes:

- General orientation to CQI
- Processes, methods, and tools for CQI
- The role of leadership
- Teamwork
- Facilitator roles
- Culture change

▶ ORGANIZATIONAL CULTURE CHANGE

CQI will change the culture of St. Mary's; however, St. Mary's will remain true to the core values of the Mercy Health System. St. Mary's work to continuously improve quality directly reflects these values in the following ways:

- *Excellence* Continually striving to improve is the means by which individuals and organizations achieve excellence.
- *Human Dignity* Respect for individuals is shown by involving those we serve and those who serve in defining quality in our efforts to improve.
- *Justice* In order to maximize creativity, the work environment must emphasize fairness, openness to different perspectives, and the freedom to speak up without risk.
- *Mercy* Delivering service with compassion is as important to us as continually improving the services we deliver
- *Sacredness of Life* Commitment to forever improving our health care services is witness to our belief in the sacredness and quality of life
- *Service* Continual improvement of services and systems yields the human and financial resources to service all people in the spirit and tradition of the Sisters of Mercy

While St. Mary's remains true to its core values, CQI differs from the traditional management previously practiced at St. Mary's. It represents a way of doing business and of managing an organization that illustrates a shift from the norm in the health care industry. The long-term success of any effort to improve quality and reduce waste requires substantial changes in the way most organizations operate. Experience has shown that these changes must go beyond changes in organization structures and technologies. They must include changes in the way people, both managers and workers, behave, think, lead, and even feel.

When asked about the progress of the executive level and the status of the program, Matijevich replied, "We have had some executive turnover and there are some new people, but there will always be turnover. There is some tendency to revert back to centralized decision making when we get into one crisis or another. I think that there is a universal 'buy-in,' which is one of the keys for our long-term survival. Certainly, that's going to be beneficial for the

Figure 10

Four-box organizational systems model

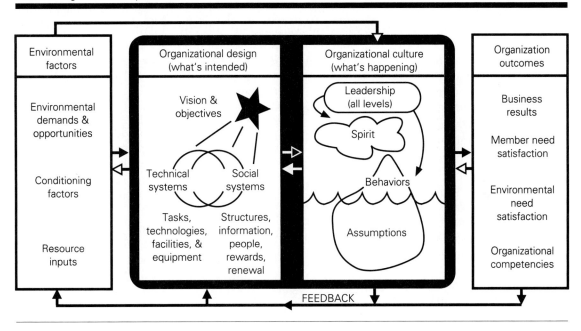

hospital in the long run, from a perspective other than just outcomes and the quality of our product."

St. Mary's leaders recognize the concept illustrated in the four-box organization systems model in Figure 10. This model indicates that the culture of an organization is inextricably linked to organization design and organization outcomes. The patterns of behavior and underlying beliefs will continually emerge to either block or enhance large-scale change efforts.

St. Mary's is trying to achieve the kinds of changes in behavior and beliefs that its leaders feel are required to implement a culture of continuous quality improvement. These changes include:

Controlling behavior of employees	Facilitating change, decision making, and problem solving
Provider focus	Customer focus
Reactive management	Proactive management
Tradition and safety	Experimentation and risk taking
Employees as expendable	Employees as customer
Blaming	Problem solving
Fear of retribution	Excitement of contribution
Cynicism	Optimism
Short-term thinking	Long-term thinking

St. Mary's CQI Implementation Plan.

Matijevich describes the culture change: "There was not real overt resistance. We were all at different places in terms of what this meant to us, i.e., how comfortable we are with it, how much of a clear understanding we have, how compatible it is with our traditional management style. Overall, it has been a couple of

From	To
Competition between departments	Cooperation between departments

steps backwards, two and a half steps forward, from time to time. The process has intermittently gained and lost momentum as other things have come up, such as organization-wide crises. But we have made progress. I think one of the better things we did was to spend as much time as it took to lay down an organizational philosophy as a framework so the program would have a halfway decent chance of getting off the ground. We had a lot of education, a lot of team building, a lot of changes in the way we interacted with our people, a lot of 'read my lips, but watch my feet.' Our managers are more aware of problems, needs, and concerns of other departments in the hospital, more aware of internal customers for other people. They are using some of that language and thought processes in making their decisions."

Resistance to change is a universal phenomenon, even among those who may desire change. But what people resist is not so much change itself, but being changed. People need to feel included in the decision to change, or, at the very least, they need to be presented with the rationale for change. This is why training, education, and getting buy-in is so important to the leaders at St. Mary's. Finally, in any change situation, the needs, fears, desires, and concerns that people have about change deserve to be listened to, responded to, and accommodated whenever possible.

Marty F. Margetts, director of continuous quality improvement at St. Mary's, acknowledges that change takes time and that the CQI program will have varying degrees of acceptance by their employees. However, the St. Mary's implementation plan has a number of strategies built into it to help reduce resistance to change:

- Changes will be phased in as training and orientation provide the rationale as well as skills to help employees feel better prepared to cope with new expectations.
- Reducing inequities in the system as the culture changes will help people feel this is a serious effort.
- Developmental work at the division and business unit levels will give many middle managers an opportunity to have some influence over how the changes will affect them.

One tool used by St. Mary's to promote this change is a storyboard, which is placed where employees can see it daily (see Figure 11). A copy is also placed in the employee training materials. The purpose of this storyboard is twofold: it is a method to inform employees about continuous quality improvement, and it is used as a teaching tool. Employees are also given the answers to questions asked on the storyboard, which helps further inform the progress of CQI at St. Mary's.

▶ FUTURE PLANS FOR CONTINUOUS IMPROVEMENT

St. Mary's Health System continues to evaluate quality in relationship to its products and services. The steering committee incorporates continuous quality improvement with the strategic planning process to link the two processes. The next step is the development of operational plans for each of the divisions and major business units. These plans will be derived from the continuous quality improvement plan and will detail the activities and timelines for implementation of continued quality improvement.

Figure 11

St. Mary's storyboard: what to look for

Step 1: Identify project	Step 2: Current situation	
• What is the area of opportunity for improvement? • What is the project statement? • Why is the project important? • Who is the customer? • Who will benefit from the improvement?	• Is there a flowchart of the process? • What are the boundaries of the project? • Do the boundaries of the flowchart align with the project statement? • What are the key quality indicators for the process? • Is there a cause and effect diagram analyzing process breakdowns?	
Team information	**Step 3: Understand problem**	
• What is the name of the project team? • Who are the team members? • Who is the guidance member? • What is the project mission statement?	• What are the possible causes of system breakdown? • Are the causes verified with data? • Is there a data collection plan? Is it clear how the data was collected? Who collected it? • What types of data were collected? • Which cause has the greatest impact on the process?	
Step 4: Selection solutions	**Plan**	**Do**

• Are there potential solutions to the process breakdown?
• How did the team select the solution for improvement?
• Are there data or other evidence to support the solution selected?
• Did the team decide to pilot the solution using the Plan-Do-Check-Act cycle?
	• What is the team's plan for piloting the improvement?
	• Does the plan indicate:
	  • the sequence of changes
	  • who will make the changes
	  • who will the changes affect
	  • how long will the changes take
	  • how to monitor the effectiveness of the changes
	  • who is to be trained on the changes
		• How was the plan for piloting the improvement executed?
		• Was the pilot monitored?
		• Who was trained on the improvement?
		• When was the pilot started?
		• How long did the pilot run?

	Act	**Check**
	• Was there data collected during the pilot? • Is the team comfortable that the pilot was long enough? • How did the data change from what was collected during Step 3? • Is there a plan to continue collecting data on the improvement?	• Did the team decide the pilot was effective? • Was the data collected able to determine the improvements? • Did the team decide to continue with the improvement?
Step 5: Results	**Step 6: Standardization**	**Step 7: Future plan**
• Did the pilot produce effective improvements? • Were the targets for improvement met? • Did the team identify other opportunities for improvement? • Did the team go through the Plan-Do-Check-Act cycle for those additional opportunities? • Did the team decide to continue with the improvement?	• Does the team have a plan to put the improvement in place beyond the pilot? • Does the team have a plan to standardize the process using the improvement? • Is there a flowchart describing the new process? • What did the team learn from the effort?	• Does the team have other opportunities for improvement? • What are the future plans of the team?

▶ QUESTIONS FOR DISCUSSION

1. Describe the measurement system St. Mary's has put in place. Does it address the various definitions of quality suggested in the discussion of Figure 2? Does it allow managers to assess the system and process improvements being worked on?

2. Imagine you are a consultant to St. Mary's. How would you suggest they design a measurement system to help meet their CQI objectives? What other infrastructure might St. Mary's need to accomplish its CQI vision?

3. What is the prognosis for CQI at St. Mary's? Will it spread infectiously or will it be a temporary flare-up?

4. St. Mary's wants CQI to become "the way to do business" rather than some activity superimposed on the normal way of doing business. Describe what the managerial activities of St. Mary's might be like once CQI becomes normalized. What would happen to the CQI structure? How would teamwork be promoted? How would improvement activities throughout St. Mary's be integrated?

▶ REFERENCES

N. Demby, "Quality Assurance and Marketing," *Dental Clinics of North America,*Vol. 29, No. 3, pp. 605–614.

W. E. Deming, *Out of the Crisis*, MIT Center for Advanced Engineering Study, Cambridge, Mass., 1986.

A. Donabedian, *Aspects of Medical Care Administration: Specifying Requirements for Health Care*, Harvard University Press for the Commonwealth Fund, Cambridge, Mass., 1973.

J. M. Juran, *Quality Control Handbook*, 3d ed., McGraw-Hill, New York, 1979.

J. Lanning and S. O'Connor, "The Health Care Quality Quagmire; Some Signposts," *Hospital and Health Services Administration*, Spring 1980, p. 41.

J. Lehtinen, "Asiakasohjautuva Palvelujarjestelkmkassitteisto je Empiirisa Sovellutuksia" ("Customer Oriented Service System"), *Acta Universitatis Tamperensis,* Vol. 160; Series A, 1983, pp. 295–316.

B. Longest, "Productivity in the Provision of Hospital Services: A Challenge to the Management Community," *Academy of Management Review,* Vol. 2, No. 3, 1977, pp. 475–483.

B. McCormick, "Innovative Programs Link Providers, Purchasers in Quality Management," *American Medical News,* Jan. 14, 1991, p. 29.

T. Marchese, "TQM Reaches the Academy," *American Association of Higher Education*, November 1991, p. 4.

"What Consumers Think of Service Quality Based on Those Experiencing Poor Service," *American Society for Quality Control*, 1985.

Toyota, Part I: The Standardization of Culture*

▶ TOYOTA QUALITY

Toyota Motor Sales, U.S.A., Inc., was organized and incorporated on October 31, 1957, as the United States sales organization for Toyota Motor Company, Japan. Operating from modest headquarters in a defunct Hollywood, California, dealership, the fledgling company offered only the Toyopet Crown. This "Tokyo Taxi" attracted only 288 customers in the first fourteen months of sales. It was a rather inauspicious beginning for a company that has since earned a healthy share of the U.S. automobile market and topped industry charts for customer satisfaction and product quality with offerings such as those from its luxury-car division, Lexus. In fact, Toyota sales now exceed one million vehicles per year (1990, 1991, 1992).

Managers at Toyota realize that customer satisfaction dictates success or failure in the highly competitive 1990s marketplace. Since satisfied Toyota customers tend to buy another Toyota, TMS managers seek to improve every aspect of the ownership experience. TMS managers also realize that customer satisfaction is more than a service; rather, it is a philosophy that should permeate all of Toyota.

Toyota leaders have repeatedly expressed their commitment to customer satisfaction. For example, Shoichiro Toyoda, president, TMC Japan, recently stated, "I intend to make this company number one in terms of customer satisfaction within the next three years. Each and every one of you, I hope, understands that customer satisfaction is the most precious asset a company can have." Tatsuro Toyoda, executive vice president, TMC Japan, concurred when he stated, "Recently, the global automotive environment has become increasingly more competitive. In order to succeed in such an environment in the 1990s, it is crucial that we become number one in customer satisfaction." Not only did these leaders express verbally their commitment, they did so with their actions.

This case describes how Toyota Motor Sales (TMS) drives a customer satisfaction philosophy throughout the organization. Part I illustrates how Toyota anchors its culture around the purpose of customer satisfaction.[1]

---

* This case was prepared by Greg Bounds.

1. This case study is based on knowledge of Toyota's customer satisfaction committee and delivery quality improvement program gained from the senior national manager or a representative of the senior national manager of each of the departments participating in the program. These people

The remaining parts illustrate specific programs and measures used to improve and standardize the delivery of high-quality, factory-fresh Toyota vehicles to customers.[2]

Total Quality Control at Toyota?

To many people, the word "quality" is synonymous with the Toyota production and management systems and Toyota products. One would think that the Toyota organization would epitomize the application of total quality control (TQC). Perhaps so at Toyota Motor Company (TMC) in Japan, but total quality control is not formally practiced at Toyota Motor Sales (TMS) in the United States.

The lack of a TQC program does not mean that there is no continuous improvement, customer orientation, or concern for quality at Toyota Motor Sales. On the contrary, these are commonplace. But these elements alone are not TQC, particularly in the eyes of Toyota leaders. Adherence to precise definitions represents a central tenet of Toyota's managerial approach. In the case of total quality control, Toyota emphasizes the word "total," which means quality control applied to the *total* organization. It means setting superordinate goals for improving quality, cost, and scheduling. It also means auditing at every level to monitor progress toward these goals (Imai, 1986). At Toyota, total quality control either exists totally or not at all.

TQC has not been fully established at TMS because its leaders have decided to more fully prepare the organization and ensure appropriate timing for TQC. The roles of managers have to be clarified, and managers have to be prepared for the roles. Explaining Toyota's corporate philosophy, Shigeru Aoki, senior managing director at Toyota Motor Company, revealed that the roles of each functional (line) department in meeting quality, cost, and scheduling goals should be well defined (see Imai, 1986, pp. 128–131). As a prerequisite for total quality control, there must be "a clear understanding of the role of each manager in achieving the predetermined business result and improving the processes." (Imai, 1986, p. 143).

The Organization of Toyota Motor Sales

Toyota Motor Sales was established as a sales and service company. Over the years, it has grown into the structure depicted in Figure 1. It encompasses and oversees Toyota Motor Distributors (ten Toyota sales divisions and two private distributors; these divisions/distributors oversee 1,100 Toyota dealers), Lexus Division, Toyota Motor Credit Corporation and Toyota Motor Insurance Services (finance and insurance), Toyota Motor Manufacturing, CALTY Research and Design, and Information (Detroit, Ann Arbor, and Washington, D.C., offices). A New York office handles information and public relations, but it is owned by TMC in Japan.

Hiroshi Imai, group vice president, manufacturing liaison and distribution, describes this organization as "really messy." He states that "before we start TQC we are trying to streamline the organization . . . to revise it and reorganize it and separate our functions . . . to form four basic functions: production, sales, finance, and information. . . . As long as a sales company owns a finance company, an insurance company, and manufacturing, it is very difficult to implement total quality control. . . . No one knows who's doing what. What is more important here, we own 80 percent of the Kentucky plant; however, we don't have anybody here who has production background. So, as far as operation is concerned, TMC Japan is controlling it completely. Under these circum-

are referred to throughout the case. The author owes a particular debt of gratitude to two TMS executives, Hiroshi Imai, group vice president, manufacturing liaison and distribution, and Robert Bennett, vice president, Vehicle Processors, Inc. These two men graciously provided the access and assistance the author needed to complete this case study.
2. Please seek the rich meanings conveyed by the use of the word "standardize" throughout this case, and do not be put off by any preconceptions.

Figure 1

Organization of Toyota Motor Sales, U.S.A., Inc.

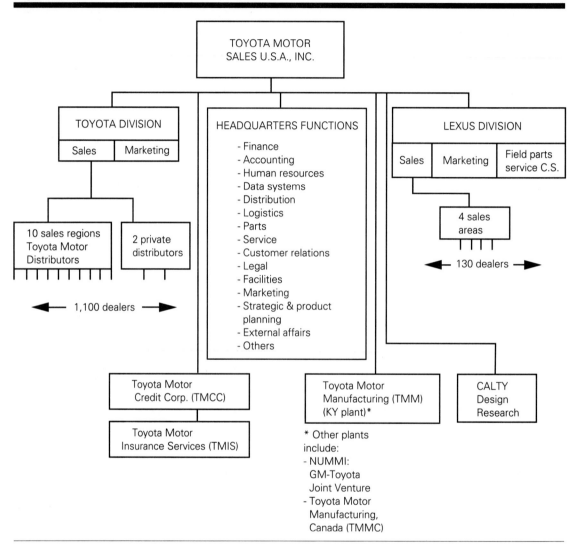

stances, TQC is a joke. . . . Once organization is clarified and once each one's job is defined, then it's easy."

Existing Cross-Functional Activity
While Toyota Motor Sales does not practice total quality control, it does have a number of cross-functional activities, some formal

and many others informal. Some of the formal cross-functional activities are briefly discussed below, including the board of general managers, chief engineer system, and improvement programs.

Board of General Managers (*Jomkai*) One of the formal cross-functional activities is a board, called *Jomkai*, which consists of about sixty members, each a general manager of a Toyota department. The board gets together every few months to set down company policies, address issues of research and development, finances, investments, and employment, and to discuss improvement programs. The top management at Toyota Motor Sales started *Jomkai* to address "communication problems" in the growing organization. As Hiroshi Imai explains, "Before Toyota became so big, we didn't have too many departments and general managers. They could have pretty free access to top management. They could always get together and work together. We did not have any communication breakdown. The company objectives were clear and the instructions were in many cases clear."

Chief Engineer Systems (*Shusa*) Another formal cross-functional activity at Toyota is the chief engineer system, called *Shusa*. In the *Shusa* system, a chief engineer assumes all responsibilities for the research, development, and engineering of one car model, e.g., Corolla, Camry, Celica, or Supra. The chief engineers report to an executive vice president in charge of all product development and engineering. The staff of the chief engineer act as coordinators to work with the various departments, such as body engineering, engine engineering, manufacturing, purchasing, and finance. They attend to mundane things like confirming the pricing of parts and making sure they fit together. And they make sure that everyone involved works as a team, working simultaneously, not sequentially. If a problem is found, they pull the appropriate team together, and solve it quickly. Each chief engineer has broad authority and a budget for making the car. Except for certain decisions which exceed prescribed limits, the chief engineer does not have to get decision approvals from his superior.

Improvement Programs Many other cross-functional activities fall into a category that

may be labeled "improvement programs." As Hiroshi Imai states, "TQC is great, but it's not a panacea. There are many other ways to improve the operation." Some of TMS's improvement programs are not formally sanctioned or monitored by top management. Some of the improvement initiatives are not cross-functional, but operate at the grass-roots level within departments. For example, many departments have established a program emphasizing the reduction of waste. Department personnel gather at a continental breakfast every few weeks to discuss ways to reduce waste. As another example, in the partners in productivity (PIP) program, each department submits solutions for improving the daily activities of the company.

Many cross-functional teams and collaborative efforts are autonomously established by managers at lower levels of the organization to address specific issues, problems, and opportunities. For example, a cross-functional team representing ten departments worked effectively for two years to implement a program to improve graphics (tape stripe) quality, saving $750,000 annually. Other improvement programs are formally sanctioned and monitored, and even led, by top management. Toyota's customer satisfaction committee is the best example.

The Delivery Quality Improvement Program Toyota Motor Sales' best example of pervasive cross-functional improvement is the delivery quality improvement (DQI) program. DQI is an outgrowth and component of Toyota's overall customer satisfaction committee activities. DQI spans the entire logistical supply chain, from production plants to the customer's garage, and commands employee attention, from the president down to the hourly worker. In fact, the delivery quality improvement program grew from the vision of executives at Toyota Motor Sales (TMS) in the United States and Toyota Motor Company (TMC) in Japan.

Despite the involvement of the highest levels of management, the implementation of improvement programs still presents many challenges, even at companies like Toyota. As Bob Bennett, vice president, Vehicle Processors, Inc., says, "You read about companies like Toyota and you think everybody is just standing there waiting to salute the next company-wide program that comes along, but the real-world facts are that they're not. Everybody doesn't agree that there is a problem with delivery quality. Everybody doesn't agree that they are part of the solution, even if they think there is a problem. They've got their own agendas, priorities, and views."

Despite western tendencies toward individualism, Toyota Motor Sales attempts to involve all relevant personnel in the cross-functional efforts to improve customer satisfaction, such as the delivery quality improvement program. The organizational culture that TMS leaders are building serves as the underlying force to involve all relevant personnel. The cultural imperative to continuously improve customer satisfaction arises from executive leadership and the customer satisfaction committee.

▶ THE CUSTOMER SATISFACTION COMMITTEE

Toyota executives lead the customer satisfaction committees at TMC and TMS. These committees help establish the link between Toyota's marketing strategy for customer satisfaction and the operational realities of the organization. Below, we discuss the development of the customer satisfaction committees, their structures, and their roles.

Development of the Customer Satisfaction Committee

One of Toyota's key indicators of its performance for customer satisfaction is "initial quality," or "the quality that's perceived by the customer in the first few months of ownership." The J. D. Power Initial Quality Survey provides feedback on initial quality to automobile producers, individual diagnostics, and comparisons to the competition. While most Toyota insiders held the impression that Toyota quality was high, Toyota was not ranked number one in customer satisfaction by J. D. Power. Indeed, Toyota had a lot of room for improvement.

In 1986, under the leadership of one of its Japanese senior vice presidents, TMS/USA made a "strong" proposal to TMC/Japan that Toyota should be ranked number one. The proposal implied that TMC should improve product quality in the plants to achieve that number one ranking. Since these issues had been brewing at TMC for a couple of years and the proposal from TMS/USA was compelling, TMC/Japan senior management was persuaded. In 1987 they began to pursue it fervently. The initiative to improve Toyota's standing to number one on J. D. Power's customer satisfaction ratings came to be referred to simply as "J1."

Establishment of TMC's Customer Satisfaction Committee

In late 1988, as they have done with other initiatives, TMC/Japan established a committee structure specifically to accomplish the J1 objective for customer satisfaction. It commanded the attention of the top managers. Shoichiro Toyoda himself chaired the customer satisfaction committee. Three subcommittees, product quality, domestic sales and service, and overseas sales and service, were established to address specific customer satisfaction issues.

Initial Effort to Improve Quality at TMC Japan

TMC's initial efforts for the J1 initiative concentrated on the work of the product quality subcommittee. They set some targets and initiated many improvements, and were 60 to

70 percent on the way toward achieving their targets when the incongruity between their "high" quality improvements and "lower" customer satisfaction ratings became obvious. TMC's product quality subcommittee relied heavily on TMS's voice-of-the-customer information, surveys of customers. TMC read the survey responses such as "door has a scratch on it," and "grease on the carpet," but their audits of the vehicles as they were leaving the plant or being loaded on the ship in Japan revealed no grease on the carpet and no scratches on the door. The damage must be occurring after the vehicles left Japan.

The J1 Boomerang In a few months, TMC executives returned to TMS with the message that product quality was improving, yet damaged vehicles continued to arrive at the dealerships. A TMC study team followed some shipments from the plant to the dealerships and discovered that the damage was indeed occurring after the vehicles left the plants in Japan, when the vehicles were the responsibility of TMS. TMC executives in Japan then reflected the "strong" proposal back to TMS that TMS itself should make some improvements for the J1 initiative.

It seems that the senior vice president who initiated J1 had the temerity (or the wisdom) to ignore the old saying, "People who live in glass houses should not throw stones." The stones now being thrown back at TMS were certainly for its own good. And TMS managers now recognize that fact. For example, regarding the boomerang effect of the J1 initiative, which came back to wrap itself around the necks of TMS managers, Bob Bennett says, "Isn't it wonderful?"

Initial Efforts to Improve Quality at TMS While the executives at TMC Japan were wrestling with the issues of product quality and customer satisfaction, as early as 1984 a small band of managers at TMS were doing the same. Even without authorization for resources, they initi-

ated efforts that would eventually serve as the preparatory work for the formal J1 challenge of 1989. They established a formal program defining standards for accessory installation processes and quality at ports of entry. Quarterly audits provided feedback and encouragement. They allowed dealership service managers to approve goodwill warranty adjustments on their own. As Bob Bennett explains, "Fortunately, these people had the foresight to have some things in place when the questions came our way. As a result of the progress we had made over the last three years, our operations were evaluated fairly well by TMC."

The TMS Customer Satisfaction Committee

TMC Japan had done their part to improve product quality. As Bob Bennett suggests, "The effort of TMC/Japan has been staggering. The senior-level managers are extremely disciplined. The way they accuse each other is ruthless at times. They demand a lot of themselves without spending a lot of money in many cases. They have put a lot of time, effort, and energy into making the product quality better. We asked for it and they did it." Now it was TMS's turn.

The J1 initiative captured the attention of TMS leaders in the United States. To lead and motivate TMS efforts to improve customer satisfaction, TMS executives established a customer satisfaction committee structure similar to that in Japan. Efforts to improve customer satisfaction were then taken up by a number of departments.

The customer satisfaction committee at TMS was established in May of 1989 to improve teamwork and communication between all departments by coordinating the development of company-wide satisfaction activities. The mission of the customer satisfaction committee can be summarized in the following chain of events:

1. To strengthen the dealer network, all TMS activities, and product quality

2. To become number one in customer satisfaction, with millions of satisfied customers and high brand image
3. To achieve and maintain a sales volume of 1.5 million annually by retaining former customers and attaining new ones[3]

Specifically, the customer satisfaction committee is responsible for ensuring the following functions are performed:

- *Collect* and analyze all customer information, making it readily accessible and actionable for each TMS department.
- *Communicate* the information through all available means (reports, presentations, special analyses) to every area of Toyota, providing data to support customer satisfaction programs in each area.
- *Coordinate* customer satisfaction efforts for all of TMS, aiding in the development, administration, and monitoring of customer satisfaction programs and policies.

As Richard Gallio, vice president, parts, service, and U.S. products, says of the customer satisfaction committee structure, "It takes the voice-of-the-customer data to tell us about product problems. Then we must analyze, prioritize, and channel it to the entity that can improve it."

The Committee Structure While committees are not so frequently used at TMS/USA, its committee structure is patterned after the ones so prevalent at TMC/Japan. The customer satisfaction committee at TMS is chaired by Bob McCurry, an executive V.P. (the second in command), who reports directly to the president of TMS, Yuki Togo.[4] Both men have expressed their commitment to customer satisfaction. For example, Yuki Togo recently stated, "Satisfying the customer is the most important thing we do. The customers we have are our best source of business for the future. Customer satisfaction has to be our number one priority." Bob McCurry says, "Customer satisfaction is the cornerstone of Toyota's business plan for the 1990s. It must be part of everything we do in order for us to be successful."

As shown in Figure 2, the customer satisfaction committee is composed of the subcommittee chairmen, Japan staff advisors, and a secretary. This committee structure is not permanent, but it has endured for over three years. While issues of customer satisfaction are likely to be paramount at Toyota for years to come, and TMS managers do not anticipate a change, the customer satisfaction committee may be replaced if Toyota priorities change. And just like anything else at Toyota, if it becomes ineffective or wasteful, it will be eliminated.

The customer satisfaction committee is driven by four major factors:

1. Input from the customer relations department provides the subcommittees with regular reports concerning customer satisfaction issues. These reports go beyond normal index and ranking information, and deal with specific issues that have been researched. The main goal is to give actionable information to the subcommittee that can be passed on to and be coordinated with the appropriate departments. In addition, customer relations also distributes information through a newsletter sent to all headquarters managers and field offices. A quarterly dealer newsletter gives customer satisfaction information to dealership staff.
2. Operational departments are involved. The customer satisfaction committee assigns ultimate responsibility for customer satisfaction to the operating departments to eliminate the misconception that customer

---

3. Toyota has subsequently lowered its sales objectives for the U.S. market.
4. In June 1992, TMS's new executive vice president, Yale Gieszl, assumed the chairmanship of the customer satisfaction committee.

Figure 2

Toyota Motor Sales customer satisfaction committee and subcommittees

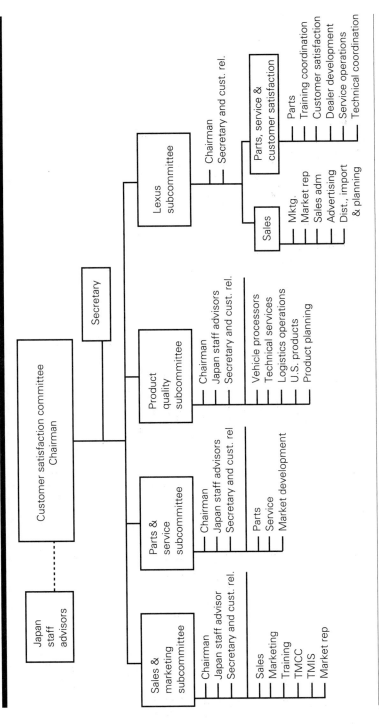

satisfaction is solely the responsibility of any one department, such as customer relations.

3. Monthly meetings of the customer satisfaction committee bring customer satisfaction issues before senior managers, often with recommendations for action. Each subcommittee reports on a quarterly basis to the president. The whole process has enhanced planning and promoted action for real progress. It also makes the appropriate departments accountable for utilizing the feedback TMS receives from customers.

4. Top management involvement ensures they benefit from this process, because it assures their understanding of the issues involved and provides a forum for discussion and support.

While the customer satisfaction committee promotes communication and continues to oversee the work of the subcommittees, the cross-functional work really gets done in the subcommittees. According to Richard Gallio, "These subcommittees have turned out to be relatively powerful in this company, as far as being able to get things done quickly." Many of the managers at TMS feel that once projects are formally established and authorized at the top level of management, after a lot of discussion and consensus building, then everybody feels obligated and committed to support them.[5]

The Subcommittees Each major operational area at TMS is represented in a subcommittee made up of members responsible for instituting improvements in customer satisfaction. These subcommittees include sales and mar-

keting, parts and service, product quality, and Lexus.[6] Each subcommittee has developed long-range plans which will contribute to the accomplishment of customer satisfaction goals. The following statements capture the substance of each subcommittee's goals.

Sales and Marketing To achieve industry-leading sales satisfaction, which will maximize initial customer satisfaction as well as capture additional repeat and conquest sales. To be number one on the Sales Satisfaction Index (SSI), an annual J. D. Power survey that measures satisfaction with the sales experience three months after purchase.

Parts and Service To achieve industry leadership in dealer after-sale customer handling and to establish a national reputation for quality and integrity in vehicle service. To be number one on the Customer Satisfaction Index (CSI), an annual J. D. Power survey that measures satisfaction with the service experience one year after purchase.

Product Quality To achieve both industry-leading product quality and product acceptance, which will maximize initial customer satisfaction as well as capture additional repeat and conquest sales. To be number one on the Initial Quality Survey (IQS), an annual J. D. Power survey that measures product quality three months after purchase. To be number one in product quality ranking by *Consumer Reports*.

Lexus To achieve unequalled customer satisfaction by placing the customer first and making certain that each Lexus's individual day-to-day performance is greater than the customer's expectations.

The Structure of the Subcommittees The subcommittees provide a forum for cross-

---

5. Members of the Japan staff feel that the commitment at TMS falls short of what they have experienced at TMC in Japan. One Japan staff person stated that at TMC in Japan when a subcommittee member goes back to his department that he's representing on the subcommittee, the staff of that department is at his command, as a resource that will support him in his role as a representative of that department.

6. Lexus is an independent division that sells and distributes vehicles, and its subcommittee interacts little with the other three subcommittees, which are more tightly aligned.

partment communications among top-level representatives from diverse operational departments and for coordinated actions to improve customer satisfaction. For example, the sales and marketing subcommittee is composed of representatives from sales, marketing, market representation (develops dealer network), TMIS (extended warranties), training, TMCC (credit), and fleet and used vehicles—all the corporate departments that directly interface with dealers. The composition of the subcommittees is fluid. At any time, the chairman can add or delete a departmental representative. For example, logistics and Vehicle Processors, Inc. (VPI), were added to the product quality subcommittee after delivery quality became a priority. Involvement of the operational departments is key to the success of the committee structure, since they bear the ultimate responsibility for customer satisfaction.

As with the customer satisfaction committee, each subcommittee has a set of Japan staff advisors who attend the subcommittee meetings and act as liaisons to Toyota Motor Company in Japan. Another key to the success of the committee structure is that each subcommittee is chaired by Toyota vice president level executives. For example, Al Wagner, the group vice president of sales, chairs the sales and marketing subcommittee. Specific people in the customer relations department provide data and information support, and a secretary coordinates and administers the activities of each subcommittee. For example, Bob Droch, national sales administration manager, acts as secretary for the sales and marketing subcommittee. All subcommittee chairmen, representatives, secretaries, and information support personnel are non-Japanese.

The executive leaders of the subcommittees are responsible for involving all affected departments in determining problems and developing action plans related to customer satisfaction. Their involvement secures support and commitment for programs that address customer satisfaction issues.

This subcommittee structure is not the organization of TMS, but a mechanism designed to overcome the separation of the various departments composing the subcommittees. It breaks down traditional barriers and allows for a free flow of communication to initiate effective customer satisfaction action plans. While there is not a great deal of formal cross-linking among the subcommittees, all three subcommittees have the common objective of making Toyota number one in customer satisfaction. Each is also involved in the delivery quality improvement program discussed in detail in Part IV. To formally build integration among the subcommittees, the subcommittee chairmen each sit in on the meetings of the other subcommittees. Further, the minutes of each subcommittee meeting are distributed to the members of all other subcommittees. Integration among the subcommittees is mostly achieved through informal means.

Information Flow through the Subcommittees The subcommittees play a major role in gathering, analyzing, reporting, and distributing actionable information that can be passed on to the appropriate departments. The subcommittee hears the customer's voice from a variety of sources, including: 1-800 phone calls, TMS survey data, external studies such as those conducted by J. D. Power and Associates and Maritz Marketing Research, and other surveys conducted by the TMS marketing research department. The customer relations department analyzes voice-of-the-customer data continually and feeds this to the customer satisfaction subcommittees through monthly reports, newsletters, and other communication. Each subcommittee has a coordinator from the customer relations department to provide this information and handle questions or data requests. The continuous flow of voice-of-the-customer information is another key to the success of the committee structure.

The subcommittees review the information and communicate it to the appropriate departments for action. This information and feedback on departmental actions are then funneled back through the subcommittee to executive management for review.[7] The customer satisfaction committee meets monthly and each subcommittee reports to president Togo on a rotating quarterly basis. This committee process ensures departmental accountability for customer satisfaction efforts. As one manager states, "If nothing else, the quarterly reporting requires that something gets done in that quarter." These reporting requirements represent another key to the success of the customer satisfaction committee structure.

Subcommittee Authority and Responsibility
Richard Gallio says of the focus of the subcommittees, "If you define the scope of responsibility too broadly, you will never get anything done." Thus, the mission of each subcommittee is narrowly defined to ensure they can function. For example, the sales and marketing subcommittee decided its mission was to improve sales satisfaction. Accordingly, it studies alternative methods to upgrade dealership facilities, improve sales professionalism, and upgrade delivery procedures, all without sacrificing sales volume.

Toyota has not restructured the company around work groups, or project teams, or any type of horizontal structure. However, the committee structure creates responsibility among the various departments to achieve objectives that are not solely affected by an individual department, somewhat parallel to Toyota's manufacturing quality management. This system denies each department, and each worker, the luxury of being able to send the problem on down to the next station and as-

sume that somewhere somebody will fix it at the end of the line. Similarly, each department on the subcommittees has some responsibility for achieving the objectives of the subcommittee.

It would be easy to get the wrong impression about the role of the committee structure. It may appear that the committee structure drives line objectives. By contrast, committee and subcommittee objectives are derived from the central objectives of the line organization, and not vice versa.[8] The committee structure ensures that the operational areas are aware of customer satisfaction problems and that they are responsible for resolving issues that fall in the normal scope of the department's objectives. The committee structure simply encourages collaboration among departments to meet line objectives that can't be met by departments working in isolation. Specifically, the subcommittees prioritize and integrate the individual actions of departments to meet objectives for being number one in customer satisfaction.

The committee structure is not designed to supplant management, but to supplement management. As Bob Daly, corporate service operations manager, puts it, "This committee system is not a substitute for good management. You have to have good managers."

The subcommittees establish their own specific plans for improving customer satisfaction, but they have no implementation power. Implementation of any action plan has to be initiated through the normal hierarchy of the organization. There are no resources in the committee to do anything other than evaluate voice-of-the-customer data, come up with a conclusion, get a consensus, and then decide on an action plan. The department managers are responsible for implementing specific actions, and they are responsible for the results.

Once a subcommittee determines a plan

---

7. The Lexus subcommittee will collect, analyze, and communicate its own information and will report concurrently with the TMS sales and marketing or parts and service subcommittee. The product quality subcommittee handles both Toyota and Lexus issues. Regional and private distributor committees establish their own schedule, but also report to executive management.

8. Basic goals of Toyota have to do with sales objectives and the aim to be number one in customer satisfaction.

for action, the department managers include those action items in their respective departmental annual plans. Subcommittee initiatives then become just a normal part of management activity, not a special program. When the subcommittee reconvenes, they review progress against objectives and make course adjustments for the implementation. As Bob Daly says, "This really means that the strategic decisions you've made to improve the company become internalized, a part of the root management structure of the organization. We like the way that works."

Regional/Private Distributor Customer Satisfaction Committees

In 1990, the customer satisfaction committee expanded with the establishment of the regional/private distributor customer satisfaction committees. The twelve groups that make up these committees are dedicated to solving problems and setting standards at the local level. As a top priority, they target high-volume, low-satisfaction dealers, contact them monthly, and urge them to follow specific customer satisfaction action plans. The regional/private distributor committee is chaired by the general manager in each field marketing area and consists of two subcommittees: sales and marketing, and parts and service. The regional/private distributor committees meet monthly and report to the customer satisfaction committee at the end of each quarter. Having these regional/private distributor committees has helped the region focus more on proactive customer satisfaction issues and less on reactive customer relations issues. Through the development of this committee, each area now focuses on target dealers, which they determine, in an effort to correct issues impacting customer satisfaction at the grass-roots level.

The committee structure is an important part of the cross-functional efforts directly aimed to improve customer satisfaction. However, it does not oversee all of Toyota's continuous improvement efforts. There are many other cross-functional project teams and departmental improvement projects not connected to the committee structure. The committee structure is just another mechanism to help make real the cultural imperative to be number one in customer satisfaction.

TMS managers are convinced that customer satisfaction will be critical in the 1990s. Over the long term, improving the processes that lead to customer satisfaction can ultimately lead to higher levels of sales. The customer relations department provides the committee members and operating managers with voice-of-the-customer data and reports about customer satisfaction issues, as discussed more thoroughly in Part II. Customer satisfaction drives continuous improvement at Toyota. The delivery quality improvement program, described more thoroughly in Part IV, represents another attempt by Toyota to improve customer satisfaction by making such process improvements. Initiatives such as the delivery quality improvement program and customer satisfaction measurement are important parts of the organizational culture at Toyota Motor Sales. This culture is more thoroughly discussed below, after a brief discussion of the delivery quality improvement program.

▶ THE DELIVERY QUALITY IMPROVEMENT PROGRAM

For the first few years following the establishment of the customer satisfaction committee, many efforts were made by individual departments to improve quality. However, by digging through the voice-of-the-customer data, TMS managers found motivation to redouble their efforts. Toyota managers observed a trend in the NVSDS survey data toward fewer defects

Figure 3

NVSDS survey data

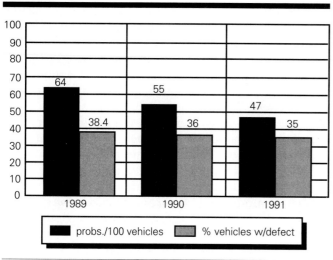

Data taken from like timeframe.

per 100 vehicles. Yet, while the overall number of defects was trending down, the number of vehicles being delivered to a customer with at least one defect was not trending down proportionately (see Figure 3). About one-third of the owners continued to get a vehicle with some defect.

Opinions varied among senior managers at TMC/Japan and TMS/USA on how to go about making improvements. Some felt that since the defects were trending down due to the efforts of many departments, there would eventually be no problem. Others felt it was a problem that needed serious attention, but that it was a product quality issue to be solved in the plants by TMC. Toyota managers wrestled with this data and issues of customer satisfaction for about nine months before concluding the problem needed a fresh approach.

The Delivery Quality Improvement Task Force

TMS had apparently addressed most of the obvious problems. They had done most of what could be done within individual departments. So they established a special task force in Feb-

ruary 1991 to get a broader cross-functional effort started to address the more intractable problems.[9] Their initial investigation revealed important opportunities throughout the delivery process, from the dealer's lot all the way back to production plants in Japan. Toyota managers decided to make small improvements in every area to integrate efforts and thereby noticeably impact customer satisfaction. The delivery quality task force split into two delivery quality working groups, each charged to formulate a comprehensive company-wide plan to improve vehicle delivery. One focused on the logistics through port processing and transportation. The other group focused on dealer involvement.

The issue of delivery quality became a top priority at TMS when it was formally addressed

---

9. TMS has neither a formal system of establishing task forces nor a sanctioning body. Any senior manager can establish or approve a task force to address special topics requiring cross-functional input or cooperation. However, they are used sparingly. Examples include a task force to build a unified owner database and a task force to coordinate the acquisition of a private distributor.

in the product quality subcommittee. With many senior managers present, the top two executives in TMS gave the mandate to the TMS vice presidents that they make it happen. All the operating departments that played a role in delivery quality were thereby drafted into the cause of improving delivery quality. Dave Zellers, the national product quality and compliance manager, accepted the responsibility to coordinate the delivery quality improvement program, or as Dave puts it, "To push it along."

With help from a full-time coordinator, Zellers scheduled meetings, kept records, and circulated memos. He had no authority to really make anything happen outside his own technical services department. But the delivery quality improvement task force, of which he was a member, did start to make things happen. This is when the cross-functional efforts intensified.

The Breakfast Club

The delivery quality improvement task force scheduled its meetings at seven in the morning. While the members worked through their agenda, they enjoyed coffee, juice, and rolls catered from the dining center. Over time, they referred to the task force as the Breakfast Club.

The Breakfast Club was regularly attended by representatives from each of the seven departments most intimately involved in the delivery quality program, including U.S. products, and the technical services, service operations, sales, logistics, vehicle processors, and customer relations departments. Managers from other areas attended periodically as needed to address particular issues. Each member of the Breakfast Club was also on one of the customer satisfaction subcommittees. So, Breakfast Club membership cut across the three subcommittees.

The executive mandate for delivery quality improvement came through the committee structure, and the subcommittees could estab-

lish directions and plans for improvement. However, implementation was done functionally or departmentally, as each manager devoted staff and resources to accomplish the cross-functional goals. Meeting each week, the Breakfast Club provided the coordination and frequent contacts needed to support the cross-functional efforts for delivery quality improvement. The Breakfast Club became the working group that made the delivery quality improvement program a reality.

Cross-Functionalism

While a great deal of the cross-functional efforts are handled through the Breakfast Club meetings, the vast majority of the communication and thinking takes place outside the walls of any conference room, through informal exchanges at the coffee machine, in halls and offices, at lunch. Rather than go up through the hierarchy or wait until the task force meets, people interact as needed, across departmental boundaries and hierarchial levels. Many of the Breakfast Club's solutions were informally developed in this manner and simply refined and approved in the weekly meetings. This informal communication pervades every level of TMS. As Dave Zellers says of two TMS vice presidents, "Richard Gallio can do more by sitting down and chatting with Al Wagner over a cup of coffee than he can by writing six memos. A lot of work gets done around here with a cup of coffee in your hand. And I don't think there is any substitute for that informal establishment of consensus."

The cross-functional mechanisms put in place by Toyota, such as the customer satisfaction committee structure, its task forces like the Breakfast Club, and informal communication networks and collaborations, are all intended to ensure teamwork for the achievement of common goals for customer satisfaction. And the information flow of voice-of-the-customer data, described in Part II, continuously gives motivation and direction for actions within those mechanisms. These features ensure that the organization is not just managed hierarchically. They also serve as the means of embedding and perpetuating Toyota's culture. Some of the key features of Toyota's culture are discussed below.

▶ THE TMS CULTURE

The following description of the culture at Toyota Motor Sales is not the product of a rigorous cultural analysis, but only some observations made by the author during the course of researching this case study. The description certainly does not apply to every person at Toyota. There is variation among areas and individuals with regard to cultural assumptions, beliefs, values, and practices. Remember that the description only lists the major tendencies observed by the author. In some cases, the description may depict ideals toward which TMS managers strive.

The following facets of culture are discussed: focus on the customer, the drive for continuous improvement, leadership and vision, responsibility, teamwork, cross-functional communication, open communication (visibility), and continuous learning. These facets of culture are interrelated, so the discussion of one may naturally flow into the other. The labels chosen for these facets of culture may seem to impose artificial barriers within the cultural description below. However, the labels are helpful in summarizing the many facets of the culture. The cultural description below uses the words of TMS's own managers as much as possible.

Focus on the Customer

Customers drive Toyota business practices primarily because managers perceive their roles to be focused on satisfying the customer. For example, Chick Ramsay states, "In my position, I take an active visible role of being interested in customers, customer satisfaction, constantly talking about it with our people, participating in meetings, and coming up with some innovative ways to approach customer satisfaction."

TMS managers realized that simple devo-

tion to customer satisfaction does not suffice. Being users of vehicles themselves, the people at Toyota could easily fall into the trap of assuming that they already know what customers value, that they are also experts who can decide whether the product is good enough to satisfy customers. However, Toyota managers do not just guess about what would satisfy customers. They go beyond their own understanding and try to confirm it with actual customers. They rely on facts, not just opinions. Perhaps being a user of vehicles helps them empathize with their customers better than managers in other industries, but as Minori Sasaki, senior executive coordinator, U.S. products and technical service, explains, "In order to improve, we have to fully understand the customers' perspective and how they use the product, and not how the engineer says it should be used. If you're going to make improvements, then you have to improve based upon what the customers say."

The survey system and other activities of the customer relations department indirectly provide facts and help to disseminate the customer voice throughout Toyota. However, Toyota managers display an uncompromising commitment to directly understanding the customer's actual use situation, an approach they call *genchi genbutsu*, which means "actual place, actual product," or more generally, "see it with your own eyes." A great deal of this hands-on learning is led by the chief engineers and their staff from TMC/Japan. They visit dealers, talk to service managers, salespeople, and customers. They get a first-hand assessment of how the new model has been accepted by customers as they're planning the next model.

Other study teams demonstrate the same

preference for *genchi genbutsu*. For example, since Toyotas are so popular, they have the dubious honor of being on the top-ten list of stolen cars. Since auto theft is not such a big problem in Japan, Toyota engineers came over to the United States for a theft awareness conference arranged by TMS to learn how to better design vehicles for theft deterrence. TMS had set up a week's worth of meetings: with staff from the National Automotive Theft Bureau (NATB), which tracks all stolen vehicles with the insurance industry; with convicted auto thieves who could demonstrate theft tools and techniques; with a Kentucky highway patrol officer who etched window glass on 80,000 high-risk vehicles. A long list of people were prepared to make presentations at the conference, but the conference format was unacceptable. The Toyota team from Japan insisted on visiting NATB in downtown Chicago, and the officer in Kentucky, and all the other experts in their own environments.

Toyota managers also realize that the pursuit of customer satisfaction must pervade the organization. They feel there must be no chinks in the armor, across levels and departments within the organization, and across time. As Bill deManincor, national port and transportation quality manager, explains: "It's not just what a single manager does here in the Toyota organization, it's what we all do from the very beginning to the very end. And the end doesn't arrive until the person stops buying Toyotas. We have to keep up that customer satisfaction to keep him coming back more and more. There's really not an end to it." Since "the global automotive environment has become increasingly more competitive," as Tatsuro Toyoda points out, keeping up customer satisfaction will require continuous improvement.

The Drive for Continuous Improvement

Part of what drives continuous improvement at Toyota is the high level of aspiration managers set. For example, Jane Baseda, national logistics planning manager, explains, "You need to set your sights very high and go for zero damage. That's what we're doing. You shouldn't be satisfied with a certain level of damage, but should always strive for more improvement."

Toyota doesn't expect to get to the top all at once. Rather, they continuously set and meet more challenging standards and goals that keep people motivated to improve. As Bob Bennett explains, "We're never satisfied with the current status. We get to a certain level, and say, 'Great, we've accomplished that. Now, how can we make it tougher next year?' We drain the swamp, identify some problems, solve them, and drain some more water out, and find some more rocks to clear out of the way."

Ironically, Toyota employees remain in a permanent state of dissatisfaction trying to achieve satisfaction for customers. As discussed in Parts III and IV, Toyota continuously improves through standardization. Employees continuously challenge existing standards, make changes for improvement, and then standardize the changes. They continuously seek to identify areas of weakness, while also raising their level of aspiration. Thus, Toyota's pursuit of perfection is indeed relentless.

People at Toyota freely pursue continuous improvement because, as Jane Baseda explains, "There is little fear of change here. Generally people welcome change because they see it as an improvement; they don't see it as threatening their job, their turf, or their personal career." Leaders determine this congenial atmosphere for change and continuous improvement with their words and actions.

Leadership and Vision

Richard Gallio suggests, "We get strong central direction from senior management." The leaders at Toyota provide direction for the organization by giving them "an overall goal, a common vision." The vision is to be number one in customer satisfaction.

The leaders at Toyota have not only established customer satisfaction as a top priority. They also created the type of organization that can continuously improve customer satisfaction. And the leadership starts at the very top of the organization. As Chick Ramsay says, "The key to success has been total management involvement from the top on down. Mr. Togo, our president, was very involved in customer satisfaction from day one. He formed committees that he would participate in and not just assign to the middle level of management. If he had not taken such an active role, the top American staff people would not have become nearly as cognizant of it. There is a total involvement here."

While top managers have led the charge, the rest of the organization has been integrated into the effort. As Joe Kane explains, "Success is achieved by top-down management. But it is also bottom-up, with people at lower levels participating in decision making and development of solutions" Leaders have not shunned their responsibility to lead by establishing vision, exemplifying commitment with their actions, and providing resources for others to fulfill their responsibilities to realize the vision. According to Minori Sasaki, "In TMS, we have many resources, compared to TMC. If we ask for some money to improve something and it is justified, we get it. So it is not very difficult to improve."

Bill deManincor elaborates on the kind of empowerment this context of leadership provides for followers: "I'm allowed to do what I know is right. If I need to do something and it's the right thing to do for Toyota, I have the resources and I have no hesitation. As managers, we usually let our people tell us how they can accomplish the goals. If they start out in the wrong direction, of course, we'd change the direction. But there is no need for us to dictate to people how they do their jobs. No two people will accomplish the same goal the same way."

Responsibility

There are several dimensions of responsibility to consider. There appears to be a strong sense of personal responsibility among Toyota managers for individual contribution to broader systems or organizational purposes. Bob Daly summarizes this sense of responsibility when he reiterates a basic Toyota production principle, "We don't send the vehicle on to the next stage if it isn't right." For managers, this sense of responsibility also means that managers do whatever is necessary to get the job done, either working within the systems or working on the systems of the organization themselves. As Bill deManincor explains, "Sometimes I am a worker and sometimes I am a manager. I choose to be a worker when the people I supervise are stretched to their limits and something needs to be done. As a manager, I'm a motivator, and my job is to find areas that need to be improved and provide that assistance. Part of my job or my responsibility to them is to give them the tools they need."

While managers feel a strong sense of personal responsibility, they are reluctant to ascribe personal blame for mistakes and failures. As Bill deManincor explains, "When someone doesn't perform, the first assumption isn't that it's their fault, but rather that the manager failed to provide them something. I truly believe if something doesn't happen, it's because somewhere along the line a member of management didn't fulfill their entire duty. You have to throw away the idea that it's somebody's fault. If it's nobody's fault, then everybody can work at fixing it. We overlap a lot in our work, and that requires us to stand up and say, 'That's my part, let me do my part.' "

The managers at TMS seem to strike a balance between personal and team responsibility, with individuals prepared to assume personal responsibility, yet reluctant to cast blame on others. Dave Zellers explains, "It's something of a blending of cultures. The Japanese have a lot of concern about establishing consensus and they are very concerned about face saving. For Americans, at least the way we typically approach business, I think most of us take the approach that when you make a mistake the best thing you can do is raise your hand and say, 'I made a mistake. I'll do my best to fix it. I'm sorry, boss,' and accept the consequences. The Japanese don't do that. They make the group responsible. That's part of this culture of establishing consensus. There's not necessarily a repression of the mistakes, but there is a repression of pinning it on an individual."[10] This balance of personal and team responsibility allows Toyota managers to avoid the classical diffusion of responsibility so common to groups.

Teamwork

Managers' sense of personal and group responsibility at Toyota help establish effective teamwork across hierarchical levels and departments. The sense of responsibility that managers have for building effective systems leads them to select people who will fit into Toyota's approach, that is, team players. Furthermore, employees are viewed as valuable assets and are treated as such. As Jane Baseda observes, "A manager's number one job is training and development of people, so you see a tremendous amount of that. Vice presidents, like Mr. Imai, walk around and talk to employees several levels below them, like David Broskow on our planning staff. They know them by name and provide day-by-day guidance, direction, and training." Coupled with managers' sense of responsibility to provide subordinates with systems, this personal attention helps to build trust among the levels of managers and a basis for vertical teamwork.

This vertical teamwork sets the stage for

horizontal teamwork, which is readily evident at Toyota. As Richard Gallio states, "There is a pervasive spirit of teamwork. While we all have our own agendas and goals, we still help other departments solve problems that we'll get no credit for." Bill deManincor explains the balance between individual and global objectives: "There are cases where you definitely have to take care of your objectives and someone else has to wait. That's the way life is. But overall, I think we all look at things globally, what's good for Toyota. It is a global atmosphere. My section has goals and objectives, and I'm going to do my best to accomplish these. But I will never hinder anyone from accomplishing theirs. I might not be in a position to help them, but I'll never hinder their progress. If you're one that stands out and fails to cooperate or you'll do anything to accomplish your objectives with no regard for the next person, your rating will be adversely affected. It matters how you meet your objectives in relation to the rest of the people."

Teamwork at Toyota is built upon a foundation of human relationships informally built among the members. Dave Zellers offers an example of the concern that managers have for human relationships: "An issue came up with respect to delivery quality. Although there had been some agreement, it was apparently forgotten. It became a very adversarial situation for a while, and one of my managers was pushing it harder than he should have. He wanted me to step in, with my grade level and my clout, and pull the reins back and get control of it for him. And I basically stalled the issue. I decided that it wasn't that important. I did not need to go cause an explosion somewhere. I let it cool down for about three or four weeks and when I felt the time was right, I went to the other person, got consensus, and it moved forward. You can approach it adversarially and write all the memos you want. But you have to establish how important something really is versus maintaining the quality of the relationships in the organization. In this

---

10. This depiction stands in contrast to the stories I've been told of TMC/Japan managers becoming accusatory and holding one another strictly accountable for failure to live up to responsibilities or achieve objectives. Perhaps the reluctance to cast blame is shed when peers, at the same hierarchical level, seek to impose discipline upon themselves as a working group to meet Toyota's challenging objectives. As Minori Sasaki hints, "We do not communicate enough here at TMS. In Japan, we accuse one another more freely. To accuse may seem bad, but this is a good meaning."

case, I viewed the relationship as more important because it will lead to further cooperation and advancement in the future. Informal management is key in the organization. A lot depends on personal relationships."

The committees and task forces help foster cross-functional teamwork at Toyota. But, as Bob Daly warns, these mechanisms must be managed carefully to avoid undermining the relationships that are the foundation of teamwork. He explains, "We try to let the organization be flexible enough to absorb the new entity and not threaten the existing structure. We use the new entity as a channel for communication, for consensus building, for encouragement, but don't try to screw up the reporting relationships. And then, when success is achieved, when we hit a major milestone in customer satisfaction, it's very important that the people who work in the departments to make it happen understand that they really did it. It wasn't just something that the customer satisfaction committee did."

Dave Zellers explains how Toyota tempers individualism to ensure teamwork in a society where most of us have been taught to push for personal achievement: "There's an old Japanese proverb that says the nail that sticks up will be hammered down. The Japanese system would rather recruit people who are either average or maybe a little above average because they're the easiest ones to mold into the cultural philosophy. For them, the superstars, fast track, hard runners tend to get out too far in front. They don't take enough time to pull the organization along with consensus. At TMS, we have lots of stand-out performers. But the way we manage those hard-chargers in this organization is always with reflection back to the Japanese philosophy of establishing consensus."

Bob Bennett elaborates on the importance of consensus: "You can't try to sell something as your program that you came up with individually. It has to be everybody's idea. You have

to make the other people heroes. You have to be humble. You have to give credit, even to people who deserve less credit. If you don't have a broad base of consensus, you don't get the multifunctional cooperation that's necessary to have something really work right."

Cross-Functional Communication

When cross-functional change is planned, the consensus process gets informally initiated rather early in the planning process. Most participants have at least heard the issues and probably given input prior to ever entering a formal meeting. Most proposals get developed and discussed so thoroughly among the involved departments that consensus forms informally prior to the meeting. Jane Baseda illustrates this cross-functional communication: "I had a conversation with the chairman of a transportation company a few months ago. He described a meeting they were about to have where all the top executives would be locked in a room to hash out a problem and not come out until it was resolved. At the same time, I had just gone through a decision process here at Toyota where I took our proposal around to about seven or eight different departments and discussed it with each staff. They in turn discussed it with their vice president or whatever level had to be involved in the decision. By the time we got to the meeting, everybody knew what the answer was going to be. There were absolutely no surprises. There was a minimum amount of discussion. Everybody understood perfectly what was going on and agreed."[11]

Toyota employees learn this approach to decision making informally. When a rookie manager proposes something to a veteran who

---

11. While many people only recognize the emphasis that the Japanese place on consensus, as one TMS manager suggests, "The Japanese are very level conscious. Their approach can be very authoritarian, with not much questioning about what top management ultimately decide."

knows the Toyota approach, the veteran asks the rookie to discuss it with certain others. Somebody always asks the rookie, "Have you talked to everybody involved?" Veterans may even ask veterans this question.

Top managers establish Toyota's emphasis on communication by setting the standard themselves. For example, as Bob Daly describes it, "In addition to regular meetings, there is a lot of informal communication. One of the things Yuki [Toyota's president] has brought to the company is the coffee meeting. Monday, Wednesday, and Friday mornings, the vice presidents and corporate managers all have coffee together for fifteen minutes. It's an opportunity to just walk up to one another and mention something or ask a question or arrange a meeting or ask, 'Hey, what is going on in such and such?' "

Toyota managers spend a lot of time in various types of meetings. Chick Ramsay suggests the costs and the benefits: "Sometimes we get frustrated that we're in meetings constantly, but at least it keeps communication lines open. It eliminates a lot of dead time trying to get things approved, or wondering what so-and-so thinks and how they will react. We get answers a lot quicker than going through the chains of command."[12]

Open Communication (Visibility)

In one regard, TMS seems to have the kind of open communication needed for continuous improvement, namely, through making problems visible. Jane Baseda summarizes it: "We have free communication of our problems. We don't hide or bury problems. The best managers are viewed as those who bring their problems to the surface and deal with them openly

rather than those who bury them and try to make it look like everything is perfect. Our chairman has said, 'Don't bring me your successes, because you can take care of those just fine. Bring me your problems, because those are the ones you need me for.' That attitude pervades the company."

However, TMS needs to improve visibility in other areas. For example, Minori Sasaki explains, "At TMS, managers do not set targets and demand that progress be made toward targets and schedule as much as in Japan. We need to make these more visible for everyone, so other people understand they are doing well or not compared to the standard. Then if the standard is not good, we can change the standard. But we have to follow the standard."

Continuous Learning

As mentioned earlier, TMC managers and engineers are inclined to learn from first-hand experience. TMS managers outside the plants increasingly take this approach. As Bob Bennett suggests, "If there is a quality problem, you don't have somebody just describe it to you with words. You go out and test drive the car, you get the actual parts. If there is a problem on the production line, they don't talk about it in the conference room or the office, they go out to the site on the plant floor and personally look at it, evaluate it, talk with the line workers, inspect the parts and the machinery, and look at the drawings, look at the standardized work procedure, and confirm that everything is being done the way it should be. They fully grasp the problem before they run off and solve the wrong problem. Quite often, it's a multifunctional approach."

Toyota devotes much time, energy, and money to study teams, which exist at all levels of Toyota, in production plants and in corporate departments. The composition of the teams varies according to the nature of the issue, including chief engineers, leading specialists, manufacturing liaisons, production

---

12. While TMS managers are becoming more like TMC managers, there are still differences. As Minori Sasaki suggests, "At TMS, we're less disciplined than TMC managers in the way we run our meetings. There is less control over the time and budget, and people tend to get off the agenda."

personnel, or suppliers, as needed. For example, an eight-person team of engineers from TMC and Panasonic came to Kansas City, Missouri, for several weeks each of two successive years to learn how to improve radio reception for Toyota customers. Along with some TMS personnel, they drove around Kansas City testing radio signal performance under actual broadcast conditions. At one point, they went on a 250-mile side trip to Kirksville, Missouri, because the team discovered interference from a Hughes Aircraft radar factory that would cause the radio to momentarily lose the signal. The engineers wanted to experience it and measure it themselves. They eventually used that particular area to test improved electronic components. Such study teams take a hands-on approach (*genchi genbutsu*) to get the facts, to see what really happens under actual operating conditions with the actual product.

Not only do Toyota managers emphasize learning as a means of making immediate improvements, they emphasize lifelong learning for individuals. Chick Ramsay states, "In this company, it's not unusual to go from one area to another, sales to logistics, or from service to sales. In other companies, you come up in one separate operation and you stay in it. So your focus is narrow. At Toyota, you move around a lot and that's good. You get a much clearer understanding of the whole business."

TMC in Japan emphasizes a type of organizational learning that TMS needs to apply to its operations. As Minori Sasaki suggests, "If we do something at TMC/Japan, like complete a project, we meet with all the key people and summarize what we learned. We keep this summary and use it for the next project." Bob Bennett elaborates: "This is a form of Deming's Plan-Do-Check-Act (PDCA) concept. The benefit for TMC is that there is a conscious building on previous know-how, and mistakes are not repeated very frequently."

As suggested earlier, TMS managers continuously learn Toyota culture by participating in it. Bob Bennett suggests, "There is extensive on-the-job training here. People come in and it just happens. If those of us at TMS who work with the Japan staff spend enough years here, we get indoctrinated automatically. Twelve years ago, when I was responsible for service merchandising, we wanted to develop a new incentive program for the dealership service departments to get them to promote more service. We couldn't get consensus with the Japan staff on the new program until we evaluated the old program and reported what worked and what didn't work. They referred to it as PDCA."

The Standardization of Culture

The culture at TMS is being put in place and developed through a variety of means. Some of these are described below. The most pervasive means is the informal contact and on-the-job enculturation that TMS managers get with Toyota veterans and the Japan staff on a daily basis. TMS managers learn the Toyota management approach by practicing it daily under the guidance of cultured veterans. Another obvious means of standardizing the Toyota culture is the participation in the committee structure, task forces, and working groups. These horizontally oriented mechanisms serve as overlays added to the vertically oriented hierarchy to ensure that TMS managers serve broader purposes, such as customer satisfaction. Finally, the most potent force for the standardization of culture appears to be that leaders lead by example. They establish a vision of the organizational purpose and the means of fulfilling that purpose. Then they follow through with their commitments by taking actions to make their vision real.

The phrase "standardization of culture" implies some known standard or definition of what the culture ought to be. Although TMS leaders appear to have a vision of the culture they are in the process of patiently developing at TMS, TMS leaders do not inflexibly pursue a set cultural standard. Rather than transplant TMC/Japan's culture to the U.S., they continuously improve their vision for TMS culture as they unfold it. This flexible unfolding of culture is consistent with their approach to management. As they discover opportunities to incorporate uniquely western elements of culture, to achieve synergies between western and Japanese approaches, or to make any type of improvement in the TMS culture, they are likely to do so. After all, continuous improvement is a key facet of the culture being standardized at TMS.

▶ **DISCUSSION QUESTIONS**

1. What components of total quality are in place and what components are missing at Toyota Motor Sales, U.S.A.? Under these circumstances, what would you do to implement total quality control at Toyota?

2. Describe the culture of TMS by listing its key values and beliefs.

3. How does TMS balance the values of individualism and teamwork?

4. Describe how Toyota is standardizing a culture at TMS. Provide examples.

5. How does Toyota's culture help it overcome the common problems of a functional structure?

Toyota, Part II: Customer Satisfaction Measurement*

▶ THE CUSTOMER RELATIONS DEPARTMENT

In 1984, TMS began putting together programs that would ultimately result in a comprehensive customer satisfaction system to gather "voice of the customer" information and communicate it throughout the organization. TMS managers were convinced that the best way to ensure customer satisfaction was to develop a sophisticated information flow for accurate and timely customer feedback. Such information would enable managers to quickly identify and correct any product deficiencies. That same year, TMS formed the customer relations department to manage the information flow and maintain good relations with Toyota customers. In 1985, customer relations managers were appointed for each of its twelve regional/private distributors, to promote and administer customer relations at the 1,250 Toyota and Lexus dealerships.

Corporate customer relations managers develop and administer the information systems. Their primary tools are surveys, a toll-free 800 number, and an arbitration system. Of these three, the surveys provide the most useful information for making improvements in direct response to customer feedback to

achieve Toyota's cultural imperative for customer satisfaction. The surveys convey the voice of the customer to Toyota managers and act as a wind that stokes the cultural fires. This part of the Toyota case discusses each of these information systems, with a main focus on Toyota's use of customer satisfaction surveys.

The 800 Number

The national 800 number receives an average of 1,200 calls per day at the Toyota customer assistance center. It yields some useful information for making improvements, but most calls from customers are inquiries or requests, not specific complaints. When a legitimate complaint is received through the 800 number, it is forwarded immediately into the field through the on-line computer system. The dealer concerned receives the message and is required to contact and respond to the customer within two days and to resolve the problem in fifteen days.

The Arbitration System

For those customers who find no satisfaction through the dealership or the 800 number, the arbitration system, administered by AAA Auto Club, provides recourse. The customer

* This case was prepared by Greg Bounds.

may submit a complaint to AAA, which inspects the situation and renders a decision that is binding for Toyota, but not for the customer, who may choose legal action if still unsatisfied.

The Customer Surveys

Since an incidence of arbitration signifies failure, Toyota would like to prevent the circumstances of customer dissatisfaction which lead to arbitration. To prevent dissatisfaction and ensure satisfaction, Toyota relies heavily on the customer surveys administered by the customer relations department. After all, satisfying customers means more than simply reacting to customer complaints. Rather, Toyota pursues a more proactive approach in order to address customer needs preventively. They hope to identify causes of problems, prevent their recurrence, and even head off problems before customers ever perceive them. To implement this approach, managers need meaningful and actionable information. The customer surveys provide part of this information.

In addition to the J. D. Power surveys, Toyota expends vast resources conducting its own surveys. Since 1984, when a customer purchases a Toyota vehicle he or she receives a new vehicle sales and delivery survey (NVSDS) within 10–45 days (see Figure 1). The NVSDS asks the customer about purchase and delivery experiences, the quality of vehicle components, and customer intentions to recommend the dealer, return to the dealer for service, and purchase another Toyota vehicle. Since 1986, TMS has sent out the Toyota service survey (TSS) to ask the customer about warranty service from the dealership (see Figure 2).[1]

During the survey process, Toyota captures the other key pieces of information: customer name and address; vehicle identification number; salesperson that dealt with the customer;

retail date or repair date; and vehicle production date. By analyzing this specific information, Toyota can achieve better insights into real causes of customer dissatisfaction. Dealers can examine specific problems regarding salespeople, using the dates when customers were dissatisfied, and manufacturing plants can relate specific mechanical problems to manufacturing date. As John McLaughlin, national customer administration manager, says, "The survey system is really the backbone of everything we do when it comes to the customer satisfaction committee. It's our primary tool." It appears that most Toyota managers share McLaughlin's sentiments. For example, Joe Kane, national export manager, states, "We really value the NVSDS and J. D. Power surveys quite a bit. If those surveys aren't working successfully, we've got a problem."

Before the survey system was put in place, Toyota had to rely on dealers reporting problems and complaints, a much slower and less reliable approach. Very few customers would, of their own accord, contact a dealer to give such detailed feedback as that gathered through surveys. And if customers did give such feedback, dealers did not always pass it on to TMS. By contrast, the survey system drives the voice of the customer throughout the organization.

Survey Participation

TMS receives over 500,000 customer surveys a year. The rates of customer participation are relatively high, 55 percent for NVSDS and 42 percent for TSS, perhaps for the following reasons. First, the surveys are fairly simple. Second, the purchase of a new vehicle represents the second highest expenditure for most people, after a home, and leads to a high level of emotional involvement. Finally, the dealers prepare customers for the survey at the dealership and follow up by calling customers at home before and after they receive the survey.[2]

---

1. Collecting data only from customers who make warranty claims ensures that dealers do not try to manipulate the data in their favor by listing bogus customers who would return falsified surveys. Dealers have to provide correct information to get reimbursed for repairs covered by warranty.

2. While customers may not realize it, the survey results are very important to the salespeople. Some dealers use survey results to determine bonus and pay schemes.

Figure 1

⊕ TOYOTA

**NEW VEHICLE
SALES AND DELIVERY SURVEY**

YOUR TELEPHONE NO.

HOME ____/____/____

WORK ____/____/____

Please mark the response boxes with an X only.

X Correct Mark

THANK YOU FOR PURCHASING A

SAMPLE   SAMPLE   SAMPLE

Did you purchase your vehicle at this dealership?   Yes ☒ No ⟶ If no, please return survey in the envelope provided.

Was the vehicle you were previously driving a Toyota?   Yes ☒ No

DEALERSHIP EVALUATION

YOUR PURCHASE EXPERIENCE

1. When you purchased your new Toyota, how satisfied were you with the performance of the dealer's sales staff on EACH of the following items?

	Very Satisfied	Somewhat Satisfied	Neither Satisfied Nor Dissatisfied	Somewhat Dissatisfied	Very Dissatisfied
Courtesy and friendliness	☒	☒	☒	☒	☒
Knowledge of Toyota products	☒	☒	☒	☒	☒
Professionalism	☒	☒	☒	☒	☒
Fulfillment to commitments made during sale	☒	☒	☒	☒	☒
Overall handling of sale by salesperson	☒	☒	☒	☒	☒

YOUR DELIVERY EXPERIENCE

2. At the time of delivery, did someone at the dealership . . .

	Yes	No	Don't Know
Explain the vehicle service maintenance schedule	☒	☒	☒
Explain the new vehicle warranty	☒	☒	☒
Provide information about the dealership's service and parts departments (such as hours open, appointments, etc.)	☒	☒	☒
Offer to demonstrate vehicle features and controls	☒	☒	☒
Give you a copy of the New Vehicle Delivery Checksheet	☒	☒	☒

3. How satisfied were you with the condition of your new Toyota at the time of delivery on EACH of the following items?

	Very Satisfied	Somewhat Satisfied	Neither Satisfied Nor Dissatisfied	Somewhat Dissatisfied	Very Dissatisfied
Cleanliness of the exterior	☒	☒	☒	☒	☒
Cleanliness of the interior	☒	☒	☒	☒	☒

DEALERSHIP CONTACT AFTER THE SALE

4. Did your salesperson or a dealership representative follow up by contacting you after delivery about your satisfaction with your overall sales experience?

In person	By phone	In writing	Response card from dealership	No contact
			☒	☒

YOUR OVERALL EXPERIENCE

5. Would you recommend this dealer to a friend as a place to buy a new vehicle?

Definitely Recommend	Probably Recommend	Might or Might Not Recommend	Probably Not Recommend	Definitely Not Recommend
		☒		

Please explain why: _____

01/93

Figure 1 (Continued)

6a. If for any reason you had to service your Toyota, do you think you would have it serviced at this dealer?

Definitely	Probably	Might or might not	Probably not	Definitely not

6b. If for any reason you had to replace your Toyota, do you think you would buy another Toyota?

Definitely	Probably	Might or might not	Probably not	Definitely not

PRODUCT EVALUATION

ABOUT YOUR NEW TOYOTA

7. Did you have any problems with your new Toyota at the time of delivery? ☐ Yes ☐ No

8. Please identify any component problems you experienced with your new Toyota.

MECHANICAL FEATURES	Specify condition within space provided next to component	INTERIOR FEATURES	Specify condition within space provided next to component
Engine (pistons, valves, radiator, lubrication, etc.)		**Interior trim** (carpets, console, upholstery, etc.)	
Engine electrical (starter, charging, ignition, etc.)		**Seats** (seatbelts, trim, etc.)	
Fuel system (carburetor, injection, emissions, etc.)		**Air conditioning/heater** (controls, compressor, hoses, etc.)	
Automatic transmission (shifting, smoothness, operation)		**Audio system** (radio, tape deck, CD, speakers, antenna, etc.)	
Manual transmission (clutch, shift levers, etc.)		**Interior switches** (light, wipers, turn signals, etc.)	
Driveline (differential, axles, etc.)		**Instrument panel** (fuel, speedometer, temperature, tach, etc.)	
Steering (wheel, linkage, alignment, etc.)		**Accessories** (cruise control, clock, etc.)	
Suspension (springs, shocks, wheels, tires, etc.)			
Brakes (rotors, drums, pedals, etc.)		**GENERAL**	

EXTERIOR FEATURES		**Water leaks** (specify location)	
		Wind noise (specify location)	
Body fit (doors, fenders, bumpers, etc.)			
Paint finish (appearance, chips, scratches, etc.)		**Squeaks/Rattles** (specify location)	
Windows (door, side, windshield, etc.)		**Other** (specify location)	
Exterior trim (mouldings, mirrors, stripe, etc.)			

If you need additional assistance with your vehicle, please contact your dealership's Customer Relations Manager or the Toyota Customer Assistance Center at 1-800-331-4331.

9. If your dealership arranged for the vehicle financing, service agreement or insurance, how satisfied were you with the treatment you received?

Very Satisfied	Somewhat Satisfied	Neither Satisfied Nor Dissatisfied	Somewhat Dissatisfied	Very Dissatisfied

10. Have you contacted the Customer Assistance Center (toll-free 800-331-4331) regarding this recent visit? ☐ Yes ☐ No

OVERALL COMMENTS

Please complete this section **only** if the name, address, phone number or social security no. shown on the front is incorrect.

TITLE   SOCIAL SECURITY/CUSTOMER REFERENCE   AREA CODE   HOME PHONE   AREA CODE   WORK PHONE   EXTENSION

FIRST NAME (PRIMARY DRIVER)   M.I.   LAST NAME (PRIMARY DRIVER)

STREET ADDRESS

Please return the completed survey directly to
Toyota Motor Sales U.S.A., Inc.,
Minneapolis, MN 55439 in the enclosed envelope.
Get more from life . . . Buckle up!

CITY   STATE   ZIP

MM92970:65

Figure 2

⊕ TOYOTA

YOUR TELEPHONE NO.

HOME _____ / _____ / _____

WORK _____ / _____ / _____

SERVICE SURVEY

THANK YOU FOR SERVICING YOUR

Please mark the response boxes with an X only.

X   Correct Mark

SAMPLE   SAMPLE   SAMPLE

Did you have your vehicle serviced at this dealership?
☒ Yes   ☒ No ⟶ If no, please return survey in the envelope provided.

DEALERSHIP EVALUATION

YOUR SERVICE EXPERIENCE

1. How satisfied were you with this Toyota dealership for each of the following service attributes?

	Very Satisfied	Somewhat Satisfied	Neither Satisfied Nor Dissatisfied	Somewhat Dissatisfied	Very Dissatisfied
Ease of getting an appointment	☒	☒	☒	☒	☒
Proper diagnosis of your service needs	☒	☒	☒	☒	☒
Overall performance of the service advisor (person who wrote the repair order)	☒	☒	☒	☒	☒
Courtesy and friendliness shown by service personnel	☒	☒	☒	☒	☒
Clear explanation of the work performed	☒	☒	☒	☒	☒
Getting the work done on time	☒	☒	☒	☒	☒
Commitment to seeing that the job is done right	☒	☒	☒	☒	☒
Willingness to stand behind or guarantee the work	☒	☒	☒	☒	☒
Appearance of the service department and customer lounge	☒	☒	☒	☒	☒
Effort of the dealership to provide parts for your vehicle **Parts Not Needed** ☒	☒	☒	☒	☒	☒

DEALERSHIP CONTACT AFTER THE SERVICE

2. Did a dealership representative follow up by contacting you after the service visit about your satisfaction with the service performed?

In person	By phone	In writing	Response card from dealership	No contact

YOUR OVERALL EXPERIENCE

3. Would you recommend this dealer to a friend as a place to have a Toyota serviced?

Definitely Recommend	Probably Recommend	Might or Might Not Recommend	Probably Not Recommend	Definitely Not Recommend
☒	☒	☒	☒	☒

Please explain why: _____

Figure 2 (Continued)

4. If for any reason you had to replace your Toyota, do you think you would buy from this dealer?

Definitely	Probably	Might or might not	Probably not	Definitely not

5. If for any reason you had to replace your Toyota, do you think you would buy another Toyota?

Definitely	Probably	Might or might not	Probably not	Definitely not

PRODUCT EVALUATION

6. How many visits were required to correct the condition(s) you were experiencing? (Please write the number of repair visits in the box on the right corresponding to the components/conditions involved.)

MECHANICAL FEATURES	NUMBER OF VISITS Condition not yet fixed	Specify condition within space provided next to component	INTERIOR FEATURES	NUMBER OF VISITS Condition not yet fixed	Specify condition within space provided next to component
Engine (pistons, valves, radiator, lubrication, etc.)			**Interior trim** (carpets, console, upholstery, etc.)		
Engine electrical (starter, charging, ignition, etc.)			**Seats** (seatbelts, trim, etc.)		
Fuel (carburetor, injection, emissions, etc.)			**Air conditioning/heater** (controls, compressor, hoses, etc.)		
Automatic transmission (shifting, smoothness, operation)			**Audio system** (radio, tape deck, speakers, antenna, etc.)		
Manual transmission (clutch, shift levers, etc.)			**Interior switches** (light, wipers, turn signals, etc.)		
Driveline (differential, axles, etc.)			**Instrument panel** (fuel, speedometer, temperature, tach, etc.)		
Steering (wheel, linkage, alignment, etc.)			**Accessories** (cruise control, clock, etc.)		
Suspension (springs, shocks, wheels, tires, etc.)			**GENERAL**		
Brakes (rotors, drums, pedals, etc.)			**Water leaks** (specify location)		
EXTERIOR FEATURES **Body fit** (doors, fenders, bumpers, etc.)			**Wind noise** (specify location)		
Paint finish (appearance, chips, scratches, etc.)			**Squeaks/Rattles** (specify location)		
Windows (door, side, windshield, etc.)			**Other** (specify location)		
Exterior trim (mouldings, mirrors, stripe, etc.)					

If you need additional assistance with your vehicle, please contact your dealership's Customer Relations Manager or the Toyota Customer Assistance Center at 1-800-331-4331.

6a. If more than one (1) visit was required, was it due to:
Condition not repaired correctly   Dealer did not have parts   Audio Re-installation   Don't know

7. For this service visit, how long did it take the dealer to correct the condition(s)?
Same Day   Next Day   3 Days   4-7 Days   More Than 1 Week

8. For this service visit, did the dealer have all the needed parts?
No parts required   Dealer had all needed parts   Dealer had to order parts (please respond to 8a.)

8a. If dealer had to order parts, how many days did you wait before you were advised that the parts were available?

9. Have you contacted the Customer Assistance Center (toll-free 800-331-4331) regarding this recent service visit?   Yes   No

OVERALL COMMENTS

Please complete this section only if the name, address, phone number or social security no. shown on the front is incorrect.

TITLE   SOCIAL SECURITY/CUSTOMER REFERENCE   AREA CODE   HOME PHONE   AREA CODE   WORK PHONE   EXTENSION

FIRST NAME (PRIMARY DRIVER)   M.I.   LAST NAME (PRIMARY DRIVER)

STREET ADDRESS

Please return the completed survey directly to Toyota Motor Sales U.S.A., Inc., Minneapolis, MN 55439 in the enclosed envelope.
Get more from life ... Buckle up!

CITY   STATE   ZIP

MM92976:054

It sometimes takes several months for all surveys to be returned to TMS. Some customers respond in a few days, others in a few months. This variation in response times from customers complicates the data analysis. The customer relations department has to decide whether to analyze monthly data according to the date the surveys were received at TMS or according to the date of the retail sale.

Any decision involves a trade-off between time delay and uniformity. For example, TMS may have to wait until March or even April to receive, analyze, and report on the surveys from the January retail sales. By contrast, analysis and reports done in the month of January for all surveys received in January are available quickly, but they may contain data from the foregoing three or four months of retail sales. This lack of uniformity in date of retail sales can make it difficult to correlate customer satisfaction data with the causes of customer satisfaction, that is, the current events in the plants, logistical systems, or dealerships. No matter how they cut the data, however, the high response rates provide TMS with a tremendous amount of customer-voice information, which the customer relations department makes available through the indexes and reports discussed below.

Customer Satisfaction Indexes

The customer relations department computes several indexes by averaging survey responses. Figure 3 shows the computation procedures for the following indexes:

1. *New Vehicle Sales and Delivery Survey (NVSDS) Index* This index measures the customer's feelings about the sales process and delivery experience. Because it tracks a salesperson's performance, many dealers want this information before they will hire new salespeople, and the dealership can also use this as a valuable counseling tool.
2. *Toyota Service Survey (TSS) Index* This index measures the customers' feelings about

their service experience. Dealers again have the flexibility to check service writer or service manager index scores in their personnel management.

3. *Owner Satisfaction Index (OSI)* This is an overall measurement of the dealership based on the "would recommend" questions from both surveys. This index is intended to measure customers' feelings toward the entire dealership and often includes feelings not measured in the NVSDS or TSS index. It is used most often in major incentive programs throughout Toyota.

4. *Delivery Quality Index (DQI)* Initiated in 1991, the DQI measures the defects observed by the customer after taking delivery of the vehicle. Toyota made a major effort in the last year to focus on delivery quality to ensure that all vehicles are delivered defect-free. This index allows Toyota to measure dealerships on their ability to succeed in this area.

TMS managers monitor these indexes over time to determine whether they are making progress toward their goals for improved customer satisfaction. For example, the sales and marketing subcommittee tracks the NVSDS index monthly. As shown in Figures 4 and 5, the NVSDS and OSI indexes have risen steadily since 1986.

Survey Routing Procedures

The customer relations department compiles all NVSDS and TSS surveys returned to Toyota, analyzes the data, and generates various reports and indexes, which they feed back to departments, subcommittees, and dealers according to their needs for information (see the survey routing procedures in Figure 6). Feedback may be given monthly, weekly, or even daily through the on-line computer system which links all dealers to regional and national headquarters.

Figure 3

NVSDS and TSS Question Scoring

Each question will be scored as follows and weighted by the number of responses:

Response Point Values

	100	80	50	20	0
5-Part Response	Very Satisfied	Somewhat Satisfied	Neither Satisfied Nor Dissatisfied	Somewhat Dissatisfied	Very Dissatisfied
3-Part Response	Yes				No
Dealer Follow-Up	Any Contact				No Contact

If a "Don't Know" response or No Response is given, the question is excluded from the survey index calculation.

NVSDS/TSS Qualifications:
• If the "Would Recommend" question and at least one other scored question (see calculation) are responded to, the entire survey is valid.
• If the "Would Recommend" question is NOT responded to, more than 50% of the scored questions must be answered for survey to be valid.

Index Calculation

$$\text{NVSDS} = \frac{\text{Total Value of the First 13 Questions}}{\text{\# Answered Questions}}$$

$$\text{TSS} = \frac{\text{Total Value of the First 11 Questions}}{\text{\# Answered Questions}}$$

$$\text{OSI} = \frac{\text{"Would Recommend" NVSDS} + \text{TSS}}{2}$$

$$\text{DQI} = \text{Percent of "No" Responses Answered for Question \#7 on the NVSDS}$$

Major Recognition Awards Customer Satisfaction Performance

Award	Description
Toyota Touch President's Award	OSI must be above certain levels depending on sales volume, or area (whichever is greater).
Board of Governors	Meeting regional or national average on OSI, whichever is lower.
Master Sales Society	NVSDS at regional average calender year-end.
Sales Society	NVSDS at regional average calender year-end.
President's Parts and Service Advisory Board	Toyota Service Survey score used as a factor of overall performance.
Toyota Touch Service Award	Toyota Service Survey score must rank within the top range of all the Region/Private Distributors' TSS scores.
Customer Satisfaction Guild	ASM TSS score must be at a minimum level.
Toyota Touch Parts Award	TSS Parts Satisfaction and Parts Availability must be at pre-established objective levels.
CR Manager Incentive Program	OSI must be above certain levels depending on sales volume.

Figure 4

New Vehicle Sales and Delivery Survey Index: month to date – receipt date

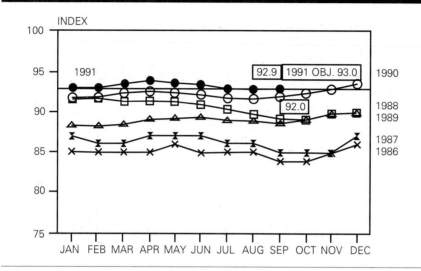

1986-1991 Report #14097.

Figure 5

Owner Satisfaction Index: month to date – receipt date

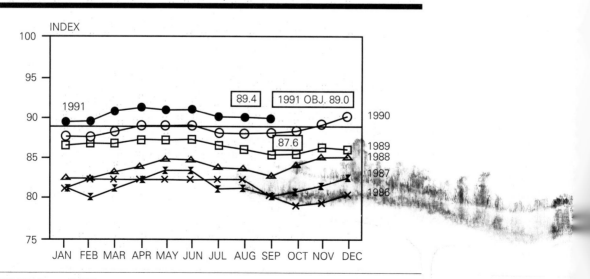

1986-1991 Report #14097.

Figure 6

Toyota customer relations survey routing procedures

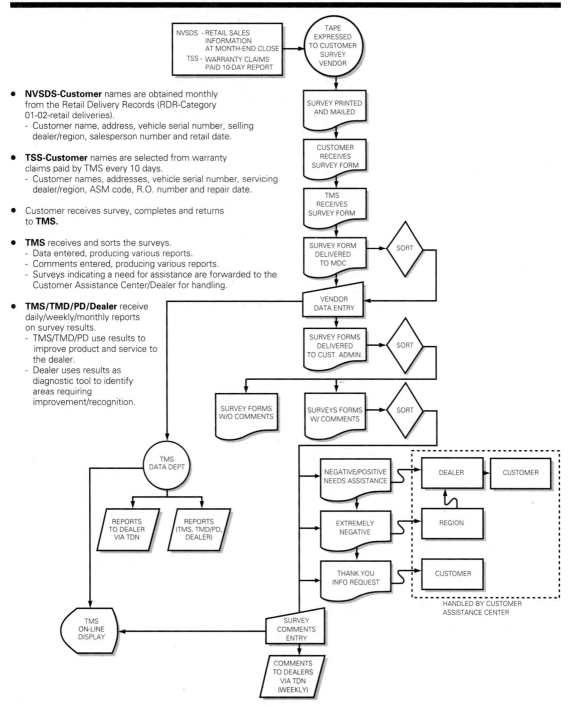

Analyzing Dealer Performance

A delivery quality report on all the dealers in the region is sent to the regional customer satisfaction committee. The report lists the one-month, three-month, and year-to-date figures for each dealer's delivery quality index, number of surveys returned, number of surveys with problems, total number of problems, number of problems per 100 vehicles, in-stock warranty claims, and first sixty days warranty claims. Regional managers use the reports to identify "problem" dealers that need special attention. The dealers can then be approached with concrete data on their performance rather than opinions from Toyota headquarters. The NVSDS and TSS reports on dealers and salespeople provide more details, including original comments from customers, to help dealers identify specific problem areas.

In addition to tracking the NVSDS, TSS, delivery quality, and overall satisfaction indexes for Toyota as a whole, the customer relations department breaks the data into analyses by regions and private distributors, with diagnostic information on each component. The regional/private distributor reports identify the top- and bottom-ranked dealers, and record an action plan and update on progress. These reports are sent to the regional customer satisfaction committees, which are responsible for developing action plans to improve regional performance.[3] The plans always target low-performing, high-volume dealers for extra attention. District sales managers will spend more time with these dealers to help them improve. Targeted dealers may even be called before the regional customer satisfaction committee to discuss the data, apparent problems, and action plans for improvement. Outstanding regional and dealership perfor-

mance in customer satisfaction is recognized with various awards (described in Figure 3).

General Customer Satisfaction Reports

The customer relations department conducts a vast array of analyses of the survey data and prepares many detailed reports for the customer satisfaction committee, subcommittees, departments, regional offices, and dealers.[4] For example, from the product evaluation section of NVSDS and TSS, they key into the computer every customer comment, conduct a content analysis of the comments, and generate condition codes to describe the problems that customers experienced with each product component. From this data, for each vehicle model, they generate a matrix of component codes and condition codes with the frequency of occurrence for each cell in the matrix (see Figure 7). For example, component code 35 is brakes, and condition code N means a noise problem (the matrix indicates there were 175 complaints about brake noise).

These data matrices are sent monthly to production plants for analysis. A quick look at the matrix reveals the major problems. For better understanding of the problems, analysts can then refer to the specific customer comments for each cell in the matrix in a companion report compiled by the customer relations department. The customer relations department serves as the antenna that receives the "voice of the customer." Therefore, the major objective is to effectively communicate this information through the company. The customer satisfaction committee is a major part of that effort.

While the people in the customer relations department are in a position to really "hit people over the head" with all this information and "demand" improvements, they play a more supportive role. John McLaughlin explains, "It

---

3. The regional customer satisfaction committees are led by the general manager of the region, with a secretary and customer relations manager as support. Similar to the TMS committee structure, the regions also have subcommittees with field personnel as members.

4. These reports may exhibit data on a national basis, as well as very specifically, for example, on an individual salesperson basis.

Figure 7

New Vehicle Sales and Delivery Survey, customer comment volume for one Toyota model through October 19, 1991, by component and condition codes

Component codes	condition codes																			
	A	B	C	D	E	F	G	H	J	K	L	N	P	Q	S	U	V	W	Z	Total
10	3	4		33		11	3	41		5	6	78	159		24	6	5			378
11	3	2			20	15	7	2	1	18		3	5	2		12				90
13	1		1	1	1	3	9		1	1		3	3	3		3				30
16	1	1	35	13			3		5	2	4	7	1	1	6	6	1			86
18		3							2		7		7			1				20
19		1					2					1		1		7				12
21	2			2	6	7	6		1	4	2	6	4							40
22	12	2			185	27	20	4	19	3	1	106	23	1	1	11	6			421
24												5				2	1			8
31	47	1	1	12	13	1	22		2			135	51	1		5	16			307
32	34	2					1		1			55	45			1				140
35	7	1			1	3	6		14	5	1	175	30			5	4			253
36	27	25					27		24		27	98	5	9	1	7	1		1	254
40	108	50			1		59		144	3	7	34	1	202		13	2		3	628
41	49	13			106	21	26		36	61	32	112	44	11		17	2		3	530
42	3								2		2	4					2			13
43	37	27			23	16	219		28	34		60	60	5		5		1		515
44	119	71			2	1	169		108	2	2	167	1	58	3	16	12		3	734
46	83	45			10	13	18		17	2	47	138	5	2		7	3		1	391
47	881	1					1							7		6			52	948
48	54																			54
51	11	8			4	6	24		19	63	24	120	256	5	7	27	2	1		577
52	19	12			5	17	83		21	139	1	53	341	29		40	8	2		771
53	25	9				3	13		6	18	2	37	63			14	2			193
54	11	10			1	2	89		6	501	1	26	84	116		71	2			920
55	1						22			8		4	18			5		36		100
56	4	1					35		2	22		2	8	3		10				86
60	20	2					41		74	1			1	6	2	5				150
65	16	1																		21
70																			1	1
99	3	1		1	2	1	13		5	1	21	553	3	3	57	2	15			681
TOTAL	1,581	293	37	63	380	153	920	47	538	893	187	1,982	1,218	465	101	304	84	40	66	9,352

would not be a team effort if we tried to force customer satisfaction through the company. Through the committee process, we feed information to the subcommittees, and it is their job to ensure the operational areas are taking action. This process makes customer satisfaction a natural part of the corporate culture and avoids the stigma that it is something extra the departments have to focus on. Our ultimate goal is to make customer satisfaction a natural part of each operational area's business plan. That can only happen if all departments operate as a team."

Specific Customer Satisfaction Reports

In addition to the general reports, the customer relations department reports on special topics. For example, they conduct specific analyses to learn more about the impact of customer satisfaction on the bottom line. They also delve into the causes of customer satisfaction, for example, the impact of salesperson turnover on customer satisfaction.

These special reports not only motivate managers by showing them the costs of dissatisfaction and the benefits of satisfaction, they also produce actionable information to help them set priorities and develop action plans to make Toyota number one in customer satisfaction. As John McLaughlin explains, "We do not just tell everybody how wonderful we are, because we're not going to get anywhere just doing that. Quite frankly, we're not wonderful in a lot of areas, and if we don't look at those areas, we're not going to fix them. So, we try to focus on the warts, because by looking at those and fixing them, you get better. . . . These special reports offer real data that managers can use to activate their departments to set up programs and make improvements."

Database Linkages In 1990, the customer relations department linked a variety of customer databases to conduct more in-depth special studies. For example, respondents from the NVSDS database were linked to the J. D. Power and Associates early buyer database by

vehicle identification number (VIN), permitting examination of previously unavailable data. Other database links, such as those listed below, enhanced their capability to provide pertinent information to all subcommittees:

- NVSDS and TSS ratings for same vehicle/owner
- Multiple TSS for same vehicle/owner
- Product problems, number of service visits, and product loyalty information
- Warranty data and TSS ratings
- Customer comments from the customer assistance center 800 number, and NVSDS and TSS survey data (link of qualitative to quantitative data)

An example of the special studies done based on these databases is discussed below, namely, the relationship between sales and service in the ownership experience.

Report on the Ownership Experience Sales and service work in tandem to provide the kind of rapport with customers that ensures future sales. By matching results from NVSDS and TSS surveys, the customer relations department studied how the customer's experiences in sales and service work alone and together to influence the ownership experience. The results shown in Figure 8 and listed below suggest that the sales experience sets the tone for service satisfaction and all other subsequent dealership contact.

(1) A majority of customers have a positive sales experience.

(2) Those with a positive sales experience (90 percent) are more likely to have a positive service experience (90 percent).

(3) Those with a negative sales experience (4 percent) are less likely to have a positive service experience (70 percent).

(4 and 5) A positive sales experience ensures a higher percentage of service business (78 percent) than does a negative sales experience (59 percent).

The relationship between the sales and

Figure 8

The ownership experience

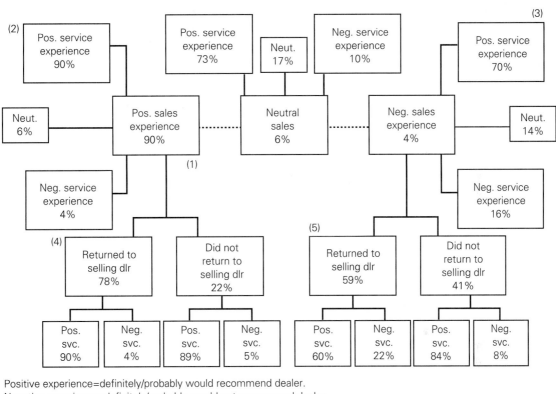

Positive experience=definitely/probably would recommend dealer.
Negative experience=definitely/probably would not recommend dealer.

1989-1991 NVSDS/TSS match.

service experience may be explained by perceptions of the customers, i.e., a customer with a bad sales experience may be predisposed to perceive the service as bad. Alternatively, dealers that give customers bad sales experiences may be more predisposed to also give them bad service experiences. In fact, Toyota has discovered that dealers with high customer satisfaction ratings tend to be those with good processes in place.

Further study revealed the importance of having in place both sales and service processes that ensure that a customer satisfaction philosophy permeates the entire dealership organization. Specifically, while satisfaction or dissat-

isfaction with any phase of the ownership experience will impact both dealer and product loyalty, the service experience, being the most recent dealership contact, has the most impact. The results shown in Figure 9 and listed below reveal the magnitude of the impact of the service experience on both dealer loyalty and product loyalty.[5] The loyalty of

5. The measure of dealer and product loyalty was the customer's stated intention to repurchase, and not actual repeat sales. Since TMS databases do not capture social security numbers, once a customer sells the Toyota vehicle, contact with him or her is lost. So these data come from a biased sample, which ignores those customers who may have had a bad experience and never returned.

Figure 9

The ownership experience (based on customers giving positive or negative responses on NVSDS and TSS surveys and returning to selling dealer for service)

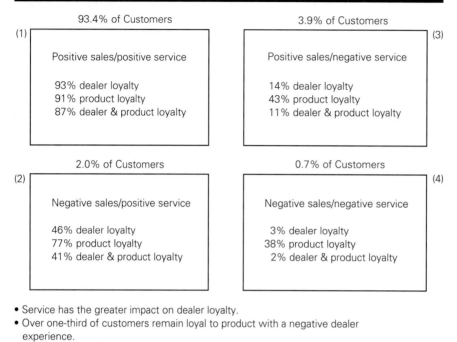

93.4% of Customers

(1)
Positive sales/positive service

93% dealer loyalty
91% product loyalty
87% dealer & product loyalty

3.9% of Customers

(3)
Positive sales/negative service

14% dealer loyalty
43% product loyalty
11% dealer & product loyalty

2.0% of Customers

(2)
Negative sales/positive service

46% dealer loyalty
77% product loyalty
41% dealer & product loyalty

0.7% of Customers

(4)
Negative sales/negative service

3% dealer loyalty
38% product loyalty
2% dealer & product loyalty

- Service has the greater impact on dealer loyalty.
- Over one-third of customers remain loyal to product with a negative dealer experience.
- Those not returning to the selling dealer (not shown here) have the same product loyalty levels based on positive or negative service.

Report #SM91008 1989-1991 NVSDS/TSS match.

those who returned to the selling dealer for service falls into one of four categories:

- Happy with sales, happy with service
- Unhappy with sales, happy with service
- Happy with sales, unhappy with service
- Unhappy with sales, unhappy with service

The majority of Toyota customers (93 percent) fall into the first category. However, the other categories, while small in percentage, represent a lot of people when projected to total sales. Toyota has opportunity for improvement, and good reason to improve because of the impact of the ownership experience on

loyalty. Toyota drew the following conclusions from these data:

- Those happy with the ownership experience have the highest loyalty overall (93 percent dealer loyal, 91 percent product loyal).
- An unhappy sales experience causes dealer loyalty to drop to 46 percent even though the service experience was happy. Product loyalty is not affected as much.
- An unhappy service experience has the biggest impact on loyalty even after a happy sales experience, with dealer loyalty dropping to 14 percent, and product

Figure 10

Product and dealer loyalty

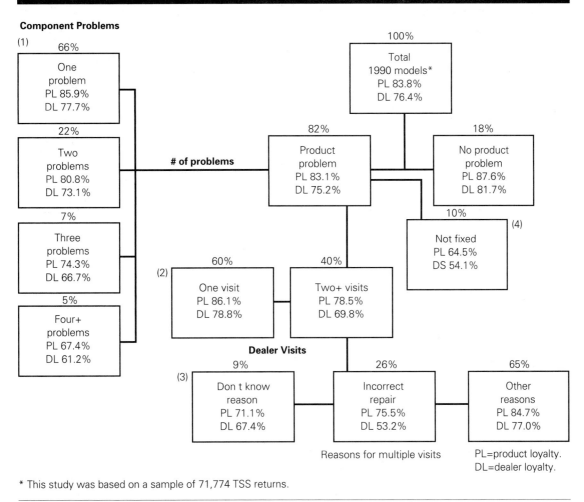

Component Problems

(1)

66%
One problem
PL 85.9%
DL 77.7%

22%
Two problems
PL 80.8%
DL 73.1%

7%
Three problems
PL 74.3%
DL 66.7%

5%
Four+ problems
PL 67.4%
DL 61.2%

# of problems

100%
Total
1990 models*
PL 83.8%
DL 76.4%

82%
Product problem
PL 83.1%
DL 75.2%

18%
No product problem
PL 87.6%
DL 81.7%

10%   (4)
Not fixed
PL 64.5%
DS 54.1%

(2)

60%
One visit
PL 86.1%
DL 78.8%

40%
Two+ visits
PL 78.5%
DL 69.8%

Dealer Visits

(3)

9%
Don t know reason
PL 71.1%
DL 67.4%

26%
Incorrect repair
PL 75.5%
DL 53.2%

65%
Other reasons
PL 84.7%
DL 77.0%

Reasons for multiple visits

PL=product loyalty.
DL=dealer loyalty.

* This study was based on a sample of 71,774 TSS returns.

1/90-7/91 returned TSS surveys for 90 Toyota models.

loyalty dropping to 43 percent. This indicates that the most recent experience can lose or win a customer for the next sale.

- A negative ownership experience makes dealer loyalty almost nil (3 percent) while product loyalty is intact for over one-third of Toyota customers (38 percent). This indicates that customers will

tend to blame the dealership, not the product, for problems, and that Toyota has a very loyal following.

To further explore the factors impacting product loyalty, information was taken from the Toyota service survey (TSS) for 1989 model-year Toyotas. As shown in Figure 10, product loyalty was measured for each of the following categories: product problem vs. no product problem; number of component problems; number of visits required to fix problem; reasons for multiple visits; and problem not fixed. The number above the box is the percentage of 1989 respondents in the category, while the number in the box is the product loyalty score (out of a maximum of 100). These results indicate the importance of avoiding component problems and quickly fixing those that do occur.

This chart shows the overall picture of the percentage of customers that are dealer and product loyal at each stage of repair activities. As you can see, the less effort required to fix a problem, the higher the loyalty figures. More specific conclusions include the following:

Number of Problems
- Of all those with a product problem on the TSS, over half had just one problem. Over one-third had more than one problem with their vehicle.
- Product and dealer loyalty are high at 85.9 and 77.7 percent, respectively, with one problem. This drops to 67.4 and 61.2 percent with four or more problems.

Number of Visits
- The more visits required to fix the problem, the lower the loyalty figures. Nearly half of all Toyota TSS customers had to return more than once to fix a problem with their vehicle. This has a great impact, with product loyalty declining from 86.1 to 78.5 percent and dealer loyalty declining from 78.8 to 69.8 percent.

Reason for the Return Visit
- This is where communication is, again, an issue. Nearly 10 percent of all customers who had to return again for service did not know the reason they had to return. This group's product loyalty is the lowest of any of the other reasons given.

- Those that had to return due to (perceived) incorrect repair felt the worst about their dealership, with loyalty declining to 53.2 percent, the lowest seen for any scenario on this chart. This is one reason that "job done right" is so highly correlated to the "would recommend" score. Customers clearly blame the dealership for the problem, not the vehicle.

Problem Not Fixed
- When a "problem not fixed" box is marked on the back of the TSS, product loyalty is at the lowest level (64.5 percent). Dealer loyalty is also low, at 54.1 percent.

The results of these studies reveal that while a company like Toyota Motor Sales may place great emphasis on setting and meeting sales objectives, as they have always done, there are other important ways to measure market success, namely, customer satisfaction.

Implications of Customer Satisfaction for Toyota and Its Dealers   Satisfied Toyota customers are a key marketing advantage. Not only are they a source of repeat sales, but the positive word of mouth they spread can be instrumental in attracting new Toyota customers and boosting brand image. Dealers know that it takes a lot of advertising money just to get potential customers through the door—industry-wide about $300 per new vehicle sold. So once customers come through the door, they should not be mishandled. Listed below are some of the potential paybacks that Toyota believes it will get for an investment in customer satisfaction:

Increased Product and Dealer Loyalty   A satisfied sales customer is more likely to return to the dealership for service, and more likely to buy a Toyota the next time from the dealer. Further, repeat customers tend to award higher ratings for the subsequent service and sales visits. A commonly held belief in marketing is that it costs five times as much to obtain a new customer as to retain an existing one. Clearly, increased loyalty not only means greater and more cost-effective sales and service business, but also higher satisfaction ratings in the bargain.

Lower Advertising Expenses Positive word of mouth is more credible, more targeted toward serious shoppers, and less expensive than traditional advertising. Further, research has shown that word of mouth has twice the impact as corporate advertising on customer purchase decisions (GE and Whirlpool, "The Information Challenge," 1983).

Improved Image A philosophy of customer satisfaction, carried out through policies and procedures at all levels of the Toyota organization, shows that Toyota and its dealers stand behind their products and services, and facilitates consumer trust in the Toyota name.

Conversely, dissatisfied customers can damage the Toyota name and cause otherwise interested consumers to consider other nameplates and/or turn to other dealerships. Dissatisfied customers can hurt the bottom line not only through negative word-of-mouth advertising, but also through loss of repeat sales, and loss of service business. One estimate by the customer relations department suggests that an unsatisfactory sales experience for just one in twenty customers of a medium-size dealership (750 units sold/year) could cost that dealership an alarming $46,930 a year in sales revenue alone (38 units lost × $1,235 gross profit per unit). This figure does not include lost revenue from negative word of mouth and lost service business. The real loss must be much greater.

Comparative Analysis of Top and Bottom NVSDS Dealers

The customer relations department at Toyota conducted a study that compared top and bot-

tom dealers.[6] The dealers were grouped based on their NVSDS performance. To ensure the two groups of dealerships were comparable, the groups included equal numbers of small-, medium-, and large-volume dealerships. Financial and diagnostic analyses were performed and overall customer satisfaction indexes examined. The results are summarized below.

Financial Analysis The business management department provided additional insight into the financial status of these two groups with the data shown in Figure 11, which specifically reveals the following:

- The overall net profit for the top dealers is almost one and one-half times as much as the bottom NVSDS dealers.
- Net profit as a percentage of total sales for the top dealers is 80 percent above that of the bottom dealers.
- Net profit per employee is 67 percent higher for the top dealers when compared to the per employee contribution of bottom dealers.
- Salesperson turnover at the bottom NVSDS dealers occurs at close to twice the rate experienced by the top dealers.

It appears that strong customer satisfaction performance, as represented by the top dealerships, not only benefits the Toyota customer, but also the Toyota dealer. Top dealers are in a stronger financial position than the bottom dealers. According to some of the characteristics of the top dealers, practicing good customer service techniques goes hand in hand with other positive aspects of running a successful business.

Diagnostic Analysis It is not surprising that the top NVSDS dealers consistently receive higher marks by their customers on all of the

---

6. The following information was taken from a bimonthly report by Tom Gauer and Vanessa Platis of the customer relations department.

Figure 11

Financial analysis of top and bottom dealers

	Top NVSDS dealers	Bottom NVSDS dealers	Difference
Net profit	$102,158	$69,693	$32,465
Net profit: % of total sale	1.61%	.89%	.72%
Net profit: per employee	$1,761	$1,056	$705
New vehicle selling expense: % of total new vehicle sales	4.72%	5.09%	.37%
Net profit: % gross profit	12.12%	6.97%	5.15%
Salesperson turnover	23.6%	41.2%	17.6%
Advertising	$79,032	$112,858	$33,826

diagnostic measures than do the bottom dealers. The interesting aspect of the discrepancy in their scores is to see the measures for which the differences in performance are the greatest. Diagnostic measures from NVSDS are presented in Figure 12. The areas where the bottom NVSDS dealers need to place the most emphasis are in the thoroughness and consistency of performing the various delivery activities.

The leading difference between the top and bottom NVSDS dealers is seen in the important procedure of follow-up with customers after the sale. Other delivery activities that are being neglected by the bottom dealers include providing copies of the new vehicle delivery check sheet, providing information about the dealership's service and parts departments, and explaining the new vehicle service maintenance schedule to the customer. On the average, the bottom NVSDS dealers score approximately ten points less than the top dealers on all of the delivery activities diagnostics. Although not as dramatic a difference as with the other delivery activities, offering to demon-

strate the vehicle features and explaining the warranty are also less likely to occur at the lower-performing dealerships.

Following the delivery activities noted above, the bottom NVSDS dealers also score considerably lower than the top performers on some of the more subjective salesperson diagnostics. The biggest discrepancy in this area is found in the salespersons' fulfillment of commitments made during the sale, followed by their overall handling of the sale and their professionalism. Although customers do not rate them significantly lower, the bottom NVSDS dealerships also score below the top-performing dealers on the salesperson skills in the areas of Toyota product knowledge as well as courtesy and friendliness.

Overall Indexes While being number one in customer satisfaction is a primary objective of Toyota Motor Sales, the lack of a "customer first" philosophy at the dealer level has a much more negative impact on the dealer himself than it does on Toyota. For example, one of the interesting things about the differences in

Figure 12
NVSDS diagnostics

Diagnostics	Top NVSDS dealers	Bottom NVSDS dealers	Difference
Follow-up	96.0	83.6	12.4
Check sheet	97.4	86.1	11.3
Service dept. info.	97.8	86.8	11.0
Exp'd. maintenance	98.4	88.0	10.4
Commitments	97.0	89.5	7.5
Demo. features	98.8	92.3	6.5
Overall handling	97.7	91.5	6.2
Professionalism	97.8	91.9	5.9
Exp'd. warranty	99.4	93.5	5.6
Staff knowledge	98.0	93.2	4.8
Staff courtesy	98.9	95.4	3.5
Clean exterior	98.6	95.2	3.4
Clean interior	98.4	95.2	3.2

BOLD type represents delivery activities.
PLAIN type represents salesperson skills.
ITALIC type represents pre-delivery activities.

diagnostic scores between the top and bottom NVSDS dealerships is that customers are much more likely to hold the dealers accountable for their lack of performance than they are to hold Toyota accountable. From the overall indexes (see Figure 13), you can see that customers of the bottom NVSDS dealers are much less likely to service their Toyota at these dealerships or to recommend these dealers as a place to buy a new vehicle. However, there is very little difference among the customers of the two dealer groups in the number who indicate they would purchase another Toyota.

More specifically, data on these overall indexes indicate that the biggest impact of a poor sales experience is seen in the customer's

Figure 13
Overall indexes

Indexes	Top NVSDS dealers	Bottom NVSDS dealers	Difference
Would svc. at dealer	90.1	85.1	8.0
Would rec. dealer	96.3	88.6	7.7
NVSDS	98.0	90.9	7.1
DQI	90.5	85.4	5.1
Product loyalty	88.2	85.2	3.0

lack of intention to service their car at that dealership (an eight-point difference), closely followed by the customer's lower likelihood of recommending that dealership to others as a place to buy a vehicle (a 7.7-point difference). Of minimum impact is the customer's perception of the Toyota product and product loyalty. As the annual ownership experience study discovered, although dealer loyalty suffers considerably, the customer's impression of the Toyota product is barely impacted by a poor sales experience. Dealers suffer higher costs of dissatisfaction due to bad sales and service experiences than Toyota Motor Sales, who represents the product.

The bottom line is that it's in the dealers' best interest to meet or exceed the expectations of their customers. Convincing dealers is easy, but getting actions for improvement requires considerably more effort. As one means to improve customer satisfaction, Toyota encourages dealers to monitor their own progress through follow-up contact with customers after the sale as well as after service visits. These contacts, if handled correctly, can yield invaluable information regarding aspects of the customers' experiences that fall short of their expectations. Such information can provide significant opportunities for dealers to address issues that might otherwise go undetected. As displayed by the financial status of the top NVSDS dealers, practicing good customer service techniques goes hand in hand with other positive aspects of running a successful business.

▶ CONCLUDING COMMENTS

Customer satisfaction is not just another program, but must be a part of the business plan of TMS and every dealership. TMS managers are convinced that customer satisfaction will be critical in the 1990s. Over the long term, improving the processes that lead to customer satisfaction can ultimately lead to higher levels of sales. Toyota attempts to improve customer satisfaction by making process improvements in its plants and its logistical systems that deliver vehicles to the dealers. These efforts are described more thoroughly in Parts III and IV.

▶ DISCUSSION QUESTIONS

1. Based on information in this part of the Toyota case, write a statement of what Toyota's long-term strategy should be for providing customer value. Provide support for the statement.
2. Summarize the evidence which indicates that customer satisfaction should be a key strategic objective for Toyota.
3. How does Toyota currently use customer satisfaction data to achieve improvement?
4. How could Toyota make better use of its customer satisfaction data?

Toyota, Part III: Toyota Production System and *Kaizen**

▶ THE TOYOTA PRODUCTION SYSTEM

Toyota Motor Manufacturing, U.S.A., Inc. (TMM), in Georgetown, Kentucky, began pilot production of the Camry sedan in May 1988, and volume production in July 1988. Toyota's $2 billion investment in Kentucky made sure the plant is outfitted with exceptional equipment, from thumbnail-size computer chips guiding robotic welders to 2,300-ton stamping presses. But it is the effort and determination of its Kentucky workers (or team members, as Toyota calls them) that are enabling this state-of-the-art facility to reach the potential for quality represented by its technology. In this setting, Toyota team members seek to build the finest-quality car at the lowest possible cost in the most efficient manner.[1]

Just like managers at Toyota plants in Japan, managers at TMM evaluate the quality of their vehicles in terms consistent with the way customers view quality. They listen to the voice of the customer, from sources such as J. D. Power surveys and Toyota's new vehicle sales and delivery survey (NVSDS). They study the reports and try to identify the processes responsible for any quality deficiencies. They form partnerships for improvement with suppliers. Plant managers lead the committees and task forces dedicated to continuous improvement, and they collaborate with corporate study teams. For example, the chief engineer teams lead improvements which begin with the design of products and processes, and encompass manufacturing, supplier development, marketing, and other functional activities. One of the most important parts of TMM's efforts to produce high-quality vehicles is known as the Toyota production system.

The Toyota production system has been refined over the years. It is made up of a number of philosophies, but not all of these philosophies focus on production. As a matter of fact, the foundation for all the philosophies that make the Toyota production system successful is the team member. Toyota invests in sophisticated technology, but knows the real key to quality is the employee.

A Respect for Human Dignity

Toyota leaders realize that if jobs are not meaningful to team members or tend to disregard their dignity as human beings, then team mem-

* This case was prepared by Greg Bounds.
1. The author thanks the following people for their special insights and contributions to this case: Kazumi Nakada, executive coordinator–production control, James White, TPS project manager, Kent Rubach, assistant project manager-production control, Michael Kinney, specialist-production control, and Kaz Sato, public affairs specialist.

bers cannot be expected to give 100 percent to their jobs or to improving their jobs. The Toyota production system is based on the philosophy of respecting human dignity. At TMM:

- Team members are led to find meaning and purpose to all work they are required to do (the company tries to make this work value-added and not wasteful of people's effort).
- People are asked to find ways to eliminate waste in their jobs, in process, time, and effort.
- People use machines, not the other way around.
- The system allows problems to become apparent to everyone, and team members are encouraged to correct them.
- People are given the opportunity to make suggestions for improving their own work.

A respect for human dignity, giving people the opportunity to be involved in improving the work they do, and the knowledge that people use machines, machines don't use people, all provide the environment for successful implementation of the philosophies of the Toyota production system. Human resource management (HRM) seeks to ensure skilled and motivated team members in support of the Toyota production system. The three dimensions of HRM at Toyota include selection, development, and support (see Figure 1).

HRM begins with a rigorous selection process to make sure new team members have the general aptitude, interpersonal skills, flexibility, desire to learn, problem-solving skills, and physical ability needed to execute the Toyota production system. Once hired, team members are developed through knowledge of the Toyota production system (including job instruction to train people on standardized work and *kaizen*). They are also developed through multiple job skills, cross-training and job rotation, problem-solving skills, involvement opportunities, internal promotion, and self-

development. Finally, team members are supported through job security, competitive wages/benefits, safe work environment, open communications, mutual trust/respect, team environment, consistent policy implementation, and a quality culture.

How a Little Line Stops a Big Line

Tour the Toyota plant in Georgetown and you'll see a low-tech feature: a rope strung above the assembly line. If any kind of problem is spotted, any team member can pull an *andon* rope, which may lead to halting production at a predetermined stop position. Except in an emergency situation, the line does not stop until a predetermined stop position because it allows the other workers on the line to complete their work task and maintain standardized work without disruption. The *andon* rope alerts the team leader through visual and audio alarms. If the problem can be fixed before the line reaches the stop position, then a release rope is pulled and the line continues without interruption. If the line does stop, the problem is resolved before the line starts up again.

The most important aspect of this process, called *jidoka* in Japanese, is the use of devices and work methods to ensure team members recognize an abnormality in the process and stop the line when necessary. The purpose of *jidoka* is to detect and prevent problems from being passed on: the problem is fixed immediately. *Jidoka* leads to further problem solving. Ideally, the real cause of a defect or problem is traced and steps are taken to prevent it from recurring.

The ability to stop a multibillion-dollar manufacturing operation is an awesome trust that most automakers invest in only a few executives. At Toyota, any team member that knows the process has that trust and responsibility.

The Pull System: Every Station a Customer

In many manufacturing facilities, each station in the manufacturing process assembles whatever is sent to it from the station before. Each

Figure 1

Human resource management in the Toyota production system

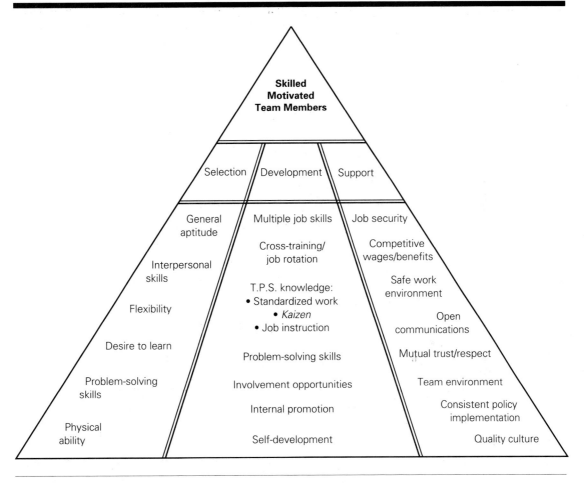

station strives to work at maximum output, "pushing" out parts and, finally, autos. Often, more parts are produced than needed, and the excess is stored.

In contrast, with the "pull" system of production at TMM, parts and autos are pulled through the system. As each station uses parts, it orders or pulls more from a preceding station. That station produces only enough to replace what was needed by the following process, subsequently minimizing inventory, and improving efficiency.

To control or implement the pull system, the *kanban* system is used. *Kanban* is the tool that enables team members to get the parts they need for each process and then reorder those parts. *Kanbans* are part information cards or production instructions that show workers what to produce, in what quantity and when, so parts will be available when needed and in the amount needed.

Toyota's simple reversal of manufacturing tradition reduces costs, and also delivers a priceless payoff: each station must treat the next one as a valued customer. If the final body line needs 300 doors from the press line, the latter is spurred to high standards by the closeness of its customer. The final body line scrutinizes the delivery. The doors are right, or they're rejected. For TMM team members, the customer isn't some stranger at a distant dealership, it's the team member just a few feet away. And that team member is no pushover, for what he or she passes on must meet the same high quality standards.

Parts Arrive as Needed

The pull system is a critical component of the just-in-time philosophy of production. And just-in-time applies to the production of components within the walls of TMM as well as to materials and components produced by suppliers on the outside. Because parts are pulled from one process to the next, only the amount needed for each process at a specific time is produced. Parts arrive just in time to be placed in or on a vehicle. For example, the seats for the Kentucky Camry are produced just a few miles away at a manufacturing facility in Georgetown. Seats are delivered sixteen times during two eight-hour shifts. They are delivered directly to the final assembly line where seats are installed at exactly the time they are needed.

Lean production and the pull system certainly enhance efficiency, with less storage space and less production lead time needed. More importantly, however, they also allow instant feedback and response to quality problems. The Toyota production system creates a work environment conducive to continuous improvement.

▶ *KAIZEN* AT TOYOTA

At Toyota, people, technology, and the constant search for a better way have been components of the improvement process. *Kaizen* is a Japanese term that means continuous improvement, always looking for a better way, a safer way, an easier way, a more efficient way. *Kaizen's* primary objectives are to identify and eliminate *"muda,"* or waste, in all areas and to ensure quality and safety. The key elements of *kaizen* emphasize: (1) making sure there is a good manufacturing system in place which is focused on optimizing overall flows and responding to customer demand, and (2) making tasks simpler and easier to perform, removing wasted motion, increasing the efficiency of the work process, maintaining a safe work environment, and constantly improving the product quality. *Kaizen* to improve the system and operations leads to ways of working that are more productive for the team member and the company.

The primary methods of achieving *kaizen* at Toyota are inextricably linked to the Toyota production system. To understand the methods of *kaizen* or continuous improvement at Toyota, you must first appreciate its context within the Toyota production system. We discuss this context in terms of the direction managers provide through the system, and the role of team members within the system. Then we illustrate Toyota's *kaizen* activities.

Managers Provide Direction through the System

Kazumi Nakada, executive coordinator–production control, says of Toyota's approach to improvement, "Every manager knows we can change the production cost by changing the methods of work, ways of producing. Human beings think 'our way is best,' but at Toyota, we are told we have to always change; we must change every three months or it's not good management. We believe there is no perfect way, so we continue to search. The goal is to break the current condition through *kaizen*."

Setting up a system conducive to *kaizen*

might be considered the primary method of improvement at Toyota. In fact, it is the most important method of improvement. General Motors realized this when it decided to start at the beginning in creating Saturn as a new organization to compete with the Japanese producers of small and medium-sized cars like Toyota. The nature of the larger system determines the way managers and workers pursue improvement within it.

Nakada explains that the Toyota production system is "the backbone of Toyota; it provides direction and helps us not to lose our way." In the Toyota production system, it is management's responsibility to provide the system and the direction. Myths about Japanese management often emphasize the importance of bottom-up management and self-managing teams. However, James White, TPS project manager, explains, "We don't have self-managing work teams. We do have suggestions, input, involvement, but a manager's role is very important, including their role in *kaizen*."

Nakada further explains: "Some people misunderstand [and believe] that Japanese management is only bottom-up, from team members. Toyota also emphasizes top-down leadership which has a good vision, knows the objectives of the company, the direction, and which can organize to reach the objective. Leaders must change methods and systems and get everyone to carry out their role appropriately. Understanding from team members is important, because they have to implement and work with the changes in their work areas. So we have a continuous cycle of input and feedback from team members, but providing direction is most important."

This responsibility for providing the system has at least two important dimensions. First, it shows concern for the good of the whole company. Second, it creates a context for improvement.

The Good of the Whole Company The Toyota production system is designed for the good of the whole company, including its suppliers, team members, and customers. Managers like Nakada and White work hard to put the Toyota production system in place because it helps to accomplish objectives that are important to Toyota corporate strategy. For example, the pull system discussed earlier helps to reduce lead time across the whole flow of production.

One of the features of the Toyota production system is that it uses an approach called leveled production. TMM gets orders of monthly sales from TMS for all combinations of model types, colors, and options. TMM divides those into a daily production plan and distributes them across the day so the total number produced equals the daily plan. If you stand and watch finished Camrys roll off the end of the assembly line, you will notice that each one in the sequence is different. Toyota does not produce batches of 100 or even ten identical cars. Each automobile may be one of three different models (four-door sedan, two-door sedan, or station wagon) and have different options, color, etc. There are various combinations of options: California emissions standards or non-California emissions standards; U.S. destination (left-hand drive) or export (right-hand drive); automatic, electronically controlled transmissions or manual transmissions. The complexity of the mix is continuing to grow; for example, the Kentucky plant recently added the production of V-6 engines into the assembly mix.

Why does Toyota do leveled production? The benefits of leveled production and the pull system extend to Toyota's suppliers by leveling their staffing requirements and helping to avoid idleness which is often associated with dedicated lines. It benefits the team member on the assembly line because it provides some diversity in work load. For example, some models and option packages require more elements of work. Station wagons require processing different from sedans. The team member whose process was affected by wagons could not keep up with the line speed if there were ten station wagons in a row. However, if a station wagon only comes along once every ten units, and is balanced between models requiring less processing, work time is equalized over a short period of time.

Leveled production shortens the lead time, or time it takes to respond to customer orders. It is concerned for the good of Toyota. If a customer places an order, Toyota can respond immediately rather than in weeks or months. The system is designed to produce vehicles in a sequence such that each is different from the one before it and the one after it. Leveled production may give up a little of the cost advantages associated with the economies of scale available in mass production (spreading costs across large batches of identical products). However, it drives Toyota to reduce costs in other ways, like avoiding costs of poor quality and costs of inventory. Most importantly, Toyota is more concerned with its overall performance in the marketplace than with cost savings in one part of the larger system. Further, the combination of leveled production with a pull system makes improvement of the overall process flow even more important.

James White explains the difficulty of promoting the good of the whole company: "The challenge of getting people to think this way is formidable, because people naturally think of their own area as opposed to the whole. They naturally think about the inputs versus changing the way they do things. They naturally accept the system versus challenging the system. It's easier to go with the flow of the system as it is rather than pull back and take a critical look at it as a whole." It is difficult to teach this philosophy, but that is exactly the job of managers like White and Nakada. For example, as Nakada explains, "Engineering people order the equipment, but they must consider the whole company, and not just do short-sighted thinking. They may be inclined

to go after the latest technology without considering whether we really need it."

Kaizen does not consist of just any change or any improvement in isolated processes. All improvements are of value, particularly as they benefit the team members. But *kaizen* requires management to consider the flow across all processes. This concern for Toyota as a whole sets the context for improvement. The Toyota production system makes it easy to see the results of production processes. As James White explains, "Managers can easily observe and judge whether production is a continuous flow. If not, then managers attack the whole, not just individual process improvements, to create a continuous flow." As discussed below, individual process improvements are designed to contribute to improving the flow.

Context for Improvement   The Toyota production system makes opportunities for improvement obvious, because it is set up to flow like a stream, which makes it easy to find problems. If a machine starts producing a defect, *the line stops* until it is fixed. Since parts are not stored in a warehouse, but are supplied just in time, when a line is producing more than is demanded, the excess *inventory stacks up* in the factory. These kinds of events are obvious indicators that reveal whether or not the whole system is flowing like a stream. At Toyota, managers and team members must process this conceptual framework before applying methods or tools for improvement; it provides the context for improvement.

Kazumi Nakada explains, "The target is to shorten the lead time and be more responsive to customer demand. The Toyota production system makes production results visible, so we can see the flow." In this context, high quality in every production process is a condition that allows short lead time and continuous flow. To achieve high quality, Toyota focuses on the methods of work used in production processes.

James White explains the emphasis on im-

proving the methods of production processes and the error that many managers make in thinking about improvement: "Typically, when managers look at production as input, processing, and output, they only think of changing the inputs (material, manpower, machine) to accomplish improvements. They do not often think about changing the methods of processing. When people are experiencing problems, they tend to think if they have more reliable material, better people, or newer and better operating equipment, they will be okay. The whole focus of TPS is on improving methods. This is at the heart of TPS." Managers are responsible for putting in place the Toyota production system and educating team members on its philosophy. When these things are in place, team members are better prepared to fulfill their roles in improving work methods.

The Role of Team Members within the System

Through *kaizen* in their own work areas, team members can eliminate wasted time, actions, materials, and energy. There's a challenge here. Team members are taught the Toyota production system, then they're asked to improve the implementation of it within their work. Toyota considers team members' minds their most important manufacturing tool and invites them to think about their work. The production system is thus not a blueprint, but a constantly evolving process.

James White explains that Toyota prepares new employees for their role as team members as soon as they are hired. "It begins in assimilation, when they first come in. We try to get some very strong messages across to them. The most important message regards their own individual responsibility in quality, which means that making an improvement and finding a better way is in their hands. People buy into this very quickly and start looking for new ways and better ways." This message gets reinforced in several different ways at Toyota:

- The importance of *kaizen* is frequently talked about.
- The next process is considered the customer.
- The suggestion system is designed toward frequent participation and small ideas (the average payout is $12–15). (Group leaders are rewarded based on dollar value of the suggestions from their team members to get them to encourage team members to submit suggestions.)[2]
- Participation in quality circles, structured problem solving focused on work-related issues and problems, not "hygiene issues." (Quality circles are generally organized around functional work teams, so their work is focused on isolated improvements. Some special-purpose quality circles do address cross-functional issues.)
- Standardized work documentation posted in the area provides opportunity for team members to see ways to suggest improvements.
- An inspection role gives team members the responsibility to call attention to problems.
- Team member input is always gathered when planning for change.

We discuss these last three points, standardized work, inspection, and team member input, in more detail below.

Standardized Work Team members are expected to identify problems and look for improvement opportunities in their own work activities. They then apply their problem-solving skills, based on the Plan-Do-Check-Act cycle, to fix the cause of the abnormality. The basis for *kaizen* by both team leaders and team

---

2. Group leaders are like first-line supervisors who supervise four or five teams. Team leaders have four or five team members on a team.

members is the documentation of standardized work.

There are many wrong ways to perform a task. Toyota has spent more than half a century developing the "right ways" and standardizing those ways as common practice. Whether it is mounting a tire, installing a seat, or a hundred other jobs, a standardized work sheet shows the proper way to perform each step, all the way to the degree of arm rotation. Toyota continually strives to organize all work around efficient human motion and to create a production sequence without any "*muda.*" Work organized and documented in such a way is called standardized work. It is made up of three elements: *takt* time, working sequence, and standardized in-process stock.

Takt time is the time which should be taken to produce one vehicle (a vehicle rolls off the end of the production line every fifty-five seconds). This timing mechanism is based on a monthly production schedule which is based on received customer orders. *Takt* time sets the assembly line speed and provides the target for the cycle times of all other production tasks. Smooth flow is accomplished when work cycles equal the *takt* time. Daily total operating time is figured on the basis of all machinery operating at 100 percent efficiency during regular working hours.

Working sequence refers to the sequence of operations in a single process which leads a floor worker to produce quality goods in the most efficient way. Standard in-process stock is the minimum quantity of parts always on hand for processing in and between subprocesses. It allows the worker to do his job continuously in a set sequence of subprocesses, repeating the same operation over and over in the same order.

To understand what standardized work means, imagine a team member in a conveyor pit under a Camry. He tightens camber bolts, sets toe adjustments, and inspects steering bolts. This requires countless moves, timed to match a teammate's efforts behind the steering wheel in the car above. Too few moves threaten the accuracy of his work; too many tire him and delay his teammate. What's needed is a harmonious balance of man and machine in time and space. Through more than fifty years and millions of vehicles, Toyota continues to refine all manufacturing motions into efficient steps for each process. The result is fewer steps, smarter moves, better cars and more of them.

Inspection: Every Team Member an Inspector

When you think of inspection, you probably think of someone examining a finished product and stamping a seal of approval, or rejecting the product due to quality problems (lack of conformance to specifications). Inspection at TMM is described by a different definition; it involves in-process inspection and does not wait until the finished product gets to the end of the production line. While there is a final inspection department that takes each vehicle through a rigorous testing process, there are thousands of inspectors throughout the facility. Because every team member is capable of stopping the line if a problem is detected, Toyota entrusts each of them with the responsibility of inspector. Inspection takes place while a vehicle is being built, during each step of the process.

Toyota's quality control during production ensures that the correct materials and parts are used and fitted with precision and accuracy. This effort is combined with thousands of rigorous inspections that occur during the production process. Employees on the line are responsible for the parts they use. Each is an inspector for their own work and the work of coworkers. As mentioned earlier, when a problem on any vehicle is spotted, any team member can pull a rope strung above the assembly line to bring attention to the problem, which may stop the line at the fixed stop position if it is not corrected immediately. Only when the problem is resolved is the line restarted. That process involves every team member in monitoring and checking the quality of every car produced. The inspection process is not used just to identify defects that need repair, as in traditional mass production approaches. It is also used to identify causes and countermeasures so defects can be avoided in the future.

When problems do occur, TPS is designed to promote immediate corrective action. James White explains, "If you have a mixed-up layout, producing in large batches, rather than just in time, you may not determine you have a problem until way downstream. But if you set up a simple process (build one and hand it to the next process) and each one is fulfilling its inspection role, then immediately you determine whether you have a quality problem. Then you get quick feedback and correct it through simple visual monitoring." When a team member finds a defect, he or she alerts the group leader, and immediately the group leader traces it back to process in their own group or wherever it goes. They either get on the phone or go personally, rather than write up a report and file it. This involves immediate and quick feedback, just as soon as it is detected.

Once the Camry reaches the end of the assembly line at TMM, it is again tested and inspected. The Camry is first started and then driven to functional inspection. In the following areas, every aspect of the vehicle is put through a demanding set of tests and inspections:

- Functional inspections are performed on tires, lights, steering wheel, horn, wheel alignment, and headlamp adjustment.
- Roll and brake tests are conducted on simulated drive, smoothness of ride, parking brake, emissions, gear shifting, braking power, instrument panel, and engine and chassis fluids.
- In the water test booth, the Camry is sprayed with high-pressure water from all angles, and every compartment is checked for water leaks.
- In the final inspection, team members probe every inch of the Camry. Both function and appearance are scrutinized.

TMM doesn't stop with thousands of inspectors or the final inspection area. About thirty-five cars are chosen randomly each day and sent to the on-site test track for a check of road performance. The test track provides an opportunity to further evaluate vehicles for performance and quality by providing simulated road surfaces and brake and function testing.

Team Member Input In traditional approaches to standardizing work, industrial engineers come in as the experts and propose changes. At Toyota, however, work methods are improved by the *kaizen* activities of team leaders and team members working together. Team leaders know how to do every job in their areas. They even fill in when a team member is absent or when a team member gets behind in his or her work. In this way, the team leader is really a part of the team, and this encourages team member input to the leader's *kaizen* activities.

Group leaders establish new standardized work methods with input from team members. They are trained on how to conduct time studies and basic problem solving. With input from the team members, they conduct analyses and develop the standardized work methods. Input comes from people in the workplace, not from an industrial engineer who comes in and tells people what the problems are, then walks off and leaves them.

Tying the Pieces Together The Toyota production system is composed of many processes linked by the pull system into a continuous flow. Each team member considers the next process on the line as his or her customer and will not pass a defective part or a problem on to that customer. Stopping the line during the process to identify a problem will lead to countermeasures. With that philosophy made real, the ultimate customer, the Toyota Camry buyer, can be assured that quality is built in. The end product reflects the processes used to accomplish it. Below, we discuss how process improvements are made within the Toyota production system.

Focused *Kaizen* at Toyota

At Toyota, ideas for *kaizen* often come from ad hoc teams dedicated to specific issues: engineering teams, production teams in a work area, maintenance teams, and managers from other sections and departments. The purpose of these teams is to learn from one another and teach ideas for *kaizen*. This approach of people studying together to make improvements is called *jishuken*. As an example of *jishuken*, TMM promotes focused *kaizen* efforts to achieve targeted improvements in a particular area over a short period of time. Led and coordinated by staff members like James White in the Toyota production system office, the focused *kaizen* efforts begin with training.

***Kaizen* Training**   Training for *kaizen* consists of review of the TPS philosophy, objectives, and examples of past *kaizen* efforts. However, it does not end with classroom instruction; it extends into actual applications in the workplace and subsequent follow-up to ensure the planned improvements were achieved. For example, the following approach was taken for achieving focused *kaizen* in the plastics department, in the areas producing glove compartment doors and instrument panels:

1. Review material and information flow (*shikumi*)
2. Select job leader/break processes up between *kaizen* members
3. Time study of process elements
4. Measuring the cycle time of machines/turntables

5. Analyze process/identify problems
6. Set *kaizen* targets and goals for change
7. Discuss ideas with team members and solicit theirs
8. Develop *kaizen* ideas
9. Try to evaluate *kaizen* ideas with team members
10. Confirm *kaizens* with others in plastics department
11. Implement *kaizens* and support team members
12. Verify impact and identify additional *kaizens* to stabilize processes
13. Identify *kaizens* not implemented and still needed for follow-up by plastics area managers
14. Report on achievement

The training also sensitized the trainees to the following main concerns: the study of ergonomics (adapting the work environment to suit the workers' needs); the importance of communication; getting support from second-shift team members; follow-up after *kaizen* activities are introduced; and quick response to suggestions.

The training was intended as a development activity. It was not just an opportunity for the staff from the TPS office to come into specific departments and impose improvements. It was intended to develop the capability of the managers and team members to achieve *kaizen* on their own by leaving them with the needed expertise after the focused training ended. After the training formally ends, the staff of the TPS office act only as consultants to assist with advice and guidance as needed.

***Kaizen* Objectives**   The objective for *kaizen* in the plastics area was a 20 percent reduction in the time it takes to produce parts in the plastics department, or man-hours per piece (MH/PC). The original condition was that plastic parts were produced using twelve processes and 0.092 MH/PC. The target was to reduce

Figure 2

Productivity analysis

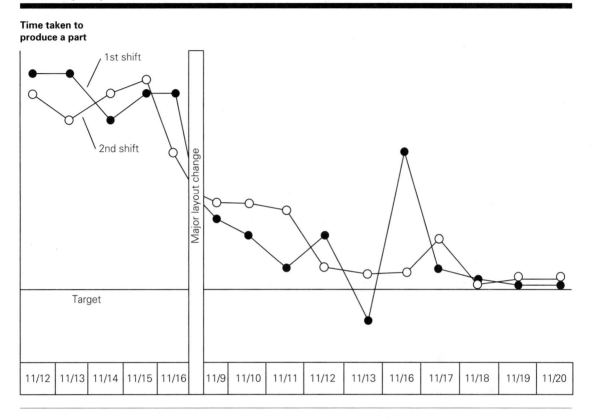

Time taken to produce a part

1st shift

2nd shift

Major layout change

Target

| 11/12 | 11/13 | 11/14 | 11/15 | 11/16 | 11/9 | 11/10 | 11/11 | 11/12 | 11/13 | 11/16 | 11/17 | 11/18 | 11/19 | 11/20 |

it to ten processes and 0.074 MH/PC, and to accomplish the target in only eight days of focused efforts. The actual result went beyond the target and reduced plastic production to nine processes (in eight days) and 0.072 MH/PC. The cycle time was also reduced for turntable one, for example, from seventy-one seconds to fifty-six seconds. The productivity analysis shown in Figure 2 illustrates the immediate effect of *kaizen* and layout changes on the amount of time required to produce a part. Below, we discuss how the *kaizen* team accomplished these improvements.

Changing Material Flows Before *kaizen*, there were two turntables which held forming ma-

chines for producing both glove compartment doors and instrument panels. As shown in the flowchart in Figure 3, a worker would stand at the workstation in front of each turntable and produce glove compartment doors and instrument panels in alternating sequence. As the turntable rotated, the parts were formed, and then removed. The parts were then recombined from the two turntables to their respective lines and passed on to subsequent trimming and assembly operations. After *kaizen*, as shown in Figure 3, each turntable was dedicated to producing only one component. This change allowed several other improvements.

Before *kaizen*, the production system was complicated and not smooth. There was a lot

Figure 3

Instrument panel and glove box material flow

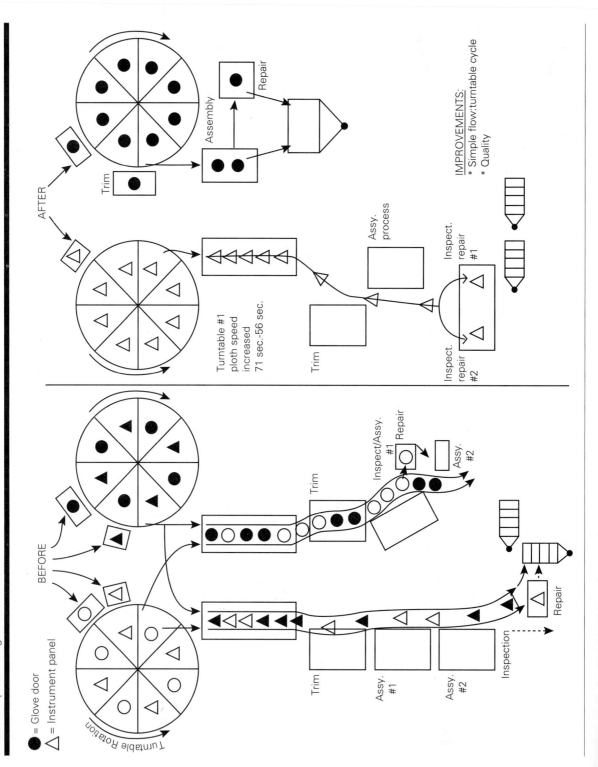

of waste in movement, such as walking, waiting, and handling parts. There was more manpower than should have been required. After *kaizen* to change the system, the product flowed through simply with a shorter cycle time. With the turntables dedicated to only one part, the flow could be made smoother with less wasted time and the support operations could be moved closer to each turntable. After the system was changed, the *kaizen* team then improved each of the operations within the system. Wasted motions were eliminated, and cycle time was further reduced. Examples of waste elimination are presented below.

Elimination of Waste The purpose of waste elimination is to improve the flow of the production process, reduce cycle time, and increase responsiveness to customers by eliminating nonvalue-added time. The methods of *kaizen* used to accomplish waste reduction are very simple. Committed to the purpose of identifying and eliminating unnecessary work, the *kaizen* team simply goes to the work site and observes the work. They look for opportunities without using sophisticated tools or methods. They rely primarily on their imagination, understanding of the principles of the Toyota production system, and the experiences gained from observing *kaizen* improvements in other work areas. They think in terms of improving flows, attacking root causes, and tackling the most obvious problems first.

They ask simple questions: What causes fluctuations in work cycle time? Because of the visibility of the work, they often find simple answers; for example, a fluctuation occurs because the machine jams and the worker has to tug on the part to get it out. Why does the machine jam? Because of the friction that builds up between the part and the machine during curing. The solution implemented by the *kaizen* team reduced the friction to release the part from the mold, by modifying the machine ejectors so the piece pops out further rather than remaining stuck in the mold. The worker can then easily lift the part from the mold. The worker suffers less fatigue and executes the work more quickly.

Many other *kaizens* focus on eliminating motion and reducing walking time, waiting time, and handling of materials. Consider some examples:

- Changing the location of a switch or turning a button panel to face the operator for easy access and reduced movement
- Installing a slide table between workstations to avoid double handling and build-up of work-in-process inventory
- Installing padding to allow operator to rest against machine instead of leaning over it trying not to touch a sharp corner
- Installing a button that opens the doors to a machine while the worker is walking over to get a part, rather than pressing the button after arriving at the machine and then waiting for the doors to open
- Installing a pressure-sensitive pad (like at the grocery store) so that when the worker steps off, the doors shut automatically; the worker does not have to stop to push a button
- Placing a hole in the worktable for disposing of cast-off material from a trimming operation into a box below the worktable rather than turning and throwing it in a box behind the worktable
- Performing inspection at a different point in the line to balance the work
- Replacing the parts supply boxes with a smaller size container to support the time reduction changes by reducing floor space required for parts

Each of these changes may save only a few seconds, but the accumulation of saved seconds across the thousands of operations throughout the system adds up to substantial savings in cycle time by the elimination of unnecessary work. When work is taken away, Toyota removes workers from the production line and reassigns them to other work. Work tasks are redistributed to workers whose work loads are reduced. This is how the *kaizen* team eliminated three of the twelve work tasks from the plastics area, as mentioned earlier.

The work eliminated does not mean that workers are laid off or fired from Toyota. Rather, they are simply removed from doing wasteful work and reassigned to work that adds value to the product. Team members appreciate that changes are being made to ensure security for all. Team members trust the intentions of managers. As one team member explained, "If they take a person away, then they have to take nonvalued work away also. They don't just make the rest of us work harder." To make sure that team members understand the proposed changes, the *kaizen* team involves the team members and communicates with them about their efforts. Certainly, Toyota encounters some skepticism from team members when changes are proposed, but these go away as the team members get used to the changes as the standard way of work.

Responsive Management   To accomplish the improvements they accomplished in eight days, the *kaizen* team and the managers above them had to react quickly to the *kaizen* opportunities they discovered. Responsive management is key to accomplishing *kaizen*. In a few days, they had to plan and approve equipment changes, schedule contractors or in-house personnel to do the equipment changes, expedite orders for parts, and execute the work over the weekend or during downtimes, so that production never missed a beat.

The Role of Statistical Theory and Data Analysis
In the Toyota production system, data analysis serves four basic roles: (1) confirmation of control, (2) operational control, (3) input to problem solving, and (4) evaluating the result of changes.

Confirmation of Control   Kazumi Nakada explains that data analysis is "like taking a pulse. If problems arise, then we look into it with more detailed analysis." Toyota managers use simple methods of data analysis to confirm that production processes are in control (taking the pulse). For instance, production performance boards on the factory floor show trend analyses on output and on defect rates. The boards show numerical comparison of planned output versus actual. Group leaders make notations for deviations. Toyota may also measure dimensional characteristics, such as location, fit, and other quality indicators, to do confirmation checks. For example, the quality department will pull a part, put it in a confirmation jig, and run a test on it. These records are plotted on run charts and fed back to the managers.

In some processes, the only way to picture a process is through data; that is, managers can't just rely on visual control. For example, in the paint process, it is important to monitor and chart data on temperature and humidity, as key indicators in order to control process performance. In this case, data analysis makes the process visible so workers know what actions to take to control its performance.

Operational Control   Toyota does not rely on confirmation checks alone to ensure quality results. The TPS philosophy is to have stabilized processes and detect abnormalities and correct them before they become a problem. Data analysis can be helpful in identifying trends so corrective action can be taken to prevent problems. Experiments and statistical analyses may also be designed to learn about how the equipment and methods of a new production process behave. This learning informs managers about how to control the process.

Input to Problem Solving   Toyota also collects data on quality and performance as a source of information for problem solving. The data allow Toyota managers to go back and trace the history of the process before making improvements, as was done in the plastics department. Data analysis is not a substitute for hands-on management. The role of the manager is primarily to see first-hand and not just sit and look at statistical reports in the office. As James White explains, "A lot of statistical analysis tools only reveal the shadow of reality. A manager's energy and time are better spent by going and seeing first-hand, not paper problem solving. We don't want the management of our processes based on statistical data reports. We want the managers to see what is going on with their own eyes and not just rely on people sending them a report." To encourage this approach to management, Toyota keeps data charts right beside the line so that as the managers walk down the line, they may see the recent history of how the line has been running over several days or weeks.

Evaluating the Results of Changes   Once Toyota managers decide to implement changes, data analysis is important in helping to evaluate the results. As Nakada explains, "Measurement is important when we are preparing improvement for the system. If we do not collect the data, we cannot know the result." For example, the results of the focused *kaizen* efforts were documented in the productivity analyses, as shown in Figure 2 above.

Managerial Responsibility for Systems
Toyota does a lot of data analysis, but it uses simple methods such as run charts, trend analysis, and Pareto charts. It does not extensively use statistical control charts to interpret varia-

tion (i.e., to differentiate special causes from common causes). Although statistical analysis is not a key part of the Toyota production system, the message underlying the statistical theory is very much a part of it. The theory of variation advocated by W. Edwards Deming suggests that managers are primarily responsible for putting in place the system that causes variation in observed production outputs. Toyota managers have taken that message to heart. They have created a production system that seeks to minimize variation and make problems visible so that managers must take immediate action when problems do arise.

How does Toyota suggest that one should attempt to get people to shift to the Toyota production system from a mass production system? Toyota often assists its suppliers in making this transition. As Nakada explains, "The first step is not to do a lot of statistical analysis, but to set up the system flow and the methods of work. Then solve the problems that emerge. You get feedback very quickly, one piece at a time, or in small lots, rather than at the end of a long production run. Immediately, when you get a part that is bad, it is easier to go back and find out what caused it rather than wait until you've got a whole lot of them."

Pretention of problems is the heart of the Toyota production system. It enables Toyota Motor Manufacturing to continuously reduce the costs of production, produce high-quality vehicles, respond quickly to customer demand, and achieve customer satisfaction in the marketplace.

▶ **DISCUSSION QUESTIONS**

1. How does the Toyota production system relate to Toyota's strategy and help accomplish Toyota's objectives for customer satisfaction?

2. What are the objectives of *kaizen* at Toyota Motor Manufacturing?

3. What is the role of standardization in the Toyota production system and *kaizen*?

4. How does the Toyota production system promote *kaizen*?

5. If you were a consultant to one of Toyota's suppliers, what are the key principles of the Toyota production system that you would try to teach them? Design a plan for implementing these principles (list a set of steps, if you wish).

Toyota, Part IV: The Culture of Standardization*

This part of the Toyota case describes the delivery quality improvement (DQI) program that was mentioned in Part I. Some of the activities of the delivery quality improvement program were initiated as preparatory work long before it was formally established in 1991. Others were recently added. Below, we describe some initiatives in each area of Toyota Motor Sales (TMS) and illustrate some improvements accomplished through standardization.

▶ QUALITY FROM THE PLANTS TO THE CUSTOMER

Toyota utilizes many resources in the research, design, and building of vehicles that should satisfy customers. In the plants, work can be standardized to fulfill Toyota plans for uniform quality levels. However, a lot happens to a vehicle between the time it rolls off the end of the production line and when it rolls off the dealer's lot in the hands of a Toyota customer (see Figure 1). It gets shipped thousands of miles, by ship, rail, and truck. It is processed at port operations and at the dealership. It is exposed to hundreds of people in different organizations, each of which has historically used nonstandardized work practices, routing the vehicle to customers all over the country. Under these conditions, the vehicles are vulnerable to damage. All efforts to produce qual-ity at the factory can be nullified in the logistical route to the customer.

The delivery quality improvement program addresses what happens to a vehicle after it leaves the factory. It intends to make sure that each vehicle is delivered to the customer in the same condition as when it left the factory. Three features of the delivery quality improvement program are evident throughout this chapter: extending Toyota production principles, uncovering causes to prevent damage, and pervasive emphasis on standardization.

Extending Toyota Production Principles

One of the fundamental principles of the Toyota production system that pervades the delivery quality improvement program is that managers should pursue problems back to their source and develop countermeasures to en-

* This case was prepared by Greg Bounds.

Figure 1

Flow of vehicles from the production plants to the dealership

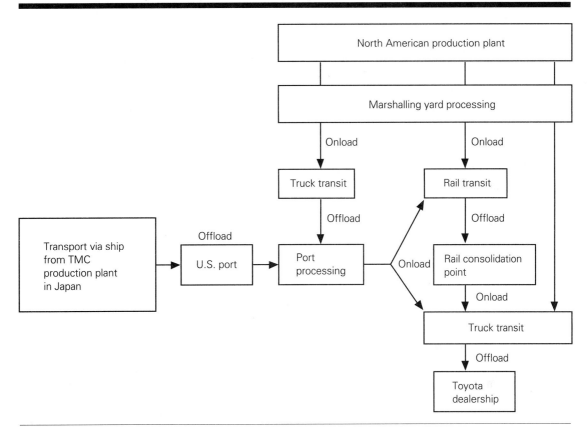

sure that problems do not happen again. Acting on this principle, TMS standardizes work processes to preserve the factory-fresh quality of Toyota vehicles and ensure customer satisfaction. In fact, TMS managers have decided that delivery quality will improve only if they view the transportation, port processing, and dealership activities as extensions of the manufacturing process to be managed just as aggressively.[1]

An interesting twist to this extension of the Toyota production system is that, to improve delivery quality, TMS managers must regard quality as more than just a matter of product design and conformance to design. To encompass more of the purchase and use experience and address all determiners of customer satisfaction, they must address the "softer side" of quality. For example, the sales experience must also be improved. So the delivery quality improvement program extends throughout not only logistical activities, where TMS attempts to deliver a vehicle with factory-fresh quality, but also throughout dealership sales and service, where dealership personnel

---

1. For several years, TMC has intensely pursued marine damage prevention and has successfully reduced damage rates to about .14 percent.

should interface with the customer in a quality manner.

Uncovering Causes to Prevent Damage

Toyota used to behave much as other automobile producers. It did not take exception to damage that occurs along the logistical route. It shipped the vehicles on to the dealerships where all the damage would then be repaired. Unfortunately, with lack of standardization at the dealerships, damaged vehicles were being passed on to customers. Toyota managers now try to identify damage where it occurs, uncover the cause, correct it, and prevent similar damage in the future. To implement this approach to damage prevention, Toyota must have a system of measurement that can link damage to its causes.

Jane Baseda, national logistics planning manager, describes the extent of surveys and process checks done by Toyota. "We do surveys throughout the whole logistics network. If we have units that are being processed at port, we'll audit them at the port before they leave to go on rail cars to make sure that there was no damage made on those vehicles before we ship them out. We will also audit them onboard the rail car. When they reach the destination, we'll audit them again on the rail car to see if there was any transit damage. We'll also audit them again on the ground to see if there was any unloading damage. Then, when we drive them away to the dealerships, we'll audit them before we put them on the truck carrier, before they're taken off the truck carrier, and once they're on the ground at the dealership."

Toyota has teamed with VASCOR, Ltd., a professional surveying company, to audit vehicles en route to dealers. VASCOR was selected because of the knowledge its people have of Toyota's approach to management, which emphasizes not just detecting damage so it can be repaired, but identifying causes so damage can be avoided. To help prevent damage, each VASCOR surveyor serves as a member of a TMS quality improvement team.

Corporate logistics managers accumulate audit data over time to reveal where damage is occurring (see Figure 2). Analysis of the data leads Toyota managers to focus investigation on causes in those particular areas. Such data analysis is useful, but Toyota managers would like to eventually reduce damage rates to the point where it becomes feasible to give immediate feedback to the preceding process. For example, as soon as an auditor finishes surveying a car load, they would key in the data for immediate transmission to the managers of the preceding process.[2]

While Toyota moves toward such real time feedback, they continue to analyze data using simple methods such as run charts and Pareto charts, to uncover the causes of damage. The auditors act as detectives, developing knowledge about the types of damage they observe and its possible causes. Given the importance of this job, Toyota faces a major challenge to find auditors with the years of experience usually required to do it well.

Toyota identifies causes of problems to prevent their recurrence and head off problems before customers ever perceive them. To implement this approach, managers need meaningful and actionable information. While customer surveys provide part of this information, the audits referred to above, and described in more detail below, provide process measures more closely related to the causes of problems.

Pervasive Emphasis on Standardization

Auditing helps identify the causes of damage and checks for standardization, i.e., assesses

---

2. Toyota managers are establishing standardized codes for auditors to describe damage conditions in as much detail as possible.

Figure 2

All routes Pareto analysis

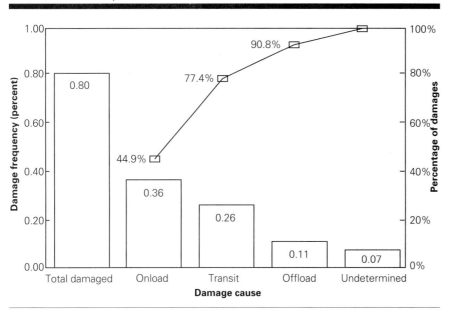

adherence to improved standards for delivery quality. Standards and standardized procedures are developed for almost everything (any potential cause of damage) that is a part of the logistics of processing, transporting, and delivering vehicles to the customer. The auditing process itself is even subject to standardization.[3]

Toyota's goal for customer satisfaction requires that they deliver to the customer a vehicle preserved "factory fresh," to meet the same high standards of quality produced in the factory. To do so, the audit standards have to match the factory standards. This presents a challenge since the various audits are performed by different people throughout the logistical flow. To improve auditing, Toyota stan-

dardizes the process and gets each auditor to judge factory freshness similarly. They do so by teaching auditors a standardized procedure for auditing and a common set of standards for identifying and assessing damage.

For example, the auditor should always start on the same side of the vehicle, go around it in the same way, conduct a prescribed sequence of checks, and spend about the same amount of time on each vehicle. To reduce variation in individual judgments, one training program, dubbed the Rainbow School, painted doors with different types of colors of paint. At the Rainbow School, auditors learned to similarly diagnose and prescribe repairs, and to identify likely causes for the different types of damage that occur on various paints. For example, vehicle standards specify the inspection method: "Vehicle body panels should be inspected from a distance of 1.5 to 3.0 feet and viewed from an angle of 30 degrees."

3. Standardized auditing helps ensure the reliability and validity of the audit data, which is important to a fact-based approach to management.

▶ PORT PROCESSING

When a vehicle arrives in the U.S. on a ship, longshoremen unload it at the port, then Vehicle Processors, Inc., (VPI), a TMS subsidiary, takes possession of it and processes it.[4] "Processing" may involve washing the vehicle and making sure it is clean, putting the appropriate price labels on it, placing the warranty booklets, and preparing it for further transportation by rail or truck. For example, the vehicle will be dewaxed if it is being trucked to a local dealership, and washed and waxed if it is to be loaded onto a rail car for shipment, for example, from Portland, Oregon, to the rail consolidation point in St. Paul, Minnesota.

VPI also accessorizes the imported vehicles: installs air conditioning, radios, CD players, trailer hitches, and other accessories in accordance with dealer orders.[5] VPI can respond much faster than the factory to rapidly changing market needs for accessories. Acting as a miniature assembly plant, VPI provides flexibility for the market and for the overseas factory. It learns about production schedules from the sales regions, and makes adjustments only a few days in advance.

VPI's ultimate goal is to get the vehicle to the dealer in "mint condition," factory fresh, with the needed accessories installed. This goal is easier set than done. Failures are reflected in the results of the J. D. Power initial quality survey (IQS) (see Figure 3). For example, it is likely that VPI contributes to problems with exterior paint/molding, interior, and body, three of the top four IQS problem areas for Toyota cars. The challenges of delivering a factory-fresh vehicle to the customer are many, but the port processors have improvement strategies for doing so.

Maintenance and Improvement Strategies

The maintenance and improvement strategies for port processing are described in Figure 4. Several of the strategic actions are not the sole responsibility of Vehicle Processors, Inc., the operations group, but also of logistics operations and U.S. Products, a support group that works with suppliers and develops accessories that VPI installs. These groups collaborate to implement the strategies for which they share responsibility.

For example, these groups collaborated to make wax coating and decoating improvements. In the past, vehicles may have arrived at the dealer with rust spots due to contamination during rail transport. Depending on the time and place, tiny iron particles, or rail dust, get sucked up from the rail beds, or fall from the walls and ceilings of the rail cars, and deposit on the horizontal surface of the vehicle. If there is no humidity, no problem occurs; the rail dust just blows off in transit or washes off easily. But humidity and heat accelerate oxidation and may cause a rust stain. The acid wash used to remove the rust stain detracts from the factory finish. The stain can even start to impregnate the paint itself, a serious problem in humid areas such as Texas and Florida.

At its Portland, Oregon, operation, Toyota piloted the use of protective coatings, much like an acrylic floor wax, to prevent rust contamination. In the future, all port processors may prepare vehicles for transport by applying a protective coating. It keeps the rail dust deposits from eating into the paint, and also provides short-term protection from acid rain. It doesn't stop acid rain from eating through but does allow more time to rinse it off before it damages the paint.

---

4. VPI acts as an agent for the TMS port operations department which controls the flow of vehicles from ocean transit through discharge, port processing, to shipping. In addition to VPI, other port processors are independently operated under contract with TMS. These independent processors are overseen by the logistics department, not by VPI.
5. The port processors do accessorize some of the vehicles produced in North America to meet customer demands, however, most are fully equipped in the factory.

Figure 3

1991 J.D. Power survey results

1991 Car IQS: Toyota
Problems/100 by problem category

	Problems/100
Problems/100 TOYOTA	89.8
Electrical/accessory	19.3
Ext. paint/molding	10.7
Interior	10.4
Body	9
Squeaks/rattles	8.6
Engine	6.1
Steering/handling	5.4
Transmission	4.5
Brakes	4.3
Temperature control	4.3
Wind noise	4.3
Water leaks	2.8

0 20 40 60 80 100
Problems/100

1991 Car IQS

Interior	Prob/100
total interior	11.2

Other	4.0
Interior soiled	1.7
Seat hard to adjust	1.0
Window trouble	0.9
Carpet wrinkled/loose	0.5
Interior door locks	0.5
Poor door panal material	0.4
Pedal operation difficult	0.4
Other instrument panel	0.4
Poor seat material	0.3
Poor glove box door	0.3

Exterior paint/molding	Prob/100
Total exterior paint/molding	10.7

Paint chips/scratch	5.8
Exterior molding/ornament	1.9
Other	1.9
Body rust corrosion	0.4
Paint thin color mismatch	0.3
Sags/run in paint	0.3

Body	Prob/100
Total body	9.0

Other	2.7
Sheet metal dents/dings	2.1
Exterior door locks	0.8
Side door fits poorly	0.8
Trunk/hatch hard to open	0.7
Side door hard to open	0.5
Sunroof does not work properly	0.5
Trunk/hatch fits poorly	0.5
Hood fits poorly	0.4

The wax coating/decoating improvement project was a good example of cross-functional collaboration for delivery quality improvement. As shown in Figure 4 (page 684), there were many port processing strategies to improve delivery quality. The most important of these strategies, the damage prevention program, is discussed in more detail below.

Damage Prevention Program

While many of the strategic actions listed in Figure 4 are group efforts, Vehicle Processors,

Figure 4

Port processing improvement strategies

Action	Description	Responsibility	Timeline
Standardized PIO process	Standardize PIO process to achieve consistently high installation quality. • Establish torques, develop process checks, installation templates and fixtures.	U.S. Products VPI Logistics Operations	Ongoing
PIO training	Expanded training of managers, supervisors and installers to assure quality processing of vehicles. • "Train the trainer" program. • Develop videos, wall posters and visual aids. • Introduced satellite teleconference to ports.	U.S. Products VPI Logistics Operations	Ongoing
Port quality assurance	• Initiated the port quality assurance program at Portland, Long Beach, and Newark. • Develop audit criteria and train port/ marshalling yard associates on audit criteria requirements. • Conduct weekly, monthly and quarterly quality audits. • Functional checks of PIO accessories and vehicles. • Quality counseling at all processing locations. • A/C installation and graphics application improvement programs.	U.S. Products VPI Logistics Operations	Ongoing
Conversion quality improvement	• Squeak and rattle course and road test. • Joint U.S.P./service POE survey • Customer telephone survey	U.S. Products	Ongoing
Facility upgrades	• Establish facility requirements for paint and body shops for Toyota port and railhead operations. • Define equipment necessary to perform PDS on fleet sales vehicles at port/ marshalling yards.	U.S. Products VPI	Ongoing
Supplier quality activities	The supplier development quality improvement plan seeks to improve the quality of supplied parts through cooperative programs.	U.S. Products	Ongoing
Wax coating/decoating improvements	Investigate and upgrade procedures and effectiveness of wax and de-wax operation to protect vehicles from iron particle contamination and industrial fallout.	U.S. Products Logistics Operations	Ongoing
Quality awards	Provide recognition and awards for excellence in vehicle processing.	VPI	Ongoing
Damage prevention program	An awareness and action program which has an objective to provide 99.9 percent damage-free processing.	VPI	June 1991

Inc., (VPI) developed and administers the damage prevention program totally on its own. Launched in mid-1991, the comprehensive damage prevention program established prevention standards and analysis tools for an aggressive campaign to reduce in-process vehicle damage rates and reduce repair costs. The compellingly clear purpose of the damage prevention program is to preserve the "factory fresh" quality finish of Toyota vehicles and thereby improve customer satisfaction. As stated in a program manual, "Damage-free vehicle processing must become the normal operating standard for VPI."

Each vehicle has the potential to be entered forty times or more on its way from the plant to the dealer. Vehicle movements, entrances, and exits, many of which take place during port processing, make vehicles highly vulnerable to damage. In an assembly plant, workers avoid moving a vehicle any more than they have to. Unfortunately, vehicle movement is an inherent part of port processing, which involves temporary storage, multiple interim stagings, accessory installations, and intermittent movement of vehicles. Each movement presents an opportunity for the vehicle interior and exterior to get dented, scratched, bumped, or dirtied. When customers see such damage, they associate it with Toyota, and not with the shipping company, the port, or the railroad. To ensure customer satisfaction, Toyota emphasizes damage prevention, which preserves the factory-fresh finish, despite all the movement, by identifying and counteracting the causes of damage.

Once damage occurs, for example, a scratch in the paint, it can be repaired. However, repairs alter the luster and never restore the factory-fresh finish which is the best finish, most likely to ensure customer satisfaction. The port processors try to reduce variation in the quality of repair through standardization, but they prefer to avoid the damage rather than fix it. After all, preventing damage could potentially save Toyota millions of dollars in repair costs.

Objectives Toyota set some challenging objectives for the damage prevention program. The first objective was to reduce the overall VPI damage rates from over 50 percent in 1990 to 0.28 percent in 1991. The damage rate objective was further reduced in 1992 to 0.21 percent. These objectives were developed from input from each operations manager and a cumulative calculation. Second, they decided to achieve 0.10 percent "yard" damage rate by the end of 1992, a challenging objective set by chairman Kaneyoshi Kusunoki based on a damage rate achieved in Japan. And third, they decided to achieve an estimated annual repair costs savings of $300,000 through the reduction of damage for 1991, a figure derived from the 0.28 percent damage rate. According to Leo Dombrowski, quality assurance manager, Vehicle Processors, Inc., and developer of the damage prevention program, the objectives were challenging, but what really motivated people to get involved was the focus on customer satisfaction. He says, "When you say customer satisfaction, everybody can relate to it because they own vehicles."

Methods The methods for achieving the above objectives include: (1) a damage awareness program, (2) prevention measures based on standards and rules, (3) statistical data tracking and analysis to determine where vehicles are most vulnerable, and (4) follow-up through process audits to discourage bad habits and reinforce good habits by all employees. The basic principle that underlies these methods is that a responsibility system should establish ownership of damage and avoid passing damage down the line to others who did not cause it. Responsibility pushes the problem to where it originates.

VPI uses a "responsibility rule": "When you take ownership, you take responsibility." So if

Figure 5

Damage prevention program overview

			Elements
PLAN	I.	Development	• Uniforms, facilities, processes, vehicle protection
		• Prevention standards	• Audits, checksheets, follow-up
		• Procedures	• Damage report form, PC software program
		• Reporting and tracking system	• Watch covers, posters, charts/PIP campaign, quarterly award
		• Awareness tools/performance recognition	
DO	II.	Implementation	• Corp. management approvals and presentation to VPI operations managers
		• Launch	
		– Corporate VPI support	• Corp. office Q.A. manager visited all locations to launch
		– VPI location "kick-off"	
		• Application	• Prevention standards enforcement, and follow-up
		– Weekly process audits (all locations)	• Operation managers sign-off of each damage
		– Damage reporting and feedback	• Watch covers, posters, trend charts displayed
		– Awareness tools	• Damage prevention PIPs, quarterly top performance award
		– Recognition awards/incentives	
CHECK	III.	Damage data tracking and analysis	• PC program to analyze damage details
		• At each VPI location	• Consolidation of damage statistics, management reports
		• At VPI corporate office	
ACTION	IV.	Continuous improvement	• Monitor trends, Toyota problem solving, audit
		• Statistical analysis and follow-up	• PIP exchange, maintain damage forms, training program
		• Upgrade standards, and objectives	

VPI gets damaged vehicles right off the ship, they must catch it and file a claim for it. The responsibility rule encourages VPI to make sure they don't unknowingly receive damaged vehicles. To prevent damage, they must separate the damage they cause from that others cause. If a vehicle comes in damaged, VPI can push upstream the responsibility for the repair cost and for identifying causes.

In the past, no one tried to determine responsibility for the causes of damage. VPI was a black hole where all undetermined damage would go. VPI absorbed the cost, and in fact, the cost was budgeted for, assuming that a certain amount of damage would occur. Whether VPI caused it or not, VPI was going to fix it. This approach was not conducive to damage prevention. Prevention requires responsibility for and understanding of the causes. Even with the responsibility rule, deter-

mining the causes is difficult to do after the fact, much like reconstructing a crime. Without the responsibility rule, it is next to impossible.

The Overall Plan   The developers of the damage prevention program set it up according to the Deming cycle: Plan, Do, Check, Action (see Figure 5 for a detailed overview). The four major components of the damage prevention program (developed in the Plan stage of Figure 5) are discussed below: prevention standards, procedures, reporting and tracking, and awareness tools/performance recognition.

Prevention Standards   By analyzing the causes of damage in port processing operations, Toyota managers discovered many opportunities for avoiding damage. For each cause, or poten-

Figure 6
Standards for first point of rest (incoming)

Vehicle side to side spacing	Left tires on bay operation lines (*8'6"* minimum bay width).
Vehicle front to rear spacing	Minimum *10"* spacing between bumpers.
Door edge protectors	Door protectors must be located and secure at the widest point of the driver's door rear edge.
Seat protectors	Seat protectors must be secure and properly located on contact area of seat back and cushion.
Carpet floor protectors	Centrally located in driver's floor area.
Damage identification	Any visible damage found should be recorded during initial damage survey and a survey document copy must be located in vehicle. The *VPI Damage Report* form must be used to identify yard and shop damage.
Windows/doors	All doors, windows, and deck lids must be fully closed.
Lot pavement surface	The FPR staging area surface must be clean and in good condition (free of potholes, broken glass, screws, sharp objects, grease, oil, or cleaning chemical puddles, etc.).

tial cause, they developed standards or rules to guide the work of employees. The standards specify what employees do and how they do it. As examples, the standards for first point of rest (incoming vehicles) and for operators are shown in Figures 6 and 7. Similar standards are specified for in-process (interim) vehicle staging, shop installation areas, car wash de-wax, and shipping loadlines (outgoing).

Consider the importance of the standards for parking. Vehicles are parked on holding lots with bay separator lines like any other parking lot. The trouble has been that vehicles were sometimes parked in the center of the lines and other times closer to one line than the other. The resulting lack of standardized spacing between parked vehicles creates potential for damage from opened doors and people squeezing between vehicles. The prevention standard simply states that the vehicle's left tires must be parked on the bay separation lines and the bay width (line separation) should be a minimum of eight feet, six inches. When adhered to, the standard creates standardized side to side spacing. A prevention standard of ten-inch spacing between the bumpers of vehicles parked end to end allows people to walk between the vehicles

without rubbing them. It also helps prevent bumping, which damages bumpers, particularly the expensive and fragile chrome bumpers on trucks.[6]

These standards are pretty basic, but unless someone puts them into writing and constantly reinforces them, they get lost in day-to-day operations. As Leo Dombrowski explains, "If a door edge protector comes off, you must put it back on. It sounds simple, but we've gone without doing it for years, and it will take constant reinforcement to make it happen." Leo further explains, "It was a career improvement for me to come to Toyota, to learn from the best. I thought, though, that it would be a lot more sophisticated and complicated. And what I really found is that quality improvement is more reliant on basics and fundamentals, whether it's in human relations, systems, or statistics."

---

6. A TMC study team followed vehicles all the way from Japan to the dealers and discovered that the dealers were the biggest offender on spacing standards. Dealers tend to park their vehicles close together on highly traversed lots, where prospective buyers, with belt buckles and rivets on blue jeans, squeeze between vehicles to look at prices and interiors.

Figure 7

Standards for operators

Clothing	Metal or hard belt buckles must not be worn or must be completely covered (taped).
	Buttons, zippers, jean rivets, ornamental studs must not be exposed to allow contact with vehicle. At a minimum, nonabrasive tape must be applied over these items when VPI uniforms are not worn.
	Pockets must not be used to hold parts, tools, or hard objects. If tool pouches are used, the material must be nonabrasive, adequately cover tools, and provide adequate padding to prevent dents.
	Soft, clean work gloves must be worn during all installations (exception: where gloves have proven to be an impediment to the installation, such as graphics). Work gloves prevent finger nail scratches, and the transfer of oils, grease, and dirt to the vehicle.
	VPI issued uniforms provide the best protection against damage from clothing!
Jewelry	Jeweled rings must not be worn. Nonjewel bands can be worn if taped or covered.
	Wrist watches must be covered. Soft cloth wrist sweatbands are acceptable protective covering.
	Bracelets must not be worn.
	Long, dangling earrings must not be worn.
	Neck chains must be contained *inside* clothing.
Processing	Guns/tools/parts should be held *close to the body* when entering and exiting vehicles.
	Lift feet to clear sill plate when entering and exiting vehicles.
	Finger-off power tool until fastener is in correct position.
	Verify correct angle of fastener *before* starting to use tool.
	No leaning on vehicle.
	Use *nylon* removal tool to remove plastic interior parts. Do not use razors or screwdrivers to pry interior parts.
Damage notification	Operators must report accidental damage *at the time of occurrence*. This is the best opportunity to investigate and implement additional preventative measures. The *VPI Damage Report* form must be used to identify yard and shop damage.
Vehicle movement	Vehicle speeds must not exceed *15* mph. Vehicle must be driven within approved driving lanes, and observe stops and caution in designated areas. There should be no cutting between rows. All vehicle drivers must receive traffic safety and damage prevention training before operating vehicles. Training certification charts should be used to document and certify individual training.

Audit Procedures To make sure workers do adhere to standards, standardized procedures were developed for audits and follow-ups to be conducted each week at each VPI location (see Figure 8). Over time, the audits reveal the impact of corrective actions. While the VPI operations managers are responsible to ensure the weekly audits are being performed, the locally designed damage prevention coordina- tor performs the audit.[7] These audits provide an ongoing, independent evaluation of damage potential within the process and identify areas needing improvement. The audit checklist (see Figure 9, page 690) records the results

7. Each location designates its own damage prevention co-ordinator. The coordinator may be a manager or hourly worker, and may be a full-time or part-time coordinator.

Figure 8
Audit procedure

Concern classification	All items listed on the audit checklist must be checked and classified by using the symbols listed below:

Symbol	Definition
○	= O.K.
△	= Needs improvement — may cause damage.
	Examples: Fresh tape should be applied to air hose connections.
	Shop floor should be marked to insure a standardized vehicle location.
X	= Noncompliance with standards — will cause damage.
	Examples: Diamond rings worn.
	Door contacts work bench when fully opened.

Audit method

- The *Damage Prevention Coordinator* will conduct a weekly "walk-through" inspection in each of the processing areas.
- The *Damage Prevention Coordinator* will rate each item listed on the audit checksheet through random observation of vehicles, operations, and operators.
- All items classified as 'X' or '△' must be fedback to the responsible supervisor immediately for confirmation and corrective action and recorded on *Audit Follow-Up Report* form.
- A copy of the completed *Audit checksheet* and *Audit Follow-Up form* must be provided to the Port Operations Manager for review.
- The *Audit Checksheet* and *Audit Follow-Up form* must be retained for record files.
- The responsible supervisor must record corrective actions and dates on *Audit Follow-Up form*.
- The Damage Prevention Coordinator will follow-up on corrective actions and record effectiveness on *Audit Follow-Up form*.

---

for each standard.[8] As indicated on the checksheet, the scope of the audit encompasses every step of port processing, from first point of rest (FPR, incoming vehicles) to shipping loadlines (outgoing).

The auditor randomly samples vehicles, operations, and operators. The audit procedures do not specify the size of the sample, but auditors are encouraged to increase or decrease their sample size depending on perceived vulnerability in each area. All items determined either to be in need of improvement

or noncompliant with standards must be fed back to the responsible supervisor and recorded on the audit follow-up report form. On the report form, the auditor describes the condition of each item and indicates the responsible supervisor. Then the responsible supervisor describes the corrective action and the planned and actual dates for correcting the problem. At the next audit, the auditor evaluates the status of the corrective action.

The weekly internal audit is intended for the VPI locations to reinforce themselves and learn about opportunities for improvement. It reveals the condition of incoming vehicles and provides a means for understanding causes of damage. The developer of the damage prevention program, Leo Dombrowski, further explains the emphasis on improvement. "I pur-

---

8. The standards established for the damage prevention program are considered minimum requirements. Additional requirements may be added by the damage prevention coordinator when damage potential is obvious or when damage history points to a cause not specified in documented standards.

Figure 9

Damage prevention program audit checklist

VPI LOCATION _____

	ITEM	F.P.R.	IN-PROCESS STAGING	WASH	SHOP	LOAD LINES
V E H I C L E	Side/Side Spacing					
	Front/Rear Spacing					
	Door Protectors					
	Seat Protectors					
	Carpet Protectors					
	Windows/Doors					
	Pavement/Floor					
	Exterior Cleanliness					
	Unreported Damage					

	ITEM	F.P.R.	IN-PROCESS STAGING	WASH	SHOP	LOAD LINES
E Q U I P M E N T	Air/Electrical Connections					
	Drill Fixtures					
	Ramps/Steps					
	Work Benches					
	Conveyor/Tire Guides					
	Towels, Mats, Rags					
	Tool/Parts Trays					

	ITEM	F.P.R.	IN-PROCESS STAGING	WASH	SHOP	LOAD LINES
O P E R A T O R	Belt Buckles					
	Buttons, ZIppers, etc.					
	Work Gloves					
	Rings					
	Watches, Bracelets					
	Dangling Earrings, Neck Chains					
	Pockets					
	Tool/Parts Handling					
	Tool/Parts Storage					
	Tool Usage, Operation					
	Entering/Exiting					
	15 MPH Speed Limit					

SUMMARY

	F.P.R.	IN-PROCESS STAGING	WASH	SHOP	LOAD LINES
Total O = OK					
Total △ = Requires Improvement					
Total° X °= Requires Correction					

AUDITOR _____

DATE _____

posely did not develop a scoring system for this, because I wanted the focus to be on the issue needing improvement, and not on the numerical score. The evaluation then is just a symbol, zero, triangle, or an X."

External audits by a corporate quality assurance manager are performed irregularly. Some locations are randomly selected, but external audits are primarily prompted by the data from the vehicle damage reports. Statistics on damage will determine what port operations and what areas of the operations will get more intensive follow-up from corporate managers. To make these determinations, corporate managers need reporting and tracking systems that provide reliable and timely information on damage.

Reporting and Tracking Each set of standards reminds workers about damage identification and reporting. For example, the standards for shop/installation areas state: "All visible damage (regardless of origin) must be reported and documented at point of discovery. Processing of damaged vehicles must not continue until damage is clearly identified and communicated on vehicle to insure control. The VPI damage report form must be used to identify yard and shop damage. Report and investigate the damage cause immediately to prevent similar reoccurrence." The yard and shop damage report describes where the damage was discovered, the nature and location of the damage (verbally and pictorially), the probable cause of the damage, investigation and countermeasures proposed.

The VPI operations manager at each location is responsible for daily summarizing and analyzing the raw data from both the damage reports by damage discovery location, damage description, and damage cause, and from corresponding damage repair reports, which describe the repair, the replacement parts used, and the repair costs. Obviously, sometimes managers are just guessing about causes and countermeasures of the damage reports, but

this requirement does continuously remind them of the objective to prevent damage. Each week, the operations managers track damage/repair data, analyze trends, chart damage statistics, and post the results for visual control.

In the early stages of the program, VPI operations manager signed each vehicle damage report and sent it to the VPI headquarters, in Torrance, California, daily for executive review. This procedure has since been revised. The quality assurance manager at headquarters no longer reviews individual damage reports, just summary reports. Each month, he collects and consolidates the damage data from all locations, tracks overall results, and publishes a management report that summarizes audit concerns for vehicle, operator, and equipment standards. These requirements for damage reporting may eventually be eliminated, but initially the reporting has effectively captured the attention of the operations managers.

Before the damage reporting and tracking system was put in place, VPI managers did not know where damage most frequently occurred or what parts of the vehicle were most susceptible to damage. Everybody had ideas and guesses, but nobody really knew. When the damage prevention program was launched in July 1991, initial findings provided some answers. For example, managers with years of experience in the industry were convinced that doors were the more frequently damaged part, but Pareto analysis revealed that bumpers are more frequently damaged. Standardized front and rear spacing in parking should help correct the problem, but awareness will also make a difference. People had just assumed that bumpers could take the punishment, so they didn't check for damage.

While bumpers were most frequently damaged, door, seat, and carpet protection were the most frequently reported concerns. Plastic door edge protectors and paper floor mats and seat covers were too frequently missing or off location. More detailed data analysis indicated

Figure 10

Vehicle protectors: percent missing or off location

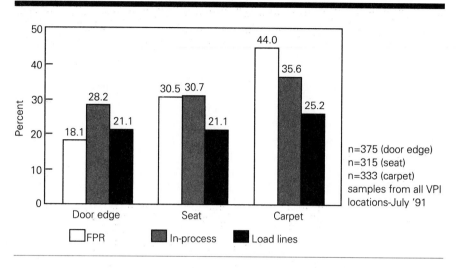

n=375 (door edge)
n=315 (seat)
n=333 (carpet)
samples from all VPI
locations-July '91

☐ FPR   ▨ In-process   ■ Load lines

where these problems most frequently occurred, first point of rest, in-process, or the load lines (see Figure 10). The data indicated that 18.1 percent of the door edge protectors were out of place by the time the vehicles had reached the first point of rest. With this kind of data, VPI managers have a better idea of where to focus their attention for damage prevention.

Sometimes the search for causes is easy. For example, the most likely cause of a scratch on the roof of a vehicle which had a roof rack installed is the installation process. Further investigation should reveal specific causes, and whether the standards were followed in installation. Other times, the search for specific causes is difficult, as with a small scratch on a front door.

The data can reveal other things about the damage prevention program. For example, if the damage reports reveal that most of the damage is being discovered at the final quality assurance checkpoint before the vehicles are loaded for outbound transport, that tells managers to put more emphasis on upstream prevention activities and auditing. By analyzing and piecing together various data on damage, an operations manager can derive an action plan for improvement based on data, not opinions.

Not only has the data been useful to identify the causes of damage and encourage better adherence to standards by workers within VPI, it has also given VPI managers a basis for attacking causes outside VPI. For example, VPI purchases and replaces vehicle protectors throughout each processing stage as a short-term fix. VPI Long Beach purchased and replaced 32,700 missing door edge protectors between January and June 1991 (29.5 percent of all vehicles processed at Long Beach). Using data from damage reports and industry studies, VPI has concluded that the door edge protectors are deficient in design. Toyota door edge protectors were inadequate compared to the domestic automakers' versions designed for the U.S. environment. VPI has obtained Toyota Motor Sales' executive support for VPI's request to Toyota in Japan for improved factory-installed protectors as a long-term solution.

The frequent occurrence of soiled vehicle interiors, revealed in the J. D. Power survey results, tempted VPI to insist that dealers do a better job of washing and cleaning interiors. However, the damage is likely related to the high rate of missing or off-location seat and carpet protectors. Again, as a short-term fix, VPI associates are asked to replace them each time they are discovered out of place. As a long-term solution for prevention, to ensure the vehicles are clean, regardless of whether the dealer washes and cleans them, VPI requested better designs from TMC Japan. They requested that TMC (1) upgrade the design for durability and retention of driver's seat protectors, (2) enlarge the floor protectors to cover the entire foot area of each model, (3) design dirt- and moisture-resistant floor protectors, and (4) add door sill and lower front door trim protection. Toyota regards the substantial costs for these protectors to be a worthy investment in overall customer satisfaction.

Awareness Tools/Performance Recognition
To launch the damage prevention program, corporate managers offered visible support for the operations managers at each VPI location. For example, the VPI quality assurance manager visited each location for the launch, trained the people on every aspect of the program, and assisted with the initial internal audits. To promote awareness of the damage prevention program, promotional items such as sweatbands/watch covers and belt covers were issued to everyone. Posters also remind workers of the causes of damage, such as uncovered shirt buttons; pencils, pens, and tools in pockets; bracelets, rings, and watches; and uncovered belt buckles.

Corporate managers also establish a special "factory fresh" campaign to solicit suggestions on damage prevention from all associates through the existing suggestion program called "partners in productivity" (PIP). For every suggestion submitted, the associates were given a gift, such as a VPI sport bag. For suggestions that were implemented, they received raffle tickets for a color TV. The campaign significantly increased the number of suggestions in the launch month, July 1991 (see Figure 11).[9] Encouraging the associates to offer suggestions fostered a lot of ideas as well as helped get the program rolling. It helped create buy-in and led to some improvements. For example, a survey revealed that one of the main reasons associates in unionized facilities choose not to use Toyota's "damage preventing" uniforms was their style and color. Since uniforms were not addressed in the current union contract, associates in unionized facilities cannot be required to wear them. In response, VPI has developed new uniforms, with preferred styles and colors, to encourage more associates to use them voluntarily. If an associate chooses not to wear the VPI uniform, his or her personal clothing must still comply with damage prevention standards (no jean rivets, exposed belt buckles, etc.).

The quality assurance manager issues a damage prevention award each quarter. The performance of each VPI operator is judged against its own damage history and year objectives.

Initial Results
The initial results of the VPI damage prevention program are positive. The overall VPI damage rate and dollars per unit processed are gradually trending down (see Figures 12 and 13). The absence of dramatic changes is both good and bad. Certainly, VPI managers would like to see more improvement; however, they feel good about the validity of the numbers they are getting and would be skeptical of numbers reflecting dramatic changes. While

---

9. This result told Toyota managers that the PIP suggestion program needs a little promotion every so often. They plan to continue with such campaigns on different themes, for example, safety.

Figure 11

VPI monthly PIP suggestions

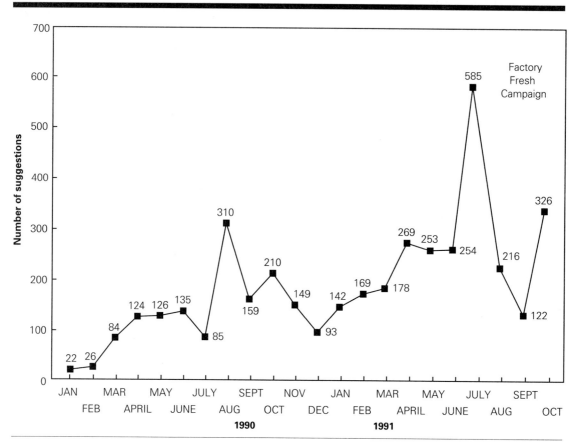

the improvements have not been dramatic from month to month, over time the change has been substantial.

Comparing the time periods before program launch (January—June 1991) to after program launch (July 1991—May 1992), the average damage rate was actually reduced by 46 percent (from .526 to .285). Damage severity from before to after was reduced by 7 percent (from 129.92 to 120.95 dollars per damage). Damage cost per unit processed was reduced by 50 percent (from .68 to .34 dollars per unit processed), for a projected cost savings of approximately $288,000.

Keeping Spirits Up

The damage prevention program relies heavily on the imposition of standards and auditing for adherence to standards. This approach might seem distasteful to some. The developer of the damage prevention program, Leo Dombrowski, explains how he tries to make it more palatable. "One key is stressing the positive. In quality, that's a tough thing to do, because you're generally talking about problems, defects. We change the terminology around a little bit and just call it 'concerns' rather than 'defects.' We say things like 'needs improvement,' rather than 'good' or 'bad'. Rather than

Figure 12

Overall VPI damage rate trend continues to decline

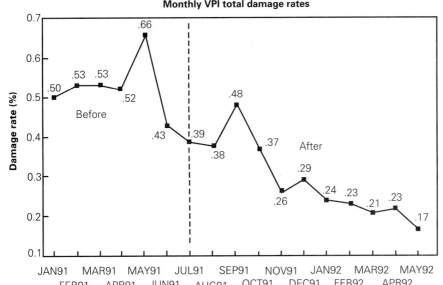

Monthly VPI total damage rates

say 'permanent dissatisfaction,' we say 'continuous improvement.' It comes from the Japanese; it's a strong factor in getting people to cooperate and have an open mind. If you talk in terms of negatives too frequently, then the defense mechanisms go up. And nobody listens to the reasons. In quality control I've always felt like the policeman or bearer of bad news, always dealing with problems. Telling someone that their system or their product is no good, especially since many times they have put a lot of sweat into it, the message isn't received too well. But to say that we can do a little better leaves the door open for a positive response."

▶ U.S. PRODUCTS (ACCESSORIES)

U.S. Products is a department of TMS that develops accessories to be manufactured in the United States and put on Toyota vehicles by VPI or dealers. These accessories include armrests, air conditioning systems, wheel covers, running boards, off road packages and bumpers for trucks, and necessities like motor oil, powertrain fluid, and brake fluid. Some of these products may be used in U.S. assembly plants to equip vehicles before they leave the plant.[10] U.S. Products also coordinates the development of protective coatings that port processors apply to vehicles prior to rail transit. It also develops procedures for application and removal of the coating.

U.S. Products does marketing, prototype development, and supplier relations. If studies

---

10. 90 percent of domestically produced vehicles are fully equipped at the plant.

Figure 13

Overall VPI damage dollars per unit processed

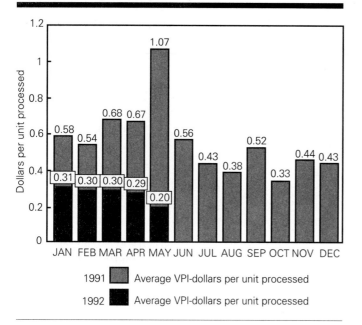

| | 1991 | Average VPI-dollars per unit processed |
| | 1992 | Average VPI-dollars per unit processed |

indicate people want an accessory on Toyota vehicles, U.S. Products designs it and tests it. Then they work closely with suppliers to establish the quality level and maintain it. U.S. Products continues to help Toyota establish a qualified U.S. supplier base. The port and dealer operations will be improved by improving the part quality as received, designing products that are "installer friendly," delivering in a timely manner, and developing products based on customer wants and needs. U.S. Products' quality improvement activities for supplier development are summarized below.

- Total quality management training

    Increased top management awareness/participation

    Organizing to support a quality production environment

    Developing long-term systems to train work force for *kaizen* activities

- *Daruma* projects/improvement themes

    Training in group activities (problem solving, product development, quality function deployment)

    Practice utilizing TQM knowledge to improve some aspect of the supplier company and use as success story to expand this practice

- Toyota production system training

    Working with key suppliers, vast strides can be made to improve the following: efficiency, material handling practices, standardized work procedures, reduced work in process/inventories, reduced scrap, and better quality

- Supplier capability audit

    A cross-discipline team reviews all business aspects of a supplier to ensure if they are the best possible candidate

    Review all functions and rate accordingly to assist supplier in improving shortcomings

- Supplier quality assurance activities
    Audit functions to assure ongoing compliance
    Assist suppliers in training, problem resolution, and product improvements

Once high-quality accessories are designed and produced, they must be installed. The cross-functional efforts to improve accessory installation are discussed in more detail below.

Accessory Installation

U.S. Products develops the installation procedures and training program for each accessory. Then U.S. Products personnel go to the ports and teach the port processors how to install these accessories. U.S. Products also provides accessory installation instructions and training to dealers to help improve delivery quality, which was never done before. In addition to conducting on-site training, U.S. Products also provides "train the trainer" programs to encourage ongoing training by personnel at the installation location. A certification program confirms the dissemination of training.

Prior to training, U.S. Products develops all the process operation sheets which tell installers exactly what to do, in sequence, and specify the type of power tools, wrenches, sockets, and screws to use. In many cases, installers have to remove parts from the vehicle, install the accessory, and then put the parts back. U.S. Products determines the best disassembly and assembly operation sequence.

The process operation sheets also explain the post-installation inspection. It specifies questions like: Are all the screws in? Are there no scratches? No grease? No handprints? Do all the parts fit back properly? Are they all tight? etc. Since the port processors get paid for installation, U.S. Products personnel establish standard times for completing each job.

Process operation sheets are not developed in the office, but on location with actual installers at a port processing center. Development proceeds through a couple of iterations between writing the instructions, trying them out in actual installations, and revising them.

The Quality Audit

As in other areas of TMS, U.S. Products conducts a quality audit to ensure that actions conform to standards. The first part of the audit focuses on the process of installation: how workers assemble and disassemble parts, where they put parts, protection of the vehicle with protective covers, the placement of parts in special trays, etc. The second part of the audit examines completed vehicles. The auditor goes into the yard and audits vehicles for functioning, parts working, parts put together properly, damage, looseness, dirtiness, lint on the carpets. The audit produces a score that TMS uses as a quality measurement for all of the processing locations: those owned by Toyota, independents, and even private distributors (e.g., southeast Toyota).

To support improvement after an audit reveals deficiencies, U.S. Products provides on-location quality counseling to help develop solutions. As Bill deManincor, national port and transportation quality manager, explains, "If somebody needs help, they can call us on the phone, they can talk to us by satellite, they can come visit us, and if it is bad enough, we'll go see them. A good, strong follow-up makes sure it happens." U.S. Products has also devoted two people, full time, to investigate instances where parts do not fit together or accessories cannot be installed properly. For example, design changes sometimes result in relocated holes or changes in bolts. As soon as they discover difficulties, these two people devise a solution and notify all other locations, often before the other locations have encountered any difficulty. They do the "firefighting" so many others will not have to.

Bill deManincor explains the supportive,

yet demanding attitude that pervades management at TMS. "We're very willing to go and provide the assistance to correct weakness. That's all part of our philosophy. I can always go there and slap somebody's hand, but it doesn't really accomplish anything. So you have to let them know that they're a little weak, show them the opportunity to improve, and give them the means to improve. That means providing the tools, whether it is a hand tool, education, exposure to certain situations, or even sending a national manager like myself to a particular location to show that we support them 100 percent. Whatever it takes to get them to improve, that's what we'll provide. Then we work as a team to take advantage of the opportunity to improve." Regarding Toyota's heavy emphasis on standardization, Bill goes on to say, "I don't think Toyota specifies standards any more than the domestic auto companies. I think the difference is the amount of training that our people get and the repetitiveness of emphasizing that things be done a certain way. Toyota is stronger at enforcing standardized work."

An Example of Cross-Functional Work

The contributions of U.S. Products to the delivery quality improvement program have required cross-functional collaboration. For example, implementing standardized instructions at dealerships required that departments collaborate cross-functionally as never before. U.S. Products could not just walk into the dealerships and implement changes without the knowledge of other departments, including regional sales organizations, which oversee dealer activities; marketing, which wants dealers to use more genuine Toyota authorized parts; and parts distribution, which is responsible for getting the parts to the dealers.

These departments assembled into an informal working group or task force to plan the implementation of the dealer training. Working together, they developed the content, such as standardized instructions, and a coordinated plan for implementation. With a lot of homework done up front, the implementation of the standards and training was done with few glitches. Each department knew its role and fulfilled it according to schedule. As Bill deManincor explains, "It helps the people that are receiving the training when they see how organized it is. And they can tell how much effort we put into it by how easy the material is to understand. They take it more seriously." Audits indicate that the training was a success. Through the coordination of this informal team, another small piece of the delivery quality improvement program was put in place.

▶ LOGISTICS: TRUCKS AND TRAINS

When an imported vehicle reaches the shores of the United States, it enters Toyota's logistics network, which is growing increasingly complex with the addition of domestic plants to numerous ports of origin and rail consolidation points. As part of their duties, logistics managers have to make routing decisions about how to get Toyota vehicles through this logistics network to the dealers. They consider things such as load make-up, cost, schedule, and quality of transportation (or damage potential). Imported vehicles arriving in Portland, Oregon, and destined for a dealer in Tacoma, Washington, are generally trucked directly to the dealer.[11] Vehicles destined for Minneapolis, Minnesota, are shipped via rail transit to St. Paul, processed at the rail consolidation point, and then trucked to the dealer.

Routing decisions are not always simple. As Ron Johnson, inland logistics manager, puts it, "The shortest distance between points A

---

11. The Portland region includes Montana, Idaho, Oregon, and Washington.

and B isn't necessarily a straight line anymore. Trucking a vehicle 700 miles may seem to make great economic sense, but it may not be the wisest way to go in a certain region of the country because of exposure to the elements. It may be better to go rail transit the first 500 miles and then truck the last leg of the trip." For example, it may be wiser to truck vehicles from the rail consolidation point in Salt Lake City to dealers in southeastern Idaho than to truck them all the way from Portland.

In addition to the traditional task of making routing decisions, logistics managers at Toyota are also involved in the effort to improve delivery quality through prevention. Although improvements have been widespread and diverse, initial efforts to improve logistical activities began with rail transit. Toyota efforts to improve rail transit performance initially concentrated on transit times.

Transit Times

When managers in the TMS logistics department started investigating rail transit times, they first discovered that nobody ever went to measure whether the transit times stated in the contracts actually happened. Toyota had relied on the railroads to report their on-time performance. Consequently, the railroads often reported 100 percent on-time performance when they were actually 50 percent late and 50 percent early. In their minds, it averaged out to 100 percent on-time.

As a necessary first step to providing an independent source of information, TMS hired an outside consultant to track actual transit times. Once they did so, TMS managers discovered tremendous variation across carriers in meeting the standards quoted in their contracts. Further analysis, by segmenting the data according to origin, destination, and carrier (e.g., Union Pacific versus Norfolk Southern), revealed which routes and which carriers were most deviant from standards. With the transit time data in hand, TMS managers started working with all of their transit suppli-

ers as partners, giving particular attention to improving the most deviant.

Using the problem solving process, TMS managers engaged with their transit partners in identifying and improving the causes of variation. They discovered, for example, that unrealistic transit times were being quoted in contracts because the marketing departments never talked to the operating departments to see what was possible. Once transit times were promised, operating departments were not informed of the performance expectations. And when schedules were known, there were no ramifications for not getting the trains out on time. Other causes pertained to incongruities between day of week for transit and capacity planning. Also, special events like track construction caused delays.

Some of the causes of variation were corrected by simply improving communication. For example, TMS explained schedules, expectations, and reasons for certain requirements to the switchmen and brakemen. As Jay Fortenberry, logistics operations manager, explained, "Having worked in the freight yards, I know the people there want to do a good job. They just need to know what is expected of them. If you don't tell them, they aren't going to seek it out. It will not get done."

By working through thorny issues and whittling away at problems and causes of variation, TMS logistics managers have been able to build more predictability into the system. For example, "on-time transit" for Union Pacific went from 62 percent to 92 percent. With reduced variability in transit times, dealers know when they order a vehicle how long it will take to get it. In addition to transit times, TMS has also worked to improve the supply and the quality of rail equipment. And as with port processing, improvements have focused on damage prevention.

Equipment Quality and Damage Prevention
Equipment in the U.S. rail industry is aging. The design of most rail cars is thirty-five years

old, and many of the rail cars are themselves that old. Often the effects of aging, such as rust, present causes of damage to Toyota vehicles in transit. Rust can damage paint's factory-fresh finish. Toyota regards rusty rail cars as dirty. And Toyota's fundamental rule in rail transit is, "Don't load dirty rail cars."

Rail Car Standards The legal document referred to in the rail transit industry as Appendix B states the standards for rail cars, including cleanliness standards. But the problem with Appendix B is, as Jay Fortenberry explains, "It is wide open to interpretation." Left to their own devices, the railroads would provide cars that comply with Appendix B, but which are deemed dirty by Toyota. It seemed to be an impossible situation to improve. To remedy this situation, Toyota developed its own set of standards for rail equipment. Toyota's rail car acceptance standards are listed below:

Unacceptable Conditions

To prevent rust contamination, the following will be enforced:

1. There will be *no* loose metal particles on any of the rail car decks (a magnet will be used on any questionable material).
2. There will be *no* metal particles left hanging from the overhead surfaces of the rail car. This includes any flaking, peeling, or "sporing" (any questionable material is *not* acceptable if it will become loose during loading or with dropping of the hinged rail car deck).
3. There will be *no* flaking, loose, or sporing rust on any of the rail car surfaces (decks, walls, roofs).

In addition, in order to prevent interior soiling or personal injuries, the following will also be enforced:

4. There will be *no* loose dirt on any of the rail car decks.

5. All equipment *must* be in proper working order. This includes: hinged decks, wheel chocks, ratchet and locking pins, hand brakes, and end-of-car cushioning devices.
6. All ratchet and idler blocks, end doors, and hinged decks must be fully lubed and easily movable, as designed.

If any of the above are not satisfied prior to spotting, the rail car will *not* be loaded. The above steps are to include inbound loaded rail cars, where the intention is to reload the rail car. It is up to the Toyota operating manager to see that these conditions are met and enforced.

Acceptable Conditions

The following will be acceptable conditions to load under:

1. Rust stains on decks, walls, and overhead surfaces of rail cars due to water staining. This does not include staining which has progressed to the flaking or peeling stages; only discoloration will be allowed.
2. Rail cars which are dusty/dirty, where dirt/dust cannot be removed with blowing equipment, will be loaded (rail cars must not have rust peeling, flaking, sporing, or contain loose metal filings).
3. Peeling paint will be allowed as long as the paint has no signs of rust/metal particles underneath or attached to it.
4. Insufficiently lubed or functioning wheel chocks, ratchets, idler blocks, end doors, and hinged decks will be loaded at the loading point Toyota operations manager's discretion.

As always, the Toyota operations manager has the last right of refusal or acceptance to the above standards.

To ensure the interpretability of the standards, pictures are used to differentiate "clean" from "dirty," "acceptable" from "unacceptable." The main focus of the pictorial standards is any loose or hanging metal particles which may become airborne or fall onto painted surfaces.

Engineering for Rail Transit   There is more to damage-free transit than just ensuring that rust and dirt do not contaminate the paint. The design of rail equipment also can contribute to damage. A long-range challenge for Toyota is to get the rail industry to upgrade their design of rail cars. After all, the automobile has evolved (e.g., without a frame and with unibody construction), while rail cars have remained essentially unchanged. In rail transit, vehicles may have to endure severe forces which can damage the vehicles in absence of any human operators.

Jay Fortenberry describes the hard lesson that Toyota engineers learned about designing vehicles for the rough ride of U.S. railroads. "I was traveling with the product engineers down in Long Beach. When they presented their planned tie-down methods for Toyota's new van, I said, 'Hey, this will never work, it'll fail.' One of them said, 'Oh no, we know about designing cars,' I said, 'Fine, it's gonna fail.' When we transported the first shipment of vans, we ripped off some tie-down brackets. Since that experience, my logistics group and the engineering group in Toyota City, Japan, have gotten really close. They came over and rode American railroads for a month, and documented with sensors almost every event that happened. The engineers performed very aggressive tests on existing products and prototypes. They got a good feel for American railroads. And from now on they will involve us at the beginning of product development, thirty-five months prior to launch. That should be enough time to alter equipment and vehicle design."

Vehicle Handling Standards   If mishandled, even a properly designed vehicle loaded onto high-quality rail equipment can result in damage. To avoid damage, TMS developed standards for handling, loading, and unloading

Toyota vehicles. These standards are assembled into a vehicle handling manual. Every person who handles a Toyota vehicle should be familiar with its contents. The first page of the manual states, "All procedures in this manual are to be followed without exception, unless notified or agreed upon (in writing) by Toyota and/or Lexus."

Similar to the detailed standards for port processing, the vehicle handling manual specifies standards for loading/unloading personnel, vehicle handling procedures, tie-down hooks, and keying procedures. The manual also specifies and illustrates tie-down procedures for each model, such as the Celica. It specifies truck-away instructions for tractor and trailor equipment, loading and unloading, and rail car instructions for transport equipment, preparation for loading, loading, wheel chock application, chain tension and unloading.

The Auditing Process   TMS did not just send the manuals out to the field and demand everyone comply. They treated the standards as an educational tool and used them to actively train all involved personnel. TMS managers publish the material and take it to the field themselves, and hold training seminars and breakfast meetings to promote improvement. They conduct audits to ensure compliance with the standards, then check to ensure that actual practices conform to standards.

TMS developed a comprehensive auditing procedure to identify areas that need improvement, including facilities, equipment, and procedures.[12] Detailed explanations of the standards for each item on the audit are available for all personnel. For example, the standard for item B1 (placement of rail cars: deck heights) states that: "The deck height differences between rail cars (bilevel and trilevel) must be no more than 3 inches."

---

12. Similar audits are conducted for trucking and dewax operations.

The standards were developed in conjunction with Toyota engineering design teams. As Ron Johnson, inland logistics manager, illustrates, "Just this year, two of the people in my department were involved in a TMC test where they actually rode on a specially equipped train from Portland to west Chicago and back again. It took about nine days. The rail cars were loaded with vehicles and all kinds of instrumentation, monitoring, closed circuit television. Sensory data was collected for the entire ride, taken back to Japan and put into what they call a shaker, a simulated rail car. What they're trying to do is emulate the ride of American rail, to ascertain the forces that go on during the transportation process." From such investigations, the engineers develop standards, which TMS managers translate into audits and support manuals. TMC also used the information to design-in the needed vehicle structural integrity for rail transport (not an issue in Japan).

Initially, these audits are performed on a monthly basis at each facility by corporate managers, and then less frequently at facilities that improve their performance. Auditors arrive unannounced and invite facility managers to accompany them for the full day that it typically requires to complete the audit. Facility personnel are also encouraged to perform the audit weekly on themselves. All audits are discussed with the facility personnel to review needs for improvement.

The Audit Score   Unlike the audit of port processing discussed earlier, the logistics audit yields an audit score based on the number of demerits accumulated for deviation from standards. After the audit is completed, demerits are totalled and subtracted from 100 to give a score for the facility (or trucking company or dewax operation). The logistics managers feel that scoring provides incentive for improvement. They tabulate and distribute monthly scores to allow each facility to see how they compare to others and to motivate them

to be the best in the country. The scores also feed problem analysis and follow-up procedures for making improvements.

The audit scores have improved, with most facilities scoring in the 90s. However, as Jay Fortenberry suggests, "We are going to have to reevaluate the audit and reweight it so that areas where we are weak get weighted more heavily. A facility can do something major [like failing to meet tie-down standards] and still get a 90 on the audit. The reweighting will push those scores back down into the 70s."

Collaboration with Other Rail Transit Customers

The most challenging obstacle to improving rail transit quality has been that, in order to hold down costs, "everybody uses everybody else's railway equipment." Each automobile producer has rail equipment assigned to it. However, Toyota may use General Motors', Ford's, or Chrysler's rail equipment, for example, in Portland where a lot of General Motors rail equipment terminates. Toyota reloads the General Motors rail equipment for shipments to the midwest. In the past, Toyota standards for rail car quality have exceeded that of the domestic automobile producers, and their choosiness in selecting rail cars has bred some resentment.

For example, the cleaning crews in the railroad collecting yards have learned to designate rail cars for Toyota that are more likely to meet Toyota standards. As Ron Johnson states, "The cleaning crew will walk through the yard and cherry-pick the cars. They will pick the ones that are easily cleanable for Toyota and tag them. Those cars that would take all day to clean, they leave for other companies."

While the cleaning crews may cherry-pick the "good" rail cars for Toyota, it is difficult to unilaterally improve the quality of rail transit without the involvement of other automobile producers. And Toyota has faced mixed responses from domestic automobile producers to their campaigns for industry cooperation.

In pursuit of industry cooperation, Toyota invited the chief executive officers of the seven major railroads to Japan for a meeting of the Japanese Automobile Manufacturing Association (JAMA). The meeting reiterated for JAMA members the nature and importance of the American railroad system in the physical distribution of vehicles.[13] The JAMA meeting also offered the first occasion where the heads of the major railroads were together. JAMA used the opportunity to get commitment from the railroads to long-term improvement in rail quality and timely delivery. The railroad CEOs responded positively. Representatives from Ford and Chrysler also attended the JAMA meeting, while General Motors was "conspicuously absent."

▶ DEALERS: SALES AND SERVICE

Once a vehicle reaches the dealer's lot, it would be easy for managers at Toyota Motor Sales to regard it as "out of our hands." However, TMS managers pursue delivery quality improvement even at the dealerships. After all, as Bob Daly, corporate service operations manager, states, "It's still our customer, and it's still our car. So we have to be very concerned about it." The TMC product quality task force uncovered many more defects per vehicle at dealerships than at the plant, port, or rail head. In fact, the number of defects per vehicle found at the dealership was more than six times greater than at the plant, more than five times greater than at the port, and about three times greater than at the rail head.

The 1991 J. D. Power new car sales satisfaction index reveals the opportunity for improvement that Toyota has within the industry.[14] The sales satisfaction index (SSI) is derived from three measures of performance: the salesperson (courtesy, knowledge, etc.), the delivery activities (operating explanations), and the initial product condition (cleanliness and problems). While Lexus ranked first, Toyota ranked fifteenth, not because of shoddy workmanship or poor quality at the plant, but because of what happened to the vehicles after they left the plant. In support of this conclusion, the 1991 J. D. Power survey on initial product condition, indicates that Toyota has only 89.8 problems per 100 vehicles, much lower than the industry average of 141 problems per 100 vehicles. (Among Toyota's major competitors, only Honda came close with 111. Saturn had 151.3, and Nissan had 159.7). However, Toyota is little different from its major competitors on ratings for clean and undamaged interiors and exteriors. It seems that vehicles are being dirtied and damaged on the way from the plant to the customer.

Quality Checks at the Dealership

In response to this data, TMS developed a dealer delivery quality improvement plan (see Figure 14). We discuss some of the more important elements of this plan below.

New Vehicle Receipt TMS extends to dealerships the principle that "we don't send the vehicle on to the next stage if it isn't right." Before the delivery quality improvement program, however, this principle was absent. For example, vehicles could arrive at the dealership with damage and nobody knew it, because many of the dealerships, particularly those with higher damage rates, had no check-in system for dealer receipt after transport. The first step to ensure delivery quality at the dealership

---

13. Vehicles are distributed exclusively through coastal ports and trucks in Japan.
14. Approximately 83,000 questionnaires were mailed to owners of cars registered for private use in November and December 1990.

Figure 14
TMS dealer delivery quality improvement plan

Program development
- Establish delivery quality index
  - ✔ Similar to OSI and TSS indexes
  - ✔ Set objective of % NVSDS returned without a problem
  - ✔ Incorporate in all future recognition/training programs
- Dealership service department support items
  - ✔ Vehicle receipt guidelines
  - ✔ Predelivery service process improvements
  - ✔ Dealer installed option guidelines
- Develop dealership sales department support items
  - ✔ Vehicle storage and handling guidelines
  - ✔ Vehicle final inspection checklist
  - ✔ Standardize-vehicle delivery process
  - ✔ Vehicle presentation enhancements

Field/dealer implementation
- TMS executive *video conference* with TMD/PD management
- Conduct kick-off meetings and provide training for dealer upgrading
  - ✔ District sales managers
  - ✔ District service managers
  - ✔ Other regional/personnel
- Launch dealer awareness/program
  - ✔ Campaign introduction letter
  - ✔ Video message from TMS executives to dealers
  - ✔ Promotional print materials: brochure, poster, etc.

Field/dealer launch
- Provide training materials to dealers
  - ✔ Vehicle receipt and PDS training to service personnel
  - ✔ Vehicle storage and delivery process training to sales personnel
- Target low performing, high volume dealers for improvement
  - ✔ Provide joint sales/service consultations
- Review all dealerships' vehicle-handling and delivery process during regular DM/DSM contacts

Additional elements
- Establish monitor dealers to report as received vehicle quality (one per district)
- Provide port and dealer paint and body repair training (est. 200 dealers—1991)
- Include delivery-quality message in sales and service training materials
- Study the feasibility of establishing sales delivery area at dealerships
- Provide PDS technician performance feedback to dealers (as currently done for salespersons)

Current actions
- TMS and region/PD awareness activities
  - ✔ TMS customer satisfaction committee involvement
  - ✔ Region/PD service/C.R. manager presentations
  - ✔ Board of directors meeting review
- Dealer awareness activities
  - ✔ Discussion at dealer council meeting
  - ✔ Parts and service advisory board meeting topic
  - ✔ New model dealer meeting topic
- Develop effective dealer measurement reports to be used by TMS regions/PDs and dealerships

---

was to have a new vehicle receipt system for checking in transported vehicles.

Through a consultation approach, TMS district managers started working with dealers, the worst offenders first, to ensure they had a new vehicle receipt system. These district managers used a consultation approach which

required them to walk through the entire vehicle handling process and evaluate the quality controls at the dealer. They used their own judgment to identify problems and develop solutions in consultation with the dealer. They indicated a yes or no response to the questions listed below, indicated whether the area needs improvement, and recorded evaluations on an evaluation form.

Questions about New Vehicle Receipt

1. Does the dealership have an established new vehicle check-in system?
2. Who is responsible for new vehicle check-in? (name/title, reports to: name/title)
3. Is there a back-up system? (describe)
4. Does the inspection include verification that options and accessories match the Monroney label?
5. Is there a separate parking area for newly received vehicles?
6. Pull twenty receipts for recently received vehicles. Does it appear that dealer personnel are doing a quality inspection?

TMS sent the dealers a booklet on procedures of how to check in a vehicle. The inspection procedures are important to Toyota's approach to identifying the causes of problems. Any problems found at new vehicle receipt are reflected back to upstream processes. Having standardized procedures for new vehicle receipt is particularly important because of the high turnover common to the job. New employees are constantly being trained for the job.

Other Evaluations In addition to the new vehicle receipt system, the district manager evaluates other areas important to delivery quality. These areas include predelivery service (inspection and repair of damage, and verification that all systems and controls are operating as designed prior to delivery to the purchaser, storage, and new vehicle delivery (the final quality check as the new vehicle is delivered to the purchaser). The evaluations are recorded on forms with questions similar to the new vehicle receipt form. The questions composing the forms are listed below. (Notice that in each area, the district manager examines twenty receipts or repair orders, and/or inspects several vehicles, to confirm that the quality checks are actually being done.)

Questions about Predelivery Service

1. Are all vehicles predelivered upon receipt?
2. Is PDS performed by line technicians?
3. Do PDS technicians report to the service manager?
4. What is the predelivery person's pay plan?
5. Who installs the in-dealership accessories? (name/title)
6. Are "due bills" created for accessories that are to be installed on new vehicles?
7. Are there provisions for weekend predelivery?
8. Is the Toyota Touch new vehicle delivery check sheet being used during predelivery?
9. Is the new vehicle predelivery area clean and well lighted?
10. Are vehicles quality checked after predelivery?
11. Pull twenty recent internal repair orders for PDS. Does it appear from the technician's comments and documentation that the technician is doing a thorough predelivery inspection?

Questions about Storage

1. Is there sufficient parking space for new vehicle inventory?
2. Is there sufficient space (at least three feet) between vehicles to prevent damage when doors are open?
3. Does the dealership utilize off-site storage for new vehicle inventory?
4. Does the dealership wash all new vehicles in inventory at least once per week?
5. Does the sales department monitor new vehicle inventory for lot damage and take corrective action prior to sale?
6. Have the sales and service managers reviewed the Toyota new vehicle storage and

handling guidelines and adopted these guidelines?

7. Walk the dealer's new vehicle inventory lot(s). Does the dealer's inventory appear to be clean, well maintained, and ready for delivery?

Questions about New Vehicle Delivery

1. Does the sales department have an established procedure for new vehicle delivery? (describe)
2. Is there a special delivery area?
3. Do salespersons inspect vehicles prior to delivery?
4. Does the inspection include verification that purchased options/accessories are installed and working?
5. Are "due bills" created for commitments that can't be fulfilled at time of delivery?
6. Are vehicles sufficiently cleaned for delivery?
7. Who is responsible for demonstration of vehicle features and operation for customers? (name/title)
8. Does the presentation include a review of warranty coverages?
9. Are service and parts operating hours, appointment system, etc., explained to customers?
10. Are customers introduced to key service and parts personnel when available?
11. Does the customer receive a dealership information brochure?
12. Is a demonstration ride offered at delivery?
13. Are Toyota new vehicle delivery check sheet forms properly completed, signed, and filed?
14. Are customers given a copy of the Toyota new vehicle delivery check sheet at delivery?
15. Inspect one or more vehicles that are ready for delivery today. In your estimation, will these vehicles meet the customer's expectations in terms of cleanliness and general preparation for delivery?

After completing evaluations in all areas, the TMS district manager fills out a delivery quality improvement plan which records all areas of concern, specific recommendations, planned and actual completion dates, individuals assigned responsibility, and the current status. The district manager uses the plan to conduct a follow-up during the next visit to the dealer.

Predelivery Service Predelivery service is particularly important to delivery quality. Performed after the new vehicle is unloaded from the transport truck, it ensures the vehicle meets a list of requirements for delivery quality before it is sold to a customer. The predelivery service includes the following:

A. *Before inspection* Install fuse(s) and outside rear-view mirrors
B. *Functional operation* Check all lights, gauges, horn, wipers, mirrors, cigarette lighter, sunroof, audio system and set clock
C. *Walk-around inspection* Check window operation, doors and locks, rear defogger, exterior and trunk lights, trim appearance, spare tire pressure, jack and tool installation, and headlight aim
D. *Under hood* Check for leaks of fluids and check engine oil and fluid levels, engine coolant level, and battery state-of-charge
E. *Under vehicle (on hoist)* Remove protective covers and spacers; install plugs, front spoiler, mudguards, tailpipe diffusers, and wheel covers; inspect tires; check for leaks
F. *Road test* Drive over a variety of road surfaces and driving conditions and check for unusual noise and driving performance
G. *Final inspection and cleaning* Remove interior protective covers and unnecessary labels; visually inspect for damage and dirt; wash and clean vehicle; inspect paint finish and exterior body parts

Many of the high-volume defects revealed

on the new vehicle sales and delivery survey (paint imperfections, squeaks and rattles, malfunctioning audio systems, wind noise, and steering problems) could be identified and fixed during predelivery service. A TMC product quality task force from Japan identified predelivery service as a top priority for improving quality at dealerships. They cited nationwide "inconsistent or incomplete methods in performing predelivery service" as a condition that had to be fixed.

In response to these findings, the TMS product quality and parts and service subcommittees launched improvement activities in 1990. For example, they issued a number of training materials dealing with the proper performance of predelivery service. As an incentive to improve product quality, TMS reimburses dealerships for performing predelivery service as well as any in-stock repairs resulting from vehicle checks. However, while predelivery service claims are made for the vast majority of vehicles sold, nonperformance of predelivery service still appears to be a prevalent problem. TMS suspects that many dealers mistakenly believe that because Toyota's quality from the factory is high, they don't have to properly perform predelivery service. These dealers tend to have a "just wash the car and it's ready to go" mentality.

New Vehicle Delivery   The new vehicle delivery check sheet ensures that salespeople follow prescribed procedures for delivery of the vehicle to the customer (see Figure 15). The procedures intend to familiarize the customer with the new vehicle, its accessories, and the dealership. Toyota wants to make sure customers get the quality they expect. Toyota also wants to ensure that customers perceive the value of what they have purchased. It would be easy to overlook, for example, the child-resistant door locks or advanced features of the digital radio. As Jim Colon, national sales administration managers, says, "A customer really doesn't understand the value of what he has received if he doesn't know how to use it." Helping a customer perceive the value of the new vehicle can, as Jim Colon says, "take the edge off the buyer's remorse, or second-guessing, that often occurs a few days down the road. If the customer focuses on the fact that there is a lot of value associated with their purchase, they will have fewer negative thoughts about how they were treated at the dealership and spend less time looking for things to be dissatisfied about."

Sales Processes

Since 45 percent of the J. D. Power sales satisfaction index (SSI) is derived from the salesperson (courtesy, knowledge, etc.), this has been an area of focus for improvement. Toyota dealers have historically spent a lot of money to train the sales force; however, a high rate of turnover (around 120 percent) for salespeople leaves dealers unmotivated to invest in training which is wasted when salespeople leave the dealership. The lack of extensive training is compounded by the lack of commitment to the customer that salespeople exhibit when they do not anticipate remaining with the dealer. Obviously, poorly trained salespeople may produce a negative sales experience and detract from customer satisfaction.

A special study by the customer relations department demonstrated the strong relationship between turnover and customer satisfaction at the dealerships. Further, they revealed some of the causes of turnover and potential solutions. For example, pay plans can reduce turnover. One pay plan common in the industry puts money, e.g., $50, into a trust fund every time the salesperson makes a sale. The salespeople must remain with the dealership for six months to get the money.

The study also revealed that salespeople want to feel self-worth, feel like they count and are a part of a team. When these things are not in place, as soon as another opportunity comes along, the salesperson will leave. Recently, Toyota has begun to work with their

Figure 15

TOYOTA

NEW VEHICLE DELIVERY CHECK SHEET

Congratulations on your new Toyota purchase. We are pleased you have chosen a Toyota vehicle and we wish you many years of enjoyable ownership. We look forward to satisfying all of your future motoring needs.

_____
Dealer/General Manager Signature

_____
Dealership Name

QUALITY INSPECTION

This check sheet is your assurance of a quality Pre-Delivery Inspection on your vehicle. Our factory-trained service professionals have verified that all systems and controls are operating as designed.

CUSTOMER SATISFACTION

I have inspected my new Toyota and acknowledge that all Pre-Delivery and Delivery Checklist items have been reviewed with me by my salesperson.

_____   _____
Customer Signature   date

_____
Name (Please Print)

_____   _____
Salesperson Signature   date

_____
Name (Please Print)

_____
Vehicle Identification Number

DELIVERY CHECKLIST

- Provide Customer with Owner's Manual
- Explain Service Maintenance Schedule
- Explain New Vehicle Warranty
- Describe Service Department Operation:
  Service Manager _____
  Business Hours _____
  Appointments and Procedures
- Describe Parts Department Operation:
  Parts Manager _____
  Business Hours _____
  Appointments and Procedures
- Conduct Dealership Walk-Through
- Demonstrate Vehicle Features and Controls
- Explain Audio and Theft Deterrent Systems
- Provide Customer with State-Required Lemon Law Materials (If Applicable)

M/N#00300-92001   91-SLS-126

dealers to build the kind of environment that will help retain salespeople. They have implemented a certification program (focused on professionalism, respect, integrity, dedication, and excellence), product knowledge testing, and incentive programs based on NVSDS performance. As John McLaughlin, national customer relations administration manager, explains, "We'll always be a people business. We deal with people as our customers, and we deal with people as our employees. Deep down inside, we all know what makes people happy, because we know what makes ourselves happy."

The delivery quality improvement program would have been incomplete had it not been extended to the dealerships. While dealers should be confident that Toyota plants and logistical systems will provide them with the high-quality vehicles they need, they should not fail to also implement the principle that "we don't send the vehicle on to the next stage if it isn't right." Toyota dealers are the last chance Toyota has to make sure that the vehicle is "right" for the customer.

▶ CONCLUDING COMMENTS

While this chapter has by no means covered all of Toyota's delivery quality improvement efforts, it has illustrated Toyota's commitment and approach to satisfying customers. Clearly, Toyota's culture is one which values standardization for the purpose of improved customer satisfaction. In its culture of standardization, Toyota continuously improves standards, which specify rules, procedures, and designs. Then it improves through standardization: it puts in place the methods and measures to ensure conformance to the improved standards.

▶ DISCUSSION QUESTIONS

1. How does the delivery quality improvement program relate to Toyota's strategy and help accomplish Toyota's objectives for customer satisfaction?
2. How does the delivery quality improvement program apply principles of the Toyota production system to Toyota's logistics and delivery system?
3. How does the delivery quality improvement program promote *kaizen*?
4. What is the role of standardization in the delivery quality improvement program?
5. What is the role of data analysis in the delivery quality improvement program?

Xerox, Part I: Establishing the Vision*

▶ THE DOCUMENT COMPANY

As the world's largest provider of copiers, duplicators, and electronic printers, Xerox deserves the self-proclaimed title "The Document Company." The slogan clearly embodies Xerox's vision to be the *best* document company, not just the largest. Xerox leaders believe that to be the best they must (1) understand their markets and customer requirements, (2) cascade customer-driven goals and objectives throughout the organization, (3) translate customer-driven goals and objectives into business processes, (4) continuously improve their business processes using facts, not opinions, and (5) do so for every product and service. This chapter tells how Xerox strives to be "The Document Company."[1]

Global Xerox

Xerox's document processing products range from desktop copiers to high performance integrated systems which handle every aspect of document creation, storage, and reproduction. In Europe, the Americas, and the Far East, Xerox manufactures over 250 equipment products which are supported by software, supplies, and accessories.

These products are marketed and distributed through geographically based marketing organizations: Rank Xerox supports Europe and Africa, USMG supports the United States, Americas Operations covers Canada and South America, and Fuji Xerox covers Japan and Asia/Pacific. Responsible for customer interface in sales and services, these marketing organizations offer the total product range in over 130 countries by a direct sales force of 15,000 and a vast network of dealers, distributors, and agents. For the majority of its products and geographies, Xerox owns the supply chain right down to the after-sales service force of 30,000.

A House Divided unto Itself

The flow of assets across vast logistical operations globally links Xerox suppliers, producers, distributors, servicers, and customers (see Figure 1). One of the major organizational dividing lines within Xerox was between the market-

* This case was prepared by Greg Bounds.
1. The first three parts of this case study represent Xerox through the fall of 1991. Part IV provides a vision of Xerox in the 1990s and beyond. The case was written from the volumes of material and hours of conversations generously provided by people in Central Logistics and Asset Management (CLAM) of the Xerox Corporation. Particular thanks are due Fred Hewitt, Graham Sweet, Bob Willard, and John Clendenin for their invaluable assistance.

Figure 1

Xerox supply chain

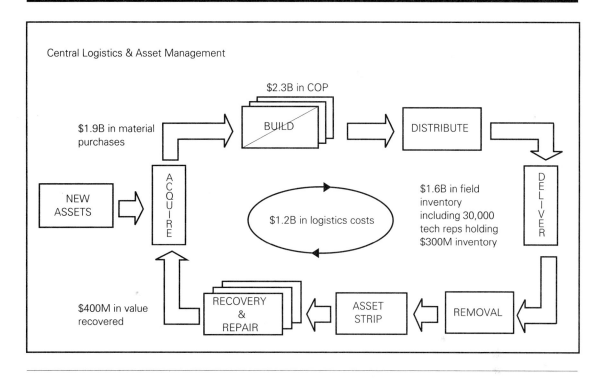

ing organizations and development and manufacturing. Another dividing line was between the supply of spare parts to service engineers, and the supply of fully configured equipment, like copiers, to customers. With the logistics fragmented accordingly, Xerox failed to integrate supply chain activities to optimally utilize its assets and serve its customers.

Added Complexity

During the 1980s, Xerox converted from a lease business to a sales business, with only 15 percent of its revenue coming from leases, reduced from 95 percent. A habit formed during its history as a leasing company continues as Xerox takes back old machines upon sale of new ones. Not only does Xerox guarantee satisfaction, by taking back any product found

to be unsatisfactory, and by teaching customers to manage paper usage, toner usage, and output, but they also promise not to leave the customer an environmentally hazardous old machine.[2]

Asset recovery and recycling old machines saves the environment, but adds complexity to the supply chain. Managers must make decisions on such issues as (1) whether to buy a new part from a reliable supplier or find an old machine, strip out a part, and rework it, (2) how to get the old machines from the point

---

2. Xerography involves many potentially hazardous chemicals, such as the heavy metals that dope the photo receptors, PCBs associated with the electronics, and many corrosive elements that are encased in stainless steel, copper, or specialty metals. Such a machine should not be dumped into a landfill.

of recovery to where they are needed around the globe, and (3) how to optimally make use of old machinery through product commonality that extends the life of a machine across multiple product generations without losing a technological edge.

Xerox's subtier supplier network also adds to its complexity. Because of necessary technology interchanges with suppliers, Xerox often specifies sourcing of components to the fourth or fifth subtier suppliers. Procurement relationships are not simply "buy from the lowest bidder."

Achieving Integration

Xerox has discovered that accomplishing corporate goals like customer satisfaction through more effective and efficient logistics and asset management requires a cross-functional approach. After a brief review of Xerox's history of quality, we will discuss Xerox's implementation of an integrated supply chain through logistics and asset management, one of Xerox's best examples of cost-functional management.

▶ HISTORY OF QUALITY

For its first fifteen years, Xerox was unmatched, best in an industry whose products were synonymous with its name. However, in the mid-1970s, foreign and U.S. competitors surpassed Xerox in both cost and quality. Xerox was not even second-best in some product categories. In 1984, led by CEO David T. Kearns and his senior management team, Xerox launched an ambitious quality improvement program. Dubbed "Leadership Through Quality," this thrust attempted to make quality improvement and, ultimately, customer satisfaction, the job of every employee. Xerox has been an American success story: winner of the 1989 Malcolm Baldrige award and one of the few companies to reverse the trend of lost world-market share in an industry targeted by the Japanese.

The Quality Process

David Kearns orchestrated the quality process by starting at the top and getting buy-in from the family group of subordinates at the next level down. The quality process cascaded down the organization, within each function, through quality objectives, but also through training. Ideally, each superior would first *learn*, then *use*, and then *teach* quality principles and tools to subordinates. The Xerox strategy for improving customer satisfaction started

with massive doses of training. All employees received at least 28 hours of training in problem solving and quality improvement techniques, which cost more than four million man hours and $125 million. (See Xerox's problem solving process in Figure 2 and the larger quality improvement process of which it is a part in Figure 3, page 714).

Team Xerox

Armed with some new tools, techniques, and a process, salaried and hourly workers were not only vested with authority over daily work decisions, but were also asked to make improvements in their work activities. Seventy-five percent of them also participated in one or more of the 7,000 quality improvement teams. These teams have saved Xerox millions of dollars and made the phrase "Team Xerox" more than an empty slogan. For example, the teams reduced scrap, tightened production schedules, and devised other efficiency and quality enhancing measures.

Xerox extended the concept of "Team Xerox" beyond their organizational boundaries to work closely with suppliers, customers, and even competitors. Xerox gave suppliers training and support in such areas as statistical process control, and ensured that suppliers' production and control processes were "process

Figure 2

Problem-solving process

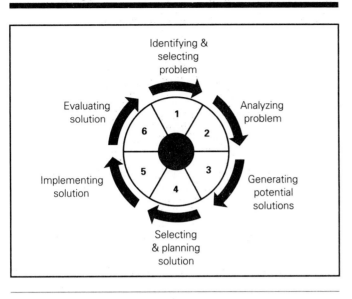

Identifying &
selecting
problem

Analyzing
problem

Generating
potential
solutions

Selecting
& planning
solution

Implementing
solution

Evaluating
solution

1 2 3 4 5 6

qualified." In a few years, Xerox reduced by 73 percent the number of defective parts reaching the production line. To develop business plans, Xerox also analyzed extensive networks of customer feedback and market surveillance data to evaluate customer requirements, behaviors, and preferences. Through competitive benchmarking, Xerox assessed its performance in over 200 key areas of product, service, and business performance. Collaborative international studies with competitors and non-competitors helped Xerox determine targets for each attribute. Targets were set at performance levels achieved by the world leaders, regardless of industry.

Xerox's dedication to quality and customer satisfaction helped them win the 1989 Malcolm Baldrige award, a crowning achievement for the turbulent business environment of the 1980s, and a tribute to the leadership of CEO David T. Kearns. In the 1980s, Xerox clearly experienced a breakthrough or turnaround in the way they did business. Despite their past accomplishments, Xerox does not rest. Under new leadership from Kearns's successor, Paul Allaire, Xerox continues the quest to satisfy customers and prosper in the business of document processing.

▶ THE CURRENT QUALITY CONTEST

Xerox has gone beyond the Baldrige award to further advance its approach to management. As the Baldrige examiners told Xerox in 1989, there is always room for improvement. Ed Leroux, then Xerox's director of education and

training, elaborates on the primary Xerox weakness revealed by the Baldrige examiners:

One of the things they talked to us about was the need for more pervasive use of what we call

Figure 3

Quality improvement process (QIP).

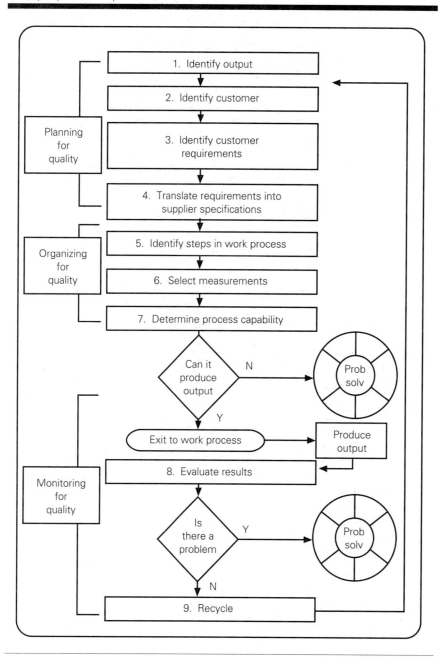

"managing by fact," that is, the use of facts in applying some basic improvement tools and the quality processes. Further, it needs to be applied across the entire spectrum of the business. We had clearly done an excellent job of letting the customer determine the business. We did so by being responsible to customer requirements, by deploying those requirements so people could ultimately relate their objectives back to the customer, and by clearly demonstrating improvement. But management by fact was still not pervasive enough.

How could it be that managers throughout Xerox could "talk a good game," but applications be pervasively absent? Many managers skipped the "use" step in the learn-use-teach implementation plan.

Lessons Learned

Further inquiry revealed that since the training provided no context for application, the applications often did not result. However, when a manager clearly defined a problem, they usually applied the training. When they defined work in terms of processes, applications were even more likely. At Xerox, "process" means the documented flow of work activities that systematically identify potential causes of business outcomes and problems. Xerox also discovered that improvement efforts tended not to flow across functional boundaries. The quality process often worked well within the functions, but not necessarily across them. The quality process did require people to identify internal customers and suppliers, which was a big step in the right direction. But it was not adequate to overcome Xerox's strong functional hierarchies. Bonus schemes, resource allocation, and information management were all hierarchically aligned. For example, Xerox had a marketing information management group and a manufacturing information management group, each with their work functionally prioritized.

The functionally cascading quality process

initiated in 1984 by Kearns fit Xerox's existing systems and culture. It seemed right for the time, as an immediate survival strategy, and perhaps it was the quickest and easiest thing to do. Certainly, some managers changed themselves and their functional processes. However, it was not a radical reorientation of Xerox culture. It was only a refinement which refocused corporate goals on the customer, and gave managers some new tools and methods to achieve those goals. Xerox leaders have recently recognized that their hierarchical culture can be changed only through conscious, comprehensive, and concerted efforts.

The New Approach to Training

In light of these lessons learned, Xerox modified its approach to training. Tools and techniques are now taught just in time for application to specific work processes to achieve market-driven goals. Figure 4 illustrates how Xerox intends to translate its market-driven goals into business processes to achieve its corporate priorities.

Process Optimization through Teamwork As "The Document Company," Xerox believes that people work better in teams and that documents really help them work more efficiently and effectively. Xerox intends to optimize their own business processes as a global showcase, to demonstrate how to optimally use information technology and document processing. Xerox has vitally focused on what they call "high impact" teams, cross-functional teams responsible for the basic processes and outputs that have significant impact on the business.[3] Ed Leroux describes the cross-functional nature of these high impact teams:

> For example, previously, we defined distribution as simply the transfer of the product from the

---

3. These process teams are high in strategic importance, not necessarily high in the hierarchy.

Figure 4
The integration of key corporate initiatives and messages

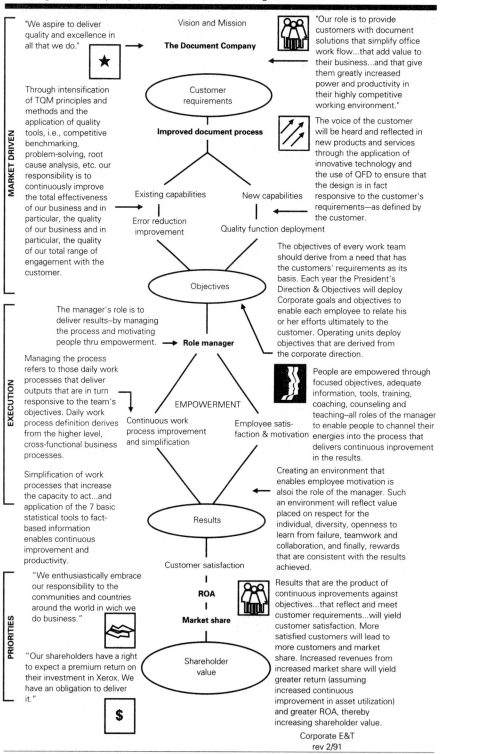

"We aspire to deliver quality and excellence in all that we do."

Through intensification of TQM principles and methods and the application of quality tools, i.e., competitive benchmarking, problem-solving, root cause analysis, etc. our responsibility is to continuously improve the total effectiveness of our business and in particular, the quality of our business and in particular, the quality of our total range of engagement with the customer.

MARKET DRIVEN

Vision and Mission

The Document Company

"Our role is to provide customers with document solutions that simplify office work flow...that add value to their business...and that give them greatly increased power and productivity in their highly competitive working environment."

Customer requirements

Improved document process

The voice of the customer will be heard and reflected in new products and services through the application of innovative technology and the use of QFD to ensure that the design is in fact responsive to the customer's requirements—as defined by the customer.

Existing capabilities   New capabilities

Error reduction improvement

Quality function deployment

The objectives of every work team should derive from a need that has the customers' requirements as its basis. Each year the President's Direction & Objectives will deploy Corporate goals and objectives to enable each employee to relate his or her efforts ultimately to the customer. Operating units deploy objectives that are derived from the corporate direction.

Objectives

The manager's role is to deliver results–by managing the process and motivating people thru empowerment. → **Role manager**

EXECUTION

Managing the process refers to those daily work processes that deliver outputs that are in turn responsive to the team's objectives. Daily work process definition derives from the higher level, cross-functional business processes.

Simplification of work processes that increase the capacity to act...and application of the 7 basic statistical tools to fact-based information enables continuous improvement and productivity.

EMPOWERMENT

Continuous work process improvement and simplification

Employee satisfaction & motivation

People are empowered through focused objectives, adequate information, tools, training, coaching, counseling and teaching–all roles of the manager to enable people to channel their energies into the process that delivers continuous inprovement in the results.

Creating an environment that enables employee motivation is alsoi the role of the manager. Such an environment will reflect value placed on respect for the individual, diversity, openness to learn from failure, teamwork and collaboration, and finally, rewards that are consistent with the results achieved.

Results

Customer satisfaction

ROA

Market share

PRIORITIES

"We enthusiastically embrace our responsibility to the communities and countries around the world in wich we do business."

"Our shareholders have a right to expect a premium return on their investment in Xerox. We have an obligation to deliver it."

Shareholder value

Results that are the product of continuous inprovements against objectives...that reflect and meet customer requirements...will yield customer satisfaction. More satisfied customers will lead to more customers and market share. Increased revenues from increased market share will yield greater return (assuming increased continuous improvement in asset utilization) and greater ROA, thereby increasing shareholder value.

$

Corporate E&T
rev 2/91

assembly line to the warehouse. But now we recognize that the distribution process touches everything, probably from the point of supplier deliveries, through where the product gets produced, to the trunk of the service representative making repairs. Now distribution has a much more cross-functional orientation. And the process teams are composed of cross-functional representatives from throughout the distribution process, like manufacturing, warehousing, and customer services.

Planned Learning Experience Xerox now provides these high impact teams with "planned learning experiences," rather than just training and educational courses. The level of knowledge and skill of the team is taken into account, so the learning experience is adjusted to fit their needs. Tools and techniques are provided as needed, just in time to be applied to a process. This approach begins with a "readiness checklist," which not only determines the knowledge and skill level of the team members for the relevant tools and techniques, but also whether the team has documented business processes to address.

Documented Processes A documented process is one that has been characterized in terms of what actually goes on and for what purpose. To understand the purpose, team members must understand the relationship of the process to the company's customer-driven goals and objectives. For workers and managers of the process, this understanding provides answers to questions like: "What is the organization trying to accomplish?" "What does this process contribute?" "What is my role in the contribution?"

To ensure the process contributes to corporate goals and objectives, team members must understand the root causes of variation in their process outputs. In order to understand the root causes of variations, or to even begin statistical studies of causal factors within the process, the team members must first know the activity sequences, decision points, inputs,

and outputs of the process. Accordingly, tools such as flow charting are used in process documentation.

Documented processes provide the basis for improvements, and define the boundary conditions for empowerment of the employees that work within the process. Empowerment is not the "manager getting out of the worker's way" or "the manager delegating authority to the point of having nothing to do." Instead, the manager frames the worker's contribution in terms of the team's objectives, and specifically communicates the scope of employee authority within the process. The manager provides workers with a process, and then facilitates their contribution to its outputs.

Process Team Coaches Coaches are assigned to assist the process team not only the readiness, but also with continuous leaning and applications. Xerox recruits coaches who already have full-time jobs, typically line mangers and not just staff professionals. Although the coaches are trained and certified, they are usually well grounded in improvement tools and statistical applications. New recruits work as apprentices with senior coaches before individually assuming coaching responsibilities.

Comprehensive Applications
In the future, Xerox employees will improve business processes throughout the organization, along multiple fronts. Broad cross-functional processes which are strategically important and greatly impact business success will command the attention of executives, and those of more limited scope will be managed by lower level managers. Even individuals at the lowest levels of the organization will improve their work processes and activities. Some of the improvement work may be integrated with the work of higher level process teams, while other improvement work is self-directed and not integrated with higher level activities.

Xerox recognizes a need to continuously improve existing processes, while also working on new processes which might render the old ones obsolete. It might seem to be a waste of time to have workers and supervisors laboring to improve their work processes only to have them eliminated through re-engineering. However, Xerox does not regard any improvement as waste. Xerox prefers to have all employees engaged in improvement all the time, even at the most atomic (or grassroots) levels of the organization, because managers can't always anticipate which activities will be kept and which eliminated.

Fundamental Directions of Process Improvement

To guide these improvements throughout the organization, Xerox has set forth two fundamental directions for change: *error reduction* and *cycle time reduction*, each of which must be consistent with a third direction: *customer satisfaction*. These directions for change ensure that, although improvement efforts are sometimes fragmented and dispersed, they will always be good for the company.

Error Reduction   Similar to Motorola's Six Sigma campaign, Xerox promotes 10X error reduction, so that whatever the rate of errors happens to be, it should be improved tenfold. Error reduction is stressed more at the atomic levels of the organization, particularly in areas of direct contact with customers.

Cycle Time Reduction   Cycle time reduction can be sought at all levels of the organization, but is particularly important in process re-engineering on bigger processes. Again, cycle time reduction through process re-engineering may totally eliminate activities at more atomic levels, despite the fact that errors may have been reduced in those activities.

Customer Satisfaction   Error reduction and cycle time improvement should drive toward customer satisfaction. For example, customer feedback indicates that the biggest irritant for customers is error in billing. So the billing team makes changes to reduce errors, despite the fact that a new process may one day eliminate the need for billing. Once error rates are reduced, Pareto analysis reveals customer concern over the time it takes for the billing statement to reach them, so the team attacks cycle times. Xerox leaders feel they can't go wrong making any such improvements in current processes in order to provide customers with products and services "faster, better, and cheaper."

In summary, Xerox intends to improve processes throughout the company to achieve improved customer satisfaction. The remainder of this chapter focuses on the implementation of cross-functional business processes led by Xerox's Central Logistics and Asset Management, or CLAM.

▶ THE EVOLUTION OF CLAM

Central Logistics and Asset Management (CLAM) is a high level group of change agents charged with ensuring the implementation of Xerox's new approach to process management to develop an integrated supply chain. CLAM evolved through the soul-searching events of the 1980s quality revolution, and represents the current stage of several parallel lines of development.

Competitive Benchmarking

As a part of Kearns's quality improvement initiatives, in 1984, Xerox undertook a corporate competitive assessment. The initial benchmarking indicated Xerox was well behind other companies in certain key areas, such as return on assets. In response, Kearns set up a task force, which ran from 1984 to 1988 and examined how leading companies managed

Figure 5

1988 inventory percent of sales diversified companies

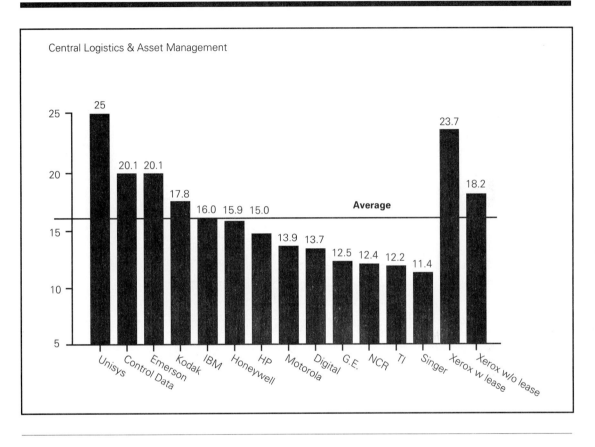

their assets (plant, machinery, fixed assets, trade receivables, etc.). The task force concluded that Xerox was far too fragmented and inefficient in use of assets, with everybody holding their own bit of inventory, doing their own hedging and balancing.

Xerox simply was not taking advantage of being a single corporation. Consider how Xerox compared to other benchmarks on inventory levels in 1988 (see Figure 5). One of Xerox's competitors, Kodak, was at 17.8 inventory as a percent of sales, while Xerox was at 23.7. To improve on such measures, Xerox would have to coordinate the worldwide use of its trading assets, that is, achieve global inventory

control and asset sharing. Such coordination would require radical changes, and perhaps even a new vision for the organization.

The Xerox Blueprint: Fourteen Basic Business Processes of Xerox Business Architecture

Xerox executives did come up with a new vision. The fourteen basic business processes that Xerox executives identified as critical are shown in Figure 6. Certainly one could debate whether there are eight or fourteen or some other number of basic processes. And Xerox executives did debate, changing the number and names of the processes several times. They settled on a vision of the company that was

Figure 6

Xerox business architecture: 14 basic business processes

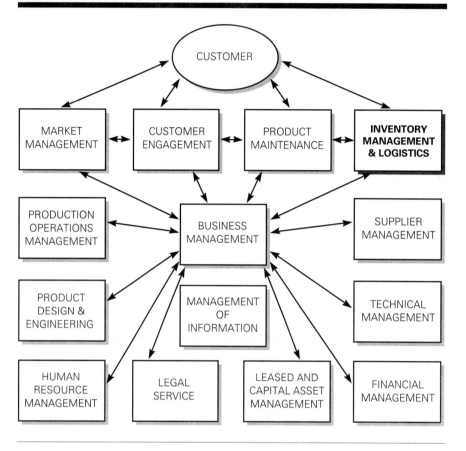

comprehensive and also inspired cross-functional change.

This new business architecture depicts Xerox in terms of the cross-functional processes that directly impact the customer. As shown in Figure 6, the four processes closest to the customer are market management, customer engagement, product maintenance, and inventory management and logistics. Supporting these key customer interface processes is business management (running the business, planning and operating), which is further supported by processes such as information management, legal services, human resource

management, and so forth. These support processes may appear to be traditional functions, but they actually span many boundaries within Xerox.

A basic business process is not simply a single sequence of activities. These fourteen processes may be more aptly described as themes that are realized through many interrelated business processes. For example, customer engagement encompasses the activities and processes that customers encounter any time they interact or do business with Xerox. In the past, customer engagement has been highly functionalized, with sales prospecting, sales administration, order entry, billing, and cash collection each handled by different functions and different people. That means four or five different interfaces for the customer, each of which knew very little about what the others were doing. At times, this disintegrated approach made Xerox a difficult company with which to do business.

Customers don't care what Xerox does internally. They just want it to be simple to deal with Xerox. Ideally, they want to see one face, one person, and if not one person, then at least one set of processes which are unified. Customers want to be certain that if they talk to one Xerox person today and to another tomorrow, each will know what's been said and decided. They do not want to relay their problem repeatedly to different people across the organization. The business architects of Xerox must build the processes of customer engagement to meet these expectations.

Process Ownership of Inventory Management and Logistics

Each of these basic business processes has a process owner or sponsor, a clearly defined mission, and associated high impact teams responsible to fulfill the mission. The responsibilities of a process sponsor are listed in Figure 7. The position of process sponsor is not usually full-time, but a collateral activity of a manager that otherwise holds a full-time corporate or line position. For example, Dr. Fred Hewitt became the sponsor of inventory management and logistics (IM&L), the process essentially responsible for "getting the right things to the right place at the right time." At the time of his appointment, Fred was director of distribution and technical services for Rank Xerox, and a pioneer in developing multinational systems for optimizing inventory levels among European operating units. Xerox gave priority to certain areas, and inventory management and logistics was one of them.

Fred Hewitt's IM&L mission is to (1) develop IM&L strategies and processes, (2) en-

sure their implementation through procedures and systems across document processing, and (3) share with the operating units the responsibility for achieving ongoing improvements in customer satisfaction, logistics costs, and asset utilization.

The Multinational Inventory Optimization Council (MIOC) As the IM&L process sponsor, Fred Hewitt leads the involvement of other key managers and executives who serve on IM&L process councils and subgroups. The Multinational Inventory Optimization Council (MIOC) is the first-tier council of the IM&L business process.[4] The MIOC executive team was originally composed of hand-picked senior managers who not only displayed the right sort of mind set, but also were significant stakeholders in the change efforts that would follow. These senior level directors and vice presidents from all different parts of Xerox corporation (from engineering, manufacturing, sales, service, from Europe, North America, Latin America, and the Far East) were charged to look for cross-functional, cross-unit opportunities.

Under Fred's leadership, the MIOC executive team developed the following integrated supply chain process vision.

- Customer satisfaction is key
  – 100 percent customer satisfaction at the lowest cost and levels of inventory
  – Customer provided an integrated solution
- Demand-driven supply chain
  – Customer orders will drive actions in all echelons of the supply chain
  – Manufacturing flexibility
  – Build/customize to order, deliver to customer in one week
- Time to customer is a competitive advantage

---

4. In 1992, MIOC was renamed the Worldwide Integrated Supply Chain Council (WISCC).

Figure 7

Xerox business architecture: business process sponsor definition (January 1991)

Responsibilities	Execution/implementation
• Provide strategic direction to business process area owners and process improvement projects	• Establish business process area goals, desired state, and critical success factors
• Initiate BAA and process improvement projects to achieve goals and desired state	• Determine projects required, commit resources and assign responsibility for process improvement projects
• Provide quality assurance to ensure that process improvement projects meet strategic and business architecture requirements	• Act as primary customer for process improvement projects outputs • Conduct periodic inspections of process improvement projects
• Demonstrate role model commitment and support for business process management	• Represent business process area (direction, resources, cross-functional and cross-organizational issues, etc.) in senior team management process
• Manage cross-process and cross-organizational/functional boundaries/ seams to ensure process integration and effectiveness	• Resolve and/or escalate cross-organizational, cross-process issues

– Removing time from the physical supply chain requires Xerox to remove time from the information pipeline

– Information pipeline is critical for quickly empowered responses

• Common product language

– Customer requirements easily translated into items to be delivered, components necessary to build these items, and raw materials necessary to assemble the components

• Complexity managed through high performance to work systems

– Complexity in our product array will be shielded from our customers and managed by our employees through high performance work systems

• Recycling is a key feature of the supply chain

– To both fully utilize all assets and meet environmental concerns, Xerox will recover and recycle whenever possible

Meeting only three times a year, MIOC addressed issues ranging from the mundane to the esoteric, through a number of subcouncils. MIOC essentially served as an advisory council to Xerox President Paul Allaire and the top five senior executive vice presidents, to give feedback on needed organizational and system changes.

The MIOC executive team significantly broadened Xerox's efforts to improve logistical systems and asset management. But MIOC had no one working full time to implement its ideas. No organization or individual owned the responsibility to make MIOC's dreams a reality. Xerox needed full-time coordination and effort toward the basic changes that were required in each area to make the IM&L process vision a reality (see the business area changes in Figure 8). This deficiency was remedied in the fall of 1988 by the appointment of Dr. Fred Hewitt as vice president of central logistics and asset management to address im-

Figure 8

Business area changes needed to realize the IM&L process vision

Business area	Current state	Changes needed
Delivery management	• Sales, administration, distribution cannot identify what components are necessary to satisfy an order. • Customer orders are split by asset type and manual linkages are made. • Xerox is often surprised when activities don't occur. • Customer doesn't know the status of the order. Delivery for customer's required date is not tracked.	• Construct an integrated customer order satisfaction process which covers assets and activities: – Explore the order into assets and establish activity work plans – Develop order routing rules – Supply chain performance monitoring to track lead times
Configuration management	• The supply chain is not supported with configuration information: – Accuracy is not there – People don't know what fits together – Some information is not there at all, so people resort to guessing • Business processes are fragmented: – Multiple processes in different organizations (over 200 data bases) – Change control is poor – Significant administrative lead time in communicating configuration information	• Integrate the information so that design, manufacturing, distribution, and marketing work from the same data. • Establish data ownership. • Involve all users of the information. • Roles and responsibilities defined for policy development and configuration management.
Inventory planning	• Forecasting inhibited by long lead times: – Difficult to adjust to actual market conditions – Forecast accuracy not tracked • Planning performed sequentially and is fragmented: – Multiple hand-offs – Second guessing • Inventory levels cover process shortfalls, and supply is unpredictable.	• Progressively move to a single supply/demand process and streamline existing processes to eliminate administrative time. • Manage inventories across all echelons in the chain. • Track and use forecast errors in the process. • Pilot new concepts before investing in large new systems and focus on leadtime reductions.
Logistics & physical distribution planning	• Strategic plans are fragmented by operating unit and asset type. • Network planning on an ad hoc basis primarily focusing on costs. • Networks are accumulations of discrete elements planned separately.	• One integrated supply chain strategic business plan, with congruent goals extension to level of service and logistics costs. • Establish information base of current network structures and performance. • Develop network modeling tools.
Logistics operations	• Assets arrive faster than data, so inventory information is "as of" the last cycle, out of date the minute it is produced. • No formal planning process. • Separate networks for the different asset types: – Warehouses – Transport – Systems	• Real time inventory information. • Planning processes put into place through "A delta T" methodology to eliminate unnecessary work steps. • Integrate asset inventories, transport, and warehousing where appropriate.

plementation.[5] This appointment gave CLAM a body, but more bodies were needed for it to really make a difference.

The Inauguration of CLAM

Although he started as a one-man band, Fred soon built the organization and human resources needed to accomplish his mission. Fred established four positions reporting to him, and quickly filled three of the positions with experienced senior employees who had managed parts of the logistics and distribution network and supply chain. These parts were recognized as the three best line organizations in Xerox. Two of the three had won the President's Award, Xerox's highest honor for improvement efforts. Fred focused his people on examining Xerox's business processes and associated decision making infrastructure.

Benchmarking the Integrated Supply Chain

Fred's group started by identifying the biggest process changes that would improve inventory turns, service level, and logistical costs. They benchmarked companies that were globally integrated and structured similarly to Xerox, as well as direct competitors, to determine what the best companies did differently in terms of business processes. Somewhat surprisingly, Xerox's direct Japanese competitors, like Canon, Minolta, and Rico, were not the best. Other companies, like NCR and Apple, proved to be leading benchmarks. After studying these companies, it became obvious to Fred's group that Xerox should focus on a concept called the "integrated supply chain." What Xerox currently had in place might be called a "disintegrated supply chain."

As Fred states, "It's really very simple. All

we are trying to do is respond to a customer requirement by buying some parts, building them into a machine, putting in some software, adding some services, and getting it all to the customer. But looking at the length of time it took to do that indicated we had a far too complex process, far too many people involved, far too much functionality, far too many hand-offs, far too many local decision making authorities in the chain, and far too many local information systems passing information among themselves." To really make it "really very simple," Fred's group quickly realized that they had to make major changes to Xerox's business processes, which would require more human resources.

The Multinational Development Council

While Central Logistics and Asset Management (CLAM) was taking root at the executive level, John Clendenin's Multinational Development Council (MDC) was developing and applying process analytical methods and change skills at the operations level. The MDC evolved from the Multinational Systems Development Center (MSDC), a systems group which worked on multinational systems of communication. MSDC primarily served lower level purchasing, logistics, distribution, and systems managers in the operating companies (USMG, Rank Xerox, Fuji Xerox, and the Americas Operations), which were in a considerable state of dysfunctionality in the 1970s. Each had different systems and approaches to data management, produced and marketed their own products, chose different hardware and software, and even named the same parts differently. If one had excess inventory of a part, another operating company might not recognize it because of different part numbers. MSDC helped sort through the disarray by developing multinational information systems that can track orders, equipment, and spare parts.

With the arrival of John Clendenin, MSDC expanded and evolved into the Multinational

---

5. Fred reported to three of the top officers in Xerox: A. Barry Rand, group vice president, USMG; Wayland Hicks, executive vice president, development and manufacturing; and Roland Magnin, head of Rank Xerox. As vice president of CLAM, after the 1992 re-organization, Fred now reports through a senior vice president within corporate strategic services.

Development Council (MDC).[6] The MDC went beyond information systems to help implement changes in any system, process, procedure, or management practice. As Fred Hewitt states, "MDC had an amazingly wide impact, given the level they worked at. But we had to lift it up about three levels and have a vice president run it." While MDC's services benefitted their users in the operating companies, and helped to save Xerox millions of dollars a year, they lacked strategic direction. As a support staff, they only reactively responded to customers' self-perceived needs. However, as change agents, they did have the operational experiences that Fred Hewitt needed to get his change agenda started in CLAM. The MDC staff viewed Xerox as a set of business processes rather than a set of functional organizations, an approach consistent with the vision of Allaire and Hewitt.

In January of 1989, Fred Hewitt took over the MDC, and its head, John Clendenin, joined the original three individual contributors of Fred's group. Along with these four contributors, and the thirty-five information systems specialists of the MDC, CLAM started to address the agenda of the new business architecture, particularly the inventory management and logistics agenda.

CLAM Reinvestments and Revisions

By April of 1989, Fred Hewitt reported progress to Paul Allaire's senior team and proposed that he expand CLAM with some new people to vigorously attack the business processes through re-engineering and simplification. Rather than just use the existing MDC staff to implement his agenda for re-engineering processes, Fred wanted to staff CLAM with hand-picked, senior-level people from diverse backgrounds and experiences. Fred boldly suggested that with these resources and the free-

dom to act, they could take a billion dollars off the balance sheet through inventory reduction. The senior team approved the idea.

The MDC got a new leader and accepted a more focused role to work on systems support. Fred then hand-picked and hired twelve people from development and manufacturing, the supply side of the house, twelve people from field sales and service, the demand side of the house and twelve people from other functions within or outside Xerox. These thirty-six people became the process architects focused on medium-term (one year to five years) and long-term, cross-functional business process improvements.

As part of the expansion, Fred hired Graham Sweet to lead CLAM's long-range planning as the strategy development manager and also to act as the secretary of the MIOC executive team. Fred hired Bob Willard from the procurement organization to oversee CLAM's implementation efforts as supply chain integration manager. Initially, Sweet and Willard joined Clendenin as CLAM's optimization managers. They focused on more localized and immediate improvements while planning long-term strategies. Later, Bob Savidge joined as CLAM's fourth optimization manager. With the cast complete, CLAM now had the resources it needed to fulfill its mission, and with top managers already involved through MIOC, it also had legitimacy.

CLAM's Organizational Alignment

Interestingly, CLAM is not located in the plush Stamford, Connecticut, corporate headquarters, with the traditional corporate staff groups. Rather, it is tucked away in comfortable, but modest facilities *down by the train tracks* in East Rochester, New York. While not formally housed in the corporate halls, CLAM derives a lot of authority and power to influence the organization from its high level connections. More importantly, the members of CLAM have significant informal power, i.e., personal relationships with Xerox executives,

---

6. See Harvard Business School Case Study #9-490-29, "Managing Xerox's Multinational Development Center," 1989.

and Fred's reputation as a skilled and dedicated leader and expert in the field of logistics contribute to CLAM's clout. CLAM's connection to top executives proved beneficial to its role as a change agent in getting buy-in on broad strategic concerns from leaders in Xerox, and motivated participation from followers.

It is difficult to classify CLAM in terms of the traditional line versus staff distinction. CLAM is not exactly a line organization because the distribution function in Europe or in Latin America, for instance, does not report to CLAM. Rather, these distribution functions report to the local management team. While CLAM appears to support the functional lines of business, it carries much more formal and informal authority than a traditional staff unit, and more responsibility for results.

► CLAM'S AGENDA

CLAM's mission statement clearly reflects its shared responsibility for achieving results along with line organizations. The mission statement follows:

> As Business Sponsors for Inventory and Logistics Management, develop integrated Inventory Management and Logistics strategies and processes and ensure their implementation through procedures and systems across Document Processing. Share with the Operating Units the responsibility for achieving ongoing improvements in customer satisfaction, logistics cost, and cash utilization.

CLAM took on the strategic role of developing and implementing better business processes. As Fred states:

> We are fundamentally, in the Xerox terminology of business processes, business engineers or business architects. The whole job is about changing the way that we handle inventory management in the corporation and associated logistics and distribution. It's totally about introducing new ways of doing business and obviously with the objective of getting a better service level, better customer satisfaction, better return on assets.

CLAM was not established only to execute the change agenda of the IM&L basic business process team and the MIOC executive team. Inventory and asset management is a core theme, but CLAM also facilitates change in other areas, particularly those that were highly integrated with the IM&L agenda. In addition to IM&L, three other basic business processes were prioritized for early attention by similar change agents: (1) customer engagement, which is important to customer satisfaction, (2) product design and engineering, which is important for improving Xerox's time to market with new and improved products on the front end of the supply chain, and (3) supplier management, which serves a just-in-time (JIT) approach by certifying suppliers, sole sourcing, and reducing the supply base down from 4,000 to 400. CLAM interfaces closely with these other groups through a business process board.

The CLAM change agents creatively provide answers, "yesable" propositions for new, re-engineered, and simplified business processes throughout the supply chain. As John Clendenin explains, CLAM provides "yesable" propositions to get people to act in the best interests of the corporation. A "yesable" proposition gives them something concrete and specific as a proposal which outlines the plans, estimated savings, and so forth. CLAM offers ideas that line managers wouldn't easily come up with on their own. So instead of just getting support and buy-in to a general idea like "let's optimize the system," CLAM provides answers. As change agents, they also help implement the answers to ensure improved processes are institutionalized in line organizations. This implementation requires a combination of salesmanship, leadership, and creative behavioral modifications. The Xerox Part III case elaborates on the change process from the point of view of the CLAM change agents.

► CULTURAL CHANGE AND STRUCTURAL CHANGE

Although Xerox wanted to manage the company through business processes that are cross-functional and strategically determined, rather than functionally organized, they left the functional structure in place for several years. While their plans for structural changes evolved, Xerox relentlessly pursued revolutionary cultural change. A major structural change was announced in February 1992, but the structural change was a result of the cultural change and not the impetus for cultural change. The new Xerox structural architecture is thoroughly described in the remarks by Paul Allaire, now chairman and chief executive officer of Xerox Corporation (see the Xerox Part IV case study). The essence of the structural change was to realign Xerox horizontally toward the customer, to better link markets and technologies, and to do away with the traditional vertically oriented structure.

Structural Change Evolves from Cultural Change

Xerox did not attempt to transform the company by starting out with formal structural organization. As Leroux warns, "You can't go into an existing infrastructure of functional units and tell them to change all the processes they are using for delivering products and services. It's just too much turmoil, too much upheaval." On the other hand, in the years prior to the major structural change, there were minor structural changes that were intended as relatively permanent. For example, the executives and managers on the basic business process teams, such as IM&L, were permanent members, and not short-term attendees to ad hoc teams.

Even after the major structural change, Xerox intends for new business process architecture to endure as a means of addressing significant cross-functional issues. With both the minor and major structural adjustments, however, the culture of Xerox was the primary target of change. The structure was simply adjusted to reflect and reinforce the cultural revolution.

Attrition and Replacement Xerox has discovered that with diligent efforts, resources, and change management skills, they can make such process changes with existing products. However, it is much easier to put the improved processes in place as they introduce new products than to revolutionize old business configurations. As new products come on line and old ones die, and as improved processes are introduced to deliver existing products, the organization will gradually be transformed. Such attrition and replacement began before the structural overhaul of 1992. In the future, attrition and replacement will be even easier. The bones of the new core structure will be fleshed out with new production and delivery systems that embody the new horizontal alignment.

Structure as an Outcome The architecture of the fourteen basic business processes (Figure 6, page 720) may or may not represent the configuration to which Xerox evolves in years to come. The structural changes of 1992 are a step in that direction. Any such picture represents only a snapshot in evolving structural concepts and realities. The plan announced in February 1992 represented the design for the core structure of Xerox, but it will certainly evolve, along with the culture, as it is implemented in a phased manner in 1993 and beyond.

Amidst all the change, one principle remains the same. Xerox leaders believe that they should not lead with structural revolution. Such rearrangements and reorganizations have proven deficient in the past. Rather, organizational structure will be an outcome, simply a by-product of applying the right tools, changing managerial behaviors, and putting in place the right business processes. In other words, organizational structure is not the solution, but will follow the solution. As Fred Hewitt states:

> Many, many times in the past we've tried, like other corporations, to drive change into the company by changing its organization. All that does is set up different dysfunctionalities than you had before. We're going to take out the dysfunctionalities and get people to operate in an integrated way across the whole supply chain. Eventually, everybody will have to change their business process, from the sales representative calling on customers, to the procurement agent buying parts from a vendor. It may require organizational and structural changes as people fit together differently. If so, then we'll change the organization.

Rather than disrupt the current operations with wholesale structural changes to achieve a new horizontal organizational alignment, new processes and systems are incrementally inserted. Over time, the traditional vertical structures are hollowed out and replaced with new processes, which means new roles, new responsibilities, new objectives, new targets, new measures, and new incentives for people. The content and focus of managerial work changes, which means cultural change. The structural overhaul in 1992 reflects and reinforces these cultural changes.

Revolutionary Cultural Change

While immediate structural change was not initially a top priority, the immediate change of culture was. Xerox's vision of using time as a competitive advantage, by implementing an integrated supply chain that is demand-driven, was revolutionary for its culture. It required such mundane changes as establishing common product languages so that product configurations could be communicated globally across the supply chain. More importantly, it required a lot of process and behavioral changes, which required new assumptions about "how Xerox should do business."

Changing Assumptions The fundamental assumptions of many managers had to change before process changes could be implemented. For example, IM&L's vision was to reduce inventory levels. However, many managers assumed that if you take out inventory, you automatically reduce the customer service level. Further, the only way to maintain service level would be to spend more on transport, i.e., air freight, because equipment would not be available at the point of need.

These managers thought in terms of cost/benefit trade-offs because they assumed that the current processes were optimal, and that the time that it took to actually get things through the chain was a given and couldn't be changed. Managers' past experiences reinforced these assumptions; for example, one said, "I remember, back in 1988, I didn't have any low volume products in stock when the market suddenly took off, and I couldn't meet demand. So I must keep inventory levels up or the service levels will suffer."

While people assumed they had to move around the fixed sides of the triangle of inventory, costs, and service, Xerox's vision was to achieve synergies by improving on all three sides of the triangle (see goals in Figure 9). For example, not only would the reduction of assets tied up in inventory help to achieve the ROA goals that Allaire had in mind (i.e., 15

Figure 9

Integrated supply chain - - route map

THE ROUTE:
Based on
benchmarking

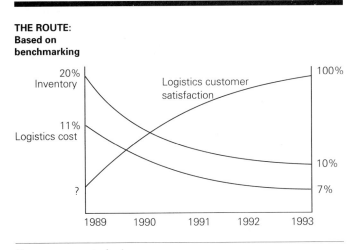

% means percent of sales.

percent), but it would also improve the service levels. Improved service would lead to more customers and more revenue, which also helped ROA. Such improvements changed processes, and ultimately changed managerial behavior. For example, marketing information on orders would have to be shared with managers further upstream in manufacturing, and information on availability would have to move downstream to the sales force.

Changing Objectives and Responsibilities
Cultural assumptions about objectives and scope of managerial responsibility are also changing at Xerox. For example, the way Xerox thinks of logistics cost has broadened significantly, which accounts for the priority placed on reducing logistics cost. Traditionally Xerox thought of logistics cost as the cost of getting products out of manufacturing and to a customer, such as manpower, warehousing, and transportation; costs which they estimated to be about 3 to 4 percent of revenue. However, when they look at all the elements of the supply chain that actually have a profit and loss impact, the figure is more like 10 percent. Other hidden costs include those associated with carrying inventory, like the costs of cash,

write-offs of obsolete material, freight, and duty.

This new conception of the logistics cost is important because most business decisions—for instance, whether or not to source products offshore—affect those costs. Decisions in one function, such as marketing, affect the performance of other functions, such as production. For example, with long lead times which require forecasting of demand over a six-month period, the accuracy of demand diminishes, manufacturing inventories go up and write-offs increase. In the future, managers of all functions will share more global responsibilities and congruent objectives for integrated supply chain performance.

An Example of Perspective Change Ideally, the changing Xerox culture will alter the perspectives of managers away from functional optimization to global optimization. Consider how Allen Vickery's perspective has changed. As director of logistics operations for Rank Xerox, Allen is responsible for equipment and parts inventories in Europe and Africa. However, Allen is no longer just targeted, measured, and paid to be the director of logistics for that part of the world. He also wears a corporate hat as part of the MIOC executive team. He must gauge every decision from the perspective of Rank Xerox and the global Xerox Corporation. As a member of two communities, with each placing tough demands upon him, Allen faces decisions that are more complicated than in the past.

In some cases the two communities are in conflict. What is good for Rank Xerox in Europe may not always seem optimal for global Xerox. For example, a lot of Xerox's sales are second and third generation sales, wherein Xerox takes a product back as they put a new one in. Since Xerox has strong market share in high-end machines, the old machine is often Xerox's own product, for example, when Xerox swaps a 5019 for an old 1090. In the past, Allen may have been inclined to say, "Well, that 1090 belongs to me, Rank Xerox. Let's put it in a corner over there and remanufacture it later when we develop a secondary market in education or elsewhere. If it doesn't sell, we'll scrap it for parts, and otherwise help Rank Xerox meet its objectives." By contrast, with a global perspective, Allen regards returned machines as Xerox Corporation assets. Even if Rank Xerox may sell it in three or four months, if Xerox has back orders for 1090s in Mexico, he should, in good faith, give the 1090 to the Latin American remanufacturing plant that supplies Mexico. He should trust that if in three months time he has an order for a 1090, he will get a 1090 from elsewhere in Xerox.

Such changes in attitude are dramatic for an organization as divided as Xerox has traditionally been. It really amounts to significant culture change. However, the culture change is driven by Xerox's vision of an integrated supply chain. In Xerox Part II, we discuss exactly how CLAM helped put in place the vision.

▶ EXERCISE

- After reading this case study, Norm Rickard, president of Xerox Business Services, offered the following personal comments from the perspective of a corporate executive who has been involved in the change process from the beginning.

1. Although with hindsight the progression from the MDC to MIOC to WISCC looks obvious and logical, it was a result of continuous fact-based reappraisal of progress against our objectives. There was no blind adherence to a master plan. The objective remained constant, but the tactical approach changed with circumstances.

2. Some people had to change very deeply held beliefs, and I am sure that this was only possible because of our use of the quality process, and continuous refocusing on end customer requirements.

3. The story is not ended. Even in logistics and asset management, we still have some way to go to be world class. In other areas, such as customer engagement and product development, we are only just beginning the journey.

4. The task now facing us is to ensure institutional learning, so that the CLAM example can be replicated more quickly in other business processes. Again, our quality focus will be of great help.

In groups of five or six people, discuss the key lessons that can be learned from Xerox's experiences. List these lessons learned and be prepared to present your group's list to the class.

Xerox, Part II: Realizing the Vision*

▶ **GLOBAL OPTIMIZATION: THE QUICK FIX**

CLAM's first steps to implement its agenda were taken by the optimization managers, including Graham Sweet, Bob Willard, John Clendenin, and Bob Savidge. These four contributors focused on localized and immediate improvements. Implementing Xerox's principle of improving existing processes even while reengineering to create new ones, the optimization managers went to work. In some cases, they attracted attention to areas that were simply neglected; in other cases, they just transplanted solutions from one part of Xerox to another.

The Optimization Managers

The four optimization managers were assigned specific areas of Xerox in which to seek immediate returns. They worked separately and assumed responsibility for different areas of Xerox, including (1) manufacturing and engineering, (2) the North American field organization, (3) the European and African field operations, and (4) Latin America and Fuji Xerox. Although these optimization managers did not have line responsibility, they did have performance objectives and bonuses tied directly to their respective operating unit's results.

With no line authority, the role of the optimization managers was not to dictate, but to identify opportunities and convince the line managers to make changes. They proved quite effective. Again, the optimization managers were not simply staff people that could easily be written off. After all, their boss, Fred Hewitt, had a very short line to the president, Paul Allaire, and the blessings of the other senior executives. And everyone knew their specific mission was to get immediate improvements. Furthermore, the optimization managers were experienced, respected, and persuasive.

It was easy for line managers to feel that the optimization managers were looking over their shoulders, second guessing them, and even blowing the whistle. The optimization managers often had to publically air some dirty laundry to get people's attention. Some line people even referred to them as the "asset police." Their intentions were not to embarrass anyone, but to attend to details that were being ignored or overlooked. They addressed issues that may have been tenth on a line manager's priority list, when the line manager only made time to address the top five or six items.

* This case was prepared by Greg Bounds.

Two optimization examples are discussed below.

Example 1: Optimization of Idle Assets

Immediate improvements came from initiatives like the "cash for inventory" task force led by Bob Savidge. The task force revealed that Xerox had a lot of unused, obsolete assets rusting or decaying in warehouses. Many of the assets were still on the balance sheet, some of them showing a high book value, undepreciated. Managers had no incentive to write them off or get rid of them. The task force broke through these artificial barriers and held warehouse sales and tent sales. If an item didn't sell, they stripped it for parts or scrapped it. Useless inventory turned into millions in cash.

Example 2: Optimization of Spare Parts Inventories

Another example comes from the parts inventory side of the house, where a supply chain provides inventory for technical representatives who maintain equipment in the field. In the early 1980s, the European operation implemented a process that dramatically improved customer service and reduced spare parts inventories. Implementing the same process in the United States and Canada with the optimization manager who had been a part of the implementation in Europe was no big challenge, except for some technical snags.[1] The experienced optimization manager knew the pitfalls and could advise, cajole, and support the U.S. and Canadian managers. He helped to make proposals to the senior management team and could honestly say, "Yes, it is going to cost you three or four million up front, but here is evidence that you'll get ten million back in the first two years."

Before the process change, each technical representative decided what trunk inventory to carry in the service vehicle. Suboptimal inventory decisions were driven by individual experiences, for example, "I got burned when I didn't have one of these parts, so I'm going to have one of these parts." The technical representative held one of those parts even if he or she only used it once a year or less. With each technical representative squirrelling away inventory, inventory levels grew.

The apparent logic behind the old process was that inventory decisions should be delegated to those responsible for service, and every technical representative in the world believed that he or she was an expert. Once a technical representative took a part out of the distribution network at his or her branch, the part was written off and assumed to be used. But in reality, parts often just sat in the trunk. Since no records were kept on actual use patterns, inventory decisions were subjective in a free-for-all type of employee involvement.

That was the process still in operation in the U.S. in the late eighties. In the early eighties, in Europe, the inventory decision process was changed. A new information system retained records of what was used each day and what remained in the trunk. Data were gathered on actual use of parts across operations, by product, by technical representative, by district, by regions, and so forth. The technical representatives were given the data, and asked to consider the facts and suggest what inventory should be in the trunk. Rather than rely on the guesses of technical representatives, inventory levels were determined empirically by pooled knowledge.

Each technical representative thus became a mobile mini-warehouse, and the process didn't discount a part until it had actually been reported as used by the technical representative. Inventory became driven by real usage. It was not just a matter of taking inventory out of the trunks, but improving the process. Some parts might be added to inventory, for example, so the technical representative could avoid having to delay repairs in order to run back

---

1. The technical information system had to be rewritten, since the European system ran on Honeywell equipment rather than IBM.

to the branch or put in an order for a new part.

It was not a question of forcing standardization, but of tailoring unique trunk inventories based on actual usage. Individual technical representatives varied in terms of their machines, level of specialization, and geographic territory. For example, technical representatives in rural Tennessee may have to fix all types of machines in fourteen counties, while a technical representative in Manhattan may fix only one type in fourteen city blocks.

With the new process, service branches no longer had parts lying around in trunks and storage rooms. In the U.S. alone, the new process saved tens of millions of dollars and paid for itself in fourteen months. More importantly, service levels improved, as measured by the percent of satisfied customers. The overall results are reflected in customers' responses to professionally administered questions such as: (1) Are you satisfied with Xerox as a vendor?, (2) Would you do business again with Xerox?, and (3) Would you recommend Xerox to a business colleague? Xerox's customer satisfaction went up dramatically on these primary measures.

Employee involvement and empowerment can certainly go awry. When the technical representatives, the so-called experts, were allowed to design their own system without a strategic focus and the right data, they achieved suboptimal results for the corporation. By contrast, the optimization manager engaged the technical representatives in employee involvement, but led it and fed it with the right statistical information the individuals might never have seen on their own.

Optimization to Leverage CLAM

The optimization managers were grabbing the low-hanging fruit, to achieve immediate and localized improvements. Fixing the obvious problem with trunk inventories led to a quarter of a billion dollar inventory reduction, with inventory as a percent of revenue reduced from 22 percent to 17 percent in little over a year. Not only were millions of dollars taken off the balance sheet, but the costs of holding inventory and throwing away obsolete materials were eliminated. And it entailed very little reengineering. It was simply internal best-practice sharing within the corporation to duplicate what was already done elsewhere.

Not only did they draw a lot of attention, but through improvements like these, the optimization managers provided the money and justification for CLAM to continue its work. CLAM was well on its way to fulfilling the promise to Paul Allaire to take a billion dollars off the balance sheet. The barrier-busting improvements that Xerox made in optimizing their after-sales process—for example, the spare parts inventory and replenishment—was impressive, but Xerox leaders realized they needed to improve many other processes through more profound and fundamental process changes.

▶ GLOBAL INTEGRATION: THE LONG HAUL

The optimization managers found improvement opportunities that proved to be easy pickings. But CLAM leaders were not content to grab the low-hanging fruit. For one thing, they realized that such fruit does not hang around for long. Once the easy pickings are gone, more diligent and creative work is required to make dramatic improvements. So, parallel to the unit optimization efforts of the individual contributors, Xerox established a vision for the supply chain of the future and a means of putting it in place. While the optimization managers would gradually disappear, the process architects would make more and more business process changes to implement CLAM's vision of an integrated supply chain. The development of that vision is discussed below.

The Vision Community

In order to implement an integrated supply chain, the vision must be shared by those in the line organizations who have to implement the changes. CLAM worked to develop a "vision community" wherein all the senior level managers and participants throughout Xerox would share the same vision and commit to making it real. The vision community includes a vast array of people. Xerox has formed partnerships with key people from the line organizations to get them involved in the vision development and reengineering efforts.[2]

Each of the CLAM change agents also helped to refine the vision. This participation helped to accomplish an important Xerox principle: the importance of getting buy-in from people involved in change. Buy-in was particularly important for the CLAM change agents, since they are the ones primarily responsible for selling it to others and facilitating change. As Fred Hewitt states:

> We continually push the vision, validate the vision, explain what we are trying to do, how it's going to help customers, how it's going to help the corporation, how it's going to help the employees. It requires changing mindsets of several thousands of people in the whole corporation and trying to orchestrate them.

One of the ways senior managers participate in the vision community is through the Multinational Inventory Optimization Council (MIOC) executive team which remained in place after the establishment of CLAM. The

continued participation of MIOC as a reference group was important for a couple of reasons. First, MIOC was composed of the senior managers and vice presidents around the world, who actually control the daily operations. Going around the MIOC table, one found the people who actually owned all 2 billion dollars of Xerox assets. Second, they were the people who had to change. They not only made sure CLAM worked on the right processes, but they also helped to devise and implement the plans of action within their line organizations.

The Vision

MIOC helped develop the IM&L process vision and game plan. Through may iterations, give and take sessions, and the electronic network, MIOC helped develop the following IM&L process vision and game plan for integrating the Xerox supply chain.

- Create a vision—competitive advantage through integrating the supply chain
  - Equipment (place parts, work in progress, finished goods)
  - Spare Parts
  - Supplies
- Develop a strategic route map to the mid-1990s which enables the vision for:
  - Customer satisfaction
  - Asset utilization
  - Logistics cost
- Develop prototype implementation plan through "showcase" teams
- Create integrated supply chain performance measures
- Integrate lessons learned into roll-out and process reengineering/systems
- Monitor/show continuous improvement in all measures

MIOC summarized the vision in the following statement:

> In support of the Xerox objectives of Customer Satisfaction, ROA and Market Share, Document

---

2. To help the Xerox community see and understand the vision, CLAM did some creative campaigning. For example, they circulated an internal video of one of the most advanced of their benchmark partners. The video concretely showed what it would be like to put the vision in place, and helped to develop understanding and promote a shared vision within Xerox.

Processing will be the Logistics Industry Benchmark in terms of Customer Service Support, Asset Utilization, and Logistics Cost in respect of all inventory elements (Equipment, Parts, Supplies and Software).

CLAM's vision was for Xerox to be the best in the business, and not just the best in customer service support, in asset utilization, or in logistical costs. Xerox intended to be the best in all three. Any proposed process changes intended to improve asset utilization and logistical costs should not jeopardize customer service, but should help improve it. To do so, process architects had to clearly understand customer requirements.

Knowing Customer Requirements To implement their approach for an integrated supply chain, Xerox executives and CLAM change agents seriously studied customer requirements. For example, one MIOC subcommittee held a roundtable discussion with customers in which they discovered that customers are not simply interested in lead time (order-to-install time) reduction. Order-to-install lead time is the time interval between when the customer signs the order and when the machine is installed. Reduced lead time is important for Xerox to match competitors, particularly for low-end and commodity products. But for high-end products, customers really want the product delivered on time, as promised. If Xerox promises delivery on September 21, then it gets delivered on the 21st, rather than rushing it on the 20th or dragging in on the 22nd.

A lot of high-end equipment is integrated into existing document processing networks, for example, a copier integrated with a huge IBM pumping out payroll slips or printing American Express bills. Such integrated networks may be dependent on the Xerox 1090 at the end of the corridor. Removal of the old 1090 must be coordinated with the arrival of the new 5090, or the customer may be without

document processing capability. Delivery has to be planned into the work process of the customer's office.

The Integrated Supply Chain Architecture CLAM not only articulated a performance vision, to be the best in the business on several measures, but also a process vision for the supply chain architecture. Fred Hewitt explains his vision with an example of the type of process changes he had in mind for the equipment side of the house.

> We would like to make it much more likely that we can give you, the customer, the machine you want, in the exact configuration you want, and install it on the day you want it. At the moment [Fall 1991] we've got an 85 to 90 percent chance at doing that, which is an improvement over the last few years.

> In the past, each branch manager assumed that in order to have the equipment available when his customers wanted it, he had to keep a full range of finished goods available locally. So he needed all the products that we make and he needed them in reasonable quantities, or unreasonable quantities, looking back at it. He needed them in every configuration that you could imagine. So our basic stocking policy was to hold fully finished, fully configured products near to the customer. The trouble is that you can't afford to do that. If you try to do that, you end up carrying vast amounts of inventory, some of which will not be sold during the year.

> If we measured from the time that we sent the machine out of the factory to when we actually installed it on the customer's premises, we would have found wide variation across products. We would have some products for which we had underestimated the demand; there were already orders there and as soon as it hit the ground we had a customer for it. Other products would sit there for a year before anybody wanted one of those strange things. The average may have rounded out to six months of supply of product;

and yet we're only getting about 75 percent service satisfaction. That was the old philosophy, the old program.

Ideally, we want to match the stocking policy to the customer's order-to-install elapsed time requirement. If the order is for one of our big products, say a quarter of a million dollar product, it may be twelve weeks plus. It takes time for financing, training, and arranging facilities, power supply, the air conditioner, or whatever it might be. If you build the equipment to order and match the elapsed time requirement, you not only give the customer the specific configuration needed, you also minimize the inventory in the pipeline.

Even with very small-end copiers or typewriters, off-the-shelf products that customers want this afternoon, the concept still applies. For example, if we sold an average of ten typewriters per week, we used to play it safe and hold twenty in stock. In the future, we will let the factory know which typewriters were sold each week, and they will take that into account when they do the scheduling in the factory.

It's just a fundamentally better way of doing business, but it requires management change unlike we have ever seen. It involves everybody in the chain, from the guy who used to hold his own stocks at the branch; to the regional warehouse that we used to have as a staging point, but which we don't need anymore; to the national warehouse which now really becomes more of an administrative center; to manufacturing who now sees real customer orders; back through to the vendors, where just-in-time is for real because now it's no longer just in time to put it into a machine which we may sell a year later, but just in time to put it into a machine that we already have an order for.

These changes may take 70 percent out of our traditional cycle times between buying parts from the supplier and having a machine with those parts installed for the customer. That in turn takes a billion dollars out of the inventory, and eliminates the 200 million dollars a year in expenses

to support that inventory. We may also raise the customer satisfaction level up from 70 to 90 percent toward the target of 100 percent, which brings you more customers and more revenue.

This vision is fleshed out below in terms of methodology, examples of processes and projects, and the architecture of the supply chain for various types of Xerox products.

The Process Analytical Methodology

CLAM's vision of implementing an integrated supply chain has led them to identify some monstrous processes. The initial task of describing those processes can be daunting. It may be difficult to tell where one process takes over and the other leaves off. Someone has to begin to understand all the entanglements before viable changes can be promoted for improvements.

Early attempts followed an approach that Bob Willard and Fred Killian of CLAM describe as business area modeling, which involves detailed decomposition of the business, modeling, and analysis. The following steps might be used to do business area modeling.

1. Divide the business into discernible business areas (e.g., the fourteen basic business processes shown earlier).
2. Gather business area experts together to define and model each of the business areas (e.g., identify the inputs, processes, and outputs, describe them graphically, and develop a computer simulation).
3. Gather data to describe these business areas numerically.
4. Run computer simulations to understand what goes on within each of the business areas and how they interact with each other.
5. Run "what ifs" to learn how to optimize each of the business areas as well as the interactions.

Xerox managers began this business area modeling; however, they quickly realized that with processes as complex as Xerox's it could take years to describe them before anything was ever done to improve them. In fact, it took Xerox a year and a half just to get through the first step. Before Xerox could have completed the remaining steps toward change, customers could have been lost.

To efficiently identify the really big problems and opportunities in the supply chain, and to avoid getting bogged down with analysis, CLAM did two things that simplified their work. First, as described later, they focused on their initial process improvement efforts on showcases. In a showcase, Xerox pulled a representative from each of the links in the integrated supply chain to be led by a showcase manager. This team devised techniques to optimize the integrated supply chain just for that showcase. So, rather than go to the corporation and suggest changing Xerox corporation, these managers isolated a showcase and made limited changes. It involved minimum risk for the corporation, because it was watched carefully and was limited in scope. Second, each process team chose process description methodologies which were simple, yet effective, and fit the process of focus.

At the kickoff meetings, the teams decided how to proceed, assisted by CLAM change agents and other process experts. They examined the issue, determined which tools were appropriate, and agreed on how to proceed. As Bob Willard states, "It's rare to get initial agreement when you get thirteen people on a team, each with different training and favorite tools. You have to sort through that pretty quickly. You don't sit around arguing over which tools to use for days." Among the many tools and techniques that CLAM used (flowcharts, Pareto charts, histograms, data stratification, brainstorming, scatter diagrams), the one most frequently used is based on elapsed times, namely, the A delta T approach described below.

Elapsed Time Analysis CLAM change agents borrowed a process methodology from Digital Equipment Corporation which focuses on the elapsed times that actually take place throughout a process. An elapsed time is just what it sounds like, the interval of time it takes to do something (produce a part, make a decision, hand off a document, transport material). "Actual" elapsed times are measured and compared to "theoretical" elapsed times (theoretical possibilities set as goals). The comparison between the actual and the theoretical reveals the amount of opportunity for cycle time reduction through process changes. Thus, the methodology is called "A delta T." Once the A delta T is described, the team must develop a plan for the transition. The CLAM change agents led and/or facilitated each of these steps toward process change.

Supply Chain Examples An example of the A delta T methodology is shown in Figure 1, where a piece of the distribution flow for the 5028 is presented. Squares represent value-contributing activities, and triangles represent waste to be eliminated. The A delta T approach is briefly summarized in four steps:

1. Document actual processes and practices in the supply chain.
2. Analyze value-added and waste against vision process model (rules and principles working document).
3. Outline process improvements, tools and barriers to move from actual to theoretical.
4. Prioritize projects based on contribution to level of service, asset utilization, and total logistics cost.

Using A delta T, CLAM leaders hoped to transform Xerox's actual supply chain, full of redundancies with safety stock and warehouses, into Xerox's theoretical supply chain, a vision of leanness.

Advantages of Elapsed Time Analysis The advantages of an elapsed time methodology include conceptual simplicity, ease of measurement, and ease of consensus on its meaning.

Figure 1

Example of a delta T methodology

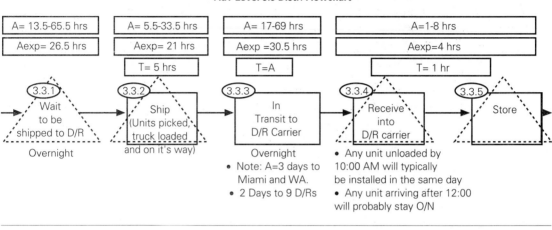

AdT Level 3.3 Distr. Flowchart

You may simply ask, "When you get one of these forms, how long does it sit on your desk before it is completed and passed on?" or "How long does it take to get this material from point A to point B?" or "How long does it take to get an answer to a question?" The elapsed time approach also fits CLAM's objectives for the supply chain. Shortened elapsed times eliminate big portions of the costs in the processes, and improves customer service levels.

Elapsed time measures get people's attention, since an A delta T ratio can be computed as the amount of wasted time versus value-contributing time (A delta T ratio = (actual/theoretical) × 100). Ratios in the hundreds, and a few in the thousands, revealed immense opportunities for cycle time reduction. The A delta T ratio often gives alarming numbers, as intended, to make waste look really bad. For example, an A delta T ratio of 2,300 reveals that it takes two days to do what should really only take two hours of value-contributing time (i.e., (46 hours/2 hours) × 100 = 2,300). Such big ratios also indicate that managers should initially eliminate waste activities rather than refine value-contributing activities.

CLAM Projects and Processes

The CLAM change agents intend to reengineer and simplify processes globally throughout the supply chain. With their roots in information system management, CLAM leaders could not forget the importance of information systems. CLAM change agents realized that all reengineered business processes must be consistent with and supported by information engineering. Thus, CLAM's improvement projects are identified, prioritized, and planned with this principle in mind. The project planning process is shown in Figure 2.

Some of the change agents have assumed responsibilities as project managers (or co-managers). As a project manager, a CLAM change agent is accountable for the objectives expectations, and deliverables of the project. The project manager manages resources and information on the project (e.g., plans and status), and coordinates with and provides information to other project teams and sponsors (internal and external to CLAM). Figure 3 lists and describes the objectives of CLAM's thirteen key projects that could be described as *push* projects, that is, projects being led and

Figure 2

CLAM s Project Planning Process

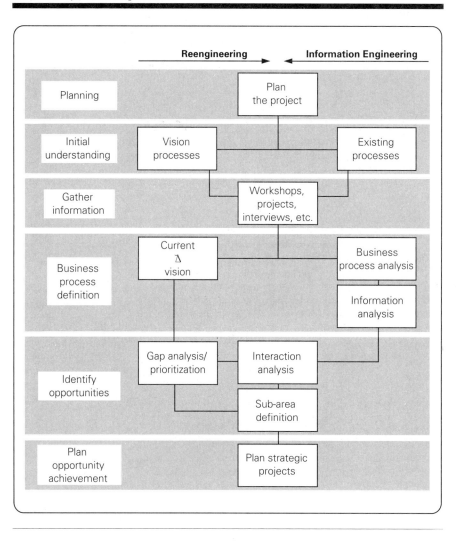

developed by CLAM with tangible CLAM outputs.

Fred Hewitt provides not only integration and barrier busting, but also inspection for the projects. Each project's status is updated and reviewed by Fred's senior staff (at a minimum) every two months. Projects are also selected for review depending on milepost dates, objectives, deliverables, costs, and needs for support,

coaching or barrier busting. Each year, a process change map shows the time-phased process implementation activities. To communicate the improvements to CLAM and others, a supply chain flash report (status report) offers success stories, process changes, business results, key activities, and future assignments.

In addition to CLAM's push projects, upon request the change agents also assist operating

Figure 3

The objectives of CLAM's 13 key projects

Asset Recovery Management (ARM): Implement asset recycling policies and principles worldwide.

Configuration Management (CONF): (1) In the near term, provide interim solutions to meet product information requirements of showcase, P3 and asset recovery projects. (2) In the long term, reengineer business processes to provide the product information required by the operational vision of the integrated supply chain supporting Xerox 2000, and establish a common language throughout the chain. Identify prioritized set of reengineered processes which provide and manage product information, test prototype business processes, and develop associated business proposals.

Congruent Goals (CONGG): Develop and implement operational metrics, including customer satisfaction and asset recycling, which drive partnerships and incorporation of best business practices between development and manufacturing, and marketing and customer operations, covering the entire integrated supply chain, to support the Xerox business objectives for inventory management and logistics for the 1990s.

Op. Co. Distribution Flexibility (OPCOFL): Perform detailed analysis of operating company (Op. Co.) current capabilities to meet customer level of service requirements. Determine the key enablers throughout the integrated supply chain that provide flexibility to achieve customer requirements.

GAINS/Data Base Development (GAINS): Provide global visibility to supply chain (activity, stock, production, and manufacturing work-in-process) with data and information that provides a means to implement consistent and timely equipment business process decisions at multinational level.

Level of Service (LOS): Define, obtain agreement, seek internalization, assist with implementation (including initial data collection and reporting) and ensure effectiveness of consistent metrics across the OpCo.s to measure the level of service provided by the parts and equipment supply chains (including, eventually, ARM).

Manufacturing Flexibility (MFGFLEX): Develop detailed analysis of manufacturing and supplier chains, assess current process capability, and lead prioritized projects for flexibility.

New Product Intercept (NPI): (1) Standardize the processes of the customization model with new products beginning in the new concept phase, to help decide the best supply chain flow alternative for new products, including manufacturing site selection. (2) Develop commitment and economic support for the North American integration center.

Order Satisfaction (OSAT): Develop a prioritized set of reengineered and implemented order satisfaction processes and associated information systems which meet the operational vision for the supply chain. This will include allowing customer orders to be routed to and tracked from any place in the supply chain and the order management of internal and supplier orders, but will not include internal production or warehouse processes.

Supply Chain Management Advisor (SCMA): Interface with most of the other CLAM projects to provide IM&L and integrated supply chain decision support and analysis tools (what-if, how-to); process engineering and reengineering support, and data, information access, filtering, presentation, and analysis.

Showcase/ISC Projects—Europe (S-EUR): Develop and implement techniques to reduce/optimize integrated supply chain operating inventory and timeline.

Showcase/ISC Projects—America (S-AMER): Develop and implement techniques to reduce/optimize integrated supply chain operating inventory and timeline. The 5090 & 5028 products are showcased with focus on inventory measurements, production planning process (P3), and A delta T techniques to improve the integrated supply chain ability to respond to demand change within P3 stated flexibility boundaries.

Spares Support Projects (SPARES): (1) Improve the new product launch spares planning process through utilization of, and funding for, excess/cancel spares. (2) Apply end of life/customer loyalty process to all products. (3) Implement hemispheres spares dredge process.

units in the application of locally developed strategies and tool sets. These projects are called *pull* projects. Whether by push or by pull, CLAM intends to achieve a number of specific process improvements within Xerox. Specific process improvements are planned for each hemisphere. For example, Xerox established process improvements for the Americas' implementation for every area of the supply chain shown in Figure 4. Some of the sub-processes or projects are mature in terms of accomplishments, like asset recovery management, while others are just getting started, like configuration management, one of the most challenging projects. Some projects are operational, for example, the revised production planning process (P3), while others serve a defining function, such as the level of service project team. Some examples are discussed below.

Level of Service The level of service project team discovered that each internal Xerox unit used different definitions to measure their level or service to customers. So data across different organizational units were not comparable and meaningful. Bob Willard recanted a story, about a manager we'll call Joe. Joe said, "I've got 97 percent level of service to my internal customer organization." Joe's customer said, "But I never got the parts I ordered." It turns out that if Joe got an order for the part, but didn't acknowledge the order, he said, "Well, I told you you couldn't have it. So I don't count that on my level of service."

Showcases After the the optimization managers grabbed the low-hanging fruit, CLAM started process reengineering through showcases. Some showcases focused on a narrow geographic range, i.e., just the U.S. rather than all of Xerox. Other showcases focused on a narrow product range, for example, new products, with CLAM change agents hoping to get it right the first time, when new processes are easier to put in place.

This "sandbox approach" allowed CLAM to get all involved people "into one arena" to expedite decisions and actions. By taking a small subset of the organization, while still encompassing cross-functional processes, CLAM could test new and reengineered processes under controlled conditions. Showcases helped them identify high problem areas and work out solutions that could be translated into standard practices, transferred to other areas, or scaled up to global processes.

In Webster, New York, CLAM did showcases for the 5028, a desk-top copier which does twenty-eight copies a minute, and the 5090, a larger floor unit that does ninety copies a minute. The 5028 showcase team started with a rigorous A delta T analysis of various business processes. For example, an A delta T analysis for manufacturing material flows determined an actual elapsed time of 123 work days and a theoretical elapsed time of 47 work days, a big opportunity for improvement.

Another analysis was conducted on the supply chain rebalance elapse time. The rebalance elapse time was computed as the interval from when underlying customer demand is recognized until the supply chain is rebalanced to accommodate that change. Note that this is not the elapsed time from customer order to installation, which is much shorter because of the buffer warehouses that provide finished inventories immediately available for purchase. Analysis revealed an actual elapsed time of 46.1 weeks, as opposed to a theoretical elapsed time of 10.6 weeks.

The showcases revealed opportunities for cycle time and inventory reductions that were astounding. For example, new systems, processes, accountabilities, and measurements of the 5090 showcase yielded dramatic reductions in inventory of finished goods days of supply. In 1990, before the P3 process, Xerox ran with an average inventory of seventy days of supply. By 1992, after Xerox had successfully introduced the showcase mode, they reduced it to thirty. They made this improvement without compromising an excellent service level, and

Figure 4

Supply chain process improvements - Americas implementation

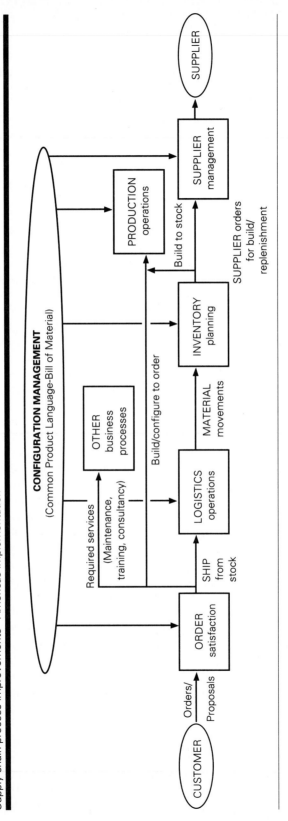

without increasing raw material and work in process inventories to do it.

CLAM leaders were careful not to invent methods that only work in the showcase sandbox. They hoped that all their learning and new processes would have expansion capability to the rest of global Xerox. As Bob Willard states, "It's easy to look good when you micromanage in the huge environment where you can pick the projects most likely to be successful."

Revised Production Planning Process (P3)
One of the first inventions that was transferred across Xerox was the revised production planning process (P3). Xerox developed P3 prototypes with new product showcases before applying them throughout Xerox.

P3 moved the manufacturing and warehousing planning away from a negotiated quarterly forecasting process. In the past, manufacturing and marketing organizations negotiated how full marketing's warehouses would be and how long it would take manufacturing to fill them. The gamesmanship that ensued always resulted in suboptimal results for the objectives of the integrated supply chain.

With P3, however, warehouses are nothing more than a central staging area which holds only replenishing stock. Inventory levels are determined on a factual basis, not on opinions. Instead of shipping according to a forecast, manufacturing ships equipment to a customer order. Equipment doesn't leave the warehouse for the field until it has a customer's name, address, and installation time attached. So production planning becomes nothing more than replenishment control, with minimum/maximum inventory levels determined statistically and empirically, based on factors such as time in the pipeline, likely need of safety stock, supplier lead times, and forecasting error. As Bob Willard puts it, "Plants don't ship to a forecasted demand; they only ship when they have an order. When that machine starts moving outward, it's not going to go sit dead in a warehouse. It's got a customer's name on it.

If it gets stopped in the pipeline and it can't be installed, there's no place to keep it out there. They have to send it back to the plant."

Changes in the supply chain such as the P3 approach require a significantly different mentality throughout all functions of Xerox. P3 teams make data-driven production decisions on the production floor, and are empowered to shut down production and send workers home or to training, without vice presidential signatures. P3 teams communicate with warehousing managers and work within the empirically determined limits for inventory levels. For some product types, warehouse inventory is nonexistent.

Part of the rationale for implementing an integrated supply chain with new products is not only to get it right the first time, but also to transform the organization through attrition. As new products come on line and old ones die off, the organization will evolve. Perhaps the new processes developed through showcases can also be transplanted or modeled in old product lines that are retained.

Configuration Management The process of order configuration is a real challenge for Xerox, one which they have just begun to address. When a salesperson writes a customer order for a large piece of equipment that is configured to the order, the product description must be translated from the salesperson's description of what was sold to the customer into something for manufacturing to build. It must be translated into a bill of materials, and flow through the levels of the production schedule.

For example, an order is placed for a Docutech, a training manual, an insurance policy, software, and a plotter from Versaterm. The Docutech may have options for a binder, a stitcher, software, and fonts. Currently, the translation process is subjectively and manually done by individuals with diverse experiences and differing understanding of the order itself. There is no common product language, and no relational database which prescribes the translation structure or spells out rules about the compatibility of options. So a machine costing hundreds of thousands of dollars may get delivered, but not do exactly what the customer wanted it to do. Xerox needed to improve their ability to talk to customers. Everyone agrees this vexing and costly problem should be addressed, but no one owned responsibility for it until the implementation of CLAM.

Other Business Processes CLAM change agents collaborate with the many other process teams dispersed throughout Xerox. The fourteen basic business processes discussed earlier span Xerox corporation by cutting across many functions and units. As we have seen with the thirteen projects of the CLAM change agents, which primarily address the inventory management and logistics (IM&L) agenda, each of the fourteen basic processes may be composed of many processes and projects. These are managed by diverse Xerox managers. High-impact teams of subordinate managers may assist the basic business process owners by improving subprocesses, or processes which are smaller in scope and contribute to the higher level processes. There may even be overlapping memberships among these different levels of high-impact teams.

High-impact teams may be cosponsored by managers of the basic business processes. For example, manufacturing resources teams (MRTs) and product development teams (PDTs) may be supported by executives who are working on the basic processes of inventory management and logistics, product design and engineering, and production operations management, and composed of people from manufacturing and design engineering units. MRTs and PDTs ensure cross-functional and early collaboration to plan the development, production, and delivery of new products. This early collaboration ensures, for example, that tooling decisions, key manufacturing investments, and process design decisions are made

in conjunction with engineering design decisions.

To integrate their work with that of these other teams, CLAM change agents advise the PDTs, for example, how to design more commonality into the processes and products, so uniqueness can be added to machines at the very last moment in production. CLAM change agents attempt to integrate their efforts with that of other teams as much as possible.

Integrating the Projects

The project manager and project team members bear the responsibility to understand their interrelationships to other processes and projects. Cross-membership of teams helps provide some integration. For example, it is common courtesy (code of honor) to give a group a seat on the process team if the work has a major impact on them. However, integration of CLAM's projects is not assumed or taken for granted. CLAM tries to avoid project isolation which would be similar to the functional isolation in traditional organizations. To help ensure that all CLAM projects were integrated appropriately, the change agents engaged in the following set of activities soon after the projects had been established:

1. Project managers identified their project's interdependencies (key alliances) with other CLAM projects. A two-dimensional matrix listing each of the projects, with rows and columns, was used to record the interdependencies (see Figure 5). The project managers indicated they were either dependent, "D," on the other project for real output to make them successful; simply an interested observe, "I"; or not interested, "—".
2. The charts were blown up to poster size and taped around the walls of the room. The project managers were then given a half-hour to walk around the room, look at all the data, make sure they were comfortable with their responses, or use a black pen for editing their own data only.

Figure 5
Dependent/interested matrix

D = Depend I = Interested – = No con'ct	ARM	CONF	CONGG	OPCOFL	GAINS	LOS	MF'GFLEX	NPI	OSAT	SCMA	S-EUR	S-AMER	SPARES
ARM	D	I	I	I	I	I	D	I	D	I	I	I	D
CONF.	–	D	I	I	D	I	D	I	D	D	I	I	D
CONG. G.	D	I	D	–	I	D	D	D	I	D	D	D	D
OPCO FL.	–	–	I	D	I	D	D	I	D	D	D	D	I
GAINS	–	D	D	I	D	I	I	–	–	D	D	D	D
LOS	I	I	D	D	I	D	D	I	I	D	I	D	I
MFG. FLEX.	D	I	I	D	I	D	D	D	I	D	D	D	D
N P INT.	–	D	I	I	I	I	I	D	D	D	D	D	D
O SAT.	–	D	–	I	I	D	O	D	D	D	I/D	I	I
SCMA	D	D	D	D	D	I	I	I	I	D	I	D	I
S-EUR	D	D	I	D	D	I	D	D	D	D	D	I	D
S-AMER	D	D	I	D	D	I	D	D	D	D	D	I	–
SPARES	I	I	I	–	–	I	I	–	D	I	I	I	D

3. For the next two hours, they walked around the room with red pens, writing questions, challenges, or agreements on other project managers' posters.

4. The project managers then taped as much supporting material around their own marked posters as needed to defend them. They had to address every red mark. If a project manager satisfied the person who made the red mark, it could be crossed off. If not, then it got recorded on an open issue sheet, to be resolved.

Not only was the process informative, but the resulting dependencies matrix reminded people of the hooks they have in each other, and the corresponding needs for collaboration and communication. The interdependencies of CLAM projects are spelled out in terms of requirements from one another. For example, the requirements from other projects for the congruent goals project are listed in Figure 6.

Supply Chain Integration Process Design
Over time, CLAM's vision of the supply chain has evolved into that shown in Figure 7 (page 747). Such refinements provide even more focus and direction for business process change in Xerox. This vision of the integrated supply chain will be implemented as "pull replenishment logistics" rather than "produce to forecast and warehouse inventories." Also, the replenishment logistics will be different for different types of products. The left side of Figure 7 shows the parts of the theoretical supply chain. The right side shows the logistical differ-

Figure 6

Project requirements/validation form

Your project name: congruent goals			
List of supplying projects	**Requirements**	**Date required**	**Planned/ not planned**
ARM Tom Lyons	• Utilization targets/measurements for commodities by Op Unit and Partnership • Off-lease inventory available for rehab by Op Unit/Commodity	Quarterly	

LOS
Susanne Guske,
then OPCO
	• Customer satisfaction
	  • Overall
	  • Post install
	  • Post service
	• Customer satisfaction
	  • Performance to customer requested delivery date
	  • Calls broken due to Parts for calls needing parts
	  • Fault free (FF) install rate
	• Inter-echelon service level metrics
		Quarterly
		
		Monthly	

MFG FLEX Ken Boudreau, then MO/Plants	• Leadtime improvements by plant/ Partnerships • Product production flexibility/ISC cost & benefits	Monthly	
NPI Dan Colbert	• Cost/benefits calculation methodology for supply chain	When developed	
SCMA Mike Thomas	• Data requirements for feeds into SCMA database • Specification of output of SCMA for inclusion into Quarterly Partnership Reporting	When developed	
EUR & AM SHOWCASES Showcase Mgrs.	• Metrics developed for tracking supply chain performance	As developed	
SPARES Project Mgr.	• Key metrics and reporting process developed as part of project	As developed	

ences, for each of these parts of the theoretical supply chain, for each type of product.

The Components of the Theoretical Supply Chain The most important component of the supply chain, customers are all those who purchase and use Xerox products and services (equipment, parts, supplies, paper, software). The customer support echelon includes all first-line customer logistical contacts (trunks,

Figure 7
Supply chain integration business process design

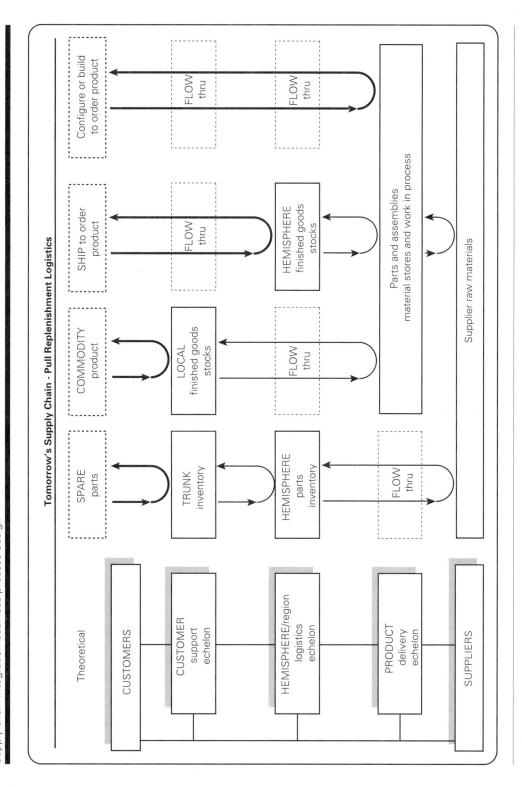

lockers, delivery/removal carrier depots). Regional logistics centers will not exist in Xerox's major markets, but will exist only under special circumstances to meet local needs (due to geography, politics, or special processes). For example, in addition to the hemisphere logistics center, national warehouses exist in Brazil, China, and India. In most cases, a hemisphere logistics center serves as the single point through which inventory is distributed to an entire hemisphere, such as America or Europe. The hemisphere logistics center provides logistics, transport, and stocking capability as well as redistribution to other hemispheres. Product delivery centers design and manufacture products to replenish logistical flows to the customer. The product delivery centers also manage the supplier base and all asset recovery and disposal operations. Suppliers are all the external (non-Xerox) suppliers of parts and services.

There will not be a single Xerox supply chain, with uniform logistical flows for every product. Rather, the supply chain will vary for different types of products and services to allow Xerox to optimally meet its objectives for customer satisfaction, asset utilization, and logistical costs. The supply chain characteristics are described below for spare parts, commodity products, ship-to-order products, and configure- or build-to-order products. Distribution processes for nonphysical products and services are not depicted here—for example, software that can be downloaded and transmitted over telephone lines.

Spare Parts   For the spare parts supply chain, the bulk of inventories will be held in two places, the technical representative's trunk and the hemisphere logistics center. For example, in the U.S., Xerox would like to replenish the technical representative's trunk daily from the hemisphere center by means of sixty or seventy conveniently located parts depots, which are only pick-up points, not stocking operations. Such overnight replenishment

means that information on part usage must be transmitted to the hemisphere center quickly, probably electronically rather than on paper order forms. Ideally, Xerox would replace the hemispheric inventory directly from the supplier as much as possible.

Commodity Products   Customers want some products as soon as possible, same day or next day. To serve these customers, local finished goods stocks are held in "reasonable" supply close to the customer. As soon as one is sold, it is replenished directly from manufacturing. So the hemisphere logistics center is simply a "flow-through" or cross-docking operation rather than a stocking location. The commodity products supply chain handles low-end products, small boxes with few options. Customers typically have a very short order-to-install (OTI) expectation for commodities: they want it to plug and play immediately. Such products as typewriters or fax machines may be sold through dealers, agents, or retail channels. In terms of sales volume, not much Xerox equipment falls into this category, but immediate availability of commodities is very important in order to achieve high service levels. Occasionally a customer wants one of the larger copiers immediately, otherwise, it's no sale. To cover such contingencies, Xerox may leave a single 5028 in each of sixty finished goods stocking locations in North America.

Ship-to-Order Products   Low- to mid-range copiers and printers are most often shipped from replenishment stock at a hemisphere center to meet a specific customer order. The customer support echelon is a flow-through, with no buffer stocks. Minimal finished goods stocks are held in the hemisphere center according to prescribed inventory levels, and stocks are replenished through the P3 process from manufacturing. Ship-to-order products have more options than commodity products, but are not so uniquely configured that there are more than a few versions available. It is only necessary to hold a couple of different configurations in stock at the hemisphere center to meet the customer's requirement. Since the customer doesn't have to have the product immediately, it can be shipped within a few days. Customers purchasing these products are more interested in reliable OTI, so the equipment is shipped according to the installation schedule. Rush orders can be shipped in one day, but at the high cost of expedited transportation.

Configure- or Build-to-Order Products Top-of-the-line products are the big, complex, highly configured systems which have lots of software options, and lots of physical options, such as stackers and binders. At this end of the product spectrum, eight to twelve weeks is the normal order-to-install expectation, although some customers need them the same day. Xerox maintains some stocks to deal with such rush orders. However, Xerox can provide much more value to the customer if it configures the equipment according to the customer's unique needs. Finished goods are shipped directly from the production plant, and no finished goods stocks are held in hemisphere logistics centers or the locations of the customer support echelon. While transportation from the production plant to the customer site may take no more than a couple of days, even across the country, it may require large, dedicated moving vans with air-ride shock absorbers to move the big systems.

For example, Xerox's Docutech system, the top-of-the-line publisher, is 28-feet long. The Docutech system runs 120 copies a minute and goes right for the heart of the off-set printer business. It has a huge memory capacity, and there are many software options; for example, the electronic publishing version of the Docutech has options for 300 font sizes and types. It takes a technical representative three or four days to physically install the machine, put it together, and get it running. Then

it may take ten working days to load all the software from floppy discs.

A customer can justifiably be frustrated when he or she pays $300,000 for a high-end publishing system only to watch a technical representative fumble with floppy discs for ten days. For one thing, the installation time means down time for customers, particularly when their old system had to be removed to make room for the new one. Xerox now prefers to load the software in a manufacturing environment with high-speed buses in under ten minutes, as opposed to doing it in the customer support echelon with rudimentary tools. In addition to software loading, CLAM is helping to set up integration centers for last-minute configuration of all equipment options.

Details of the Supply Chain Vision

CLAM leaders Fred Hewitt, Graham Sweet, and Bob Willard have fleshed out detailed plans for every aspect of the integrated supply chain. For example, Figure 8 shows a flow diagram of the 1990s supply chain for spare parts.

Figure 9 shows CLAM's vision for supplying, manufacturing, distribution, and customer interface of the equipment side of the house. Again, the equipment network will look slightly different for each type of product.

For example, the manufacturing strategy to configure mid-volume products to a customer order allows Xerox to assemble the product into its final configuration as late as possible and thus quickly react to customer requirements. As Graham Sweet explains:

> Some finished goods are language sensitive, software sensitive, voltage sensitive, and cycle sensitive, for different worldwide markets. The minute you make a 240 volt, 60 cycle, Greek language, typewriter, that's where it goes, to Greece. We prefer to leave it in sub-assembly form until the order for a Greek typewriter, or a Spanish typewriter, or a Mexican or Canadian one comes in, then tailor it. We will build it to a level where it's

Figure 8

1990's spares supply chain

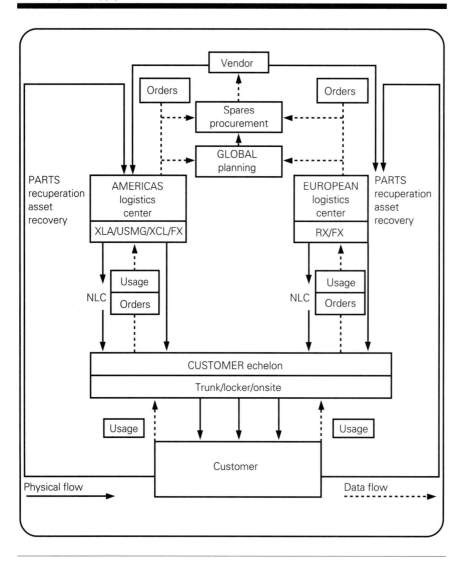

generic, and then configure it and finish it when we have an order for it. We may have to hold a little more work in process inventory back in the plant, but we can certainly avoid holding lots of finished options out in the field.

Consenting to hold a little work-in-process inventory in the plant does not totally obviate just-in-time (JIT) principles, Rather, it implies that cycle time reduction and JIT are important throughout the supply chain, not just within the walls of a manufacturing plant. It makes no sense to save three hours in JIT manufacturing if the finished product waits for

Figure 9

1990's equipment network

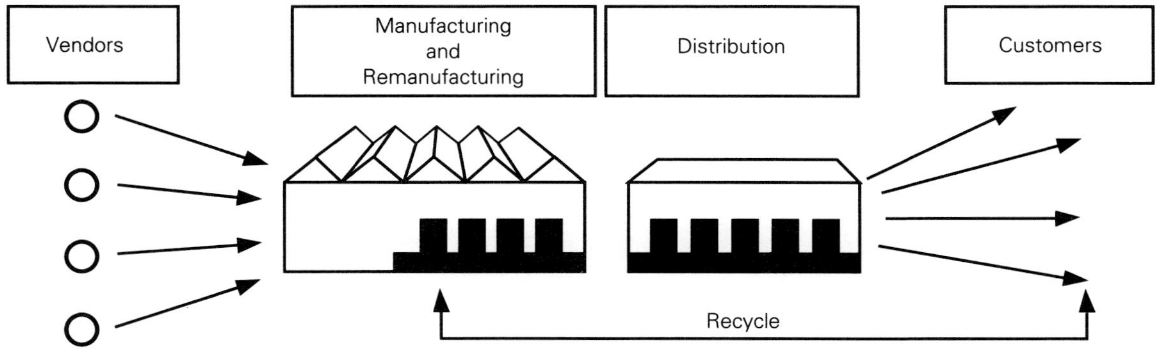

General	Sourcing	Manufacture	Distribution	Customer Interface
HIGH volume EP complex networks	Balanced sourcing/ manufacturer	Full product assembly	Single touch distribution	Competitive order to installation 100% delivery to customer Committed date
MID volume	Local sourcing Preference	Build to order	Zero stock	Fully configured customized product
COMMODITY products workstations	Local sourcing	Configure to order	Minimal neutral Finished goods	Late addition of customization
ASSET recovery management	Local Sourcing/OEM	Build To Full Configuration/ OEM	Commodity stocks held close to customer but single echelon	FULLY configured product (plug and play)
	Parts strip for new build substitutes	RE manufacturing	MINIMAL stock	Local turn around of trials, dustoffs

nine months in the field because there is no immediate demand.

Tomorrrow's Certified Business Processes

Reducing cycle time and removing inventory through this vision of an integrated supply chain obviously achieves economic improvements through cost reduction. However, to also ensure improved customer service, execution of the leaner supply chain must approach perfection. With little buffer stock, there is little margin for error. All elements must come together for a successful installation or successful service call: the right material, in the right configuration, in the right condition, at the right place, at the right time. Success means the business processes of the supply chain, such as those listed below, must be certified to approach perfection:

1. Customize install/service to site and customer conditions
2. Damage-free transport
3. Logistics reliability and accuracy
4. Configuration and quality
5. Ship to order

Xerox measures fault-free installation, where everything comes together at the right place at the right time, for a totally successful machine installation. Currently fault-free installations occur about 30 to 40 percent of the time.[3] Flaws occur 60 to 70 percent of the time. Each flaw triggers a corrective action process by the technical representatives and installers who have to fix the problems. For example, they must hunt down missing parts, because the order was transmitted incorrectly or the installation kit is incomplete. They must sometimes race back to the branch and pick up

three parts, or steal an installation kit from another machine 's ready to go. Requiring the customer support echelon to correct internal problems misuses resources. Xerox needs these employees focused on customer-unique conditions, tailoring products and services to specific customer needs, and not focused on fixing avoidable problems.

In the past, the customer support echelon had to do rework because the nature of the supply chain increased the likelihood of defects. For example, manufacturing builds processors; xerographic engines; sorters, stackers, output trays, and binders that give various output options; and the document handlers and paper trays that give various input options. The field orders all these parts independently from different manufacturing plants or different stocking locations. Somehow, through scattered distribution processes, all the right parts are supposed to come together at the right place, at the right time, at the customer service level. But rarely does it happen. When a delivery removal carrier, a contract employee who installs machines, arrives at a customer site, he or she expects to have all the pieces of the order available. If something is missing such as a sorter, a customer care kit, the documentation, or the processor, he or she can't complete the installation.

To drive defects to a parts per million level, Xerox plans to stop collating parts in the customer support echelon. When this many sites are involved, it's much easier to certify the configuration process in one location, the manufacturing plant. In a manufacturing environment, the tools and quality process are available to oversee the collation process. Under this new approach, all parts are configured in the manufacturing plant, and one load is shipped with everything needed for installation. It's much more difficult to certify processes in sixty-five random locations and warehouses across the country.

If manufacturing provides the right material, in the right configuration, then logistics

---

3. That sounds less than optimal, but since Xerox's exception processes (for handling problems) are good overall, customers are satisfied with the installation process 95 to 96 percent of the time. Sometimes the customers never see minor flaws which are corrected fast enough. Even though customers are satisfied, the costs of not doing it right the first time can be quite high.

simply has to provide defect-free transport of the equipment package. They should not introduce any defects or damage it. They can't touch the equipment, or even open the box. If logistics provides this damage-free transport, then certified processes for logistics reliability and accuracy and ship-to-order capability will ensure that the equipment gets to the right place, at the right time.

Consider the changes that were made in the 5090 series. Xerox previously built unique machines for the U.S. and Canadian markets. The Canadian models had multinational symbols, three languages, and standard international panels, which are not back-lighted. The U.S. models had English-only wording on the front, no multinational symbols, with back-lighted panels for use in a dark room. Producing and validating these unique configurations, creating unique machines, used to require 200 extra hours. There were inventories in Canada for Canadian machines, and inventories in the U.S. for U.S. machines.

In reality, after assembly, the only real difference is about sixty cents worth of labels, and one eprom, which was written in French. So Xerox changed the processes. Designers reduced the uniqueness and made all the parts the same creating a common machine, and at the last minute, when it's going out the door, it is customized. If it has a Canadian customer's name on it, a French kit is slipped into the package, just sixty cents worth of labels and the eprom for the machine software. All the uniqueness that drove unique stock locations is eliminated. Xerox no longer has thousands of assets, uniquely configured, sitting in warehouses. The Canadian salespeople never get to a site and have the wrongly labeled machine. And it only costs $6 and two minutes of time.

Managerial Changes

Xerox has initiated a change process that has already yielded remarkable business results, for customers and for other stakeholders. The change process is driven by a clear vision of what the organization needs to do. However, this new vision will not be realized without extensive cultural, managerial, and process changes. The change process that CLAM's change agents are leading and facilitating is discussed in the Xerox Part III case.

▶ **EXERCISE**

- Assemble into groups of five or six people and complete the following exercise. Figure 3 in the chapter on "Organizing to Improve Systems" lists several approaches used to address cross-functional systems. For each of the approaches listed below, describe an example from the Xerox case which illustrates the use of the approach. Indicate what cross-functional system (or cross-functional issue) was being addressed with the approach, how it was being addressed, and what was accomplished.

Approach	Xerox example
1. Ad hoc teams	1.
2. Committee structure	2.
3. Internal customer concept	3.
4. Cross-functional systems	4.
5. Systems focused on products	5.
6. Systems focused on customers	6.

Describe other ways Xerox could apply these approaches to accomplish its integrated supply chain vision.

Xerox, Part III: Accomplishing Behavioral Change*

▶ PROVIDING LEADERSHIP

The business process changes being implemented through Central Logistics and Asset Management (CLAM) at Xerox are broad and pervasive, tugging at every corner of the cultural fabric. Such changes require new behaviors from managers. The CLAM change agents work full time on changing processes and behaviors. Fred Hewitt, vice president of CLAM, explains the rationale for devoting full-time change agents to this task.

> The instigation of the change, generally speaking, has come through this particular organization [CLAM]. The implementation task has been carried forward by the line organization. Our job is to get the line operations to take ownership of the change . . . to leave behind the new process sufficiently owned by and embedded in the line functions.
>
> We have come to the conclusion that it's very difficult for people to play simultaneously the operational role [in functional line management] and at the same time be a multifunctional process change agent. We've got a lot of people who can play either role, but you really do put some very

strange pressures on people, even if you ask the most confident person to play both roles simultaneously. Our president Paul Allaire experienced this when we were simultaneously going through the leadership through quality exercise and going through the Malcolm Baldrige exercise. He said he found it very hard because it suddenly put him in two different positions. During most of his time as the head of Xerox, he was being awfully critical about the organization, looking for our faults, insisting on removing the blemishes. And then periodically he would have to sit in front of the Baldrige award team to say how good we are and how far we've come, to say that, although we're not perfect, we're probably the most customer-oriented company that you could find. He found that very, very difficult.

> It's similar to being the head of the manufacturing enterprise, within the corporation, and at the same time to be asked to take a view that manufacturing is only a part of the broader supply chain extending from the supplier to the customer. We've got to fundamentally change the way we do business, change all the barometers we measure ourselves on, and maybe change accounting systems because idle capacity may not be a bad thing after all. It is difficult to do these

* This case was prepared by Greg Bounds.

kinds of things when you're also asked to run five or six major factories around the world and make sure that you get production out of them. I'm sure a person can occasionally do both, but whether that person can effectively do both, simultaneously, from day to day, is questionable.

Thus, Xerox acknowledges the difficulties that line managers have with "breaking away from the treadmill of control," by having full-time change agents help them break away. The CLAM change agents are instigators and facilitators as well as leaders and participants in the implementation. CLAM change agents pro-vide strategic direction and vision, as the strategic consciousness of Xerox. But they also aim to make leaders out of line managers by involving them in developing the vision and implementing viable solutions.

This part of the case study explores the process and nature of behavioral change at Xerox, getting line managers to lead change. Below, we will briefly discuss how CLAM change agents view the change curve, explore a model of the behavioral changes they are facilitating, and then hear, in their own words, how the change agents facilitate change.

▶ THE CHANGE CURVE

The CLAM change agents bear the responsibility not only for coming up with proposals for new and improved business processes. They are also responsible for putting them in place. The goal of CLAM change agents is for their proposed process changes to be institutionalized and internalized, that is, to become an embedded part of the cultural fabric that doesn't easily get washed out. Thus, they are involved in process change from the initial stages of contacting the potential stakeholders. Their involvement continues until the process of change is absorbed by line managers and operators, who then have the resources and commitment to sustain the change.

The development of an effective change management strategy is one of the greatest challenges that the CLAM change agents face. Although CLAM change agents do not follow a lock-step procedure, they do refer to the model in Figure 1 to help them anticipate and understand the likely stages of progress in implementing a process or system change. Figure 1 depicts the likely reactions of stakeholders, or line manager implementors, to change proposals. For example, change agents should expect the initial confusion that results once stakeholders are made aware of the proposed change. Although the change agents use data and the quality process throughout the various stages of change, these are particularly important in the initial stages, to achieve awareness and understanding. Even with good information, it takes some time for the stakeholders to understand the change. Once the stakeholders understand the change, confusion may turn into negative perceptions. The change curve helps change agents realize that the change process can be lengthy and require much time and attention to work through each stage. If change agents get stuck with the downside arrows in the change curve, the change gets thwarted and never becomes a permanent part of the organization.

To move as quickly as possible toward internalization, the change agents must realize which stage of change they face and take action accordingly. Consider, for example, the diverse stakeholders that may need to be involved in the change process. In the initial stages of contact, the change agents must build alliances with key stakeholders (decision makers) to build awareness, understanding, and eventual approval of the change. However, when it comes time for installation, there may be other key stakeholders (implementers and

Figure 1

Change curve of progress

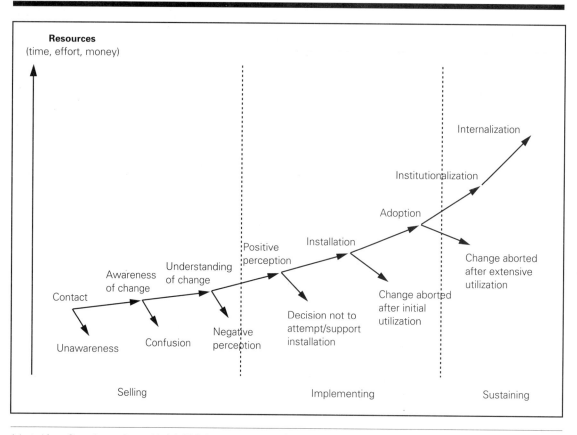

Resources
(time, effort, money)

Internalization

Institutionalization

Adoption

Installation

Positive
perception

Change aborted
after extensive
utilization

Understanding
of change

Awareness
of change

Contact

Change aborted
after initial
utilization

Decision not to
attempt/support
installation

Confusion

Negative
perception

Unawareness

Selling   Implementing   Sustaining

Adapted from Commitment Stages Model, ODR, Inc., Atlanta, Georgia.

operators) with whom alliances must be built, including some who may never be directly involved in its operation. Even after the change has been adopted, change agents must not pretend that they can hand it over to operators as if it has been internalized. Initial operational buy-in of a change does not necessarily lead to internalization for the long term. Rather, it needs nurturing, perhaps from other key stakeholders (operators, facilitators and supporters) to help it through its early phases.

CLAM's projects are at various stages of

progress toward internalization. Some are just achieving awareness, while others are being institutionalized. The change curve is one of the many tools change agents use. The CLAM change agents have not written out a prescription for what to do at each of these stages. Rather, they hold project reviews of progress and study them as a team.[1] They draw from their own collective wisdom.

---

1. All projects fit into an overall architecture and prioritized sequence of what CLAM wants to accomplish in the integrated supply chain each year.

▶ MANAGERIAL BEHAVIOR CHANGE

The curve in Figure 1 describes the general stages a change agent faces in getting managerial stakeholders to internalize a change in the organization. However, the change curve does not describe the behavior changes required to integrate Xerox's supply chain. The framework presented below elaborates on the nature of these behavioral changes.

To integrate the supply chain and improve basic business processes across all of Xerox Corporation, managers will have to move away from a functional approach toward the improvement of cross-functionally integrated systems (or business processes). This movement requires significant changes in the behavior of individual managers. These behaviors can be generally described in terms of three dimensions: breadth of involvement, level of competency, and depth of involvement. The cube in Figure 2 shows these three dimensions, each of which is described below.

Breadth of Involvement

The breadth of involvement of a manager in the management of an organization may be described as ranging across five levels, from a narrow orientation at one extreme (isolates functions) to a broad orientation at the other extreme (optimizes systems). Other terms might be substituted for the term "function," for example, department, unit, area, division, work group, or some other term for pieces of an organization. A "system" is broader in that it spans or transcends these narrower pieces of an organization. Other terms may be used to convey system, for example, Xerox uses the term "business process." The concept of the integrated supply chain may be seen as a system. For convenience, we use the term "function" to convey narrowness and the term "system" to convey breadth along this dimension labeled "breadth of involvement." The positions on this dimension include:

1. Isolates functions
2. Bargains
3. Cooperates
4. Contributes
5. Optimizes systems

Isolates Functions   The functionally oriented manager isolates his or her function and attempts to optimize the performance of the function. Functional managers remain detached and do not collaborate with other functions. Unfortunately, such functional optimization often leads to system suboptimization. Some functional managers simply inherit existing systems and processes and run them as they are, with little understanding of how or why they arose, and little effort to improve. Other functional managers may make improvements, but the improvements are also aimed at achieving functional goals; for example, a production department pursues machine utilization and labor rates rather than external customer satisfaction.

Bargains   The bargaining manager is functionally focused; however, he or she sees the need for functional neighbors to sometimes accommodate each other. These managers only accommodate others if they can get something out of it to advance their own functional agenda. So the accommodation is self-serving and is not motivated by higher-order goals. Relationships are contractual, "tit for tat."

Cooperates   An intermediate position, between functional orientation and systems orientation, is that of the manager who willingly interfaces and cooperates with other functions. They are not totally self-serving. They coordinate activities with other functions, and may build internal supplier/customer relationships. They cooperate with others, perhaps out of genuine concern for the performance of the whole organization.

Figure 2

The management cube

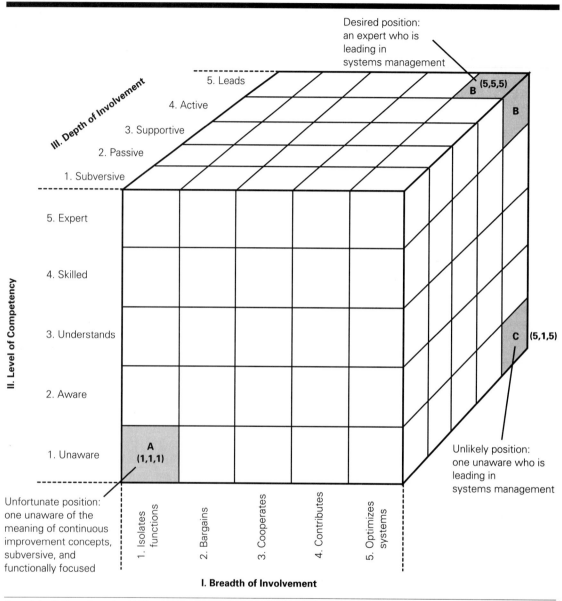

Copyright © Greg Bounds, 1992.

Contributes The contributing manager recognizes the existence of cross-functional systems which fulfill higher order goals, such as providing superior value to external customers. The contributing managers do not place functional concerns above system concerns. Rather, they willingly serve the purposes of higher order systems and integrate their efforts to optimize systems performance.

Systems Optimization System managers go well beyond the concept of internal customers, and do not simply contribute to systems. They assume personal ownership and responsibility for cross-functional systems (cross-departmental, cross-unit, or cross-divisional). The systems optimization managers may work in teams of owners or as individual owners. These systems are purposefully managed and integrated to serve strategic organizational objectives, such as serving external customers. System managers collaborate with other managers to build integrated systems to optimize organizational performance.

Level of Knowledge and Skill

The knowledge and skill we refer to specifically pertain to systems and continuous improvement concepts, tools, and techniques.[2] The level of knowledge and skill of a manager may be described as ranging across five levels:

1. Unaware
2. Aware
3. Understands
4. Skilled
5. Expert

Unaware The unaware manager is not aware of the significance of such concepts as continuous improvement, systems management, and superior customer value. This manager is unaware of any personal roles he or she might play in implementing these concepts, and does not possess the tools or techniques needed.

Aware The aware manager is aware of these concepts, but does not really understand them,

having minimal knowledge of tools and techniques and no skill in using them.

Understands The understanding managers know the significance of these concepts and understand how to apply them using appropriate tools and techniques; however, they have little, if any, behavioral experience and skill.

Skilled The skilled manager has behavioral experience and fairly good skill in applying various tools, techniques, and concepts.

Expert The expert manager not only has mastered an understanding of the concepts, and has extensive behavioral experience, but can practice the concepts expertly.

Depth of Involvement

Managers may involve themselves in prospective changes in various ways. The depth of involvement of a manager in improving an organization may be described as ranging across five levels:

1. Subversive
2. Passive
3. Supportive
4. Active
5. Leader

Subversive The subversive manager acts as an adversary to change through disruptive, diversionary, and/or noncooperative actions. He or she refuses to personally change his or her behavior and undermines the efforts of others to change theirs. The subversive activity may be overt, such as disrupting team meetings, or covert, such as in refusing to fund the education of key subordinates or staff.

Passive The passive manager does not engage in either personal role changes or corresponding organizational changes. Although

---

2. In the following section, some quotations from change agents refer also to the level of functional specialization a person has.

not openly subversive, he or she is reluctant to tamper with the status quo, and does not encourage subordinates or staff to change. Passive managers may go along with changes initiated by others.

Supportive The supportive manager encourages improvement activities by others, particularly subordinates and staff. However, he or she is not personally involved in any improvement activities, such as the analytical use of tools and techniques or the development of plans and strategies. The supportive manager delegates improvement work and responds to the suggestions of others with supportive resources and approvals.

Active The active manager is actively and personally involved in improvement activities. Not only does he or she support and respond to the improvement efforts of others, the active manager takes personal responsibility for applying the concepts, tools, and techniques for continuous improvement.

Leader A leader is not only actively involved in improvement activities, but also leads others in making improvements. He or she accepts ownership and responsibility for specific areas of improvement, formulates and shares his or her vision for improvement, and inspires and motivates others to get involved. He or she addresses interpersonal relations to enhance the participation, communication, and teamwork needed to implement improvements.

The Management Cube

These three dimensions can be combined into a cube that represents the different combinations that might be used to describe managerial behavior (see Figure 1).

Examples of Positions The position labeled A on the cube represents a functional manager, unaware of continuous improvement concepts, and subversive of changes for improve-

ment. This position is at level 1 on all three dimensions (position 1,1,1), an undesirable and unfortunate position. By contrast, the position labeled B on the cube represents a systems manager, expertly knowledgeable and skilled at continuous improvement, and leading system improvement activities. This very desirable position is at level 5 on all three dimensions (position 5,5,5).

The position labeled C indicates a position on the cube that is not likely to be observed by the change agent. It represents a manager who is managing systems, unaware of continuous improvement concepts and techniques, yet who is leading improvement (position 5,1,5). There are other positions on the cube that are not likely to occur; some of the positional combinations of the three dimensions may be mutually exclusive.

You may recognize other positions on the cube as descriptive of people you have observed, for example, people who may be described as amiable toward continuous improvement, but deceptive (i.e., position 1,3,1: isolates functions, understands, subversive). This type of person understands continuous improvement, and can talk a good game, but lacks true conviction. He or she fails to support talk with action, and even blocks progress by indirectly resisting the efforts of others, particularly cross-functional efforts.

As another example, you may recognize the position of mediocrity (3,3,3: cooperative, understands, supportive). This manager cooperates with other functions, understands continuous improvement, but doesn't personally practice it. He or she simply delegates improvement activities to subordinates and supports them with resources. As a result, any improvements may not be strategically linked to system optimization, and thus may even add cost and compromise system optimization. This position of mediocrity is one of the most insidious for organizations. The mediocre manager can be perceived as a good person, but he or she misses wonderful opportunities for strategic improvement and systems integration. Too many managers believe their job is to be on the sidelines, cooperative, understanding, and supportive.

Generality of the Categories The dimensions and positions that compose the cube are general categories which can be used to describe the "behavioral facts." These categories are general enough to allow some diversity within them with regard to other factors not considered on this cube, such as attitudes, feelings, motivations, and other causes of behavior. For example, one manager may be passive because he lacks conviction about continuous improvement. Another may be passive because he lacks self-confidence, and fears that he would fail miserably in trying to act on his conviction that continuous improvement is important.

A Practical Framework This cube is not intended to depict all the diversity of managerial behavior that can be observed in an organization. But it offers a general framework to give order to our observations. Furthermore, it suggests a goal for managerial behavior, that is, to generally move managers away from Position A (1,1,1: isolates functions, unware, subversive) and toward Position B (5,5,5: optimizes systems, expert, leader).

Change agents need to discover how to move people toward this behavioral goal, that is, to develop a practical guide to implementing behavioral change. Certainly, the prescriptions will vary with the starting position of the individual manager, and the feasibility of the various paths that may lead from that starting position to the more desired positions in the region of Position B. Furthermore, as mentioned above, the general nature of the positions in the cube is limited when it comes to understanding the causes of the behavior. The cube is simply a framework for the behavioral facts, which are outcomes of a number of causes. The challenge to the change agent is

to understand the underlying causes of the observed behavior.

Proposed Learning Agenda
To get stakeholders to internalize proposed system changes, CLAM change agents must delve below the level of behavioral description to unearth causes of stakeholder behavior. The behaviors per se are different from the causes of the behaviors. The behaviors are facts, the outputs of results of some complex system of causes, which are the leverage points for behavioral change. As discussed above, there may be many different causes of quite similar behaviors. For example:

1. *Attitudes* may be determined by personal values, beliefs, and goals.
2. *Motivation* may be determined by self-perceived ability, skills, and organizational appraisal systems, rewards, sanctions, cultural norms, and goals.
3. *Ability* may be determined by education, job experiences, life experiences, job training, and developmental experiences.
4. *Constraints* such as company policies and the availability of resources may *discourage* people from behaving in certain ways.
5. *Enablers* such as the availability of resources, methods, technologies, and broader systems may *help* people to behave in certain ways.

The change agent must learn to first recognize the behaviors and then to diagnose the causes of the behaviors. Understanding the causes can give clues about how to change the behavior. The experienced CLAM change agents have learned valuable lessons about what tends to work and not work in particular situations and positions on the cube. The agenda for this part of the Xerox case study is to learn from these experiences.

To learn about the change process at Xerox, I engaged in many hours of conversation with CLAM change agents. Using the cube as a framework for these conversations, I attempted to learn about the change process (e.g., interpersonal dynamics, timing issues, sequences of changes in leverage points). This learning can be shared with other change agents and managers to improve their effectiveness in accomplishing behavioral change.[3]

Questions for Change Agents

The change agents were given an overview of the cube (written and verbally) before exploring the following questions through conversation.

1. Describe the behavior of some of the managers you have encountered while implementing cross-functionally integrated systems. It might help to think of the behavior of specific people at various positions on the cube. (If the dimensions of the cube are not useful, then suggest how it should be changed to reflect your experiences.)

2. What were some of the consequences of the managerial behavior you just described? How did the managerial behavior impede or facilitate your efforts to implement integrated systems?

3. How did you deal with this behavior? What leverage points (causal factors) did you use to encourage behavior change? What worked and did not work in dealing with this behavior (leverage points, sequences, process of change)?

4. What paths of behavioral change have you observed? If a person is in a given position in the cube, what is the most likely next move en route to the most desirable corner of the cube (position 5,5,5)? What paths have proven treacherous? What paths have proven effective?

▶ THE THOUGHTS OF THE CHANGE AGENTS

The following examples, observations, and thoughts (some are quotations and others are paraphrases) are drawn from conversations with CLAM change agents.[4] Selected content of these interviews is organized below according to the causes and leverages of the types of managerial behavior shown in the cube.[5]

- Accountability/authority
- Complacency
- Credibility of the change agents

- Credibility of the proposed change
- Goals, measures, and rewards
- Infrastructure/autonomy/empowerment
- Organizational level and position
- Participation
- Personal preparedness
- Vision/perspective/leadership

In most of the excerpts below, my comments are deleted, and those of the change agents are edited into one paragraph. However, since the comments are drawn from conversational give and take, in some places it was necessary to insert my own comments in brackets [additional comments] to provide context and flow. Although I tried not to put words into the mouths of the change agents, I certainly did lead some of their responses with my part of the conversation. The reader needs to see the context of some of these re-

---

3. Although the learning gathered from a handful of experienced change agents will be biased and limited in scope, it does provide a starting point for capturing CLAM's collective knowledge about the change process.

4. The content here was drawn from several hundred pages of transcribed conversations, and has been edited heavily for brevity and clarity.

5. I debated on how much to process this information for the reader. I decided that hearing these messages from the change agents in their own words would be more robust, interesting, and powerful than reading general principles.

sponses.[6] Some of these excerpts are contradictory, and others are controversial. After all, these are individual beliefs, so they may vary according to an individual's experience.

Accountability/Authority

1. "Somebody has to start it off most of the time. Somebody really has to say, 'I am going to put the effort into this thing, recruit the people, get the meetings together, publish the minutes, and push this thing forward.' "

2. "Fred [the vice president of CLAM] clears the way to make a lot of things happen that we couldn't make happen at lower levels. A lot of times, we make these recommendations and realize there is no way the team can have any impact. When Fred sees that happening, he clears the way to make things happen so the team will in fact have the power to do it. Many times, just mentioning his name seems to help make things happen, because everybody knows how supportive he is of his operation."

3. [How do you get someone who has the capacity to be a leader to actually be one?] "Well, one way is to specifically charter them and give them the authority." [Make it their job.] "Yes. And let the people know they have authority. If Paul Allaire [Xerox president] says to Fred, 'You do whatever is necessary for inventory levels,' that's going to help him get it done. Fred could be the world's best person and really be passionate about inventory levels. But if Allaire had not said to the people in the other organizations, 'I want Fred to do this,' Fred wouldn't have necessarily been authorized. That's part of empowering or enabling.' "

4. "It gets back to the kind of change. If you're talking about dramatic, radical change, nobody except the very senior people can deal with that unless somebody enables them to. It's like beating their head against the wall. They might have the idea down there, but the only way they're going to make that idea happen is to consult somebody up here who actually has the power to make it happen."

5. "I have this spares manager who is critical to my project. I can't get the spare parts I need without him. I've not been able to pressure him too much, and we are behind schedule. I've got to be on his side, because he is helping me to get the job done. So, I'm the good cop. And then I've got the bad cop, a marketing manager. We all go into a PDT meeting, with a bunch of other people, including the chief engineer. The spares guy gives his status report, and it's not good. Instead of me giving in and saying that I screwed up, the marketing guy, the bad cop, gets up and blasts at him. Then the chief engineer starts blasting him because the customer is not happy. And I sit over there playing sympathetic. I go to him and say, 'I'm sorry, but he is right. I didn't want to say anything, I was going to work with you a little bit more.' So, I'm still the good cop. Sometimes we reverse the role, and I play bad cop on behalf of the other fellow."

6. "If you are not getting what you want, what you do is write a memo to the person you are having a problem with. You say to him, 'OK, here is where I think our level of agreement is. Here is where I think you are wrong and why I think I'm right and why we've got to do something about that.' And you lay it out in a factual straightforward manner, without emotions. You just say, 'Here is the situation as I see it.' And then you [send a written] copy to the guy's boss. So that if the boss is rather objective, and he reads the factual content, hopefully he will agree with you and say to the person, 'This guy is right. We really ought to do it.'

---

6. Note also that these interviews were conducted in November 1991, prior to the structural reorganization announced at Xerox in February 1992.

7. "Without embarrassing the person or making him look terrible, I change his objective in front of his boss. I invite him to the meeting, along with his boss—say, the chief engineer—and make sure he's at the meeting when I make the pitch. I keep staring at the chief engineer's eyes, to see if he has accepted it or not. If the chief engineer accepts it, then it's almost a no-brainer, the other guy has accepted it. It applies the pressure downward, even if it's not direct."

8. "Fred Hewitt is the business process champion for logistics and asset management for Xerox worldwide, across all functions. He would like to listen to you, to understand you, and get ideas from you. He would like to come to agreement with you. But at the end of the day, he says how we're going to run this part of the business. He has the authority and mandate to optimize the system. It's an interesting balance."

Complacency

1. "In a nutshell, the biggest resistance is that people don't like to change. That's the way they've been doing business for twenty years and that's the way they'd like to continue doing business. But do they understand why they do it that way? No, because when you ask why, the answer is, 'We've been doing it all along and it seems like it's working.'" [So, one way to motivate someone to change is to attack their complacency.] "That's one way, by maybe sharing with them some kind of data that reveals their way isn't adequate. The other way is to offer changes, and make them understand why we're changing, why it will be better. Maybe show them the kind of dollars we impact."

2. "We use external benchmarking to depoliticize things. When people say, "That can't be done,' then you politely take them and show them that it is being done. That tends to defuse it. When you get to the next stage, which is, 'Well, that's fine for them, but we can't do it here,' then you show them

someone doing it in the same environment. Then it keeps moving along. Competitive benchmarks are especially important, because that tends to get everybody wanting to work together against a common enemy."

3. "We can show them Apple, NCR, Control Data, and Corning, companies that are better than us on some things, and compare ourselves to companies in industries close to ours, and it becomes tough to refute or say we aren't driving the right way."

Credibility of the Change Agents

1. "I try to approach it with the finance guys in a quantitative approach. They understand data and think in terms of trends. The logistics guys may be more comfortable talking about fewer warehouses, or maybe a visible velocity stream. But for the finance guys, you have to come back to the facts, and that means numbers. We had a very good year last year, surprised a lot of people, took a lot of money out of inventory. We established our credibility with that very good year. And that has been something we have been able to use through 1991 to push some projects. When top management blesses you at the end of the year, that halo hangs around for a long time."

2. "If you're trying to convince somebody by logical argument, it is crucial to say the same thing every time the subject comes up. It seems a very simple point, but it can be very, very difficult to maintain absolute consistency. It has to become virtually a knee jerk reaction: every time a question is asked, the answer is always the same. One thing I've found, both in Europe and over here, is that people don't understand a new concept the first time you present it to them. Many people don't understand the concept the second time, or the third, or the fourth. Sometimes it has to be presented a minimum of six times before some people will understand it. And the presentation has to be exactly the same every time. Although they

don't understand it, they remember everything you've said in the previous occasions. So if you vary one iota from what you presented previously, they'll hook on to that, especially the subversive people. The expert subversives hook on to that and use it to try and tear the whole thing apart." [That flies in the face of the conventional wisdom that says if they don't understand it when you say it one way, then say it a different way.] "I've tried that before, and it doesn't work. If you change your approach, they use that to tear the whole thing apart."

3. "It makes a difference how well you know the person and for how long. If I've known him for twenty years, I can call on that personal relationship and I know how to handle him better. I can be blunt and say, 'Come on, you know this is the right thing to do. How can you not go in this direction?' But you have to have a good reputation and be respected and knowledgeable. It really helps, especially if the person is subversive. Then you have to make sure that they understand the long-range goal, and you've got to back it up with the required information to support your position. Without that, in a world of finances, you aren't going any place."

Credibility of the Proposed Change

1. "The first approach for me is to increase the person's understanding of what's happening, because if the other person is not on the same level of understanding, you're not going anyplace."

2. "You have to understand their process. Like with the finance process, which has been established for awhile, people are doing things monthly, weekly, yearly, based on that. You have to carefully consider when to intersect it to enable the change. You can intersect it at a certain point, but you cause all kinds of waves. That's why in the 1992 plan, when we knew we wanted to establish inventory as a percent of revenue as

the metric across the partnerships, we had to get in right on June 1, with our pitch, knowing that by July 1, the target letter would come out. If we had come in much later, we might have missed it by a year."

3. [What do you show them to convince them it really works?] "It can be as simple as taking them to a site that they can actually see. Let them touch and feel the systems and processes and show them the results. Letting them talk to the people that are really using the system is the most important thing. You can show reports that it's doing everything perfectly, but the type of people that are in that situation, the overtly subversive people, don't normally trust reports unless they can go and talk to the real users and have free rein to ask them any questions they like. That works very well to convert them, but you can't always do that. If it's something totally new then there's no experience to show them."

4. "You can put together something that looks factual, but the first time you take it out to three groups, two of them are going to say, 'Oh no, it's such and such, and that's just not true.' You killed your credibility. So when you're managing change, you have to be extremely careful that what you present to people is recognizable to them, it is fact-based, it is real. You might get away with a certain amount of giving them something that looks factual, but as soon as it proves not to be, then the next time you go back it will be more difficult. You could create enemies."

Goals, Measures, and Rewards

1. "The reason [managers] are subversive is because, behaviorally, they get reinforced for being very loyal to other purposes."

2. "Their behaviors are influenced by the ways in which their particular performance is measured by the management, which may be suboptimal to the company, but that's how they get paid, the way their bonuses

are calculated. So they are very much interested in their functional performance first and foremost."

3. "If two people are otherwise inclined, because of the roles they play, to pull in opposite directions, then giving them a joint goal, and some money for the achievement of that joint goal, is probably the quickest way of getting them onto the same team. But be careful that it doesn't then set them as one team against yet another part of the organization. You do get some debates on that."

4. "Both manufacturing and marketing were measured on inventory, days of supply, once a year. The problem was that manufacturing would do better at the end of the year if they threw the inventory across to the marketing company. And, of course, the marketing company would do better if several months before the end of the year it told manufacturing, 'I don't want to take what I told you I needed.' We changed that. We established partnerships, for example, so that a manufacturing guy and a marketing guy here in the U.S. are now evaluated on the same inventory number, combined inventory across manufacturing and marketing.

5. "For example, the USMG vice president and the head of manufacturing share a common metric. They used to be trying to minimize their respective days of supply at the expense of the other fellow. Now manufacturing has to be concerned about producing things that are not needed, to reduce finished goods, but also to be responsive. Since inventory is to be reduced throughout the chain, he can't rely on safety stock. Functional measures, like manufacturing inventory, are still looked at as a second-tier measurement, and tracked over time to help managers understand the dynamics. But it's not top priority. Global optimization is top priority."

6. "It always has to get down to actions, where

people do things differently from how they have traditionally done them. And there has to be a measurement of the results that things are done differently, and a communication of those results."

7. "On one particular program we wanted the manufacturing people to include an activity that they did not want to include. It turned out that the reason they did not want to include it was they had an objective for this particular program, and maybe all programs, to be 95 percent value added to that program, and only 5 percent for inspection and other things that are not value added. The activity was not value added in their metric, but it was in ours. [The manufacturing manager] had a family. He wasn't going to take a hit on his performance. We went to his boss's boss, up two levels, and got his objective waived for that particular program. When we got the objective waived for this guy, that barrier went away, and he immediately became supportive. He was happy to do it."

8. "One of the fellows from the warehouse did some work for us and I gave him a dinner certificate for two, not very much, $25, and said sincerely 'Thanks a lot. We really appreciate your help.' That guy would kill for me now, because no one ever did that for him before. Another time, we gave pizza to the whole group. Sometimes it's just a pat on the back. Sometimes I don't go directly to the person to say thank you. It's a lot nicer when I go to the boss or write to the boss, and the boss passes it along. Or I may thank the guy in front of the boss. People like to be told that they did a good job, if you tell them sincerely. If you just pass these things out, it loses its significance." [It still seems somewhat manipulative.] "But if you sincerely tell somebody, 'Hey, you did a nice job. I really appreciate what you did for me,' that sincerity comes across. At the same time, it establishes credibility, because I'm going to fight for you just as much as I'm

going to fight for everything else. And if you are wrong, I will tell you you are wrong. If you are right, I will tell you you are right." [These meager rewards help build enthusiasm, but they probably wouldn't work with a subversive person.]

9. "These requirements put people under a lot of pressure. It's tempting to just say, 'Come on now, you're a big boy, you're a big girl, you're paid a lot of money in this corporation. Yes, life's tough, but that's what we pay you for.' And we do say that, but we also put in place things to support and encourage these changes, for example, congruent goals, which re-orient managers toward performance across the chain and not just in their little piece of it. We've had a lot of success embedding congruent goals for customer satisfaction and inventory, but developing measures for cost is more difficult. With the many different budget centers worldwide, it can be a nightmare getting reliable base data and tracking it correctly."

Infrastructure/Autonomy/Empowerment

1. "When we talk about empowering people, we're really not talking about empowering people who want to isolate their function and be more strong there. We want to empower people who are trying to do the things that are consistent with the corporate strategy and the corporate good."

2. "You don't really want everybody coming up with changes and saying, 'Oh, we'll change this, we'll change that.' You want to be able to say, this is the strategy, this is who gets to decide. And you need an information flow to figure out which change and in what order. It must be well thought out, and that's why project managers actually follow a process all the way through."

3. "We need to modify our business processes and systems. Right now, a lot of our systems do not support the new way of doing busi-

ness. They are a little disjointed. For example, Europe doesn't use the same system we use. To support the new business processes like the sharing of material inventories, we need systems to tell what's available, where it's available, and how we can move it around the world. We need to know each other's goals, so we can negotiate customer requirements, supplier specifications. Those are key things."

4. "So, one way to get things to happen is to have organizations like this [CLAM]. We pave the way and put the energy into developing ideas enough so they can be deployed by the line organizations. It's clearly not enough just to do the brain work, and to have the discussions, the meetings, and say, 'Isn't this a wonderful idea,' with the expected outcome that all of those line managers are going to go back to their offices and deploy those ideas. It isn't going to happen that way. Deployment is the real issue. The most important thing is that you attack at the right level, know to whom you have to go, and find those people who can incorporate your ideas into their vision and into their deployment ideas for the next business year. You've got to know where resource decision making takes place, to get projects funded. You have to attack with the right people, with the right credentials. Often times we need to get Fred into the picture. Fred has the right credentials, operates at the right level, to get into certain offices, to twist certain arms, to get commitment to resources from certain management. Individually I can't do that."

5. "Often people won't take risks because of short-term payback requirements. If you find a problem that would take two years to change, and the management insists that every project has to have payback within one financial year, that makes it rather difficult. Since you can't justify the two-year project, you have to try and do it with

short-term fixes. And there are some problems that short-term fixes will never work on. It often needs to be a long-term project. Even when you finally get agreement for a three-year project and the business proposal is signed off, at the end of that financial year you would have to go and beg for the money to do the second year. There can be a lot of pressure to show immediate results. Often you can't show any benefits the first year because it is all development time, and unfortunately these are the projects that don't get done, but really need to be done more than any other."

6. "Other than personal behaviors, the biggest systemic problem that we have had is that we are great at planning and talking about the benefits of a project without ever really implementing the resources or enabling the project. We build a big set of plans and targets and say, 'Oh yes, we can save $50 million here and $50 million there.' But somewhere down the line we kind of forget about the $5 million worth of capital to implement and that it took some enablers, ten dedicated people, to make it happen. All of a sudden you find yourself committed to these visions without any capability to go out and implement them."

7. "An organizational environment with many levels of hierarchy can cause impairment to the lower levels. In most cases, they are standing in front of an eighteen wheeler. The eighteen wheeler is doing 55 mph towards them, and they are having a committee to decide, not which way to jump, but even if they should jump. In most cases the top managers don't know that this is what they are doing to the organization. The top management think they have fully empowered the organization, and that they've got good people doing the job perfectly. They don't know they are in trouble, because the organization

is so large and there is no management information, there is no detail that comes through to show them that they are dying."

8. "If you really are trying to implement a dramatic change, then almost all of your personnel systems, cultural systems, also have to be revised. Human resources are not set up for that right now. They're set up to manage current policies. [To hire and fire.] Yes. Think of the system changes. Instead of having this person that takes an order and this person that keys it in and this person that goes off and tells manufacturing they need it, and this person who fills the order, maybe you even have only one person that does all of it. If so, you have to change how you compensate people. You have to change job descriptions."

9. [You simply cannot expect some people to lead changes because they just don't have the capacity for it. But they may be good followers.] "That's right. When you implement change, it affects everyone. So you don't want the people who are doing it to throw a wrench into the works. You want them to want to do it the new way. So you help them understand why it's important, train them exactly how to do it, and give them the tools. Tools are, I think, a major enabler."

10. "There are some people who are just very competitive people, turf builders, and resources do not necessarily make them cooperate. They might use the resources to do more empire building." [How do you avoid that?] "Well, there are ways you can provide resources only for a certain purpose. That kind of goes against what people like to say about empowerment. But empowerment doesn't work unless you have infrastructure that provides you with the support mechanisms. If you don't have a basic infrastructure, what you get is chaos instead of effective interrelated business. Any time you optimize business processes

that flow in a continuum across a global company or across a broad geographic area, there's some infrastructure you absolutely have to have, like available and reliable information across this process, the technology that provides it, all those business processes that manage the information."

11. "A couple of years ago, we were trying to convince line people to take their resources and make a trade-off, whereas now we have a central group. So Graham can now come up with a yesable strategy and get the buy-in, and he also has a group of people that can develop it as opposed to approaching one of the VPs and saying, 'Please take some of your people and develop a worldwide strategy.' "

12. "We go through these terrible budgeting discussions. And people will say, All bets are off, I know I promised that, but I can't do it. I'm not funded, I don't have the resources, I need more people. And you go through all those discussions, and for a little while you come to a screeching halt."

13. [Regarding change management] "It is an extremely stressful situation. It is a very intense work environment. And if we bring you in as a change agent, train you and you can make it through a project, and then we say, 'Okay, your reward for finishing this one is that you get to do it again in another area with new people.' And you start over again. Then you finish that one; your reward is that you get to do it again. These are really, really intense; and it's often really confrontational. Burnout is a real environmental risk. We will need to have personnel policies that provide for things like sabbaticals, going back to school and getting your brain refreshed, getting new ideas, having contact with people in other companies."

14. "Change agents, they only get their reward in heaven. They initiate change and fade away before anyone realizes who initiated the change."

Organizational Level and Position

1. "Your power level can have a lot to do with your depth of involvement. You might firmly believe in business process management, and you might be very expert at it, but if you have no power to make it happen, then you probably wouldn't be subversive, but you might be passive or just supportive. Your power base just wouldn't allow you to do it."

2. "It is not just people, it's also the place the people have in the total structure, in the company. The way you fit in that cube also is a result of where you are in the organization and the ins and outs of that organization."

3. "There's a guy named Joe, in a position created a year and a half ago, a pretty senior level manager, who has been around Xerox for a long time. He is very much a change agent, but somewhat self-chosen. He understands very clearly what we are trying to accomplish with these logistics initiatives and why it's important. He is very actively involved. He is looking to optimize the system as opposed to his own functional area. And he is doing a lot of leading. The role he is in requires him to be involved with a number of different functional groups around the country. So, his role is not narrowly defined. His job is broadly defined." [Does the role make him that way, or was he picked because he is that type of person?] "Well, I think in this case it is a combination of both. He is the right fellow to be in that job, because of his energy and enthusiasm and his desire to optimize the system for the corporation. At the same time, his job definition and his boundary conditions let him be that kind of change agent. He is less constrained by the achievement of day-to-day deliverables than some of the other people."

4. "People come at the job of making changes

in their organizations from limited perspectives. It is something we should expect from a functionally aligned company. They have reached positions of decision-making authority and responsibility because they have demonstrated to their superiors good, solid capabilities to do those things over the years. They certainly are not afraid of making decisions and taking action. Yet, their frame of reference, unless they are the unusual person that has spent time in a lot of different parts of the company, will reflect the functional growth that they had in the corporation."

5. "Fred comes closest, of anybody I know, to being in the 5,5,5 box. He was put in this position because he is a change agent. He is a leader of change. It's encouraging to see that the most senior management in this company has allowed Fred Hewitt to do the job that he is doing. They have put him in a role so he can be a person that will fit into the 5,5,5 box in the model."

6. "You have to be careful. You don't want everybody to migrate up those dimensions. For example, we want experts that lead in an isolated function, too. You need those in the company."

Participation

1. "It's the middle level and below that does most of the day-to-day work. You have to really get in bed with them to make the changes. We must work with the sergeants and lieutenants, or it doesn't matter what the generals are talking about."

2. "Some of Fred's people are on these other teams. Fred contributes people with knowledge in certain areas. It also enables him to make sure that these other teams are aware of our strategic direction for the supply chain, and make sure everything fits and doesn't do something counter to the total vision."

3. [Regarding the position in the center of the cube, 3,3,3.] "They'll do just enough to ensure that it doesn't fail, but they won't go the extra mile to make sure that it succeeds. They do just what they're asked to do. The emphasis is on covering their asses. We actually wrote a letter for one of these guys to allow him to say, 'Although I'm signing off on this project, if it fails, I didn't have anything to do with it.' These are the classic fence sitters. They do cooperate. They do exactly what's needed, but you have to spell it out exactly. You have to become the expert in their side of the business, so that when you ask them to do something, you have asked them for everything they could possibly do to contribute. They're not going to put themselves forward or offer anything more. It takes longer and takes more effort, but you do get results. The other thing is that you document everything you've asked them to do. In that situation, they can be very good at actioning items out of meetings. They can be a good contributor to the overall change, but you can miss opportunities because of them."

4. "Some of it is training. Some of it is letting people know why, and the second part is letting them participate. If it's their idea, they move up this dimension toward active involvement."

5. "Deciding something before knowing all the facts doesn't work. Somebody will say, 'Of course, if you had just asked me, I could have told you.' That's one of the reasons why it's risky to proceed without pulling everybody in, especially in a company that's very functional or very decentralized. If you come up with the best answer yourself and present it to people, you will not get the response that you would get if they developed it with you. You won't even come close. It might take you a lot longer."

6. "CLAM change agents are primarily the visionaries, while line managers are implementors. But there is an overlap zone, where our visionaries assist with implementing and where the implementors are also visionaries. The line managers come up with some of the best ideas. And they partici-

pate in the MIOC as a visioning team, which is good because it keeps us grounded in reality and gets buy-in from them."

7. "We know the things that don't work. Management fiat doesn't work. Writing a memo to the VP of that other organization never gets you anywhere, because nobody will ever dictate anything until they appreciate it, so, we do the work bottom-up. Quality improvement teams are built into our culture now. If a team wants to make a major change that has an impact on you, the team is almost required to allow you to put a member on the team. It's a code of honor. You can't ignore them or stonewall them."

Personal Preparedness

1. "What the boss says and how hard he pushes it isn't going to affect whether or not a person becomes skilled at managing change. That depends on whether or not they have the skills."

2. "These people are successful people. They are not disloyal to the corporation just because they are not change agents or leaders. They have their little mission in life. So you've got to understand how to get along with different types of people and still get the change. You can't make everybody the same type."

3. "It helps if the change agents have interdisciplinary backgrounds, because then they can speak more than one language. They relate to a fairly wide body of people and are not locked into one specialty. The person who is the top change agent is absolutely key. Fred's makeup is such that he can deal with the longer-term divisions, like R&D, and with the practical day-to-day, like manufacturing. His background is mixed, with finance, logistics, and other areas. The top change agent is absolutely important."

4. "You must sell at the right level. And that is hard, because not everybody thinks on a global basis. Some people think on a day-to-day or practical basis. You have to speak

their language. That's the trick, to cascade it down." [To relate the global to their specific concerns.] "Right, and try and make up an example. I've always felt that if I can show an example, first of all, I knew what I was speaking about, and second, I could teach it to somebody."

5. "You need a certain amount of time, even yourself as a change agent, to go through the logic process. CLAM's changes have cascaded from Fred down to his management, and down to the next level. It took me time to get comfortable with the changes he professed. There is a time factor. I have a learning curve; if I hear a speech, I can't go out and sell it the next day, but must understand it myself. And then the other person has a learning curve, so don't shortchange the time required. Maybe if it was a less layered organization, it would have less of a learning curve."

6. "One of the biggest catalysts has been training on the leadership through quality approach, and some of what came out of the Baldrige award. It opened a lot of eyes. With leadership through quality, we talk the same language: quality improvement, problem solving, identification of goals, customer requirements, supplier specifications."

7. "We needed a good hands-on, nuts and bolts kind of manufacturing manager to lead it. And this fellow was appointed that had not had any involvement with the kind of work we are doing. He has spent most of his time working in manufacturing. So his view of the company was somewhat limited. After about four months, he has a very broad view of the company. And he has told me that this work has really opened his eyes. When he's done with it, he is going to be successful. Several of us are working behind the scenes to ensure that he is going to be successful. He is going to be in a different place in your model than when he started, simply because he has a better understanding of the

business system. And he's had to move up in terms of skill. In the future, with a successful completion, he will be more inclined to be actively involved in projects like this."

8. "To be a skilled change agent, you really have to deal with the complexity of a lot of factors, many of which seem outside your control. A lot of people don't perceive that they can influence things, and other people perceive that almost anything can be influenced or changed. Depending on which you are, you can get to different levels on the cube."

9. "When somebody is subversive, they might be subversive because they don't have the time or the resources to do anything other than what they're doing right now. Or they might be subversive because in some way they're threatened."

10. "Very few people will fit comfortably in all places. Some people will want to just have a very specific isolated role."

11. "The key is to get the change embedded into the operations as quickly as possible. To do that, we may actually transfer people into operations (from CLAM) to take what they have been working on with them."

12. "The rotation of line managers from operating companies to CLAM helps implement change at all levels of an operating company. Once back in line management, the broad experience allows a manager to translate the vision of the company into operations and higher level systems."

Vision/Perspective/Leadership

1. "We purposely put people into a role which says you have to be both the corporate citizen and the local guy. We develop a worldwide perspective at a local level, and integrate local contributions through a worldwide strategy for re-engineered processes. Operationally, these changes have to be made to work through the partnerships across the chain, and it has to be consistent with what needs to be done at the local level. Otherwise, it will break down."

2. "Initially, we try to keep the debate on the process level rather than on the organizational pieces. We focus on what we, collectively, should be doing and not who should be doing what. And we focus externally on the customer. If you can stay on an abstract level, and say, 'Don't you think it would be right if this is the way that we, Xerox, were delivering product to our customer?' Rather than say, 'Don't you think that you guys in distribution ought to do this, that, or the other, or ought to be more reactive, or ought to be faster?' This is a bit more pejorative, and more difficult to accept. Until we get buy-in, we delay the discussion on who does what."

3. [Why are these people mediocre on each dimension?] "Because they perceive that to be the safe spot. That has changed now because part of riding the fence is that you have your own little world. And we don't have our own little world anymore. The fence is going away. Again, you have to communicate to them what they are doing and its impact on the whole business."

4. "First, they must understand the total picture, not just their area, but how their operation fits into the total corporation. Second, they must understand that the negative impact, i.e., a couple extra days of supply in inventory, will be overshadowed by a positive impact someplace else. Another thing, change is happening so quickly, you should really be seen as someone who is a change agent, supportive of it, or else when the change comes you may not be in a good position anymore. So you might as well be on the forefront, even though it seemingly is going to hurt a little now. As things change, you may be in a better position. People are realizing now that change is imminent and that is important."

5. "The senior management of this corporation has for years made it clear that change

is inevitable. They have not preached standardization and the idea that 'once you have it right you don't ever have to re-engineer it or rework it.' They have promoted the opposite idea, that change is inevitable and that the success of the company is very much dependent on our being able to effectively change and improve."

6. "It is important to push ideas at all levels and not pass up opportunities to market the ideas, to get the soapbox out and talk to people. I have in my mind the changes that are important at all times, and listen to the conversations of others. When I hear key thoughts expressed, key words, I jump in to link those to these bigger ideas. It builds up a foundation of support for these ideas. If they hear it enough and they think about it enough, they can relate that idea to things that they are responsible for day to day. In their own ways, they begin to influence change. Communication is extremely important in all this. Memos, letters, articles in magazines, you just have to get it out there. It's a marketing campaign to stimulate the thinking, keep it stirred all the time."

7. "If you're dealing with processes, people can be very isolated until they see where they fit into the bigger picture. So you can get a similar kind of jump, as with the subversives, as soon as they understand. They can jump up to being a contributor or optimizer."

8. "All of the isolation is caused by legend and folklore and not talking to the other organizations. Most of it is a communication breakdown that builds on itself, so that the less communications you have, the less you want to have, and a death spiral starts. But the way to work through the breadth of involvement dimension is to get people to communicate. Get a roundtable going to understand one another's problems. The communication process solves it virtually instantaneously. One of the biggest things is defining terms, because peo-

ple have different names for the same things, and also clarifying assumptions. You almost need an interpreter."

9. "You go through the same script, every time, even if it's someone else doing it. That's one of the powers of having a vision when you're dealing with a new concept. That vision is what makes you consistent. Also, a vision seems to be better if someone actually speaks it, reads it out aloud. Written, it's okay, but it really should be dynamic enough and forceful enough that it needs to be read with the right emphasis put on each particular word the same way every time."

10. "We tend to get people that go from subversive directly to active, without passing through these other steps. It can happen suddenly, halfway through a meeting or because of some event in the implementation, where they suddenly stop being subversive and become so positive for it, because they've seen the light. It's a very dramatic jump." [Correspondingly, have you noticed the tendency for those who are passive simply to become supportive?] "Yes. The passive people tend to move one step at a time. But the subversive may go right up to leading, because the reason the people are subversive is because they feel so strongly about the situation. So once you have convinced them, then they go strongly positive, just as much as they were strongly negative in the first place.

11. "Vision is one of the empowering tools. You have to give people an idea and authorize them to develop it and accept it yourself if you're the senior people. People have to know what direction going." [or else there's no telling which direction they'll go.] "Especially if you have lots of people changing lots of things. You have to have something that unifies it and puts it together, like the integrated supply chain vision. As we were doing priorities for major change projects, we very specifically went out and looked at other groups' vi-

sions to make sure we understood their requirements and were in sync with them. So when we went to them with our vision, they would recognize it and say, 'Oh yeah, that's what we want.' They saw their own vision in ours."

12. "If you're in a mode of fire-fighting or dealing with today's crisis, you don't necessarily have time to stop and think. If someone provides you with the education, then you know the circumstances outside have changed, the customer has changed, the business has changed, requirements have changed. Once you become aware of it and understand how it relates to you, then you move."

13. "To the functional manager it might seem like a change is working. And it might be working within his own area. But it affects all the other surrounding or downstream activities. I rationally explain to him where we are, what we're trying to do, and then discuss what the future is going to look like. I give them a perspective of what the bigger system is."

14. "What really makes a difference is whether the person at the top gives very clear direction that he expects these people to participate. The boss must walk the talk. Everything he does must make it obvious what the priority is. And the performance mea-

sures, the resources, and the communications have to line up with that. The boss has to always give a consistent message."

15. "To optimize the supply chain globally, Xerox needed its managers to act responsibly and take into account how their actions would affect their partners in the other parts of the supply chain, in other functions as well as in other geographic locations. Ideally, every manager would ask of himself or herself, 'If I moved over and swapped jobs with my partners, would I be comfortable with the decisions I just made in the last six months? Partnerships are intended to change managerial behaviors and decisions toward a more global perspective. Changing the behaviors of the leaders sends out a message to everybody else in the organization. Partnerships create the opportunity for such role modeling because they are not just composed of two people. For example, in Europe, the VP of logistics and the VP of manufacturing formed a partnership which includes their family groups as well. The family groups meet every four weeks as a team. So the subordinates see the behavioral changes in a collaborative work situation. The two top guys don't just have a lunch together and maybe play a little golf, and pretend that they have sorted out their problems."

▶ **EXERCISE**

1. After reading the "Thoughts of the Change Agents," write a set of guidelines or principles for change agents that addresses (a) each of the themes, and (b) what change agents need to know about the dynamics of moving people along these dimensions of the cube (such as path issues and the interactions and interdependencies of the dimensions).

2. Based upon the comments of the change agents, describe the Xerox culture before CLAM started making changes in the integrated supply chain. Contrast that prior culture with the culture CLAM is trying to put in place.

Xerox, Part IV: Xerox 2000: Putting It Together "Building the New Xerox"

This communique from Paul Allaire, Chairman and Chief Executive Officer, Xerox Corporation, articulates Xerox's plans for structural reorganization and cultural change alluded to in Parts I through III of the Xerox case.

▶ INTRODUCTION

During the coming months, we will be engaged in a major effort to fundamentally change the way we conduct our business. We will change our organizational structure, we will change our processes, we will change job assignments, we will change the way we empower and reward people. Perhaps most importantly, we will be changing how we think about our businesses and how we behave as we lead our businesses day to day.

I have said on a number of occasions that we will need to change Xerox more in the next five years than we have in the past ten. The shape of that change is becoming clearer to us as the result of the work that we've been doing since 1989 when I announced our "change agenda." In 1990, the senior management of the company participated in a set of activities called the Xerox 2000 strategic planning process. As that strategic work was reaching its conclusions, I initiated the second effort, using the quality process, to understand how we could run the company more effectively to achieve the Xerox 2000 vision.

As a result of our work over the past fifteen months on the nature and shape of this new Xerox, we have decided to move forward. During 1992, we will be implementing a major change of the governance, structure, process, and leadership of our company. Since this change is a direct outgrowth of the Xerox 2000 strategic work, we should think about this as a second phase of Xerox 2000, where we will be "putting it together." We will be working together to create an enterprise that builds on the improvements we've achieved in the past five years to ensure growth and competitive success in the 1990s.

The changes required are significant. But there are things that absolutely will not change! First are the Xerox corporate values. They are the bedrock of Xerox. They go back to Joe Wilson—they are what make Xerox special. The second is quality as our basic business principle. Leadership through quality enabled us to survive in the 80s. We've used the quality process to design these changes and will now use it to implement them.

The change is significant, but the opportunity is even greater. Effective implementation of these changes will enable us to:

- Provide our customers with better offerings—products and services that fully meet their needs in a more timely and more effective manner.

- Provide our shareholders with improved value by being significantly more productive—increasing both growth and returns.

- Provide Xerox employees with a more satisfying and rewarding experience that fully utilizes their talents.

▶ WHAT MUST WE DO?

My objective is to fundamentally change the way that we run the company. There are a number of factors that have made this change an imperative. First, the Xerox 2000 strategic work helped us understand the tremendous opportunities of the global document market. We recognized that our concept of The Document Company is valid and powerful. We confirmed that our strategic intent is "to be the leader in the document market by providing document services that enhance business productivity." However, the businesses that we see making up the document market in the second half of this decade are significantly different from the way we define our business today. Therefore, our corporate strategic intent leads us to changing the shape of our company. Second, we have realized that the market and customer environment is changing at an even faster rate. There are basic changes in customer needs, in competitive actions, and even in who our competitors are. This requires us to be even more market and customer focused than we have been. It demands that we better understand customer needs at every step of the process of developing and delivering our offerings. Third, technology changes are coming at an even faster rate than we had anticipated a few years ago. This requires an ability to develop and manage technology more effectively and closely linked to market needs.

To achieve our vision, Xerox must become an enterprise that is unequaled in the ability to link markets and technologies. The core of our success will be the ability to bring together emerging document technologies with the current or latent needs of the marketplace to create offerings that yield high value to the customer.

These thoughts about change are not new. Back in 1989, we recognized the challenges and the need to change when we began to talk about the "change agenda" for the company. We've made good progress

on that change agenda, but it has been incremental progress. We've built a solid base—now we must accelerate our pace.

During the past year of study, observation, benchmarking and problem analysis, it's become apparent that if we are to accelerate the rate of change, then we must change our basic approach to managing the company. For decades, we've run the organization as a large functional machine, which is governed by decisions made at the center. We've created a system that is complex and which prevents people from taking responsibility. We've overburdened the top of the organization with the requirements to make a lot of operational decisions that it is not well equipped to make.

I've therefore come to the conclusion that we need to basically restructure the way that we run the business. We need to create discontinuous change; incremental changes will not get us to our vision.

Specifically:

- We need to focus our efforts more on the customer, the marketplace, and competition, as opposed to managing internal boundaries.
- We need to give people more "end to end" accountability, with a clear line of sight to the customer.
- We need to provide people with the capacity to act, and then clearly reward, counsel, or penalize individuals based on their performance.
- We need to enable people to manage quality, customer satisfaction, employee satisfaction, market share, and growth for their own pieces of the business.
- We need to make the company a whole lot simpler. There is inherent complexity in

our offerings and our markets, but we've made it even more complex by how we run our business.

- We need to unleash the entrepreneurial spirit that I know exists within the company.

- We need to radically increase the "clock speed" of the organization, with the objective of significantly reducing the time that it takes us to get to market, ahead of the competition, with offerings that meet or exceed customer requirements.

▶ REENGINEERING THE ENTERPRISE

A key catalyst in this change in the way we run the business is a change in the basic architecture of our organization. We should all be clear that organization structure in and of itself is not the answer. I do believe, however, that structure can stand in the way of change or, conversely, be an important catalyst for change. By changing our basic organization structure, we can signal major change in how we run the company, create the basis for accountability, provide a platform for reducing time to market, and help develop a generation of management that thinks like entrepreneurial business leaders, rather than functional administrators.

Organizational structure change is necessary, but not sufficient to achieve the changes that we need. If we change the structure, but still try to run the company the way that we have in the past, we will fail. So the structural change must be accompanied by changes in management process, in our management style, in our systems, in our processes, in our rewards approach, and in our behavior. We might think of these elements as the *software* which must be changed along with the *hardware* of the structure. The changes in behavior apply to all of us, but in particular to the senior management group, including myself. We need to develop a different set of roles and different ways for senior management to lead and direct the growth of the business.

▶ ORGANIZATION—WHAT WE'VE DONE SO FAR

Approximately fifteen months ago, as we neared completion of the Xerox 2000 strategic work. I began to suspect that our organization was getting in the way of achieving the changes we required. I was getting messages to that effect from a variety of sources, including presidential reviews, senior management meetings, discussions with new hires, customers, and benchmark visits.

All of these pointed to a need to basically rethink how we're organized. Rather than jump to a conclusion about what we should do. I formed a quality implementation team (QIT) to help gain more understanding. We chartered a group of some of the best and brightest of our managers from different functions and geographies. Most of these people were a couple of levels down in the organization from my direct team. We asked them to look at our organization, to do problem solving, and to help us understand the nature of the problems and our alternatives.

We did not constrain the team. We asked them to look broadly at what I called the organizational architecture of Xerox, including both the hardware and software. Since this group was charged to look at our future organizational architecture, they called themselves the "Future-tecture" team.

The team built criteria for assessment of alternative approaches and assessed different potential solutions. They identified Xerox-specific design criteria to use as a basis for evaluating different approaches. This design criteria focused on:

- Capitalizing on employee energy
- Reducing time to market
- Simplifying the running of the business
- Increasing customer focus
- Improving competitiveness

They then developed four different approaches to the organizational architecture of Xerox, which included a business divisions structure, an improved marketing structure, a geographical/transnational structure, and optimizing our current approach. After a good deal of analysis, they came to the conclusion that the business divisions model would provide the best platform for Xerox for the 1990s.

The approach they presented was an architecture for running the company, rather than merely an organizational structure. The Future-tecture team recommended major changes in how we run the company, including changes in behavior, changes in process, and changes in structure.

During the summer of 1991, my direct team and I spent time working with a core group of the Future-tecture team to move their approach to the next level of detail and resolve the key open questions.

We then convened a group of key managers representing different functions, geographies, and points of view in the corporation to help us finish the design of this new Xerox, and to work with us to plan the transition. We called this group the Organization Transition Board (OTB), and it was made up of fifteen senior levels managers from throughout the company.

From early fall 1991 until today, this group literally spent hundreds of hours piecing together the new organization, designing the necessary new processes, and describing the required new behaviors. They called upon many others in the organization to participate through subteams and other QITs. During this time, OTB representatives also met regularly with my direct team. The new approach, therefore, has been shaped by more than fifty people working in different configurations over the past fifteen months. It represents our use of the creative energies of some of our best people, employing the quality tools and processes to design a new way of working together for Xerox.

▶ THE CONCEPT OF THE NEW XEROX— PUTTING IT TOGETHER

At the core of our new approach is a recognition that we need to do a better job linking markets and technologies. We believe that the key to doing this is to create entities—units and teams—which have complete "end to end" responsibility for a Xerox offering. We believe that we can do a better job of developing our technology into offerings that meet or exceed customer requirements when the different functions—research, development, manufacturing, marketing, customer operations, etc.—can come together and work with each other on a day-by-day basis. We believe that people in such configurations will do a better job of putting it together, and putting it together faster, than can any senior management structure directing effort from a distance.

Therefore, the basic approach can be thought of as in Figure 1. We will be breaking the company into a set of business divisions each having end to end responsibilities for a set of Xerox offerings, targeted at a particular set of market needs. If Xerox were made up of distinctly different and separate offerings, drawing on different technologies and serving different markets, then this "break-up" of the company would be sufficient. We all know, however, that we are linked together through common technologies and markets. In fact, this has and can continue to be a great strength and competitive advantage for the company. Therefore, in addition to the creation of business units, we recognized the need for putting them together, without damaging their autonomy, their freedom to act, and their ability to manage themselves. We thought carefully about where there was true value for the customer and the shareholder by coordination of cross-business activities.

The approach is illustrated in Figure 2. There are three key points of coordination and leverage among the business divisions. First, we must maintain our focus on the customer, our commitment to customer satisfaction, and our ability to provide customers with the full range of Xerox products and services in a seamless manner. Therefore, a key component of this new approach is the customer operations division. These units will have the primary responsibility for direct interactions with Xerox customers and for ensuring customer satisfaction. As indicated in Figure 2, some business divisions may go directly to the market through their own sales forces or sales channels, but we expect most divisions to leverage our competencies

Figure 1

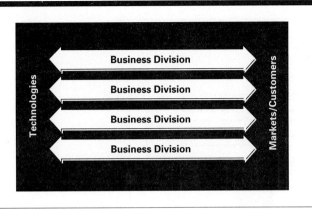

in sales, service, and administration by working through customer operations.

Second, it is critical that we wisely and creatively leverage our technology resources through common technology architecture, nurtured core competencies, and thoughtful advanced development. We need to create an effective linkage between our research centers and the business divisions. We also need to ensure that the developments of one business division have the potential to be used across other business divisions. We therefore have designed a technology management process to accomplish these objectives.

Third, we need to make sure that we do not throw away the strategic advantages that stem from the size and scope of the Xerox Corporation, even as we break ourselves into smaller, more autonomous, and more responsive units. We therefore have created a set of strategic services, which are intended to support the business divisions, particularly in the areas of manufacturing, logistics, supplies (materials), and strategic relationships.

Finally, we face another challenge of putting it together by allocating our resources effectively over time. We've designed a new approach to corporate governance, including a new corporate office and a refocused corporate staff.

Figure 2

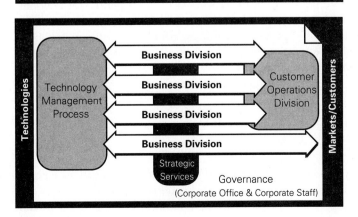

Figure 3

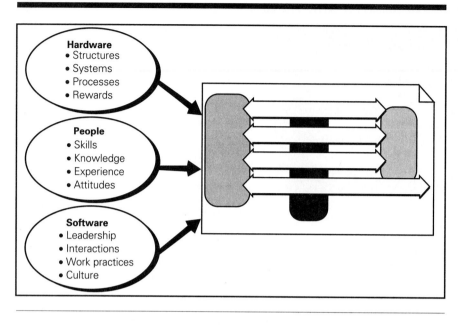

It would be a mistake to think about this new approach merely in terms of organizational structure. We have given as much or more thought to how we will operate and work together as we have to the formal organizational arrangements we will be putting in place. In fact, we see the new Xerox as being shaped by three key factors, as shown in Figure 3. Clearly, one element of this new approach is the organizational hardware, the structures, systems, processes, and rewards that we will put in place. A second critical element is people. The types of individuals that we put in key roles will have a major impact on our ability to succeed. A third element, and perhaps the most important in the long term, is what we've called software. This involves how we actually work together and behave on a day-by-day basis. It includes the patterns of leadership, the way we interact with each other, the

work practices that we develop, and finally the type of organizational culture that we create and transmit to all of our people.

All three of these elements are critical factors in shaping the new Xerox. Again, if we cannot put together the hardware, the people, and software effectively, we will not succeed. We must pay attention to each one of these key elements. Each is necessary for us to change, but the key is working on all three at the same time.

In the remainder of this paper, I want to briefly review some of the key features of each of these three elements—hardware, people, and software. My objective is to provide the basic concepts and intent, rather than a detailed description. My goal here is to provide only an orientation to the new approach.

▶ HARDWARE

We have implemented the new Xerox approach by structuring the company around three basic value-added levels of organization. Starting at the "top" and closest to the customer is the operational management

level. Day-to-day management of operations focused on the development and delivery of offerings to our customers will be done here by business teams and districts (or operating companies overseas). The pri-

Figure 4

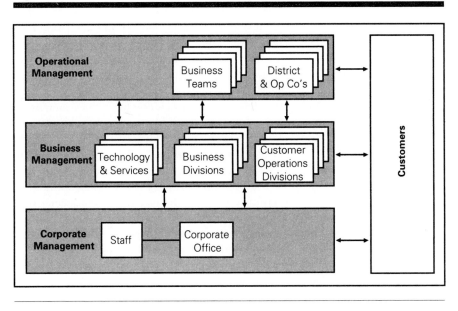

mary focus for the management of the organization is the business management level, and specifically the business divisions and customer operations divisions. Finally, strategic direction, resource allocation, and policy will be the responsibility of the corporate management level. These three levels can be thought of graphically as in Figure 4.

This approach to the organization has a number of features which should be noted:

- Figure 4 is oriented differently from the traditional organization chart. At the "top" are the business teams and districts. The levels below all have the basic role of supporting those at the top of the chart.
- All three of these levels need to be connected to and focused on the customer. While the primary responsibility for the

customer is with the business teams and the districts, all levels and functions need to be customer focused.

- The core funding of the organization is through the business division.
- The intent is to run the organization with these three levels. While there may be "linking pin" positions to coordinate between these three levels, there will be no intermediate organizations or staff. These linkages will be done through positions filled by line managers, drawing staff support from one or more of the three primary value-added levels of the organization.

To understand this organization concept, the key components will be discussed in more detail in the following sections.

▶ THE BUSINESS DIVISION

The primary focus for management of the organization is the business division. The basic intent of the organization design is to move decision making out

from the corporate center to the business divisions, and thus closer to the customer. The goal is to empower people throughout the organization to act with an entrepreneurial spirit, to increase customer responsiveness, decrease time to market, and thus improve competitive performance.

A business division is a set of activities, people, and assets that approximate a complete "end to end" business with an income statement and a balance sheet. A business division is therefore an identifiable surrogate for a stand-alone business, including:

- A clear set of offerings (products and services)
- A set of primary markets towards which those offerings are targeted
- An identifiable set of competitors
- An identifiable "business model"—or an economic case

The mission of the business division is to develop, acquire, and ensure delivery of world class offerings that delight customers, and ensure a dominant position in its designated market. The business division is also charged to manage its assigned businesses to produce acceptable shareholder results, and to achieve sustained results through the use of a motivated team, using quality tools and processes to win in the marketplace.

A business division has effective control over the complete value-added chain including business planning, product planning, development, manufacturing, distribution, marketing, sales (including control of its own sales force/channel), and customer service and support. While the business division has initial and primary control over all the elements of the value-added chain, business divisions may decide to conclude agreements with other units to provide for services, on a contracted basis. For example:

- Manufacturing through "focused factories" that are supported by a manufacturing utility
- Sales through a sales force that is shared with other business divisions
- Customer support that is contracted from the customer operations divisions.

A business division is managed by a business division president and his/her team. They are responsible for the results of the business (customer satisfaction,

employee motivation and satisfaction, ROA, market share), for developing and achieving the strategic plan of the business, and for resource allocation within the business division.

At the core of the business division is a set of "business teams," led by business team general managers. The mission of the business team is the aggressive development/acquisition of products and/or solutions which delight designated customers and which achieve quality, cost, and delivery (QCD) benchmarks to win in the marketplace. The business team is responsible for an offering, or a set of offerings, in an "end to end" manner. The team is responsible for lifetime performance of the offering, including customer satisfaction, market share, and profit (ROA). The business team general manager is envisioned as the primary general management job at the operations level. It also will serve as a key developmental position for future senior managers of the corporation.

In different business divisions, the business team may be organized around different activities. However, the primary device for managing the business division is the business team, which in itself includes a microcosm of the functions of the enterprise.

The typical structure for a business division will be as in Figure 5. The work of Future-tecture and the OTB led us to create nine business divisions. They are as follows:

Personal Document Products This division will aggressively pursue our participation in the growing retail, direct mail, and catalog market segments for a major push to capture a position in the small business and individual consumer market worldwide.

Office Document Systems This division will define and become the leading vendor of office document printers while actively participating in the generic office page printer market. The division will work to achieve this mission by focusing on high-value, document-oriented features, exploiting full color applications and evolving towards distributed document services.

Office Document Products The mission for this division is to grow our share of the office light lens reprographics market. It will aggressively lead the industry

Figure 5

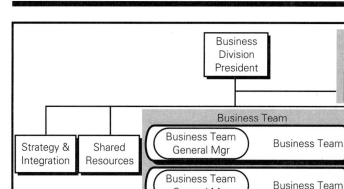

transition from light lens to stand-alone digital copying through high-value extended functions such as color. It will also lead our participation in the plain paper fax market and merge this functionally into digital copiers.

X-Soft   As a stand-alone business, X-Soft will work to realize its mission to commercialize market-driven, pioneering, document-oriented software products focused on collaborative document applications and management services for key business process productivity. X-Soft will also develop software solutions for other business divisions to use as part of a total solutions offering. Targeted markets are office, publishing, and low-end document applications.

Advanced Office Document Services   This organization will develop advanced document services for the office market. It may eventually become a full division as these offerings approach the market.

Document Production Systems   Through this division, we will become the premier vendor of business productivity solutions in the dedicated operator printing market. The DocuTech and 5090 families are the flagship product lines of this division, which will allow us to continue to drive the transfer of offset printing to reprographics. The print-on-demand and short-run spot color market segments will be directly targeted by this division.

Printing Systems   This division will be charged with increasing our market share in large data center direct connect printing by emphasizing high-value transaction-based applications. It will make Xerox the premier vendor of non-impact printing solutions to small and medium data centers and make us a player in the remote data center printing market and the major player n the MICR market.

Xerox Engineering Systems   As an existing division, XES will continue its charter to be the leading vendor of productivity solutions to the engineering document market. This includes the design, manufacture, marketing, and support of a line of products that facilitate engineering document processing.

Xerox Business Services   As a new stand-alone entry, XBS will respond worldwide to market demand for full vendor accountability for services and outsourcing based on Xerox technolnogy and appropriate non-Xerox hardware and software. Its mission encompasses the management, operation, and delivery of value-added document services at the customer's location and through Xerox sites.

The current ISO organization will transfer to U.S. customer operations. However, business strategy will study the desirability of a document systems integration division to address worldwide customer systems integration opportunities.

▶ THE CUSTOMER OPERATIONS DIVISION

Another primary focus of the organization is the customer operations division. Customer operations divisions are responsible for support of all activities which relate to the customer, including service, administration, integration of major customer relationships, sales support, and providing local administration for the business division sales force.

Customer operations divisions are responsible for customers in a specified geography. They have responsibility for customer satisfaction. They are accountable to business units to provide the services which they have contracted to provide. They are particularly responsible for integration of Xerox's sales, service, customer support, and administration activities so that Xerox provides a consistent face to the customer and is easy to do business with. Customer operations activities are funded through contracts with the business divi-sions. Customer operations, therefore, are responsible to optimize the profitability of their assigned territory within the business divisions' strategy.

Business divisions may contract with other channels, as necessary, to distribute and support its offerings, although there is a bias towards "staying within the family," other things being equal.

The business division and the customer operations division therefore play different, but complementary roles in relation to the customer. Therefore, both organizations will need to work collaboratively to ensure that Xerox is able to respond quickly and effectively to the customer's requirements. The development of the business division/customer operations relationship will be one of the critical success factors for the new approach.

▶ THE CORPORATE OFFICE

Business divisions and customer operations divisions will report in to the corporate office, which will be responsible for leadership of the corporation. The corporate office will be primarily responsible for strategic direction, interbusiness division resource allocation, support of business divisions, maintenance of the values of the company, and the creation of a context that enhances the ability of business divisions and customer operations divisions to be effective.

In general, operating decisions will not come to the corporate office. Several members of the corporate office will be designated as operations executives. Each of the operations executives with primary operating responsibilities will have a set of business divisions and a customer operations division reporting to him/her, while other executives in the corporate office will have elements of corporate services.

The operations executives will be responsible for:

- Serving as coaches to ensure the success of the business division and customer operation division presidents

- Providing strategic support to business divisions, to ensure that the business division's core offerings, business model, etc., are adjusted over time to reflect the realities of the marketplace and technology
- Focusing on emerging business opportunities and identifying new opportunities where business divisions need to be created
- Serving as a member of the corporate office and thus to participate in strategic planning and resource allocation among business divisions

While the operations executive will have primary responsibility for the business divisions and customer operations division that report in to him/her, the corporate office as a whole is responsible for ensuring the performance of all the business units.

Operations executives also will serve as "corporate champions" for certain issues or functions, such as sales competency, service, etc., drawing upon staff in business divisions or customer operations divisions to work on these issues.

There will be no aggregation of results or activities across business divisions that report to a single operations executive. Operations executives in the corporate office will have no dedicated staff. The corporate office will probably spend approximately one week each month working together.

Two other executives in the corporate office will have specific roles in support of the business divisions and customer operations divisions. One executive will have responsibility for research, technology, and architecture. As such, he will be the lead executive responsible for the company's technology management process. He also will be accountable for the identification, nurturance, and development of critical technology-based core competencies for the corporation.

Another executive will have responsibility for strategic services. These are units that will be providing services to business divisions, including manufacturing support, logistics management, management of the supplies (materials) activities, and coordination of strategic relationships.

Finally, a number of corporate staff executives will report into the corporate office. The primary role of the corporate staff is to support the corporate office in the strategic direction of the company as well as providing required support for the management of Xerox as a corporate legal entity.

Putting all of these together, the basic organizational structure of the new Xerox is as shown in Figure 6.

▶ PEOPLE

The second major element of the new Xerox is people. Clearly Xerox today has a group of tremendously talented and motivated people. Our people have been a competitive strength and will continue to be in the future. At the same time, this new environment is going to require new skills, knowledge, and experience. Perhaps even more importantly, it will require new attitudes on the part of many managers.

There are five requirements in the people area. For the new Xerox to succeed we need people with the following characteristics:

General Management Experience/Skills   We need individuals who understand what it takes to run a business, how to bring together all of the functions from development through customer support, and how to maintain customer focus while promoting innovation and drastically reducing time to market.

Systems Capabilities   Our offerings are quickly moving to being digitally based and ultimately all of our activities will be tied up in the systems world and systems environments. We need individuals who understand systems, not only in the development end of the business, but in all functions.

Market Orientation   We must continue to be customer and market oriented, and we must become more market oriented in the early stages of the development of offerings. Thus, all of our people, not only

Figure 6

Document processing organization

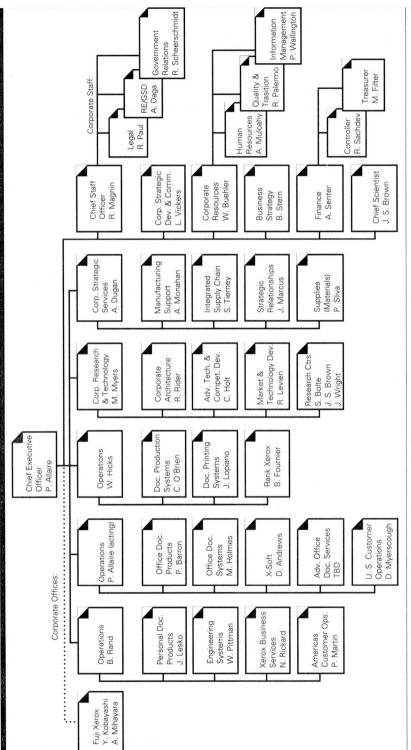

Note: This chart is illustrative only and does not show all organizations or reporting relations.

in the customer operations organizations, but in all functions, must be market oriented.

Ability to Delegate and Empower Our approach is based on the core concept that we will be empowering individuals and teams throughout the organization, and moving decision making closer to the point where we develop the offering and support the customer. Our people must have the capacity and skills to manage in different ways which empower people.

Cross-Organizational Teamwork Our people must have the skills to work across boundaries and units. We are breaking up the company, but at the same time we are focusing on putting it together, both within units and between units. Teamwork skills will be required.

The reality is that we don't have all the people we need today with these capacities. The implication is that we will need to make a major effort to develop and find managerial talent. We have identified twenty-three specific leadership attributes that are needed to succeed in our new environment. We will need to draw on those in the current management who display these capacities or who have the potential to develop them. We will also need to reach out into the organization and promote individuals who have great promise, but have not yet been given a chance to serve as general managers. Finally, we will need to continue to bring in managers from the outside, as we have over the past year. These individuals have and will bring valuable experience, skills, and perspectives that add to the richness and capabilities of our management team.

Because we don't have all of the experience and skills we need, this new Xerox will be an undertaking which requires learning on all our parts. In particular, during 1992 and 1993, each of us will be engaged in a major learning experience. We will individually and collectively need to learn from our successes and our failures. We will need to create an environment where we reflect our actions and learn from them, where productive failures and productive successes are understood and leveraged across the enterprise.

▶ SOFTWARE

In the long run, the benefit of our new approach will come from how we work together. While the hardware and people elements are critical, if we create a new structure and import or develop people, but continue to work together as we have in the past, we will fail. Putting it together implies a whole new way of working together. It requires a new approach to leading and managing. It demands a new type of organizational culture for Xerox. Ultimately, it is the actions of each of us, individually, that will create this new environment.

We have spent a good deal of time since 1989 attempting to understand the culture of Xerox and how it can be both leveraged and changed to support our success in the future. Before focusing on what needs to change, we should be clear about what needs to be preserved and strengthened. Three things are of particular value. First, we must preserve and strengthen the Xerox corporate values. This way of thinking about the enterprise can be traced back to Joe Wilson. Last year, we spent some time reviewing the values, and I felt so strongly that these are as important as ever that I had booklets on the values created and distributed to our employees.

We take these values very seriously. They have defined Xerox as being more than just another big company, rather as a place that is special. Not only are the values still valid, but they are even more critical as we move into this next period of the company's life.

Second, we must reaffirm our commitment to leadership through quality. I have said many times that the quality is what enabled Xerox to survive in the 1980s. Our quality process and quality tools have been critical to the recovery of the business, and they have gained us recognition from customers, suppliers, and the business community at large. In fact, our work in quality should now help us to make this change.

Figure 7

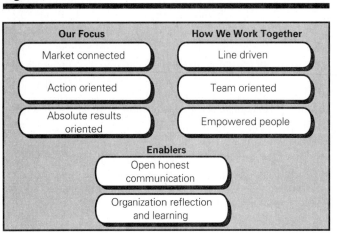

Third, our concept of The Document Company is very valid. In fact, these changes stem from the Xerox 2000 strategy and The Document Company concept. In 1992, we are not changing direction, rather, we are changing how we work in order to better implement our vision and strategy.

While there are many positive aspects of the culture of Xerox, there are also many things which need to change if we are to succeed in this new and challenging environment.

With the help of the OTB, I've identified eight dimensions which characterize the organizational culture that we're seeking to create. During the coming months, we will all need to work together to understand these dimensions. Each of us will need to work to understand how our own actions and behavior either contributes to or diverts us from creating the culture that we require to succeed.

The eight dimensions of the required culture can be thought of as in Figure 7. I think about these in three groups. First, we need to all be focused towards the same type of environment, one where we are market connected, action oriented, and working to ensure absolute results (results in external business terms, rather than results against plan). Second, we need to change how we work together for the good of the common team. We need to empower our people.

Third, there are some key enablers that we need to build into our way of working. We need to have open and honest communication, even if it causes embarrassment and discomfort. We need constructive conflict or productive collision, rather than collusion. We also need to create an environment where we are constantly reflecting on what we do and learning from it.

I recognize that it is easy to put together a list of dimensions and to exhort people to change. In reality, change is very, very difficult. We tend to focus on the hardware of organization change, ironically, because it is easy to work on. This software is more difficult to change. As some have said, "The soft stuff is the hard stuff."

However, I am determined that we must change, we can change, and we will change. Therefore, we will be devoting significant time and effort, starting with the corporate office, on the software and culture issues during 1992. We will use many of the approaches that we found to be successful in implementing leadership through quality almost a decade ago. We will modify our reward systems to encourage the new required behavior. We will promote those who manage in a way consistent with the new approach and coach, counsel, or ultimately penalize those who do not.

▶ WHERE TO FROM HERE?— IMPLEMENTATION AND TIMING

The challenge now is implementation, in its broadest terms. An architecture and design for the core of the structure has been created, but much work remains to be done. We need to make the transition from where we are today to this new Xerox, without disadvantaging the customer or our shareholders in the short term.

We will be moving to the new organizational structure in a phased manner. The process has begun in the U.S. We may not complete the process until 1993, although we will begin financial reporting by business divisions in 1992. Rank Xerox and Americas Operations will begin the process of reporting financial results by business divisions in late 1992 with full implementation to be carried out in a phased manner in 1993. Both entities will also begin the process of aligning their headquarters and operating companies resources to more effectively interface with the business divisions. We will also engage Fuji Xerox to determine how we can use our new approach to work together for the greater good of both Fuji Xerox and Xerox Corporation.

Staffing of the new organization in the U.S. is in progress. Employees in our units that will be immediately involved have been identified and a process for mapping people into positions in the new organization has been developed. That process is underway. Most affected will be people from marketing and development and manufacturing units who may be reassigned into business divisions or corporate staff services. Least affected will be sales, service, and administrative employees whose day-to-day assignments will remain the same.

Although we are moving to nine new business divisions, we will not be adding incrementally to headcount. We will draw from our existing talent pool and, over time, I expect our indirect headcount to decrease as we become more focused and productive. As we will be shifting from a functional, staff-oriented organization to a more streamlined, line-oriented organization, we should be able to operate more efficiently with less indirect people.

▶ XEROX 2000: PUTTING IT TOGETHER

As I mentioned at the start, I am announcing more than another reorganization of Xerox. I am announcing a profound change in the way we intend to manage, which will allow us to realize our Xerox 2000 strategy and "put it together" for customers, for shareholders, and for us.

Everything we do from now on is aimed at increasing the intensity of our focus on the customer and the speed with which we respond to the customer. This increase in focus and speed should move us more rapidly toward our vision of becoming one of the most innovative, productive, and admired companies in the world. We want to be a proof case inside for what we sell outside. The foundation for our success will be a deep commitment to creating new value for and with our customers, and to leveraging all our resources—

capital, technology and especially people—so that the total Xerox is always more than the sum total of its parts.

With our new organization and management approach, we will align our technical and human resources to intensify our market focus and to strengthen our connection with customers. We will radically simplify our work and business processes to decrease time-to-market and to increase the time we spend with and for our customers. We will disperse decision making to those who are the most knowledgeable—those closest to the work and closest to our customers.

"Putting it together" will create a climate that fosters "communities of work"—work groups that can assume ownership and embrace responsibility for what they do and bring out and recognize the best in each of us—work groups that can build and sustain entrepreneurial initiative and risk taking—work groups that foster creative learning from their environment and what they do. And we will marshal the productive power of diverse contributions by focusing these groups on a shared goal, a set of core values and the power of an idea—The Document Company.

The hallmark of our leadership will be "Xerox 2000: Putting It Together."

The task ahead of us is a major one, and at times it can feel daunting. We've taken on a tremendous challenge. The last time we tried anything of this proportion was when we initiated leadership through quality in 1983. This may be an even larger undertaking. But as we learned from quality, there was a payoff from doing it right the first time. We need to be thoughtful, deliberate, and disciplined, but we also need to be determined in our conviction that the company must change, the company can change, and the company will change. We also must make these changes in a manner that neither the shareholder or customer is hurt in the short term. We must make our 1992 objectives as well as these changes. With this new approach, a bright future awaits us as we implement the Xerox 2000 direction, and realize our Document Company vision.

▶ EXERCISES

1. What lessons can be learned from the approach Xerox used to develop the new structure?
2. Describe how the structural changes at Xerox are designed to support the culture its leaders are trying to develop.
3. What are some of the potential limitations or problems that might be associated with this structure?
4. What other structural alternatives would you suggest the Xerox leaders consider? Explain your reasoning for these suggestions.

Glossary

acceptance sampling Checking a certain number of items for a specified lot size, counting the number of defective items, and consulting sampling tables (based on probability theory) to decide whether or not the entire lot should be rejected.

ad hoc team A group of people put together to address specific problems.

anomaly A stage of paradigm shift when unexpected events challenge management's assumptions about business. Normal conditions are disrupted.

anticipated value The value that customers predict they will get in the future if they purchase and use a particular product. Choice is often based upon anticipation of the benefits and sacrifices, and customers may make relative comparisons of product alternatives.

artifacts Observable products and patterns of behavior.

assumptions Over time, fundamental values and beliefs become so taken for granted that they are assumed true and never questioned.

attitudes Involve evaluating an object or event as either good or bad, liked or disliked, positive or negative.

Baldrige Award National quality award competition by the U.S. government.

behavioral analysis The on-site observation and probing of the use processes of customers.

beliefs Perceived associations between two or more objects, events, attributes, or outcomes that may affect an individual's behavior.

breakthrough A big improvement accomplished through radical departure from past practices; accomplished through creativity and innovation.

buyer value Defines value as a function of buyer performance (in economic terms) and buyer cost.

categorical data Data obtained by classifying each of a group of individuals, items, or events into one of two or more categories; the data are counts of how many of the group were classified into each category.

cause and effect diagram A diagram showing current thinking about possible causes for an effect under study.

committee structure Provides a forum for communication, coordination, and participation; provides a coordinating body to guide ad hoc teams and make sure their work fits together well enough to serve the organization's purposes.

common causes Causes of variation imbedded in the design and daily operating practices of the organizational system.

continuous improvement A constant striving to change and make things better. It is one of the three themes of the emerging paradigm.

control chart A graphical display of a series of results with statistical control limits.

core capability A set of differentiated skills, complementary assets, and routines that provide the basis for a firm's competitive capacities and sustainable advantage in a particular business.

core competence A distinctive competence that is a key source of the value attributed by customers to the product or service; a core competence adds to the perceived end-product benefits that customers value, makes many more markets accessible, and is difficult to imitate.

core product/service That product or service most valued by customers. Core products often account for the largest part of either sales or gross profit; a core product may be a key component which is protected by patent or proprietary position.

core technology That combination of know-how, hardware, and software that is the basis of a core competence.

counts of events in space or time Data obtained by observing an event in time or in some volume or area of physical material.

crisis resolution (firefighting) Represents fixing the immediate situation just so normal operations can continue. It puts out the fire for now, but the fire may recur.

critical incidents Historical events that may have come about as a result of a major obstacle, threat, or opportunity—milestones which lead a group to shared understandings by providing a focus for the group.

critical path to change A change sequence which begins with a redefinition of roles, responsibilities, and relationships; structural change is the last phase of the change process.

cross-functional system An organization's informal structure for integrating and coordinating processes involving several functions that have a direct impact on a common customer need.

cross-functional system approach General approach based on definition of systems as horizontal flows of work and resources that serve customers; assigns ownership which redefines managerial roles and responsibilities in terms of systems to integrate a collection of system elements scattered throughout the organizaton. Integrates activities throughout the organization for improving toward strategic objectives.

cultural values Provide a context within which individual attitudes and behaviors are formed. Cultural values are shared among the members of a group and may offer a source of common meaning, identity, and cohesion for the members.

cultural view of organizations Managers pursue the organization's purpose in a more enlightened way and acknowledge the realities of human nature. It helps provide managers with an understanding of the causes of human behavior that are locked inside the heads of people—the thoughts, interpretations, expectations, and habits—and gives managers insight into how to change them.

culture A pattern of artifacts, behaviors, values, beliefs, and assumptions that a group develops as it learns to cope with internal and external problems of survival and prosperity. This definition encompasses both the outward and inward views.

customer-focused system Organizes horizontal flows of work around customers.

customer value Defines value as benefits minus sacrifices; perceptions of value may be affected by the customer/supplier relationship.

customer value strategy The business plan for offering value to customers, including product characteristics, attributes, mode of delivery, support services, and so on. It is one of the three themes of the emerging paradigm.

Deming cycle (Plan, Do, Study, Act) A scientific method for learning how to make improvements.

design strategy Organizing the means of producing and delivering value.

domains of accomplishment The object or the part of the organization that is being acted upon; these range from strategy, through systems, to operations.

double loop learning Learning through challenging or questioning the assumptions about the context within which action is taking place; leads to transformational change because it alters the socially construed meanings people share.

eclectic approach Draws from all the approaches discussed elsewhere; uses a mixture of approaches as needed.

employability security Having the opportunity for developing skills which will enhance an employee's chances of remaining employable either within or outside the company.

employee involvement A process for empowering members of organizations to make decisions and solve problems appropriate to their levels in the organization.

espoused theories What people think and say they do.

event explanations Explanations of results or occurrences that point to an event that occurred at nearly the same time.

execution Taking action to directly accomplish an intended purpose.

external adaptation Coping with the environment by developing cultural solutions.

FATSUDS An acronym for the activities of the use process: find, acquire, transport, store, use, dispose of, and stop the ongoing use of a product or service.

focus group technique An unstructured interview technique for encouraging a group of customers to discuss their feelings, attitudes, and perceptions about a particular topic.

formal process The formal description of how a process works.

frame-breaking change Revolutionary changes of the organizational system as opposed to incremental changes in the system. It begins with a new vision from senior management. Structural change occurs early in the process. Subsequent changes in roles and responsibilities within the new structure are critical to the change process.

generic strategy A firm's strategic position, relative to its competitors, on total delivered cost, differentiation, and market focus.

goal A statement of the strategic direction pursued by managers.

grand strategy The integrating basis of a firm's coordinated and sustained efforts designed to achieve its long-term objectives.

hierarchical management In a hierarchical structure, people are focused on completing their assigned tasks and meeting their own specialized objectives. Managerial attitudes, responsibilities, approaches, and objectives are also fragmented. Managers do not work collaboratively as team members.

hierarchical structure Divides the work of an organization into a sequence of separate and narrowly defined tasks, and reaggregates the people performing those tasks into departments. This results in an organization that is divided into specialized functions, units, or departments.

hierarchical team Consists of a manager and his or her immediate subordinates.

histogram A graphical display of the distribution of a collection of measurements.

implementation Any device (e.g., systems, policy, structure, culture) used by a manager to install new strategy or reinforce existing strategy.

incrementalism Small inprovements accomplished through adjustments and slight alterations.

indicators of organizational performance Traditional measures of costs, schedule attainment, quality, profit, and so on, used to evaluate organizational performance.

informal process The way a process actually works; often different from the formal process.

inspection Examination of products to detect flaws and separate the good from the bad.

interdependencies Relationships among parts of a system.

internal customer Within the organization, encourages workers to think of the next process as the customer; encourages workers to be sensitive to problems or inconveniences they cause others downstream; requires every individual to resolve never to pass on a problem to the next process.

internal integration Ensuring the cohesion of a group, how members are able to work together to fulfill the group's mission by developing cultural solutions.

inward view of culture Stresses the process through which behavior is learned and the ideas, beliefs, symbolism, and evaluative aspects of culture. Views culture as a set of implicit rules that govern behavior.

job-based compensation systems Pay the individual employee on the basis of the specific job he or she is actually doing at a particular point in time.

job enrichment A form of job redesign that seeks to provide employees with jobs that are more intrinsically motivating to perform. This is done through designing the job so that each employee has more responsibility, receives recognition, and has more achievement potential.

Juran's Trilogy An approach to cross-functional management that is composed of the three managerial processes of planning, control, and improvement.

kaizen A number of undramatic and subtle improvements gradually and cumulatively raising the level of performance without interruption (or continuous advancement).

labor-management action teams Temporary parallel problem-solving units which acknowledge the role of the union.

laddering An associative, probing procedure for relating verbal responses to uncover relationships among the components of customer value that avoids the bias of focusing on particular aspects that might confirm the interviewer's preconceptions.

leverage points for change Aspects of the organizational setting that provide opportunities for reinforcing change.

linking pins Middle managers play different roles in each of two hierarchical teams, as a leader in the lower group and a subordinate member in the up-

per group. To be effective in this linking pin role, the middle manager must be able to exert influence upward on his or her own boss as well as downward to lead subordinates.

local solutions Problem solutions arrived at by dealing with causes that exist in the process where the problem arises; local solutions do not address causes that exist elsewhere in the organization.

logic flow diagram A diagram describing actions and decisions in a process.

maintenance Fully sustains and controls the existing system (and mode) of execution, with no changes in its architecture; ensures that the system consistently produces valued goods and services for customers. Crises are resolved immediately to maintain system performance; preventive actions are taken to avoid problems and to ensure consistency in the future.

Management Activity Topograph (MAT) A two-dimensional framework that describes managerial role responsibilities in terms of types and domains of accomplishment.

managerial paradigm The way people think and act in conducting business.

manufacturing-based view of quality Focuses on manufacturing and engineering practices, emphasizes conformance to specified requirements, and relies on statistical analysis to measure quality.

market segmentation The division of a product market into actionable subgroups of customers based on similar needs within groups and different needs between groups.

market segments Groupings of customers which represent a compromise between treating each customer as unique and treating all customers as the same. While each customer is unique, needs do overlap to some degree. Customers are grouped according to criteria that can differentiate them.

market test Having target customers try the product, usually under the same circumstances in which they would use similar products.

mass market approach Tries to meet every person's need with one product.

matrix management Leaves the hierarchy in place but superimposes a horizontal structure in order to achieve some coordination and integration. A product or project manager assumes responsibility for the horizontal flow.

means/ends model Suggests that customers buy products (means) to accomplish some purpose or fulfill a need (ends) and that customer value increases with the match between product use consequences and customer needs.

mission The fundamental purpose of an organization in terms of customer need, core product or service, target market, and technology used to satisfy the need stated in a way that sets the organization apart from others of its type.

modern control and improvement process Incorporates some of the elements of the traditional control process along with the statistical approach to the study of variation and its causes (Deming's Plan, Do, Study, Act cycle). It is built around four basic building blocks that very simply describe the *process of performance.* These building blocks are input, transformation, output, and customer.

monetary value Equates the value of something with its price.

need A term often used for brevity to refer to a host of desired end states (including needs, goals, wants, personal values, and self-concept) that affect customer value.

normalcy A stage of paradigm shift when managerial practices are firmly based upon principles or truths that the management community believes in. Thought and action proceed as normal.

objective A quantified business or corporate-level performance target to be reached in a specified timeframe.

operations Work performed by people and machines on materials or information; a discrete stage at which a person may work on different products at a particular workstation over time. Transforms input into an output; includes operational tasks for doing the work and operating methods guiding that work.

optimization Achievement of the aim or purpose of a system or subsystem.

organizational systems The means that provide customer value. These systems broadly include material and human inputs, process technology, operating methods and work practices, streams of work activity, information flows, and decision making. It is one of the three themes of the emerging paradigm.

outward view of culture Focuses on behavior and those things about culture that are directly observable such as artifacts, patterns of behavior, speech, formal laws, and technical know-how.

p **chart** A control chart used to analyze the variation in categorical data.

paradigm The organizational realities (such as values, beliefs, traditional practices, methods, tools, etc.) that members of a social group construct to integrate the thoughts and actions of its members. It provides rules and standards as well as accepted examples of managerial practice, laws, theories, applications, and instrumentation.

paradigm shift When many beliefs and actions change in concert within an organization.

Pareto diagram A type of bar graph constructed from counts of occurrences, such as defects.

PDSA (Plan, Do, Study, Act) cycle A systematic method to learn and to improve, as described by Deming.

policies General statements or principles intended to guide individual thinking, decision making, and action, or define the domain of decision making by designating authority and limitations.

problem solving Represents finding the cause of the problem and addressing the cause so that the problem does not return. It removes the source of the fire, the smoldering embers.

process The flow of products, materials, or information from one worker or operation to another to transport input into output for customers; composed of four phenomena: *processing* (or machining), *inspection, transport,* and *delay;* two types of processes are production processes and business processes.

product-based view of quality Argues that the quality of a manufactured product may be described in terms of a set of characteristics.

product-focused system Organizes horizontal flows of work around products.

Protocol analysis or content analysis A data collection and analysis technique in which a researcher first records a conversation with an individual respondent, transcribes it, then develops a coding system for patterns in the responses.

pull model of employee involvement Managers create an environment where employees are routinely included in continuous improvement. Involvement efforts are aligned with the customer value strategy.

push model of employee involvement Employee involvement is promoted as an end in itself. Involvement efforts are not aligned with the customer value strategy.

quality A principle that encourages excellence in everything: products, strategies, systems, processes, and people. There are many ways in which quality can be pursued and realized.

quality assurance era When the concept of quality in the United States evolved from a narrow, manufacturing-based discipline to one with implications for management throughout a firm. Quality remained focused on defect prevention, but with a more proactive approach and some new tools.

quality circle A group of employees from the same work unit who volunteer to meet regularly to solve productivity and quality-related problems, or to improve the existing level of product quality in their work area. Generally, the number of participants ranges from six to twelve, plus a facilitator.

quality function deployment (QFD) A structured format for translating customer value requirements into specific company systems and processes, product/service characteristics, and detailed technical requirements across all stages of the activity chain to provide the valued products and services.

rational view of organizations Members pursue the organization's purposes or goals, and the professional manager's job is to make sure the organization achieves its purposes by focusing on goals, formal roles, and technologies.

realized value Actual customer value realized once the customer acquires and uses the product.

reliability engineering An approach to quality that sought to assure acceptable product performance over time. Engineers developed mathematical models for predicting equipment performance over time for different products under different operating conditions.

replacement A stage of paradigm shift when new theories, principles, and practices replace the old ones. Managers achieve a new consensus on the fundamentals of business and management, the questions that should be asked, and the techniques that should be employed in seeking solutions.

resourcefulness A firm's ability to quickly acquire the technology to radically or continuously improve customer value.

role accomplishments The outcomes of role behaviors.

role behaviors Actions to accomplish the role perceptions.

role perceptions Reside in the minds of people as beliefs about what should be done.

role systems The interrelated role perceptions and behaviors of the people in the organization; the bridge between the inward and outward sides of culture.

role values Unique to their job position or interpersonal role in the group. These may differ from personal values and from other role values in a different group.

roles The responsibilities, behaviors, or performance accomplishments expected of a person in a position.

routinization Standardized changes are fine-tuned, balanced, and mastered by those subordinates responsible for operations. The "bugs are worked out," so execution becomes more predictable, and initial performance variations are explained and reduced over time (a subordinate's responsibility).

run chart A time sequence plot of a series of results.

segmentation The iterative and ongoing process of grouping customers into segments which define the structure of a market.

seven tools for quality control Methods for studying processes used in Japan and in the U.S.

shared understanding A communication system with shared meaning.

single loop learning Learning that involves correcting variance in cause and effect relationships so a desired outcome is achieved.

skill-based pay Pay based on the skills an employee has demonstrated and can potentially use while contributing to the work unit.

socialization Individual learning becomes shared as people help one another interpret and understand events. For the new member, it means "learning the ropes," formally and informally.

special causes Causes that act intermittently to produce variation in addition to that which would exist given the action of common causes.

stable variation Variation of a consistent magnitude showing random fluctuations around a steady average.

standardization To verify the operability and performance of a change before releasing it for use, the manager must transmit information, educate people, and demonstrate that the change works as intended. The resulting standardized change displays the right strategic focus, statistical capability, and predictability for stable, on-target system performance (a superior's responsibility).

statistical control limits Limits of stable variation derived by applying appropriate statistical formulas to a series of results.

statistically controlled variation Stable variation.

statistical quality control Requires that numbers derived from measures of processes or products be analyzed according to theories of statistical probability.

strategic management The process managers use to formulate and implement strategies for providing best customer value that will achieve the objectives of the organization.

strategic quality management era Top managers view quality positively as a competitive weapon, and they address it in their strategic planning processes which are focused on customer value.

strategy The pattern of organizational moves and managerial approaches used to achieve organizational objectives and pursue the organization's mission.

streamlining General task of eliminating waste and inefficiency.

strong culture   Consensus on expected behaviors, values, beliefs, and assumptions.

subcultures   A culture specific to a subgroup within the organization (divisions, functions, departments).

suboptimization   Failure to achieve the aim or purpose of a system or subsystem.

subsystem   Partitions an organization into horizontal slices, including strategic, technological, human-cultural, structural, and managerial.

system   Consists of an integrated collection of personnel, knowledge, abilities, motivations, equipment, machinery, methods, measures, processes, and task activities; collection of cause factors, including material, machine, measurement, method, and manpower (the five Ms); includes domains of policies, motivators, processes, technology, and operations; everything that affects customer value; elements organized into aligned subsystems and horizontal flows to serve customers.

system improvement   Requires rethinking of the system. The system is not just repaired and maintained but changed even in the absence of a crisis or a problem. Managers do not wait for a fire.

system ownership   Acknowledges the existence of horizontal systems and redefines managerial roles and responsibilities accordingly to overcome many of the deficiencies of hierarchical management.

systems view   Describes an organization as an *open system* in flux with its environment through a work flow of input, conversion, and output, with interrelated parts.

task forces   Mechanisms for addressing problems and making decisions that have multifunctional implications.

teams   Groups of employees who are collectively responsible for some carefully delineated, complete piece of the work process. Sometimes they are referred to as self-directed work teams, autonomous work groups, or self-regulating work groups.

technology   The elements of applied science needed for doing the work to provide value in the goods and services produced; used to convert inputs into outputs. Includes two components: knowledge and tools.

theories in use   What people actually do or how they act regardless of what they say they do.

Total Quality Management (TQM)   A people-focused management system that aims at continual increase in customer satisfaction at continually lower real cost. TQ is a total system approach (not a separate area or program) and an integral part of high-level strategy. It works horizontally across functions and departments, involving all employees, top to bottom, and extends backward and forward to include the supply chain and the customer chain.

Toyota Production System   A revolutionary approach that has been adopted by many Japanese companies in the aftermath of the 1973 oil shock. Its primary purpose is to completely eliminate unnecessary elements in production to achieve cost reduction and satisfy consumer needs at the lowest possible cost.

trade-off analysis   Using a matrix format to have customers make relative comparisons among a set of attributes and indicate which attributes are most important to them.

traditional control theory   Defines controlling as a systematic effort by business management to compare performance with predetermined standards, plans, or objectives to determine whether performance is in line with these standards and presumably to take any remedial action required to see that human and other corporate resources are being used in the most effective and efficient way possible in achieving corporate objectives.

transcendent view of quality   Implies that high quality is something timeless and enduring, an essence that transcends or rises above individual tastes or styles. It often regards quality as an unanalyzable property that people learn to recognize through experience.

transformational change   Change in the cultural paradigm of the organization.

types of accomplishments   Categories of role accomplishments that vary in the degree of change exhibited or required; these range from consistent execution (no change in systems) to breakthroughs (unprecedented, radical change in systems).

u chart   A control chart used to analyze the variation in counts of events in space or time.

unstable variation   Variation not of a consistent magnitude, having a changing average or exhibiting systematic (nonrandom) patterns of fluctuation.

upstream control   Emphasizes taking action on systems and processes to prevent failure and ensure success in the future.

use process   All the activities that customers go through in using a product or service.

user-based view of quality   Popular with people in marketing, presumes that quality rests in "the eyes of the beholder," the user of the product.

valuation process   Concerns how the customer perceives product attributes and infers means/ends relationships, and then assimilates this information into memory to influence behaviors.

value added   Selling price less the cost of purchased raw materials; a concept used to distinguish end users from all others in the industrial chain according to whether they add value to the product as it passes along the chain or whether they consume value.

value-based strategy   The pattern of decisions and

actions in which managers take responsibility for (1) delivering products/services that provide best net value for defined needs and (2) creating strategic systems to continuously improve that value and satisfy the obligations of the enterprise.

value chain   Disaggregates a firm into its strategically relevant activities to understand costs and sources of differentiation.

values   State what is important or convey a sense of what "ought to be."

variables data   Data produced by measuring a quantitative characteristic on some continuous scale; for example, length, weight, or time.

variation   Fluctuation in events or outcomes over time; differences in results or characteristics of a collection of items or individuals.

X and moving R charts   Control charts used to analyze the variation in a collection of variables data that consist of single measurements.

X-bar and R charts   Control charts used to analyze the variation in a collection of variables data grouped into subgroups of two or more measurements.

zero defects   Focused on management expectations, human relations, and workers' motivation and awareness, with the goal to promote a constant, conscious desire to do a job (any job) right the first time.

Name and Company Index

Ackoff, R. L., 307
Adams, M., 214, 491
Advanced Computer Technology (ACT), 478–481
Advanta Corporation, 289–290
Airbus, 5, 20
Ajzen, I., 102, 190, 199
Albrecht, K., 283
Alcoa, 141–142
Alden, S. D., 184, 266
Alderfer, C. P., 186
Allaire, Paul A., 117–119, 154
Allstate Insurance, 444
Amalgamated Clothing and Textile Workers Union (ACTWU), 466
American Express, 228
American Quality Foundation, 27
Ames Rubber, 162
Analog Devices, 433–435
Anderson, P., 224
Ansoff, I., 239
Apple Computer, 103, 148, 200–201
Archibald, Nolan D., 296
Argyris, Chris, 103, 352, 503, 504
Arnold, Bill, 450
Arnold, M. B., 288
Arnold, T., 98
Aronson, E., 191
Arthur D. Little Consulting, 477
Artzt, Edwin L., 176–177
Assael, H., 196
Atmospheric Processing, 337
AT&T, 44, 148, 276, 333, 334n.
Automatic Data Processing, 148

Babbage, Charles, 97
Badovick, G. J., 194
Bailey, J., 258
Baldwin, T. T., 455
Banc One, 470
Bandura, A., 133
Barley, S. R., 497
Barnard, G. I., 98
Barney, J. B., 124
Barnouw, V., 100
Bartlett, C. A., 320
Bay Banks, 151–152
Beatty, S. E., 194
Becker, Selwyn W., 43n.
Beedle, Jack, 22–23
Beer, Michael, 125, 482, 487–489, 495
Bell, C. H., 96n., 125
Bell Labs, 44, 48, 52, 53
Bennett, Thomas E., 269
Bennis, Warren, 115

Berry, L. L., 283n.
Bieber, Owen, 456–457
Blackler, F. H. M., 493
Boeing, 5, 14, 20
Bogan, C. E., 484
Bonoma, T. V., 181
Bounds, Gregory M., 79, 136, 139, 140, 155–158, 181, 182, 259, 355–356, 448, 467–469, 501
Bounds, Tuck, 296n.
Bowander, B., 18, 20
Bowditch, J. L., 101
Boyle, D., 144
Brache, A. T., 233
Bradford, L. J., 283
Brassard, M., 329, 332n.
Broadhead, James, 484–486, 490
Brogden, James M., 346–347
Brookfield, S. D., 499, 500
Brown, C., 454, 493
Brown, R. H., 100
Brown, T., 220–221
Browning Ferris Industries, 258, 262
Brunswick, E., 184
Buono, A. F., 101
Burns, M. J., 187, 192, 202, 264, 265, 285–288
Burr, I. W., 392n., 412n.
Business Week, 21, 22, 28, 90, 142, 146n., 148, 151, 162, 183, 239, 337, 493
Byham, W. C., 454

Cadillac, 49, 111, 178, 265, 323, 336
Cadotte, E., 283
Capon, N., 215
Carlson, B., 342n.
Carothers, H. G., 181, 214, 259
Carrol, S. J., 136
Case, J., 13
Caterpillar, 12–13
Centennial Medical Center, 450
Ceridian Corporation, 95–96
Chambers, D. S., 365, 392n.
Champy, J., 316n.
Chandler, A., 213n.
Chandler, C., 238
Chang, R. Y., 449, 470
Cherns, A. B., 446
Chevrolet, 49, 230, 336
Child, J., 319
Cho, Fujio, 462–463
Chrysler Corporation, 5, 10, 66, 162, 180, 322–323, 456
Citicorp, 289
Civil Aeronautics Board, 253
Clark, K. B., 16

Clarkson, Thomas F., 444
Clausing, D., 276, 277
Clemons, D. S., 192, 195, 264, 265, 266, 285–288
Clinton, Bill, 89
Coca-Cola, 10, 146, 229, 492
Codex, 163
Coggin, Robert W., 253
Cole, Albert J., 132–133, 175n.
Cole, R. E., 276, 278, 447, 461
Conner Peripherals, 147–148
Consumer Reports, 271
Conway, Earl, 182, 255, 273–274
Cooney, Barry D., 121
Cormetech, 470
Cornfield, B., 45
Corning Glass, 148, 470
Costanza, A., 466
Cravens, D., 222
Cravens, Hills, and Woodruff, 188, 196, 197, 221
Crayola crayons, 45
Cronin, J. J., Jr., 283n.
Crosby, Philip B., 59, 160, 484
Crozier, M., 124
Cummings, M. C., 194
Curry, D. J., 63
Cyert, R. M., 216n.
Cyrix, 239

Daft, R., 224n.
David, F., 226
Davis, F. W., 179
Davis, L. E., 446
Dawn, 177
De Bobadilla, Diego, 172
Deal, T. E., 97, 100
Dechant, Kathleen, 125, 503
Del Norte Technology, 449, 465
Dell Computers, 234, 275, 290
Delta Air Lines, 186, 253
Deming, W. Edwards, 4, 41, 50n., 51n., 52n., 53, 54, 55, 56n., 60, 64, 72–77, 106, 134, 160, 214, 237, 246, 276, 302–303, 319, 334, 342, 357, 358n., 361, 362, 363n., 392n., 393, 439, 468, 484, 485
Dennison, W. E., 481
Deutsche Bank, 19, 20
Deutscher, I., 103
Devanna, M. A., 467
Dewhirst, H. D., 501
Digital Equipment Corporation, 276, 478
Disk Lavier, 203
Disney, Walt, 329
Dobbert, M. L., 499
Dobbins, G. H., 79, 136, 182
Dodge, 180, 230
Dodge, Harold, 52
Dover, P., 283
Doz, Y. L., 240
Drucker, Peter F., 202
Du Pont, 111
Dumaine, B., 162

Duncan, W. J., 123
Dunt, D., 264

Edwards, O., 45
Eisenstat, R. A., 482, 487–489
Ernst & Young, 27, 151
Escort, 178
Eulberg, J. R., 134
Evans, P., 164
Excel Industries, 22

F-16, 183
FACOM, 304–305
Faris, C. W., 194
Farley, J. U., 215
Faulds, D. J., 63
Fayol, Henri, 104, 136–138, 308
Feder, Barnaby J., 163
Federal Express, 181, 186, 511–537
Feigenbaum, Armand V., 53, 55, 56, 57, 60, 61, 78
Fennell, Geraldine, 187
Ferdows, K., 17
Fetterman, D. M., 499
Finnigan, Jerome P., 61–62
Firestone Tire and Rubber, 60
First Bank System, 470
Fishbein, M., 102, 190, 199
Fites, Donald V., 12–13
Florida Power and Light (FPL), 162, 484–486, 490
Fombrun, C. J., 467
Forbes, 298
Ford, Henry, 7, 48, 141
Ford Motor Company, 5, 10, 22, 66, 178, 230, 276, 456, 481
Forker, L. B., 17
Fortun, Wayne M., 28
Fortune, 14, 22–23, 27, 91, 115n., 142, 147, 149, 153, 158, 308, 325, 328
Fredrickson, J. W., 212
French, W. L., 96n., 125
Fuchsberg, G., 41, 215

Galbraith, Frank, 7, 214, 314, 319, 464
Galvin, Robert, 94, 237, 248, 484
Gardial, S. F., 192, 264, 265, 285–288
Garvin, D. A., 45, 46, 47, 49, 63, 65, 179, 258, 273, 484
Geertz, C., 103
General Dynamics, 183
General Electric, 14, 329, 465
General Motors, 5, 10, 27, 111, 146, 160–161, 276, 298, 306, 323, 336, 432, 454, 455–456, 459, 481
Georgia-Pacific, 111, 323–325
Gerth, H., 97
Gilbert, K. C., 355–356
Gilbreth, Frank B., 97, 304
Gillen, D. J., 136
Gitlow, Howard S., 69
Gitlow, Shelley J., 69
Globe Metallurgical, 486–487

Gluck, F., 211, 212
Goffman, E., 122
Government Accounting Office, 255
Graen, G., 133
Granbois, D. H., 196
Greenawalt, Richard, 290
Gregory, K. L., 122
Griffin, A., 278, 279, 281
Grigsby, D., 242
Guteck, B. A., 144
Gutman, J., 184, 266
GVO, 148

Hackman, J. R., 154n., 457, 458, 494
Hall, R. H., 493
Hallmark Cards, 327–328
Halpin, James F., 58–59
Hambrick, D. C., 215n.
Hamel, G., 1, 202, 218, 220, 232, 240
Hammer, M., 298, 309, 311, 316n., 328
Hanan, M., 268
Handberg, Roger E., 95–96
Harari, Oren, 42, 43n.
Harrington, H. J., 150, 306, 316, 335–336
Harrison, R., 96
Hart, C. W. L., 186, 484
Harvard Business Review, 484
Haskett, J. L., 186
Hatsopoulos, G. N., 15
Hauser, J. R., 276, 277
Hausknecht, D. R., 283, 285
Hayes, R. H., 16
Hayes, T. J., 265
Heinz, 153
Hering, Gail, 337–338
Hershey's Kisses, 45, 48
Herzberg, F., 154n., 457
Hewlett-Packard, 100–101, 276, 575–595
Highway Loss Institute, 271
Hills, G., 222
Hirohito, Emperor, 54n.
Hitachi, 19
Hoenig, S., 215
Hofer, C. W., 215n.
Hoffner, A., 466
Hollander, E. P., 124
Home Depot, 199–200
Honeywell, 28
Howard, J. A., 184, 196
Howard, R., 154
Huge, E. C., 244
Hughes Aircraft, 142, 145
Hunt, V. Daniel, 81n.
Hurricane Andrew, 484–485
Hutchinson Technology, 28

IBM, 5, 28, 62–63, 69, 91, 115, 148, 150, 305–306, 432, 478
IBM Rochester, 113, 120, 538–574
Imai, M., 61, 68, 69, 70, 78, 80, 214, 244, 281, 310, 318, 320, 321, 393

Inc., 337
Ingersoll-Dresser Pump Company, 269
Intel, 22, 148, 239
Ishikawa, Kaoru, 41, 54, 55, 61, 65, 78, 80, 142, 209, 214, 277–278, 299–300, 301, 304, 309, 318, 320, 393, 459, 461
Iverson, Kenneth, 164–165
Izard, C. E., 288

J. B. Hunt Transport Services, 186
J. C. Penney, 290
J. D. Power Initial Quality Survey, 271
Jacques, E., 96
James, Lee Ann, 156n., 240
Janson, R., 457, 458
Japanese Ministry of Labor, 461
Japanese Union of Scientists and Engineers (JUSE), 485
Jenkins, R., 283
Jennings, K., 194
Joiner, Brian, 355n.
Johnson, R. M., 266
Jones, Bill, 193–194
Jorgensen, D. L., 499
Journal of Business Strategy, 212
Judge, J. M., 450
Juran, Joseph M., 40, 53, 55–56, 60, 66–68, 75, 76, 77, 309, 317

Kahan, G., 144
Kahle, L., 187
Kahn, R. L., 133, 135, 299
Kaplan, R. S., 493
Karp, P., 268
Kast, Fremont E., 302
Katz, D., 133, 135, 299
Kaufman, S., 211, 212
Kelleher, Larry, 485
Kelly, David, 90
Kelly, John, 454
Kennedy, A. A., 97, 100
Kentucky Fried Chicken ("KFC"), 65
Keough, Donald R., 492
Kiehl, Marie, 282
Kiernan, M. J., 213
Kilpatrick, F. P., 194
Kindel, Stephen, 22
King, B., 244, 277
Kirby, K. E., 332–333
Kluckhohn, C., 100
Kmart, 164, 290
Kohler, Robert J., 219–220
Komatsu, 12
Kroeber, A. L., 100
Krugman, P. R., 15
Kuhn, Thomas S., 6, 100

Lamont, L. M., 187
Lau, L. J., 211
Lawler, E. E., III, 454, 458, 460, 461, 464, 470, 482, 492, 501
Lazes, P., 466
Lean Cuisine, 202

Ledford, G. E., 458, 461, 470, 482, 501
Lehmann, D. R., 181
Lei, D., 215*n.*
Leonard-Barton, D., 234
Leonardo da Vinci, 329
Levitt, R., 184
Lewin, K., 481, 501
Lewis, J. W., III, 101
Lexus, 93
Lieberman, M., 211
Likert, R., 308
Limited, The, 214
Lincoln Electric, 214, 218, 228
Linton, R., 100
Little, J. H., 213
Locker, D., 264
Lu, D., 142, 209, 300, 309, 320

McCormick & Company, 144
McCurdy, D. W., 100
McDonald's, 143, 182
McDonnell Douglas, 5, 20
McGrath, J. E., 133
Machiavelli, 476, 477
McKenna, Michael, J., 130
Magjuka, R. J., 455
Manrodt, K. B., 175, 179
March, J. G., 216*n.*
Marketing News, 202, 257
Marriott Corporation, 186
Marshall, R., 498, 505
Marsick, Victoria J., 125, 503, 504
Martin, J., 101, 123
Martin, S., 325
Martin, Tom, 275
Martin Company, 58–59
Maruta, Y., 240
Maslow, A., 186
Mason, J., 200
Master Industries, 346–347
MasterCard, 289
Matsushita, 148
Matsushita, K., 240
Mayo, J. S., 44
Mercedes-Benz, 19
Merrills, Roy, 330–331
Mezirow, J., 504
Millenson, J. R., 144
Miller, Cyndee, 22
Miller, G., 17, 214
Miller, J. A., 271, 283, 285
Milliken, Robert, 248
Mills, C. W., 97
Minnesota Council for Quality, 28
Mintzberg, H., 136–137, 138, 213*n.*, 216*n.*
Mitchell, G. D., 100
Mitsubishi, 19, 20, 276, 470
Miyake, T., 18, 20
Mizuno, S., 329, 332*n.*
Mockler, R. J., 105
Moen, R. D., 392*n.*, 439*n.*

Mohrman, A. M., Jr., 482, 501
Mohrman, S., 458, 460, 461, 464, 470, 482, 501
Monden, Yasuhiro, 8
Montgomery Ward, 104
Morgan, G., 100, 307
Morita, Masaki, 225–226
Motorola, 22, 28, 73, 163, 214, 234, 236, 237, 482, 484
Mutual Benefit Life (MBL), 328
Myers, J. H., 184, 185

Nader, Ralph, 60
Nadler, D. A., 489–490, 495
Nakane, J., 17
Narver, J. C., 201, 202, 224
National Geographic, 172
Newman, W. H., 489–490
Newsweek, 6*n.*, 21
Nicol, R., 327
Nintendo, 192, 241
Nippon Steel, 20
Nissan, 19, 22
Nolan, T. W., 392*n.*, 439*n.*
Nolan, Tom, 274*n.*
Nordstrom's, 214
North American Phillips, 259
Northern Telecom, 330–331
Nucor Corporation, 164–165, 303
NUMMI, 454, 456

O'Connor, E. J., 134
Ohmae, Kenichi, 203, 241
Ohno, Taiichi, 144, 459
Olander, F., 286
Oldham, G. R., 154*n.*, 457, 458
Oliver, R. L., 283, 287
Olshavsky, R. W., 196, 285
Olson, J. C., 283
O'Neill, Paul H., 141–142
Ore-Ida, 153
Ostby, Sharon A., 95–96
Ott, J. S., 101, 102
Ouchi, William G., 98, 122*n.*

Pace, L. A., 139, 296, 447, 451, 452, 466–469
Pae, P., 290
Parasuraman, A., 283*n.*
Parsons, T., 100
Pascale, R., 150
Pasmore, W. A., 299
Passell, P., 45
Paul, W. J., 154*n.*
Pearce, J., 226
Pearson, A. E., 212, 220, 226–227, 232, 245, 247
Pelto, P. J., 498
Pepsico, 10, 226–227, 229
Perkins, W. S., 184
Perrow, C., 97, 493
Peters, Jeff, 93*n.*
Peters, L. H., 134
Pettigrew, A. M., 121, 500
Pirelli, Thomas, 91

Pirsig, Robert M., 45
Pisano, G., 234
Plaspac, 446–451, 459, 464, 468, 470, 471
Plato, 45
Polaroid, 162
Porter, C. W., 494
Porter, Michael, 124, 173–175, 213, 228, 233
Postal Service, U.S., 282
Power, C., 255, 257, 289
Prahalad, C. K., 1, 202, 218, 220, 232, 240
Procter & Gamble, 255, 273–274, 276, 328, 330
Provost, L. P., 274*n.*, 392*n.*, 439*n.*
Purdy, K., 457, 458
Putnam, R., 503

Quality Progress, 274*n.*
Quinn, J. 213*n.*, 216*n.*

Radcliffe-Brown, A. R., 101
Radford, G. S., 48
Ragland, T. C., 257
Rain Bird Sales, 449
Rampey, J., 4
Ranney, Gipsie, 342*n.*, 427*n.*
Ransom, Cindy, 157–158
Rath and Strong Consulting, 478
Rayner, B., 486
Reader's Digest, 282
Reagan, Ronald, 10
Redeployment Issues, 485
Reebok, 147
Reeve, Jim, 296*n.*, 355–356
Reich, D. M., 454
Reich, Robert, 7*n.*
Reilly, M. D., 283
Reimann, B. C., 218, 234
Reimann, Curt W., 23–26
Rescorla, R. A., 192
Reynolds, T. J., 184
Rhyne, L., 212
Ricoh Company, 90
Riley, D., 449
Riley, P., 124
Robert, M., 179*n.*, 289
Roberts, H., 4
Robertson, K. B., 154*n.*
Robinson, P. J. 194
Rohan, T. M., 161
Rokeach, M., 187, 264
Romig, Harry, 52
Rosenberg, M. J., 263
Rosenzweig, James E., 302
Ross, L., 45
Rubbermaid, 234
Ruckleshaus, William, 258
Rumelt, R, 239, 241
Rummler, G., 233
Rumpeltes, L., 466
Runyon, Marvin, 282

St. Cyr, Kenneth L., 200–201
St. Mary's Medical Center, 596–619
Sanday, P. P., 498
Sandberg, W., 241
Sasser, W. E., Jr., 186
Sathe, V., 101, 121, 124
Saturn, 455–456, 470
Schein, Edgar H., 101–104, 113, 114, 116, 119, 120, 125,
    194, 299, 480, 497, 498, 500, 501
Schmidt, Warren H., 61–62
Schneider, C., 449
Schneider, H. L., 449
Schneiderman, Arthur M., 68*n.*
Scholtes, Peter, 437*n.*
Schon, D. A., 103, 503, 504
Schonberger, R. J., 213, 215, 237, 245, 256, 309, 325–326
Schriber, J. B., 144
Schuler, R. S., 468–469
Schumann, D. W., 192, 264, 265, 285–288
Schwartz, H. S., 91
Schwartz, Stephen B., 62–63
Schweiger, D., 241
Scott, J. E., 187
Scott, W. R.., 97
Sears Roebuck, 104, 214, 290
Selznick, P., 98
Senge, Peter M., 299, 303, 306–307, 308*n.*, 356, 401, 415*n.*,
    432*n.*, 498*n.*
Shanmugan, A. V., 101
Shelton, James, E., 162
Shephard, J., 241
Shewhart, Walter A., 44–45, 48–54, 60, 72, 353, 357–361,
    392*n.*, 393, 397, 422, 439
Shingo, Shigeo, 142, 150, 304, 305, 459
Shocker, A. D., 184, 185
Shuen, A., 234
Shulman, L. E., 164
Sidlik, Thomas W., 322–323
Shiel, C., 123
Sims, Arden, 486
Sirgy, M. J., 285
Sirkin, H., 327
Skinner, W., 326
Slater, S. F., 201, 202, 224
Smith, D. M., 503
Smith, Roger, 298
Smothers, N., 215, 228
Solomon, R. L., 119
Sony, 141, 145, 148, 192, 224, 226, 231, 260
Space Communications Corp., 19
Spector, B., 482, 487–489
Sperlich, Hal, 66
Spradley, J. P., 100
Spreng, R. A., 285
Stalk, George, Jr., 164, 186*n.*, 234
Stata, Ray, 433–435
Stealth, 180
Steingraber, Fred G., 60, 79
Stevens, Candice, 22
Stouffer, 202
Stout, Thomas M., 186*n.*

Strickland, A., 213n.
Sullivan, L. P., 278
Sun Microcomputers, 147
Sun Microsystems, 234
Sun Tzu, 241
Suzaki, K., 311n.
Swan, J. E., 283
Swiss Army knives, 45

Taguchi, Genichi, 72, 73
Tanka, Y., 100
Tasma, C., 325
Tastee Freeze, 182
Tathum, C. B., 265
Taylor, Frederick W., 7, 10, 48, 97
Taylor, Lauren P., 104
Taylor, S. A. 283n.
Teece, D., 234
Teixeira, D., 152
TelePad Corporation, 148
Tennessee Eastman, 464
Tennessee Valley Authority, 149
Texas Instruments, 22
Thomas, K. W., 455
Thompson, A., 213n.
Thompson, J. D., 97
3M, 28, 218, 335
Thurow, Lester, 11, 16, 18, 20, 23
Tichy, N. M., 113, 124, 467
Tide, 330
Tokyo Buisness Today, 17, 21
Tolman, E. C., 192
Toshiba, 19
Toyoda, Shoichiro, 55n., 148
Toyota, 5, 7, 8, 19, 21, 22, 113–114, 121, 146, 148–149,
   150, 230, 238, 276, 278, 299, 320, 321, 335, 454, 461–
   464, 620–709
Triandis, H. C., 100
Truell, G. F., 454
TRW, 219–220
Tuckman, B. W., 455
Tushman, M. I., 489–490

United Auto Workers (UAW), 456–457
University of Michigan Hospital, 183
UPS, 186

Van Gigch, J. P., 301
Vassilou, G., 100
Vassilou, V., 100
Video Storyboard Tests, 290
Vinson, D. E., 187
Visa, 289
Volkswagen Beetle, 45
Vollmann, T. E., 17
Vroom, V. H., 190

Wall Street Journal, 290, 470

Wallace Co., 27
Wallach, A. S., 211, 212
Wallach, Ellen J., 98, 194
Wal-Mart, 114, 164, 213–214, 218, 245, 290, 328, 330
Walt Disney Corporation, 186, 214
Walton, Mary, 3n.
Walton, Sam, 114, 214, 245
Warren, Nancy, 3n.
Waste Management, 258
Waters, D., 213n.
Watervliet Arsenal, 181, 322, 332
Watkins, K. E., 504
Watson, Tom, Sr., 115
Wausau Insurance, 234
WEAF Group, 13
Weber, Max, 97, 98
Webster, F. E., 202
Wellins, R. S., 453–454
Westbrook, R. A., 264, 283, 287
Western Electric, 48n.
Wheeler, D. W., 365, 392n.
Wheeling-Pittsburgh Steel Corp., 226, 227
Wheelwright, S. C., 16
Whirlpool, 286
White, J. B., 238
Whitsett, David A., 122, 446n., 457, 482, 493, 494
Wilkins, Alan L., 98, 103
Williams, Frank, 478, 479
Williams, M. D., 211
Wilson, J. M., 454
Wind, Y., 194
Winer, R. S., 181
Wohlking, Wallace, 125
Wolcott, H., 498
Womack, James P., 7, 149n.
Woodruff, D., 215
Woodruff, R. B., 187, 192, 195, 202, 222, 264, 265, 283,
   285–287
Woolman, C. E., 253
Wynne, L. C., 119

Xerox, 116–119, 220, 237, 466, 482, 710–790

Yamaha, 202–203
Yin, R. K., 144
Yorks, Lyle, 446n., 457, 482, 493, 494, 505
Yoshida, Kosaku, 19, 20, 21
Young, John, 100

Zaleznik, Abraham, 161, 310
Zangwill, W. I., 260
Zarowitz, Ron, 162
Zawacki, R. A., 96n., 125
Zeithaml, V. A., 175, 283n.
Zemke, Ron, 186
Zenith, 14
Ziskin, J., 152
Zytec Corporation, 28

Subject Index

Absolutes of Quality Management, 59
Acceptable quality levels (AQL), 53, 59, 70
Acceptance sampling, 52, 55
Accomplishments for improvement, 141–144
Accomplishments for stabilization, 141, 144–145
Accountability, hierarchical management and, 308–309
Achievement motivation, 61
Action plans, 242–244
Activity analysis, 234
Ad hoc teams, 315–317
Administrative processes, 305n.
Aesthetics, 180
Affinity diagram, 329
After-sale feedback, 268
American Society for Quality Control (ASQC), 53
Analytical methodology, 307
Annual objectives, 242
Anomalies stage of managerial paradigm shift, 13–28
    competitive responses, 21–23
    defined, 9
    evidence of a shift, 13–14
    explanations for, 14–16
        head-to-head competition, 16
        normal responses to the macroeconomic climate, 14–15
        poor management, 16
    Japanese competitiveness and (see Japanese competitiveness)
    small and midsize companies and, 27–28
Anticipated value, 188
Apple Quality Management (AQM), 103
Approach and continuous improvement, 32, 33
Arbitrary standards, 354–356, 423–425
Artifacts of culture, 101, 102, 111–112
Assumptions and culture, 103–104, 111–112
Attention, diversion of, 12
Attitude formation, 189–191
    binary decisions and cutoffs, 196
    prioritized criteria, 196
    simplification of mental processing, 195
Attributes, 186, 263–264
    assessing specific, 288
Authority and continuous improvement, 33–34
Autonomation, 8
Autonomous work groups, 157, 453–456
Avoidable costs, 55–56

Baldrige award (see Malcolm Baldrige National Quality Award [MBNQA])
Barriers to entry, 228
Behavioral analysis, 263
Behavioral learning, 119–120
Behavioral roles, 138
Beliefs, 190
    interrelatedness of cultural levels and, 111–112
    inward view of culture and, 102–103

Benchmarks, competitive, 234
    choosing, 286–287
Beneficiary, 180
Benefits, 175, 186, 190–191
Bernoulli model, 367n.
Best, The (Passell and Ross), 45
Beta test, 266–267
Breakthroughs, 67–70, 141–142
Build and grow strategies, 239
Bureaucracy, 97, 98
    theory of, 10
Business processes, 150, 305–306
Buyer value, 173–175
Buyers, power of, 229
Buying roles, 181
Buying situations, 194–195
By-products, 92

Call records, 267
Case studies:
    Federal Express, 511–537
    Hewlett-Packard, 575–595
    IBM Rochester, 538–574
    St. Mary's Medical Center, 596–619
    Toyota, 620–709
    Xerox, 710–790
Categorical data, 366
    p chart to analyze, 367–370
Cause/effect diagram, 55, 299–301, 381–382
Centralization, 416
    illustrated, 417
Channel customers, 193
Characteristics, 186
Charisma, 115
Cold War, 11
Commanding, 136
    planning and, 136–137
Commercial customer value, 268–270
Committee structure, 315, 317
Common causes of variation, 360–361
    mistakes of interpretation and, 360–362, 422–423
Communication, constrained, 309
Company-Wide Quality Control (CWQC), 61, 78
Competitive advantage, 233–234
Competitive benchmarks, 234
    choosing, 286–287
Competitive strategy, 240
Competitor analysis, 230–231
Competitor orientation, 241
Complaint data, 268
Component motions, 138
Concurrent control, 109
Concurrent engineering, 323
Confirming, customer value and, 259, 262–263
Conformance, 180
    quality of, 65
        economics of, 66–67

Consensus, cultural, 121–122
Consumer products, variation in, 348–349
Consumer services, variation in, 349
Consumer value concept, 63–65, 79
    toward a, 81–82
Consumption, 181
Content analysis, 264–265
Continuous improvement, 32–34, 66–79, 247
    approach and, 32, 33
    authority and, 33–34
    breakthroughs versus increments, 67–70
    continuous learning and, 504–505
    control and, 33, 34, 106
    costs and, 66–67
    crisis resolution and, 79
    cross-functional systems approach and, 74–79
    decision-making perspective and, 33
    defined, 67–69
    evaluation and control for, 248
    at every level of the organization, 94–95
    external analysis and, 228
    focus and, 34
    management responsibility for systems and processes,
        74–79
    managerial roles and, 33, 138–139
    means and, 34
    occasion and, 32, 33
    problem solving and, 79
    reducing variation, 69–74
    response to error, 33
    system improvement and, 79
    teamwork for, 162–163
    types of accomplishments and (see Types of accom-
        plishments)
    working to specification versus, 93
Control, 308
Control chart, 358–360
    statistical (see Statistical control charts)
Control matrix, 279
Control theory, 104–111
    continuous improvement and, 33, 34, 106
    knowledge development and, 106
    modern control and improvement process, 106–110
    traditional, 104–105
        deficiencies of, 105–106
        steps in, 105
    upstream control and, 110–111
Controlling, 104–105, 136
    planning and, 136–137
Cooperation, 23
Cooperative strategy, 240
Coordinating, 136
    planning and, 136–137
Core capability, 234
Core competencies, 218
Core products, 218
Core technologies, 218
Corporate accounts payable, 412–418
Corporate culture, 61, 100
    (See also Organizational culture)
Corporate policies, 149

Corporate values, 218, 226–227
Costs of quality, 55–56
Countercultures, 123
Counts of events or occurrences in space or time, 366
    u chart to analyze, 371–375
Creative thinking, 8
Crisis resolution, 79
Critical incidents, 120
    analysis of, 500
Critical path of change, 487–489
Cross-docking, 164
Cross-functional systems approach, 31, 74–79, 149, 161,
        233–234, 298
    ad hoc teams and, 315–317
    benefits and drawbacks of, 315
    hierarchical management and, 309–310, 325
    horizontal reductionism and, 303
    key elements of (see Systems view of organizations,
        key elements of)
    satisfaction/dissatisfaction measurement and, 288–289
    system ownership and, 315, 320–325
        product design/redesign, 323
        provisioning systems, 322
        value specification systems, 323–325
Cross-functional teams, 464–465
Cross-training, 470
Cultural insurance, 124
Cultural values, 194
Cultural view of organizations, 98–99
    (See also Organizational culture)
Culture, 100–112
    defined, 89n., 100–101
    holistic view of, 101–104
        artifacts, 101, 102
        underlying assumptions, 103–104
        values and beliefs, 102–103
    interrelatedness of levels of, 111–112
    inward view of, 100–101
    organizational (see Organizational culture)
    organizational systems and, 32
    outward view of, 100
    role systems and, 134–135
Customer benefit, 241
Customer Focused Quality, 444
Customer-focused systems, 328–330
    advantages of, 329–330
    creating, 329
    examples of, 328
    flexible use of, 330
Customer knowledge, 344–345
Customer orientation, 90–91
    competitor orientation versus, 241
    organizational culture and, 92
Customer satisfaction, 231
    (See also Satisfaction/dissatisfaction measurement)
Customer value, 29, 106, 170–208, 254–263
    anticipated value and, 188
    attitude formation and, 189–191
        abbreviated, 195–196
    as benefits minus sacrifices, 175
    choice and, influence of norms on, 198–199

Customer value (*continued*)
  concept of, 172–176
  conclusion, 203–204
  defined, 172, 178
  determining, 90
  focusing on, 254–263
  garbage business and, 258–259
  idiosyncratic nature of, 192
  learning about, 259–263
    confirming, 259, 262–263
    discovering, 259, 262
    invalidating, 259, 261–262
    projecting, 259, 260–261
  market segmentation and, 178–180
  as a means/ends relationship (*see* Means/ends model)
  measuring (*see* Measuring customer value)
  model of, 256
  modern control and improvement process and, 106–110
  needs, quality, satisfaction and, 255–259
  organizational valuation and, 192–195
    cultural values, 194
    role values, 194–195
  purchase behavior and, 199–200
  realized value and, 188
  relationship between supplier and customer and, 175
  relative nature of, 191–192
  superior, 91, 178
  use experience and, 200
  use of product and, 180–181
  use process and, 181–183
  valuation process, 189–192, 196–198
    extensive valuation, 198
    extent of involvement and, 196
    familiarity with the product and, 196–197
    learned shortcuts, 197–198
    steps in, 189
Customer value strategy, 29–30, 147–153, 201–204
  domains of accomplishment and (*see* Domains of accomplishments)
  implementing, 203
  key stakeholder and, 29, 30
  measurement and, 29, 30
  positioning and, 29, 30
  product design and, 29, 30
  quality and, 29–30
  revitalized demand and, 202–203
Customers, 178–183
  characteristics of, 183
  defined, 180
  market segmentation, 178
    refinement of, 178–180
  use of product or service and, 180–181
    broader use process, 181–183
Cycle times, 239

Damage control, 110
Decider role, 180, 181
Decision making and continuous improvement, 33
Decisional roles, 137
Defect-free production, 256
Delay, 304, 305

Delivery Quality Improvement Program, 321, 335
Deming Cycle, 54, 106, 334, 439–441
Deming Guide to Quality and Competitive Position, The (Deming), 69
Deming Prize, 484, 485
Deming's fourteen points for management, 74
Departmental policies, 149
Derating, 58
Design for quick response, 259–260
Design matrix, 279
Design/redesign (*see* Product design/redesign)
Design strategy, 30, 147–148
Deviations, 106
Direct observation, 267
Disconfirming experiences, 490–491, 496, 497
Discovering, customer value and, 259, 262
Dispersion analysis, 300–301
Dissemination role, 137
Distinctive competence, 233
Distribution processes, 305
Disturbance handler role, 137
Division of labor, 97
"Do the right thing the right way the first time," 276
Domains of accomplishments, 139, 145–153
  combining types and, 139–141
  design strategy and, 147–148
  motivators and, 150
  operations and, 152–153
  policies and, 149–150
  processes and, 150–151
  systems and, 148–149
  technology and, 151–152
Double loop learning, 503–504
Durability, 180

Eclectic approach, 334–335
Ecological trends, 228
Economic Control of Quality of Manufactured Product (Shewhart), 48–54
Economic trends, 228
Economic value, 173
Education, 436
  paradigms and, 7
Employability security, 470–471
Employee involvement, 61, 444–475
  in action, 446
  adjusting averages and, 450
  cross-functional teams, 464–465
  defined, 447
  implementing changes and, 451
  introduction, 445, 447
  job enrichment, 457–459
  MAT framework for, 447–450
  mistakes to be avoided when implementing, 466–467
  operational proficiency, improving, 450–451
  organizational forms of, 452–453
  organizational systems and, 31
  pull model of, 451–452
  push model of, 451–452, 453
  quality circles, 459–464
  reducing variation and, 450

Employee involvement (*continued*)
  within a strategic context, 447
  suggesting changes and, 450
  task forces, 464–465
  work teams, 453–456
  (*See also* Human resource implications of employee
    involvement)
Empowerment, 94
Enablement, 94
Enhancing subcultures, 123
Enriched jobs, 457–459
Entrepreneur role, 137
Espoused theory, 503
European Economic Community (EEC), 17
Event explanations, 432
Excellence, 43, 45–46
Exchange rates, 15
  Japanese response to unfavorable, 20
Execution, 145
Experimentation for knowledge, 92
External adaptation, 112–113
External analysis, 227–232
  competitor, 230–231
  forecasting and prioritizing, 231–232
  industry, 228–230
  remote, 227–228
External stakeholders, 224
Extras, 326

Failure mode and effect analysis (FMEA), 58
Familiarity with a product, 196–197
FATSUDS activities:
  benefits, sacrifices and, 186
  customer value and, 182
  defined, 181–182
  role values and, 194
Features, 180
Feedback information, 110–111
  after-sale, 268
Fifth Discipline, The (Senge), 356
Figurehead role, 137
Financial planning processes, 306
Fire fighting, 79
First-line supervisor, 157
Fishbone diagram, 55, 299–301, 381–382
Five Ms, 300
Fixation on events, 356
Flexible manufacturing system, 289, 312–313
Flexible work groups, 454
Flexible workforce, 8
Focus and continuous improvement, 33, 34
Focus group technique, 265–266
Focused differentiation, 240
Focused factories, 326
Forecasting, 231–232
Foreman, 157
Formal process, 406–407
Formal roles, 133
Formal socialization, 121
Forming stage of teams, 455
Fragmentation, 306

Frame-breaking change, 489–490
Function analysis, 233–234
Functional team, 91
Future conditions, variation in, 350–351

Gap analysis, 236
Garbage business, 258–259
Gatekeeper role, 181
Generic strategy, 213–214
Global cooperation, 20
Global strategy, 241
Goals, 186, 218
  operative, 492–494
  strategic objectives and, 237–239
Good soldiers, 124
Grand strategy, 213, 214
  build and grow, 239
  hold and maintain, 239, 240
  retrenchment, 239, 240
Group dynamics, 61
Guidance teams, 246
Guide to Quality Control (Ishikawa), 393

Head-to-head competition, 16
Hierarchical management, 307–313
  advantages to, 307
  defined, 298–299, 307
  growing complexity of, 311–313
    just-in-time strategies, 312
    marketing promotions, 311
    procurement practices, 311–312
    upstream processes impeding improvement, 312–313
  horizontal linkages to patch, 313–318
    ad hoc teams, 315–317
    committee structure, 315, 317
    internal customers, 315, 317–318
    organizational learning disabilities and, 314
    streamlining, 316
  inadequacy of hierarchical teams, 310–311
  problems with, 308–310
    constrained communication, 309
    excessive control, 308
    imposed results, delegated means, 309
    inhibiting customer value, 310
    lack of cross-functional responsibility, 309–310
    narrow accountability, 308–309
    partitioning into vertical slices, 310
    social isolation, 309
Hierarchical structures, 298, 307
  problems of, 297
Hierarchical teams, 308
  benefits and drawbacks of, 315
  inadequacy of, 310–311
Histograms, 395–396
Hold-and-maintain strategy, 239
Hollow corporations, 14
Horizontal *keiretsu*, 19
Horizontal linkages to patch the hierarchy, 313–318
Horizontal reductionism, 303
Horizontal slice, 303

Horizontal work flows, 302–303
    vertical flow integrated with, 303–304
Hoshin planning, 243–244
House of quality matrix, 277–281
Human resource implications of employee involvement,
    467–471
    employment relationship, 470–471
    new focus, 468–469
    skilled-based pay and, 469–470
    traditional perspective, 467–468
    training and, 470
Human resource management (HRM), 31–32
    strategic management and, 246–247
Human Theories of Control, 352–353

Idiosyncratic customer value, 192
Improvement, action for, 435–441
    barriers to, identification of, 439
    education, 436
    identification and prioritization of, 436–437
    modeling by managers, 436
    organization-wide, 435–439
    responsibility, clear understanding of, 436
    review of, 437–439
    sharing learning, 439
    strategic importance of, 436
    systematic learning, 439–441
    systematic method of, 437
    training, 437
Improvement processes, responsibilities for, 332–334
In Search of Excellence, 432
Incremental changes, 67–70, 142
Indicators of organizational performance, interpreting,
    421–435
    arbitrary targets, 423–425
    common causes, 422–432
    evaluating performance of systems and people, 432–433
    hypothetical factory, 426–432
    interdependence of organizational results, 426–432
    special causes, 422–423
        action on, 425–426
Individual component analysis, 58
Individuality, 124
Industrial chain, 173–175
Industry analysis, 228–230
Influencer role, 181
Informal process, 406–407
Informal roles, 133
Informal socialization, 121
Informational roles, 137
Initiator role, 181
Innovative changes, 67–70, 141–142
Input, 106–111
Inspection, 304, 305
Inspection era, 47–48
    formalizing the inspection function, 48
    identifying characteristics, 47
    mass production and inspection, 47–48
Interdependencies, 402–443
    defined, 404
    examples of, 404–421

Internal analysis, 232–235
    function, activity, and process, 233–234
    performance, 232–233
    portfolio, 235
Internal consistency, 241
Internal customer orientation, 78
    as horizontal linkage, 315, 317–318
Internal integration, 113–114
Internal invisibility, overcoming, 497–498
Internal learning, 402–443
Internal stakeholders, 224
International Quality Study, 27
International Standards Organization (ISO-9000), 22, 212
Interpersonal roles, 137
Interviews, 264
Intuitive/inductive approach to decision making, 216*n.*
Invalidating, customer value and, 259, 261–262
Involvement with a product, 196
Inward view of culture, 100–101
    holistic, 101–102
    roles and, 134–135
Irrational side of organizational life, 98
Ishikawa diagram, 54, 299–301, 381–382

Japan:
    continuous improvement and, 94–95
    exchange rates and, 15
    quality circles and, 459–464
    statistical quality control era in, 53–55
    value-based strategies and, 214–215
"Japan bashing," 21
Japanese competitiveness, 16–21, 230–231
    competitive advantage and, 241
    global cooperation, 20
    government cooperation and leadership, 19–20
    Keiretsu industrial groupings, 19
    response to pressure, 20–21
    sequence of priorities in manufacturing, 17–18
    technology strategies, 18–19
    U.S. emulation of, 22
Job-based compensation systems, 469
Job enrichment, 457–459
Juran's Trilogy, 75–77
Jury of expert opinion, 267
Just-in-time manufacturing, 8, 42, 305
    implementing, 312

Kaizen concept, 68–70, 80, 320
Kanban system, 8
Keiretsu industrial groupings, 19, 21, 175
Key stakeholder and customer value strategy, 30
Knowledge, 151
    types of, 344–345
Knowledge development, 106

Labor-management action teams, 465–466
Laddering, 266
Leader role, 137
Leadership and management, 244–245
Learning, mistakes leading to organizational, 93
Learning curve, 144

Learning disabilities, organizational, 314, 356
Learning process, 119–120
  abstract concepts, 120
  behavioral, 119–120
  improvement and (*see* Improvement, action for)
  internal, 402–443
  systematic, 439–441
Leverage points for driving transformational change,
    490–495
  allocating rewards and status, 494
  disconfirming experiences and, 491
  operative goals, 492–494
  staffing decisions, 494–495
  training and development, 495
Liason role, 137
Linking-pin concept of organizations, 61, 308
Local solutions, 411
Logic flow diagram, 407–408
  illustrated, 409
Long-term strategies, 239–240

Machine That Changed the World, The (Womack), 7
Macroenvironment, 183
Maintenance, 144–145
Malcolm Baldrige National Quality Award (MBNQA),
    23–26, 41, 162
  conceptual model of, 23–25
    core values, 24
    criteria characteristics, 25
    criteria structure, 24–25
  criticism of, 26–27
  institutional strategy, 25–26
    assessment capability, 26
    communications, 25–26
    involvement in the award program, 26
  role of, in the paradigm shift, 26–27
  as a trigger for change, 483–487
Management Accomplishment Topograph (MAT),
    139–141
  domains of accomplishments and, 145–153
  employee involvement and, 447–450
  role systems and, 153–166
    inadequacies in, 160–162
    key to culture change, 166
    nature of, 162–164
    responsibility and, 154–160
  types of accomplishments and, 141–145
Management by exceptions, 106
Management by objectives (MBO), 10, 97
Management by policy (management by planning)
    (MBP), 243–244
Management role responsibilities, 130–169
  continuous improvement and, 138–139
  culture and role systems, 134–135
  decisional, 137
  depicting, 154–160
  differences, 154, 159
  framework for, 136–153
  importance of, 131–135
  informational, 137
  interpersonal, 137

Management role responsibilities (*continued*)
  key to culture change, 166
  MAT framework for, 153–166
  nature of, 162–164
    flexible team participation, 163
    integration for synergy, 163–164
    teamwork for continuous improvement, 162–163
  performance and, 133–134
  responsibilities for prescribing, 159–160
  role accomplishments and (*see* Domains of accomplish-
    ments; Types of accomplishments))
  system inadequacies, 160–162
    failure of quality circles, 160–161
    lack of leadership, 161
    loss of market opportunities, 162
    waste of resources, 162
  team, 159
  traditional, 136–138
Managerial Breakthrough (Juran), 68
Managerial paradigm, 6
  shifts in (*see* Paradigm shifts)
Managerial roles and continuous improvement, 33
Managerial subculture, 123
Managing upstream, 78
Manufacturing-based view of quality, 49–51
Market-Driven Quality, 5, 113, 115, 120
Market fragmentation, 289
Market opportunity analysis (MOA), 221–224
Market segmentation, 178
  dimensions of quality and, 179–180
  refinement of, 178–180
  satisfaction/dissatisfaction measurement and, 289
Market share, 232–233
Market test, 266–267
Marketing promotions, complexity and, 311
Marketing research, 290
Mass market approach, 178, 179
Material requirements planning (MRP), 9
Matrix management, 319–320
  benefits and drawbacks of, 315
Mavericks, 124
Means and continuous improvement, 33, 34
Means/ends model, 183–187, 256
  assessing, 288
  attitude formation and, 189–190
  components of, 183–184
  concern for end use, 184–185
  end states and evaluative criteria, 186–187
  illustrated, 184, 185
  product attributes and characteristics, 185–186
Measurement and customer value strategy, 30, 185
Measuring commerical customer value, 268–270
Measuring customer value, 263–295
  principles of measurement, 270–273
    avoiding errors in, 272–273
    behavior over attitudes or purchase intentions, 271
    direct and indirect measures of key constructs,
      271–272
    multiple measures of each construct, 270–271
    quantitative results and qualitative studies, 272
    timing of measurement, 272

Measuring customer value, principles of measurement
  (*continued*)
  validating intrusive methods with nonintrusive tech-
    niques, 272
  satisfaction/dissatisfaction (*see* Satisfaction/dissatisfaction
    measurement)
  techniques for, 263–273
    after-sale feedback, 268
    direct observation, 267
    focus groups, 265–266
    laddering, 266
    market test, 266–267
    other sources of data, 267
    personal interviews, 264
    protocol analysis, 264–265
    trade-off analysis, 266
  using the measures, 273–282
    improvement of systems and processes, 281–282
    methods for improving system performance, 275–276
    quality function deployment, 276–282
    translating learning into strategy and systems, 273–275
Middle managers, 154, 156
Military strategy, 240
Ministry of International Trade and Industry (MITI)
    (Japan), 19–20
Mission, 218
Mission statement, 218, 220, 227
Modeling by managers, 436
Modern control and improvement process, 106–110
  action, 108
  illustrated, 107
  measurement, 108
  performance control and, 108–110
  standards for, 107–108
  study, 108
Modified rebuy, 195
Monetary value, 172–173
Money, diversion of, 11–12
Monitor role, 137
Monitoring of field failures, 58
Motivators:
  customer value strategy and, 150
  systems and, 306
Moving R charts, 383–392

Need, 186, 255–258
Negotiator role, 137
New Economics for Industry, Education and Government, The
  (Deming), 363*n.*
New information, openness to, 92
New leadership theory, 61
New task, 194–195
Ningen kankej, 121*n.*
Nonconformity:
  group, 122–123
  individual, 123–124
  strong culture and, 124
Normalcy stage of managerial paradigm shift, 10–13
  attention, diversion of, 12
  Cold War and, 11–12

Normalcy stage of managerial paradigm shift (*continued*)
  defined, 7, 9
  money, diversion of, 11–12
  traditional management and, 10–11
Norming stage of teams, 455–456
Norms, 198–199

Objectives, 237
  annual, 242
  strategic, 237–239
Occasion and continuous improvement, 32, 33
Open systems, 299, 304
  interrelated subsystems and, 302
Operating matrix, 279
Operating methods, 152–153
Operational tasks, 152
Operations, 304
  customer value strategy and, 152–153
  improving proficiency of, 450–451
  processes versus, 304–305
Operative goals, 492–494
Operators, 154–157
Opportunities and threats, 231–232
Optimization, 404
Order-flow system, 326–327
Organizational architecture, 154
Organizational culture, 87–95
  assessing, 497–501
    critical incident analysis, 500
    data gathering, 498–501
    group self-analysis, 500
    individual interviews, 499–500
    observation, 499
    overseers of, 497–498
    questionnaires, 500–501
  change and, 480–483
    difficulty of triggering, 481–482
    impediments to, 495–497
    as a paradigm shift, 482–483
    (*See also* Transformational change)
  control theory and (*see* Control theory)
  development of, 114–121
    critical incidents, 120
    as a learning process, 119–120
    mechanisms for, 116–117
    role of founders and leaders, 114–115
    shared understandings, 120–121
    socialization, 120–121
  emergence of, 112–114
    external adaptation and, 112–113
    internal integration and, 113–114
  as a guide to behavior, 121–125
    consensus and, 121–122
    cultural change and, 124–125
    group nonconformity and, 122–123
    individual nonconformity and, 123–124
    strong culture and, 124
  organizational purpose and, 96–99
    cultural view of, 98–99
    rational view of, 97–98
  strategic management and, 246–247

Organizational culture (*continued*)
　supporting the emerging paradigm, 89–95
　　continuous improvement, 93, 94–95
　　customer value, determining, 90
　　customer versus organizational focus, 90–91
　　experimentation for knowledge, 92
　　openness to new information, 92
　　organizational learning, mistakes leading to, 93
　　organizational performance, optimizing, 92
　　performance improvement, 93–94
　　process/system improvement, 93–94
　　processes and systems that cause results, 92
　　(*See also* Culture)
Organizational Development (OD), 61, 96, 125
Organizational inputs, variation in, 349–350
Organizational learning and transformational change,
　　501–505
　continuous improvement, 504–505
　double loops versus single loop, 503–504
　espoused theory and, 503
　theory in use and, 503
Organizational learning disabilities, 314
Organizational performance, optimizing, 92
Organizational purpose, 139
Organizational systems, 30–32
　cross-functional approach and, 31
　culture and, 31, 32
　employee involvement and, 31
　human resource management and, 31–32
　role definition and 31, 32
　structure and, 31, 32
　technology and, 31
Organizational theory in use, 503
Organizational valuation, 192–195
　cultural values, 194
　role values, 194–195
Organizing, 136
　to improve systems (*see* Hierarchical management;
　　System ownership; Systems view of organizations)
　planning and, 136–137
Orthogonal subcultures, 123
Out of the Crisis (Deming), 358*n*.
Output, 106–111
Outward view of culture, 100
　holistic, 102–104
　roles and, 134–135

p chart, 367–370
Paradigm:
　defined, 6, 89*n*.
　toward normalcy of, 82
Paradigm shifts, 1–34
　cultural change as, 482–483
　defined, 4–7
　education and, 7
　nature of, 6–7, 82–83
　organizational culture and (*see* Organizational culture)
　pervasive change and, 5–10
　stages of (*see* Anomalies stage of managerial paradigm
　　shift; Normalcy stage of managerial paradigm shift;
　　Replacement stage of managerial paradigm shift)

Paradigm shifts (*continued*)
　strategic management and (*see* Strategic management)
　TQM and, 3–5
Pareto analysis, 393–394
Pareto diagram, 374–375
Pareto principle, 326
Patterns of behavior, 101,102
Peer review system, 470
People, quality of, 80
Perceived quality, 180
Perceived value, 283
Perfection, 58–59
Performance, 180
　analysis of, 232–233
　quality of, 65
　　role responsibilities and, 133–134
Performance control, 108–110
　concurrent control, 109
　damage control, 110
　preliminary control, 109
　rework control, 109–110
Performance improvement, 93–94
Performing stage of teams, 455–456
Personal interviews, 264
Personal values, 187
Philosophy, corporate, 218, 226–227
　statements of, 103
Plan, Do, Study, Action (PDSA) cycle, 54, 106, 334,
　　439–441
Planned obsolescence, 231
Planning, 136, 137–138
　types of, 211–212
Poisson model, 371*n*.
Policies, 243
　customer value strategy and, 149–150
　systems and, 306
Policy deployment, 243–244
Political and regulatory climate, 228
Political/behavioral approach to decision making,
　　216*n*.
Poor management, 16
Portfolio analysis, 235
Positioning and customer value strategy, 30
Possession value, 187
Preliminary control, 109
Pride in workmanship, 91
Principles, corporate, 226–227
Prioritizing products, 326
Problem solving, 79
　focus on, 241
Problems versus symptoms, 235–237, 241
Process control chart, 51–52
Process of performance, 106
Process-oriented management, 78
Process Quality Management and Improvement Guidelines
　　(AT&T), 334*n*.
Processes, 74–79
　analysis of, 233–234
　components of, 304–305
　customer value strategy and, 150–151
　defined, 304

Processes (*continued*)
  formal and informal, 406–407
  improvement in, 93–94
    root causes and, 94
  operations versus, 304–305
  systems versus, 306
  that cause results, 92
  upstream, impeding improvement, 312–313
Processing, 304
Procurement practices, complexity and, 311–312
Product-based view of quality, 49
Product design/redesign, 323
  customer value strategy and, 30, 147–148
  quality of, 64, 65
Product-focused systems, 325–328
  greeting cards, 327–328
  insurance company, 327
  order flow system and, 326–327
  prioritizing products and, 326
Product-market hierarchy, 221–224
Production as a system, 75–79
Production control processes, 306
Production processes, 150, 305–306
Products of behavior, 101, 102
Projecting, customer value and, 259, 260–261
Protectionism, 21, 22
Protocol analysis, 264–265
Provisioning systems, 322
Pull model of employee involvement, 451–452
Purchase behavior, 199–200
Purchaser rule, 181
Purchasing processes, 306
Push model of employee involvement, 451–452, 453

Qualitative measures of satisfaction/dissatisfaction, 287–288
Quality, 41–84
  concept of, 44–46
  customer value strategy and, 29–30
  defined, 43
  evolution of approaches to (*see* Inspection era; Quality assurance era; Statistical quality control era; Strategic Quality Management era)
  manufacturing-based view of, 49–51
  market segmentation and dimensions of, 179–180
  of people, 80
  product-based view of, 49
  role systems and, 135
  service, 259
    survey of, 260–261
  transcendent view of, 45
    critique of, 45–46
  user-based view of, 51
  variation and, 404–412
Quality assurance era, 55–59
  costs of quality and, 55–56
  identifying characteristics, 47
  reliability engineering and, 56, 58
  Total Quality Control and, 56, 57
  zero defects and, 58–59

Quality circles, 41
  employee involvement and, 459–464
  failure of, 160–161
Quality control, 77
Quality function deployment (QFD), 276–282
  implementing, 278–281
  improvement of systems and processes and, 281–282
Quality improvement, 77
Quality improvement boards, 246
Quality Improvement Process (QIP), 485–486
Quality in Action, 12–13, 23–26, 44, 62–63, 95–96, 132–133, 164–165, 175–176, 200–201, 219–220, 269, 275, 322–323, 330–331, 346–348, 433–435, 492
Quality Is Free (Crosby), 59
Quality management, 213
"Quality or Else," 44–45
Quality planning, 76–77
Quality Without Tears (Crosby), 59
Quintessence: The Quality of Having It (Cornfeld and Edwards), 45

R charts, 375–383
Ranking (rating) performance, 367, 432–433
Rational/analytical approach to decision making, 216*n.*
Rational view of organizations, 97–98
Realistic strategy, 241
Realized value, 188
Rebels, 123–124
Reductionism, 303, 307
Redundancy, 58
Relative deprivation, 191–192
Relative value, 287
Reliability, 180
Reliability engineering, 56, 58
Remote environmental analysis, 227–228
Replacement stage of managerial paradigm shift, 28–34
  defined, 9
  themes of (*see* Continuous improvement; Customer value strategy; Organizational systems)
Resource allocation role, 137
Response to error and continuous improvement, 33
Responsibility, clear understanding of, 436
Responsible management, 135
  (*See also* Management role responsibilities)
Retrenchment strategies, 239, 240
Returns data, 268
Revitalized demand, 202–203
Rework control, 109–110
Rivalry, 229–230
Role accomplishments, 139
  diversity of, 139
  domains of (*see* Domains of accomplishments)
  types of (*see* Types of accomplishments)
Role behaviors, 135
Role definition and organizational systems, 32
Role perceptions, 134–135
Role systems, 134–135
Role value, 194–195
Roles:
  behavioral, 138

Roles (*continued*)
buying, 181
culture and, 134–135
defined, 133
(*See also* Management role responsibilities)
Root causes, 94
Routinization, 144

Sacrifices, 175, 186, 190–191
Sales promotions, 418–421
Sampling techniques, 52–53
Sam's rules for building and business, 245
Satisfaction, 255–258
Satisfaction/dissatisfaction measurement, 282–291
cross-functional participation and, 288–289
dynamics of value and, 286–287
competitive benchmarks, 286–287
relative value, 287
examples of, 284–285
implications for strategy, 289–291
meaning of, 285–286
means/ends relationship and, 288
qualitative measures, 287–288
reactions to perceived value, 283
refining, 287–289
specific objects/attributes and, 288
tailored measurement systems and, 288
types of standards, 283, 285
Scientific management, 10, 61, 97
Scientific study, 255
Segmentation, 178–180
Self-concept (self-image), 187
Self-directed work teams, 453–456
Self-insurance, 124
Self knowledge, 345
Self-managing teams, 157
Self-regulated work groups, 453–456
Service activities, production function of, 419n.
Serviceability, 180
Seven New QC Tools (Seven Management and Planning
Tools) (7MP Tools), 332n., 393, 397
Shared understandings, 120–121
Shewhart's theory and method to interpret variation, 357–
393, 422–423
stable versus unstable variation, 357–358
statistical control charts (*see* Statistical control charts)
statistically controlled variation, 358
use of information, 392–393
Simultaneous engineering (SE), 323
Single loop learning, 503–504
Six Sigma, 73
Skill-based pay, 469–470
Smooth Surface, 324–325
Social dramas, 500
Social isolation, 309
Social matrix, 482
Social trends, 227–228
Socialization, 120–121
Sociotechnical systems, 61

Special causes of variation, 360–361
action on, 425–426
mistakes of interpretation and, 360–362, 422–423
Specialists, 158
Specialization, 97
Spokesman role, 137
Stable variation, 357–358
Stakeholder analysis, 224–225
Standardization, 142–144
Starlets, 326
Stars, 326
Statistical control, 51
Statistical control charts, 358–362
common causes of variation and, 360–361
constructing, 365–392
control limits on, 363
interpreting, 363–365
mistakes in, 360–362
minimizing economic loss through, 360–361
moving R, 383–392
p, 367–370
R, 375–383
special causes of variation and, 360–361
tampering and, 361
u, 371–375
use of information contained in, 392–393
X, 383–392
X-bar, 375–383, 389–392
Statistical process control chart, 51–52
Statistical process control (SPC), 42, 420n., 423n.
Statistical quality control era, 48–55
indentifying characteristics, 47
manufacturing-based view of quality, 49–51
post-war Japan and, 53–55
process variation and control and, 51–52
product-based view of quality, 49
sampling techniques and, 52–53
Shewhart's views of quality, 48–54
user-based view of quality, 51
World War II and, 53
Statistically controlled variation, 358, 405
Steering Committee, 317
Storming stage of teams, 455–456
Storyboarding, 329
Straight rebuy, 195
Strategic business units (SBUs), 235
Strategic customer focus, 65–66
Strategic intent, 220
Strategic leaders, 154, 155–156
Strategic management, 209–252
activities in process of, 216
defined, 213–215
defining the business, 218–227
corporate values/philosophy/principles and, 226–227
market opportunity analysis and, 221–224
mission statement, 218, 220, 227
product-market hierarchy and, 221–224
stakeholder analysis and, 224–225
vision statement, 220–221
emerging paradigm and, 215–216

Strategic management (*continued*)
  evaluation and control for continuous improvement, 248
  external analysis (*see* External analysis)
  growing role of, 211–213
  internal analysis (*see* Internal analysis)
  introduction, 211–216
  involvement in, 215
  key problems and, 235–237
  model of process of, 216–217
  strategic alternatives, 237–242
    competitive versus cooperative, 240, 241
    evaluating, 241–242
    goals and objectives, 237–239
    long-term, 239–240
  strategic choice and implementation, 242–248
    action plans and policies, 243–244
    annual objectives, 242
    human resource management, 247–248
    leadership and management, 244–245
    organizational culture, 246–247
    systems and structure, 245–246
Strategic planning, 61
Strategic quality focus, 66
Strategic Quality Management era, 60–84
  conclusion, 83–84
  consumer value concept and, 63–65
  continuous improvement philosophy and (*see* Continuous improvement)
  identifying characteristics, 47
  nature of the paradigm shift and, 82–83
  strategic customer focus and, 65–66
  strategic quality focus and, 66
  Total Quality Management (*see* Total Quality Management [TQM] [Total Quality])
  total view of quality and, 79–80
Strategy, 213–215
  employee involvement and, 447
  implementation, 248
  improvement and, 436
  translating measurements of customer value into, 273–275, 289–291
Streamlining, 316
Structural devices for improving system performance, 275–276
Structure, 245–246
  organizational systems and, 32
Subculture, 122–123
Subject matter knowledge, 345
Subjectivity bias, 497
Suboptimization, 404
Substitutes, 229
Subsystems, 301–302
Superordinate goal strategy, 276, 320
Suppliers, power of, 229
Support staff, 158
Survey of service quality, 259, 260–261
System improvement, 79
  structure and, 245–246
System ownership, 299, 318–338
  advantages of, 332

System ownership (*continued*)
  benefits and drawbacks of, 315
  beyond structural change, 337–338
  clarified responsibilities and, 332–334
  cross-functional systems approach, 315, 320–325
  customer focus and (*see* Customer-focused systems)
  eclectic approach, 334–335
  limitations of, 336–337
  managers creating their own realities, 335–336
  matrix management, 315, 319–320
  product focus and (*see* Product-focused systems)
Systems, 74–79, 299
  customer value strategy and, 148–149
  domains of, 301
  hierarchical structures and, 297–298
  improvement in, 93–94
    methods for, 275–276
    root causes and, 94
  processes versus, 306
  roles and, 133–135
  that cause results, 92
  translating learning into, 273–275
Systems thinking, 306–307
Systems view of organizations, 299–307
  aligned subsystems, 301–302
  combined horizontal and vertical flows, 303–304
  horizontal work flows to serve customers, 302–303
  Ishikawa's cause and effect diagram, 299–301
  key elements of, 304–307
    policies, motivators and technology, 306
    processes versus operations, 304–305
    production versus business processes, 305–306
    systems thinking, 306–307
    systems versus processes, 306
  open systems, 302

Taguchi loss function, 72–73
Tampering, 361
Task forces, 464–465
Teams:
  cross-functional, 464–465
  labor-management action, 465–466
  task forces, 464–465
  training and, 470
  work, 453–456
Technology:
  core, 218
  customer value strategy and, 151–152
  Japanese strategies concerning, 18–19
  organizational system and, 31
  systems and, 306
  trends in, 228
  vital, 13–14
Theories in use, 103, 503
3C Policy (customers, company, communities), 225–226
Tools, 151
Total Quality Control (TQC), 56, 61, 78
  matrix, 56, 57
Total Quality Forum, 4, 81

Total Quality Management (TQM) (Total Quality), 60–62, 274*n*.
  antithetical practices, 62
  at AT&T, 44
  beyond, 80–82
  defined, 3–5, 60–61
  disappointment with, 6
  failure of "programs," 42–43
  rational approach to, 98–99
  roots of, 61
Total view of quality, 79–80
Toyota Production System, 8
Trade-off analysis, 266
Traditional management, 10–11
Training and development, 61, 437
  as leverage point for driving transformational change, 495
  team responsibility for, 470
Transcendant view of quality, 45
  critique of, 45–46
Transformation, 106–111
Transformational change, 476–509
  causing, 483–497
    Baldridge award, 483–487
    critical path of change, 487–489
    cultural impediments to, 495–497
    frame-breaking change, 489–490
    leverage points (*see* Leverage points for driving transformational change)
    introduction, 477–478
    organizational culture, and, 480–483
      change as a paradigm shift, 482–483
      difficulty of triggering change, 481–482
    organizational learning and (*see* Organizational learning and transformational change)
  Total Quality Management, 478–480
Transport, 304, 305
Types of accomplishments, 139
  breakthrough and, 141–142
  combining domains and, 139–141
  execution and, 145
  incrementation and, 142
  maintenance and, 144–145
  routinization and, 144
  standardization and, 142–144

u chart, 371–375, 404*n*.
Unavoidable costs, 55–56
Unfreezing, 481–482
Union of Japanese Scientists and Engineers (JUSE), 53, 54
Unstable variation, 357–358
Upstream control, 110–111
Use experience, 200
Use process, 181–183
Use situations, 187
User-based view of quality, 51
User role, 181

Valuation process (*see* Customer value, valuation process)

Value, 255
  customer (*see* Customer value)
  dynamics of, and measurement, 286–287
Value added, 173
Value-adder, 268–269
Value-based measures of quality, 63–65
Value-based strategy, 214–215
Value chain, 173–175
Value specific systems, 323–325
Value strategy, 214
Values:
  anticipated, 188
  buyer, 173–175
  corporate, 218, 226–227
  cultural, 194
  customer (*see* Customer value)
  interrelatedness of cultural levels and, 111–112
  inward view of culture and, 102–103
  monetary, 172–173
  personal, 187
  possession, 187
  realized, 188
  role, 194–195
Values gap, 226–227
Variables data, 366–367
  charts to analyze, 375–392
Variation, 51–52, 342–443
  in consumer products, 348–349
  in consumer services, 349
  defined, 343
  effects of, 348–352
  employee involvement and, 450–451
  in future conditions, 350–351
  histograms and, 394–396
  inside the organization, 351–352
  introduction, 343–345, 402–404
  key ideas, 345–346, 403–404
  linked to causes, 404–421
    corporate accounts payable, 412–418
    product quality, 404–412
    sales promotion, 418–421
  in organizational inputs, 349–350
  Pareto analysis and, 393–394
  recognizing and interpreting, 345–346
  reduction of, 69–74
  remarks on the use of tools, 397
  theories for interpreting the meaning of, 352–357
    ignoring variation, 353–354
    imposing arbitrary standards, 354–356
    overreacting to variation, 356
    Shewhart's theory (*see* Shewhart's theory and method to interpret variation)
    summary of, 353
  (*See also* Indicators of organizational performace, interpreting)
Vertical *keiretsu*, 19
Vertical reductionism, 303
Vertical slice, 299, 310
Vertical work flows, 303–304
Vision statement, 220–221

Wall Street Journal, The, 13n., 22n., 41n., 43n.
Want, 186
Warranty claims, 268
What-how matrix, 276–281
Wobbling, 300–301
Work ethic, 16
Work teams, 453–456
    stages of development of, 455–456

Working to specification versus continuous improvement, 93

X-bar charts, 375–383, 389–392
X charts, 383–392

Zen and the Art of Motorcycle Maintenance (Pirsig), 45
Zero defects, 58–59, 68–69